GUIDE TO THE PCAOB INTERNAL CONTROL STANDARD

A. WAYNE AVELLANET
Certified Management Accountant

Warren, Gorham & Lamont

Table of Contents

WG
&L Warren, Gorham & Lamont

¶ i. Organization of the Book

¶ ii—Contents. A complete list of topics discussed, arranged by paragraph.

¶ iii—Introduction. An overview of PCAOB Auditing Standard No. 2 and an introduction to the analysis.

¶ iv—Glossary. Definitions of key terms, using the exact wording promulgated by the PCAOB.

¶ 100 to ¶ 122—Analysis of PCAOB Auditing Standard No. 2: An Audit of Internal Control Over Financial Reporting Performed in Conjunction with an Audit of Financial Statements. Each paragraph of the auditing standard is described and analyzed. The author provides:

- Analysis of each paragraph's requirements.
- Comments on internal control.
- Who is affected by each requirement.
- Actions that must be taken.
- Rules and regulations cited in the standard.
- Suggested references for further reading.
- Sample client letters, interoffice memoranda, and audit reports.

¶ 200—Annotated PCAOB Auditing Standard No. 2: An Audit of Internal Control Over Financial Reporting Performed in Conjunction with an Audit of Financial Statements. This annotated version of the auditing standard provides cites to the analysis for quick reference.

¶ 300—Cross-Reference Tables. These are useful tools that highlight who is affected, the effect of the standard, applicable rules and regulations, actions that must be taken, and suggested references.

¶ 400—PCAOB Auditing Standard No. 2: An Audit of Internal Control Over Financial Reporting Performed in Conjunction with an Audit of Financial Statements. This is the full text of the standard adopted by the PCAOB on March 9, 2004.

¶ 500—PCAOB Release No. 2003-017: Proposed Auditing Standard— An Audit of Internal Control Over Financial Reporting Performed in Conjunction with an Audit of Financial Statements. This is the full text of the proposed standard as it was issued on October 7, 2003.

¶ 600—Selected Public Comments on the Proposed Standard. The PCAOB received 193 public comments on the proposed standard. This section includes a representative selection of 40 letters.

¶ 700—PCAOB Briefing Paper for the Roundtable on Reporting on Internal Control. This briefing paper, issued July 10, 2003, was prepared by the PCAOB as its initial outline for its July 29, 2003 roundtable on reporting on internal control. It provides a list of discussion questions that highlight the main issues the PCAOB set out to address during the process of developing a new auditing standard on internal control.

¶ 800—PCAOB Briefing Paper for the Public Meeting of the Board Regarding Proposed Auditing Standard—An Audit of Internal Control Over Financial Reporting Performed in Conjunction with an Audit of Financial Statements. This briefing paper, issued October 7, 2003, was prepared by the PCAOB for the public meeting at which the PCAOB issued the new auditing standard in its proposed form. It outlines the thinking behind the PCAOB's development of the new standard.

¶ 900—PCAOB Briefing Paper for the Public Meeting of the Board: Board Considers Adopting Standard for Audits of Internal Control Over Financial Reporting. This briefing paper, issued March 9, 2004, was prepared by the PCAOB for the public meeting at which the PCAOB issued and adopted the final version of the new auditing standard on internal control over financial reporting. It provides some feedback on the public comments that the PCAOB received after issuing the proposed version of the standard, and summarizes the PCAOB's decisions to change some parts of the standard and leave other parts just as they appeared in the proposed version.

¶ 1000—SEC Release No. 33-8238—Final Rule: Management's Reports on Internal Control Over Financial Reporting and Certification of Disclosure in Exchange Act Periodic Reports. This is the SEC rule that governs management's reports on internal control and certifications of disclosure in Exchange Act periodic reports. This guidance outlines what management must do in order to comply with Sarbanes-Oxley Act Section 404's reporting requirements.

¶ 1100—SEC Release No. 33-8392—Final Rule: Management's Reports on Internal Control Over Financial Reporting and Certification of Disclosure in Exchange Act Periodic Reports. This SEC rule extended the compliance dates for Sec Release No. 33-8238 until November 15, 2004 for accelerated filers and July 15, 2005 for other issuers.

¶ 1200—Text of the Sarbanes-Oxley Act of 2002. The complete text of the Sarbanes-Oxley Act is included for easy reference.

¶ 1300—Index. A detailed index directs the reader to the appropriate analysis in the book.

¶ ii. Contents

WG
&L Warren, Gorham & Lamont

CONTENTS

¶ iii. Introduction

Guide to the PCAOB Internal Control Standard

When the Public Company Accounting Oversight Board (PCAOB) took on the task of writing the auditing standard for the new requirement that management assess the effectiveness of internal control over financial reporting and auditors evaluate that assessment, the Board received a historic opportunity to improve generally accepted auditing standards (GAAS). GAAS as it applied to internal control over financial reporting, though robust in theory, had become diluted in its application and was to some extent blamed, fairly or unfairly, as a contributing factor in the financial reporting debacles of the early 2000s.

The PCAOB's primary contribution to GAAS, via this auditing standard, is to firmly incorporate the COSO framework (i.e., the Committee of Sponsoring Organizations of the Treadway Commission's *Internal Control—Integrated Framework*) into the thinking of corporate leadership. Management is now required to apply the COSO framework and GAAS to something that it had never been rigorously applied to before—internal control over financial reporting. No longer is it acceptable for management to simply produce financial statements that can pass an audit. Now management must take responsibility for and assess the effectiveness of the company's internal controls over the processes it uses to prepare the financial reporting it issues. That assessment must then pass its own audit. That audit, or attestation as some might refer to it, by the external auditor is governed by this auditing standard.

While some might argue that this auditing standard does not go far enough in its pursuit of financial reporting improvement, others would surely argue that it goes too far. The rest of us will be satisfied with the PCAOB's newly clarified guidance on how internal controls should be applied to ensure the accuracy of public companies' financial reporting, and will hope that the new auditing requirements help restore the public's confidence in the U.S. accounting and auditing industries.

In any event, few would argue that this auditing standard does not accomplish its objective. That objective is set forth in the Sarbanes-Oxley Act and is focused on improving the quality and reliability of published financial reports. This auditing standard adds an entire layer of external audit oversight. It requires an audit of management's assessment of the internal control over financial reporting and an audit of the actual effectiveness of the issuer's internal controls over financial reporting. That audit must also incorporate an audit of the company's financial statements. As the PCAOB states in the introduction to the new standard, "The one audit cannot be separated from the other. The information the auditor learns as a result of auditing the company's financial statements has a direct and important bearing on the auditor's conclusion about the effectiveness of the company's internal control over financial reporting." The implementation of this auditing standard should raise the quality and reliability of financial reporting to a whole new level.

The Benefits of Internal Control Over Financial Reporting

The strengthening of public companies' internal control over financial reporting will help to restore investor confidence in publicly issued financial reporting. The PCAOB has issued this auditing standard with the intent of improving the quality and reliability of the financial statements issued by publicly traded companies. In the end, however, internal control over financial reporting is a process conducted by people. People invariably make mistakes, so no system of internal control is absolutely foolproof. That said, the anticipation is that as the internal controls over the processes that management uses to produce financial statements improve, the quality of those financial statements themselves will inevitably improve as a result.

More and more companies are realizing the importance of effective, documented policies and procedures and the need for consistent application of generally accepted accounting principles (GAAP). In addition, strong internal controls will help companies prevent and detect errors and fraud and safeguard assets that, when all is said and done, belong to the shareholders. The PCAOB has chosen to base this auditing standard on the requirements of the COSO framework, and elements of that framework are incorporated throughout the standard.

Background of the Standard

The PCAOB was required by the Sarbanes-Oxley Act to issue this new auditing standard for an audit of internal control over financial reporting performed in conjunction with an audit of financial statements. The PCAOB issued the proposed version of the standard as PCAOB Release 2003-017 on October 7, 2003. Following a public comment period, the PCAOB issued the final auditing standard on March 9, 2004.

Section 404(a) of the Sarbanes-Oxley Act requires management to assess and report on the effectiveness of a company's internal control over financial reporting. Section 404(b) requires that the company's external auditor attest to that assessment. Section 404(b) also stipulates that the auditor's attestation must be performed in conjunction with the audit of the financial statements themselves. In general, that attestation involves the external auditor validating the assertions made by management regarding the effectiveness of the firm's internal controls.

In April 2003, the PCAOB adopted interim attestation standards in PCAOB Rule 3300T, which included the existing standard covering the auditor's attestation on internal control materials. The PCAOB convened a roundtable on July 29, 2003, to discuss topics and positions related to reviews of internal control. The participants at the roundtable represented a variety of positions. The result of the roundtable discussion was that the PCAOB determined that the existing standard covering attestations of internal control was insufficient to effectively implement Section 404's requirements. For the PCAOB to adequately discharge its duties under Section 103(a) of the Sarbanes-Oxley Act, the board members felt that the PCAOB must develop this new auditing standard.

On October 7, 2003, the proposed version of the auditing standard was issued for public comment. The PCAOB received and reviewed an unprecedented 193 public comment letters from a variety of organizations and individuals. The final version of the new standard—Auditing Standard No. 2, *An Audit of Internal Control Over Financial Reporting Performed in Conjunction with an Audit of Financial Statements*—was adopted by the PCAOB at a public meeting on March 9, 2004. The PCAOB incorporated some of the suggestions it received from the public in the final version of the standard, and issued an explanation of the staff's reasoning in Appendix E of the new standard.

The Nature of an Audit of Internal Control Over Financial Reporting

Under the new standard, a company's external auditor must evaluate the processes that management used to prepare the company's externally published financial statements. The internal controls over financial reporting must provide high, though not necessarily absolute, assurance regarding the company's objectives in the area of financial reporting accuracy and reliability.

There was much discussion among the comment letters the PCAOB received as to whether this standard was an auditing standard or an attestation standard. In recognizing the scope and expectations of the work to be performed, the PCAOB established this as an auditing standard and not as an attestation standard. The PCAOB explained its position by stating, "An auditing process restricted to evaluating what management has done would not provide the auditor with a sufficiently high level of assurance that management's conclusion is correct. The auditor needs to evaluate management's assessment process to be satisfied that management has an appropriate basis for its conclusion. The auditor, however, also needs to test the effectiveness of internal control to be satisfied that management's conclusion is correct and, therefore, fairly stated."

An Integrated Audit of the Financial Statements and Internal Control Over Financial Reporting

Section 404(b) of the Sarbanes-Oxley Act provides that the auditor's attestation of management's report should not be the subject of a separate engagement. The external auditor must evaluate the processes management uses to prepare the company's financial statements and must gather and review evidence regarding the operating effectiveness of the company's internal control over financial reporting in order to attest as to whether management's own assessment is fair and accurate. This attestation must be performed in conjunction with an audit of the financial statements. These audits must be performed together.

The PCAOB embraces the practical reality that it would be virtually impossible to assess the effectiveness of internal controls over financial reporting separately from the financial reporting itself. It therefore created this standard based on the innovative concept that the internal controls over financial reporting and the financial reporting itself are intertwined. The inseparable nature of internal controls and financial reporting necessitate an integrated standard. However, the PCAOB states in its introduction to the standard, "Notwithstanding the fact that the two audits are interrelated, the integrated audit results in two separate objectives: to express an opinion on management's assessment of the effectiveness of the company's internal control over financial reporting and to express an opinion on whether the financial statements are fairly stated."

The Cost of the New Requirements

The PCAOB received numerous comments on the proposed standard that expressed concerns about the costs of implementing the new auditing requirements. Regardless of the cost, the PCAOB deems internal control over financial reporting to result in benefits of improved financial reporting to the investment community. The result is expected to be improved financial reporting for the investment community and reduced litigation costs across the accounting industry.

Higher audit fees are expected as a result of the new auditing requirements, and some would say they are inevitable given the extent of testing and assessment required in the new standard. There are also greater out-of-pocket expenses associated with compliance work leading up to the audit of internal control over financial reporting. To the investing public, however, the costs of compliance, estimated to be some millions in many cases, are supremely preferable to wholesale corporate failures that result in losses of many billions.

To further ease the costs of compliance, the PCAOB made efforts to accommodate public companies' management and the public accounting industry. These appeasements include allowing auditors to use the work of others and broad auditor discretion in the determination of necessary tests. The expectation is that the auditor will only perform those tests that are appropriate for the company in question. The result is expected to be that costs for small companies will be much lower than costs for large companies. The PCAOB also indicates that, based on all available information, the greatest costs will be incurred in the first year of compliance. After that, it anticipates the costs to be less burdensome.

The PCAOB also stresses that it does not expect that internal control over financial reporting and the COSO framework to be a one-size-fits-all solution in their application to small firms. The PCAOB expects auditors to tailor the scope of the audit down for smaller issuers. During the March 9, 2004 public meeting at which the standard was adopted, PCAOB Chairman William J. McDonough commented, "As we heard from many public companies, these requirements are tough, and they will entail extra work and cost. That said, the Board will be watching and listening closely to learn whether companies, especially small and medium-sized companies, are being unduly charged for these audit services. The internal controls necessary for one company may not be necessary for all companies."

A New Kind of Audit Process

In this auditing standard, the PCAOB greatly increases the scope and complexity of the traditional audit. The audit of internal control over financial reporting is an extensive process requiring substantial skill and expertise. The external auditor must conduct a detailed audit covering a wide variety of material. The auditor must plan the audit, evaluate management's assessment of internal control over financial reporting, and evaluate the design and operation of the issuer's internal controls.

The PCAOB also introduces complexity by referring to internal control throughout the auditing standard as a process. Traditionally, almost all audit literature focused on the validation of transactions and balances at a point in time. Until now, the auditor was rarely, if ever, required to consider the effects of accounting activities or internal controls in a fluid way.

Evaluating Management's Assessment

The objective of an audit of internal control over financial reporting is to form an opinion as to whether management's assessment of the effectiveness of the registrant's internal control over financial reporting is fairly stated in all material respects. The Sarbanes-Oxley Act also requires the auditor's report to present an evaluation of whether the internal control structure provides reasonable assurance that the financial reports are accurate. In order to do this, the auditing standard requires the auditor to evaluate management's assessment process. In order to accomplish this task, the auditor must test the effectiveness of the company's internal controls. The auditor must gather and review evidence regarding the operating effectiveness of the company's internal control over financial reporting and attest as to whether management's own assessment is fair and accurate. The standard requires that documentation of internal controls must exist for an auditor to have validated the controls' effectiveness. This creates a hurdle for the issuer that requires the presence of adequate internal control documentation.

Obtaining an Understanding of Internal Control Over Financial Reporting

The independent auditor must conduct testing sufficient to obtain an understanding of the company's internal control over financial reporting. The standard allows the auditor to use the work performed by others, including management and internal auditors, to a certain degree. This allowance should greatly reduce the amount of work done by the auditor.

The auditor must understand how the internal controls over financial reporting are designed and also how they operate in practice. The auditing standard requires that the auditor:

- Make inquiries of management and staff.
- Observe the operation of the controls by the personnel performing them on a routine basis.

- Review documents that are used in, and that result from, the application of the controls.

- Compare supporting documentation and documents (for example, sales invoices, contracts, and bills of lading) to the accounting records.

- Perform walkthroughs of the transactions through the accounting systems.

The standard states, "In a walkthrough, the auditor traces a transaction from each major class of transactions from origination, through the company's accounting and information systems and financial report preparation processes, to it being reported in the company's financial statements." The PCAOB requires the auditor to perform walkthroughs in each annual audit, and does not allow the auditor to rely on walkthroughs performed by others, such as management or internal auditors, beyond the use of such work as additional evidence. In fact, the PCAOB places such emphasis on walkthroughs that it requires "appropriately experienced auditors" to perform them, rather than less experienced personnel.

The auditor has wide discretion in determining which controls should be tested. The standard only requires that the auditor obtain evidence to validate significant accounts for purposes of the audit of internal control over financial reporting. The auditor is expected to start by evaluating the accounts at the financial-statement or note-disclosure level. The auditor then expands the evaluation to include qualitative risk factors. The expectation is that, based on the auditor's non-specific quantitative and qualitative assessments of financial reporting risk, a certain quantity of transactional tests will be identified and conducted. The results of these validation tests are required for the auditor to attest to management's assertion about the effectiveness of internal control over financial reporting.

Identifying Significant Accounts and Relevant Assertions

The PCAOB allows that the auditor does not have to test every single account or assertion. The auditor must only test those that are significant. In this regard, the PCAOB defers to GAAS, which inherently recognizes that some accounts, assertions, and classes of transactions are more significant than others. The two key concepts to keep in mind are significant accounts and relevant assertions:

- *Significant accounts.* These are accounts that are capable of affecting the financial statements quantitatively at a caption or note-disclosure level. This is expanded to include qualitative factors such as differing risks, organizational structure, and other factors.

- *Relevant assertions.* These are the primary underlying assumptions and are specific to the firm.

Experienced auditors are familiar with the process of identifying significant accounts, classes of transactions, and relevant assertions as part of the normal audit process. Those same techniques should be applied to the audit of internal control over financial reporting.

Testing and Evaluating the Effectiveness of the Design of Controls

During the audit, the auditor must determine if the internal controls are designed to provide a reasonable level of assurance over the accurate and reliable preparation of financial reporting. The auditor must examine the controls and determine if they would work based solely on their design. This is referred to as design effectiveness. Design effectiveness is a crucial aspect of internal control validation. According to the PCAOB, "The procedures an auditor performs to test and evaluate design effectiveness include inquiries of company personnel, observation of internal controls, walkthroughs, and a specific evaluation of whether the controls are likely to prevent or detect financial statement misstatements if they operate as designed."

Testing Operating Effectiveness

Given the proper design of the internal controls, the auditor must collect enough evidence to attest that the internal controls are operationally effective in providing reasonable assurance of accurate, reliable financial reporting. This auditing standard requirement speaks to the quantity, timing, and frequency of internal control validation testing to be performed by the auditor.

The auditing standard starts by requiring the auditor to obtain sufficient evidence about the design and operating effectiveness of controls related to financial statement preparation. The standard also requires the auditor to actually perform those tests. But then the standard begins to articulate the limitations of the scope of the audit. Some of the limits set forth in the auditing standard are:

- It is only necessary to apply tests to controls that are "important" to fairly present the relevant assertions in the financial statements.
- It is not necessary to test all controls.
- It is not necessary to test redundant controls.
- Focus should be on "relevant assertions" rather than "significant controls." (While open to considerable interpretation, the goal is to focus on judgments that affect financial statement results.)
- Rotating tests of controls are acceptable. (The standard advises that the auditor should vary testing from year-to-year. This testing should not be predictable and should be in response to operational or internal control changes made at the company. This encompasses common audit practices where workpapers are recreated for subsequent audits with only minor variations in testing.)
- Testing need not be extensive; however, each year's audit must stand on its own. (The auditor must obtain evidence of the effectiveness of con-

trols for all relevant assertions for all significant accounts and disclosures every year.)

Timing of Testing

The Sarbanes-Oxley Act requires management's assessment and the auditor's opinion to address the effectiveness of internal control as of the end of the company's most recent fiscal year. This assessment is as of a point in time. However, it would not be practical or appropriate to conduct all of the validation testing as of a single point in time, such as December 31. The auditing standard allows the auditor to conduct the audit tests over the course of the year, provided that the auditor updates and validates those tests as of the end of the issuer's fiscal year.

Using the Work of Others

Under the auditing standard, the auditor is allowed to use (and in some cases is required to consider) the work of others that is related to internal controls over financial reporting. This includes the work of management, the company's internal auditors, and the work of other auditors. The auditor should also consider the results of others' tests of internal controls in the design of the audit plan. However, while taking the work of others into consideration, the auditor's own work must provide the principal evidence for the audit opinion. The PCAOB clearly intended for the auditing standard to provide flexibility in using the work of others and also prevent inappropriate over-reliance on the work of others.

The auditing standard particularly emphasizes the use of the work of a company's internal auditors. It states, "Internal auditors are expected to have greater competence with regard to internal control over financial reporting and objectivity than other company personnel. Therefore, the auditor may be able to use their work to a greater extent than the work of other company personnel .... If internal auditors have performed an extensive amount of relevant work and the auditor determines they possess a high degree of competence and objectivity, the auditor could use their work to the greatest extent an auditor could use the work of others." The standard goes on to outline what factors might influence the levels of objectivity and competency of a company's internal audit function. This judgment is based on the internal audit department's use of IIA standards and a reporting relationship with the audit committee rather than reporting solely to management.

Fraud Considerations in an Audit of Internal Control Over Financial Reporting

The auditing standard emphasizes that the auditor must review controls that are designed to prevent or detect fraud. The PCAOB continues to delineate its logic with regard to internal control by emphasizing the detection and prevention of fraud in financial reporting to protect the investing public. The auditor is required to personally test these controls and is not allowed to rely on the work of others in this area. Appendix C of the standard specifically addresses the safeguarding of assets.

Evaluating the Results of Testing

The auditing standard defines reportable conditions as internal control deficiencies, significant deficiencies, and material weaknesses in internal control over financial reporting. The issuer's management and auditors will almost inevitably identify internal control deficiencies. The auditing standard defines and classifies these deficiencies. Those deficiencies that do not allow the company's management or employees, in the normal course of business, to prevent or detect financial misstatements on a timely basis are called internal control deficiencies. A deficiency, or combination of deficiencies, that allows more than the remote likelihood of a misstatement in the company's financial statements that is more than inconsequential in amount and will not be prevented or detected is termed a significant deficiency. Further, the auditing standard provides that a significant deficiency should be classified as a material weakness if it results in more than a remote likelihood that a material misstatement in the company's annual or interim financial statements will not be prevented or detected.

The auditing standard provides for all significant deficiencies and material weaknesses in internal control to be reported in writing to the audit committee. The auditor is also required to communicate all internal control deficiencies to management in writing and to notify the audit committee that this communication has been made. The auditor is not required to communicate to the audit committee in writing the internal control deficiencies that do not cross the threshold of significant deficiencies or material weaknesses.

Identifying Significant Deficiencies

The auditing standard defines a few extreme, very unlikely, situations that would be considered significant deficiencies as well as strong indicators that a material weakness exists. These are:

- *Ineffective oversight of the company's external financial reporting and internal control over financial reporting by the company's audit committee.* The auditing standard points out that a company's board of directors is responsible for supervising the audit committee. So while the standard requires the auditors to assess of the effectiveness of the audit committee's oversight as part of the evaluation of the control environment and monitoring components of internal control, if the auditors conclude that the oversight provided by the audit committee is ineffective, they are required to communicate this specific significant deficiency, or material weakness as the case may be, in writing to the board of directors. Some may think this requirement presents a conflict of interest because the audit committee is responsible for hiring and overseeing the company's external auditors. The PCAOB responds by stating that "this type of conflict is one that experienced auditors are accustomed to bearing and that investors expect an auditor to address: when the auditor determines that its overseer is ineffective, . . . the auditor must speak up."

- *Material misstatement in the financial statements not initially identified by the company's internal controls.* This would require, given evidence of material misstatements in the financial statements, that the auditor conclude that the internal controls over the preparation of those same financial statements was ineffective.

- *Timing differences that affect the financial statements.* Any timing differences related to preliminary financial statements must be evaluated and the final effect taken into consideration by the auditor. These may rise to the level of significant deficiencies, but are not always material weaknesses.

- *Significant deficiencies that have been communicated to management and the audit committee, but that remain uncorrected after reasonable periods of time.* This requirement speaks to the likelihood that the significant deficiencies identified by the auditor will contribute to a material weakness in internal control over financial reporting at some time in the future.

Forming an Opinion and Reporting

The auditing standard states that the auditor may express an unqualified opinion only if the auditor has identified no material weaknesses in internal control, having performed all of the procedures the auditor considers necessary given the circumstances (i.e., there has been no unreasonable limitation of the scope of the audit). The auditor's report is to include two opinions as a result of the audit of internal control over financial reporting: one on management's assessment and one on the effectiveness of internal control over financial reporting.

In general, the PCAOB gives both management and auditors broad discretion in deciding which internal control deficiencies are classified as significant deficiencies versus material weaknesses. This discretion is bound somewhat by the language in the auditing standard that addresses combinations of significant deficiencies.

The auditing standard does not increase the level of strictness or conservatism of internal controls over financial reporting that it expects issuers to apply. Nor does the auditing standard impose any penalties for issuers that have a large number of minor internal control deficiencies. As long as both management and the auditor do not raise a significant internal control deficiency or combination of deficiencies to the level of material weakness, then the issuer receives an unqualified audit opinion.

WG
                                                            &L   Warren, Gorham & Lamont

Disclosure of Significant Deficiencies Not Required

The auditor's assessment of internal control over financial reporting must follow the same guidelines as management's assessment of internal control over financial reporting. That is, only material weaknesses in internal control must be disclosed. The PCAOB notes, however, that a combination of significant deficiencies may itself rise to the level of a material weakness, in which case disclosure would be required.

Material Weaknesses Result in an Adverse Opinion on Internal Control

Material weaknesses in internal control will result in adverse audit opinions. Further, if a material weakness exists, and management's report does not identify it, then the auditor must not qualify the audit opinion but must instead render an adverse opinion. These brief examples help clarify the possibilities:

- *A material weakness exists and management concludes that internal control is effective.* "Management is not permitted to conclude that the registrant's internal control over financial reporting is effective if there are one or more material weaknesses in the registrant's internal control over financial reporting." Therefore, in this case the auditor must issue an adverse opinion on management's assessment. The auditor is not able to provide a qualified opinion.
- *A material weakness exists and management acknowledges the weakness in its assessment.* The auditor is allowed to provide an unqualified opinion on management's assessment and an adverse opinion on the effectiveness of internal control.

The introduction to the standard stipulates, "If the auditor and management disagree about whether a material weakness exists (i.e., the auditor concludes a material weakness exists but management does not and therefore makes the conclusion in its assessment that internal control is effective), then the auditor would render an adverse opinion on management's assessment."

Effective Date

Companies considered accelerated filers (seasoned U.S. companies with public float exceeding $75 million) are required to comply with the internal control reporting and disclosure requirements of Section 404(a) of the Act for fiscal years ending on or after November 15, 2004. Other companies (including smaller companies, foreign private issuers, and companies with only registered debt securities) have until fiscal years ending on or after July 15, 2005, to comply with these internal control reporting and disclosure requirements.

¶ iv. Glossary

Note: This glossary provides the definitions of the listed key terms as they are defined by the PCAOB in Auditing Standard No. 2, *An Audit of Internal Control Over Financial Reporting Performed in Conjunction with an Audit of the Financial Statements.* The paragraph numbers in parentheses after the definitions refer to the location in the standard of the PCAOB's definition.

Term	The PCAOB's Definition
auditor	Public accounting firm registered with the PCAOB and associated persons thereof. (¶ 1)
attestation of management's assessment of the effectiveness of internal control over financial reporting	The result of an audit of internal control over financial reporting. (¶ 3) The auditing standard also uses the term "audit of internal control over financial reporting" to refer to the attestation, saying that both terms "refer to the same professional service."
audit of internal control over financial reporting	The process that results in an attestation of management's assessment of the effectiveness of internal control over financial reporting, as required by Sarbanes-Oxley Act Section 404(b). (¶ 3) The auditing standard also uses the term "audit of internal control over financial reporting" to refer to the attestation of management's assessment of the effectiveness of internal control over financial reporting, saying that both terms "refer to the same professional service."
control deficiency	Exists when the design or operation of a control does not allow management or employees, in the normal course of performing their assigned functions, to prevent or detect misstatements on a timely basis. (¶ 8)
deficiency in design	Exists when a control necessary to meet the control objective is missing or an existing control is not properly designed so that, even if the control operates as designed, the control objective is not always met. (¶ 8)
deficiency in operation	Exists when a properly designed control does not operate as designed, or when the person performing the control does not possess the necessary authority or qualifications to perform the control effectively. (¶ 8)
design deficiency	See *deficiency in design.*
detective controls	Controls that have the objective of detecting errors or fraud that have already occurred that could result in a misstatement of the financial statements. (¶ 11)
estimation transactions	Activities that involve management judgments or assumptions in formulating account balances in the absence of a precise means of measurement (e.g., determining the allowance for doubtful accounts, establishing warranty reserves, or assessing assets for impairment). (¶ 72)

inconsequential misstatement

A reasonable person would conclude, after considering the possibility of further undetected misstatements, that the misstatement, either individually or aggregated with other misstatements, would clearly be immaterial to the financial statements. (¶ 9) See also *more than inconsequential misstatement.*

internal control over financial reporting

A process designed by, or under the supervision of, the company's principal executive and principal financial officers, or persons performing similar functions, and effected by the company's board of directors, management, and other personnel, to provide reasonable assurance regarding the reliability of financial reporting and the preparation of financial statements for external purposes in accordance with GAAP and includes those policies and procedures that: (1) pertain to the maintenance of records that, in reasonable detail, accurately and fairly reflect the transactions and dispositions of the assets of the company; (2) provide reasonable assurance that transactions are recorded as necessary to permit preparation of financial statements in accordance with GAAP, and that receipts and expenditures of the company are being made only in accordance with authorizations of management and directors of the company; and (3) provide reasonable assurance regarding prevention or timely detection of unauthorized acquisition, use, or disposition of the company's assets that could have a material effect on the financial statements. (¶ 7)

issuer

An issuer (as defined in Section 3 of the Securities Exchange Act of 1934), the securities of which are registered under Section 12 of that Act, or that is required to file reports under Section 15(d) of that Act, or that files or has filed a registration statement with the SEC that has not yet become effective under the Securities Act of 1933, and that it has not withdrawn. (¶ 2) Section 3 of the Securities Exchange Act of 1934 defines issuer as "any person who issues or proposes to issue any security; except that with respect to certificates of deposit for securities, voting-trust certificates, or collateral-trust certificates, or with respect to certificates of interest or shares in an unincorporated investment trust not having a board of directors or of the fixed, restricted management, or unit type, the term "issuer" means the person or persons performing the acts and assuming the duties of depositor or manager pursuant to the provisions of the trust or other agreement or instrument under which such securities are issued; and except that with respect to equipment-trust certificates or like securities, the term "issuer" means the person by whom the equipment or property is, or is to be, used."

material weakness

A significant deficiency or combination of significant deficiencies that results in more than a remote likelihood that a material misstatement of the annual or interim financial statements will not be prevented or detected. (¶ 10)

more than inconsequential misstatement	A reasonable person is unable to conclude, after considering the possibility of further undetected misstatements, that the misstatement, either individually or aggregated with other misstatements, would clearly be immaterial to the financial statements. (¶ 9) See also *inconsequential misstatement.*
more than remote likelihood	The likelihood of a future event or events occurring is either reasonably possible or probable. (¶ 9) See also *remote likelihood.*
nonroutine transactions	Activities that occur only periodically (e.g., taking physical inventory, calculating depreciation expense, or adjusting for foreign currencies). Data involved are generally not part of the routine flow of transactions. (¶ 72)
operation deficiency	See *deficiency in operation.*
preventative controls	Controls that have the objective of preventing errors or fraud that could result in the misstatement of the financial statements. (¶ 11)
reasonable assurance	A high level of assurance, though not absolute assurance, that there is a remote likelihood that material misstatements will not be prevented or detected in a timely manner. (¶ 17)
relevant assertion	An assertion that has a meaningful bearing on whether an account is fairly stated in the financial statements. (¶ 70)
remote likelihood	The chance that future event or events occurring is slight, as opposed to reasonably possible or probable. (¶ 9) See also *more than remote likelihood.*
routine transactions	Recurring financial activities reflected in the accounting records in the normal course of business (e.g., sales, purchases, cash receipts, cash disbursements, and payroll). (¶ 72)
senior management	The principal executive and financial officers signing the company's certifications as required under Section 302 of the Sarbanes-Oxley Act, as well as any other member of management who plays a significant role in the company's financial reporting process. (¶ 140)
significant deficiency	A control deficiency or combination of control deficiencies that adversely affects the company's ability to initiate, authorize, record, process, or report external financial data reliably in accordance with GAAP, such that it is reasonably possible or probable that a misstatement of the company's annual or interim financial statements that is more than inconsequential will not be prevented or detected. (¶ 9)
walkthrough	The auditor traces a transaction from origination through the company's information systems until it is reflected in the company's financial reports. (¶ 79)

¶ 100. Analysis of PCAOB Auditing Standard No. 2: An Audit of Internal Control Over Financial Reporting Performed in Conjunction with an Audit of Financial Statements

¶ 100. Applicability of the Standard

As stated in ¶ 1 of the auditing standard, the standard "establishes requirements and provides directions that apply when an auditor is engaged to audit both a company's financial statements and management's assessment of the effectiveness of internal control over financial reporting." These requirements apply to all public company issuers.

Section 404(a) of the Sarbanes-Oxley Act requires public issuers to include in their annual reports a report by management on the company's internal control over financial reporting. Section 404(b) requires the public company's auditor to attest to the report on the effectiveness of internal controls made by management. The public company is then required to include the auditor's attestation as part of its annual report.

Under Section 103(a)(2)(A)(iii) of the Sarbanes-Oxley Act, the PCAOB was required to issue this auditing standard so that issuers and their auditors can comply with Section 404(b) of the Act.

Compliance with this auditing standard is required for all issuers.

Auditing Standard Paragraphs: ¶s 1–3

Persons Affected:

Management, Directors, Audit Committee Members, Auditors, Internal Auditors, Accounting Staff, Accounting Management, Attorneys Preparing SEC Reporting, Financial Statement Users, Investors, Creditors, Regulators (in specialized industries, such as banking or insurance).

Effect:

The PCAOB has proposed another auditing standard that amends or supersedes many other interim auditing standards as a result of the adoption of this standard (see PCAOB Release No. 2004-002, March 9, 2004). Of particular importance is the fact that AU Section 325, *Communication of Internal Control Related Matters Noted in an Audit*, and AT Section 501, *Reporting on an Entity's Internal Control Over Financial Reporting*, will be superseded by PCAOB Auditing Standard No. 2 as of November 15, 2004. In addition, the following interim standards will be amended to conform with Auditing Standard No. 2:

- AU Section 310, *Appointment of the Independent Auditor*
- AU Section 311, *Planning and Supervision*

- AU Section 312, *Audit Risk and Materiality in Conducting an Audit*
- AU Section 313, *Substantive Tests Prior to the Balance Sheet Date*
- AU Section 316, *Consideration of Fraud in a Financial Statement Audit*
- AU Section 319, *Consideration of Internal Control in a Financial Statement Audit*
- AU Section 322, *The Auditor's Consideration of the Internal Audit Function in an Audit of Financial Statements*
- AU Section 324, *Service Organizations*
- AU Section 326, *Evidential Matter*
- AU Section 329, *Analytical Procedures*
- AU Section 332, *Auditing Derivative Instruments, Hedging Activities, and Investments in Securities*
- AU Section 333, *Management Representations*
- AU Section 339, *Audit Documentation*
- AU Section 342, *Auditing Accounting Estimates*
- AU Section 508, *Reports on Audited Financial Statements*
- AU Section 530, *Dating of the Independent Auditor's Report*
- AU Section 543, *Part of Audit Performed by Other Independent Auditors*
- AU Section 560, *Subsequent Events*
- AU Section 561, *Subsequent Discovery of Facts Existing at the Date of the Auditor's Report*
- AU Section 711, *Filings Under Federal Securities Statutes*
- AU Section 722, *Interim Financial Information*
- ET Section 101, *Independence*

Action:

Auditors must comply with this new auditing standard when performing the newly required audit of internal control over financial reporting in conjunction with an audit of financial statements. They should also take into account the conforming amendments to the interim standards proposed in PCAOB Release No. 2004-002.

Rules and Regulations Cited:

Sarbanes-Oxley Act Sections 103(a)(2)(A)(iii) and 404 Securities Exchange Act of 1934 Sections 3, 12, and 15(d) (15 USCS 78c, 15 USCS 78l, 15 USCS 78o-1(d)); Securities Act of 1933 (15 USCS 77a).

Suggested References:

"Auditing Standard No. 2—Audit of Internal Control Over Financial Reporting in Conjunction with an Audit of Financial Statements," *SEC Accounting & Reporting Update* 2004-13 (April 2004).

"A Proposed Auditing Standard—Conforming Amendments to Interim Standards Adopted by the Board," *SEC Accounting & Reporting Update* 2004-14 (April 2004).

"PCAOB Adopts Internal Control Auditing Standard," *Internal Auditing Report* (April 2004).

"SEC Finalizes Rules on Internal Control Reports," *Internal Auditing Report* (July 2003).

"Management's Responsibility for Internal Control Under Section 404," *Bank Auditing and Accounting Report* (March 2004).

"PCAOB Adopts Guidance for Audits of Internal Control Over Financial Reporting," *SEC Compliance: Financial Reporting and Forms* ¶ 4.6 (2004).

Practical Guide to Corporate Governance and Accounting: Implementing the Requirements of the Sarbanes-Oxley Act (2004 Edition).

¶ 101. The Auditor's Objective in an Audit of Internal Control Over Financial Reporting

Paragraphs 4, 5, and 6 of the auditing standard lay out the auditor's objective in an audit of internal control over financial reporting. The auditor must conduct an audit of management's assessment of internal control over financial reporting that the auditor can use as a basis for expressing an opinion on management's assessment. In order to express an opinion on management's assessment, the auditor must also audit the issuer's financial statements for that same period. The goal is to provide a basis, at the level of reasonable assurance, on which the auditor can base its opinion.

The auditor must evaluate management's assessment of internal control over financial reporting in order to determine whether the issuer's internal controls over financial reporting were operating effectively over the course of the time period to which management's assessment applies, usually one year. The objective is to determine whether any material weaknesses exist as of the date specified in management's assessment.

The audit of internal control over financial reporting is intended to provide the external users of the issuer's financial statements with the confidence and assurance that they can rely on these financial statements. In this regard, the auditor should take into account any specific early warning signs or industry-specific concerns that users of the financial statements need for that reliance.

In order to achieve the objective of an audit of internal control over financial reporting, the company's auditor must:

- Plan and perform the audit.

- Conduct the examination at a level that provides reasonable assurance about management's assessment of internal control over financial reporting. (Reasonable assurance, not absolute assurance, is the objective.)

- Evaluate management's assessment.

- Obtain and evaluate evidence about whether the company's internal controls are efficient and effective.

- Audit the issuer's financial statements that cover the same time period as management's assessment.

Auditing Standard Paragraphs: ¶s 4–6

Persons Affected:

Management, Auditors

Effect:

The issuer's auditor must express an opinion on management's assessment of the effectiveness of internal controls over financial reporting. The auditor's review of management's assessment must provide a level of reasonable assurance that the company's financial statements are materially accurate. The auditor must also audit the company's financial statements as of the date specified in management's assessment.

Action:

Management must evaluate, test, and document the company's system of internal control over financial reporting, then prepare an assessment. The company's auditor must evaluate management's assessment as well as obtain and evaluate evidence that the company's internal control over financial reporting is designed and operating effectively. In order to do this, the auditor must also audit the company's financial statements for the same time period covered by management's assessment of internal control.

Rules and Regulations Cited:

Sarbanes-Oxley Act Section 302; 17 CFR §240.13a-14(a); 17 CFR §240.15d-14(a).

¶ 102. Definitions Related to Internal Control Over Financial Reporting

The PCAOB provides some specific definitions for the primary terms used throughout the auditing standard.

"Internal control over financial reporting" is defined as a process that is designed by, or under the supervision of, the company's CEO and CFO or employees performing similar functions, and implemented by management, the board of directors, and other personnel. The primary objective is to provide reasonable assurance that the financial statements are reliable and comply with GAAP. The internal control process should include policies and procedures that:

- Address the maintenance and retention of transactional records.
- Provide reasonable assurance that transactions are recorded in accordance with GAAP.
- Ensure that receipts and expenditures are authorized by management and the board.
- Allow for the detection and prevention of material, unauthorized acquisition, disposition, and use of the company's assets.

An "internal control deficiency" exists when the design or operation of a control does not result in the prevention or detection of misstatements on a timely basis. Two types of internal control deficiencies are defined in the standard:

- A "deficiency in design" exists when the control is missing or improperly constructed.
- A "deficiency in operation" exists when a properly designed control does not work correctly or when the person responsible for implementing the control is not properly qualified or authorized.

A "significant deficiency" is an internal control deficiency (or combination of deficiencies) that adversely affects the company's ability to initiate, record, process, or report external financial data reliably in accordance with GAAP. This results in more than a slight chance that a misstatement of the annual or interim financial statements that is more than inconsequential in amount will not be prevented or detected. The auditor is expected to evaluate the effect of compensating controls when determining whether a significant deficiency exists.

A "material weakness" is a significant internal control deficiency that results in more than a remote likelihood that a material misstatement of the annual or interim financial statements will not be prevented or detected. The key word in this part of the definition is "material misstatement" versus simply "misstatement" in the definition of significant deficiency.

Internal controls over financial reporting are defined by the PCAOB as either "preventive controls" or "detective controls." Preventive controls are designed to prevent errors or fraud that could result in a financial misstatement from ever occurring. Detective controls are expected to detect errors or fraud that could result in a financial misstatement after the transaction occurs but before the financial statements are complete. Effective internal controls over financial reporting include a combination of both preventive and detective controls.

Neither the auditor's procedures associated with the audit of internal control over financial reporting nor the audit of financial statements can be considered part of a company's system of internal control over financial reporting.

Auditing Standard Paragraphs: ¶s 7–12

See Also Auditing Standard Paragraphs: ¶s 23, 130–137

Persons Affected:

Auditors

Effect:

The terms "internal control over financial reporting," "control deficiency," "deficiency in design," "deficiency in operation," "significant deficiency," "material weakness," "preventative control," and "detective control" are defined.

Action:

Those involved with internal control over financial reporting should become familiar with the definitions in order to avoid any confusion.

Rules and Regulations Cited:

17 CFR §240.13a-15(f); 17 CFR §240.15d-15(f); FAS No. 5, *Accounting for Contingencies.*

¶ 103. The Framework Used by Management to Conduct Its Assessment

In this part of the auditing standard, the PCAOB is reacting to the broad support of internal control over financial reporting offered by the Committee of Sponsoring Organizations of the Treadway Commission's *Internal Control—Integrated Framework*, otherwise known as the COSO report or the COSO framework. The COSO framework is considered by many to be both high-level and qualitative in nature and should have significant impact on the quality of internal control over financial reporting. The PCAOB based the requirements of this auditing standard on the requirements of the COSO framework.

The PCAOB establishes the COSO framework as a "suitable and available framework for purposes of management's assessment" by drawing on some of its primary strengths. As required, the COSO report is:

- *A suitable, recognized control framework.* In order to be recognized, an internal control framework would have to have been in existence for some time. In fact, the COSO framework was originally published in 1992. The COSO material reflects timeless applicability for current internal control issues like stock option expensing, "pump and dump" schemes, and excessive executive compensation.

- *Established by a body of experts that followed due-process procedures, including the broad distribution of the framework for public comment.* The COSO framework was written by a broad range of professionals who represented the primary constituencies of financial reporting. COSO is made up of representatives from the American Institute of Certified Public Accountants (AICPA), the Institute of Internal Auditors (IIA), Financial Executives International (FEI), the American Accounting Association (AAA), and the Institute of Management Accountants (IMA). While input was provided by a steering committee, all of the members of that steering committee directly represented diverse user interests and the public accounting industry. There was also input from the public investment community and from corporate practitioners of internal control.

The COSO report addresses the efficiency and effectiveness of operations, financial reporting, and compliance as three separate elements. In the auditing standard, however, the PCAOB emphasizes that these three objectives often overlap, and that accounting controls are not the only types of controls that need to be considered in an audit of internal control over financial reporting. As the standard points out in ¶ 15, "all controls that could materially affect financial reporting, including controls that focus primarily on the effectiveness and efficiency of operations or compliance with laws and regulations and also have a material effect on the reliability of financial reporting, are a part of internal control over financial reporting."

The auditing standard allows for the use of other internal control frameworks published in other countries or that may be developed in the future. Given the broad acceptance of the COSO framework in the United States, however, it is hard to imagine that any alternative internal control framework will dethrone COSO any time soon. This will certainly not occur in the near or intermediate term. However, the opportunity does exist for firms that understand their financial reporting liability to supplement the COSO framework with more robust methodologies in order to greatly reduce their risks of financial reporting misstatement, fraud, and related litigation. That is, the auditing standard certainly does allow for internal controls in excess of the required minimums to be implemented by conscientious issuers.

The auditing standard for internal control over financial reporting in combination with the implementation of the COSO framework do not, in any way, alter the fundamental structure of the issuer's internal control over financial reporting. They merely institute a risk assessment of those controls in accordance with the COSO framework, combined with an audit of the controls as defined in this auditing standard. There are no internal control requirements, improvements, or modifications specified in this auditing standard beyond those in the COSO framework.

Auditing Standard Paragraphs: ¶s 13–15

See Also Auditing Standard Paragraph: ¶ 16

Persons Affected:

Management, Auditors

Effect:

The auditing standard defines the characteristics of acceptable internal control frameworks that can be used to assess compliance with Sections 302 and 404 of the Sarbanes-Oxley Act. The characteristics are defined so narrowly that only the COSO framework can possibly be used by U.S. issuers for compliance with the Act at this time.

Action:

Companies that have not already done so should ensure that they are implementing at least the components of the COSO framework that relate to financial reporting, though certain aspects of the efficiency and effectiveness of operations and compliance with laws and regulations will also fall under the purview of internal control over financial reporting.

Rules and Regulations Cited:

SAS No. 95, *Generally Accepted Auditing Standards*; AU Section 319, *Consideration of Internal Control in a Financial Statement Audit*; PCAOB Rule 3200T, *Interim Auditing Standards*.

Suggested References:

"Management Internal Control Reports Over Financial Reporting," *Handbook of SEC Accounting and Disclosure* § 18.

"Management Internal Control Reports and Related Certification Matters," *SEC Accounting and Reporting Update* 2003-29 (June 2003).

"Internal Control," *Handbook of Accounting and Auditing* § B4.

"Reports on Internal Control," *Accounting and Auditing Disclosure Manual* § 90.

"COSO: More Relevant Now Than Ever," *Internal Auditing* (July/August 2003).

"Section 404 Compliance: Meeting the Challenges," *Internal Auditing* (July/August 2003).

"SEC Finalizes Rules on Internal Control Reports," *Internal Auditing Report* (July 2003).

"Management's Responsibility for Internal Control Under Section 404," *Bank Auditing and Accounting Report* (March 2004).

¶ 104. Inherent Limitations in Internal Control Over Financial Reporting

Following the discussion of the COSO framework, the PCAOB lowers the expectations for internal control over financial reporting somewhat by pointing out what it sees as "inherent limitations." The shortcomings itemized by the PCAOB are all associated with the human element of internal control: human error, lapses in judgment, fraud by collusion, and management override. Thus, while internal controls may reduce the risk of financial misstatements, they will never completely eliminate that risk. The discussion in this paragraph and the next section on the concept of reasonable assurance directly reflect the limitations of internal control outlined in Chapter 7 of the COSO report.

By codifying perceived shortcomings of internal control in the auditing standard, the PCAOB may be trying to limit the potential liability of the public accounting industry, which might otherwise be held liable for inadequate internal control reviews. For instance, if an issuer's financial statements and internal controls are given an unqualified audit opinion subsequent to implementation of the auditing standard, and those financial statements are later found to contain a material misstatement, then the public audit firm, absent a codified excuse, would probably be held liable for not having found the internal control weakness.

Auditing Standard Paragraph: ¶ 16

Persons Affected:

Management, Auditors

Effect:

Internal control over financial reporting is not expected to completely prevent or detect all material misstatements, due to inherent limitations.

Action:

Establish realistic expectations for internal control over financial reporting, and, as much as is feasible, introduce safeguards against human error and fraud in order to minimize the risk of financial misstatements.

Rules and Regulations Cited:

None cited.

¶ 105. The Concept of Reasonable Assurance

After having hedged its position slightly by codifying the fallibility of internal control in auditing standard ¶ 16, the PCAOB defines what it means by "reasonable assurance." The effect of ¶s 17 through 19 is to state that:

- Reasonable assurance is the best that can be done by either auditors or management in the area of internal control over financial reporting.
- Reasonable assurance means that the risk of material misstatement is relatively low—there is a slight chance that the internal controls will not prevent or detect material misstatements.
- Reasonable assurance is a high, though not absolute, level of assurance.
- There are inherent limitations in how much assurance can be provided by an auditor's review of management's assessment of internal control over financial reporting—professional judgment is a factor and an audit is by definition somewhat limited in scope.
- The auditor is providing the same level of reasonable assurance and performing the same level of work, via testing, whether the auditor is expressing an opinion on management's assessment or an opinion on the effectiveness of the internal controls themselves.
- The auditor's assessment is based on independent review and testing done by the auditor.
- The auditor's assurance does not relieve management of responsibility for assuring users of the company's financial reports about the effectiveness of internal controls over financial reporting.

Auditing Standard Paragraphs: ¶s 17–19

Persons Affected:

Management, Auditors

Effect:

The auditing standard requires the management assessment and auditor attestation of internal control over financial reporting to be at the level of reasonable, not absolute, assurance.

Action:

Management and the company's auditors should understand the inherent l imitations involved with internal control and should discuss the remote likelihood that material misstatements will not be detected or prevented by management's assessment and the audit of internal control over financial reporting. Management should have a plan in place to address this possibility. Management should also take primary responsibility for conveying the effectiveness of the company's internal over financial reporting to users of the company's financial reports.

Rules and Regulations Cited:

SEC Release No. 33-8238 *Final Rule: Management's Reports on Internal Control Over Financial Reporting and Certification of Disclosure in Exchange Act Periodic Reports* (June 5, 2003).

¶ 106. Management's Responsibilities in an Audit of Internal Control Over Financial Reporting

The auditing standard presents the minimum requirements that management must meet in order to discharge its responsibility under Section 404 of the Sarbanes-Oxley Act. Management must:

- Accept responsibility for and assess the effectiveness of internal control over financial reporting.
- Assemble sufficient documentation as evidence of this assessment.
- Present a written assessment as of the end of the company's fiscal year.

If the documentation and/or assessment report are not present and adequate, then the auditor must conclude that management has not fulfilled its responsibilities under Section 404(a) of the Sarbanes-Oxley Act. The auditor is then required to communicate its negative findings in writing to management and the audit committee.

This documentation standard presents the auditors with a firewall that they can retreat behind if the auditor faces pressure from the issuer's management to provide an attestation that is not deserved. While management's assessment report itself could conceivably be written in a few hours, all of the documentation required to support the assessment would have to have been assembled by many people over several months. It is likely that the auditors on some engagements will be pressured to provide an attestation for management's assessment of the effectiveness of internal control over financial reporting where no such validation is clearly deserved. This portion of the auditing standard provides linkage between the need for physical documentation and the more theoretical acceptance of responsibility by management. For management to have truly accepted the theoretical responsibility for effective internal control over financial reporting, the auditor would necessarily expect to find a substantial amount of documentary evidence to support such a claim. For the auditor to find an insufficient amount of documentation to support such a claim of responsibility is for that same auditor to necessarily conclude that, in reality, management has never acted on nor implemented that responsibility for internal control over financial reporting which they may have otherwise claimed to accept. Without this specification in the auditing standard, the auditor might be forced to attest to poorly documented management assessments that it would otherwise judge incomplete.

Auditing Standard Paragraphs: ¶s 20–21

See Also Auditing Standard Paragraphs: ¶s 40–46

Persons Affected:

Management, Audit Committee Members, Auditors

Effect:

Sufficient documentation is required to pass an audit of internal control over financial reporting. Management must accept responsibility for and assess the effectiveness of the internal controls over financial reporting. Documentation serves as evidence of this responsibility and assessment and is therefore an essential requirement in an audit of internal control over financial reporting.

Action:

Management must accept responsibility for and assess the effectiveness of the internal controls over financial reporting. During management's assessment, proper and complete documentation of the effectiveness of the company's internal controls must be compiled. A written assessment of the effectiveness of the company's internal control over financial reporting must be prepared by management at the end of each fiscal year. The auditor must notify management and the audit committee in writing if the auditor finds that management has not fulfilled its responsibilities with regard to this assessment process.

Rules and Regulations Cited:

17 CFR §228.308(a) and 17 CFR §228.308(c); 17 CFR §229.308(a) and 17 CFR §229.308(c) (Items 308(a) and of Regulation S-B and S-K, respectively).

Suggested References:

"Management Internal Control Reports Over Financial Reporting," *Handbook of SEC Accounting and Disclosure* § I8.

"Management Internal Control Reports and Related Certification Matters," *SEC Accounting and Reporting Update* 2003-29 (June 2003).

"SEC Finalizes Rules on Internal Control Reports," *Internal Auditing Report* (July 2003).

"Management's Responsibility for Internal Control Under Section 404," *Bank Auditing and Accounting Report* (March 2004).

¶ 107. Materiality Considerations in an Audit of Internal Control Over Financial Reporting

The PCAOB here divides the concept of materiality into the financial-statement level and the individual account-balance level. Materiality at the account-balance level is assigned a lower priority by the PCAOB than materiality at the financial-statement level, though the standard states that both are relevant to audit planning. The PCAOB also addresses both quantitative and qualitative considerations with regard to materiality, but does not go into great detail here, stating simply that the quantitative and qualitative considerations that apply to an audit of financial statements also apply to an audit of internal control over financial reporting.

In its brief discussion of materiality in an audit of internal control over financial reporting, the PCAOB has squandered an opportunity to correct a significant problem in auditing: the off-hand dismissal of issues that are immaterial at the account level but material at the financial statement level. For example, a $100 billion issuer can easily dismiss accounting problems of $5 million at each $10 billion division level for a single account. But when aggregated, this same $100 billion company might normally report no more than $50 million in profit. As a percentage of profit, what was immaterial at the account level becomes material—in the 100 percent range—at the financial-statement level. What happens in practice is that materiality is measured against revenues and assets when it should be judged against profits. The easiest way in accounting to hide a problem or pump up profits is to, for instance in the example above, take $50 million out of expense by scattering it all across a $100 billion company. This is the motive behind the "pump and dump" schemes of recent history—the very problems that the Sarbanes-Oxley Act was designed to address.

Materiality is a complicated concept, and the Achilles heel of the whole audit function is the determination of materiality relative to the financial-statement profit level. What the PCAOB did was reiterate the existing audit literature that allows materiality to be judged at the (much higher) financial-statement level for adjustments made at that level—and almost no adjustments or journal entries are made at that level. The standard states, "Materiality at the account-balance level is necessarily lower than materiality at the financial-statement level." This does not provide an adequate solution to the materiality dilemma. The account-level materiality test should be to compare the account-level "problem" to the financial statement profit figures, not to the division-level account figures. The PCAOB presents definitions of quantitative and qualitative materiality considerations but does not specifically mandate the relative testing that it probably should have required auditors to perform.

The standard also stresses that materiality is relevant to the regulatory environment of the issuer. In ¶ 140, the standard states that, for complex entities in highly regulated industries, an ineffective regulatory compliance function should be regarded as at least a significant deficiency and a strong indicator that a material weakness exists. The standard stipulates that this requirement "relates solely to those aspects of the ineffective regulatory compliance function in which associated violations of laws and regulations could have a material effect on the reliability of financial reporting."

The issue of materiality speaks to the concept of the usefulness of financial reporting. That is, financial reports should be useful to the intended readers for decision making purposes. In this regard, a financial report is judged inadequate if it omits information that would be required for ordinary users of the report to actually use it. The PCAOB failed to seize the opportunity to have a substantive discussion about improved financial reporting by segment, product, or geography. This is a common complaint that investors have about financial reporting. For example, among pharmaceutical companies it is common knowledge that a small percentage of products drive a large percentage of revenues and profits. But the segment reporting provided by pharmaceutical companies is of no use in determining which products are the winners and which are the losers. The reader is left to rely on the "hyped up" marketing portion of the annual report or on reporting assembled externally, such as information compiled by market research firms and published in periodicals.

Auditing Standard Paragraphs: ¶s 22–23

See Also Auditing Standard Paragraphs: ¶s 6, 140

Persons Affected:

Management, Auditors

Effect:

Auditors are to use the same definition of materiality and the same quantitative and qualitative judgments in an audit of the effectiveness of internal controls over financial reporting that they would use in an audit of financial statements.

Action:

Management and the company's auditors should establish defined levels of materiality with regard to the financial reporting at both the financial-statement level and the individual account-balance level.

Rules and Regulations Cited:

AU Section 312, *Audit Risk and Materiality in Conducting an Audit.*

Suggested References:

"Materiality," *Handbook of SEC Accounting and Disclosure* § A10.

"The Ethics of Materiality in Financial Reporting," *Internal Auditing* (January/February 2002).

¶ 108. Fraud Considerations in an Audit of Internal Control Over Financial Reporting

The PCAOB references the COSO framework's approach to preventing and detecting fraud but omits any specific methods for actually detecting or preventing fraud—the objective here is simply to examine the controls in place to detect and prevent fraud. The auditing standard requires the auditor to:

- Examine controls specifically designed to restrain the inappropriate use of company assets.
- Review the company's risk assessment process. (**Note:** Risk assessment processes generally tend to suffer the same materiality consideration problems that all audits suffer from.)
- Understand the company's code of ethics.
- Evaluate the adequacy of the company's internal audit activities, internal audit's reporting relationship to the audit committee, and the audit committee's involvement and interaction with internal audit.
- Consider the adequacy of the company's procedures for handling complaints and confidential submissions of concerns about questionable accounting and auditing practices.

The PCAOB specifies that, through these evaluations, the auditor should be able to assess the "tone at the top" of the organization. This is a concept taken directly from the COSO framework, which states, "In any organization, 'the buck stops' with the chief executive. He or she has ultimate ownership responsibility for the internal control system. One of the most important aspects of carrying out this responsibility is to ensure the existence of a positive control environment. More than any other individual or function, the chief executive sets the 'tone at the top' that affects control environment factors and other components of internal control." (COSO, *Internal Control—Integrated Framework*, p. 84.) According to the framework, the board of directors and the audit committee also play a role in the tone at the top. The main factors in setting the tone at the top are ensuring an adequate system of internal control exists and establishing a corporate culture based on integrity and honesty. The auditor's evaluation of the tone at the top of the organization will impact the overall assessment of internal control over financial reporting.

The practical application of these evaluations is less clear. It is difficult to imagine that any issuer would not have a code of ethics. It is also difficult to imagine that issuers would openly divulge shortcomings in policies and procedures for risk assessment and complaint handling. The PCAOB might have served the goal of internal control over financial reporting better by offering some specific testing requirements for evaluating controls related to the detection and prevention of fraud rather than simply providing a marginally modified version of GAAS. Management, audit committee members, and auditors should be sure to consult the COSO framework for more specific guidelines, since the PCAOB guidance provided here is based on that framework.

Auditing Standard Paragraphs: ¶s 24–26

See Also Auditing Standard Paragraph: ¶ 49

Persons Affected:

Management, Directors, Audit Committee Members, Internal Auditors, Ethics Officers, Auditors

Effect:

Auditors are required to place a special emphasis on their examination of controls designed to detect and prevent fraud.

Action:

The auditor should evaluate the company's control environment, risk assessment processes, codes of ethics, internal audit activities, and management's procedures for handling complaints. Management should ensure that the company's system of internal control is designed specifically to prevent, deter, and detect fraud. Management, directors, and audit committee members should confirm their commitment to the "tone at the top" concept as outlined in the COSO framework.

Rules and Regulations Cited:

AU Section 316, *Consideration of Fraud in a Financial Statement Audit.*

Suggested References:

"More Organizations Are Detecting Fraud," *Internal Auditing Report* (January 2004).

"Ten Questions to Jump-Start a Fraud Risk Assessment," *Internal Auditing Report* (December 2002).

"Will You Detect Fraud If You Think You Can?," *Internal Auditing* (July/August 2003).

"Preventing Revenue Recognition Problems: Internal Controls and Best Practices," *Internal Auditing* (May/June 2003).

"What Kind of CPA Detects Fraud?," *Internal Auditing* (September/October 2002).

"When Earnings Management Becomes Fraud," *Internal Auditing* (July/August 2002).

"Internal Auditors' Roles in the Prevention, Detection, and Correction of Financial Statement Fraud," *Internal Auditing* (May/June 2002).

"How Financial Executives Can Promote Quality Financial Reporting," *Internal Auditing* (January/February 2002).

"Auditing Journal Entries and Other Adjustments," *Accounting and Auditing Update 2003-21* (June 2003).

"Consideration of Fraud in a Financial Statement Audit," *Accounting and Auditing Update* 2002-35 (November 2002).

¶ 109. Performing an Audit of Internal Control Over Financial Reporting

Given the short development time frame for this auditing standard, it is hard to imagine that the PCAOB could possibly have developed entirely new general auditing standards. The PCAOB's broad acceptance of almost all existing GAAS as interim auditing standards seems to indicate that the PCAOB does not think there is much within GAAS that needs to be fixed, and that the status quo is adequate, at least for now. GAAS is, of course, the longstanding work of the AICPA.

As laid out in the new auditing standard, in an audit of internal control over financial reporting, the auditor is required to:

- Plan the engagement (certainly no surprise here).
- Evaluate management's assessment process. (Note the recurring theme of "assessment as a process.")
- Obtain an understanding of the company's internal control over financial reporting.
- Test and evaluate the design effectiveness of the company's internal control over financial reporting. (The key term here is "design effectiveness." This is the normal review of the design of the internal controls.)
- Test and evaluate the operating effectiveness of the company's internal control over financial reporting. (The key term here is "operating effectiveness." This is the validation that the controls are actually working as designed.)
- Form an opinion on the effectiveness of the company's internal control over financial reporting. (This is the culmination of the testing and involves writing the audit report and presenting the audit findings.)

This is not a sequential process. Some, if not most, of these steps will be conducted concurrently.

Here, in ¶ 27, the PCAOB reiterates the importance of materiality and reasonable assurance: "The auditor must plan and perform the audit to obtain reasonable assurance that deficiencies that, individually or in the aggregate, would represent material weaknesses are identified. Thus, *the audit is not designed to detect deficiencies in internal control over financial reporting that, individually or in the aggregate, are less severe than a material weakness.*" (Emphasis added.)

Auditing Standard Paragraphs: ¶s 27–141

See Also Auditing Standard Paragraph: ¶ 145

Persons Affected:

Management, Auditors

Effect:

The audit of internal control over financial reporting must be done in conjunction with an audit of the financial statements. All of the traditional auditing standards and considerations are applicable to this auditing standard as well.

Action:

Auditors should apply all of the general and applicable fieldwork standards that would be appropriate to an audit of financial statements to an audit of internal control over financial reporting.

Rules and Regulations Cited:

See ¶ 109.1–¶ 109.8.2 of this discussion for rules and regulations cited.

¶ 109.1. Applying General, Fieldwork, and Reporting Standards

In April 2003, the PCAOB adopted the preexisting GAAS on an interim basis so that the auditing industry would not be without standards while the PCAOB goes through the lengthy process of adopting its own auditing standards (see PCAOB Rule 3200T). Thus, in this standard, the PCAOB made the existing basic GAAS requirements for auditors applicable to the audit of internal control over financial reporting. At a primary level the PCAOB requires that auditors be technically trained and competent. They must also act independently in fact and appearance. In addition, auditors must exercise due professional care, which includes exercising adequate skepticism during the audit.

Auditing Standard Paragraphs: ¶s 30–38

See Also Auditing Standard Paragraphs: ¶s 22–23

Persons Affected:

Auditors

Effect:

All of the traditional general auditing standards and considerations are applicable to an audit of internal control over financial reporting.

Action:

Auditors can leverage existing skills and methods.

Rules and Regulations Cited:

AU Section 150, *Generally Accepted Auditing Standards*; 17 CFR §210.2-01 (Rule 2-01 of Regulation S-X).

¶ 109.1.1. Technical Training and Proficiency

The PCAOB provides a requirement that auditors who perform audits of internal control over financial reporting must be technically trained and proficient on the topic of internal control over financial reporting. However, the standard does not specify what constitutes technical proficiency. Given the adoption of the COSO framework as the basis for internal control over financial reporting, the PCAOB appears to defer to the continuing education industry to provide guidance as to what constitutes adequate training on the COSO framework.

Auditing Standard Paragraph: ¶ 31

Persons Affected:

Auditors

Effect:

The auditor must have competence in the subject matter of internal control over financial reporting.

Action:

Auditors must obtain training in the subject matter of internal control over financial reporting prior to commencing audits of internal control over financial reporting. Auditors should be well-versed in the COSO framework.

Rules and Regulations Cited:

None cited.

¶ 109.1.2. Independence

Section 201 of the Sarbanes-Oxley Act provides a list of non-audit services that audit firms are prohibited from providing to their audit clients, including "management functions" and "internal audit outsourcing services." The gist of Section 201 is generally construed to be that there is an inherent conflict of interest present in the situation where an auditor provides certain services to its audit clients. An example of this was Enron, where Arthur Anderson provided internal audit services as well as external audit services. So it is somewhat difficult to understand why the PCAOB wrote specific language into ¶s 32 through 35 that specifically allows audit firms to provide internal control services to their audit clients with audit committee pre-approval.

Perhaps the PCAOB was under pressure from issuers to allow their audit firms to tell them, in a lot of detail, what they needed to do for that same auditor to provide them an unqualified opinion on internal control over financial reporting. One would think that, since there are only four large public accounting firms providing the lion's share of audit services, the internal control consulting work would be interchangeable. That is, an issuer could get guidance on internal control from one audit firm and that guidance would pass the audit of any other audit firm. But perhaps that is not the case. Public companies may have been intent on being able to receive guidance on how to construct internal controls by their same audit firm that was going to audit those internal controls.

The PCAOB does limit the scope and approval parameters of the auditor's internal control engagement, however. Under the Sarbanes-Oxley Act, all non-audit professional services provided by the auditor must be preapproved by the audit committee, and this requirement is reiterated in the auditing standard. The PCAOB seeks to limit the role of the auditor in non-audit, internal control-related services by requiring that:

- The auditor must not function in the role of management and must not audit his or her own work.
- Management must be extensively and actively involved and cannot delegate responsibility.
- The audit committee must pre-approve the internal control-related services provided by the auditor.
- The auditor and the audit committee must diligently review the nature and extent of the services provided in order to maintain the appropriate level of auditor independence.
- Management's acceptance of responsibility for documentation and testing performed by the auditor is not enough to satisfy the independence requirements.

In contrast, there are also indications that the PCAOB sought to give auditors substantial control over the design and implementation of the internal controls over financial reporting. The standard does not preclude the auditor from making "substantive recommendations as to how management may improve the design or operation of the company's internal controls as a by-product of an audit." (¶ 32.)

Auditing Standard Paragraphs: ¶s 32–35

Persons Affected:

Management, Audit Committee Members, Auditors

Effect:

The auditor must not function in the role of management and must not audit his or her own work, but may provide substantive recommendations regarding the design or operation of internal control over financial reporting as a by-product of the audit.

Action:

Management should remain actively involved in the design, documentation, and testing of internal control over financial reporting and must not delegate all responsibility for these matters to the auditor. Audit committees must pre-approve internal control-related services provided by the company's auditor. Auditors and audit committee members should be vigilant about any appearance of compromised auditor independence. Auditors may provide internal control services that are pre-approved by the audit committee.

Rules and Regulations Cited:

AU Section 150, *Generally Accepted Auditing Standards*; 17 CFR §210.2-01 (Rule 2-01 of Regulation S-X).

Suggested References:

"Disclosures Made to Audit Committees Regarding Matters of Independence," *Accounting and Auditing Disclosure Manual* § 107.

"Accountants' Independence," *Handbook of SEC Accounting and Disclosure* § 12.

"Accountants' Independence," *SEC Accounting and Reporting Manual* § 14.03.

"Guidance on the Application of the Commission's New Rules for Auditor Independence," *SEC Accounting and Reporting Update* 2003-37 (August 2003).

"Auditor Independence and Related Matters," *SEC Accounting and Reporting Update* 2003-08 (February 2003).

¶ 109.1.3. Due Professional Care

The auditing standard requires that auditors exercise the same standards of professional skepticism and due professional care in an audit of internal control over financial reporting as that required in an audit of financial statements. Professional skepticism is one of the key reasons that an auditor probably should not be involved in providing internal control services for an audit client. If the auditor has substantial input into the design and implementation of internal controls over financial reporting, regardless of the level of management's involvement, the auditor is inherently less likely to have sufficient professional skepticism when auditing those same controls.

Auditing Standard Paragraph: ¶ 36

Persons Affected:

Auditors

Effect:

Auditors must exercise professional skepticism in an audit of internal control over financial reporting.

Action:

The auditor must conduct a critical assessment of the work that management has performed in evaluating and testing controls.

Rules and Regulations Cited:

None cited.

¶ 109.1.4. Fieldwork and Reporting Standards

Rather than relying on existing standards of fieldwork and reporting, the PCAOB states that such standards as they apply to an audit of internal control over financial reporting are established by this auditing standard, and that the concept of materiality should guide the application of the general and fieldwork standards.

Auditing Standard Paragraphs: ¶s 37–38

See Also Auditing Standard Paragraphs: ¶s 22–23

Persons Affected:

Auditors

Effect:

The fieldwork and reporting standards for an audit of internal control over financial reporting are established by this auditing standard.

Action:

The auditor should carefully review the fieldwork and reporting requirements outlined in this auditing standard, and should apply the concept of materiality when following the general and fieldwork standards.

Rules and Regulations Cited:

None cited.

¶ 109.2. Planning the Engagement

Paragraph 39 of the auditing standard employs nearly the same language as the first general fieldwork standard in AT Section 101, *Attest Engagements*, when it says, "The audit of internal control over financial reporting should be properly planned and assistants, if any, are to be properly supervised." The PCAOB provides additional guidance that the auditor should take into consideration in planning the audit of internal control over financial reporting. These considerations include:

- Information about the company's internal controls gained during other engagements.

- Information about the company's industry (e.g., financial reporting practices, economic conditions, laws and regulations, and technological changes) and any legal or regulatory matters of which the company is aware.

- How the company conducts its business (e.g., its organization, operating characteristics, capital structure, and distribution methods) and any recent changes in the company, its operations, or its internal control over financial reporting.

- The number of significant business locations or units, including management's documentation and monitoring of controls over such locations or business units.

- Management's process for assessing the effectiveness of the company's internal control over financial reporting.

- The type and extent of available evidence related to the effectiveness of the company's internal control over financial reporting.

- Internal control deficiencies previously communicated to the audit committee or management.

- Preliminary judgments about materiality, risk, and other factors relating to the determination of material weaknesses, as well as the effectiveness of the company's internal control over financial reporting.

Auditing Standard Paragraph: ¶ 39

See Also Auditing Standard Paragraphs: Appendix B, ¶s B1–B17

Persons Affected:

Auditors

Effect:

The guidance on planning the audit engagement is very similar to existing guidance in the existing audit literature, with specific details added with regard to internal control over financial reporting.

Action:

When planning the audit engagement, auditors are required to consider various aspects of a company's internal controls and operations, management's assessment of internal control effectiveness, and preliminary judgments about the company's controls and levels of risk.

Rules and Regulations Cited:

None cited.

¶ 109.3. Evaluating Management's Assessment Process

The guidance provided in ¶s 40 through 46 of the auditing standard is incremental to that in the existing audit literature, but also provides a detailed list of what elements management should consider when preparing an assessment of the company's internal control over financial reporting. The guidance lays out some of the areas that management should address in the assessment process. This includes determining which controls should be tested, such as controls over relevant assertions related to all significant accounts and disclosures in the financial statements. Some specific areas where controls need to be tested include:

- *Controls over initiating, recording, processing, and reporting significant accounts and disclosures and related assertions embodied in the financial statements.* This includes the normal consolidation processes where financial statements get rolled up.

- *Controls over the selection and application of accounting policies that are in conformity with GAAP.* All policies and procedures should be in conformance with GAAP. GAAP conformance is not usually the issue. The more common issue is the consistency of policies across operating divisions of large companies. For instance; all divisions may use a loss reserve, but most companies usually can be found to have a wide variety of detail variations within the application of that common policy. One division may reserve 1 percent of inventory as a loss reserve, while a separate though similar division may reserve 3 percent of inventory as a loss reserve.

- *Antifraud programs and controls.* This would also include the procedures that the company uses to allow employees to report suspected accounting improprieties.

- *Controls, including IT general controls, on which other controls are dependent.* This is typically the weakest of all audit validation areas. Auditors typically take the majority of the accounting system controls for granted. There is no way for the auditor to test each and every IT general control. It is important for management to include this information in the internal control assessment.

- *Controls over significant nonroutine and nonsystematic transactions, such as accounts involving judgments and estimates.* This presents a significant problem for auditors. The evaluation of the accounting judgments that support the largest nonroutine transactions is simply beyond the capability of some auditors, given time and training requirements. Perhaps the PCAOB should have either established a minimum documentation standard that allowed for audit management review of all accounting judgments or put some sort of minimum experience requirement in place so that the audit firms could not send inexperienced auditors to evaluate accounting judgments and estimates. Traditionally, problems associated with failed audits can frequently be traced to either the failure of an inexperienced auditor to identify an accounting problem or the failure of that same inexperienced auditor to properly document the judgment for the accounting entry so that members of the audit supervisory team could review and validate the underlying judgment. Clearly, this area of the audit of internal control over financial reporting should be treated with extra care and scrutiny.

- *The company-level control environment.* This includes the COSO objectives discussed in ¶ 108 of this discussion and in auditing standard ¶s 24–26.

- *Controls over the period-end financial reporting process (both quarterly and annual), including controls over procedures used to enter transaction totals into the general ledger; to initiate, record, and process journal entries in the general ledger; and to record recurring and nonrecurring adjustments to the financial statements.* This is meant to address the timing of transactions. Traditionally, firms have been able to pull revenue from later periods into the current period as well as shift expenses from the current period to later periods. The controls over the period-end financial reporting process are critical to controlling the proper timing of financial

---

reporting. These controls tend to require testing of the accounting systems. The accounting system must be tested to see what abilities are available to the firm to backdate and postdate transactions.

The auditing standard also takes into account the COSO framework's risk assessment strategy by requiring the auditor to determine whether management has evaluated the likelihood that failure of any particular control will result in a misstatement and the degree to which other controls, if effective, would achieve the same control objectives. This step allows the auditor to assess the risk associated with a particular internal control failure. In the event that other controls compensate for a possible failure of a single, specific control, the odds become much lower that a misstatement could occur. What the auditor and management should be looking for then is overlapping and compensating controls. Overlap and compensation should be built into the internal controls over financial reporting.

The auditor also needs to review the process management uses to determine the locations or business units it includes in its assessment. This is covered in detail in Appendix B of the auditing standard, which mandates tests that are to be performed by the auditor when a company has multiple locations or business units. (See ¶ 118 of this discussion for more on Appendix B.)

For each and every control tested, the auditor needs to assess management's design of the control. The assessment of the design of the control needs to consider at a minimum:

- The likely effectiveness of the control to detect or prevent the error or fraud.
- The capability of the control to withstand an attempt to defeat it.
- The ability of other controls to detect that this control was defeated or to compensate for the control's failure.

The auditor should also determine whether management has evaluated the operating effectiveness of the controls—whether they are actually working as designed. The standard allows management to rely on the testing of controls by others, such as internal audit, when looking at operating effectiveness. In addition, as part of the auditor's evaluation of management's assessment of internal control, the auditor is expected to obtain an understanding of the results of procedures performed by others, because those results are part of the basis of management's assessment.

Management should determine the magnitude and likelihood of occurrence of any control deficiencies discovered during its assessment, and is expected to evaluate whether they are significant deficiencies or material weaknesses and report these findings to the company's external auditor. The auditor is required by the standard to evaluate whether management has included this information in the control assessment.

The standard specifically states in ¶ 41 that management "cannot use the auditor's procedures as part of the basis for its assessment of the effectiveness of internal control over financial reporting." Therefore, while management may base its assessment in part on the internally performed procedures, such as testing done by internal audit, they cannot use the results of the external audit of internal control over financial reporting as evidence for their own assessment.

Auditing Standard Paragraphs: ¶s 40–46

See Also Auditing Standard Paragraphs: ¶s 49, 53, 138, Appendix B, ¶s B1–B29, Appendix C, ¶s C1–C6

Persons Affected:

Management, Internal Auditors, Auditors

Effect:

The standard outlines what elements of a company's internal control structure should have been addressed by management in its assessment of internal control over financial reporting.

Action:

The auditor must examine sufficient evidence and obtain an understanding of management's process for assessing the effectiveness of the company's internal control over financial reporting. Management should ensure that its assessment of internal control over financial reporting addresses the elements that the auditor is expected to cover in its audit of management's assessment.

Rules and Regulations Cited:

None cited.

Suggested References:

"Management Internal Control Reports Over Financial Reporting," *Handbook of SEC Accounting and Disclosure* § 18.

"Management Internal Control Reports and Related Certification Matters," *SEC Accounting and Reporting Update* 2003-29 (June 2003).

"Internal Control," *Handbook of Accounting and Auditing* § B4.

"Reports on Internal Control," *Accounting and Auditing Disclosure Manual* § 90.

"Section 404 Compliance: Meeting the Challenges," *Internal Auditing* (July/August 2003).

"SEC Finalizes Rules on Internal Control Reports," *Internal Auditing Report* (July 2003).

"Management's Responsibility for Internal Control Under Section 404," *Bank Auditing and Accounting Report* (March 2004).

¶ 109.3.1. Management's Documentation

The auditor must review the documentation gathered by management for its assessment of the company's internal control over financial reporting.

Management's evidence should include documentation of the design of controls over relevant assertions related to all significant accounts and disclosures in the financial statements. These controls should clearly incorporate the five COSO components (control environment, risk assessment, control activities, information and communication, and monitoring).

Information should also be included in the documentation about how significant transactions are initiated, recorded, processed, and reported. The best way for a company to accomplish this is to construct uniform documentation of policies and procedures. Without a consistent and complete format, the issuer will find it difficult to assemble adequate documentation of its internal control over financial reporting.

Management's documentation should include enough information about the flow of transactions to identify where material misstatements due to error or fraud could occur, i.e., control points. However, it may not be enough for an auditor to simply understand the transactional flows where material misstatements or fraud could occur. This is because fraud and material misstatements can occur anywhere in any of the transactional flows. Large, material misstatements can be broken down into a large number of small transactions and scattered across a number of different transactional flows. By only looking at large transactions or specific transactional flows, the auditor invariably excludes massive quantities of transactional activities from consideration. A financial fraud can occur in any account and can consist of any number of small, medium, or large individual transactions. The company's risk assessment should address this possibility.

Management must document the company's controls that are specifically designed to prevent or detect fraud, including who performs the controls and the related segregation of duties. Detective controls generally include management-level reviews of accounting transactions. Most detective controls do not operate at the transaction level, but rather at the account level. Detective controls made up of management reviews, while often designed properly, are rarely performed on a routine basis in practice. In large corporations management reviews rarely, if ever, go up more than one level. This creates a problem because the auditor has no way to validate that the controls are being performed on a routine basis. But the even larger problem is that the purpose of the control itself, to prevent financial fraud, is sometimes easily circumvented by the person who is supposed to be performing the control. This issue underscores the importance of the segregation of duties. If the financial manager is perpetrating a financial fraud and that same manager is responsible for reviewing the transactions at the account level, there is almost no way that an internal or external auditor can obtain any verification that the manager performed the control correctly.

Controls over period-end financial reporting processes and over safeguarding of assets must also be documented by management. The period-end controls are intended to ensure that revenue is not pulled in from later periods and expenses are not pushed out to later periods. Accounting and auditing practices are fairly effective at protecting cash, merchandise, inventory, and fixed assets. Where accounting and auditing have been substantially ineffective is safeguarding financial and transactional assets like accounting reserves, booked revenues, work order systems, accruals, stock options, contracts, intellectual property, and derivatives. The complexity of these types of assets is such that even experienced lawyers, accountants, and auditors can debate what constitutes adequate documentation or even what that documentation means. One could surmise that this is what happened at Enron. Enron's lawyers created very complex special purpose entities. Unless very skilled lawyers were involved in the audit, it is unlikely that even the partner Anderson had on the engagement could have accurately interpreted the impact of those legal entities. The point is, legal documentation can sometimes obfuscate the underlying purpose of the document. What auditors should do when they encounter complex legal assets is consult legal counsel to professionally and objectively assess those legal assets.

Management's documentation must also demonstrate the results of management's own testing and evaluation of internal control over financial reporting.

Many large organizations are conducting their management assessment of the effectiveness of their internal control over financial reporting by relying on their internal audit departments to document and test controls. If the auditor is required to review management's assessment, then management is required to open up its internal audit results to the external auditors. This can create a problem at companies where internal audit departments, during the normal course of an internal audit, uncover significant problems that management has no intention of disclosing to its auditors but instead intends to remedy prior to the audit of internal control over financial reporting. This, and other requirements in this auditing standard that require the auditor to review the results of internal audits, indicates why larger corporations should consider separating their internal control function from their internal audit function. The internal control function within an organization should function on behalf of the operational accounting departments and "clear the way" for internal audit. In this way, the significant deficiencies in internal control over financial reporting can be identified and corrected prior to the internal audit. The alternative is that the traditional internal audit will find these deficiencies and, even though they may be corrected before the external audit, they would nevertheless have to be disclosed to the external auditors. When the external auditors come in contact with these deficiencies, even though they may have been corrected, the auditors would have to document and possibly disclose them as changes in internal control that oc-curred during the interim period.

The auditing standard provides that documentation can take many forms (e.g., electronic, paper, and other media) and will include many different types of information (e.g., policy manuals, process models, flowcharts, job descriptions, documents, and forms). There is not any one particular form of documentation required, and the extent of documentation is not stipulated. Here the PCAOB squandered an opportunity to standardize the chaos that constitutes most audit workpapers. The standard could have provided some specific requirements for documentation, and this would have made both management's assessment and the audit process much more predictable. However, this oversight is good in some respects. Smaller and less complex organizations are not required to do the same level of compliance work as larger and more complex organizations. Nonetheless, by leaving the minimum documentation requirements open to interpretation, the PCAOB also left the requirements open to interpretation.

Inadequate documentation of internal control over financial reporting is grounds for the auditor to find that management's assessment is invalid or, at least, that it cannot attest to management's assertions. However, the auditor can conclude that the deficiency is "only a deficiency" or that it constitutes a significant deficiency or material weakness. The standard leaves management and the auditor one "out" here, in that the auditor can determine that management can demonstrate the adequacy of the monitoring component of internal control over financial reporting in the absence of adequate documentation. According to the COSO framework, the monitoring component is "accomplished through ongoing monitoring activities, separate evaluations or a combination of the two. Ongoing monitoring occurs in the course of operations. It includes regular management and supervisory activities, and other actions personnel take in performing their duties. The scope and frequency of separate evaluations will depend primarily on an assessment of risks and the effectiveness of ongoing monitoring procedures. Internal control deficiencies should be reported upstream, with serious matters reported to top management and the board." (COSO, *Internal Control—Integrated Framework*, p. 5.)

By allowing the monitoring component to affect whether the auditor decides that inadequate documentation results in a significant deficiency or material weakness, the standard seems to imply that management can claim, in lieu of documentation, that it checked the accounting results that were incorporated into the financial statements. This is fortunate for both management and the auditors in that it allows the auditor to attest to management's assessment even when management did not adequately document their own assessment, but to some it might appear as a potential loophole in the otherwise strict documentation requirements.

Another alternative provided in the auditing standard is that, given a shortage of documentation, the auditor can limit the scope of the audit to only that which can be validated. This is an unlikely outcome however, because it would result in the auditor essentially withholding an unqualified audit opinion.

Auditing Standard Paragraphs: ¶s 42–46

See Also Auditing Standard Paragraphs: ¶s 49, 53, 138, Appendix C, ¶s C1–C6

Persons Affected:

 Management, Internal Auditors, Auditors

Effect:

The auditor is required to evaluate the adequacy of management's documentation in support of its assessment of internal control over financial reporting.

Action:

Management should become familiar with the documentation requirements provided by the standard. The auditor must review the issuer's documentation of management's assessment of internal control over financial reporting. Given a substantial absence of documentation of internal control over financial reporting on the part of the issuer, the auditor must withhold the attestation or limit the scope of the audit of internal control over financial reporting.

Rules and Regulations Cited:

None cited.

Suggested References:

 "Management Internal Control Reports Over Financial Reporting," *Handbook of SEC Accounting and Disclosure* § I8.

 "Management Internal Control Reports and Related Certification Matters," *SEC Accounting and Reporting Update* 2003-29 (June 2003).

 "Internal Control," *Handbook of Accounting and Auditing* § B4.

 "Reports on Internal Control," *Accounting and Auditing Disclosure Manual* § 90.

 "SEC Finalizes Rules on Internal Control Reports," *Internal Auditing Report* (July 2003).

 "Management's Responsibility for Internal Control Under Section 404," *Bank Auditing and Accounting Report* (March 2004).

¶ 109.4. Obtaining an Understanding of Internal Control Over Financial Reporting

The standard requires that the auditor perform specific inquiries, inspect company documents, observe the application of specific controls, and trace transactions through the company's accounting systems in order to obtain an understanding of the design of specific controls.

The standard requires the auditor to make "inquiries of appropriate management, supervisory, and staff personnel." (¶ 47.) This procedure highlights the need for organizations to conduct training for all personnel, both accounting and operational, who perform any administrative-type functions that could have an impact on the financial statements. If the issuer does not educate all of its administrative personnel about internal controls—including their design, function, and implementation—there is a chance that the auditor will encounter personnel who, even though they may be doing the right things, are unable to provide the right answers to the auditor's questions. The likely minimum result of any incorrect answer is further testing in that area and increased audit costs to the issuer. The maximum result is that the auditor might uncover some significant deficiency that was somehow undetected by management. Education serves additional purposes as well. If all administrative personnel are trained about internal control, they can help the issuer identify and correct real internal control deficiencies. Most firms' compliance efforts are limited primarily to accounting and finance personnel in their organizations, while the audit will surely encompass other administrative functions.

The documentation requirements discussed in ¶ 109.3.1 (and addressed in ¶s 42 through 46 of the auditing standard) tie in to the requirement that auditors inspect company documents in order to obtain an understanding of the design of specific controls. Most firms are adept at maintaining policy manuals and records like purchase order authorizations. Those same firms are not always as adept at documenting processes and transactional flows. Especially important for large, complex organizations is documentation of how their financial statements are rolled up and consolidated.

The auditor is required to observe the application of specific controls. This involves validation testing that the controls are actually being performed. Education will pay off handsomely for the issuer in this area. If the administrative personnel have been trained correctly prior to an audit, they will understand what the auditor is looking for and will be much more able to provide correct answers and demonstrate the effective implementation of the controls in question.

The auditor must trace specific transactions through the information system relevant to financial reporting. Interestingly, the PCAOB only requires the examination of systems that it deems relevant to financial reporting and not the equally important transactional systems where transactions are created. More critically, the PCAOB cannot escape the historical GAAS focus on examining individual transactions. Some would argue that the PCAOB should have shifted some of the focus to large groups of transactions. For example, ERP systems at large organizations process millions of transactions per day and could potentially suffer from weak internal controls that would not be caught during this type of audit process.

This part of the standard reiterates the requirement that the auditor assess the company's internal controls based on the COSO model of five components: control environment, risk assessment, control activities, information and communication, and monitoring.

Control Environment

The COSO report includes the following definition of control environment: "The control environment sets the tone of an organization, influencing the control consciousness of its people. It is the foundation for all other components of internal control, providing discipline and structure. Control environment factors include integrity, ethical values and competence of the entity's people; management's philosophy and operating style: the way management assigns authority and responsibility, and organizes and develops its people; and the attention and direction provided by the board of directors." (COSO, *Internal Control—Integrated Framework,* p. 23.) This is the organizational context that influences the effectiveness of all of the other internal control elements. The primary tangible tools and techniques for articulating the "tone at the top" are policies, procedures, and codes of conduct. Some would refer to these sorts of controls as "hard controls," as opposed to the related but less tangible "soft controls" such as integrity, ethical values, and an expectation of competence.

According to the COSO framework, the functional categories of the control environment include:

- *Integrity and ethical values.* These are "essential elements of the control environment," according to the COSO report. (COSO, *Internal Control—Integrated Framework,* p. 23.) Unfortunately, in practice companies often espouse integrity and ethical values but reward financial results (e.g., quarterly results via stock options). Internal control is nothing more than applied integrity. If a company truly values integrity and ethics, then in practice, it would remove the temptations to act unethically. Regarding incentives and temptations, the COSO report points out that employees "may engage in dishonest, illegal or unethical acts simply because their organizations give them strong incentives or temptations to do so . . . . Removing or reducing these incentives and temptations can go a long way toward diminishing undesirable behavior." (COSO, *Internal Control—Integrated Framework,* pp. 24–25.) Auditors should look for the presence of financial rewards for financial fraud, no matter how well-intentioned.

- *Commitment to competence.* "Competence should reflect the knowledge and skills needed to accomplish tasks that define the individual's job."(COSO, *Internal Control—Integrated Framework,* p. 26.) In practice, once a company has filled the specialized jobs, the key leadership posts are sometimes based solely on politics. The key component of competence that a firm should consider in selecting executives is the honesty and integrity of the candidate. Ideally, the auditor could look for a pattern of honesty and integrity in the executives, but this is clearly not part of a traditional audit.

- *Management's philosophy and operating style.* The key point related to management's philosophy and operating style is the selection and promotion of either a more liberal or more conservative accounting strategy. The auditor needs to understand what policy the issuer has selected. They have either selected a liberal or conservative policy set. In the alternative that they have selected neither, then by default they have selected an ultra-liberal set of accounting policies because, in fact, they have none at all. Policy development should be based on one approach and consistently applied over the long term. This is one of the top issues in internal control that the auditor should consider. In practice, some firms adopt liberal or conservative primary accounting approaches based on what suits them in a particular quarter. If they are having a bad quarter and need earnings, they adopt a policy with more liberal interpretations and greater management flexibility. If they are having a good quarter, they adopt a policy with a more conservative interpretation that lets them build reserves up for the bad times. Unfortunately, this topic is not addressed head on in the COSO framework. From an internal control standpoint, management's philosophy and operating style should mean that one of the approaches should be selected and applied consistently year-over-year so that financial statements are comparable. This failure to address the long-term variability of primary accounting approaches, either liberal or conservative, and the requirement for comparability of financial statements year-over-year is one of the largest single failures of the COSO framework.

- *Organizational structure.* The COSO framework discusses direct versus indirect or matrix management styles and their relative levels of control. Direct styles yield greater control. The auditor should evaluate which style is used by management. However, an organizational structure with more direct control does not necessarily mean a more conservative approach to accounting. Any organizational structure can be paired with either a good or bad internal control structure.

- *Assignment of authority and responsibility.* "The control environment is greatly influenced by the extent to which individuals recognize that they will be held accountable." (COSO, *Internal Control—Integrated Framework,* p. 29.) One of the major problems contributing to financial fraud is the rotation of executives through division-level management jobs because of the inherent lack of accountability. Auditors would be wise to consider it a red flag if a company's executives are rotated to different positions on a regular basis.

- *Human resources policies and practices.* The COSO framework indicates that effective human resource policies and practices can be used to hire ethical people and educate them about the ethics policies of the firm. The auditor should review what kinds of background checks are done when executives and others who can impact financial results are hired. A company's training practices should be scrutinized—is an ongoing education program in place?

As the COSO report points out, "Since no two operating divisions or foreign or domestic subsidiaries are managed in the same way, it is unlikely that control environments will be the same . . . . The impact of an ineffective control environment could be far reaching, possibly resulting in a financial loss . . . or business failure." (COSO, *Internal Control—Integrated Framework,* p. 30.) In terms of Section 404 compliance, this means that internal controls can vary from site to site and still be considered adequate. This makes compliance much easier for the issuer. From a risk perspective though, it means that the executives either must accept the differences in the internal controls or try to figure them out and bring them into alignment. These differences can represent a major risk. Auditors will have difficulty auditing an organization with varying controls across sites, because they would be required to relearn the internal control structure for each division. The risk is that an adequate understanding of internal controls is buried in the complexity and that a substantial financial problem could exist. Regarding the control environment, the auditing standard requires that "Weaknesses in the control environment should cause the auditor to alter the nature, timing, or extent of tests of operating effectiveness that otherwise would have been performed in the absence of the weaknesses." (¶ 49.)

Risk Assessment

Regarding risk assessment, the COSO report states, "Every entity faces a variety of risks from external and internal sources that must be assessed. A precondition to risk assessment is establishment of objectives, linked at different levels and internally consistent. Risk assessment is the identification and analysis of relevant risks to achievement of objectives, forming a basis for determining how the risks should be managed. Because economic, industry, regulatory and operating conditions will continue to change, mechanisms are needed to identify and deal with the special risks associated with change." (COSO, *Internal Control—Integrated Framework,* p. 33.)

There are two major parts of this definition. The first deals with objectives and the risk that the firm will not achieve those objectives. Issuers will essentially be in compliance with the objectives portion of the COSO framework as it relates to internal control over financial reporting if they have decent budgeting systems and methods. The auditor is required to assess the budgeting and reporting systems as part of its examination. Typically, the budgeting variance and reporting systems constitute the primary tools of management's internal control over financial reporting. The second part of the definition deals with risk assessment. This section of COSO compliance is going to be the primary activity that most issuers will need to undertake to comply with Section 404 of the Sarbanes-Oxley Act.

Most firms know where the financial risks lie within their firms but have not documented them for a variety of reasons. One reason is because they do not want to provide evidence to potential litigants. Another is that these problems may have been hidden from external auditors, perhaps intentionally, for many years. Alternatively, management may think they know where their problems are but are not sure. Now that executives face the new risk of, perhaps, going to jail if a financial fraud is found, they are more anxious to understand what sort of latent financial problems their firm possesses. The solution for the issuer is to create an internal control structure that addresses internal control weakness remediation prior to the internal audit. The auditing standard requires the auditor to review the results of the internal audit. Management's objective is to address all concerns regarding weak internal controls even before the internal auditors can find them.

The external auditors are also driving risk assessment because they do not know where the risks are within the client firm. The auditors, naturally, want to know what the problems are and which internal controls deserve more careful scrutiny than others. A proper risk assessment will identify the significant accounts and disclosures and related assertions that affect the accuracy of the financial statements, and will highlight controls designed to prevent and detect errors and fraud.

Control Activities

The COSO report states, "Control activities are the policies and procedures that help ensure management directives are carried out. They help ensure that necessary actions are taken to address risks to achievement of the entity's objectives. Control activities occur throughout the organization, at all levels and in all functions. They include a range of activities as diverse as approvals, authorizations, verifications, reconciliations, reviews of operating performance, security of assets and segregation of duties." (COSO, *Internal Control—Integrated Framework*, p. 49.)

Portions of the control activities interrelate most closely with the risk assessment. That is, the risk assessment reviews the control activities, looking for missing or ineffective controls. For most companies concerned with this auditing standard and Section 404 certification, the control activities, or "control points" as they are generally called, will usually require some documentation and remediation.

According to the COSO framework, control activities can be loosely categorized into the following groups:

- *Top level reviews.* These are high-level budget and operating performance reviews. All large companies have some kinds of budget and operating reviews. From a compliance perspective, this should not be an issue for most issuers. Auditors will find that sufficient documentation exists and that management uses these reports as detective controls.

- *Direct functional or activity management.* This refers to management reviews of transaction processing. This is one of the hardest areas for an auditor to validate. Even given checklists, the auditor should keep in mind that the accounting management at the operating division level is rarely second-guessed by upper management, especially at the transaction level.

- *Information processing.* Most issuers will not have a problem with the information processing areas related to this auditing standard and Section 404 certification. Unfortunately, both the auditing standard and the COSO report are a little bit dated in this area. References in the COSO report to technologies such as CASE, end user computing, artificial intelligence, minicomputers, distributing data and computer power, job set-up and scheduling, and job control language were out-of-date relatively shortly after the report's publication in 1992. Personal computers and PC accounting software had begun to displace much of the mainframe and minicomputer accounting software. PCs attached to computer networks then rapidly replaced these minicomputers and mainframes. It has been suggested that computer technology has not advanced the cause of internal control or either internal or external auditing in many years. This auditing standard and the COSO framework could have been updated, as some of the public comment letters suggested during the proposal phase, to reflect the changes in accounting software and technology prior to acceptance as the standard by the PCAOB.

- *Physical controls.* With regard to physical controls, the COSO report states, "Equipment, inventories, securities, cash and other assets are secured physically, and periodically counted and compared with amounts shown on control records." (COSO, *Internal Control—Integrated Framework,* p. 50.) Accounting policies and procedures typically excel at these types of physical controls. Except in some extreme examples of fraud and blatant oversight failures, these controls are usually not a major problem for issuers.

- *Performance indicators.* The COSO framework describes, in very general terms, indicators like purchase price variance, percentage of rush orders, and returns, but does not define the specific details that should be familiar to most auditors. Given the variety of industry practices and the vagueness of the COSO framework on this topic, it is probably not very likely that companies will encounter many compliance issues based on this category. Unfortunately, issuers will probably face a wide variety of enforcement interpretations from various audit firms. Some auditors may insist on strict interpretations while others may be quite liberal. The PCAOB provides no specific guidance on this topic. What the framework is alluding to here has, in the last 10 years, become known as key performance indicators (KPIs). This term is especially well-known in the fields of business process reengineering and total quality management. This sort of management reporting is the easiest of all corporate reporting to manipulate. Furthermore, within this class of easily manipulated management reporting, KPIs are, by far, the easiest thing to manipulate. KPIs may not be reconciled or even checked for accuracy. They may be more accurately considered as internal marketing literature rather than true indicators of performance. This is because they are not a subset of financial reporting and are not intended for external consumption. Auditors should take into account the intended audience when reviewing management reporting.

- *Segregation of duties.* With regard to the segregation of duties, the COSO report states, "Duties are divided, or segregated, among different people to reduce the risk of error or inappropriate actions." (COSO, *Internal Control—Integrated Framework,* p. 51.) Again, here is an example of a control activity where accounting policies and procedures typically excel. These controls are generally well understood and checked.

According to the PCAOB, during an audit of internal control over financial reporting, "the auditor's understanding of control activities encompasses a broader range of accounts and disclosures than what is normally obtained for the financial statement audit." (¶ 49.)

Information and Communication

With respect to information and communication, the COSO report says, "Pertinent information must be identified, captured and communicated in a form and timeframe that enables people to carry out their responsibilities. Information systems produce reports, containing operational, financial and compliance-related information, that make it possible to run and control the business. They deal not only with internally generated data, but also information about external events, activities and conditions necessary to informed business decision-making and external reporting. Effective communication also must occur in a broader sense, flowing down, across and up the organization. All personnel must receive a clear message from top management that control responsibilities must be taken seriously. They must understand their own role in the internal control system, as well as how individual activities relate to the work of others. They must have a means of communicating significant information upstream. There also needs to be effective communication with external parties, such as customers, suppliers, regulators and shareholders." (COSO, *Internal Control—Integrated Framework*, p. 59.)

From an auditing standard perspective, most firms have sufficient internal and external reporting structures to be in compliance. The COSO framework's discussion on this topic describes, in general terms, some of the different types and applications of communications and their relationship to business transactions and financial reporting. The framework also describes, again in general terms, some auditing considerations of information and communication. The guidance is general enough that pretty much anything in written form will pass as documentation. Fortunately there are not any more specific requirements for information and communication systems in the auditing standard. This will make the compliance efforts for this area straightforward.

Monitoring

As the COSO report points out, "Internal control systems need to be monitored—a process that assesses the quality of the system's performance over time. This is accomplished through ongoing monitoring activities, separate evaluations or a combination of the two. Ongoing monitoring occurs in the course of operations. It includes regular management and supervisory activities, and other actions personnel take in performing their duties. The scope and frequency of separate evaluations will depend primarily on an assessment of risks and the effectiveness of ongoing monitoring procedures. Internal control deficiencies should be reported upstream, with serious matters reported to top management and the board." (COSO, *Internal Control—Integrated Framework*, p. 69.)

The key points regarding the auditing standard's stance on monitoring are:

- Ongoing monitoring relies on the existing accounting and management reporting apparatus and requires no additional effort for most issuers. Auditors must, however, review this documentation.
- Separate evaluations are focused on the same risk assessment exercise referenced in the other COSO framework components. The auditor should review the risk assessment done by management.

The COSO framework's requirements are general and, provided a proper risk assessment is done, should not present problems for audit compliance for most issuers. The requirements of the framework are not further clarified or altered very much by the PCAOB's auditing standard. Most issuers with a plethora of management reporting should not have much of a problem complying with the COSO-based requirements in the standard.

It is important that the auditor consider internal controls in conjunction with one another. The combination of company-wide controls is important in the auditor's overall evaluation of management's assessment. Compensating or overlapping controls can affect the impact of a control deficiency that would otherwise rise to the level of significant deficiency or material weakness.

Auditing Standard Paragraphs: ¶s 47–87

Persons Affected:

Management, Auditors

Effect:

Based on the COSO framework, the auditing standard defines specific steps the auditor must perform to evaluate the documentation and establish an understanding of internal control over financial reporting.

Action:

The auditor must perform certain tasks and procedures to evaluate management's documentation and to establish an understanding of the company's internal control over financial reporting. These tasks and procedures follow the model put forth in the COSO framework. Management is expected to implement the five basic COSO components: control environment, risk assessment, control activities, information and communication, and monitoring.

Rules and Regulations Cited:

See ¶ 109.4.1–¶ 109.4.8 of this discussion for rules and regulations cited.

Suggested References:

"Management Internal Control Reports Over Financial Reporting," *Handbook of SEC Accounting and Disclosure* § 18.

"Management Internal Control Reports and Related Certification Matters," *SEC Accounting and Reporting Update* 2003-29 (June 2003).

"Internal Control," *Handbook of Accounting and Auditing* § B4.

"Reports on Internal Control," *Accounting and Auditing Disclosure Manual* § 90.

"Tools and Techniques for Documenting Accounting Systems," *Internal Auditing* (September/October 2003).

"COSO: More Relevant Now Than Ever," *Internal Auditing* (July/August 2003).

"Section 404 Compliance: Meeting the Challenges," *Internal Auditing* (July/August 2003).

"SEC Finalizes Rules on Internal Control Reports," *Internal Auditing Report* (July 2003).

"Management's Responsibility for Internal Control Under Section 404," *Bank Auditing and Accounting Report* (March 2004).

¶ 109.4.1. Identifying Company-Level Controls

The standard itemizes certain types of company-level controls, but qualifies that list by saying that it is not intended to be a complete list, nor is a company required to have all of the company-level controls specified. "However," the standard states, "ineffective company-level controls are a deficiency that will affect the scope of work performed, particularly when a company has multiple locations or business units." (¶ 53.) Company-level controls listed in ¶ 53 of the auditing standard include:

- Controls within the company's control environment, including tone at the top, the assignment of authority and responsibility, consistent policies and procedures, and company-wide programs, such as codes of conduct and fraud prevention, that apply to all locations and business units. (See ¶ 109.4 of this discussion for more on the control environment.)

- Management's risk assessment process. (See ¶ 109.4 of this discussion for more on risk assessment.)

- Centralized processing and controls, including shared service environments.

- Monitoring results of operations. (See ¶ 109.4 of this discussion for more on monitoring.)

- Monitoring other controls, including activities of the internal audit function, the audit committee, and self-assessment programs. This is the not the first mention of self-assessment programs in the auditing standard— it first appears in passing in ¶ 40. Self-assessment programs are so new that many companies do not perform them at this time. The topic of self-assessment, also known as control self-assessment (CSA), is covered in literature published by the Institute of Internal Auditors (IIA). A CSA is somewhat similar to an internal audit that focuses on controls.

- The period-end financial reporting process. (See ¶ 109.3 and ¶ 109.3.1 of this discussion for more on period-end controls.)

- Board-approved policies that address significant business control and risk management practices. Here the PCAOB introduces, for the first time, the concept that the external auditor should review the policies that the company's board of directors has approved to direct how much risk the company bears. Overall, broad, general, non-specific policies that unduly restrict risk would fail an audit review.

Because the company-level controls affect everything else involved in the audit, it is practical that the auditor assess these company-wide controls first. If the company-wide controls appear lax and ineffective, then the auditors should realize that they probably will find lax and ineffective internal controls over financial reporting throughout the organization. However, most companies are more adept and addressing these high-level, qualitative internal control requirements than they are at addressing the low- and intermediate-level, more quantitative internal control requirements.

The auditing standard specifically states in ¶ 54 that, even though the auditor evaluates company-level controls, this evaluation alone is not sufficient for the purpose of expressing an opinion on the effectiveness of a company's internal control over financial reporting. The implication here is that, even if the company-wide controls are judged to be effective, the auditor still must audit other, more specific internal controls over financial reporting.

Auditing Standard Paragraphs: ¶s 52–54

See Also Auditing Standard Paragraphs: ¶s 113–115, Appendix B ¶s B1–B31

Persons Affected:

Management, Internal Auditors, Auditors

Effect:

The auditing standard recommends that auditors test those controls that affect primarily the control environment and pervade all other controls first, i.e., the company-level controls. Auditors should evaluate the results of the evaluation of the company-wide controls when creating the audit plan for the rest of the company's controls over financial reporting.

Action:

Identification and testing of company-level controls by the external auditor is required. Management should ensure that proper documentation of company-wide controls exists.

Rules and Regulations Cited:

None cited.

Suggested Reference:

"IT Governance Institute Publishes IT Internal Controls Guidance," *Internal Auditing Report* (December 2003).

¶ 109.4.2. Evaluating the Effectiveness of the Audit Committee's Oversight of the Company's External Financial Reporting and Internal Control Over Financial Reporting

The auditing standard requires the company's auditor to review and evaluate the effectiveness of the audit committee in its oversight role. This was an issue of some contention during the public comment phase of the proposed standard. Many comments on the proposed standard expressed concern about requiring that the auditor, having been hired and overseen by the audit committee, evaluate the effectiveness of that same audit committee. Some saw this as an apparent conflict of interest. (See the auditing standard's Appendix E, ¶ E61–¶ E69, for a discussion of the comments received and the PCAOB's response.)

Section 301 of the Sarbanes-Oxley Act requires publicly traded firms to establish independent audit committees. In the past, not all companies have had audit committees. Among those that did have audit committees, some were not composed of independent board members. So the Sarbanes-Oxley requirement creates substantial work on the part of some issuers to identify potential independent board members, elect them to the board of directors, and appoint them to the audit committee. Given the effective dates of the legislation, most companies should already have accomplished this by the end of 2003. However some issuers may still be struggling with this requirement. Additionally, among the firms that have been able to address the new requirements, there may still be the question of whether the audit committee oversight function is effective. The company's external auditor must determine and assess what level of documentation is required to validate effective oversight.

Section 301 of the Sarbanes-Oxley Act reads, in part:

(2) RESPONSIBILITIES RELATING TO REGISTERED PUBLIC ACCOUNTING FIRMS—The audit committee of each issuer, in its capacity as a committee of the board of directors, shall be directly responsible for the appointment, compensation, and oversight of the work of any registered public accounting firm employed by that issuer (including resolution of disagreements between management and the auditor regarding financial reporting) for the purpose of preparing or issuing an audit report or related work, and each such registered public accounting firm shall report directly to the audit committee.

(3) INDEPENDENCE

(A) IN GENERAL—Each member of the audit committee of the issuer shall be a member of the board of directors of the issuer, and shall otherwise be independent.

(B) CRITERIA—In order to be considered to be independent for purposes of this paragraph, a member of an audit committee of an issuer may not, other than in his or her capacity as a member of the audit committee, the board of directors, or any other board committee—

(i) accept any consulting, advisory, or other compensatory fee from the issuer; or

(ii) be an affiliated person of the issuer or any subsidiary thereof.

We can briefly compare and contrast the requirements established by Congress via the Sarbanes-Oxley Act to the following regulatory rules adopted by the SEC to comply with the congressional directives. In this particular case, the SEC chose to adopt the rules proposed by the NYSE and NASD instead of writing its own regulations. The auditor will have to evaluate the effectiveness against the requirements of these regulations.

The following is the NYSE regulation as adopted by the SEC (SEC Release No. 34-48745.):

6. Audit Committee

a. Composition

NYSE Sections 303A(6) and 303A(7) would require each NYSE-listed company to have a minimum three-person audit committee composed entirely of directors that meet the independence standards of both NYSE Section 303A(2) and Rule 10A-3 . . . . In addition, the Commentary to NYSE Section 303A(7)(a) would require that each member of the audit committee be financially literate, as such qualification is interpreted by the board in its business judgment, or must become financially literate within a reasonable period of time after his or her appointment to the audit committee. In addition, at least one member of the audit committee would be required to have accounting or related financial management expertise, as the company's board interprets such qualification in its business judgment. The NYSE also proposes to clarify that while the Exchange does not require that a listed company's audit committee include a person who satisfies the definition of audit committee financial expert set forth in Item 401(e) of Regulation S-K (17 CFR §229.401(e)), a board may presume that such a person has accounting or related financial management experience.

If an audit committee member simultaneously serves on the audit committee of more than three public companies, and the listed company does not limit the number of audit committees on which its audit committee members serve, each board would be required to determine that such simultaneous service would not impair the ability of such member to effectively serve on the listed company's audit committee and to disclose such determination.

In summary, the NYSE requires:

- At least a three-person audit committee.
- Financial literacy (this is only vaguely defined).
- At least one financial expert (this is only vaguely defined).

- Specific permission for a single audit committee member to serve on more than three audit committees.

The NYSE was successful in limiting the requirement to state simply that the person must be financially literate or become financially literate at some future, unspecified, date. The auditor should bear this requirement in mind as it deals with the audit committee members.

The NYSE further outlines the audit committee charter and responsibilities (SEC Release No. 34-48745.):

b. Audit Committee Charter and Responsibilities

NYSE Section 303A(7)(c) would require the audit committee of each listed company to have a written audit committee charter that addresses: (i) the committee's purpose; (ii) an annual performance evaluation of the audit committee; and (iii) the duties and responsibilities of the audit committee ("NYSE Audit Committee Charter Provision").

The NYSE Audit Committee Charter Provision provides details as to the duties and responsibilities of the audit committee that must be addressed. These include, at a minimum, those set out in Rule 10A-3(b)(2), (3), (4) and (5), as well as the responsibility to annually obtain and review a report by the independent auditor; discuss the company's annual audited financial statement and quarterly financial statements with management and the independent auditor; discuss the company's earnings press releases, as well as financial information and earnings guidance provided to analysts and rating agencies; discuss policies with respect to risk assessment and risk management; meet separately, periodically, with management, with internal auditors (or other personnel responsible for the internal audit function), and with independent auditors; review with the independent auditors any audit problems or difficulties and management's response; set clear hiring policies for employees or former employees of the independent auditors; and report regularly to the board.

The NYSE also requires the audit committee to "discuss the company's earnings press releases, as well as financial information and earnings guidance provided to analysts and rating agencies." (SEC Release No. 34-48745.) This takes into account that goal of the Sarbanes-Oxley Act to provide oversight of the financial reporting function via the independent audit committee. The auditor should note whether the company's audit committee has reviewed these documents prior to their publication.

The relevant requirements from the Nasdaq are very similar (SEC Release No. 34-48745.):

6. Audit Committee Charter and Responsibilities

NASD Rule 4350(d) would retain the requirement that each issuer adopt a formal written audit committee charter, and the proposed amendment to the rule would require the charter to specify the committee's purpose of overseeing the accounting and financial reporting processes and the audits of the financial statements of the issuer. The written charter also would be required to include specific audit committee responsibilities and authority, as set forth in the proposed amendment to Rule 4350(d)(3). Nasdaq also proposes to state in Interpretive Material to Rule 4350(d) that the written charter set forth the scope of the audit committee's responsibilities and the means by which the committee carries out those responsibilities; the outside auditor's accountability to the committee; and the committee's responsibility to ensure the independence of the outside auditors.

7. Audit Committee Composition

NASD Rule 4350(d) would retain the requirement that each listed issuer have an audit committee composed of at least three members. However, under the proposed requirements, each audit committee member would be required to: (1) be independent, as defined under NASD Rule 4200; (2) meet the criteria for independence set forth in Rule 10A-3 (subject to the exceptions provided in Rule 10A-3(c)); and (3) not have participated in the preparation of the financial statements of the company or any current subsidiary of the company at any time during the past three years, in addition to satisfying the current requirement that the member be able to read and understand fundamental financial statements, including a company's balance sheet, income statement, and cash flow statement ("Nasdaq Audit Committee Provision").

One director who is not independent as defined in NASD Rule 4200 and meets the criteria set forth in Section 10A(m)(3) of the Exchange Act (15 USCS 78j-1) and the rules hereunder, and is not a current officer or employee of the company or a Family Member of such person, may be appointed to the audit committee if the board, under exceptional and limited circumstances, determines that membership on the committee by the individual is required by the best interests of the company and its shareholders, and the board discloses, in the next annual proxy statement subsequent to such determination (or, if the issuer does not file a proxy, in its Form 10-K or 20-F), the nature of the relationship and the reasons for that determination. A member appointed under this exception would not be permitted to serve longer than two years and would not be permitted to chair the audit committee. Nasdaq proposes to add to Interpretive Material the recommendation that an issuer disclose in its annual proxy (or, if the issuer does not file a proxy, in its Form 10-K or 20-F) if any director is deemed independent but falls outside the safe harbor provisions of Rule 10A-3(e)(1)(ii).

In addition, Nasdaq will retain the requirement that at least one member of the audit committee have past employment experience in finance or accounting, requisite professional certification in accounting, or any other comparable experience or background which results in the individual's financial sophistication, including being or having been a chief executive officer, chief financial officer or other senior officer with financial oversight responsibilities.

Nasdaq proposes to delete from the Interpretive Material the discussion relating to determining whether a person is an affiliate solely by virtue of stock ownership.

8. Cure Periods

Nasdaq proposes to add a cure period provision, as follows: (1) if a listed issuer fails to comply with the audit committee composition requirements under Rule 10A-3 and NASD Rule 4350(d)(2), because an audit committee member ceases to be independent for reasons outside the member's reasonable control, the audit committee member could remain on the committee until the earlier of the issuer's next annual shareholders meeting or one year from the occurrence of the event that caused the failure to comply with the requirements; and (2) if an issuer fails to comply with the audit committee composition requirements due to one vacancy on the audit committee, and the aforementioned cure period is not otherwise being relied upon for another audit committee member, the issuer would have until the earlier of the next annual shareholders meeting or one year from the occurrence of the event that caused the failure to comply with this requirement. An issuer relying on either of these provisions would be required to provide notice to Nasdaq immediately upon learning of the event or circumstance that caused the non-compliance.

9. Notification of Noncompliance

Nasdaq proposes to require that an issuer provide Nasdaq with prompt notification after an executive officer of the issuer becomes aware of any material noncompliance by the issuer with the requirements of NASD Rule 4350.

When evaluating the effectiveness of the audit committee's oversight of the company's external financial reporting and internal control over financial reporting, the auditor should consider:

- *The independence of the audit committee as set forth in the SRO requirements.*

- *The clarity with which the audit committee's responsibilities are articulated and how well the audit committee understands those responsibilities.* This implies that the auditor should question the audit committee members in some detail. In practice this may be difficult to implement in a detailed way. It is very difficult to imagine that the audit committee members would tolerate any sort of interrogation about their understanding of their job or their qualifications for that job. This is especially true given that the audit committee hires and fires the auditor. The auditor is unlikely to be eager to say or ask anything that might irritate the audit committee members. It remains to be seen how this potentially touchy situation is handled in practice.

- *The level of involvement and interaction with the independent auditor.* Again, the audit committee hires the auditor and pre-approves any internal control-related services provided by the auditor, so the auditor's evaluation of this might be overshadowed by that relationship. One thing the auditor should consider is whether the audit committee asks questions that indicate the members understand the company's accounting policies. The auditor should also note how responsive the audit committee is to issues raised by the auditor.

- *The level of involvement and interaction with internal audit.* Does internal audit report directly to the audit committee? Does the chief audit executive meet regularly with the audit committee?

- *The level of interaction with key members of financial management (e.g., the CFO and accounting management).* Again, does the audit committee demonstrate an understanding of the company's accounting policies? Do committee members question judgmental accounting estimates?

- *Compliance with the requirements of Section 301 of the Sarbanes-Oxley Act, as described above.*

Indicating the PCAOB's emphasis on the importance of the audit committee, in the event that the auditor finds that the audit committee's oversight of the company's external financial reporting or internal control over financial reporting is ineffective, this would constitute at least a significant deficiency, and may indicate the presence of a material weakness in the company's internal control over financial reporting.

Auditing Standard Paragraphs: ¶s 55–59

Persons Affected:

Directors, Audit Committee Members, Internal Auditors, Auditors

Effect:

The auditor must review and assess the effectiveness of the audit committee's oversight of the company's external financial reporting and internal control over financial reporting.

Action:

The auditor must review the audit committee's involvement in detail and assess the effectiveness of the audit committee's oversight of the company's external financial reporting and internal control over financial reporting. The auditor must also assess the relative effectiveness of the audit committee's oversight role. If the auditor finds that the audit committee is ineffective in the oversight role, then this constitutes a significant deficiency. Boards of directors should ensure that their audit committees are in compliance with the requirements of Section 301 of the Sarbanes-Oxley Act, as well as the applicable SRO corporate governance rules.

Rules and Regulations Cited:

15 USCS 78c; 15 USCS 7201(a)(3); 17 CFR §240.10A-3; (Securities Exchange Act Rule 10A-3); 17 CFR §240.10A-3(c)(2) (Securities Exchange Act Rule 10A-3(c)(2)); 17 CFR §210.2-01(c)(7) (Regulation S-X Rule 2-01(c)(7)).

Suggested References:

"Standards for Listed Company Audit Committees," *Handbook of SEC Accounting and Disclosure* § E32.

"Audit Committee Reporting," *Handbook of SEC Accounting and Disclosure* § E25.

"SEC Approves Corporate Governance Proposals," *SEC Accounting and Reporting Manual.*

"Standards for Listed Company Audit Committees," *SEC Accounting and Reporting Update* 2003-17 (April 2003).

"Audit Committees," *SEC Compliance: Financial Reporting and Forms* ¶ 17,229.

"The Audit Committee," *Handbook of Accounting and Auditing,* Chapter B2.

"Corporate Governance: The Changed Environment: Challenges and Opportunities in 2004," *Corporate Finance Review* (January/February 2004).

"Audit Committees Focus on Risk Management," *Internal Auditing* (July/August 2002).

"Where Was the Audit Committee?," *Internal Auditing* (May/June 2002).

¶ 109.4.3. Identifying Significant Accounts

With regard to accounts, the specific requirements in the auditing standard are:

- Identification of significant accounts, starting at the financial-statement level.
- Then at the account level.
- Or at the disclosure level.

An account is deemed to be significant if:

- There is a "more than remote likelihood that the account could contain misstatements that individually, or when aggregated with others, could have a material effect on the financial statements." (¶ 61.)

- On a qualitative basis, the account is relevant to a financial statement users (e.g., the account represents an important performance measure).

- Components of the account balance are subject to inherent and control risks due to the nature of the account. Reserve accounts would fall into this category. Inventory accounts would also fall into this category because they are the result of different processes.

- The account has a likely exposure to unrecognized obligations. This would include accounts used to record loss reserves.

All of the account types included in these requirements are those that would normally be covered in a traditional audit. Given the scenarios laid out by the PCAOB in Appendix D of the auditing standard (Examples of Significant Deficiencies and Material Weaknesses), it appears that all accounts, even insignificant ones, can contribute to a material weakness. Besides the size of the account, the auditor is also required to consider qualitative factors, such as the susceptibility of the account to errors or fraud, the complexity of the transactions that are processed through the account, the existence of related-party transactions in the account, and changes from the prior period in account characteristics. The standard cites fixed asset accounts as an example where the accounts may be deemed insignificant during an audit of the financial statements, but significant during and audit of internal control over financial reporting.

It appears that organizations will fall into one of the following categories:

		Relative Quality of the Organization's Reconciliations and Internal Controls	
		High Quality Work and Effective in All Respects	**Less Than High Quality Work and Not Necessarily Effective in All Respects**
Relative Severity of the Auditor's Evaluation Process—Strictly Interprets the Scenarios in Appendix D	**Very Exacting**	Passes the audit, performed all work to very high standards.	Material weaknesses noted, unable to take adequate corrective measures prior to issuance of audit report, essentially fails the audit.
	Less than Very Exacting	Passes the audit, but performed to standards that were higher than necessary. Firms in this category performed "extra" work that was not necessary to pass the audit and wasted resources in doing so.	Passes the audit, performed all work to acceptable standards, but performed no "extra" work.

These requirements probably have a lot to do with the PCAOB's reasoning for expanding the scope of internal control services that can be provided by the audit firm to the issuer. If the issuers are forced to guess what level of internal controls the auditor is going to require, they would stand a very high chance that they performed too little remediation work on their internal controls, and thus they would fail the audit. Or in the alternative, they would spend more resources than necessary on modifying their internal controls and would thus waste significant resources unnecessarily fixing problems that did not need to be fixed in order to pass the audit.

Auditing Standard Paragraphs: ¶s 60–67

Persons Affected:

Accounting Staff, Accounting Management, Auditors

Effect:

After considering both quantitative and qualitative factors, the company's auditors must identify significant accounts.

Action:

Auditors must identify all significant accounts within the financial statements. This includes a quantitative and qualitative assessment and is significant when there is a more than remote likelihood that the account could contain misstatements.

Rules and Regulations Cited:

None cited.

¶ 109.4.4. Identifying Relevant Financial Statement Assertions

The auditing standard requires that the auditor evaluate the judgment underlying the primary financial statement assertions. The standard directs the auditor to AU Section 326, *Evidential Matter*, for additional guidance. As listed in Auditing Standard No. 2 and in AU Section 326, these financial statement assertions include:

- *Existence or occurrence.* The financial statements assert that an asset or liability exists at a given date and state whether transactions have occurred during a given period.
- *Completeness.* All transactions and accounts that should be presented in the financial statements are indeed included there.
- *Valuation or allocation.* All assets, liabilities, equity, revenue, and expenses are valued appropriately and in accordance with GAAP.
- *Rights and obligations.* Assets properly represent rights owned by the issuer and liabilities represent obligations of the issuer.
- *Presentation and disclosure.* Accounts and related information are properly classified, described, and disclosed.

In order to figure out which assertions are more likely to result in potential misstatements for each significant account, the auditor should consider:

- *The nature of the assertion.* What is the "story"? Is it plausible? Does it make sense? Is it consistent with the control environment of the company, other divisions, and the company's historical practices?

- *The volume of data and transactions related to the assertion.* Does management have a solid understanding of how their accounting processes actually affect their transactional flows? Do they understand how their systems work? Is it generally considered a good system, or is it buggy and problematic? Is there good system documentation? Are there millions of transactions in this account each month? Each week? Every day?

- *The nature and complexity of the systems and technology the company uses and the controls over that supporting technology.*

Regarding the information technology and systems by which the company processes and controls information that supports the financial statement assertions, the auditor might want to consider the following step-by-step process:

- *Start with an overview of the implementation.* How and when was it implemented? What is the underlying technology platform? Is it considered current technology, or is it leftover from a bygone era with nonexistent support or documentation?

- *Identify the processes involved.* Are they identified at a high level?

- *Identify the transactional systems associated with each process.* Does the process documentation correlate to the transactional systems showing cause and effect?

- *Document the processes.* Are the processes thoroughly understood and documented? Are the systems' data models documented?

- *Look at the data warehouse tools and documentation used for summarizations.* What kinds of tools are used to reconcile the systems' transactional activities to the financial statements? Are they only tested on an individual transaction "walkthrough" basis when there are, literally, millions of transactions being processed per accounting period?

- *Checklist the transactional summaries for each process.* Are checklists prepared that are used to validate that all of the processes are generating the anticipated transactional activity?

- *Checklist the transactional summaries to the financial statements and vice versa from the financial statements back through the transactions to the process summaries.* Are checklists prepared that are used to validate that all of the transactions generated result in the anticipated financial statement activity? Conversely, is all of the financial statement activity validated back to its supposed sources?

Auditing Standard Paragraphs: ¶s 68–70

Persons Affected:

Accounting Staff, Accounting Management, Auditors

Effect:

Auditors must identify all relevant financial statement assertions.

Action:

Auditors must identify, examine, and determine the relevance of each assertion underlying each significant account. The auditor must determine the source of likely misstatements in each account.

Rules and Regulations Cited:

AU Section 326, *Evidential Matter.*

Suggested Reference:

"Tools and Techniques for Documenting Accounting Systems," *Internal Auditing* (September/October 2003).

¶ 109.4.5. Identifying Significant Processes and Major Classes of Transactions

Regarding the requirement that auditors identify significant processes and major classes of transactions, the PCAOB made great improvements to the conventional auditing standards espoused in AU Section 319, *Consideration of Internal Control in a Financial Statement Audit.* The auditing standard starts by requiring the auditor to identify each significant process over each major class of transactions affecting significant accounts or groups of accounts.

Here is an example of an initial process identification worksheet (for an oil and gas company, in this example):

	Processes—Division A	Processes—Division B	Processes—Division C
Purchasing			
Receiving of materials and equipment			
Project tracking			
Inventory—consumable drilling materials			
Inventory—produced oil and gas			
Assets—drilling equipment			
Assets—surface equipment			
Assets—land and leases			
Distribution tracking			
Accounts receivable			
Accounts payable—contract drillers			
Accounts payable—travel expenses			
Payroll			
General ledger			
Database			
Budgeting			
Forecasting			
Consolidations			
Geophysical engineering			
Well performance tracking			

The auditing standard includes requirements that, for each significant process, the auditor should:

- *Understand the flow of transactions, including how transactions are initiated, recorded, processed, and reported.* This understanding can be gained during the auditor's performance of walkthroughs. (See ¶ 109.4.7 of this discussion for more on walkthroughs.)

- *Identify the points within the process where a misstatement, including a misstatement due to fraud, related to each relevant financial statement assertion could arise.* This is basic process analysis from an internal control standpoint—what are the essential control points?

- *Identify the controls that management has implemented to address these potential misstatements.* This requires proper process documentation that incorporates a focus on where misstatements could occur and the internal controls over them. Management should have identified these issues during its risk assessment.

- *Identify the controls that management has implemented to prevent and detect unauthorized acquisition, use, or disposition of the company's as-*

sets. This requires proper process documentation that incorporates a focus on administrative functions that might allow unauthorized transactions to occur and the internal controls set up to prevent and detect fraud.

Information technology's impact on a company's internal control over financial reporting is touched on briefly in ¶ 75 of the standard, but only insofar as
to say that the "nature and characteristics of a company's use of information
technology in its information system affect the company's internal control over
financial reporting." The standard then refers the reader to AU Section 319,
Consideration of Internal Control in a Financial Statement Audit for further information. AU Section 319 states, in part:

> **.16** An entity's use of IT may affect any of the five components of internal
> control relevant to the achievement of the entity's financial reporting, oper-
> ations, or compliance objectives, and its operating units or business func-
> tions. For example, an entity may use IT as part of discrete systems that
> support only particular business units, functions, or activities, such as a
> unique accounts receivable system for a particular business unit or a sys-
> tem that controls the operation of factory equipment. Alternatively, an en-
> tity may have complex, highly integrated systems that share data and that
> are used to support all aspects of the entity's financial reporting, opera-
> tions, and compliance objectives.
>
> **.17** The use of IT also affects the fundamental manner in which transac-
> tions are initiated, recorded, processed, and reported. In a manual system,
> an entity uses manual procedures and records in paper format (for example,
> individuals may manually record sales orders on paper forms or journals,
> authorize credit, prepare shipping reports and invoices, and maintain ac-
> counts receivable records). Controls in such a system also are manual and
> may include such procedures as approvals and reviews of activities, and
> reconciliations and follow-up of reconciling items. Alternatively, an entity
> may have information systems that use automated procedures to initiate, re-
> cord, process, and report transactions, in which case records in electronic
> format replace such paper documents as purchase orders, invoices, shipping
> documents, and related accounting records. Controls in systems that use IT
> consist of a combination of automated controls (for example, controls em-
> bedded in computer programs) and manual controls. Further, manual con-
> trols may be independent of IT, may use information produced by IT, or
> may be limited to monitoring the effective functioning of IT and of auto-
> mated controls, and to handling exceptions. An entity's mix of manual and
> automated controls varies with the nature and complexity of the entity's
> use of IT.
>
> **.18** IT provides potential benefits of effectiveness and efficiency for an en-
> tity's internal control because it enables an entity to—
>
>   • Consistently apply predefined business rules and perform complex cal-
>   culations in processing large volumes of transactions or data.

- Enhance the timeliness, availability, and accuracy of information.
- Facilitate the additional analysis of information.
- Enhance the ability to monitor the performance of the entity's activities and its policies and procedures.
- Reduce the risk that controls will be circumvented.
- Enhance the ability to achieve effective segregation of duties by implementing security controls in applications, databases, and operating systems.

.19 IT also poses specific risks to an entity's internal control, including—

- Reliance on systems or programs that are inaccurately processing data, processing inaccurate data, or both.
- Unauthorized access to data that may result in destruction of data or improper changes to data, including the recording of unauthorized or nonexistent transactions or inaccurate recording of transactions.
- Unauthorized changes to data in master files.
- Unauthorized changes to systems or programs.
- Failure to make necessary changes to systems or programs.
- Inappropriate manual intervention.
- Potential loss of data.

.20 The extent and nature of these risks to internal control vary depending on the nature and characteristics of the entity's information system. For example, multiple users, either external or internal, may access a common database of information that affects financial reporting. In such circumstances, a lack of control at a single user entry point might compromise the security of the entire database, potentially resulting in improper changes to or destruction of data. When IT personnel or users are given, or can gain, access privileges beyond those necessary to perform their assigned duties, a breakdown in segregation of duties can occur. This could result in unauthorized transactions or changes to programs or data that affect the financial statements. Therefore, the nature and characteristics of an entity's use of IT in its information system affect the entity's internal control.

****

.30 In making a judgment about the understanding of internal control necessary to plan the audit, the auditor also considers IT risks that could result in misstatements. For example, if an entity uses IT to perform complex calculations, the entity receives the benefit of having the calculations consistently performed. However, the use of IT also presents risks, such as the risk that improperly authorized, incorrectly defined, or improperly implemented changes to the system or programs performing the calculations, or to related program tables or master files, could result in consistently performing those calculations inaccurately. As an entity's operations and systems become more complex and sophisticated, it becomes more likely that the auditor would need to increase his or her understanding of the internal control components to obtain the understanding necessary to design tests of controls, when applicable, and substantive tests.

.31 The auditor should consider whether specialized skills are needed for the auditor to determine the effect of IT on the audit, to understand the IT controls, or to design and perform tests of IT controls or substantive tests. A professional possessing IT skills may be either on the auditor's staff or an outside professional. In determining whether such a professional is needed on the audit team, the auditor considers factors such as the following:

- The complexity of the entity's systems and IT controls and the manner in which they are used in conducting the entity's business
- The significance of changes made to existing systems, or the implementation of new systems
- The extent to which data is shared among systems
- The extent of the entity's participation in electronic commerce
- The entity's use of emerging technologies
- The significance of audit evidence that is available only in electronic form

.32 Procedures that the auditor may assign to a professional possessing IT skills include inquiring of an entity's IT personnel how data and transactions are initiated, recorded, processed, and reported and how IT controls are designed; inspecting systems documentation; observing the operation of IT controls; and planning and performing tests of IT controls. If the use of a professional possessing IT skills is planned, the auditor should have sufficient IT-related knowledge to communicate the audit objectives to the professional, to evaluate whether the specified procedures will meet the auditor's objectives, and to evaluate the results of the procedures as they relate to the nature, timing, and extent of other planned audit procedures.

****

.77 In designing tests of automated controls, the auditor should consider the need to obtain evidence supporting the effective operation of controls directly related to the assertions as well as other indirect controls on which these controls depend. For example, the auditor may identify a "user review of an exception report of credit sales over a customer's authorized credit limit" as a direct control related to an assertion. In such cases, the auditor should consider the effectiveness of the user review of the report and also the controls related to the accuracy of the information in the report (for example, the general controls).

.78 Because of the inherent consistency of IT processing, the auditor may be able to reduce the extent of testing of an automated control. For example, a programmed application control should function consistently unless the program (including the tables, files, or other permanent data used by the program) is changed. Once the auditor determines that an automated control is functioning as intended (which could be done at the time the control is initially implemented or at some other date), the auditor should consider performing tests to determine that the control continues to function effectively. Such tests might include determining that changes to the program are not made without being subject to the appropriate program change controls, that the authorized version of the program is used for processing transactions, and that other relevant general controls are effective. Such tests also might include determining that changes to the programs have not been made, as may be the case when the entity uses packaged software applications without modifying or maintaining them.

.79 To test automated controls, the auditor may need to use techniques that are different from those used to test manual controls. For example, computer-assisted audit techniques may be used to test automated controls or data related to assertions. Also, the auditor may use other automated tools or reports produced by IT to test the operating effectiveness of general controls, such as program change controls, access controls, and system software controls. The auditor should consider whether specialized skills are needed to design and perform such tests of controls.

Auditing Standard Paragraphs: ¶s 71–75

See Also: ¶ 79

Persons Affected:

Accounting Staff, Accounting Management, Auditors

Effect:

Auditors must identify each significant process over each major class of transactions affecting significant accounts or groups of accounts. The auditor must consider the nature and characteristics of the company's information system in relation to internal control over financial reporting.

Action:

Auditors must identify, review, and evaluate each significant process over each major class of transactions affecting significant accounts or groups of accounts. The auditor must understand the flow of transactions, including how transactions are initiated, authorized, recorded, processed, and reported. This can be achieved during a walkthrough. The auditor must consider the nature and characteristics of the company's information system in relation to internal control over financial reporting.

Rules and Regulations Cited:

AU Section 319, *Consideration of Internal Control in a Financial Statement Audit.*

Suggested Reference:

"Tools and Techniques for Documenting Accounting Systems," *Internal Auditing* (September/October 2003).

¶ 109.4.6. Understanding the Period-End Financial Reporting Process

The PCAOB specifies that the period-end financial reporting process includes:

- *The procedures used to enter transactions into the general ledger.* Who enters the transactions? How are the transactions developed, authorized, and checked?

- *The procedures used to initiate, record, and process journal entries in the general ledger.* How is the processing done? How are the journal entries developed, authorized, and checked?

- *Other procedures used to record recurring and nonrecurring adjustments to the financial statements, such as consolidating adjustments, report combinations, and classifications.* This requirement refers to rollups. Rollups, or consolidations, are one of the most problematic areas in financial reporting. It also refers to period-end adjusting entries and the clearing of reserve balances. Both of these items require substantial judgment and evaluation to properly assess.

- *Procedures for drafting financial statements and related disclosures.* This is the process companies use to transfer figures from internal accounting reports to externally published financial reports.

As part of the evaluation of the period-end reporting process, the company's auditors are required to evaluate:

- *The inputs, procedures performed, and outputs of the processes the company uses to produce its financial statements.* This requires high-quality process documentation. This sort of documentation should be part of the company's policies and procedures.

- *The extent of information technology involvement in each period-end financial reporting process element.* This is not explained as well as it could be in the auditing standard. The extent of information technology involvement could be something like 100 percent, depending on how the auditor examines the topic. While there are manual inputs at period-end, such as journal entries, the period-end processing is normally 100 percent automated. Here the PCAOB is incorporating an elemental concept that involves defining the transactional data flow and then summarizing and checking it all.

- *Who participates from management.* Are the proper people involved in period-end decision making?

- *The number of locations involved.* The more locations there are, the more complex the period-end financial reporting process becomes.

- *Types of adjusting entries (e.g., standard, nonstandard, eliminating, or consolidating).* Adjusting entries should receive careful attention from the auditor.

- *The nature and extent of the oversight of the process by appropriate parties, including management, the board of directors, and the audit committee.* This speaks to the company's overall control environment.

This part of the auditing standard is meant to address the timing of transactions. Many firms have been able to pull revenue from later periods into the current period as well as shift expenses from the current period to later periods. The controls over the period-end financial reporting process are critical to controlling the proper timing of financial reporting. These controls tend to require testing of the accounting systems. The accounting system must be tested to see what abilities are available to the firm to backdate and postdate transactions.

Auditing Standard Paragraphs:　¶s 76–78

Persons Affected:

Management, Directors, Audit Committee Members, Accounting Staff, Accounting Management, Auditors

Effect:

Auditors must obtain an understanding of and evaluate the period-end financial reporting process.

Action:

Auditors must review and evaluate the period-end financial reporting processes to ensure that transactions are recorded in their proper periods. The impact of the company's control environment on period-end financial reporting should be taken into account by the auditor. Management, the board, and the audit committee should ensure proper oversight of the period-end process.

Rules and Regulations Cited:

None cited.

Suggested Reference:

"Auditing Revenue Recognition," *Internal Auditing* (January/February 2003).

¶ 109.4.7. Performing Walkthroughs

The auditing standard requires the company's auditor to "perform at least one walkthrough for each major class of transactions . . . . In a walkthrough, the auditor traces a transaction from origination through the company's information systems until it is reflected in the company's financial reports." (¶ 79.) The major classes of transactions are covered in ¶ 71 of the standard. (See ¶ 109.4.5 of this discussion.) Companies can simplify the walkthrough process by maintaining and providing to the auditor thorough documentation of accounting policies and procedures.

This requirement for auditor walkthroughs created some controversy during the public comment period of the proposed auditing standard. While some commenters expressed support for the requirement, others were concerned that requiring walkthroughs would result in drastically increased audit fees. Some were also concerned that by requiring the auditor to walkthrough each major class of transactions, the PCAOB was discouraging or disregarding the work of others, particularly the internal audit function. However, the PCAOB concluded that audit walkthroughs are a necessary component of an effective audit of internal control over financial reporting, and that, although auditors are allowed to rely on the work of others to some extent, the audit objectives achieved by walkthroughs could not be achieved secondhand. The PCAOB did, however, narrow the definition of the required walkthroughs in the final version of the standard. Unlike the proposed standard, the final version allows the company's auditors to incorporate professional judgments about the level of risk and materiality in a given transaction in order to determine if the transaction requires a walkthrough.

During a walkthrough, the auditor should examine the entire process of initiating, authorizing, recording, processing, and reporting individual transactions and controls for each of the significant processes identified. Controls that are designed to address the risk of fraud should receive special attention. According to the standard, "During the walkthrough, at each point at which important processing procedures or controls occur, the auditor should question the company's personnel about their understanding of what is required by the company's prescribed procedures and controls and determine whether the processing procedures are performed as originally understood and on a timely basis." (¶ 80.) Accordingly, management would be wise to ensure that all administrative employees whose tasks have an impact on the company's financial statements receive adequate training on the company's policies and procedures.

The standard is quite specific about the level of detail the auditor should be looking for during a walkthrough. It mandates that the auditor "should follow the process flow of actual transactions using the same documents and information technology that company personnel use and make inquiries of relevant personnel involved in significant aspects of the process or controls." (¶ 81.) The auditor is required to ask company personnel very specific questions about how they perform their tasks and how they respond to anomalies. The walkthrough should be performed in such a way that it uncovers control override situations and determines the effectiveness of internal controls that are designed to detect and prevent error and fraud.

Auditing Standard Paragraphs: ¶s 79–83

See Also Auditing Standard Paragraphs: ¶s 71, 108–126

Persons Affected:

Management, Accounting Staff, Accounting Management, Auditors

Effect:

The auditor is required to validate that the company's accounting systems and controls are working properly by walking transactions through the accounting system to make sure it is working as intended and employees understand the control activities they are required to perform.

Action:

The auditor is required to perform at least one walkthrough for each major class of transactions. Company personnel will be required to respond to the auditor's queries about their understanding of what is required by the company's policies, procedures, and controls. Management should ensure that the controls and procedures relevant to all significant accounts are properly documented, and that employees are adequately trained with regard to controls, exception handling, and company policies.

Rules and Regulations Cited:

None cited.

Suggested Reference:

"Tools and Techniques for Documenting Accounting Systems," *Internal Auditing* (September/October 2003).

¶ 109.4.8. Identifying Controls to Test

According to the standard, the company's auditor must obtain evidence that validates the effectiveness of controls for all relevant assertions related to all significant accounts and disclosures in the financial statements. The standard mandates that the auditor should evaluate the following to identify the controls to be tested:

- The process points where fraud could occur (i.e., the control points).
- The type and nature of the controls implemented by management.
- The relative significance of each control in achieving the objectives of the control criteria and the relative level of overlap for compensating controls.

- The risk that the controls might not be operating effectively.

No matter how well the company's controls are designed, their effective operation can be affected by:

- *Changes in the volume and nature of transactions being processed by the accounting systems.* For example, controls designed to validate a small number of transactions per period may not be effective when the transactional system is suddenly processing millions of transactions.

- *Changes to the design of the controls.* If the controls are redesigned without sufficient planning and testing, there is a risk that they will be ineffective in operation.

- *Overlapping and compensating controls.* Many controls are not very effective in isolation. The company's overall control environment and general IT controls may compensate for risks associated with more specific controls. In addition, when designing controls, management should ensure that high-risk activities (especially activities at risk of fraud or error) have ample compensating controls to ensure an acceptable level of risk is maintained.

- *Changes in the personnel responsible for performing controls and ensuring that the company's controls are operating as designed.* Management should ensure that consistent documentation is maintained so that new supervisory personnel are properly trained in how to ensure the company's controls are correctly implemented. In addition, all key employees responsible for performing controls should receive adequate training and must be informed of any changes to the control procedures.

- *Whether the control is manual or automated.* If controls are fully automated, management must ensure that the company's general IT controls are sufficient to ensure the proper operation of the automated controls. In turn, manual implementation of controls leaves the implementation of these controls open to human error. Compensating controls will be especially important if this is the case.

- *How complex the underlying material is and the required level of complexity embedded in the control.* More complex controls are more difficult to maintain and validate. Again, management should ensure an adequate level of compensating controls are in place for particularly complex controls. Management should also ensure that a proper level of documentation for complex controls is made available to the company's auditor.

The auditing standard requires the company's auditor to clearly link, via documentation, the individual controls with the significant accounts and assertions to which they relate. Management can help ensure a smooth audit process by ensuring that the documentation on which it bases its assessment of the company's internal control over financial reporting adequately links controls with the relevant accounts and assertions.

Because effective internal control often includes a combination of preventive controls (e.g., authorizations) and detective controls (e.g., reconciliations or variance reports), the auditor will need to test the combination of both types of controls to determine their effectiveness. The standard provides some guidance as to the scope of the auditor's testing of these controls by stating, "It is neither necessary to test all controls nor is it necessary to test redundant controls (that is, controls that duplicate other controls that achieve the same objective and already have been tested), unless redundancy is itself a control objective, as in the case of certain computer controls." (¶ 86.)

The standard allows the auditor to rely to some extent on the work of others, such as internal auditors, when determining which controls will need to be tested.

Auditing Standard Paragraphs: ¶s 83–87

See Also Auditing Standard Paragraphs: ¶s 23, 130–137, Appendix B, ¶s B1–B17

Persons Affected:

Management, Internal Auditors, Auditors

Effect:

The company's auditor must obtain evidence that validates the effectiveness of controls over financial reporting.

Action:

The auditor should obtain evidence of the effectiveness of controls on which to base its opinion. The auditor must either perform these tests himself or herself or may rely, to some extent, on the work of others, such as the company's internal auditors. Management should ensure that adequate documentation exists of the company's significant control points, the nature of the controls implemented by management, the significance of each control, and the level of risk that the controls might not be operating as designed.

Rules and Regulations Cited:

None cited.

Suggested References:

"Auditing Internal Controls Under Sarbanes-Oxley," *Bank Auditing and Accounting Report* (January 2004).

"Internal Control," *Handbook of Accounting and Auditing* Chapter B4.

¶ 109.5. Testing and Evaluating Design Effectiveness

The PCAOB reiterates its guidance regarding the effectiveness of the design of internal controls over financial reporting in ¶s 88 through 91 of the auditing standard. Controls should be designed to effectively prevent or detect errors or fraud that could result in material misstatements in the company's financial statements. In determining the effectiveness of the company's internal controls, the auditor is required to:

- Identify the control objectives in each area.

- Identify the controls that satisfy each objective.

- Determine whether the controls will be effective if they operate as designed.

The auditor's evaluation of the design of the company's internal controls also provides the auditor with evidence of the controls' effectiveness in operation.

Auditing Standard Paragraphs: ¶s 88–91

Persons Affected:

Auditors

Effect:

The company's auditor must test and evaluate the design of the company's internal controls over financial reporting.

Action:

Through procedures such as inquiry, observation, walkthroughs, inspection of relevant documentation, and an evaluation of whether the controls are likely to prevent or detect errors or fraud if they operate as designed, the auditor must test and evaluate the design of the company's internal controls over financial reporting.

Rules and Regulations Cited:

None cited.

Suggested References:

"Auditing Internal Controls Under Sarbanes-Oxley," *Bank Auditing and Accounting Report* (January 2004).

"Internal Control," *Handbook of Accounting and Auditing* Chapter B4.

¶ 109.6. Testing and Evaluating Operating Effectiveness

The PCAOB reiterates its guidance regarding the operating effectiveness of internal controls over financial reporting in ¶s 92 through 107 of the auditing standard, but adds some details about the nature, timing, and extent of the auditor's tests of the controls. The auditor is required to determine whether the company's controls are operating as designed and whether the employees performing the controls have the necessary authority and qualifications to perform the controls effectively. See ¶ 109.6.1–¶ 109.6.4 of this discussion for more on the auditor's testing of operating effectiveness.

Auditing Standard Paragraphs: ¶s 92–107

See Also Auditing Standard Paragraphs: ¶s 179, 207

Persons Affected:

Auditors

Effect:

The company's auditor must test and evaluate the operating effectiveness of the company's internal controls over financial reporting.

Action:

The auditor must validate the operating effectiveness of internal controls over financial reporting by using a mix of inquiries, inspection, observation, testing, and reperformance. The auditor must verify that the employees performing the controls have the necessary authority and qualifications to perform the controls effectively.

Rules and Regulations Cited:

None cited.

Suggested References:

"Auditing Internal Controls Under Sarbanes-Oxley," *Bank Auditing and Accounting Report* (January 2004).

"Internal Control," *Handbook of Accounting and Auditing* Chapter B4.

¶ 109.6.1. Nature of Tests of Controls

The requirement that auditors test and evaluate the design effectiveness prior to testing the operating effectiveness is straightforward. The key factor in an effective design evaluation is the training and experience of the auditor. The auditor needs to know what they are looking for beyond the documentation they are offered for review by the issuer.

The auditor's tests should include:

- Inquiries of the personnel responsible for the effective operation of the control. (These can be performed concurrently with the requisite walk-throughs, and can be written or oral.)
- Inspection of relevant documentation.
- Observation of the company's operations.
- Reperformance of the application of the control.

Auditing Standard Paragraphs: ¶s 93–97

Persons Affected:

Auditors

Effect:

In order to test and evaluate the operating effectiveness of the company's internal controls over financial reporting, the company's auditor must utilize a mix of inquiry, observation, documentation review, and reperformance.

Action:

The auditor's tests of the operating effectiveness of the company's internal controls over financial reporting should include written and/or oral inquiry, direct observation, documentation review, and reperformance of key controls.

Rules and Regulations Cited:

None cited.

Suggested References:

"Auditing Internal Controls Under Sarbanes-Oxley," *Bank Auditing and Accounting Report* (January 2004).

"Internal Control," *Handbook of Accounting and Auditing* Chapter B4.

¶ 109.6.2. Timing of Tests of Controls

Tests of controls should cover an adequate time period to corroborate the claims made in management's report. The auditor's testing of the operating effectiveness of the controls should occur when the controls are operating. It is virtually impossible to validate an operational test on a control that is no longer active. There is no way to be sure that the documentation was not simply backdated and that the controls were never really performed.

When auditors report on the effectiveness of controls "as of" a specific date and are trying to apply that evaluation to a later, interim, period, they should consider:

- The results of the tests of the controls prior to the last "as of" date.
- How much evidence exists about the effectiveness of the controls prior to the last "as of" date.

- How much time has elapsed since the last "as of" date.

- The likelihood or possibility that there have been significant changes made in internal control over financial reporting since the last "as of" date.

The most likely scenario that many auditors will face in this situation is that the control did not really exist prior to passage of the Sarbanes-Oxley Act and subsequent risk assessment and internal control remediation efforts. The auditor then has to ask the right questions to determine if the controls in question were operating effectively during prior periods. The standard provides some guidance is this regard when it states, "Prior to the date specified in management's report, management might implement changes to the company's controls to make them more effective or efficient or to address control deficiencies. In that case, the auditor might not need to evaluate controls that have been superseded . . . . In addition, the auditor should evaluate how the design and operating effectiveness of the superseded controls relates to the auditor's reliance on controls for financial statement audit purposes." (¶s 102–103.)

Timing issues are actually much more pervasive in internal control than many auditors realize. One of the easiest ways to find inconsistent accounting is to look at certain items on a trend basis covering multiple accounting years. Some examples of how to spot games in the financial reporting include:

- List the inventory reserves by dollar value and percent of inventory over the last 10 years.

- List all reserves by dollar value and a percentage of profit over the last 10 years.

- List the profits for each of the last 10 years.

- List all other accounting entries that are based on judgments, estimates, or valuations.

- Now put all these figures on the same trend report. See if the profit does not somehow correspond to any of these other accounting entries. This is the best way to spot timing issues in internal controls.

Auditing Standard Paragraphs: ¶s 98–103

See Also Auditing Standard Paragraphs: ¶s 179, 207

Persons Affected:

Auditors

Effect:

The auditor must consider time and timing issues related to tests of controls.

Action:

The auditor should evaluate the time periods covered by controls, the timing of tests of controls, and when the controls were put in place.

Rules and Regulations Cited:

None cited.

¶ 109.6.3. Extent of Tests of Controls

The high level of assurance that the auditors must provide requires that they consider certain aspects of each internal control over financial reporting that they are evaluating. Those aspects include:

- *The nature of the control.* Is the control manual or automatic? How complex is the control? Is a high level of competence required to correctly implement the control? An auditor may be able to validate an automated control with fewer observations than would be required for a manual control. Also, an auditor can evaluate a simple control much faster than a more complex control.

- *The frequency of the operation of the control.* It is easier for an auditor to validate a manual control that is performed frequently because there are more opportunities to observe the control in action. Whereas a less frequently performed control, like a reconciliation, might only be performed once a month. For example, if materials are received on a dock continuously all day long, an auditor could review the internal controls over receiving many times in a single day. On the other hand, if the general ledger account for inventory is reconciled monthly, there is only one opportunity per month for the auditor to validate that control. On the other hand, the more frequently a control must be performed, the more opportunities there are for error or fraud to occur. Thus, frequently performed controls will probably require more extensive testing than occasional ones. Sampling may be an appropriate testing method in the case of frequently performed controls.

- *The importance of the control.* It makes sense that the more important the control, the more thoroughly it should be tested. Controls that affect many financial statement significant accounts or assertions should be tested very thoroughly. Also, detective controls that the issuer relies on to overlap with and compensate for other internal controls should be well tested.

The PCAOB requires the auditor to vary the nature, timing, and extent of control testing from year to year to avoid predictability and to respond to changes in the company's internal control over financial reporting.

Auditing Standard Paragraphs: ¶s 104–105

Persons Affected:

Auditors

Effect:

The auditor must obtain sufficient evidence about whether the company's internal control over financial reporting is operating effectively.

Action:

The nature and extent of testing for each control must be determined by the auditor by taking into consideration the nature of the control, its frequency of operation, and the importance of the control.

Rules and Regulations Cited:

None cited.

Suggested References:

"Auditing Internal Controls Under Sarbanes-Oxley," *Bank Auditing and Accounting Report* (January 2004).

"Internal Control," *Handbook of Accounting and Auditing* Chapter B4.

¶ 109.6.4. Use of Professional Skepticism When Evaluating the Results of Testing

The auditor must conduct the audit of internal control over financial reporting with professional skepticism. The PCAOB requires that auditors exercise the same standards of professional skepticism and due professional care in an audit of internal control over financial reporting as that required in an audit of financial statements. The auditor must have a "questioning mind" with which to conduct a critical assessment of audit evidence.

The skepticism standard is one of the key reasons that an auditor probably should not be involved in providing an audit client internal control-related services. If the auditor has substantial input into the design and implementation of internal control over financial reporting, regardless of management's level of involvement, the auditors are inherently less likely to have sufficient professional skepticism when auditing those same controls. Even though a control might have been functioning properly in the past, that does not ensure that the same control, even being performed by the same person, is still effective. It is the auditor's professional skepticism that provides the attitude necessary to validate that the controls are still functioning correctly now.

Given a situation where the auditor identifies an internal control deficiency, the auditor should use professional skepticism to think through what other aspects of the environment are also affected and what other controls might be failing. For example, if a preventive authorization control is failing to operate effectively, then the associated detective controls (e.g., variance reporting) are probably not being correctly implemented either.

Auditing Standard Paragraphs: ¶s 106–107

Persons Affected:

Auditors

Effect:

The auditor must conduct the audit of internal control over financial reporting and the audit of the financial statements with professional skepticism.

Action:

The auditor needs to have a "questioning mind" and must conduct a critical assessment of audit evidence. When the auditor identifies exceptions to the company's control procedures, he or she should determine, using professional skepticism, the effect of the exception. Additional testing may be appropriate or necessary.

Rules and Regulations Cited:

None cited.

¶ 109.7. Using the Work of Others

Paragraphs 108 through 126 of the auditing standard reflect the PCAOB's reaction to public company representatives who commented during the proposal phase of the standard that Section 404 compliance will require substantial retesting and wasted cost. It also reflects concern about the experience of federal bank regulators where the external auditors used the work of internal auditors to an inappropriately high degree. There were problematic cases where the auditors did not independently validate the internal controls over financial reporting.

The standard mandates that "the auditor must perform enough of the testing himself or herself so that the auditor's own work provides the principal evidence for the auditor's opinion. The auditor may, however, use the work of others to alter the nature, timing, or extent of the work he or she otherwise would have performed." (¶ 108.) Despite allowing the use of the work of others, the standard emphasizes that the auditor's direct personal knowledge, observations, reperformance of key control steps, and inspection take precedence over information provided by others.

The "others" the standard is referring to include:

- Internal auditors. (The standard refers auditors to AU Section 322, *The Auditor's Consideration of the Internal Audit Function in an Audit of Financial Statements*, for further guidance.)
- Other company personnel.

- Third parties working under the direction of management or the audit committee.

When deciding to use the work of others, the auditor is required to evaluate the nature of the controls subjected to the work of others (see ¶ 109.7.1 of this discussion), evaluate the competence and objectivity of the persons who performed the work (see ¶ 109.7.2 of this discussion), and test some of the work to evaluate its quality and effectiveness (see ¶ 109.7.3 of this discussion).

Auditing Standard Paragraphs: ¶s 108–126

See Also Auditing Standard Paragraphs: ¶s 9, 40, 79

Persons Affected:

Internal Auditors, Auditors

Effect:

Auditors can use the work of others to a certain extent when performing the audit. The auditing standard clarifies the ability of the auditor to use the work of others and reiterates that the auditor's opinion must be based solely on work done by the auditor or the auditor's direct validation of any work done by others.

Action:

Auditors can use the work of others but the auditors' own work must be substantial enough to form the basis for the auditors' opinion on the effectiveness of the company's internal control over financial reporting. Auditors are required to evaluate and test the work of others upon which they plan to rely. Internal auditors may provide the results of their work on the company's internal controls over financial reporting to the external auditors for use during the audit of the company's financial statements and internal control over financial reporting.

Rules and Regulations Cited:

AU Section 319, *Internal Control in a Financial Statement Audit*; AU Section 322, *The Auditor's Consideration of the Internal Audit Function in an Audit of Financial Statements*; FAS No. 5, *Accounting for Contingencies; the Institute of Internal Auditors International Standards for the Professional Practice of Internal Auditing.*

Suggested References:

"Relationships with Third-Party Users of Internal Auditing Work Products," *Internal Auditing Manual* Chapter I1.

"Internal Auditors' Roles in the Prevention, Detection, and Correction of Financial Statement Fraud," *Internal Auditing* (May/June 2002).

¶ 109.7.1. Evaluating the Nature of the Controls Subjected to the Work of Others

When using the work of others, the auditor is required to evaluate the nature of the controls subjected to the work, such as:

- *The materiality and the risk of misstatement in these particular accounts and disclosures.* The riskier and more material the accounts and amounts, the less the auditor can rely on the work of others. The auditors must be especially careful to conduct for themselves the testing of all controls specifically designed to detect or prevent fraud that is at least reasonably possible to result in material misstatements.

- *The degree of judgment required to evaluate the operating effectiveness of the control.* The more judgment required, then the less the auditor can rely on the work of others. If the only way to test the control is via subjective evaluation, then the auditor cannot rely on the work of others. On the other hand, if the control is subject to substantial objective testing, then the auditor can rely more on the work of others.

- *The pervasiveness of the control.* If the control affects many different accounts and amounts, then the auditor must not rely on the work of others as extensively as when the control does not affect many accounts.

- *The level of judgment or estimation that is required in the account or disclosure.* The higher the level of judgment or estimation, the less the auditor can rely on the work of others.

- *The potential for management override and manipulation of the control.* As a general rule, any account that involves judgments, valuations, or estimates should be directly validated by the auditor.

The auditing standard advises that the auditor should pay special attention to the results of tests of the company's control environment and should not rely on the work of others to reduce the amount of work in this area, though the auditor can consult such work in order to help determine the level of testing required with regard to the control environment. (See ¶ 109.4 of this discussion for more on the control environment.)

The control environment of the organization pervades all other controls. It includes both hard and soft controls, such as those over:

- *Integrity and ethical values.* The auditor should make initial judgments regarding the culture of the firm. This should take into account any known history of the firm's management and its relationship with other auditors in the past.

- *Commitment to competence.* What level of education and experience does management and the audit committee possess?

- *Board of directors or audit committee participation.* Does this firm have competent leadership, and are the board members and audit committee members actively participating in the company's financial reporting decisions?

- *Management's philosophy and operating style.* Is this basically a financially conservative firm or a financially liberal firm? What level of risk is considered appropriate?

- *Organizational structure.* Is the company centralized or geographically dispersed? What are the relevant reporting relationships?

- *Assignment of authority and responsibility.* Is there tight, centralized control, or is the company decentralized?

- *Human resource policies and procedures.* Are thorough background checks conducted on all personnel? Are employees adequately trained in company policies, procedures, and controls?

The auditor must perform walkthroughs but can also gain additional evidence by reviewing the work of others who have performed and documented walkthroughs. This is a difficult issue given the complexity of accounting software currently in use. The challenge becomes, given the auditor's limited capabilities with unfamiliar software, how do they limit their reliance on the work of others and still collect the necessary evidence? Thorough documentation of all control policies and procedures will assist the auditor in this regard.

Auditing Standard Paragraphs: ¶s 112–116

See Also Auditing Standard Paragraphs: ¶s 9, 79

Persons Affected:

Internal Auditors, Auditors

Effect:

Auditors must evaluate the nature of the controls subjected to the work of others before the auditors rely on that work.

Action:

Auditors must evaluate the nature of the controls subjected to the work of others before the auditors rely on that work. Auditors should not rely on the work of others when evaluating the company's overall control environment. Auditors must perform walkthroughs themselves but may obtain additional evidence from walkthroughs performed by others.

Rules and Regulations Cited:

AU Section 319, *Internal Control in a Financial Statement Audit*; FAS No. 5, *Accounting for Contingencies.*

¶ 109.7.2. Evaluating the Competency and Objectivity of Others

The degree of competence and objectivity of the individuals performing the work on which the auditor may potentially rely must be evaluated. Though this may seem like a purely judgmental determination, based on the guidance in AU Section 322, *The Auditor's Consideration of the Internal Audit Function in an Audit of Financial Statements*, there are some specific factors that the auditor can consider, including:

- The individual's educational level, professional experience, professional certification, and continuing education.
- Company practices regarding employee assignments, supervisory and review practices, and performance evaluations.
- Documentation of the individual's work.
- The organizational status of individuals responsible for the work of others (i.e., the testing authority).
- The company's policies intended to maintain the individuals' objectivity about the areas being tested (e.g., policies prohibiting an employee from testing an area where the employee's relative is responsible for controls and prohibiting employees from testing controls in areas where they were recently assigned).

The standard makes it clear that the company's external auditor can rely on the work of the company's internal audit function. This addresses a point raised by many of the public comments received by the PCAOB during the proposed phase of the standard. Many commenters were concerned that the PCAOB was discounting the work of internal auditors by requiring the external auditors to perform so many of the testing procedures themselves. The standard in its final form allays some of these concerns by stating: "Internal auditors are expected to have greater competence with regard to internal control over financial reporting and objectivity than other company personnel. Therefore, the auditor may be able to use their work to a greater extent than the work of other company personnel . . . . If internal auditors have performed an extensive amount of relevant work and the auditor determines they possess a high degree of competence and objectivity, the auditor could use their work to the greatest extent an auditor could use the work of others." (¶ 121.) This endorsement of the work of internal auditors is accompanied by one caveat: if the internal audit function reports solely to management rather than the audit committee or full board, their work should be relied upon to a lesser extent.

The PCAOB refers to AU Section 322, *The Auditor's Consideration of the Internal Audit Function in an Audit of Financial Statements*, as being useful guidance to the auditor considering using the work of internal auditors. In summary, Section 322 instructs the external auditors to:

- Assess the competence and objectivity of the internal audit function.

- Determine the effect of the internal audit function on understanding internal control, the assessed risk, and the design of substantive procedures.
- Determine the degree of reliance on the internal audit function.
- Evaluate the internal audit work.

The quality of an internal auditing department cannot be equated with the quality of the issuer's internal controls. A good internal auditing department is not necessarily indicative of high-quality internal controls, nor is a low-quality internal audit department indicative of substandard internal controls. Internal auditing and internal control are separate functions that are generally developed, implemented, and monitored by completely separate functional departments. Management, not the internal auditing function, is ultimately responsible for the design and monitoring of the company's internal controls.

Here is a list of questions that auditors can use to help them evaluate the quality of the issuer's internal audit function:

(1) What is the level of internal auditing expertise in the department?

(2) How many years of experience does each internal auditor have, or what is the average number of years of experience of the entire department?

(3) Does the internal audit function report to the audit committee?

(4) Are the internal auditors members of the Institute of Internal Auditors (IIA), which would require them to comply with the IIA's Code of Ethics?

(5) Do the internal auditors follow the IIA's *International Standards for the Professional Practice of Internal Auditing*?

(6) Does the internal audit function vigilantly guard its independence within the company?

(7) Can management and the external auditors look to the internal audit department for direction on strong versus weak areas of the company?

(8) What level of testing does the internal audit function perform?

(9) Are the internal auditors testing only a fraction of the transactions that affect the financial statements, or are they conducting more thorough, comprehensive tests?

(10) What are the technical skill levels of the internal audit staff?

(11) Does the internal audit function have dedicated IT auditors on staff?

Auditing Standard Paragraphs: ¶s 117–122

See Also Auditing Standard Paragraph: ¶ 112

Persons Affected:

Internal Auditors, Auditors

Effect:

Auditors must evaluate the competence and objectivity of others before using their work.

Action:

By looking at factors such as educational level, professional experience, professional certification, continuing education, work assignments, supervision, documentation, and performance evaluations, auditors must evaluate the competence and objectivity of others before using their work. External auditors may rely on the work of qualified and objective internal auditors more heavily than the work of other parties, unless the internal auditors report solely to management.

Rules and Regulations Cited:

International Standards for the Professional Practice of Internal Auditing

Suggested References:

"Relationships with Third-Party Users of Internal Auditing Work Products," *Internal Auditing Manual* Chapter 11.

"Affirming Independence, Integrity, and Objectivity in Enron's Shadow," *Internal Auditing Report* (April 2002).

"Internal Auditors' Roles in Overcoming the Financial Reporting Crisis," *Internal Auditing* (November/December 2002).

¶ 109.7.3. Testing the Work of Others

The PCAOB provides some fairly detailed guidance about what level of testing the auditor should perform when using the work of others in an audit of internal control over financial reporting. The "others" referred to in these paragraphs are the company's personnel, especially the issuer's internal audit department. The goal of the auditing standard is to allow auditors to use as much of the work of others as possible where reliance on that work is warranted. To that end, the PCAOB provides evaluation criteria and examples for the auditor to use as guidance when planning a validation testing plan. The standard states that the auditor should test some of the controls that others tested or similar controls not actually tested by others.

The type and extent of testing that the auditor performs on the work of others can vary, but should be sufficient given the nature, circumstances, and extent of testing required to cover the material. In all cases, the overall level of testing performed by the auditor must be sufficient to form the basis of the auditor's opinion on the effectiveness of internal control over financial reporting.

Foremost in the auditor's evaluation should be the competence and objectivity of the company's personnel performing the work. In addition, the auditor should evaluate whether:

- *The scope of work is appropriate to meet the objectives.* Was a broad enough testing sample performed under the circumstances?

- *Work programs are adequate.* Was the testing thorough?

- *Work performed is adequately documented, including evidence of supervision and review.* Is the documentation sufficient for review without further work being required, and is it clear that the appropriate level of supervision and review has taken place?

- *Conclusions are appropriate in the circumstances.* Are the interpretations of the test results valid?

- *Reports are consistent with the results of the work performed.* Is there consistency between the work plan and the reporting of results?

The auditing standard provides some specific examples as guidance for the auditor with regard to:

- *Controls over the period-end financial reporting process.* Due to the risks involved, the auditors should probably perform most of these tests themselves. According to the standard, "the auditor might use the work of internal auditors to some extent but not the work of others within the company." (¶ 126.)

- *IT general controls.* The standard deems these controls to have a low degree of judgment and, due to their pervasiveness, a high impact on the control environment. Therefore, the auditor can usually use the work of others in this area to a moderate extent.

- *Management self-assessment of controls.* The standard points out that, since these controls are self-assessed by the persons responsible for performing the controls, the self-assessments should not be used because they may lack objectivity.

- *Controls over the calculation of depreciation of fixed assets.* The standard allows that, due to the repetitive nature of this material, the auditor can rely on the work of others "perhaps entirely" as long as the competence and objectivity of those performing the work is adequate and there is a low potential for management override of the associated controls. There is a caveat here though—the depreciation of the fixed assets is usually not the issue. A primary audit issue in the fixed assets arena is what makes up the book value of those assets. A common financial fraud is for the company to shift operating expenses, through the work order system, to the balance sheet as assets. The auditor should certainly validate that this is not occurring.

- *Alternating tests of controls.* The standard uses accounts payable, including controls over cash disbursements, as an example and allows that these controls involve a low degree of judgment and have a low potential for management override. The standard allows that the auditors can rely on the work of others to a large extent, "perhaps entirely," based, of course, on the objectivity and competence of those performing the work.

Auditing Standard Paragraphs: ¶s 123–126

See Also Auditing Standard Paragraph: ¶ 40

Persons Affected:

Management, Internal Auditors, Auditors

Effect:

Auditors must test some of the work of others in order to evaluate the quality and effectiveness of the work. The standard provides specific guidance regarding controls over period-end financial reporting, IT general controls, management self-assessment, controls over the calculation of the depreciation of assets, and alternating tests of controls.

Action:

By looking at factors such as scope of the work, adequacy of procedures, adequacy of documentation, appropriateness of conclusions, and consistency of reports, auditors must evaluate the quality and effectiveness of the work of others before using the work. Management should consult the standard's guidance regarding the auditor's use of the work of others in specific situations related to controls over period-end financial reporting, IT general controls, management self-assessment, controls over the calculation of the depreciation of assets, and alternating tests of controls.

Rules and Regulations Cited:

None cited.

¶ 109.8. Forming an Opinion on the Effectiveness of Internal Control Over Financial Reporting

Before forming an opinion, the auditor must evaluate all of the information that was gathered during the audit from all sources. This includes:

- *The adequacy of management's assessment of internal control over financial reporting.*
- *The results of the testing of internal controls conducted by the auditors.* This would include the results of inquiries, documentation, reperformance of controls, and walkthroughs.
- *The results of the financial statement audit.* If misstatements or material errors are found in the financial statements, this serves as practical evidence that the internal controls over financial reporting are not wholly effective and may contain significant deficiencies.

- *Any identified internal control deficiencies.* Significant deficiencies or material weaknesses, whether corrected or not, should be considered in forming an overall opinion.

- *All reports issued by the internal audit department that address internal control over financial reporting.* Any findings or reports prepared by the internal audit department should be taken into consideration. According to the standard, this is not limited to financial audits conducted by internal auditors, but rather includes "reports issued by internal audit as a result of operational audits or specific reviews of key processes if those reports address controls related to internal control over financial reporting." (¶ 128.) Any internal control deficiencies identified by internal audit, or similar departments such as a loan review department at a bank, should be taken into consideration by the auditor when forming the opinion.

Auditing Standard Paragraphs: ¶s 127–141

See Also Auditing Standard Paragraphs: ¶s 9–10, 55–59, 175, 178

Persons Affected:

Internal Auditors, Auditors

Effect:

Auditors must evaluate information from all relevant sources, particularly the company's internal audit function, when forming an opinion on internal control over financial reporting.

Action:

Auditors must evaluate evidence from all relevant sources, including management's assessment of internal control over financial reporting, negative results of substantive procedures performed during the financial statement audit, any identified control deficiencies, and all relevant reports issued by the company's internal audit function. Internal audit departments must be prepared to provide the company's external auditors with copies of all reports issued during the year that have even a tangential relevancy to internal control over financial reporting.

Rules and Regulations Cited:

SEC Staff Accounting Bulletin Topic 1M2, *Immaterial Misstatements That Are Intentional*; Sarbanes-Oxley Act Section 302.

Suggested Reference:

"Relationships with Third-Party Users of Internal Auditing Work Products," *Internal Auditing Manual* Chapter I1.

¶ 109.8.1. Issuing an Unqualified Opinion

Of course, every company's goal is to receive an unqualified opinion from its auditors. The PCAOB sets the hurdle high when it states that the auditor may issue an unqualified opinion "only when there are no identified material weaknesses and when there have been no restrictions in the scope of the auditor's work. The existence of a material weakness requires the auditor to express an adverse opinion ... while a scope limitation requires the auditor to express a qualified opinion or a disclaimer of opinion, depending on the significance of the limitation in scope." (¶ 129.)

Assuming both the auditor and issuer are acting reputably, the standard of "no material weakness" is very high indeed. The majority of firms will, with the assistance of their auditors, no doubt find many internal control deficiencies, particularly during their first audit of internal control over financial reporting. These will have to be corrected immediately so that companies can validate the effectiveness of the remediation prior to publication of the financial statements. Even then, under the auditing standard, significant deficiencies that were present during the interim periods might have to be disclosed as changes in internal control over financial reporting.

The issue of whether a problem with an internal control rises to the level of a material weakness or significant deficiency is sure to cause some conflict between companies and their auditors as issuers struggle to meet these requirements. See ¶ 107 of this discussion for more on the issue of materiality.

Auditing Standard Paragraph: ¶ 129

See Also Auditing Standard Paragraphs: ¶s 175, 178

Persons Affected:

Management, Auditors

Effect:

The company's auditor can issue an unqualified opinion on the company's internal control over financial reporting only if there are no identified material weaknesses and there have been no restrictions on the scope of the audit.

Action:

The auditor must determine that there are no material weaknesses or scope restrictions in order to provide an unqualified opinion.

Rules and Regulations Cited:

None cited.

Suggested References:

"Unqualified Opinions," *Accounting and Auditing Disclosure Manual* § 70.

"Adverse Opinions," *Accounting and Auditing Disclosure Manual* § 73.

"Disclaimer of Opinion," *Accounting and Auditing Disclosure Manual* § 74.

¶ 109.8.2. Evaluating Deficiencies in Internal Control Over Financial Reporting

Given identified deficiencies, the auditor must assess and evaluate the significance of these deficiencies individually and in the aggregate. This evaluation should address the likelihood that the deficiency or combination of deficiencies will result in a misstatement, as well as the magnitude of the potential misstatement that would result.

In evaluating these deficiencies in internal control over financial reporting, the potential for a misstatement determines the significance of the deficiency. It is the *potential* for misstatement that the auditor is focused on, as opposed to actual misstatement. From an internal control standpoint, the goal is to identify where misstatements could occur. This is a higher safety threshold for financial reporting than is the identification of actual financial reporting misstatements and is closely associated with the company's risk assessment and control points.

Several factors affect the likelihood that a deficiency, or combination of deficiencies, could result in a misstatement of an account balance or disclosure, including:

- *The nature of the financial statement accounts or disclosures.* For example, reserves, valuations, suspense accounts, and related-party transactions inherently involve greater risks.

- *The susceptibility of the related assets or liabilities to loss or fraud.* Greater susceptibility increases risk. An example of an asset that is not highly susceptible to loss or fraud is industrial chemicals. Most are very application-specific and are often customized. That is, there is no ready market for the asset if it were stolen. In comparison, cash in a cash register, general merchandise, and stocks of food in a restaurant are all likely to be stolen and all have ready uses to the average thief. But nonetheless, companies should be very careful about controls over all assets that could have value whether that be monetary value to a thief or destructive value to a terrorist.

- *The subjectivity, complexity, and extent of judgment involved.* The more subjectivity, complexity, and judgment associated with an internal control, the greater the risk that there could be an error or fraud that could cause a misstatement.

- *The cause and frequency of known or detected exceptions for the control.* Some controls have known variances. A control with an observed non-negligible deviation rate is a deficiency.

- *The interaction of the control with other overlapping and compensating controls.* Given that a particular control may not be very effective, the risk that the failure of the control would result in a misstatement can be minimized by well-designed overlapping and compensating controls.

- *Interaction of deficiencies.* Some combinations of deficiencies could create a significant deficiency. That is, some controls, if not performed properly, are exacerbated by design weaknesses and operational deficiencies of other internal controls. For example, if certain reconciliations have not been performed for an extended period of time in one area, then a manager perpetrating a financial reporting fraud that has eluded other internal controls over financial reporting may have taken advantage and caused the financial impact of the ignored reconciliation to increase to a material level.

- *Possible future consequences of a deficiency.* The auditor should take into account the growth rate of the underlying activity and what will happen in the future if the deficiency is allowed to continue.

Other concerns that the auditor should take into account when evaluating the risk of an account include:

- *The underlying nature of the accounts, processes, and disclosures.* In each industry, there are certain known "red flag" accounts and practices. For example, sales contracts in the software industry often include contingencies, warranties, or satisfaction guarantees that prevent the booking of the sale, or at least the full sale amount. In retailing, merchandise loss reserves, health insurance reserves (especially 125K self-insurance plans), and forced discounts can cause problems. In healthcare, billing scams are an issue. The auditor must identify these types of red flag issues and provide those areas with a thorough evaluation based on the greater degree of risk associated with those items.

- *Known operational problems with operating controls.* When the auditor encounters problems with the design or operating effectiveness of an internal control, the auditor must evaluate the cause and likely frequency of the failure of that control. For instance, when a problem exists in one area of a large organization, it becomes more likely that this same problem exists in other divisions of that same firm. Systemic problems in large companies can be clustered around similar types of operations that have similar accounting software implementations and similar organizational philosophies. Another key way for the auditor to track internal control problems through a company is, once an internal control issue is identified, for the auditor to follow the career path of the manager that created the internal control problem to the other operating divisions of the firm. Management personnel often spend only a few years in each job. The auditor is likely to find the same behavioral patterns, relating to internal control over financial reporting, follow those same managers.

The existence and likely effect of overlapping and compensating controls should be understood. In most cases there may be overlapping or compensating general controls that mitigate the severity of the deficiency. The auditing standard recognizes that some controls are designed to work as a group of controls with the same control objective.

The auditor should consider the relevant size and impact of the misstatement likely to occur as the result of a deficient control. Factors that affect the magnitude of the misstatement that could result from a deficiency in controls include:

- *The financial statement amounts, potential amounts, or total of transactions exposed to the internal control deficiency.* The smaller the amounts, or potential amounts, the less severe the weakness.

- *The volume of activity in the account in the current period or expected in the future.* If an organization had a problem with petty cash in the current period, but eliminates the petty cash account, then the future volume of activity would be expected to be zero.

In evaluating the size of any potential misstatement, the auditor can take into account the maximum possible misstatement, or misstatement by omission, of that particular account. The audit standard refers to the level of assurance that the auditor should strive for as a level of detail "that would satisfy prudent officials ... that they have reasonable assurance that transactions are recorded as necessary to permit the preparation of financial statements in conformity with" GAAP. This "prudent official" qualification has its origins in the SEC requirements for reasonable assurance and reasonable detail. (See, for example, 15 USCS 78m.)

Inadequate documentation of the design and intended functioning of internal control over financial reporting is a control deficiency. This places a high premium on documentation, given that a simple lack of documentation engenders a discussion about the significance of the deficiency. Many organizations have the remediation of their documentation as one of their primary Section 404 compliance objectives. This makes perfect sense because it is very difficult for higher levels of management to evaluate anything that is not documented. The auditor must determine the extent of the missing documentation to determine the significance of the deficiency.

The auditor is also expected to evaluate the qualitative and quantitative controls associated with each account. According to the standard, deficiencies in the following areas would likely be found to be significant deficiencies:

- *Controls over the selection and application of accounting policies that are in conformance with GAAP.* In practice, this is probably not a problem for most companies. Even Enron's chief accountant, in his legal defense, could claim that all of their accounting conformed to GAAP. Just because policies conform to GAAP does not mean that their application fairly or accurately represents the financial condition of the firm. The auditor should be looking for consistency in the application of policies over a consecutive period spanning several years. The most common failure in the area of policy selection and application is the inconsistent application of policies. Policy application often fails to be consistent between operating divisions of the same company and across a span of consecutive years for that same company. Wide variations in policy application give the operating executives substantial leeway in manipulating the financial results, all under the auspices of GAAP compliance.

- *Antifraud programs and controls.* All firms will be espousing compliance with the whistleblower protections contained in the Sarbanes-Oxley Act. The auditor should be focused on finding evidence, either positive or negative, that the whistleblower protections are being taken seriously. If the auditor finds no evidence of any whistleblower program, this should serve as practical evidence that the firm has no such program in existence.

- *Controls over non-routine and non-systematic transactions.* These include reserves, valuations, and estimates. These are the red flag accounts that all companies have. In specific industries there will be specific issues that are the bogeymen of that industry. Experienced auditors will keep an extensive list of problems known to exist within each specific industry.

- *Controls over the period-end financial reporting process, including controls over procedures used to enter transaction totals in into the general ledger; initiate, authorize, record, and process journal entries into the general ledger; and record recurring and nonrecurring adjustments to the financial statements.* If qualitative weakness is found in conjunction with quantitative weakness in any of the critical manual rollup processes, the auditor should conclude that there are significant deficiencies. The rollup and consolidation of financial reporting is one of the most problematic areas in all of accounting and is also one of the hardest areas to check.

In ¶ 140, the auditing standard also presents a long list of items that the auditor should consider as at least a significant deficiency and as a strong indicator that a material weakness in internal control over financial reporting exists:

- *Restatement of a previously issued financial statement to reflect the correction of a misstatement due to error or fraud.* Just because a previously issued financial statement may not have been correct does not necessarily mean that a future financial statement will be erroneous. However, the PCAOB does feel it is a red flag to be considered.

- *Identification by the auditor of a material misstatement in financial statements in the current period that was not initially identified by the company's internal control over financial reporting.* This is still a strong indicator of material weakness even if management corrects the misstatement. This makes sense—if the auditor catches an error in the financial statements that the issuer missed, then there is evidently a breakdown somewhere in the internal control structure.

- *Ineffective audit committee oversight of the company's external financial reporting and internal control over external financial reporting.* This must be reported to the full board of directors. See ¶ 109.4.2 of this discussion for more on the auditor's evaluation of audit committee effectiveness.

- *An ineffective internal audit function or risk assessment function.* This is more important than perhaps it was previously because now the auditor is able to rely very heavily on the work done by others, such as internal auditors.

- *An ineffective regulatory compliance function.* This concern is especially pronounced in industries with intense regulation, such as banking, insurance, and healthcare.

- *Fraud of any magnitude on the part of senior management.* Should the auditor become aware of fraud on the part of management, whether material or immaterial in nature, this would clearly be a strong indicator that material weaknesses may exist in the issuer's internal control over financial reporting. According to the standard, "The auditor is required to plan and perform procedures to obtain reasonable assurance that material misstatement caused by fraud is detected." (¶ 140.)

- *Uncorrected significant deficiencies that were communicated to management and the audit committee some time ago.* While this might appear very obvious—that this type of item should be remediated immediately—some issues are very difficult and time-consuming to address. Some internal control problems might require massive commitments of time and effort to resolve. The auditor should attempt to understand the complexity and magnitude of an existing deficiency before making a judgment. The standard stipulates that these issues must have remained uncorrected "after some reasonable period of time" before becoming a cause for additional concern.

- *An ineffective control environment.* This is often a difficult concept for the auditor to assess. It is based on the myriad considerations laid out in the COSO framework. See ¶ 109.4 of this discussion for more on the auditor's assessment of the control environment.

Appendix D of the auditing standard provides a few examples of significant deficiencies and material weaknesses, but the discussion there is brief.

Auditing Standard Paragraphs: ¶s 130–141

See Also Auditing Standard Paragraphs: ¶s 9–10, 55–59, Appendix D ¶s D1–D3

Persons Affected:

Management, Internal Auditors, Accounting Management, Compliance Officers, Audit Committee Members, Auditors

Effect:

Auditors must evaluate deficiencies in the company's internal control over financial reporting and determine whether the deficiencies, individually or in combination, rise to the level of significant deficiencies or material weaknesses.

Action:

The auditor must look at all of the company's internal control deficiencies and determine, based on certain criteria, if the deficiencies constitute significant deficiencies or material weaknesses.

Rules and Regulations Cited:

SEC Staff Accounting Bulletin Topic 1M2, *Immaterial Misstatements That Are Intentional*; Sarbanes-Oxley Act Section 302.

Suggested References:

"Materiality," *Handbook of SEC Accounting and Disclosure* § A10.

"The Ethics of Materiality in Financial Reporting," *Internal Auditing* (January/February 2002).

¶ 110. The Requirement for Written Representations

The PCAOB requires the auditor to obtain written representations from management. The specific items that must be included in the management representation letter are stipulated in the auditing standard as statements:

- *Acknowledging that management has responsibility for establishing and maintaining effective internal control over financial reporting.* Considering the requirements of the Sarbanes-Oxley Act, management should have no issue with signing off on this point.

- *Stating that management has performed an evaluation of the effectiveness of the company's internal control over financial reporting and specifying the control criteria.* The evaluation part of this statement is straightforward. Specifying the control criteria probably means building the COSO framework components and objectives into the letter. Since the COSO framework is the only clearly acceptable criteria, it is difficult to imagine any other criteria would appear in this part of the letter.

- *Stating that management did not use the auditor's procedures performed during the audits of internal control over financial reporting or the financial statements as part of the basis for management's assessment of the effectiveness of internal control over financial reporting.* This is a reiteration of the prohibition in ¶ 41 of the standard.

• *Stating management's conclusion about the effectiveness of the company's internal control over financial reporting based on the control criteria as of a specified date.* To provide any answer other than that the internal controls over financial reporting are effective would preclude the issuance of an unqualified opinion.

• *Stating that management has disclosed to the auditor all deficiencies in the design or operation of internal control over financial reporting identified as part of management's assessment, and separately disclosed significant deficiencies and material weaknesses.* This leaves management with little leeway—all deficiencies must be disclosed, regardless of whether management feels they are significant deficiencies or material weaknesses. The separate disclosure of deficiencies that management believes to be significant deficiencies or material weaknesses in internal control over financial reporting will alert the company's auditors to the need to look at these specific issues closely.

• *Describing any material fraud and any other fraud that, although not material, involves senior management or management or other employees who have a significant role in the company's internal control over financial reporting.* This requirement sounds good but it remains to be seen to what extent management will be willing to divulge what has traditionally been handled as discreetly as possible. Hopefully, in the post-Sarbanes-Oxley world, this sort of disclosure will become the norm.

• *Stating whether control deficiencies identified and communicated to the audit committee during previous engagements have been resolved, and specifically identifying any that have not.* This provides a follow-up mechanism for the auditor from year to year. Paragraph 207 of the auditing standard requires the auditor to communicate in writing to management and the audit committee all significant deficiencies and material weaknesses identified during the audit. Determining whether these reported issues have been addressed will be key during the audit planning phase.

• *Stating whether there were, subsequent to the date being reported on, any changes in internal control over financial reporting or other factors that might significantly affect internal control over financial reporting, including any corrective actions taken by management with regard to significant deficiencies and material weaknesses.* Particularly in the first year of implementation, some companies may be faced with the need to change their internal controls over financial reporting or take corrective action with regard to significant deficiencies and material weaknesses. Not all companies will achieve these changes and corrective actions in time to include this information in the initial report, and will then need to provide this information in the management representation letter, as required. In future years, this should be avoided if possible, as it simply raises red flags from the very beginning of the audit.

In summary then, the failure to obtain written representations from management, including management's refusal to furnish them, constitutes a limitation on the scope of the audit and precludes an unqualified opinion. The representation letter should be signed by the CEO and CFO, or others with equivalent positions in the company.

Auditing Standard Paragraphs: ¶s 142–144

See Also Auditing Standard Paragraphs: ¶s 178, 207

Persons Affected:

Management, Auditors

Effect:

The auditor is required to obtain certain management representations specific to the audit of internal control over financial reporting.

Action:

As in all audits, the auditor must receive certain written representations from the company's CEO and CFO.

Rules and Regulations Cited:

AU Section 333, *Management Representations.*

¶ 111. The Relationship of an Audit of Internal Control Over Financial Reporting to an Audit of Financial Statements

The internal controls over financial reporting are, of course, interrelated with the financial statements themselves. It would be redundant to a large extent for audits to be done for internal control and then done separately for financial statements. The PCAOB responded to the input it received, especially from issuers, that requiring two separate audits would double the cost of the annual audit without any incremental benefit. On the other hand, audits of internal control over financial reporting were part of the existing GAAS related to financial statement audits for many years. Yet the audits of internal control over financial reporting that were conducted prior to the PCAOB's establishment of this auditing standard do not appear to have had an enormous effect on the reliability or usefulness of financial statements. At any rate, the issuers got part of what they wanted in that they do not have to pay for two completely separate audits. It remains to be seen what the audit firms will charge companies for their audit of internal control over financial reporting that is performed in conjunction with their audit of financial statements. Audit fees are sure to increase—the PCAOB acknowledged this fact when it released the final standard—but by how much is uncertain.

The standard points out that although the audit of the financial statements is integrated with the audit of internal control over financial reporting, the objectives and procedures are not identical. Because the objectives of each audit are interrelated, the auditor is expected to coordinate them, effectively conducting both audits simultaneously.

Auditing Standard Paragraphs: ¶s 145–158

See Also Auditing Standard Paragraphs: ¶s 26, 160

Persons Affected:

Auditors

Effect:

The audit of internal control over financial reporting should be integrated with the audit of the issuer's financial statements.

Action:

The auditor must integrate the audit of internal control over financial reporting with the audit of financial statements.

Rules and Regulations Cited:

AU Section 316, *Consideration of Fraud in a Financial Statement Audit*; AU Section 330, *The Confirmation Process*; AU Section 331, *Inventories*.

¶ 111.1. Tests of Controls in an Audit of internal Control Over Financial Reporting

The auditor must obtain evidence about the company's internal control over financial reporting as of "a point in time" and "taken as a whole" in order to issue an opinion on whether management's assessment of the effectiveness of the company's internal control over financial reporting is fairly stated:

- *As of a point in time.* The auditor should obtain evidence that internal control over financial reporting has operated effectively for a sufficient period of time. This is ordinarily the year covered by the company's financial statements.

- *As a whole.* The auditor should obtain evidence about the effectiveness of controls related to all relevant assertions for all significant accounts and disclosures in the financial statements. This requires a lot more testing than what would normally be required of the auditor to provide an opinion on the financial statements at a single point in time.

Therefore the scope of the audit over both internal control and the financial statements is much broader than in the past. The financial statement audit could be said to require an opinion that the financial statements fairly represent the financial condition of the issuer as of a point in time. This new auditing standard requires the auditor to state as such, but also to state an opinion about the way those financial statements were assembled.

Auditing Standard Paragraphs: ¶s 147–149

Persons Affected:

Auditors

Effect:

The auditor's opinion on whether management's assessment of the effectiveness of the company's internal control over financial reporting is fairly stated must relate the effectiveness of the company's internal control over financial reporting as of a point in time and taken as a whole.

Action:

The auditor has different testing standards for the effectiveness of the company's internal control over financial reporting at a point in time versus the financial statements taken as a whole.

Rules and Regulations Cited:

None cited.

¶ 111.2. Tests of Controls in an Audit of Financial Statements

According to the standard, "To assess control risk for specific financial statement assertions at less than the maximum, the auditor is required to obtain evidence that the relevant controls operated effectively during the *entire* period upon which the auditor plans to place reliance on those controls." (¶ 150.) Thus, in a financial statement audit, the auditor does not have to assess that the risk associated with an internal control failure is very high if the auditor can show that the internal control was functioning properly for the entire period. This means that, especially given the examples in Appendix D of the standard, the PCAOB has effectively raised the standards for auditing financial statements. This occurs because the audit of internal control over financial reporting is required to be performed in conjunction with the audit of financial statements and the new auditing standard for the former is more robust than the previous standard for the latter.

Auditing Standard Paragraphs: ¶s 150–151

See Also Auditing Standard Paragraphs: ¶s 147–149, 160

Persons Affected:

Auditors

Effect:

Tests of controls in an audit of financial statements are different than those in an audit of internal control over financial reporting.

Action:

Auditors ordinarily perform tests of controls and substantive procedures in an audit of financial statements. The auditor is required to assess control risk during the audit of the financial statements and determine whether relevant controls operated effectively during the entire period upon which the auditor plans to place reliance on the effectiveness of those controls.

Rules and Regulations Cited:

None cited.

Suggested References:

"Auditing Internal Controls Under Sarbanes-Oxley," *Bank Auditing and Accounting Report* (January 2004).

"Performing the Audit," *Handbook of Accounting and Auditing* Chapter B3.

¶ 111.3. The Effect of Tests of Controls on Substantive Procedures

The PCAOB states that the auditor must continue to perform tests of controls on substantive procedures in the financial statement audit—this requirement is not in any way diminished by the requirement that the tests of substantive procedures be done for the audit of internal control over financial reporting. That is, the auditor was always required to perform tests of substantive procedures covering how the issuer assembles its financial statements. The PCAOB is making it clear that, although the auditors now have to do a lot more testing of substantive procedures involved with the audit of internal control over financial reporting, they still have to do this work in association with an audit of financial statements. This is an interesting presentation by the PCAOB. Consider that the tests of substantive procedures associated with financial statements involve the auditor testing the details of transactions and balances, and internal controls over all of these. If these tests had worked effectively in the past, auditors would have identified and possibly prevented many of the large financial frauds. But, given the litany of financial frauds and misstatements in recent years, these tests of substantive procedures did not, apparently, work very well in the past.

In addition to testing the details of transactions and balances and performing analytical procedures, the auditor is specifically required to:

- Reconcile the financial statements to the accounting records.
- Evaluate the risk of management override of controls, particularly with regard to period-end controls.

- Examine material adjustments made during the preparation of the financial statements.

- Perform specific tests of details in the financial statements (e.g., request the confirmation of accounts receivable, observe the inventories, etc.).

Auditing Standard Paragraphs: ¶s 152–156

Persons Affected:

Auditors

Effect:

Tests of controls on substantive procedures in an audit of financial statements are germane in an audit of internal controls over financial reporting.

Action:

The auditor is required to continue performing tests of controls on substantive procedures.

Rules and Regulations Cited:

AU Section 316, *Consideration of Fraud in a Financial Statement Audit*; AU Section 330, *The Confirmation Process*; AU Section 331, *Inventories*.

¶ 111.4. The Effect of Substantive Procedures on the Auditor's Conclusions About the Operating Effectiveness of Controls

In case it was not already clear, the PCAOB mandates that the auditor must consider the impact of the findings of the audit of the company's financial statements on the effectiveness of the company's internal control over financial reporting. The standard goes so far as to delineate certain weaknesses found in the financial statement audit that must be evaluated in the audit of internal control over financial reporting. These are:

- The auditor's risk evaluations, especially those related to fraud.

- Findings with respect to illegal acts and related-party transactions.

- Indications of management bias in making accounting estimates and in selecting accounting principles.

- Any misstatements detected by the auditor's substantive procedures.

Auditing Standard Paragraphs: ¶s 157–158

See Also Auditing Standard Paragraph: ¶ 26

Persons Affected:

Auditors

Effect:

The auditor must evaluate the results of the tests of substantive procedures performed for the financial statements and apply them to conclusions about the operating effectiveness of internal control over financial reporting.

Action:

The auditor should evaluate the effect of findings in the financial statement audit on the operating effectiveness of the company's internal control over financial reporting. Particular attention must be paid to substantive procedures related to fraud, illegal acts, related-party transactions, accounting estimates, the selection of accounting principles, and misstatements.

Rules and Regulations Cited:

None cited.

¶ 112. Documentation Requirements

The PCAOB should be commended for seizing this opportunity to improve the discipline of financial auditing. It imposes the same documentation requirements used by auditors traditionally but makes additions to those requirements. In addition to the standard audit documentation, the auditor is required to document:

- *The results of the auditor's evaluation of each of the five components of the company's internal control over financial reporting.* This means that the auditor has to document the results of the issuer's compliance with the COSO framework. The five COSO framework components are: (1) control environment, (2) risk assessment, (3) control activities, (4) information and communication, and (5) monitoring.

- *The process used to determine significant accounts, classes of transactions, disclosures, and locations or business units tested.* This presents a potentially dangerous proposition for the auditor. It is likely that, in the future, auditors will be enveloped in any litigation resulting from financial fraud or even financial restatements by issuers. It is common for issuers to be sued by shareholders in a class action when stock prices drop drastically. If the auditor documents the process for selecting what it deems as significant in terms of the audit, the auditor creates a trail of evidence that ultimately can be used against it in a class-action lawsuit about why it did not choose some account—an account that turns out later to have been the one that contained the material weakness.

- *The identification of points at which misstatements related to relevant financial statement assertions could occur within significant accounts and disclosures and major classes of transactions.* This will require vastly improved process documentation on the part of management and the auditor.

- *The extent to which the auditor relied upon the work performed by management or others and the auditor's assessment of their competence and objectivity.* Auditors can rely on the work of others to a certain extent but must base the audit opinion on their own work.

- *The evaluation of any deficiencies noted as the result of the auditor's testing.* Auditors are required to determine if deficiencies or groups of deficiencies rise to the level of significant deficiencies or material weaknesses, which would affect the auditor's ability to issue an unqualified opinion.

- *Other findings that could result in a modification to the auditor's report.* A limit in the scope of the audit is an example of a finding that could result in a modification of the report.

The PCAOB anticipates that auditors for issuers with effective internal controls will be able to perform sufficient testing of those controls to be able to assess risk related to significant accounts and disclosures at a low level. If the auditor assesses risk as other than low the auditor should document the reasons for that determination. The standard presents two examples of situations where auditors should not conclude that the control risk is low:

- *When a control over a relevant assertion related to a significant account or disclosure was superseded late in the year and only the new control was tested for operating effectiveness.* This is likely to be the case when an issuer has no controls in a particular area, or no documentation of a control, and then remediates the situation. A situation like this would be more likely to occur in the first year of Section 404 compliance than in subsequent years, when companies' internal controls should be in better shape. This is very bad news for any issuer that did not start remediating internal controls over financial reporting early in the game.

- *When a material weakness existed during the period under audit and was corrected by the end of the period.* This results in a required disclosure of a change in internal control over financial reporting. This is black eye on the annual external financial reports. The result is a red flag to all who would use those financial statements for previous and interim periods.

The auditing standard requires the auditor to document the effect of a conclusion that control risk is other than low for any relevant assertions for any significant accounts on his or her opinion on the audit of internal control over financial reporting. That means that the auditor must document how the problem he or she found in the financial statements affected his or her opinion on the company's internal control over financial reporting.

Auditing Standard Paragraphs: ¶s 159–161

Persons Affected:

Auditors

Effect:

The documentation standard is raised from that in AU Section 339, *Audit Documentation.* The documentation requirements in this auditing standard reinforce the connection between the audit of the financial statements and the audit of internal control over financial reporting.

Action:

The auditor must adhere to the audit documentation standards set forth in AU Section 339, *Audit Documentation*, and must also include additional documentation covering all aspects of the audit of internal control over financial reporting.

Rules and Regulations Cited:

AU Section 339, *Audit Documentation.*

Suggested Reference:

"A Proposed Auditing Standard on Audit Documentation and a Proposed Amendment to the Board's Interim Standards Concerning Documentation by Principal Auditors," *SEC Accounting and Reporting Update* 2003-51 (December 2003).

¶ 113. Reporting on Internal Control Over Financial Reporting

Paragraphs 162 through 199 of the auditing standard present the primary aspects of the reporting requirements, covering management's report, the auditor's evaluation of management's report, and the auditor's report.

This part of the auditing standard also presents the primary operative rules associated with the auditing standard:

- *Management cannot conclude that the company's internal control over financial reporting is effective if there are one or more material weaknesses.* This is not a major leap for most issuers. Executives of most large companies are probably comfortable concluding that their internal controls are effective and any weaknesses are less than material.

- *Management is required to disclose all material weaknesses that exist as of the end of the most recent fiscal year.* This will probably prove a little more difficult for many executives than the effectiveness assessment. Proper documentation is key here.

- *If one or more material weaknesses exist in the issuer's internal control over financial reporting, the auditor must express an adverse, or negative, opinion on the company's internal control over financial reporting.* Auditors are going to sift through a much broader scoped audit than ever before. In the context of increased oversight by the PCAOB and a very litigious societal environment, the auditors can be expected to play it straight. The largest challenge for both management and the auditor is to uncover the big problems quickly and get them fixed so that the remediation can be in place long enough for the auditor to conclude that they are effective prior to the filing date.

- *If there are any restrictions on the scope of the audit of internal control over financial reporting, the auditor must withhold an unqualified opinion.* Management should ensure that auditors have access to all the information they need for the audit of internal control over financial reporting—limiting the scope of the audit should not even be considered an option.

- *Given a scope limitation for any reason, the auditor's only options are to withdraw from the engagement, disclaim an opinion, or express a qualified opinion.* This is where the PCAOB links the concepts together: (1) Management has to positively assess the effectiveness of the company's internal control over financial reporting. (2) Management cannot assess positively if there are any, even one, material weaknesses. (3) If there are any material weaknesses, the auditor cannot give the issuer an unqualified opinion. (4) If the issuer tries to hide a problem by excluding it from consideration, the auditor cannot give the issuer an unqualified opinion.

Auditing Standard Paragraphs: ¶s 162–199

See Also Auditing Standard Paragraphs: ¶s 7, 10, 14, 130–142, 200, 206, Appendix A, Examples A-3 and A-4, Appendix B, ¶ B15

Persons Affected:

Management, Auditors

Effect:

Management must issue a report on the effectiveness of the company's internal control over financial reporting. The auditor must evaluate that report and, if it agrees with management's assessment, issue a report attesting to management's assertions.

Action:

Management is required to issue a report on the effectiveness of the company's internal control over financial reporting. The auditor is required to review and evaluate this report. Then, based on its independent assessment of the effectiveness of internal control over the issuer's financial reporting, the auditor issues its attestation of management's report. Any limit in the scope of the audit of internal control over financial reporting requires the auditor to, at a minimum, issue a qualified opinion. Management must ensure that the scope of the audit is not limited.

Rules and Regulations Cited:

See ¶s 113.1–113.3.12 for rules and regulations.

Suggested References:

"Management Internal Control Reports Over Financial Reporting," *Handbook of SEC Accounting and Disclosure* § I8.

"Reports of Independent Auditors," *SEC Accounting and Reporting Manual* § 10.40.

"Management Internal Control Reports and Related Certification Matters," *SEC Accounting and Reporting Update* 2003-29 (June 2003).

"Certification of chief executive officer pursuant to Section 302 of the Sarbanes-Oxley Act of 2002," *SEC Compliance: Financial Reporting and Forms* ¶ 4655.

"Certification of chief financial officer pursuant to Section 302 of the Sarbanes-Oxley Act of 2002," *SEC Compliance: Financial Reporting and Forms* ¶ 4656.

"Rule 2-02. Accountants' reports and attestation reports on management's assessment of internal control over financial reporting," *SEC Compliance: Financial Reporting and Forms* ¶ 20,072.02.

"SEC Adopts Rule Requiring Internal Control Report," *SEC Accounting Report* (August 2003).

"Management's Responsibility for Internal Control Under Section 404," *Bank Auditing and Accounting Report* (March 2004).

¶ 113.1. Management's Report

Sarbanes-Oxley Act Section 302 requires management (specifically the company's CEO and CFO or persons performing similar functions) to certify in each annual report that they:

- Are responsible for establishing and maintaining internal controls.
- Have designed such controls to ensure that material information is made known to such officers by others.
- Have evaluated the effectiveness of the issuer's internal controls as of a date within 90 days prior to the issuance of the report.
- Have presented their conclusions about the effectiveness of the issuer's internal controls as of that date.
- Have disclosed to the issuer's auditors and audit committee all significant deficiencies in the design and operation of internal controls which

could adversely affect the issuer's ability to record, process, summarize, and report financial data; have identified to the auditors any material weaknesses in internal controls; and have disclosed to the auditors and audit committee any fraud, material or not, perpetrated by management or other employees who have a significant role in the issuer's internal controls.

- Have indicated whether or not there were significant changes in internal controls subsequent to the date of their evaluation, including any corrective actions with regard to significant deficiencies and material weaknesses.

Section 404 of the Sarbanes-Oxley Act reinforces the requirement.

The auditing standard reiterates the requirements of Sections 302 and 404 in ¶s 162–165, but incorporates the requirements outlined by the SEC in Item 308 of Regulation S-B and Regulation S-K (17 CFR §228.308 and 17 CFR §229.308, respectively), which adds a requirement that management include a statement identifying the framework used by management to conduct the required assessment of the effectiveness of the company's internal control over financial reporting. For most if not all companies, this would mean the COSO framework. A statement that the registered public accounting firm that audited the financial statements included in the annual report has issued an attestation report on management's assessment of the company's internal control over financial reporting must also be included.

Management cannot state that its internal control over financial reporting is effective if there are one or more material weaknesses identified by either the company or the auditor. However, management is allowed to say that internal control over financial reporting, as of the end of the company's most recent year, is effective even if one or more material weaknesses existed during the period if management has fixed the deficient control sufficiently in advance of the "as of" date to have satisfactorily tested the effectiveness of the now-repaired internal control. If the effectiveness of the deficient control can be tested over a period of time that is adequate for management to determine whether, as of the end of the fiscal year, the design and operation of the internal control over financial reporting is effective, then management can give a positive assessment of internal control over financial reporting. This means that management must commence their assessment of the company's internal control prior to year end if they want to improve their chances of identifying and repairing deficient internal controls.

Auditing Standard Paragraphs: ¶s 162–165

See Also Auditing Standard Paragraph: ¶ 200

Persons Affected:

Management

Effect:

The auditing standard reiterates the requirements put forth in Sections 302 and 404 of the Sarbanes-Oxley Act and SEC Release No. 33-8238.

Action:

Management is required to include its assessment of the effectiveness of the company's internal control over financial reporting in its annual report required under SEC reporting regulations. Management must take responsibility for the company's internal controls. Management must identify the framework (i.e., COSO) used to conduct its assessment of the internal controls. If one or more material weaknesses are discovered by management during the assessment of the company's internal controls, management must change the internal control to eliminate the material weakness sufficiently in advance of the "as of" date and must test the effectiveness of the revised control in order to determine whether it is effective.

Rules and Regulations Cited:

17 CFR §228.308(a) and 17 CFR §229.308(a) (Item 308(a) of Regulation S-B and Regulation S-K, respectively); 17 CFR §240.13a-14(a) and 17 CFR §240.15d-14(a) (Securities Exchange Act Rules 13a-14(a) and 15d-14(a), respectively).

Suggested References:

"Management Internal Control Reports Over Financial Reporting," *Handbook of SEC Accounting and Disclosure* § 18.

"Management Internal Control Reports and Related Certification Matters," *SEC Accounting and Reporting Update* 2003-29 (June 2003).

"Certification of chief executive officer pursuant to Section 302 of the Sarbanes-Oxley Act of 2002," *SEC Compliance: Financial Reporting and Forms* ¶ 4655.

"Certification of chief financial officer pursuant to Section 302 of the Sarbanes-Oxley Act of 2002," *SEC Compliance: Financial Reporting and Forms* ¶ 4656.

"SEC Adopts Rule Requiring Internal Control Report," *SEC Accounting Report* (August 2003).

"Management's Responsibility for Internal Control Under Section 404," *Bank Auditing and Accounting Report* (March 2004).

¶ 113.2. The Auditor's Evaluation of Management's Report

The auditor should evaluate management's assessment of the company's internal control over financial reporting and determine whether:

- *Management establishes its responsibility for internal control.* This responsibility cannot be delegated or assigned.

- *Management used the proper framework.* The PCAOB makes clear earlier in the standard that it intends that in most cases the COSO framework should be used for internal control assessments.

- *Management presented its assessment in an acceptable form.* Management must state whether the company's internal control over financial reporting is effective. A negative assurance statement is not acceptable. (That is, management cannot state that nothing has come to their attention that indicates substandard internal controls. They must affirm the effectiveness of the controls.) Management cannot conclude that internal control over financial reporting is effective if there are one or more material weaknesses.

- *Whether any material weaknesses that existed during the period, but were corrected, are properly disclosed.*

Auditing Standard Paragraph: ¶ 166

See Also Auditing Standard Paragraphs: ¶s 14, 206

Persons Affected:

Management, Auditors

Effect:

The auditor must evaluate management's assessment of the effectiveness of internal control over financial reporting.

Action:

The auditor should evaluate management's assessment and determine that management establishes its responsibility for internal control, used the proper framework (i.e., COSO), and presented its assessment in an acceptable form.

Rules and Regulations Cited:

None cited.

Suggested References:

"Management Internal Control Reports Over Financial Reporting," *Handbook of SEC Accounting and Disclosure* § 18.

"Reports of Independent Auditors," *SEC Accounting and Reporting Manual* § 10.40.

"Management Internal Control Reports and Related Certification Matters," *SEC Accounting and Reporting Update* 2003-29 (June 2003).

"Certification of chief executive officer pursuant to Section 302 of the Sarbanes-Oxley Act of 2002," *SEC Compliance: Financial Reporting and Forms* ¶ 4655.

"Certification of chief financial officer pursuant to Section 302 of the Sarbanes-Oxley Act of 2002," *SEC Compliance: Financial Reporting and Forms* ¶ 4656.

"Rule 2-02. Accountants' reports and attestation reports on management's assessment of internal control over financial reporting," *SEC Compliance: Financial Reporting and Forms* ¶ 20,072.02.

"SEC Adopts Rule Requiring Internal Control Report," *SEC Accounting Report* (August 2003).

"Management's Responsibility for Internal Control Under Section 404," *Bank Auditing and Accounting Report* (March 2004).

¶ 113.3. The Auditor's Report on Management's Assessment of Internal Control Over Financial Reporting

The auditing standard presents the requirements for the auditor's report on management's assessment of internal control over financial reporting. The minimum requirements include:

- *The word "independent" must appear in the title.* The primary function of the auditor's work is an "independent" attestation of management's assessment. The PCAOB appears to have felt that the investing public would benefit by requiring the auditor's assessment to be clearly defined as independent.

- *The identification of management's conclusion about the effectiveness of the company's internal control over financial reporting as of a specified date, based on specific control criteria.* The "as of" date is usually the end of the issuer's current fiscal year. The only clearly acceptable criteria is the COSO framework.

- *An identification in the title of the management report that includes management's assessment.* The auditor should use the same description of the company's internal control as management uses in its report.

- *A statement that the assessment is the responsibility of management.* Management cannot delegate its responsibility for internal control to the auditor or any third party. This underscores the requirement that management take responsibility for the company's internal control in its assessment.

- *A statement that the auditor's responsibility is to express an opinion on management's assessment and on the company's internal control over fi-*

nancial reporting based on the audit. All audit opinions must have the basis for the opinion stated.

- *A definition of internal control over financial reporting.* The definition should be the one provided by the PCAOB in ¶ 7 of the standard. (See ¶ 102 of this discussion.) This makes the subject matter uniform for all issuers and makes issuers and auditors adhere to a common standard of internal control.

- *A statement that the audit was conducted in accordance with the standards of the PCAOB.* This is new and it establishes the supremacy of the PCAOB in setting auditing standards. In the past this paragraph would reference the standards promulgated by the AICPA via GAAP and GAAS.

- *A statement that the PCAOB standards require that the auditor plan and perform the audit to obtain reasonable assurance about whether effective internal control over financial reporting was maintained in all material respects.* This introduces the concepts of reasonable assurance and materiality as basic elements of the audit.

- *A statement that an audit includes obtaining an understanding of internal control over financial reporting, evaluating management's assessment, testing and evaluating the design and operating effectiveness of internal control, and performing such other procedures as the auditor considered necessary in the circumstances.* This outlines the audit, explains what the auditor did, and validates, by discussing the work performed, the conclusion presented in a later paragraph.

- *A statement that the auditor believes the audit provides a reasonable basis for his or her opinion.* This links the audit work conducted to the conclusion drawn in a later paragraph.

- *A paragraph stating that, because of inherent limitations, internal control over financial reporting may not prevent or detect misstatements and that projections of any evaluation of effectiveness to future periods are subject to the risk that controls may become inadequate because of changes in conditions, or that the degree of compliance with the policies or procedures may deteriorate.* This is standard CPA disclaimer material. Disclaimers serve the purpose of defining scope limitations of the audit discipline.

- *The auditor's opinion on whether management's assessment of the effectiveness of the company's internal control over financial reporting as of the specified date is fairly stated, in all material respects, based on the control criteria.* This is the thumbs-up or thumbs-down result. It is either a pass or it is failure. The control criteria are the five components of the COSO framework—control environment, risk assessment, control activities, information and communication, and monitoring.

- *The auditor's opinion on whether the company maintained, in all material respects, effective internal control over financial reporting as of the specified date.* This is based on the issuer's acceptable implementation of the COSO control criteria.

- *The usual housekeeping.* This includes the manual or printed signature of the auditor's firm, the city and state (or city and country, for non-U.S. issuers) from which the auditor's report has been issued, and the date of the audit report.

Auditing Standard Paragraphs: ¶s 167–199

See Also Auditing Standard Paragraphs: ¶s 7, 10, 130–142, 162, Appendix A, Examples A-1, A-3, and A-4, Appendix B, ¶ B15

Persons Affected:

Auditors

Effect:

Every auditor's report on management's assessment of the effectiveness of internal control over financial reporting must include certain uniform elements.

Action:

Auditors must incorporate all of the listed requirements into their opinion on the effectiveness of the issuer's internal control over financial reporting. Examples of attestation statements are included in the appendices as examples for auditors to follow.

Rules and Regulations Cited:

See ¶s 113.3.1–113.3.12 for rules and regulations.

Suggested References:

"Management Internal Control Reports Over Financial Reporting," *Handbook of SEC Accounting and Disclosure* § 18.

"Reports of Independent Auditors," *SEC Accounting and Reporting Manual* § 10.40.

"Management Internal Control Reports and Related Certification Matters," *SEC Accounting and Reporting Update* 2003-29 (June 2003).

"Certification of chief executive officer pursuant to Section 302 of the Sarbanes-Oxley Act of 2002," *SEC Compliance: Financial Reporting and Forms* ¶ 4655.

"Certification of chief financial officer pursuant to Section 302 of the Sarbanes-Oxley Act of 2002," *SEC Compliance: Financial Reporting and Forms* ¶ 4656.

"Rule 2-02. Accountants' reports and attestation reports on management's assessment of internal control over financial reporting," *SEC Compliance: Financial Reporting and Forms* ¶ 20,072.02.

"SEC Adopts Rule Requiring Internal Control Report," *SEC Accounting Report* (August 2003).

"Management's Responsibility for Internal Control Under Section 404," *Bank Auditing and Accounting Report* (March 2004).

¶ 113.3.1. Separate or Combined Reports

Though the audit of internal control over financial reporting is performed in conjunction with the audit of the financial statements, the auditor is allowed to issue either a combined report or separate reports. Examples of both separate and combined reports are presented in the standard's appendices. Auditors will most likely use the exact wording, or nearly exact wording, when writing their actual audit reports.

In the event the auditor does decide to issue separate reports, he or she should include the following paragraph to the audit opinion of the financial statements:

> We also have audited, in accordance with the standards of the Public Company Accounting Oversight Board (United States), the effectiveness of W Company's internal control over financial reporting as of December 31, 20X3, based on [*identify control criteria*] and our report dated [*date of report, which should be the same as the date of the report on the financial statements*] expressed [*include nature of opinion*].

Then the auditor should also add this paragraph to the report on the company's internal control over financial reporting:

> We have also audited, in accordance with the standards of the Public Company Accounting Oversight Board (United States), the [*identify financial statements*] of W Company and our report dated [*date of report, which should be the same as the date of the report on the effectiveness of internal control over financial reporting*] expressed [*include nature of opinion*].

This will effectively link the two separate opinions together. This will also make it easier for the users of the financial statements to know that the other piece is not missing.

Auditing Standard Paragraphs: ¶s 169–170

See Also Auditing Standard Paragraph: Appendix A, Example A-7

Persons Affected:

Auditors

Effect:

The auditor can issue either separate or combined reports.

Action:

The auditor's report can be combined for both the audit of the financial statements and the audit of internal control over financial reporting. The auditor may also issue the reports separately. If the reports are issued separately, specific language provided in the standard must be included in each report.

Rules and Regulations Cited:

None cited.

¶ 113.3.2. Report Date

The audit opinion on the financial statements addresses multiple time periods. However, the audit of internal control over financial reporting addresses only the end of the most recent fiscal year. The following paragraph from Example A-7 in the standard's appendices specifies how the dates should be presented:

> In our opinion, the financial statements referred to above present fairly, in all material respects, the financial position of W Company as of December 31, 20X3 and 20X2, and the results of its operations and its cash flows for each of the years in the three-year period ended December 31, 20X3 in conformity with accounting principles generally accepted in the United States of America. Also in our opinion, management's assessment that W Company maintained effective internal control over financial reporting as of December 31, 20X3, is fairly stated, in all material respects, based on [*Identify criteria, for example, "criteria established in Internal Control— Integrated Framework issued by the Committee of Sponsoring Organizations of the Treadway Commission (COSO)."*].

Note that the reports should be dated identically.

Auditing Standard Paragraphs: ¶s 171–172

See Also Auditing Standard Paragraph: Appendix A, Example A-7

Persons Affected:

Auditors

Effect:

The dates of the financial statement audit and the audit of internal control over financial reporting should be dated the same even though they may cover differing periods.

Action:

The audit of internal control over financial reporting must be done in conjunction with the audit of financial statements. Therefore the dates on the reports, whether separate or combined, should be the same.

Rules and Regulations Cited:

None cited.

¶ 113.3.3. Report Modifications

In certain cases, the auditor is required to modify the standard report to reflect particular conditions. In the event the auditor identifies any of the following, the audit report must reflect the situation:

- *Management's assessment is inadequate or management's report is inappropriate.* (See ¶ 113.3.4 of this discussion for more on this topic.)
- *There is a material weakness in the company's internal control over financial reporting.* (See ¶ 113.3.5 of this discussion for more on this topic.)
- *There is a restriction on the scope of the engagement.* (See ¶ 113.3.6 of this discussion for more on this topic.)
- *The auditor decides to refer to the report of other auditors as the basis, in part, for the auditor's own report.* (See ¶ 113.3.7 of this discussion for more on this topic.)
- *A significant subsequent event has occurred since the date being reported on.* (See ¶ 113.3.8 of this discussion for more on this topic.)
- *There is other information contained in management's report on internal control over financial reporting.* (See ¶ 113.3.9 of this discussion for more on this topic.)

Auditing Standard Paragraph: ¶ 173

See Also Auditing Standard Paragraphs: ¶ 174–192

Persons Affected:

Auditors

Effect:

Under certain circumstances the auditor is required to modify the standard report.

Action:

The auditor should modify the standard report to reflect an inadequate assessment of internal control by management, a material weakness in the company's internal controls, a scope restriction, the use of other auditors' work, significant subsequent events, or other information contained in management's report on internal control over financial reporting.

Rules and Regulations Cited:

None cited.

¶ 113.3.4. Management's Assessment Inadequate or Report Inappropriate

If the auditor determines that management's process for assessing internal control over financial reporting is inadequate, the auditor should modify his or her opinion for a scope limitation. The key term here is "process." The auditor must look at and evaluate the process that management used to assess the effectiveness of internal control. If the auditor determines that management's report is inappropriate, if management reached the wrong conclusion, the auditor should modify his or her report to include an explanation of the reasons for the auditor's conclusion that management is wrong.

Auditing Standard Paragraph: ¶ 174

See Also Auditing Standard Paragraph: ¶ 178

Persons Affected:

Management, Auditors

Effect:

The auditor must modify the audit opinion if the auditor determines that management's assessment process is inadequate or if the auditor determines that management's report is inappropriate.

Action:

The auditor must modify the audit opinion if the auditor determines that management's assessment process is inadequate or if the auditor determines that management's report is inappropriate. At a minimum, this means adding an explanatory paragraph describing the reasons for this conclusion. Management should make every effort to ensure that the process used for evaluating the company's internal control over financial reporting is adequate, i.e., that the process meets the requirements outlined in this auditing standard and in the SEC's requirements.

Rules and Regulations Cited:

None cited.

Suggested References:

"Management Internal Control Reports Over Financial Reporting," *Handbook of SEC Accounting and Disclosure* § I8.

"Management Internal Control Reports and Related Certification Matters," *SEC Accounting and Reporting Update* 2003-29 (June 2003).

"Certification of chief executive officer pursuant to Section 302 of the Sarbanes-Oxley Act of 2002," *SEC Compliance: Financial Reporting and Forms* ¶ 4655.

"Certification of chief financial officer pursuant to Section 302 of the Sarbanes-Oxley Act of 2002," *SEC Compliance: Financial Reporting and Forms* ¶ 4656.

"SEC Adopts Rule Requiring Internal Control Report," *SEC Accounting Report* (August 2003).

"Management's Responsibility for Internal Control Under Section 404," *Bank Auditing and Accounting Report* (March 2004).

¶ 113.3.5. Material Weaknesses

If there are significant deficiencies that, individually or in combination, result in one or more material weaknesses, management cannot conclude that internal control over financial reporting is effective. (See ¶ 109.8.2 of this discussion for more on significant deficiencies.) In this case, the auditor must express a negative opinion on the company's internal control over financial reporting.

In the event that the auditor identifies a material weakness, the auditor must modify his or her report to include:

- *This definition of a material weakness:* "A material weakness is a significant deficiency that, by itself, or in combination with other significant deficiencies, results in more than a remote likelihood that a material misstatement of the annual or interim financial statements will not be prevented or detected."

- *A statement should be added to the auditor's report that a material weakness has been identified and included in management's assessment.* In the event that the material weakness has not been included in management's assessment, this sentence should be modified to state that the material weakness has been identified but not included in management's assessment. In this case, the auditor also is required to communicate in writing to the audit committee that the material weakness was not disclosed or identified as a material weakness in management's report.

- *The auditor should also modify the report to include a description of any material weaknesses identified.* This description should provide the users of the audit report with specific information about the material weakness, and its actual and potential effect on the presentation of the company's financial statements issued during the existence of the weakness. This is likely to be a subjective assessment of the actual or potential effects on the financial statements. This is due to the nature of internal control weaknesses.

The auditor may express both an unqualified opinion and an other-than-unqualified opinion within the same report on internal control over financial reporting. In the event that management makes an adverse assessment because a material weakness has been identified and not corrected ("internal control over financial reporting is not effective"), the auditor would express an unqualified opinion on management's assessment ("management's assessment that internal control over financial reporting is not effective is fairly stated, in all material respects"). At the same time, the auditor would express an adverse opinion about the effectiveness of internal control over financial reporting ("In our opinion, because of the effect of the material weakness described, the company's internal control over financial reporting is not effective.").

Auditing Standard Paragraphs:　¶s 175–177

See Also Auditing Standard Paragraphs:　¶s 10, 130–141, 194, Appendix A, Examples A-2 and A-6

Persons Affected:

Management, Auditors

Effect:

If there are one or more material weaknesses in the company's internal control over financial reporting, then the auditor must express an adverse opinion. In this case, management is also precluded from concluding that internal control over financial reporting is effective.

Action:

In the event there are any uncorrected material weaknesses at the end of the reporting year, then the auditor must express an adverse opinion on internal control over financial reporting.

Rules and Regulations Cited:

None cited.

Suggested References:

"Materiality," *Handbook of SEC Accounting and Disclosure* § A10.

"The Ethics of Materiality in Financial Reporting," *Internal Auditing* (January/February 2002).

¶ 113.3.6. Scope Limitations

The auditor must have been able to apply all of the audit procedures deemed necessary for the audit in order to express an unqualified opinion on management's assessment of internal control over financial reporting and on the effectiveness of internal control over financial reporting. According to the PCAOB, "If there are restrictions on the scope of the engagement imposed by the circumstances, the auditor should withdraw from the engagement, disclaim an opinion, or express a qualified opinion. The auditor's decision depends on his or her assessment of the importance of the omitted procedure(s) to his or her ability to form an opinion . . . . However, when the restrictions are imposed by management, the auditor should withdraw from the engagement or disclaim an opinion." (¶ 178.)

The real issue here is the ability of the auditor to expand the current practical scope limitations of the audit. What the PCAOB is saying here is that they want more areas checked than were being checked previously under the audit of financial statements. They want the internal controls for not necessarily every single one but most substantive processes associated with or underlying the preparation of financial statements to be tested and in proper working order. Traditionally, auditors validated not only a small fraction of all the systems but within those systems, only a small number of actual transactions. Given the growth of technology since most of GAAS was published, it is unfathomable that an auditor testing a small number of transactions could validate the proper functioning of these massive ERP systems that are processing, in many cases, millions of transactions per day. The number of comment letters the PCAOB received objecting to system walkthroughs was surprising. The discussion of scope limitations necessarily digresses to a discussion of technology because that is how accounting is done at this point in the 21st century. Thousands of very large firms create many millions of transactions that are processed by tens of thousands of personnel scattered, literally, around the world.

If the auditor plans to disclaim an opinion because of scope limitations but the limited procedures that the auditor was able to perform uncovered one or more material weaknesses, the auditor is expected to report on those material weaknesses.

Here is the example of a situation from ¶ 179 of the auditing standard, probably the most common situation that would be grounds for a scope limitation:

> For example, management might have identified a material weakness in its internal control over financial reporting prior to the date specified in its report and implemented controls to correct it. If management believes that the new controls have been operating for a sufficient period of time to determine that they are both effectively designed and operating, management would be able to include in its assessment its conclusion that internal control over financial reporting is effective as of the date specified. However, if the auditor disagrees with the sufficiency of the time period, he or she would be unable to obtain sufficient evidence that the new controls have been operating effectively for a sufficient period. In that case, the auditor should modify the opinion on the effectiveness of internal control over financial reporting and the opinion on management's assessment of internal control over financial reporting because of a scope limitation.

What the PCAOB and the industry expects is that, given examples like that in the auditing standard, issuers that failed to fix specific controls fast enough will receive adverse opinions based on scope limitations. This is as it should be. Problems with internal control over financial reporting have been low in priority or ignored completely for many years and the issuers that do not deal with weaknesses in internal controls over financial reporting effectively should now lose their unqualified audit opinions and face the consequences.

Auditing Standard Paragraphs: ¶s 178–181

See Also Auditing Standard Paragraphs: ¶s 10, 194, Appendix A, Examples A-3 and A-4

Persons Affected:

Management, Auditors

Effect:

Limitations on the scope of the audit result in a qualified opinion at best.

Action:

Given any limitation in the scope of the audit, the auditor is unable to express an unqualified opinion. Even if the scope of the audit is limited, if the auditor uncovers a material weakness, that weakness must be reported. Management should do their best to ensure the auditor is able to apply all the procedures necessary in the circumstances, with no interference from management or employees of the company.

Rules and Regulations Cited:

None cited.

¶ 113.3.7. Opinions Based, in Part, on the Report of Another Auditor

It is common for auditors to rely on the work of other independent auditors who, for various reasons, have audited some portion of the organization. This auditing standard allows auditors to continue that practice. Here are some of the situations where this practice makes sense:

- *Geographical dispersion.* If the auditor has no ability to audit the firm's operations in a foreign country, it may rely on a local independent auditor. This reduces the cost to both the auditor and the issuer.

- *Service bureaus.* If issuers use the services of a service bureau (e.g., a payroll service), it would not make sense for every one of the payroll service's clients to spend the time and effort to audit the payroll service's internal controls. Given that the payroll service performs payroll processing for the issuers, it would make sense that all of the payroll service's clients rely on the payroll service's independent auditor's conclusions instead of duplicating this audit effort many times over.

In any event, the auditor's own work must be sufficient to support the audit opinion. Therefore the auditor must decide whether or not to rely on the work of other independent auditors. When an auditor decides to use the report of another auditor as part of the basis for his or her opinion, the auditor should disclose this when describing the scope of the audit and should refer to the report of the other auditor when expressing his or her opinion.

When using the work of other independent auditors, an auditor can express his or her own opinion on either the assessment or directly on the subject matter itself. This means that the auditor can either:

- *Say that he or she agrees with the other independent auditor's assessment.* This is riskier and requires more faith.

- *Discuss the work the auditor did and how and why they believe the work is valid.* This is less risky because it shows that the auditor evaluated the other independent auditor's work and drew his or her own conclusions.

However, given an example like an issuer that uses the services of a large service bureau, it is more likely that, assuming the service bureau received their audit from a major accounting firm, the issuer's auditor would just incorporate the other independent auditor's assessment, because nobody would doubt that the work was done correctly.

When relying on the report of another auditor, the auditor should decide whether to make reference in the report on internal control over financial reporting to the audit of internal control over financial reporting performed by the other auditor. The auditor's decision should be based on an evaluation similar to that of the independent auditor who uses the work and reports of other independent auditors when reporting on a company's financial statements, as described in AU Section 543, *Part of Audit Performed by Other Independent Auditors.*

Auditing Standard Paragraphs: ¶s 182–185

See Also Auditing Standard Paragraph: Appendix B, ¶ B15

Persons Affected:

Auditors

Effect:

The auditor may rely on reports from other independent auditors to a certain extent.

Action:

The auditor can rely on the work of other independent auditors but determine whether or not disclose their reliance on that work in conformance with AU Section 543, *Part of Audit Performed by Other Independent Auditors.*

Rules and Regulations Cited:

AU Section 543, *Part of Audit Performed by Other Independent Auditors.*

¶ 113.3.8. Subsequent Events

The auditor is required to inquire of management whether there were any changes in internal control over financial reporting that might significantly affect internal control over financial reporting subsequent to the end of the audit but before the date of the auditor's report. This is a standard requirement in all audit engagements. Management is required to provide a representation letter saying that if anything changes after the audit is complete, but before the report is published, that they will inform the auditor.

The PCAOB articulates some specific items that the auditor should inquire about, and certainly examine if they are found:

- *Relevant internal audit reports (or similar functions, such as loan review in a financial institution) issued during the subsequent period.* This refers to new internal information that appears during the interim between conclusion of the audit and publication of the auditor's report.

- *Independent auditor reports (if other than the auditor's) of significant deficiencies or material weaknesses.* Other auditors might issue their reports subsequent to the end date of the audit of internal control over financial reporting. If these are received before the auditor's current report is issued, and they bring to light significant deficiencies or material weaknesses in internal control, the auditor should make note of them in the audit report.

- *Regulatory agency reports on the company's internal control over financial reporting.* This refers to new information from regulatory bodies that may come to light.

- *Information about the effectiveness of the company's internal control over financial reporting obtained through other engagements.* This requirement is interesting because it implies that the auditor should take into account information it receives from one its audit clients and use it to evaluate its opinion regarding a completely separate audit client. This is a new twist. Given that, according to published reports, the Big Four have the vast majority of the large audit clients in the United States, it is very likely that they could obtain and use information in this fashion. What is so stunning about this is that it is completely anathema to the AICPA's Code of Ethics, which protects issuers from information obtained via other engagements via the concept of confidentiality written throughout the code. So that the PCAOB would change that tenet of public audit practice is a major development.

Example: Giant Company A sells materials to Giant Company B. Company A's audit of internal control over financial reporting is complete with no material weaknesses identified. Meanwhile, over at Company B, the same auditor is busy with the audit. During the course of the audit at Company B, it is discovered that they cannot validate a receivable for the cylinders they receive their materials in from Company A. Because Company B pays substantial dollar deposits on each and every one of these very specialized cylinders to Company A, the auditor requires that Company B substantiate its receivable from Company A. Upon further examination and requests it is discovered that Company A has no capacity whatsoever to account for many millions of dollars worth of its cylinders that are being transported around the country at any given time. Since this represents a material weakness for both Company A and Company B for that matter, the auditor for Company B informs the auditor for Company A, who both work for the same firm, that there is a material weakness. Once notified of this material weakness, it becomes obligatory that the auditor for Company A either get the control rectified immediately or issue an adverse opinion.

An interesting question occurs—what is the expected level of cooperation between members of the same audit firm? What is the duty of, and liability for, the auditor to pass information regarding material weaknesses of internal control over financial reporting amongst its audit teams? Perhaps the PCAOB should have been clearer on this issue.

Auditing Standard Paragraphs: ¶s 186–189

See Also Auditing Standard Paragraphs: ¶s 142, 190

Persons Affected:

Management, Internal Auditors, Regulators, Auditors

Effect:

Auditors must take subsequent events into consideration if they reflect changes in internal control over financial reporting that occur after the audit but before the auditor's opinion is issued.

Action:

If a subsequent event occurs after the audit but before issuance of the auditor's report, the auditor must evaluate the event and determine its impact. Management must disclose subsequent events to the auditor in the representation letter. This includes internal audit reports and regulatory agency reports that are relevant to internal control over financial reporting.

Rules and Regulations Cited:

AU Section 560, *Subsequent Events.*

¶ 113.3.9. Management's Report Containing Additional Information

Management's report on the effectiveness of the company's internal control over financial reporting might sometimes include tangential information that does not apply precisely to internal control over financial reporting. Examples of this type of information include:

- *Disclosures about corrective actions taken after the date of management's assessment was concluded.* This is more likely to occur during the first year of compliance, as some companies scramble to document and implement previously lacking internal controls.

- *The company's future plans to implement new internal controls.* Perhaps companies that disclose this sort of information are trying to emphasize the fact that they are committed to improving their internal control over financial reporting.

- *A statement that management believes the cost of correcting a material weakness would exceed the benefits.* This is a common complaint about internal control over financial reporting—do the benefits outweigh the costs or vice versa?

If management's report includes this sort of extraneous material, the auditor should use language presented in the auditing standard to disclaim the additional information. In this example the auditor is responding to a hypothetical comment from an issuer that refuses to perform some internal control because it costs more than the issuer thinks that it is worth: "We do not express an opinion or any other form of assurance on management's statement referring to the costs and related benefits of implementing new controls." However, if the auditor believes that management's additional information is incorrect, the auditor is expected to discuss the matter with management. If the issue is not resolved at this level, the auditor is expected to notify management and the audit committee in writing that the auditor believes the information contains a material misstatement of fact.

Auditing Standard Paragraphs: ¶s 190–192

Persons Affected:

Management, Audit Committee Members, Auditors

Effect:

Management may add additional information to its report on the assessment of internal control over financial reporting that is not necessarily relevant to the audit of internal control over financial reporting. The auditor is expected to disclaim an opinion on the additional information.

Action:

If management adds any extraneous information to the standard format of the report, the auditor should disclaim this information. If the auditor believes the extra information includes a material misstatement of fact, the auditor is expected to discuss the issue with management directly. If this does not resolve the issue, the auditor is required to notify management and the audit committee in writing of its concerns regarding the information.

Rules and Regulations Cited:

Section 10A of the Securities Exchange Act of 1934 (15 USCS 78j-1).

Suggested References:

"Management Internal Control Reports Over Financial Reporting," *Handbook of SEC Accounting and Disclosure* § I8.

"Management Internal Control Reports and Related Certification Matters," *SEC Accounting and Reporting Update* 2003-29 (June 2003)

"Certification of chief executive officer pursuant to Section 302 of the Sarbanes-Oxley Act of 2002," *SEC Compliance: Financial Reporting and Forms* ¶ 4655.

"Certification of chief financial officer pursuant to Section 302 of the Sarbanes-Oxley Act of 2002," *SEC Compliance: Financial Reporting and Forms* ¶ 4656.

"SEC Adopts Rule Requiring Internal Control Report," *SEC Accounting Report* (August 2003).

"Management's Responsibility for Internal Control Under Section 404," *Bank Auditing and Accounting Report* (March 2004).

¶ 113.3.10. The Effect of the Auditor's Adverse Opinion on Internal Control Over Financial Reporting on the Opinion on Financial Statements

The auditing standard allows that the auditor can find a material weakness during the audit of internal control over financial reporting but somehow not rely on that internal control when evaluating the financial statements. This is difficult to understand. If an internal control deficiency constitutes a material weakness, but it did not affect the financial statements in question, then why did the auditor consider it a material weakness? If the auditor could have relied on some other control to determine that the financial statements are correct, then, in a practical sense there must have been an overlapping or compensating control. The presence of the overlapping or compensating control would have downgraded the internal control in question from a material weakness to a mere deficiency. According to the auditing standard, the auditor is required to perform "additional substantive procedures to determine whether there was a material misstatement in the account related to the control. If, as a result of these procedures, the auditor determines that there was not a material misstatement in the account, he or she would be able to express an unqualified opinion on the financial statements." (¶ 193.)

That said, in the event the auditor finds cause to reach an affirmative conclusion on the financial statements but a negative conclusion about management's assessment of internal control over financial reporting, it should include a paragraph about the material weakness and that paragraph should include this language in order to ensure that financial statement users understand the reasons behind the unqualified opinion:

> This material weakness was considered in determining the nature, timing, and extent of audit tests applied in our audit of the 20X3 financial statements, and this report does not affect our report dated [*date of report*] on those financial statements. [*Revise this wording appropriately for use in a combined report.*].

Auditing Standard Paragraphs: ¶s 193–196

Persons Affected:

Auditors

Effect:

The auditor can conclude that the financial statements deserve an unqualified opinion and simultaneously conclude that the assessment of internal control over financial reporting does not receive an unqualified opinion.

Action:

Even given a material weakness in the internal control over financial reporting, the auditor can conclude that the related financial statements are nonetheless accurate. This conclusion must be based on additional substantive procedures to determine if there was a material misstatement related to the ineffective control.

Rules and Regulations Cited:

None cited.

Suggested Reference:

"Adverse Opinions," *Accounting and Auditing Disclosure Manual* § 73.

¶ 113.3.11. Subsequent Discovery of Information Existing at the Date of the Auditor's Report on Internal Control Over Financial Reporting

The same standards apply in this situation as the auditor would apply in an audit of financial statements. If reliable new information becomes known about a material weakness that existed in the issuer's internal control over financial reporting at the date of the auditor's report that would have altered the auditor's conclusions, then the auditor must recall and reissue the opinion. This recall and reissue should be done according to the same detailed audit procedures that apply to this situation involving financial statements, as described in AU Section 561, *Subsequent Discovery of Facts Existing at the Date of the Auditor's Report.*

Auditing Standard Paragraph: ¶ 197

Persons Affected:

Auditors

Effect:

If reliable information becomes known about a material weakness that existed at the date of the auditor's report that would have altered the auditor's conclusions, then the auditor must recall and reissue the audit opinion.

Action:

If new information becomes known about a material weakness that existed at the date of the auditor's report that would have altered the auditor's conclusions then the auditor must recall and reissue the opinion. This recall and reissue should be done according to the detailed requirements of AU Section 561, *Subsequent Discovery of Facts Existing at the Date of the Auditor's Report.*

Rules and Regulations Cited:

AU Section 561, *Subsequent Discovery of Facts Existing at the Date of the Auditor's Report.*

¶ 113.3.12. Filings Under Federal Securities Statutes

The auditor should obtain written representations from officers and other executives responsible for financial and accounting matters about whether any events have occurred that have a material effect on the audited financial statements. This requirement is extended by the auditing standard to matters that could have a material effect on management's assessment of internal control over financial reporting.

When the auditor has received all of the required representations from management and is ready to sign off on the inclusion of their report on management's assessment of the effectiveness of internal control over financial reporting in the securities filing, the auditor's consent should clearly indicate that both the audit report on financial statements and the audit report on management's assessment of the effectiveness of internal control over financial reporting (or both opinions if a combined report is issued) are included in his or her consent.

Auditing Standard Paragraphs: ¶s 198–199

Persons Affected:

Auditors

Effect:

The auditor should apply the rules under AU Section 711, *Filings Under Federal Securities Statutes*, when the auditor's report is to be included in federal filings.

Action:

The auditor should apply the rules under AU Section 711, *Filings Under Federal Securities Statutes*, when the auditor's report is to be included in federal filings. The auditor should also apply AU Section 711 with respect to the auditor's report on management's assessment of the effectiveness of internal control over financial reporting included in such filings.

Rules and Regulations Cited:

AU Section 711, *Filings Under Federal Securities Statutes.*

¶ 114. The Auditor's Responsibilities for Evaluating Management's Certification Disclosures About Internal Control Over Financial Reporting

As mentioned previously in ¶ 113.1 of this discussion, management is required to make certain disclosures and certifications under Section 302 of the Sarbanes-Oxley Act. One of those requirements is that management must disclose any changes in internal control over financial reporting required to cure a material weakness in financial reporting. In turn, the company's auditor is required to evaluate the reason for the change in internal controls. The SEC's Final Rule, *Management's Reports on Internal Control Over Financial Reporting and Certification of Disclosure in Exchange Act Periodic Reports*, SEC Release No. 33-8238 (June 5, 2003), states: "Although the final rules do not explicitly require the company to disclose the reasons for any change that occurred during a fiscal quarter, or to otherwise elaborate about the change, a company will have to determine, on a facts and circumstances basis, whether the reasons for the change, or other information about the circumstances surrounding the change, constitute material information necessary to make the disclosure about the change not misleading."

Auditors are also required to conduct limited procedures quarterly to provide a basis for determining whether any changes in the company's internal controls are material to management's compliance with Section 302 of the Sarbanes-Oxley Act. These procedures include inquiries, evaluation of the implications of misstatements that have been identified, and determinations of materiality.

Auditing Standard Paragraphs: ¶s 200–206

Persons Affected:

Management, Auditors

Effect:

Management is required to make disclosures under Section 302. The auditor is required to evaluate the need for any possible disclosures related to changes in internal control over financial reporting. The auditor is required to conduct limited quarterly procedures.

Action:

Management must issue the statements required by Section 302 of the Sarbanes-Oxley Act. The auditor is required to evaluate the need for any possible disclosures related to changes in internal control over financial reporting. The auditor is required to conduct quarterly inquiries and evaluations regarding the materiality of changes to internal control and any misstatements that have been discovered.

Rules and Regulations Cited:

Sarbanes-Oxley Act Section 302; 15 USCS 78j-1 (Section 10A of the Securities Exchange Act of 1934); 17 CFR §240.13a-14a and 17 CFR §240.15d-14a (Securities Exchange Act Rules 13a-14(a) and 15d-14(a), respectively); Securities Exchange Act Rule 12b-20 (17 CFR §240.12b-20); AU Section 317, *Illegal Acts by Clients*; AU Section 722, *Interim Financial Information.*

Suggested References:

"Management Internal Control Reports Over Financial Reporting," *Handbook of SEC Accounting and Disclosure* § I8.

"Management Internal Control Reports and Related Certification Matters," *SEC Accounting and Reporting Update* 2003-29 (June 2003).

"Certification of chief executive officer pursuant to Section 302 of the Sarbanes-Oxley Act of 2002," *SEC Compliance: Financial Reporting and Forms* ¶ 4655.

"Certification of chief financial officer pursuant to Section 302 of the Sarbanes-Oxley Act of 2002," *SEC Compliance: Financial Reporting and Forms* ¶ 4656.

"SEC Adopts Rule Requiring Internal Control Report," *SEC Accounting Report* (August 2003).

"Management's Responsibility for Internal Control Under Section 404," *Bank Auditing and Accounting Report* (March 2004).

¶ 114.1. Required Management Certifications

As stated in the auditing standard, the required management certifications in Sarbanes-Oxley Act Section 302 that relate to internal control over financial reporting are:

- A statement that the certifying officers are responsible for establishing and maintaining internal control over financial reporting.

- A statement that the certifying officers have designed such internal control over financial reporting, or caused such internal control over financial reporting to be designed under their supervision, to provide reasonable assurance regarding the reliability of financial reporting and the preparation of financial statements for external purposes in accordance with GAAP.

- A statement that the report discloses any changes in the company's internal control over financial reporting that occurred during the most recent fiscal quarter (the company's fourth fiscal quarter in the case of an annual report) that have materially affected, or are reasonably likely to materially affect, the company's internal control over financial reporting.

In the event that the reason for a change in internal control over financial reporting is the correction of a material weakness, the auditor should evaluate if that material weakness is subject to disclosure.

These are the portions of Section 302 designed to improve financial reporting by improving the internal controls over the processes that companies use to prepare their financial statements. The more specific objective of these required management certifications is to assign specific accountability to the executives of the issuer for the financial reporting of that same issuer. Many would argue that this accountability already existed, but at a minimum, these requirements strengthen that accountability.

Auditing Standard Paragraphs: ¶s 200–201

Persons Affected:

Management, Auditors

Effect:

Section 302 of the Sarbanes-Oxley Act requires management to make certain disclosures certifying the accuracy and reliability of the issuer's financial statements. One of those disclosures is a statement certifying that the officers of the issuer have implemented internal controls over financial reporting that are effective.

Action:

Management must certify that the internal control over the company's financial reporting is effective. Management must also issue a statement that discloses any changes in the company's internal control over financial reporting that occurred during the most recent fiscal quarter. Management must also certify that it has responsibility for internal control over financial reporting. The auditor is required to evaluate the need for any possible disclosures related to changes in internal control over financial reporting.

Rules and Regulations Cited:

Sarbanes-Oxley Act Section 302; 17 CFR §240.13a-14a and 17 CFR §15d-14a (Securities Exchange Act Rules 13a-14(a) and 15d-14(a), respectively); Securities Exchange Act Rule 12b-20 (17 CFR §240.12b-20).

Suggested References:

"Management Internal Control Reports Over Financial Reporting," *Handbook of SEC Accounting and Disclosure* § I8.

"Management Internal Control Reports and Related Certification Matters," *SEC Accounting and Reporting Update* 2003-29 (June 2003).

"Certification of chief executive officer pursuant to Section 302 of the Sarbanes-Oxley Act of 2002," *SEC Compliance: Financial Reporting and Forms* ¶ 4655.

"Certification of chief financial officer pursuant to Section 302 of the Sarbanes-Oxley Act of 2002," *SEC Compliance: Financial Reporting and Forms* ¶ 4656.

"SEC Adopts Rule Requiring Internal Control Report," *SEC Accounting Report* (August 2003).

"Management's Responsibility for Internal Control Under Section 404," *Bank Auditing and Accounting Report* (March 2004).

¶ 114.2. Auditor Evaluation Responsibilities

It is not practical for the auditor to test all substantive procedures on a quarterly basis. Therefore the PCAOB allows that the auditor only needs to perform limited procedures on a quarterly basis. During these limited quarterly procedures, the auditor needs to watch for changes in internal control over financial reporting that could be material enough to constitute a required disclosure. On a quarterly basis the auditor should:

- *Inquire of management and other personnel about any significant changes to the design or operation of internal control over financial re-*

porting as it relates to the preparation of annual and interim financial information. The auditor should be looking for material changes that have been implemented since the last audit or interim review.

- *Evaluate the implications of misstatements identified by the auditor during the interim review.* The auditor should consider whether the misstatements that he or she identifies will impact the effectiveness of internal control over financial reporting.

- *Determine whether any change in internal control has materially affected or is likely to affect internal control over financial reporting.* The auditor is really concerned with whether any changes introduce a significant deficiency or material weakness into the design of any internal control over financial reporting.

In the situation where the auditor reviews interim changes to the internal control over financial reporting and determines that a change represents a new significant deficiency or material weakness, the auditor should communicate this to the appropriate level of management immediately. In the event management does not respond appropriately within a reasonable time period, the auditor should inform the audit committee. In the unlikely event that the audit committee does not respond appropriately, then the auditor would have no choice but to proceed under the responsibilities outlined in AU Section 317, *Illegal Acts by Clients*, and Section 10A of the Securities Exchange Act of 1934 (15 USCS 78j-1). These auditor actions would in no way diminish management's responsibilities for reporting under Section 302 of the Act.

Auditing Standard Paragraphs: ¶s 202–206

Persons Affected:

Management, Audit Committee Members, Auditors

Effect:

Interim quarterly auditor evaluations of internal control over financial reporting can be based on limited procedures.

Action:

Auditors need only perform limited procedures on a quarterly basis to validate their annual assessment. In performing the quarterly procedures, the auditor is looking for material modifications that could become a required disclosure about changes in internal control over financial reporting in order for management's certifications to be accurate. The auditor is required to notify management of any material matters. If management does not respond appropriately, the auditor must notify the audit committee.

Rules and Regulations Cited:

Sarbanes-Oxley Act Section 302; AU Section 722, *Interim Financial Information*; AU Section 317, *Illegal Acts by Clients*; 17 CFR §240.13a-14(a) and 17 CFR §240.15d-14(a) (Securities Exchange Act Rules 13a-14(a) and 15d-14(a), respectively); 15 USCS 78j-1 (Section 10A of the Securities Exchange Act of 1934).

¶ 115. Required Communications in an Audit of Internal Control Over Financial Reporting

Prior to the auditor issuing its report on internal control over financial reporting, the auditor must notify management and the audit committee, in writing, of any significant deficiencies or material weakness that the auditor identifies. This report from the auditor must clearly distinguish between significant deficiencies and material weaknesses. In the event the auditor concludes that the audit committee's oversight of the internal control function constitutes a significant deficiency or material weakness, then the auditor must communicate this specific deficiency, in writing, to the board of directors.

The standard further states that the auditor is, specifically, not required to perform procedures sufficient to identify all control deficiencies. This is the only time this statement appears in the standard in such direct language. Paragraph 209 goes a long way to limiting potential litigation exposure for the public accounting industry.

The auditor should communicate to management, in writing, all deficiencies that do not rise to the level of significant deficiencies in internal control over financial reporting that have been identified during the audit. The auditing standard requires that the auditor inform the audit committee when these communications are made, but does not require the auditor to directly inform the audit committee about these deficiencies. The auditor does not have to rehash the details of each and every deficiency and may just refer to them by title and date if they have been included in other written communications from the auditor, internal auditors, or other personnel. This plays into the requirement that the company have a process in place for internal auditors and others to notify management of internal control deficiencies in a timely way.

These communications from the auditor should include:

- A statement that the communication is intended solely for the information and the use of the board of directors, audit committee, management, and others within the organization.
- If governmental authorities require the company's auditors to furnish these reports, specific reference to the regulatory agencies in question.
- Definitions of control deficiencies, significant deficiencies, and material weaknesses.

In the event that the auditor comes across evidence of fraud or illegal acts, they must be brought to the attention of the appropriate level of management. That level varies depending on the nature of the fraud or illegal act. If senior management is implicated, the auditor must communicate the matter to the audit committee. In this instance, the auditor should follow the guidance in AU Section 316, *Consideration of Fraud in a Financial Statement Audit.* If the matter involves illegal acts, the auditor should follow the guidance in AU Section 317, *Illegal Acts by Clients.* The auditor should also determine his or her responsibilities under Section 10A of the Securities Exchange Act of 1934 (15 USCS 78j-1). This guidance generally follows the track that the auditor notifies successively higher levels of management, then the audit committee. If the audit committee or the board of directors does not react appropriately in a timely fashion, then the auditor is basically left with the option of resigning.

When important communications are required to be made by the auditor regarding findings of fraud or illegal acts, they may be made during the audit instead of only at the end. For most auditors this would go without saying, but the audit standard specifically allows for this optional communication timing when the issues are relevant and material. The auditor is expected to take into consideration the significance of the matter and whether the matter requires immediate follow-up.

Auditing Standard Paragraphs: ¶s 207–214

See Also Auditing Standard Paragraphs: ¶s 9–10

Persons Affected:

Management, Directors, Audit Committee Members, Auditors

Effect:

The auditor is required to communicate in writing to management and the audit committee all significant deficiencies and material weaknesses identified during the audit. The auditor is also required to make certain communications with management and the audit committee when the auditor becomes aware of fraud or illegal acts.

Action:

The auditor is required to communicate in writing to management and the audit committee all significant deficiencies and material weaknesses identified during the audit. The auditor is also required to make certain communications with management and the audit committee when the auditor becomes aware of fraud or illegal acts. The auditor must notify the board of directors if the audit committee is ineffectively overseeing the internal control function.

Rules and Regulations Cited:

AU Section 316, *Consideration of Fraud in a Financial Statement Audit*; AU Section 317, *Illegal Acts by Clients*; 15 USCS 78j-1 (Section 10A of the Securities Exchange Act of 1934).

¶ 116. Effective Date

The SEC originally stipulated that Section 404's requirements would apply to fiscal years ending after June 15, 2004, for most companies. Just prior to issuance of this auditing standard, the SEC extended the effective date for most companies from June 15, 2004, to November 15, 2004. (See SEC Release No. 33-8392.) This was a direct result of protests that the SEC received that claimed it was unreasonable for accelerated filers to implement an auditing standard for a fiscal year that was going to be, for many filers, more than halfway complete by the time this auditing standard was even issued.

The PCAOB has aligned the effective date for Auditing Standard No. 2 with the dates the SEC has established for Section 302 and 404 compliance. Thus, accelerated filers must comply with this standard for fiscal years ending on or after November 15, 2004, and all other companies have until fiscal years ending on or after July 15, 2005, to comply. Early compliance is, of course, permitted.

However, the standard states, "The auditor's responsibilities for evaluating management's certification disclosures about internal control over financial reporting described in paragraphs 202 through 206 take effect beginning with the first quarter after the auditor's first audit report on the company's internal control over financial reporting." (¶ 215.) This refers to the limited procedures that the auditor is required to perform with regard to management's quarterly certifications of internal control over financial reporting.

Auditing Standard Paragraphs: ¶s 215–216

See Also Auditing Standard Paragraphs: ¶s 202–206

Persons Affected:

Management, Directors, Audit Committee Members, Auditors, Internal Auditors, Accounting Staff, Accounting Management, Attorneys Preparing SEC Reporting, Financial Statement Users, Investors, Creditors, Regulators (in specialized industries, such as banking or insurance).

Effect:

Companies and auditors are required to comply with PCAOB Auditing Standard No. 2 for their the internal control reporting for fiscal years ending on or after November 15, 2004 (accelerated filers) or July 15, 2005 (other companies).

Action:

Auditors of companies considered accelerated filers (seasoned U.S. companies with public float exceeding $75 million) are required to comply with PCAOB Auditing Standard No. 2 for fiscal years ending on or after November 15, 2004. Auditors of other companies (including smaller companies, foreign private issuers and companies with only registered debt securities) have until fiscal years ending on or after July 15, 2005, to comply with PCAOB Auditing Standard No. 2.

Rules and Regulations Cited:

Sarbanes-Oxley Act Section 404; 17 CFR §240.12b-2 (Securities Exchange Act Rule 12b-2).

¶ 117. Illustrative Reports on Internal Control Over Financial Reporting

The auditing standard provides the auditor with examples of the exact text they need to properly construct the final report of the auditor's opinion. There are actually three different areas that the auditor is expressing an opinion on:

- Management's assessment of the effectiveness of internal control over financial reporting.
- The effectiveness of internal control over financial reporting.
- The financial statements.

The auditor's options for the opinions are: unqualified, qualified, and disclaiming or adverse.

Here is a summary of the different examples presented in Appendix A of the standard and an indication of their appropriate use:

- *Example A-1—Expressing an Unqualified Opinion on Management's Assessment of the Effectiveness of Internal Control Over Financial Reporting and an Unqualified Opinion on the Effectiveness of Internal Control Over Financial Reporting (Separate Report).* This is an example of a positive assurance for both management's assessment and the effectiveness of the internal controls. The auditor has the option, as in this example, of issuing two separate reports. This example is for the audits of management's assessment and the effectiveness of internal control as one report and the opinion on the financial statements as a second report. This is referred to as separate reports. A combined report would cover all three topics.

- *Example A-2—Expressing an Unqualified Opinion on Management's Assessment of the Effectiveness of Internal Control Over Financial Reporting and an Adverse Opinion on the Effectiveness of Internal Control Over Financial Reporting Because of the Existence of a Material Weakness.* In this example a material weakness exists in the internal control over financial reporting. Management is aware of the material weakness and includes it in their assessment. The auditor agrees with this and thus issues an unqualified opinion of management's assessment while simultaneously issuing an adverse opinion over the effectiveness of the internal controls over financial reporting. In this example the financial statement opinion is the subject of a separate opinion. It would be possible that, even though a material weakness exists in the internal control over financial reporting, this issuer could receive an unqualified opinion on their financial statements if the auditor were able to not rely on that internal control for its audit of the financial statements.

- *Example A-3—Expressing a Qualified Opinion on Management's Assessment of the Effectiveness of Internal Control Over Financial Reporting and a Qualified Opinion on the Effectiveness of Internal Control Over Financial Reporting Because of a Limitation on the Scope of the Audit.* This will likely occur when a company rectifies a material weakness too late in its fiscal year for the auditor to assess its effectiveness over the previous interim periods. The auditor faced with this situation declares a scope limitation because the auditors have no ability to validate the effectiveness of that internal control over financial reporting backward in time from the correction date.

- *Example A-4—Disclaiming an Opinion on Management's Assessment of the Effectiveness of Internal Control Over Financial Reporting and Disclaiming an Opinion on the Effectiveness of Internal Control Over Financial Reporting Because of a Limitation on the Scope of the Audit.* This is a polite way for an auditor to not issue an adverse opinion. From a practical standpoint, this is probably the worst possible opinion an issuer could get from an auditor that completes an audit. It is much more likely that an auditor would resign from an audit where the issuer had multiple material weaknesses too massive to downgrade, remediate, or ignore.

- *Example A-5—Expressing an Unqualified Opinion on Management's Assessment of the Effectiveness of Internal Control Over Financial Reporting That Refers to the Report of Other Auditors As a Basis, in Part, for the Auditor's Opinion and an Unqualified Opinion on the Effectiveness of Internal Control Over Financial Reporting.* This is a very likely outcome for many large companies that use outside service organizations. This is because the outside service organizations are likely to have perfectly acceptable audits that the issuer's auditor is comfortable relying on for assurance. This outline and sample language would be applicable in this situation.

- *Example A-6—Expressing an Adverse Opinion on Management's Assessment of the Effectiveness of Internal Control Over Financial Reporting and an Adverse Opinion on the Effectiveness of Internal Control Over Financial Reporting Because of the Existence of a Material Weakness.* In the event that the auditor does not agree with either management's assessment of internal control over financial reporting or the effectiveness of internal control over financial reporting, this is the type of opinion the auditor would issue. In this event, it is most likely that the auditor would be having issues with the financial statement audit as well. In these situations, from a practical standpoint, the auditor usually resigns or is fired before they are forced to write an adverse opinion like this. But if they did complete the audit and material weaknesses could not be reconciled with management, then this is the sort of audit opinion that they would be required to issue.

- *Example A-7—Expressing an Unqualified Opinion on Financial Statements, an Unqualified Opinion on Management's Assessment of the Effectiveness of Internal Control Over Financial Reporting, and an Unqualified Opinion on the Effectiveness of Internal Control Over Financial Reporting (Combined Report).* This is surely the most desirable opinion an issuer can receive. The goal for all issuers is to transition from the old unqualified financial statement opinion to the new combined unqualified audit opinion. It is very likely that most issuers will accomplish this goal.

Auditing Standard Paragraph: Appendix A, ¶ A1

See Also Auditing Standard Paragraphs: ¶s 10, 167–199

Persons Affected:

Auditors

Effect:

Appendix A of the auditing standard provides sample text to guide auditors in writing opinions on internal control over financial reporting.

Action:

Auditors should consult the illustrative examples in Appendix A of the auditing standard when writing their reports on internal control over financial reporting.

Rules and Regulations Cited:

None cited.

¶ 118. Additional Performance Requirements and Directions; Extent-of-Testing Examples

Each subsection of Appendix B of the auditing standard covers a different area of audit testing. The primary areas covered are:

- Tests to be performed when a company has multiple locations or business units.
- Use of service organizations.

- Examples of extent-of-testing decisions.

Tests to be Performed When a Company Has Multiple Locations or Business Units

According to the PCAOB, when a company has multiple locations or business units, the main consideration is the business unit or location's relative financial significance. The auditor should also consider the risk of material misstatement that could result from that location or business unit. For each significant location or business unit, the auditor should evaluate the company's documentation and controls and test controls over significant accounts and disclosures. If there are any unique risks associated with any business unit, the auditor should assess the documentation of controls over that risk and test those controls for each specific risk identified.

The standard points out that the auditor should also take into account which other locations or business units that, when aggregated, represent a group with a level of financial significance that could create a material misstatement in the financial statements. For the group, the auditor should review whether there are company-wide controls in place. If there are company-wide controls in place, then the auditor should evaluate the documentation and test the company-wide controls. If there are not company-wide controls in place, then the auditor should perform tests of controls at some of the locations or business units.

The auditing standard allows that the auditor does not need to perform any additional testing on the remaining locations and businesses as long as they are not able to create, either individually or collectively, a material misstatement in the financial statements. This will come as a huge relief to both auditors and management. Given the vast dispersal of business units and operating locations that most large companies have, it would have been an enormous task to try to physically audit them all. The auditing standard allows that, generally, a small number of locations or business units will cover a large portion of a company's operations and financial position, making them financially significant. This is meaningful in that it tends to indicate that the PCAOB does not expect the auditors to perform testing at a large percentage of the issuer's locations.

Anytime there is a unique, specific risk associated with a business unit, the auditor should evaluate the controls over that risk and determine the likelihood of a material misstatement arising from that risk. The auditing standard allows that, just because the auditor must evaluate a unique specific risk at a business location, the auditor need not test controls over all relevant assertions for all significant accounts at these locations or business units.

When determining the locations or business units to visit and the controls to test, the auditor should evaluate the following factors:

- *The relative financial significance of each location or business unit.* If the location or business unit is unable to have a material impact on the company's financial statements, it is a low priority and does not require additional testing. As the PCAOB points out, generally, "a relatively small number of locations or business units will encompass a large portion of a company's operations and financial position." (¶ B4.)

- *The risk of material misstatement arising from each location or business unit.* This is the auditor's primary concern.

- *The similarity of business operations and internal control over financial reporting at the various locations or business units.* The more similar they are, then the less testing needs to be done.

- *The degree of centralization of processes and financial reporting applications.* The more centralized the processing, the more company-wide controls will be present and the more standardized the processing is likely to be.

- *The effectiveness of the control environment, particularly management's direct control over the exercise of authority delegated to others and its ability to effectively supervise activities at the various locations or business units.* An ineffective control environment over the locations or business units might constitute a material weakness.

- *The nature and amount of transactions executed and related assets at the various locations or business units.* Higher volumes of more various types of transactions will generate more risk.

- *The potential for material unrecognized obligations to exist at a location or business unit and to what degree the location or business unit could create an obligation on the part of the company.* This is the hardest thing for the auditor to figure out in a vacuum. The auditors will typically conduct inquiries, but if nobody tells them about an issue, they must rely on their knowledge of the industry and how this company functions within that industry to figure out what sorts of omissions they should be looking for.

- *Management's risk assessment process and analysis for excluding a location or business unit from its assessment of internal control over financial reporting.* This does not preclude the auditor from determining for himself or herself the level of risk involved.

Testing company-level controls is not a substitute for the auditor's testing of controls over a large portion of the company's operations or financial position. If the auditor cannot test a large portion of the company's operations and financial position by selecting a relatively small number of locations or business units, the auditor should expand the number of locations or business units selected to effectively evaluate internal control over financial reporting.

Use of Service Organizations

The PCAOB offers specific guidance for audits of companies that use service organizations, referring the auditor to AU Section 324, *Service Organizations*. The standard also states that it is appropriate for management to apply the relevant concepts from AU Section 324 during its assessment of the company's internal control over financial reporting.

Management and the auditor should obtain an understanding of the controls at the service organization that are relevant to the company's internal control. In turn, the company should have internal controls in place to monitor the activities of the service organization. The use of a service organization does not reduce management's responsibility to maintain effective internal controls.

Management and the auditor should have clear evidence that these controls are operating effectively. This evidence can be gained by performing tests of the company's controls over the activities of the service organization, performing tests of the service organization's controls, or obtaining a service auditor's report that specifically addresses the effectiveness of the service organization's internal controls. Appendix B of the auditing standard provides specific procedures management and the auditor should undertake to ensure the service auditor's report fulfills the PCAOB's requirements regarding internal control over financial reporting. It should be noted, however, that the auditor is not permitted to refer to the service auditor's report when expressing an opinion on the company's internal control over financial reporting.

If the company's auditor does not feel that enough evidence is available to prove the effective operation of controls at the service organization, the standard requires the auditor to:

- Evaluate the procedures performed by management and the results of those procedures.
- Contact the service organization, through the company, to obtain more specific information.
- Request that a service auditor be engaged to perform additional procedures.
- Visit the service organization and perform such procedures.

Examples of Extent-of-Testing Decisions

Appendix B provides some specific examples of the extent of testing this auditing standard requires. The examples presented are similar to the conventional audit plan an auditor would use for the scenarios provided. Here are some of the highlights from the selected examples:

- *Example B-1—Daily Programmed Application Control and Daily Information Technology-Dependent Manual Control.* The auditor is examining, evaluating, and testing the lockbox procedures for a company's cash receipts and applications. The issuer uses third-party software to apply cash to customer accounts. Unmatched cash receipts are noted on a standard report. The auditor is required, in this example, to validate the software is the correct version, compare the compiled software to the executable files actually running, then confirm that the software is generating the proper results using a single walkthrough example. This is either more or less research than would have normally been required under old GAAS depending on who was interpreting it. For most auditors, this constitutes additional work. The audit of internal control over financial reporting requires that the auditor validate the functionality of the software and that all data and system access is properly secured. Then the auditor checks the manual follow procedures for 25 unapplied cash items with the administrative personnel to verify that they are reconciled properly. The other interim steps involve inquiries and documentation reviews on the part of the auditor that would have been normally required under GAAS anyway. The primary change to conventional auditing introduced in this example of the auditing standard is the walkthrough of the transaction through the accounting software. This example allows for a lot of faith in the software in that only one example is walked through a system that potentially handles millions of transactions.

- *Example B-2—Monthly Manual Reconciliation.* The auditor in this example is reconciling a trade accounts receivable account. The auditor makes inquiries of the personnel performing the reconciliation and then performs a routine review and validation of the reconciliation. In this example, the issuer's staff could have easily done all of the reconciliations for the year just prior to the auditor's arrival and back-dated them. There would have been no possible way for the auditor to tell the difference unless it was disclosed during the auditor's inquiries of the staff or unless the auditor had reviewed this control during one of the interim periods. There is no difference between this example in the auditing standard and traditional GAAS procedures.

- *Example B-3—Daily Manual Preventative Control.* In this example the auditor is testing a manual three-way match for an accounts payable process between the invoice, receiver, and purchase order. The auditor randomly selects 25 samples and tests them. These tests are conducted at an interim date. At year-end the auditor validates that the internal control is still functioning properly by conducting the walkthrough of a single example through the process. There is no difference between this example in the auditing standard and GAAS procedures except for the single walkthrough example at year-end.

- *Example B-4—Programmed Prevent Control and Weekly Information Technology-Dependent Manual Detective Control.* This example involves the auditor validating a computerized three-way match process. The computer match is a programmed application control, while the review and follow up of the unmatched records is a detective control. The auditor validates the version, size, and access to the application via general computer controls. The auditor then tests, in detail, the intended functionality of the software applications involved. To test the manual controls related to reconciliation of the unmatched items, the auditor reperforms the tests on five examples of unmatched items. To ensure that the controls were functioning properly at year-end, the auditor scanned the unmatched items report to determine that the control was performed on a timely basis. This example has the auditor validating the functionality of the software in much detail, but the rest of the audit procedure would have been the same prior to this auditing standard. This example, where the auditor tests that the software is working properly by testing the screens and the other examples that included a single walkthrough illustrate the high level of technical expertise and expectations of the audit profession. The field of internal control has been advanced significantly by technological innovations in the last four decades. The field of accounting in general has been advanced dramatically by technology along with the field of audit and internal control. Every time a new accounting technology has been introduced, the related techniques for how to audit it have been developed as well.

Auditing Standard Paragraphs: Appendix B, ¶s B1–B31

See Also Auditing Standard Paragraphs: ¶s 53, 83–107, 204–205

Persons Affected:

Auditors, Service Auditors, Service Organizations

Effect:

Appendix B provides additional guidance on tests to be performed when a company has multiple locations or business units and when a company obtains services from a service organization. It also provides detailed examples of the extent of testing required by the standard.

Action:

Auditors should refer to the guidance in Appendix B when auditing companies with multiple locations or business units or companies that use service organizations. Auditors should also familiarize themselves with the examples laid out by the PCAOB of the extent of testing required to determine the effectiveness of a company's internal control over financial reporting.

Rules and Regulations Cited:

AU Section 324, *Service Organizations*; AU Section 543, *Part of Audit Performed by Other Independent Auditors.*

Suggested References:

"Service Organizations," *Accounting and Auditing Disclosure Manual* § 91.

"Responsibilities of Service Auditors and of Service Organizations," *Accounting and Auditing Update* 2002-03 (January 2002).

"How the Use of a Service Organization Affects Internal Control Considerations," *Accounting and Auditing Update* 1999-15 (July 1999).

¶ 119. Safeguarding of Assets

The definition of safeguarding of assets used in this auditing standard is consistent with the definition provided in the COSO report's addendum, *Reporting to External Parties*, which provides the following definition of internal control over safeguarding of assets:

> Internal control over safeguarding of assets against unauthorized acquisition, use or disposition is a process, effected by an entity's board of directors, management and other personnel, designed to provide reasonable assurance regarding prevention or timely detection of unauthorized acquisition, use, or disposition of the entity's assets that could have a material effect on the financial statements. Such internal control can be judged effective if the board of directors and management have reasonable assurance that unauthorized acquisition, use or disposition of the entity's assets that could have a material effect on the financial statements is being prevented or detected on a timely basis. (COSO, *Internal Control—Integrated Framework*, p. 155.)

Therefore, a material weakness would only exist when the company does not have effective controls—considering safeguarding, overlapping, and compensating controls—to prevent or detect a material misstatement of the financial statements.

The PCAOB notes that management's future plans have no impact on the company's current abilities to initiate, authorize, record, process, or report financial data and are therefore irrelevant in any discussion of internal control over financial reporting. Likewise, the company's possession of insurance or a disaster recovery plan has no effect on internal control over financial reporting even though they may provide loss relief or remediation in certain cases.

Some might question why there is a discussion of safeguarding of assets in the auditing standard at all. One purpose of Appendix C is to establish one of the primary objectives of the entire auditing standard. That objective is to safeguard the assets that hold the underlying value of the company on behalf of the shareholders. To that end, the PCAOB defers its definition to that in the COSO framework and referenced, to some extent, in ¶ 7.

Here is some expansion of the definitions referenced in Appendix C that are included in the COSO framework:

> Internal control is not one event or circumstance, but a series of actions that permeate an entity's activities .... Business processes, which are conducted within or across organization units or functions, are managed through the basic management processes of planning, executing and monitoring. Internal control is a part of these processes and is integrated with them .... The internal control system is intertwined with an entity's operating activities and exists for fundamental business reasons. Internal controls are most effective when they are build into the entity's infrastructure and are part of the essence of the enterprise. They should be "built in" rather than "built on." (COSO, *Internal Control—Integrated Framework*, p. 14.)

This is a very important point. It implies that internal controls must be incorporated seamlessly into the policies, processes, and systems used by the company. The COSO report also states, "Thus, internal control would include, for example, actions of an entity's board of directors, management or other personnel, including internal auditors, but would exclude actions of regulators and external auditors." (COSO, *Internal Control—Integrated Framework*, p. 105.)

Auditing Standard Paragraphs: Appendix C, ¶s C1–C6

See Also Auditing Standard Paragraph: ¶ 7

Persons Affected:

Management, Auditors

Effect:

Appendix C reiterates the PCAOB's emphasis on the importance of controls that operate to safeguard the company's assets, and defers to the COSO report for guidance on the safeguarding of assets as it relates to internal control over financial reporting.

Action:

Auditors should use the COSO framework as their guideline in determining the scope of the audit of internal controls intended to safeguard the company's assets. Management must realize that plans that could potentially affect financial reporting in future periods are not controls in the present. Business continuity plans are also not considered part of internal control over financial reporting. Management should ensure that the company has compensatory and overlapping controls in place where there is a risk of error or fraud that could affect the safeguarding of the company's assets.

Rules and Regulations Cited:

None cited.

¶ 120. Examples of Significant Deficiencies and Material Weaknesses

In Appendix D, the auditing standard provides three examples to help the auditor determine the difference between a significant deficiency and a material weakness in internal control over financial reporting. All of these examples deal with the same core principles.

Example D-1 presents two similar cases of inadequate intercompany reconciliations. The difference between a significant deficiency and a material weakness in the example hinges on the application of the standard's definitions of significant deficiency, remote likelihood, and material weakness (see Glossary at ¶ iv for the PCAOB's definitions). To paraphrase the standard, a material weakness is present when the likelihood of a material misstatement is more than remote.

In studying this and the other examples in Appendix D, the auditor should keep in mind the three levels of potential misstatement: inconsequential, more than inconsequential but less than material, and material. The auditor should also keep in mind the three levels of likelihood:

- Probable (the future event or events are likely to occur).
- Reasonably possible (the chance of the future event or events occurring is more than remote but less than likely).
- Remote (the chance of the future events or events occurring is slight).

The auditor need only focus on the characteristics of the deficiency to classify it as a significant deficiency or as a material weakness.

The examples in Appendix D all apply different combinations of the key concepts above. One way for the auditor to understand this would be to construct a point system based on the number of each item below. Note in the scoring that a score of 5 or above equals a material weakness, 4 equals a significant deficiency, and 3 or below is a mere deficiency.

Potential misstatement:

1 point.	Inconsequential.
2 points.	More than inconsequential but less than material.
3 points.	Material.

Levels of likelihood:

1 point.	Remote—the chance of the future events or events occurring is slight.
2 points.	Reasonably possible—the chance of the future event or events occurring is more than remote but less than likely.
3 points.	Probable—the future event or events are likely to occur.

If the auditor were to apply the point scale above to the scenarios provided in Appendix D, the following scores would result:

- Example D-1, Scenario A: misstatement more than inconsequential (2), plus likelihood more than remote (2) = 4 = significant deficiency.

- Example D-1, Scenario B: misstatement material (3), plus likelihood more than remote (2) = 5 = material weakness.

- Example D-2, Scenario A: misstatement more than inconsequential (2), plus likelihood more than remote (2) = 4 = significant deficiency.

- Example D-2, Scenario B: misstatement material (3), plus likelihood more than remote (2) = 5 = material weakness.

- Example D-3, Scenario A: misstatement more than inconsequential (2), plus likelihood more than remote (2) = 4 = significant deficiency, *plus* misstatement more than inconsequential (2), plus likelihood more than remote (2) = 4 = significant deficiency, *plus* misstatement more than inconsequential (2), plus likelihood more than remote (2) = 4 = significant deficiency. The scenario has multiple (3) significant deficiencies, and the result is a total score of 12 and a material weakness.

- Example D-3, Scenario B: misstatement more than inconsequential (2), plus likelihood more than remote (2) = 4 = significant deficiency, *plus* misstatement more than inconsequential (2), plus likelihood more than remote (2) = 4 = significant deficiency. The scenario has multiple (2) significant deficiencies, and the result is a total score of 8 and a material weakness.

What we have here is a standard that is somewhat subjective and relatively vague evaluation criteria based on, essentially, the judgment of the auditor and the audit firm's management. There is a lot of latitude provided here for the auditor pass judgment on materiality. In Example D-1, for instance, from a practical standpoint it is impossible to know, or even guess, about the likelihood that an intercompany reconciliation was correct for some months that were not reconciled unless those months were reviewed in an interim period by the auditor. There are a few common issues that are often difficult or impossible to sort out in an intercompany reconciliation, including intercompany pricing disputes, system interfaces connecting disparate legacy accounting systems, and manual processing errors.

Auditing Standard Paragraphs: Appendix D, ¶s D1–D3

See Also Auditing Standard Paragraphs: ¶s 8–10, 22–23, 130–140

Persons Affected:

Auditors

Effect:

Appendix D provides detailed examples as guidance for the auditor to differentiate between a significant deficiency and a material weakness in internal control over financial reporting.

Action:

Auditors should use Appendix D as a guide when they cannot determine the difference between a significant deficiency and a material weakness. The implementation of a simple point system to score potential misstatements and levels of likelihood might also prove useful.

Rules and Regulations Cited:

None cited.

¶ 121. Background and Basis for Conclusions

The proposed version of this auditing standard generated 193 public comments. The level of feedback the PCAOB received about the standard was as unprecedented as the standard itself. Appendix E represents the PCAOB's attempt to explain how and why it came to the conclusions it did when preparing the final version of the standard. As such, Appendix E includes discussion relevant to:

- *An introduction.* The PCAOB summarizes the purpose of this appendix, which is to present its thoughts on how it reached the conclusions presented in this auditing standard.

- *Background.* The PCAOB presents the background issues underlying this standard. Primary among those issues is the goal of implementing Section 404 of the Sarbanes-Oxley Act to protect the interests of the public regarding the integrity of financial reporting. The standard specifically references the "spectacular audit failures and corporate malfeasance that led to the passage of the Act."

- *The fundamental scope of the auditors' work in an audit of internal control over financial reporting.* The PCAOB discusses the many comments it received from issuers and others protesting the level of work required to be performed. In the end, the PCAOB states that requiring a lesser level of work would not adequately discharge its responsibility as it was directed by Congress. The PCAOB further responds to the protestations about cost with the argument that the majority of the costs incurred would be incurred by companies to implement internal controls over financial reporting, not to audit those internal controls.

- *Audit vs. attestation.* The PCAOB considered the protestations of those who, citing specific "attestation" language in Section 404, felt that the scope of the auditing standard went beyond that required under the Sarbanes-Oxley Act. Since the level and scope of the work required was closer to that of an audit than an attestation, the PCAOB chose to use the word "audit" in the standard.

- *Form of the auditor's opinion.* The auditing standard requires the auditor to express two opinions: one on management's assessment of the effectiveness of the company's internal control over financial reporting and a separate opinion on the effectiveness of the internal control over financial reporting. (There is also a third opinion on the financial statements.) The PCAOB selected this final format to minimize confusion, especially in the case where management assessed that there was a material weakness. The final form allows the auditor to differentiate between management's assessment of internal control over financial reporting and the effectiveness of that internal control over financial reporting.

- *Use of the work of others.* The PCAOB explains why it expanded the limits on auditors' use of the work of others. The GAAS in this area allows wide latitude, and the PCAOB's proposed version of this standard did not. The commenters protested that raising the existing GAAS standard was unfair and a waste of perfectly good internal audit work. The PCAOB incorporates a number of judgment tests into the final version. But the PCAOB, essentially, succumbed to these arguments and allowed an expansion of the use of the work of others, particularly internal audit, in the final version of the auditing standard.

- *Walkthroughs.* The PCAOB acknowledges the argument that walkthroughs are necessary and required procedures but then goes on to support its decision to narrow the scope and limit the number of procedures required. The scope was narrowed to "major classes of transactions." Further liberalizing the walkthrough requirement, the PCAOB allows the auditor to determine what constitutes a major class of transactions.

- *Small business issues.* The PCAOB emphasizes that the COSO framework provides sufficient guidance for small businesses. The PCAOB did not want to create a two-tier system of internal control requirements, one for large companies and a second for small companies, but at the same time recognizes that "one sizes does not fit all."

- *Evaluation of the effectiveness of the audit committee.* The PCAOB reacted to the argument that the auditor, who was formerly hired by management but is now hired by the audit committee, would again have a conflict of interest if required to evaluate the effectiveness of the audit committee's oversight of financial reporting and internal control. In the end, the PCAOB retained the requirement that the auditor evaluate the effectiveness of the audit committee. If the auditor considers the audit committee's functionality a material weakness, then the auditor must report this to the board of directors.

- *Definitions of significant deficiency and material weakness.* The PCAOB discusses the various arguments regarding the language used to determine the level of deficiency required to be considered significant or to be considered a material weakness. The PCAOB's standard is the same as the SEC's, or at least as close as they could get it. Auditing and disclosure determination is a very imprecise science. Terms like "more than inconsequential in amount" and "the likelihood is more than remote" are, perhaps, as good as can be developed today. Perhaps in the future someone will develop a comprehensive, quantitative approach to validating the accuracy of the mass of transactions that underlie financial reporting.

- *Strong indicators of material weaknesses and de facto significant deficiencies.* The PCAOB, in its original proposed standard, intended to identify those indicators, which if brought to the attention of the auditors, were strong indicators of material weaknesses. The PCAOB received numerous arguments that generally sought to clarify the examples and reduce any additional assessment requirements. This is especially true in the realm of the "control environment." The PCAOB entertains arguments about what the auditor should and should not consider to affect the control environment and to what degree the auditor should or should not consider them. What the PCAOB was trying to do was provide guidance to auditors, with examples of what to look for when trying to determine, on a contextual basis, whether there is likely to be a material weakness in the internal control over financial reporting. The PCAOB tried its best to clarify the situation.

- *Independence.* The PCAOB grappled with arguments, pro and con, about the level of internal control-related services that the auditor can offer its audit clients.

- *Requirement for adverse opinion when a material weakness exists.* The PCAOB was deliberating over the point that the auditor be allowed to provide a qualified opinion in the event of a material weakness, essentially an "except for" situation instead of only an adverse opinion. The PCAOB decided that this was incongruent with the SEC's standards and maintained the requirement that, given a material weakness, the auditor must issue an adverse opinion. In the event of a scope limitation, the auditor may issue a qualified opinion.

- *Rotating tests of controls.* The PCAOB held its ground here by maintaining the principle that each year's audit must stand on its own. The argument was made that, for various reasons, controls do not need to be tested every year. This is indicative of why GAAS failed to prevent "the spectacular audit failures and corporate malfeasance that led to the passage of the Act." Some very major aspects of the financial statements were only tested every few years. The PCAOB did not state the entirety of its reasoning for raising the standard but it should be commended nonetheless.

- *Mandatory integration with the audit of the financial statements.* Section 404 provides that the auditor's attestation of management's assessment of internal control over financial reporting shall not be the subject of a separate engagement. The PCAOB also follows the argument that it would not make sense for the issuer to engage separate audit firms, one for the financial statement audit and one for the audit of internal controls. Finally, the PCAOB recognizes that it is necessary for the same firm to audit both the financial statements and the issuer's internal controls because the findings of either audit necessarily affect the other.

Auditing Standard Paragraphs: Appendix E, ¶s E1–E130

See Also Auditing Standard Paragraphs: ¶s 10, 15, 76–77, 112, Appendix B, Appendix D

Persons Affected:

Management, Directors, Audit Committee Members, Auditors, Internal Auditors, Accounting Staff, Accounting Management, Attorneys Preparing SEC Reporting, Financial Statement Users, Investors, Creditors, Regulators (in specialized industries, such as banking or insurance).

Effect:

The PCAOB issued a proposed version of this auditing standard in October 2003. In Appendix E, the PCAOB provides its explanation of the consideration it gave to the various viewpoints submitted during the comment period.

Action:

Management and auditors should read Appendix E so they can understand the relevant thought processes that underlie the PCAOB's intent regarding various aspects of the audit of internal control over financial reporting.

Rules and Regulations Cited:

Sarbanes-Oxley Act Sections 103 and 404; AU Section 312, *Audit Risk and Materiality in Conducting an Audit*; AU Section 322, *The Auditor's Consideration of the Internal Audit Function in an Audit of Financial Statements*; AU Section 325, *Communication of Internal Control Related Matters Noted in an Audit*; SSAE No. 10, *Attestation Standards: Revision and Recodification* (AT Section 501); SEC Release No. 33-8238, *Final Rule: Management's Reports on Internal Control Over Financial Reporting and Certification of Disclosure in Exchange Act Periodic Reports* (June 5, 2003); 15 USCS 78j-1 (Section 10A of the Securities Exchange Act of 1934); FAS No. 5, *Accounting for Contingencies*; Staff Accounting Bulletin (SAB) No. 99, *Materiality*; IAS No. 200, *Objective and Principles Governing an Audit of Financial Statements*; PCAOB Rule 3300T; Federal Deposit Insurance Corporation Improvement Act of 1991 (FDCIA).

¶ 122. Client Letters, Interoffice Memoranda, and Sample Auditor Reports

The following sample client letters and interoffice memoranda can be used to notify affected parties of the changes resulting from the PCAOB's adoption of Auditing Standard No. 2, *An Audit of Internal Control Over Financial Reporting Performed in Conjunction With an Audit of Financial Statements* These include:

- Interoffice Memo to Staff of an Accounting Firm That Audits Public Companies
- Interoffice Memo to Internal Audit Department of a Public Company
- Interoffice Memo to Accounting Management of a Public Company
- Letter From CFO or Accountant to the Audit Committee of a Public Company

- Letter From Consultant Offering Internal Control Design and Evaluation Services

- Letter From Consultant Offering Internal Audit Department Evaluation and Consulting Services to Non-Audit Client

In addition, the sample auditor reports provided in Appendix A of the auditing standard are included here for easy reference.

¶ 122.1. Interoffice Memo to Staff of an Accounting Firm That Audits Public Companies

To: All Professional Staff

From: Managing Partner

Subject: Compliance with PCAOB Release No. 2004-001—Auditing Standard No. 2, *An Audit of Internal Control Over Financial Reporting Performed in Conjunction With an Audit of Financial Statements*

The PCAOB has adopted Auditing Standard No. 2, *An Audit of Internal Control Over Financial Reporting Performed in Conjunction With an Audit of Financial Statements.* This new auditing standard will mandate significant changes to the way we conduct audits in the future. The following changes are effective immediately:

1. Audit of Internal Control Over Financial Reporting—General Description

We, as an independent auditor, must evaluate (1) the client's management's assessment of the company's internal control over financial reporting; (2) the company's internal control over financial reporting; and (3) the company's financial statements. This will be an integrated audit that examines, in part, the processes a client's management uses to prepare the company's financial statements that are published externally to the organization. The internal controls involved must provide high, though not necessarily absolute, assurance regarding the firm's objectives in the area of financial reporting accuracy and reliability. Therefore, in recognizing the scope and expectations of the work to be performed, the PCAOB established this as an auditing standard and not as an attestation standard.

2. Scope of the Audit of Internal Control Over Financial Reporting

We must evaluate the processes management uses to prepare the client's financial statements. Auditors must gather and review evidence regarding the operating effectiveness of the client's internal control over financial reporting and attest as to whether management's own assessment is fair and accurate. This attestation must be performed in conjunction with an audit of the financial statements. The internal control and financial statement audits must be performed together.

3. Testing Requirements Include Walkthroughs

We must evaluate the design and application of internal control processes that management uses to prepare the client's financial statements. Auditors must make inquiries, test controls using walkthroughs, and review evidence regarding the operating effectiveness of the client's internal control over financial reporting.

4. Assessment of Internal Control Design Effectiveness

Given the design of the internal controls, auditors must collect enough evidence to attest that the internal controls are operationally effective in providing reasonable assurance of accurate, reliable financial reporting. Auditors are required to review and understand the results of procedures performed by management, internal auditors, and third parties to ensure the effectiveness of internal control over financial reporting. Auditors should also consider the results of those tests in the design of the audit plan.

5. Using the Work of Others

While taking the work of others into consideration, the auditor's own work must provide the principal evidence for the audit opinion. The PCAOB specifically allows auditors to rely more heavily on the work of a company's internal auditors than on other personnel.

6. Evaluating the Results of the Audit

The client's management and the auditors will identify internal control deficiencies. The auditing standard defines and classifies these deficiencies. Those deficiencies that do not allow the client's management or employees, in the normal course of business, to prevent or detect financial misstatements on a timely basis are considered internal control deficiencies. A deficiency, or combination of deficiencies, that allow *more than the remote likelihood* of a misstatement in the company's financial statements that is *more than inconsequential* in amount is termed a significant deficiency. Further, the auditing standard provides that a significant deficiency should be classified as a material weakness if it results in more than a remote likelihood that a material misstatement in the company's annual or interim financial statements will not be prevented or detected.

7. Reporting on Internal Control Over Financial Reporting

The auditor's assessment of internal control over financial reporting must follow the same guidelines as management's assessment of internal control over financial reporting. That is, only material weaknesses in internal control result in adverse audit opinions. The auditor is not required to disclose significant deficiencies, only material weaknesses. The auditor's report is to include two opinions as a result of the audit of internal control over financial reporting: one on management's assessment and one on the effectiveness of internal control over financial reporting. The auditor's report can be combined for both the financial statements and the assessment of internal control over financial reporting, or the auditor can issue the reports separately.

8. Audit of Internal Control Must Be Done in Conjunction With the Audit of the Financial Statements

The audit of the client's internal control over financial reporting must be done in conjunction with the audit of the client's financial statements. Therefore the dates on the reports, whether separate or combined, should be the same. The audit opinion on the financial statements addresses multiple time periods. However, the audit of management's assessment of the effectiveness of internal control over financial reporting addresses only the end of the most recent fiscal year.

9. Adverse Opinion

In the event there are any uncorrected material weaknesses at the end of the reporting year, then the auditor must express an adverse opinion on internal control over financial reporting.

10. Other Than Unqualified Opinion

Given any limitation in the scope of the audit at all, the auditor is unable to express an unqualified opinion.

¶ 122.2. Interoffice Memo to Internal Audit Department of a Public Company

To: Chief Audit Executive

From: CEO or CFO

Subject: Compliance with PCAOB Release No. 2004-001—Auditing Standard No. 2, *An Audit of Internal Control Over Financial Reporting Performed in Conjunction With an Audit of Financial Statements*

The PCAOB has adopted Auditing Standard No. 2, *An Audit of Internal Control Over Financial Reporting Performed in Conjunction With an Audit of Financial Statements.* The standard addresses both the work that is required to audit internal control over financial reporting and the relationship of that audit to the audit of financial statements. This auditing standard will mandate significant changes to the way we conduct our internal audits in the future. The following changes are effective immediately:

1. External Auditor's Ability to Use the Work of Others

The company's external auditors can use the work of others but should not over-rely on that work. The auditor's own work must be substantial enough to form the basis for the auditor's opinion on internal control over financial reporting. The auditing standard clarifies the ability of the auditor to use the work of others and reiterates that the auditor's opinion must be based solely on work done by the auditor or the auditor's direct validation of any work done by others. The auditing standard establishes criteria that the auditor must evaluate when using the work of others.

2. Limitations on Auditor's Use of the Work of Others

The PCAOB specifically limits all reliance on the work of others however by stipulating that the auditor's own work must provide the principal evidence for the audit opinion. The auditing standard defines three classes of controls and the extent to which the external auditor can rely on the work of others. These three classes are:

- *Controls for which the auditor should not rely on the work of others.* These are environmental controls and those specifically intended to prevent or detect fraud. Environmental controls like codes of ethics are, by far, the most difficult to test. It makes sense that the auditor would not rely on the work of others. It also follows that there would not be much reliance on testing done by others on environmental controls.

- *Controls for which the auditor may rely on the work of others but that reliance should be limited.* Examples include controls over non-routine transactions that involve judgments and estimates. While the auditing standard allows limited reliance on the work of others, it is anticipated that judgments and estimates involving significant dollar amounts would be tested for validity.

- *Controls for which the auditor's reliance on the work of others is not specifically limited.* Examples include controls over routine processing of significant accounts. The auditing standard allows for reliance on the work of others in the areas of routine processing. However the auditing standard does require that walkthroughs of the transaction processing systems be performed by the external auditors.

3. The External Auditor's Use of the Work of the Internal Audit Department

The PCAOB intended for the auditing standard to provide flexibility in using the work of others and also prevent inappropriate over-reliance on the work of others. The standard relies on the auditor's judgment to determine when tests over internal controls must be validated. The auditor is allowed to rely more heavily on the work of the internal auditors if the internal audit department is judged to be capable of high-quality work. It states, "Internal auditors are expected to have greater competence with regard to internal control over financial reporting and objectivity than other company personnel. Therefore, the auditor may be able to use their work to a greater extent than the work of other company personnel . . . . If internal auditors have performed an extensive amount of relevant work and the auditor determines they possess a high degree of competence and objectivity, the auditor could use their work to the greatest extent an auditor could use the work of others." The standard goes on to outline what factors might influence the levels of objectivity and competency of a company's internal audit function. This judgment is based on the internal audit department's use of IIA standards and a reporting relationship to the audit committee rather than reporting solely to management.

4. The External Auditor's Evaluation of the Internal Audit Department's Work

This auditing standard describes the criteria that the external auditor should use to evaluate the quality of the internal auditor's work when relying on that work. It is important that the external auditors are able to rely on the work of the internal auditors because it will reduce the amount of work that must be done by the external auditors and save our company money.

The auditing standard refers to AU Section 322, *The Auditor's Consideration of the Internal Audit Function in an Audit of Financial Statements*, as being useful guidance to the auditor considering using the work of others. All members of the internal audit staff should be familiar with the requirements of AU Section 322. In summary, Section 322 instructs the external auditors to:

- Assess the competence and objectivity of the internal audit function.
- Determine the effect of the internal audit function on understanding internal control.
- Determine the effect of the internal audit function on the assessed risk.
- Determine the effect of the internal audit function on the design of substantive procedures.
- Determine the degree of reliance on the internal audit function.
- Evaluate the internal audit work.

The external auditors are required to evaluate the adequacy of our internal audit activities, internal audit's reporting relationship to the audit committee, and the audit committee's involvement and interaction with internal audit.

5. Disclosures to Auditors

The external auditors will be relying on our internal audits for some aspects of their opinion. In some areas their reliance on the work of others is limited while in other areas it will be extensive. The standard also requires the external auditors to evaluate "reports issued by internal audit as a result of operational audits or specific reviews of key processes if those reports address controls related to internal control over financial reporting." This means that we need to use the utmost accuracy in our written communications. In everything we document or write relating to internal control over financial reporting, we must remember that the external auditors are likely to both examine and rely upon this documentation.

6. The Goal of Using the Work of Others

The goal of the auditing standard is to allow auditors to use as much of the work of others as possible where reliance on that work is warranted. To that end, the PCAOB provides evaluation criteria and examples to use as guidance for the auditor when they are planning their validation testing plan. In any event, the external auditor should actually test, themselves, both some of the examples where testing has been performed and examples where testing has not been performed by others. The type and extent of testing that the auditor performs on the work of others can vary, but should be sufficient given the nature, circumstances and extent of testing required to cover the material. In all cases, the overall level of testing performed by the auditor must be sufficient to form the basis of the auditor's opinion on the effectiveness of internal control over financial reporting. The goal of using the work of others is to avoid unnecessary retesting and to lower the overall cost and time requirement of the audit.

7. Cooperation Is Expected

Fortunately, because this company's internal audit function adheres to the IIA's *International Standards for the Professional Practice of Internal Auditing* and you report directly to our audit committee, our audit firm will be able to rely on your work to the greatest extent allowed by the PCAOB. I anticipate that the audit committee will provide you with further instruction on the level of cooperation needed during the upcoming audit of internal control over financial reporting, and I thank you in advance for your assistance in this matter.

¶ 122.3. Interoffice Memo to Accounting Management of a Public Company

To: All Professional Staff

From: CFO

Subject: Compliance with PCAOB Release No. 2004-001—Auditing Standard No. 2, *An Audit of Internal Control Over Financial Reporting Performed in Conjunction With an Audit of Financial Statements*

The PCAOB has adopted Auditing Standard No. 2, *An Audit of Internal Control Over Financial Reporting Performed in Conjunction With an Audit of Financial Statements.* This auditing standard will mandate significant changes to the way we conduct our internal controls relating to accounting and operations in the future. The following changes are effective immediately:

1. Management is required to assess the effectiveness of internal control over financial reporting using an acceptable standard.

Section 404(a) of the Sarbanes-Oxley Act requires that management assess the effectiveness of internal control over financial reporting. Section 404(b) requires the external auditor to attest to management's assessment. Section 103 of the Act requires that the PCAOB provide guidance to the accounting industry in conducting the audit of management's assessment of internal control over financial reporting. This auditing standard provides that guidance.

The standard mandates that the COSO framework should be used by U.S. issuers for compliance with the Act. The COSO framework is considered by many to be both high-level and qualitative in nature and should have significant impact on the quality of internal control over financial reporting. The Board establishes the COSO framework as the standard that management should use to assess its internal control over financial reporting. The COSO framework is currently the only acceptable framework on which to base internal controls over financial reporting at this time. All accounting managers are expected to familiarize themselves with the contents of the COSO report, *Internal Control—Integrated Framework*. Please consult the summary provided on the company's intranet immediately if you have not already done so.

2. The external auditor is required to attest to management's assessment and conduct its own audit to validate the effectiveness of internal control over financial reporting.

The Sarbanes-Oxley Act and the PCAOB's new auditing standard require that management must accept responsibility for and assess the effectiveness of the company's internal controls over financial reporting. Documentation serves as evidence of this responsibility and assessment. The auditing standard presents the minimum requirements that management must meet in order to discharge its responsibility under Section 404 of the Act. If the required documentation or assessment report are not present, then the auditor must conclude that management has not fulfilled its responsibilities under Section 404(a) of the Act.

Management and the auditors will identify internal control deficiencies. The auditing standard defines and classifies these deficiencies. Those deficiencies that do not allow the company's management or employees, in the normal course of business, to prevent or detect financial misstatements on a timely basis are called internal control deficiencies. A deficiency, or combination of deficiencies, that allow more than the remote likelihood of a misstatement in the company's financial statements that is more than inconsequential in amount and will not be prevented or detected is termed a significant deficiency. Further, the auditing standard provides that a significant deficiency should be classified as a material weakness if it results in more than a remote likelihood that a material misstatement in the company's annual or interim financial statements will not be prevented or detected.

3. Control deficiencies and weaknesses must be reported.

Management is required to disclose material weaknesses in internal control in its assessment, and the auditor is required to disclose material weaknesses in internal controls over financial reporting that relate to interim financial reporting. Accordingly, accounting managers are required to report any known deficiencies or weaknesses in the company's internal controls to the CFO immediately upon their discovery.

Staff should use the Internal Control Alert form posted on the company's intranet to notify appropriate levels of management of any issues or concerns regarding the company's internal controls. Managers are expected to train staff with regard to the internal controls they are responsible for, and they must inform staff of the company's "no tolerance" policy regarding the failure to perform a control effectively or the attempted override of a control. Employees who do not feel comfortable notifying their managers about control deficiencies or suspected override of controls should report their concerns to the internal audit department or the Employee Concerns Hotline, which is completely confidential.

¶ 122.4. Letter From CFO or Accountant to the Audit Committee of a Public Company

To: Audit Committee Members

From: CFO or Public Accountant

Subject: Compliance with PCAOB Release No. 2004-001—Auditing Standard No. 2, *An Audit of Internal Control Over Financial Reporting Performed in Conjunction With an Audit of Financial Statements*

The PCAOB has adopted Auditing Standard No. 2, *An Audit of Internal Control Over Financial Reporting Performed in Conjunction With an Audit of Financial Statements.* This auditing standard will mandate significant changes to the way we conduct our external audits in the future. The following changes are effective immediately:

1. Audit Committee Manages External Audit Function

As a result of the Sarbanes-Oxley Act, the external audit function now reports to the audit committee. Part of this external audit function is a requirement in Section 404(b) that the auditor evaluate management's assessment of internal control over financial reporting. The auditor is also required to assess the effectiveness of internal control over financial reporting. This auditing standard contains the regulations that cover audit engagements related to *An Audit of Internal Control Over Financial Reporting Performed in Conjunction With an Audit of Financial Statements.* The auditor's report is to include two opinions as a result of the audit of internal control over financial reporting: one on management's assessment and one on the effectiveness of internal control over financial reporting.

2. Minimum Disclosure Requirements

The auditor's assessment of internal control over financial reporting must follow the same guidelines as management's assessment of internal control over financial reporting. That is, only material weaknesses in internal control result in adverse audit opinions. The auditor is not required to disclose significant deficiencies, only material weaknesses.

The external auditor must evaluate the processes management uses to prepare the company's financial statements. The auditor must gather and review evidence regarding the operating effectiveness of the company's internal control over financial reporting and attest as to whether management's own assessment is fair and accurate. This attestation must be performed in conjunction with an audit of the financial statements. The internal control and financial statement audits must be performed together.

3. The Auditor Must Evaluate the Effectiveness of the Audit Committee's Oversight

If the auditors determine that the audit committee's oversight of internal control over financial reporting is ineffective, they must report this to the full board of directors. The auditor must review audit committee involvement in detail and assess the effectiveness of the audit committee's oversight of the company's external financial reporting and internal control over financial reporting. The auditor must also assess the relative effectiveness of the audit committee's oversight role with regard to the internal audit function. If the auditor finds that the audit committee is ineffective in its oversight role, then this constitutes a significant deficiency.

4. Required Communications

Prior to the auditor issuing the report on internal control over financial reporting, the auditor must notify management and the audit committee, in writing, of any significant deficiencies or material weakness that the auditor identifies. This report from the auditor must delineate between significant deficiencies and material weaknesses. In the event the auditor concludes that the audit committee's oversight of the internal control function constitutes a significant deficiency or material weakness, then the auditor must communicate this specific deficiency, in writing, to the board of directors.

The auditor should communicate to management, in writing, all deficiencies in internal control over financial reporting that they identify during the audit. The auditing standard says that the auditor should inform the audit committee when these communications are made.

¶ 122.5. Letter From Consultant Offering Internal Control Design and Evaluation Services

To: Prospective Client Company Management

From: Consultant

Subject: Internal control design and evaluation services to aid your company with compliance with PCAOB Release No. 2004-001—Auditing Standard No. 2, *An Audit of Internal Control Over Financial Reporting Performed in Conjunction With an Audit of Financial Statements*

The PCAOB has adopted Auditing Standard No. 2, *An Audit of Internal Control Over Financial Reporting Performed in Conjunction With an Audit of Financial Statements.* This auditing standard will mandate significant changes to the way you design, operate, document, and manage your internal control over financial reporting in the future. Due to restrictions imposed by the PCAOB, the firm that conducts your financial statement audits may not be able to help you design or evaluate your internal controls.

As you probably already know, management of your company is required to assess the effectiveness of internal control over financial reporting. The acceptable standards required under Section 404(a) of the Sarbanes-Oxley Act are set forth in the COSO framework. The COSO framework should be used by U.S. issuers for compliance with the Act. The COSO framework is considered by many to be both high-level and qualitative in nature and should have significant impact on the quality of internal control over financial reporting. However for many firms, the COSO framework is new and requires assistance for proper implementation.

That is where our firm, [*insert firm name here*], can help. We have success-fully implemented the COSO framework for several other clients. Our client list includes [*insert client names here*]. Like you, they understood the severe conse-quences of non-compliance with Sarbanes-Oxley and sought out the experience and knowledge of our firm to assist them with their implementations.

One of the primary concerns that companies like yours have is documenta-tion. Management must accept responsibility for and assess the effectiveness of the internal controls over financial reporting. Documentation serves as evidence of this responsibility and assessment. If the documentation is inadequate, then the auditor must conclude that management has not fulfilled its responsibilities under Section 404(a) of the Act. While management's assessment report itself can probably be written in a few hours, all of the documentation required to support the assessment would have to have been assembled by many people over several months. This is where [*insert firm name here*] can help. We are ex-perts at preparing the documentation you need to pass your audit of internal control over financial reporting.

Another area of concern for most issuers is the identification and remediation of internal control deficiencies. The auditors will identify internal control defi-ciencies. The auditing standard defines and classifies these deficiencies. Those deficiencies that do not allow the company's management or employees, in the normal course of business, to prevent or detect financial misstatements on a timely basis are called internal control deficiencies. A deficiency, or combina-tion of deficiencies, that allow more than the remote likelihood of a misstate-ment in the company's financial statements that is more than inconsequential in amount and will not be prevented or detected is termed a significant deficiency. Further, the auditing standard provides that a significant deficiency should be classified as a material weakness if it results in more than a remote likelihood that a material misstatement in the company's annual or interim financial state-ments will not be prevented or detected. The presence of one or more material weaknesses will result in an adverse audit opinion on internal control over fi-nancial reporting. Our firm can help you identify and remediate internal control deficiencies before the audit begins.

¶ 122.6. Letter From Consultant Offering Internal Audit Depart-ment Evaluation and Consulting Services to Non-Audit Client

To: Prospective Client Company Management

From: Consultant

Subject: Is Your Internal Audit Department Ready for PCAOB Auditing Standard No. 2?

The PCAOB has adopted Auditing Standard No. 2, *An Audit of Internal Con-trol Over Financial Reporting Performed in Conjunction With an Audit of Fi-nancial Statements.* A key aspect of this new auditing standard is that the audi-tor will now rely on the work of others in preparing their audit opinion. The "others" referred to in the auditing standard are predominantly the members of your internal audit department. But how does your internal audit department measure up? How do you rate them in the following areas:

- Competence?
- Education?
- Experience?
- Objectivity?
- Independence?

This is where we at, [insert firm name here], can help. We know how to evaluate your internal audit department. We can evaluate your staff and provide the training and supplemental skills they might need. Topics we cover in our training include:

- The COSO framework.
- Internal control over financial reporting—testing and evaluation.
- Walkthroughs.
- Auditing service organizations.
- Audit report writing.

¶ 122.7. Auditor's Report Expressing an Unqualified Opinion on Management's Assessment of the Effectiveness of Internal Control Over Financial Reporting and an Unqualified Opinion on the Effectiveness of Internal Control Over Financial Reporting (Separate Report)

Note: *This sample auditor's report appears in Appendix A, Example A-1 of the auditing standard.*

Report of Independent Registered Public Accounting Firm

[Introductory paragraph]

We have audited management's assessment, included in the accompanying [*title of management's report*], that W Company maintained effective internal control over financial reporting as of December 31, 20X3, based on [*Identify control criteria, for example, "criteria established in Internal Control—Integrated Framework issued by the Committee of Sponsoring Organizations of the Treadway Commission (COSO)."*]. W Company's management is responsible for maintaining effective internal control over financial reporting and for its assessment of the effectiveness of internal control over financial reporting. Our responsibility is to express an opinion on management's assessment and an opinion on the effectiveness of the company's internal control over financial reporting based on our audit.

[Scope paragraph]

We conducted our audit in accordance with the standards of the Public Company Accounting Oversight Board (United States). Those standards require that we plan and perform the audit to obtain reasonable assurance about whether effective internal control over financial reporting was maintained in all material respects. Our audit included obtaining an understanding of internal control over financial reporting, evaluating management's assessment, testing and evaluating the design and operating effectiveness of internal control, and performing such other procedures as we considered necessary in the circumstances. We believe that our audit provides a reasonable basis for our opinion.

[*Definition paragraph*]

A company's internal control over financial reporting is a process designed to provide reasonable assurance regarding the reliability of financial reporting and the preparation of financial statements for external purposes in accordance with generally accepted accounting principles. A company's internal control over financial reporting includes those policies and procedures that (1) pertain to the maintenance of records that, in reasonable detail, accurately and fairly reflect the transactions and dispositions of the assets of the company; (2) provide reasonable assurance that transactions are recorded as necessary to permit preparation of financial statements in accordance with generally accepted accounting principles, and that receipts and expenditures of the company are being made only in accordance with authorizations of management and directors of the company; and (3) provide reasonable assurance regarding prevention or timely detection of unauthorized acquisition, use, or disposition of the company's assets that could have a material effect on the financial statements.

[*Inherent limitations paragraph*]

Because of its inherent limitations, internal control over financial reporting may not prevent or detect misstatements. Also, projections of any evaluation of effectiveness to future periods are subject to the risk that controls may become inadequate because of changes in conditions, or that the degree of compliance with the policies or procedures may deteriorate.

[*Opinion paragraph*]

In our opinion, management's assessment that W Company maintained effective internal control over financial reporting as of December 31, 20X3, is fairly stated, in all material respects, based on [*Identify control criteria, for example, "criteria established in Internal Control—Integrated Framework issued by the Committee of Sponsoring Organizations of the Treadway Commission (COSO)."*]. Also in our opinion, W Company maintained, in all material respects, effective internal control over financial reporting as of December 31, 20X3, based on [*Identify control criteria, for example, "criteria established in Internal Control—Integrated Framework issued by the Committee of Sponsoring Organizations of the Treadway Commission (COSO)."*].

[*Explanatory paragraph*]

We have also audited, in accordance with the standards of the Public Company Accounting Oversight Board (United States), the [*identify financial state-*

ments] of W Company and our report dated [*date of report, which should be the same as the date of the report on the effectiveness of internal control over financial reporting*] expressed [*include nature of opinion*].

[*Signature*]

[*City and State or Country*]

[*Date*]

¶ 122.8. Auditor's Report Expressing an Unqualified Opinion on Management's Assessment of the Effectiveness of Internal Control Over Financial Reporting and an Adverse Opinion on the Effectiveness of Internal Control Over Financial Reporting Because of the Existence of a Material Weakness

Note: *This sample auditor's report appears in Appendix A, Example A-2 of the auditing standard.*

Report of Independent Registered Public Accounting Firm

[*Introductory paragraph*]

We have audited management's assessment, included in the accompanying [*title of management's report*], that W Company did not maintain effective internal control over financial reporting as of December 31, 20X3, because of the effect of [*material weakness identified in management's assessment*], based on [*Identify criteria, for example, "criteria established in Internal Control—Integrated Framework issued by the Committee of Sponsoring Organizations of the Treadway Commission (COSO)."*]. W Company's management is responsible for maintaining effective internal control over financial reporting and for its assessment of the effectiveness of internal control over financial reporting. Our responsibility is to express an opinion on management's assessment and an opinion on the effectiveness of the company's internal control over financial reporting based on our audit.

[*Scope paragraph*]

We conducted our audit in accordance with the standards of the Public Company Accounting Oversight Board (United States). Those standards require that we plan and perform the audit to obtain reasonable assurance about whether effective internal control over financial reporting was maintained in all material respects. Our audit included obtaining an understanding of internal control over financial reporting, evaluating management's assessment, testing and evaluating the design and operating effectiveness of internal control, and performing such other procedures as we considered necessary in the circumstances. We believe that our audit provides a reasonable basis for our opinion

[*Definition paragraph*]

A company's internal control over financial reporting is a process designed to provide reasonable assurance regarding the reliability of financial reporting and the preparation of financial statements for external purposes in accordance with generally accepted accounting principles. A company's internal control over financial reporting includes those policies and procedures that (1) pertain to the maintenance of records that, in reasonable detail, accurately and fairly reflect the transactions and dispositions of the assets of the company; (2) provide reasonable assurance that transactions are recorded as necessary to permit preparation of financial statements in accordance with generally accepted accounting principles, and that receipts and expenditures of the company are being made only in accordance with authorizations of management and directors of the company; and (3) provide reasonable assurance regarding prevention or timely detection of unauthorized acquisition, use, or disposition of the company's assets that could have a material effect on the financial statements.

[*Inherent limitations paragraph*]

Because of its inherent limitations, internal control over financial reporting may not prevent or detect misstatements. Also, projections of any evaluation of effectiveness to future periods are subject to the risk that controls may become inadequate because of changes in conditions, or that the degree of compliance with the policies or procedures may deteriorate.

[*Explanatory paragraph*]

A material weakness is a control deficiency, or combination of control deficiencies, that results in more than a remote likelihood that a material misstatement of the annual or interim financial statements will not be prevented or detected. The following material weakness has been identified and included in management's assessment. [*Include a description of the material weakness and its effect on the achievement of the objectives of the control criteria.*] This material weakness was considered in determining the nature, timing, and extent of audit tests applied in our audit of the 20X3 financial statements, and this report does not affect our report dated [*date of report, which should be the same as the date of this report on internal control*] on those financial statements.

[*Opinion paragraph*]

In our opinion, management's assessment that W Company did not maintain effective internal control over financial reporting as of December 31, 20X3, is fairly stated, in all material respects, based on [*Identify control criteria, for example, "criteria established in Internal Control—Integrated Framework issued by the Committee of Sponsoring Organizations of the Treadway Commission (COSO)."*]. Also, in our opinion, because of the effect of the material weakness described above on the achievement of the objectives of the control criteria, W Company has not maintained effective internal control over financial reporting as of December 31, 20X3, based on [*Identify control criteria, for example, "criteria established in Internal Control—Integrated Framework issued by the Committee of Sponsoring Organizations of the Treadway Commission (COSO)."*].

[*Signature*]

[*City and State or Country*]

[*Date*]

¶ 122.9. Auditor's Report Expressing a Qualified Opinion on Management's Assessment of the Effectiveness of Internal Control Over Financial Reporting and a Qualified Opinion on the Effectiveness of Internal Control Over Financial Reporting Because of a Limitation on the Scope of the Audit

Note: *This sample auditor's report appears in Appendix A, Example A-3 of the auditing standard.*

Report of Independent Registered Public Accounting Firm

[*Introductory paragraph*]

We have audited management's assessment, included in the accompanying [*title of management's report*], that W Company maintained effective internal control over financial reporting as of December 31, 20X3, based on [*Identify control criteria, for example, "criteria established in Internal Control—Integrated Framework issued by the Committee of Sponsoring Organizations of the Treadway Commission (COSO)."*]. W Company's management is responsible for maintaining effective internal control over financial reporting and for its assessment of the effectiveness of internal control over financial reporting. Our responsibility is to express an opinion on management's assessment and an opinion on the effectiveness of the company's internal control over financial reporting based on our audit.

[*Scope paragraph*]

Except as described below, we conducted our audit in accordance the standards of the Public Company Accounting Oversight Board (United States). Those standards require that we plan and perform the audit to obtain reasonable assurance about whether effective internal control over financial reporting was maintained in all material respects. Our audit included obtaining an understanding of internal control over financial reporting, evaluating management's assessment, testing and evaluating the design and operating effectiveness of internal control, and performing such other procedures as we considered necessary in the circumstances. We believe that our audit provides a reasonable basis for our opinion.

[*Explanatory paragraph that describes scope limitation*]

A material weakness is a control deficiency, or combination of control deficiencies, that results in more than a remote likelihood that a material misstatement of the annual or interim financial statements will not be prevented or detected. The following material weakness has been identified and included in management's assessment. Prior to December 20, 20X3, W Company had an inadequate system for recording cash receipts, which could have prevented the Company from recording cash receipts on accounts receivable completely and properly. Therefore, cash received could have been diverted for unauthorized use, lost, or otherwise not properly recorded to accounts receivable. We believe this condition was a material weakness in the design or operation of the internal control of W Company in effect prior to December 20, 20X3. Although the Company implemented a new cash receipts system on December 20, 20X3, the system has not been in operation for a sufficient period of time to enable us to obtain sufficient evidence about its operating effectiveness.

[*Definition paragraph*]

A company's internal control over financial reporting is a process designed to provide reasonable assurance regarding the reliability of financial reporting and the preparation of financial statements for external purposes in accordance with generally accepted accounting principles. A company's internal control over financial reporting includes those policies and procedures that (1) pertain to the maintenance of records that, in reasonable detail, accurately and fairly reflect the transactions and dispositions of the assets of the company; (2) provide reasonable assurance that transactions are recorded as necessary to permit preparation of financial statements in accordance with generally accepted accounting principles, and that receipts and expenditures of the company are being made only in accordance with authorizations of management and directors of the company; and (3) provide reasonable assurance regarding prevention or timely detection of unauthorized acquisition, use, or disposition of the company's assets that could have a material effect on the financial statements.

[*Inherent limitations paragraph*]

Because of its inherent limitations, internal control over financial reporting may not prevent or detect misstatements. Also, projections of any evaluation of effectiveness to future periods are subject to the risk that controls may become inadequate because of changes in conditions, or that the degree of compliance with the policies or procedures may deteriorate.

[*Opinion paragraph*]

In our opinion, except for the effect of matters we might have discovered had we been able to examine evidence about the effectiveness of the new cash receipts system, management's assessment that W Company maintained effective internal control over financial reporting as of December 31, 20X3, is fairly stated, in all material respects, based on [*Identify control criteria, for example,* "criteria established in Internal Control—Integrated Framework issued by the Committee of Sponsoring Organizations of the Treadway Commission (COSO)."]. Also, in our opinion, except for the effect of matters we might have discovered had we been able to examine evidence about the effectiveness of the new cash receipts system, W Company maintained, in all material respects, effective internal control over financial reporting as of December 31, 20X3, based on [*Identify control criteria, for example, "criteria established in Internal Control—Integrated Framework issued by the Committee of Sponsoring Organizations of the Treadway Commission (COSO)."*].

[*Explanatory paragraph*]

We have also audited, in accordance with the standards of the Public Company Accounting Oversight Board (United States), the [*identify financial statements*] of W Company and our report dated [*date of report, which should be the same as the date of the report on the effectiveness of internal control over financial reporting*] expressed [*include nature of opinion*].

[*Signature*]

[*City and State or Country*]

[*Date*]

¶ 122.10. Auditor's Report Disclaiming an Opinion on Management's Assessment of the Effectiveness of Internal Control Over Financial Reporting and Disclaiming an Opinion on the Effectiveness of Internal Control Over Financial Reporting Because of a Limitation on the Scope of the Audit

Note: *This sample auditor's report appears in Appendix A, Example A-4 of the auditing standard.*

Report of Independent Registered Public Accounting Firm

[*Introductory paragraph*]

We were engaged to audit management's assessment included in the accompanying [*title of management's report*] that W Company maintained effective internal control over financial reporting as of December 31, 20X3 based on [*Identify control criteria, for example, "criteria established in Internal Control—Integrated Framework issued by the Committee of Sponsoring Organizations of the Treadway Commission (COSO)."*]. W Company's management is responsible for maintaining effective internal control over financial reporting and for its assessment of the effectiveness of internal control over financial reporting.

[*Omit scope paragraph*]

[*Explanatory paragraph that describes scope limitation*]

[*Definition paragraph*]

A company's internal control over financial reporting is a process designed to provide reasonable assurance regarding the reliability of financial reporting and the preparation of financial statements for external purposes in accordance with generally accepted accounting principles. A company's internal control over financial reporting includes those policies and procedures that (1) pertain to the maintenance of records that, in reasonable detail, accurately and fairly reflect the transactions and dispositions of the assets of the company; (2) provide reasonable assurance that transactions are recorded as necessary to permit preparation of financial statements in accordance with generally accepted accounting principles, and that receipts and expenditures of the company are being made only in accordance with authorizations of management and directors of the company; and (3) provide reasonable assurance regarding prevention or timely detection of unauthorized acquisition, use, or disposition of the company's assets that could have a material effect on the financial statements.

[*Inherent limitations paragraph*]

Because of its inherent limitations, internal control over financial reporting may not prevent or detect misstatements. Also, projections of any evaluation of effectiveness to future periods are subject to the risk that controls may become inadequate because of changes in conditions, or that the degree of compliance with the policies or procedures may deteriorate.

[*Opinion paragraph*]

Since management [*describe scope restrictions*] and we were unable to apply other procedures to satisfy ourselves as to the effectiveness of the company's internal control over financial reporting, the scope of our work was not sufficient to enable us to express, and we do not express, an opinion either on management's assessment or on the effectiveness of the company's internal control over financial reporting.

[*Explanatory paragraph*]

We have also audited, in accordance with the standards of the Public Company Accounting Oversight Board (United States), the [*identify financial statements*] of W Company and our report dated [*date of report, which should be the same as the date of the report on the effectiveness of internal control over financial reporting*] expressed

[*include nature of opinion*].

[*Signature*]

[*City and State or Country*]

[*Date*]

¶ 122.11. Auditor's Report Expressing an Unqualified Opinion on Management's Assessment of the Effectiveness of Internal Control Over Financial Reporting That Refers to the Report of Other Auditors as a Basis, in Part, for the Auditor's Opinion and an Unqualified Opinion on the Effectiveness of Internal Control Over Financial Reporting

Note: *This sample auditor's report appears in Appendix A, Example A-5 of the auditing standard.*

Report of Independent Registered Public Accounting Firm

[*Introductory paragraph*]

We have audited management's assessment, included in the accompanying [*title of management's report*], that W Company maintained effective internal control over financial reporting as of December 31, 20X3, based on [*Identify control criteria, for example, "criteria established in Internal Control—Integrated Framework issued by the Committee of Sponsoring Organizations of the Treadway Commission (COSO)."*]. W Company's management is responsible for maintaining effective internal control over financial reporting and for its assessment of the effectiveness of internal control over financial reporting. Our responsibility is to express an opinion on management's assessment and an opinion on the effectiveness of the company's internal control over financial reporting based on our audit. We did not examine the effectiveness of internal control over financial reporting of B Company, a wholly owned subsidiary, whose financial statements reflect total assets and revenues constituting 20 and 30 percent, respectively, of the related consolidated financial statement amounts as of and for the year ended December 31, 20X3. The effectiveness of B Company's internal control over financial reporting was audited by other auditors whose report has been furnished to us, and our opinion, insofar as it relates to the effectiveness of B Company's internal control over financial reporting, is based solely on the report of the other auditors.

[*Scope paragraph*]

We conducted our audit in accordance with the standards of the Public Company Accounting Oversight Board (United States). Those standards require that we plan and perform the audit to obtain reasonable assurance about whether effective internal control over financial reporting was maintained in all material respects. Our audit included obtaining an understanding of internal control over financial reporting, evaluating management's assessment, testing and evaluating the design and operating effectiveness of internal control, and performing such other procedures as we considered necessary in the circumstances. We believe that our audit and the report of the other auditors provide a reasonable basis for our opinion.

[*Definition paragraph*]

A company's internal control over financial reporting is a process designed to provide reasonable assurance regarding the reliability of financial reporting and the preparation of financial statements for external purposes in accordance with generally accepted accounting principles. A company's internal control over financial reporting includes those policies and procedures that (1) pertain to the maintenance of records that, in reasonable detail, accurately and fairly reflect the transactions and dispositions of the assets of the company; (2) provide reasonable assurance that transactions are recorded as necessary to permit preparation of financial statements in accordance with generally accepted accounting principles, and that receipts and expenditures of the company are being made only in accordance with authorizations of management and directors of the company; and (3) provide reasonable assurance regarding prevention or timely detection of unauthorized acquisition, use, or disposition of the company's assets that could have a material effect on the financial statements.

[*Inherent limitations paragraph*]

Because of its inherent limitations, internal control over financial reporting may not prevent or detect misstatements. Also, projections of any evaluation of effectiveness to future periods are subject to the risk that controls may become inadequate because of changes in conditions, or that the degree of compliance with the policies or procedures may deteriorate.

[*Opinion paragraph*]

In our opinion, based on our audit and the report of the other auditors, management's assessment that W Company maintained effective internal control over financial reporting as of December 31, 20X3, is fairly stated, in all material respects, based on [*Identify control criteria, for example, "criteria established in Internal Control—Integrated Framework issued by the Committee of Sponsoring Organizations of the Treadway Commission (COSO)."*]. Also, in our opinion, based on our audit and the report of the other auditors, W Company maintained, in all material respects, effective internal control over financial reporting as of December 31, 20X3, based on [*Identify control criteria, for example, "criteria established in Internal Control—Integrated Framework issued by the Committee of Sponsoring Organizations of the Treadway Commission (COSO)."*].

[*Explanatory paragraph*]

We have also audited, in accordance with the standards of the Public Company Accounting Oversight Board (United States), the [*identify financial statements*] of W Company and our report dated [*date of report, which should be the same as the date of the report on the effectiveness of internal control over financial reporting*] expressed [*include nature of opinion*].

[*Signature*]

[*City and State or Country*]

[*Date*]

¶ 122.12. Auditor's Report Expressing an Adverse Opinion on Management's Assessment of the Effectiveness of Internal Control Over Financial Reporting and an Adverse Opinion on the Effectiveness of Internal Control Over Financial Reporting Because of the Existence of a Material Weakness

Note: *This sample auditor's report appears in Appendix A, Example A-6 of the auditing standard.*

Report of Independent Registered Public Accounting Firm

[*Introductory paragraph*]

We have audited management's assessment, included in the accompanying [*title of management's report*], that W Company maintained effective internal control over financial reporting as of December 31, 20X3, based on [*Identify control criteria, for example, "criteria established in Internal Control—Integrated Framework issued by the Committee of Sponsoring Organizations of the Treadway Commission (COSO)."*]. W Company's management is responsible for maintaining effective internal control over financial reporting and for its assessment of the effectiveness of internal control over financial reporting. Our responsibility is to express an opinion on management's assessment and an opinion on the effectiveness of the company's internal control over financial reporting based on our audit.

[*Scope paragraph*]

We conducted our audit in accordance with the standards of the Public Company Accounting Oversight Board (United States). Those standards require that we plan and perform the audit to obtain reasonable assurance about whether effective internal control over financial reporting was maintained in all material respects. Our audit included obtaining an understanding of internal control over financial reporting, evaluating management's assessment, testing and evaluating the design and operating effectiveness of internal control, and performing such other procedures as we considered necessary in the circumstances. We believe that our audit provides a reasonable basis for our opinion.

[*Definition paragraph*]

A company's internal control over financial reporting is a process designed to provide reasonable assurance regarding the reliability of financial reporting and the preparation of financial statements for external purposes in accordance with generally accepted accounting principles. A company's internal control over financial reporting includes those policies and procedures that (1) pertain to the maintenance of records that, in reasonable detail, accurately and fairly reflect the transactions and dispositions of the assets of the company; (2) provide reasonable assurance that transactions are recorded as necessary to permit preparation of financial statements in accordance with generally accepted accounting principles, and that receipts and expenditures of the company are being made only in accordance with authorizations of management and directors of the company; and (3) provide reasonable assurance regarding prevention or timely detection of unauthorized acquisition, use, or disposition of the company's assets that could have a material effect on the financial statements.

[*Inherent limitations paragraph*]

Because of its inherent limitations, internal control over financial reporting may not prevent or detect misstatements. Also, projections of any evaluation of effectiveness to future periods are subject to the risk that controls may become inadequate because of changes in conditions, or that the degree of compliance with the policies or procedures may deteriorate.

[*Explanatory paragraph*]

A material weakness is a control deficiency, or combination of control deficiencies, that results in more than a remote likelihood that a material misstatement of the annual or interim financial statements will not be prevented or detected. We have identified the following material weakness that has not been identified as a material weakness in management's assessment [*Include a description of the material weakness and its effect on the achievement of the objectives of the control criteria.*] This material weakness was considered in determining the nature, timing, and extent of audit tests applied in our audit of the 20X3 financial statements, and this report does not affect our report dated [*date of report, which should be the same as the date of this report on internal control*] on those financial statements.

[*Opinion paragraph*]

In our opinion, because of the effect of the material weakness described above on the achievement of the objectives of the control criteria, management's assessment that W Company maintained effective internal control over financial reporting as of December 31, 20X3, is not fairly stated, in all material respects, based on [*Identify control criteria, for example, "criteria established in Internal Control—Integrated Framework issued by the Committee of Sponsoring Organizations of the Treadway Commission (COSO)."*]. Also, in our opinion, because of the effect of the material weakness described above on the achievement of the objectives of the control criteria, W Company has not maintained effective internal control over financial reporting as of December 31, 20X3, based on [*Identify control criteria, for example, "criteria established in Internal Control—Integrated Framework issued by the Committee of Sponsoring Organizations of the Treadway Commission (COSO)."*].

[*Signature*]

[*City and State or Country*]

[*Date*]

¶ 122.13. Auditor's Combined Report Expressing an Unqualified Opinion on Financial Statements, an Unqualified Opinion on Management's Assessment of the Effectiveness of Internal Control Over Financial Reporting and an Unqualified Opinion on the Effectiveness of Internal Control Over Financial Reporting

Note: *This sample auditor's report appears in Appendix A, Example A-7 of the auditing standard.*

Report of Independent Registered Public Accounting Firm

[*Introductory paragraph*]

We have audited the accompanying balance sheets of W Company as of December 31, 20X3 and 20X2, and the related statements of income, stockholders' equity and comprehensive income, and cash flows for each of the years in the three-year period ended December 31, 20X3. We also have audited management's assessment, included in the accompanying [*title of management's report*], that W Company maintained effective internal control over financial reporting as of December 31, 20X3, based on [*Identify control criteria, for example, "criteria established in Internal Control—Integrated Framework issued by the Committee of Sponsoring Organizations of the Treadway Commission (COSO)."*]. W Company's management is responsible for these financial statements, for maintaining effective internal control over financial reporting, and for its assessment of the effectiveness of internal control over financial reporting. Our responsibility is to express an opinion on these financial statements, an opinion on management's assessment, and an opinion on the effectiveness of the company's internal control over financial reporting based on our audits.

[*Scope paragraph*]

We conducted our audits in accordance with the standards of the Public Company Accounting Oversight Board (United States). Those standards require that we plan and perform the audits to obtain reasonable assurance about whether the financial statements are free of material misstatement and whether effective internal control over financial reporting was maintained in all material respects. Our audit of financial statements included examining, on a test basis, evidence supporting the amounts and disclosures in the financial statements, assessing the accounting principles used and significant estimates made by management, and evaluating the overall financial statement presentation. Our audit of internal control over financial reporting included obtaining an understanding of internal control over financial reporting, evaluating management's assessment, testing and evaluating the design and operating effectiveness of internal control, and performing such other procedures as we considered necessary in the circumstances. We believe that our audits provide a reasonable basis for our opinions.

[*Definition paragraph*]

A company's internal control over financial reporting is a process designed to provide reasonable assurance regarding the reliability of financial reporting and the preparation of financial statements for external purposes in accordance with generally accepted accounting principles. A company's internal control over financial reporting includes those policies and procedures that (1) pertain to the maintenance of records that, in reasonable detail, accurately and fairly reflect the transactions and dispositions of the assets of the company; (2) provide reasonable assurance that transactions are recorded as necessary to permit preparation of financial statements in accordance with generally accepted accounting principles, and that receipts and expenditures of the company are being made only in accordance with authorizations of management and directors of the company; and (3) provide reasonable assurance regarding prevention or timely detection of unauthorized acquisition, use, or disposition of the company's assets that could have a material effect on the financial statements.

[*Inherent limitations paragraph*]

Because of its inherent limitations, internal control over financial reporting may not prevent or detect misstatements. Also, projections of any evaluation of effectiveness to future periods are subject to the risk that controls may become inadequate because of changes in conditions, or that the degree of compliance with the policies or procedures may deteriorate.

[*Opinion paragraph*]

In our opinion, the financial statements referred to above present fairly, in all material respects, the financial position of W Company as of December 31, 20X3 and 20X2, and the results of its operations and its cash flows for each of the years in the three-year period ended December 31, 20X3 in conformity with accounting principles generally accepted in the United States of America. Also in our opinion, management's assessment that W Company maintained effective internal control over financial reporting as of December 31, 20X3, is fairly stated, in all material respects, based on [*Identify control criteria, for example, "criteria established in Internal Control—Integrated Framework issued by the Committee of Sponsoring Organizations of the Treadway Commission (COSO)."*]. Furthermore, in our opinion, W Company maintained, in all material respects, effective internal control over financial reporting as of December 31, 20X3, based on [*Identify control criteria, for example, "criteria established in Internal Control—Integrated Framework issued by the Committee of Sponsoring Organizations of the Treadway Commission (COSO)."*].

[*Signature*]

[*City and State or Country*]

[*Date*]

¶ 200. Annotated PCAOB Auditing Standard No. 2: An Audit of Internal Control Over Financial Reporting Performed in Conjunction with an Audit of Financial Statements

Note: This section of *Guide to the PCAOB Internal Control Standard* reproduces PCAOB Auditing Standard No. 2: *An Audit of Internal Control Over Financial Reporting Performed in Conjunction with an Audit of Financial Statements.* The endnotes refer the reader to RIA's analysis of the standard. The full text of the standard without annotations appears in ¶ 400.

¶ 200.A.I. *Applicability of Standard*

200.A.1.I This standard establishes requirements and provides directions that apply when an auditor is engaged to audit both a company's financial statements and management's assessment of the effectiveness of internal control over financial reporting.

> **Note:** The term *auditor* includes both public accounting firms registered with the Public Company Accounting Oversight Board ("PCAOB" or the "Board") and associated persons thereof.

For Analysis, see ¶ 100.

200.A.2.I A company subject to the reporting requirements of the Securities Exchange Act of 1934 (an "issuer") is required to include in its annual report a report of management on the company's internal control over financial reporting. Registered investment companies, issuers of asset-backed securities, and nonpublic companies are not subject to the reporting requirements mandated by Section 404 of the Sarbanes-Oxley Act of 2002 (the "Act") (PL 107-204). The report of management is required to contain management's assessment of the effectiveness of the company's internal control over financial reporting as of the end of the company's most recent fiscal year, including a statement as to whether the company's internal control over financial reporting is effective. The auditor that audits the company's financial statements included in the annual report is required to attest to and report on management's assessment. The company is required to file the auditor's attestation report as part of the annual report.

> **Note:** The term issuer means an issuer (as defined in Section 3 of the Securities Exchange Act of 1934), the securities of which are registered under Section 12 of that Act, or that is required to file reports under Section 15(d) of that Act, or that files or has filed a registration statement with the Securities and Exchange Commission ("SEC" or "Commission") that has not yet become effective under the Securities Act of 1933, and that it has not withdrawn.

Note: Various parts of this standard summarize legal requirements imposed on issuers by the SEC, as well as legal requirements imposed on auditors by regulatory authorities other than the PCAOB. These parts of the standard are intended to provide context and to promote the auditor's understanding of the relationship between his or her obligations under this standard and his or her other legal responsibilities. The standard does not incorporate these legal requirements by reference and is not an interpretation of those other requirements and should not be so construed. (This Note does not apply to references in the standard to the existing professional standards and the Board's interim auditing and related professional practice standards.)

For Analysis, see ¶ 100.

200.A.3.I This standard is the standard on attestation engagements referred to in Section 404(b) of the Act. This standard is also the standard referred to in Section 103(a)(2)(A)(iii) of the Act. Throughout this standard, the auditor's attestation of management's assessment of the effectiveness of internal control over financial reporting required by Section 404(b) of the Act is referred to as the *audit of internal control over financial reporting.*

Note: The two terms *audit of internal control over financial reporting* and *attestation of management's assessment of the effectiveness of internal control over financial reporting* refer to the same professional service. The first refers to the process, and the second refers to the result of that process.

For Analysis, see ¶ 100.

¶ 200.A.II. *Auditor's Objective in an Audit of Internal Control Over Financial Reporting*

200.A.4.II The auditor's objective in an audit of internal control over financial reporting is to express an opinion on management's assessment of the effectiveness of the company's internal control over financial reporting. To form a basis for expressing such an opinion, the auditor must plan and perform the audit to obtain reasonable assurance about whether the company maintained, in all material respects, effective internal control over financial reporting as of the date specified in management's assessment. The auditor also must audit the company's financial statements as of the date specified in management's assessment because the information the auditor obtains during a financial statement audit is relevant to the auditor's conclusion about the effectiveness of the company's internal control over financial reporting. Maintaining effective internal control over financial reporting means that no material weaknesses exist; therefore, the objective of the audit of internal control over financial reporting is to obtain reasonable assurance that no material weaknesses exist as of the date specified in management's assessment.

For Analysis, see ¶ 101.

200.A.5.II To obtain reasonable assurance, the auditor evaluates the assessment performed by management and obtains and evaluates evidence about whether the internal control over financial reporting was designed and operated effectively. The auditor obtains this evidence from a number of sources, including using the work performed by others and performing auditing procedures himself or herself.

For Analysis, see ¶ 101.

200.A.6.II The auditor should be aware that persons who rely on the information concerning internal control over financial reporting include investors, creditors, the board of directors and audit committee, and regulators in specialized industries, such as banking or insurance. The auditor should be aware that external users of financial statements are interested in information on internal control over financial reporting because it enhances the quality of financial reporting and increases their confidence in financial information, including financial information issued between annual reports, such as quarterly information. Information on internal control over financial reporting is also intended to provide an early warning to those inside and outside the company who are in a position to insist on improvements in internal control over financial reporting, such as the audit committee and regulators in specialized industries. Additionally, Section 302 of the Act and Securities Exchange Act Rule 13a-14(a) or 15d-14(a),[1] whichever applies, require management, with the participation of the principal executive and financial officers, to make quarterly and annual certifications with respect to the company's internal control over financial reporting.

For Analysis, see ¶ 101.

¶ 200.A.III. *Definitions Related to Internal Control Over Financial Reporting*

200.A.7.III For purposes of management's assessment and the audit of internal control over financial reporting in this standard, *internal control over financial reporting* is defined as follows:

> A process designed by, or under the supervision of, the company's principal executive and principal financial officers, or persons performing similar functions, and effected by the company's board of directors, management, and other personnel, to provide reasonable assurance regarding the reliability of financial reporting and the preparation of financial statements for external purposes in accordance with generally accepted accounting principles and includes those policies and procedures that:

---

1. See 17 C.F.R. 240.13a-14(a) or 17 C.F.R. 240.15d-14(a), whichever applies.

---

(1) Pertain to the maintenance of records that, in reasonable detail, accurately and fairly reflect the transactions and dispositions of the assets of the company;

(2) Provide reasonable assurance that transactions are recorded as necessary to permit preparation of financial statements in accordance with generally accepted accounting principles, and that receipts and expenditures of the company are being made only in accordance with authorizations of management and directors of the company; and

(3) Provide reasonable assurance regarding prevention or timely detection of unauthorized acquisition, use or disposition of the company's assets that could have a material effect on the financial statements.

Note: This definition is the same one used by the SEC in its rules requiring management to report on internal control over financial reporting, except the word "registrant" has been changed to "company" to conform to the wording in this standard. (See Securities Exchange Act Rules 13a-15(f) and 15d-15(f).[2])

Note: Throughout this standard, *internal control over financial reporting* (singular) refers to the process described in this paragraph. Individual controls or subsets of controls are referred to as *controls* or *controls over financial reporting.*

For Analysis, see ¶ 102.

200.A.8.III A *control deficiency* exists when the design or operation of a control does not allow management or employees, in the normal course of performing their assigned functions, to prevent or detect misstatements on a timely basis.

- A deficiency in *design* exists when (a) a control necessary to meet the control objective is missing or (b) an existing control is not properly designed so that, even if the control operates as designed, the control objective is not always met.

- A deficiency in *operation* exists when a properly designed control does not operate as designed, or when the person performing the control does not possess the necessary authority or qualifications to perform the control effectively.

For Analysis, see ¶ 102.

200.A.9.III A *significant deficiency* is a control deficiency, or combination of control deficiencies, that adversely affects the company's ability to initiate, authorize, record, process, or report external financial data reliably in accordance with generally accepted accounting principles such that there is more than a re-

---

2. See 17 C.F.R. 240, 13a-15(f) and 15d-15(f).

mote likelihood that a misstatement of the company's annual or interim financial statements that is more than inconsequential will not be prevented or detected.

Note: The term "remote likelihood" as used in the definitions of *significant deficiency* and *material weakness* (paragraph 10) has the same meaning as the term "remote" as used in Financial Accounting Standards Board Statement No. 5, *Accounting for Contingencies* ("FAS No. 5"). Paragraph 3 of FAS No. 5 states:

When a loss contingency exists, the likelihood that the future event or events will confirm the loss or impairment of an asset or the incurrence of a liability can range from probable to remote. This Statement uses the terms *probable, reasonably possible,* and *remote* to identify three areas within that range, as follows:

a. *Probable.* The future event or events are likely to occur.

b. *Reasonably possible.* The chance of the future event or events occurring is more than remote but less than likely.

c. *Remote.* The chance of the future events or events occurring is slight.

Therefore, the likelihood of an event is "more than remote" when it is either reasonably possible or probable.

Note: A misstatement is *inconsequential* if a reasonable person would conclude, after considering the possibility of further undetected misstatements, that the misstatement, either individually or when aggregated with other misstatements, would clearly be immaterial to the financial statements. If a reasonable person could not reach such a conclusion regarding a particular misstatement, that misstatement is *more than inconsequential.*

For Analysis, see ¶ 102.

200.A.10.III A *material weakness* is a significant deficiency, or combination of significant deficiencies, that results in more than a remote likelihood that a material misstatement of the annual or interim financial statements will not be prevented or detected.

Note: In evaluating whether a control deficiency exists and whether control deficiencies, either individually or in combination with other control deficiencies, are significant deficiencies or material weaknesses, the auditor should consider the definitions in paragraphs 8, 9 and 10, and the directions in paragraphs 130 through 137. As explained in paragraph 23, the evaluation of the materiality of the control deficiency should include both quantitative and qualitative considerations. Qualitative factors that might be important in this evaluation include the nature of the financial statement accounts and assertions involved and the reasonably possible future consequences of the deficiency. Furthermore, in determining whether a control deficiency or combination of deficiencies is a significant deficiency or a material weakness, the auditor should evaluate the effect of compensating controls and whether such compensating controls are effective.

For Analysis, see ¶ 102, ¶ 107, and ¶ 109.8.2.

200.A.11.III Controls over financial reporting may be *preventive controls* or *detective controls.*

- Preventive controls have the objective of preventing errors or fraud from occurring in the first place that could result in a misstatement of the financial statements.

- Detective controls have the objective of detecting errors or fraud that have already occurred that could result in a misstatement of the financial statements.

For Analysis, see ¶ 102.

200.A.12.III Even well-designed controls that are operating as designed might not prevent a misstatement from occurring. However, this possibility may be countered by overlapping preventive controls or partially countered by detective controls. Therefore, effective internal control over financial reporting often includes a combination of preventive and detective controls to achieve a specific control objective. The auditor's procedures as part of either the audit of internal control over financial reporting or the audit of the financial statements are not part of a company's internal control over financial reporting.

For Analysis, see ¶ 102.

¶ 200.A.IV. *Framework Used by Management to Conduct Its Assessment*

200.A.13.IV Management is required to base its assessment of the effectiveness of the company's internal control over financial reporting on a suitable, recognized control framework established by a body of experts that followed due-process procedures, including the broad distribution of the framework for public comment. In addition to being available to users of management's reports, a framework is suitable only when it:

- Is free from bias;

- Permits reasonably consistent qualitative and quantitative measurements of a company's internal control over financial reporting;

- Is sufficiently complete so that those relevant factors that would alter a conclusion about the effectiveness of a company's internal control over financial reporting are not omitted; and

- Is relevant to an evaluation of internal control over financial reporting.

For Analysis, see ¶ 103.

¶ 200.A.IV.a. Committee of Sponsoring Organizations Framework

200.A.14.IV.a In the United States, the Committee of Sponsoring Organizations ("COSO") of the Treadway Commission has published *Internal Control—Integrated Framework*. Known as the COSO report, it provides a suitable and available framework for purposes of management's assessment. For that reason, the performance and reporting directions in this standard are based on the COSO framework. Other suitable frameworks have been published in other countries and may be developed in the future. Such other suitable frameworks may be used in an audit of internal control over financial reporting. Although different frameworks may not contain exactly the same elements as COSO, they should have elements that encompass, in general, all the themes in COSO. Therefore, the auditor should be able to apply the concepts and guidance in this standard in a reasonable manner.

For Analysis, see ¶ 103.

200.A.15.IV.a The COSO framework identifies three primary objectives of internal control: efficiency and effectiveness of operations, financial reporting, and compliance with laws and regulations. The COSO perspective on internal control over financial reporting does not ordinarily include the other two objectives of internal control, which are the effectiveness and efficiency of operations and compliance with laws and regulations. However, the controls that management designs and implements may achieve more than one objective. Also, operations and compliance with laws and regulations directly related to the presentation of and required disclosures in financial statements are encompassed in internal control over financial reporting. Additionally, not all controls relevant to financial reporting are accounting controls. Accordingly, all controls that could materially affect financial reporting, including controls that focus primarily on the effectiveness and efficiency of operations or compliance with laws and regulations and also have a material effect on the reliability of financial reporting, are a part of internal control over financial reporting. More information about the COSO framework is included in the COSO report and in AU sec. 319, Consideration of Internal Control in a Financial Statement Audit.[3] The COSO report also discusses special considerations for internal control over financial reporting for small and medium-sized companies.

For Analysis, see ¶ 103.

---

3. The Board adopted the generally accepted auditing standards, as described in the AICPA Auditing Standards Board's ("ASB") Statement on Auditing Standards No. 95, *Generally Accepted Auditing Standards*, as in existence on April 16, 2003, on an initial, transitional basis. The Statements on Auditing Standards promulgated by the ASB have been codified into the AICPA *Professional Standards*, Volume 1, as AU sections 100 through 900. References in this standard to AU sections refer to those generally accepted auditing standards, as adopted on an interim basis in PCAOB Rule 3200T.

¶ 200.A.V. *Inherent Limitations in Internal Control Over Financial Reporting*

200.A.16.V Internal control over financial reporting cannot provide absolute assurance of achieving financial reporting objectives because of its inherent limitations. Internal control over financial reporting is a process that involves human diligence and compliance and is subject to lapses in judgment and breakdowns resulting from human failures. Internal control over financial reporting also can be circumvented by collusion or improper management override. Because of such limitations, there is a risk that material misstatements may not be prevented or detected on a timely basis by internal control over financial reporting. However, these inherent limitations are known features of the financial reporting process. Therefore, it is possible to design into the process safeguards to reduce, though not eliminate, this risk.

For Analysis, see ¶ 104.

¶ 200.A.VI. *The Concept of Reasonable Assurance*

200.A.17.VI Management's assessment of the effectiveness of internal control over financial reporting is expressed at the level of *reasonable assurance.* The concept of reasonable assurance is built into the definition of internal control over financial reporting and also is integral to the auditor's opinion.[4] Reasonable assurance includes the understanding that there is a remote likelihood that material misstatements will not be prevented or detected on a timely basis. Although not absolute assurance, reasonable assurance is, nevertheless, a high level of assurance.

For Analysis, see ¶ 105.

200.A.18.VI Just as there are inherent limitations on the assurance that effective internal control over financial reporting can provide, as discussed in paragraph 16, there are limitations on the amount of assurance the auditor can obtain as a result of performing his or her audit of internal control over financial reporting. Limitations arise because an audit is conducted on a test basis and requires the exercise of professional judgment. Nevertheless, the audit of internal control over financial reporting includes obtaining an understanding of internal control over financial reporting, testing and evaluating the design and operating effectiveness of internal control over financial reporting, and performing such other procedures as the auditor considers necessary to obtain reasonable assurance about whether internal control over financial reporting is effective.

For Analysis, see ¶ 104 and ¶ 105.

200.A.19.VI There is no difference in the level of work performed or assurance obtained by the auditor when expressing an opinion on management's as-

---

4. See *Final Rule: Management's Reports on Internal Control Over Financial Reporting and Certification of Disclosure in Exchange Act Periodic Reports,* Securities and Exchange Commission Release No. 33-8238 (June 5, 2003) [68 FR 36636] for further discussion of reasonable assurance.

---

sessment of effectiveness or when expressing an opinion directly on the effectiveness of internal control over financial reporting. In either case, the auditor must obtain sufficient evidence to provide a reasonable basis for his or her opinion and the use and evaluation of management's assessment is inherent in expressing either opinion.

> **Note:** The auditor's report on internal control over financial reporting does not relieve management of its responsibility for assuring users of its financial reports about the effectiveness of internal control over financial reporting.

For Analysis, see ¶ 105.

¶ 200.A.VII. *Management's Responsibilities in an Audit of Internal Control Over Financial Reporting*

200.A.20.VII For the auditor to satisfactorily complete an audit of internal control over financial reporting, management must do the following:[5]

a. Accept responsibility for the effectiveness of the company's internal control over financial reporting;

b. Evaluate the effectiveness of the company's internal control over financial reporting using suitable control criteria;

c. Support its evaluation with sufficient evidence, including documentation; and

d. Present a written assessment of the effectiveness of the company's internal control over financial reporting as of the end of the company's most recent fiscal year.

For Analysis, see ¶ 106.

200.A.21.VII If the auditor concludes that management has not fulfilled the responsibilities enumerated in the preceding paragraph, the auditor should communicate, in writing, to management and the audit committee that the audit of internal control over financial reporting cannot be satisfactorily completed and that he or she is required to disclaim an opinion. Paragraphs 40 through 46 provide information for the auditor about evaluating management's process for assessing internal control over financial reporting.

For Analysis, see ¶ 106 and ¶ 109.3.

---

5. Management is required to fulfill these responsibilities. See Items 308(a) and (c) of Regulation S-B and S-K, 17 C.F.R. 228.308(a) and (c) and 229.308(a) and (c), respectively.

¶ 200.A.VIII. *Materiality Considerations in an Audit of Internal Control Over Financial Reporting*

200.A.22.VIII The auditor should apply the concept of materiality in an audit of internal control over financial reporting at both the financial-statement level and at the individual account-balance level. The auditor uses materiality at the financial-statement level in evaluating whether a deficiency, or combination of deficiencies, in controls is a significant deficiency or a material weakness. Materiality at both the financial-statement level and the individual account-balance level is relevant to planning the audit and designing procedures. Materiality at the account-balance level is necessarily lower than materiality at the financial-statement level.

For Analysis, see ¶ 107.

200.A.23.VIII The same conceptual definition of materiality that applies to financial reporting applies to information on internal control over financial reporting, including the relevance of both quantitative and qualitative considerations.[6]

- The quantitative considerations are essentially the same as in an audit of financial statements and relate to whether misstatements that would not be prevented or detected by internal control over financial reporting, individually or collectively, have a quantitatively material effect on the financial statements.

- The qualitative considerations apply to evaluating materiality with respect to the financial statements and to additional factors that relate to the perceived needs of reasonable persons who will rely on the information. Paragraph 6 describes some qualitative considerations.

For Analysis, see ¶ 101 and ¶ 107.

¶ 200.A.IX. *Fraud Considerations in an Audit of Internal Control Over Financial Reporting*

200.A.24.IX The auditor should evaluate all controls specifically intended to address the risks of fraud that have at least a reasonably possible likelihood of having a material effect on the company's financial statements. These controls may be a part of any of the five components of internal control over financial reporting, as discussed in paragraph 49. Controls related to the prevention and detection of fraud often have a pervasive effect on the risk of fraud. Such controls include, but are not limited to, the:

- Controls restraining misappropriation of company assets that could result in a material misstatement of the financial statements;
- Company's risk assessment processes;

---

6. AU sec. 312, *Audit Risk and Materiality in Conducting an Audit,* provides additional explanation of materiality.

- Code of ethics/conduct provisions, especially those related to conflicts of interest, related party transactions, illegal acts, and the monitoring of the code by management and the audit committee or board;

- Adequacy of the internal audit activity and whether the internal audit function reports directly to the audit committee, as well as the extent of the audit committee's involvement and interaction with internal audit; and

- Adequacy of the company's procedures for handling complaints and for accepting confidential submissions of concerns about questionable accounting or auditing matters.

For Analysis, see ¶ 108 and ¶ 109.4.

200.A.25.IX Part of management's responsibility when designing a company's internal control over financial reporting is to design and implement programs and controls to prevent, deter, and detect fraud. Management, along with those who have responsibility for oversight of the financial reporting process (such as the audit committee), should set the proper tone; create and maintain a culture of honesty and high ethical standards; and establish appropriate controls to prevent, deter, and detect fraud. When management and those responsible for the oversight of the financial reporting process fulfill those responsibilities, the opportunities to commit fraud can be reduced significantly.

For Analysis, see ¶ 108.

200.A.26.IX In an audit of internal control over financial reporting, the auditor's evaluation of controls is interrelated with the auditor's evaluation of controls in a financial statement audit, as required by AU sec. 316, *Consideration of Fraud in a Financial Statement Audit.* Often, controls identified and evaluated by the auditor during the audit of internal control over financial reporting also address or mitigate fraud risks, which the auditor is required to consider in a financial statement audit. If the auditor identifies deficiencies in controls designed to prevent and detect fraud during the audit of internal control over financial reporting, the auditor should alter the nature, timing, or extent of procedures to be performed during the financial statement audit to be responsive to such deficiencies, as provided in paragraphs .44 and .45 of AU sec. 316.

For Analysis, see ¶ 108.

¶ 200.A.X. *Performing an Audit of Internal Control Over Financial Reporting*

200.A.27.X In an audit of internal control over financial reporting, the auditor must obtain sufficient competent evidence about the design and operating effectiveness of controls over all relevant financial statement assertions related to all significant accounts and disclosures in the financial statements. The auditor must plan and perform the audit to obtain reasonable assurance that deficiencies that, individually or in the aggregate, would represent material weaknesses are identified. Thus, the audit is not designed to detect deficiencies in internal control over financial reporting that, individually or in the aggregate, are less severe than a material weakness. Because of the potential significance of the information obtained during the audit of the financial statements to the auditor's conclusions about the effectiveness of internal control over financial reporting, the auditor cannot audit internal control over financial reporting without also auditing the financial statements.

> **Note:** However, the auditor may audit the financial statements without also auditing internal control over financial reporting, for example, in the case of certain initial public offerings by a company. See the discussion beginning at paragraph 145 for more information about the importance of auditing both internal control over financial reporting as well as the financial statements when the auditor is engaged to audit internal control over financial reporting.

For Analysis, see ¶ 109 and ¶ 111.

200.A.28.X The auditor must adhere to the general standards (See paragraphs 30 through 36) and fieldwork and reporting standards (See paragraph 37) in performing an audit of a company's internal control over financial reporting. This involves the following:

a. Planning the engagement;

b. Evaluating management's assessment process;

c. Obtaining an understanding of internal control over financial reporting;

d. Testing and evaluating design effectiveness of internal control over financial reporting;

e. Testing and evaluating operating effectiveness of internal control over financial reporting; and

f. Forming an opinion on the effectiveness of internal control over financial reporting.

For Analysis, see ¶ 109 and ¶ 109.1.

200.A.29.X Even though some requirements of this standard are set forth in a manner that suggests a sequential process, auditing internal control over financial reporting involves a process of gathering, updating, and analyzing information. Accordingly, the auditor may perform some of the procedures and evaluations described in this section on "Performing an Audit of Internal Control Over Financial Reporting" concurrently.

For Analysis, see ¶ 109.

¶ 200.A.X.a. Applying General, Fieldwork, and Reporting Standards

200.A.30.X.a The general standards (See AU sec. 150, *Generally Accepted Auditing Standards*) are applicable to an audit of internal control over financial reporting. These standards require technical training and proficiency as an auditor, independence in fact and appearance, and the exercise of due professional care, including professional skepticism.

For Analysis, see ¶ 109 and ¶ 109.1.

200.A.31.X.a *Technical Training and Proficiency.* To perform an audit of internal control over financial reporting, the auditor should have competence in the subject matter of internal control over financial reporting.

For Analysis, see ¶ 109, ¶ 109.1, and ¶ 109.1.1.

200.A.32.X.a *Independence.* The applicable requirements of independence are largely predicated on four basic principles: (1) an auditor must not act as management or as an employee of the audit client, (2) an auditor must not audit his or her own work, (3) an auditor must not serve in a position of being an advocate for his or her client, and (4) an auditor must not have mutual or conflicting interests with his or her audit client.[7] If the auditor were to design or implement controls, that situation would place the auditor in a management role and result in the auditor auditing his or her own work. These requirements, however, do not preclude the auditor from making substantive recommendations as to how management may improve the design or operation of the company's internal controls as a by-product of an audit.

For Analysis, see ¶ 109, ¶ 109.1, and ¶ 109.1.2.

200.A.33.X.a The auditor must not accept an engagement to provide internal control-related services to an issuer for which the auditor also audits the financial statements unless that engagement has been specifically pre-approved by the audit committee. For any internal control services the auditor provides, management must be actively involved and cannot delegate responsibility for these matters to the auditor. Management's involvement must be substantive and extensive. Management's acceptance of responsibility for documentation and testing performed by the auditor does not by itself satisfy the independence requirements.

For Analysis, see ¶ 109, ¶ 109.1, and ¶ 109.1.2.

200.A.34.X.a Maintaining independence, in fact and appearance, requires careful attention, as is the case with all independence issues when work concerning internal control over financial reporting is performed. Unless the auditor and the audit committee are diligent in evaluating the nature and extent of ser-

---

7. See the Preliminary Note of Rule 2-01 of Regulation S-X, 17 C.F.R. 210.2-01.

vices provided, the services might violate basic principles of independence and cause an impairment of independence in fact or appearance.

For Analysis, see ¶ 109, ¶ 109.1, and ¶ 109.1.2.

200.A.35.X.a The independent auditor and the audit committee have significant and distinct responsibilities for evaluating whether the auditor's services impair independence in fact or appearance. The test for independence in fact is whether the activities would impede the ability of anyone on the engagement team or in a position to influence the engagement team from exercising objective judgment in the audits of the financial statements or internal control over financial reporting. The test for independence in appearance is whether a reasonable investor, knowing all relevant facts and circumstances, would perceive an auditor as having interests which could jeopardize the exercise of objective and impartial judgments on all issues encompassed within the auditor's engagement.

For Analysis, see ¶ 109, ¶ 109.1, and ¶ 109.1.2.

200.A.36.X.a *Due Professional Care.* The auditor must exercise due professional care in an audit of internal control over financial reporting. One important tenet of due professional care is exercising professional skepticism. In an audit of internal control over financial reporting, exercising professional skepticism involves essentially the same considerations as in an audit of financial statements, that is, it includes a critical assessment of the work that management has performed in evaluating and testing controls.

For Analysis, see ¶ 109, ¶ 109.1, and ¶ 109.1.3.

200.A.37.X.a *Fieldwork and Reporting Standards.* This standard establishes the fieldwork and reporting standards applicable to an audit of internal control over financial reporting.

For Analysis, see ¶ 109, ¶ 109.1, and ¶ 109.4.

200.A.38.X.a The concept of materiality, as discussed in paragraphs 22 and 23, underlies the application of the general and fieldwork standards.

For Analysis, see ¶ 107, ¶ 109, ¶ 109.1, and ¶ 109.1.4.

¶ 200.A.X.b. Planning the Engagement

200.A.39.X.b The audit of internal control over financial reporting should be properly planned and assistants, if any, are to be properly supervised. When planning the audit of internal control over financial reporting, the auditor should evaluate how the following matters will affect the auditor's procedures:

- Knowledge of the company's internal control over financial reporting obtained during other engagements.

- Matters affecting the industry in which the company operates, such as financial reporting practices, economic conditions, laws and regulations, and technological changes.

- Matters relating to the company's business, including its organization, operating characteristics, capital structure, and distribution methods.

- The extent of recent changes, if any, in the company, its operations, or its internal control over financial reporting.

- Management's process for assessing the effectiveness of the company's internal control over financial reporting based upon control criteria.

- Preliminary judgments about materiality, risk, and other factors relating to the determination of material weaknesses.

- Control deficiencies previously communicated to the audit committee or management.

- Legal or regulatory matters of which the company is aware.

- The type and extent of available evidence related to the effectiveness of the company's internal control over financial reporting.

- Preliminary judgments about the effectiveness of internal control over financial reporting.

- The number of significant business locations or units, including management's documentation and monitoring of controls over such locations or business units. (Appendix B, paragraphs B1 through B17, discusses factors the auditor should evaluate to determine the locations at which to perform auditing procedures.)

For Analysis, see ¶ 109, ¶ 109.2, and ¶ 118.

¶ 200.A.X.c. Evaluating Management's Assessment Process

200.A.40.X.c The auditor must obtain an understanding of, and evaluate, management's process for assessing the effectiveness of the company's internal control over financial reporting. When obtaining the understanding, the auditor should determine whether management has addressed the following elements:

- Determining which controls should be tested, including controls over all relevant assertions related to all significant accounts and disclosures in the financial statements. Generally, such controls include:

  —Controls over initiating, authorizing, recording, processing, and reporting significant accounts and disclosures and related assertions embodied in the financial statements.

  —Controls over the selection and application of accounting policies that are in conformity with generally accepted accounting principles.

  —Antifraud programs and controls.

—Controls, including information technology general controls, on which other controls are dependent.

—Controls over significant nonroutine and nonsystematic transactions, such as accounts involving judgments and estimates.

—Company level controls (as described in paragraph 53), including:

    —The control environment and

    —Controls over the period-end financial reporting process, including controls over procedures used to enter transaction totals into the general ledger; to initiate, authorize, record, and process journal entries in the general ledger; and to record recurring and nonrecurring adjustments to the financial statements (for example, consolidating adjustments, report combinations, and reclassifications).

Note: References to the period-end financial reporting process in this standard refer to the preparation of both annual and quarterly financial statements.

- Evaluating the likelihood that failure of the control could result in a misstatement, the magnitude of such a misstatement, and the degree to which other controls, if effective, achieve the same control objectives.

- Determining the locations or business units to include in the evaluation for a company with multiple locations or business units (See paragraphs B1 through B17).

- Evaluating the design effectiveness of controls.

- Evaluating the operating effectiveness of controls based on procedures sufficient to assess their operating effectiveness. Examples of such procedures include testing of the controls by internal audit, testing of controls by others under the direction of management, using a service organization's reports (See paragraphs B18 through B29), inspection of evidence of the application of controls, or testing by means of a selfassessment process, some of which might occur as part of management's ongoing monitoring activities. Inquiry alone is not adequate to complete this evaluation. To evaluate the effectiveness of the company's internal control over financial reporting, management must have evaluated controls over all relevant assertions related to all significant accounts and disclosures.

- Determining the deficiencies in internal control over financial reporting that are of such a magnitude and likelihood of occurrence that they constitute significant deficiencies or material weaknesses.

- Communicating findings to the auditor and to others, if applicable.

- Evaluating whether findings are reasonable and support management's assessment.

For Analysis, see ¶ 109, ¶ 109.3, ¶ 109.4.1, and ¶ 118.

200.A.41.X.c As part of the understanding and evaluation of management's process, the auditor should obtain an understanding of the results of procedures performed by others. Others include internal audit and third parties working under the direction of management, including other auditors and accounting professionals engaged to perform procedures as a basis for management's assessment. Inquiry of management and others is the beginning point for obtaining an understanding of internal control over financial reporting, but inquiry alone is not adequate for reaching a conclusion on any aspect of internal control over financial reporting effectiveness.

> **Note:** Management cannot use the auditor's procedures as part of the basis for its assessment of the effectiveness of internal control over financial reporting.

For Analysis, see ¶ 109 and ¶ 109.3.

200.A.42.X.c *Management's Documentation.* When determining whether management's documentation provides reasonable support for its assessment, the auditor should evaluate whether such documentation includes the following:

- The design of controls over all relevant assertions related to all significant accounts and disclosures in the financial statements. The documentation should include the five components of internal control over financial reporting as discussed in paragraph 49, including the control environment and company-level controls as described in paragraph 53;

- Information about how significant transactions are initiated, authorized, recorded, processed and reported;

- Sufficient information about the flow of transactions to identify the points at which material misstatements due to error or fraud could occur;

- Controls designed to prevent or detect fraud, including who performs the controls and the related segregation of duties;

- Controls over the period-end financial reporting process;

- Controls over safeguarding of assets (See paragraphs C1 through C6); and

- The results of management's testing and evaluation.

For Analysis, see ¶ 109, ¶ 109.3, ¶ 109.3.1, ¶ 109.4, ¶ 109.4.1, and ¶ 119.

200.A.43.X.c Documentation might take many forms, such as paper, electronic files, or other media, and can include a variety of information, including policy manuals, process models, flowcharts, job descriptions, documents, and forms. The form and extent of documentation will vary depending on the size, nature, and complexity of the company.

For Analysis, see ¶ 109, ¶ 109.3, and ¶ 109.3.1.

200.A.44.X.c Documentation of the design of controls over relevant assertions related to significant accounts and disclosures is evidence that controls related to management's assessment of the effectiveness of internal control over financial reporting, including changes to those controls, have been identified, are capable of being communicated to those responsible for their performance, and are capable of being monitored by the company. Such documentation also provides the foundation for appropriate communication concerning responsibilities for performing controls and for the company's evaluation of and monitoring of the effective operation of controls.

For Analysis, see ¶ 109, ¶ 109.3, and ¶ 109.3.1.

200.A.45.X.c Inadequate documentation of the design of controls over relevant assertions related to significant accounts and disclosures is a deficiency in the company's internal control over financial reporting. As discussed in paragraph 138, the auditor should evaluate this documentation deficiency. The auditor might conclude that the deficiency is only a deficiency, or that the deficiency represents a significant deficiency or a material weakness. In evaluating the deficiency as to its significance, the auditor should determine whether management can demonstrate the monitoring component of internal control over financial reporting.

For Analysis, see ¶ 109, ¶ 109.3, ¶ 109.3.1, and ¶ 109.8.2.

200.A.46.X.c Inadequate documentation also could cause the auditor to conclude that there is a limitation on the scope of the engagement.

For Analysis, see ¶ 109, ¶ 109.3, and ¶ 109.3.1.

¶ 200.A.X.d. Obtaining an Understanding of Internal Control Over Financial Reporting

200.A.47.X.d The auditor should obtain an understanding of the design of specific controls by applying procedures that include:

- Making inquiries of appropriate management, supervisory, and staff personnel;
- Inspecting company documents;
- Observing the application of specific controls; and
- Tracing transactions through the information system relevant to financial reporting.

For Analysis, see ¶ 109 and ¶ 109.4.

200.A.48.X.d The auditor could also apply additional procedures to obtain an understanding of the design of specific controls.

For Analysis, see ¶ 109 and ¶ 109.4.

200.A.49.X.d The auditor must obtain an understanding of the design of controls related to each component of internal control over financial reporting, as discussed below.

- *Control Environment.* Because of the pervasive effect of the control environment on the reliability of financial reporting, the auditor's preliminary judgment about its effectiveness often influences the nature, timing, and extent of the tests of operating effectiveness considered necessary. Weaknesses in the control environment should cause the auditor to alter the nature, timing, or extent of tests of operating effectiveness that otherwise should have been performed in the absence of the weaknesses.

- *Risk Assessment.* When obtaining an understanding of the company's risk assessment process, the auditor should evaluate whether management has identified the risks of material misstatement in the significant accounts and disclosures and related assertions of the financial statements and has implemented controls to prevent or detect errors or fraud that could result in material misstatements. For example, the risk assessment process should address how management considers the possibility of unrecorded transactions or identifies and analyzes significant estimates recorded in the financial statements. Risks relevant to reliable financial reporting also relate to specific events or transactions.

- *Control Activities.* The auditor's understanding of control activities relates to the controls that management has implemented to prevent or detect errors or fraud that could result in material misstatement in the accounts and disclosures and related assertions of the financial statements. For the purposes of evaluating the effectiveness of internal control over financial reporting, the auditor's understanding of control activities encompasses a broader range of accounts and disclosures than what is normally obtained for the financial statement audit.

- *Information and Communication.* The auditor's understanding of management's information and communication involves understanding the same systems and processes that he or she addresses in an audit of financial statements. In addition, this understanding includes a greater emphasis on comprehending the safeguarding controls and the processes for authorization of transactions and the maintenance of records, as well as the period-end financial reporting process (discussed further beginning at paragraph 76).

- *Monitoring.* The auditor's understanding of management's monitoring of controls extends to and includes its monitoring of all controls, including control activities, which management has identified and designed to prevent or detect material misstatement in the accounts and disclosures and related assertions of the financial statements.

For Analysis, see ¶ 109, ¶ 109.4, and ¶ 109.4.6.

200.A.50.X.d Some controls (such as company-level controls, described in paragraph 53) might have a pervasive effect on the achievement of many over-all objectives of the control criteria. For example, information technology general controls over program development, program changes, computer operations, and access to programs and data help ensure that specific controls over the processing of transactions are operating effectively. In contrast, other controls are designed to achieve specific objectives of the control criteria. For example, management generally establishes specific controls, such as accounting for all shipping documents, to ensure that all valid sales are recorded.

For Analysis, see ¶ 109, ¶ 109.4, and ¶ 109.4.1.

200.A.51.X.d The auditor should focus on combinations of controls, in addition to specific controls in isolation, in assessing whether the objectives of the control criteria have been achieved. The absence or inadequacy of a specific control designed to achieve the objectives of a specific criterion might not be a deficiency if other controls specifically address the same criterion. Further, when one or more controls achieve the objectives of a specific criterion, the auditor might not need to evaluate other controls designed to achieve those same objectives.

For Analysis, see ¶ 109 and ¶ 109.4.

200.A.52.X.d *Identifying Company-Level Controls.* Controls that exist at the company-level often have a pervasive impact on controls at the process, transaction, or application level. For that reason, as a practical consideration, it may be appropriate for the auditor to test and evaluate the design effectiveness of company-level controls first, because the results of that work might affect the way the auditor evaluates the other aspects of internal control over financial reporting.

For Analysis, see ¶ 109, ¶ 109.4, and ¶ 109.4.1.

200.A.53.X.d Company-level controls are controls such as the following:

- Controls within the control environment, including tone at the top, the assignment of authority and responsibility, consistent policies and procedures, and company-wide programs, such as codes of conduct and fraud prevention, that apply to all locations and business units (See paragraphs 113 through 115 for further discussion);
- Management's risk assessment process;
- Centralized processing and controls, including shared service environments;
- Controls to monitor results of operations;
- Controls to monitor other controls, including activities of the internal audit function, the audit committee, and self-assessment programs;
- The period-end financial reporting process; and

- Board-approved policies that address significant business control and risk management practices.

Note: The controls listed above are not intended to be a complete list of company-level controls nor is a company required to have all the controls in the list to support its assessment of effective company-level controls. However, ineffective company-level controls are a deficiency that will affect the scope of work performed, particularly when a company has multiple locations or business units, as described in Appendix B.

For Analysis, see ¶ 109, ¶ 109.4, ¶ 109.4.1, ¶ 109.7.1, and ¶ 118.

200.A.54.X.d Testing company-level controls alone is not sufficient for the purpose of expressing an opinion on the effectiveness of a company's internal control over financial reporting.

For Analysis, see ¶ 109, ¶ 109.4, and ¶ 109.4.1.

200.A.55.X.d *Evaluating the Effectiveness of the Audit Committee's Oversight of the Company's External Financial Reporting and Internal Control Over Financial Reporting.* The company's audit committee plays an important role within the control environment and monitoring components of internal control over financial reporting. Within the control environment, the existence of an effective audit committee helps to set a positive tone at the top. Within the monitoring component, an effective audit committee challenges the company's activities in the financial arena.

Note: Although the audit committee plays an important role within the control environment and monitoring components of internal control over financial reporting, management is responsible for maintaining effective internal control over financial reporting. This standard does not suggest that this responsibility has been transferred to the audit committee.

Note: If no such committee exists with respect to the company, all references to the audit committee in this standard apply to the entire board of directors of the company.[8] The auditor should be aware that companies whose securities are not listed on a national securities exchange or an automated inter-dealer quotation system of a national securities association (such as the New York Stock Exchange, American Stock Exchange, or NASDAQ) may not be required to have independent directors for their audit committees. In this case, the auditor should not consider the lack of independent directors at these companies indicative, by itself, of a control deficiency. Likewise, the independence requirements of Securities Exchange Act Rule 10A-3[9] are not applicable to the listing of non-equity securities of a consolidated or at least 50 percent beneficially owned subsidiary of a listed issuer that is subject to the requirements of Securities Exchange Act

---

8. See 15 U.S.C. 78c(a)58 and 15 U.S.C. 7201(a)(3).
9. See 17 C.F.R. 240.10A-3.

Rule 10A-3(c)(2).[10] Therefore, the auditor should interpret references to the audit committee in this standard, as applied to a subsidiary registrant, as being consistent with the provisions of Securities Exchange Act Rule 10A-3(c)(2).[11] Furthermore, for subsidiary registrants, communications required by this standard to be directed to the audit committee should be made to the same committee or equivalent body that pre-approves the retention of the auditor by or on behalf of the subsidiary registrant pursuant to Rule 2-01(c)(7) of Regulation S-X[12] (which might be, for example, the audit committee of the subsidiary registrant, the full board of the subsidiary registrant, or the audit committee of the subsidiary registrant's parent). In all cases, the auditor should interpret the terms "board of directors" and "audit committee" in this standard as being consistent with provisions for the use of those terms as defined in relevant SEC rules.

For Analysis, see ¶ 109, ¶ 109.4, and ¶ 109.4.2.

200.A.56.X.d The company's board of directors is responsible for evaluating the performance and effectiveness of the audit committee; this standard does not suggest that the auditor is responsible for performing a separate and distinct evaluation of the audit committee. However, because of the role of the audit committee within the control environment and monitoring components of internal control over financial reporting, the auditor should assess the effectiveness of the audit committee as part of understanding and evaluating those components.

For Analysis, see ¶ 109, ¶ 109.4, and ¶ 109.4.2.

200.A.57.X.d The aspects of the audit committee's effectiveness that are important may vary considerably with the circumstances. The auditor focuses on factors related to the effectiveness of the audit committee's oversight of the company's external financial reporting and internal control over financial reporting, such as the independence of the audit committee members from management and the clarity with which the audit committee's responsibilities are articulated (for example, in the audit committee's charter) and how well the audit committee and management understand those responsibilities. The auditor might also consider the audit committee's involvement and interaction with the independent auditor and with internal auditors, as well as interaction with key members of financial management, including the chief financial officer and chief accounting officer.

For Analysis, see ¶ 109, ¶ 109.4, and ¶ 109.4.2.

200.A.58.X.d The auditor might also evaluate whether the right questions are raised and pursued with management and the auditor, including questions that

---

10. See 17 C.F.R. 240.10A-3(c)(2).
11. See 17 C.F.R. 240.10A-3(c)(2).
12. See 17 C.F.R. 210.2-01(c)(7).

indicate an understanding of the critical accounting policies and judgmental accounting estimates, and the responsiveness to issues raised by the auditor.

For Analysis, see ¶ 109, ¶ 109.4, and ¶ 109.4.2.

200.A.59.X.d Ineffective oversight by the audit committee of the company's external financial reporting and internal control over financial reporting should be regarded as at least a significant deficiency and is a strong indicator that a material weakness in internal control over financial reporting exists.

For Analysis, see ¶ 109, ¶ 109.4, and ¶ 109.4.2.

200.A.60.X.d *Identifying Significant Accounts.* The auditor should identify significant accounts and disclosures, first at the financial-statement level and then at the account or disclosure-component level. Determining specific controls to test begins by identifying significant accounts and disclosures within the financial statements. When identifying significant accounts, the auditor should evaluate both quantitative and qualitative factors.

For Analysis, see ¶ 109, ¶ 109.4, and ¶ 109.4.3.

200.A.61.X.d An account is significant if there is more than a remote likelihood that the account could contain misstatements that individually, or when aggregated with others, could have a material effect on the financial statements, considering the risks of both overstatement and understatement. Other accounts may be significant on a qualitative basis based on the expectations of a reasonable user. For example, investors might be interested in a particular financial statement account even though it is not quantitatively large because it represents an important performance measure.

> **Note:** For purposes of determining significant accounts, the assessment as to likelihood should be made without giving any consideration to the effectiveness of internal control over financial reporting.

For Analysis, see ¶ 109, ¶ 109.4, and ¶ 109.4.3.

200.A.62.X.d Components of an account balance subject to differing risks (inherent and control) or different controls should be considered separately as potential significant accounts. For instance, inventory accounts often consist of raw materials (purchasing process), work in process (manufacturing process), finished goods (distribution process), and an allowance for obsolescence.

For Analysis, see ¶ 109, ¶ 109.4, and ¶ 109.4.3.

200.A.63.X.d In some cases, separate components of an account might be a significant account because of the company's organizational structure. For example, for a company that has a number of separate business units, each with different management and accounting processes, the accounts at each separate business unit are considered individually as potential significant accounts.

For Analysis, see ¶ 109, ¶ 109.4, and ¶ 109.4.3.

200.A.64.X.d An account also may be considered significant because of the exposure to unrecognized obligations represented by the account. For example, loss reserves related to a self-insurance program or unrecorded contractual obligations at a construction contracting subsidiary may have historically been insignificant in amount, yet might represent a more than remote likelihood of material misstatement due to the existence of material unrecorded claims.

For Analysis, see ¶ 109, ¶ 109.4, and ¶ 109.4.3.

200.A.65.X.d When deciding whether an account is significant, it is important for the auditor to evaluate both quantitative and qualitative factors, including the:

- Size and composition of the account;
- Susceptibility of loss due to errors or fraud;
- Volume of activity, complexity, and homogeneity of the individual transactions processed through the account;
- Nature of the account (for example, suspense accounts generally warrant greater attention);
- Accounting and reporting complexities associated with the account;
- Exposure to losses represented by the account (for example, loss accruals related to a consolidated construction contracting subsidiary);
- Likelihood (or possibility) of significant contingent liabilities arising from the activities represented by the account;
- Existence of related party transactions in the account; and
- Changes from the prior period in account characteristics (for example, new complexities or subjectivity or new types of transactions).

For Analysis, see ¶ 109, ¶ 109.4, and ¶ 109.4.3.

200.A.66.X.d For example, in a financial statement audit, the auditor might not consider the fixed asset accounts significant when there is a low volume of transactions and when inherent risk is assessed as low, even though the balances are material to the financial statements. Accordingly, he or she might decide to perform only substantive procedures on such balances. In an audit of internal control over financial reporting, however, such accounts are significant accounts because of their materiality to the financial statements.

For Analysis, see ¶ 109, ¶ 109.4, and ¶ 109.4.3.

200.A.67.X.d As another example, the auditor of the financial statements of a financial institution might not consider trust accounts significant to the institution's financial statements because such accounts are not included in the institution's balance sheet and the associated fee income generated by trust activities is not material. However, in determining whether trust accounts are a significant account for purposes of the audit of internal control over financial reporting, the auditor should assess whether the activities of the trust department are significant to the institution's financial reporting, which also would include considering the contingent liabilities that could arise if a trust department failed to fulfill its fiduciary responsibilities (for example, if investments were made that were not in accordance with stated investment policies). When assessing the significance of possible contingent liabilities, consideration of the amount of assets under the trust department's control may be useful. For this reason, an auditor who has not considered trust accounts significant accounts for purposes of the financial statement audit might determine that they are significant for purposes of the audit of internal control over financial reporting.

For Analysis, see ¶ 109, ¶ 109.4, and ¶ 109.4.3.

200.A.68.X.d Identifying Relevant Financial Statement Assertions. For each significant account, the auditor should determine the relevance of each of these financial statement assertions:[13]

- Existence or occurrence;
- Completeness;
- Valuation or allocation;
- Rights and obligations; and
- Presentation and disclosure.

For Analysis, see ¶ 109, ¶ 109.4, and ¶ 109.4.4.

200.A.69.X.d To identify relevant assertions, the auditor should determine the source of likely potential misstatements in each significant account. In determining whether a particular assertion is relevant to a significant account balance or disclosure, the auditor should evaluate:

- The nature of the assertion;
- The volume of transactions or data related to the assertion; and
- The nature and complexity of the systems, including the use of information technology by which the company processes and controls information supporting the assertion.

For Analysis, see ¶ 109, ¶ 109.4, and ¶ 109.4.4.

200.A.70.X.d *Relevant assertions* are assertions that have a meaningful bearing on whether the account is fairly stated. For example, valuation may not be relevant to the cash account unless currency translation is involved; however, existence and completeness are always relevant. Similarly, valuation may not be relevant to the gross amount of the accounts receivable balance, but is relevant to the related allowance accounts. Additionally, the auditor might, in some circumstances, focus on the presentation and disclosure assertion separately in connection with the period-end financial reporting process.

---

13. See AU sec. 326, *Evidential Matter*, which provides additional information on financial statement assertions.

For Analysis, see ¶ 109, ¶ 109.4, and ¶ 109.4.4.

200.A.71.X.d *Identifying Significant Processes and Major Classes of Transactions.* The auditor should identify each significant process over each major class of transactions affecting significant accounts or groups of accounts. Major classes of transactions are those classes of transactions that are significant to the company's financial statements. For example, at a company whose sales may be initiated by customers through personal contact in a retail store or electronically through use of the internet, these types of sales would be two major classes of transactions within the sales process if they were both significant to the company's financial statements. As another example, at a company for which fixed assets is a significant account, recording depreciation expense would be a major class of transactions.

For Analysis, see ¶ 109, ¶ 109.4, and ¶ 109.4.5.

200.A.72.X.d Different types of major classes of transactions have different levels of inherent risk associated with them and require different levels of management supervision and involvement. For this reason, the auditor might further categorize the identified major classes of transactions by transaction type: routine, nonroutine, and estimation.

- Routine transactions are recurring financial activities reflected in the accounting records in the normal course of business (for example, sales, purchases, cash receipts, cash disbursements, payroll).

- Nonroutine transactions are activities that occur only periodically (for example, taking physical inventory, calculating depreciation expense, adjusting for foreign currencies). A distinguishing feature of nonroutine transactions is that data involved are generally not part of the routine flow of transactions.

- Estimation transactions are activities that involve management judgments or assumptions in formulating account balances in the absence of a precise means of measurement (for example, determining the allowance for doubtful accounts, establishing warranty reserves, assessing assets for impairment).

For Analysis, see ¶ 109, ¶ 109.4, and ¶ 109.4.5.

200.A.73.X.d Most processes involve a series of tasks such as capturing input data, sorting and merging data, making calculations, updating transactions and master files, generating transactions, and summarizing and displaying or reporting data. The processing procedures relevant for the auditor to understand the flow of transactions generally are those activities required to initiate, authorize, record, process and report transactions. Such activities include, for example, initially recording sales orders, preparing shipping documents and invoices, and updating the accounts receivable master file. The relevant processing procedures also include procedures for correcting and reprocessing previously rejected transactions and for correcting erroneous transactions through adjusting journal entries.

For Analysis, see ¶ 109, ¶ 109.4, and ¶ 109.4.5.

200.A.74.X.d For each significant process, the auditor should:

- Understand the flow of transactions, including how transactions are initiated, authorized, recorded, processed, and reported.
- Identify the points within the process at which a misstatement — including a misstatement due to fraud — related to each relevant financial statement assertion could arise.
- Identify the controls that management has implemented to address these potential misstatements.
- Identify the controls that management has implemented over the prevention or timely detection of unauthorized acquisition, use, or disposition of the company's assets.

Note: The auditor frequently obtains the understanding and identifies the controls described above as part of his or her performance of walkthroughs (as described beginning in paragraph 79).

For Analysis, see ¶ 109, ¶ 109.4, ¶ 109.4.5, and ¶ 109.4.7.

200.A.75.X.d The nature and characteristics of a company's use of information technology in its information system affect the company's internal control over financial reporting. AU sec. 319, *Consideration of Internal Control in a Financial Statement Audit,* paragraphs .16 through .20, .30 through .32, and .77 through .79, discuss the effect of information technology on internal control over financial reporting.

For Analysis, see ¶ 109, ¶ 109.4, and ¶ 109.4.5.

200.A.76.X.d *Understanding the Period-end Financial Reporting Process.* The period-end financial reporting process includes the following:

- The procedures used to enter transaction totals into the general ledger;
- The procedures used to initiate, authorize, record, and process journal entries in the general ledger;
- Other procedures used to record recurring and nonrecurring adjustments to the annual and quarterly financial statements, such as consolidating adjustments, report combinations, and classifications; and
- Procedures for drafting annual and quarterly financial statements and related disclosures.

For Analysis, see ¶ 109, ¶ 109.4, and ¶ 109.4.6.

200.A.77.X.d As part of understanding and evaluating the period-end financial reporting process, the auditor should evaluate:

- The inputs, procedures performed, and outputs of the processes the company uses to produce its annual and quarterly financial statements;
- The extent of information technology involvement in each period-end financial reporting process element;
- Who participates from management;
- The number of locations involved;
- Types of adjusting entries (for example, standard, nonstandard, eliminating, and consolidating); and
- The nature and extent of the oversight of the process by appropriate parties, including management, the board of directors, and the audit committee.

For Analysis, see ¶ 109, ¶ 109.4, and ¶ 109.4.6.

200.A.78.X.d The period-end financial reporting process is always a significant process because of its importance to financial reporting and to the auditor's opinions on internal control over financial reporting and the financial statements. The auditor's understanding of the company's period-end financial reporting process and how it interrelates with the company's other significant processes assists the auditor in identifying and testing controls that are the most relevant to financial statement risks.

For Analysis, see ¶ 109, ¶ 109.4, and ¶ 109.4.6.

200.A.79.X.d *Performing Walkthroughs.* The auditor should perform at least one walkthrough for each major class of transactions (as identified in paragraph 71). In a walkthrough, the auditor traces a transaction from origination through the company's information systems until it is reflected in the company's financial reports. Walkthroughs provide the auditor with evidence to:

- Confirm the auditor's understanding of the process flow of transactions;
- Confirm the auditor's understanding of the design of controls identified for all five components of internal control over financial reporting, including those related to the prevention or detection of fraud;
- Confirm that the auditor's understanding of the process is complete by determining whether all points in the process at which misstatements related to each relevant financial statement assertion that could occur have been identified;
- Evaluate the effectiveness of the design of controls; and
- Confirm whether controls have been placed in operation.

Note: The auditor can often gain an understanding of the transaction flow, identify and understand controls, and conduct the walkthrough simultaneously.

For Analysis, see ¶ 109, ¶ 109.4, ¶ 109.4.5, and ¶ 109.4.7.

200.A.80.X.d The auditor's walkthroughs should encompass the entire process of initiating, authorizing, recording, processing, and reporting individual transactions and controls for each of the significant processes identified, including controls intended to address the risk of fraud. During the walkthrough, at each point at which important processing procedures or controls occur, the auditor should question the company's personnel about their understanding of what is required by the company's prescribed procedures and controls and determine whether the processing procedures are performed as originally understood and on a timely basis. (Controls might not be performed regularly but still be timely.) During the walkthrough, the auditor should be alert for exceptions to the company's prescribed procedures and controls.

For Analysis, see ¶ 109, ¶ 109.4, and ¶ 109.4.7.

200.A.81.X.d While performing a walkthrough, the auditor should evaluate the quality of the evidence obtained and perform walkthrough procedures that produce a level of evidence consistent with the objectives listed in paragraph 79. Rather than reviewing copies of documents and making inquiries of a single person at the company, the auditor should follow the process flow of actual transactions using the same documents and information technology that company personnel use and make inquiries of relevant personnel involved in significant aspects of the process or controls. To corroborate information at various points in the walkthrough, the auditor might ask personnel to describe their understanding of the previous and succeeding processing or control activities and to demonstrate what they do. In addition, inquiries should include followup questions that could help identify the abuse of controls or indicators of fraud. Examples of follow-up inquiries include asking personnel:

- What they do when they find an error or what they are looking for to determine if there is an error (rather than simply asking them if they perform listed procedures and controls); what kind of errors they have found; what happened as a result of finding the errors, and how the errors were resolved. If the person being interviewed has never found an error, the auditor should evaluate whether that situation is due to good preventive controls or whether the individual performing the control lacks the necessary skills.
- Whether they have ever been asked to override the process or controls, and if so, to describe the situation, why it occurred, and what happened.

For Analysis, see ¶ 109, ¶ 109.4, and ¶ 109.4.7.

200.A.82.X.d During the period under audit, when there have been significant changes in the process flow of transactions, including the supporting computer applications, the auditor should evaluate the nature of the change(s) and the effect on related accounts to determine whether to walk through transactions that were processed both before and after the change.

Note: Unless significant changes in the process flow of transactions, including the supporting computer applications, make it more efficient for the auditor to prepare new documentation of a walkthrough, the auditor may carry his or her documentation forward each year, after updating it for any changes that have taken place.

For Analysis, see ¶ 109, ¶ 109.4, and ¶ 109.4.7.

200.A.83.X.d *Identifying Controls to Test.* The auditor should obtain evidence about the effectiveness of controls (either by performing tests of controls himself or herself, or by using the work of others)[14] for all relevant assertions related to all significant accounts and disclosures in the financial statements. After identifying significant accounts, relevant assertions, and significant processes, the auditor should evaluate the following to identify the controls to be tested:

- Points at which errors or fraud could occur;
- The nature of the controls implemented by management;
- The significance of each control in achieving the objectives of the control criteria and whether more than one control achieves a particular objective or whether more than one control is necessary to achieve a particular objective; and
- The risk that the controls might not be operating effectively. Factors that affect whether the control might not be operating effectively include the following:

  —Whether there have been changes in the volume or nature of transactions that might adversely affect control design or operating effectiveness;

  —Whether there have been changes in the design of controls;

  —The degree to which the control relies on the effectiveness of other controls (for example, the control environment or information technology general controls);

  —Whether there have been changes in key personnel who perform the control or monitor its performance;

  —Whether the control relies on performance by an individual or is automated; and

  —The complexity of the control.

For Analysis, see ¶ 109, ¶ 109.4, ¶ 109.4.8, and ¶ 109.7.

200.A.84.X.d The auditor should clearly link individual controls with the significant accounts and assertions to which they relate.

For Analysis, see ¶ 109, ¶ 109.4, and ¶ 109.4.8.

---

14. See paragraphs 108 through 126 for additional direction on using the work of others.

200.A.85.X.d The auditor should evaluate whether to test preventive controls, detective controls, or a combination of both for individual relevant assertions related to individual significant accounts. For instance, when performing tests of preventive and detective controls, the auditor might conclude that a deficient preventive control could be compensated for by an effective detective control and, therefore, not result in a significant deficiency or material weakness. For example, a monthly reconciliation control procedure, which is a detective control, might detect an out-of-balance situation resulting from an unauthorized transaction being initiated due to an ineffective authorization procedure, which is a preventive control. When determining whether the detective control is effective, the auditor should evaluate whether the detective control is sufficient to achieve the control objective to which the preventive control relates.

> **Note:** Because effective internal control over financial reporting often includes a combination of preventive and detective controls, the auditor ordinarily will test a combination of both.

For Analysis, see ¶ 109, ¶ 109.4, and ¶ 109.4.8.

200.A.86.X.d The auditor should apply tests of controls to those controls that are important to achieving each control objective. It is neither necessary to test all controls nor is it necessary to test redundant controls (that is, controls that duplicate other controls that achieve the same objective and already have been tested), unless redundancy is itself a control objective, as in the case of certain computer controls.

For Analysis, see ¶ 109, ¶ 109.4, and ¶ 109.4.8.

200.A.87.X.d Appendix B, paragraphs B1 through B17, provide additional direction to the auditor in determining which controls to test when a company has multiple locations or business units. In these circumstances, the auditor should determine significant accounts and their relevant assertions, significant processes, and major classes of transactions based on those that are relevant and significant to the consolidated financial statements. Having made those determinations in relation to the consolidated financial statements, the auditor should then apply the directions in Appendix B.

For Analysis, see ¶ 109, ¶ 109.4, ¶ 109.4.8, and ¶ 118.

¶ 200.A.X.e. Testing and Evaluating Design Effectiveness

200.A.88.X.e Internal control over financial reporting is effectively designed when the controls complied with would be expected to prevent or detect errors or fraud that could result in material misstatements in the financial statements. The auditor should determine whether the company has controls to meet the objectives of the control criteria by:

- Identifying the company's control objectives in each area;
- Identifying the controls that satisfy each objective; and

- Determining whether the controls, if operating properly, can effectively prevent or detect errors or fraud that could result in material misstatements in the financial statements.

For Analysis, see ¶ 109 and ¶ 109.5.

200.A.89.X.e Procedures the auditor performs to test and evaluate design effectiveness include inquiry, observation, walkthroughs, inspection of relevant documentation, and a specific evaluation of whether the controls are likely to prevent or detect errors or fraud that could result in misstatements if they are operated as prescribed by appropriately qualified persons.

For Analysis, see ¶ 109 and ¶ 109.5.

200.A.90.X.e The procedures that the auditor performs in evaluating management's assessment process and obtaining an understanding of internal control over financial reporting also provide the auditor with evidence about the design effectiveness of internal control over financial reporting.

For Analysis, see ¶ 109 and ¶ 109.5.

200.A.91.X.e The procedures the auditor performs to test and evaluate design effectiveness also might provide evidence about operating effectiveness.

For Analysis, see ¶ 109 and ¶ 109.5.

¶ 200.A.X.f. Testing and Evaluating Operating Effectiveness

200.A.92.X.f An auditor should evaluate the operating effectiveness of a control by determining whether the control is operating as designed and whether the person performing the control possesses the necessary authority and qualifications to perform the control effectively.

For Analysis, see ¶ 109 and ¶ 109.6.

200.A.93.X.f *Nature of Tests of Controls.* Tests of controls over operating effectiveness should include a mix of inquiries of appropriate personnel, inspection of relevant documentation, observation of the company's operations, and reperformance of the application of the control. For example, the auditor might observe the procedures for opening the mail and processing cash receipts to test the operating effectiveness of controls over cash receipts. Because an observation is pertinent only at the point in time at which it is made, the auditor should supplement the observation with inquiries of company personnel and inspection of documentation about the operation of such controls at other times. These inquiries might be made concurrently with performing walkthroughs.

For Analysis, see ¶ 109, ¶ 109.6, and ¶ 109.6.1.

200.A.94.X.f Inquiry is a procedure that consists of seeking information, both financial and nonfinancial, of knowledgeable persons throughout the company. Inquiry is used extensively throughout the audit and often is complementary to performing other procedures. Inquiries may range from formal written inquiries to informal oral inquiries.

For Analysis, see ¶ 109, ¶ 109.6, and ¶ 109.6.1.

200.A.95.X.f Evaluating responses to inquiries is an integral part of the inquiry procedure. Examples of information that inquiries might provide include the skill and competency of those performing the control, the relative sensitivity of the control to prevent or detect errors or fraud, and the frequency with which the control operates to prevent or detect errors or fraud. Responses to inquiries might provide the auditor with information not previously possessed or with corroborative evidence. Alternatively, responses might provide information that differs significantly from other information the auditor obtains (for example, information regarding the possibility of management override of controls). In some cases, responses to inquiries provide a basis for the auditor to modify or perform additional procedures.

For Analysis, see ¶ 109, ¶ 109.6, and ¶ 109.6.1.

200.A.96.X.f Because inquiry alone does not provide sufficient evidence to support the operating effectiveness of a control, the auditor should perform additional tests of controls. For example, if the company implements a control activity whereby its sales manager reviews and investigates a report of invoices with unusually high or low gross margins, inquiry of the sales manager as to whether he or she investigates discrepancies would be inadequate. To obtain sufficient evidence about the operating effectiveness of the control, the auditor should corroborate the sales manager's responses by performing other procedures, such as inspecting reports or other documentation used in or generated by the performance of the control, and evaluate whether appropriate actions were taken regarding discrepancies.

For Analysis, see ¶ 109, ¶ 109.6, and ¶ 109.6.1.

200.A.97.X.f The nature of the control also influences the nature of the tests of controls the auditor can perform. For example, the auditor might examine documents regarding controls for which documentary evidence exists. However, documentary evidence regarding some aspects of the control environment, such as management's philosophy and operating style, might not exist. In circumstances in which documentary evidence of controls or the performance of controls does not exist and is not expected to exist, the auditor's tests of controls would consist of inquiries of appropriate personnel and observation of company activities. As another example, a signature on a voucher package to indicate that the signer approved it does not necessarily mean that the person carefully reviewed the package before signing. The package may have been signed based on only a cursory review (or without any review). As a result, the quality of the evidence regarding the effective operation of the control might not be sufficiently persuasive. If that is the case, the auditor should reperform the control (for example, checking prices, extensions, and additions) as part of the test of the control. In addition, the auditor might inquire of the person responsible for approving voucher packages what he or she looks for when approving packages and how many errors have been found within voucher packages. The auditor also might inquire of supervisors whether they have any knowledge of errors that the person responsible for approving the voucher packages failed to detect.

For Analysis, see ¶ 109, ¶ 109.6, and ¶ 109.6.1.

200.A.98.X.f *Timing of Tests of Controls.* The auditor must perform tests of controls over a period of time that is adequate to determine whether, as of the date specified in management's report, the controls necessary for achieving the objectives of the control criteria are operating effectively. The period of time over which the auditor performs tests of controls varies with the nature of the controls being tested and with the frequency with which specific controls operate and specific policies are applied. Some controls operate continuously (for example, controls over sales), while others operate only at certain times (for example, controls over the preparation of monthly or quarterly financial statements and controls over physical inventory counts).

For Analysis, see ¶ 109, ¶ 109.6, and ¶ 109.6.2.

200.A.99.X.f The auditor's testing of the operating effectiveness of such controls should occur at the time the controls are operating. Controls "as of" a specific date encompass controls that are relevant to the company's internal control over financial reporting "as of" that specific date, even though such controls might not operate until after that specific date. For example, some controls over the period-end financial reporting process normally operate only after the "as of" date. Therefore, if controls over the December 31, 20X4 period-end financial reporting process operate in January 20X5, the auditor should test the control operating in January 20X5 to have sufficient evidence of operating effectiveness "as of" December 31, 20X4.

For Analysis, see ¶ 109, ¶ 109.6, and ¶ 109.6.2.

200.A.100.X.f When the auditor reports on the effectiveness of controls "as of" a specific date and obtains evidence about the operating effectiveness of controls at an interim date, he or she should determine what additional evidence to obtain concerning the operation of the control for the remaining period. In making that determination, the auditor should evaluate:

- The specific controls tested prior to the "as of" date and the results of those tests;

- The degree to which evidence about the operating effectiveness of those controls was obtained;

- The length of the remaining period; and

- The possibility that there have been any significant changes in internal control over financial reporting subsequent to the interim date.

For Analysis, see ¶ 109, ¶ 109.6, and ¶ 109.6.2.

200.A.101.X.f For controls over significant nonroutine transactions, controls over accounts or processes with a high degree of subjectivity or judgment in measurement, or controls over the recording of period-end adjustments, the auditor should perform tests of controls closer to or at the "as of" date rather than at an interim date. However, the auditor should balance performing the tests of controls closer to the "as of" date with the need to obtain sufficient evidence of operating effectiveness.

For Analysis, see ¶ 109, ¶ 109.6, and ¶ 109.6.2.

200.A.102.X.f Prior to the date specified in management's report, management might implement changes to the company's controls to make them more effective or efficient or to address control deficiencies. In that case, the auditor might not need to evaluate controls that have been superseded. For example, if the auditor determines that the new controls achieve the related objectives of the control criteria and have been in effect for a sufficient period to permit the auditor to assess their design and operating effectiveness by performing tests of controls,[15] he or she will not need to evaluate the design and operating effectiveness of the superseded controls for purposes of expressing an opinion on internal control over financial reporting.

For Analysis, see ¶ 109, ¶ 109.6, ¶ 109.6.2, and ¶ 113.3.6.

200.A.103.X.f As discussed in paragraph 207, however, the auditor must communicate all identified significant deficiencies and material weaknesses in controls to the audit committee in writing. In addition, the auditor should evaluate how the design and operating effectiveness of the superseded controls relates to the auditor's reliance on controls for financial statement audit purposes.

For Analysis, see ¶ 109, ¶ 109.6, ¶ 109.6.2, and ¶ 115.

200.A.104.X.f *Extent of Tests of Controls.* Each year the auditor must obtain sufficient evidence about whether the company's internal control over financial reporting, including the controls for all internal control components, is operating effectively. This means that each year the auditor must obtain evidence about the effectiveness of controls for all relevant assertions related to all significant accounts and disclosures in the financial statements. The auditor also should vary from year to year the nature, timing, and extent of testing of controls to introduce unpredictability into the testing and respond to changes in circumstances. For example, each year the auditor might test the controls at a different interim period; increase or reduce the number and types of tests performed; or change the combination of procedures used.

For Analysis, see ¶ 109, ¶ 109.6, and ¶ 109.6.3.

---

15. Paragraph 179 provides reporting directions in these circumstances when the auditor has not been able to obtain evidence that the new controls were appropriately designed or have been operating effectively for a sufficient period of time.

200.A.105.X.f In determining the extent of procedures to perform, the auditor should design the procedures to provide a high level of assurance that the control being tested is operating effectively. In making this determination, the auditor should assess the following factors:

- *Nature of the control.* The auditor should subject manual controls to more extensive testing than automated controls. In some circumstances, testing a single operation of an automated control may be sufficient to obtain a high level of assurance that the control operated effectively, provided that information technology general controls also are operating effectively. For manual controls, sufficient evidence about the operating effectiveness of the controls is obtained by evaluating multiple operations of the control and the results of each operation. The auditor also should assess the complexity of the controls, the significance of the judgments that must be made in connection with their operation, and the level of competence of the person performing the controls that is necessary for the control to operate effectively. As the complexity and level of judgment increase or the level of competence of the person performing the control decreases, the extent of the auditor's testing should increase.

- *Frequency of operation.* Generally, the more frequently a manual control operates, the more operations of the control the auditor should test. For example, for a manual control that operates in connection with each transaction, the auditor should test multiple operations of the control over a sufficient period of time to obtain a high level of assurance that the control operated effectively. For controls that operate less frequently, such as monthly account reconciliations and controls over the period-end financial reporting process, the auditor may test significantly fewer operations of the control. However, the auditor's evaluation of each operation of controls operating less frequently is likely to be more extensive. For example, when evaluating the operation of a monthly exception report, the auditor should evaluate whether the judgments made with regard to the disposition of the exceptions were appropriate and adequately supported.

Note: When sampling is appropriate and the population of controls to be tested is large, increasing the population size does not proportionately increase the required sample size.

- *Importance of the control.* Controls that are relatively more important should be tested more extensively. For example, some controls may address multiple financial statement assertions, and certain period-end detective controls might be considered more important than related preventive controls. The auditor should test more operations of such controls or, if such controls operate infrequently, the auditor should evaluate each operation of the control more extensively.

For Analysis, see ¶ 109, ¶ 109.6, and ¶ 109.6.3.

200.A.106.X.f *Use of Professional Skepticism when Evaluating the Results of Testing.* The auditor must conduct the audit of internal control over financial reporting and the audit of the financial statements with professional skepticism, which is an attitude that includes a questioning mind and a critical assessment of audit evidence. For example, even though a control is performed by the same employee whom the auditor believes performed the control effectively in prior periods, the control may not be operating effectively during the current period because the employee could have become complacent, distracted, or otherwise not be effectively carrying out his or her responsibilities. Also, regardless of any past experience with the entity or the auditor's beliefs about management's honesty and integrity, the auditor should recognize the possibility that a material misstatement due to fraud could be present. Furthermore, professional skepticism requires the auditor to consider whether evidence obtained suggests that a material misstatement due to fraud has occurred. In exercising professional skepticism in gathering and evaluating evidence, the auditor must not be satisfied with less-than-persuasive evidence because of a belief that management is honest.

For Analysis, see ¶ 109, ¶ 109.6, and ¶ 109.6.4.

200.A.107.X.f When the auditor identifies exceptions to the company's prescribed control procedures, he or she should determine, using professional skepticism, the effect of the exception on the nature and extent of additional testing that may be appropriate or necessary and on the operating effectiveness of the control being tested. A conclusion that an identified exception does not represent a control deficiency is appropriate only if evidence beyond what the auditor had initially planned and beyond inquiry supports that conclusion.

For Analysis, see ¶ 109, ¶ 109.6, and ¶ 109.6.4.

¶ 200.A.X.g. Using the Work of Others

200.A.108.X.g In all audits of internal control over financial reporting, the auditor must perform enough of the testing himself or herself so that the auditor's own work provides the principal evidence for the auditor's opinion. The auditor may, however, use the work of others to alter the nature, timing, or extent of the work he or she otherwise would have performed. For these purposes, the work of others includes relevant work performed by internal auditors, company personnel (in addition to internal auditors), and third parties working under the direction of management or the audit committee that provides information about the effectiveness of internal control over financial reporting.

Note: Because the amount of work related to obtaining sufficient evidence to support an opinion about the effectiveness of controls is not susceptible to precise measurement, the auditor's judgment about whether he or she has obtained the principal evidence for the opinion will be qualitative as well as quantitative. For example, the auditor might give more weight to work he or she performed on pervasive controls and in areas such as the control environment than on other controls, such as controls over low-risk, routine transactions.

For Analysis, see ¶ 109 and ¶ 109.7.

200.A.109.X.g The auditor should evaluate whether to use the work performed by others in the audit of internal control over financial reporting. To determine the extent to which the auditor may use the work of others to alter the nature, timing, or extent of the work the auditor would have otherwise performed, in addition to obtaining the principal evidence for his or her opinion, the auditor should:

a. Evaluate the nature of the controls subjected to the work of others (See paragraphs 112 through 116);

b. Evaluate the competence and objectivity of the individuals who performed the work (See paragraphs 117 through 122); and

c. Test some of the work performed by others to evaluate the quality and effectiveness of their work (See paragraphs 123 through 125).

Note: AU sec. 322, *The Auditor's Consideration of the Internal Audit Function in an Audit of Financial Statements,* applies to using the work of internal auditors in an audit of the financial statements. The auditor may apply the relevant concepts described in that section to using the work of others in the audit of internal control over financial reporting.

For Analysis, see ¶ 109, ¶ 109.7, ¶ 109.7.1, ¶ 109.7.2, and ¶ 109.7.3.

200.A.110.X.g The auditor must obtain sufficient evidence to support his or her opinion. Judgments about the sufficiency of evidence obtained and other factors affecting the auditor's opinion, such as the significance of identified control deficiencies, should be those of the auditor. Evidence obtained through the auditor's direct personal knowledge, observation, reperformance, and inspection is generally more persuasive than information obtained indirectly from others, such as from internal auditors, other company personnel, or third parties working under the direction of management.

For Analysis, see ¶ 109 and ¶ 109.7.

200.A.111.X.g The requirement that the auditor's own work must provide the principal evidence for the auditor's opinion is one of the boundaries within which the auditor determines the work he or she must perform himself or herself in the audit of internal control over financial reporting. Paragraphs 112 through 125 provide more specific and definitive direction on how the auditor makes this determination, but the directions allow the auditor significant flexibility to use his or her judgment to determine the work necessary to obtain the principal evidence and to determine when the auditor can use the work of others rather than perform the work himself or herself. Regardless of the auditor's determination of the work that he or she must perform himself or herself, the auditor's responsibility to report on the effectiveness of internal control over financial reporting rests solely with the auditor; this responsibility cannot be shared with the other individuals whose work the auditor uses. Therefore, when the auditor uses the work of others, the auditor is responsible for the results of their work.

For Analysis, see ¶ 109, ¶ 109.7, and ¶ 109.7.1.

200.A.112.X.g *Evaluating the Nature of the Controls Subjected to the Work of Others.* The auditor should evaluate the following factors when evaluating the nature of the controls subjected to the work of others. As these factors increase in significance, the need for the auditor to perform his or her own work on those controls increases. As these factors decrease in significance, the need for the auditor to perform his or her own work on those controls decreases.

- The materiality of the accounts and disclosures that the control addresses and the risk of material misstatement.
- The degree of judgment required to evaluate the operating effectiveness of the control (that is, the degree to which the evaluation of the effectiveness of the control requires evaluation of subjective factors rather than objective testing).
- The pervasiveness of the control.
- The level of judgment or estimation required in the account or disclosure.
- The potential for management override of the control.

For Analysis, see ¶ 109, ¶ 109.7, and ¶ 109.7.1.

200.A.113.X.g Because of the nature of the controls in the control environment, the auditor should not use the work of others to reduce the amount of work he or she performs on controls in the control environment. The auditor should, however, consider the results of work performed in this area by others because it might indicate the need for the auditor to increase his or her work.

For Analysis, see ¶ 109, ¶ 109.7, and ¶ 109.7.1.

200.A.114.X.g The control environment encompasses the following factors:[16]

- Integrity and ethical values;
- Commitment to competence;
- Board of directors or audit committee participation;
- Management's philosophy and operating style;
- Organizational structure;
- Assignment of authority and responsibility; and

---

16. See the COSO report and paragraph .110 of AU sec. 319, *Internal Control in a Financial Statement Audit,* for additional information about the factors included in the control environment.

- Human resource policies and procedures.

For Analysis, see ¶ 109, ¶ 109.7, and ¶ 109.7.1.

200.A.115.X.g Controls that are part of the control environment include, but are not limited to, controls specifically established to prevent and detect fraud that is at least reasonably possible to result in material misstatement of the financial statements.

> **Note:** The term "reasonably possible" has the same meaning as in FAS No. 5. See the first note to paragraph 9 for further discussion.

For Analysis, see ¶ 102, ¶ 109, ¶ 109.7, and ¶ 109.7.1.

200.A.116.X.g The auditor should perform the walkthroughs (as discussed beginning at paragraph 79) himself or herself because of the degree of judgment required in performing this work. However, to provide additional evidence, the auditor may also review the work of others who have performed and documented walkthroughs. In evaluating whether his or her own evidence provides the principal evidence, the auditor's work on the control environment and in performing walkthroughs constitutes an important part of the auditor's own work.

For Analysis, see ¶ 109, ¶ 109.4.7, ¶ 109.7, and ¶ 109.7.1.

200.A.117.X.g *Evaluating the Competence and Objectivity of Others.* The extent to which the auditor may use the work of others depends on the degree of competence and objectivity of the individuals performing the work. The higher the degree of competence and objectivity, the greater use the auditor may make of the work; conversely, the lower the degree of competence and objectivity, the less use the auditor may make of the work. Further, the auditor should not use the work of individuals who have a low degree of objectivity, regardless of their level of competence. Likewise, the auditor should not use the work of individuals who have a low level of competence regardless of their degree of objectivity.

For Analysis, see ¶ 109, ¶ 109.7, and ¶ 109.7.2.

200.A.118.X.g When evaluating the competence and objectivity of the individuals performing the tests of controls, the auditor should obtain, or update information from prior years, about the factors indicated in the following paragraph. The auditor should determine whether to test the existence and quality of those factors and, if so, the extent to which to test the existence and quality of those factors, based on the intended effect of the work of others on the audit of internal control over financial reporting.

For Analysis, see ¶ 109, ¶ 109.7, and ¶ 109.7.2.

200.A.119.X.g Factors concerning the competence of the individuals performing the tests of controls include:

- Their educational level and professional experience.
- Their professional certification and continuing education.
- Practices regarding the assignment of individuals to work areas.
- Supervision and review of their activities.
- Quality of the documentation of their work, including any reports or recommendations issued.
- Evaluation of their performance.

For Analysis, see ¶ 109, ¶ 109.7, and ¶ 109.7.2.

200.A.120.X.g Factors concerning the objectivity of the individuals performing the tests of controls include:

- The organizational status of the individuals responsible for the work of others ("testing authority") in testing controls, including—

  a. Whether the testing authority reports to an officer of sufficient status to ensure sufficient testing coverage and adequate consideration of, and action on, the findings and recommendations of the individuals performing the testing.

  b. Whether the testing authority has direct access and reports regularly to the board of directors or the audit committee.

  c. Whether the board of directors or the audit committee oversees employment decisions related to the testing authority.

- Policies to maintain the individuals' objectivity about the areas being tested, including—

  a. Policies prohibiting individuals from testing controls in areas in which relatives are employed in important or internal controlsensitive positions.

  b. Policies prohibiting individuals from testing controls in areas to which they were recently assigned or are scheduled to be assigned upon completion of their controls testing responsibilities.

For Analysis, see ¶ 109, ¶ 109.7, and ¶ 109.7.2.

200.A.121.X.g Internal auditors normally are expected to have greater competence with regard to internal control over financial reporting and objectivity than other company personnel. Therefore, the auditor may be able to use their work to a greater extent than the work of other company personnel. This is particularly true in the case of internal auditors who follow the *International Standards for the Professional Practice of Internal Auditing* issued by the Institute of Internal Auditors. If internal auditors have performed an extensive amount of relevant work and the auditor determines they possess a high degree of competence and objectivity, the auditor could use their work to the greatest extent an auditor could use the work of others. On the other hand, if the internal audit function reports solely to management, which would reduce internal auditors' objectivity, or if limited resources allocated to the internal audit function result in very limited testing procedures on its part or reduced competency of the internal auditors, the auditor should use their work to a much lesser extent and perform more of the testing himself or herself.

For Analysis, see ¶ 109, ¶ 109.7, and ¶ 109.7.2.

200.A.122.X.g When determining how the work of others will alter the nature, timing, or extent of the auditor's work, the auditor should assess the interrelationship of the nature of the controls, as discussed in paragraph 112, and the competence and objectivity of those who performed the work, as discussed in paragraphs 117 through 121. As the significance of the factors listed in paragraph 112 increases, the ability of the auditor to use the work of others decreases at the same time that the necessary level of competence and objectivity of those who perform the work increases. For example, for some pervasive controls, the auditor may determine that using the work of internal auditors to a limited degree would be appropriate and that using the work of other company personnel would not be appropriate because other company personnel do not have a high enough degree of objectivity as it relates to the nature of the controls.

For Analysis, see ¶ 109, ¶ 109.7, ¶ 109.7.1, ¶ 109.7.2, and ¶ 109.7.3.

200.A.123.X.g *Testing the Work of Others.* The auditor should test some of the work of others to evaluate the quality and effectiveness of the work. The auditor's tests of the work of others may be accomplished by either (a) testing some of the controls that others tested or (b) testing similar controls not actually tested by others.

For Analysis, see ¶ 109, ¶ 109.7, and ¶ 109.7.3.

200.A.124.X.g The nature and extent of these tests depend on the effect of the work of others on the auditor's procedures but should be sufficient to enable the auditor to make an evaluation of the overall quality and effectiveness of the work the auditor is considering. The auditor also should assess whether this evaluation has an effect on his or her conclusions about the competence and objectivity of the individuals performing the work.

For Analysis, see ¶ 109, ¶ 109.7, and ¶ 109.7.3.

200.A.125.X.g In evaluating the quality and effectiveness of the work of others, the auditor should evaluate such factors as to whether the:

- Scope of work is appropriate to meet the objectives.
- Work programs are adequate.
- Work performed is adequately documented, including evidence of supervision and review.
- Conclusions are appropriate in the circumstances.
- Reports are consistent with the results of the work performed.

For Analysis, see ¶ 109, ¶ 109.7, and ¶ 109.7.3.

200.A.126.X.g The following examples illustrate how to apply the directions discussed in this section:

- *Controls over the period-end financial reporting process.* Many of the controls over the period-end financial reporting process address significant risks of misstatement of the accounts and disclosures in the annual and quarterly financial statements, may require significant judgment to evaluate their operating effectiveness, may have a higher potential for management override, and may affect accounts that require a high level of judgment or estimation. Therefore, the auditor could determine that, based on the nature of controls over the period-end financial reporting process, he or she would need to perform more of the tests of those controls himself or herself. Further, because of the nature of the controls, the auditor should use the work of others only if the degree of competence and objectivity of the individuals performing the work is high; therefore, the auditor might use the work of internal auditors to some extent but not the work of others within the company.

- *Information technology general controls.* Information technology general controls are part of the control activities component of internal control; therefore, the nature of the controls might permit the auditor to use the work of others. For example, program change controls over routine maintenance changes may have a highly pervasive effect, yet involve a low degree of judgment in evaluating their operating effectiveness, can be subjected to objective testing, and have a low potential for management override. Therefore, the auditor could determine that, based on the nature of these program change controls, the auditor could use the work of others to a moderate extent so long as the degree of competence and objectivity of the individuals performing the test is at an appropriate level. On the other hand, controls to detect attempts to override controls that prevent unauthorized journal entries from being posted may have a highly pervasive effect, may involve a high degree of judgment in evaluating their operating effectiveness, may involve a subjective evaluation, and may have a reasonable possibility for management override. Therefore, the auditor could determine that, based on the nature of these controls over systems access, he or she would need to perform more of the tests of those controls himself or herself. Further, because of the nature of the controls, the auditor should use the work of others only if the degree of competence and objectivity of the individuals performing the tests is high.

- *Management self-assessment of controls.* As described in paragraph 40, management may test the operating effectiveness of controls using a selfassessment process. Because such an assessment is made by the same personnel who are responsible for performing the control, the individuals performing the self-assessment do not have sufficient objectivity as it relates to the subject matter. Therefore, the auditor should not use their work.

- *Controls over the calculation of depreciation of fixed assets.* Controls over the calculation of depreciation of fixed assets are usually not pervasive, involve a low degree of judgment in evaluating their operating effectiveness, and can be subjected to objective testing. If these conditions describe the controls over the calculation of depreciation of fixed assets and if there is a low potential for management override, the auditor could determine that, based on the nature of these controls, the auditor could use the work of others to a large extent (perhaps entirely) so long as the degree of competence and objectivity of the individuals performing the test is at an appropriate level.

- *Alternating tests of controls.* Many of the controls over accounts payable, including controls over cash disbursements, are usually not pervasive, involve a low degree of judgment in evaluating their operating effectiveness, can be subjected to objective testing, and have a low potential for management override. When these conditions describe the controls over accounts payable, the auditor could determine that, based on the nature of these controls, he or she could use the work of others to a large extent (perhaps entirely) so long as the degree of competence and objectivity of the individuals performing the test is at an appropriate level. However, if the company recently implemented a major information technology change that significantly affected controls over cash disbursements, the auditor might decide to use the work of others to a lesser extent in the audit immediately following the information technology change and then return, in subsequent years, to using the work of others to a large extent in this area. As another example, the auditor might use the work of others for testing controls over the depreciation of fixed assets (as described in the point above) for several years' audits but decide one year to perform some extent of the work himself or herself to gain an understanding of these controls beyond that provided by performing a walkthrough.

For Analysis, see ¶ 109, ¶ 109.3, ¶ 109.7, and ¶ 109.7.3.

¶ 200.A.X.h. Forming an Opinion on the Effectiveness of Internal Control Over Financial Reporting

200.A.127.X.h When forming an opinion on internal control over financial reporting, the auditor should evaluate all evidence obtained from all sources, including:

- The adequacy of the assessment performed by management and the results of the auditor's evaluation of the design and tests of operating effectiveness of controls;

- The negative results of substantive procedures performed during the financial statement audit (for example, recorded and unrecorded adjustments identified as a result of the performance of the auditing procedures); and

- Any identified control deficiencies.

For Analysis, see ¶ 109 and ¶ 109.8.

200.A.128.X.h As part of this evaluation, the auditor should review all reports issued during the year by internal audit (or similar functions, such as loan review in a financial institution) that address controls related to internal control over financial reporting and evaluate any control deficiencies identified in those reports. This review should include reports issued by internal audit as a result of operational audits or specific reviews of key processes if those reports address controls related to internal control over financial reporting.

For Analysis, see ¶ 109 and ¶ 109.8.

200.A.129.X.h *Issuing an Unqualified Opinion.* The auditor may issue an unqualified opinion only when there are no identified material weaknesses and when there have been no restrictions on the scope of the auditor's work. The existence of a material weakness requires the auditor to express an adverse opinion on the effectiveness of internal control over financial reporting (See paragraph 175), while a scope limitation requires the auditor to express a qualified opinion or a disclaimer of opinion, depending on the significance of the limitation in scope (See paragraph 178).

For Analysis, see ¶ 109, ¶ 109.8, and ¶ 109.8.1, ¶ 113.3.5, and ¶ 113.3.6.

200.A.130.X.h *Evaluating Deficiencies in Internal Control Over Financial Reporting.* The auditor must evaluate identified control deficiencies and determine whether the deficiencies, individually or in combination, are significant deficiencies or material weaknesses. The evaluation of the significance of a deficiency should include both quantitative and qualitative factors.

For Analysis, see ¶ 109, ¶ 109.8, and ¶ 109.8.2.

200.A.131.X.h The auditor should evaluate the significance of a deficiency in internal control over financial reporting initially by determining the following:

- The likelihood that a deficiency, or a combination of deficiencies, could result in a misstatement of an account balance or disclosure; and

- The magnitude of the potential misstatement resulting from the deficiency or deficiencies.

For Analysis, see ¶ 109, ¶ 109.8, and ¶ 109.8.2.

200.A.132.X.h The significance of a deficiency in internal control over financial reporting depends on the *potential* for a misstatement, not on whether a misstatement actually has occurred.

For Analysis, see ¶ 109, ¶ 109.8, and ¶ 109.8.2.

200.A.133.X.h Several factors affect the *likelihood* that a deficiency, or a combination of deficiencies, could result in a misstatement of an account balance or disclosure. The factors include, but are not limited to, the following:

- The nature of the financial statement accounts, disclosures, and assertions involved; for example, suspense accounts and related party transactions involve greater risk.

- The susceptibility of the related assets or liability to loss or fraud; that is, greater susceptibility increases risk.

- The subjectivity, complexity, or extent of judgment required to determine the amount involved; that is, greater subjectivity, complexity, or judgment, like that related to an accounting estimate, increases risk.

- The cause and frequency of known or detected exceptions for the operating effectiveness of a control; for example, a control with an observed non-negligible deviation rate is a deficiency.

- The interaction or relationship of the control with other controls; that is, the interdependence or redundancy of the control.

- The interaction of the deficiencies; for example, when evaluating a combination of two or more deficiencies, whether the deficiencies could affect the same financial statement accounts and assertions.

- The possible future consequences of the deficiency.

For Analysis, see ¶ 109, ¶ 109.8, and ¶ 109.8.2.

200.A.134.X.h When evaluating the likelihood that a deficiency or combination of deficiencies could result in a misstatement, the auditor should evaluate how the controls interact with other controls. There are controls, such as information technology general controls, on which other controls depend. Some controls function together as a group of controls. Other controls overlap, in the sense that these other controls achieve the same objective.

For Analysis, see ¶ 109, ¶ 109.8, and ¶ 109.8.2.

200.A.135.X.h Several factors affect the magnitude of the misstatement that could result from a deficiency or deficiencies in controls. The factors include, but are not limited to, the following:

- The financial statement amounts or total of transactions exposed to the deficiency.

- The volume of activity in the account balance or class of transactions exposed to the deficiency that has occurred in the current period or that is expected in future periods.

For Analysis, see ¶ 109, ¶ 109.8, and ¶ 109.8.2.

200.A.136.X.h In evaluating the magnitude of the potential misstatement, the auditor should recognize that the maximum amount that an account balance or total of transactions can be overstated is generally the recorded amount. However, the recorded amount is not a limitation on the amount of potential understatement. The auditor also should recognize that the risk of misstatement might be different for the maximum possible misstatement than for lesser possible amounts.

For Analysis, see ¶ 109, ¶ 109.8, and ¶ 109.8.2.

200.A.137.X.h When evaluating the significance of a deficiency in internal control over financial reporting, the auditor also should determine the level of detail and degree of assurance that would satisfy prudent officials in the conduct of their own affairs that they have reasonable assurance that transactions are recorded as necessary to permit the preparation of financial statements in conformity with generally accepted accounting principles. If the auditor determines that the deficiency would prevent prudent officials in the conduct of their own affairs from concluding that they have reasonable assurance,[17] then the auditor should deem the deficiency to be at least a significant deficiency. Having determined in this manner that a deficiency represents a significant deficiency, the auditor must further evaluate the deficiency to determine whether individually, or in combination with other deficiencies, the deficiency is a material weakness.

Note: Paragraphs 9 and 10 provide the definitions of significant deficiency and material weakness, respectively.

For Analysis, see ¶ 102, ¶ 109, ¶ 109.8, and ¶ 109.8.2.

200.A.138.X.h Inadequate documentation of the design of controls and the absence of sufficient documented evidence to support management's assessment of the operating effectiveness of internal control over financial reporting are control deficiencies. As with other control deficiencies, the auditor should evaluate these deficiencies as to their significance.

For Analysis, see ¶ 109, ¶ 109.8, and ¶ 109.8.2.

200.A.139.X.h The interaction of qualitative considerations that affect internal control over financial reporting with quantitative considerations ordinarily results in deficiencies in the following areas being at least significant deficiencies in internal control over financial reporting:

- Controls over the selection and application of accounting policies that are in conformity with generally accepted accounting principles;
- Antifraud programs and controls;
- Controls over non-routine and non-systematic transactions; and
- Controls over the period-end financial reporting process, including controls over procedures used to enter transaction totals into the general

---

17. See SEC Staff Accounting Bulletin Topic 1M2, *Immaterial Misstatements That Are Intentional,* for further discussion about the level of detail and degree of assurance that would satisfy prudent officials in the conduct of their own affairs.

ledger; initiate, authorize, record, and process journal entries into the general ledger; and record recurring and nonrecurring adjustments to the financial statements

For Analysis, see ¶ 109, ¶ 109.8, and ¶ 109.8.2.

200.A.140.X.h Each of the following circumstances should be regarded as at least a significant deficiency and as a strong indicator that a material weakness in internal control over financial reporting exists:

- Restatement of previously issued financial statements to reflect the correction of a misstatement.

Note: The correction of a misstatement includes misstatements due to error or fraud; it does not include restatements to reflect a change in accounting principle to comply with a new accounting principle or a voluntary change from one generally accepted accounting principle to another generally accepted accounting principle.

- Identification by the auditor of a material misstatement in financial statements in the current period that was not initially identified by the company's internal control over financial reporting. (This is a strong indicator of a material weakness even if management subsequently corrects the misstatement.)

- Oversight of the company's external financial reporting and internal control over financial reporting by the company's audit committee is ineffective. (Paragraphs 55 through 59 present factors to evaluate when determining whether the audit committee is ineffective.)

- The internal audit function or the risk assessment function is ineffective at a company for which such a function needs to be effective for the company to have an effective monitoring or risk assessment component, such as for very large or highly complex companies.

Note: The evaluation of the internal audit or risk assessment functions is similar to the evaluation of the audit committee, as described in paragraphs 55 through 59, that is, the evaluation is made within the context of the monitoring and risk assessment components. The auditor is not required to make a separate evaluation of the effectiveness and performance of these functions. Instead, the auditor should base his or her evaluation on evidence obtained as part of evaluating the monitoring and risk assessment components of internal control over financial reporting.

- For complex entities in highly regulated industries, an ineffective regulatory compliance function. This relates solely to those aspects of the ineffective regulatory compliance function in which associated violations of laws and regulations could have a material effect on the reliability of financial reporting.

- Identification of fraud of any magnitude on the part of senior management.

Note: The auditor is required to plan and perform procedures to obtain reasonable assurance that material misstatement caused by fraud is detected by the auditor. However, for the purposes of evaluating and reporting deficiencies in internal control over financial reporting, the auditor should evaluate fraud of any magnitude (including fraud resulting in immaterial misstatements) on the part of senior management of which he or she is aware. Furthermore, for the purposes of this circumstance, "senior management" includes the principal executive and financial officers signing the company's certifications as required under Section 302 of the Act as well as any other member of management who play a significant role in the company's financial reporting process.

- Significant deficiencies that have been communicated to management and the audit committee remain uncorrected after some reasonable period of time.

- An ineffective control environment.

For Analysis, see ¶ 109, ¶ 109.4.2, ¶ 109.8, and ¶ 109.8.2.

200.A.141.X.h Appendix D provides examples of significant deficiencies and material weaknesses.

For Analysis, see ¶ 109, ¶ 109.8, ¶ 109.8.2, and ¶ 120.

¶ 200.A.XI. *Requirement for Written Representations*

200.A.142.XI In an audit of internal control over financial reporting, the auditor should obtain written representations from management:

a. Acknowledging management's responsibility for establishing and maintaining effective internal control over financial reporting;

b. Stating that management has performed an assessment of the effectiveness of the company's internal control over financial reporting and specifying the control criteria;

c. Stating that management did not use the auditor's procedures performed during the audits of internal control over financial reporting or the financial statements as part of the basis for management's assessment of the effectiveness of internal control over financial reporting;

d. Stating management's conclusion about the effectiveness of the company's internal control over financial reporting based on the control criteria as of a specified date;

e. Stating that management has disclosed to the auditor all deficiencies in the design or operation of internal control over financial reporting identified as part of management's assessment, including separately disclosing to the auditor all such deficiencies that it believes to be significant deficiencies or material weaknesses in internal control over financial reporting;

f. Describing any material fraud and any other fraud that, although not material, involves senior management or management or other employees who have a significant role in the company's internal control over financial reporting;

g. Stating whether control deficiencies identified and communicated to the audit committee during previous engagements pursuant to paragraph 207 have been resolved, and specifically identifying any that have not; and

h. Stating whether there were, subsequent to the date being reported on, any changes in internal control over financial reporting or other factors that might significantly affect internal control over financial reporting, including any corrective actions taken by management with regard to significant deficiencies and material weaknesses.

For Analysis, see ¶ 110 and ¶ 115.

200.A.143.XI The failure to obtain written representations from management, including management's refusal to furnish them, constitutes a limitation on the scope of the audit sufficient to preclude an unqualified opinion. As discussed further in paragraph 178, when management limits the scope of the audit, the auditor should either withdraw from the engagement or disclaim an opinion. Further, the auditor should evaluate the effects of management's refusal on his or her ability to rely on other representations, including, if applicable, representations obtained in an audit of the company's financial statements.

For Analysis, see ¶ 110 and ¶ 113.3.6.

200.A.144.XI AU sec. 333, *Management Representations,* explains matters such as who should sign the letter, the period to be covered by the letter, and when to obtain an updating letter.

For Analysis, see ¶ 110.

¶ 200.A.XII. *Relationship of an Audit of Internal Control over Financial Reporting to an Audit of Financial Statements*

200.A.145.XII The audit of internal control over financial reporting should be integrated with the audit of the financial statements. The objectives of the procedures for the audits are not identical, however, and the auditor must plan and perform the work to achieve the objectives of both audits.

For Analysis, see ¶ 111.

200.A.146.XII The understanding of internal control over financial reporting the auditor obtains and the procedures the auditor performs for purposes of expressing an opinion on management's assessment are interrelated with the internal control over financial reporting understanding the auditor obtains and procedures the auditor performs to assess control risk for purposes of expressing an opinion on the financial statements. As a result, it is efficient for the auditor to coordinate obtaining the understanding and performing the procedures.

For Analysis, see ¶ 111.

¶ 200.A.XII.a. Tests of Controls in an Audit of Internal Control Over Financial Reporting

200.A.147.XII.a The objective of the tests of controls in an audit of internal control over financial reporting is to obtain evidence about the effectiveness of controls to support the auditor's opinion on whether management's assessment of the effectiveness of the company's internal control over financial reporting is fairly stated. The auditor's opinion relates to the effectiveness of the company's internal control over financial reporting as of a *point in time* and *taken as a whole.*

For Analysis, see ¶ 111 and ¶ 111.1.

200.A.148.XII.a To express an opinion on internal control over financial reporting effectiveness as of a *point in time,* the auditor should obtain evidence that internal control over financial reporting has operated effectively for a sufficient period of time, which may be less than the entire period (ordinarily one year) covered by the company's financial statements. To express an opinion on internal control over financial reporting effectiveness *taken as a whole,* the auditor must obtain evidence about the effectiveness of controls over all relevant assertions related to all significant accounts and disclosures in the financial statements. This requires that the auditor test the design and operating effectiveness of controls he or she ordinarily would not test if expressing an opinion only on the financial statements.

For Analysis, see ¶ 111 and ¶ 111.1.

200.A.149.XII.a When concluding on the effectiveness of internal control over financial reporting for purposes of expressing an opinion on management's assessment, the auditor should incorporate the results of any additional tests of controls performed to achieve the objective related to expressing an opinion on the financial statements, as discussed in the following section.

For Analysis, see ¶ 111 and ¶ 111.1.

¶ 200.A.XII.b. Tests of Controls in an Audit of Financial Statements

200.A.150.XII.b To express an opinion on the financial statements, the auditor ordinarily performs tests of controls and substantive procedures. The objective of the tests of controls the auditor performs for this purpose is to assess control risk. To assess control risk for specific financial statement assertions at less than the maximum, the auditor is required to obtain evidence that the relevant controls operated effectively during the *entire period* upon which the auditor plans to place reliance on those controls. However, the auditor is not required to assess control risk at less than the maximum for *all* relevant assertions and, for a variety of reasons, the auditor may choose not to do so.[18]

For Analysis, see ¶ 111, ¶ 111.2, and ¶ 112.

200.A.151.XII.b When concluding on the effectiveness of controls for the purpose of assessing control risk, the auditor also should evaluate the results of any additional tests of controls performed to achieve the objective related to expressing an opinion on management's assessment, as discussed in paragraphs 147 through 149. Consideration of these results may require the auditor to alter the nature, timing, and extent of substantive procedures and to plan and perform further tests of controls, particularly in response to identified control deficiencies.

For Analysis, see ¶ 111, ¶ 111.1, and ¶ 111.2.

¶ 200.A.XII.c. Effect of Tests of Controls on Substantive Procedures

200.A.152.XII.c Regardless of the assessed level of control risk or the assessed risk of material misstatement in connection with the audit of the financial statements, the auditor should perform substantive procedures for all relevant assertions related to all significant accounts and disclosures. Performing procedures to express an opinion on internal control over financial reporting does not diminish this requirement.

For Analysis, see ¶ 111 and ¶ 111.3.

200.A.153.XII.c The substantive procedures that the auditor should perform consist of tests of details of transactions and balances and analytical procedures. Before using the results obtained from substantive analytical procedures, the auditor should either test the design and operating effectiveness of controls over financial information used in the substantive analytical procedures or perform other procedures to support the completeness and accuracy of the underlying information. For significant risks of material misstatement, it is unlikely that audit evidence obtained from substantive analytical procedures alone will be sufficient.

For Analysis, see ¶ 111 and ¶ 111.3.

200.A.154.XII.c When designing substantive analytical procedures, the auditor also should evaluate the risk of management override of controls. As part of this process, the auditor should evaluate whether such an override might have allowed adjustments outside of the normal period-end financial reporting process to have been made to the financial statements. Such adjustments might have resulted in artificial changes to the financial statement relationships being analyzed, causing the auditor to draw erroneous conclusions. For this reason, substantive analytical procedures alone are not well suited to detecting fraud.

---

18. See paragraph 160 for additional documentation requirements when the auditor assesses control risk as other than low.

For Analysis, see ¶ 111 and ¶ 111.3.

200.A.155.XII.c The auditor's substantive procedures must include reconciling the financial statements to the accounting records. The auditor's substantive procedures also should include examining material adjustments made during the course of preparing the financial statements. Also, other auditing standards require auditors to perform specific tests of details in the financial statement audit. For instance, AU sec. 316, *Consideration of Fraud in a Financial Statement Audit,* requires the auditor to perform certain tests of details to further address the risk of management override, whether or not a specific risk of fraud has been identified. Paragraph .34 of AU Sec. 330, *The Confirmation Process,* states that there is a presumption that the auditor will request the confirmation of accounts receivable. Similarly, paragraph .01 of AU Sec. 331, *Inventories,* states that observation of inventories is a generally accepted auditing procedure and that the auditor who issues an opinion without this procedure "has the burden of justifying the opinion expressed."

For Analysis, see ¶ 111 and ¶ 111.3.

200.A.156.XII.c If, during the audit of internal control over financial reporting, the auditor identifies a control deficiency, he or she should determine the effect on the nature, timing, and extent of substantive procedures to be performed to reduce the risk of material misstatement of the financial statements to an appropriately low level.

For Analysis, see ¶ 111 and ¶ 111.3.

¶ 200.A.XII.d. Effect of Substantive Procedures on the Auditor's Conclusions About the Operating Effectiveness of Controls

200.A.157.XII.d In an audit of internal control over financial reporting, the auditor should evaluate the effect of the findings of all substantive auditing procedures performed in the audit of financial statements on the effectiveness of internal control over financial reporting. This evaluation should include, but not be limited to:

- The auditor's risk evaluations in connection with the selection and application of substantive procedures, especially those related to fraud (See paragraph 26);

- Findings with respect to illegal acts and related party transactions;

- Indications of management bias in making accounting estimates and in selecting accounting principles; and

- Misstatements detected by substantive procedures. The extent of such misstatements might alter the auditor's judgment about the effectiveness of controls.

For Analysis, see ¶ 108, ¶ 111 and ¶ 111.4.

200.A.158.XII.d However, the absence of misstatements detected by substantive procedures does not provide evidence that controls related to the assertion being tested are effective.

For Analysis, see ¶ 111 and ¶ 111.4.

¶ 200.A.XIII. *Documentation Requirements*

200.A.159.XIII In addition to the documentation requirements in AU sec. 339, *Audit Documentation,* the auditor should document:

- The understanding obtained and the evaluation of the design of each of the five components of the company's internal control over financial reporting;
- The process used to determine significant accounts and disclosures and major classes of transactions, including the determination of the locations or business units at which to perform testing;
- The identification of the points at which misstatements related to relevant financial statement assertions could occur within significant accounts and disclosures and major classes of transactions;
- The extent to which the auditor relied upon work performed by others as well as the auditor's assessment of their competence and objectivity;
- The evaluation of any deficiencies noted as a result of the auditor's testing; and
- Other findings that could result in a modification to the auditor's report.

For Analysis, see ¶ 112.

200.A.160.XIII For a company that has effective internal control over financial reporting, the auditor ordinarily will be able to perform sufficient testing of controls to be able to assess control risk for all relevant assertions related to significant accounts and disclosures at a low level. If, however, the auditor assesses control risk as other than low for certain assertions or significant accounts, the auditor should document the reasons for that conclusion. Examples of when it is appropriate to assess control risk as other than low include:

- When a control over a relevant assertion related to a significant account or disclosure was superseded late in the year and only the new control was tested for operating effectiveness.
- When a material weakness existed during the period under audit and was corrected by the end of the period.

For Analysis, see ¶ 112.

200.A.161.XIII The auditor also should document the effect of a conclusion that control risk is other than low for any relevant assertions related to any significant accounts in connection with the audit of the financial statements on his or her opinion on the audit of internal control over financial reporting.

For Analysis, see ¶ 112.

¶ 200.A.XIV. *Reporting on Internal Control Over Financial Reporting*

¶ 200.A.XIV.a. Management's Report

200.A.162.XIV.a Management is required to include in its annual report its assessment of the effectiveness of the company's internal control over financial reporting in addition to its audited financial statements as of the end of the most recent fiscal year. Management's report on internal control over financial reporting is required to include the following:[19]

- A statement of management's responsibility for establishing and maintaining adequate internal control over financial reporting for the company;
- A statement identifying the framework used by management to conduct the required assessment of the effectiveness of the company's internal control over financial reporting;
- An assessment of the effectiveness of the company's internal control over financial reporting as of the end of the company's most recent fiscal year, including an explicit statement as to whether that internal control over financial reporting is effective; and
- A statement that the registered public accounting firm that audited the financial statements included in the annual report has issued an attestation report on management's assessment of the company's internal control over financial reporting.

For Analysis, see ¶ 113 and ¶ 113.1.

200.A.163.XIV.a Management should provide, both in its report on internal control over financial reporting and in its representation letter to the auditor, a written conclusion about the effectiveness of the company's internal control over financial reporting. The conclusion about the effectiveness of a company's internal control over financial reporting can take many forms; however, management is required to state a direct conclusion about whether the company's internal control over financial reporting is effective. This standard, for example, includes the phrase "management's assessment that W Company maintained effective internal control over financial reporting as of [*date*]" to illustrate such a conclusion. Other phrases, such as "management's assessment that W Company's internal control over financial reporting as of [*date*] is sufficient to meet the stated objectives," also might be used. However, the conclusion should not be so subjective (for example, "very effective internal control") that people having competence in and using the same or similar criteria would not ordinarily be able to arrive at similar conclusions.

---

19. See Item 308(a) of Regulation S-B and S-K, 17 C.F.R. 228.308(a) and 17 C.F.R. 229.308(a), respectively.

For Analysis, see ¶ 113 and ¶ 113.1.

200.A.164.XIV.a Management is precluded from concluding that the company's internal control over financial reporting is effective if there are one or more material weaknesses.[20] In addition, management is required to disclose all material weaknesses that exist as of the end of the most recent fiscal year.

For Analysis, see ¶ 113 and ¶ 113.1.

200.A.165.XIV.a Management might be able to accurately represent that internal control over financial reporting, as of the end of the company's most recent fiscal year, is effective even if one or more material weaknesses existed during the period. To make this representation, management must have changed the internal control over financial reporting to eliminate the material weaknesses sufficiently in advance of the "as of" date and have satisfactorily tested the effectiveness over a period of time that is adequate for it to determine whether, as of the end of the fiscal year, the design and operation of internal control over financial reporting is effective.[21]

For Analysis, see ¶ 113, ¶ 113.1, and ¶ 114.1.

¶ 200.A.XIV.b. Auditor's Evaluation of Management's Report

200.A.166.XIV.b With respect to management's report on its assessment, the auditor should evaluate the following matters:

a. Whether management has properly stated its responsibility for establishing and maintaining adequate internal control over financial reporting.

b. Whether the framework used by management to conduct the evaluation is suitable. (As discussed in paragraph 14, the framework described in COSO constitutes a suitable and available framework.)

c. Whether management's assessment of the effectiveness of internal control over financial reporting, as of the end of the company's most recent fiscal year, is free of material misstatement.

d. Whether management has expressed its assessment in an acceptable form.

—Management is required to state whether the company's internal control over financial reporting is effective.

—A negative assurance statement indicating that, "Nothing has come to management's attention to suggest that the company's internal control over financial reporting is not effective," is not acceptable.

—Management is not permitted to conclude that the company's internal control over financial reporting is effective if there are one or more ma-

---

20. See Item 308(a)(3) of Regulation S-B and S-K, 17 C.F.R. 228.308(a) and 17 C.F.R. 229.308(a), respectively.

21. However, when the reason for a change in internal control over financial reporting is the correction of a material weakness, management and the auditor should evaluate whether the reason for the change and the circumstances surrounding the change are material information necessary to make the disclosure about the change not misleading in a filing subject to certification under Securities Exchange Act Rule 13a-14(a) or 15d-14(a), 17 C.F.R. 240.13a-14(a) or 17 C.F.R. 240.15d-14(a). See discussion beginning at paragraph 200 for further direction.

terial weaknesses in the company's internal control over financial reporting.

e. Whether material weaknesses identified in the company's internal control over financial reporting, if any, have been properly disclosed, including material weaknesses corrected during the period.[22]

For Analysis, see ¶ 103, ¶ 113, ¶ 113.2, and ¶ 114.2.

¶ 200.A.XIV.c. Auditor's Report on Management's Assessment of Internal Control Over Financial Reporting

200.A.167.XIV.c The auditor's report on management's assessment of the effectiveness of internal control over financial reporting must include the following elements:

a. A title that includes the word *independent;*

b. An identification of management's conclusion about the effectiveness of the company's internal control over financial reporting as of a specified date based on the control criteria [for example, criteria established in *Internal Control—Integrated Framework* issued by the Committee of Sponsoring Organizations of the Treadway Commission (COSO)];

c. An identification of the title of the management report that includes management's assessment (the auditor should use the same description of the company's internal control over financial reporting as management uses in its report);

d. A statement that the assessment is the responsibility of management;

e. A statement that the auditor's responsibility is to express an opinion on the assessment and an opinion on the company's internal control over financial reporting based on his or her audit;

f. A definition of internal control over financial reporting as stated in paragraph 7;

g. A statement that the audit was conducted in accordance with the standards of the Public Company Accounting Oversight Board (United States);

h. A statement that the standards of the Public Company Accounting Oversight Board require that the auditor plan and perform the audit to obtain reasonable assurance about whether effective internal control over financial reporting was maintained in all material respects;

i. A statement that an audit includes obtaining an understanding of internal control over financial reporting, evaluating management's assessment, testing and evaluating the design and operating effectiveness of internal control, and performing such other procedures as the auditor considered necessary in the circumstances;

---

22. See paragraph 206 for direction when a material weakness was corrected during the fourth quarter and the auditor believes that modification to the disclosures about changes in internal control over financial reporting are necessary for the annual certifications to be accurate and to comply with the requirements of Section 302 of the Act.

j. A statement that the auditor believes the audit provides a reasonable basis for his or her opinions;

k. A paragraph stating that, because of inherent limitations, internal control over financial reporting may not prevent or detect misstatements and that projections of any evaluation of effectiveness to future periods are subject to the risk that controls may become inadequate because of changes in conditions, or that the degree of compliance with the policies or procedures may deteriorate;

l. The auditor's opinion on whether management's assessment of the effectiveness of the company's internal control over financial reporting as of the specified date is fairly stated, in all material respects, based on the control criteria (See discussion beginning at paragraph 162);

m. The auditor's opinion on whether the company maintained, in all material respects, effective internal control over financial reporting as of the specified date, based on the control criteria;

n. The manual or printed signature of the auditor's firm;

o. The city and state (or city and country, in the case of non-U.S. auditors) from which the auditor's report has been issued; and

p. The date of the audit report.

For Analysis, see ¶ 102, ¶ 113, ¶ 113.1, and ¶ 113.3.

200.A.168.XIV.c Example A-1 in Appendix A is an illustrative auditor's report for an unqualified opinion on management's assessment of the effectiveness of the company's internal control over financial reporting and an unqualified opinion on the effectiveness of the company's internal control over financial reporting.

For Analysis, see ¶ 113, ¶ 113.3, and ¶ 117.

200.A.169.XIV.c *Separate or Combined Reports.* The auditor may choose to issue a combined report (that is, one report containing both an opinion on the financial statements and the opinions on internal control over financial reporting) or separate reports on the company's financial statements and on internal control over financial reporting. Example A-7 in Appendix A is an illustrative combined audit report on internal control over financial reporting. Appendix A also includes examples of separate reports on internal control over financial reporting.

For Analysis, see ¶ 113, ¶ 113.3, ¶ 113.3.1, and ¶ 117.

200.A.170.XIV.c If the auditor chooses to issue a separate report on internal control over financial reporting, he or she should add the following paragraph to the auditor's report on the financial statements:

We also have audited, in accordance with the standards of the Public Company Accounting Oversight Board (United States), the effectiveness of W

Company's internal control over financial reporting as of December 31, 20X3, based on [*identify control criteria*] and our report dated [*date of report, which should be the same as the date of the report on the financial statements*] expressed [*include nature of opinions*].

and add the following paragraph to the report on internal control over financial reporting:

We have also audited, in accordance with the standards of the Public Company Accounting Oversight Board (United States), the [*identify financial statements*] of W Company and our report dated [*date of report, which should be the same as the date of the report on the effectiveness of internal control over financial reporting*] expressed [*include nature of opinion*].

For Analysis, see ¶ 113, ¶ 113.3, and ¶ 113.3.1.

200.A.171.XIV.c *Report Date.* As stated previously, the auditor cannot audit internal control over financial reporting without also auditing the financial statements. Therefore, the reports should be dated the same.

For Analysis, see ¶ 113, ¶ 113.3, and ¶ 113.3.2.

200.A.172.XIV.c When the auditor elects to issue a combined report on the audit of the financial statements and the audit of internal control over financial reporting, the audit opinion will address multiple reporting periods for the financial statements presented but only the end of the most recent fiscal year for the effectiveness of internal control over financial reporting and management's assessment of the effectiveness of internal control over financial reporting. See a combined report in Example A-7 in Appendix A.

For Analysis, see ¶ 113, ¶ 113.3, ¶ 113.3.2, and ¶ 117.

200.A.173.XIV.c *Report Modifications.* The auditor should modify the standard report if any of the following conditions exist.

a. Management's assessment is inadequate or management's report is inappropriate. (See paragraph 174.)

b. There is a material weakness in the company's internal control over financial reporting. (See paragraphs 175 through 177.)

c. There is a restriction on the scope of the engagement. (See paragraphs 178 through 181.)

d. The auditor decides to refer to the report of other auditors as the basis, in part, for the auditor's own report. (See paragraphs 182 through 185.)

e. A significant subsequent event has occurred since the date being reported on. (See paragraphs 186 through 189.)

f. There is other information contained in management's report on internal control over financial reporting. (See paragraphs 190 through 192.)

For Analysis, see ¶ 113, ¶ 113.3, ¶ 113.3.3, ¶ 113.3.4, ¶ 113.3.5, ¶ 113.3.6, ¶ 113.3.7, ¶ 113.3.8, and ¶ 113.3.9.

200.A.174.XIV.c *Management's Assessment Inadequate or Report Inappropriate.* If the auditor determines that management's process for assessing internal control over financial reporting is inadequate, the auditor should modify his or her opinion for a scope limitation (discussed further beginning at paragraph 178). If the auditor determines that management's report is inappropriate, the auditor should modify his or her report to include, at a minimum, an explanatory paragraph describing the reasons for this conclusion.

For Analysis, see ¶ 113, ¶ 113.3, ¶ 113.3.4, and ¶ 113.3.6.

200.A.175.XIV.c *Material Weaknesses.* Paragraphs 130 through 141 describe significant deficiencies and material weaknesses. If there are significant deficiencies that, individually or in combination, result in one or more material weaknesses, management is precluded from concluding that internal control over financial reporting is effective. In these circumstances, the auditor must express an adverse opinion on the company's internal control over financial reporting.

For Analysis, see ¶ 109.8.2, ¶ 113, ¶ 113.3, and ¶ 113.3.5.

200.A.176.XIV.c When expressing an adverse opinion on the effectiveness of internal control over financial reporting because of a material weakness, the auditor's report must include:

- The definition of a material weakness, as provided in paragraph 10.

- A statement that a material weakness has been identified and included in management's assessment. (If the material weakness has not been included in management's assessment, this sentence should be modified to state that the material weakness has been identified but not included in management's assessment. In this case, the auditor also is required to communicate in writing to the audit committee that the material weakness was not disclosed or identified as a material weakness in management's report.)

- A description of any material weaknesses identified in a company's internal control over financial reporting. This description should provide the users of the audit report with specific information about the nature of any material weakness, and its actual and potential effect on the presentation of the company's financial statements issued during the existence of the weakness. This description also should address requirements described in paragraph 194.

For Analysis, see ¶ 102, ¶ 113, ¶ 113.3, ¶ 113.3.5, and ¶ 113.3.10.

200.A.177.XIV.c Depending on the circumstances, the auditor may express both an unqualified opinion and an other-than-unqualified opinion within the same report on internal control over financial reporting. For example, if management makes an adverse assessment because a material weakness has been identified and not corrected ("...internal control over financial reporting is not effective..."), the auditor would express an unqualified opinion on management's assessment ("...management's assessment that internal control over financial reporting is not effective is fairly stated, in all material respects..."). At the same time, the auditor would express an adverse opinion about the effectiveness of internal control over financial reporting ("In our opinion, because of the effect of the material weakness described, the company's internal control over financial reporting is not effective."). Example A-2 in Appendix A illustrates the form of the report that is appropriate in this situation. Example A-6 in Appendix A illustrates a report that reflects disagreement between management and the auditor that a material weakness exists.

For Analysis, see ¶ 113, ¶ 113.3, ¶ 113.3.5, and ¶ 117.

200.A.178.XIV.c *Scope Limitations.* The auditor can express an unqualified opinion on management's assessment of internal control over financial reporting and an unqualified opinion on the effectiveness of internal control over financial reporting only if the auditor has been able to apply all the procedures necessary in the circumstances. If there are restrictions on the scope of the engagement imposed by the circumstances, the auditor should withdraw from the engagement, disclaim an opinion, or express a qualified opinion. The auditor's decision depends on his or her assessment of the importance of the omitted procedure(s) to his or her ability to form an opinion on management's assessment of internal control over financial reporting and an opinion on the effectiveness of the company's internal control over financial reporting. However, when the restrictions are imposed by management, the auditor should withdraw from the engagement or disclaim an opinion on management's assessment of internal control over financial reporting and the effectiveness of internal control over financial reporting.

For Analysis, see ¶ 113, ¶ 113.3, and ¶ 113.3.6.

200.A.179.XIV.c For example, management might have identified a material weakness in its internal control over financial reporting prior to the date specified in its report and implemented controls to correct it. If management believes that the new controls have been operating for a sufficient period of time to determine that they are both effectively designed and operating, management would be able to include in its assessment its conclusion that internal control over financial reporting is effective as of the date specified. However, if the auditor disagrees with the sufficiency of the time period, he or she would be unable to obtain sufficient evidence that the new controls have been operating effectively for a sufficient period. In that case, the auditor should modify the opinion on the effectiveness of internal control over financial reporting and the opinion on management's assessment of internal control over financial reporting because of a scope limitation.

For Analysis, see ¶ 113, ¶ 113.3, and ¶ 113.3.6.

200.A.180.XIV.c When the auditor plans to disclaim an opinion and the limited procedures performed by the auditor caused the auditor to conclude that a material weakness exists, the auditor's report should include:

- The definition of a material weakness, as provided in paragraph 10.

- A description of any material weaknesses identified in the company's internal control over financial reporting. This description should provide the users of the audit report with specific information about the nature of any material weakness, and its actual and potential effect on the presentation of the company's financial statements issued during the existence of the weakness. This description also should address the requirements in paragraph 194.

For Analysis, see ¶ 102, ¶ 113, ¶ 113.3, ¶ 113.3.6, and ¶ 113.3.10.

200.A.181.XIV.c Example A-3 in Appendix A illustrates the form of report when there is a limitation on the scope of the audit causing the auditor to issue qualified opinions. Example A-4 illustrates the form of report when restrictions on the scope of the audit cause the auditor to disclaim opinions.

For Analysis, see ¶ 113, ¶ 113.3, ¶ 113.3.6, and ¶ 117.

200.A.182.XIV.c *Opinions Based, in Part, on the Report of Another Auditor.* When another auditor has audited the financial statements and internal control over financial reporting of one or more subsidiaries, divisions, branches, or components of the company, the auditor should determine whether he or she may serve as the principal auditor and use the work and reports of another auditor as a basis, in part, for his or her opinions. AU sec. 543, *Part of Audit Performed by Other Independent Auditors,* provides direction on the auditor's decision of whether to serve as the principal auditor of the financial statements. If the auditor decides it is appropriate to serve as the principal auditor of the financial statements, then that auditor also should be the principal auditor of the company's internal control over financial reporting. This relationship results from the requirement that an audit of the financial statements must be performed to audit internal control over financial reporting; only the principal auditor of the financial statements can be the principal auditor of internal control over financial reporting. In this circumstance, the principal auditor of the financial statements needs to participate sufficiently in the audit of internal control over financial reporting to provide a basis for serving as the principal auditor of internal control over financial reporting.

For Analysis, see ¶ 113, ¶ 113.3, and ¶ 113.3.7.

200.A.183.XIV.c When serving as the principal auditor of internal control over financial reporting, the auditor should decide whether to make reference in the report on internal control over financial reporting to the audit of internal control over financial reporting performed by the other auditor. In these circumstances, the auditor's decision is based on factors similar to those of the independent auditor who uses the work and reports of other independent auditors when reporting on a company's financial statements as described in AU sec. 543.

For Analysis, see ¶ 113, ¶ 113.3, and ¶ 113.3.7.

200.A.184.XIV.c The decision about whether to make reference to another auditor in the report on the audit of internal control over financial reporting might differ from the corresponding decision as it relates to the audit of the financial statements. For example, the audit report on the financial statements may make reference to the audit of a significant equity investment performed by another independent auditor, but the report on internal control over financial reporting might not make a similar reference because management's evaluation of internal control over financial reporting ordinarily would not extend to controls at the equity method investee.[23]

For Analysis, see ¶ 113, ¶ 113.3, ¶ 113.3.7, and ¶ 118.

200.A.185.XIV.c When the auditor decides to make reference to the report of the other auditor as a basis, in part, for his or her opinions, the auditor should refer to the report of the other auditor when describing the scope of the audit and when expressing the opinions.

For Analysis, see ¶ 113, ¶ 113.3, and ¶ 113.3.7.

200.A.186.XIV.c *Subsequent Events.* Changes in internal control over financial reporting or other factors that might significantly affect internal control over financial reporting might occur subsequent to the date as of which internal control over financial reporting is being audited but before the date of the auditor's report. The auditor should inquire of management whether there were any such changes or factors. As described in paragraph 142, the auditor should obtain written representations from management relating to such matters. Additionally, to obtain information about whether changes have occurred that might affect the effectiveness of the company's internal control over financial reporting and, therefore, the auditor's report, the auditor should inquire about and examine, for this subsequent period, the following:

- Relevant internal audit reports (or similar functions, such as loan review in a financial institution) issued during the subsequent period;
- Independent auditor reports (if other than the auditor's) of significant deficiencies or material weaknesses;
- Regulatory agency reports on the company's internal control over financial reporting; and
- Information about the effectiveness of the company's internal control over financial reporting obtained through other engagements.

For Analysis, see ¶ 110, ¶ 113, ¶ 113.3, and ¶ 113.3.8.

---

23. See Appendix B, paragraph B15, for further discussion of the evaluation of the controls over financial reporting for an equity method investment.

200.A.187.XIV.c The auditor could inquire about and examine other documents for the subsequent period. Paragraphs .01 through .09 of AU sec. 560, *Subsequent Events,* provides direction on subsequent events for a financial statement audit that also may be helpful to the auditor performing an audit of internal control over financial reporting.

For Analysis, see ¶ 113, ¶ 113.3, and ¶ 113.3.8.

200.A.188.XIV.c If the auditor obtains knowledge about subsequent events that materially and adversely affect the effectiveness of the company's internal control over financial reporting as of the date specified in the assessment, the auditor should issue an adverse opinion on the effectiveness of internal control over financial reporting (and issue an adverse opinion on management's assessment of internal control over financial reporting if management's report does not appropriately assess the affect of the subsequent event). If the auditor is unable to determine the effect of the subsequent event on the effectiveness of the company's internal control over financial reporting, the auditor should disclaim opinions. As described in paragraph 190, the auditor should disclaim an opinion on management's disclosures about corrective actions taken by the company after the date of management's assessment, if any.

For Analysis, see ¶ 113, ¶ 113.3, ¶ 113.3.8, and ¶ 113.3.9.

200.A.189.XIV.c The auditor may obtain knowledge about subsequent events with respect to conditions that did not exist at the date specified in the assessment but arose subsequent to that date. If a subsequent event of this type has a material effect on the company, the auditor should include in his or her report an explanatory paragraph describing the event and its effects or directing the reader's attention to the event and its effects as disclosed in management's report. Management's consideration of such events to be disclosed in its report should be limited to a change that has materially affected, or is reasonably likely to materially affect, the company's internal control over financial reporting.

For Analysis, see ¶ 113, ¶ 113.3, and ¶ 113.3.8.

200.A.190.XIV.c *Management's Report Containing Additional Information.* Management's report on internal control over financial reporting may contain information in addition to management's assessment of the effectiveness of its internal control over financial reporting. Such information might include, for example:

- Disclosures about corrective actions taken by the company after the date of management's assessment;
- The company's plans to implement new controls; and
- A statement that management believes the cost of correcting a material weakness would exceed the benefits to be derived from implementing new controls.

For Analysis, see ¶ 113, ¶ 113.3, and ¶ 113.3.9.

200.A.191.XIV.c If management's assessment includes such additional information, the auditor should disclaim an opinion on the information. For example, the auditor should use the following language as the last paragraph of the report to disclaim an opinion on management's cost-benefit statement:

> We do not express an opinion or any other form of assurance on management's statement referring to the costs and related benefits of implementing new controls.

For Analysis, see ¶ 113, ¶ 113.3, and ¶ 113.3.9.

200.A.192.XIV.c If the auditor believes that management's additional information contains a material misstatement of fact, he or she should discuss the matter with management. If the auditor concludes that there is a valid basis for concern, he or she should propose that management consult with some other party whose advice might be useful, such as the company's legal counsel. If, after discussing the matter with management and those management has consulted, the auditor concludes that a material misstatement of fact remains, the auditor should notify management and the audit committee, in writing, of the auditor's views concerning the information. The auditor also should consider consulting the auditor's legal counsel about further actions to be taken, including the auditor's responsibility under Section 10A of the Securities Exchange Act of 1934.[24]

> **Note:** If management makes the types of disclosures described in paragraph 190 outside its report on internal control over financial reporting and includes them elsewhere within its annual report on the company's financial statements, the auditor would not need to disclaim an opinion, as described in paragraph 191. However, in that situation, the auditor's responsibilities are the same as those described in paragraph 192 if the auditor believes that the additional information contains a material misstatement of fact.

For Analysis, see ¶ 113, ¶ 113.3, and ¶ 113.3.9.

200.A.193.XIV.c *Effect of Auditor's Adverse Opinion on Internal Control Over Financial Reporting on the Opinion on Financial Statements.* In some cases, the auditor's report on internal control over financial reporting might describe a material weakness that resulted in an adverse opinion on the effectiveness of internal control over financial reporting while the audit report on the financial statements remains unqualified. Consequently, during the audit of the financial statements, the auditor did not rely on that control. However, he or she performed additional substantive procedures to determine whether there was a material misstatement in the account related to the control. If, as a result of these procedures, the auditor determines that there was not a material misstate-

---

24. See Section 10A of the Securities Exchange Act of 1934, 15 U.S.C. 78j-1.

---

ment in the account, he or she would be able to express an unqualified opinion on the financial statements.

For Analysis, see ¶ 113, ¶ 113.3, and ¶ 113.3.10.

200.A.194.XIV.c When the auditor's opinion on the financial statements is unaffected by the adverse opinion on the effectiveness of internal control over financial reporting, the report on internal control over financial reporting (or the combined report, if a combined report is issued) should include the following or similar language in the paragraph that describes the material weakness:

> This material weakness was considered in determining the nature, timing, and extent of audit tests applied in our audit of the 20X3 financial statements, and this report does not affect our report dated [*date of report*] on those financial statements. [*Revise this wording appropriately for use in a combined report.*]

For Analysis, see ¶ 113, ¶ 113.3, and ¶ 113.3.10.

200.A.195.XIV.c Such disclosure is important to ensure that users of the auditor's report on the financial statements understand why the auditor issued an unqualified opinion on those statements.

For Analysis, see ¶ 113, ¶ 113.3, and ¶ 113.3.10.

200.A.196.XIV.c Disclosure is also important when the auditor's opinion on the financial statements is affected by the adverse opinion on the effectiveness of internal control over financial reporting. In that circumstance, the report on internal control over financial reporting (or the combined report, if a combined report is issued) should include the following or similar language in the paragraph that describes the material weakness:

> This material weakness was considered in determining the nature, timing, and extent of audit tests applied in our audit of the 20X3 financial statements.

For Analysis, see ¶ 113, ¶ 113.3, and ¶ 113.3.10.

200.A.197.XIV.c *Subsequent Discovery of Information Existing at the Date of the Auditor's Report on Internal Control Over Financial Reporting.* After the issuance of the report on internal control over financial reporting, the auditor may become aware of conditions that existed at the report date that might have affected the auditor's opinions had he or she been aware of them. The auditor's evaluation of such subsequent information is similar to the auditor's evaluation of information discovered subsequent to the date of the report on an audit of financial statements, as described in AU sec. 561, *Subsequent Discovery of Facts Existing at the Date of the Auditor's Report.* That standard requires the auditor to determine whether the information is reliable and whether the facts existed at the date of his or her report. If so, the auditor should determine (1) whether the facts would have changed the report if he or she had been aware of them and

(2) whether there are persons currently relying on or likely to rely on the auditor's report. For instance, if previously issued financial statements and the auditor's report have been recalled and reissued to reflect the correction of a misstatement, the auditor should presume that his or her report on the company's internal control over financial reporting as of same specified date also should be recalled and reissued to reflect the material weakness that existed at that date. Based on these considerations, paragraph .06 of AU sec. 561 provides detailed requirements for the auditor.

For Analysis, see ¶ 113, ¶ 113.3, and ¶ 113.3.11.

200.A.198.XIV.c *Filings Under Federal Securities Statutes.* AU sec. 711, *Filings Under Federal Securities Statutes,* describes the auditor's responsibilities when an auditor's report is included in registration statements, proxy statements, or periodic reports filed under the federal securities statutes. The auditor should also apply AU sec. 711 with respect to the auditor's report on management's assessment of the effectiveness of internal control over financial reporting included in such filings. In addition, the direction in paragraph .10 of AU sec. 711 to inquire of and obtain written representations from officers and other executives responsible for financial and accounting matters about whether any events have occurred that have a material effect on the audited financial statements should be extended to matters that could have a material effect on management's assessment of internal control over financial reporting.

For Analysis, see ¶ 113, ¶ 113.3, and ¶ 113.3.12.

200.A.199.XIV.c When the auditor has fulfilled these responsibilities and intends to consent to the inclusion of his or her report on management's assessment of the effectiveness of internal control over financial reporting in the securities filing, the auditor's consent should clearly indicate that both the audit report on financial statements and the audit report on management's assessment of the effectiveness of internal control over financial reporting (or both opinions if a combined report is issued) are included in his or her consent.

For Analysis, see ¶ 113, ¶ 113.3, and ¶ 113.3.12.

¶ 200.A.XV. *Auditor's Responsibilities for Evaluating Management's Certification Disclosures About Internal Control Over Financial Reporting*

¶ 200.A.XV.a. Required Management Certifications

200.A.200.XV.a Section 302 of the Act, and Securities Exchange Act Rule 13a-14(a) or 15d-14(a), whichever applies,[25] requires a company's management, with the participation of the principal executive and financial officers (the certifying officers), to make the following quarterly and annual certifications with respect to the company's internal control over financial reporting:

---

25. See 17 C.F.R., 240.13a-14a or 15d-14a, whichever applies.

- A statement that the certifying officers are responsible for establishing and maintaining internal control over financial reporting;

- A statement that the certifying officers have designed such internal control over financial reporting, or caused such internal control over financial reporting to be designed under their supervision, to provide reasonable assurance regarding the reliability of financial reporting and the preparation of financial statements for external purposes in accordance with generally accepted accounting principles; and

- A statement that the report discloses any changes in the company's internal control over financial reporting that occurred during the most recent fiscal quarter (the company's fourth fiscal quarter in the case of an annual report) that have materially affected, or are reasonably likely to materially affect, the company's internal control over financial reporting.

For Analysis, see ¶ 114 and ¶ 114.1.

200.A.201.XV.a When the reason for a change in internal control over financial reporting is the correction of a material weakness, management has a responsibility to determine and the auditor should evaluate whether the reason for the change and the circumstances surrounding that change are material information necessary to make the disclosure about the change not misleading.[26]

For Analysis, see ¶ 114 and ¶ 114.1.

¶ 200.A.XV.b. Auditor Evaluation Responsibilities

200.A.202.XV.b The auditor's responsibility as it relates to management's quarterly certifications on internal control over financial reporting is different from the auditor's responsibility as it relates to management's annual assessment of internal control over financial reporting. The auditor should perform limited procedures quarterly to provide a basis for determining whether he or she has become aware of any material modifications that, in the auditor's judgment, should be made to the disclosures about changes in internal control over financial reporting in order for the certifications to be accurate and to comply with the requirements of Section 302 of the Act.

For Analysis, see ¶ 114 and ¶ 114.2.

200.A.203.XV.b To fulfill this responsibility, the auditor should perform, on a quarterly basis, the following procedures:

- Inquire of management about significant changes in the design or operation of internal control over financial reporting as it relates to the preparation of annual as well as interim financial information that could have occurred subsequent to the preceding annual audit or prior review of interim financial information;

---

26. See Securities Exchange Act Rule 12b-20, 17 C.F.R. 240.12b-20.

- Evaluate the implications of misstatements identified by the auditor as part of the auditor's required review of interim financial information (See AU sec. 722, *Interim Financial Information*) as it relates to effective internal control over financial reporting; and

- Determine, through a combination of observation and inquiry, whether any change in internal control over financial reporting has materially affected, or is reasonably likely to materially affect, the company's internal control over financial reporting.

Note: Foreign private issuers filing Forms 20-F and 40-F are not subject to quarterly reporting requirements, therefore, the auditor's responsibilities would extend only to the certifications in the annual report of these companies.

For Analysis, see ¶ 114 and ¶ 114.2.

200.A.204.XV.b When matters come to auditor's attention that lead him or her to believe that modification to the disclosures about changes in internal control over financial reporting is necessary for the certifications to be accurate and to comply with the requirements of Section 302 of the Act and Securities Exchange Act Rule 13a-14(a) or 15d-14(a), whichever applies,[27] the auditor should communicate the matter(s) to the appropriate level of management as soon as practicable.

For Analysis, see ¶ 114 and ¶ 114.2.

200.A.205.XV.b If, in the auditor's judgment, management does not respond appropriately to the auditor's communication within a reasonable period of time, the auditor should inform the audit committee. If, in the auditor's judgment, the audit committee does not respond appropriately to the auditor's communication within a reasonable period of time, the auditor should evaluate whether to resign from the engagement. The auditor should evaluate whether to consult with his or her attorney when making these evaluations. In these circumstances, the auditor also has responsibilities under AU sec. 317, *Illegal Acts by Clients,* and Section 10A of the Securities Exchange Act of 1934.[28] The auditor's responsibilities for evaluating the disclosures about changes in internal control over financial reporting do not diminish in any way management's responsibility for ensuring that its certifications comply with the requirements of Section 302 of the Act and Securities Exchange Act Rule 13a-14(a) or 15d-14(a), whichever applies.[29]

For Analysis, see ¶ 114 and ¶ 114.2.

200.A.206.XV.b If matters come to the auditor's attention as a result of the audit of internal control over financial reporting that lead him or her to believe that modifications to the disclosures about changes in internal control over fi-

---

27. See 17 C.F.R. 240.13a-14(a) or 17 C.F.R. 240.15d-14(a), whichever applies.
28. See 15 U.S.C. 78j-1.
29. See 17 C.F.R. 240.13a-14(a) or 17 C.F.R. 240.15d-14(a), whichever applies.

---

nancial reporting (addressing changes in internal control over financial reporting occurring during the fourth quarter) are necessary for the annual certifications to be accurate and to comply with the requirements of Section 302 of the Act and Securities Exchange Act Rule 13a-14(a) or 15d-14(a), whichever applies,[30] the auditor should follow the same communication responsibilities as described in paragraphs 204 and 205. However, if management and the audit committee do not respond appropriately, in addition to the responsibilities described in the preceding two paragraphs, the auditor should modify his or her report on the audit of internal control over financial reporting to include an explanatory paragraph describing the reasons the auditor believes management's disclosures should be modified.

For Analysis, see ¶ 114 and ¶ 114.2.

¶ 200.A.XVI. *Required Communications in An Audit of Internal Control Over Financial Reporting*

200.A.207.XVI The auditor must communicate in writing to management and the audit committee all significant deficiencies and material weaknesses identified during the audit. The written communication should be made prior to the issuance of the auditor's report on internal control over financial reporting. The auditor's communication should distinguish clearly between those matters considered to be significant deficiencies and those considered to be material weaknesses, as defined in paragraphs 9 and 10, respectively.

For Analysis, see ¶ 102 and ¶ 115.

200.A.208.XVI If a significant deficiency or material weakness exists because the oversight of the company's external financial reporting and internal control over financial reporting by the company's audit committee is ineffective, the auditor must communicate that specific significant deficiency or material weakness in writing to the board of directors.

For Analysis, see ¶ 115.

200.A.209.XVI In addition, the auditor should communicate to management, in writing, all deficiencies in internal control over financial reporting (that is, those deficiencies in internal control over financial reporting that are of a lesser magnitude than significant deficiencies) identified during the audit and inform the audit committee when such a communication has been made. When making this communication, it is not necessary for the auditor to repeat information about such deficiencies that have been included in previously issued written communications, whether those communications were made by the auditor, internal auditors, or others within the organization. Furthermore, the auditor is not required to perform procedures sufficient to identify all control deficiencies; rather, the auditor should communicate deficiencies in internal control over financial reporting of which he or she is aware.

---

30. See 17 C.F.R. 240.13a-14(a) or 17 C.F.R. 240.15d-14(a), whichever applies.

Note: As part of his or her evaluation of the effectiveness of internal control over financial reporting, the auditor should determine whether control deficiencies identified by internal auditors and others within the company, for example, through ongoing monitoring activities and the annual assessment of internal control over financial reporting, are reported to appropriate levels of management in a timely manner. The lack of an internal process to report deficiencies in internal control to management on a timely basis represents a control deficiency that the auditor should evaluate as to severity.

For Analysis, see ¶ 115.

200.A.210.XVI These written communications should state that the communication is intended solely for the information and use of the board of directors, audit committee, management, and others within the organization. When there are requirements established by governmental authorities to furnish such reports, specific reference to such regulatory agencies may be made.

For Analysis, see ¶ 115.

200.A.211.XVI These written communications also should include the definitions of control deficiencies, significant deficiencies, and material weaknesses and should clearly distinguish to which category the deficiencies being communicated relate.

For Analysis, see ¶ 115.

200.A.212.XVI Because of the potential for misinterpretation of the limited degree of assurance associated with the auditor issuing a written report representing that no significant deficiencies were noted during an audit of internal control over financial reporting, the auditor should not issue such representations.

For Analysis, see ¶ 115.

200.A.213.XVI When auditing internal control over financial reporting, the auditor may become aware of fraud or possible illegal acts. If the matter involves fraud, it must be brought to the attention of the appropriate level of management. If the fraud involves senior management, the auditor must communicate the matter directly to the audit committee as described in AU sec. 316, *Consideration of Fraud in a Financial Statement Audit.* If the matter involves possible illegal acts, the auditor must assure himself or herself that the audit committee is adequately informed, unless the matter is clearly inconsequential, in accordance with AU sec. 317, *Illegal Acts by Clients.* The auditor also must determine his or her responsibilities under Section 10A of the Securities Exchange Act of 1934.[31]

For Analysis, see ¶ 115.

---

31. See 15 U.S.C. 78j-1.

200.A.214.XVI When timely communication is important, the auditor should communicate the preceding matters during the course of the audit rather than at the end of the engagement. The decision about whether to issue an interim communication should be determined based on the relative significance of the matters noted and the urgency of corrective follow-up action required.

For Analysis, see ¶ 115.

¶ 200.A.XVII. *Effective Date*

200.A.215.XVII Companies considered accelerated filers under Securities Exchange Act Rule 12b-2[32] are required to comply with the internal control reporting and disclosure requirements of Section 404 of the Act *for fiscal years ending on or after November 15, 2004.* (Other companies have until fiscal years ending on or after July 15, 2005, to comply with these internal control reporting and disclosure requirements.) Accordingly, independent auditors engaged to audit the financial statements of accelerated filers for fiscal years ending on or after November 15, 2004, also are required to audit and report on the company's internal control over financial reporting as of the end of such fiscal year. This standard is required to be complied with for such engagements, except as it relates to the auditor's responsibilities for evaluating management's certification disclosures about internal control over financial reporting. The auditor's responsibilities for evaluating management's certification disclosures about internal control over financial reporting described in paragraphs 202 through 206 take effect beginning with the first quarter after the auditor's first audit report on the company's internal control over financial reporting.

For Analysis, see ¶ 114.2 and ¶ 116.

200.A.216.XVII Early compliance with this standard is permitted.

For Analysis, see ¶ 116.

¶ 201. *APPENDIX A—Illustrative Reports on Internal Control Over Financial Reporting*

201.A1 Paragraphs 167 through 199 of this standard provide direction on the auditor's report on management's assessment of internal control over financial reporting. The following examples illustrate how to apply that direction in several different situations.

* * *

For Analysis of Appendix A, see ¶ 102, ¶ 113.3, and ¶ 117.

---

32.   See 17 C.F.R. 240.12b-2.

Example A-1

ILLUSTRATIVE REPORT EXPRESSING AN UNQUALIFIED OPINION ON MANAGEMENT'S ASSESSMENT OF THE EFFECTIVENESS OF INTERNAL CONTROL OVER FINANCIAL REPORTING AND AN UNQUALIFIED OPINION ON THE EFFECTIVENESS OF INTERNAL CONTROL OVER FINANCIAL REPORTING (SEPARATE REPORT)[1]

Report of Independent Registered Public Accounting Firm

[Introductory paragraph]

We have audited management's assessment, included in the accompanying *[title of management's report]*, that W Company maintained effective internal control over financial reporting as of December 31, 20X3, based on *[Identify control criteria, for example, "criteria established in Internal Control—Integrated Framework issued by the Committee of Sponsoring Organizations of the Treadway Commission (COSO)."]*. W Company's management is responsible for maintaining effective internal control over financial reporting and for its assessment of the effectiveness of internal control over financial reporting. Our responsibility is to express an opinion on management's assessment and an opinion on the effectiveness of the company's internal control over financial reporting based on our audit.

[Scope paragraph]

We conducted our audit in accordance with the standards of the Public Company Accounting Oversight Board (United States). Those standards require that we plan and perform the audit to obtain reasonable assurance about whether effective internal control over financial reporting was maintained in all material respects. Our audit included obtaining an understanding of internal control over financial reporting, evaluating management's assessment, testing and evaluating the design and operating effectiveness of internal control, and performing such other procedures as we considered necessary in the circumstances. We believe that our audit provides a reasonable basis for our opinion.

[Definition paragraph]

A company's internal control over financial reporting is a process designed to provide reasonable assurance regarding the reliability of financial reporting and the preparation of financial statements for external purposes in accordance with generally accepted accounting principles. A company's internal control over financial reporting includes those policies and procedures that (1) pertain to the maintenance of records that, in reasonable detail, accurately and fairly reflect the transactions and dispositions of the assets of the company; (2) provide reasonable assurance that transactions are recorded as necessary to permit prepa-

---

1. If the auditor issues separate reports on the audit of internal control over financial reporting and the audit of the financial statements, both reports should include a statement that the audit was conducted in accordance with standards of the Public Company Accounting Oversight Board (United States).

ration of financial statements in accordance with generally accepted accounting principles, and that receipts and expenditures of the company are being made only in accordance with authorizations of management and directors of the company; and (3) provide reasonable assurance regarding prevention or timely detection of unauthorized acquisition, use, or disposition of the company's assets that could have a material effect on the financial statements.

[*Inherent limitations paragraph*]

Because of its inherent limitations, internal control over financial reporting may not prevent or detect misstatements. Also, projections of any evaluation of effectiveness to future periods are subject to the risk that controls may become inadequate because of changes in conditions, or that the degree of compliance with the policies or procedures may deteriorate.

[*Opinion paragraph*]

In our opinion, management's assessment that W Company maintained effective internal control over financial reporting as of December 31, 20X3, is fairly stated, in all material respects, based on [*Identify control criteria, for example, "criteria established in Internal Control—Integrated Framework issued by the Committee of Sponsoring Organizations of the Treadway Commission (COSO)."*]. Also in our opinion, W Company maintained, in all material respects, effective internal control over financial reporting as of December 31, 20X3, based on [*Identify control criteria, for example, "criteria established in Internal Control—Integrated Framework issued by the Committee of Sponsoring Organizations of the Treadway Commission (COSO)."*].

[*Explanatory paragraph*]

We have also audited, in accordance with the standards of the Public Company Accounting Oversight Board (United States), the [*identify financial statements*] of W Company and our report dated [*date of report, which should be the same as the date of the report on the effectiveness of internal control over financial reporting*] expressed [*include nature of opinion*].

[*Signature*]

[*City and State or Country*]

[*Date*]

Example A-2

ILLUSTRATIVE REPORT EXPRESSING AN UNQUALIFIED OPINION ON MANAGEMENT'S ASSESSMENT OF THE EFFECTIVENESS OF INTERNAL CONTROL OVER FINANCIAL REPORTING AND AN ADVERSE OPINION ON THE EFFECTIVENESS OF INTERNAL CONTROL OVER FINANCIAL REPORTING BECAUSE OF THE EXISTENCE OF A MATERIAL WEAKNESS

Report of Independent Registered Public Accounting Firm

[*Introductory paragraph*]

We have audited management's assessment, included in the accompanying [*title of management's report*], that W Company did not maintain effective internal control over financial reporting as of December 31, 20X3, because of the effect of [*material weakness identified in management's assessment*], based on [*Identify criteria, for example, "criteria established in Internal Control—Integrated Framework issued by the Committee of Sponsoring Organizations of the Treadway Commission (COSO)."*]. W Company's management is responsible for maintaining effective internal control over financial reporting and for its assessment of the effectiveness of internal control over financial reporting. Our responsibility is to express an opinion on management's assessment and an opinion on the effectiveness of the company's internal control over financial reporting based on our audit.

[*Scope paragraph*]

We conducted our audit in accordance with the standards of the Public Company Accounting Oversight Board (United States). Those standards require that we plan and perform the audit to obtain reasonable assurance about whether effective internal control over financial reporting was maintained in all material respects. Our audit included obtaining an understanding of internal control over financial reporting, evaluating management's assessment, testing and evaluating the design and operating effectiveness of internal control, and performing such other procedures as we considered necessary in the circumstances. We believe that our audit provides a reasonable basis for our opinion.

[*Definition paragraph*]

A company's internal control over financial reporting is a process designed to provide reasonable assurance regarding the reliability of financial reporting and the preparation of financial statements for external purposes in accordance with generally accepted accounting principles. A company's internal control over financial reporting includes those policies and procedures that (1) pertain to the maintenance of records that, in reasonable detail, accurately and fairly reflect the transactions and dispositions of the assets of the company; (2) provide reasonable assurance that transactions are recorded as necessary to permit preparation of financial statements in accordance with generally accepted accounting principles, and that receipts and expenditures of the company are being made only in accordance with authorizations of management and directors of the company; and (3) provide reasonable assurance regarding prevention or timely detection of unauthorized acquisition, use, or disposition of the company's assets that could have a material effect on the financial statements.

[Inherent limitations paragraph]

Because of its inherent limitations, internal control over financial reporting may not prevent or detect misstatements. Also, projections of any evaluation of effectiveness to future periods are subject to the risk that controls may become inadequate because of changes in conditions, or that the degree of compliance with the policies or procedures may deteriorate.

[Explanatory paragraph]

A material weakness is a control deficiency, or combination of control deficiencies, that results in more than a remote likelihood that a material misstatement of the annual or interim financial statements will not be prevented or detected. The following material weakness has been identified and included in management's assessment. [*Include a description of the material weakness and its effect on the achievement of the objectives of the control criteria.*] This material weakness was considered in determining the nature, timing, and extent of audit tests applied in our audit of the 20X3 financial statements, and this report does not affect our report dated [*date of report, which should be the same as the date of this report on internal control*] on those financial statements.[1]

[Opinion paragraph]

In our opinion, management's assessment that W Company did not maintain effective internal control over financial reporting as of December 31, 20X3, is fairly stated, in all material respects, based on [*Identify control criteria, for example, "criteria established in Internal Control—Integrated Framework issued by the Committee of Sponsoring Organizations of the Treadway Commission (COSO)."*]. Also, in our opinion, because of the effect of the material weakness described above on the achievement of the objectives of the control criteria, W Company has not maintained effective internal control over financial reporting as of December 31, 20X3, based on [*Identify control criteria, for example, "criteria established in Internal Control—Integrated Framework issued by the Committee of Sponsoring Organizations of the Treadway Commission (COSO)."*].

[Signature]

[City and State or Country]

[Date]

---

1. Modify this sentence when the auditor's opinion on the financial statements is affected by the adverse opinion on the effectiveness of internal control over financial reporting, as described in paragraph 196.

Example A-3

ILLUSTRATIVE REPORT EXPRESSING A QUALIFIED OPINION ON MANAGEMENT'S ASSESSMENT OF THE EFFECTIVENESS OF INTERNAL CONTROL OVER FINANCIAL REPORTING AND A QUALIFIED OPINION ON THE EFFECTIVENESS OF INTERNAL CONTROL OVER FINANCIAL REPORTING BECAUSE OF A LIMITATION ON THE SCOPE OF THE AUDIT

Report of Independent Registered Public Accounting Firm

[*Introductory paragraph*]

We have audited management's assessment, included in the accompanying [*title of management's report*], that W Company maintained effective internal control over financial reporting as of December 31, 20X3, based on [*Identify control criteria, for example, "criteria established in Internal Control—Integrated Framework issued by the Committee of Sponsoring Organizations of the Treadway Commission (COSO)."*]. W Company's management is responsible for maintaining effective internal control over financial reporting and for its assessment of the effectiveness of internal control over financial reporting. Our responsibility is to express an opinion on management's assessment and an opinion on the effectiveness of the company's internal control over financial reporting based on our audit.

[*Scope paragraph*]

Except as described below, we conducted our audit in accordance the standards of the Public Company Accounting Oversight Board (United States). Those standards require that we plan and perform the audit to obtain reasonable assurance about whether effective internal control over financial reporting was maintained in all material respects. Our audit included obtaining an understanding of internal control over financial reporting, evaluating management's assessment, testing and evaluating the design and operating effectiveness of internal control, and performing such other procedures as we considered necessary in the circumstances. We believe that our audit provides a reasonable basis for our opinion.

[*Explanatory paragraph that describes scope limitation*]

A material weakness is a control deficiency, or combination of control deficiencies, that results in more than a remote likelihood that a material misstatement of the annual or interim financial statements will not be prevented or detected. The following material weakness has been identified and included in management's assessment.[1] Prior to December 20, 20X3, W Company had an inadequate system for recording cash receipts, which could have prevented the Company from recording cash receipts on accounts receivable completely and

---

1. If the auditor has identified a material weakness that is not included in management's assessment, add the following wording to the report: "In addition, we have identified the following material weakness that has not been identified as a material weakness in management's assessment."

properly. Therefore, cash received could have been diverted for unauthorized use, lost, or otherwise not properly recorded to accounts receivable. We believe this condition was a material weakness in the design or operation of the internal control of W Company in effect prior to December 20, 20X3. Although the Company implemented a new cash receipts system on December 20, 20X3, the system has not been in operation for a sufficient period of time to enable us to obtain sufficient evidence about its operating effectiveness.

[*Definition paragraph*]

A company's internal control over financial reporting is a process designed to provide reasonable assurance regarding the reliability of financial reporting and the preparation of financial statements for external purposes in accordance with generally accepted accounting principles. A company's internal control over financial reporting includes those policies and procedures that (1) pertain to the maintenance of records that, in reasonable detail, accurately and fairly reflect the transactions and dispositions of the assets of the company; (2) provide reasonable assurance that transactions are recorded as necessary to permit preparation of financial statements in accordance with generally accepted accounting principles, and that receipts and expenditures of the company are being made only in accordance with authorizations of management and directors of the company; and (3) provide reasonable assurance regarding prevention or timely detection of unauthorized acquisition, use, or disposition of the company's assets that could have a material effect on the financial statements.

[*Inherent limitations paragraph*]

Because of its inherent limitations, internal control over financial reporting may not prevent or detect misstatements. Also, projections of any evaluation of effectiveness to future periods are subject to the risk that controls may become inadequate because of changes in conditions, or that the degree of compliance with the policies or procedures may deteriorate.

[*Opinion paragraph*]

In our opinion, except for the effect of matters we might have discovered had we been able to examine evidence about the effectiveness of the new cash receipts system, management's assessment that W Company maintained effective internal control over financial reporting as of December 31, 20X3, is fairly stated, in all material respects, based on [*Identify control criteria, for example, "criteria established in Internal Control—Integrated Framework issued by the Committee of Sponsoring Organizations of the Treadway Commission (COSO)."*]. Also, in our opinion, except for the effect of matters we might have discovered had we been able to examine evidence about the effectiveness of the new cash receipts system, W Company maintained, in all material respects, effective internal control over financial reporting as of December 31, 20X3, based on [*Identify control criteria, for example, "criteria established in Internal Con-*

trol—Integrated Framework issued by the Committee of Sponsoring Organizations of the Treadway Commission (COSO)."].

[*Explanatory paragraph*]

We have also audited, in accordance with the standards of the Public Company Accounting Oversight Board (United States), the [*identify financial statements*] of W Company and our report dated [*date of report, which should be the same as the date of the report on the effectiveness of internal control over financial reporting*] expressed [*include nature of opinion*].

[*Signature*]

[*City and State or Country*]

[*Date*]

Example A-4

ILLUSTRATIVE REPORT DISCLAIMING AN OPINION ON MANAGEMENT'S ASSESSMENT OF THE EFFECTIVENESS OF INTERNAL CONTROL OVER FINANCIAL REPORTING AND DISCLAIMING AN OPINION ON THE EFFECTIVENESS OF INTERNAL CONTROL OVER FINANCIAL REPORTING BECAUSE OF A LIMITATION ON THE SCOPE OF THE AUDIT

Report of Independent Registered Public Accounting Firm

[*Introductory paragraph*]

We were engaged to audit management's assessment included in the accompanying [*title of management's report*] that W Company maintained effective internal control over financial reporting as of December 31, 20X3 based on [*Identify control criteria, for example, "criteria established in Internal Control— Integrated Framework issued by the Committee of Sponsoring Organizations of the Treadway Commission (COSO)."*]. W Company's management is responsible for maintaining effective internal control over financial reporting and for its assessment of the effectiveness of internal control over financial reporting.

[*Omit scope paragraph*]

[*Explanatory paragraph that describes scope limitation*][1]

[*Definition paragraph*]

A company's internal control over financial reporting is a process designed to provide reasonable assurance regarding the reliability of financial reporting and the preparation of financial statements for external purposes in accordance with generally accepted accounting principles. A company's internal control over financial reporting includes those policies and procedures that (1) pertain

---

1. If, through the limited procedures performed, the auditor concludes that a material weakness exists, the auditor should add the definition of material weakness (as provided in paragraph 10) to the explanatory paragraph. In addition, the auditor should include a description of the material weakness and its effect on the achievement of the objectives of the control criteria.

to the maintenance of records that, in reasonable detail, accurately and fairly reflect the transactions and dispositions of the assets of the company; (2) provide reasonable assurance that transactions are recorded as necessary to permit preparation of financial statements in accordance with generally accepted accounting principles, and that receipts and expenditures of the company are being made only in accordance with authorizations of management and directors of the company; and (3) provide reasonable assurance regarding prevention or timely detection of unauthorized acquisition, use, or disposition of the company's assets that could have a material effect on the financial statements.

[Inherent limitations paragraph]

Because of its inherent limitations, internal control over financial reporting may not prevent or detect misstatements. Also, projections of any evaluation of effectiveness to future periods are subject to the risk that controls may become inadequate because of changes in conditions, or that the degree of compliance with the policies or procedures may deteriorate.

[Opinion paragraph]

Since management *[describe scope restrictions]* and we were unable to apply other procedures to satisfy ourselves as to the effectiveness of the company's internal control over financial reporting, the scope of our work was not sufficient to enable us to express, and we do not express, an opinion either on management's assessment or on the effectiveness of the company's internal control over financial reporting.

[Explanatory paragraph]

We have also audited, in accordance with the standards of the Public Company Accounting Oversight Board (United States), the *[identify financial statements]* of W Company and our report dated *[date of report, which should be the same as the date of the report on the effectiveness of internal control over financial reporting]* expressed *[include nature of opinion]*.

[Signature]

[City and State or Country]

[Date]

Example A-5

ILLUSTRATIVE REPORT EXPRESSING AN UNQUALIFIED OPINION ON MANAGEMENT'S ASSESSMENT OF THE EFFECTIVENESS OF INTERNAL CONTROL OVER FINANCIAL REPORTING THAT REFERS TO THE REPORT OF OTHER AUDITORS AS A BASIS, IN PART, FOR THE AUDITOR'S OPINION AND AN UNQUALIFIED OPINION ON THE EFFECTIVENESS OF INTERNAL CONTROL OVER FINANCIAL REPORTING

Report of Independent Registered Public Accounting Firm

[Introductory paragraph]

We have audited management's assessment, included in the accompanying *[title of management's report]*, that W Company maintained effective internal control over financial reporting as of December 31, 20X3, based on *[Identify control criteria, for example, "criteria established in Internal Control—Integrated Framework issued by the Committee of Sponsoring Organizations of the Treadway Commission (COSO)."]*. W Company's management is responsible for maintaining effective internal control over financial reporting and for its assessment of the effectiveness of internal control over financial reporting. Our responsibility is to express an opinion on management's assessment and an opinion on the effectiveness of the company's internal control over financial reporting based on our audit. We did not examine the effectiveness of internal control over financial reporting of B Company, a wholly owned subsidiary, whose financial statements reflect total assets and revenues constituting 20 and 30 percent, respectively, of the related consolidated financial statement amounts as of and for the year ended December 31, 20X3. The effectiveness of B Company's internal control over financial reporting was audited by other auditors whose report has been furnished to us, and our opinion, insofar as it relates to the effectiveness of B Company's internal control over financial reporting, is based solely on the report of the other auditors.

[Scope paragraph]

We conducted our audit in accordance with the standards of the Public Company Accounting Oversight Board (United States). Those standards require that we plan and perform the audit to obtain reasonable assurance about whether effective internal control over financial reporting was maintained in all material respects. Our audit included obtaining an understanding of internal control over financial reporting, evaluating management's assessment, testing and evaluating the design and operating effectiveness of internal control, and performing such other procedures as we considered necessary in the circumstances. We believe that our audit and the report of the other auditors provide a reasonable basis for our opinion.

[*Definition paragraph*]

A company's internal control over financial reporting is a process designed to provide reasonable assurance regarding the reliability of financial reporting and the preparation of financial statements for external purposes in accordance with generally accepted accounting principles. A company's internal control over financial reporting includes those policies and procedures that (1) pertain to the maintenance of records that, in reasonable detail, accurately and fairly reflect the transactions and dispositions of the assets of the company; (2) provide reasonable assurance that transactions are recorded as necessary to permit preparation of financial statements in accordance with generally accepted accounting principles, and that receipts and expenditures of the company are being made only in accordance with authorizations of management and directors of the company; and (3) provide reasonable assurance regarding prevention or timely detection of unauthorized acquisition, use, or disposition of the company's assets that could have a material effect on the financial statements.

[*Inherent limitations paragraph*]

Because of its inherent limitations, internal control over financial reporting may not prevent or detect misstatements. Also, projections of any evaluation of effectiveness to future periods are subject to the risk that controls may become inadequate because of changes in conditions, or that the degree of compliance with the policies or procedures may deteriorate.

[*Opinion paragraph*]

In our opinion, based on our audit and the report of the other auditors, management's assessment that W Company maintained effective internal control over financial reporting as of December 31, 20X3, is fairly stated, in all material respects, based on [*Identify control criteria, for example, "criteria established in Internal Control—Integrated Framework issued by the Committee of Sponsoring Organizations of the Treadway Commission (COSO)."*]. Also, in our opinion, based on our audit and the report of the other auditors, W Company maintained, in all material respects, effective internal control over financial reporting as of December 31, 20X3, based on [*Identify control criteria, for example, "criteria established in Internal Control—Integrated Framework issued by the Committee of Sponsoring Organizations of the Treadway Commission (COSO)."*].

[*Explanatory paragraph*]

We have also audited, in accordance with the standards of the Public Company Accounting Oversight Board (United States), the [*identify financial statements*] of W Company and our report dated [*date of report, which should be the same as the date of the report on the effectiveness of internal control over financial reporting]* expressed *[include nature of opinion]*.

[Signature]

[City and State or Country]

[Date]

Example A-6

ILLUSTRATIVE REPORT EXPRESSING AN ADVERSE OPINION ON MANAGEMENT'S ASSESSMENT OF THE EFFECTIVENESS OF INTERNAL CONTROL OVER FINANCIAL REPORTING AND AN ADVERSE OPINION ON THE EFFECTIVENESS OF INTERNAL CONTROL OVER FINANCIAL REPORTING BECAUSE OF THE EXISTENCE OF A MATERIAL WEAKNESS

Report of Independent Registered Public Accounting Firm

[Introductory paragraph]

We have audited management's assessment, included in the accompanying *[title of management's report]*, that W Company maintained effective internal control over financial reporting as of December 31, 20X3, based on *[Identify control criteria, for example, "criteria established in Internal Control—Integrated Framework issued by the Committee of Sponsoring Organizations of the Treadway Commission (COSO)."]*. W Company's management is responsible for maintaining effective internal control over financial reporting and for its assessment of the effectiveness of internal control over financial reporting. Our responsibility is to express an opinion on management's assessment and an opinion on the effectiveness of the company's internal control over financial reporting based on our audit.

[Scope paragraph]

We conducted our audit in accordance with the standards of the Public Company Accounting Oversight Board (United States). Those standards require that we plan and perform the audit to obtain reasonable assurance about whether effective internal control over financial reporting was maintained in all material respects. Our audit included obtaining an understanding of internal control over financial reporting, evaluating management's assessment, testing and evaluating the design and operating effectiveness of internal control, and performing such other procedures as we considered necessary in the circumstances. We believe that our audit provides a reasonable basis for our opinion.

[Definition paragraph]

A company's internal control over financial reporting is a process designed to provide reasonable assurance regarding the reliability of financial reporting and the preparation of financial statements for external purposes in accordance with generally accepted accounting principles. A company's internal control over financial reporting includes those policies and procedures that (1) pertain to the maintenance of records that, in reasonable detail, accurately and fairly reflect the transactions and dispositions of the assets of the company; (2) provide reasonable assurance that transactions are recorded as necessary to permit preparation of financial statements in accordance with generally accepted accounting principles, and that receipts and expenditures of the company are being made only in accordance with authorizations of management and directors of the company; and (3) provide reasonable assurance regarding prevention or timely detection of unauthorized acquisition, use, or disposition of the company's assets that could have a material effect on the financial statements.

[Inherent limitations paragraph]

Because of its inherent limitations, internal control over financial reporting may not prevent or detect misstatements. Also, projections of any evaluation of effectiveness to future periods are subject to the risk that controls may become inadequate because of changes in conditions, or that the degree of compliance with the policies or procedures may deteriorate.

[Explanatory paragraph]

A material weakness is a control deficiency, or combination of control deficiencies, that results in more than a remote likelihood that a material misstatement of the annual or interim financial statements will not be prevented or detected. We have identified the following material weakness that has not been identified as a material weakness in management's assessment [*Include a description of the material weakness and its effect on the achievement of the objectives of the control criteria.*] This material weakness was considered in determining the nature, timing, and extent of audit tests applied in our audit of the 20X3 financial statements, and this report does not affect our report dated [*date of report, which should be the same as the date of this report on internal control*] on those financial statements.[1]

[Opinion paragraph]

In our opinion, because of the effect of the material weakness described above on the achievement of the objectives of the control criteria, management's assessment that W Company maintained effective internal control over financial reporting as of December 31, 20X3, is not fairly stated, in all material respects, based on [*Identify control criteria, for example, "criteria established in Internal Control—Integrated Framework issued by the Committee of Sponsoring Organizations of the Treadway Commission (COSO)."*]. Also, in our opinion, because of the effect of the material weakness described above on the achievement of the objectives of the control criteria, W Company has not maintained effective internal control over financial reporting as of December 31,

---

1. Modify this sentence when the auditor's opinion on the financial statements is affected by the adverse opinion on the effectiveness of internal control over financial reporting.

20X3, based on [*Identify control criteria, for example, "criteria established in Internal Control—Integrated Framework issued by the Committee of Sponsoring Organizations of the Treadway Commission (COSO)."*].

[*Signature*]

[*City and State or Country*]

[*Date*]

Example A-7

ILLUSTRATIVE COMBINED REPORT EXPRESSING AN UN-QUALIFIED OPINION ON FINANCIAL STATEMENTS, AN UNQUALI-FIED OPINION ON MANAGEMENT'S ASSESSMENT OF THE EFFEC-TIVENESS OF INTERNAL CONTROL OVER FINANCIAL REPORTING AND AN UNQUALIFIED OPINION ON THE EFFECTIVE-NESS OF INTERNAL CONTROL OVER FINANCIAL REPORTING

Report of Independent Registered Public Accounting Firm

[*Introductory paragraph*]

We have audited the accompanying balance sheets of W Company as of December 31, 20X3 and 20X2, and the related statements of income, stockholders' equity and comprehensive income, and cash flows for each of the years in the three-year period ended December 31, 20X3. We also have audited management's assessment, included in the accompanying [*title of management's report*], that W Company maintained effective internal control over financial reporting as of December 31, 20X3, based on [*Identify control criteria, for example, "criteria established in Internal Control—Integrated Framework issued by the Committee of Sponsoring Organizations of the Treadway Commission (COSO)."*]. W Company's management is responsible for these financial statements, for maintaining effective internal control over financial reporting, and for its assessment of the effectiveness of internal control over financial reporting. Our responsibility is to express an opinion on these financial statements, an opinion on management's assessment, and an opinion on the effectiveness of the company's internal control over financial reporting based on our audits.

[*Scope paragraph*]

We conducted our audits in accordance with the standards of the Public Company Accounting Oversight Board (United States). Those standards require that we plan and perform the audits to obtain reasonable assurance about whether the financial statements are free of material misstatement and whether effective internal control over financial reporting was maintained in all material respects. Our audit of financial statements included examining, on a test basis, evidence supporting the amounts and disclosures in the financial statements, assessing the accounting principles used and significant estimates made by management, and evaluating the overall financial statement presentation. Our audit of internal control over financial reporting included obtaining an understanding of internal control over financial reporting, evaluating management's assessment, testing and evaluating the design and operating effectiveness of internal control, and performing such other procedures as we considered necessary in the circumstances. We believe that our audits provide a reasonable basis for our opinions.

[*Definition paragraph*]

A company's internal control over financial reporting is a process designed to provide reasonable assurance regarding the reliability of financial reporting and the preparation of financial statements for external purposes in accordance with generally accepted accounting principles. A company's internal control over financial reporting includes those policies and procedures that (1) pertain to the maintenance of records that, in reasonable detail, accurately and fairly reflect the transactions and dispositions of the assets of the company; (2) provide reasonable assurance that transactions are recorded as necessary to permit preparation of financial statements in accordance with generally accepted accounting principles, and that receipts and expenditures of the company are being made only in accordance with authorizations of management and directors of the company; and (3) provide reasonable assurance regarding prevention or timely detection of unauthorized acquisition, use, or disposition of the company's assets that could have a material effect on the financial statements.

[*Inherent limitations paragraph*]

Because of its inherent limitations, internal control over financial reporting may not prevent or detect misstatements. Also, projections of any evaluation of effectiveness to future periods are subject to the risk that controls may become inadequate because of changes in conditions, or that the degree of compliance with the policies or procedures may deteriorate.

[*Opinion paragraph*]

In our opinion, the financial statements referred to above present fairly, in all material respects, the financial position of W Company as of December 31, 20X3 and 20X2, and the results of its operations and its cash flows for each of the years in the three-year period ended December 31, 20X3 in conformity with accounting principles generally accepted in the United States of America. Also in our opinion, management's assessment that W Company maintained effective internal control over financial reporting as of December 31, 20X3, is fairly stated, in all material respects, based on [*Identify control criteria, for example, "criteria established in Internal Control—Integrated Framework issued by the Committee of Sponsoring Organizations of the Treadway Commission (COSO)."*]. Furthermore, in our opinion, W Company maintained, in all material respects, effective internal control over financial reporting as of December 31, 20X3, based on [*Identify control criteria, for example, "criteria established in Internal Control—Integrated Framework issued by the Committee of Sponsoring Organizations of the Treadway Commission (COSO)."*].

[*Signature*]

[*City and State or Country*]

[*Date*]

¶ 202. *APPENDIX B—Additional Performance Requirements and Directions; Extent-of-Testing Examples*

For Analysis of Appendix B, see ¶ 109.4.1, ¶ 109.4.8, ¶ 109.5, ¶ 109.6, ¶ 114.2, and ¶ 118.

¶ 202.I. *Tests to be Performed When a Company Has Multiple Locations or Business Units*

202.B1.I To determine the locations or business units for performing audit procedures, the auditor should evaluate their relative financial significance and the risk of material misstatement arising from them. In making this evaluation, the auditor should identify the locations or business units that are individually important, evaluate their documentation of controls, and test controls over significant accounts and disclosures. For locations or business units that contain specific risks that, by themselves, could create a material misstatement, the auditor should evaluate their documentation of controls and test controls over the specific risks.

202.B2.I The auditor should determine the other locations or business units that, when aggregated, represent a group with a level of financial significance that could create a material misstatement in the financial statements. For that group, the auditor should determine whether there are company-level controls in place. If so, the auditor should evaluate the documentation and test such company-level controls. If not, the auditor should perform tests of controls at some of the locations or business units.

202.B3.I No further work is necessary on the remaining locations or businesses, provided that they are not able to create, either individually or in the aggregate, a material misstatement in the financial statements.

¶ 202.I.a. Locations or Business Units That Are Financially Significant

202.B4.I.a Because of the importance of financially significant locations or business units, the auditor should evaluate management's documentation of and perform tests of controls over all relevant assertions related to significant accounts and disclosures at each financially significant location or business unit, as discussed in paragraphs 83 through 105. Generally, a relatively small number of locations or business units will encompass a large portion of a company's operations and financial position, making them financially significant.

202.B5.I.a In determining the nature, timing, and extent of testing at the individual locations or business units, the auditor should evaluate each entity's involvement, if any, with a central processing or shared service environment.

¶ 202.I.b. Locations or Business Units That Involve Specific Risks

202.B6.I.b Although a location or business unit might not be individually financially significant, it might present specific risks that, by themselves, could create a material misstatement in the company's financial statements. The auditor should test the controls over the specific risks that could create a material misstatement in the company's financial statements. The auditor need not test controls over all relevant assertions related to all significant accounts at these locations or business units. For example, a business unit responsible for foreign exchange trading could expose the company to the risk of material misstatement, even though the relative financial significance of such transactions is low.

¶ 202.I.c. Locations or Business Units That Are Significant Only When Aggregated with Other Locations and Business Units

202.B7.I.c In determining the nature, timing, and extent of testing, the auditor should determine whether management has documented and placed in operation companylevel controls (See paragraph 53) over individually unimportant locations and business units that, when aggregated with other locations or business units, might have a high level of financial significance. A high level of financial significance could create a greater than remote risk of material misstatement of the financial statements.

202.B8.I.c For the purposes of this evaluation, company-level controls are controls management has in place to provide assurance that appropriate controls exist throughout the organization, including at individual locations or business units.

202.B9.I.c The auditor should perform tests of company-level controls to determine whether such controls are operating effectively. The auditor might conclude that he or she cannot evaluate the operating effectiveness of such controls without visiting some or all of the locations or business units.

202.B10.I.c If management does not have company-level controls operating at these locations and business units, the auditor should determine the nature, timing, and extent of procedures to be performed at each location, business unit, or combination of locations and business units. When determining the locations or business units to visit and the controls to test, the auditor should evaluate the following factors:

- The relative financial significance of each location or business unit.
- The risk of material misstatement arising from each location or business unit.

- The similarity of business operations and internal control over financial reporting at the various locations or business units.
- The degree of centralization of processes and financial reporting applications.
- The effectiveness of the control environment, particularly management's direct control over the exercise of authority delegated to others and its ability to effectively supervise activities at the various locations or business units. An ineffective control environment over the locations or business units might constitute a material weakness.
- The nature and amount of transactions executed and related assets at the various locations or business units.
- The potential for material unrecognized obligations to exist at a location or business unit and the degree to which the location or business unit could create an obligation on the part of the company.
- Management's risk assessment process and analysis for excluding a location or business unit from its assessment of internal control over financial reporting.

202.B11.I.c Testing company-level controls is not a substitute for the auditor's testing of controls over a large portion of the company's operations or financial position. If the auditor cannot test a large portion of the company's operations and financial position by selecting a relatively small number of locations or business units, he or she should expand the number of locations or business units selected to evaluate internal control over financial reporting.

> **Note:** The evaluation of whether controls over a large portion of the company's operations or financial position have been tested should be made at the overall level, not at the individual significant account level.

¶ 202.I.d. Locations and Business Units That Do Not Require Testing

202.B12.I.d No testing is required for locations or business units that individually, and when aggregated with others, could not result in a material misstatement to the financial statements.

¶ 202.I.e. Multi-Location Testing Considerations Flowchart

202.B13.I.e Illustration B-1 depicts how to apply the directions in this section to a hypothetical company with 150 locations or business units, along with the auditor's testing considerations for those locations or business units.

Illustration B-1

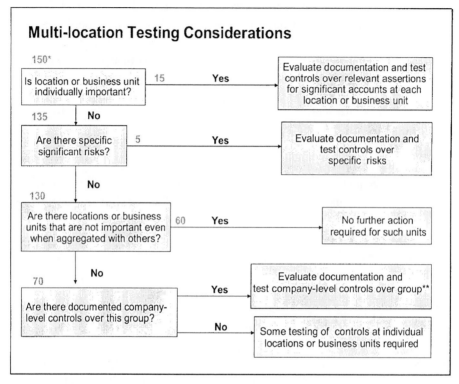

Multi-location Testing Considerations

150*
Is location or business unit individually important? —15— **Yes** → Evaluate documentation and test controls over relevant assertions for significant accounts at each location or business unit

135 **No**
Are there specific significant risks? —5— **Yes** → Evaluate documentation and test controls over specific risks

No
130
Are there locations or business units that are not important even when aggregated with others? —60— **Yes** → No further action required for such units

No
70
Are there documented company-level controls over this group? → **Yes** → Evaluate documentation and test company-level controls over group**

→ **No** → Some testing of controls at individual locations or business units required

* Numbers represent number of locations affected.
** See paragraph B7.

¶ 202.I.f. Special Situations

202.B14.I.f The scope of the evaluation of the company's internal control over financial reporting should include entities that are acquired on or before the date of management's assessment and operations that are accounted for as discontinued operations on the date of management's assessment. The auditor should consider this multiple locations discussion in determining whether it will be necessary to test controls at these entities or operations.

202.B15.I.f For equity method investments, the evaluation of the company's internal control over financial reporting should include controls over the reporting in accordance with generally accepted accounting principles, in the company's financial statements, of the company's portion of the investees' income or loss, the investment balance, adjustments to the income or loss and investment balance, and related disclosures. The evaluation ordinarily would not extend to controls at the equity method investee.

202.B16.I.f In situations in which the SEC allows management to limit its assessment of internal control over financial reporting by excluding certain entities, the auditor may limit the audit in the same manner and report without reference to the limitation in scope. However, the auditor should evaluate the reasonableness of management's conclusion that the situation meets the criteria of the SEC's allowed exclusion and the appropriateness of any required disclosure related to such a limitation. If the auditor believes that management's disclosure about the limitation requires modification, the auditor should follow the same communication responsibilities as described in paragraphs 204 and 205. If management and the audit committee do not respond appropriately, in addition to fulfilling those responsibilities, the auditor should modify his or her report on the audit of internal control over financial reporting to include an explanatory paragraph describing the reasons why the auditor believes management's disclosure should be modified.

202.B17.I.f For example, for entities that are consolidated or proportionately consolidated, the evaluation of the company's internal control over financial reporting should include controls over significant accounts and processes that exist at the consolidated or proportionately consolidated entity. In some instances, however, such as for some variable interest entities as defined in Financial Accounting Standards Board Interpretation No. 46, *Consolidation of Variable Interest Entities,* management might not be able to obtain the information necessary to make an assessment because it does not have the ability to control the entity. If management is allowed to limit its assessment by excluding such entities,[1] the auditor may limit the audit in the same manner and report without reference to the limitation in scope. In this case, the evaluation of the company's internal control over financial reporting should include evaluation of controls over the reporting in accordance with generally accepted accounting principles, in the company's financial statements, of the company's portion of the entity's income or loss, the investment balance, adjustments to the income or loss and investment balances, and related disclosures. However, the auditor should evaluate the reasonableness of management's conclusion that it does not have the ability to obtain the necessary information as well as the appropriateness of any required disclosure related to such a limitation.

¶ 202.II. *Use of Service Organizations*

202.B18.II AU sec. 324, *Service Organizations,* applies to the audit of financial statements of a company that obtains services from another organization that are part of its information system. The auditor may apply the relevant concepts described in AU sec. 324 to the audit of internal control over financial reporting. Further, although AU sec. 324 was designed to address auditor-to-auditor communications as part of the audit of financial statements, it also is

---

1. It is our understanding that the SEC Staff may conclude that management can limit the scope of its assessment if it does not have the authority to affect, and therefore cannot assess, the controls in place over certain amounts. This would relate to entities that are consolidated or proportionately consolidated when the issuer does not have sufficient control over the entity to assess and affect controls. If management's report on its assessment of the effectiveness of internal control over financial reporting is limited in that manner, the SEC staff may permit the company to disclose this fact as well as information about the magnitude of the amounts included in the financial statements from entities whose controls cannot be assessed. This disclosure would be required in each filing, but outside of management's report on its assessment of the effectiveness of internal control over financial reporting.

---

appropriate for management to apply the relevant concepts described in that standard to its assessment of internal control over financial reporting.

202.B19.II Paragraph .03 of AU sec. 324 describes the situation in which a service organization's services are part of a company's information system. If the service organization's services are part of a company's information system, as described therein, then they are part of the information and communication component of the company's internal control over financial reporting. When the service organization's services are part of the company's internal control over financial reporting, management should consider the activities of the service organization in making its assessment of internal control over financial reporting, and the auditor should consider the activities of the service organization in determining the evidence required to support his or her opinion.

> **Note:** The use of a service organization does not reduce management's responsibility to maintain effective internal control over financial reporting.

202.B20.II Paragraphs .07 through .16 in AU sec. 324 describe the procedures that management and the auditor should perform with respect to the activities performed by the service organization. The procedures include:

> a. Obtaining an understanding of the controls at the service organization that are relevant to the entity's internal control and the controls at the user organization over the activities of the service organization, and

> b. Obtaining evidence that the controls that are relevant to management's assessment and the auditor's opinion are operating effectively.

202.B21.II Evidence that the controls that are relevant to management's assessment and the auditor's opinion are operating effectively may be obtained by following the procedures described in paragraph .12 of AU sec. 324. These procedures include:

> a. Performing tests of the user organization's controls over the activities of the service organization (for example, testing the user organization's independent reperformance of selected items processed by the service organization or testing the user organization's reconciliation of output reports with source documents).

> b. Performing tests of controls at the service organization.

> c. Obtaining a service auditor's report on controls placed in operation and tests of operating effectiveness, or a report on the application of agreed-upon procedures that describes relevant tests of controls.

> **Note:** The service auditor's report referred to above means a report with the service auditor's opinion on the service organization's description of the design of its controls, the tests of controls, and results of those tests performed by the service auditor, and the service auditor's opinion on whether the controls tested were operating effectively during the specified period (in other words, "reports on controls placed in operation and tests

of operating effectiveness" described in paragraph .24b of AU sec. 324). A service auditor's report that does not include tests of controls, results of the tests, and the service auditor's opinion on operating effectiveness (in other words, "reports on controls placed in operation" described in paragraph .24a of AU sec. 324) does not provide evidence of operating effectiveness. Furthermore, if the evidence regarding operating effectiveness of controls comes from an agreed-upon procedures report rather than a service auditor's report issued pursuant to AU sec. 324, management and the auditor should evaluate whether the agreed-upon procedures report provides sufficient evidence in the same manner described in the following paragraph.

202.B22.II If a service auditor's report on controls placed in operation and tests of operating effectiveness is available, management and the auditor may evaluate whether this report provides sufficient evidence to support the assessment and opinion, respectively. In evaluating whether such a service auditor's report provides sufficient evidence, management and the auditor should consider the following factors:

- The time period covered by the tests of controls and its relation to the date of management's assessment,
- The scope of the examination and applications covered, the controls tested, and the way in which tested controls relate to the company's controls,
- The results of those tests of controls and the service auditor's opinion on the operating effectiveness of the controls.

Note: These factors are similar to factors the auditor would consider in determining whether the report provides sufficient evidence to support the auditor's assessed level of control risk in an audit of the financial statements as described in paragraph .16 of AU sec. 324.

202.B23.II If the service auditor's report on controls placed in operation and tests of operating effectiveness contains a qualification that the stated control objectives might be achieved only if the company applies controls contemplated in the design of the system by the service organization, the auditor should evaluate whether the company is applying the necessary procedures. For example, completeness of processing payroll transactions might depend on the company's validation that all payroll records sent to the service organization were processed by checking a control total.

202.B24.II In determining whether the service auditor's report provides sufficient evidence to support management's assessment and the auditor's opinion, management and the auditor should make inquiries concerning the service auditor's reputation, competence, and independence. Appropriate sources of information concerning the professional reputation of the service auditor are discussed in paragraph .10a of AU sec. 543, *Part of Audit Performed by Other Independent Auditors.*

202.B25.II When a significant period of time has elapsed between the time period covered by the tests of controls in the service auditor's report and the date of management's assessment, additional procedures should be performed. The auditor should inquire of management to determine whether management has identified any changes in the service organization's controls subsequent to the period covered by the service auditor's report (such as changes communicated to management from the service organization, changes in personnel at the service organization with whom management interacts, changes in reports or other data received from the service organization, changes in contracts or service level agreements with the service organization, or errors identified in the service organization's processing). If management has identified such changes, the auditor should determine whether management has performed procedures to evaluate the effect of such changes on the effectiveness of the company's internal control over financial reporting. The auditor also should consider whether the results of other procedures he or she performed indicate that there have been changes in the controls at the service organization that management has not identified.

202.B26.II The auditor should determine whether to obtain additional evidence about the operating effectiveness of controls at the service organization based on the procedures performed by management or the auditor and the results of those procedures and on an evaluation of the following factors. As these factors increase in significance, the need for the auditor to obtain additional evidence increases.

- The elapsed time between the time period covered by the tests of controls in the service auditor's report and the date of management's assessment,

- The significance of the activities of the service organization,

- Whether there are errors that have been identified in the service organization's processing, and

- The nature and significance of any changes in the service organization's controls identified by management or the auditor.

202.B27.II If the auditor concludes that additional evidence about the operating effectiveness of controls at the service organization is required, the auditor's additional procedures may include:

- Evaluating the procedures performed by management and the results of those procedures.

- Contacting the service organization, through the user organization, to obtain specific information.

- Requesting that a service auditor be engaged to perform procedures that will supply the necessary information.

- Visiting the service organization and performing such procedures.

202.B28.II Based on the evidence obtained, management and the auditor should determine whether they have obtained sufficient evidence to obtain the reasonable assurance necessary for their assessment and opinion, respectively.

202.B29.II The auditor should not refer to the service auditor's report when expressing an opinion on internal control over financial reporting.

¶ 202.III. *Examples of Extent-of-Testing Decisions*

202.B30.III As discussed throughout this standard, determining the effectiveness of a company's internal control over financial reporting includes evaluating the design and operating effectiveness of controls over all relevant assertions related to all significant accounts and disclosures in the financial statements. Paragraphs 88 through 107 provide the auditor with directions about the nature, timing, and extent of testing of the design and operating effectiveness of internal control over financial reporting.

202.B31.III Examples B-1 through B-4 illustrate how to apply this information in various situations. These examples are for illustrative purposes only.

Example B-1 — *Daily Programmed Application Control and Daily Information Technology-Dependent Manual Control*

The auditor has determined that cash and accounts receivable are significant accounts to the audit of XYZ Company's internal control over financial reporting. Based on discussions with company personnel and review of company documentation, the auditor learned that the company had the following procedures in place to account for cash received in the lockbox:

a. The company receives a download of cash receipts from the banks.

b. The information technology system applies cash received in the lockbox to individual customer accounts.

c. Any cash received in the lockbox and not applied to a customer's account is listed on an exception report (Unapplied Cash Exception Report).

- Therefore, the application of cash to a customer's account is a programmed application control, while the review and follow-up of unapplied cash from the exception report is a manual control.

To determine whether misstatements in cash (existence assertion) and accounts receivable (existence, valuation, and completeness) would be prevented or detected on a timely basis, the auditor decided to test the controls provided by the system in the daily reconciliation of lock box receipts to customer accounts, as well as the control over reviewing and resolving unapplied cash in the Unapplied Cash Exception Report.

Nature, Timing, and Extent of Procedures. To test the programmed application control, the auditor:

- Identified, through discussion with company personnel, the software used to receive the download from the banks and to process the transactions and determined that the banks supply the download software.

  —The company uses accounting software acquired from a third-party supplier. The software consists of a number of modules. The client modifies the software only for upgrades supplied by the supplier.

- Determined, through further discussion with company personnel, that the cash module operates the lockbox functionality and the posting of cash to the general ledger. The accounts receivable module posts the cash to individual customer accounts and produces the Unapplied Cash Exception Report, a standard report supplied with the package. The auditor agreed this information to the supplier's documentation.

- Identified, through discussions with company personnel and review of the supplier's documentation, the names, file sizes (in bytes), and locations of the executable files (programs) that operate the functionality under review. The auditor then identified the compilation dates of these programs and agreed them to the original installation date of the application.

- Identified the objectives of the programs to be tested. The auditor wanted to determine whether only appropriate cash items are posted to customers' accounts and matched to customer number, invoice number, amount, etc., and that there is a listing of inappropriate cash items (that is, any of the above items not matching) on the exception report.

In addition, the auditor had evaluated and tested general computer controls, including program changes (for example, confirmation that no unauthorized changes are undertaken) and logical access (for example, data file access to the file downloaded from the banks and user access to the cash and accounts receivable modules) and concluded that they were operating effectively.

To determine whether such programmed controls were operating effectively, the auditor performed a walkthrough in the month of July. The computer controls operate in a systematic manner, therefore, the auditor concluded that it was sufficient to perform a walkthrough for only the one item. During the walkthrough, the auditor performed and documented the following items:

a. Selected one customer and agreed the amount billed to the customer to the cash received in the lockbox.

b. Agreed the total of the lockbox report to the posting of cash receipts in the general ledger.

c. Agreed the total of the cash receipt download from the bank to the lockbox report and supporting documentation.

d. Selected one customer's remittance and agreed amount posted to the customer's account in the accounts receivable subsidiary ledger.

To test the detective control of review and follow up on the Daily Unapplied Cash Exception Report, the auditor:

a. *Made inquiries of company personnel.* To understand the procedures in place to ensure that all unapplied items are resolved, the time frame in which such resolution takes place, and whether unapplied items are handled properly within the system, the auditor discussed these matters with the employee responsible for reviewing and resolving the Daily Unapplied Cash Exception Reports. The auditor learned that, when items appear on the Daily-Unapplied Cash Exception Report, the employee must manually enter the correction into the system. The employee typically performs the resolution procedures the next business day. Items that typically appear on the Daily Unapplied Cash Exception Report relate to payments made by a customer without reference to an invoice number/purchase order number or to underpayments of an invoice due to quantity or pricing discrepancies.

b. *Observed personnel performing the control.* The auditor then observed the employee reviewing and resolving a Daily Unapplied Cash Exception Report. The day selected contained four exceptions three related to payments made by a customer without an invoice number, and one related to an underpayment due to a pricing discrepancy.

- For the pricing discrepancy, the employee determined, through discussions with a sales person, that the customer had been billed an incorrect price; a price break that the sales person had granted to the customer was not reflected on the customer's invoice. The employee resolved the pricing discrepancy, determined which invoices were being paid, and entered a correction into the system to properly apply cash to the customer's account and reduce accounts receivable and sales accounts for the amount of the price break.

c. *Reperformed the control.* Finally, the auditor selected 25 Daily Unapplied Cash Exception Reports from the period January to September. For the reports selected, the auditor reperformed the follow-up procedures that the employee performed. For instance, the auditor inspected the documents and sources of information used in the follow-up and determined that the transaction was properly corrected in the system. The auditor also scanned other Daily Unapplied Cash Exception Reports to determine that the control was performed throughout the period of intended reliance.

Because the tests of controls were performed at an interim date, the auditor had to determine whether there were any significant changes in the controls from interim to year-end. Therefore, the auditor asked company personnel about the procedures in place at year-end. Such procedures had not changed from the interim period, therefore, the auditor observed that the controls were still in place by scanning Daily Unapplied Cash Exception Reports to determine the control was performed on a timely basis during the period from September to year-end.

Based on the auditor's procedures, the auditor concluded that the employee was clearing exceptions in a timely manner and that the control was operating effectively as of year-end.

Example B-2 — *Monthly Manual Reconciliation*

The auditor determined that accounts receivable is a significant account to the audit of XYZ Company's internal control over financial reporting. Through discussions with company personnel and review of company documentation, the auditor learned that company personnel reconcile the accounts receivable subsidiary ledger to the general ledger on a monthly basis. To determine whether misstatements in accounts receivable (existence, valuation, and completeness) would be detected on a timely basis, the auditor decided to test the control provided by the monthly reconciliation process.

Nature, Timing, and Extent of Procedures. The auditor tested the company's reconciliation control by selecting a sample of reconciliations based upon the number of accounts, the dollar value of the accounts, and the volume of transactions affecting the account. Because the auditor considered all other receivable accounts immaterial, and because such accounts had only minimal transactions flowing through them, the auditor decided to test only the reconciliation for the trade accounts receivable account. The auditor elected to perform the tests of controls over the reconciliation process in conjunction with the auditor's substantive procedures over the accounts receivable confirmation procedures, which were performed in July.

To test the reconciliation process, the auditor:

a. *Made inquiries of personnel performing the control.* The auditor asked the employee performing the reconciliation a number of questions, including the following:

- What documentation describes the account reconciliation process?
- How long have you been performing the reconciliation work?
- What is the reconciliation process for resolving reconciling items?
- How often are the reconciliations formally reviewed and signed off?
- If significant issues or reconciliation problems are noticed, to whose attention do you bring them?
- On average, how many reconciling items are there?
- How are old reconciling items treated?
- If need be, how is the system corrected for reconciling items?
- What is the general nature of these reconciling items?

b. *Observed the employee performing the control.* The auditor observed the employee performing the reconciliation procedures. For nonrecurring reconciling items, the auditor observed whether each item included a clear explanation as to its nature, the action that had been taken to resolve it, and whether it had been resolved on a timely basis.

c. *Reperformed the control.* Finally, the auditor inspected the reconciliations and reperfomed the reconciliation procedures. For the May and July reconciliations, the auditor traced the reconciling amounts to the source documents on a test basis. The only reconciling item that appeared on these reconciliations was cash received in the lockbox the previous day that had not been applied yet to the customer's account. The auditor pursued the items in each month's reconciliation to determine that the reconciling item cleared the following business day. The auditor also scanned through the file of all reconciliations prepared during the year and noted that they had been performed on a timely basis. To determine that the company had not made significant changes in its reconciliation control procedures from interim to year-end, the auditor made inquiries of company personnel and determined that such procedures had not changed from interim to year-end. Therefore, the auditor verified that controls were still in place by scanning the monthly account reconciliations to determine that the control was performed on a timely basis during the interim to year-end period.

Based on the auditor's procedures, the auditor concluded that the reconciliation control was operating effectively as of year-end.

Example B-3 — *Daily Manual Preventive Control*

The auditor determined that cash and accounts payable were significant accounts to the audit of the company's internal control over financial reporting. Through discussions with company personnel, the auditor learned that company personnel make a cash disbursement only after they have matched the vendor invoice to the receiver and purchase order. To determine whether misstatements in cash (existence) and accounts payable (existence, valuation, and completeness) would be prevented on a timely basis, the auditor tested the control over making a cash disbursement only after matching the invoice with the receiver and purchase.

Nature, Timing, and Extent of Procedures. On a haphazard basis, the auditor selected 25 disbursements from the cash disbursement registers from January through September. In this example, the auditor deemed a test of 25 cash disbursement transactions an appropriate sample size because the auditor was testing a manual control performed as part of the routine processing of cash disbursement transactions through the system. Furthermore, the auditor expected no errors based on the results of company-level tests performed earlier. [If, however, the auditor had encountered a control exception, the auditor would have attempted to identify the root cause of the exception and tested an additional number of items. If another control exception had been noted, the auditor would have decided that this control was not effective. As a result, the auditor would have decided to increase the extent of substantive procedures to be performed in connection with the financial statement audit of the cash and accounts payable accounts.]

a. After obtaining the related voucher package, the auditor examined the invoice to see if it included the signature or initials of the accounts payable clerk, evidencing the clerk's performance of the matching control. However, a signature on a voucher package to indicate signor approval does not necessarily mean that the person carefully reviewed it before signing. The voucher package may have been signed based on only a cursory review, or without any review.

b. The auditor decided that the quality of the evidence regarding the effective operation of the control evidenced by a signature or initials was not sufficiently persuasive to ensure that the control operated effectively during the test period. In order to obtain additional evidence, the auditor reperformed the matching control corresponding to the signature, which included examining the invoice to determine that (a) its items matched to the receiver and purchase order and (b) it was mathematically accurate.

Because the auditor performed the tests of controls at an interim date, the auditor updated the testing through the end of the year (initial tests are through September to December) by asking the accounts payable clerk whether the control was still in place and operating effectively. The auditor confirmed that understanding by performing a walkthrough of one transaction in December.

Based on the auditor's procedures, the auditor concluded that the control over making a cash disbursement only after matching the invoice with the receiver and purchase was operating effectively as of year-end.

Example B-4 — *Programmed Prevent Control and Weekly Information Technology-Dependent Manual Detective Control*

The auditor determined that cash, accounts payable, and inventory were significant accounts to the audit of the company's internal control over financial reporting. Through discussions with company personnel, the auditor learned that the company's computer system performs a three-way match of the receiver, purchase order, and invoice. If there are any exceptions, the system produces a list of unmatched items that employees review and follow up on weekly.

In this case, the computer match is a programmed application control, and the review and follow-up of the unmatched items report is a detective control. To determine whether misstatements in cash (existence) and accounts payable/inventory (existence, valuation, and completeness) would be prevented or detected on a timely basis, the auditor decided to test the programmed application control of matching the receiver, purchase order, and invoice as well as the review and follow-up control over unmatched items.

Nature, Timing, and Extent of Procedures. To test the programmed application control, the auditor:

a. Identified, through discussion with company personnel, the software used to process receipts and purchase invoices. The software used was a third-party package consisting of a number of modules.

b. Determined, through further discussion with company personnel, that they do not modify the core functionality of the software, but sometimes make personalized changes to reports to meet the changing needs of the business. From previous experience with the company's information technology environment, the auditor believes that such changes are infrequent and that information technology process controls are well established.

c. Established, through further discussion, that the inventory module operated the receiving functionality, including the matching of receipts to open purchase orders. Purchase invoices were processed in the accounts payable module, which matched them to an approved purchase order against which a valid receipt has been made. That module also produced the Unmatched Items Report, a standard report supplied with the package to which the company has not made any modifications. That information was agreed to the supplier's documentation and to documentation within the information technology department.

d. Identified, through discussions with the client and review of the supplier's documentation, the names, file sizes (in bytes), and locations of the executable files (programs) that operate the functionality under review. The auditor then identified the compilation dates of the programs and agreed them to the original installation date of the application. The compilation date of the report code was agreed to documentation held within the information technology department relating to the last change made to that report (a change in formatting).

e. Identified the objectives of the programs to be tested. The auditor wanted to determine whether appropriate items are received (for example, match a valid purchase order), appropriate purchase invoices are posted (for example, match a valid receipt and purchase order, non-duplicate reference numbers) and unmatched items (for example, receipts, orders or invoices) are listed on the exception report. The auditor then reperformed all those variations in the packages on a test-of-one basis to determine that the programs operated as described.

In addition, the auditor had evaluated and tested general computer controls, including program changes (for example, confirmation that no unauthorized changes are undertaken to the functionality and that changes to reports are appropriately authorized, tested, and approved before being applied) and logical access (for example, user access to the inventory and accounts payable modules and access to the area on the system where report code is maintained), and concluded that they were operating effectively. (Since the computer is deemed to operate in a systematic manner, the auditor concluded that it was sufficient to perform a walkthrough for only the one item.)

To determine whether the programmed control was operating effectively, the auditor performed a walkthrough in the month of July. As a result of the walkthrough, the auditor performed and documented the following items:

a. Receiving cannot record the receipt of goods without matching the receipt to a purchase order on the system. The auditor tested that control by attempting to record the receipt of goods into the system without a purchase order. However, the system did not allow the auditor to do that. Rather, the system produced an error message stating that the goods could not be recorded as received without an active purchase order.

b. An invoice will not be paid unless the system can match the receipt and vendor invoice to an approved purchase order. The auditor tested that control by attempting to approve an invoice for payment in the system. The system did not allow the auditor to do that. Rather, it produced an error message indicating that invoices could not be paid without an active purchase order and receiver.

c. The system disallows the processing of invoices with identical vendor and identical invoice numbers. In addition, the system will not allow two invoices to be processed against the same purchase order unless the sum of the invoices is less than the amount approved on the purchase order. The auditor tested that control by attempting to process duplicate invoices. However, the system produced an error message indicating that the invoice had already been processed.

d. The system compares the invoice amounts to the purchase order. If there are differences in quantity/extended price, and such differences fall outside a preapproved tolerance, the system does not allow the invoice to be processed. The auditor tested that control by attempting to process an invoice that had quantity/price differences outside the tolerance level of 10 pieces, or $1,000. The system produced an error message indicating that the invoice could not be processed because of such differences.

e. The system processes payments only for vendors established in the vendor master file. The auditor tested that control by attempting to process an invoice for a vendor that was not established in the vendor master file. However, the system did not allow the payment to be processed.

f. The auditor tested user access to the vendor file and whether such users can make modifications to such file by attempting to access and make changes to the vendor tables. However, the system did not allow the auditor to perform that function and produced an error message stating that the user was not authorized to perform that function.

g. The auditor verified the completeness and accuracy of the Unmatched Items Report by verifying that one unmatched item was on the report and one matched item was not on the report.

Note: It is inadvisable for the auditor to have uncontrolled access to the company's systems in his or her attempts described above to record the receipt of goods without a purchase order, approve an invoice for payment, process duplicate invoices, etc. These procedures ordinarily are performed in the presence of appropriate company personnel so that they can be notified immediately of any breach to their systems.

To test the detect control of review and follow up on the Unmatched Items Report, the auditor performed the following procedures in the month of July for the period January to July:

a. *Made inquiries of company personnel.* To gain an understanding of the procedures in place to ensure that all unmatched items are followed-up properly and that corrections are made on a timely basis, the auditor made inquiries of the employee who follows up on the weekly-unmatched items reports. On a weekly basis, the control required the employee to review the Unmatched Items Report to determine why items appear on it. The employee's review includes proper followup on items, including determining whether:

- All open purchase orders are either closed or voided within an acceptable amount of time.

- The requesting party is notified periodically of the status of the purchase order and the reason for its current status.

- The reason the purchase order remains open is due to incomplete shipment of goods and, if so, whether the vendor has been notified.

- There are quantity problems that should be discussed with purchasing.

b. *Observed the performance of the control.* The auditor observed the employee performing the control for the Unmatched Items Reports generated during the first week in July.

c. *Reperformed the control.* The auditor selected five weekly Unmatched Items Reports, selected several items from each, and reperformed the procedures that the employee performed. The auditor also scanned other Unmatched Items Reports to determine that the control was performed throughout the period of intended reliance.

To determine that the company had not made significant changes in their controls from interim to year-end, the auditor discussed with company personnel the procedures in place for making such changes. Since the procedures had not changed from interim to year-end, the auditor observed that the controls were still in place by scanning the weekly Unmatched Items Reports to determine that the control was performed on a timely basis during the interim to year-end period.

Based on the auditor's procedures, the auditor concluded that the employee was clearing exceptions in a timely manner and that the control was operating effectively as of year-end.

¶ 203. *APPENDIX C—Safeguarding of Assets*

For Analysis of Appendix C, see ¶ 102 and ¶ 119.

203.C1 *Safeguarding of assets* is defined in paragraph 7 as those policies and procedures that "provide reasonable assurance regarding prevention or timely detection of unauthorized acquisition, use or disposition of the company's assets that could have a material effect on the financial statements." This definition is consistent with the definition provided in the Committee of Sponsoring Organizations (COSO) of the Treadway Commission's Addendum, *Reporting to External Parties*, which provides the following definition of internal control over safeguarding of assets:

> Internal control over safeguarding of assets against unauthorized acquisition, use or disposition is a process, effected by an entity's board of directors, management and other personnel, designed to provide reasonable assurance regarding prevention or timely detection of unauthorized acquisition, use, or disposition of the entity's assets that could have a material effect on the financial statements. Such internal control can be judged effective if the board of directors and management have reasonable assurance that unauthorized acquisition, use or disposition of the entity's assets that could have a material effect on the financial statements is being prevented or detected on a timely basis.

203.C2 For example, a company has safeguarding controls over inventory tags (preventive controls) and also performs periodic physical inventory counts (detective control) timely in relation to its quarterly and annual financial reporting dates. Although the physical inventory count does not safeguard the inventory from theft or loss, it prevents a material misstatement to the financial statements if performed effectively and timely.

203.C3 Therefore, given that the definitions of material weakness and significant deficiency relate to the likelihood of misstatement of the financial statements, the failure of a preventive control such as inventory tags will not result in a significant deficiency or material weakness if the detective control (physical inventory) prevents a misstatement of the financial statements. The COSO Addendum also indicates that to the extent that such losses might occur, controls over financial reporting are effective if they provide reasonable assurance that those losses are properly reflected in the financial statements, thereby alerting financial statement users to consider the need for action.

> **Note:** *Properly reflected* in the financial statements includes both correctly recording the loss and adequately disclosing the loss.

203.C4 Material weaknesses relating to controls over the safeguarding of assets would only exist when the company does not have effective controls (considering both safeguarding and other controls) to prevent or detect a material misstatement of the financial statements.

203.C5 Furthermore, management's plans that could potentially affect financial reporting in future periods are not controls. For example, a company's business continuity or contingency planning has no effect on the company's current abilities to initiate, authorize, record, process, or report financial data. Therefore, a company's business continuity or contingency planning is not part of internal control over financial reporting.

203.C6 The COSO Addendum provides further information about safeguarding of assets as it relates to internal control over financial reporting.

¶ 204. APPENDIX D—Examples of Significant Deficiencies and Material Weaknesses

For Analysis of Appendix D, see ¶ 102, ¶ 107, ¶ 109.8.2, and ¶ 120.

204.D1 Paragraph 8 of this standard defines a control deficiency. Paragraphs 9 and 10 go on to define a significant deficiency and a material weakness, respectively.

204.D2 Paragraphs 22 through 23 of this standard discuss materiality in an audit of internal control over financial reporting, and paragraphs 130 through 140 provide additional direction on evaluating deficiencies in internal control over financial reporting.

204.D3 The following examples illustrate how to evaluate the significance of internal control deficiencies in various situations. These examples are for illustrative purposes only.

Example D-1—*Reconciliations of Intercompany Accounts Are Not Performed on a Timely Basis*

Scenario A — Significant Deficiency. The company processes a significant number of routine intercompany transactions on a monthly basis. Individual intercompany transactions are not material and primarily relate to balance sheet activity, for example, cash transfers between business units to finance normal operations.

A formal management policy requires monthly reconciliation of intercompany accounts and confirmation of balances between business units. However, there is not a process in place to ensure performance of these procedures. As a result, detailed reconciliations of intercompany accounts are not performed on a timely basis. Management does perform monthly procedures to investigate selected large-dollar intercompany account differences. In addition, management prepares a detailed monthly variance analysis of operating expenses to assess their reasonableness.

Based only on these facts, the auditor should determine that this deficiency represents a significant deficiency for the following reasons: The magnitude of a financial statement misstatement resulting from this deficiency would reasonably be expected to be more than inconsequential, but less than material, because individual intercompany transactions are not material, and the compensating controls operating monthly should detect a material misstatement. Furthermore, the transactions are primarily restricted to balance sheet accounts. However, the compensating detective controls are designed only to detect material misstatements. The controls do not address the detection of misstatements that are more than inconsequential but less than material. Therefore, the likelihood that a misstatement that was more than inconsequential, but less than material, could occur is more than remote.

Scenario B — Material Weakness. The company processes a significant number of intercompany transactions on a monthly basis. Intercompany transactions relate to a wide range of activities, including transfers of inventory with intercompany profit between business units, allocation of research and development costs to business units and corporate charges. Individual intercompany transactions are frequently material.

A formal management policy requires monthly reconciliation of intercompany accounts and confirmation of balances between business units. However, there is not a process in place to ensure that these procedures are performed on a consistent basis. As a result, reconciliations of intercompany accounts are not performed on a timely basis, and differences in intercompany accounts are frequent and significant. Management does not perform any alternative controls to investigate significant intercompany account differences.

Based only on these facts, the auditor should determine that this deficiency represents a material weakness for the following reasons: The magnitude of a financial statement misstatement resulting from this deficiency would reasonably be expected to be material, because individual intercompany transactions are frequently material and relate to a wide range of activities. Additionally, actual unreconciled differences in intercompany accounts have been, and are, material. The likelihood of such a misstatement is more than remote because such misstatements have frequently occurred and compensating controls are not effective, either because they are not properly designed or not operating effectively. Taken together, the magnitude and likelihood of misstatement of the financial statements resulting from this internal control deficiency meet the definition of a material weakness.

Example D-2—*Modifications to Standard Sales Contract Terms Not Reviewed To Evaluate Impact on Timing and Amount of Revenue Recognition*

Scenario A — Significant Deficiency. The company uses a standard sales contract for most transactions. Individual sales transactions are not material to the entity. Sales personnel are allowed to modify sales contract terms. The company's accounting function reviews significant or unusual modifications to the sales contract terms, but does not review changes in the standard shipping terms. The changes in the standard shipping terms could require a delay in the timing of revenue recognition. Management reviews gross margins on a monthly basis and investigates any significant or unusual relationships. In addition, management reviews the reasonableness of inventory levels at the end of each accounting period. The entity has experienced limited situations in which revenue has been inappropriately recorded in advance of shipment, but amounts have not been material.

Based only on these facts, the auditor should determine that this deficiency represents a significant deficiency for the following reasons: The magnitude of a financial statement misstatement resulting from this deficiency would reasonably be expected to be more than inconsequential, but less than material, because individual sales transactions are not material and the compensating detective controls operating monthly and at the end of each financial reporting period should reduce the likelihood of a material misstatement going undetected. Furthermore, the risk of material misstatement is limited to revenue recognition errors related to shipping terms as opposed to broader sources of error in revenue recognition. However, the compensating detective controls are only designed to detect material misstatements. The controls do not effectively address the detection of misstatements that are more than inconsequential but less than material, as evidenced by situations in which transactions that were not material were improperly recorded. Therefore, there is a more than remote likelihood that a misstatement that is more than inconsequential but less than material could occur.

Scenario B — Material Weakness. The company has a standard sales contract, but sales personnel frequently modify the terms of the contract. The nature of the modifications can affect the timing and amount of revenue recognized. Individual sales transactions are frequently material to the entity, and the gross margin can vary significantly for each transaction.

The company does not have procedures in place for the accounting function to regularly review modifications to sales contract terms. Although management reviews gross margins on a monthly basis, the significant differences in gross margins on individual transactions make it difficult for management to identify potential misstatements. Improper revenue recognition has occurred, and the amounts have been material.

Based only on these facts, the auditor should determine that this deficiency represents a material weakness for the following reasons: The magnitude of a financial statement misstatement resulting from this deficiency would reasonably be expected to be material, because individual sales transactions are frequently material, and gross margin can vary significantly with each transaction (which would make compensating detective controls based on a reasonableness review ineffective). Additionally, improper revenue recognition has occurred, and the amounts have been material. Therefore, the likelihood of material misstatements occurring is more than remote. Taken together, the magnitude and likelihood of misstatement of the financial statements resulting from this internal control deficiency meet the definition of a material weakness.

Scenario C — Material Weakness. The company has a standard sales contract, but sales personnel frequently modify the terms of the contract. Sales personnel frequently grant unauthorized and unrecorded sales discounts to customers without the knowledge of the accounting department. These amounts are deducted by customers in paying their invoices and are recorded as outstanding balances on the accounts receivable aging. Although these amounts are individually insignificant, they are material in the aggregate and have occurred consistently over the past few years.

Based on only these facts, the auditor should determine that this deficiency represents a material weakness for the following reasons: The magnitude of a financial statement misstatement resulting from this deficiency would reasonably be expected to be material, because the frequency of occurrence allows insignificant amounts to become material in the aggregate. The likelihood of material misstatement of the financial statements resulting from this internal control deficiency is more than remote (even assuming that the amounts were fully reserved for in the company's allowance for uncollectible accounts) due to the likelihood of material misstatement of the gross accounts receivable balance. Therefore, this internal control deficiency meets the definition of a material weakness.

Example D-3—*Identification of Several Deficiencies*

Scenario A — Material Weakness. During its assessment of internal control over financial reporting, management identified the following deficiencies. Based on the context in which the deficiencies occur, management and the auditor agree that these deficiencies individually represent significant deficiencies:

- Inadequate segregation of duties over certain information system access controls.

- Several instances of transactions that were not properly recorded in subsidiary ledgers; transactions were not material, either individually or in the aggregate.

- A lack of timely reconciliations of the account balances affected by the improperly recorded transactions.

Based only on these facts, the auditor should determine that the combination of these significant deficiencies represents a material weakness for the following reasons: Individually, these deficiencies were evaluated as representing a more than remote likelihood that a misstatement that is more than inconsequential, but less than material, could occur. However, each of these significant deficiencies affects the same set of accounts. Taken together, these significant deficiencies represent a more than remote likelihood that a material misstatement could occur and not be prevented or detected. Therefore, in combination, these significant deficiencies represent a material weakness.

Scenario B — Material Weakness. During its assessment of internal control over financial reporting, management of a financial institution identifies deficiencies in: the design of controls over the estimation of credit losses (a critical accounting estimate); the operating effectiveness of controls for initiating, processing, and reviewing adjustments to the allowance for credit losses; and the operating effectiveness of controls designed to prevent and detect the improper recognition of interest income. Management and the auditor agree that, in their overall context, each of these deficiencies individually represent a significant deficiency.

In addition, during the past year, the company experienced a significant level of growth in the loan balances that were subjected to the controls governing credit loss estimation and revenue recognition, and further growth is expected in the upcoming year.

Based only on these facts, the auditor should determine that the combination of these significant deficiencies represents a material weakness for the following reasons:

- The balances of the loan accounts affected by these significant deficiencies have increased over the past year and are expected to increase in the future.

- This growth in loan balances, coupled with the combined effect of the significant deficiencies described, results in a more than remote likelihood that a material misstatement of the allowance for credit losses or interest income could occur.

Therefore, in combination, these deficiencies meet the definition of a material weakness.

¶ 205. *APPENDIX E—BACKGROUND AND BASIS FOR CONCLUSIONS*

For Analysis of Appendix E, see ¶ 102, ¶ 103, ¶ 109.4.6, ¶ 109.7.1, ¶ 118, ¶ 120, and ¶ 121.

* * *

¶ 205.I. *Introduction*

205.E1.I This appendix summarizes factors that the Public Company Accounting Oversight Board (the "Board") deemed significant in reaching the conclusions in the standard. This appendix includes reasons for accepting certain views and rejecting others.

¶ 205.II. *Background*

205.E2.II Section 404(a) of the Sarbanes-Oxley Act of 2002 (the "Act"), and the Securities and Exchange Commission's (SEC) related implementing rules, require the management of a public company to assess the effectiveness of the company's internal control over financial reporting, as of the end of the company's most recent fiscal year. Section 404(a) of the Act also requires management to include in the company's annual report to shareholders management's conclusion as a result of that assessment of whether the company's internal control over financial reporting is effective.

205.E3.II Sections 103(a)(2)(A) and 404(b) of the Act direct the Board to establish professional standards governing the independent auditor's attestation and reporting on management's assessment of the effectiveness of internal control over financial reporting.

205.E4.II The backdrop for the development of the Board's first major auditing standard was, of course, the spectacular audit failures and corporate malfeasance that led to the passage of the Act. Although all of the various components of the Act work together to help restore investor confidence and help prevent the types of financial reporting breakdowns that lead to the loss of investor confidence, Section 404 of the Act is certainly one of the most visible and tangible changes required by the Act.

205.E5.II The Board believes that effective controls provide the foundation for reliable financial reporting. Congress believed this too, which is why the new reporting by management and the auditor on the effectiveness of internal control over financial reporting received such prominent attention in the Act. Internal control over financial reporting enhances a company's ability to produce fair and complete financial reports. Without reliable financial reports, making good judgments and decisions about a company becomes very difficult for anyone, including the board of directors, management, employees, investors, lenders, customers, and regulators. The auditor's reporting on management's assessment of the effectiveness of internal control over financial reporting provides users of that report with important assurance about the reliability of the company's financial reporting.

205.E6.II The Board's efforts to develop this standard were an outward expression of the Board's mission, "to protect the interests of investors and further the public interest in the preparation of informative, fair, and independent audit reports." As part of fulfilling that mission as it relates to this standard, the Board considered the advice that respected groups had offered to other auditing standards setters in the past. For example, the Public Oversight Board's Panel on Audit Effectiveness recommended that "auditing standards need to provide clear, concise and definitive imperatives for auditors to follow."[1] As another example, the International Organization of Securities Commissioners advised the

---

1. Panel on Audit Effectiveness, *Report and Recommendations*, sec. 2.228 (August 31, 2000).

International Auditing and Assurance Standards Board "that the IAASB must take care to avoid language that could inadvertently encourage inappropriate shortcuts in audits, at a time when rigorous audits are needed more than ever to restore investor confidence."[2]

205.E7.II The Board understood that, to effectively fulfill its mission and for this standard to achieve its ultimate goal of restoring investor confidence by increasing the reliability of public company financial reporting, the Board's standard must contain clear directions to the auditor consistent with investor's expectations that the reliability of financial reporting be significantly improved. Just as important, the Board recognized that this standard must appropriately balance the costs to implement the standard's directions with the benefits of achieving these important goals. As a result, all of the Board's decisions about this standard were guided by the additional objective of creating a rational relationship between costs and benefits.

205.E8.II When the Board adopted its interim attestation standards in Rule 3300T on an initial, transitional basis, the Board adopted a pre-existing standard governing an auditor's attestation on internal control over financial reporting.[3] As part of the Board's process of evaluating that pre-existing standard, the Board convened a public roundtable discussion on July 29, 2003 to discuss issues and hear views related to reporting on internal control over financial reporting. The participants at the roundtable included representatives from public companies, accounting firms, investor groups, and regulatory organizations. Based on comments made at the roundtable, advice from the Board's staff, and other input the Board received, the Board determined that the preexisting standard governing an auditor's attestation on internal control over financial reporting was insufficient for effectively implementing the requirements of Section 404 of the Act and for the Board to appropriately discharge its standard-setting obligations under Section 103(a) of the Act. In response, the Board developed and issued, on October 7, 2003, a proposed auditing standard titled, *An Audit of Internal Control Over Financial Reporting Performed in Conjunction with An Audit of Financial Statements.*

205.E9.II The Board received 189 comment letters on a broad array of topics from a variety of commenters, including auditors, investors, internal auditors, issuers, regulators, and others. Those comments led to changes in the standard, intended to make the requirements of the standard clearer and more operational. This appendix summarizes significant views expressed in those comment letters and the Board's responses.

---

2. April 8, 2003 comment letter from the International Organization of Securities Commissions to the International Auditing and Assurance Standards Board regarding the proposed international standards on audit risk (Amendment to ISA 200, "Objective and Principles Governing an Audit of Financial Statements;" proposed ISAs, "Understanding the Entity and Its Environment and Assessing the Risks of Material Misstatement;" "Auditor's Procedures in Response to Assessed Risks;" and "Audit Evidence").

3. The pre-existing standard is Chapter 5, "*Reporting on an Entity's Internal Control Over Financial Reporting*" of Statement on Standards for Attestation Engagements (SSAE) No. 10, *Attestation Standards: Revision and Recodification*(AICPA, *Professional Standards*, Vol. 1, AT sec. 501). SSAE No. 10 has been codified into AICPA Professional Standards, Volume 1, as AT sections 101 through 701.

¶ 205.III. *Fundamental Scope of the Auditor's Work in an Audit of Internal Control over Financial Reporting*

205.E10.III The proposed standard stated that the auditor's objective in an audit of internal control over financial reporting was to express an opinion on management's assessment of the effectiveness of the company's internal control over financial reporting. To render such an opinion, the proposed standard required the auditor to obtain reasonable assurance about whether the company maintained, in all material respects, effective internal control over financial reporting as of the date specified in management's report. To obtain reasonable assurance, the auditor was required to evaluate both management's process for making its assessment and the effectiveness of internal control over financial reporting.

205.E11.III Virtually all investors and auditors who submitted comment letters expressed support for this approach. Other commenters, primarily issuers, expressed concerns that this approach was contrary to the intent of Congress and, therefore, beyond what was specifically required by Section 404 of the Act. Further, issuers stated their views that this approach would lead to unnecessary and excessive costs. Some commenters in this group suggested the auditor's work should be limited to evaluating management's assessment process and the testing performed by management and internal audit. Others acknowledged that the auditor would need to test at least some controls directly in addition to evaluating and testing management's assessment process. However, these commenters described various ways in which the auditor's own testing could be significantly reduced from the scope expressed in the proposed standard. For instance, they proposed that the auditor could be permitted to use the work of management and others to a much greater degree; that the auditor could use a "risk analysis" to identify only a few controls to be tested; and a variety of other methods to curtail the extent of the auditor's work. Of those opposed to the scope, most cited their belief that the scope of work embodied in the standard would lead to a duplication of effort between management and the auditor which would needlessly increase costs without adding significant value.

205.E12.III After considering the comments, the Board retained the approach described in the proposed standard. The Board concluded that the approach taken in the standard is consistent with the intent of Congress. Also, to provide the type of report, at the level of assurance called for in Sections 103 and 404, the Board concluded that the auditor must evaluate both management's assessment process and the effectiveness of internal control over financial reporting. Finally, the Board noted the majority of the cost to be borne by companies (and ultimately investors) results directly from the work the company will have to perform to maintain effective internal control over financial reporting and to comply with Section 404(a) of the Act. The cost of the auditor's work as described in this standard ultimately will represent a smaller portion of the total cost to companies of implementing Section 404.

205.E13.III The Board noted that large, federally insured financial institutions have had a similar internal control reporting requirement for over ten years. The Federal Deposit Insurance Corporation Improvement Act of 1991 (FDICIA) has required, since 1993, managements of large financial institutions to make an assessment of internal control over financial reporting effectiveness and the institution's independent auditor to issue an attestation report on management's assessment.

205.E14.III The attestation standards under which FDICIA engagements are currently performed are clear that, when performing an examination of management's assertion on the effectiveness of internal control over financial reporting (management's report on the assessment required by Section 404(a) of the Act must include a statement as to whether the company's internal control over financial reporting is effective), the auditor may express an opinion either on management's assertion (that is, whether management's assessment about the effectiveness of the internal control over financial reporting is fairly stated) or directly on the subject matter (that is, whether the internal control over financial reporting is effective) because the level of work that must be performed is the same in either case.

205.E15.III The Board observed that Congress indicated an intent to require an examination level of work in Section 103(a) of the Act, which states, in part, that each registered public accounting firm shall:

describe in each audit report the scope of the auditor's testing of the internal control structure and procedures of the issuer, required by Section 404(b), and present (in such report or in a separate report)—

(I) the findings of the auditor from such testing;

(II) an evaluation of whether such internal control structure and procedures—

(aa) include maintenance of records that in reasonable detail accurately reflect the transactions and dispositions of the assets of the issuer;

(bb) provide reasonable assurance that transactions are recorded as necessary to permit preparation of financial statements in accordance with generally accepted accounting principles, and that receipts and expenditures of the issuer are being made only in accordance with authorizations of management and directors of the issuer; and

(III) a description, at a minimum, of material weaknesses in such internal controls, and of any material noncompliance found on the basis of such testing. [emphasis added].

205.E16.III The Board concluded that the auditor must test internal control over financial reporting directly, in the manner and extent described in the standard, to make the evaluation described in Section 103. The Board also interpreted Section 103 to provide further support that the intent of Congress was to require an opinion on the effectiveness of internal control over financial reporting.

205.E17.III The Board concluded that the auditor must obtain a high level of assurance that the conclusion expressed in management's assessment is correct to provide an opinion on management's assessment. An auditing process restricted to evaluating what management has done would not provide the auditor with a sufficiently high level of assurance that management's conclusion is correct. Instead, it is necessary for the auditor to evaluate management's assessment process to be satisfied that management has an appropriate basis for its statement, or assertion, about the effectiveness of the company's internal control over financial reporting. It also is necessary for the auditor to directly test the effectiveness of internal control over financial reporting to be satisfied that management's conclusion is correct, and that management's assertion is fairly stated.

205.E18.III This testing takes on added importance with the public nature of the internal control reporting. Because of the auditor's association with a statement by management that internal control over financial reporting is effective, it is reasonable for a user of the auditor's report to expect that the auditor tested the effectiveness of internal control over financial reporting. For the auditor to do otherwise would create an expectation gap, in which the assurance that the auditor obtained is less than what users reasonably expect.

205.E19.III Auditors, investors, and the Federal bank regulators reaffirmed in their comment letters on the proposed auditing standard that the fundamental approach taken by the Board was appropriate and necessary. Investors were explicit in their expectation that the auditor must test the effectiveness of controls directly in addition to evaluating management's assessment process. Investors further recognized that this kind of assurance would come at a price and expressed their belief that the cost of the anticipated benefits was reasonable. The federal banking regulators, based on their experience examining financial institutions' internal control assessments and independent auditors' attestation reports under FDICIA, commented that the proposed auditing standard was a significant improvement over the existing attestation standard.

¶ 205.IV. *Reference to Audit vs. Attestation*

205.E20.IV The proposed standard referred to the attestation required by Section 404(b) of the Act as the *audit* of internal control over financial reporting instead of an *attestation* of management's assessment. The proposed standard took that approach both because the auditor's objective is to express an opinion on management's assessment of the effectiveness of internal control over financial reporting, just as the auditor's objective in an audit of the financial statements is to express an opinion on the fair presentation of the financial statements, and because the level of assurance obtained by the auditor is the same in both cases. Furthermore, the proposed standard described an *integrated* audit of the financial statements and internal control over financial reporting and allowed the auditor to express his or her opinions on the financial statements and on the effectiveness of internal control in separate reports or in a single, combined report.

205.E21.IV Commenters' views on this matter frequently were related to their views on whether the proposed scope of the audit was appropriate. Those who agreed that the scope in the proposed standard was appropriate generally agreed that referring to the engagement as an *audit* was appropriate. On the other hand, commenters who objected to the scope of work described in the proposed standard often drew an important distinction between an *audit* and an *attestation.* Because Section 404 calls for an attestation, they believed it was inappropriate to call the engagement anything else (or to mandate a scope that called for a more extensive level of work).

205.E22.IV Based, in part, on the Board's decisions about the scope of the audit of internal control over financial reporting, the Board concluded that the engagement should continue to be referred to as an "audit." This term emphasizes the nature of the auditor's objective and communicates that objective most clearly to report users. Use of this term also is consistent with the integrated approach described in the standard and the requirement in Section 404 of the Act that this reporting not be subject to a separate engagement.

205.E23.IV Because the Board's standard on internal control is an auditing standard, it is preferable to use the term *audit* to describe the engagement rather than the term *examination,* which is used in the attestation standards to describe an engagement designed to provide a high level of assurance.

205.E24.IV Finally, the Board believes that using the term *audit* helps dispel the misconception that an audit of internal control over financial reporting is a different level of service than an attestation of management's assessment of internal control over financial reporting.

¶ 205.V. *Form of the Auditor's Opinion*

205.E25.V The proposed auditing standard required that the auditor's opinion in his or her report state whether management's assessment of the effectiveness of the company's internal control over financial reporting as of the specified date is fairly stated, in all material respects, based on the control criteria. However, the proposed standard also stated that nothing precluded the auditor from auditing management's assessment and opining directly on the effectiveness of internal control over financial reporting. This is because the scope of the work, as defined by the proposed standard, was the same, regardless of whether the auditor reports on management's assessment or directly on the effectiveness of internal control over financial reporting. The form of the opinion was essentially interchangeable between the two.

205.E26.V However, if the auditor planned to issue other than an unqualified opinion, the proposed standard required the auditor to report directly on the effectiveness of the company's internal control over financial reporting rather than on management's assessment. The Board initially concluded that expressing an opinion on management's assessment, in these circumstances, did not most effectively communicate the auditor's conclusion that internal control was not effective. For example, if management expresses an adverse assessment because a material weakness exists at the date of management's assessment ("...internal control over financial reporting is not effective...") and the auditor expresses his or her opinion on management's assessment ("...management's assessment that internal control over financial reporting is not effective is fairly stated, in all material respects..."), a reader might not be clear about the results of the auditor's testing and about the auditor's conclusions. The Board initially decided that reporting directly on the effectiveness of the company's internal control over financial reporting better communicates to report users the effect of such conditions, because direct reporting more clearly states the auditor's conclusions about the effectiveness of internal control over financial reporting ("In our opinion, because of the effect of the material weakness described..., the Company's internal control over financial reporting is not effective.").

205.E27.V A number of commenters were supportive of the model described in the previous paragraph, as they agreed with the Board's reasoning. However, several commenters believed that report users would be confused as to why the form of the auditor's opinion would be different in various circumstances. These commenters thought that the auditor's opinion should be consistently expressed in all reports. Several auditors recommended that auditors always report directly on the effectiveness of the company's internal control over financial reporting. They reasoned that the scope of the audit— which always would require the auditor to obtain reasonable assurance about whether the internal control over financial reporting was effective—would be more clearly communicated, in all cases, by the auditor reporting directly on the effectiveness of internal control over financial reporting. Other commenters suggested that the auditor always should express two opinions: one on management's assessment and one directly on the effectiveness of internal control over financial reporting. They believed the Act called for two opinions: Section 404 calls for an opinion on management's assessment, while Section 103 calls for an opinion directly on the effectiveness of internal control over financial reporting.

205.E28.V The Board believes that the reporting model in the proposed standard is appropriate. However, the Board concluded that the expression of two opinions — one on management's assessment and one on the effectiveness of internal control over financial reporting — in all reports is a superior approach that balances the concerns of many different interested parties. This approach is consistent with the scope of the audit, results in more consistent reporting in differing circumstances, and makes the reports more easily understood by report users. Therefore, the standard requires that the auditor express two opinions in all reports on internal control over financial reporting.

¶ 205.VI. *Use of the Work of Others*

205.E29.VI After giving serious consideration to a rational relationship between costs and benefits, the Board decided to change the provisions in the proposed standard regarding using the work of others. The proposed standard required the auditor to evaluate whether to use the work of others, such as internal auditors and others working under the direction of management, and described an evaluation process focused on the competence and objectivity of the persons who performed the work that the auditor was required to use when determining the extent to which he or she could use the work of others.

205.E30.VI The proposed standard also described two principles that limited the auditor's ability to use of the work of others. First, the proposed standard defined three categories of controls and the extent to which the auditor could use the work of others in each of those categories:

- Controls for which the auditor should not rely on the work of others, such as controls in the control environment and controls specifically intended to prevent or detect fraud that is reasonably likely to have a material effect on the company's financial statements,

- Controls for which the auditor may rely on the work of others, but his or her reliance on the work of others should be limited, such as controls over nonroutine transactions that are considered high risk because they involve judgments and estimates, and

- Controls for which the auditor's reliance on the work of others is not specifically limited, such as controls over routine processing of significant accounts.

205.E31.VI Second, the proposed standard required that, on an overall basis, the auditor's own work must provide the principal evidence for the audit opinion (this is referred to as the *principal evidence provision*).

205.E32.VI In the proposed standard, these two principles provided the auditor with flexibility in using the work of others while preventing him or her from placing inappropriate overreliance on the work of others. Although the proposed standard required the auditor to reperform some of the tests performed by others to use their work, it did not establish specific requirements for the extent of the reperformance. Rather, it allowed the auditor to use his or her judgment and the directions provided by the two principles discussed in the previous two paragraphs to determine the appropriate extent of reperformance.

205.E33.VI The Board received a number of comments that agreed with the proposed three categories of controls and the principal evidence provision. However, most commenters expressed some level of concern with the categories, the principal evidence provision, or both.

205.E34.VI Comments opposing or criticizing the categories of controls varied from general to very specific. In general terms, many commenters (particularly issuers) expressed concern that the categories described in the proposed standard were too restrictive. They believed the auditor should be able to use his or her judgment to determine in which areas and to what extent to rely on the work of others. Other commenters indicated that the proposed standard did not place enough emphasis on the work of internal auditors whose competence and objectivity, as well as adherence to professional standards of internal auditing, should clearly set their work apart from the work performed by others in the organization (such as management or third parties working under management's direction). Further, these commenters believed that the standard should clarify that the auditor should be able to use work performed by internal auditors extensively. In that case, their concerns about excessive cost also would be partially alleviated.

205.E35.VI Other commenters expressed their belief that the proposed standard repudiated the approach established in AU sec. 322, *The Auditor's Consideration of the Internal Audit Function in an Audit of Financial Statements,* for the auditor's use of the work of internal auditors in a financial statement audit. Commenters also expressed very specific and pointed views on the three categories of controls. As defined in the proposed standard, the first category (in which the auditor should not use the work of others at all) included:

- Controls that are part of the control environment, including controls specifically established to prevent and detect fraud that is reasonably likely to result in material misstatement of the financial statements.

- Controls over the period-end financial reporting process, including controls over procedures used to enter transaction totals into the general ledger; to initiate, record, and process journal entries in the general ledger; and to record recurring and nonrecurring adjustments to the financial statements (for example, consolidating adjustments, report combinations, and reclassifications).

- Controls that have a pervasive effect on the financial statements, such as certain information technology general controls on which the operating effectiveness of other controls depend.

- Walkthroughs.

205.E36.VI Commenters expressed concern that the prohibition on using the work of others in these areas would (a) drive unnecessary and excessive costs, (b) not give appropriate recognition to those instances in which the auditor evaluated internal audit as having a high degree of competence and objectivity, and (c) be impractical due to resource constraints at audit firms. Although each individual area was mentioned, the strongest and most frequent objections were to the restrictions imposed over the inclusion in the first category of walkthroughs, controls over the period-end financial reporting process, and information technology general controls. Some commenters suggested the Board should consider moving these areas from the first category to the second category (in which using the work of others would be limited, rather than prohibited); others suggested removing any limitation on using the work of others in these areas altogether.

205.E37.VI Commenters also expressed other concerns with respect to the three control categories. Several commenters asked for clarification on what constituted *limited* use of the work of others for areas included in the second category. Some commenters asked for clarification about the extent of reperformance necessary for the auditor to use the work of others. Other commenters questioned the meaning of the term *without specific limitation* in the third category by asking, did this mean that the auditor could use the work of others in these areas without performing or reperforming any work in those areas?

205.E38.VI Although most commenters suggested that the principal evidence threshold for the auditor's own work be retained, some commenters objected to the principal evidence provision. Although many commenters identified the broad array of areas identified in the first category (in which the auditor should not use the work of others at all) as the key driver of excessive costs, others identified the principal evidence provision as the real source of their excessive cost concerns. Even if the categories were redefined in such a way as to permit the auditor to use the work of others in more areas, any associated decrease in audit cost would be limited by the principal evidence provision which, if retained, would still require significant original work on the part of the auditor. On the other hand, both investors and auditors generally supported retaining the principal evidence provision as playing an important role in ensuring the independence of the auditor's opinion and preventing inappropriate overreliance on the work of internal auditors and others.

205.E39.VI Commenters who both supported and opposed the principal evidence provision indicated that implementing it would be problematic because the nature of the work in an audit of internal control over financial reporting does not lend itself to a purely quantitative measurement. Thus, auditors would be forced to use judgment when determining whether the principal evidence provision has been satisfied.

205.E40.VI In response to the comments, the Board decided that some changes to the guidance on using the work of others were necessary. The Board did not intend to reject the concepts in AU sec. 322 and replace them with a different model. Although AU sec. 322 is designed to apply to an audit of financial statements, the Board concluded that the concepts contained in AU sec. 322 are sound and should be used in an audit of internal control over financial reporting, with appropriate modification to take into account the differences in the nature of the evidence necessary to support an opinion on financial statements and the evidence necessary to support an opinion on internal control effectiveness. The Board also wanted to make clear that the concepts in AU sec. 322 also may be applied, with appropriate auditor judgment, to the relevant work of others.

205.E41.VI The Board remained concerned, however, with the possibility that auditors might overrely on the work of internal auditors and others. Inappropriate overreliance can occur in a variety of ways. For example, an auditor might rely on the work of a highly competent and objective internal audit function for proportionately too much of the evidence that provided the basis for the auditor's opinion. Inappropriate overreliance also occurs when the auditor incorrectly concludes that internal auditors have a high degree of competence and objectivity when they do not, perhaps because the auditor did not exercise professional skepticism or due professional care when making his or her evaluation. In either case, the result is the same: unacceptable risk that the auditor's conclusion that internal control over financial reporting is effective is incorrect. For example, federal bank regulators commented that, in their experience with FDICIA, auditors have a tendency to rely too heavily on the work of management and others, further noting that this situation diminishes the independence of the auditor's opinion on control effectiveness.

205.E42.VI The Board decided to revise the categories of controls by focusing on the nature of the controls being tested, evaluating the competence and objectivity of the individuals performing the work, and testing the work of others. This allows the auditor to exercise substantial judgment based on the outcome of this work as to the extent to which he or she can make use of the work of internal auditors or others who are suitably qualified.

205.E43.VI This standard emphasizes the direct relationship between the assessed level of competence and objectivity and the extent to which the auditor may use the work of others. The Board included this clarification to highlight the special status that a highly competent and objective internal auditor has in the auditor's work as well as to caution against inappropriate overreliance on the work of management and others who would be expected to have lower degrees of competence and objectivity in assessing controls. Indeed, the Board noted that, with regard to internal control over financial reporting, internal auditors would normally be assessed as having a higher degree of competence and objectivity than management or others and that an auditor will be able to rely to a greater extent on the work of a highly competent and objective internal auditor than on work performed by others within the company.

205.E44.VI The Board concluded that the principal evidence provision is critical to preventing overreliance on the work of others in an audit of internal control over financial reporting. The requirement for the auditor to perform enough of the control testing himself or herself so that the auditor's own work provides the principal evidence for the auditor's opinion is of paramount importance to the auditor's assurance providing the level of reliability that investors expect. However, the Board also decided that the final standard should articulate clearly that the auditor's judgment about whether he or she has obtained the principal evidence required is qualitative as well as quantitative. Therefore, the standard now states, "Because the amount of work related to obtaining sufficient evidence to support an opinion about the effectiveness of controls is not susceptible to precise measurement, the auditor's judgment about whether he or she has obtained the principal evidence for the opinion will be qualitative as well as quantitative. For example, the auditor might give more weight to work performed on pervasive controls and in areas such as the control environment than on other controls, such as controls over low-risk, routine transactions."

205.E45.VI The Board also concluded that a better balance could be achieved in the standard by instructing the auditor to factor into the determination of the extent to which to use the work of others an evaluation of the nature of the controls on which others performed their procedures.

205.E46.VI Paragraph 112 of the standard provides the following factors the auditor should consider when evaluating the nature of the controls subjected to the work of others:

- The materiality of the accounts and disclosures that the control addresses and the risk of material misstatement.
- The degree of judgment required to evaluate the operating effectiveness of the control (that is, the degree to which the evaluation of the effectiveness of the control requires evaluation of subjective factors rather than objective testing).
- The pervasiveness of the control.
- The level of judgment or estimation required in the account or disclosure.
- The potential for management override of the control.

205.E47.VI As these factors increase in significance, the need for the auditor to perform his or her own work on those controls increases. As these factors decrease in significance, the auditor may rely more on the work of others. Because of the nature of controls in the control environment, however, the standard does not allow the auditor to use the work of others to reduce the amount of work he or she performs on such controls. In addition, the standard also does not allow the auditor to use the work of others in connection with the performance of walkthroughs of major classes of transactions because of the high degree of judgment required when performing them (See separate discussion in paragraphs E51 through E57).

205.E48.VI The Board decided that this approach was responsive to those who believed that the auditor should be able to use his or her judgment in determining the extent to which to use the work of others. The Board designed the requirement that the auditor's own work must provide the principal evidence for the auditor's opinion as one of the boundaries within which the auditor determines the work he or she must perform himself or herself in the audit of internal control over financial reporting. The other instructions about using the work of others provide more specific direction about how the auditor makes this determination, but allow the auditor significant flexibility to use his or her judgment to determine the work necessary to obtain the principal evidence, and to determine when the auditor can use the work of others rather than perform the work himself or herself. Although some of the directions are specific and definitive, such as the directions for the auditor to perform tests of controls in the control environment and walkthroughs himself or herself, the Board decided that these areas were of such audit importance that the auditor should always perform this testing as part of obtaining the principal evidence for his or her opinion. The Board concluded that this approach appropriately balances the use of auditor judgment and the risk of inappropriate overreliance.

205.E49.VI The Board was particularly concerned by comments that issuers might choose to reduce their internal audit staff or the extent of internal audit testing in the absence of a significant change in the proposed standard that would significantly increase the extent to which the auditor may use the work of internal auditors. The Board believes the standard makes clear that an effective internal audit function does permit the auditor to reduce the work that otherwise would be necessary.

205.E50.VI Finally, as part of clarifying the linkage between the degree of competence and objectivity of the others and the ability to use their work, the Board decided that additional clarification should be provided on the extent of testing that should be required of the work of others. The Board noted that the interaction of the auditor performing walkthroughs of every significant process and the retention of the principal evidence provision precluded the need for the auditor to test the work of others in every significant account. However, testing the work of others is an important part of an ongoing assessment of their competence and objectivity. Therefore, as part of the emphasis on the direct relationship between the assessed level of competence and objectivity to the extent of the use of the work of others, additional provisions were added discussing how the results of the testing of the work of others might affect the auditor's assessment of competence and objectivity. The Board also concluded that testing the work of others should be clearly linked to an evaluation of the quality and effectiveness of their work.

¶ 205.VII. *Walkthroughs*

205.E51.VII The proposed standard included a requirement that the auditor perform walkthroughs, stating that the auditor should perform a walkthrough for all of the company's significant processes. In the walkthrough, the auditor was to trace all types of transactions and events, both recurring and unusual, from origination through the company's information systems until they were included in the company's financial reports. As stated in the proposed standard, walkthroughs provide the auditor with evidence to:

- Confirm the auditor's understanding of the process flow of transactions;

- Confirm the auditor's understanding of the design of controls identified for all five components of internal control over financial reporting, including those related to the prevention or detection of fraud;

- Confirm that the auditor's understanding of the process is complete by determining whether all points in the process at which misstatements related to each relevant financial statement assertion that could occur have been identified;

- Evaluate the effectiveness of the design of controls; and

- Confirm whether controls have been placed in operation.

205.E52.VII A number of commenters expressed strong support for the requirement for the auditor to perform walkthroughs as described in the proposed standard. They agreed that auditors who did not already perform the type of walkthrough described in the proposed standard should perform them as a matter of good practice. These commenters further recognized that the first-hand understanding an auditor obtains from performing these walkthroughs puts the auditor in a much better position to design an effective audit and to evaluate the quality and effectiveness of the work of others. They considered the walkthrough requirement part of "getting back to basics," which they viewed as a positive development.

205.E53.VII Some commenters expressed general support for walkthroughs as required procedures, but had concerns about the scope of the work. A number of commenters suggested that requiring walkthroughs of *all* significant processes and *all* types of transactions would result in an overwhelming and unreasonable number of walkthroughs required. Commenters made various suggestions for alleviating this problem, including permitting the auditor to determine, using broad auditor judgment, which classes of transactions to walk through or refining the scope of "all types of transactions" to include some kind of consideration of risk and materiality.

205.E54.VII Other commenters believed that required walkthroughs would result in excessive cost if the auditor were prohibited from using the work of others. These commenters suggested that the only way that required walkthroughs would be a reasonable procedure is to permit the auditor to use the work of others. Although commenters varied on whether the auditor's use of the work of others for walkthroughs should be liberal or limited, and whether it should include management or be limited to internal auditors, a large number of commenters suggested that limiting walkthroughs to only the auditor himself or herself was impractical.

205.E55.VII The Board concluded that the objectives of the walkthroughs cannot be achieved second-hand. For the objectives to be effectively achieved, the auditor must perform the walkthroughs himself or herself. Several commenters who objected to the prohibition on using the work of internal auditors for walkthroughs described situations in which internal auditors would be better able to effectively perform walkthroughs because internal auditors understood the company's business and controls better than the external auditor and because the external auditor would struggle in performing walkthroughs due to a lack of understanding. The Board observed that these commenters' perspectives support the importance of requiring the external auditor to perform walkthroughs. If auditors struggle to initially perform walkthroughs because their knowledge of the company and its controls is weak, then that situation would only emphasize the necessity for the auditor to increase his or her level of understanding. After considering the nature and extent of the procedures that would be required to achieve these objectives, the Board concluded that performing walkthroughs would be the most efficient means of doing so. The first-hand understanding the auditor will obtain of the company's processes and its controls through the walkthroughs will translate into increased effectiveness and quality throughout the rest of the audit, in a way that cannot be achieved otherwise.

205.E56.VII The Board also decided that the scope of the transactions that should be subjected to walkthroughs should be more narrowly defined. To achieve the objectives the Board intended for walkthroughs to accomplish, the auditor should not be forced to perform walkthroughs on what many commenters reasoned was an unreasonably large population. The Board decided that the auditor should be able to use judgment in considering risk and materiality to determine which transactions and events within a given significant process to walk through. As a result, the directions in the standard on determining significant processes and major classes of transactions were expanded, and the population of transactions for which auditors will be required to walk through narrowed by replacing "all types of transactions" with "major classes of transactions."

205.E57.VII Although judgments of risk and materiality are inherent in identifying major classes of transactions, the Board decided to also remove from the standard the statement, "walkthroughs are required procedures" as a means of further clarifying that auditor judgment plays an important role in determining the major classes of transactions for which to perform a walkthrough. The Board observed that leading off the discussion of walkthroughs in the standard with such a sentence could be read as setting a tone that diminished the role of judgment in selecting the transactions to walk through. As a result, the directions in the standard on performing walkthroughs begin with, "The auditor should perform at least one walkthrough for each major class of transactions..." The Board's decision to eliminate the statement "walkthroughs are required procedures" should not be viewed as an indication that performing walkthroughs are optional under the standard's directions. The Board believes the auditor might be able to achieve the objectives of a walkthrough by performing a combination of procedures, including inquiry, inspection, observation, and reperformance; however, performing a walkthrough represents the most efficient and effective means of doing so. The auditor's work on the control environment and walkthroughs is an important part of the principal evidence that the auditor must obtain himself or herself.

¶ 205.VIII. *Small Business Issues*

205.E58.VIII Appendix E of the proposed standard discussed small and medium-sized company considerations. Comments were widely distributed on this topic. A number of commenters indicated that the proposed standard gave adequate consideration to how internal control is implemented in, and how the audit of internal control over financial reporting should be conducted at, small and medium-sized companies. Other commenters, particularly smaller issuers and smaller audit firms, indicated that the proposed standard needed to provide much more detail on how internal control over financial reporting could be different at a small or medium-sized issuer and how the auditor's approach could differ. Some of these commenters indicated that the concepts articulated in the Board's proposing release concerning accommodations for small and medium-sized companies were not carried through to the proposed standard itself.

205.E59.VIII On the other hand, other commenters, particularly large audit firms and investors, expressed views that the proposed standard went too far in creating too much of an accommodation for small and medium-sized issuers. In fact, many believed that the proposed standard permitted those issuers to have less effective internal control over financial reporting than larger issuers, while providing guidance to auditors permitting them to perform less extensive testing at those small and medium-sized issuers than they might have at larger issuers. These commenters stressed that effective internal control over financial reporting is equally important at small and medium-sized issuers. Some commenters also expressed concerns that the guidance in proposed Appendix E appeared to emphasize that the actions of senior management, if carried out with integrity, could offset deficiencies in internal control over financial reporting, such as the lack of written policies and procedures. Because the risk of management override of controls is higher in these types of environments, such commenters were concerned that the guidance in proposed Appendix E might result in an increased fraud risk at small and medium-sized issuers. At a minimum, they argued, the interpretation of Appendix E might result in a dangerous expectation gap for users of their internal control reports. Some commenters who were of this view suggested that Appendix E be deleted altogether or replaced with a reference to the report of the Committee of Sponsoring Organizations (COSO) of the Treadway Commission, *Internal Control—Integrated Framework*, which they felt contained sufficient guidance on small and medium-sized company considerations.

205.E60.VIII Striking an appropriate balance regarding the needs of smaller issuers is particularly challenging. The Board considered cautionary views about the difficulty in expressing accommodations for small and medium-sized companies without creating an inappropriate second class of internal control effectiveness and audit assurance. Further, the Board noted that the COSO framework currently provides management and the auditor with more guidance and flexibility regarding small and medium-sized companies than the Board had provided in the proposed Appendix E. As a result, the Board eliminated proposed Appendix E and replaced the appendix with a reference to COSO in paragraph 15 of the standard. The Board believes providing internal control criteria for small and medium-sized companies within the internal control framework is more appropriately within the purview of COSO. Furthermore, the COSO report was already tailored for special small and medium-sized company considerations. The Board decided that emphasizing the existing guidance within COSO was the best way of recognizing the special considerations that can and should be given to small and medium-sized companies without inappropriately weakening the standard to which these smaller entities should, nonetheless, be held. If additional tailored guidance on the internal control framework for small and medium-sized companies is needed, the Board encourages COSO, or some other appropriate body, to develop this guidance.

¶ 205.IX. *Evaluation of the Effectiveness of the Audit Committee*

205.E61.IX The proposed standard identified a number of circumstances that, because of their likely significant negative effect on internal control over financial reporting, are significant deficiencies as well as *strong indicators* that a material weakness exists. A particularly notable significant deficiency and strong indicator of a material weakness was the ineffective oversight by the audit committee of the company's external financial reporting and internal control over financial reporting. In addition, the proposed standard required the auditor to evaluate factors related to the effectiveness of the audit committee's oversight of the external financial reporting process and the internal control over financial reporting.

205.E62.IX This provision related to evaluating the effectiveness of the audit committee was included in the proposed standard for two primary reasons. First, the Board initially decided that, because of the significant role that the audit committee has in the control environment and monitoring components of internal control over financial reporting, an ineffective audit committee is a gravely serious control weakness that is strongly indicative of a material weakness. Most auditors should have already been reaching this conclusion when confronted with an obviously ineffective audit committee. Second, highlighting the adverse consequences of an ineffective audit committee would, perhaps, further encourage weak audit committees to improve.

205.E63.IX Investors supported this provision. They expressed an expectation that the auditor would evaluate the audit committee's effectiveness and speak up if the audit committee was determined to be ineffective. Investors drew a link among restoring their confidence, audit committees having new and enhanced responsibilities, and the need for assurance that audit committees are, in fact, meeting their responsibilities.

205.E64.IX Auditors also were generally supportive of such an evaluation. However, many requested that the proposed standard be refined to clearly indicate that the auditor's responsibility to evaluate the effectiveness of the audit committee's oversight of the company's external financial reporting and internal control over financial reporting is not a separate and distinct evaluation. Rather, the evaluation is one element of the auditor's overall understanding and assessment of the company's control environment and monitoring components. Some commenters suggested that, in addition to needing clarification of the auditor's responsibility, the auditor would have difficulty in evaluating all of the factors listed in the proposed standard, because the auditor's normal interaction with the audit committee would not provide sufficient basis to conclude on some of those factors.

205.E65.IX Issuers and some others were opposed to the auditor evaluating the effectiveness of the audit committee on the fundamental grounds that such an evaluation would represent an unacceptable conflict of interest. Several commenters shared the view that this provision would reverse an important improvement in governance and audit quality. Whereas the auditor was formerly retained and compensated by management, the Act made clear that these responsibilities should now be those of the audit committee. In this way, commenters saw a conflict of interest being remedied. Requiring the auditor to evaluate the effectiveness of the audit committee led commenters to conclude that the same kind of conflict of interest was being reestablished. These commenters also believed that the auditor would not have a sufficient basis on which to evaluate the effectiveness of the audit committee because the auditor does not have complete and free access to the audit committee, does not have appropriate expertise to evaluate audit committee members (who frequently are more experienced businesspeople than the auditor), does not have the legal expertise to make determinations about some of the specific factors listed in the proposed standard, and other shortcomings. These commenters also emphasized that the board of directors' evaluation of the audit committee is important and that the proposed standard could be read to supplant this important evaluation with that of the auditor's.

205.E66.IX The Board concluded that this provision should be retained but decided that clarification was needed to emphasize that the auditor's evaluation of the audit committee was not a separate evaluation but, rather, was made as part of the auditor's evaluation of the control environment and monitoring components of internal control over financial reporting. The Board reasoned that clarifying both this context and limitation on the auditor's evaluation of the audit committee would also address, to some degree, the conflict-of-interest concerns raised by other commenters. The Board also observed, however, that conflict is, to some extent, inherent in the duties that society expects of auditors.

Just as auditors were expected in the past to challenge management when the auditor believed a material misstatement of the financial statements or material weakness in internal control over financial reporting existed, the auditor similarly is expected to speak up when he or she believes the audit committee is ineffective in its oversight.

205.E67.IX The Board decided that when the auditor is evaluating the control environment and monitoring components, if the auditor concludes that the audit committee's oversight of the company's external financial reporting and internal control over financial reporting is ineffective, the auditor should be strongly encouraged to consider that situation a material weakness and, at a minimum, a significant deficiency. The objective of the evaluation is not to grade the effectiveness of the audit committee along a scale. Rather, in the course of performing procedures related to evaluating the effectiveness of the control environment and monitoring components, including evaluating factors related to the effectiveness of the audit committee's oversight, if the auditor concludes that the audit committee's oversight of the external financial reporting and internal control over financial reporting is ineffective, then the auditor should consider that a strong indicator of a material weakness.

205.E68.IX The Board concluded that several refinements should be made to this provision. As part of emphasizing that the auditor's evaluation of the audit committee is to be made as part of evaluating the control environment and not as a separate evaluation, the Board determined that the evaluation factors should be modified. The factors that addressed compliance with listing standards and sections of the Act were deleted, because those factors were specifically criticized in comment letters as being either outside the scope of the auditor's expertise or outside the scope of internal control over financial reporting. The Board also believed that those factors were not significant to the type of evaluation the auditor was expected to make of the audit committee. The Board decided to add the following factors, which are based closely on factors described in COSO, as relevant to evaluating those who govern, including the audit committee:

- Extent of direct and independent interaction with key members of financial management, including the chief financial officer and chief accounting officer.

- Degree to which difficult questions are raised and pursued with management and the auditor, including questions that indicate an understanding of the critical accounting policies and judgmental accounting estimates.

- Level of responsiveness to issues raised by the auditor, including those required to be communicated by the auditor to the audit committee.

205.E69.IX The Board also concluded that the standard should explicitly acknowledge that the board of directors is responsible for evaluating the effectiveness of the audit committee and that the auditor's evaluation of the control environment is not intended to supplant those evaluations. In addition, the Board concluded that, in the event the auditor determines that the audit committee's oversight is ineffective, the auditor should communicate that finding to the full board of directors. This communication should occur regardless of whether the auditor concludes that the condition represents a significant deficiency or a material weakness, and the communication should take place in addition to the normal communication requirements that attach to those deficiencies.

¶ 205.X. *Definitions of Significant Deficiency and Material Weakness*

205.E70.X As part of developing the proposed standard, the Board evaluated the existing definitions of significant deficiency (which the SEC defined as being the same as a reportable condition) and material weakness to determine whether they would permit the most effective implementation of the internal control reporting requirements of the Act.

205.E71.X AU sec. 325, *Communication of Internal Control Related Matters Noted in an Audit,* defined a material weakness as follows:

> A *material weakness* in internal control is a reportable condition in which the design or operation of one or more of the internal control components does not reduce to a *relatively low level* the risk that misstatements caused by error or fraud in amounts that would be material in relation to the financial statements being audited may occur and not be detected within a timely period by employees in the normal course of performing their assigned functions.

205.E72.X The framework that defined a material weakness focused on likelihood of and magnitude for evaluating a weakness. The Board decided that this framework would facilitate effective implementation of the Act's internal control reporting requirements; therefore, the Board's proposed definitions focused on likelihood and magnitude. However, as part of these deliberations, the Board decided that likelihood and magnitude needed to be defined in terms that would encourage more consistent application.

205.E73.X Within the existing definition of material weakness, the magnitude of "material in relation to the financial statements" was well supported by the professional standards, SEC rules and guidance, and other literature. However, the Board decided that the definition of likelihood would be improved if it used "more than remote" instead of "relatively low level." FASB Statement No. 5, *Accounting for Contingencies* (FAS No. 5) defines "remote." The Board decided that, because auditors were familiar with the application of the likelihood definitions in FAS No. 5, using "more than remote" in the definition of material weakness would infuse the evaluation of whether a control deficiency was a material weakness with the additional consistency that the Board wanted to encourage.

205.E74.X AU sec. 325 defined *reportable conditions* as follows:

...matters coming to the auditor's attention that, in his judgment, should be communicated to the audit committee because they represent significant deficiencies in the design or operation of internal control, which could adversely affect the organization's ability to initiate, record, process, and report financial data consistent with the assertions of management in the financial statements.

205.E75.X The Board observed that this definition makes the determination of whether a condition is reportable solely a matter of the auditor's judgment. The Board believed that this definition was insufficient for purposes of the Act because management also needs a definition to determine whether a deficiency is significant and that the definition should be the same as the definition used by the auditor. Furthermore, using this existing definition, the auditor's judgment could never be questioned.

205.E76.X The Board decided that the same framework that represented an appropriate framework for defining a material weakness also should be used for defining a significant deficiency. Although auditor judgment is integral and essential to the audit process (including in determining the severity of control weaknesses), auditors, nonetheless, must be accountable for their judgments. Increasing the accountability of auditors for their judgments about whether a condition represents a significant deficiency and increasing the consistency with which those judgments are made are interrelated. Hence, the same framework of likelihood and magnitude were applied in the Board's proposed definition of significant deficiency.

205.E77.X In applying the likelihood and magnitude framework to defining a significant deficiency, the Board decided that the "more than remote" likelihood of occurrence used in the definition of material weakness was the best benchmark. In terms of magnitude, the Board decided that "more than inconsequential" should be the threshold for a significant deficiency.

205.E78.X A number of commenters were supportive of the definitions in the proposed standard. These commenters believed the definitions were an improvement over the previous definitions, used terms familiar to auditors, and would promote increased consistency in evaluations.

205.E79.X Most commenters, however, objected to these definitions. The primary, overarching objection was that these definitions set too low a threshold for the reporting of significant deficiencies. Some commenters focused on "more than remote" likelihood as the driver of an unreasonably low threshold, while others believed "more than inconsequential" in the definition of significant deficiency was the main culprit. While some commenters understood "more than inconsequential" well enough, others indicated significant concerns that this represented a new term of art that needed to be accompanied by a clear definition of "inconsequential" as well as supporting examples. Several commenters suggested retaining the likelihood and magnitude approach to a definition but suggested alternatives for likelihood (such as reasonably likely, reasonably possible, more likely than not, probable) and magnitude (such as material, significant, insignificant).

205.E80.X Some commenters suggested that the auditing standard retain the existing definitions of material weakness and significant deficiency, consistent with the SEC's final rules implementing Section 404. In their final rules, the SEC tied management's assessment to the existing definitions of material weakness and significant deficiency (through the existing definition of a reportable condition) in AU sec. 325. These commenters suggested that, if the auditing standard used a different definition, a dangerous disconnect would result, whereby management would be using one set of definitions under the SEC's rules and auditors would be using another set under the Board's auditing standards. They further suggested that, absent rulemaking by the SEC to change its definitions, the Board should simply defer to the existing definitions.

205.E81.X A number of other commenters questioned the reference to "a misstatement of the annual or interim financial statements" in the definitions, with the emphasis on why "interim" financial statements were included in the definition, since Section 404 required only an annual assessment of internal control over financial reporting effectiveness, made as of year-end. They questioned whether this definition implied that the auditor was required to identify deficiencies that could result in a misstatement in interim financial statements; they did not believe that the auditor should be required to plan his or her audit of internal control over financial reporting at a materiality level of the interim financial statements.

205.E82.X The Board ultimately concluded that focusing the definitions of material weakness and significant deficiency on likelihood of misstatement and magnitude of misstatement provides the best framework for evaluating deficiencies. Defaulting to the existing definitions would not best serve the public interest nor facilitate meaningful and effective implementation of the auditing standard.

205.E83.X The Board observed that the SEC's final rules requiring management to report on internal control over financial reporting define material weakness, for the purposes of the final rules, as having "the same meaning as the definition under GAAS and attestation standards." Those rules state:

> The term "significant deficiency" has the same meaning as the term "reportable condition" as used in AU §325 and AT §501. The terms "material weakness" and "significant deficiency" both represent deficiencies in the design or operation of internal control that could adversely affect a company's ability to record, process, summarize and report financial data consistent with the assertions of management in the company's financial statements, with a "material weakness" constituting a greater deficiency than a "significant deficiency." Because of this relationship, it is our judgment

that an aggregation of significant deficiencies could constitute a material weakness in a company's internal control over financial reporting.[4]

205.E84.X The Board considered the SEC's choice to cross-reference to generally accepted auditing standards (GAAS) and the attestation standards as the means of defining these terms, rather than defining them outright within the final rules, noteworthy as it relates to the question of whether any disconnect could result between auditors' and managements' evaluations if the Board changed the definitions in its standards. Because the standard changes the definition of these terms within the interim standards, the Board believes the definitions are, therefore, changed for both auditors' and managements' purposes.

205.E85.X The Board noted that commenters who were concerned that the definitions in the proposed standard set too low of a threshold for significant deficiencies and material weaknesses believed that the proposed standard required that each control deficiency be evaluated in isolation. The intent of the proposed standard was that control deficiencies should first be evaluated individually; the determination as to whether they are significant deficiencies or material weaknesses should be made considering the effects of compensating controls. The effect of compensating controls should be taken into account when assessing the likelihood of a misstatement occurring and not being prevented or detected. The proposed standard illustrated this type of evaluation, including the effect of compensating controls when assessing likelihood, in the examples in Appendix D. Based on the comments received, however, the Board determined that additional clarification within the standard was necessary to emphasize the importance of considering compensating controls when evaluating the likelihood of a misstatement occurring. As a result, the note to paragraph 10 was added.

205.E86.X The Board concluded that considering the effect of compensating controls on the likelihood of a misstatement occurring and not being prevented or detected sufficiently addressed the concerns that the definitions set too low a threshold. For example, several issuer commenters cited concerns that the proposed definitions precluded a rational cost-benefit analysis of whether to correct a deficiency. These issuers believed they would be compelled to correct deficiencies (because the deficiencies would be considered to be at least significant deficiencies) in situations in which management had made a previous conscious decision that the costs of correcting the deficiency outweighed the benefits. The Board observed that, in cases in which management has determined not to correct a known deficiency based on a cost-benefit analysis, effective compensating controls usually lie at the heart of management's decision. The standard's use of "likelihood" in the definition of a significant deficiency or material weakness accommodates such a consideration of compensating controls. If a deficiency is effectively mitigated by compensating controls, then the

---

4. See footnote 73 to *Final Rule: Management's Reports on Internal Control Over Financial Reporting and Certification of Disclosure in Exchange Act Periodic Reports,* Securities and Exchange Commission Release No. 33-8238 (June 5, 2003) [68 FR 36636].

likelihood of a misstatement occurring and not being prevented or detected may very well be remote.

205.E87.X The Board disagreed with comments that "more than inconsequential" was too low a threshold; however, the Board decided the term "inconsequential" needed additional clarity. The Board considered the term "inconsequential" in relation to the SEC's guidance on audit requirements and materiality. Section 10A(b)(1)(B)[5] describes the auditor's communication requirements when the auditor detects or otherwise becomes aware of information indicating that an illegal act has or may have occurred, "unless the illegal act is clearly inconsequential." Staff Accounting Bulletin (SAB) No. 99, *Materiality,* provides the most recent and definitive guidance on the concept of materiality as it relates to the financial reporting of a public company. SAB No. 99 uses the term "inconsequential" in several places to draw a distinction between amounts that are not material. SAB No. 99 provides the following guidance to assess the significance of a misstatement:

> Though the staff does not believe that registrants need to make finely calibrated determinations of significance with respect to immaterial items, plainly it is "reasonable" to treat misstatements whose effects are clearly inconsequential differently than more significant ones.

205.E88.X The discussion in the previous paragraphs provided the Board's context for using "material" and "more than inconsequential" for the magnitude thresholds in the standard's definitions. "More than inconsequential" indicates an amount that is less than material yet has significance.

205.E89.X The Board also considered the existing guidance in the Board's interim standards for evaluating materiality and accumulating audit differences in a financial statement audit. Paragraph .41 of AU sec. 312, *Audit Risk and Materiality in Conducting an Audit,* states:

> In aggregating likely misstatements that the entity has not corrected, pursuant to paragraphs .34 and .35, the auditor may designate an amount below which misstatements need not be accumulated. This amount should be set so that any such misstatements, either individually or when aggregated with other such misstatements, would not be material to the financial statements, after the possibility of further undetected misstatements is considered.

205.E90.X The Board considered the discussion in AU sec. 312 that spoke specifically to evaluating differences individually *and in the aggregate,* as well as to considering the possibility of additional undetected misstatements, important distinguishing factors that should be carried through to the evaluation of whether a control deficiency represents a significant deficiency because the magnitude of the potential misstatement is more than inconsequential.

---

5. See Section 10A of the Securities Exchange Act of 1934, 15 U.S.C., 78j-1.

205.E91.X The Board combined its understanding of the salient concepts in AU sec. 312 and the SEC guidance on materiality to develop the following definition of inconsequential:

> A misstatement is *inconsequential* if a reasonable person would conclude, after considering the possibility of further undetected misstatements, that the misstatement, either individually or when aggregated with other misstatements, would clearly be immaterial to the financial statements. If a reasonable person could not reach such a conclusion regarding a particular misstatement, that misstatement is *more than inconsequential.*

205.E92.X Finally, the inclusion of *annual or interim financial statements* in the definitions rather than just "annual financial statements" was intentional and, in the Board's opinion, closely aligned with the spirit of what Section 404 seeks to accomplish. However, the Board decided that this choice needed clarification within the auditing standard. The Board did not intend the inclusion of the interim financial statements in the definition to require the auditor to perform *an audit of internal control over financial reporting* at each interim date. Rather, the Board believed that the SEC's definition of internal control over financial reporting included all financial reporting that a public company makes publicly available. In other words, internal control over financial reporting includes controls over the preparation of annual and quarterly financial statements. Thus, an evaluation of internal control over financial reporting as of yearend encompasses controls over the annual financial reporting and quarterly financial reporting as such controls exist at that point in time.

205.E93.X Paragraphs 76 and 77 of the standard clarify this interpretation, as part of the discussion of the period-end financial reporting process. The period-end financial reporting process includes procedures to prepare both annual and quarterly financial statements.

¶ 205.XI. *Strong Indicators of Material Weaknesses and DeFacto Significant Deficiencies*

205.E94.XI The proposed standard identified a number of circumstances that, because of their likely significant negative effect on internal control over financial reporting, are significant deficiencies as well as strong indicators that a material weakness exists. The Board developed this list to promote increased rigor and consistency in auditors' evaluations of weaknesses. For the implementation of Section 404 of the Act to achieve its objectives, the public must have confidence that all material weaknesses that exist as of the company's year-end will be publicly reported. Historically, relatively few material weaknesses have been reported by the auditor to management and the audit committee. That condition is partly due to the nature of a financial statement audit. In an audit of only the financial statements, the auditor does not have a detection responsibility for material weaknesses in internal control; such a detection responsibility is being newly introduced for all public companies through Sections 103 and 404 of the Act. However, the Board was concerned about instances in which auditors had identified a condition that should have been, but was not, communicated as a material weakness. The intention of including the list of strong indicators of material weaknesses in the proposed standard was to bring further clarity to conditions that were likely to be material weaknesses in internal control and to create more consistency in auditors' evaluations.

205.E95.XI Most commenters were generally supportive of a list of significant deficiencies and strong indicators of the existence of material weaknesses. They believed such a list provided instructive guidance to both management and the auditor. Some commenters, however, disagreed with the proposed approach of providing such a list. They believed that the determination of the significance of a deficiency should be left entirely to auditor judgment. A few commenters requested clarification of the term "strong indicator" and specific guidance on how and when a "strong indicator" could be overcome. A number of commenters expressed various concerns with individual circumstances included in the list.

- *Restatement of previously issued financial statements to reflect the correction of a misstatement.* Some commenters expressed concern about the kinds of restatements that would trigger this provision. A few mentioned the specific instance in which the restatement reflected the SEC's subsequent view of an accounting matter when the auditor, upon reevaluation, continued to believe that management had reasonable support for its original position. They believed this specific circumstance would not necessarily indicate a significant deficiency in internal control over financial reporting. Others commented that a restatement of previously issued financial statements would indicate a significant deficiency and strong indicator of a material weakness in the prior period but not necessarily in the current period.

- *Identification by the auditor of a material misstatement in financial statements in the current period that was not initially identified by the company's internal control over financial reporting (even if management subsequently corrects the misstatement).* Several commenters, issuers and auditors alike, expressed concern about including this circumstance on the list. They explained that, frequently, management is completing the preparation of the financial statements at the same time that the auditor is completing his or her auditing procedures. In the face of this "strong indicator" provision, a lively debate of "who found it first" would ensue whenever the auditor identifies a misstatement that management subsequently corrects. Another argument is that the company's controls would have detected a misstatement identified by the auditor if the controls had an opportunity to operate (that is, the auditor performed his or her testing before the company's controls had an opportunity to operate). Several issuers indicated that they would prevent this latter situation by delaying the auditor's work until the issuers had clearly completed their entire period-end financial reporting process — a delay they viewed as detrimental.

- *For larger, more complex entities, the internal audit function or the risk assessment function is ineffective.* Several commenters asked for specific factors the auditor was expected to use to assess the effectiveness of these functions.

- *For complex entities in highly regulated industries, an ineffective regulatory compliance function.* Several commenters, particularly issuers in highly regulated industries, objected to the inclusion of this circumstance because they believed this to be outside the scope of internal control over financial reporting. (They agreed that this would be an internal control-related matter, but one that falls into operating effectiveness and compliance with laws and regulations, not financial reporting.) Many of these commenters suggested that this circumstance be deleted from the list altogether. Fewer commenters suggested that this problem could be addressed by simply clarifying that this circumstance is limited to situations in which the ineffective regulatory function relates solely to those aspects for which related violations of laws and regulations could have a direct and material effect on the financial statements.

- *Identification of fraud of any magnitude on the part of senior management.* Several commenters expressed concern that the inclusion of this circumstance created a detection responsibility for the auditor such that the auditor would have to plan and perform procedures to detect fraud of *any magnitude* on the part of senior management. Others expressed concern that identification of fraud on the part of senior management by the company's system of internal control over financial reporting might indicate that controls were operating effectively rather than indicating a significant deficiency or material weakness. Still others requested clarification on how to determine who constituted "senior management."

205.E96.XI A couple of commenters also suggested that an ineffective control environment should be added to the list.

205.E97.XI The Board concluded that the list of significant deficiencies and strong indicators of material weakness should be retained. Such a list will promote consistency in auditors' and managements' evaluations of deficiencies consistent with the definitions of significant deficiency and material weakness. The Board also decided to retain the existing structure of the list. Although the standard leaves auditor judgment to determine whether those deficiencies are material weaknesses, the existence of one of the listed deficiencies is by definition a significant deficiency. Furthermore, the "strong indicator" construct allows the auditor to factor extenuating or unique circumstances into the evaluation and possibly to conclude that the situation does not represent a material weakness, rather, only a significant deficiency.

205.E98.XI The Board decided that further clarification was not necessary within the standard itself addressing specifically how and when a "strong indicator" can be overcome. The term "strong indicator" was selected as opposed to the stronger "presumption" or other such term precisely because the Board did not intend to provide detailed instruction on how to overcome such a presumption. It is, nevertheless, the Board's view that auditors should be biased toward considering the listed circumstances as material weaknesses.

205.E99.XI The Board decided to clarify several circumstances included in the list:

- *Restatement of previously issued financial statements to reflect the correction of a misstatement.* The Board observed that the circumstance in which a restatement reflected the SEC's subsequent view of an accounting matter, when the auditor concluded that management had reasonable support for its original position, might present a good example of only a significant deficiency and not a material weakness. However, the Board concluded that requiring this situation to, nonetheless, be considered by definition a significant deficiency is appropriate, especially considering that the primary result of the circumstance being considered a significant deficiency is the communication of the matter to the audit committee. Although the audit committee might already be well aware of the circumstances of any restatement, a restatement to reflect the SEC's view on an accounting matter at least has implications for the quality of the company's accounting principles, which is already a required communication to the audit committee.

With regard to a restatement being a strong indicator of a material weakness in the prior period but not necessarily the current period, the Board disagreed with these comments. By virtue of the restatement occurring during the current period, the Board views it as appropriate to consider that circumstance a strong indicator that a material weakness existed during the current period. Depending on the circumstances of the restatement, however, the material weakness may also have been corrected during the current period. The construct of the standard does not preclude management and the auditor from determining that the circumstance was corrected prior to year-end and, therefore, that a material weakness did not exist at year-end. The emphasis here is that the circumstance is a strong indicator that a material weakness exists; management and the auditor will separately need to determine whether it has been corrected. The Board decided that no further clarification was needed in this regard.

- *Identification by the auditor of a material misstatement in financial statements in the current period that was not initially identified by the company's internal control over financial reporting (even if management subsequently corrects the misstatement).* Regarding the "who-found-it-first" dilemma, the Board recognizes that this circumstance will present certain implementation challenges. However, the Board decided that none of those challenges were so significant as to require eliminating this circumstance from the list.

When the Board developed the list of strong indicators, the Board observed that it is not uncommon for the financial statement auditor to identify material misstatements in the course of the audit that are corrected by management prior to the issuance of the company's financial statements. In some cases, management has relied on the auditor to identify misstatements in certain financial statement items and to propose corrections in amount, classification, or disclosure. With the introduction of the requirement for management and the auditor to report on the effectiveness of internal control over financial reporting, it becomes obvious that this situation is unacceptable, unless management is willing to accept other than an unqualified report on the internal control effectiveness. (This situation also raises the question as to the extent management may rely on the annual audit to produce accurate and fair financial statements without impairing the auditor's independence.) This situation is included on the list of strong indicators because the Board believes it will encourage management and auditors to evaluate this situation with intellectual honesty and to recognize, first, that the company's internal control should provide reasonable assurance that the company's financial statements are presented fairly in accordance with generally accepted accounting principles.

Timing might be a concern for some issuers. However, to the extent that management takes additional steps to ensure that the financial information is correct prior to providing it to their auditors, this may, at times, result in an improved control environment. When companies and auditors work almost simultaneously on completing the preparation of the annual financial statements and the audit, respectively, the role of the auditor can blur with the responsibility of management. In the year-end rush to complete the annual report, some companies might have come to rely on their auditors as a "control" to further ensure no misstatements are accidentally reflected in the financial statements. The principal burden seems to be for management's work schedule and administration of their financial reporting deadlines to allow the auditor sufficient time to complete his or her procedures.

Further, if the auditor initially identified a material misstatement in the financial statements but, given the circumstances, determined that management ultimately would have found the misstatement, the auditor could determine that the circumstance was a significant deficiency but not a material weakness. The Board decided to retain the provision that this circumstance is at least a significant deficiency because reporting such a circumstance to the audit committee would always be appropriate.

- *For larger, more complex entities, the internal audit function or the risk assessment function is ineffective.* Relatively few commenters requested clarification on how to evaluate these functions. The Board expects that most auditors will not have trouble making this evaluation. Similar to the audit committee evaluation, this evaluation is not a separate evaluation of the internal audit or risk assessment functions but, rather, is a way of requiring the auditor to speak up if either of these functions is obviously ineffective at an entity that needs them to have an effective monitoring or risk assessment component. Unlike the audit committee discussion, most commenters seemed to have understood that this was the context for the internal audit and risk assessment function evaluation. Nonetheless, the Board decided to add a clarifying note to this circumstance emphasizing the context.

- *For complex entities in highly regulated industries, an ineffective regulatory compliance function.* The Board decided that this circumstance, as described in the proposed standard, would encompass aspects that are outside internal control over financial reporting (which would, of course, be inappropriate for purposes of this standard given its definition of internal control over financial reporting). The Board concluded that this circumstance should be retained, though clarified, to only apply to those aspects of an ineffective regulatory compliance function that could have a material effect on the financial statements.

- *Identification of fraud of any magnitude on the part of senior management.* The Board did not intend to create any additional detection responsibility for the auditor; rather, it intended that this circumstance apply to fraud on the part of senior management that came to the auditor's attention, regardless of amount. The Board decided to clarify the standard to make this clear. The Board noted that identification of fraud by the company's system of internal control over financial reporting might indicate that controls were operating effectively, except when that fraud involves senior management. Because of the critical role of tone-at-the-top in the overall effectiveness of the control environment and due to the significant negative evidence that fraud of any magnitude on the part of senior management reflects on the control environment, the Board decided that it is appropriate to include this circumstance in the list, regardless of whether the company's controls detected the fraud. The Board also decided to clarify who is included in "senior management" for this purpose.

205.E100.XI The Board agreed that an ineffective control environment was a significant deficiency and a strong indicator that a material weakness exists and decided to add it to the list.

¶ 205.XII. *Independence*

205.E101.XII The proposed standard explicitly prohibited the auditor from accepting an engagement to provide an internal control-related service to an audit client that has not been specifically pre-approved by the audit committee. In other words, the audit committee would not be able to pre-approve internal control-related services as a category. The Board did not propose any specific guidance on permissible internal control-related services in the proposed standard but, rather, indicated its intent to conduct an in-depth evaluation of independence requirements in the future and highlighted its ability to amend the independence information included in the standard pending the outcome of that analysis.

205.E102.XII Comments were evenly split among investors, auditors, and issuers who believed the existing guidance was sufficient versus those who believed the Board should provide additional guidance. Commenters who believed existing guidance was sufficient indicated that the SEC's latest guidance on independence needed to be given more time to take effect given its recency and because existing guidance was clear enough. Commenters who believed more guidance was necessary suggested various additions, from more specificity about permitted and prohibited services to a sweeping ban on any internal control-related work for an audit client. Other issuers commented about auditors participating in the Section 404 implementation process at their audit clients in a manner that could be perceived as affecting their independence.

205.E103.XII Some commenters suggested that the SEC should change the pre-approval requirements on internal control-related services to specific pre-approval. Another commenter suggested that specific pre-approval of all internal control-related services would pose an unreasonable burden on the audit committee and suggested reverting to pre-approval by category.

205.E104.XII The Board clearly has the authority to set independence standards as it may deem necessary or appropriate in the public interest or for the protection of investors. Given ongoing concerns about the appropriateness of auditors providing these types of services to audit clients, the fact-specific nature of each engagement, and the critical importance of ongoing audit committee oversight of these types of services, the Board continues to believe that specific pre-approval of internal control-related services is a logical step that should not pose a burden on the audit committee beyond that which effective oversight of financial reporting already entails. Therefore, the standard retains this provision unchanged.

¶ 205.XIII. *Requirement for Adverse Opinion When a Material Weakness Exists*

205.E105.XIII The existing attestation standard (AT sec. 501) provides that, when the auditor has identified a material weakness in internal control over financial reporting, depending on the significance of the material weakness and its effect on the achievement of the objectives of the control criteria, the auditor may qualify his or her opinion ("except for the effect of the material weakness, internal control over financial reporting was effective") or express an adverse opinion ("internal control over financial reporting was not effective").

205.E106.XIII The SEC's final rules implementing Section 404 state that, "Management is not permitted to conclude that the registrant's internal control over financial reporting is effective if there are one or more material weaknesses in the registrant's internal control over financial reporting." In other words, in such a case, management must conclude that internal control over financial reporting is not effective (that is, a qualified or "except-for" conclusion is not acceptable).

205.E107.XIII The Board initially decided that the reporting model for the auditor should follow the required reporting model for management. Therefore, because management is required to express an "adverse" conclusion in the event a material weakness exists, the auditor's opinion also must be adverse. The proposed standard did not permit a qualified audit opinion in the event of a material weakness.

205.E108.XIII Comments received on requiring an adverse opinion when a material weakness exists were split. A large number affirmed that this seemed to be the only logical approach, based on a philosophical belief that if a material weakness exists, then internal control over financial reporting is ineffective. These commenters suggested that permitting a qualified opinion would be akin to creating another category of control deficiency material weaknesses that were really material (resulting in an adverse opinion) and material weaknesses that weren't so material (resulting in a qualified opinion).

205.E109.XIII A number of commenters agreed that the auditor's report must follow the same model as management' reporting, but they believe strongly that the SEC's guidance for management accommodated either a qualified or adverse opinion when a material weakness existed.

205.E110.XIII These commenters cited Section II.B.3.c of the SEC Final Rule and related footnote no. 72:

> The final rules therefore preclude management from determining that a company's internal control over financial reporting is effective if it identifies one or more material weaknesses in the company's internal control over financial reporting. This is consistent with interim attestation standards. See AT sec. 501.

205.E111.XIII They believe this reference to the interim attestation standard in the SEC Final Rule is referring to paragraph .37 of AT sec. 501, which states, in part,

> Therefore, the presence of a material weakness will preclude the practitioner from concluding that the entity has effective internal control. However, depending on the significance of the material weakness and its effect on the achievement of the objectives of the control criteria, the practitioner may qualify his or her opinion (that is, express an opinion that internal control is effective "except for" the material weakness noted) or may express an adverse opinion.

205.E112.XIII Their reading of the SEC Final Rule and the interim attestation standard led them to conclude that it would be appropriate for the auditor to express either an adverse opinion or a qualified "except-for" opinion about the effectiveness of the company's internal control over financial reporting depending on the circumstances.

205.E113.XIII Some commenters responded that they thought a qualified opinion would be appropriate in certain cases, such as an acquisition close to year-end (too close to be able to assess controls at the acquiree).

205.E114.XIII After additional consultation with the SEC staff about this issue, the Board decided to retain the proposed reporting model in the standard. The primary reason for that decision was the Board's continued understanding that the SEC staff would expect only an adverse conclusion from management (not a qualified conclusion) in the event a material weakness existed as of the date of management's report.

205.E115.XIII The commenters who suggested that a qualified opinion should be permitted in certain circumstances, such as an acquisition close to year-end, were essentially describing scope limitations. The standard permits a qualified opinion, a disclaimer of opinion, or withdrawal from the engagement if there are restrictions on the scope of the engagement. As it relates specifically to acquisitions near year-end, this is another case in which the auditor's model needs to follow the model that the SEC sets for management. The standard added a new paragraph to Appendix B permitting the auditor to limit the scope of his or her work (without referring to a scope limitation in the auditor's report) in the same manner that the SEC permits management to limit its assessment. In other words, if the SEC permits management to exclude an entity acquired late in the year from a company's assessment of internal control over financial reporting, then the auditor could do the same.

¶ 205.XIV. *Rotating Tests of Controls*

205.E116.XIV The proposed standard directed the auditor to perform tests of controls on "relevant assertions" rather than on "significant controls." To comply with those requirements, the auditor would be required to apply tests to those controls that are important to presenting each relevant assertion in the financial statements. The proposed standard emphasized controls that affect relevant assertions because those are the points at which misstatements could occur. However, it is neither necessary to test all controls nor to test redundant controls (unless redundancy is itself a control objective, as in the case of certain computer controls). Thus, the proposed standard encouraged the auditor to identify and test controls that addressed the primary areas in which misstatements could occur, yet limited the auditor's work to only the necessary controls.

205.E117.XIV Expressing the extent of testing in this manner also simplified other issues involving extent of testing decisions from year to year (the so-called "rotating tests of controls" issue). The proposed standard stated that the auditor should vary testing from year to year, both to introduce unpredictability into the testing and to respond to changes at the company. However, the proposed standard maintained that each year's audit must stand on its own. Therefore, the auditor must obtain evidence of the effectiveness of controls over all relevant assertions related to all significant accounts and disclosures every year.

205.E118.XIV Auditors and investors expressed support for these provisions as described in the proposed standard. In fact, some commenters compared the notion of rotating tests of control in an audit of internal control over financial reporting to an auditor testing accounts receivable only once every few years in a financial statement audit. Permitting so-called rotation of testing would compromise the auditor's ability to obtain reasonable assurance that his or her opinion was correct.

205.E119.XIV Others, especially issuers concerned with limiting costs, strongly advocated some form of rotating tests of controls. Some commenters suggested that the auditor should have broad latitude to perform some cursory procedures to determine whether any changes had occurred in controls and, if not, to curtail any further testing in that area. Some suggested that testing as described in the proposed standard should be required in the first year of the audit (the "baseline" year) and that in subsequent years the auditor should be able to reduce the required testing. Others suggested progressively less aggressive strategies for reducing the amount of work the auditor should be required to perform. In fact, several commenters (primarily internal auditors) described "baselining" controls as an important strategy to retain. They argued, for example, that IT application controls, once tested, could be relied upon (without additional testing) in subsequent years as long as general controls over program changes and access controls were effective and continued to be tested.

205.E120.XIV The Board concluded that each year's audit must stand on its own. Cumulative audit knowledge is not to be ignored; some natural efficiencies will emerge as the auditor repeats the audit process. For example, the auditor will frequently spend less time to obtain the requisite understanding of the company's internal control over financial reporting in subsequent years compared with the time necessary in the first year's audit of internal control over financial reporting. Also, to the extent that the auditor has previous knowledge of control weaknesses, his or her audit strategy should, of course, reflect that knowledge. For example, a pattern of mistakes in prior periods is usually a good indicator of the areas in which misstatements are likely to occur. However, the absence of fraud in prior periods is not a reasonable indicator of the likelihood of misstatement due to fraud.

205.E121.XIV However, the auditor needs to test controls every year, regardless of whether controls have obviously changed. Even if nothing else changed about the company — no changes in the business model, employees, organization, etc. — controls that were effective last year may not be effective this year due to error, complacency, distraction, and other human conditions that result in the inherent limitations in internal control over financial reporting.

205.E122.XIV What several commenters referred to as "baselining" (especially as it relates to IT controls) is more commonly referred to by auditors as "benchmarking." This type of testing strategy for application controls is not precluded by the standard. However, the Board believes that providing a description of this approach is beyond the scope of this standard. For these reasons, the standard does not address it.

¶ 205.XV. *Mandatory Integration with the Audit of the Financial Statements*

205.E123.XV Section 404(b) of the Act provides that the auditor's attestation of management's assessment of internal control shall not be the subject of a separate engagement. Because the objectives of and work involved in performing both an attestation of management's assessment of internal control over financial reporting and an audit of the financial statements are closely interrelated, the proposed auditing standard introduced an integrated audit of internal control over financial reporting and audit of financial statements.

205.E124.XV However, the proposed standard went even further. Because of the potential significance of the information obtained during the audit of the financial statements to the auditor's conclusions about the effectiveness of internal control over financial reporting, the proposed standard stated that the auditor could not audit internal control over financial reporting without also auditing the financial statements. (However, the proposed standard retained the auditor's ability to audit *only* the financial statements, which might be necessary in the case of certain initial public offerings.)

205.E125.XV Although the Board solicited specific comment on whether the auditor should be prohibited from performing an audit of internal control over financial reporting without also performing an audit of the financial statements, few commenters focused on the significance of the potentially negative evidence that would be obtained during the audit of the financial statements or the implications of this prohibition. Most commenters focused on the wording of Section 404(b), which indicates that the auditor's attestation of management's assessment of internal control over financial reporting shall not be the subject of a separate engagement. Based on this information, most commenters saw the prohibition in the proposed standard as superfluous and benign.

205.E126.XV Several commenters recognized the importance of the potentially negative evidence that might be obtained as part of the audit of the financial statements and expressed strong support for requiring that an audit of financial statements be performed to audit internal control over financial reporting.

205.E127.XV Others recognized the implications of this prohibition and expressed concern: What if a company wanted or needed an opinion on the effectiveness of internal control over financial reporting as of an interim date? For the most part, these commenters (primarily issuers) objected to the implication that an auditor would have to audit a company's financial statements as of an interim date to enable him or her to audit and report on its internal control over financial reporting as of that same interim date. Other issuers expressed objections related to their desires to engage one auditor to provide an opinion on the effectiveness of internal control over financial reporting and another to audit the financial statements. Others requested clarification about which guidance would apply when other forms of internal control work were requested by companies.

205.E128.XV The Board concluded that an auditor should perform an audit of internal control over financial reporting only when he or she has also audited company's financial statements. The auditor must audit the financial statements to have a high level of assurance that his or her conclusion on the effectiveness of internal control over financial reporting is correct. Inherent in the reasonable assurance provided by the auditor's opinion on internal control over financial reporting is a responsibility for the auditor to plan and perform his or her work to obtain reasonable assurance that material weaknesses, if they exist, are detected. As previously discussed, this standard states that the identification by the auditor of a *material misstatement* in the financial statements that was not initially identified by the company's internal control over financial reporting, is a strong indicator of a material weakness. Without performing a financial statement audit, the auditor would not have reasonable assurance that he or she had detected all material misstatements. The Board believes that allowing the auditor to audit internal control over financial reporting without also auditing the financial statements would not provide the auditor with a high level of assurance and would mislead investors in terms of the level of assurance obtained.

205.E129.XV In response to other concerns, the Board noted that an auditor can report on the effectiveness of internal control over financial reporting using existing AT sec. 501 for purposes other than satisfying the requirements of Section 404. This standard supersedes AT sec. 501 only as it relates to complying with Section 404 of the Act.

205.E130.XV Although reporting under the remaining provisions of AT sec. 501 is currently permissible, the Board believes reports issued for public companies under the remaining provisions of AT sec. 501 will be infrequent. In any event, additional rulemaking might be necessary to prevent confusion that might arise from reporting on internal control engagements under two different standards. For example, explanatory language could be added to reports issued under AT sec. 501 to clarify that an audit of financial statements was not performed in conjunction with the attestation on internal control over financial reporting and that such a report is not the report resulting from an audit of internal control over financial reporting performed in conjunction with an audit of the financial statements under this standard. This report modification would alert report readers, particularly if such a report were to appear in an SEC filing or otherwise be made publicly available, that the assurance obtained by the auditor in that engagement is different from the assurance that would have been obtained by the auditor for Section 404 purposes. Another example of the type of change that might be necessary in separate rulemaking to AT sec. 501 would be to supplement the performance directions to be comparable to those in this standard. Auditors should remain alert for additional rulemaking by the Board that affects AT sec. 501.

¶ 300. Cross Reference Tables

¶ 301. Standard Section

Standard ¶	Analysis ¶	Rules and Regulations	Who is Affected	Effect	Action
1 through 3	100	Sarbanes-Oxley Act Sections 103(a)(2)(A)(iii) and 404 Securities Exchange Act of 1934 Sections 3, 12, and 15(d); Securities Act of 1933.	Management, Directors, Audit Committee Members, Auditors, Internal Auditors, Accounting Staff, Accounting Management, Attorneys Preparing SEC Reporting, Financial Statement Users, Investors, Creditors, Regulators (in specialized industries, such as banking or insurance)	The PCAOB has proposed another auditing standard that amends or supersedes many other interim auditing standards as a result of the adoption of this standard (see PCAOB Release No. 2004-002, March 9, 2004). Of particular importance is the fact that AU Section 325, *Communication of Internal Control Related Matters Noted in an Audit*, and AT Section 501, *Reporting on an Entity's Internal Control Over Financial Reporting*, will be superseded by PCAOB Auditing Standard No. 2 as of November 15, 2004. In addition, the following interim standards will be amended to conform with Auditing Standard No. 2: • AU Section 310, *Appointment of the Independent Auditor* • AU Section 311, *Planning and Supervision* • AU Section 312, *Audit Risk and Materiality in Conducting an Audit* • AU Section 313, *Substantive Tests Prior to the Balance Sheet Date*	

Standard ¶	Analysis ¶	Rules and Regulations	Who is Affected	Effect	Action
				• AU Section 316, *Consideration of Fraud in a Financial Statement Audit* • AU Section 319, *Consideration of Internal Control in a Financial Statement Audit* • AU Section 322, *The Auditor's Consideration of the Internal Audit Function in an Audit of Financial Statements* • AU Section 324, *Service Organizations* • AU Section 326, *Evidential Matter* • AU Section 329, *Analytical Procedures* • AU Section 332, *Auditing Derivative Instruments, Hedging Activities, and Investments in Securities* • AU Section 333, *Management Representation* • AU Section 339, *Audit Documentation* • AU Section 342, *Auditing Accounting Estimates* • AU Section 508, *Reports on Audited Financial Statements* • AU Section 530, *Dating of the Independent Auditor's Report* • AU Section 543, *Part of Audit Performed by Other Independent Auditors* • AU Section	Auditors must comply with this new auditing standard when performing the newly required audit of internal control over financial reporting in conjunction with an audit of financial statements. They should also take into account the conforming amendments to the interim standards proposed in PCAOB Release No. 2004-002.

WG&L Warren, Gorham & Lamont

Standard ¶	Analysis ¶	Rules and Regulations	Who is Affected	Effect	Action
				560, *Subsequent Events* • AU Section 561, *Subsequent Discovery of Facts Existing at the Date of the Auditor's Report* • AU Section 711, *Filings Under Federal Securities Statutes* • AU Section 722, *Interim Financial Information* • ET Section 101, *Independence*	
4 through 6	101	Sarbanes-Oxley Act Section 302; 17 CFR §240.13a-14(a); 17 CFR §240.15d-14(a).	Management, Auditors	The issuer's auditor must express an opinion on management's assessment of the effectiveness of internal controls over financial reporting. The auditor's review of management's assessment must provide a level of reasonable assurance that the company's financial statements are materially accurate. The auditor must also audit the company's financial statements as of the date specified in management's assessment.	Management must evaluate, test, and document the company's system of internal control over financial reporting, then prepare an assessment. The company's auditor must evaluate management's assessment as well as obtain and evaluate evidence that the company's internal control over financial reporting is designed and operating effectively. In order to do this, the auditor must also audit the company's financial statements for the same time period covered by management's assessment of internal control.

Standard ¶	Analysis ¶	Rules and Regulations	Who is Affected	Effect	Action
7 through 12	102	17 CFR 240.13a-15(f) and 17 CFR 240.15d-15(f); FAS No. 5, *Accounting for Contingencies.*	Auditors	The terms "internal control over financial reporting," "control deficiency," "deficiency in design," "deficiency in operation," "significant deficiency," "material weakness," "preventative control," and "detective control" are defined.	Those involved with internal control over financial reporting should become familiar with the definitions in order to avoid any confusion.
13 through 15	103	Statement on Auditing Standards (SAS) No. 95SAS No. 95, *Generally Accepted Auditing Standards;* AU Section 319, *Consideration of Internal Control in a Financial Statement Audit;* PCAOB Rule 3300T *Interim Auditing Standards.*	Management, Auditors	The auditing standard defines the characteristics of acceptable internal control frameworks that can be used to assess compliance with Sections 302 and 404 of the Sarbanes-Oxley Act. The characteristics are defined so narrowly that only the COSO framework can possibly be used by U.S. issuers for compliance with the Act at this time.	Companies that have not already done so should ensure that they are implementing at least the components of the COSO framework that relate to financial reporting, though certain aspects of the efficiency and effectiveness of operations and compliance with laws and regulations will also fall under the purview of internal control over financial reporting.
16	104	None cited	Management, Auditors	Internal control over financial reporting is not expected to completely prevent or detect all material misstatements, due to inherent limitations.	Establish realistic expectations for internal control over financial reporting, and, as much as is feasible, introduce safeguards against human error and fraud in order to minimize the risk of financial misstatements.

Standard ¶	Analysis ¶	Rules and Regulations	Who is Affected	Effect	Action
17 through 19	105	SEC Release No. 33-8238, *Final Rule: Management's Reports on Internal Control Over Financial Reporting and Certification of Disclosure in Exchange Act Periodic Reports* (June 5, 2003).	Management, Auditors	The auditing standard requires the management assessment and auditor attestation of internal control over financial reporting to be at the level of reasonable, not absolute, assurance.	Management and the company's auditors should understand the inherent limitations involved with internal control and should discuss the remote likelihood that material misstatements will not be detected or prevented by management's assessment and the audit of internal control over financial reporting. Management should have a plan in place to address this possibility. Management should also take primary responsibility for conveying the effectiveness of the company's internal over financial reporting to users of the company's financial reports.

Standard ¶	Analysis ¶	Rules and Regulations	Who is Affected	Effect	Action
20 through 21	106	17 CFR 228.308(a) and 17 CFR 228.308(c), (Items 308(a) and (c) of Regulation S-B and S-K, respectively).	Management, Audit Committee Members, Auditors	Sufficient documentation is required to pass an audit of internal control over financial reporting. Management must accept responsibility for and assess the effectiveness of the internal controls over financial reporting. Documentation serves as evidence of this responsibility and assessment and is therefore an essential requirement in an audit of internal control over financial reporting.	Management must accept responsibility for and assess the effectiveness of the internal controls over financial reporting. During management's assessment, proper and complete documentation of the effectiveness of the company's internal controls must be compiled. A written assessment of the effectiveness of the company's internal control over financial reporting must be prepared by management at the end of each fiscal year. The auditor must notify management and the audit committee in writing if the auditor finds that management has not fulfilled its responsibilities with regard to this assessment process.
22 through 23	107	AU Section 312, *Audit Risk and Materiality in Conducting an Audit.*	Management, Auditors	Auditors are to use the same definition of materiality and the same quantitative and qualitative judgments in an audit of the effectiveness of internal controls over financial reporting that they would use in an audit of financial statements.	Management and the company's auditors should establish defined levels of materiality with regard to the financial reporting at both the financial-statement level and the individual account-balance level.

Standard ¶	Analysis ¶	Rules and Regulations	Who is Affected	Effect	Action
24 through 26	108	AU Section 316, *Consideration of Fraud in a Financial Statement Audit.*	Management, Directors, Audit Committee Members, Internal Auditors, Ethics Officers, Auditors	Auditors are required to place a special emphasis on their examination of controls designed to detect and prevent fraud.	The auditor should evaluate the company's control environment, risk assessment processes, codes of ethics, internal audit activities, and management's procedures for handling complaints. Management should ensure that the company's system of internal control is designed specifically to prevent, deter, and detect fraud. Management, directors, and audit committee members should confirm their commitment to the "tone at the top" concept as outlined in the COSO framework.
27 through 141	109	See ¶s 109.1– 109.8.2 for rules and regulations cited.	Management, Auditors	The audit of internal control over financial reporting must be done in conjunction with an audit of the financial statements. All of the traditional auditing standards and considerations are applicable to this auditing standard as well.	Auditors should apply all of the general and applicable fieldwork standards that would be appropriate to an audit of financial statements to an audit of internal control over financial reporting.
30 through 38	109.1	AU Section 150, *Generally Accepted Auditing Standards;* 17 CFR 210.2-01 (Rule 2-01 of Regulation S-X).	Auditors	All of the traditional general auditing standards and considerations are applicable to an audit of internal control over financial reporting.	Auditors can leverage existing skills and methods.

Standard ¶	Analysis ¶	Rules and Regulations	Who is Affected	Effect	Action
31	109.1.1	None cited.	Auditors	The auditor must have competence in the subject matter of internal control over financial reporting.	Auditors must obtain training in the subject matter of internal control over financial reporting prior to commencing audits of internal control over financial reporting. Auditors should be well-versed in the COSO framework.
32 through 35	109.1.2	AU Section 150, *Generally Accepted Auditing Standards;* 17 CFR 210.2-01 (Rule 2-01 of Regulation S-X).	Management, Audit Committee Members, Auditors	The auditor must not function in the role of management and must not audit his or her own work, but may provide substantive recommendations regarding the design or operation of internal control over financial reporting as a by-product of the audit.	Management should remain actively involved in the design, documentation, and testing of internal control over financial reporting and must not delegate all responsibility for these matters to the auditor. Audit committees must pre-approve internal control-related services provided by the company's auditor. Auditors and audit committee members should be vigilant about any appearance of compromised auditor independence. Auditors may provide internal control services that are pre-approved by the audit committee.
36	109.1.3	None cited	Auditors	Auditors must exercise professional skepticism in an audit of internal control over financial reporting.	The auditor must conduct a critical assessment of the work that management has performed in evaluating and testing controls.

WG
&L Warren, Gorham & Lamont

Standard ¶	Analysis ¶	Rules and Regulations	Who is Affected	Effect	Action
37 through 38	109.1.4	None cited	Auditors	The fieldwork and reporting standards for an audit of internal control over financial reporting are established by this auditing standard.	The auditor should carefully review the fieldwork and reporting requirements outlined in this auditing standard, and should apply the concept of materiality when following the general and fieldwork standards.
39	109.2	None cited	Auditors	The guidance on planning the audit engagement is very similar to existing guidance in the existing audit literature, with specific details added with regard to internal control over financial reporting.	When planning the audit engagement, auditors are required to consider various aspects of a company's internal controls and operations, management's assessment of internal control effectiveness, and preliminary judgments about the company's controls and levels of risk.
40 through 46	109.3	None cited	Management, Internal Auditors, Auditors	The standard outlines what elements of a company's internal control structure should have been addressed by management in its assessment of internal control over financial reporting.	The auditor must examine sufficient evidence and obtain an understanding of management's process for assessing the effectiveness of the company's internal control over financial reporting. Management should ensure that its assessment of internal control over financial reporting addresses the elements that the auditor is expected to cover in its audit of management's assessment.

Standard ¶	Analysis ¶	Rules and Regulations	Who is Affected	Effect	Action
42 through 46	109.3.1	None cited	Management, Internal Auditors, Auditors	The auditor is required to evaluate the adequacy of management's documentation in support of its assessment of internal control over financial reporting.	Management should become familiar with the documentation requirements provided by the standard. The auditor must review the issuer's documentation of management's assessment of internal control over financial reporting. Given a substantial absence of documentation of internal control over financial reporting on the part of the issuer, the auditor must withhold the attestation or limit the scope of the audit of internal control over financial reporting.
47 through 87	109.4	See ¶s 109.4.1– 109.4.8 for rules and regulations cited.	Management, Auditors	Based on the COSO framework, the auditing standard defines specific steps the auditor must perform to evaluate the documentation and establish an understanding of internal control over financial reporting.	The auditor must perform certain tasks and procedures to evaluate management's documentation and to establish an understanding of the company's internal control over financial reporting. These tasks and procedures follow the model put forth in the COSO framework. Management is expected to implement the five basic COSO components: control environment, risk assessment, control activities, information and communication, and monitoring

Standard ¶	Analysis ¶	Rules and Regulations	Who is Affected	Effect	Action
52 through 54	109.4.1	None cited.	Management, Internal Auditors, Auditors	The auditing standard recommends that auditors test those controls that affect primarily the control environment and pervade all other controls first, i.e., the company-level controls. Auditors should evaluate the results of the evaluation of the company-wide controls when creating the audit plan for the rest of the company's controls over financial reporting.	Identification and testing of company-level controls by the external auditor is required. Management should ensure that proper documentation of company-wide controls exists.

Standard ¶	Analysis ¶	Rules and Regulations	Who is Affected	Effect	Action
55 through 59	109.4.2	15 USC 78c; 15 USC 7201(a)(3); 17 CFR 240.10A-3 (Securities Exchange Act Rule 10A-3); 17 CFR 240.10A-3(c)(2) (Securities Exchange Act Rule 10A-3(c)(2)); 17 CFR 210.2-01(c)(7) (Regulation S-X Rule 2-01(c)(7)).	Directors, Audit Committee Members, Internal Auditors, Auditors	The auditor must review and assess the effectiveness of the audit committee's oversight of the company's external financial reporting and internal control over financial reporting.	The auditor must review the audit committee's involvement in detail and assess the effectiveness of the audit committee's oversight of the company's external financial reporting and internal control over financial reporting. The auditor must also assess the relative effectiveness of the audit committee's oversight role. If the auditor finds that the audit committee is ineffective in the oversight role, then this constitutes a significant deficiency. Boards of directors should ensure that their audit committees are in compliance with the requirements of Section 301 of the Sarbanes-Oxley Act, as well as the applicable SRO corporate governance rules.
60 through 67	109.4.3	None cited	Accounting Staff, Accounting Management, Auditors	After considering both quantitative and qualitative factors, the company's auditors must identify significant accounts.	Auditors must identify all significant accounts within the financial statements. This includes a quantitative and qualitative assessment and is significant when there is a more than remote likelihood that the account could contain misstatements.

Standard ¶	Analysis ¶	Rules and Regulations	Who is Affected	Effect	Action
68 through 70	109.4.4	AU Section 326, *Evidential Matter.*	Accounting Staff, Accounting Management, Auditors	Auditors must identify all relevant financial statement assertions.	Auditors must identify, examine, and determine the relevance of each assertion underlying each significant account. The auditor must determine the source of likely misstatements in each account.
71 through 75	109.4.5	AU Section 319, *Consideration of Internal Control in a Financial Statement Audit.*	Accounting Staff, Accounting Management, Auditors	Auditors must identify each significant process over each major class of transactions affecting significant accounts or groups of accounts. The auditor must consider the nature and characteristics of the company's information system in relation to internal control over financial reporting.	Auditors must identify, review, and evaluate each significant process over each major class of transactions affecting significant accounts or groups of accounts. The auditor must understand the flow of transactions, including how transactions are initiated, authorized, recorded, processed, and reported. This can be achieved during a walkthrough. The auditor must consider the nature and characteristics of the company's information system in relation to internal control over financial reporting.

Standard ¶	Analysis ¶	Rules and Regulations	Who is Affected	Effect	Action
76 through 78	109.4.6	None cited	Management, Directors, Audit Committee Members, Accounting Staff, Accounting Management, Auditors	Auditors must obtain an understanding of and evaluate the period-end financial reporting process.	Auditors must review and evaluate the period-end financial reporting processes to ensure that transactions are recorded in their proper periods. The impact of the company's control environment on period-end financial reporting should be taken into account by the auditor. Management, the board, and the audit committee should ensure proper oversight of the period-end process.

Standard ¶	Analysis ¶	Rules and Regulations	Who is Affected	Effect	Action
79 through 83	109.4.7	None cited	Management, Accounting Staff, Accounting Management, Auditors	The auditor is required to validate that the company's accounting systems and controls are working properly by walking transactions through the accounting system to make sure it is working as intended and employees understand the control activities they are required to perform.	The auditor is required to perform at least one walkthrough for each major class of transactions. Company personnel will be required to respond to the auditor's queries about their understanding of what is required by the company's policies, procedures, and controls. Management should ensure that the controls and procedures relevant to all significant accounts are properly documented, and that employees are adequately trained with regard to controls, exception handling, and company policies.

Standard ¶	Analysis ¶	Rules and Regulations	Who is Affected	Effect	Action
83 through 87	109.4.8	None cited	Management, Internal Auditors, Auditors	The company's auditor must obtain evidence that validates the effectiveness of controls over financial reporting.	The auditor should obtain evidence of the effectiveness of controls on which to base its opinion. The auditor must either perform these tests himself or herself or may rely, to some extent, on the work of others, such as the company's internal auditors. Management should ensure that adequate documentation exists of the company's significant control points, the nature of the controls implemented by management, the significance of each control, and the level of risk that the controls might not be operating as designed.
88 through 91	109.5	None cited	Auditors	The company's auditor must test and evaluate the design of the company's internal controls over financial reporting.	Through procedures such as inquiry, observation, walkthroughs, inspection of relevant documentation, and an evaluation of whether the controls are likely to prevent or detect errors or fraud if they operate as designed, the auditor must test and evaluate the design of the company's internal controls over financial reporting.

Standard ¶	Analysis ¶	Rules and Regulations	Who is Affected	Effect	Action
92 through 107	109.6	None cited	Auditors	The company's auditor must test and evaluate the operating effectiveness of the company's internal controls over financial reporting.	The auditor must validate the operating effectiveness of internal controls over financial reporting by using a mix of inquiries, inspection, observation, testing, and reperformance. The auditor must verify that the employees performing the controls have the necessary authority and qualifications to perform the controls effectively.
93 through 97	109.6.1	None cited	Auditors	In order to test and evaluate the operating effectiveness of the company's internal controls over financial reporting, the company's auditor must utilize a mix of inquiry, observation, documentation review, and reperformance.	The auditor's tests of the operating effectiveness of the company's internal controls over financial reporting should include written and/or oral inquiry, direct observation, documentation review, and reperformance of key controls.
98 through 103	109.6.2	None cited	Auditors	The auditor must consider time and timing issues related to tests of controls.	The auditor should evaluate the time periods covered by controls, the timing of tests of controls, and when the controls were put in place.
104 through 105	109.6.3	None cited	Auditors	The auditor must obtain sufficient evidence about whether the company's internal control over financial reporting is operating effectively.	The nature and extent of testing for each control must be determined by the auditor by taking into consideration the nature of the control, its frequency of operation, and the importance of the control.

Standard ¶	Analysis ¶	Rules and Regulations	Who is Affected	Effect	Action
106 through 107	109.6.4.	None cited	Auditors	The auditor must conduct the audit of internal control over financial reporting and the audit of the financial statements with professional skepticism.	The auditor needs to have a "questioning mind" and must conduct a critical assessment of audit evidence. When the auditor identifies exceptions to the company's control procedures, he or she should determine, using professional skepticism, the effect of the exception. Additional testing may be appropriate or necessary.
108 through 126	109.7	AU Section 319, *Internal Control in a Financial Statement Audit;* AU Section 322, *The Auditor's Consideration of the Internal Audit Function in an Audit of Financial Statements;* FAS No. 5, *Accounting for Contingencies;* The Institute of Internal Auditors, *International Standards for the Professional Practice of Internal Auditing.*	Internal Auditors, Auditors	Auditors can use the work of others to a certain extent when performing the audit. The auditing standard clarifies the ability of the auditor to use the work of others and reiterates that the auditor's opinion must be based solely on work done by the auditor or the auditor's direct validation of any work done by others.	Auditors can use the work of others but the auditors' own work must be substantial enough to form the basis for the auditors' opinion on the effectiveness of the company's internal control over financial reporting. Auditors are required to evaluate and test the work of others upon which they plan to rely. Internal auditors may provide the results of their work on the company's internal controls over financial reporting to the external auditors for use during the audit of the company's financial statements and internal control over financial reporting.

Standard ¶	Analysis ¶	Rules and Regulations	Who is Affected	Effect	Action
112 through 116	109.7.1	AU Section 319, *Internal Control in a Financial Statement Audit*; FAS No. 5, *Accounting for Contingencies.*	Internal Auditors, Auditors	Auditors must evaluate the nature of the controls subjected to the work of others before the auditors rely on that work.	Auditors must evaluate the nature of the controls subjected to the work of others before the auditors rely on that work. Auditors should not rely on the work of others when evaluating the company's overall control environment. Auditors must perform walkthroughs themselves but may obtain additional evidence from walkthroughs performed by others.
117 through 122	109.7.2	*International Standards for the Professional Practice of Internal Auditing*	Internal Auditors, Auditors	Auditors must evaluate the competence and objectivity of others before using their work.	By looking at factors such as educational level, professional experience, professional certification, continuing education, work assignments, supervision, documentation, and performance evaluations, auditors must evaluate the competence and objectivity of others before using their work. External auditors may rely on the work of qualified and objective internal auditors more heavily than the work of other parties, unless the internal auditors report solely to management.

Standard ¶	Analysis ¶	Rules and Regulations	Who is Affected	Effect	Action
123 through 126	109.7.3	None cited	Management, Internal Auditors, Auditors	Auditors must test some of the work of others in order to evaluate the quality and effectiveness of the work. The standard provides specific guidance regarding controls over period-end financial reporting, IT general controls, management self-assessment, controls over the calculation of the depreciation of assets, and alternating tests of controls.	By looking at factors such as scope of the work, adequacy of procedures, adequacy of documentation, appropriateness of conclusions, and consistency of reports, auditors must evaluate the quality and effectiveness of the work of others before using the work. Management should consult the standard's guidance regarding the auditor's use of the work of others in specific situations related to controls over period-end financial reporting, IT general controls, management self-assessment, controls over the calculation of the depreciation of assets, and alternating tests of controls.

Standard ¶	Analysis ¶	Rules and Regulations	Who is Affected	Effect	Action
127 through 141	109.8	SEC Staff Accounting Bulletin Topic 1M2, *Immaterial Misstatements That Are Intentional;* Sarbanes-Oxley Act Section 302.	Internal Auditors, Auditors	Auditors must evaluate information from all relevant sources, particularly the company's internal audit function, when forming an opinion on internal control over financial reporting.	Auditors must evaluate evidence from all relevant sources, including management's assessment of internal control over financial reporting, negative results of substantive procedures performed during the financial statement audit, any identified control deficiencies, and all relevant reports issued by the company's internal audit function. Internal audit departments must be prepared to provide the company's external auditors with copies of all reports issued during the year that have even a tangential relevancy to internal control over financial reporting.
129	109.8.1	None cited	Management, Auditors	The company's auditor can issue an unqualified opinion on the company's internal control over financial reporting only if there are no identified material weaknesses and there have been no restrictions on the scope of the audit.	The auditor must determine that there are no material weaknesses or scope restrictions in order to provide an unqualified opinion.

Standard ¶	Analysis ¶	Rules and Regulations	Who is Affected	Effect	Action
130 through 141	109.8.2	SEC Staff Accounting Bulletin Topic 1M2, *Immaterial Misstatements That Are Intentional;* Sarbanes-Oxley Act Section 302.	Management, Internal Auditors, Accounting Management, Compliance Officers, Audit Committee Members, Auditors	Auditors must evaluate deficiencies in the company's internal control over financial reporting and determine whether the deficiencies, individually or in combination, rise to the level of significant deficiencies or material weaknesses.	The auditor must look at all of the company's internal control deficiencies and determine, based on certain criteria, if the deficiencies constitute significant deficiencies or material weaknesses.
142 through 144	110	AU Section 333, *Management Representations.*	Management, Auditors	The auditor is required to obtain certain management representations specific to the audit of internal control over financial reporting.	As in all audits, the auditor must receive certain written representations from the company's CEO and CFO.
145 through 158	111	AU Section 316, *Consideration of Fraud in a Financial Statement Audit;* AU Section 330, *The Confirmation Process;* AU Section 331, *Inventories.*	Auditors	The audit of internal control over financial reporting should be integrated with the audit of the issuer's financial statements.	The auditor must integrate the audit of internal control over financial reporting with the audit of financial statements.
147 through 149	111.1	None cited	Auditors	The auditor's opinion on whether management's assessment of the effectiveness of the company's internal control over financial reporting is fairly stated must relate the effectiveness of the company's internal control over financial reporting as of a point in time and taken as a whole.	The auditor has different testing standards for the effectiveness of the company's internal control over financial reporting at a point in time versus the financial statements taken as a whole.

Standard ¶	Analysis ¶	Rules and Regulations	Who is Affected	Effect	Action
150 through 151	111.2	None cited	Auditors	Tests of controls in an audit of financial statements are different than those in an audit of internal control over financial reporting.	Auditors ordinarily perform tests of controls and substantive procedures in an audit of financial statements. The auditor is required to assess control risk during the audit of the financial statements and determine whether relevant controls operated effectively during the entire period upon which the auditor plans to place reliance on the effectiveness of those controls.
152 through 156	111.3	AU Section 316, *Consideration of Fraud in a Financial Statement Audit;* AU Section 330, *The Confirmation Process;* AU Section 331, *Inventories.*	Auditors	Tests of controls on substantive procedures in an audit of financial statements are germane in an audit of internal controls over financial reporting.	The auditor is required to continue performing tests of controls on substantive procedures.
157 through 158	111.4	None cited	Auditors	The auditor must evaluate the results of the tests of substantive procedures performed for the financial statements and apply them to conclusions about the operating effectiveness of internal control over financial reporting.	The auditor should evaluate the effect of findings in the financial statement audit on the operating effectiveness of the company's internal control over financial reporting. Particular attention must be paid to substantive procedures related to fraud, illegal acts, related-party transactions, accounting estimates, the selection of accounting principles, and misstatements.

Standard ¶	Analysis ¶	Rules and Regulations	Who is Affected	Effect	Action
159 through 161	112	AU Section 339, *Audit Documentation.*	Auditors	The documentation standard is raised from that in AU Section 339, *Audit Documentation.* The documentation requirements in this auditing standard reinforce the connection between the audit of the financial statements and the audit of internal control over financial reporting.	The auditor must adhere to the audit documentation standards set forth in AU Section 339, *Audit Documentation,* and must also include additional documentation covering all aspects of the audit of internal control over financial reporting.
162 through 199	113	See ¶s 113.1– 113.3.12 for rules and regulations.	Management, Auditors	Management must issue a report on the effectiveness of the company's internal control over financial reporting. The auditor must evaluate that report and, if it agrees with management's assessment, issue a report attesting to management's assertions.	Management is required to issue a report on the effectiveness of the company's internal control over financial reporting. The auditor is required to review and evaluate this report. Then, based on its independent assessment of the effectiveness of internal control over the issuer's financial reporting, the auditor issues its attestation of management's report. Any limit in the scope of the audit of internal control over financial reporting requires the auditor to, at a minimum, issue a qualified opinion. Management must ensure that the scope of the audit is not limited.

WG
&L Warren, Gorham & Lamont

Standard ¶	Analysis ¶	Rules and Regulations	Who is Affected	Effect	Action
162 through 165	113.1	17 CFR 228.308(a) and 17 CFR229.308(a) (Item 308(a) of Regulation S-B and Regulation S-K, respectively); 17 CFR 240.13a-14(a) and 17 CFR 240.15d-14(a) (Securities Exchange Act Rules 13a-14(a) and 15d-14(a), respectively).	Management	The auditing standard reiterates the requirements put forth in Sections 302 and 404 of the Sarbanes-Oxley Act and SEC Release No. 33-8238.	Management is required to include its assessment of the effectiveness of the company's internal control over financial reporting in its annual report required under SEC reporting regulations. Management must take responsibility for the company's internal controls. Management must identify the framework (i.e., COSO) used to conduct its assessment of the internal controls. If one or more material weaknesses are discovered by management during the assessment of the company's internal controls, management must change the internal control to eliminate the material weakness sufficiently in advance of the "as of" date and must test the effectiveness of the revised control in order to determine whether it is effective.

Standard ¶	Analysis ¶	Rules and Regulations	Who is Affected	Effect	Action
166	113.2	None cited	Management, Auditors	The auditor must evaluate management's assessment of the effectiveness of internal control over financial reporting.	The auditor should evaluate management's assessment and determine that management establishes its responsibility for internal control, used the proper framework (i.e., COSO), and presented its assessment in an acceptable form.
167 through 199	113.3	See ¶s 113.3.1 – 113.3.12 for rules and regulations.	Auditors	Every auditor's report on management's assessment of the effectiveness of internal control over financial reporting must include certain uniform elements.	Auditors must incorporate all of the listed requirements into their opinion on the effectiveness of the issuer's internal control over financial reporting. Examples of attestation statements are included in the appendices as examples for auditors to follow.
169 through 170	113.3.1	None cited	Auditors	The auditor can issue either separate or combined reports.	The auditor's report can be combined for both the audit of the financial statements and the audit of internal control over financial reporting. The auditor may also issue the reports separately. If the reports are issued separately, specific language provided in the standard must be included in each report.

WG
&L Warren, Gorham & Lamont

Standard ¶	Analysis ¶	Rules and Regulations	Who is Affected	Effect	Action
171 through 172	113.3.2	None cited	Auditors	The dates of the financial statement audit and the audit of internal control over financial reporting should be dated the same even though they may cover differing periods.	The audit of internal control over financial reporting must be done in conjunction with the audit of financial statements. Therefore the dates on the reports, whether separate or combined, should be the same.
173	113.3.3	None cited	Auditors	Under certain circumstances the auditor is required to modify the standard report.	The auditor should modify the standard report to reflect an inadequate assessment of internal control by management, a material weakness in the company's internal controls, a scope restriction, the use of other auditors' work, significant subsequent events, or other information contained in management's report on internal control over financial reporting.

Standard ¶	Analysis ¶	Rules and Regulations	Who is Affected	Effect	Action
174	113.3.4	None cited	Management, Auditors	The auditor must modify the audit opinion if the auditor determines that management's assessment process is inadequate or if the auditor determines that management's report is inappropriate.	The auditor must modify the audit opinion if the auditor determines that management's assessment process is inadequate or if the auditor determines that management's report is inappropriate. At a minimum, this means adding an explanatory paragraph describing the reasons for this conclusion. Management should make every effort to ensure that the process used for evaluating the company's internal control over financial reporting is adequate, i.e., that the process meets the requirements outlined in this auditing standard and in the SEC's requirements.
175 through 177	113.3.5	None cited	Management, Auditors	If there are one or more material weaknesses in the company's internal control over financial reporting, then the auditor must express an adverse opinion. In this case, management is also precluded from concluding that internal control over financial reporting is effective.	In the event there are any uncorrected material weaknesses at the end of the reporting year, then the auditor must express an adverse opinion on internal control over financial reporting.

Standard ¶	Analysis ¶	Rules and Regulations	Who is Affected	Effect	Action
178 through 181	113.3.6	None cited	Management, Auditors	Limitations on the scope of the audit result in a qualified opinion at best.	Given any limitation in the scope of the audit, the auditor is unable to express an unqualified opinion. Even if the scope of the audit is limited, if the auditor uncovers a material weakness, that weakness must be reported. Management should do their best to ensure the auditor is able to apply all the procedures necessary in the circumstances, with no interference from management or employees of the company.
182 through 185	113.3.7	AU Section 543, *Part of Audit Performed by Other Independent Auditors.*	Auditors	The auditor may rely on reports from other independent auditors to a certain extent.	The auditor can rely on the work of other independent auditors but determine whether or not disclose their reliance on that work in conformance with AU Section 543, *Part of Audit Performed by Other Independent Auditors.*

Standard ¶	Analysis ¶	Rules and Regulations	Who is Affected	Effect	Action
186 through 189	113.3.8	AU Section 560, *Subsequent Events.*	Management, Internal Auditors, Regulators, Auditors	Auditors must take subsequent events into consideration if they reflect changes in internal control over financial reporting that occur after the audit but before the auditor's opinion is issued.	If a subsequent event occurs after the audit but before issuance of the auditor's report, the auditor must evaluate the event and determine its impact. Management must disclose subsequent events to the auditor in the representation letter. This includes internal audit reports and regulatory agency reports that are relevant to internal control over financial reporting.
190 through 192	113.3.9	15 USC 78j-1 (Section 10A of the Securities Exchange Act of 1934).	Management, Audit Committee Members, Auditors	Management may add additional information to its report on the assessment of internal control over financial reporting that is not necessarily relevant to the audit of internal control over financial reporting. The auditor is expected to disclaim an opinion on the additional information.	If management adds any extraneous information to the standard format of the report, the auditor should disclaim this information. If the auditor believes the extra information includes a material misstatement of fact, the auditor is expected to discuss the issue with management directly. If this does not resolve the issue, the auditor is required to notify management and the audit committee in writing of its concerns regarding the information.

Standard ¶	Analysis ¶	Rules and Regulations	Who is Affected	Effect	Action
193 through 196	113.3.10	None cited	Auditors	The auditor can conclude that the financial statements deserve an unqualified opinion and simultaneously conclude that the assessment of internal control over financial reporting does not receive an unqualified opinion.	Even given a material weakness in the internal control over financial reporting, the auditor can conclude that the related financial statements are nonetheless accurate. This conclusion must be based on additional substantive procedures to determine if there was a material misstatement related to the ineffective control.
197	113.3.11	AU Section 561, *Subsequent Discovery of Facts Existing at the Date of the Auditor's Report.*	Auditors	If reliable information becomes known about a material weakness that existed at the date of the auditor's report that would have altered the auditor's conclusions, then the auditor must recall and reissue the audit opinion.	If new information becomes known about a material weakness that existed at the date of the auditor's report that would have altered the auditor's conclusions then the auditor must recall and reissue the opinion. This recall and reissue should be done according to the detailed requirements of AU Section 561, *Subsequent Discovery of Facts Existing at the Date of the Auditor's Report.*

Standard ¶	Analysis ¶	Rules and Regulations	Who is Affected	Effect	Action
198 through 199	113.3.12	AU Section 711, *Filings Under Federal Securities Statutes.*	Auditors	The auditor should apply the rules under AU Section 711, *Filings Under Federal Securities Statutes,* when the auditor's report is to be included in federal filings.	The auditor should apply the rules under AU Section 711, *Filings Under Federal Securities Statutes,* when the auditor's report is to be included in federal filings. The auditor should also apply AU Section 711 with respect to the auditor's report on management's assessment of the effectiveness of internal control over financial reporting included in such filings.
200 through 206	114	Sarbanes-Oxley Act Section 302; 15 USC 78j-1 (Section 10A of the Securities Exchange Act of 1934); 17 CFR 240.13a-14a and 17 CFR 15d-14a (Securities Exchange Act Rules 13a-14(a) and 15d-14(a), respectively); 17 CFR 240.12b-20 (Securities Exchange Act Rule 12b-20); AU Section 317, *Illegal Acts by Clients;* AU Section 722, *Interim Financial Information.*	Management, Auditors	Management is required to make disclosures under Section 302. The auditor is required to evaluate the need for any possible disclosures related to changes in internal control over financial reporting. The auditor is required to conduct limited quarterly procedures.	Management must issue the statements required by Section 302 of the Sarbanes-Oxley Act. The auditor is required to evaluate the need for any possible disclosures related to changes in internal control over financial reporting. The auditor is required to conduct quarterly inquiries and evaluations regarding the materiality of changes to internal control and any misstatements that have been discovered.

WG &L Warren, Gorham & Lamont

Standard ¶	Analysis ¶	Rules and Regulations	Who is Affected	Effect	Action
200 through 201	114.1	Sarbanes-Oxley Act Section 302); 17 CFR 240.13a-14a and 17 CFR 15d-14a (Securities Exchange Act Rules 13a-14(a) and 15d-14(a), respectively); 17 CFR 240.12b-20 (Securities Exchange Act Rule 12b-20).	Management, Auditors	Section 302 of the Sarbanes-Oxley Act requires management to make certain disclosures certifying the accuracy and reliability of the issuer's financial statements. One of those disclosures is a statement certifying that the officers of the issuer have implemented internal controls over financial reporting that are effective.	Management must certify that the internal control over the company's financial reporting is effective. Management must also issue a statement that discloses any changes in the company's internal control over financial reporting that occurred during the most recent fiscal quarter. Management must also certify that it has responsibility for internal control over financial reporting. The auditor is required to evaluate the need for any possible disclosures related to changes in internal control over financial reporting.

Standard ¶	Analysis ¶	Rules and Regulations	Who is Affected	Effect	Action
202 through 206	114.2	Sarbanes-Oxley Act Section 302; AU Section 722, *Interim Financial Information*; AU Section 317, *Illegal Acts by Clients*; 17 CFR 240.13a-14(a) and 17 CFR 240.15d-14(a) (Securities Exchange Act Rules 13a-14(a) and 15d-14(a), respectively); (Section 10A of the Securities Exchange Act of 1934).	Management, Audit Committee Members, Auditors	Interim quarterly auditor evaluations of internal control over financial reporting can be based on limited procedures.	Auditors need only perform limited procedures on a quarterly basis to validate their annual assessment. In performing the quarterly procedures, the auditor is looking for material modifications that could become a required disclosure about changes in internal control over financial reporting in order for management's certifications to be accurate. The auditor is required to notify management of any material matters. If management does not respond appropriately, the auditor must notify the audit committee.

Standard ¶	Analysis ¶	Rules and Regulations	Who is Affected	Effect	Action
207 through 214	115	AU Section 316, *Consideration of Fraud in a Financial Statement Audit*; AU Section 317, *Illegal Acts by Clients*; 15 USC 78j-1 (Section 10A of the Securities Exchange Act of 1934).	Management, Directors, Audit Committee Members, Auditors	The auditor is required to communicate in writing to management and the audit committee all significant deficiencies and material weaknesses identified during the audit. The auditor is also required to make certain communications with management and the audit committee when the auditor becomes aware of fraud or illegal acts.	The auditor is required to communicate in writing to management and the audit committee all significant deficiencies and material weaknesses identified during the audit. The auditor is also required to make certain communications with management and the audit committee when the auditor becomes aware of fraud or illegal acts. The auditor must notify the board of directors if the audit committee is ineffectively overseeing the internal control function.

Standard ¶	Analysis ¶	Rules and Regulations	Who is Affected	Effect	Action
215 through 216	116	Sarbanes-Oxley Act Section 404; 17 CFR 240.12b-2 (Securities Exchange Act Rule 12b-2).	Management, Directors, Audit Committee Members, Auditors, Internal Auditors, Accounting Staff, Accounting Management, Attorneys Preparing SEC Reporting, Financial Statement Users, Investors, Creditors, Regulators (in specialized industries, such as banking or insurance).	Companies and auditors are required to comply with PCAOB Auditing Standard No. 2 for their the internal control reporting for fiscal years ending on or after November 15, 2004 (accelerated filers) or July 15, 2005 (other companies).	Auditors of companies considered accelerated filers (seasoned U.S. companies with public float exceeding $75 million) are required to comply with PCAOB Auditing Standard No. 2 for fiscal years ending on or after November 15, 2004. Auditors of other companies (including smaller companies, foreign private issuers and companies with only registered debt securities) have until fiscal years ending on or after July 15, 2005, to comply with PCAOB Auditing Standard No. 2.
Appendix A	117	None cited	Auditors	Appendix A of the auditing standard provides sample text to guide auditors in writing opinions on internal control over financial reporting.	Auditors should consult the illustrative examples in Appendix A of the auditing standard when writing their reports on internal control over financial reporting

Standard ¶	Analysis ¶	Rules and Regulations	Who is Affected	Effect	Action
Appendix B	118	AU Section 324, *Service Organizations*; AU Section 543, *Part of Audit Performed by Other Independent Auditors.*	Auditors, Service Auditors, Service Organizations	Appendix B provides additional guidance on tests to be performed when a company has multiple locations or business units and when a company obtains services from a service organization. It also provides detailed examples of the extent of testing required by the standard.	Auditors should refer to the guidance in Appendix B when auditing companies with multiple locations or business units or companies that use service organizations. Auditors should also familiarize themselves with the examples laid out by the PCAOB of the extent of testing required to determine the effectiveness of a company's internal control over financial reporting.

Standard ¶	Analysis ¶	Rules and Regulations	Who is Affected	Effect	Action
Appendix C	119	None cited	Management, Auditors	Appendix C reiterates the PCAOB's emphasis on the importance of controls that operate to safeguard the company's assets, and defers to the COSO report for guidance on the safeguarding of assets as it relates to internal control over financial reporting.	Auditors should use the COSO framework as their guideline in determining the scope of the audit of internal controls intended to safeguard the company's assets. Management must realize that plans that could potentially affect financial reporting in future periods are not controls in the present. Business continuity plans are also not considered part of internal control over financial reporting. Management should ensure that the company has compensatory and overlapping controls in place where there is a risk of error or fraud that could affect the safeguarding of the company's assets.
Appendix D	120	None cited	Auditors	Appendix D provides detailed examples as guidance for the auditor to differentiate between a significant deficiency and a material weakness in internal control over financial reporting.	Auditors should use Appendix D as a guide when they cannot determine the difference between a significant deficiency and a material weakness. The implementation of a simple point system to score potential misstatements and levels of likelihood might also prove useful.

Standard ¶	Analysis ¶	Rules and Regulations	Who is Affected	Effect	Action
Appendix E	121	Sarbanes-Oxley Act Sections 103 and 404; AU Section 312, *Audit Risk and Materiality in Conducting an Audit;* AU Section 322, *The Auditor's Consideration of the Internal Audit Function in an Audit of Financial Statements;* AU Section 325, *Communication of Internal Control Related Matters Noted in an Audit;* SSAE No. 10, *Attestation Standards: Revision and Recodification* (AT Section 501); SEC Release No. 33-8238, *Final Rule: Management's Reports on Internal Control Over Financial Reporting and Certification of Disclosure in Exchange Act Periodic Reports* (June 5, 2003); 15 USC (Section 10A of the Securities Exchange Act of 1934); FAS No. 5, *Accounting for Contingencies;* Staff Accounting Bulletin (SAB) No. 99, *Materiality;* IAS No. 200, *Objective and Principles Governing an Audit of Financial Statements;* PCAOB Rule 3300T; *Federal Deposit Insurance Corporation*	Management, Directors, Audit Committee Members, Auditors, Internal Auditors, Accounting Staff, Accounting Management, Attorneys Preparing SEC Reporting, Financial Statement Users, Investors, Creditors, Regulators (in specialized industries, such as banking or insurance).	The PCAOB issued a proposed version of this auditing standard in October 2003. In Appendix E, the PCAOB provides its explanation of the consideration it gave to the various viewpoints submitted during the comment period.	Management and auditors should read Appendix E so they can understand the relevant thought processes that underlie the PCAOB's intent regarding various aspects of the audit of internal control over financial reporting.

Standard ¶	Analysis ¶	Rules and Regulations	Who is Affected	Effect	Action
		Improvement Act of 1991 (FDCIA)			

¶ 302. Who Is Affected

Who is Affected	Standard ¶	Analysis ¶	Rules and Regulations	Effect	Action
Accounting Management	1 through 3	100	Sarbanes-Oxley Act Sections 103(a)(2)(A)(iii) and 404; Securities Exchange Act of 1934 Sections 3, 12, and 15(d); Securities Act of 1933.	The PCAOB has proposed another auditing standard that amends or supersedes many other interim auditing standards as a result of the adoption of this standard (see PCAOB Release No. 2004-002, March 9, 2004). Of particular importance is the fact that AU Section 325, *Communication of Internal Control Related Matters Noted in an Audit,* and AT Section 501, *Reporting on an Entity's Internal Control Over Financial Reporting,* will be superseded by PCAOB Auditing Standard No. 2 as of November 15, 2004. In addition, the following interim standards will be amended to conform with Auditing Standard No. 2: • AU Section 310, *Appointment of the Independent Auditor* • AU Section 311, *Planning and Supervision* • AU Section 312, *Audit Risk and Materiality in Conducting an Audit* • AU Section 313, *Substantive Tests Prior to the Balance Sheet Date* • AU Section 316, *Consideration of Fraud in a Financial Statement Audit*	

Who is Affected	Standard ¶	Analysis ¶	Rules and Regulations	Effect	Action
				• AU Section 319, *Consideration of Internal Control in a Financial Statement Audit* • AU Section 322, *The Auditor's Consideration of the Internal Audit Function in an Audit of Financial Statements* • AU Section 324, *Service Organizations* • AU Section 326, *Evidential Matter* • AU Section 329, *Analytical Procedures* • AU Section 332, *Auditing Derivative Instruments, Hedging Activities, and Investments in Securities* • AU Section 333, *Management Representation* • AU Section 339, *Audit Documentation* • AU Section 342, *Auditing Accounting Estimates* • AU Section 508, *Reports on Audited Financial Statements* • AU Section 530, *Dating of the Independent Auditor's Report* • AU Section 543, *Part of Audit Performed by Other Independent Auditors* • AU Section 560, *Subsequent Events* • AU Section 561, *Subsequent Discovery of Facts Existing at the Date of the Auditor's Report* • AU Section 711, *Filings Under Federal Securities Statutes* • AU Section 722, *Interim Financial*	Auditors must comply with this new auditing standard when performing the newly required audit of internal control over financial reporting in conjunction with an audit of financial statements. They should also take into account the conforming amendments to the interim standards proposed in PCAOB Release No. 2004-002.

Who is Affected	Standard ¶	Analysis ¶	Rules and Regulations	Effect	Action
				Information • ET Section 101, *Independence*	
Accounting Management	60 through 67	109.4.3	None cited	After considering both quantitative and qualitative factors, the company's auditors must identify significant accounts.	Auditors must identify all significant accounts within the financial statements. This includes a quantitative and qualitative assessment and is significant when there is a more than remote likelihood that the account could contain misstatements.
Accounting Management	68 through 70	109.4.4	AU Section 326, *Evidential Matter*	Auditors must identify all relevant financial statement assertions.	Auditors must identify, examine, and determine the relevance of each assertion underlying each significant account. The auditor must determine the source of likely misstatements in each account.

Who is Affected	Standard ¶	Analysis ¶	Rules and Regulations	Effect	Action
Accounting Management	71 through 75	109.4.5	AU Section 319, *Consideration of Internal Control in a Financial Statement Audit.*	Auditors must identify each significant process over each major class of transactions affecting significant accounts or groups of accounts. The auditor must consider the nature and characteristics of the company's information system in relation to internal control over financial reporting.	Auditors must identify, review, and evaluate each significant process over each major class of transactions affecting significant accounts or groups of accounts. The auditor must understand the flow of transactions, including how transactions are initiated, authorized, recorded, processed, and reported. This can be achieved during a walkthrough. The auditor must consider the nature and characteristics of the company's information system in relation to internal control over financial reporting.
Accounting Management	76 through 78	109.4.6	None cited	Auditors must obtain an understanding of and evaluate the period-end financial reporting process.	Auditors must review and evaluate the period-end financial reporting processes to ensure that transactions are recorded in their proper periods. The impact of the company's control environment on period-end financial reporting should be taken into account by the auditor. Management, the board, and the audit committee should ensure proper oversight of the period-end process.

WG&L Warren, Gorham & Lamont

Who is Affected	Standard ¶	Analysis ¶	Rules and Regulations	Effect	Action
Accounting Management	79 through 83	109.4.7	None cited	The auditor is required to validate that the company's accounting systems and controls are working properly by walking transactions through the accounting system to make sure it is working as intended and employees understand the control activities they are required to perform.	The auditor is required to perform at least one walkthrough for each major class of transactions. Company personnel will be required to respond to the auditor's queries about their understanding of what is required by the company's policies, procedures, and controls. Management should ensure that the controls and procedures relevant to all significant accounts are properly documented, and that employees are adequately trained with regard to controls, exception handling, and company policies.
Accounting Management	130 through 141	109.8.2	SEC Staff Accounting Bulletin Topic 1M2, *Immaterial Misstatements That Are Intentional;* Sarbanes-Oxley Act Section 302.	Auditors must evaluate deficiencies in the company's internal control over financial reporting and determine whether the deficiencies, individually or in combination, rise to the level of significant deficiencies or material weaknesses.	The auditor must look at all of the company's internal control deficiencies and determine, based on certain criteria, if the deficiencies constitute significant deficiencies or material weaknesses.

Who is Affected	Standard ¶	Analysis ¶	Rules and Regulations	Effect	Action
Accounting Management	215 through 216	116	Sarbanes-Oxley Act Section 404; 17 CFR 240.12b-2 (Securities Exchange Act Rule 12b-2).	Companies and auditors are required to comply with PCAOB Auditing Standard No. 2 for their the internal control reporting for fiscal years ending on or after November 15, 2004 (accelerated filers) or July 15, 2005 (other companies).	Auditors of companies considered accelerated filers (seasoned U.S. companies with public float exceeding $75 million) are required to comply with PCAOB Auditing Standard No. 2 for fiscal years ending on or after November 15, 2004. Auditors of other companies (including smaller companies, foreign private issuers and companies with only registered debt securities) have until fiscal years ending on or after July 15, 2005, to comply with PCAOB Auditing Standard No. 2.

Who is Affected	Standard ¶	Analysis ¶	Rules and Regulations	Effect	Action
Accounting Management	Appendix E	121	Sarbanes-Oxley Act Sections 103 and 404; AU Section 312, *Audit Risk and Materiality in Conducting an Audit*; AU Section 322, *The Auditor's Consideration of the Internal Audit Function in an Audit of Financial Statements*; AU Section 325, *Communication of Internal Control Related Matters Noted in an Audit*; SSAE No. 10, *Attestation Standards: Revision and Recodification* (AT Section 501); SEC Release No. 33-8238, *Final Rule: Management's Reports on Internal Control Over Financial Reporting and Certification of Disclosure in Exchange Act Periodic Reports* (June 5, 2003); Section 10A of the Securities Exchange Act of 1934; FAS No. 5, *Accounting for Contingencies*; Staff Accounting Bulletin (SAB) No. 99, *Materiality*; IAS No. 200, *Objective and Principles Governing an Audit of Financial Statements*; PCAOB Rule 3300T; *Federal Deposit Insurance Corporation Improvement Act of 1991 (FDCIA)*	The PCAOB issued a proposed version of this auditing standard in October 2003. In Appendix E, the PCAOB provides its explanation of the consideration it gave to the various viewpoints submitted during the comment period.	Management and auditors should read Appendix E so they can understand the relevant thought processes that underlie the PCAOB's intent regarding various aspects of the audit of internal control over financial reporting.

Who is Affected	Standard ¶	Analysis ¶	Rules and Regulations	Effect	Action
Accounting Staff	1 through 3	100	Sarbanes-Oxley Act Sections 103(a)(2)(A)(iii) and 404; Securities Exchange Act of 1934 Sections 3, 12, and 15(d); Securities Act of 1933.	The PCAOB has proposed another auditing standard that amends or supersedes many other interim auditing standards as a result of the adoption of this standard (see PCAOB Release No. 2004-002, March 9, 2004). Of particular importance is the fact that AU Section 325, *Communication of Internal Control Related Matters Noted in an Audit,* and AT Section 501, *Reporting on an Entity's Internal Control Over Financial Reporting,* will be superseded by PCAOB Auditing Standard No. 2 as of November 15, 2004. In addition, the following interim standards will be amended to conform with Auditing Standard No. 2: • AU Section 310, *Appointment of the Independent Auditor* • AU Section 311, *Planning and Supervision* • AU Section 312, *Audit Risk and Materiality in Conducting an Audit* • AU Section 313, *Substantive Tests Prior to the Balance Sheet Date* • AU Section 316, *Consideration of Fraud in a Financial Statement Audit* • AU Section 319, *Consideration of Internal Control in a Financial*	Auditors must comply with this new auditing standard when performing the newly required audit of internal control over financial reporting in conjunction with an audit of financial statements. They should also take into account the conforming amendments to the interim standards proposed in PCAOB Release No. 2004-002.

Who is Affected	Standard ¶	Analysis ¶	Rules and Regulations	Effect	Action
				Statement Audit • AU Section 322, *The Auditor's Consideration of the Internal Audit Function in an Audit of Financial Statements* • AU Section 324, *Service Organizations* • AU Section 326, *Evidential Matter* • AU Section 329, *Analytical Procedures* • AU Section 332, *Auditing Derivative Instruments, Hedging Activities, and Investments in Securities* • AU Section 333, *Management Representation* • AU Section 339, *Audit Documentation* • AU Section 342, *Auditing Accounting Estimates* • AU Section 508, *Reports on Audited Financial Statements* • AU Section 530, *Dating of the Independent Auditor's Report* • AU Section 543, *Part of Audit Performed by Other Independent Auditors* • AU Section 560, *Subsequent Events* • AU Section 561, *Subsequent Discovery of Facts Existing at the Date of the Auditor's Report* • AU Section 711, *Filings Under Federal Securities Statutes* • AU Section 722, *Interim Financial Information* • ET Section 101, *Independence*	

Who is Affected	Standard ¶	Analysis ¶	Rules and Regulations	Effect	Action
Accounting Staff	60 through 67	109.4.3	None cited	After considering both quantitative and qualitative factors, the company's auditors must identify significant accounts.	Auditors must identify all significant accounts within the financial statements. This includes a quantitative and qualitative assessment and is significant when there is a more than remote likelihood that the account could contain misstatements.
Accounting Staff	68 through 70	109.4.4	AU Section 326, *Evidential Matter*	Auditors must identify all relevant financial statement assertions.	Auditors must identify, examine, and determine the relevance of each assertion underlying each significant account. The auditor must determine the source of likely misstatements in each account.

WG
&L Warren, Gorham & Lamont

Who is Affected	Standard ¶	Analysis ¶	Rules and Regulations	Effect	Action
Accounting Staff	71 through 75	109.4.5	AU Section 319, *Consideration of Internal Control in a Financial Statement Audit.*	Auditors must identify each significant process over each major class of transactions affecting significant accounts or groups of accounts. The auditor must consider the nature and characteristics of the company's information system in relation to internal control over financial reporting.	Auditors must identify, review, and evaluate each significant process over each major class of transactions affecting significant accounts or groups of accounts. The auditor must understand the flow of transactions, including how transactions are initiated, authorized, recorded, processed, and reported. This can be achieved during a walkthrough. The auditor must consider the nature and characteristics of the company's information system in relation to internal control over financial reporting.
Accounting Staff	76 through 78	109.4.6	None cited	Auditors must obtain an understanding of and evaluate the period-end financial reporting process.	Auditors must review and evaluate the period-end financial reporting processes to ensure that transactions are recorded in their proper periods. The impact of the company's control environment on period-end financial reporting should be taken into account by the auditor. Management, the board, and the audit committee should ensure proper oversight of the period-end process.

Who is Affected	Standard ¶	Analysis ¶	Rules and Regulations	Effect	Action
Accounting Staff	79 through 83	109.4.7	None cited	The auditor is required to validate that the company's accounting systems and controls are working properly by walking transactions through the accounting system to make sure it is working as intended and employees understand the control activities they are required to perform.	The auditor is required to perform at least one walkthrough for each major class of transactions. Company personnel will be required to respond to the auditor's queries about their understanding of what is required by the company's policies, procedures, and controls. Management should ensure that the controls and procedures relevant to all significant accounts are properly documented, and that employees are adequately trained with regard to controls, exception handling, and company policies.

Who is Affected	Standard ¶	Analysis ¶	Rules and Regulations	Effect	Action
Accounting Staff	215 through 216	116	Sarbanes-Oxley Act Section 404; 17 CFR 240.12b-2 (Securities Exchange Act Rule 12b-2).	Companies and auditors are required to comply with PCAOB Auditing Standard No. 2 for their the internal control reporting for fiscal years ending on or after November 15, 2004 (accelerated filers) or July 15, 2005 (other companies).	Auditors of companies considered accelerated filers (seasoned U.S. companies with public float exceeding $75 million) are required to comply with PCAOB Auditing Standard No. 2 for fiscal years ending on or after November 15, 2004. Auditors of other companies (including smaller companies, foreign private issuers and companies with only registered debt securities) have until fiscal years ending on or after July 15, 2005, to comply with PCAOB Auditing Standard No. 2.

Who is Affected	Standard ¶	Analysis ¶	Rules and Regulations	Effect	Action
Accounting Staff	Appendix E	121	Sarbanes-Oxley Act Sections 103 and 404; AU Section 312, *Audit Risk and Materiality in Conducting an Audit;* AU Section 322, *The Auditor's Consideration of the Internal Audit Function in an Audit of Financial Statements;* AU Section 325, *Communication of Internal Control Related Matters Noted in an Audit;* SSAE No. 10, *Attestation Standards: Revision and Recodification* (AT Section 501); SEC Release No. 33-8238, *Final Rule: Management's Reports on Internal Control Over Financial Reporting and Certification of Disclosure in Exchange Act Periodic Reports* (June 5, 2003); Section 10A of the Securities Exchange Act of 1934; FAS No. 5, *Accounting for Contingencies;* Staff Accounting Bulletin (SAB) No. 99, *Materiality;* IAS No. 200, *Objective and Principles Governing an Audit of Financial Statements;* PCAOB Rule 3300T; Federal Deposit Insurance Corporation Improvement Act of 1991 (FDCIA)	The PCAOB issued a proposed version of this auditing standard in October 2003. In Appendix E, the PCAOB provides its explanation of the consideration it gave to the various viewpoints submitted during the comment period.	Management and auditors should read Appendix E so they can understand the relevant thought processes that underlie the PCAOB's intent regarding various aspects of the audit of internal control over financial reporting.

Who is Affected	Standard ¶	Analysis ¶	Rules and Regulations	Effect	Action
Attorneys Preparing SEC Reporting	1 through 3	100	Sarbanes-Oxley Act Sections 103(a)(2)(A)(iii) and 404; Securities Exchange Act of 1934 Sections 3, 12, and 15(d); Securities Act of 1933.	The PCAOB has proposed another auditing standard that amends or supersedes many other interim auditing standards as a result of the adoption of this standard (see PCAOB Release No. 2004-002, March 9, 2004). Of particular importance is the fact that AU Section 325, *Communication of Internal Control Related Matters Noted in an Audit,* and AT Section 501, *Reporting on an Entity's Internal Control Over Financial Reporting,* will be superseded by PCAOB Auditing Standard No. 2 as of November 15, 2004. In addition, the following interim standards will be amended to conform with Auditing Standard No. 2: • AU Section 310, *Appointment of the Independent Auditor* • AU Section 311, *Planning and Supervision* • AU Section 312, *Audit Risk and Materiality in Conducting an Audit* • AU Section 313, *Substantive Tests Prior to the Balance Sheet Date* • AU Section 316, *Consideration of Fraud in a Financial Statement Audit* • AU Section 319, *Consideration of Internal Control in a Financial Statement Audit*	Auditors must comply with this new auditing standard when performing the newly required audit of internal control over financial reporting in conjunction with an audit of financial statements. They should also take into account the conforming amendments to the interim standards proposed in PCAOB Release No. 2004-002.

Who is Affected	Standard ¶	Analysis ¶	Rules and Regulations	Effect	Action
				• AU Section 322, *The Auditor's Consideration of the Internal Audit Function in an Audit of Financial Statements* • AU Section 324, *Service Organizations* • AU Section 326, *Evidential Matter* • AU Section 329, *Analytical Procedures* • AU Section 332, *Auditing Derivative Instruments, Hedging Activities, and Investments in Securities* • AU Section 333, *Management Representation* • AU Section 339, *Audit Documentation* • AU Section 342, *Auditing Accounting Estimates* • AU Section 508, *Reports on Audited Financial Statements* • AU Section 530, *Dating of the Independent Auditor's Report* • AU Section 543, *Part of Audit Performed by Other Independent Auditors* • AU Section 560, *Subsequent Events* • AU Section 561, *Subsequent Discovery of Facts Existing at the Date of the Auditor's Report* • AU Section 711, *Filings Under Federal Securities Statutes* • AU Section 722, *Interim Financial Information* • ET Section 101, *Independence*	

Who is Affected	Standard ¶	Analysis ¶	Rules and Regulations	Effect	Action
Attorneys Preparing SEC Reporting	215 through 216	116	Sarbanes-Oxley Act Section 404; 17 CFR 240.12b-2 (Securities Exchange Act Rule 12b-2).	Companies and auditors are required to comply with PCAOB Auditing Standard No. 2 for their the internal control reporting for fiscal years ending on or after November 15, 2004 (accelerated filers) or July 15, 2005 (other companies).	Auditors of companies considered accelerated filers (seasoned U.S. companies with public float exceeding $75 million) are required to comply with PCAOB Auditing Standard No. 2 for fiscal years ending on or after November 15, 2004. Auditors of other companies (including smaller companies, foreign private issuers and companies with only registered debt securities) have until fiscal years ending on or after July 15, 2005, to comply with PCAOB Auditing Standard No. 2.

Who is Affected	Standard ¶	Analysis ¶	Rules and Regulations	Effect	Action
Attorneys Preparing SEC Reporting	Appendix E	121	Sarbanes-Oxley Act Sections 103 and 404; AU Section 312, *Audit Risk and Materiality in Conducting an Audit;* AU Section 322, *The Auditor's Consideration of the Internal Audit Function in an Audit of Financial Statements;* AU Section 325, *Communication of Internal Control Related Matters Noted in an Audit;* SSAE No. 10, *Attestation Standards: Revision and Recodification* (AT Section 501); SEC Release No. 33-8238, *Final Rule: Management's Reports on Internal Control Over Financial Reporting and Certification of Disclosure in Exchange Act Periodic Reports* (June 5, 2003); Section 10A of the Securities Exchange Act of 1934; FAS No. 5, *Accounting for Contingencies;* Staff Accounting Bulletin (SAB) No. 99, *Materiality;* IAS No. 200, *Objective and Principles Governing an Audit of Financial Statements;* PCAOB Rule 3300T; Federal Deposit Insurance Corporation Improvement Act of 1991 (FDCIA)	The PCAOB issued a proposed version of this auditing standard in October 2003. In Appendix E, the PCAOB provides its explanation of the consideration it gave to the various viewpoints submitted during the comment period.	Management and auditors should read Appendix E so they can understand the relevant thought processes that underlie the PCAOB's intent regarding various aspects of the audit of internal control over financial reporting.

Who is Affected	Standard ¶	Analysis ¶	Rules and Regulations	Effect	Action
Audit Committee Members	1 through 3	100	Sarbanes-Oxley Act Sections 103(a)(2)(A)(iii) and 404; Securities Exchange Act of 1934 Sections 3, 12, and 15(d); Securities Act of 1933.	The PCAOB has proposed another auditing standard that amends or supersedes many other interim auditing standards as a result of the adoption of this standard (see PCAOB Release No. 2004-002, March 9, 2004). Of particular importance is the fact that AU Section 325, *Communication of Internal Control Related Matters Noted in an Audit*, and AT Section 501, *Reporting on an Entity's Internal Control Over Financial Reporting*, will be superseded by PCAOB Auditing Standard No. 2 as of November 15, 2004. In addition, the following interim standards will be amended to conform with Auditing Standard No. 2: • AU Section 310, *Appointment of the Independent Auditor* • AU Section 311, *Planning and Supervision* • AU Section 312, *Audit Risk and Materiality in Conducting an Audit* • AU Section 313, *Substantive Tests Prior to the Balance Sheet Date* • AU Section 316, *Consideration of Fraud in a Financial Statement Audit* • AU Section 319, *Consideration of Internal Control in a Financial Statement Audit*	Auditors must comply with this new auditing standard when performing the newly required audit of internal control over financial reporting in conjunction with an audit of financial statements. They should also take into account the conforming amendments to the interim standards proposed in PCAOB Release No. 2004-002.

Who is Affected	Standard ¶	Analysis ¶	Rules and Regulations	Effect	Action
				• AU Section 322, *The Auditor's Consideration of the Internal Audit Function in an Audit of Financial Statements*	
				• AU Section 324, *Service Organizations*	
				• AU Section 326, *Evidential Matter*	
				• AU Section 329, *Analytical Procedures*	
				• AU Section 332, *Auditing Derivative Instruments, Hedging Activities, and Investments in Securities*	
				• AU Section 333, *Management Representation*	
				• AU Section 339, *Audit Documentation*	
				• AU Section 342, *Auditing Accounting Estimates*	
				• AU Section 508, *Reports on Audited Financial Statements*	
				• AU Section 530, *Dating of the Independent Auditor's Report*	
				• AU Section 543, *Part of Audit Performed by Other Independent Auditors*	
				• AU Section 560, *Subsequent Events*	
				• AU Section 561, *Subsequent Discovery of Facts Existing at the Date of the Auditor's Report*	
				• AU Section 711, *Filings Under Federal Securities Statutes*	
				• AU Section 722, *Interim Financial Information*	
				• ET Section 101, *Independence*	

Who is Affected	Standard ¶	Analysis ¶	Rules and Regulations	Effect	Action
Audit Committee Members	20 through 21	106	17 CFR 228.308(a) and 17 CFR 228.308(c); 17 CFR 229.308(a) and 17 CFR 229.308(c) (Items 308(a) and (c) of Regulation S-B and S-K, respectively).	Sufficient documentation is required to pass an audit of internal control over financial reporting. Management must accept responsibility for and assess the effectiveness of the internal controls over financial reporting. Documentation serves as evidence of this responsibility and assessment and is therefore an essential requirement in an audit of internal control over financial reporting.	Management must accept responsibility for and assess the effectiveness of the internal controls over financial reporting. During management's assessment, proper and complete documentation of the effectiveness of the company's internal controls must be compiled. A written assessment of the effectiveness of the company's internal control over financial reporting must be prepared by management at the end of each fiscal year. The auditor must notify management and the audit committee in writing if the auditor finds that management has not fulfilled its responsibilities with regard to this assessment process.

Who is Affected	Standard ¶	Analysis ¶	Rules and Regulations	Effect	Action
Audit Committee Members	24 through 26	108	AU Section 316, *Consideration of Fraud in a Financial Statement Audit.*	Auditors are required to place a special emphasis on their examination of controls designed to detect and prevent fraud.	The auditor should evaluate the company's control environment, risk assessment processes, codes of ethics, internal audit activities, and management's procedures for handling complaints. Management should ensure that the company's system of internal control is designed specifically to prevent, deter, and detect fraud. Management, directors, and audit committee members should confirm their commitment to the "tone at the top" concept as outlined in the COSO framework.

WG &L Warren, Gorham & Lamont

Who is Affected	Standard ¶	Analysis ¶	Rules and Regulations	Effect	Action
Audit Committee Members	32 through 35	109.1.2	AU Section 150, *Generally Accepted Auditing Standards;* 17 CFR 210.2-01 (Rule 2-01 of Regulation S-X).	The auditor must not function in the role of management and must not audit his or her own work, but may provide substantive recommendations regarding the design or operation of internal control over financial reporting as a by-product of the audit.	Management should remain actively involved in the design, documentation, and testing of internal control over financial reporting and must not delegate all responsibility for these matters to the auditor. Audit committees must pre-approve internal control-related services provided by the company's auditor. Auditors and audit committee members should be vigilant about any appearance of compromised auditor independence. Auditors may provide internal control services that are pre-approved by the audit committee.

Who is Affected	Standard ¶	Analysis ¶	Rules and Regulations	Effect	Action
Audit Committee Members	55 through 59	109.4.2	15 U.S.C. 78c; 15 U.S.C. 7201(a)(3); 17 CFR 240.10A-3 (Securities Exchange Act Rule 10A-3); 17 CFR 240.10A-3(c)(2) (Securities Exchange Act Rule 10A-3(c)(2)); 17 CFR 210.2-01(c)(7) (Regulation S-X Rule 2-01(c)(7)).	The auditor must review and assess the effectiveness of the audit committee's oversight of the company's external financial reporting and internal control over financial reporting.	The auditor must review the audit committee's involvement in detail and assess the effectiveness of the audit committee's oversight of the company's external financial reporting and internal control over financial reporting. The auditor must also assess the relative effectiveness of the audit committee's oversight role. If the auditor finds that the audit committee is ineffective in the oversight role, then this constitutes a significant deficiency. Boards of directors should ensure that their audit committees are in compliance with the requirements of Section 301 of the Sarbanes-Oxley Act, as well as the applicable SRO corporate governance rules.

WG&L Warren, Gorham & Lamont

Who is Affected	Standard ¶	Analysis ¶	Rules and Regulations	Effect	Action
Audit Committee Members	76 through 78	109.4.6	None cited	Auditors must obtain an understanding of and evaluate the period-end financial reporting process.	Auditors must review and evaluate the period-end financial reporting processes to ensure that transactions are recorded in their proper periods. The impact of the company's control environment on period-end financial reporting should be taken into account by the auditor. Management, the board, and the audit committee should ensure proper oversight of the period-end process.
Audit Committee Members	130 through 141	109.8.2	SEC Staff Accounting Bulletin Topic 1M2, *Immaterial Misstatements That Are Intentional;* Sarbanes-Oxley Act Section 302.	Auditors must evaluate deficiencies in the company's internal control over financial reporting and determine whether the deficiencies, individually or in combination, rise to the level of significant deficiencies or material weaknesses.	The auditor must look at all of the company's internal control deficiencies and determine, based on certain criteria, if the deficiencies constitute significant deficiencies or material weaknesses.

Who is Affected	Standard ¶	Analysis ¶	Rules and Regulations	Effect	Action
Audit Committee Members	190 through 192	113.3.9	Section 10A of the Securities Exchange Act of 1934.	Management may add additional information to its report on the assessment of internal control over financial reporting that is not necessarily relevant to the audit of internal control over financial reporting. The auditor is expected to disclaim an opinion on the additional information.	If management adds any extraneous information to the standard format of the report, the auditor should disclaim this information. If the auditor believes the extra information includes a material misstatement of fact, the auditor is expected to discuss the issue with management directly. If this does not resolve the issue, the auditor is required to notify management and the audit committee in writing of its concerns regarding the information.
Audit Committee Members	202 through 206	114.2	Sarbanes-Oxley Act Section 302; AU Section 722, *Interim Financial Information*; AU Section 317, *Illegal Acts by Clients*; 17 CFR 240.13a-14(a) and 17 CFR 240.15d-14(a) (Securities Exchange Act Rules 13a-14(a) and 15d-14(a), respectively); Section 10A of the Securities Exchange Act of 1934.	Interim quarterly auditor evaluations of internal control over financial reporting can be based on limited procedures.	Auditors need only perform limited procedures on a quarterly basis to validate their annual assessment. In performing the quarterly procedures, the auditor is looking for material modifications that could become a required disclosure about changes in internal control over financial reporting in order for management's certifications to be accurate. The auditor is required to notify management of any material matters. If management does not respond appropriately, the auditor must notify the audit committee.

WG
&L Warren, Gorham & Lamont

Who is Affected	Standard ¶	Analysis ¶	Rules and Regulations	Effect	Action
Audit Committee Members	207 through 214	115	AU Section 316, *Consideration of Fraud in a Financial Statement Audit*; AU Section 317, *Illegal Acts by Clients*; Section 10A of the Securities Exchange Act of 1934.	The auditor is required to communicate in writing to management and the audit committee all significant deficiencies and material weaknesses identified during the audit. The auditor is also required to make certain communications with management and the audit committee when the auditor becomes aware of fraud or illegal acts.	The auditor is required to communicate in writing to management and the audit committee all significant deficiencies and material weaknesses identified during the audit. The auditor is also required to make certain communications with management and the audit committee when the auditor becomes aware of fraud or illegal acts. The auditor must notify the board of directors if the audit committee is ineffectively overseeing the internal control function.
Audit Committee Members	215 through 216	116	Sarbanes-Oxley Act Section 404; 17 CFR 240.12b-2 (Securities Exchange Act Rule 12b-2).	Companies and auditors are required to comply with PCAOB Auditing Standard No. 2 for their the internal control reporting for fiscal years ending on or after November 15, 2004 (accelerated filers) or July 15, 2005 (other companies).	Auditors of companies considered accelerated filers (seasoned U.S. companies with public float exceeding $75 million) are required to comply with PCAOB Auditing Standard No. 2 for fiscal years ending on or after November 15, 2004. Auditors of other companies (including smaller companies, foreign private issuers and companies with only registered debt securities) have until fiscal years ending on or after July 15, 2005, to comply with PCAOB Auditing Standard No. 2.

Who is Affected	Standard ¶	Analysis ¶	Rules and Regulations	Effect	Action
Audit Committee Members	Appendix E	121	Sarbanes-Oxley Act Sections 103 and 404; AU Section 312, *Audit Risk and Materiality in Conducting an Audit;* AU Section 322, *The Auditor's Consideration of the Internal Audit Function in an Audit of Financial Statements;* AU Section 325, *Communication of Internal Control Related Matters Noted in an Audit;* SSAE No. 10, *Attestation Standards: Revision and Recodification* (AT Section 501); SEC Release No. 33-8238, *Final Rule: Management's Reports on Internal Control Over Financial Reporting and Certification of Disclosure in Exchange Act Periodic Reports* (June 5, 2003); Section 10A of the Securities Exchange Act of 1934; FAS No. 5, *Accounting for Contingencies;* Staff Accounting Bulletin (SAB) No. 99, *Materiality;* IAS No. 200, *Objective and Principles Governing an Audit of Financial Statements;* PCAOB Rule 3300T; *Federal Deposit Insurance Corporation Improvement Act of 1991 (FDCIA).*	The PCAOB issued a proposed version of this auditing standard in October 2003. In Appendix E, the PCAOB provides its explanation of the consideration it gave to the various viewpoints submitted during the comment period.	Management and auditors should read Appendix E so they can understand the relevant thought processes that underlie the PCAOB's intent regarding various aspects of the audit of internal control over financial reporting.

Who is Affected	Standard ¶	Analysis ¶	Rules and Regulations	Effect	Action
Auditors	1 through 3	100	Sarbanes-Oxley Act Sections 103(a)(2)(A)(iii) and 404; Securities Exchange Act of 1934 Sections 3, 12, and 15(d); Securities Act of 1933.	The PCAOB has proposed another auditing standard that amends or supersedes many other interim auditing standards as a result of the adoption of this standard (see PCAOB Release No. 2004-002, March 9, 2004). Of particular importance is the fact that AU Section 325, *Communication of Internal Control Related Matters Noted in an Audit,* and AT Section 501, *Reporting on an Entity's Internal Control Over Financial Reporting,* will be superseded by PCAOB Auditing Standard No. 2 as of November 15, 2004. In addition, the following interim standards will be amended to conform with Auditing Standard No. 2: • AU Section 310, *Appointment of the Independent Auditor* • AU Section 311, *Planning and Supervision* • AU Section 312, *Audit Risk and Materiality in Conducting an Audit* • AU Section 313, *Substantive Tests Prior to the Balance Sheet Date* • AU Section 316, *Consideration of Fraud in a Financial Statement Audit* • AU Section 319, *Consideration of Internal Control in a Financial Statement Audit*	Auditors must comply with this new auditing standard when performing the newly required audit of internal control over financial reporting in conjunction with an audit of financial statements. They should also take into account the conforming amendments to the interim standards proposed in PCAOB Release No. 2004-002.

Who is Affected	Standard ¶	Analysis ¶	Rules and Regulations	Effect	Action
				• AU Section 322, *The Auditor's Consideration of the Internal Audit Function in an Audit of Financial Statements*	
				• AU Section 324, *Service Organizations*	
				• AU Section 326, *Evidential Matter*	
				• AU Section 329, *Analytical Procedures*	
				• AU Section 332, *Auditing Derivative Instruments, Hedging Activities, and Investments in Securities*	
				• AU Section 333, *Management Representation*	
				• AU Section 339, *Audit Documentation*	
				• AU Section 342, *Auditing Accounting Estimates*	
				• AU Section 508, *Reports on Audited Financial Statements*	
				• AU Section 530, *Dating of the Independent Auditor's Report*	
				• AU Section 543, *Part of Audit Performed by Other Independent Auditors*	
				• AU Section 560, *Subsequent Events*	
				• AU Section 561, *Subsequent Discovery of Facts Existing at the Date of the Auditor's Report*	
				• AU Section 711, *Filings Under Federal Securities Statutes*	
				• AU Section 722, *Interim Financial Information*	
				• ET Section 101, *Independence*	

Who is Affected	Standard ¶	Analysis ¶	Rules and Regulations	Effect	Action
Auditors	4 through 6	101	Sarbanes-Oxley Act Section 302; 17 CFR 240.13a-14(a); 17 CFR 240.15d-14(a).	The issuer's auditor must express an opinion on management's assessment of the effectiveness of internal controls over financial reporting. The auditor's review of management's assessment must provide a level of reasonable assurance that the company's financial statements are materially accurate. The auditor must also audit the company's financial statements as of the date specified in management's assessment.	Management must evaluate, test, and document the company's system of internal control over financial reporting, then prepare an assessment. The company's auditor must evaluate management's assessment as well as obtain and evaluate evidence that the company's internal control over financial reporting is designed and operating effectively. In order to do this, the auditor must also audit the company's financial statements for the same time period covered by management's assessment of internal control.
Auditors	7 through 12	102	17 CFR 240; 17 CFR 13a-15(f); 17 CFR 15d-15(f); FAS No. 5, *Accounting for Contingencies.*	The terms "internal control over financial reporting," "control deficiency," "deficiency in design," "deficiency in operation," "significant deficiency," "material weakness," "preventative control," and "detective control" are defined.	Those involved with internal control over financial reporting should become familiar with the definitions in order to avoid any confusion.

Who is Affected	Standard ¶	Analysis ¶	Rules and Regulations	Effect	Action
Auditors	13 through 15	103	SAS No. 95SAS No. 95, *Generally Accepted Auditing Standards;* AU Section 319, *Consideration of Internal Control in a Financial Statement Audit;* PCAOB Rule 3200T, *Interim Auditing Standards.*	The auditing standard defines the characteristics of acceptable internal control frameworks that can be used to assess compliance with Sections 302 and 404 of the Sarbanes-Oxley Act. The characteristics are defined so narrowly that only the COSO framework can possibly be used by U.S. issuers for compliance with the Act at this time.	Companies that have not already done so should ensure that they are implementing at least the components of the COSO framework that relate to financial reporting, though certain aspects of the efficiency and effectiveness of operations and compliance with laws and regulations will also fall under the purview of internal control over financial reporting.
Auditors	16	104	None cited	Internal control over financial reporting is not expected to completely prevent or detect all material misstatements, due to inherent limitations.	Establish realistic expectations for internal control over financial reporting, and, as much as is feasible, introduce safeguards against human error and fraud in order to minimize the risk of financial misstatements.

Who is Affected	Standard ¶	Analysis ¶	Rules and Regulations	Effect	Action
Auditors	17 through 19	105	SEC Release No. 33-8238, *Final Rule: Management's Reports on Internal Control Over Financial Reporting and Certification of Disclosure in Exchange Act Periodic Reports* (June 5, 2003).	The auditing standard requires the management assessment and auditor attestation of internal control over financial reporting to be at the level of reasonable, not absolute, assurance.	Management and the company's auditors should understand the inherent limitations involved with internal control and should discuss the remote likelihood that material misstatements will not be detected or prevented by management's assessment and the audit of internal control over financial reporting. Management should have a plan in place to address this possibility. Management should also take primary responsibility for conveying the effectiveness of the company's internal over financial reporting to users of the company's financial reports.

Who is Affected	Standard ¶	Analysis ¶	Rules and Regulations	Effect	Action
Auditors	20 through 21	106	17 CFR 228.308(a) and 17 CFR 228.308(c); 17 CFR 229.308(a) and 17 CFR 229.308(c) (Items 308(a) and (c) of Regulation S-B and S-K, respectively).	Sufficient documentation is required to pass an audit of internal control over financial reporting. Management must accept responsibility for and assess the effectiveness of the internal controls over financial reporting. Documentation serves as evidence of this responsibility and assessment and is therefore an essential requirement in an audit of internal control over financial reporting.	Management must accept responsibility for and assess the effectiveness of the internal controls over financial reporting. During management's assessment, proper and complete documentation of the effectiveness of the company's internal controls must be compiled. A written assessment of the effectiveness of the company's internal control over financial reporting must be prepared by management at the end of each fiscal year. The auditor must notify management and the audit committee in writing if the auditor finds that management has not fulfilled its responsibilities with regard to this assessment process.
Auditors	22 through 23	107	AU Section 312, *Audit Risk and Materiality in Conducting an Audit.*	Auditors are to use the same definition of materiality and the same quantitative and qualitative judgments in an audit of the effectiveness of internal controls over financial reporting that they would use in an audit of financial statements.	Management and the company's auditors should establish defined levels of materiality with regard to the financial reporting at both the financial-statement level and the individual account-balance level.

Who is Affected	Standard ¶	Analysis ¶	Rules and Regulations	Effect	Action
Auditors	24 through 26	108	AU Section 316, *Consideration of Fraud in a Financial Statement Audit.*	Auditors are required to place a special emphasis on their examination of controls designed to detect and prevent fraud.	The auditor should evaluate the company's control environment, risk assessment processes, codes of ethics, internal audit activities, and management's procedures for handling complaints. Management should ensure that the company's system of internal control is designed specifically to prevent, deter, and detect fraud. Management, directors, and audit committee members should confirm their commitment to the "tone at the top" concept as outlined in the COSO framework.
Auditors	27 through 141	109	See ¶s 109.1– 109.8.2 for rules and regulations cited.	The audit of internal control over financial reporting must be done in conjunction with an audit of the financial statements. All of the traditional auditing standards and considerations are applicable to this auditing standard as well.	Auditors should apply all of the general and applicable fieldwork standards that would be appropriate to an audit of financial statements to an audit of internal control over financial reporting.
Auditors	30 through 38	109.1	AU Section 150, *Generally Accepted Auditing Standards;* 17 CFR 210.2-01 (Rule 2-01 of Regulation S-X).	All of the traditional general auditing standards and considerations are applicable to an audit of internal control over financial reporting.	Auditors can leverage existing skills and methods.

Who is Affected	Standard ¶	Analysis ¶	Rules and Regulations	Effect	Action
Auditors	31	109.1.1	None cited.	The auditor must have competence in the subject matter of internal control over financial reporting.	Auditors must obtain training in the subject matter of internal control over financial reporting prior to commencing audits of internal control over financial reporting. Auditors should be well-versed in the COSO framework.
Auditors	32 through 35	109.1.2	AU Section 150, *Generally Accepted Auditing Standards;* 17 CFR 210.2-01 (Rule 2-01 of Regulation S-X).	The auditor must not function in the role of management and must not audit his or her own work, but may provide substantive recommendations regarding the design or operation of internal control over financial reporting as a by-product of the audit.	Management should remain actively involved in the design, documentation, and testing of internal control over financial reporting and must not delegate all responsibility for these matters to the auditor. Audit committees must pre-approve internal control-related services provided by the company's auditor. Auditors and audit committee members should be vigilant about any appearance of compromised auditor independence. Auditors may provide internal control services that are pre-approved by the audit committee.
Auditors	36	109.1.3	None cited	Auditors must exercise professional skepticism in an audit of internal control over financial reporting.	The auditor must conduct a critical assessment of the work that management has performed in evaluating and testing controls.

W̶G̶ &E̶ **Warren, Gorham & Lamont**

Who is Affected	Standard ¶	Analysis ¶	Rules and Regulations	Effect	Action
Auditors	37 through 38	109.1.4	None cited	The fieldwork and reporting standards for an audit of internal control over financial reporting are established by this auditing standard.	The auditor should carefully review the fieldwork and reporting requirements outlined in this auditing standard, and should apply the concept of materiality when following the general and fieldwork standards.
Auditors	39	109.2	None cited	The guidance on planning the audit engagement is very similar to existing guidance in the existing audit literature, with specific details added with regard to internal control over financial reporting.	When planning the audit engagement, auditors are required to consider various aspects of a company's internal controls and operations, management's assessment of internal control effectiveness, and preliminary judgments about the company's controls and levels of risk.
Auditors	40 through 46	109.3	None cited	The standard outlines what elements of a company's internal control structure should have been addressed by management in its assessment of internal control over financial reporting.	The auditor must examine sufficient evidence and obtain an understanding of management's process for assessing the effectiveness of the company's internal control over financial reporting. Management should ensure that its assessment of internal control over financial reporting addresses the elements that the auditor is expected to cover in its audit of management's assessment.

Who is Affected	Standard ¶	Analysis ¶	Rules and Regulations	Effect	Action
Auditors	42 through 46	109.3.1	None cited	The auditor is required to evaluate the adequacy of management's documentation in support of its assessment of internal control over financial reporting.	Management should become familiar with the documentation requirements provided by the standard. The auditor must review the issuer's documentation of management's assessment of internal control over financial reporting. Given a substantial absence of documentation of internal control over financial reporting on the part of the issuer, the auditor must withhold the attestation or limit the scope of the audit of internal control over financial reporting.
Auditors	47 through 87	109.4	See ¶s 109.4.1– 109.4.8 for rules and regulations cited.	Based on the COSO framework, the auditing standard defines specific steps the auditor must perform to evaluate the documentation and establish an understanding of internal control over financial reporting.	The auditor must perform certain tasks and procedures to evaluate management's documentation and to establish an understanding of the company's internal control over financial reporting. These tasks and procedures follow the model put forth in the COSO framework. Management is expected to implement the five basic COSO components: control environment, risk assessment, control activities, information and communication, and monitoring.

Who is Affected	Standard ¶	Analysis ¶	Rules and Regulations	Effect	Action
Auditors	52 through 54	109.4.1	None cited.	The auditing standard recommends that auditors test those controls that affect primarily the control environment and pervade all other controls first, i.e., the company-level controls. Auditors should evaluate the results of the evaluation of the company-wide controls when creating the audit plan for the rest of the company's controls over financial reporting.	Identification and testing of company-level controls by the external auditor is required. Management should ensure that proper documentation of company-wide controls exists.

Who is Affected	Standard ¶	Analysis ¶	Rules and Regulations	Effect	Action
Auditors	55 through 59	109.4.2	15 U.S.C. 78c; 15 U.S.C. 7201(a)(3); 17 CFR 240.10A-3 (Securities Exchange Act Rule 10A-3); 17 CFR 240.10A-3(c)(2) (Securities Exchange Act Rule 10A-3(c)(2)); 17 CFR 210.2-01(c)(7) (Regulation S-X Rule 2-01(c)(7)).	The auditor must review and assess the effectiveness of the audit committee's oversight of the company's external financial reporting and internal control over financial reporting.	The auditor must review the audit committee's involvement in detail and assess the effectiveness of the audit committee's oversight of the company's external financial reporting and internal control over financial reporting. The auditor must also assess the relative effectiveness of the audit committee's oversight role. If the auditor finds that the audit committee is ineffective in the oversight role, then this constitutes a significant deficiency. Boards of directors should ensure that their audit committees are in compliance with the requirements of Section 301 of the Sarbanes-Oxley Act, as well as the applicable SRO corporate governance rules.
Auditors	60 through 67	109.4.3	None cited	After considering both quantitative and qualitative factors, the company's auditors must identify significant accounts.	Auditors must identify all significant accounts within the financial statements. This includes a quantitative and qualitative assessment and is significant when there is a more than remote likelihood that the account could contain misstatements.

WG&L Warren, Gorham & Lamont

Who is Affected	Standard ¶	Analysis ¶	Rules and Regulations	Effect	Action
Auditors	68 through 70	109.4.4	AU Section 326, *Evidential Matter.*	Auditors must identify all relevant financial statement assertions.	Auditors must identify, examine, and determine the relevance of each assertion underlying each significant account. The auditor must determine the source of likely misstatements in each account.
Auditors	71 through 75	109.4.5	AU Section 319, *Consideration of Internal Control in a Financial Statement Audit.*	Auditors must identify each significant process over each major class of transactions affecting significant accounts or groups of accounts. The auditor must consider the nature and characteristics of the company's information system in relation to internal control over financial reporting.	Auditors must identify, review, and evaluate each significant process over each major class of transactions affecting significant accounts or groups of accounts. The auditor must understand the flow of transactions, including how transactions are initiated, authorized, recorded, processed, and reported. This can be achieved during a walkthrough. The auditor must consider the nature and characteristics of the company's information system in relation to internal control over financial reporting.

Who is Affected	Standard ¶	Analysis ¶	Rules and Regulations	Effect	Action
Auditors	76 through 78	109.4.6	None cited	Auditors must obtain an understanding of and evaluate the period-end financial reporting process.	Auditors must review and evaluate the period-end financial reporting processes to ensure that transactions are recorded in their proper periods. The impact of the company's control environment on period-end financial reporting should be taken into account by the auditor. Management, the board, and the audit committee should ensure proper oversight of the period-end process.
Auditors	79 through 83	109.4.7	None cited	The auditor is required to validate that the company's accounting systems and controls are working properly by walking transactions through the accounting system to make sure it is working as intended and employees understand the control activities they are required to perform.	The auditor is required to perform at least one walkthrough for each major class of transactions. Company personnel will be required to respond to the auditor's queries about their understanding of what is required by the company's policies, procedures, and controls. Management should ensure that the controls and procedures relevant to all significant accounts are properly documented, and that employees are adequately trained with regard to controls, exception handling, and company policies.

WG&L Warren, Gorham & Lamont

Who is Affected	Standard ¶	Analysis ¶	Rules and Regulations	Effect	Action
Auditors	83 through 87	109.4.8	None cited	The company's auditor must obtain evidence that validates the effectiveness of controls over financial reporting.	The auditor should obtain evidence of the effectiveness of controls on which to base its opinion. The auditor must either perform these tests himself or herself or may rely, to some extent, on the work of others, such as the company's internal auditors. Management should ensure that adequate documentation exists of the company's significant control points, the nature of the controls implemented by management, the significance of each control, and the level of risk that the controls might not be operating as designed.
Auditors	88 through 91	109.5	None cited	The company's auditor must test and evaluate the design of the company's internal controls over financial reporting.	Through procedures such as inquiry, observation, walkthroughs, inspection of relevant documentation, and an evaluation of whether the controls are likely to prevent or detect errors or fraud if they operate as designed, the auditor must test and evaluate the design of the company's internal controls over financial reporting.

Who is Affected	Standard ¶	Analysis ¶	Rules and Regulations	Effect	Action
Auditors	92 through 107	109.6	None cited	The company's auditor must test and evaluate the operating effectiveness of the company's internal controls over financial reporting.	The auditor must validate the operating effectiveness of internal controls over financial reporting by using a mix of inquiries, inspection, observation, testing, and reperformance. The auditor must verify that the employees performing the controls have the necessary authority and qualifications to perform the controls effectively.
Auditors	93 through 97	109.6.1	None cited	In order to test and evaluate the operating effectiveness of the company's internal controls over financial reporting, the company's auditor must utilize a mix of inquiry, observation, documentation review, and reperformance.	The auditor's tests of the operating effectiveness of the company's internal controls over financial reporting should include written and/or oral inquiry, direct observation, documentation review, and reperformance of key controls.
Auditors	98 through 103	109.6.2	None cited	The auditor must consider time and timing issues related to tests of controls.	The auditor should evaluate the time periods covered by controls, the timing of tests of controls, and when the controls were put in place.
Auditors	104 through 105	109.6.3	None cited	The auditor must obtain sufficient evidence about whether the company's internal control over financial reporting is operating effectively.	The nature and extent of testing for each control must be determined by the auditor by taking into consideration the nature of the control, its frequency of operation, and the importance of the control.

Who is Affected	Standard ¶	Analysis ¶	Rules and Regulations	Effect	Action
Auditors	106 through 107	109.6.4	None cited	The auditor must conduct the audit of internal control over financial reporting and the audit of the financial statements with professional skepticism.	The auditor needs to have a "questioning mind" and must conduct a critical assessment of audit evidence. When the auditor identifies exceptions to the company's control procedures, he or she should determine, using professional skepticism, the effect of the exception. Additional testing may be appropriate or necessary.
Auditors	108 through 126	109.7	AU Section 319, *Internal Control in a Financial Statement Audit;* AU Section 322, *The Auditor's Consideration of the Internal Audit Function in an Audit of Financial Statements;* FAS No. 5, *Accounting for Contingencies;* The Institute of Internal Auditors, *International Standards for the Professional Practice of Internal Auditing.*	Auditors can use the work of others to a certain extent when performing the audit. The auditing standard clarifies the ability of the auditor to use the work of others and reiterates that the auditor's opinion must be based solely on work done by the auditor or the auditor's direct validation of any work done by others.	Auditors can use the work of others but the auditors' own work must be substantial enough to form the basis for the auditors' opinion on the effectiveness of the company's internal control over financial reporting. Auditors are required to evaluate and test the work of others upon which they plan to rely. Internal auditors may provide the results of their work on the company's internal controls over financial reporting to the external auditors for use during the audit of the company's financial statements and internal control over financial reporting.

Who is Affected	Standard ¶	Analysis ¶	Rules and Regulations	Effect	Action
Auditors	112 through 116	109.7.1	AU Section 319, *Internal Control in a Financial Statement Audit;* FAS No. 5, *Accounting for Contingencies.*	Auditors must evaluate the nature of the controls subjected to the work of others before the auditors rely on that work.	Auditors must evaluate the nature of the controls subjected to the work of others before the auditors rely on that work. Auditors should not rely on the work of others when evaluating the company's overall control environment. Auditors must perform walkthroughs themselves but may obtain additional evidence from walkthroughs performed by others.
Auditors	117 through 122	109.7.2	*International Standards for the Professional Practice of Internal Auditing*	Auditors must evaluate the competence and objectivity of others before using their work.	By looking at factors such as educational level, professional experience, professional certification, continuing education, work assignments, supervision, documentation, and performance evaluations, auditors must evaluate the competence and objectivity of others before using their work. External auditors may rely on the work of qualified and objective internal auditors more heavily than the work of other parties, unless the internal auditors report solely to management.

WG&L Warren, Gorham & Lamont

Who is Affected	Standard ¶	Analysis ¶	Rules and Regulations	Effect	Action
Auditors	123 through 126	109.7.3	None cited	Auditors must test some of the work of others in order to evaluate the quality and effectiveness of the work. The standard provides specific guidance regarding controls over period-end financial reporting, IT general controls, management self-assessment, controls over the calculation of the depreciation of assets, and alternating tests of controls.	By looking at factors such as scope of the work, adequacy of procedures, adequacy of documentation, appropriateness of conclusions, and consistency of reports, auditors must evaluate the quality and effectiveness of the work of others before using the work. Management should consult the standard's guidance regarding the auditor's use of the work of others in specific situations related to controls over period-end financial reporting, IT general controls, management self-assessment, controls over the calculation of the depreciation of assets, and alternating tests of controls.

Who is Affected	Standard ¶	Analysis ¶	Rules and Regulations	Effect	Action
Auditors	127 through 141	109.8	SEC Staff Accounting Bulletin Topic 1M2, *Immaterial Misstatements That Are Intentional;* Sarbanes-Oxley Act Section 302.	Auditors must evaluate information from all relevant sources, particularly the company's internal audit function, when forming an opinion on internal control over financial reporting.	Auditors must evaluate evidence from all relevant sources, including management's assessment of internal control over financial reporting, negative results of substantive procedures performed during the financial statement audit, any identified control deficiencies, and all relevant reports issued by the company's internal audit function. Internal audit departments must be prepared to provide the company's external auditors with copies of all reports issued during the year that have even a tangential relevancy to internal control over financial reporting.
Auditors	129	109.8.1	None cited	The company's auditor can issue an unqualified opinion on the company's internal control over financial reporting only if there are no identified material weaknesses and there have been no restrictions on the scope of the audit.	The auditor must determine that there are no material weaknesses or scope restrictions in order to provide an unqualified opinion.

Who is Affected	Standard ¶	Analysis ¶	Rules and Regulations	Effect	Action
Auditors	130 through 141	109.8.2	SEC Staff Accounting Bulletin Topic 1M2, *Immaterial Misstatements That Are Intentional;* Sarbanes-Oxley Act Section 302.	Auditors must evaluate deficiencies in the company's internal control over financial reporting and determine whether the deficiencies, individually or in combination, rise to the level of significant deficiencies or material weaknesses.	The auditor must look at all of the company's internal control deficiencies and determine, based on certain criteria, if the deficiencies constitute significant deficiencies or material weaknesses.
Auditors	142 through 144	110	AU Section 333, *Management Representations.*	The auditor is required to obtain certain management representations specific to the audit of internal control over financial reporting.	As in all audits, the auditor must receive certain written representations from the company's CEO and CFO.
Auditors	145 through 158	111	AU Section 316, *Consideration of Fraud in a Financial Statement Audit;* AU Section 330, *The Confirmation Process;* AU Section 331, *Inventories.*	The audit of internal control over financial reporting should be integrated with the audit of the issuer's financial statements.	The auditor must integrate the audit of internal control over financial reporting with the audit of financial statements.
Auditors	147 through 149	111.1	None cited	The auditor's opinion on whether management's assessment of the effectiveness of the company's internal control over financial reporting is fairly stated must relate the effectiveness of the company's internal control over financial reporting as of a point in time and taken as a whole.	The auditor has different testing standards for the effectiveness of the company's internal control over financial reporting at a point in time versus the financial statements taken as a whole.

Who is Affected	Standard ¶	Analysis ¶	Rules and Regulations	Effect	Action
Auditors	150 through 151	111.2	None cited	Tests of controls in an audit of financial statements are different than those in an audit of internal control over financial reporting.	Auditors ordinarily perform tests of controls and substantive procedures in an audit of financial statements. The auditor is required to assess control risk during the audit of the financial statements and determine whether relevant controls operated effectively during the entire period upon which the auditor plans to place reliance on the effectiveness of those controls.
Auditors	152 through 156	111.3	AU Section 316, *Consideration of Fraud in a Financial Statement Audit;* AU Section 330, *The Confirmation Process;* AU Section 331, *Inventories.*	Tests of controls on substantive procedures in an audit of financial statements are germane in an audit of internal controls over financial reporting.	The auditor is required to continue performing tests of controls on substantive procedures.
Auditors	157 through 158	111.4	None cited	The auditor must evaluate the results of the tests of substantive procedures performed for the financial statements and apply them to conclusions about the operating effectiveness of internal control over financial reporting.	The auditor should evaluate the effect of findings in the financial statement audit on the operating effectiveness of the company's internal control over financial reporting. Particular attention must be paid to substantive procedures related to fraud, illegal acts, related-party transactions, accounting estimates, the selection of accounting principles, and misstatements.

Who is Affected	Standard ¶	Analysis ¶	Rules and Regulations	Effect	Action
Auditors	159 through 161	112	AU Section 339, *Audit Documentation.*	The documentation standard is raised from that in AU Section 339, *Audit Documentation.* The documentation requirements in this auditing standard reinforce the connection between the audit of the financial statements and the audit of internal control over financial reporting.	The auditor must adhere to the audit documentation standards set forth in AU Section 339, *Audit Documentation,* and must also include additional documentation covering all aspects of the audit of internal control over financial reporting.
Auditors	162 through 199	113	See ¶s 113.1– 113.3.12 for rules and regulations.	Management must issue a report on the effectiveness of the company's internal control over financial reporting. The auditor must evaluate that report and, if it agrees with management's assessment, issue a report attesting to management's assertions.	Management is required to issue a report on the effectiveness of the company's internal control over financial reporting. The auditor is required to review and evaluate this report. Then, based on its independent assessment of the effectiveness of internal control over the issuer's financial reporting, the auditor issues its attestation of management's report. Any limit in the scope of the audit of internal control over financial reporting requires the auditor to, at a minimum, issue a qualified opinion. Management must ensure that the scope of the audit is not limited.

Who is Affected	Standard ¶	Analysis ¶	Rules and Regulations	Effect	Action
Auditors	166	113.2	None cited	The auditor must evaluate management's assessment of the effectiveness of internal control over financial reporting.	The auditor should evaluate management's assessment and determine that management establishes its responsibility for internal control, used the proper framework (i.e., COSO), and presented its assessment in an acceptable form.
Auditors	167 through 199	113.3	See ¶s 113.3.1– 113.3.12 for rules and regulations.	Every auditor's report on management's assessment of the effectiveness of internal control over financial reporting must include certain uniform elements.	Auditors must incorporate all of the listed requirements into their opinion on the effectiveness of the issuer's internal control over financial reporting. Examples of attestation statements are included in the appendices as examples for auditors to follow.
Auditors	169 through 170	113.3.1	None cited	The auditor can issue either separate or combined reports.	The auditor's report can be combined for both the audit of the financial statements and the audit of internal control over financial reporting. The auditor may also issue the reports separately. If the reports are issued separately, specific language provided in the standard must be included in each report.

WG
&L Warren, Gorham & Lamont

Who is Affected	Standard ¶	Analysis ¶	Rules and Regulations	Effect	Action
Auditors	171 through 172	113.3.2	None cited	The dates of the financial statement audit and the audit of internal control over financial reporting should be dated the same even though they may cover differing periods.	The audit of internal control over financial reporting must be done in conjunction with the audit of financial statements. Therefore the dates on the reports, whether separate or combined, should be the same.
Auditors	173	113.3.3	None cited	Under certain circumstances the auditor is required to modify the standard report.	The auditor should modify the standard report to reflect an inadequate assessment of internal control by management, a material weakness in the company's internal controls, a scope restriction, the use of other auditors' work, significant subsequent events, or other information contained in management's report on internal control over financial reporting.

Who is Affected	Standard ¶	Analysis ¶	Rules and Regulations	Effect	Action
Auditors	174	113.3.4	None cited	The auditor must modify the audit opinion if the auditor determines that management's assessment process is inadequate or if the auditor determines that management's report is inappropriate.	The auditor must modify the audit opinion if the auditor determines that management's assessment process is inadequate or if the auditor determines that management's report is inappropriate. At a minimum, this means adding an explanatory paragraph describing the reasons for this conclusion. Management should make every effort to ensure that the process used for evaluating the company's internal control over financial reporting is adequate, i.e., that the process meets the requirements outlined in this auditing standard and in the SEC's requirements.
Auditors	175 through 177	113.3.5	None cited	If there are one or more material weaknesses in the company's internal control over financial reporting, then the auditor must express an adverse opinion. In this case, management is also precluded from concluding that internal control over financial reporting is effective.	In the event there are any uncorrected material weaknesses at the end of the reporting year, then the auditor must express an adverse opinion on internal control over financial reporting.

WG&L Warren, Gorham & Lamont

Who is Affected	Standard ¶	Analysis ¶	Rules and Regulations	Effect	Action
Auditors	178 through 181	113.3.6	None cited	Limitations on the scope of the audit result in a qualified opinion at best.	Given any limitation in the scope of the audit, the auditor is unable to express an unqualified opinion. Even if the scope of the audit is limited, if the auditor uncovers a material weakness, that weakness must be reported. Management should do their best to ensure the auditor is able to apply all the procedures necessary in the circumstances, with no interference from management or employees of the company.
Auditors	182 through 185	113.3.7	AU Section 543, *Part of Audit Performed by Other Independent Auditors.*	The auditor may rely on reports from other independent auditors to a certain extent.	The auditor can rely on the work of other independent auditors but determine whether or not disclose their reliance on that work in conformance with AU Section 543, *Part of Audit Performed by Other Independent Auditors.*

Who is Affected	Standard ¶	Analysis ¶	Rules and Regulations	Effect	Action
Auditors	186 through 189	113.3.8	AU Section 560, *Subsequent Events*.	Auditors must take subsequent events into consideration if they reflect changes in internal control over financial reporting that occur after the audit but before the auditor's opinion is issued.	If a subsequent event occurs after the audit but before issuance of the auditor's report, the auditor must evaluate the event and determine its impact. Management must disclose subsequent events to the auditor in the representation letter. This includes internal audit reports and regulatory agency reports that are relevant to internal control over financial reporting.
Auditors	190 through 192	113.3.9	Section 10A of the Securities Exchange Act of 1934.	Management may add additional information to its report on the assessment of internal control over financial reporting that is not necessarily relevant to the audit of internal control over financial reporting. The auditor is expected to disclaim an opinion on the additional information.	If management adds any extraneous information to the standard format of the report, the auditor should disclaim this information. If the auditor believes the extra information includes a material misstatement of fact, the auditor is expected to discuss the issue with management directly. If this does not resolve the issue, the auditor is required to notify management and the audit committee in writing of its concerns regarding the information.

Who is Affected	Standard ¶	Analysis ¶	Rules and Regulations	Effect	Action
Auditors	193 through 196	113.3.10	None cited	The auditor can conclude that the financial statements deserve an unqualified opinion and simultaneously conclude that the assessment of internal control over financial reporting does not receive an unqualified opinion.	Even given a material weakness in the internal control over financial reporting, the auditor can conclude that the related financial statements are nonetheless accurate. This conclusion must be based on additional substantive procedures to determine if there was a material misstatement related to the ineffective control.
Auditors	197	113.3.11	AU Section 561, *Subsequent Discovery of Facts Existing at the Date of the Auditor's Report.*	If reliable information becomes known about a material weakness that existed at the date of the auditor's report that would have altered the auditor's conclusions, then the auditor must recall and reissue the audit opinion.	If new information becomes known about a material weakness that existed at the date of the auditor's report that would have altered the auditor's conclusions then the auditor must recall and reissue the opinion. This recall and reissue should be done according to the detailed requirements of AU Section 561, *Subsequent Discovery of Facts Existing at the Date of the Auditor's Report.*

Who is Affected	Standard ¶	Analysis ¶	Rules and Regulations	Effect	Action
Auditors	198 through 199	113.3.12	AU Section 711, *Filings Under Federal Securities Statutes.*	The auditor should apply the rules under AU Section 711, *Filings Under Federal Securities Statutes,* when the auditor's report is to be included in federal filings.	The auditor should apply the rules under AU Section 711, *Filings Under Federal Securities Statutes,* when the auditor's report is to be included in federal filings. The auditor should also apply AU Section 711 with respect to the auditor's report on management's assessment of the effectiveness of internal control over financial reporting included in such filings.
Auditors	200 through 206	114	Sarbanes-Oxley Act Section 302; Section 10A of the Securities Exchange Act of 1934; 17 CFR 240.13a-14a and 17 CFR 15d-14a (Securities Exchange Act Rules 13a-14(a) and 15d-14(a), respectively); 17 CFR 240.12b-20 (Securities Exchange Act Rule 12b-20); AU Section 317, *Illegal Acts by Clients;* AU Section 722, *Interim Financial Information.*	Management is required to make disclosures under Section 302. The auditor is required to evaluate the need for any possible disclosures related to changes in internal control over financial reporting. The auditor is required to conduct limited quarterly procedures.	Management must issue the statements required by Section 302 of the Sarbanes-Oxley Act. The auditor is required to evaluate the need for any possible disclosures related to changes in internal control over financial reporting. The auditor is required to conduct quarterly inquiries and evaluations regarding the materiality of changes to internal control and any misstatements that have been discovered.

WG&L Warren, Gorham & Lamont

Who is Affected	Standard ¶	Analysis ¶	Rules and Regulations	Effect	Action
Auditors	200 through 201	114.1	Sarbanes-Oxley Act Section 302; 17 CFR 240.13a-14a and 17 CFR 15d-14a (Securities Exchange Act Rules 13a-14(a) and 15d-14(a), respectively); 17 CFR 240.12b-20 (Securities Exchange Act Rule 12b-20).	Section 302 of the Sarbanes-Oxley Act requires management to make certain disclosures certifying the accuracy and reliability of the issuer's financial statements. One of those disclosures is a statement certifying that the officers of the issuer have implemented internal controls over financial reporting that are effective.	Management must certify that the internal control over the company's financial reporting is effective. Management must also issue a statement that discloses any changes in the company's internal control over financial reporting that occurred during the most recent fiscal quarter. Management must also certify that it has responsibility for internal control over financial reporting. The auditor is required to evaluate the need for any possible disclosures related to changes in internal control over financial reporting.

Who is Affected	Standard ¶	Analysis ¶	Rules and Regulations	Effect	Action
Auditors	202 through 206	114.2	Sarbanes-Oxley Act Section 302; AU Section 722, *Interim Financial Information;* AU Section 317, *Illegal Acts by Clients;* 17 CFR 240.13a-14(a) and 17 CFR 240.15d-14(a) (Securities Exchange Act Rules 13a-14(a) and 15d-14(a), respectively); Section 10A of the Securities Exchange Act of 1934.	Interim quarterly auditor evaluations of internal control over financial reporting can be based on limited procedures.	Auditors need only perform limited procedures on a quarterly basis to validate their annual assessment. In performing the quarterly procedures, the auditor is looking for material modifications that could become a required disclosure about changes in internal control over financial reporting in order for management's certifications to be accurate. The auditor is required to notify management of any material matters. If management does not respond appropriately, the auditor must notify the audit committee.

Who is Affected	Standard ¶	Analysis ¶	Rules and Regulations	Effect	Action
Auditors	207 through 214	115	AU Section 316, *Consideration of Fraud in a Financial Statement Audit;* AU Section 317, *Illegal Acts by Clients;* Section 10A of the Securities Exchange Act of 1934.	The auditor is required to communicate in writing to management and the audit committee all significant deficiencies and material weaknesses identified during the audit. The auditor is also required to make certain communications with management and the audit committee when the auditor becomes aware of fraud or illegal acts.	The auditor is required to communicate in writing to management and the audit committee all significant deficiencies and material weaknesses identified during the audit. The auditor is also required to make certain communications with management and the audit committee when the auditor becomes aware of fraud or illegal acts. The auditor must notify the board of directors if the audit committee is ineffectively overseeing the internal control function.
Auditors	215 through 216	116	Sarbanes-Oxley Act Section 404; 17 CFR 240.12b-2 (Securities Exchange Act Rule 12b-2).	Companies and auditors are required to comply with PCAOB Auditing Standard No. 2 for their the internal control reporting for fiscal years ending on or after November 15, 2004 (accelerated filers) or July 15, 2005 (other companies).	Auditors of companies considered accelerated filers (seasoned U.S. companies with public float exceeding $75 million) are required to comply with PCAOB Auditing Standard No. 2 for fiscal years ending on or after November 15, 2004. Auditors of other companies (including smaller companies, foreign private issuers and companies with only registered debt securities) have until fiscal years ending on or after July 15, 2005, to comply with PCAOB Auditing Standard No. 2.

Who is Affected	Standard ¶	Analysis ¶	Rules and Regulations	Effect	Action
Auditors	Appendix A	117	None cited	Appendix A of the auditing standard provides sample text to guide auditors in writing opinions on internal control over financial reporting.	Auditors should consult the illustrative examples in Appendix A of the auditing standard when writing their reports on internal control over financial reporting
Auditors	Appendix B	118	AU Section 324, *Service Organizations*; AU Section 543, *Part of Audit Performed by Other Independent Auditors.*	Appendix B provides additional guidance on tests to be performed when a company has multiple locations or business units and when a company obtains services from a service organization. It also provides detailed examples of the extent of testing required by the standard.	Auditors should refer to the guidance in Appendix B when auditing companies with multiple locations or business units or companies that use service organizations. Auditors should also familiarize themselves with the examples laid out by the PCAOB of the extent of testing required to determine the effectiveness of a company's internal control over financial reporting.

Who is Affected	Standard ¶	Analysis ¶	Rules and Regulations	Effect	Action
Auditors	Appendix C	119	None cited	Appendix C reiterates the PCAOB's emphasis on the importance of controls that operate to safeguard the company's assets, and defers to the COSO report for guidance on the safeguarding of assets as it relates to internal control over financial reporting.	Auditors should use the COSO framework as their guideline in determining the scope of the audit of internal controls intended to safeguard the company's assets. Management must realize that plans that could potentially affect financial reporting in future periods are not controls in the present. Business continuity plans are also not considered part of internal control over financial reporting. Management should ensure that the company has compensatory and overlapping controls in place where there is a risk of error or fraud that could affect the safeguarding of the company's assets.
Auditors	Appendix D	120	None cited	Appendix D provides detailed examples as guidance for the auditor to differentiate between a significant deficiency and a material weakness in internal control over financial reporting.	Auditors should use Appendix D as a guide when they cannot determine the difference between a significant deficiency and a material weakness. The implementation of a simple point system to score potential misstatements and levels of likelihood might also prove useful.

Who is Affected	Standard ¶	Analysis ¶	Rules and Regulations	Effect	Action
Auditors	Appendix E	121	Sarbanes-Oxley Act Sections 103 and 404; AU Section 312, *Audit Risk and Materiality in Conducting an Audit*; AU Section 322, *The Auditor's Consideration of the Internal Audit Function in an Audit of Financial Statements*; AU Section 325, *Communication of Internal Control Related Matters Noted in an Audit*; SSAE No. 10, *Attestation Standards: Revision and Recodification* (AT Section 501); SEC Release No. 33-8238, *Final Rule: Management's Reports on Internal Control Over Financial Reporting and Certification of Disclosure in Exchange Act Periodic Reports* (June 5, 2003); Section 10A of the Securities Exchange Act of 1934; FAS No. 5, *Accounting for Contingencies*; Staff Accounting Bulletin (SAB) No. 99, *Materiality*; IAS No. 200, *Objective and Principles Governing an Audit of Financial Statements*; PCAOB Rule 3300T; Federal Deposit Insurance Corporation Improvement Act of 1991 (FDCIA).	The PCAOB issued a proposed version of this auditing standard in October 2003. In Appendix E, the PCAOB provides its explanation of the consideration it gave to the various viewpoints submitted during the comment period.	Management and auditors should read Appendix E so they can understand the relevant thought processes that underlie the PCAOB's intent regarding various aspects of the audit of internal control over financial reporting.

Who is Affected	Standard ¶	Analysis ¶	Rules and Regulations	Effect	Action
Compliance Officers	130 through 141	109.8.2	SEC Staff Accounting Bulletin Topic 1M2, *Immaterial Misstatements That Are Intentional;* Sarbanes-Oxley Act Section 302.	Auditors must evaluate deficiencies in the company's internal control over financial reporting and determine whether the deficiencies, individually or in combination, rise to the level of significant deficiencies or material weaknesses	The auditor must look at all of the company's internal control deficiencies and determine, based on certain criteria, if the deficiencies constitute significant deficiencies or material weaknesses.

Who is Affected	Standard ¶	Analysis ¶	Rules and Regulations	Effect	Action
Creditors	1 through 3	100	Sarbanes-Oxley Act Sections 103(a)(2)(A)(iii) and 404; Securities Exchange Act of 1934 Sections 3, 12, and 15(d); Securities Act of 1933.	The PCAOB has proposed another auditing standard that amends or supersedes many other interim auditing standards as a result of the adoption of this standard (see PCAOB Release No. 2004-002, March 9, 2004). Of particular importance is the fact that AU Section 325, *Communication of Internal Control Related Matters Noted in an Audit*, and AT Section 501, *Reporting on an Entity's Internal Control Over Financial Reporting*, will be superseded by PCAOB Auditing Standard No. 2 as of November 15, 2004. In addition, the following interim standards will be amended to conform with Auditing Standard No. 2: • AU Section 310, *Appointment of the Independent Auditor* • AU Section 311, *Planning and Supervision* • AU Section 312, *Audit Risk and Materiality in Conducting an Audit* • AU Section 313, *Substantive Tests Prior to the Balance Sheet Date* • AU Section 316, *Consideration of Fraud in a Financial Statement Audit* • AU Section 319, *Consideration of Internal Control in a Financial*	Auditors must comply with this new auditing standard when performing the newly required audit of internal control over financial reporting in conjunction with an audit of financial statements. They should also take into account the conforming amendments to the interim standards proposed in PCAOB Release No. 2004-002.

WG
&L Warren, Gorham & Lamont

Who is Affected	Standard ¶	Analysis ¶	Rules and Regulations	Effect	Action
				Statement Audit • AU Section 322, *The Auditor's Consideration of the Internal Audit Function in an Audit of Financial Statements* • AU Section 324, *Service Organizations* • AU Section 326, *Evidential Matter* • AU Section 329, *Analytical Procedures* • AU Section 332, *Auditing Derivative Instruments, Hedging Activities, and Investments in Securities* • AU Section 333, *Management Representation* • AU Section 339, *Audit Documentation* • AU Section 342, *Auditing Accounting Estimates* • AU Section 508, *Reports on Audited Financial Statements* • AU Section 530, *Dating of the Independent Auditor's Report* • AU Section 543, *Part of Audit Performed by Other Independent Auditors* • AU Section 560, *Subsequent Events* • AU Section 561, *Subsequent Discovery of Facts Existing at the Date of the Auditor's Report* • AU Section 711, *Filings Under Federal Securities Statutes* • AU Section 722, *Interim Financial Information* • ET Section 101, *Independence*	

Who is Affected	Standard ¶	Analysis ¶	Rules and Regulations	Effect	Action
Creditors	215 through 216	116	Sarbanes-Oxley Act Section 404; 17 CFR 240.12b-2 (Securities Exchange Act Rule 12b-2).	Companies and auditors are required to comply with PCAOB Auditing Standard No. 2 for their the internal control reporting for fiscal years ending on or after November 15, 2004 (accelerated filers) or July 15, 2005 (other companies).	Auditors of companies considered accelerated filers (seasoned U.S. companies with public float exceeding $75 million) are required to comply with PCAOB Auditing Standard No. 2 for fiscal years ending on or after November 15, 2004. Auditors of other companies (including smaller companies, foreign private issuers and companies with only registered debt securities) have until fiscal years ending on or after July 15, 2005, to comply with PCAOB Auditing Standard No. 2.

Who is Affected	Standard ¶	Analysis ¶	Rules and Regulations	Effect	Action
Creditors	Appendix E	121	Sarbanes-Oxley Act Sections 103 and 404; AU Section 312, *Audit Risk and Materiality in Conducting an Audit;* AU Section 322, *The Auditor's Consideration of the Internal Audit Function in an Audit of Financial Statements;* AU Section 325, *Communication of Internal Control Related Matters Noted in an Audit;* SSAE No. 10, *Attestation Standards: Revision and Recodification* (AT Section 501); SEC Release No. 33-8238, *Final Rule: Management's Reports on Internal Control Over Financial Reporting and Certification of Disclosure in Exchange Act Periodic Reports* (June 5, 2003); Section 10A of the Securities Exchange Act of 1934; FAS No. 5, *Accounting for Contingencies;* Staff Accounting Bulletin (SAB) No. 99, *Materiality;* IAS No. 200, *Objective and Principles Governing an Audit of Financial Statements;* PCAOB Rule 3300T; *Federal Deposit Insurance Corporation Improvement Act of 1991 (FDCIA)*	The PCAOB issued a proposed version of this auditing standard in October 2003. In Appendix E, the PCAOB provides its explanation of the consideration it gave to the various viewpoints submitted during the comment period.	Management and auditors should read Appendix E so they can understand the relevant thought processes that underlie the PCAOB's intent regarding various aspects of the audit of internal control over financial reporting.

Who is Affected	Standard ¶	Analysis ¶	Rules and Regulations	Effect	Action
Directors	1 through 3	100	Sarbanes-Oxley Act Sections 103(a)(2)(A)(iii) and 404; Securities Exchange Act of 1934 Sections 3, 12, and 15(d); Securities Act of 1933.	The PCAOB has proposed another auditing standard that amends or supersedes many other interim auditing standards as a result of the adoption of this standard (see PCAOB Release No. 2004-002, March 9, 2004). Of particular importance is the fact that AU Section 325, *Communication of Internal Control Related Matters Noted in an Audit*, and AT Section 501, *Reporting on an Entity's Internal Control Over Financial Reporting*, will be superseded by PCAOB Auditing Standard No. 2 as of November 15, 2004. In addition, the following interim standards will be amended to conform with Auditing Standard No. 2: • AU Section 310, *Appointment of the Independent Auditor* • AU Section 311, *Planning and Supervision* • AU Section 312, *Audit Risk and Materiality in Conducting an Audit* • AU Section 313, *Substantive Tests Prior to the Balance Sheet Date* • AU Section 316, *Consideration of Fraud in a Financial Statement Audit* • AU Section 319, *Consideration of Internal Control in a Financial*	Auditors must comply with this new auditing standard when performing the newly required audit of internal control over financial reporting in conjunction with an audit of financial statements. They should also take into account the conforming amendments to the interim standards proposed in PCAOB Release No. 2004-002.

Who is Affected	Standard ¶	Analysis ¶	Rules and Regulations	Effect	Action
				Statement Audit • AU Section 322, *The Auditor's Consideration of the Internal Audit Function in an Audit of Financial Statements* • AU Section 324, *Service Organizations* • AU Section 326, *Evidential Matter* • AU Section 329, *Analytical Procedures* • AU Section 332, *Auditing Derivative Instruments, Hedging Activities, and Investments in Securities* • AU Section 333, *Management Representation* • AU Section 339, *Audit Documentation* • AU Section 342, *Auditing Accounting Estimates* • AU Section 508, *Reports on Audited Financial Statements* • AU Section 530, *Dating of the Independent Auditor's Report* • AU Section 543, *Part of Audit Performed by Other Independent Auditors* • AU Section 560, *Subsequent Events* • AU Section 561, *Subsequent Discovery of Facts Existing at the Date of the Auditor's Report* • AU Section 711, *Filings Under Federal Securities Statutes* • AU Section 722, *Interim Financial Information* • ET Section 101, *Independence*	

Who is Affected	Standard ¶	Analysis ¶	Rules and Regulations	Effect	Action
Directors	24 through 26	108	AU Section 316, *Consideration of Fraud in a Financial Statement Audit.*	Auditors are required to place a special emphasis on their examination of controls designed to detect and prevent fraud.	The auditor should evaluate the company's control environment, risk assessment processes, codes of ethics, internal audit activities, and management's procedures for handling complaints. Management should ensure that the company's system of internal control is designed specifically to prevent, deter, and detect fraud. Management, directors, and audit committee members should confirm their commitment to the "tone at the top" concept as outlined in the COSO framework.

WG &LE Warren, Gorham & Lamont

Who is Affected	Standard ¶	Analysis ¶	Rules and Regulations	Effect	Action
Directors	55 through 59	109.4.2	15 U.S.C. 78c; 15 U.S.C. 7201(a)(3); 17 CFR 240.10A-3 (Securities Exchange Act Rule 10A-3); 17 CFR 240.10A-3(c)(2) (Securities Exchange Act Rule 10A-3(c)(2)); 17 CFR 210.2-01(c)(7) (Regulation S-X Rule 2-01(c)(7)).	The auditor must review and assess the effectiveness of the audit committee's oversight of the company's external financial reporting and internal control over financial reporting.	The auditor must review the audit committee's involvement in detail and assess the effectiveness of the audit committee's oversight of the company's external financial reporting and internal control over financial reporting. The auditor must also assess the relative effectiveness of the audit committee's oversight role. If the auditor finds that the audit committee is ineffective in the oversight role, then this constitutes a significant deficiency. Boards of directors should ensure that their audit committees are in compliance with the requirements of Section 301 of the Sarbanes-Oxley Act, as well as the applicable SRO corporate governance rules.

Who is Affected	Standard ¶	Analysis ¶	Rules and Regulations	Effect	Action
Directors	76 through 78	109.4.6	None cited	Auditors must obtain an understanding of and evaluate the period-end financial reporting process.	Auditors must review and evaluate the period-end financial reporting processes to ensure that transactions are recorded in their proper periods. The impact of the company's control environment on period-end financial reporting should be taken into account by the auditor. Management, the board, and the audit committee should ensure proper oversight of the period-end process.
Directors	207 through 214	115	AU Section 316, *Consideration of Fraud in a Financial Statement Audit;* AU Section 317, *Illegal Acts by Clients;* Section 10A of the Securities Exchange Act of 1934.	The auditor is required to communicate in writing to management and the audit committee all significant deficiencies and material weaknesses identified during the audit. The auditor is also required to make certain communications with management and the audit committee when the auditor becomes aware of fraud or illegal acts.	The auditor is required to communicate in writing to management and the audit committee all significant deficiencies and material weaknesses identified during the audit. The auditor is also required to make certain communications with management and the audit committee when the auditor becomes aware of fraud or illegal acts. The auditor must notify the board of directors if the audit committee is ineffectively overseeing the internal control function.

W︦G︦&L Warren, Gorham & Lamont

Who is Affected	Standard ¶	Analysis ¶	Rules and Regulations	Effect	Action
Directors	215 through 216	116	Sarbanes-Oxley Act Section 404; 17 CFR 240.12b-2 (Securities Exchange Act Rule 12b-2).	Companies and auditors are required to comply with PCAOB Auditing Standard No. 2 for their the internal control reporting for fiscal years ending on or after November 15, 2004 (accelerated filers) or July 15, 2005 (other companies).	Auditors of companies considered accelerated filers (seasoned U.S. companies with public float exceeding $75 million) are required to comply with PCAOB Auditing Standard No. 2 for fiscal years ending on or after November 15, 2004. Auditors of other companies (including smaller companies, foreign private issuers and companies with only registered debt securities) have until fiscal years ending on or after July 15, 2005, to comply with PCAOB Auditing Standard No. 2.

Who is Affected	Standard ¶	Analysis ¶	Rules and Regulations	Effect	Action
Directors	Appendix E	121	Sarbanes-Oxley Act Sections 103 and 404; AU Section 312, *Audit Risk and Materiality in Conducting an Audit;* AU Section 322, *The Auditor's Consideration of the Internal Audit Function in an Audit of Financial Statements;* AU Section 325, *Communication of Internal Control Related Matters Noted in an Audit;* SSAE No. 10, *Attestation Standards: Revision and Recodification* (AT Section 501); SEC Release No. 33-8238, *Final Rule: Management's Reports on Internal Control Over Financial Reporting and Certification of Disclosure in Exchange Act Periodic Reports* (June 5, 2003); Section 10A of the Securities Exchange Act of 1934; FAS No. 5, *Accounting for Contingencies;* Staff Accounting Bulletin (SAB) No. 99, *Materiality;* IAS No. 200, *Objective and Principles Governing an Audit of Financial Statements;* PCAOB Rule 3300T; Federal Deposit Insurance Corporation Improvement Act of 1991 (FDCIA)	The PCAOB issued a proposed version of this auditing standard in October 2003. In Appendix E, the PCAOB provides its explanation of the consideration it gave to the various viewpoints submitted during the comment period.	Management and auditors should read Appendix E so they can understand the relevant thought processes that underlie the PCAOB's intent regarding various aspects of the audit of internal control over financial reporting.

Who is Affected	Standard ¶	Analysis ¶	Rules and Regulations	Effect	Action
Ethics Officers	24 through 26	108	AU Section 316, *Consideration of Fraud in a Financial Statement Audit.*	Auditors are required to place a special emphasis on their examination of controls designed to detect and prevent fraud.	The auditor should evaluate the company's control environment, risk assessment processes, codes of ethics, internal audit activities, and management's procedures for handling complaints. Management should ensure that the company's system of internal control is designed specifically to prevent, deter, and detect fraud. Management, directors, and audit committee members should confirm their commitment to the "tone at the top" concept as outlined in the COSO framework.

Who is Affected	Standard ¶	Analysis ¶	Rules and Regulations	Effect	Action
Financial Statement Users	1 through 3	100	Sarbanes-Oxley Act Sections 103(a)(2)(A)(iii) and 404; Securities Exchange Act of 1934 Sections 3, 12, and 15(d); Securities Act of 1933.	The PCAOB has proposed another auditing standard that amends or supersedes many other interim auditing standards as a result of the adoption of this standard (see PCAOB Release No. 2004-002, March 9, 2004). Of particular importance is the fact that AU Section 325, *Communication of Internal Control Related Matters Noted in an Audit*, and AT Section 501, *Reporting on an Entity's Internal Control Over Financial Reporting*, will be superseded by PCAOB Auditing Standard No. 2 as of November 15, 2004. In addition, the following interim standards will be amended to conform with Auditing Standard No. 2: • AU Section 310, *Appointment of the Independent Auditor* • AU Section 311, *Planning and Supervision* • AU Section 312, *Audit Risk and Materiality in Conducting an Audit* • AU Section 313, *Substantive Tests Prior to the Balance Sheet Date* • AU Section 316, *Consideration of Fraud in a Financial Statement Audit* • AU Section 319, *Consideration of Internal Control in a Financial*	Auditors must comply with this new auditing standard when performing the newly required audit of internal control over financial reporting in conjunction with an audit of financial statements. They should also take into account the conforming amendments to the interim standards proposed in PCAOB Release No. 2004-002.

Who is Affected	Standard ¶	Analysis ¶	Rules and Regulations	Effect	Action
				Statement Audit • AU Section 322, *The Auditor's Consideration of the Internal Audit Function in an Audit of Financial Statements* • AU Section 324, *Service Organizations* • AU Section 326, *Evidential Matter* • AU Section 329, *Analytical Procedures* • AU Section 332, *Auditing Derivative Instruments, Hedging Activities, and Investments in Securities* • AU Section 333, *Management Representation* • AU Section 339, *Audit Documentation* • AU Section 342, *Auditing Accounting Estimates* • AU Section 508, *Reports on Audited Financial Statements* • AU Section 530, *Dating of the Independent Auditor's Report* • AU Section 543, *Part of Audit Performed by Other Independent Auditors* • AU Section 560, *Subsequent Events* • AU Section 561, *Subsequent Discovery of Facts Existing at the Date of the Auditor's Report* • AU Section 711, *Filings Under Federal Securities Statutes* • AU Section 722, *Interim Financial Information* • ET Section 101, *Independence*	

Who is Affected	Standard ¶	Analysis ¶	Rules and Regulations	Effect	Action
Financial Statement Users	215 through 216	116	Sarbanes-Oxley Act Section 404; 17 CFR 240.12b-2 (Securities Exchange Act Rule 12b-2).	Companies and auditors are required to comply with PCAOB Auditing Standard No. 2 for their the internal control reporting for fiscal years ending on or after November 15, 2004 (accelerated filers) or July 15, 2005 (other companies).	Auditors of companies considered accelerated filers (seasoned U.S. companies with public float exceeding $75 million) are required to comply with PCAOB Auditing Standard No. 2 for fiscal years ending on or after November 15, 2004. Auditors of other companies (including smaller companies, foreign private issuers and companies with only registered debt securities) have until fiscal years ending on or after July 15, 2005, to comply with PCAOB Auditing Standard No. 2.

Who is Affected	Standard ¶	Analysis ¶	Rules and Regulations	Effect	Action
Financial Statement Users	Appendix E	121	Sarbanes-Oxley Act Sections 103 and 404; AU Section 312, *Audit Risk and Materiality in Conducting an Audit;* AU Section 322, *The Auditor's Consideration of the Internal Audit Function in an Audit of Financial Statements;* AU Section 325, *Communication of Internal Control Related Matters Noted in an Audit;* SSAE No. 10, *Attestation Standards: Revision and Recodification* (AT Section 501); SEC Release No. 33-8238, *Final Rule: Management's Reports on Internal Control Over Financial Reporting and Certification of Disclosure in Exchange Act Periodic Reports* (June 5, 2003); Section 10A of the Securities Exchange Act of 1934; FAS No. 5, *Accounting for Contingencies;* Staff Accounting Bulletin (SAB) No. 99, *Materiality;* IAS No. 200, *Objective and Principles Governing an Audit of Financial Statements;* PCAOB Rule 3300T; *Federal Deposit Insurance Corporation Improvement Act of 1991 (FDCIA)*	The PCAOB issued a proposed version of this auditing standard in October 2003. In Appendix E, the PCAOB provides its explanation of the consideration it gave to the various viewpoints submitted during the comment period.	Management and auditors should read Appendix E so they can understand the relevant thought processes that underlie the PCAOB's intent regarding various aspects of the audit of internal control over financial reporting.

Who is Affected	Standard ¶	Analysis ¶	Rules and Regulations	Effect	Action
Internal Auditors	1 through 3	100	Sarbanes-Oxley Act Sections 103(a)(2)(A)(iii) and 404; Securities Exchange Act of 1934 Sections 3, 12, and 15(d); Securities Act of 1933.	The PCAOB has proposed another auditing standard that amends or supersedes many other interim auditing standards as a result of the adoption of this standard (see PCAOB Release No. 2004-002, March 9, 2004). Of particular importance is the fact that AU Section 325, *Communication of Internal Control Related Matters Noted in an Audit,* and AT Section 501, *Reporting on an Entity's Internal Control Over Financial Reporting,* will be superseded by PCAOB Auditing Standard No. 2 as of November 15, 2004. In addition, the following interim standards will be amended to conform with Auditing Standard No. 2: • AU Section 310, *Appointment of the Independent Auditor* • AU Section 311, *Planning and Supervision* • AU Section 312, *Audit Risk and Materiality in Conducting an Audit* • AU Section 313, *Substantive Tests Prior to the Balance Sheet Date* • AU Section 316, *Consideration of Fraud in a Financial Statement Audit* • AU Section 319, *Consideration of Internal Control in a Financial*	Auditors must comply with this new auditing standard when performing the newly required audit of internal control over financial reporting in conjunction with an audit of financial statements. They should also take into account the conforming amendments to the interim standards proposed in PCAOB Release No. 2004-002.

Who is Affected	Standard ¶	Analysis ¶	Rules and Regulations	Effect	Action
				Statement Audit • AU Section 322, *The Auditor's Consideration of the Internal Audit Function in an Audit of Financial Statements* • AU Section 324, *Service Organizations* • AU Section 326, *Evidential Matter* • AU Section 329, *Analytical Procedures* • AU Section 332, *Auditing Derivative Instruments, Hedging Activities, and Investments in Securities* • AU Section 333, *Management Representation* • AU Section 339, *Audit Documentation* • AU Section 342, *Auditing Accounting Estimates* • AU Section 508, *Reports on Audited Financial Statements* • AU Section 530, *Dating of the Independent Auditor's Report* • AU Section 543, *Part of Audit Performed by Other Independent Auditors* • AU Section 560, *Subsequent Events* • AU Section 561, *Subsequent Discovery of Facts Existing at the Date of the Auditor's Report* • AU Section 711, *Filings Under Federal Securities Statutes* • AU Section 722, *Interim Financial Information* • ET Section 101, *Independence*	

Who is Affected	Standard ¶	Analysis ¶	Rules and Regulations	Effect	Action
Internal Auditors	24 through 26	108	AU Section 316, *Consideration of Fraud in a Financial Statement Audit.*	Auditors are required to place a special emphasis on their examination of controls designed to detect and prevent fraud.	The auditor should evaluate the company's control environment, risk assessment processes, codes of ethics, internal audit activities, and management's procedures for handling complaints. Management should ensure that the company's system of internal control is designed specifically to prevent, deter, and detect fraud. Management, directors, and audit committee members should confirm their commitment to the "tone at the top" concept as outlined in the COSO framework.
Internal Auditors	40 through 46	109.3	None cited	The standard outlines what elements of a company's internal control structure should have been addressed by management in its assessment of internal control over financial reporting.	The auditor must examine sufficient evidence and obtain an understanding of management's process for assessing the effectiveness of the company's internal control over financial reporting. Management should ensure that its assessment of internal control over financial reporting addresses the elements that the auditor is expected to cover in its audit of management's assessment.

WG
&L Warren, Gorham & Lamont

Who is Affected	Standard ¶	Analysis ¶	Rules and Regulations	Effect	Action
Internal Auditors	42 through 46	109.3.1	None cited	The auditor is required to evaluate the adequacy of management's documentation in support of its assessment of internal control over financial reporting.	Management should become familiar with the documentation requirements provided by the standard. The auditor must review the issuer's documentation of management's assessment of internal control over financial reporting. Given a substantial absence of documentation of internal control over financial reporting on the part of the issuer, the auditor must withhold the attestation or limit the scope of the audit of internal control over financial reporting.
Internal Auditors	52 through 54	109.4.1	None cited.	The auditing standard recommends that auditors test those controls that affect primarily the control environment and pervade all other controls first, i.e., the company-level controls. Auditors should evaluate the results of the evaluation of the company-wide controls when creating the audit plan for the rest of the company's controls over financial reporting.	Identification and testing of company-level controls by the external auditor is required. Management should ensure that proper documentation of company-wide controls exists.

Who is Affected	Standard ¶	Analysis ¶	Rules and Regulations	Effect	Action
Internal Auditors	55 through 59	109.4.2	15 U.S.C. 78c; 15 U.S.C. 7201(a)(3); 17 CFR 240.10A-3 (Securities Exchange Act Rule 10A-3); 17 CFR 240.10A-3(c)(2) (Securities Exchange Act Rule 10A-3(c)(2)); 17 CFR 210.2-01(c)(7) (Regulation S-X Rule 2-01(c)(7)).	The auditor must review and assess the effectiveness of the audit committee's oversight of the company's external financial reporting and internal control over financial reporting.	The auditor must review the audit committee's involvement in detail and assess the effectiveness of the audit committee's oversight of the company's external financial reporting and internal control over financial reporting. The auditor must also assess the relative effectiveness of the audit committee's oversight role. If the auditor finds that the audit committee is ineffective in the oversight role, then this constitutes a significant deficiency. Boards of directors should ensure that their audit committees are in compliance with the requirements of Section 301 of the Sarbanes-Oxley Act, as well as the applicable SRO corporate governance rules.

WG&L Warren, Gorham & Lamont

Who is Affected	Standard ¶	Analysis ¶	Rules and Regulations	Effect	Action
Internal Auditors	83 through 87	109.4.8	None cited	The company's auditor must obtain evidence that validates the effectiveness of controls over financial reporting.	The auditor should obtain evidence of the effectiveness of controls on which to base its opinion. The auditor must either perform these tests himself or herself or may rely, to some extent, on the work of others, such as the company's internal auditors. Management should ensure that adequate documentation exists of the company's significant control points, the nature of the controls implemented by management, the significance of each control, and the level of risk that the controls might not be operating as designed.

Who is Affected	Standard ¶	Analysis ¶	Rules and Regulations	Effect	Action
Internal Auditors	108 through 126	109.7	AU Section 319, *Internal Control in a Financial Statement Audit*; AU Section 322, *The Auditor's Consideration of the Internal Audit Function in an Audit of Financial Statements*; FAS No. 5, *Accounting for Contingencies*; The Institute of Internal Auditors, *International Standards for the Professional Practice of Internal Auditing*.	Auditors can use the work of others to a certain extent when performing the audit. The auditing standard clarifies the ability of the auditor to use the work of others and reiterates that the auditor's opinion must be based solely on work done by the auditor or the auditor's direct validation of any work done by others.	Auditors can use the work of others but the auditors' own work must be substantial enough to form the basis for the auditors' opinion on the effectiveness of the company's internal control over financial reporting. Auditors are required to evaluate and test the work of others upon which they plan to rely. Internal auditors may provide the results of their work on the company's internal controls over financial reporting to the external auditors for use during the audit of the company's financial statements and internal control over financial reporting.
Internal Auditors	112 through 116	109.7.1	AU Section 319, *Internal Control in a Financial Statement Audit*; FAS No. 5, *Accounting for Contingencies*.	Auditors must evaluate the nature of the controls subjected to the work of others before the auditors rely on that work.	Auditors must evaluate the nature of the controls subjected to the work of others before the auditors rely on that work. Auditors should not rely on the work of others when evaluating the company's overall control environment. Auditors must perform walkthroughs themselves but may obtain additional evidence from walkthroughs performed by others.

Who is Affected	Standard ¶	Analysis ¶	Rules and Regulations	Effect	Action
Internal Auditors	117 through 122	109.7.2	*International Standards for the Professional Practice of Internal Auditing*	Auditors must evaluate the competence and objectivity of others before using their work.	By looking at factors such as educational level, professional experience, professional certification, continuing education, work assignments, supervision, documentation, and performance evaluations, auditors must evaluate the competence and objectivity of others before using their work. External auditors may rely on the work of qualified and objective internal auditors more heavily than the work of other parties, unless the internal auditors report solely to management.

Who is Affected	Standard ¶	Analysis ¶	Rules and Regulations	Effect	Action
Internal Auditors	123 through 126	109.7.3	None cited	Auditors must test some of the work of others in order to evaluate the quality and effectiveness of the work. The standard provides specific guidance regarding controls over period-end financial reporting, IT general controls, management self-assessment, controls over the calculation of the depreciation of assets, and alternating tests of controls.	By looking at factors such as scope of the work, adequacy of procedures, adequacy of documentation, appropriateness of conclusions, and consistency of reports, auditors must evaluate the quality and effectiveness of the work of others before using the work. Management should consult the standard's guidance regarding the auditor's use of the work of others in specific situations related to controls over period-end financial reporting, IT general controls, management self-assessment, controls over the calculation of the depreciation of assets, and alternating tests of controls.

Who is Affected	Standard ¶	Analysis ¶	Rules and Regulations	Effect	Action
Internal Auditors	127 through 141	109.8	SEC Staff Accounting Bulletin Topic 1M2, *Immaterial Misstatements That Are Intentional*; Sarbanes-Oxley Act Section 302.	Auditors must evaluate information from all relevant sources, particularly the company's internal audit function, when forming an opinion on internal control over financial reporting.	Auditors must evaluate evidence from all relevant sources, including management's assessment of internal control over financial reporting, negative results of substantive procedures performed during the financial statement audit, any identified control deficiencies, and all relevant reports issued by the company's internal audit function. Internal audit departments must be prepared to provide the company's external auditors with copies of all reports issued during the year that have even a tangential relevancy to internal control over financial reporting.
Internal Auditors	130 through 141	109.8.2	SEC Staff Accounting Bulletin Topic 1M2, *Immaterial Misstatements That Are Intentional*; Sarbanes-Oxley Act Section 302.	Auditors must evaluate deficiencies in the company's internal control over financial reporting and determine whether the deficiencies, individually or in combination, rise to the level of significant deficiencies or material weaknesses	The auditor must look at all of the company's internal control deficiencies and determine, based on certain criteria, if the deficiencies constitute significant deficiencies or material weaknesses.

Who is Affected	Standard ¶	Analysis ¶	Rules and Regulations	Effect	Action
Internal Auditors	186 through 189	113.3.8	AU Section 560, *Subsequent Events*.	Auditors must take subsequent events into consideration if they reflect changes in internal control over financial reporting that occur after the audit but before the auditor's opinion is issued.	If a subsequent event occurs after the audit but before issuance of the auditor's report, the auditor must evaluate the event and determine its impact. Management must disclose subsequent events to the auditor in the representation letter. This includes internal audit reports and regulatory agency reports that are relevant to internal control over financial reporting.
Internal Auditors	215 through 216	116	Sarbanes-Oxley Act Section 404; 17 CFR 240.12b-2 (Securities Exchange Act Rule 12b-2).	Companies and auditors are required to comply with PCAOB Auditing Standard No. 2 for their the internal control reporting for fiscal years ending on or after November 15, 2004 (accelerated filers) or July 15, 2005 (other companies).	Auditors of companies considered accelerated filers (seasoned U.S. companies with public float exceeding $75 million) are required to comply with PCAOB Auditing Standard No. 2 for fiscal years ending on or after November 15, 2004. Auditors of other companies (including smaller companies, foreign private issuers and companies with only registered debt securities) have until fiscal years ending on or after July 15, 2005, to comply with PCAOB Auditing Standard No. 2.

WG &LE **Warren, Gorham & Lamont**

Who is Affected	Standard ¶	Analysis ¶	Rules and Regulations	Effect	Action
Internal Auditors	Appendix E	121	Sarbanes-Oxley Act Sections 103 and 404; AU Section 312, *Audit Risk and Materiality in Conducting an Audit;* AU Section 322, *The Auditor's Consideration of the Internal Audit Function in an Audit of Financial Statements;* AU Section 325, *Communication of Internal Control Related Matters Noted in an Audit;* SSAE No. 10, *Attestation Standards: Revision and Recodification* (AT Section 501); SEC Release No. 33-8238, *Final Rule: Management's Reports on Internal Control Over Financial Reporting and Certification of Disclosure in Exchange Act Periodic Reports* (June 5, 2003); Section 10A of the Securities Exchange Act of 1934; FAS No. 5, *Accounting for Contingencies;* Staff Accounting Bulletin (SAB) No. 99, *Materiality;* IAS No. 200, *Objective and Principles Governing an Audit of Financial Statements;* PCAOB Rule 3300T; *Federal Deposit Insurance Corporation Improvement Act of 1991 (FDCIA)*	The PCAOB issued a proposed version of this auditing standard in October 2003. In Appendix E, the PCAOB provides its explanation of the consideration it gave to the various viewpoints submitted during the comment period.	Management and auditors should read Appendix E so they can understand the relevant thought processes that underlie the PCAOB's intent regarding various aspects of the audit of internal control over financial reporting.

Who is Affected	Standard ¶	Analysis ¶	Rules and Regulations	Effect	Action
Investors	1 through 3	100	Sarbanes-Oxley Act Sections 103(a)(2)(A)(iii) and 404; Securities Exchange Act of 1934 Sections 3, 12, and 15(d); Securities Act of 1933.	The PCAOB has proposed another auditing standard that amends or supersedes many other interim auditing standards as a result of the adoption of this standard (see PCAOB Release No. 2004-002, March 9, 2004). Of particular importance is the fact that AU Section 325, *Communication of Internal Control Related Matters Noted in an Audit*, and AT Section 501, *Reporting on an Entity's Internal Control Over Financial Reporting*, will be superseded by PCAOB Auditing Standard No. 2 as of November 15, 2004. In addition, the following interim standards will be amended to conform with Auditing Standard No. 2: • AU Section 310, *Appointment of the Independent Auditor* • AU Section 311, *Planning and Supervision* • AU Section 312, *Audit Risk and Materiality in Conducting an Audit* • AU Section 313, *Substantive Tests Prior to the Balance Sheet Date* • AU Section 316, *Consideration of Fraud in a Financial Statement Audit* • AU Section 319, *Consideration of Internal Control in a Financial*	Auditors must comply with this new auditing standard when performing the newly required audit of internal control over financial reporting in conjunction with an audit of financial statements. They should also take into account the conforming amendments to the interim standards proposed in PCAOB Release No. 2004-002.

Who is Affected	Standard ¶	Analysis ¶	Rules and Regulations	Effect	Action
				Statement Audit • AU Section 322, *The Auditor's Consideration of the Internal Audit Function in an Audit of Financial Statements* • AU Section 324, *Service Organizations* • AU Section 326, *Evidential Matter* • AU Section 329, *Analytical Procedures* • AU Section 332, *Auditing Derivative Instruments, Hedging Activities, and Investments in Securities* • AU Section 333, *Management Representation* • AU Section 339, *Audit Documentation* • AU Section 342, *Auditing Accounting Estimates* • AU Section 508, *Reports on Audited Financial Statements* • AU Section 530, *Dating of the Independent Auditor's Report* • AU Section 543, *Part of Audit Performed by Other Independent Auditors* • AU Section 560, *Subsequent Events* • AU Section 561, *Subsequent Discovery of Facts Existing at the Date of the Auditor's Report* • AU Section 711, *Filings Under Federal Securities Statutes* • AU Section 722, *Interim Financial Information* • ET Section 101, *Independence*	

Who is Affected	Standard ¶	Analysis ¶	Rules and Regulations	Effect	Action
Investors	215 through 216	116	Sarbanes-Oxley Act Section 404; 17 CFR 240.12b-2 (Securities Exchange Act Rule 12b-2).	Companies and auditors are required to comply with PCAOB Auditing Standard No. 2 for their the internal control reporting for fiscal years ending on or after November 15, 2004 (accelerated filers) or July 15, 2005 (other companies).	Auditors of companies considered accelerated filers (seasoned U.S. companies with public float exceeding $75 million) are required to comply with PCAOB Auditing Standard No. 2 for fiscal years ending on or after November 15, 2004. Auditors of other companies (including smaller companies, foreign private issuers and companies with only registered debt securities) have until fiscal years ending on or after July 15, 2005, to comply with PCAOB Auditing Standard No. 2.

Who is Affected	Standard ¶	Analysis ¶	Rules and Regulations	Effect	Action
Investors	Appendix E	121	Sarbanes-Oxley Act Sections 103 and 404; AU Section 312, *Audit Risk and Materiality in Conducting an Audit;* AU Section 322, *The Auditor's Consideration of the Internal Audit Function in an Audit of Financial Statements;* AU Section 325, *Communication of Internal Control Related Matters Noted in an Audit;* SSAE No. 10, *Attestation Standards: Revision and Recodification* (AT Section 501); SEC Release No. 33-8238, *Final Rule: Management's Reports on Internal Control Over Financial Reporting and Certification of Disclosure in Exchange Act Periodic Reports* (June 5, 2003); Section 10A of the Securities Exchange Act of 1934; FAS No. 5, *Accounting for Contingencies;* Staff Accounting Bulletin (SAB) No. 99, *Materiality;* IAS No. 200, *Objective and Principles Governing an Audit of Financial Statements;* PCAOB Rule 3300T; *Federal Deposit Insurance Corporation Improvement Act of 1991 (FDCIA)*	The PCAOB issued a proposed version of this auditing standard in October 2003. In Appendix E, the PCAOB provides its explanation of the consideration it gave to the various viewpoints submitted during the comment period.	Management and auditors should read Appendix E so they can understand the relevant thought processes that underlie the PCAOB's intent regarding various aspects of the audit of internal control over financial reporting.

Who is Affected	Standard ¶	Analysis ¶	Rules and Regulations	Effect	Action
Management	1 through 3	100	Sarbanes-Oxley Act Sections 103(a)(2)(A)(iii) and 404; Securities Exchange Act of 1934 Sections 3, 12, and 15(d); Securities Act of 1933.	The PCAOB has proposed another auditing standard that amends or supersedes many other interim auditing standards as a result of the adoption of this standard (see PCAOB Release No. 2004-002, March 9, 2004). Of particular importance is the fact that AU Section 325, *Communication of Internal Control Related Matters Noted in an Audit*, and AT Section 501, *Reporting on an Entity's Internal Control Over Financial Reporting*, will be superseded by PCAOB Auditing Standard No. 2 as of November 15, 2004. In addition, the following interim standards will be amended to conform with Auditing Standard No. 2: • AU Section 310, *Appointment of the Independent Auditor* • AU Section 311, *Planning and Supervision* • AU Section 312, *Audit Risk and Materiality in Conducting an Audit* • AU Section 313, *Substantive Tests Prior to the Balance Sheet Date* • AU Section 316, *Consideration of Fraud in a Financial Statement Audit* • AU Section 319, *Consideration of Internal Control in a Financial*	Auditors must comply with this new auditing standard when performing the newly required audit of internal control over financial reporting in conjunction with an audit of financial statements. They should also take into account the conforming amendments to the interim standards proposed in PCAOB Release No. 2004-002.

WG&L Warren, Gorham & Lamont

Who is Affected	Standard ¶	Analysis ¶	Rules and Regulations	Effect	Action
				Statement Audit • AU Section 322, *The Auditor's Consideration of the Internal Audit Function in an Audit of Financial Statements* • AU Section 324, *Service Organizations* • AU Section 326, *Evidential Matter* • AU Section 329, *Analytical Procedures* • AU Section 332, *Auditing Derivative Instruments, Hedging Activities, and Investments in Securities* • AU Section 333, *Management Representation* • AU Section 339, *Audit Documentation* • AU Section 342, *Auditing Accounting Estimates* • AU Section 508, *Reports on Audited Financial Statements* • AU Section 530, *Dating of the Independent Auditor's Report* • AU Section 543, *Part of Audit Performed by Other Independent Auditors* • AU Section 560, *Subsequent Events* • AU Section 561, *Subsequent Discovery of Facts Existing at the Date of the Auditor's Report* • AU Section 711, *Filings Under Federal Securities Statutes* • AU Section 722, *Interim Financial Information* • ET Section 101, *Independence*	

Who is Affected	Standard ¶	Analysis ¶	Rules and Regulations	Effect	Action
Management	4 through 6	101	Sarbanes-Oxley Act Section 302; 17 CFR 240.13a-14(a); 17 CFR 240.15d-14(a).	The issuer's auditor must express an opinion on management's assessment of the effectiveness of internal controls over financial reporting. The auditor's review of management's assessment must provide a level of reasonable assurance that the company's financial statements are materially accurate. The auditor must also audit the company's financial statements as of the date specified in management's assessment.	Management must evaluate, test, and document the company's system of internal control over financial reporting, then prepare an assessment. The company's auditor must evaluate management's assessment as well as obtain and evaluate evidence that the company's internal control over financial reporting is designed and operating effectively. In order to do this, the auditor must also audit the company's financial statements for the same time period covered by management's assessment of internal control.
Management	13 through 15	103	SAS No. 95SAS No. 95, *Generally Accepted Auditing Standards;* AU Section 319, *Consideration of Internal Control in a Financial Statement Audit;* PCAOB Rule 3200T, *Interim Auditing Standards*	The auditing standard defines the characteristics of acceptable internal control frameworks that can be used to assess compliance with Sections 302 and 404 of the Sarbanes-Oxley Act. The characteristics are defined so narrowly that only the COSO framework can possibly be used by U.S. issuers for compliance with the Act at this time.	Companies that have not already done so should ensure that they are implementing at least the components of the COSO framework that relate to financial reporting, though certain aspects of the efficiency and effectiveness of operations and compliance with laws and regulations will also fall under the purview of internal control over financial reporting.

Who is Affected	Standard ¶	Analysis ¶	Rules and Regulations	Effect	Action
Management	16	104	None cited	Internal control over financial reporting is not expected to completely prevent or detect all material misstatements, due to inherent limitations.	Establish realistic expectations for internal control over financial reporting, and, as much as is feasible, introduce safeguards against human error and fraud in order to minimize the risk of financial misstatements.
Management	17 through 19	105	SEC Release No. 33-8238, *Final Rule: Management's Reports on Internal Control Over Financial Reporting and Certification of Disclosure in Exchange Act Periodic Reports* (June 5, 2003).	The auditing standard requires the management assessment and auditor attestation of internal control over financial reporting to be at the level of reasonable, not absolute, assurance.	Management and the company's auditors should understand the inherent limitations involved with internal control and should discuss the remote likelihood that material misstatements will not be detected or prevented by management's assessment and the audit of internal control over financial reporting. Management should have a plan in place to address this possibility. Management should also take primary responsibility for conveying the effectiveness of the company's internal over financial reporting to users of the company's financial reports.

Who is Affected	Standard ¶	Analysis ¶	Rules and Regulations	Effect	Action
Management	20 through 21	106	17 CFR 228.308(a) and 17 CFR 228.308(c); 17 CFR 229.308(a) and 17 CFR 229.308(c) (Items 308(a) and (c) of Regulation S-B and S-K, respectively).	Sufficient documentation is required to pass an audit of internal control over financial reporting. Management must accept responsibility for and assess the effectiveness of the internal controls over financial reporting. Documentation serves as evidence of this responsibility and assessment and is therefore an essential requirement in an audit of internal control over financial reporting.	Management must accept responsibility for and assess the effectiveness of the internal controls over financial reporting. During management's assessment, proper and complete documentation of the effectiveness of the company's internal controls must be compiled. A written assessment of the effectiveness of the company's internal control over financial reporting must be prepared by management at the end of each fiscal year. The auditor must notify management and the audit committee in writing if the auditor finds that management has not fulfilled its responsibilities with regard to this assessment process.
Management	22 through 23	107	AU Section 312, *Audit Risk and Materiality in Conducting an Audit.*	Auditors are to use the same definition of materiality and the same quantitative and qualitative judgments in an audit of the effectiveness of internal controls over financial reporting that they would use in an audit of financial statements.	Management and the company's auditors should establish defined levels of materiality with regard to the financial reporting at both the financial-statement level and the individual account-balance level.

Who is Affected	Standard ¶	Analysis ¶	Rules and Regulations	Effect	Action
Management	24 through 26	108	AU Section 316, *Consideration of Fraud in a Financial Statement Audit.*	Auditors are required to place a special emphasis on their examination of controls designed to detect and prevent fraud.	The auditor should evaluate the company's control environment, risk assessment processes, codes of ethics, internal audit activities, and management's procedures for handling complaints. Management should ensure that the company's system of internal control is designed specifically to prevent, deter, and detect fraud. Management, directors, and audit committee members should confirm their commitment to the "tone at the top" concept as outlined in the COSO framework.
Management	27 through 141	109	See ¶s 109.1– 109.8.2 for rules and regulations cited.	The audit of internal control over financial reporting must be done in conjunction with an audit of the financial statements. All of the traditional auditing standards and considerations are applicable to this auditing standard as well.	Auditors should apply all of the general and applicable fieldwork standards that would be appropriate to an audit of financial statements to an audit of internal control over financial reporting.

Who is Affected	Standard ¶	Analysis ¶	Rules and Regulations	Effect	Action
Management	32 through 35	109.1.2	AU Section 150, *Generally Accepted Auditing Standards;* 17 CFR 210.2-01 (Rule 2-01 of Regulation S-X).	The auditor must not function in the role of management and must not audit his or her own work, but may provide substantive recommendations regarding the design or operation of internal control over financial reporting as a by-product of the audit.	Management should remain actively involved in the design, documentation, and testing of internal control over financial reporting and must not delegate all responsibility for these matters to the auditor. Audit committees must pre-approve internal control-related services provided by the company's auditor. Auditors and audit committee members should be vigilant about any appearance of compromised auditor independence. Auditors may provide internal control services that are pre-approved by the audit committee.
Management	40 through 46	109.3	None cited	The standard outlines what elements of a company's internal control structure should have been addressed by management in its assessment of internal control over financial reporting.	The auditor must examine sufficient evidence and obtain an understanding of management's process for assessing the effectiveness of the company's internal control over financial reporting. Management should ensure that its assessment of internal control over financial reporting addresses the elements that the auditor is expected to cover in its audit of management's assessment.

WG&L Warren, Gorham & Lamont

Who is Affected	Standard ¶	Analysis ¶	Rules and Regulations	Effect	Action
Management	42 through 46	109.3.1	None cited	The auditor is required to evaluate the adequacy of management's documentation in support of its assessment of internal control over financial reporting.	Management should become familiar with the documentation requirements provided by the standard. The auditor must review the issuer's documentation of management's assessment of internal control over financial reporting. Given a substantial absence of documentation of internal control over financial reporting on the part of the issuer, the auditor must withhold the attestation or limit the scope of the audit of internal control over financial reporting.
Management	47 through 87	109.4	See ¶s 109.4.1 – 109.4.8 for rules and regulations cited.	Based on the COSO framework, the auditing standard defines specific steps the auditor must perform to evaluate the documentation and establish an understanding of internal control over financial reporting.	The auditor must perform certain tasks and procedures to evaluate management's documentation and to establish an understanding of the company's internal control over financial reporting. These tasks and procedures follow the model put forth in the COSO framework. Management is expected to implement the five basic COSO components: control environment, risk assessment, control activities, information and communication, and monitoring.

Who is Affected	Standard ¶	Analysis ¶	Rules and Regulations	Effect	Action
Management	52 through 54	109.4.1	None cited.	The auditing standard recommends that auditors test those controls that affect primarily the control environment and pervade all other controls first, i.e., the company-level controls. Auditors should evaluate the results of the evaluation of the company-wide controls when creating the audit plan for the rest of the company's controls over financial reporting.	Identification and testing of company-level controls by the external auditor is required. Management should ensure that proper documentation of company-wide controls exists.
Management	76 through 78	109.4.6	None cited	Auditors must obtain an understanding of and evaluate the period-end financial reporting process.	Auditors must review and evaluate the period-end financial reporting processes to ensure that transactions are recorded in their proper periods. The impact of the company's control environment on period-end financial reporting should be taken into account by the auditor. Management, the board, and the audit committee should ensure proper oversight of the period-end process.

WG&L Warren, Gorham & Lamont

Who is Affected	Standard ¶	Analysis ¶	Rules and Regulations	Effect	Action
Management	79 through 83	109.4.7	None cited	The auditor is required to validate that the company's accounting systems and controls are working properly by walking transactions through the accounting system to make sure it is working as intended and employees understand the control activities they are required to perform.	The auditor is required to perform at least one walkthrough for each major class of transactions. Company personnel will be required to respond to the auditor's queries about their understanding of what is required by the company's policies, procedures, and controls. Management should ensure that the controls and procedures relevant to all significant accounts are properly documented, and that employees are adequately trained with regard to controls, exception handling, and company policies.

Who is Affected	Standard ¶	Analysis ¶	Rules and Regulations	Effect	Action
Management	83 through 87	109.4.8	None cited	The company's auditor must obtain evidence that validates the effectiveness of controls over financial reporting.	The auditor should obtain evidence of the effectiveness of controls on which to base its opinion. The auditor must either perform these tests himself or herself or may rely, to some extent, on the work of others, such as the company's internal auditors. Management should ensure that adequate documentation exists of the company's significant control points, the nature of the controls implemented by management, the significance of each control, and the level of risk that the controls might not be operating as designed.

Who is Affected	Standard ¶	Analysis ¶	Rules and Regulations	Effect	Action
Management	123 through 126	109.7.3	None cited	Auditors must test some of the work of others in order to evaluate the quality and effectiveness of the work. The standard provides specific guidance regarding controls over period-end financial reporting, IT general controls, management self-assessment, controls over the calculation of the depreciation of assets, and alternating tests of controls.	By looking at factors such as scope of the work, adequacy of procedures, adequacy of documentation, appropriateness of conclusions, and consistency of reports, auditors must evaluate the quality and effectiveness of the work of others before using the work. Management should consult the standard's guidance regarding the auditor's use of the work of others in specific situations related to controls over period-end financial reporting, IT general controls, management self-assessment, controls over the calculation of the depreciation of assets, and alternating tests of controls.
Management	129	109.8.1	None cited	The company's auditor can issue an unqualified opinion on the company's internal control over financial reporting only if there are no identified material weaknesses and there have been no restrictions on the scope of the audit.	The auditor must determine that there are no material weaknesses or scope restrictions in order to provide an unqualified opinion.

Who is Affected	Standard ¶	Analysis ¶	Rules and Regulations	Effect	Action
Management	130 through 141	109.8.2	SEC Staff Accounting Bulletin Topic 1M2, *Immaterial Misstatements That Are Intentional;* Sarbanes-Oxley Act Section 302.	Auditors must evaluate deficiencies in the company's internal control over financial reporting and determine whether the deficiencies, individually or in combination, rise to the level of significant deficiencies or material weaknesses	The auditor must look at all of the company's internal control deficiencies and determine, based on certain criteria, if the deficiencies constitute significant deficiencies or material weaknesses.
Management	142 through 144	110	AU Section 333, *Management Representations*	The auditor is required to obtain certain management representations specific to the audit of internal control over financial reporting.	As in all audits, the auditor must receive certain written representations from the company's CEO and CFO.
Management	162 through 199	113	See ¶s 113.1– 113.3.12 for rules and regulations.	Management must issue a report on the effectiveness of the company's internal control over financial reporting. The auditor must evaluate that report and, if it agrees with management's assessment, issue a report attesting to management's assertions.	Management is required to issue a report on the effectiveness of the company's internal control over financial reporting. The auditor is required to review and evaluate this report. Then, based on its independent assessment of the effectiveness of internal control over the issuer's financial reporting, the auditor issues its attestation of management's report. Any limit in the scope of the audit of internal control over financial reporting requires the auditor to, at a minimum, issue a qualified opinion. Management must ensure that the scope of the audit is not limited.

Who is Affected	Standard ¶	Analysis ¶	Rules and Regulations	Effect	Action
Management	162 through 165	113.1	17 CFR 228.308(a) and 17 CFR 229.308(a) (Item 308(a) of Regulation S-B and Regulation S-K, respectively); 17 CFR 240.13a-14(a) and 17 CFR 240.15d-14(a) (Securities Exchange Act Rules 13a-14(a) and 15d-14(a), respectively).	The auditing standard reiterates the requirements put forth in Sections 302 and 404 of the Sarbanes-Oxley Act and SEC Release No. 33-8238.	Management is required to include its assessment of the effectiveness of the company's internal control over financial reporting in its annual report required under SEC reporting regulations. Management must take responsibility for the company's internal controls. Management must identify the framework (i.e., COSO) used to conduct its assessment of the internal controls. If one or more material weaknesses are discovered by management during the assessment of the company's internal controls, management must change the internal control to eliminate the material weakness sufficiently in advance of the "as of" date and must test the effectiveness of the revised control in order to determine whether it is effective.
Management	166	113.2	None cited	The auditor must evaluate management's assessment of the effectiveness of internal control over financial reporting.	The auditor should evaluate management's assessment and determine that management establishes its responsibility for internal control, used the proper framework (i.e., COSO), and presented its assessment in an acceptable form.

Who is Affected	Standard ¶	Analysis ¶	Rules and Regulations	Effect	Action
Management	174	113.3.4	None cited	The auditor must modify the audit opinion if the auditor determines that management's assessment process is inadequate or if the auditor determines that management's report is inappropriate.	The auditor must modify the audit opinion if the auditor determines that management's assessment process is inadequate or if the auditor determines that management's report is inappropriate. At a minimum, this means adding an explanatory paragraph describing the reasons for this conclusion. Management should make every effort to ensure that the process used for evaluating the company's internal control over financial reporting is adequate, i.e., that the process meets the requirements outlined in this auditing standard and in the SEC's requirements.
Management	175 through 177	113.3.5	None cited	If there are one or more material weaknesses in the company's internal control over financial reporting, then the auditor must express an adverse opinion. In this case, management is also precluded from concluding that internal control over financial reporting is effective.	In the event there are any uncorrected material weaknesses at the end of the reporting year, then the auditor must express an adverse opinion on internal control over financial reporting.

WG&L Warren, Gorham & Lamont

Who is Affected	Standard ¶	Analysis ¶	Rules and Regulations	Effect	Action
Management	178 through 181	113.3.6	None cited	Limitations on the scope of the audit result in a qualified opinion at best.	Given any limitation in the scope of the audit, the auditor is unable to express an unqualified opinion. Even if the scope of the audit is limited, if the auditor uncovers a material weakness, that weakness must be reported. Management should do their best to ensure the auditor is able to apply all the procedures necessary in the circumstances, with no interference from management or employees of the company.
Management	186 through 189	113.3.8	AU Section 560, *Subsequent Events*.	Auditors must take subsequent events into consideration if they reflect changes in internal control over financial reporting that occur after the audit but before the auditor's opinion is issued.	If a subsequent event occurs after the audit but before issuance of the auditor's report, the auditor must evaluate the event and determine its impact. Management must disclose subsequent events to the auditor in the representation letter. This includes internal audit reports and regulatory agency reports that are relevant to internal control over financial reporting.

Who is Affected	Standard ¶	Analysis ¶	Rules and Regulations	Effect	Action
Management	190 through 192	113.3.9	Section 10A of the Securities Exchange Act of 1934.	Management may add additional information to its report on the assessment of internal control over financial reporting that is not necessarily relevant to the audit of internal control over financial reporting. The auditor is expected to disclaim an opinion on the additional information.	If management adds any extraneous information to the standard format of the report, the auditor should disclaim this information. If the auditor believes the extra information includes a material misstatement of fact, the auditor is expected to discuss the issue with management directly. If this does not resolve the issue, the auditor is required to notify management and the audit committee in writing of its concerns regarding the information.
Management	200 through 206	114	Sarbanes-Oxley Act Section 302; Section 10A of the Securities Exchange Act of 1934; 17 CFR 240.13a-14a and 17 CFR 15d-14a (Securities Exchange Act Rules 13a-14(a) and 15d-14(a), respectively); 17 CFR 240.12b-20 (Securities Exchange Act Rule 12b-20); AU Section 317, *Illegal Acts by Clients;* AU Section 722, *Interim Financial Information.*	Management is required to make disclosures under Section 302. The auditor is required to evaluate the need for any possible disclosures related to changes in internal control over financial reporting. The auditor is required to conduct limited quarterly procedures.	Management must issue the statements required by Section 302 need for any possible disclosures related to changes in internal control over financial reporting. The auditor is required to conduct quarterly inquiries and evaluations regarding the materiality of changes to internal control and any misstatements that have been discovered.

Who is Affected	Standard ¶	Analysis ¶	Rules and Regulations	Effect	Action
Management	200 through 201	114.1	Sarbanes-Oxley Act Section 302; 17 CFR 240.13a-14a and 17 CFR 15d-14a (Securities Exchange Act Rules 13a-14(a) and 15d-14(a), respectively); 17 CFR 240.12b-20 (Securities Exchange Act Rule 12b-20).	Section 302 of the Sarbanes-Oxley Act requires management to make certain disclosures certifying the accuracy and reliability of the issuer's financial statements. One of those disclosures is a statement certifying that the officers of the issuer have implemented internal controls over financial reporting that are effective.	Management must certify that the internal control over the company's financial reporting is effective. Management must also issue a statement that discloses any changes in the company's internal control over financial reporting that occurred during the most recent fiscal quarter. Management must also certify that it has responsibility for internal control over financial reporting. The auditor is required to evaluate the need for any possible disclosures related to changes in internal control over financial reporting.

Who is Affected	Standard ¶	Analysis ¶	Rules and Regulations	Effect	Action
Management	202 through 206	114.2	Sarbanes-Oxley Act Section 302; AU Section 722, *Interim Financial Information;* AU Section 317, *Illegal Acts by Clients*; 17 CFR 240.13a-14(a) and 17 CFR 240.15d-14(a) (Securities Exchange Act Rules 13a-14(a) and 15d-14(a), respectively); Section 10A of the Securities Exchange Act of 1934.	Interim quarterly auditor evaluations of internal control over financial reporting can be based on limited procedures.	Auditors need only perform limited procedures on a quarterly basis to validate their annual assessment. In performing the quarterly procedures, the auditor is looking for material modifications that could become a required disclosure about changes in internal control over financial reporting in order for management's certifications to be accurate. The auditor is required to notify management of any material matters. If management does not respond appropriately, the auditor must notify the audit committee.

Who is Affected	Standard ¶	Analysis ¶	Rules and Regulations	Effect	Action
Management	207 through 214	115	AU Section 316, *Consideration of Fraud in a Financial Statement Audit;* AU Section 317, *Illegal Acts by Clients;* Section 10A of the Securities Exchange Act of 1934.	The auditor is required to communicate in writing to management and the audit committee all significant deficiencies and material weaknesses identified during the audit. The auditor is also required to make certain communications with management and the audit committee when the auditor becomes aware of fraud or illegal acts.	The auditor is required to communicate in writing to management and the audit committee all significant deficiencies and material weaknesses identified during the audit. The auditor is also required to make certain communications with management and the audit committee when the auditor becomes aware of fraud or illegal acts. The auditor must notify the board of directors if the audit committee is ineffectively overseeing the internal control function.
Management	215 through 216	116	Sarbanes-Oxley Act Section 404; 17 CFR 240.12b-2 (Securities Exchange Act Rule 12b-2).	Companies and auditors are required to comply with PCAOB Auditing Standard No. 2 for their the internal control reporting for fiscal years ending on or after November 15, 2004 (accelerated filers) or July 15, 2005 (other companies).	Auditors of companies considered accelerated filers (seasoned U.S. companies with public float exceeding $75 million) are required to comply with PCAOB Auditing Standard No. 2 for fiscal years ending on or after November 15, 2004. Auditors of other companies (including smaller companies, foreign private issuers and companies with only registered debt securities) have until fiscal years ending on or after July 15, 2005, to comply with PCAOB Auditing Standard No. 2.

Who is Affected	Standard ¶	Analysis ¶	Rules and Regulations	Effect	Action
Management	Appendix C	119	None cited	Appendix C reiterates the PCAOB's emphasis on the importance of controls that operate to safeguard the company's assets, and defers to the COSO report for guidance on the safeguarding of assets as it relates to internal control over financial reporting	Auditors should use the COSO framework as their guideline in determining the scope of the audit of internal controls intended to safeguard the company's assets. Management must realize that plans that could potentially affect financial reporting in future periods are not controls in the present. Business continuity plans are also not considered part of internal control over financial reporting. Management should ensure that the company has compensatory and overlapping controls in place where there is a risk of error or fraud that could affect the safeguarding of the company's assets.

Who is Affected	Standard ¶	Analysis ¶	Rules and Regulations	Effect	Action
Management	Appendix E	121	Sarbanes-Oxley Act Sections 103 and 404; AU Section 312, *Audit Risk and Materiality in Conducting an Audit;* AU Section 322, *The Auditor's Consideration of the Internal Audit Function in an Audit of Financial Statements;* AU Section 325, *Communication of Internal Control Related Matters Noted in an Audit;* SSAE No. 10, *Attestation Standards: Revision and Recodification* (AT Section 501); SEC Release No. 33-8238, *Final Rule: Management's Reports on Internal Control Over Financial Reporting and Certification of Disclosure in Exchange Act Periodic Reports* (June 5, 2003); Section 10A of the Securities Exchange Act of 1934; FAS No. 5, *Accounting for Contingencies;* Staff Accounting Bulletin (SAB) No. 99, *Materiality;* IAS No. 200, *Objective and Principles Governing an Audit of Financial Statements;* PCAOB Rule 3300T; *Federal Deposit Insurance Corporation Improvement Act of 1991 (FDCIA)*	The PCAOB issued a proposed version of this auditing standard in October 2003. In Appendix E, the PCAOB provides its explanation of the consideration it gave to the various viewpoints submitted during the comment period.	Management and auditors should read Appendix E so they can understand the relevant thought processes that underlie the PCAOB's intent regarding various aspects of the audit of internal control over financial reporting.

Who is Affected	Standard ¶	Analysis ¶	Rules and Regulations	Effect	Action
Regulators	1 through 3	100	Sarbanes-Oxley Act Sections 103(a)(2)(A)(iii) and 404; Securities Exchange Act of 1934 Sections 3, 12, and 15(d); Securities Act of 1933.	The PCAOB has proposed another auditing standard that amends or supersedes many other interim auditing standards as a result of the adoption of this standard (see PCAOB Release No. 2004-002, March 9, 2004). Of particular importance is the fact that AU Section 325, *Communication of Internal Control Related Matters Noted in an Audit,* and AT Section 501, *Reporting on an Entity's Internal Control Over Financial Reporting,* will be superseded by PCAOB Auditing Standard No. 2 as of November 15, 2004. In addition, the following interim standards will be amended to conform with Auditing Standard No. 2: • AU Section 310, *Appointment of the Independent Auditor* • AU Section 311, *Planning and Supervision* • AU Section 312, *Audit Risk and Materiality in Conducting an Audit* • AU Section 313, *Substantive Tests Prior to the Balance Sheet Date* • AU Section 316, *Consideration of Fraud in a Financial Statement Audit* • AU Section 319, *Consideration of Internal Control in a Financial*	Auditors must comply with this new auditing standard when performing the newly required audit of internal control over financial reporting in conjunction with an audit of financial statements. They should also take into account the conforming amendments to the interim standards proposed in PCAOB Release No. 2004-002.

Who is Affected	Standard ¶	Analysis ¶	Rules and Regulations	Effect	Action
				Statement Audit • AU Section 322, *The Auditor's Consideration of the Internal Audit Function in an Audit of Financial Statements* • AU Section 324, *Service Organizations* • AU Section 326, *Evidential Matter* • AU Section 329, *Analytical Procedures* • AU Section 332, *Auditing Derivative Instruments, Hedging Activities, and Investments in Securities* • AU Section 333, *Management Representation* • AU Section 339, *Audit Documentation* • AU Section 342, *Auditing Accounting Estimates* • AU Section 508, *Reports on Audited Financial Statements* • AU Section 530, *Dating of the Independent Auditor's Report* • AU Section 543, *Part of Audit Performed by Other Independent Auditors* • AU Section 560, *Subsequent Events* • AU Section 561, *Subsequent Discovery of Facts Existing at the Date of the Auditor's Report* • AU Section 711, *Filings Under Federal Securities Statutes* • AU Section 722, *Interim Financial Information* • ET Section 101, *Independence*	

Who is Affected	Standard ¶	Analysis ¶	Rules and Regulations	Effect	Action
Regulators	186 through 189	113.3.8	AU Section 560, *Subsequent Events.*	Auditors must take subsequent events into consideration if they reflect changes in internal control over financial reporting that occur after the audit but before the auditor's opinion is issued.	If a subsequent event occurs after the audit but before issuance of the auditor's report, the auditor must evaluate the event and determine its impact. Management must disclose subsequent events to the auditor in the representation letter. This includes internal audit reports and regulatory agency reports that are relevant to internal control over financial reporting.
Regulators	215 through 216	116	Sarbanes-Oxley Act Section 404; 17 CFR 240.12b-2 (Securities Exchange Act Rule 12b-2).	Companies and auditors are required to comply with PCAOB Auditing Standard No. 2 for their the internal control reporting for fiscal years ending on or after November 15, 2004 (accelerated filers) or July 15, 2005 (other companies).	Auditors of companies considered accelerated filers (seasoned U.S. companies with public float exceeding $75 million) are required to comply with PCAOB Auditing Standard No. 2 for fiscal years ending on or after November 15, 2004. Auditors of other companies (including smaller companies, foreign private issuers and companies with only registered debt securities) have until fiscal years ending on or after July 15, 2005, to comply with PCAOB Auditing Standard No. 2.

Who is Affected	Standard ¶	Analysis ¶	Rules and Regulations	Effect	Action
Regulators	Appendix E	121	Sarbanes-Oxley Act Sections 103 and 404; AU Section 312, *Audit Risk and Materiality in Conducting an Audit*; AU Section 322, *The Auditor's Consideration of the Internal Audit Function in an Audit of Financial Statements*; AU Section 325, *Communication of Internal Control Related Matters Noted in an Audit*; SSAE No. 10, *Attestation Standards: Revision and Recodification* (AT Section 501); SEC Release No. 33-8238, *Final Rule: Management's Reports on Internal Control Over Financial Reporting and Certification of Disclosure in Exchange Act Periodic Reports* (June 5, 2003); Section 10A of the Securities Exchange Act of 1934; FAS No. 5, *Accounting for Contingencies*; Staff Accounting Bulletin (SAB) No. 99, *Materiality*; IAS No. 200, *Objective and Principles Governing an Audit of Financial Statements*; PCAOB Rule 3300T; *Federal Deposit Insurance Corporation Improvement Act of 1991 (FDCIA)*	The PCAOB issued a proposed version of this auditing standard in October 2003. In Appendix E, the PCAOB provides its explanation of the consideration it gave to the various viewpoints submitted during the comment period.	Management and auditors should read Appendix E so they can understand the relevant thought processes that underlie the PCAOB's intent regarding various aspects of the audit of internal control over financial reporting.

Who is Affected	Standard ¶	Analysis ¶	Rules and Regulations	Effect	Action
Service Auditors	Appendix B	118	AU Section 324, *Service Organizations*; AU Section 543, *Part of Audit Performed by Other Independent Auditors.*	Appendix B provides additional guidance on tests to be performed when a company has multiple locations or business units and when a company obtains services from a service organization. It also provides detailed examples of the extent of testing required by the standard.	Auditors should refer to the guidance in Appendix B when auditing companies with multiple locations or business units or companies that use service organizations. Auditors should also familiarize themselves with the examples laid out by the PCAOB of the extent of testing required to determine the effectiveness of a company's internal control over financial reporting.
Service Organizations	Appendix B	118	AU Section 324, *Service Organizations*; AU Section 543, *Part of Audit Performed by Other Independent Auditors.*	Appendix B provides additional guidance on tests to be performed when a company has multiple locations or business units and when a company obtains services from a service organization. It also provides detailed examples of the extent of testing required by the standard.	Auditors should refer to the guidance in Appendix B when auditing companies with multiple locations or business units or companies that use service organizations. Auditors should also familiarize themselves with the examples laid out by the PCAOB of the extent of testing required to determine the effectiveness of a company's internal control over financial reporting.

WG&L Warren, Gorham & Lamont

¶ 303. Suggested References

Standard ¶	Effect	Suggested References
1 through 3	The PCAOB has proposed another auditing standard that amends or supersedes many other interim auditing standards as a result of the adoption of this standard (see PCAOB Release No. 2004-002, March 9, 2004). Of particular importance is the fact that AU Section 325, *Communication of Internal Control Related Matters Noted in an Audit*, and AT Section 501, *Reporting on an Entity's Internal Control Over Financial Reporting*, will be superseded by PCAOB Auditing Standard No. 2 as of November 15, 2004. In addition, the following interim standards will be amended to conform with Auditing Standard No. 2: • AU Section 310, *Appointment of the Independent Auditor* • AU Section 311, *Planning and Supervision* • AU Section 312, *Audit Risk and Materiality in Conducting an Audit* • AU Section 313, *Substantive Tests Prior to the Balance Sheet Date* • AU Section 316, *Consideration of Fraud in a Financial Statement Audit* • AU Section 319, *Consideration of Internal Control in a Financial Statement Audit* • AU Section 322, *The Auditor's Consideration of the Internal Audit Function in an Audit of Financial Statements* • AU Section 324, *Service Organizations* • AU Section 326, *Evidential Matter* • AU Section 329, *Analytical Procedures* • AU Section 332, *Auditing Derivative Instruments, Hedging Activities, and Investments in Securities* • AU Section 333, *Management Representation* • AU Section 339, *Audit Documentation* • AU Section 342, *Auditing Accounting Estimates* • AU Section 508, *Reports on Audited Financial Statements* • AU Section 530, *Dating of the Independent Auditor's Report* • AU Section 543, *Part of Audit Performed by Other Independent Auditors* • AU Section 560, *Subsequent Events* • AU Section 561, *Subsequent Discovery of Facts Existing at the Date of the Auditor's Report* • AU Section 711, *Filings Under Federal Securities Statutes* • AU Section 722, *Interim Financial Information* • ET Section 101, *Independence*	"Auditing Standard No. 2—Audit of Internal Control Over Financial Reporting in Conjunction with an Audit of Financial Statements," *SEC Accounting and Reporting Update* 2004-13 (April 2004). "A Proposed Auditing Standard—Conforming Amendments to Interim Standards Adopted by the Board," *SEC Accounting and Reporting Update* 2004-14 (April 2004). "PCAOB Adopts Internal Control Auditing Standard," *Internal Auditing Report* (April 2004). "SEC Finalizes Rules on Internal Control Reports," *Internal Auditing Report* (July 2003). "Management's Responsibility for Internal Control Under Section 404," *Bank Auditing and Accounting Report* (March 2004). "PCAOB Adopts Guidance for Audits of Internal Control Over Financial Reporting," *SEC Compliance: Financial Reporting and Forms* ¶ 4.6 (2004). *Practical Guide to Corporate Governance and Accounting: Implementing the Requirements of the Sarbanes-Oxley Act (2004 Edition).*

Standard ¶	Effect	Suggested References
13 through 15	The auditing standard defines the characteristics of acceptable internal control frameworks that can be used to assess compliance with Sections 302 and 404 of the Sarbanes-Oxley Act. The characteristics are defined so narrowly that only the COSO framework can possibly be used by U.S. issuers for compliance with the Act at this time.	"Management Internal Control Reports Over Financial Reporting," *Handbook of SEC Accounting and Disclosure* § I8. "Management Internal Control Reports and Related Certification Matters," *SEC Accounting and Reporting Update* 2003-29 (June 2003). "Internal Control," *Handbook of Accounting and Auditing* § B4. "Reports on Internal Control," *Accounting and Auditing Disclosure Manual* § 90. "COSO: More Relevant Now Than Ever," *Internal Auditing* (July/August 2003). "Section 404 Compliance: Meeting the Challenges," *Internal Auditing* (July/August 2003). "SEC Finalizes Rules on Internal Control Reports," *Internal Auditing Report* (July 2003). "Management's Responsibility for Internal Control Under Section 404," *Bank Auditing and Accounting Report* (March 2004).
20 through 21	Sufficient documentation is required to pass an audit of internal control over financial reporting. Management must accept responsibility for and assess the effectiveness of the internal controls over financial reporting. Documentation serves as evidence of this responsibility and assessment and is therefore an essential requirement in an audit of internal control over financial reporting.	"Management Internal Control Reports Over Financial Reporting," *Handbook of SEC Accounting and Disclosure* § I8. "Management Internal Control Reports and Related Certification Matters," *SEC Accounting and Reporting Update* 2003-29 (June 2003). "SEC Finalizes Rules on Internal Control Reports," *Internal Auditing Report* (July 2003). "Management's Responsibility for Internal Control Under Section 404," *Bank Auditing and Accounting Report* (March 2004).
22 through 23	Auditors are to use the same definition of materiality and the same quantitative and qualitative judgments in an audit of the effectiveness of internal controls over financial reporting that they would use in an audit of financial statements.	"Materiality," *Handbook of SEC Accounting and Disclosure* § A10. "The Ethics of Materiality in Financial Reporting," *Internal Auditing* (January/February 2002).

Standard ¶	Effect	Suggested References
24 through 26	Auditors are required to place a special emphasis on their examination of controls designed to detect and prevent fraud.	"More Organizations Are Detecting Fraud," *Internal Auditing Report* (January 2004). "Ten Questions to Jump-Start a Fraud Risk Assessment," *Internal Auditing Report* (December 2002). "Will You Detect Fraud If You Think You Can?," *Internal Auditing* (July/August 2003). "Preventing Revenue Recognition Problems: Internal Controls and Best Practices," *Internal Auditing* (May/June 2003). "What Kind of CPA Detects Fraud?," *Internal Auditing* (September/October 2002). "When Earnings Management Becomes Fraud," *Internal Auditing* (July/August 2002). "Internal Auditors' Roles in the Prevention, Detection, and Correction of Financial Statement Fraud," *Internal Auditing* (May/June 2002). "How Financial Executives Can Promote Quality Financial Reporting," *Internal Auditing* (January/February 2002). "Auditing Journal Entries and Other Adjustments," *Accounting and Auditing Update 2003-21* (June 2003). "Consideration of Fraud in a Financial Statement Audit," *Accounting and Auditing Update* 2002-35 (November 2002).
32 through 35	The auditor must not function in the role of management and must not audit his or her own work, but may provide substantive recommendations regarding the design or operation of internal control over financial reporting as a by-product of the audit.	"Disclosures Made to Audit Committees Regarding Matters of Independence," *Accounting and Auditing Disclosure Manual* § 107. "Accountants' Independence," *Handbook of SEC Accounting and Disclosure* § 12. "Accountants' Independence," *SEC Accounting and Reporting Manual* § 14.03. "Guidance on the Application of the Commission's New Rules for Auditor Independence," *SEC Accounting and Reporting Update* 2003-37 (August 2003). "Auditor Independence and Related Matters," *SEC Accounting and Reporting Update* 2003-08 (February 2003).
40 through 46	The standard outlines what elements of a company's internal control structure should have been addressed by management in its assessment of internal control over financial reporting.	"Management Internal Control Reports Over Financial Reporting," *Handbook of SEC Accounting and Disclosure* § 18. "Management Internal Control Reports and Related Certification Matters," *SEC Accounting and Reporting Update* 2003-29 (June 2003). "Internal Control," *Handbook of Accounting and Auditing* § B4. "Reports on Internal Control," *Accounting and Auditing Disclosure Manual* § 90. "SEC Finalizes Rules on Internal Control Reports," *Internal Auditing Report* (July 2003). "Management's Responsibility for Internal Control Under Section 404," *Bank Auditing and Accounting Report* (March 2004).

Standard ¶	Effect	Suggested References
42 through 46	The auditor is required to evaluate the adequacy of management's documentation in support of its assessment of internal control over financial reporting.	"Management Internal Control Reports Over Financial Reporting," *Handbook of SEC Accounting and Disclosure* § 18. "Management Internal Control Reports and Related Certification Matters," *SEC Accounting and Reporting Update* 2003-29 (June 2003). "Internal Control," *Handbook of Accounting and Auditing* § B4. "Reports on Internal Control," *Accounting and Auditing Disclosure Manual* § 90. "Section 404 Compliance: Meeting the Challenges," *Internal Auditing* (July/August 2003). "SEC Finalizes Rules on Internal Control Reports," *Internal Auditing Report* (July 2003). "Management's Responsibility for Internal Control Under Section 404," *Bank Auditing and Accounting Report* (March 2004).
47 through 87	Based on the COSO framework, the auditing standard defines specific steps the auditor must perform to evaluate the documentation and establish an understanding of internal control over financial reporting.	"Management Internal Control Reports Over Financial Reporting," *Handbook of SEC Accounting and Disclosure* § 18. "Management Internal Control Reports and Related Certification Matters," *SEC Accounting and Reporting Update* 2003-29 (June 2003). "Internal Control," *Handbook of Accounting and Auditing* § B4. "Reports on Internal Control," *Accounting and Auditing Disclosure Manual* § 90. "Tools and Techniques for Documenting Accounting Systems," *Internal Auditing* (September/October 2003). "COSO: More Relevant Now Than Ever," *Internal Auditing* (July/August 2003). "Section 404 Compliance: Meeting the Challenges," *Internal Auditing* (July/August 2003). "SEC Finalizes Rules on Internal Control Reports," *Internal Auditing Report* (July 2003). "Management's Responsibility for Internal Control Under Section 404," *Bank Auditing and Accounting Report* (March 2004).
52 through 54	The auditing standard recommends that auditors test those controls that affect primarily the control environment and pervade all other controls first, i.e., the company-level controls. Auditors should evaluate the results of the evaluation of the company-wide controls when creating the audit plan for the rest of the company's controls over financial reporting.	"IT Governance Institute Publishes IT Internal Controls Guidance," *Internal Auditing Report* (December 2003).

Standard ¶	Effect	Suggested References
55 through 59	The auditor must review and assess the effectiveness of the audit committee's oversight of the company's external financial reporting and internal control over financial reporting.	"Standards for Listed Company Audit Committees," *Handbook of SEC Accounting and Disclosure* § E32. "Audit Committee Reporting," *Handbook of SEC Accounting and Disclosure* § E25. "SEC Approves Corporate Governance Proposals," *SEC Accounting and Reporting Manual.* "Standards for Listed Company Audit Committees," *SEC Accounting and Reporting Update* 2003-17 (April 2003). "Audit Committees," *SEC Compliance: Financial Reporting and Forms* ¶ 17,229. "The Audit Committee," *Handbook of Accounting and Auditing*, Chapter B2. "Corporate Governance: The Changed Environment: Challenges and Opportunities in 2004," *Corporate Finance Review* (January/February 2004). "Audit Committees Focus on Risk Management," *Internal Auditing* (July/August 2002). "Where Was the Audit Committee?," *Internal Auditing* (May/June 2002).
68 through 70	Auditors must identify all relevant financial statement assertions.	"Tools and Techniques for Documenting Accounting Systems," *Internal Auditing* (September/October 2003).
71 through 75	Auditors must identify each significant process over each major class of transactions affecting significant accounts or groups of accounts. The auditor must consider the nature and characteristics of the company's information system in relation to internal control over financial reporting.	"Tools and Techniques for Documenting Accounting Systems," *Internal Auditing* (September/October 2003).
76 through 78	Auditors must obtain an understanding of and evaluate the period-end financial reporting process.	"Auditing Revenue Recognition," *Internal Auditing* (January/February 2003).
79 through 83	The auditor is required to validate that the company's accounting systems and controls are working properly by walking transactions through the accounting system to make sure it is working as intended and employees understand the control activities they are required to perform.	"Tools and Techniques for Documenting Accounting Systems," *Internal Auditing* (September/October 2003).
83 through 87	The company's auditor must obtain evidence that validates the effectiveness of controls over financial reporting.	"Auditing Internal Controls Under Sarbanes-Oxley," *Bank Auditing and Accounting Report* (January 2004). "Internal Control," *Handbook of Accounting and Auditing* Chapter B4.
88 through 91	The company's auditor must test and evaluate the design of the company's internal controls over financial reporting.	"Auditing Internal Controls Under Sarbanes-Oxley," *Bank Auditing and Accounting Report* (January 2004). "Internal Control," *Handbook of Accounting and Auditing* Chapter B4.
92 through 107	The company's auditor must test and evaluate the operating effectiveness of the company's internal controls over financial reporting.	"Auditing Internal Controls Under Sarbanes-Oxley," *Bank Auditing and Accounting Report* (January 2004). "Internal Control," *Handbook of Accounting and Auditing* Chapter B4.

Standard ¶	Effect	Suggested References
93 through 97	In order to test and evaluate the operating effectiveness of the company's internal controls over financial reporting, the company's auditor must utilize a mix of inquiry, observation, documentation review, and reperformance.	"Auditing Internal Controls Under Sarbanes-Oxley," *Bank Auditing and Accounting Report* (January 2004). "Internal Control," *Handbook of Accounting and Auditing* Chapter B4.
104 through 105	The auditor must obtain sufficient evidence about whether the company's internal control over financial reporting is operating effectively.	"Auditing Internal Controls Under Sarbanes-Oxley," *Bank Auditing and Accounting Report* (January 2004). "Internal Control," *Handbook of Accounting and Auditing* Chapter B4.
108 through 126	Auditors can use the work of others to a certain extent when performing the audit. The auditing standard clarifies the ability of the auditor to use the work of others and reiterates that the auditor's opinion must be based solely on work done by the auditor or the auditor's direct validation of any work done by others.	"Relationships with Third-Party Users of Internal Auditing Work Products," *Internal Auditing Manual* Chapter I1. "Internal Auditors' Roles in the Prevention, Detection, and Correction of Financial Statement Fraud," *Internal Auditing* (May/June 2002).
117 through 122	Auditors must evaluate the competence and objectivity of others before using their work.	"Relationships with Third-Party Users of Internal Auditing Work Products," *Internal Auditing Manual* Chapter I1. "Affirming Independence, Integrity, and Objectivity in Enron's Shadow," *Internal Auditing Report* (April 2002). "Internal Auditors' Roles in Overcoming the Financial Reporting Crisis," *Internal Auditing* (November/December 2002).
127 through 141	Auditors must evaluate information from all relevant sources, particularly the company's internal audit function, when forming an opinion on internal control over financial reporting.	"Relationships with Third-Party Users of Internal Auditing Work Products," *Internal Auditing Manual* Chapter I1.
129	The company's auditor can issue an unqualified opinion on the company's internal control over financial reporting only if there are no identified material weaknesses and there have been no restrictions on the scope of the audit.	"Unqualified Opinions," *Accounting and Auditing Disclosure Manual* § 70. "Adverse Opinions," *Accounting and Auditing Disclosure Manual* § 73. "Disclaimer of Opinion," *Accounting and Auditing Disclosure Manual* § 74.
130 through 141	Auditors must evaluate deficiencies in the company's internal control over financial reporting and determine whether the deficiencies, individually or in combination, rise to the level of significant deficiencies or material weaknesses	"Materiality," *Handbook of SEC Accounting and Disclosure* § A10. "The Ethics of Materiality in Financial Reporting," *Internal Auditing* (January/February 2002).
150 through 151	Tests of controls in an audit of financial statements are different than those in an audit of internal control over financial reporting.	"Auditing Internal Controls Under Sarbanes-Oxley," *Bank Auditing and Accounting Report* (January 2004). "Performing the Audit," *Handbook of Accounting and Auditing* Chapter B3.
159 through 161	The documentation standard is raised from that in AU Section 339, *Audit Documentation.* The documentation requirements in this auditing standard reinforce the connection between the audit of the financial statements and the audit of internal control over financial reporting.	"A Proposed Auditing Standard on Audit Documentation and a Proposed Amendment to the Board's Interim Standards Concerning Documentation by Principal Auditors," *SEC Accounting and Reporting Update* 2003-51 (December 2003).

Standard ¶	Effect	Suggested References
162 through 199	Management must issue a report on the effectiveness of the company's internal control over financial reporting. The auditor must evaluate that report and, if it agrees with management's assessment, issue a report attesting to management's assertions.	"Management Internal Control Reports Over Financial Reporting," *Handbook of SEC Accounting and Disclosure* § 18. "Reports of Independent Auditors," *SEC Accounting and Reporting Manual* § 10.40. "Management Internal Control Reports and Related Certification Matters," *SEC Accounting and Reporting Update* 2003-29 (June 2003). "Certification of chief executive officer pursuant to Section 302 of the Sarbanes-Oxley Act of 2002," *SEC Compliance: Financial Reporting and Forms* ¶ 4655. "Certification of chief financial officer pursuant to Section 302 of the Sarbanes-Oxley Act of 2002," *SEC Compliance: Financial Reporting and Forms* ¶ 4656. "Rule 2-02. Accountants' reports and attestation reports on management's assessment of internal control over financial reporting," *SEC Compliance: Financial Reporting and Forms* ¶ 20,072.02. "SEC Adopts Rule Requiring Internal Control Report," *SEC Accounting Report* (August 2003). "Management's Responsibility for Internal Control Under Section 404," *Bank Auditing and Accounting Report* (March 2004).
162 through 165	The auditing standard reiterates the requirements put forth in Sections 302 and 404 of the Sarbanes-Oxley Act and SEC Release No. 33-8238.	"Management Internal Control Reports Over Financial Reporting," *Handbook of SEC Accounting and Disclosure* § 18. "Management Internal Control Reports and Related Certification Matters," *SEC Accounting and Reporting Update* 2003-29 (June 2003). "Certification of chief executive officer pursuant to Section 302 of the Sarbanes-Oxley Act of 2002," *SEC Compliance: Financial Reporting and Forms* ¶ 4655. "Certification of chief financial officer pursuant to Section 302 of the Sarbanes-Oxley Act of 2002," *SEC Compliance: Financial Reporting and Forms* ¶ 4656. "SEC Adopts Rule Requiring Internal Control Report," *SEC Accounting Report* (August 2003). "Management's Responsibility for Internal Control Under Section 404," *Bank Auditing and Accounting Report* (March 2004).

Standard ¶	Effect	Suggested References
166	The auditor must evaluate management's assessment of the effectiveness of internal control over financial reporting.	"Management Internal Control Reports Over Financial Reporting," *Handbook of SEC Accounting and Disclosure* § 18. "Reports of Independent Auditors," *SEC Accounting and Reporting Manual* § 10.40. "Management Internal Control Reports and Related Certification Matters," *SEC Accounting and Reporting Update* 2003-29 (June 2003). "Certification of chief executive officer pursuant to Section 302 of the Sarbanes-Oxley Act of 2002," *SEC Compliance: Financial Reporting and Forms* ¶ 4655. "Certification of chief financial officer pursuant to Section 302 of the Sarbanes-Oxley Act of 2002," *SEC Compliance: Financial Reporting and Forms* ¶ 4656. "Rule 2-02. Accountants' reports and attestation reports on management's assessment of internal control over financial reporting," *SEC Compliance: Financial Reporting and Forms* ¶ 20,072.02. "SEC Adopts Rule Requiring Internal Control Report," *SEC Accounting Report* (August 2003). "Management's Responsibility for Internal Control Under Section 404," *Bank Auditing and Accounting Report* (March 2004).

Standard ¶	Effect	Suggested References
167 through 199	Every auditor's report on management's assessment of the effectiveness of internal control over financial reporting must include certain uniform elements	"Management Internal Control Reports Over Financial Reporting," *Handbook of SEC Accounting and Disclosure* § I8. "Reports of Independent Auditors," *SEC Accounting and Reporting Manual* § 10.40. "Management Internal Control Reports and Related Certification Matters," *SEC Accounting and Reporting Update* 2003-29 (June 2003). "Certification of chief executive officer pursuant to Section 302 of the Sarbanes-Oxley Act of 2002," *SEC Compliance: Financial Reporting and Forms* ¶ 4655. "Certification of chief financial officer pursuant to Section 302 of the Sarbanes-Oxley Act of 2002," *SEC Compliance: Financial Reporting and Forms* ¶ 4656. "Rule 2-02. Accountants' reports and attestation reports on management's assessment of internal control over financial reporting," *SEC Compliance: Financial Reporting and Forms* ¶ 20,072.02. "SEC Adopts Rule Requiring Internal Control Report," *SEC Accounting Report* (August 2003). "Management's Responsibility for Internal Control Under Section 404," *Bank Auditing and Accounting Report* (March 2004).
174	The auditor must modify the audit opinion if the auditor determines that management's assessment process is inadequate or if the auditor determines that management's report is inappropriate	"Management Internal Control Reports Over Financial Reporting," *Handbook of SEC Accounting and Disclosure* § I8. "Management Internal Control Reports and Related Certification Matters," *SEC Accounting and Reporting Update* 2003-29 (June 2003). "Certification of chief executive officer pursuant to Section 302 of the Sarbanes-Oxley Act of 2002," *SEC Compliance: Financial Reporting and Forms* ¶ 4655. "Certification of chief financial officer pursuant to Section 302 of the Sarbanes-Oxley Act of 2002," *SEC Compliance: Financial Reporting and Forms* ¶ 4656. "SEC Adopts Rule Requiring Internal Control Report," *SEC Accounting Report* (August 2003). "Management's Responsibility for Internal Control Under Section 404," *Bank Auditing and Accounting Report* (March 2004).
175 through 177	If there are one or more material weaknesses in the company's internal control over financial reporting, then the auditor must express an adverse opinion. In this case, management is also precluded from concluding that internal control over financial reporting is effective.	"Materiality," *Handbook of SEC Accounting and Disclosure* § A10. "The Ethics of Materiality in Financial Reporting," *Internal Auditing* (January/February 2002).

Standard ¶	Effect	Suggested References
190 through 192	Management may add additional information to its report on the assessment of internal control over financial reporting that is not necessarily relevant to the audit of internal control over financial reporting. The auditor is expected to disclaim an opinion on the additional information.	"Management Internal Control Reports Over Financial Reporting," *Handbook of SEC Accounting and Disclosure* § 18. "Management Internal Control Reports and Related Certification Matters," *SEC Accounting and Reporting Update* 2003-29 (June 2003) "Certification of chief executive officer pursuant to Section 302 of the Sarbanes-Oxley Act of 2002," *SEC Compliance: Financial Reporting and Forms* ¶ 4655. "Certification of chief financial officer pursuant to Section 302 of the Sarbanes-Oxley Act of 2002," *SEC Compliance: Financial Reporting and Forms* ¶ 4656. "SEC Adopts Rule Requiring Internal Control Report," *SEC Accounting Report* (August 2003). "Management's Responsibility for Internal Control Under Section 404," *Bank Auditing and Accounting Report* (March 2004).
193 through 196	The auditor can conclude that the financial statements deserve an unqualified opinion and simultaneously conclude that the assessment of internal control over financial reporting does not receive an unqualified opinion.	"Adverse Opinions," *Accounting and Auditing Disclosure Manual* § 73.
200 through 206	Management is required to make disclosures under Section 302. The auditor is required to evaluate the need for any possible disclosures related to changes in internal control over financial reporting. The auditor is required to conduct limited quarterly procedures.	"Management Internal Control Reports Over Financial Reporting," *Handbook of SEC Accounting and Disclosure* § 18. "Management Internal Control Reports and Related Certification Matters," *SEC Accounting and Reporting Update* 2003-29 (June 2003). "Certification of chief executive officer pursuant to Section 302 of the Sarbanes-Oxley Act of 2002," *SEC Compliance: Financial Reporting and Forms* ¶ 4655. "Certification of chief financial officer pursuant to Section 302 of the Sarbanes-Oxley Act of 2002," *SEC Compliance: Financial Reporting and Forms* ¶ 4656. "SEC Adopts Rule Requiring Internal Control Report," *SEC Accounting Report* (August 2003). "Management's Responsibility for Internal Control Under Section 404," *Bank Auditing and Accounting Report* (March 2004).

WG&L Warren, Gorham & Lamont

Standard ¶	Effect	Suggested References
200 through 201	Section 302 of the Sarbanes-Oxley Act requires management to make certain disclosures certifying the accuracy and reliability of the issuer's financial statements. One of those disclosures is a statement certifying that the officers of the issuer have implemented internal controls over financial reporting that are effective.	"Management Internal Control Reports Over Financial Reporting," *Handbook of SEC Accounting and Disclosure* § 18. "Management Internal Control Reports and Related Certification Matters," *SEC Accounting and Reporting Update* 2003-29 (June 2003). "Certification of chief executive officer pursuant to Section 302 of the Sarbanes-Oxley Act of 2002," *SEC Compliance: Financial Reporting and Forms* ¶ 4655. "Certification of chief financial officer pursuant to Section 302 of the Sarbanes-Oxley Act of 2002," *SEC Compliance: Financial Reporting and Forms* ¶ 4656. "SEC Adopts Rule Requiring Internal Control Report," *SEC Accounting Report* (August 2003). "Management's Responsibility for Internal Control Under Section 404," *Bank Auditing and Accounting Report* (March 2004).
Appendix B	Appendix B provides additional guidance on tests to be performed when a company has multiple locations or business units and when a company obtains services from a service organization. It also provides detailed examples of the extent of testing required by the standard.	"Service Organizations," *Accounting and Auditing Disclosure Manual* § 91. "Responsibilities of Service Auditors and of Service Organizations," *Accounting and Auditing Update* 2002-03 (January 2002). "How the Use of a Service Organization Affects Internal Control Considerations," *Accounting and Auditing Update* 1999-15 (July 1999).

¶ 400. PCAOB Release No. 2004-001: PCAOB Auditing Standard No. 2: An Audit of Internal Control Over Financial Reporting Performed in Conjunction With an Audit of Financial Statements

Summary:

After public comment, the Public Company Accounting Oversight Board (the "Board" or "PCAOB") has adopted Auditing Standard No. 2, An Audit of Internal Control Over Financial Reporting Performed in Conjunction With an Audit of Financial Statements. This standard is the standard on attestation engagements referred to in Section 404(b) as well as Section 103(a)(2)(A) of the Sarbanes-Oxley Act of 2002 (the "Sarbanes-Oxley Act" or "the Act"). The Board will submit this standard to the Securities and Exchange Commission ("Commission" or "SEC") for approval pursuant to Section 107 of the Sarbanes-Oxley Act of 2002 (the "Act"). This standard will not take effect unless approved by the Commission.

Board Contacts:

Thomas Ray, Deputy Chief Auditor (202/207-9112; rayt@pcaobus.org), Laura Phillips, Associate Chief Auditor (202/207-9111; phillipsl@pcaobus.org).

*   *   *

The series of business failures that began with Enron in late 2001 exposed serious weaknesses in the system of checks and balances that were intended to protect the interests of shareholders, pension beneficiaries and employees of public companies — and to protect the confidence of the American public in the stability and fairness of U.S. capital markets.

From the boardroom to the executive suite, to the offices of accountants and lawyers, the historic gatekeepers of this confidence were found missing or, worse, complicit in the breaches of the public trust.

Congress responded to the corporate failures with the Sabanes-Oxley Act of 2002, creating a broad, new oversight regime for auditors of public companies while prescribing specific steps to address specific failures and codifying the responsibilities of corporate executives, corporate directors, lawyers and accountants.

The merits, benefits, cost and wisdom of each of the prescriptions can and will fuel debate. But the context for the passage of the Sarbanes-Oxley Act, and the President's signing it into law on July 30, 2002, cannot be ignored: Corporate leaders and advisors failed. People lost their livelihoods and their life savings. The faith of America and the world in U.S. markets was shaken to the core.

In that context, the PCAOB adopted the standard for auditors to use when assessing whether managers of a public company have accurately reported on companies' internal controls over financial reporting.

Failures in internal control, particularly over financial reporting, were among the specific concerns addressed by Congress in the Sarbanes-Oxley Act. Congress required not just that management report on a company's internal control over financial reporting, but that auditors attest to the accuracy of management's report.

The bottom line for Congress, and for the PCAOB, is the reliability of the company's financial statements — statements relied on by shareholders, management, directors, regulators, lenders, investors and the market at large.

To achieve reliable financial statements, internal controls must be in place to see that records accurately and fairly reflect transactions in and dispositions of a company's assets; to provide assurance that the records of transactions are sufficient to prepare financial statements in accordance with generally accepted accounting principles, and that receipts and expenditures are made only as authorized by management and directors; and to make sure that steps are in place to prevent or detect theft, unauthorized use or disposition of the company's assets of a value that could have a material effect on the financial statements.

In the simplest terms, investors can have much more confidence in the reliability of a corporate financial statement if corporate management demonstrates that it exercises adequate internal control over bookkeeping, the sufficiency of books and records for the preparation of accurate financial statements, adherence to rules about the use of company assets and the possibility of misappropriation of company assets.

The Sarbanes-Oxley Act, in Section 404, requires company management to assess and report on the company's internal control. It also requires a company's independent, outside auditors to issue an "attestation" to management's assessment—in other words, to provide shareholders and the public at large with an independent reason to rely on management's description of the company's internal control over financial reporting.

Reliable financial reporting is too important to relegate an auditor's attestation to a rubber-stamped endorsement of management's report on internal controls. As a result, the PCAOB is requiring that auditors perform an audit of internal control over financial reporting and to perform that audit in conjunction with the audit of a company's financial statements.

The one audit cannot be separated from the other. The information the auditor learns as a result of auditing the company's financial statements has a direct and important bearing on the auditor's conclusion about the effectiveness of the company's internal control over financial reporting.

Section 404 and the Board's requirements will entail extra work and, for companies, extra expense, particularly in the first year of implementation. The PCAOB will be vigilant in its inspections of accounting firms and conversations with issuers, particularly small and medium-sized companies, to see that expense isn't increased for its own sake.

The Board does not underestimate the demands this auditing standard will impose on auditors and public companies. But in the end, the Board, public companies and the accounting profession answer to the higher demand of accuracy, reliability and fairness in the financial statements that provide the basis for trust in our financial markets.

A. The Benefits of Effective Internal Control Over Financial Reporting

Companies use internal controls as checks on a variety of processes, including financial reporting, operating efficiency and effectiveness, and compliance with applicable laws and regulations. The Sarbanes-Oxley Act focuses on companies' internal control over financial reporting.

Internal control over financial reporting consists of company policies and procedures that are designed and operated to provide reasonable assurance about the reliability of a company's financial reporting and its process for preparing and fairly presenting financial statements in accordance with generally accepted accounting principles. It includes policies and procedures for maintaining accounting records, authorizing receipts and disbursements, and the safeguarding of assets.

Effective internal control over financial reporting is essential for a company to effectively manage its affairs and to fulfill its obligation to its investors. A company's management, its owners — public investors — and others must be able to rely on the financial information reported by companies to make decisions.

Strong internal controls also provide better opportunities to detect and deter fraud. For example, many frauds resulting in financial statement restatement relied upon the ability of management to exploit weaknesses in internal control. To the extent that internal control reporting can help restore investor confidence by improving the effectiveness of internal controls (and reducing the incidence of fraud), assessments of internal controls over financial reporting should emphasize controls that prevent or detect errors as well as fraud.

Evaluating a company's internal control over financial reporting is not without cost, but it provides many far-reaching benefits. Regular assessments, and reporting on those assessments, can help management develop, maintain and improve existing internal control. Assessments can identify cost-ineffective procedures, reduce costs of processing accounting information, increase productivity of the company's financial function, and simplify financial control systems. It also may result in fewer financial statement restatements and less litigation.

The primary benefit of evaluations, however, is to provide the company, its management, its board and audit committee, and its owners and other stakeholders with a reasonable basis on which to rely on the company's financial reporting. The integrity of financial reporting represents the foundation upon which this country's public markets are built.

As with many endeavors, internal control over financial reporting is a process that involves human diligence and compliance and, consequently, can be intentionally circumvented. As a result, no system of internal control over financial reporting, regardless of how well it is designed and operating, can provide absolute assurance that a company's financial statements are accurate.

Nevertheless, as companies develop processes to assist management in assessing internal control and as auditors perform their evaluations, the assessment process should result in a continuous strengthening of internal control over financial reporting.

B. Basis for Internal Control Reporting and the Board's Standard

Section 404(a) of the Sarbanes-Oxley Act requires the management of a public company to assess the effectiveness of the company's internal control over financial reporting as of the end of the company's most recent fiscal year and to include in the company's annual report to shareholders management's conclusion, as a result of that assessment, about whether the company's internal control is effective. The SEC implemented Section 404(a) in a rule on June 5, 2003.[1]

Section 404(b) of the Act requires the company's auditor to attest to and report on the assessment made by the company's management. Sections 103(a)(2)(A) and 404(b) of the Act direct the PCAOB to establish professional standards governing the independent auditor's attestation.

In April 2003, the Board adopted pre-existing professional standards as the Board's interim standards, including a standard governing an auditor's attestation on internal control. Mindful of the requirements of the Sarbanes-Oxley Act and the need to evaluate the pre-existing stan-

---

1. *See* Management's Reports on Internal Control Over Financial Reporting and Certification of Disclosure in Exchange Act Periodic Reports, Securities and Exchange Commission Release No. 33-8238 (June 5, 2003) [68 FR 36636].

---

dard, the Board convened a public roundtable discussion on July 29, 2003, to discuss issues and hear views related to reporting on internal control. The participants included representatives from public companies, accounting firms, investor groups, and regulatory organizations.

As a result of comments made at the roundtable, advice from the Board's staff, and other input, the Board determined that the pre-existing standard governing an auditor's attestation on internal control was insufficient for purposes of effectively implementing the requirements of Section 404(b) of the Act and for the Board to appropriately discharge the Board's standard-setting obligations under Section 103 of the Act. In response, the Board developed and issued, on October 7, 2003, a proposed auditing standard titled "An Audit of Internal Control over Financial Reporting in Conjunction with An Audit of Financial Statements."

The Board received 193 comment letters from a variety of interested parties, including auditors, investors, internal auditors, issuers, regulators, and others on a broad array of topics. Those comments led to changes in the proposed standard, intended to make the requirements of the standard clearer and more operational.

The Board has approved PCAOB Auditing Standard No. 2, implementing the requirements of the Sarbanes-Oxley Act and incorporating comments received.

This release summarizes the process involved in conducting an audit of internal control over financial reporting, other significant provisions of PCAOB Auditing Standard No. 2 and some of the significant considerations of the Board when it initially proposed this standard and when it evaluated the comments it received. The Board's detailed analysis of the comments received and the Board's responses are contained in Appendix E to the standard.

C. The Audit of Internal Control Over Financial Reporting

In preparing PCAOB Auditing Standard No. 2, the Board was guided by a number of broad considerations that have effect throughout the standard. Those broad considerations included: that "attestation" is insufficient to describe the process of assessing management's report on internal controls; that an audit of internal control over financial reporting must be integrated with an audit of the company's financial statements; and that the costs of the internal control audit be appropriate in consideration of the expected benefits to investors of improved internal control over financial reporting.

D. Attestation vs. Audit

Throughout Auditing Standard No. 2, the auditor's attestation of management's assessment of the effectiveness of internal control is referred to as the audit of internal control over financial reporting. The Board has noted, in comment letters and in other communications, that some people have drawn a distinction between an "audit" and an "attestation," suggesting that an attestation is a different type of engagement that involves a lesser amount of work than an audit. This idea is erroneous. An attestation engagement to examine management's assessment of internal control requires the same level of work as an audit of internal control over financial reporting.

The objective of an audit of internal control over financial reporting is to form an opinion "as to whether management's assessment of the effectiveness of the registrant's internal control over financial reporting is fairly stated in all material respects."[2] Further, Section 103(a)(2)(A)(iii) of the Act requires the auditor's report to present an evaluation of whether the internal control structure provides reasonable assurance that transactions are recorded as necessary, among other requirements.

---

2. *See* SEC Regulation S-X 2-02(f), 17 C.F.R. 210.2-02(f).

Importantly, the auditor's conclusion will pertain directly to whether the auditor can agree with management that internal control is effective, not just to the adequacy of management's process for determining whether internal control is effective.

An auditing process restricted to evaluating what management has done would not provide the auditor with a sufficiently high level of assurance that management's conclusion is correct. The auditor needs to evaluate management's assessment process to be satisfied that management has an appropriate basis for its conclusion. The auditor, however, also needs to test the effectiveness of internal control to be satisfied that management's conclusion is correct and, therefore, fairly stated. Indeed, as the Board heard at the internal control roundtable and in comment letters, investors expect the independent auditor to test whether the company's internal control over financial reporting is effective, and Auditing Standard No. 2 requires the auditor to do so.

E. Integrated Audit

PCAOB Auditing Standard No. 2 describes an integrated audit of the financial statements and internal control over financial reporting. Accordingly, it is an integrated standard that (1) addresses both the work that is required to audit internal control over financial reporting and the relationship of that audit to the audit of the financial statements and (2) refers to the attestation of management's assessment of the effectiveness of the internal control as the audit of internal control over financial reporting.

The Board decided that these audits should be integrated because the objectives of, and work involved in performing, an audit of internal control over financial reporting and an audit of the financial statements are closely related. Furthermore, Section 404(b) of the Sarbanes-Oxley Act provides that the auditor's attestation of management's assessment of internal control shall not be the subject of a separate engagement.

Each audit provides the auditor with information relevant to the auditor's evaluation of the results of the other audit. For example, the auditor's discovery of misstatements in the financial statements while performing financial statement auditing procedures indicates that there may be weaknesses in the company's internal control over financial reporting. Because of the significance of this interrelationship, the Board has made it clear that, to conduct and report on the results of an audit of internal control over financial reporting pursuant to Auditing Standard No. 2, the auditor also must audit the company's financial statements.

Notwithstanding the fact that the two audits are interrelated, the integrated audit results in two separate objectives: to express an opinion on management's assessment of the effectiveness of the company's internal control over financial reporting and to express an opinion on whether the financial statements are fairly stated.

F. Cost

The Board is sensitive to the costs Section 404 and Auditing Standard No. 2 may impose on all companies, particularly some small and medium-sized companies. The Board anticipates that most companies of all sizes will experience the highest cost of complying with Section 404 during the first year of implementation.

Internal control is not "one-size-fits-all," and the nature and extent of controls that are necessary depend, to a great extent, on the size and complexity of the company. Large, complex, multi-national companies, for example, are likely to need extensive and sophisticated internal control systems.

In smaller companies, or in companies with less complex operations, the ethical behavior and core values of a senior management group that is directly involved in daily interactions with both internal and external parties might reduce the need for elaborate internal control systems. The Board expects that the auditor will exercise reasonable professional judgment in determining the extent of the audit of internal control and perform only those tests that are necessary to ascertain the effectiveness of the company's internal control.

Management is required to base its assessment of the effectiveness of the company's internal control over financial reporting on a suitable, recognized control framework established by a body of experts that followed due-process procedures to develop the framework. In the United States, the Committee of Sponsoring Organizations ("COSO") of the Treadway Commission has published Internal Control—Integrated Framework. COSO's publication (also referred to simply as COSO) provides a suitable framework for purposes of management's assessment.

The directions in Auditing Standard No. 2 are based on the internal control framework established by COSO because of the frequency with which management of public companies are expected to use that framework for their assessments. Other suitable frameworks have been published in other countries and likely will be published in the future. Although different frameworks may not contain exactly the same elements as COSO, they should have elements that encompass all of COSO's general themes. The auditor should therefore be able to apply the concepts and guidance in Auditing Standard No. 2 in a reasonable manner if management uses a suitable framework other than COSO.

The Board believes that the special considerations for small and medium-sized companies included within COSO provide well for the auditor's use of such judgment, more so than the appendix that the Board's proposed standard originally included. For this reason, the proposed appendix was removed from Auditing Standard No. 2 and replaced with a direct reference to the special considerations within COSO.

The Board also was cognizant of audit costs in its consideration of the appropriate extent to which the auditor may use the work of internal auditors and others to support the auditor's opinion on internal control effectiveness. Auditing Standard No. 2 provides the auditor with significant flexibility in using the relevant work of highly competent and objective personnel, while also requiring the auditor to obtain through his or her own auditing procedures a meaningful portion of the evidence that supports the auditor's opinion. The Board believes it has achieved an appropriate balance of work between the auditor and others that will ensure a high quality audit of internal control and that have the complementary benefit of encouraging companies to invest in competent and objective internal audit functions.

G. The Audit Process

An audit of internal control over financial reporting is an extensive process involving several steps, including planning the audit, evaluating the process management used to perform its assessment of internal control effectiveness, obtaining an understanding of the internal control, evaluating the effectiveness of both the design and operation of the internal control, and forming an opinion about whether internal control over financial reporting is effective.

The auditor's objective is to express an opinion about whether management's assessment, or conclusion, on the effectiveness of internal control over financial reporting is stated fairly, in all material respects. To support his or her opinion, the auditor must obtain evidence about whether internal control over financial reporting is effective. The auditor obtains this evidence in several ways, including evaluating and testing management's assessment process;

evaluating and testing work on internal control performed by others, such as internal auditors; and testing the effectiveness of the controls himself or herself.

H. Auditor Independence

The Sarbanes-Oxley Act, and the SEC rules implementing Section 404(a) of the Act, require the auditor to be independent to perform an audit of internal control over financial reporting. Under the SEC's Rule 2-01 on auditor independence, an auditor impairs his or her independence if the auditor audits his or her own work, including any work on designing or implementing an audit client's internal control system. PCAOB Auditing Standard No. 2 explicitly prohibits the auditor from accepting an engagement to provide an audit client with an internal control-related service that has not been specifically pre-approved by the audit committee. That is, the audit committee cannot pre-approve internal control-related services as a category, but must approve each service.

I. Key Provisions of Audit Standard No. 2

1. Evaluating Management's Assessment

The natural starting place for the audit of a company's internal control over financial reporting is management's assessment. By evaluating management's assessment, an auditor can have confidence that management has a basis for expressing its conclusion on the effectiveness of internal control. Such an evaluation also provides information that will help the auditor understand the company's internal control, helps the auditor plan the work necessary to complete the audit, and provides some of the evidence the auditor will use to support his or her opinion.

The work that management performs in connection with its assessment can have a significant effect on the nature, timing, and extent of the work the independent auditor will need to perform. Auditing Standard No. 2 allows the auditor to use, to a reasonable degree, the work performed by others. The more extensive and reliable management's assessment is, the less extensive and costly the auditor's work will need to be.

Also, the more clearly management documents its internal control over financial reporting, the process used to assess the effectiveness of the internal control, and the results of that process, the easier it will be for the auditor to understand the internal control, confirm that understanding, evaluate management's assessment, and plan and perform the audit of internal control over financial reporting. This too should translate into reduced professional fees for the audit of internal control over financial reporting.

2. Obtaining an Understanding of Internal Control Over Financial Reporting, Including Performing Walkthroughs

The auditor should understand how internal control over financial reporting is designed and operates to evaluate and test its effectiveness. The auditor obtains a substantial amount of this understanding when evaluating management's assessment process.

The auditor also should be satisfied, however, that the controls actually have been implemented and are operating as designed. Thus, while inquiry of company personnel and a review of management's assessment process provide the auditor with an understanding of how the system of internal control is designed and operates, they are insufficient by themselves. Other procedures are necessary for the auditor to confirm his or her understanding.

Auditing Standard No. 2 directs the auditor to confirm his or her understanding by performing procedures that include making inquiries of and observing the personnel who actually perform the controls; reviewing documents that are used in, and that result from, the application of the controls; and comparing supporting documents (for example, sales invoices, contracts, and bills of lading) to the accounting records.

The most effective means of accomplishing this objective is for the auditor to perform "walkthroughs" of the company's significant processes. To introduce a powerful efficiency, and because of the importance of several other objectives that walkthroughs accomplish, Auditing Standard No. 2 requires the auditor to perform walkthroughs in each annual audit of internal control over financial reporting.

In a walkthrough, the auditor traces a transaction from each major class of transactions from origination, through the company's accounting and information systems and financial report preparation processes, to it being reported in the company's financial statements. Walkthroughs provide the auditor with audit evidence that supports or refutes his or her understanding of the process flow of transactions, the design of controls, and whether controls are in operation. Walkthroughs also help the auditor to determine whether his or her understanding is complete and provide information necessary for the auditor to evaluate the effectiveness of the design of the internal control over financial reporting.

Because of the judgment that a walkthrough requires and the significance of the objectives that walkthroughs allow the auditor to achieve, Auditing Standard No. 2 requires the auditor to perform the walkthroughs himself or herself. In other words, Auditing Standard No. 2 does not allow the auditor to use the work performed by management or others to satisfy the requirement to perform walkthroughs. However, to provide additional evidence, the auditor may also review walkthroughs that have been performed and documented by others.

The walkthroughs also must be done in each annual audit of internal control over financial reporting. Important objectives of walkthroughs are to confirm that the auditor's understanding of the controls is correct and complete. Without actually "walking" transactions through the significant processes each year, there is too high a risk that changes to the processes would go undetected by the auditor.

Because of the significance of the objectives they are intended to achieve, and the judgment necessary to their effective performance, walkthroughs should be performed by appropriately experienced auditors. Inexperienced audit personnel who participate in walkthroughs should be supervised closely so that the conditions encountered in the walkthroughs are considered appropriately and that the information obtained in the walkthroughs is appropriately documented.

3. Identifying Significant Accounts and Relevant Assertions

As a part of obtaining an understanding of internal control, the auditor also determines which controls should be tested, either by the auditor, management, or others. Auditing Standard No. 2 requires that the auditor obtain evidence about the operating effectiveness of internal control over financial reporting for all relevant assertions for all significant accounts or disclosures. This requirement relies heavily on two concepts: significant account and relevant assertion.

Auditing standards implicitly recognize that some accounts are more significant than others. Auditing Standard No. 2 provides additional direction on how to determine significant accounts for purposes of the audit of internal control over financial reporting. In short, the auditor begins by performing a quantitative evaluation of accounts at the financial-statement caption or note-disclosure level. Then the auditor expands the evaluation to include qualitative factors, such as differing risks, company organization structure, and other factors, which would likely result in additional accounts being identified as significant.

Financial statement amounts and disclosures embody financial statement assertions. Does the asset exist, or did the transaction occur? Has the company included all loans outstanding in its loans payable account? Have marketable investments been valued properly? Does the company have the rights to the accounts receivable, and are the loans payable the proper obligation of the company? Are the amounts in the financial statements appropriately presented, and is there adequate disclosure about them? Answering these questions helps the auditor to identify the relevant financial statement assertions for which the company should have controls.

Identifying "relevant" assertions is a familiar process for experienced auditors, and because of the importance relevant assertions play in the required extent of testing, Auditing Standard No. 2 provides additional direction.

Similarly, experienced auditors are familiar with identifying significant processes and major classes of transactions. Major classes of transactions are those groupings of transactions that are significant to the company's financial statements. For example, at a company for which sales may be initiated by customers through personal contract in a retail store or electronically using the Internet, these would be two major classes of transactions within the sales process (if they were both significant to the company's financial statements). Because of the importance of significant processes and major classes of transaction in the design of the auditor's procedures, Auditing Standard No. 2 provides additional direction here, too.

4. Testing and Evaluating the Effectiveness of the Design of Controls

To be effective, internal controls must be designed properly, and all the controls necessary to provide reasonable assurance about the fairness of a company's financial statements should be in place and performed by appropriately qualified people who have the authority to implement them. At some point during the internal control audit, the auditor will need to make a determination as to whether the controls would be effective if they were operated as designed, and whether all the necessary controls are in place. This is known as design effectiveness.

The procedures the auditor performs to test and evaluate design effectiveness include inquiries of company personnel, observation of internal controls, walkthroughs, and a specific evaluation of whether the controls are likely to prevent or detect financial statement misstatements if they operate as designed. Auditing Standard No. 2 adopts these methods of testing and evaluating design effectiveness. The last step is especially important because it calls for the auditor to apply professional judgment and knowledge of and experience with internal control over financial reporting to his or her understanding of the company's controls.

5. Testing Operating Effectiveness

Auditing Standard No. 2 requires the auditor to obtain evidence about the operating effectiveness of controls related to all relevant financial statement assertions for all significant accounts and disclosures in the financial statements.

For this reason, in addition to being satisfied as to the effectiveness of the design of the internal controls, the auditor performs tests of controls to obtain evidence about the operating effectiveness of the controls. These tests include a mix of inquiries of appropriate company personnel, inspection of relevant documentation, such as sales orders and invoices, observation of the controls in operation, and reperformance of the application of the control.

Auditing Standard No. 2 directs required tests of controls to "relevant assertions" rather than to "significant controls." To comply with the requirements of Auditing Standard No. 2, the auditor would apply tests to those controls that are important to fairly presenting each relevant assertion in the financial statements. It is neither necessary to test all controls nor is it necessary to test redundant controls (unless redundancy is itself a control objective, as in the case of certain computer controls). However, the emphasis is better placed on addressing relevant assertions (because those are the points where misstatements could occur) rather than significant controls. This emphasis encourages the auditor to identify and test controls that address the primary areas where misstatements could occur, yet limits the auditor's work to the necessary controls.

Expressing the extent of testing in this manner also resolves the issue of the extent of testing from year to year (the "rotating tests of controls" issue). Auditing Standard No. 2 states that the auditor should vary testing from year to year, both to introduce unpredictability into the testing and to respond to changes at the company. However, each year's audit must stand on its own. Therefore, the auditor must obtain evidence of the effectiveness of controls for all relevant assertions for all significant accounts and disclosures every year.

At the Board's roundtable, public company representatives and auditors indicated that providing examples of extent-of-testing decisions would be helpful. The proposed auditing standard included several examples, which have been retained in Appendix B of Auditing Standard No. 2.

6. Timing of Testing

The Act requires management's assessment and the auditor's opinion to address whether internal control was effective as of the end of the company's most recent fiscal year, in other words, as of a point-in-time. Performing all of the testing on December 31 is neither practical nor appropriate, however. To form a basis to express an opinion about whether internal control was effective as of a point in time requires the auditor to obtain evidence that the internal control operated effectively over an appropriate period of time. Auditing Standard No. 2 recognizes this and allows the auditor to obtain evidence about operating effectiveness at different times throughout the year, provided that the auditor updates those tests or obtains other evidence that the controls still operated effectively at the end of the company's fiscal year.

7. Using the Work of Others

The auditor must consider other relevant and available information about internal control when evaluating internal control effectiveness. In this regard, Auditing Standard No. 2 requires the auditor to understand the results of procedures performed by others, for example, internal auditors, other company personnel, and third parties working under the direction of management, on internal control over financial reporting.

At a minimum, the auditor should consider the results of those tests in designing the audit approach and ultimately in forming an opinion on the effectiveness of internal control over financial reporting. To this end, Auditing Standard No. 2 requires the auditor to review all reports issued during the year by internal audit (or similar functions, such as loan review in a financial institution) that address internal controls over financial reporting and evaluate any internal control deficiencies identified in those reports.

Additionally, the auditor may use the results of testing by others to alter the nature, timing, and extent of his or her tests of controls. At the Board's roundtable and in comment letters, public companies indicated their concern that at some point, the Board's standard could require an excessive amount of retesting by the auditor in order to use the work of others, especially internal auditors, and would inappropriately restrict the auditor's ability to use the work of internal auditors and others.

Public companies were particularly sensitive to this issue because of its direct bearing on the cost of complying with Section 404. On the other hand, the federal bank regulators indicated that experience with the Federal Deposit Insurance Corporation Improvement Act of 1991 ("FDICIA"), which requires internal control reporting similar to Section 404 of the Act, revealed instances in which the auditor used the work of internal auditors to an inappropriately high degree, where the auditor himself or herself did not perform sufficient work to provide a reasonable basis for his or her opinion.

The directions in Auditing Standard No. 2 for using the work of others are based on the same concepts as Statement on Auditing Standards ("SAS") No. 65, Auditor's Consideration of the Internal Audit Function in an Audit of the Financial Statements.[3] However, because the subject matter in an audit of internal control — the effectiveness of the controls — is different from the subject matter in an audit of financial statements — the reliability of the financial amounts and disclosures — some adaptation of SAS No. 65 was required.

The competence and objectivity factors described in SAS No. 65 were adapted to the evaluation of persons other than internal auditors, such as members of financial management, and the evaluation of the nature of the items tested by others was adapted to the context of an audit of internal control over financial reporting rather than an audit of financial statements. Additionally, Auditing Standard No. 2 creates an overall boundary on the use of the work of others in an audit of internal control over financial reporting not contained in SAS No. 65 by requiring that the auditor's own work provide the principal evidence for the audit opinion.

Auditing Standard No. 2 describes an evaluation process, focusing on the nature of the controls subject to the work of others and the competence and objectivity of the persons who performed the work, that the auditor should use in determining the extent to which he or she may use the work of others.

For example, based on the nature of the controls in the control environment, the auditor should not use the work of others to reduce the amount of work he or she performs on the control environment. On the other hand, the auditor could use the work of others to test controls over the period-end financial reporting process. However, given the nature of these controls, the auditor would normally determine that he or she should perform more of these tests himself or herself, and that for any of the work of others the auditor used, the degree of competence and objectivity of the individuals performing the work should be high. Therefore, the auditor might use the work of internal auditors in this area to some degree but not the work of others within the company. Because of the importance of these decisions, Auditing Standard No. 2 provides additional direction.

Auditing Standard No. 2 also requires that, on an overall basis, the auditor's own work must provide the principal evidence for the audit opinion. Because the amount of work related to obtaining sufficient evidence to support an opinion about the effectiveness of controls is not susceptible to precise measurement, the auditor's judgment as to whether he or she has obtained the principal evidence for the opinion will be qualitative as well as quantitative. For example, the auditor might give more weight to work performed on pervasive controls and in

---

3. The Board adopted the generally accepted auditing standards, as described in the American Institute of Certified Public Accountants' ("AICPA") Auditing Standards Board's ("ASB") SAS No. 95, *Generally Accepted Auditing Standards*, as in existence on April 16, 2003, on an initial, transitional basis. SAS No. 65 is one of those standards.

areas such as the control environment than on other controls such as controls over routine, low-risk transactions. Also, the work the auditor performs in the control environment and walkthroughs provide an important part of the principal evidence the auditor needs to obtain.

These principles interact to provide the auditor with considerable flexibility in using the work of others and also prevent inappropriate over-reliance on the work of others. Although Auditing Standard No. 2 requires that the auditor reperform some of the tests performed by others in order to use their work, it does not set any specific requirement on the extent of the reperformance. For example, the standard does not require that the auditor reperform tests of controls over all significant accounts for which the auditor uses the work of others. Rather, Auditing Standard No. 2 relies on the auditor's judgment, such that the re-testing is sufficient to enable the auditor to evaluate the quality and effectiveness of the work.

This considerable flexibility in using the work of others should translate into a strong encouragement for companies to develop high-quality internal audit, compliance, and other such functions. The more highly competent and objective these functions are, and the more thorough their testing, the more the auditor will be able to use their work.

8. Evaluating the Results of Testing

Both management and the auditor may identify deficiencies in internal control over financial reporting. A control deficiency exists when the design or operation of a control does not allow the company's management or employees, in the normal course of performing their assigned functions, to prevent or detect misstatements on a timely basis.

Auditing Standard No. 2 requires the auditor to evaluate the severity of all identified control deficiencies because such deficiencies can have an effect on the auditor's overall conclusion about whether internal control is effective. The auditor also has a responsibility to make sure that certain parties, such as the audit committee, are aware of control deficiencies that rise to a certain level of severity.

Under Auditing Standard No. 2, a control deficiency (or a combination of internal control deficiencies) should be classified as a significant deficiency if, by itself or in combination with other control deficiencies, it results in more than a remote likelihood of a misstatement of the company's annual or interim financial statements that is more than inconsequential will not be prevented or detected. A significant deficiency should be classified as a material weakness if, by itself or in combination with other control deficiencies, it results in more than a remote likelihood that a material misstatement in the company's annual or interim financial statements will not be prevented or detected.

The definitions of significant deficiency and material weakness focus on likelihood and magnitude as the framework for evaluating deficiencies. The Board anticipates that this framework will bring increased consistency to these evaluations yet preserve an appropriate degree of judgment. Additionally, Auditing Standard No. 2 includes examples of how these definitions would be applied in several different scenarios.

Auditing Standard No. 2 requires the auditor to communicate in writing to the company's audit committee all significant deficiencies and material weaknesses of which the auditor is aware. The auditor also is required to communicate to the company's management, in writing, all control deficiencies of which he or she is aware that have not previously been communicated in writing to management and to notify the audit committee that such communication has been made.

---

9. Identifying Significant Deficiencies

Auditing Standard No. 2 identifies a number of circumstances that, because of their likely significant negative effect on internal control over financial reporting, are significant deficiencies as well as strong indicators that a material weakness exists, including—

- Ineffective oversight of the company's external financial reporting and internal control over financial reporting by the company's audit committee. Effective oversight by the company's board of directors, including its audit committee, is essential to the company's achievement of its objectives and is an integral part of a company's monitoring of internal control. In addition to requiring the audit committee to oversee the company's external financial reporting and internal control over financial reporting, the Act makes the audit committee directly responsible for the appointment, compensation, and oversight of the work of the auditor. Thus, an ineffective audit committee can have detrimental effects on the company and its internal control over financial reporting, as well as on the independent audit. Auditing Standard No. 2 requires that, as part of evaluating the control environment and monitoring components of internal control, the auditor assess the effectiveness of the audit committee's oversight of the external financial reporting process and internal control over financial reporting.

To be sure, the company's board of directors is responsible for evaluating the performance and effectiveness of the audit committee. Auditing Standard No. 2 does not suggest that the auditor is responsible for performing a separate and distinct evaluation of the audit committee. If the auditor concludes that oversight by the audit committee is ineffective, however, the auditor must communicate that specific significant deficiency, or material weakness as the case may be, in writing to the board of directors.

Normally, the auditor's interests and the audit committee's interests will be aligned: both should be interested in fairly presented financial statements, effective internal control over financial reporting, and an effective audit process. The Board recognizes that a theoretical conflict of interest results from the audit committee's responsibility to hire and fire the auditor. However, this type of conflict is one that experienced auditors are accustomed to bearing and that investors expect an auditor to address: when the auditor determines that its overseer is ineffective (which significantly impairs the effectiveness of the financial reporting process), the auditor must speak up.

- Material misstatement in the financial statements not initially identified by the company's internal controls. As previously stated, the audit of internal control over financial reporting and the audit of the company's financial statements are an integrated activity and are required by the Act to be a single engagement. The results of the work performed in a financial statement audit provide evidence to support the auditor's conclusions on the effectiveness of internal control, and vice-versa. Therefore, if the auditor discovers a material misstatement in the financial statements as a part of the audit of the financial statements, the auditor should consider whether internal control over financial reporting is effective. That the company's internal controls did not first detect the misstatement is, therefore, a strong indicator that the company's internal control over financial reporting is ineffective.

Timing might be a concern for some issuers, particularly as it relates to making preliminary drafts of the financial statements available to the auditor. However, changes to the financial statement preparation process that increase the likelihood that the financial information is correct prior to providing it to the auditors likely will result in an improved control environment. The auditor also must exercise judgment when performing this evaluation. For example, if the auditor initially identified a material misstatement in the financial statements but, given the circumstances, determined that management would have found the misstatement on a timely basis before the financial statements were made publicly available, the auditor might appropriately determine that the circumstance was a significant deficiency but not a material weakness.

- Significant deficiencies that have been communicated to management and the audit committee, but that remain uncorrected after reasonable periods of time. Significant deficiencies in internal control that are not also determined to be material weaknesses, as defined in the proposed auditing standard, are not so severe as to require the auditor to conclude that internal control is ineffective. However, these deficiencies are, nonetheless, significant, and the auditor should expect the company to correct them. If, however, management fails to correct significant deficiencies within a reasonable period of time, that situation reflects poorly on tone-at-the-top, and directly on the control environment as a whole. Additionally, the significance of the deficiency can change over time (for example, major changes in sales volume or added complexity in sales transaction structures might increase the severity of a significant deficiency affecting sales).

10. Forming an Opinion and Reporting

Auditing Standard No. 2 permits the auditor to express an unqualified opinion if the auditor has identified no material weaknesses in internal control after having performed all of the procedures that the auditor considers necessary in the circumstances. In the event that the auditor cannot perform all of the procedures that the auditor considers necessary in the circumstances, Auditing Standard No. 2 permits the auditor to either qualify or disclaim an opinion. If an overall opinion cannot be expressed, Auditing Standard No. 2 requires the auditor to explain why.[4]

In addition, the auditor's report is to include two opinions as a result of the audit of internal control over financial reporting: one on management's assessment and one on the effectiveness of internal control over financial reporting. The Board decided that two opinions will most clearly communicate to report readers the nature and results of the work performed and most closely track with the requirements of Sections 404 and 103 of the Act.

11. No Disclosure of Significant Deficiencies

The auditor's report must follow the same disclosure model as management's assessment. The SEC's final rules implementing Section 404(a) require management's assessment to disclose only material weaknesses, not significant deficiencies. Therefore, because management's assessment will disclose only material weaknesses, the auditor's report may disclose only material weaknesses.[5]

---

4. See also SEC Regulation S-X 2-02(f), 17 C.F.R. § 212.2-02(f) ("The attestation report on management's assessment of internal control over financial reporting shall be dated, signed manually, identify the period covered by the report and clearly state the opinion of the accountant as to whether management's assessment of the effectiveness of the registrant's internal control over financial reporting is fairly stated in all material respects, or must include an opinion to the effect that an overall opinion cannot be expressed. If an overall opinion cannot be expressed, explain why.").

5. It should be noted, however, that the final rules indicated that an aggregation of significant deficiencies may constitute a material weakness in a company's internal control over financial reporting, in which case disclosure would

12. Material Weaknesses Result in Adverse Opinion on Internal Control

The previously existing attestation standard provided that when the auditor identified a material weakness in internal control, depending on the significance of the material weakness and its effect on the achievement of the objectives of the control criteria, the auditor might qualify his or her opinion ("except for the effect of the material weakness, internal control was effective") or might express an adverse opinion ("internal control over financial reporting was not effective").

The SEC's final rules implementing Section 404(a) state that "Management is not permitted to conclude that the registrant's internal control over financial reporting is effective if there are one or more material weaknesses in the registrant's internal control over financial reporting." In other words, in such a case, management must conclude that internal control is not effective (*i.e.*, a qualified or "except for" conclusion is not allowed).

Similar to the reporting of significant deficiencies, the reporting model for the auditor must follow the required reporting model for management. Therefore, because management is required to express an "adverse" conclusion in the event a material weakness exists, the auditor's opinion on the effectiveness of internal control over financial reporting must also be adverse; Auditing Standard No. 2 does not permit a qualified opinion in the event of a material weakness. However, Auditing Standard No. 2 also requires an opinion on management's assessment in every audit report.

In the event of a material weakness, the auditor could express an unqualified opinion on management's assessment, so long as management properly identified the material weakness and concluded in their assessment that internal control was not effective.

If the auditor and management disagree about whether a material weakness exists (*i.e.*, the auditor concludes a material weakness exists but management does not and therefore makes the conclusion in its assessment that internal control is effective), then the auditor would render an adverse opinion on management's assessment.

The Board chose for the auditor's report to express two opinions in part because it would be more informative when a material weakness exists.

13. Testing Controls Intended to Prevent or Detect Fraud

Strong internal controls provide better opportunities to detect and deter fraud. For example, many frauds resulting in financial statement restatement relied upon the ability of management to exploit weaknesses in internal control. To the extent that the internal control reporting required by Section 404 can help restore investor confidence by improving the effectiveness of internal controls (and reducing the incidence of fraud), the auditing standard on performing the audit of internal control over financial reporting should emphasize controls that prevent or detect errors as well as fraud. For this reason, Auditing Standard No. 2 specifically addresses and emphasizes the importance of controls over possible fraud and requires the auditor to test controls specifically intended to prevent or detect fraud that is reasonably possible to result in material misstatement of the financial statements.

*   *   *

On the 9th day of March, in the year 2004, the foregoing was, in accordance with the bylaws of the Public Company Accounting Oversight Board,

---

be required. *See* Final Rule: Management's Reports in Internal Control Over Financial Reporting and Certification of Disclosure in Exchange Act Periodic Reports, Securities and Exchange Commission Release No. 33-8238, (June 5, 2003) [68 FR 36636].

ADOPTED BY THE BOARD.

/s/ J. Gordon Seymour

Acting Secretary

March 9, 2004

Auditing Standard No. 2—An Audit of Internal Control Over Financial Reporting Performed in Conjunction with an Audit of Financial Statements

Applicability of Standard

1. This standard establishes requirements and provides directions that apply when an auditor is engaged to audit both a company's financial statements and management's assessment of the effectiveness of internal control over financial reporting.

> **Note:** The term *auditor* includes both public accounting firms registered with the Public Company Accounting Oversight Board ("PCAOB" or the "Board") and associated persons thereof.

2. A company subject to the reporting requirements of the Securities Exchange Act of 1934 (an "issuer") is required to include in its annual report a report of management on the company's internal control over financial reporting. Registered investment companies, issuers of asset-backed securities, and nonpublic companies are not subject to the reporting requirements mandated by Section 404 of the Sarbanes-Oxley Act of 2002 (the "Act") (PL 107-204). The report of management is required to contain management's assessment of the effectiveness of the company's internal control over financial reporting as of the end of the company's most recent fiscal year, including a statement as to whether the company's internal control over financial reporting is effective. The auditor that audits the company's financial statements included in the annual report is required to attest to and report on management's assessment. The company is required to file the auditor's attestation report as part of the annual report.

> **Note:** The term issuer means an issuer (as defined in Section 3 of the Securities Exchange Act of 1934), the securities of which are registered under Section 12 of that Act, or that is required to file reports under Section 15(d) of that Act, or that files or has filed a registration statement with the Securities and Exchange Commission ("SEC" or "Commission") that has not yet become effective under the Securities Act of 1933, and that it has not withdrawn.

> **Note:** Various parts of this standard summarize legal requirements imposed on issuers by the SEC, as well as legal requirements imposed on auditors by regulatory authorities other than the PCAOB. These parts of the standard are intended to provide context and to promote the auditor's understanding of the relationship between his or her obligations under this standard and his or her other legal responsibilities. The standard does not incorporate these legal requirements by reference and is not an interpretation of those other requirements and should not be so construed. (This Note does not apply to refer-

ences in the standard to the existing professional standards and the Board's interim auditing and related professional practice standards.)

3. This standard is the standard on attestation engagements referred to in Section 404(b) of the Act. This standard is also the standard referred to in Section 103(a)(2)(A)(iii) of the Act. Throughout this standard, the auditor's attestation of management's assessment of the effectiveness of internal control over financial reporting required by Section 404(b) of the Act is referred to as the *audit of internal control over financial reporting.*

> **Note:** The two terms *audit of internal control over financial reporting* and *attestation of management's assessment of the effectiveness of internal control over financial reporting* refer to the same professional service. The first refers to the process, and the second refers to the result of that process.

Auditor's Objective in an Audit of Internal Control Over Financial Reporting

4. The auditor's objective in an audit of internal control over financial reporting is to express an opinion on management's assessment of the effectiveness of the company's internal control over financial reporting. To form a basis for expressing such an opinion, the auditor must plan and perform the audit to obtain reasonable assurance about whether the company maintained, in all material respects, effective internal control over financial reporting as of the date specified in management's assessment. The auditor also must audit the company's financial statements as of the date specified in management's assessment because the information the auditor obtains during a financial statement audit is relevant to the auditor's conclusion about the effectiveness of the company's internal control over financial reporting. Maintaining effective internal control over financial reporting means that no material weaknesses exist; therefore, the objective of the audit of internal control over financial reporting is to obtain reasonable assurance that no material weaknesses exist as of the date specified in management's assessment.

5. To obtain reasonable assurance, the auditor evaluates the assessment performed by management and obtains and evaluates evidence about whether the internal control over financial reporting was designed and operated effectively. The auditor obtains this evidence from a number of sources, including using the work performed by others and performing auditing procedures himself or herself.

6. The auditor should be aware that persons who rely on the information concerning internal control over financial reporting include investors, creditors, the board of directors and audit committee, and regulators in specialized industries, such as banking or insurance. The auditor should be aware that external users of financial statements are interested in information on internal control over financial reporting because it enhances the quality of financial reporting and increases their confidence in financial information, including financial information issued between annual reports, such as quarterly information. Information on internal control over financial reporting is also intended to provide an early warning to those inside and outside the company who are in a position to insist on improvements in internal control over financial reporting, such as the audit committee and regulators in specialized industries. Additionally, Section 302 of the Act and Securities Exchange Act Rule 13a-14(a) or 15d-14(a),[1] whichever applies, require management, with the participation of the principal executive and financial officers, to make quarterly and annual certifications with respect to the company's internal control over financial reporting.

---

1. See 17 C.F.R. 240.13a-14(a) or 17 C.F.R. 240.15d-14(a), whichever applies.

Definitions Related to Internal Control Over Financial Reporting

7. For purposes of management's assessment and the audit of internal control over financial reporting in this standard, *internal control over financial reporting* is defined as follows:

> A process designed by, or under the supervision of, the company's principal executive and principal financial officers, or persons performing similar functions, and effected by the company's board of directors, management, and other personnel, to provide reasonable assurance regarding the reliability of financial reporting and the preparation of financial statements for external purposes in accordance with generally accepted accounting principles and includes those policies and procedures that:
>
> (1) Pertain to the maintenance of records that, in reasonable detail, accurately and fairly reflect the transactions and dispositions of the assets of the company;
>
> (2) Provide reasonable assurance that transactions are recorded as necessary to permit preparation of financial statements in accordance with generally accepted accounting principles, and that receipts and expenditures of the company are being made only in accordance with authorizations of management and directors of the company; and
>
> (3) Provide reasonable assurance regarding prevention or timely detection of unauthorized acquisition, use or disposition of the company's assets that could have a material effect on the financial statements.
>
> **Note:** This definition is the same one used by the SEC in its rules requiring management to report on internal control over financial reporting, except the word "registrant" has been changed to "company" to conform to the wording in this standard. (See Securities Exchange Act Rules 13a-15(f) and 15d-15(f).[2])
>
> **Note:** Throughout this standard, *internal control over financial reporting* (singular) refers to the process described in this paragraph. Individual controls or subsets of controls are referred to as *controls* or *controls over financial reporting.*

8. A *control deficiency* exists when the design or operation of a control does not allow management or employees, in the normal course of performing their assigned functions, to prevent or detect misstatements on a timely basis.

- A deficiency in *design* exists when (a) a control necessary to meet the control objective is missing or (b) an existing control is not properly designed so that, even if the control operates as designed, the control objective is not always met.

- A deficiency in *operation* exists when a properly designed control does not operate as designed, or when the person performing the control does not possess the necessary authority or qualifications to perform the control effectively.

9. A *significant deficiency* is a control deficiency, or combination of control deficiencies, that adversely affects the company's ability to initiate, authorize, record, process, or report external financial data reliably in accordance with generally accepted accounting principles such that there is more than a remote likelihood that a misstatement of the company's annual or interim financial statements that is more than inconsequential will not be prevented or detected.

---

2. See 17 C.F.R. 240, 13a-15(f) and 15d-15(f).

Note: The term "remote likelihood" as used in the definitions of *significant deficiency* and *material weakness* (paragraph 10) has the same meaning as the term "remote" as used in Financial Accounting Standards Board Statement No. 5, *Accounting for Contingencies* ("FAS No. 5"). Paragraph 3 of FAS No. 5 states:

> When a loss contingency exists, the likelihood that the future event or events will confirm the loss or impairment of an asset or the incurrence of a liability can range from probable to remote. This Statement uses the terms *probable*, *reasonably possible*, and *remote* to identify three areas within that range, as follows:
>
> a. *Probable.* The future event or events are likely to occur.
>
> b. *Reasonably possible.* The chance of the future event or events occurring is more than remote but less than likely.
>
> c. *Remote.* The chance of the future events or events occurring is slight.

Therefore, the likelihood of an event is "more than remote" when it is either reasonably possible or probable.

Note: A misstatement is *inconsequential* if a reasonable person would conclude, after considering the possibility of further undetected misstatements, that the misstatement, either individually or when aggregated with other misstatements, would clearly be immaterial to the financial statements. If a reasonable person could not reach such a conclusion regarding a particular misstatement, that misstatement is *more than inconsequential*.

10. A *material weakness* is a significant deficiency, or combination of significant deficiencies, that results in more than a remote likelihood that a material misstatement of the annual or interim financial statements will not be prevented or detected.

Note: In evaluating whether a control deficiency exists and whether control deficiencies, either individually or in combination with other control deficiencies, are significant deficiencies or material weaknesses, the auditor should consider the definitions in paragraphs 8, 9 and 10, and the directions in paragraphs 130 through 137. As explained in paragraph 23, the evaluation of the materiality of the control deficiency should include both quantitative and qualitative considerations. Qualitative factors that might be important in this evaluation include the nature of the financial statement accounts and assertions involved and the reasonably possible future consequences of the deficiency. Furthermore, in determining whether a control deficiency or combination of deficiencies is a significant deficiency or a material weakness, the auditor should evaluate the effect of compensating controls and whether such compensating controls are effective.

11. Controls over financial reporting may be *preventive controls* or *detective controls.*

- Preventive controls have the objective of preventing errors or fraud from occurring in the first place that could result in a misstatement of the financial statements.

- Detective controls have the objective of detecting errors or fraud that have already occurred that could result in a misstatement of the financial statements.

12. Even well-designed controls that are operating as designed might not prevent a misstatement from occurring. However, this possibility may be countered by overlapping preventive controls or partially countered by detective controls. Therefore, effective internal control over financial reporting often includes a combination of preventive and detective controls to achieve a specific control objective. The auditor's procedures as part of either the audit of internal control over financial reporting or the audit of the financial statements are not part of a company's internal control over financial reporting.

Framework Used by Management to Conduct Its Assessment

13. Management is required to base its assessment of the effectiveness of the company's internal control over financial reporting on a suitable, recognized control framework established by a body of experts that followed due-process procedures, including the broad distribution of the framework for public comment. In addition to being available to users of management's reports, a framework is suitable only when it:

- Is free from bias;

- Permits reasonably consistent qualitative and quantitative measurements of a company's internal control over financial reporting;

- Is sufficiently complete so that those relevant factors that would alter a conclusion about the effectiveness of a company's internal control over financial reporting are not omitted; and

- Is relevant to an evaluation of internal control over financial reporting.

Committee of Sponsoring Organizations Framework

14. In the United States, the Committee of Sponsoring Organizations ("COSO") of the Treadway Commission has published *Internal Control—Integrated Framework.* Known as the COSO report, it provides a suitable and available framework for purposes of management's assessment. For that reason, the performance and reporting directions in this standard are based on the COSO framework. Other suitable frameworks have been published in other countries and may be developed in the future. Such other suitable frameworks may be used in an audit of internal control over financial reporting. Although different frameworks may not contain exactly the same elements as COSO, they should have elements that encompass, in general, all the themes in COSO. Therefore, the auditor should be able to apply the concepts and guidance in this standard in a reasonable manner.

15. The COSO framework identifies three primary objectives of internal control: efficiency and effectiveness of operations, financial reporting, and compliance with laws and regulations. The COSO perspective on internal control over financial reporting does not ordinarily include the other two objectives of internal control, which are the effectiveness and efficiency of operations and compliance with laws and regulations. However, the controls that management designs and implements may achieve more than one objective. Also, operations and compliance with laws and regulations directly related to the presentation of and required disclosures in financial statements are encompassed in internal control over financial reporting. Additionally, not all controls relevant to financial reporting are accounting controls. Accordingly, all controls that could materially affect financial reporting, including controls that focus primarily on the effectiveness and efficiency of operations or compliance with laws and regulations and also have a material effect on the reliability of financial reporting, are a part of internal control over financial reporting. More information about the COSO framework is included in the COSO report and in AU sec. 319, Consideration of Internal Control in a Financial Statement Audit.[3] The COSO report also discusses special considerations for internal control over financial reporting for small and medium-sized companies.

---

3. The Board adopted the generally accepted auditing standards, as described in the AICPA Auditing Standards Board's ("ASB") Statement on Auditing Standards No. 95, *Generally Accepted Auditing Standards,* as in existence on April 16, 2003, on an initial, transitional basis. The Statements on Auditing Standards promulgated by the ASB

Inherent Limitations in Internal Control Over Financial Reporting

16. Internal control over financial reporting cannot provide absolute assurance of achieving financial reporting objectives because of its inherent limitations. Internal control over financial reporting is a process that involves human diligence and compliance and is subject to lapses in judgment and breakdowns resulting from human failures. Internal control over financial reporting also can be circumvented by collusion or improper management override. Because of such limitations, there is a risk that material misstatements may not be prevented or detected on a timely basis by internal control over financial reporting. However, these inherent limitations are known features of the financial reporting process. Therefore, it is possible to design into the process safeguards to reduce, though not eliminate, this risk.

The Concept of Reasonable Assurance

17. Management's assessment of the effectiveness of internal control over financial reporting is expressed at the level of *reasonable assurance*. The concept of reasonable assurance is built into the definition of internal control over financial reporting and also is integral to the auditor's opinion.[4] Reasonable assurance includes the understanding that there is a remote likelihood that material misstatements will not be prevented or detected on a timely basis. Although not absolute assurance, reasonable assurance is, nevertheless, a high level of assurance.

18. Just as there are inherent limitations on the assurance that effective internal control over financial reporting can provide, as discussed in paragraph 16, there are limitations on the amount of assurance the auditor can obtain as a result of performing his or her audit of internal control over financial reporting. Limitations arise because an audit is conducted on a test basis and requires the exercise of professional judgment. Nevertheless, the audit of internal control over financial reporting includes obtaining an understanding of internal control over financial reporting, testing and evaluating the design and operating effectiveness of internal control over financial reporting, and performing such other procedures as the auditor considers necessary to obtain reasonable assurance about whether internal control over financial reporting is effective.

19. There is no difference in the level of work performed or assurance obtained by the auditor when expressing an opinion on management's assessment of effectiveness or when expressing an opinion directly on the effectiveness of internal control over financial reporting. In either case, the auditor must obtain sufficient evidence to provide a reasonable basis for his or her opinion and the use and evaluation of management's assessment is inherent in expressing either opinion.

> **Note:** The auditor's report on internal control over financial reporting does not relieve management of its responsibility for assuring users of its financial reports about the effectiveness of internal control over financial reporting.

---

have been codified into the AICPA *Professional Standards*, Volume 1, as AU sections 100 through 900. References in this standard to AU sections refer to those generally accepted auditing standards, as adopted on an interim basis in PCAOB Rule 3200T.

4. See *Final Rule: Management's Reports on Internal Control Over Financial Reporting and Certification of Disclosure in Exchange Act Periodic Reports*, Securities and Exchange Commission Release No. 33-8238 (June 5, 2003) [68 FR 36636] for further discussion of reasonable assurance.

Management's Responsibilities in an Audit of Internal Control Over Financial Reporting

20. For the auditor to satisfactorily complete an audit of internal control over financial reporting, management must do the following:[5]

a. Accept responsibility for the effectiveness of the company's internal control over financial reporting;

b. Evaluate the effectiveness of the company's internal control over financial reporting using suitable control criteria;

c. Support its evaluation with sufficient evidence, including documentation; and

d. Present a written assessment of the effectiveness of the company's internal control over financial reporting as of the end of the company's most recent fiscal year.

21. If the auditor concludes that management has not fulfilled the responsibilities enumerated in the preceding paragraph, the auditor should communicate, in writing, to management and the audit committee that the audit of internal control over financial reporting cannot be satisfactorily completed and that he or she is required to disclaim an opinion. Paragraphs 40 through 46 provide information for the auditor about evaluating management's process for assessing internal control over financial reporting.

Materiality Considerations in an Audit of Internal Control Over Financial Reporting

22. The auditor should apply the concept of materiality in an audit of internal control over financial reporting at both the financial-statement level and at the individual account-balance level. The auditor uses materiality at the financial-statement level in evaluating whether a deficiency, or combination of deficiencies, in controls is a significant deficiency or a material weakness. Materiality at both the financial-statement level and the individual account-balance level is relevant to planning the audit and designing procedures. Materiality at the account-balance level is necessarily lower than materiality at the financial-statement level.

23. The same conceptual definition of materiality that applies to financial reporting applies to information on internal control over financial reporting, including the relevance of both quantitative and qualitative considerations.[6]

- The quantitative considerations are essentially the same as in an audit of financial statements and relate to whether misstatements that would not be prevented or detected by internal control over financial reporting, individually or collectively, have a quantitatively material effect on the financial statements.

- The qualitative considerations apply to evaluating materiality with respect to the financial statements and to additional factors that relate to the perceived needs of reasonable persons who will rely on the information. Paragraph 6 describes some qualitative considerations.

Fraud Considerations in an Audit of Internal Control Over Financial Reporting

24. The auditor should evaluate all controls specifically intended to address the risks of fraud that have at least a reasonably possible likelihood of having a material effect on the company's financial statements. These controls may be a part of any of the five components of internal control over financial reporting, as discussed in paragraph 49. Controls related to the

---

5. Management is required to fulfill these responsibilities. See Items 308(a) and (c) of Regulation S-B and S-K, 17 C.F.R. 228.308(a) and (c) and 229.308(a) and (c), respectively.

6. AU sec. 312, *Audit Risk and Materiality in Conducting an Audit,* provides additional explanation of materiality.

prevention and detection of fraud often have a pervasive effect on the risk of fraud. Such controls include, but are not limited to, the:

- Controls restraining misappropriation of company assets that could result in a material misstatement of the financial statements;

- Company's risk assessment processes;

- Code of ethics/conduct provisions, especially those related to conflicts of interest, related party transactions, illegal acts, and the monitoring of the code by management and the audit committee or board;

- Adequacy of the internal audit activity and whether the internal audit function reports directly to the audit committee, as well as the extent of the audit committee's involvement and interaction with internal audit; and

- Adequacy of the company's procedures for handling complaints and for accepting confidential submissions of concerns about questionable accounting or auditing matters.

25. Part of management's responsibility when designing a company's internal control over financial reporting is to design and implement programs and controls to prevent, deter, and detect fraud. Management, along with those who have responsibility for oversight of the financial reporting process (such as the audit committee), should set the proper tone; create and maintain a culture of honesty and high ethical standards; and establish appropriate controls to prevent, deter, and detect fraud. When management and those responsible for the oversight of the financial reporting process fulfill those responsibilities, the opportunities to commit fraud can be reduced significantly.

26. In an audit of internal control over financial reporting, the auditor's evaluation of controls is interrelated with the auditor's evaluation of controls in a financial statement audit, as required by AU sec. 316, *Consideration of Fraud in a Financial Statement Audit*. Often, controls identified and evaluated by the auditor during the audit of internal control over financial reporting also address or mitigate fraud risks, which the auditor is required to consider in a financial statement audit. If the auditor identifies deficiencies in controls designed to prevent and detect fraud during the audit of internal control over financial reporting, the auditor should alter the nature, timing, or extent of procedures to be performed during the financial statement audit to be responsive to such deficiencies, as provided in paragraphs .44 and .45 of AU sec. 316.

Performing an Audit of Internal Control Over Financial Reporting

27. In an audit of internal control over financial reporting, the auditor must obtain sufficient competent evidence about the design and operating effectiveness of controls over all relevant financial statement assertions related to all significant accounts and disclosures in the financial statements. The auditor must plan and perform the audit to obtain reasonable assurance that deficiencies that, individually or in the aggregate, would represent material weaknesses are identified. Thus, the audit is not designed to detect deficiencies in internal control over financial reporting that, individually or in the aggregate, are less severe than a material weakness. Because of the potential significance of the information obtained during the audit of the financial statements to the auditor's conclusions about the effectiveness of internal control over financial reporting, the auditor cannot audit internal control over financial reporting without also auditing the financial statements.

> **Note:** However, the auditor may audit the financial statements without also auditing internal control over financial reporting, for example, in the case of certain initial public

offerings by a company. See the discussion beginning at paragraph 145 for more information about the importance of auditing both internal control over financial reporting as well as the financial statements when the auditor is engaged to audit internal control over financial reporting.

28. The auditor must adhere to the general standards (See paragraphs 30 through 36) and fieldwork and reporting standards (See paragraph 37) in performing an audit of a company's internal control over financial reporting. This involves the following:

a. Planning the engagement;

b. Evaluating management's assessment process;

c. Obtaining an understanding of internal control over financial reporting;

d. Testing and evaluating design effectiveness of internal control over financial reporting;

e. Testing and evaluating operating effectiveness of internal control over financial reporting; and

f. Forming an opinion on the effectiveness of internal control over financial reporting.

29. Even though some requirements of this standard are set forth in a manner that suggests a sequential process, auditing internal control over financial reporting involves a process of gathering, updating, and analyzing information. Accordingly, the auditor may perform some of the procedures and evaluations described in this section on "Performing an Audit of Internal Control Over Financial Reporting" concurrently.

Applying General, Fieldwork, and Reporting Standards

30. The general standards (See AU sec. 150, *Generally Accepted Auditing Standards*) are applicable to an audit of internal control over financial reporting. These standards require technical training and proficiency as an auditor, independence in fact and appearance, and the exercise of due professional care, including professional skepticism.

31. *Technical Training and Proficiency.* To perform an audit of internal control over financial reporting, the auditor should have competence in the subject matter of internal control over financial reporting.

32. *Independence.* The applicable requirements of independence are largely predicated on four basic principles: (1) an auditor must not act as management or as an employee of the audit client, (2) an auditor must not audit his or her own work, (3) an auditor must not serve in a position of being an advocate for his or her client, and (4) an auditor must not have mutual or conflicting interests with his or her audit client.[7] If the auditor were to design or implement controls, that situation would place the auditor in a management role and result in the auditor auditing his or her own work. These requirements, however, do not preclude the auditor from making substantive recommendations as to how management may improve the design or operation of the company's internal controls as a by-product of an audit.

33. The auditor must not accept an engagement to provide internal control-related services to an issuer for which the auditor also audits the financial statements unless that engagement has been specifically pre-approved by the audit committee. For any internal control services the auditor provides, management must be actively involved and cannot delegate responsibility for these matters to the auditor. Management's involvement must be substantive and ex-

---

7. See the Preliminary Note of Rule 2-01 of Regulation S-X, 17 C.F.R. 210.2-01.

tensive. Management's acceptance of responsibility for documentation and testing performed by the auditor does not by itself satisfy the independence requirements.

34. Maintaining independence, in fact and appearance, requires careful attention, as is the case with all independence issues when work concerning internal control over financial reporting is performed. Unless the auditor and the audit committee are diligent in evaluating the nature and extent of services provided, the services might violate basic principles of independence and cause an impairment of independence in fact or appearance.

35. The independent auditor and the audit committee have significant and distinct responsibilities for evaluating whether the auditor's services impair independence in fact or appearance. The test for independence in fact is whether the activities would impede the ability of anyone on the engagement team or in a position to influence the engagement team from exercising objective judgment in the audits of the financial statements or internal control over financial reporting. The test for independence in appearance is whether a reasonable investor, knowing all relevant facts and circumstances, would perceive an auditor as having interests which could jeopardize the exercise of objective and impartial judgments on all issues encompassed within the auditor's engagement.

36. *Due Professional Care.* The auditor must exercise due professional care in an audit of internal control over financial reporting. One important tenet of due professional care is exercising professional skepticism. In an audit of internal control over financial reporting, exercising professional skepticism involves essentially the same considerations as in an audit of financial statements, that is, it includes a critical assessment of the work that management has performed in evaluating and testing controls.

37. *Fieldwork and Reporting Standards.* This standard establishes the fieldwork and reporting standards applicable to an audit of internal control over financial reporting.

38. The concept of materiality, as discussed in paragraphs 22 and 23, underlies the application of the general and fieldwork standards.

Planning the Engagement

39. The audit of internal control over financial reporting should be properly planned and assistants, if any, are to be properly supervised. When planning the audit of internal control over financial reporting, the auditor should evaluate how the following matters will affect the auditor's procedures:

- Knowledge of the company's internal control over financial reporting obtained during other engagements.
- Matters affecting the industry in which the company operates, such as financial reporting practices, economic conditions, laws and regulations, and technological changes.
- Matters relating to the company's business, including its organization, operating characteristics, capital structure, and distribution methods.
- The extent of recent changes, if any, in the company, its operations, or its internal control over financial reporting.
- Management's process for assessing the effectiveness of the company's internal control over financial reporting based upon control criteria.
- Preliminary judgments about materiality, risk, and other factors relating to the determination of material weaknesses.
- Control deficiencies previously communicated to the audit committee or management.

- Legal or regulatory matters of which the company is aware.

- The type and extent of available evidence related to the effectiveness of the company's internal control over financial reporting.

- Preliminary judgments about the effectiveness of internal control over financial reporting.

- The number of significant business locations or units, including management's documentation and monitoring of controls over such locations or business units. (Appendix B, paragraphs B1 through B17, discusses factors the auditor should evaluate to determine the locations at which to perform auditing procedures.)

Evaluating Management's Assessment Process

40. The auditor must obtain an understanding of, and evaluate, management's process for assessing the effectiveness of the company's internal control over financial reporting. When obtaining the understanding, the auditor should determine whether management has addressed the following elements:

- Determining which controls should be tested, including controls over all relevant assertions related to all significant accounts and disclosures in the financial statements. Generally, such controls include:

  —Controls over initiating, authorizing, recording, processing, and reporting significant accounts and disclosures and related assertions embodied in the financial statements.

  —Controls over the selection and application of accounting policies that are in conformity with generally accepted accounting principles.

  —Antifraud programs and controls.

  —Controls, including information technology general controls, on which other controls are dependent.

  —Controls over significant nonroutine and nonsystematic transactions, such as accounts involving judgments and estimates.

  —Company level controls (as described in paragraph 53), including:

    —The control environment and

    —Controls over the period-end financial reporting process, including controls over procedures used to enter transaction totals into the general ledger; to initiate, authorize, record, and process journal entries in the general ledger; and to record recurring and nonrecurring adjustments to the financial statements (for example, consolidating adjustments, report combinations, and reclassifications).

    Note: References to the period-end financial reporting process in this standard refer to the preparation of both annual and quarterly financial statements.

- Evaluating the likelihood that failure of the control could result in a misstatement, the magnitude of such a misstatement, and the degree to which other controls, if effective, achieve the same control objectives.

- Determining the locations or business units to include in the evaluation for a company with multiple locations or business units (See paragraphs B1 through B17).

- Evaluating the design effectiveness of controls.

- Evaluating the operating effectiveness of controls based on procedures sufficient to assess their operating effectiveness. Examples of such procedures include testing of the controls by internal audit, testing of controls by others under the direction of management, using a service organization's reports (See paragraphs B18 through B29), inspection of evidence of the application of controls, or testing by means of a selfassessment process, some of which might occur as part of management's ongoing monitoring activities. Inquiry alone is not adequate to complete this evaluation. To evaluate the effectiveness of the company's internal control over financial reporting, management must have evaluated controls over all relevant assertions related to all significant accounts and disclosures.

- Determining the deficiencies in internal control over financial reporting that are of such a magnitude and likelihood of occurrence that they constitute significant deficiencies or material weaknesses.

- Communicating findings to the auditor and to others, if applicable.

- Evaluating whether findings are reasonable and support management's assessment.

41. As part of the understanding and evaluation of management's process, the auditor should obtain an understanding of the results of procedures performed by others. Others include internal audit and third parties working under the direction of management, including other auditors and accounting professionals engaged to perform procedures as a basis for management's assessment. Inquiry of management and others is the beginning point for obtaining an understanding of internal control over financial reporting, but inquiry alone is not adequate for reaching a conclusion on any aspect of internal control over financial reporting effectiveness.

Note: Management cannot use the auditor's procedures as part of the basis for its assessment of the effectiveness of internal control over financial reporting.

42. *Management's Documentation.* When determining whether management's documentation provides reasonable support for its assessment, the auditor should evaluate whether such documentation includes the following:

- The design of controls over all relevant assertions related to all significant accounts and disclosures in the financial statements. The documentation should include the five components of internal control over financial reporting as discussed in paragraph 49, including the control environment and company-level controls as described in paragraph 53;

- Information about how significant transactions are initiated, authorized, recorded, processed and reported;

- Sufficient information about the flow of transactions to identify the points at which material misstatements due to error or fraud could occur;

- Controls designed to prevent or detect fraud, including who performs the controls and the related segregation of duties;

- Controls over the period-end financial reporting process;

- Controls over safeguarding of assets (See paragraphs C1 through C6); and

- The results of management's testing and evaluation.

43. Documentation might take many forms, such as paper, electronic files, or other media, and can include a variety of information, including policy manuals, process models, flowcharts, job descriptions, documents, and forms. The form and extent of documentation will vary depending on the size, nature, and complexity of the company.

44. Documentation of the design of controls over relevant assertions related to significant accounts and disclosures is evidence that controls related to management's assessment of the effectiveness of internal control over financial reporting, including changes to those controls, have been identified, are capable of being communicated to those responsible for their performance, and are capable of being monitored by the company. Such documentation also provides the foundation for appropriate communication concerning responsibilities for performing controls and for the company's evaluation of and monitoring of the effective operation of controls.

45. Inadequate documentation of the design of controls over relevant assertions related to significant accounts and disclosures is a deficiency in the company's internal control over financial reporting. As discussed in paragraph 138, the auditor should evaluate this documentation deficiency. The auditor might conclude that the deficiency is only a deficiency, or that the deficiency represents a significant deficiency or a material weakness. In evaluating the deficiency as to its significance, the auditor should determine whether management can demonstrate the monitoring component of internal control over financial reporting.

46. Inadequate documentation also could cause the auditor to conclude that there is a limitation on the scope of the engagement.

Obtaining an Understanding of Internal Control Over Financial Reporting

47. The auditor should obtain an understanding of the design of specific controls by applying procedures that include:

- Making inquiries of appropriate management, supervisory, and staff personnel;
- Inspecting company documents;
- Observing the application of specific controls; and
- Tracing transactions through the information system relevant to financial reporting.

48. The auditor could also apply additional procedures to obtain an understanding of the design of specific controls.

49. The auditor must obtain an understanding of the design of controls related to each component of internal control over financial reporting, as discussed below.

- *Control Environment.* Because of the pervasive effect of the control environment on the reliability of financial reporting, the auditor's preliminary judgment about its effectiveness often influences the nature, timing, and extent of the tests of operating effectiveness considered necessary. Weaknesses in the control environment should cause the auditor to alter the nature, timing, or extent of tests of operating effectiveness that otherwise should have been performed in the absence of the weaknesses.

- *Risk Assessment.* When obtaining an understanding of the company's risk assessment process, the auditor should evaluate whether management has identified the risks of material misstatement in the significant accounts and disclosures and related assertions of the financial statements and has implemented controls to prevent or detect errors or fraud that could result in material misstatements. For example, the risk assessment process should address how management considers the possibility of unrecorded transactions or identifies and analyzes significant estimates recorded in the financial statements. Risks relevant to reliable financial reporting also relate to specific events or transactions.

- *Control Activities.* The auditor's understanding of control activities relates to the controls that management has implemented to prevent or detect errors or fraud that could result in material misstatement in the accounts and disclosures and related assertions of the financial statements. For the purposes of evaluating the effectiveness of internal control over financial reporting, the auditor's understanding of control activities encompasses a broader range of accounts and disclosures than what is normally obtained for the financial statement audit.

- *Information and Communication.* The auditor's understanding of management's information and communication involves understanding the same systems and processes that he or she addresses in an audit of financial statements. In addition, this understanding includes a greater emphasis on comprehending the safeguarding controls and the processes for authorization of transactions and the maintenance of records, as well as the period-end financial reporting process (discussed further beginning at paragraph 76).

- *Monitoring.* The auditor's understanding of management's monitoring of controls extends to and includes its monitoring of all controls, including control activities, which management has identified and designed to prevent or detect material misstatement in the accounts and disclosures and related assertions of the financial statements.

50. Some controls (such as company-level controls, described in paragraph 53) might have a pervasive effect on the achievement of many overall objectives of the control criteria. For example, information technology general controls over program development, program changes, computer operations, and access to programs and data help ensure that specific controls over the processing of transactions are operating effectively. In contrast, other controls are designed to achieve specific objectives of the control criteria. For example, management generally establishes specific controls, such as accounting for all shipping documents, to ensure that all valid sales are recorded.

51. The auditor should focus on combinations of controls, in addition to specific controls in isolation, in assessing whether the objectives of the control criteria have been achieved. The absence or inadequacy of a specific control designed to achieve the objectives of a specific criterion might not be a deficiency if other controls specifically address the same criterion. Further, when one or more controls achieve the objectives of a specific criterion, the auditor might not need to evaluate other controls designed to achieve those same objectives.

52. *Identifying Company-Level Controls.* Controls that exist at the company-level often have a pervasive impact on controls at the process, transaction, or application level. For that reason, as a practical consideration, it may be appropriate for the auditor to test and evaluate the design effectiveness of company-level controls first, because the results of that work might affect the way the auditor evaluates the other aspects of internal control over financial reporting.

53. Company-level controls are controls such as the following:

- Controls within the control environment, including tone at the top, the assignment of authority and responsibility, consistent policies and procedures, and company-wide programs, such as codes of conduct and fraud prevention, that apply to all locations and business units (See paragraphs 113 through 115 for further discussion);

- Management's risk assessment process;
- Centralized processing and controls, including shared service environments;
- Controls to monitor results of operations;
- Controls to monitor other controls, including activities of the internal audit function, the audit committee, and self-assessment programs;
- The period-end financial reporting process; and
- Board-approved policies that address significant business control and risk management practices.

Note: The controls listed above are not intended to be a complete list of company-level controls nor is a company required to have all the controls in the list to support its assessment of effective company-level controls. However, ineffective company-level controls are a deficiency that will affect the scope of work performed, particularly when a company has multiple locations or business units, as described in Appendix B.

54. Testing company-level controls alone is not sufficient for the purpose of expressing an opinion on the effectiveness of a company's internal control over financial reporting.

55. *Evaluating the Effectiveness of the Audit Committee's Oversight of the Company's External Financial Reporting and Internal Control Over Financial Reporting.* The company's audit committee plays an important role within the control environment and monitoring components of internal control over financial reporting. Within the control environment, the existence of an effective audit committee helps to set a positive tone at the top. Within the monitoring component, an effective audit committee challenges the company's activities in the financial arena.

Note: Although the audit committee plays an important role within the control environment and monitoring components of internal control over financial reporting, management is responsible for maintaining effective internal control over financial reporting. This standard does not suggest that this responsibility has been transferred to the audit committee.

Note: If no such committee exists with respect to the company, all references to the audit committee in this standard apply to the entire board of directors of the company.[8] The auditor should be aware that companies whose securities are not listed on a national securities exchange or an automated inter-dealer quotation system of a national securities association (such as the New York Stock Exchange, American Stock Exchange, or NASDAQ) may not be required to have independent directors for their audit committees. In this case, the auditor should not consider the lack of independent directors at these companies indicative, by itself, of a control deficiency. Likewise, the independence requirements of Securities Exchange Act Rule 10A-3[9] are not applicable to the listing of non-equity securities of a consolidated or at least 50 percent beneficially owned subsidiary of a listed issuer that is subject to the requirements of Securities Exchange Act Rule 10A-3(c)(2).[10] Therefore, the auditor should interpret references to the audit committee in this standard, as applied to a subsidiary registrant, as being consistent with the provisions of Securities Exchange Act Rule 10A-3(c)(2).[11] Furthermore, for subsidiary regis-

8. See 15 U.S.C. 78c(a)58 and 15 U.S.C. 7201(a)(3).
9. See 17 C.F.R. 240.10A-3.
10. See 17 C.F.R. 240.10A-3(c)(2).
11. See 17 C.F.R. 240.10A-3(c)(2).

trants, communications required by this standard to be directed to the audit committee should be made to the same committee or equivalent body that pre-approves the retention of the auditor by or on behalf of the subsidiary registrant pursuant to Rule 2-01(c)(7) of Regulation S-X[12] (which might be, for example, the audit committee of the subsidiary registrant, the full board of the subsidiary registrant, or the audit committee of the subsidiary registrant's parent). In all cases, the auditor should interpret the terms "board of directors" and "audit committee" in this standard as being consistent with provisions for the use of those terms as defined in relevant SEC rules.

56. The company's board of directors is responsible for evaluating the performance and effectiveness of the audit committee; this standard does not suggest that the auditor is responsible for performing a separate and distinct evaluation of the audit committee. However, because of the role of the audit committee within the control environment and monitoring components of internal control over financial reporting, the auditor should assess the effectiveness of the audit committee as part of understanding and evaluating those components.

57. The aspects of the audit committee's effectiveness that are important may vary considerably with the circumstances. The auditor focuses on factors related to the effectiveness of the audit committee's oversight of the company's external financial reporting and internal control over financial reporting, such as the independence of the audit committee members from management and the clarity with which the audit committee's responsibilities are articulated (for example, in the audit committee's charter) and how well the audit committee and management understand those responsibilities. The auditor might also consider the audit committee's involvement and interaction with the independent auditor and with internal auditors, as well as interaction with key members of financial management, including the chief financial officer and chief accounting officer.

58. The auditor might also evaluate whether the right questions are raised and pursued with management and the auditor, including questions that indicate an understanding of the critical accounting policies and judgmental accounting estimates, and the responsiveness to issues raised by the auditor.

59. Ineffective oversight by the audit committee of the company's external financial reporting and internal control over financial reporting should be regarded as at least a significant deficiency and is a strong indicator that a material weakness in internal control over financial reporting exists.

60. *Identifying Significant Accounts.* The auditor should identify significant accounts and disclosures, first at the financial-statement level and then at the account or disclosure-component level. Determining specific controls to test begins by identifying significant accounts and disclosures within the financial statements. When identifying significant accounts, the auditor should evaluate both quantitative and qualitative factors.

61. An account is significant if there is more than a remote likelihood that the account could contain misstatements that individually, or when aggregated with others, could have a material effect on the financial statements, considering the risks of both overstatement and understatement. Other accounts may be significant on a qualitative basis based on the expectations of a reasonable user. For example, investors might be interested in a particular financial statement account even though it is not quantitatively large because it represents an important performance measure.

---

12. See 17 C.F.R. 210.2-01(c)(7).

Note: For purposes of determining significant accounts, the assessment as to likelihood should be made without giving any consideration to the effectiveness of internal control over financial reporting.

62. Components of an account balance subject to differing risks (inherent and control) or different controls should be considered separately as potential significant accounts. For instance, inventory accounts often consist of raw materials (purchasing process), work in process (manufacturing process), finished goods (distribution process), and an allowance for obsolescence.

63. In some cases, separate components of an account might be a significant account because of the company's organizational structure. For example, for a company that has a number of separate business units, each with different management and accounting processes, the accounts at each separate business unit are considered individually as potential significant accounts.

64. An account also may be considered significant because of the exposure to unrecognized obligations represented by the account. For example, loss reserves related to a self-insurance program or unrecorded contractual obligations at a construction contracting subsidiary may have historically been insignificant in amount, yet might represent a more than remote likelihood of material misstatement due to the existence of material unrecorded claims.

65. When deciding whether an account is significant, it is important for the auditor to evaluate both quantitative and qualitative factors, including the:

- Size and composition of the account;
- Susceptibility of loss due to errors or fraud;
- Volume of activity, complexity, and homogeneity of the individual transactions processed through the account;
- Nature of the account (for example, suspense accounts generally warrant greater attention);
- Accounting and reporting complexities associated with the account;
- Exposure to losses represented by the account (for example, loss accruals related to a consolidated construction contracting subsidiary);
- Likelihood (or possibility) of significant contingent liabilities arising from the activities represented by the account;
- Existence of related party transactions in the account; and
- Changes from the prior period in account characteristics (for example, new complexities or subjectivity or new types of transactions).

66. For example, in a financial statement audit, the auditor might not consider the fixed asset accounts significant when there is a low volume of transactions and when inherent risk is assessed as low, even though the balances are material to the financial statements. Accordingly, he or she might decide to perform only substantive procedures on such balances. In an audit of internal control over financial reporting, however, such accounts are significant accounts because of their materiality to the financial statements.

67. As another example, the auditor of the financial statements of a financial institution might not consider trust accounts significant to the institution's financial statements because such accounts are not included in the institution's balance sheet and the associated fee income generated by trust activities is not material. However, in determining whether trust accounts are a significant account for purposes of the audit of internal control over financial reporting, the auditor should assess whether the activities of the trust department are significant to the institution's financial reporting, which also would include considering the contingent liabilities that could arise if a trust department failed to fulfill its fiduciary responsibilities (for example, if investments were made that were not in accordance with stated investment policies). When assessing the significance of possible contingent liabilities, consideration of the amount of assets under the trust department's control may be useful. For this reason, an auditor who has not considered trust accounts significant accounts for purposes of the financial statement audit might determine that they are significant for purposes of the audit of internal control over financial reporting.

68. Identifying Relevant Financial Statement Assertions. For each significant account, the auditor should determine the relevance of each of these financial statement assertions:[13]

- Existence or occurrence;
- Completeness;
- Valuation or allocation;
- Rights and obligations; and
- Presentation and disclosure.

69. To identify relevant assertions, the auditor should determine the source of likely potential misstatements in each significant account. In determining whether a particular assertion is relevant to a significant account balance or disclosure, the auditor should evaluate:

- The nature of the assertion;
- The volume of transactions or data related to the assertion; and
- The nature and complexity of the systems, including the use of information technology by which the company processes and controls information supporting the assertion.

70. *Relevant assertions* are assertions that have a meaningful bearing on whether the account is fairly stated. For example, valuation may not be relevant to the cash account unless currency translation is involved; however, existence and completeness are always relevant. Similarly, valuation may not be relevant to the gross amount of the accounts receivable balance, but is relevant to the related allowance accounts. Additionally, the auditor might, in some circumstances, focus on the presentation and disclosure assertion separately in connection with the period-end financial reporting process.

71. *Identifying Significant Processes and Major Classes of Transactions.* The auditor should identify each significant process over each major class of transactions affecting significant accounts or groups of accounts. Major classes of transactions are those classes of transactions that are significant to the company's financial statements. For example, at a company whose sales may be initiated by customers through personal contact in a retail store or electronically through use of the internet, these types of sales would be two major classes of transactions within the sales process if they were both significant to the company's financial statements. As another example, at a company for which fixed assets is a significant account, recording depreciation expense would be a major class of transactions.

72. Different types of major classes of transactions have different levels of inherent risk associated with them and require different levels of management supervision and involvement.

---

13. See AU sec. 326, *Evidential Matter,* which provides additional information on financial statement assertions.

For this reason, the auditor might further categorize the identified major classes of transactions by transaction type: routine, nonroutine, and estimation.

- Routine transactions are recurring financial activities reflected in the accounting records in the normal course of business (for example, sales, purchases, cash receipts, cash disbursements, payroll).

- Nonroutine transactions are activities that occur only periodically (for example, taking physical inventory, calculating depreciation expense, adjusting for foreign currencies). A distinguishing feature of nonroutine transactions is that data involved are generally not part of the routine flow of transactions.

- Estimation transactions are activities that involve management judgments or assumptions in formulating account balances in the absence of a precise means of measurement (for example, determining the allowance for doubtful accounts, establishing warranty reserves, assessing assets for impairment).

73. Most processes involve a series of tasks such as capturing input data, sorting and merging data, making calculations, updating transactions and master files, generating transactions, and summarizing and displaying or reporting data. The processing procedures relevant for the auditor to understand the flow of transactions generally are those activities required to initiate, authorize, record, process and report transactions. Such activities include, for example, initially recording sales orders, preparing shipping documents and invoices, and updating the accounts receivable master file. The relevant processing procedures also include procedures for correcting and reprocessing previously rejected transactions and for correcting erroneous transactions through adjusting journal entries.

74. For each significant process, the auditor should:

- Understand the flow of transactions, including how transactions are initiated, authorized, recorded, processed, and reported.

- Identify the points within the process at which a misstatement — including a misstatement due to fraud — related to each relevant financial statement assertion could arise.

- Identify the controls that management has implemented to address these potential misstatements.

- Identify the controls that management has implemented over the prevention or timely detection of unauthorized acquisition, use, or disposition of the company's assets.

Note: The auditor frequently obtains the understanding and identifies the controls described above as part of his or her performance of walkthroughs (as described beginning in paragraph 79).

75. The nature and characteristics of a company's use of information technology in its information system affect the company's internal control over financial reporting. AU sec. 319, *Consideration of Internal Control in a Financial Statement Audit,* paragraphs .16 through .20, .30 through .32, and .77 through .79, discuss the effect of information technology on internal control over financial reporting.

76. *Understanding the Period-end Financial Reporting Process.* The period-end financial reporting process includes the following:

- The procedures used to enter transaction totals into the general ledger;

- The procedures used to initiate, authorize, record, and process journal entries in the general ledger;

- Other procedures used to record recurring and nonrecurring adjustments to the annual and quarterly financial statements, such as consolidating adjustments, report combinations, and classifications; and

- Procedures for drafting annual and quarterly financial statements and related disclosures.

77. As part of understanding and evaluating the period-end financial reporting process, the auditor should evaluate:

- The inputs, procedures performed, and outputs of the processes the company uses to produce its annual and quarterly financial statements;

- The extent of information technology involvement in each period-end financial reporting process element;

- Who participates from management;

- The number of locations involved;

- Types of adjusting entries (for example, standard, nonstandard, eliminating, and consolidating); and

- The nature and extent of the oversight of the process by appropriate parties, including management, the board of directors, and the audit committee.

78. The period-end financial reporting process is always a significant process because of its importance to financial reporting and to the auditor's opinions on internal control over financial reporting and the financial statements. The auditor's understanding of the company's period-end financial reporting process and how it interrelates with the company's other significant processes assists the auditor in identifying and testing controls that are the most relevant to financial statement risks.

79. *Performing Walkthroughs.* The auditor should perform at least one walkthrough for each major class of transactions (as identified in paragraph 71). In a walkthrough, the auditor traces a transaction from origination through the company's information systems until it is reflected in the company's financial reports. Walkthroughs provide the auditor with evidence to:

- Confirm the auditor's understanding of the process flow of transactions;

- Confirm the auditor's understanding of the design of controls identified for all five components of internal control over financial reporting, including those related to the prevention or detection of fraud;

- Confirm that the auditor's understanding of the process is complete by determining whether all points in the process at which misstatements related to each relevant financial statement assertion that could occur have been identified;

- Evaluate the effectiveness of the design of controls; and

- Confirm whether controls have been placed in operation.

Note: The auditor can often gain an understanding of the transaction flow, identify and understand controls, and conduct the walkthrough simultaneously.

80. The auditor's walkthroughs should encompass the entire process of initiating, authorizing, recording, processing, and reporting individual transactions and controls for each of the significant processes identified, including controls intended to address the risk of fraud. During the walkthrough, at each point at which important processing procedures or controls occur, the auditor should question the company's personnel about their understanding of what is required by the company's prescribed procedures and controls and determine whether the processing procedures are performed as originally understood and on a timely basis. (Controls might not be performed regularly but still be timely.) During the walkthrough, the auditor should be alert for exceptions to the company's prescribed procedures and controls.

81. While performing a walkthrough, the auditor should evaluate the quality of the evidence obtained and perform walkthrough procedures that produce a level of evidence consistent with the objectives listed in paragraph 79. Rather than reviewing copies of documents and making inquiries of a single person at the company, the auditor should follow the process flow of actual transactions using the same documents and information technology that company personnel use and make inquiries of relevant personnel involved in significant aspects of the process or controls. To corroborate information at various points in the walkthrough, the auditor might ask personnel to describe their understanding of the previous and succeeding processing or control activities and to demonstrate what they do. In addition, inquiries should include followup questions that could help identify the abuse of controls or indicators of fraud. Examples of follow-up inquiries include asking personnel:

- What they do when they find an error or what they are looking for to determine if there is an error (rather than simply asking them if they perform listed procedures and controls); what kind of errors they have found; what happened as a result of finding the errors, and how the errors were resolved. If the person being interviewed has never found an error, the auditor should evaluate whether that situation is due to good preventive controls or whether the individual performing the control lacks the necessary skills.

- Whether they have ever been asked to override the process or controls, and if so, to describe the situation, why it occurred, and what happened.

82. During the period under audit, when there have been significant changes in the process flow of transactions, including the supporting computer applications, the auditor should evaluate the nature of the change(s) and the effect on related accounts to determine whether to walk through transactions that were processed both before and after the change.

> **Note:** Unless significant changes in the process flow of transactions, including the supporting computer applications, make it more efficient for the auditor to prepare new documentation of a walkthrough, the auditor may carry his or her documentation forward each year, after updating it for any changes that have taken place.

83. *Identifying Controls to Test.* The auditor should obtain evidence about the effectiveness of controls (either by performing tests of controls himself or herself, or by using the work of others)[14] for all relevant assertions related to all significant accounts and disclosures in the financial statements. After identifying significant accounts, relevant assertions, and significant processes, the auditor should evaluate the following to identify the controls to be tested:

- Points at which errors or fraud could occur;

---

14. See paragraphs 108 through 126 for additional direction on using the work of others.

- The nature of the controls implemented by management;

- The significance of each control in achieving the objectives of the control criteria and whether more than one control achieves a particular objective or whether more than one control is necessary to achieve a particular objective; and

- The risk that the controls might not be operating effectively. Factors that affect whether the control might not be operating effectively include the following:

  —Whether there have been changes in the volume or nature of transactions that might adversely affect control design or operating effectiveness;

  —Whether there have been changes in the design of controls;

  —The degree to which the control relies on the effectiveness of other controls (for example, the control environment or information technology general controls);

  —Whether there have been changes in key personnel who perform the control or monitor its performance;

  —Whether the control relies on performance by an individual or is automated; and

  —The complexity of the control.

84. The auditor should clearly link individual controls with the significant accounts and assertions to which they relate.

85. The auditor should evaluate whether to test preventive controls, detective controls, or a combination of both for individual relevant assertions related to individual significant accounts. For instance, when performing tests of preventive and detective controls, the auditor might conclude that a deficient preventive control could be compensated for by an effective detective control and, therefore, not result in a significant deficiency or material weakness. For example, a monthly reconciliation control procedure, which is a detective control, might detect an out-of-balance situation resulting from an unauthorized transaction being initiated due to an ineffective authorization procedure, which is a preventive control. When determining whether the detective control is effective, the auditor should evaluate whether the detective control is sufficient to achieve the control objective to which the preventive control relates.

> **Note:** Because effective internal control over financial reporting often includes a combination of preventive and detective controls, the auditor ordinarily will test a combination of both.

86. The auditor should apply tests of controls to those controls that are important to achieving each control objective. It is neither necessary to test all controls nor is it necessary to test redundant controls (that is, controls that duplicate other controls that achieve the same objective and already have been tested), unless redundancy is itself a control objective, as in the case of certain computer controls.

87. Appendix B, paragraphs B1 through B17, provide additional direction to the auditor in determining which controls to test when a company has multiple locations or business units. In these circumstances, the auditor should determine significant accounts and their relevant assertions, significant processes, and major classes of transactions based on those that are relevant and significant to the consolidated financial statements. Having made those determinations in relation to the consolidated financial statements, the auditor should then apply the directions in Appendix B.

Testing and Evaluating Design Effectiveness

88. Internal control over financial reporting is effectively designed when the controls complied with would be expected to prevent or detect errors or fraud that could result in material misstatements in the financial statements. The auditor should determine whether the company has controls to meet the objectives of the control criteria by:

- Identifying the company's control objectives in each area;
- Identifying the controls that satisfy each objective; and
- Determining whether the controls, if operating properly, can effectively prevent or detect errors or fraud that could result in material misstatements in the financial statements.

89. Procedures the auditor performs to test and evaluate design effectiveness include inquiry, observation, walkthroughs, inspection of relevant documentation, and a specific evaluation of whether the controls are likely to prevent or detect errors or fraud that could result in misstatements if they are operated as prescribed by appropriately qualified persons.

90. The procedures that the auditor performs in evaluating management's assessment process and obtaining an understanding of internal control over financial reporting also provide the auditor with evidence about the design effectiveness of internal control over financial reporting.

91. The procedures the auditor performs to test and evaluate design effectiveness also might provide evidence about operating effectiveness.

Testing and Evaluating Operating Effectiveness

92. An auditor should evaluate the operating effectiveness of a control by determining whether the control is operating as designed and whether the person performing the control possesses the necessary authority and qualifications to perform the control effectively.

93. *Nature of Tests of Controls.* Tests of controls over operating effectiveness should include a mix of inquiries of appropriate personnel, inspection of relevant documentation, observation of the company's operations, and reperformance of the application of the control. For example, the auditor might observe the procedures for opening the mail and processing cash receipts to test the operating effectiveness of controls over cash receipts. Because an observation is pertinent only at the point in time at which it is made, the auditor should supplement the observation with inquiries of company personnel and inspection of documentation about the operation of such controls at other times. These inquiries might be made concurrently with performing walkthroughs.

94. Inquiry is a procedure that consists of seeking information, both financial and nonfinancial, of knowledgeable persons throughout the company. Inquiry is used extensively throughout the audit and often is complementary to performing other procedures. Inquiries may range from formal written inquiries to informal oral inquiries.

95. Evaluating responses to inquiries is an integral part of the inquiry procedure. Examples of information that inquiries might provide include the skill and competency of those performing the control, the relative sensitivity of the control to prevent or detect errors or fraud, and the frequency with which the control operates to prevent or detect errors or fraud. Responses to inquiries might provide the auditor with information not previously possessed or with corroborative evidence. Alternatively, responses might provide information that differs significantly from other information the auditor obtains (for example, information regarding the possibility of management override of controls). In some cases, responses to inquiries provide a basis for the auditor to modify or perform additional procedures.

96. Because inquiry alone does not provide sufficient evidence to support the operating effectiveness of a control, the auditor should perform additional tests of controls. For example, if the company implements a control activity whereby its sales manager reviews and investigates a report of invoices with unusually high or low gross margins, inquiry of the sales manager as to whether he or she investigates discrepancies would be inadequate. To obtain sufficient evidence about the operating effectiveness of the control, the auditor should corroborate the sales manager's responses by performing other procedures, such as inspecting reports or other documentation used in or generated by the performance of the control, and evaluate whether appropriate actions were taken regarding discrepancies.

97. The nature of the control also influences the nature of the tests of controls the auditor can perform. For example, the auditor might examine documents regarding controls for which documentary evidence exists. However, documentary evidence regarding some aspects of the control environment, such as management's philosophy and operating style, might not exist. In circumstances in which documentary evidence of controls or the performance of controls does not exist and is not expected to exist, the auditor's tests of controls would consist of inquiries of appropriate personnel and observation of company activities. As another example, a signature on a voucher package to indicate that the signer approved it does not necessarily mean that the person carefully reviewed the package before signing. The package may have been signed based on only a cursory review (or without any review). As a result, the quality of the evidence regarding the effective operation of the control might not be sufficiently persuasive. If that is the case, the auditor should reperform the control (for example, checking prices, extensions, and additions) as part of the test of the control. In addition, the auditor might inquire of the person responsible for approving voucher packages what he or she looks for when approving packages and how many errors have been found within voucher packages. The auditor also might inquire of supervisors whether they have any knowledge of errors that the person responsible for approving the voucher packages failed to detect.

98. *Timing of Tests of Controls.* The auditor must perform tests of controls over a period of time that is adequate to determine whether, as of the date specified in management's report, the controls necessary for achieving the objectives of the control criteria are operating effectively. The period of time over which the auditor performs tests of controls varies with the nature of the controls being tested and with the frequency with which specific controls operate and specific policies are applied. Some controls operate continuously (for example, controls over sales), while others operate only at certain times (for example, controls over the preparation of monthly or quarterly financial statements and controls over physical inventory counts).

99. The auditor's testing of the operating effectiveness of such controls should occur at the time the controls are operating. Controls "as of" a specific date encompass controls that are relevant to the company's internal control over financial reporting "as of" that specific date, even though such controls might not operate until after that specific date. For example, some controls over the period-end financial reporting process normally operate only after the "as of" date. Therefore, if controls over the December 31, 20X4 period-end financial reporting process operate in January 20X5, the auditor should test the control operating in January 20X5 to have sufficient evidence of operating effectiveness "as of" December 31, 20X4.

100. When the auditor reports on the effectiveness of controls "as of" a specific date and obtains evidence about the operating effectiveness of controls at an interim date, he or she should determine what additional evidence to obtain concerning the operation of the control for the remaining period. In making that determination, the auditor should evaluate:

- The specific controls tested prior to the "as of" date and the results of those tests;
- The degree to which evidence about the operating effectiveness of those controls was obtained;
- The length of the remaining period; and
- The possibility that there have been any significant changes in internal control over financial reporting subsequent to the interim date.

101. For controls over significant nonroutine transactions, controls over accounts or processes with a high degree of subjectivity or judgment in measurement, or controls over the recording of period-end adjustments, the auditor should perform tests of controls closer to or at the "as of" date rather than at an interim date. However, the auditor should balance performing the tests of controls closer to the "as of" date with the need to obtain sufficient evidence of operating effectiveness.

102. Prior to the date specified in management's report, management might implement changes to the company's controls to make them more effective or efficient or to address control deficiencies. In that case, the auditor might not need to evaluate controls that have been superseded. For example, if the auditor determines that the new controls achieve the related objectives of the control criteria and have been in effect for a sufficient period to permit the auditor to assess their design and operating effectiveness by performing tests of controls,[15] he or she will not need to evaluate the design and operating effectiveness of the superseded controls for purposes of expressing an opinion on internal control over financial reporting.

103. As discussed in paragraph 207, however, the auditor must communicate all identified significant deficiencies and material weaknesses in controls to the audit committee in writing. In addition, the auditor should evaluate how the design and operating effectiveness of the superseded controls relates to the auditor's reliance on controls for financial statement audit purposes.

104. *Extent of Tests of Controls.* Each year the auditor must obtain sufficient evidence about whether the company's internal control over financial reporting, including the controls for all internal control components, is operating effectively. This means that each year the auditor must obtain evidence about the effectiveness of controls for all relevant assertions related to all significant accounts and disclosures in the financial statements. The auditor also should vary from year to year the nature, timing, and extent of testing of controls to introduce unpredictability into the testing and respond to changes in circumstances. For example, each year the auditor might test the controls at a different interim period; increase or reduce the number and types of tests performed; or change the combination of procedures used.

105. In determining the extent of procedures to perform, the auditor should design the procedures to provide a high level of assurance that the control being tested is operating effectively. In making this determination, the auditor should assess the following factors:

- *Nature of the control.* The auditor should subject manual controls to more extensive testing than automated controls. In some circumstances, testing a single operation of

---

15. Paragraph 179 provides reporting directions in these circumstances when the auditor has not been able to obtain evidence that the new controls were appropriately designed or have been operating effectively for a sufficient period of time.

---

an automated control may be sufficient to obtain a high level of assurance that the control operated effectively, provided that information technology general controls also are operating effectively. For manual controls, sufficient evidence about the operating effectiveness of the controls is obtained by evaluating multiple operations of the control and the results of each operation. The auditor also should assess the complexity of the controls, the significance of the judgments that must be made in connection with their operation, and the level of competence of the person performing the controls that is necessary for the control to operate effectively. As the complexity and level of judgment increase or the level of competence of the person performing the control decreases, the extent of the auditor's testing should increase.

- *Frequency of operation.* Generally, the more frequently a manual control operates, the more operations of the control the auditor should test. For example, for a manual control that operates in connection with each transaction, the auditor should test multiple operations of the control over a sufficient period of time to obtain a high level of assurance that the control operated effectively. For controls that operate less frequently, such as monthly account reconciliations and controls over the period-end financial reporting process, the auditor may test significantly fewer operations of the control. However, the auditor's evaluation of each operation of controls operating less frequently is likely to be more extensive. For example, when evaluating the operation of a monthly exception report, the auditor should evaluate whether the judgments made with regard to the disposition of the exceptions were appropriate and adequately supported.

Note: When sampling is appropriate and the population of controls to be tested is large, increasing the population size does not proportionately increase the required sample size.

- *Importance of the control.* Controls that are relatively more important should be tested more extensively. For example, some controls may address multiple financial statement assertions, and certain period-end detective controls might be considered more important than related preventive controls. The auditor should test more operations of such controls or, if such controls operate infrequently, the auditor should evaluate each operation of the control more extensively.

106. *Use of Professional Skepticism when Evaluating the Results of Testing.* The auditor must conduct the audit of internal control over financial reporting and the audit of the financial statements with professional skepticism, which is an attitude that includes a questioning mind and a critical assessment of audit evidence. For example, even though a control is performed by the same employee whom the auditor believes performed the control effectively in prior periods, the control may not be operating effectively during the current period because the employee could have become complacent, distracted, or otherwise not be effectively carrying out his or her responsibilities. Also, regardless of any past experience with the entity or the auditor's beliefs about management's honesty and integrity, the auditor should recognize the possibility that a material misstatement due to fraud could be present. Furthermore, professional skepticism requires the auditor to consider whether evidence obtained suggests that a material misstatement due to fraud has occurred. In exercising professional skepticism in gathering and evaluating evidence, the auditor must not be satisfied with less-than-persuasive evidence because of a belief that management is honest.

107. When the auditor identifies exceptions to the company's prescribed control procedures, he or she should determine, using professional skepticism, the effect of the exception on the nature and extent of additional testing that may be appropriate or necessary and on the operating effectiveness of the control being tested. A conclusion that an identified exception does not represent a control deficiency is appropriate only if evidence beyond what the auditor had initially planned and beyond inquiry supports that conclusion.

Using the Work of Others

108. In all audits of internal control over financial reporting, the auditor must perform enough of the testing himself or herself so that the auditor's own work provides the principal evidence for the auditor's opinion. The auditor may, however, use the work of others to alter the nature, timing, or extent of the work he or she otherwise would have performed. For these purposes, the work of others includes relevant work performed by internal auditors, company personnel (in addition to internal auditors), and third parties working under the direction of management or the audit committee that provides information about the effectiveness of internal control over financial reporting.

> **Note:** Because the amount of work related to obtaining sufficient evidence to support an opinion about the effectiveness of controls is not susceptible to precise measurement, the auditor's judgment about whether he or she has obtained the principal evidence for the opinion will be qualitative as well as quantitative. For example, the auditor might give more weight to work he or she performed on pervasive controls and in areas such as the control environment than on other controls, such as controls over low-risk, routine transactions.

109. The auditor should evaluate whether to use the work performed by others in the audit of internal control over financial reporting. To determine the extent to which the auditor may use the work of others to alter the nature, timing, or extent of the work the auditor would have otherwise performed, in addition to obtaining the principal evidence for his or her opinion, the auditor should:

> a. Evaluate the nature of the controls subjected to the work of others (See paragraphs 112 through 116);
>
> b. Evaluate the competence and objectivity of the individuals who performed the work (See paragraphs 117 through 122); and
>
> c. Test some of the work performed by others to evaluate the quality and effectiveness of their work (See paragraphs 123 through 125).

> **Note:** AU sec. 322, *The Auditor's Consideration of the Internal Audit Function in an Audit of Financial Statements,* applies to using the work of internal auditors in an audit of the financial statements. The auditor may apply the relevant concepts described in that section to using the work of others in the audit of internal control over financial reporting.

110. The auditor must obtain sufficient evidence to support his or her opinion. Judgments about the sufficiency of evidence obtained and other factors affecting the auditor's opinion, such as the significance of identified control deficiencies, should be those of the auditor. Evidence obtained through the auditor's direct personal knowledge, observation, reperformance, and inspection is generally more persuasive than information obtained indirectly from others, such as from internal auditors, other company personnel, or third parties working under the direction of management.

111. The requirement that the auditor's own work must provide the principal evidence for the auditor's opinion is one of the boundaries within which the auditor determines the work he or she must perform himself or herself in the audit of internal control over financial reporting. Paragraphs 112 through 125 provide more specific and definitive direction on how the auditor makes this determination, but the directions allow the auditor significant flexibility to use his or her judgment to determine the work necessary to obtain the principal evidence and to determine when the auditor can use the work of others rather than perform the work himself or herself. Regardless of the auditor's determination of the work that he or she must perform himself or herself, the auditor's responsibility to report on the effectiveness of internal control over financial reporting rests solely with the auditor; this responsibility cannot be shared with the other individuals whose work the auditor uses. Therefore, when the auditor uses the work of others, the auditor is responsible for the results of their work.

112. *Evaluating the Nature of the Controls Subjected to the Work of Others.* The auditor should evaluate the following factors when evaluating the nature of the controls subjected to the work of others. As these factors increase in significance, the need for the auditor to perform his or her own work on those controls increases. As these factors decrease in significance, the need for the auditor to perform his or her own work on those controls decreases.

- The materiality of the accounts and disclosures that the control addresses and the risk of material misstatement.
- The degree of judgment required to evaluate the operating effectiveness of the control (that is, the degree to which the evaluation of the effectiveness of the control requires evaluation of subjective factors rather than objective testing).
- The pervasiveness of the control.
- The level of judgment or estimation required in the account or disclosure.
- The potential for management override of the control.

113. Because of the nature of the controls in the control environment, the auditor should not use the work of others to reduce the amount of work he or she performs on controls in the control environment. The auditor should, however, consider the results of work performed in this area by others because it might indicate the need for the auditor to increase his or her work.

114. The control environment encompasses the following factors:[16]

- Integrity and ethical values;
- Commitment to competence;
- Board of directors or audit committee participation;
- Management's philosophy and operating style;
- Organizational structure;
- Assignment of authority and responsibility; and
- Human resource policies and procedures.

115. Controls that are part of the control environment include, but are not limited to, controls specifically established to prevent and detect fraud that is at least reasonably possible to result in material misstatement of the financial statements.

---

16. See the COSO report and paragraph .110 of AU sec. 319, *Internal Control in a Financial Statement Audit,* for additional information about the factors included in the control environment.

Note: The term "reasonably possible" has the same meaning as in FAS No. 5. See the first note to paragraph 9 for further discussion.

116. The auditor should perform the walkthroughs (as discussed beginning at paragraph 79) himself or herself because of the degree of judgment required in performing this work. However, to provide additional evidence, the auditor may also review the work of others who have performed and documented walkthroughs. In evaluating whether his or her own evidence provides the principal evidence, the auditor's work on the control environment and in performing walkthroughs constitutes an important part of the auditor's own work.

117. *Evaluating the Competence and Objectivity of Others.* The extent to which the auditor may use the work of others depends on the degree of competence and objectivity of the individuals performing the work. The higher the degree of competence and objectivity, the greater use the auditor may make of the work; conversely, the lower the degree of competence and objectivity, the less use the auditor may make of the work. Further, the auditor should not use the work of individuals who have a low degree of objectivity, regardless of their level of competence. Likewise, the auditor should not use the work of individuals who have a low level of competence regardless of their degree of objectivity.

118. When evaluating the competence and objectivity of the individuals performing the tests of controls, the auditor should obtain, or update information from prior years, about the factors indicated in the following paragraph. The auditor should determine whether to test the existence and quality of those factors and, if so, the extent to which to test the existence and quality of those factors, based on the intended effect of the work of others on the audit of internal control over financial reporting.

119. Factors concerning the competence of the individuals performing the tests of controls include:

- Their educational level and professional experience.
- Their professional certification and continuing education.
- Practices regarding the assignment of individuals to work areas.
- Supervision and review of their activities.
- Quality of the documentation of their work, including any reports or recommendations issued.
- Evaluation of their performance.

120. Factors concerning the objectivity of the individuals performing the tests of controls include:

- The organizational status of the individuals responsible for the work of others ("testing authority") in testing controls, including —

  a. Whether the testing authority reports to an officer of sufficient status to ensure sufficient testing coverage and adequate consideration of, and action on, the findings and recommendations of the individuals performing the testing.

  b. Whether the testing authority has direct access and reports regularly to the board of directors or the audit committee.

  c. Whether the board of directors or the audit committee oversees employment decisions related to the testing authority.

- Policies to maintain the individuals' objectivity about the areas being tested, including—

  a. Policies prohibiting individuals from testing controls in areas in which relatives are employed in important or internal controlsensitive positions.

  b. Policies prohibiting individuals from testing controls in areas to which they were recently assigned or are scheduled to be assigned upon completion of their controls testing responsibilities.

121. Internal auditors normally are expected to have greater competence with regard to internal control over financial reporting and objectivity than other company personnel. Therefore, the auditor may be able to use their work to a greater extent than the work of other company personnel. This is particularly true in the case of internal auditors who follow the *International Standards for the Professional Practice of Internal Auditing* issued by the Institute of Internal Auditors. If internal auditors have performed an extensive amount of relevant work and the auditor determines they possess a high degree of competence and objectivity, the auditor could use their work to the greatest extent an auditor could use the work of others. On the other hand, if the internal audit function reports solely to management, which would reduce internal auditors' objectivity, or if limited resources allocated to the internal audit function result in very limited testing procedures on its part or reduced competency of the internal auditors, the auditor should use their work to a much lesser extent and perform more of the testing himself or herself.

122. When determining how the work of others will alter the nature, timing, or extent of the auditor's work, the auditor should assess the interrelationship of the nature of the controls, as discussed in paragraph 112, and the competence and objectivity of those who performed the work, as discussed in paragraphs 117 through 121. As the significance of the factors listed in paragraph 112 increases, the ability of the auditor to use the work of others decreases at the same time that the necessary level of competence and objectivity of those who perform the work increases. For example, for some pervasive controls, the auditor may determine that using the work of internal auditors to a limited degree would be appropriate and that using the work of other company personnel would not be appropriate because other company personnel do not have a high enough degree of objectivity as it relates to the nature of the controls.

123. *Testing the Work of Others.* The auditor should test some of the work of others to evaluate the quality and effectiveness of the work. The auditor's tests of the work of others may be accomplished by either (a) testing some of the controls that others tested or (b) testing similar controls not actually tested by others.

124. The nature and extent of these tests depend on the effect of the work of others on the auditor's procedures but should be sufficient to enable the auditor to make an evaluation of the overall quality and effectiveness of the work the auditor is considering. The auditor also should assess whether this evaluation has an effect on his or her conclusions about the competence and objectivity of the individuals performing the work.

125. In evaluating the quality and effectiveness of the work of others, the auditor should evaluate such factors as to whether the:

- Scope of work is appropriate to meet the objectives.
- Work programs are adequate.
- Work performed is adequately documented, including evidence of supervision and review.

- Conclusions are appropriate in the circumstances.

- Reports are consistent with the results of the work performed.

126. The following examples illustrate how to apply the directions discussed in this section:

- *Controls over the period-end financial reporting process.* Many of the controls over the period-end financial reporting process address significant risks of misstatement of the accounts and disclosures in the annual and quarterly financial statements, may require significant judgment to evaluate their operating effectiveness, may have a higher potential for management override, and may affect accounts that require a high level of judgment or estimation. Therefore, the auditor could determine that, based on the nature of controls over the period-end financial reporting process, he or she would need to perform more of the tests of those controls himself or herself. Further, because of the nature of the controls, the auditor should use the work of others only if the degree of competence and objectivity of the individuals performing the work is high; therefore, the auditor might use the work of internal auditors to some extent but not the work of others within the company.

- *Information technology general controls.* Information technology general controls are part of the control activities component of internal control; therefore, the nature of the controls might permit the auditor to use the work of others. For example, program change controls over routine maintenance changes may have a highly pervasive effect, yet involve a low degree of judgment in evaluating their operating effectiveness, can be subjected to objective testing, and have a low potential for management override. Therefore, the auditor could determine that, based on the nature of these program change controls, the auditor could use the work of others to a moderate extent so long as the degree of competence and objectivity of the individuals performing the test is at an appropriate level. On the other hand, controls to detect attempts to override controls that prevent unauthorized journal entries from being posted may have a highly pervasive effect, may involve a high degree of judgment in evaluating their operating effectiveness, may involve a subjective evaluation, and may have a reasonable possibility for management override. Therefore, the auditor could determine that, based on the nature of these controls over systems access, he or she would need to perform more of the tests of those controls himself or herself. Further, because of the nature of the controls, the auditor should use the work of others only if the degree of competence and objectivity of the individuals performing the tests is high.

- *Management self-assessment of controls.* As described in paragraph 40, management may test the operating effectiveness of controls using a selfassessment process. Because such an assessment is made by the same personnel who are responsible for performing the control, the individuals performing the self-assessment do not have sufficient objectivity as it relates to the subject matter. Therefore, the auditor should not use their work.

- *Controls over the calculation of depreciation of fixed assets.* Controls over the calculation of depreciation of fixed assets are usually not pervasive, involve a low degree of judgment in evaluating their operating effectiveness, and can be subjected to objective testing. If these conditions describe the controls over the calculation of depreciation of fixed assets and if there is a low potential for management override, the auditor could determine that, based on the nature of these controls, the auditor could use the work of others to a large extent (perhaps entirely) so long as the degree of competence and objectivity of the individuals performing the test is at an appropriate level.

- *Alternating tests of controls.* Many of the controls over accounts payable, including controls over cash disbursements, are usually not pervasive, involve a low degree of judgment in evaluating their operating effectiveness, can be subjected to objective testing, and have a low potential for management override. When these conditions describe the controls over accounts payable, the auditor could determine that, based on the nature of these controls, he or she could use the work of others to a large extent (perhaps entirely) so long as the degree of competence and objectivity of the individuals performing the test is at an appropriate level. However, if the company recently implemented a major information technology change that significantly affected controls over cash disbursements, the auditor might decide to use the work of others to a lesser extent in the audit immediately following the information technology change and then return, in subsequent years, to using the work of others to a large extent in this area. As another example, the auditor might use the work of others for testing controls over the depreciation of fixed assets (as described in the point above) for several years' audits but decide one year to perform some extent of the work himself or herself to gain an understanding of these controls beyond that provided by performing a walkthrough.

Forming an Opinion on the Effectiveness of Internal Control Over Financial Reporting

127. When forming an opinion on internal control over financial reporting, the auditor should evaluate all evidence obtained from all sources, including:

- The adequacy of the assessment performed by management and the results of the auditor's evaluation of the design and tests of operating effectiveness of controls;

- The negative results of substantive procedures performed during the financial statement audit (for example, recorded and unrecorded adjustments identified as a result of the performance of the auditing procedures); and

- Any identified control deficiencies.

128. As part of this evaluation, the auditor should review all reports issued during the year by internal audit (or similar functions, such as loan review in a financial institution) that address controls related to internal control over financial reporting and evaluate any control deficiencies identified in those reports. This review should include reports issued by internal audit as a result of operational audits or specific reviews of key processes if those reports address controls related to internal control over financial reporting.

129. *Issuing an Unqualified Opinion.* The auditor may issue an unqualified opinion only when there are no identified material weaknesses and when there have been no restrictions on the scope of the auditor's work. The existence of a material weakness requires the auditor to express an adverse opinion on the effectiveness of internal control over financial reporting (See paragraph 175), while a scope limitation requires the auditor to express a qualified opinion or a disclaimer of opinion, depending on the significance of the limitation in scope (See paragraph 178).

130. *Evaluating Deficiencies in Internal Control Over Financial Reporting.* The auditor must evaluate identified control deficiencies and determine whether the deficiencies, individually or in combination, are significant deficiencies or material weaknesses. The evaluation of the significance of a deficiency should include both quantitative and qualitative factors.

---

131. The auditor should evaluate the significance of a deficiency in internal control over financial reporting initially by determining the following:

- The likelihood that a deficiency, or a combination of deficiencies, could result in a misstatement of an account balance or disclosure; and

- The magnitude of the potential misstatement resulting from the deficiency or deficiencies.

132. The significance of a deficiency in internal control over financial reporting depends on the *potential* for a misstatement, not on whether a misstatement actually has occurred.

133. Several factors affect the *likelihood* that a deficiency, or a combination of deficiencies, could result in a misstatement of an account balance or disclosure. The factors include, but are not limited to, the following:

- The nature of the financial statement accounts, disclosures, and assertions involved; for example, suspense accounts and related party transactions involve greater risk.

- The susceptibility of the related assets or liability to loss or fraud; that is, greater susceptibility increases risk.

- The subjectivity, complexity, or extent of judgment required to determine the amount involved; that is, greater subjectivity, complexity, or judgment, like that related to an accounting estimate, increases risk.

- The cause and frequency of known or detected exceptions for the operating effectiveness of a control; for example, a control with an observed non-negligible deviation rate is a deficiency.

- The interaction or relationship of the control with other controls; that is, the interdependence or redundancy of the control.

- The interaction of the deficiencies; for example, when evaluating a combination of two or more deficiencies, whether the deficiencies could affect the same financial statement accounts and assertions.

- The possible future consequences of the deficiency.

134. When evaluating the likelihood that a deficiency or combination of deficiencies could result in a misstatement, the auditor should evaluate how the controls interact with other controls. There are controls, such as information technology general controls, on which other controls depend. Some controls function together as a group of controls. Other controls overlap, in the sense that these other controls achieve the same objective.

135. Several factors affect the magnitude of the misstatement that could result from a deficiency or deficiencies in controls. The factors include, but are not limited to, the following:

- The financial statement amounts or total of transactions exposed to the deficiency.

- The volume of activity in the account balance or class of transactions exposed to the deficiency that has occurred in the current period or that is expected in future periods.

136. In evaluating the magnitude of the potential misstatement, the auditor should recognize that the maximum amount that an account balance or total of transactions can be overstated is generally the recorded amount. However, the recorded amount is not a limitation on the amount of potential understatement. The auditor also should recognize that the risk of misstatement might be different for the maximum possible misstatement than for lesser possible amounts.

137. When evaluating the significance of a deficiency in internal control over financial reporting, the auditor also should determine the level of detail and degree of assurance that would satisfy prudent officials in the conduct of their own affairs that they have reasonable assurance that transactions are recorded as necessary to permit the preparation of financial statements in conformity with generally accepted accounting principles. If the auditor determines that the deficiency would prevent prudent officials in the conduct of their own affairs from concluding that they have reasonable assurance,[17] then the auditor should deem the deficiency to be at least a significant deficiency. Having determined in this manner that a deficiency represents a significant deficiency, the auditor must further evaluate the deficiency to determine whether individually, or in combination with other deficiencies, the deficiency is a material weakness.

> **Note:** Paragraphs 9 and 10 provide the definitions of significant deficiency and material weakness, respectively.

138. Inadequate documentation of the design of controls and the absence of sufficient documented evidence to support management's assessment of the operating effectiveness of internal control over financial reporting are control deficiencies. As with other control deficiencies, the auditor should evaluate these deficiencies as to their significance.

139. The interaction of qualitative considerations that affect internal control over financial reporting with quantitative considerations ordinarily results in deficiencies in the following areas being at least significant deficiencies in internal control over financial reporting:

- Controls over the selection and application of accounting policies that are in conformity with generally accepted accounting principles;
- Antifraud programs and controls;
- Controls over non-routine and non-systematic transactions; and
- Controls over the period-end financial reporting process, including controls over procedures used to enter transaction totals into the general ledger; initiate, authorize, record, and process journal entries into the general ledger; and record recurring and non-recurring adjustments to the financial statements.

140. Each of the following circumstances should be regarded as at least a significant deficiency and as a strong indicator that a material weakness in internal control over financial reporting exists:

- Restatement of previously issued financial statements to reflect the correction of a misstatement.

> **Note:** The correction of a misstatement includes misstatements due to error or fraud; it does not include restatements to reflect a change in accounting principle to comply with a new accounting principle or a voluntary change from one generally accepted accounting principle to another generally accepted accounting principle.

- Identification by the auditor of a material misstatement in financial statements in the current period that was not initially identified by the company's internal control over

---

17. See SEC Staff Accounting Bulletin Topic 1M2, *Immaterial Misstatements That Are Intentional,* for further discussion about the level of detail and degree of assurance that would satisfy prudent officials in the conduct of their own affairs.

---

financial reporting. (This is a strong indicator of a material weakness even if management subsequently corrects the misstatement.)

- Oversight of the company's external financial reporting and internal control over financial reporting by the company's audit committee is ineffective. (Paragraphs 55 through 59 present factors to evaluate when determining whether the audit committee is ineffective.)

- The internal audit function or the risk assessment function is ineffective at a company for which such a function needs to be effective for the company to have an effective monitoring or risk assessment component, such as for very large or highly complex companies.

Note: The evaluation of the internal audit or risk assessment functions is similar to the evaluation of the audit committee, as described in paragraphs 55 through 59, that is, the evaluation is made within the context of the monitoring and risk assessment components. The auditor is not required to make a separate evaluation of the effectiveness and performance of these functions. Instead, the auditor should base his or her evaluation on evidence obtained as part of evaluating the monitoring and risk assessment components of internal control over financial reporting.

- For complex entities in highly regulated industries, an ineffective regulatory compliance function. This relates solely to those aspects of the ineffective regulatory compliance function in which associated violations of laws and regulations could have a material effect on the reliability of financial reporting.

- Identification of fraud of any magnitude on the part of senior management.

Note: The auditor is required to plan and perform procedures to obtain reasonable assurance that material misstatement caused by fraud is detected by the auditor. However, for the purposes of evaluating and reporting deficiencies in internal control over financial reporting, the auditor should evaluate fraud of any magnitude (including fraud resulting in immaterial misstatements) on the part of senior management of which he or she is aware. Furthermore, for the purposes of this circumstance, "senior management" includes the principal executive and financial officers signing the company's certifications as required under Section 302 of the Act as well as any other member of management who play a significant role in the company's financial reporting process.

- Significant deficiencies that have been communicated to management and the audit committee remain uncorrected after some reasonable period of time.

- An ineffective control environment.

141. Appendix D provides examples of significant deficiencies and material weaknesses.

Requirement for Written Representations

142. In an audit of internal control over financial reporting, the auditor should obtain written representations from management:

a. Acknowledging management's responsibility for establishing and maintaining effective internal control over financial reporting;

b. Stating that management has performed an assessment of the effectiveness of the company's internal control over financial reporting and specifying the control criteria;

c. Stating that management did not use the auditor's procedures performed during the audits of internal control over financial reporting or the financial statements as part of the basis for management's assessment of the effectiveness of internal control over financial reporting;

d. Stating management's conclusion about the effectiveness of the company's internal control over financial reporting based on the control criteria as of a specified date;

e. Stating that management has disclosed to the auditor all deficiencies in the design or operation of internal control over financial reporting identified as part of management's assessment, including separately disclosing to the auditor all such deficiencies that it believes to be significant deficiencies or material weaknesses in internal control over financial reporting;

f. Describing any material fraud and any other fraud that, although not material, involves senior management or management or other employees who have a significant role in the company's internal control over financial reporting;

g. Stating whether control deficiencies identified and communicated to the audit committee during previous engagements pursuant to paragraph 207 have been resolved, and specifically identifying any that have not; and

h. Stating whether there were, subsequent to the date being reported on, any changes in internal control over financial reporting or other factors that might significantly affect internal control over financial reporting, including any corrective actions taken by management with regard to significant deficiencies and material weaknesses.

143. The failure to obtain written representations from management, including management's refusal to furnish them, constitutes a limitation on the scope of the audit sufficient to preclude an unqualified opinion. As discussed further in paragraph 178, when management limits the scope of the audit, the auditor should either withdraw from the engagement or disclaim an opinion. Further, the auditor should evaluate the effects of management's refusal on his or her ability to rely on other representations, including, if applicable, representations obtained in an audit of the company's financial statements.

144. AU sec. 333, *Management Representations,* explains matters such as who should sign the letter, the period to be covered by the letter, and when to obtain an updating letter.

Relationship of an Audit of Internal Control over Financial Reporting to an Audit of Financial Statements

145. The audit of internal control over financial reporting should be integrated with the audit of the financial statements. The objectives of the procedures for the audits are not identical, however, and the auditor must plan and perform the work to achieve the objectives of both audits.

146. The understanding of internal control over financial reporting the auditor obtains and the procedures the auditor performs for purposes of expressing an opinion on management's assessment are interrelated with the internal control over financial reporting understanding the auditor obtains and procedures the auditor performs to assess control risk for purposes of expressing an opinion on the financial statements. As a result, it is efficient for the auditor to coordinate obtaining the understanding and performing the procedures.

Tests of Controls in an Audit of Internal Control Over Financial Reporting

147. The objective of the tests of controls in an audit of internal control over financial reporting is to obtain evidence about the effectiveness of controls to support the auditor's opinion on whether management's assessment of the effectiveness of the company's internal control over financial reporting is fairly stated. The auditor's opinion relates to the effectiveness of the company's internal control over financial reporting as of a *point in time* and *taken as a whole.*

148. To express an opinion on internal control over financial reporting effectiveness as of a *point in time,* the auditor should obtain evidence that internal control over financial reporting has operated effectively for a sufficient period of time, which may be less than the entire period (ordinarily one year) covered by the company's financial statements. To express an opinion on internal control over financial reporting effectiveness *taken as a whole,* the auditor must obtain evidence about the effectiveness of controls over all relevant assertions related to all significant accounts and disclosures in the financial statements. This requires that the auditor test the design and operating effectiveness of controls he or she ordinarily would not test if expressing an opinion only on the financial statements.

149. When concluding on the effectiveness of internal control over financial reporting for purposes of expressing an opinion on management's assessment, the auditor should incorporate the results of any additional tests of controls performed to achieve the objective related to expressing an opinion on the financial statements, as discussed in the following section.

Tests of Controls in an Audit of Financial Statements

150. To express an opinion on the financial statements, the auditor ordinarily performs tests of controls and substantive procedures. The objective of the tests of controls the auditor performs for this purpose is to assess control risk. To assess control risk for specific financial statement assertions at less than the maximum, the auditor is required to obtain evidence that the relevant controls operated effectively during the *entire period* upon which the auditor plans to place reliance on those controls. However, the auditor is not required to assess control risk at less than the maximum for *all* relevant assertions and, for a variety of reasons, the auditor may choose not to do so.[18]

151. When concluding on the effectiveness of controls for the purpose of assessing control risk, the auditor also should evaluate the results of any additional tests of controls performed to achieve the objective related to expressing an opinion on management's assessment, as discussed in paragraphs 147 through 149. Consideration of these results may require the auditor to alter the nature, timing, and extent of substantive procedures and to plan and perform further tests of controls, particularly in response to identified control deficiencies.

Effect of Tests of Controls on Substantive Procedures

152. Regardless of the assessed level of control risk or the assessed risk of material misstatement in connection with the audit of the financial statements, the auditor should perform substantive procedures for all relevant assertions related to all significant accounts and disclosures. Performing procedures to express an opinion on internal control over financial reporting does not diminish this requirement.

153. The substantive procedures that the auditor should perform consist of tests of details of transactions and balances and analytical procedures. Before using the results obtained from substantive analytical procedures, the auditor should either test the design and operating effectiveness of controls over financial information used in the substantive analytical procedures or perform other procedures to support the completeness and accuracy of the underly-

---

18. See paragraph 160 for additional documentation requirements when the auditor assesses control risk as other than low.

---

ing information. For significant risks of material misstatement, it is unlikely that audit evidence obtained from substantive analytical procedures alone will be sufficient.

154. When designing substantive analytical procedures, the auditor also should evaluate the risk of management override of controls. As part of this process, the auditor should evaluate whether such an override might have allowed adjustments outside of the normal period-end financial reporting process to have been made to the financial statements. Such adjustments might have resulted in artificial changes to the financial statement relationships being analyzed, causing the auditor to draw erroneous conclusions. For this reason, substantive analytical procedures alone are not well suited to detecting fraud.

155. The auditor's substantive procedures must include reconciling the financial statements to the accounting records. The auditor's substantive procedures also should include examining material adjustments made during the course of preparing the financial statements. Also, other auditing standards require auditors to perform specific tests of details in the financial statement audit. For instance, AU sec. 316, *Consideration of Fraud in a Financial Statement Audit,* requires the auditor to perform certain tests of details to further address the risk of management override, whether or not a specific risk of fraud has been identified. Paragraph .34 of AU Sec. 330, *The Confirmation Process,* states that there is a presumption that the auditor will request the confirmation of accounts receivable. Similarly, paragraph .01 of AU Sec. 331, *Inventories,* states that observation of inventories is a generally accepted auditing procedure and that the auditor who issues an opinion without this procedure "has the burden of justifying the opinion expressed."

156. If, during the audit of internal control over financial reporting, the auditor identifies a control deficiency, he or she should determine the effect on the nature, timing, and extent of substantive procedures to be performed to reduce the risk of material misstatement of the financial statements to an appropriately low level.

Effect of Substantive Procedures on the Auditor's Conclusions About the Operating Effectiveness of Controls

157. In an audit of internal control over financial reporting, the auditor should evaluate the effect of the findings of all substantive auditing procedures performed in the audit of financial statements on the effectiveness of internal control over financial reporting. This evaluation should include, but not be limited to:

- The auditor's risk evaluations in connection with the selection and application of substantive procedures, especially those related to fraud (See paragraph 26);

- Findings with respect to illegal acts and related party transactions;

- Indications of management bias in making accounting estimates and in selecting accounting principles; and

- Misstatements detected by substantive procedures. The extent of such misstatements might alter the auditor's judgment about the effectiveness of controls.

158. However, the absence of misstatements detected by substantive procedures does not provide evidence that controls related to the assertion being tested are effective.

Documentation Requirements

159. In addition to the documentation requirements in AU sec. 339, *Audit Documentation,* the auditor should document:

- The understanding obtained and the evaluation of the design of each of the five components of the company's internal control over financial reporting;

- The process used to determine significant accounts and disclosures and major classes of transactions, including the determination of the locations or business units at which to perform testing;

- The identification of the points at which misstatements related to relevant financial statement assertions could occur within significant accounts and disclosures and major classes of transactions;

- The extent to which the auditor relied upon work performed by others as well as the auditor's assessment of their competence and objectivity;

- The evaluation of any deficiencies noted as a result of the auditor's testing; and

- Other findings that could result in a modification to the auditor's report.

160. For a company that has effective internal control over financial reporting, the auditor ordinarily will be able to perform sufficient testing of controls to be able to assess control risk for all relevant assertions related to significant accounts and disclosures at a low level. If, however, the auditor assesses control risk as other than low for certain assertions or significant accounts, the auditor should document the reasons for that conclusion. Examples of when it is appropriate to assess control risk as other than low include:

- When a control over a relevant assertion related to a significant account or disclosure was superseded late in the year and only the new control was tested for operating effectiveness.

- When a material weakness existed during the period under audit and was corrected by the end of the period.

161. The auditor also should document the effect of a conclusion that control risk is other than low for any relevant assertions related to any significant accounts in connection with the audit of the financial statements on his or her opinion on the audit of internal control over financial reporting.

Reporting on Internal Control Over Financial Reporting

Management's Report

162. Management is required to include in its annual report its assessment of the effectiveness of the company's internal control over financial reporting in addition to its audited financial statements as of the end of the most recent fiscal year. Management's report on internal control over financial reporting is required to include the following:[19]

- A statement of management's responsibility for establishing and maintaining adequate internal control over financial reporting for the company;

- A statement identifying the framework used by management to conduct the required assessment of the effectiveness of the company's internal control over financial reporting;

- An assessment of the effectiveness of the company's internal control over financial reporting as of the end of the company's most recent fiscal year, including an explicit statement as to whether that internal control over financial reporting is effective; and

---

19. See Item 308(a) of Regulation S-B and S-K, 17 C.F.R. 228.308(a) and 17 C.F.R. 229.308(a), respectively.

- A statement that the registered public accounting firm that audited the financial statements included in the annual report has issued an attestation report on management's assessment of the company's internal control over financial reporting.

163. Management should provide, both in its report on internal control over financial reporting and in its representation letter to the auditor, a written conclusion about the effectiveness of the company's internal control over financial reporting. The conclusion about the effectiveness of a company's internal control over financial reporting can take many forms; however, management is required to state a direct conclusion about whether the company's internal control over financial reporting is effective. This standard, for example, includes the phrase "management's assessment that W Company maintained effective internal control over financial reporting as of [*date*]" to illustrate such a conclusion. Other phrases, such as "management's assessment that W Company's internal control over financial reporting as of [*date*] is sufficient to meet the stated objectives," also might be used. However, the conclusion should not be so subjective (for example, "very effective internal control") that people having competence in and using the same or similar criteria would not ordinarily be able to arrive at similar conclusions.

164. Management is precluded from concluding that the company's internal control over financial reporting is effective if there are one or more material weaknesses.[20] In addition, management is required to disclose all material weaknesses that exist as of the end of the most recent fiscal year.

165. Management might be able to accurately represent that internal control over financial reporting, as of the end of the company's most recent fiscal year, is effective even if one or more material weaknesses existed during the period. To make this representation, management must have changed the internal control over financial reporting to eliminate the material weaknesses sufficiently in advance of the "as of" date and have satisfactorily tested the effectiveness over a period of time that is adequate for it to determine whether, as of the end of the fiscal year, the design and operation of internal control over financial reporting is effective.[21]

Auditor's Evaluation of Management's Report

166. With respect to management's report on its assessment, the auditor should evaluate the following matters:

a. Whether management has properly stated its responsibility for establishing and maintaining adequate internal control over financial reporting.

b. Whether the framework used by management to conduct the evaluation is suitable. (As discussed in paragraph 14, the framework described in COSO constitutes a suitable and available framework.)

c. Whether management's assessment of the effectiveness of internal control over financial reporting, as of the end of the company's most recent fiscal year, is free of material misstatement.

d. Whether management has expressed its assessment in an acceptable form.

---

20. See Item 308(a)(3) of Regulation S-B and S-K, 17 C.F.R. 228.308(a) and 17 C.F.R. 229.308(a), respectively.
21. However, when the reason for a change in internal control over financial reporting is the correction of a material weakness, management and the auditor should evaluate whether the reason for the change and the circumstances surrounding the change are material information necessary to make the disclosure about the change not misleading in a filing subject to certification under Securities Exchange Act Rule 13a-14(a) or 15d-14(a), 17 C.F.R. 240.13a-14(a) or 17 C.F.R. 240.15d-14(a). See discussion beginning at paragraph 200 for further direction.

—Management is required to state whether the company's internal control over financial reporting is effective.

—A negative assurance statement indicating that, "Nothing has come to management's attention to suggest that the company's internal control over financial reporting is not effective," is not acceptable.

—Management is not permitted to conclude that the company's internal control over financial reporting is effective if there are one or more material weaknesses in the company's internal control over financial reporting.

e. Whether material weaknesses identified in the company's internal control over financial reporting, if any, have been properly disclosed, including material weaknesses corrected during the period.[22]

Auditor's Report on Management's Assessment of Internal Control Over Financial Reporting

167. The auditor's report on management's assessment of the effectiveness of internal control over financial reporting must include the following elements:

a. A title that includes the word *independent;*

b. An identification of management's conclusion about the effectiveness of the company's internal control over financial reporting as of a specified date based on the control criteria [for example, criteria established in *Internal Control—Integrated Framework* issued by the Committee of Sponsoring Organizations of the Treadway Commission (COSO)];

c. An identification of the title of the management report that includes management's assessment (the auditor should use the same description of the company's internal control over financial reporting as management uses in its report);

d. A statement that the assessment is the responsibility of management;

e. A statement that the auditor's responsibility is to express an opinion on the assessment and an opinion on the company's internal control over financial reporting based on his or her audit;

f. A definition of internal control over financial reporting as stated in paragraph 7;

g. A statement that the audit was conducted in accordance with the standards of the Public Company Accounting Oversight Board (United States);

h. A statement that the standards of the Public Company Accounting Oversight Board require that the auditor plan and perform the audit to obtain reasonable assurance about whether effective internal control over financial reporting was maintained in all material respects;

i. A statement that an audit includes obtaining an understanding of internal control over financial reporting, evaluating management's assessment, testing and evaluating the design and operating effectiveness of internal control, and performing such other procedures as the auditor considered necessary in the circumstances;

---

22. See paragraph 206 for direction when a material weakness was corrected during the fourth quarter and the auditor believes that modification to the disclosures about changes in internal control over financial reporting are necessary for the annual certifications to be accurate and to comply with the requirements of Section 302 of the Act.

WG
                                                        &L   **Warren, Gorham & Lamont**

j. A statement that the auditor believes the audit provides a reasonable basis for his or her opinions;

k. A paragraph stating that, because of inherent limitations, internal control over financial reporting may not prevent or detect misstatements and that projections of any evaluation of effectiveness to future periods are subject to the risk that controls may become inadequate because of changes in conditions, or that the degree of compliance with the policies or procedures may deteriorate;

l. The auditor's opinion on whether management's assessment of the effectiveness of the company's internal control over financial reporting as of the specified date is fairly stated, in all material respects, based on the control criteria (See discussion beginning at paragraph 162);

m. The auditor's opinion on whether the company maintained, in all material respects, effective internal control over financial reporting as of the specified date, based on the control criteria;

n. The manual or printed signature of the auditor's firm;

o. The city and state (or city and country, in the case of non-U.S. auditors) from which the auditor's report has been issued; and

p. The date of the audit report.

168. Example A-1 in Appendix A is an illustrative auditor's report for an unqualified opinion on management's assessment of the effectiveness of the company's internal control over financial reporting and an unqualified opinion on the effectiveness of the company's internal control over financial reporting.

169. *Separate or Combined Reports.* The auditor may choose to issue a combined report (that is, one report containing both an opinion on the financial statements and the opinions on internal control over financial reporting) or separate reports on the company's financial statements and on internal control over financial reporting. Example A-7 in Appendix A is an illustrative combined audit report on internal control over financial reporting. Appendix A also includes examples of separate reports on internal control over financial reporting.

170. If the auditor chooses to issue a separate report on internal control over financial reporting, he or she should add the following paragraph to the auditor's report on the financial statements:

> We also have audited, in accordance with the standards of the Public Company Accounting Oversight Board (United States), the effectiveness of W Company's internal control over financial reporting as of December 31, 20X3, based on [*identify control criteria*] and our report dated [*date of report, which should be the same as the date of the report on the financial statements*] expressed [*include nature of opinions*].

and add the following paragraph to the report on internal control over financial reporting:

> We have also audited, in accordance with the standards of the Public Company Accounting Oversight Board (United States), the [*identify financial statements*] of W Company and our report dated [*date of report, which should be the same as the date of the report on the effectiveness of internal control over financial reporting*] expressed [*include nature of opinion*].

171. *Report Date.* As stated previously, the auditor cannot audit internal control over financial reporting without also auditing the financial statements. Therefore, the reports should be dated the same.

172. When the auditor elects to issue a combined report on the audit of the financial statements and the audit of internal control over financial reporting, the audit opinion will address multiple reporting periods for the financial statements presented but only the end of the most recent fiscal year for the effectiveness of internal control over financial reporting and management's assessment of the effectiveness of internal control over financial reporting. See a combined report in Example A-7 in Appendix A.

173. *Report Modifications.* The auditor should modify the standard report if any of the following conditions exist.

a. Management's assessment is inadequate or management's report is inappropriate. (See paragraph 174.)

b. There is a material weakness in the company's internal control over financial reporting. (See paragraphs 175 through 177.)

c. There is a restriction on the scope of the engagement. (See paragraphs 178 through 181.)

d. The auditor decides to refer to the report of other auditors as the basis, in part, for the auditor's own report. (See paragraphs 182 through 185.)

e. A significant subsequent event has occurred since the date being reported on. (See paragraphs 186 through 189.)

f. There is other information contained in management's report on internal control over financial reporting. (See paragraphs 190 through 192.)

174. *Management's Assessment Inadequate or Report Inappropriate.* If the auditor determines that management's process for assessing internal control over financial reporting is inadequate, the auditor should modify his or her opinion for a scope limitation (discussed further beginning at paragraph 178). If the auditor determines that management's report is inappropriate, the auditor should modify his or her report to include, at a minimum, an explanatory paragraph describing the reasons for this conclusion.

175. *Material Weaknesses.* Paragraphs 130 through 141 describe significant deficiencies and material weaknesses. If there are significant deficiencies that, individually or in combination, result in one or more material weaknesses, management is precluded from concluding that internal control over financial reporting is effective. In these circumstances, the auditor must express an adverse opinion on the company's internal control over financial reporting.

176. When expressing an adverse opinion on the effectiveness of internal control over financial reporting because of a material weakness, the auditor's report must include:

• The definition of a material weakness, as provided in paragraph 10.

• A statement that a material weakness has been identified and included in management's assessment. (If the material weakness has not been included in management's assessment, this sentence should be modified to state that the material weakness has been identified but not included in management's assessment. In this case, the auditor also is required to communicate in writing to the audit committee that the material weakness was not disclosed or identified as a material weakness in management's report.)

- A description of any material weaknesses identified in a company's internal control over financial reporting. This description should provide the users of the audit report with specific information about the nature of any material weakness, and its actual and potential effect on the presentation of the company's financial statements issued during the existence of the weakness. This description also should address requirements described in paragraph 194.

177. Depending on the circumstances, the auditor may express both an unqualified opinion and an other-than-unqualified opinion within the same report on internal control over financial reporting. For example, if management makes an adverse assessment because a material weakness has been identified and not corrected ("...internal control over financial reporting is not effective..."), the auditor would express an unqualified opinion on management's assessment ("...management's assessment that internal control over financial reporting is not effective is fairly stated, in all material respects..."). At the same time, the auditor would express an adverse opinion about the effectiveness of internal control over financial reporting ("In our opinion, because of the effect of the material weakness described..., the company's internal control over financial reporting is not effective."). Example A-2 in Appendix A illustrates the form of the report that is appropriate in this situation. Example A-6 in Appendix A illustrates a report that reflects disagreement between management and the auditor that a material weakness exists.

178. *Scope Limitations.* The auditor can express an unqualified opinion on management's assessment of internal control over financial reporting and an unqualified opinion on the effectiveness of internal control over financial reporting only if the auditor has been able to apply all the procedures necessary in the circumstances. If there are restrictions on the scope of the engagement imposed by the circumstances, the auditor should withdraw from the engagement, disclaim an opinion, or express a qualified opinion. The auditor's decision depends on his or her assessment of the importance of the omitted procedure(s) to his or her ability to form an opinion on management's assessment of internal control over financial reporting and an opinion on the effectiveness of the company's internal control over financial reporting. However, when the restrictions are imposed by management, the auditor should withdraw from the engagement or disclaim an opinion on management's assessment of internal control over financial reporting and the effectiveness of internal control over financial reporting.

179. For example, management might have identified a material weakness in its internal control over financial reporting prior to the date specified in its report and implemented controls to correct it. If management believes that the new controls have been operating for a sufficient period of time to determine that they are both effectively designed and operating, management would be able to include in its assessment its conclusion that internal control over financial reporting is effective as of the date specified. However, if the auditor disagrees with the sufficiency of the time period, he or she would be unable to obtain sufficient evidence that the new controls have been operating effectively for a sufficient period. In that case, the auditor should modify the opinion on the effectiveness of internal control over financial reporting and the opinion on management's assessment of internal control over financial reporting because of a scope limitation.

180. When the auditor plans to disclaim an opinion and the limited procedures performed by the auditor caused the auditor to conclude that a material weakness exists, the auditor's report should include:

- The definition of a material weakness, as provided in paragraph 10.

- A description of any material weaknesses identified in the company's internal control over financial reporting. This description should provide the users of the audit report with specific information about the nature of any material weakness, and its actual and potential effect on the presentation of the company's financial statements issued during the existence of the weakness. This description also should address the requirements in paragraph 194.

181. Example A-3 in Appendix A illustrates the form of report when there is a limitation on the scope of the audit causing the auditor to issue qualified opinions. Example A-4 illustrates the form of report when restrictions on the scope of the audit cause the auditor to disclaim opinions.

182. *Opinions Based, in Part, on the Report of Another Auditor.* When another auditor has audited the financial statements and internal control over financial reporting of one or more subsidiaries, divisions, branches, or components of the company, the auditor should determine whether he or she may serve as the principal auditor and use the work and reports of another auditor as a basis, in part, for his or her opinions. AU sec. 543, *Part of Audit Performed by Other Independent Auditors,* provides direction on the auditor's decision of whether to serve as the principal auditor of the financial statements. If the auditor decides it is appropriate to serve as the principal auditor of the financial statements, then that auditor also should be the principal auditor of the company's internal control over financial reporting. This relationship results from the requirement that an audit of the financial statements must be performed to audit internal control over financial reporting; only the principal auditor of the financial statements can be the principal auditor of internal control over financial reporting. In this circumstance, the principal auditor of the financial statements needs to participate sufficiently in the audit of internal control over financial reporting to provide a basis for serving as the principal auditor of internal control over financial reporting.

183. When serving as the principal auditor of internal control over financial reporting, the auditor should decide whether to make reference in the report on internal control over financial reporting to the audit of internal control over financial reporting performed by the other auditor. In these circumstances, the auditor's decision is based on factors similar to those of the independent auditor who uses the work and reports of other independent auditors when reporting on a company's financial statements as described in AU sec. 543.

184. The decision about whether to make reference to another auditor in the report on the audit of internal control over financial reporting might differ from the corresponding decision as it relates to the audit of the financial statements. For example, the audit report on the financial statements may make reference to the audit of a significant equity investment performed by another independent auditor, but the report on internal control over financial reporting might not make a similar reference because management's evaluation of internal control over financial reporting ordinarily would not extend to controls at the equity method investee.[23]

185. When the auditor decides to make reference to the report of the other auditor as a basis, in part, for his or her opinions, the auditor should refer to the report of the other auditor when describing the scope of the audit and when expressing the opinions.

186. *Subsequent Events.* Changes in internal control over financial reporting or other factors that might significantly affect internal control over financial reporting might occur subsequent to the date as of which internal control over financial reporting is being audited but before

---

23. See Appendix B, paragraph B15, for further discussion of the evaluation of the controls over financial reporting for an equity method investment.

---

the date of the auditor's report. The auditor should inquire of management whether there were any such changes or factors. As described in paragraph 142, the auditor should obtain written representations from management relating to such matters. Additionally, to obtain information about whether changes have occurred that might affect the effectiveness of the company's internal control over financial reporting and, therefore, the auditor's report, the auditor should inquire about and examine, for this subsequent period, the following:

- Relevant internal audit reports (or similar functions, such as loan review in a financial institution) issued during the subsequent period;

- Independent auditor reports (if other than the auditor's) of significant deficiencies or material weaknesses;

- Regulatory agency reports on the company's internal control over financial reporting; and

- Information about the effectiveness of the company's internal control over financial reporting obtained through other engagements.

187. The auditor could inquire about and examine other documents for the subsequent period. Paragraphs .01 through .09 of AU sec. 560, *Subsequent Events,* provides direction on subsequent events for a financial statement audit that also may be helpful to the auditor performing an audit of internal control over financial reporting.

188. If the auditor obtains knowledge about subsequent events that materially and adversely affect the effectiveness of the company's internal control over financial reporting as of the date specified in the assessment, the auditor should issue an adverse opinion on the effectiveness of internal control over financial reporting (and issue an adverse opinion on management's assessment of internal control over financial reporting if management's report does not appropriately assess the affect of the subsequent event). If the auditor is unable to determine the effect of the subsequent event on the effectiveness of the company's internal control over financial reporting, the auditor should disclaim opinions. As described in paragraph 190, the auditor should disclaim an opinion on management's disclosures about corrective actions taken by the company after the date of management's assessment, if any.

189. The auditor may obtain knowledge about subsequent events with respect to conditions that did not exist at the date specified in the assessment but arose subsequent to that date. If a subsequent event of this type has a material effect on the company, the auditor should include in his or her report an explanatory paragraph describing the event and its effects or directing the reader's attention to the event and its effects as disclosed in management's report. Management's consideration of such events to be disclosed in its report should be limited to a change that has materially affected, or is reasonably likely to materially affect, the company's internal control over financial reporting.

190. *Management's Report Containing Additional Information.* Management's report on internal control over financial reporting may contain information in addition to management's assessment of the effectiveness of its internal control over financial reporting. Such information might include, for example:

- Disclosures about corrective actions taken by the company after the date of management's assessment;

- The company's plans to implement new controls; and

- A statement that management believes the cost of correcting a material weakness would exceed the benefits to be derived from implementing new controls.

191. If management's assessment includes such additional information, the auditor should disclaim an opinion on the information. For example, the auditor should use the following language as the last paragraph of the report to disclaim an opinion on management's cost-benefit statement:

> We do not express an opinion or any other form of assurance on management's statement referring to the costs and related benefits of implementing new controls.

192. If the auditor believes that management's additional information contains a material misstatement of fact, he or she should discuss the matter with management. If the auditor concludes that there is a valid basis for concern, he or she should propose that management consult with some other party whose advice might be useful, such as the company's legal counsel. If, after discussing the matter with management and those management has consulted, the auditor concludes that a material misstatement of fact remains, the auditor should notify management and the audit committee, in writing, of the auditor's views concerning the information. The auditor also should consider consulting the auditor's legal counsel about further actions to be taken, including the auditor's responsibility under Section 10A of the Securities Exchange Act of 1934.[24]

> **Note:** If management makes the types of disclosures described in paragraph 190 outside its report on internal control over financial reporting and includes them elsewhere within its annual report on the company's financial statements, the auditor would not need to disclaim an opinion, as described in paragraph 191. However, in that situation, the auditor's responsibilities are the same as those described in paragraph 192 if the auditor believes that the additional information contains a material misstatement of fact.

193. *Effect of Auditor's Adverse Opinion on Internal Control Over Financial Reporting on the Opinion on Financial Statements.* In some cases, the auditor's report on internal control over financial reporting might describe a material weakness that resulted in an adverse opinion on the effectiveness of internal control over financial reporting while the audit report on the financial statements remains unqualified. Consequently, during the audit of the financial statements, the auditor did not rely on that control. However, he or she performed additional substantive procedures to determine whether there was a material misstatement in the account related to the control. If, as a result of these procedures, the auditor determines that there was not a material misstatement in the account, he or she would be able to express an unqualified opinion on the financial statements.

194. When the auditor's opinion on the financial statements is unaffected by the adverse opinion on the effectiveness of internal control over financial reporting, the report on internal control over financial reporting (or the combined report, if a combined report is issued) should include the following or similar language in the paragraph that describes the material weakness:

> This material weakness was considered in determining the nature, timing, and extent of audit tests applied in our audit of the 20X3 financial statements, and this report does not affect our report dated [*date of report*] on those financial statements. [*Revise this wording appropriately for use in a combined report.*]

195. Such disclosure is important to ensure that users of the auditor's report on the financial statements understand why the auditor issued an unqualified opinion on those statements.

---

24. See Section 10A of the Securities Exchange Act of 1934, 15 U.S.C. 78j-1.

---

196. Disclosure is also important when the auditor's opinion on the financial statements is affected by the adverse opinion on the effectiveness of internal control over financial reporting. In that circumstance, the report on internal control over financial reporting (or the combined report, if a combined report is issued) should include the following or similar language in the paragraph that describes the material weakness:

> This material weakness was considered in determining the nature, timing, and extent of audit tests applied in our audit of the 20X3 financial statements.

197. *Subsequent Discovery of Information Existing at the Date of the Auditor's Report on Internal Control Over Financial Reporting.* After the issuance of the report on internal control over financial reporting, the auditor may become aware of conditions that existed at the report date that might have affected the auditor's opinions had he or she been aware of them. The auditor's evaluation of such subsequent information is similar to the auditor's evaluation of information discovered subsequent to the date of the report on an audit of financial statements, as described in AU sec. 561, *Subsequent Discovery of Facts Existing at the Date of the Auditor's Report.* That standard requires the auditor to determine whether the information is reliable and whether the facts existed at the date of his or her report. If so, the auditor should determine (1) whether the facts would have changed the report if he or she had been aware of them and (2) whether there are persons currently relying on or likely to rely on the auditor's report. For instance, if previously issued financial statements and the auditor's report have been recalled and reissued to reflect the correction of a misstatement, the auditor should presume that his or her report on the company's internal control over financial reporting as of same specified date also should be recalled and reissued to reflect the material weakness that existed at that date. Based on these considerations, paragraph .06 of AU sec. 561 provides detailed requirements for the auditor.

198. *Filings Under Federal Securities Statutes.* AU sec. 711, *Filings Under Federal Securities Statutes,* describes the auditor's responsibilities when an auditor's report is included in registration statements, proxy statements, or periodic reports filed under the federal securities statutes. The auditor should also apply AU sec. 711 with respect to the auditor's report on management's assessment of the effectiveness of internal control over financial reporting included in such filings. In addition, the direction in paragraph .10 of AU sec. 711 to inquire of and obtain written representations from officers and other executives responsible for financial and accounting matters about whether any events have occurred that have a material effect on the audited financial statements should be extended to matters that could have a material effect on management's assessment of internal control over financial reporting.

199. When the auditor has fulfilled these responsibilities and intends to consent to the inclusion of his or her report on management's assessment of the effectiveness of internal control over financial reporting in the securities filing, the auditor's consent should clearly indicate that both the audit report on financial statements and the audit report on management's assessment of the effectiveness of internal control over financial reporting (or both opinions if a combined report is issued) are included in his or her consent.

Auditor's Responsibilities for Evaluating Management's Certification Disclosures About Internal Control Over Financial Reporting

Required Management Certifications

200. Section 302 of the Act, and Securities Exchange Act Rule 13a-14(a) or 15d-14(a), whichever applies,[25] requires a company's management, with the participation of the principal executive and financial officers (the certifying officers), to make the following quarterly and annual certifications with respect to the company's internal control over financial reporting:

- A statement that the certifying officers are responsible for establishing and maintaining internal control over financial reporting;

- A statement that the certifying officers have designed such internal control over financial reporting, or caused such internal control over financial reporting to be designed under their supervision, to provide reasonable assurance regarding the reliability of financial reporting and the preparation of financial statements for external purposes in accordance with generally accepted accounting principles; and

- A statement that the report discloses any changes in the company's internal control over financial reporting that occurred during the most recent fiscal quarter (the company's fourth fiscal quarter in the case of an annual report) that have materially affected, or are reasonably likely to materially affect, the company's internal control over financial reporting.

201. When the reason for a change in internal control over financial reporting is the correction of a material weakness, management has a responsibility to determine and the auditor should evaluate whether the reason for the change and the circumstances surrounding that change are material information necessary to make the disclosure about the change not misleading.[26]

Auditor Evaluation Responsibilities

202. The auditor's responsibility as it relates to management's quarterly certifications on internal control over financial reporting is different from the auditor's responsibility as it relates to management's annual assessment of internal control over financial reporting. The auditor should perform limited procedures quarterly to provide a basis for determining whether he or she has become aware of any material modifications that, in the auditor's judgment, should be made to the disclosures about changes in internal control over financial reporting in order for the certifications to be accurate and to comply with the requirements of Section 302 of the Act.

203. To fulfill this responsibility, the auditor should perform, on a quarterly basis, the following procedures:

- Inquire of management about significant changes in the design or operation of internal control over financial reporting as it relates to the preparation of annual as well as interim financial information that could have occurred subsequent to the preceding annual audit or prior review of interim financial information;

- Evaluate the implications of misstatements identified by the auditor as part of the auditor's required review of interim financial information (See AU sec. 722, *Interim Fi-*

---

25. See 17 C.F.R., 240.13a-14a or 15d-14a, whichever applies.
26. See Securities Exchange Act Rule 12b-20, 17 C.F.R. 240.12b-20.

nancial Information) as it relates to effective internal control over financial reporting; and

- Determine, through a combination of observation and inquiry, whether any change in internal control over financial reporting has materially affected, or is reasonably likely to materially affect, the company's internal control over financial reporting.

Note: Foreign private issuers filing Forms 20-F and 40-F are not subject to quarterly reporting requirements, therefore, the auditor's responsibilities would extend only to the certifications in the annual report of these companies.

204. When matters come to auditor's attention that lead him or her to believe that modification to the disclosures about changes in internal control over financial reporting is necessary for the certifications to be accurate and to comply with the requirements of Section 302 of the Act and Securities Exchange Act Rule 13a-14(a) or 15d-14(a), whichever applies,[27] the auditor should communicate the matter(s) to the appropriate level of management as soon as practicable.

205. If, in the auditor's judgment, management does not respond appropriately to the auditor's communication within a reasonable period of time, the auditor should inform the audit committee. If, in the auditor's judgment, the audit committee does not respond appropriately to the auditor's communication within a reasonable period of time, the auditor should evaluate whether to resign from the engagement. The auditor should evaluate whether to consult with his or her attorney when making these evaluations. In these circumstances, the auditor also has responsibilities under AU sec. 317, *Illegal Acts by Clients,* and Section 10A of the Securities Exchange Act of 1934.[28] The auditor's responsibilities for evaluating the disclosures about changes in internal control over financial reporting do not diminish in any way management's responsibility for ensuring that its certifications comply with the requirements of Section 302 of the Act and Securities Exchange Act Rule 13a-14(a) or 15d-14(a), whichever applies.[29]

206. If matters come to the auditor's attention as a result of the audit of internal control over financial reporting that lead him or her to believe that modifications to the disclosures about changes in internal control over financial reporting (addressing changes in internal control over financial reporting occurring during the fourth quarter) are necessary for the annual certifications to be accurate and to comply with the requirements of Section 302 of the Act and Securities Exchange Act Rule 13a-14(a) or 15d-14(a), whichever applies,[30] the auditor should follow the same communication responsibilities as described in paragraphs 204 and 205. However, if management and the audit committee do not respond appropriately, in addition to the responsibilities described in the preceding two paragraphs, the auditor should modify his or her report on the audit of internal control over financial reporting to include an explanatory paragraph describing the reasons the auditor believes management's disclosures should be modified.

Required Communications in An Audit of Internal Control Over Financial Reporting

207. The auditor must communicate in writing to management and the audit committee all significant deficiencies and material weaknesses identified during the audit. The written communication should be made prior to the issuance of the auditor's report on internal control

---

27. See 17 C.F.R. 240.13a-14(a) or 17 C.F.R. 240.15d-14(a), whichever applies.
28. See 15 U.S.C. 78j-1.
29. See 17 C.F.R. 240.13a-14(a) or 17 C.F.R. 240.15d-14(a), whichever applies.
30. See 17 C.F.R. 240.13a-14(a) or 17 C.F.R. 240.15d-14(a), whichever applies.

over financial reporting. The auditor's communication should distinguish clearly between those matters considered to be significant deficiencies and those considered to be material weaknesses, as defined in paragraphs 9 and 10, respectively.

208. If a significant deficiency or material weakness exists because the oversight of the company's external financial reporting and internal control over financial reporting by the company's audit committee is ineffective, the auditor must communicate that specific significant deficiency or material weakness in writing to the board of directors.

209. In addition, the auditor should communicate to management, in writing, all deficiencies in internal control over financial reporting (that is, those deficiencies in internal control over financial reporting that are of a lesser magnitude than significant deficiencies) identified during the audit and inform the audit committee when such a communication has been made. When making this communication, it is not necessary for the auditor to repeat information about such deficiencies that have been included in previously issued written communications, whether those communications were made by the auditor, internal auditors, or others within the organization. Furthermore, the auditor is not required to perform procedures sufficient to identify all control deficiencies; rather, the auditor should communicate deficiencies in internal control over financial reporting of which he or she is aware.

> **Note:** As part of his or her evaluation of the effectiveness of internal control over financial reporting, the auditor should determine whether control deficiencies identified by internal auditors and others within the company, for example, through ongoing monitoring activities and the annual assessment of internal control over financial reporting, are reported to appropriate levels of management in a timely manner. The lack of an internal process to report deficiencies in internal control to management on a timely basis represents a control deficiency that the auditor should evaluate as to severity.

210. These written communications should state that the communication is intended solely for the information and use of the board of directors, audit committee, management, and others within the organization. When there are requirements established by governmental authorities to furnish such reports, specific reference to such regulatory agencies may be made.

211. These written communications also should include the definitions of control deficiencies, significant deficiencies, and material weaknesses and should clearly distinguish to which category the deficiencies being communicated relate.

212. Because of the potential for misinterpretation of the limited degree of assurance associated with the auditor issuing a written report representing that no significant deficiencies were noted during an audit of internal control over financial reporting, the auditor should not issue such representations.

213. When auditing internal control over financial reporting, the auditor may become aware of fraud or possible illegal acts. If the matter involves fraud, it must be brought to the attention of the appropriate level of management. If the fraud involves senior management, the auditor must communicate the matter directly to the audit committee as described in AU sec. 316, *Consideration of Fraud in a Financial Statement Audit.* If the matter involves possible illegal acts, the auditor must assure himself or herself that the audit committee is adequately informed, unless the matter is clearly inconsequential, in accordance with AU sec. 317, *Illegal Acts by Clients.* The auditor also must determine his or her responsibilities under Section 10A of the Securities Exchange Act of 1934.[31]

---

31. See 15 U.S.C. 78j-1.

214. When timely communication is important, the auditor should communicate the preceding matters during the course of the audit rather than at the end of the engagement. The decision about whether to issue an interim communication should be determined based on the relative significance of the matters noted and the urgency of corrective follow-up action required.

Effective Date

215. Companies considered *accelerated filers* under Securities Exchange Act Rule 12b-2[32] are required to comply with the internal control reporting and disclosure requirements of Section 404 of the Act *for fiscal years ending on or after November 15, 2004.* (Other companies have until fiscal years ending on or after July 15, 2005, to comply with these internal control reporting and disclosure requirements.) Accordingly, independent auditors engaged to audit the financial statements of accelerated filers for fiscal years ending on or after November 15, 2004, also are required to audit and report on the company's internal control over financial reporting as of the end of such fiscal year. This standard is required to be complied with for such engagements, except as it relates to the auditor's responsibilities for evaluating management's certification disclosures about internal control over financial reporting. The auditor's responsibilities for evaluating management's certification disclosures about internal control over financial reporting described in paragraphs 202 through 206 take effect beginning with the first quarter after the auditor's first audit report on the company's internal control over financial reporting.

216. Early compliance with this standard is permitted.

APPENDIX A

Illustrative Reports on Internal Control Over Financial Reporting

A1. Paragraphs 167 through 199 of this standard provide direction on the auditor's report on management's assessment of internal control over financial reporting. The following examples illustrate how to apply that direction in several different situations.

ILLUSTRATIVE REPORT

Example A-1—*Expressing an Unqualified Opinion on Management's Assessment of the Effectiveness of Internal Control Over Financial Reporting and an Unqualified Opinion on the Effectiveness of Internal Control Over Financial Reporting (Separate Report)*

Example A-2—*Expressing an Unqualified Opinion on Management's Assessment of the Effectiveness of Internal Control Over Financial Reporting and an Adverse Opinion on the Effectiveness of Internal Control Over Financial Reporting Because of the Existence of a Material Weakness*

Example A-3—*Expressing a Qualified Opinion on Management's Assessment of the Effectiveness of Internal Control Over Financial Reporting and a Qualified Opinion on the Effectiveness of Internal Control Over Financial Reporting Because of a Limitation on the Scope of the Audit*

Example A-4—*Disclaiming an Opinion on Management's Assessment of the Effectiveness of Internal Control Over Financial Reporting and Disclaiming an Opinion on the Effectiveness of Internal Control Over Financial Reporting Because of a Limitation on the Scope of the Audit*

Example A-5—*Expressing an Unqualified Opinion on Management's Assessment of the Effectiveness of Internal Control Over Financial Reporting That Refers to the Report of*

---

32. See 17 C.F.R. 240.12b-2.

Other Auditors As a Basis, in Part, for the Auditor's Opinion and an Unqualified Opinion on the Effectiveness of Internal Control Over Financial Reporting

Example A-6—*Expressing an Adverse Opinion on Management's Assessment of the Effectiveness of Internal Control Over Financial Reporting and an Adverse Opinion on the Effectiveness of Internal Control Over Financial Reporting Because of the Existence of a Material Weakness*

Example A-7—*Expressing an Unqualified Opinion on Financial Statements, an Unqualified Opinion on Management's Assessment of the Effectiveness of Internal Control Over Financial Reporting, and an Unqualified Opinion on the Effectiveness of Internal Control Over Financial Reporting (Combined Report)*

Example A-1

ILLUSTRATIVE REPORT EXPRESSING AN UNQUALIFIED OPINION ON MANAGEMENT'S ASSESSMENT OF THE EFFECTIVENESS OF INTERNAL CONTROL OVER FINANCIAL REPORTING AND AN UNQUALIFIED OPINION ON THE EFFECTIVENESS OF INTERNAL CONTROL OVER FINANCIAL REPORTING (SEPARATE REPORT)[1]

Report of Independent Registered Public Accounting Firm

[Introductory paragraph]

We have audited management's assessment, included in the accompanying [*title of management's report*], that W Company maintained effective internal control over financial reporting as of December 31, 20X3, based on [*Identify control criteria, for example, "criteria established in Internal Control—Integrated Framework issued by the Committee of Sponsoring Organizations of the Treadway Commission (COSO)."*]. W Company's management is responsible for maintaining effective internal control over financial reporting and for its assessment of the effectiveness of internal control over financial reporting. Our responsibility is to express an opinion on management's assessment and an opinion on the effectiveness of the company's internal control over financial reporting based on our audit.

[Scope paragraph]

We conducted our audit in accordance with the standards of the Public Company Accounting Oversight Board (United States). Those standards require that we plan and perform the audit to obtain reasonable assurance about whether effective internal control over financial reporting was maintained in all material respects. Our audit included obtaining an understanding of internal control over financial reporting, evaluating management's assessment, testing and evaluating the design and operating effectiveness of internal control, and performing such other procedures as we considered necessary in the circumstances. We believe that our audit provides a reasonable basis for our opinion.

[Definition paragraph]

A company's internal control over financial reporting is a process designed to provide reasonable assurance regarding the reliability of financial reporting and the preparation of financial statements for external purposes in accordance with generally accepted accounting principles. A company's internal control over financial reporting includes those policies and

---

1. If the auditor issues separate reports on the audit of internal control over financial reporting and the audit of the financial statements, both reports should include a statement that the audit was conducted in accordance with standards of the Public Company Accounting Oversight Board (United States).

procedures that (1) pertain to the maintenance of records that, in reasonable detail, accurately and fairly reflect the transactions and dispositions of the assets of the company; (2) provide reasonable assurance that transactions are recorded as necessary to permit preparation of financial statements in accordance with generally accepted accounting principles, and that receipts and expenditures of the company are being made only in accordance with authorizations of management and directors of the company; and (3) provide reasonable assurance regarding prevention or timely detection of unauthorized acquisition, use, or disposition of the company's assets that could have a material effect on the financial statements.

[Inherent limitations paragraph]

Because of its inherent limitations, internal control over financial reporting may not prevent or detect misstatements. Also, projections of any evaluation of effectiveness to future periods are subject to the risk that controls may become inadequate because of changes in conditions, or that the degree of compliance with the policies or procedures may deteriorate.

[Opinion paragraph]

In our opinion, management's assessment that W Company maintained effective internal control over financial reporting as of December 31, 20X3, is fairly stated, in all material respects, based on [Identify control criteria, for example, "criteria established in Internal Control—Integrated Framework issued by the Committee of Sponsoring Organizations of the Treadway Commission (COSO)."]. Also in our opinion, W Company maintained, in all material respects, effective internal control over financial reporting as of December 31, 20X3, based on [Identify control criteria, for example, "criteria established in Internal Control—Integrated Framework issued by the Committee of Sponsoring Organizations of the Treadway Commission (COSO)."].

[Explanatory paragraph]

We have also audited, in accordance with the standards of the Public Company Accounting Oversight Board (United States), the [identify financial statements] of W Company and our report dated [date of report, which should be the same as the date of the report on the effectiveness of internal control over financial reporting] expressed [include nature of opinion].

[Signature]

[City and State or Country]

[Date]

Example A-2

ILLUSTRATIVE REPORT EXPRESSING AN UNQUALIFIED OPINION ON MANAGEMENT'S ASSESSMENT OF THE EFFECTIVENESS OF INTERNAL CONTROL OVER FINANCIAL REPORTING AND AN ADVERSE OPINION ON THE EFFECTIVENESS OF INTERNAL CONTROL OVER FINANCIAL REPORTING BECAUSE OF THE EXISTENCE OF A MATERIAL WEAKNESS

Report of Independent Registered Public Accounting Firm

[Introductory paragraph]

We have audited management's assessment, included in the accompanying [title of management's report], that W Company did not maintain effective internal control over financial reporting as of December 31, 20X3, because of the effect of [material weakness identified in management's assessment], based on [Identify criteria, for example, "criteria established in

Internal Control—Integrated Framework issued by the Committee of Sponsoring Organizations of the Treadway Commission (COSO)."]. W Company's management is responsible for maintaining effective internal control over financial reporting and for its assessment of the effectiveness of internal control over financial reporting. Our responsibility is to express an opinion on management's assessment and an opinion on the effectiveness of the company's internal control over financial reporting based on our audit.

[*Scope paragraph*]

We conducted our audit in accordance with the standards of the Public Company Accounting Oversight Board (United States). Those standards require that we plan and perform the audit to obtain reasonable assurance about whether effective internal control over financial reporting was maintained in all material respects. Our audit included obtaining an understanding of internal control over financial reporting, evaluating management's assessment, testing and evaluating the design and operating effectiveness of internal control, and performing such other procedures as we considered necessary in the circumstances. We believe that our audit provides a reasonable basis for our opinion.

[*Definition paragraph*]

A company's internal control over financial reporting is a process designed to provide reasonable assurance regarding the reliability of financial reporting and the preparation of financial statements for external purposes in accordance with generally accepted accounting principles. A company's internal control over financial reporting includes those policies and procedures that (1) pertain to the maintenance of records that, in reasonable detail, accurately and fairly reflect the transactions and dispositions of the assets of the company; (2) provide reasonable assurance that transactions are recorded as necessary to permit preparation of financial statements in accordance with generally accepted accounting principles, and that receipts and expenditures of the company are being made only in accordance with authorizations of management and directors of the company; and (3) provide reasonable assurance regarding prevention or timely detection of unauthorized acquisition, use, or disposition of the company's assets that could have a material effect on the financial statements.

[*Inherent limitations paragraph*]

Because of its inherent limitations, internal control over financial reporting may not prevent or detect misstatements. Also, projections of any evaluation of effectiveness to future periods are subject to the risk that controls may become inadequate because of changes in conditions, or that the degree of compliance with the policies or procedures may deteriorate.

[*Explanatory paragraph*]

A material weakness is a control deficiency, or combination of control deficiencies, that results in more than a remote likelihood that a material misstatement of the annual or interim financial statements will not be prevented or detected. The following material weakness has been identified and included in management's assessment. [*Include a description of the material weakness and its effect on the achievement of the objectives of the control criteria.*] This material weakness was considered in determining the nature, timing, and extent of audit tests applied in our audit of the 20X3 financial statements, and this report does not affect our report dated [*date of report, which should be the same as the date of this report on internal control*] on those financial statements.[1]

[*Opinion paragraph*]

In our opinion, management's assessment that W Company did not maintain effective internal control over financial reporting as of December 31, 20X3, is fairly stated, in all material respects, based on [*Identify control criteria, for example, "criteria established in Internal Control—Integrated Framework issued by the Committee of Sponsoring Organizations of the Treadway Commission (COSO)."*]. Also, in our opinion, because of the effect of the material weakness described above on the achievement of the objectives of the control criteria, W Company has not maintained effective internal control over financial reporting as of December 31, 20X3, based on [*Identify control criteria, for example, "criteria established in Internal Control—Integrated Framework issued by the Committee of Sponsoring Organizations of the Treadway Commission (COSO)."*].

[*Signature*]

[*City and State or Country*]

[*Date*]

Example A-3

ILLUSTRATIVE REPORT EXPRESSING A QUALIFIED OPINION ON MANAGEMENT'S ASSESSMENT OF THE EFFECTIVENESS OF INTERNAL CONTROL OVER FINANCIAL REPORTING AND A QUALIFIED OPINION ON THE EFFECTIVENESS OF INTERNAL CONTROL OVER FINANCIAL REPORTING BECAUSE OF A LIMITATION ON THE SCOPE OF THE AUDIT

Report of Independent Registered Public Accounting Firm

[*Introductory paragraph*]

We have audited management's assessment, included in the accompanying [*title of management's report*], that W Company maintained effective internal control over financial reporting as of December 31, 20X3, based on [*Identify control criteria, for example, "criteria established in Internal Control—Integrated Framework issued by the Committee of Sponsoring Organizations of the Treadway Commission (COSO)."*]. W Company's management is responsible for maintaining effective internal control over financial reporting and for its assessment of the effectiveness of internal control over financial reporting. Our responsibility is to express an opinion on management's assessment and an opinion on the effectiveness of the company's internal control over financial reporting based on our audit.

[*Scope paragraph*]

Except as described below, we conducted our audit in accordance the standards of the Public Company Accounting Oversight Board (United States). Those standards require that we plan and perform the audit to obtain reasonable assurance about whether effective internal control over financial reporting was maintained in all material respects. Our audit included obtaining an understanding of internal control over financial reporting, evaluating management's assessment, testing and evaluating the design and operating effectiveness of internal control, and

---

1. Modify this sentence when the auditor's opinion on the financial statements is affected by the adverse opinion on the effectiveness of internal control over financial reporting, as described in paragraph 196.

---

performing such other procedures as we considered necessary in the circumstances. We believe that our audit provides a reasonable basis for our opinion.

[Explanatory paragraph that describes scope limitation]

A material weakness is a control deficiency, or combination of control deficiencies, that results in more than a remote likelihood that a material misstatement of the annual or interim financial statements will not be prevented or detected. The following material weakness has been identified and included in management's assessment.[1] Prior to December 20, 20X3, W Company had an inadequate system for recording cash receipts, which could have prevented the Company from recording cash receipts on accounts receivable completely and properly. Therefore, cash received could have been diverted for unauthorized use, lost, or otherwise not properly recorded to accounts receivable. We believe this condition was a material weakness in the design or operation of the internal control of W Company in effect prior to December 20, 20X3. Although the Company implemented a new cash receipts system on December 20, 20X3, the system has not been in operation for a sufficient period of time to enable us to obtain sufficient evidence about its operating effectiveness.

[Definition paragraph]

A company's internal control over financial reporting is a process designed to provide reasonable assurance regarding the reliability of financial reporting and the preparation of financial statements for external purposes in accordance with generally accepted accounting principles. A company's internal control over financial reporting includes those policies and procedures that (1) pertain to the maintenance of records that, in reasonable detail, accurately and fairly reflect the transactions and dispositions of the assets of the company; (2) provide reasonable assurance that transactions are recorded as necessary to permit preparation of financial statements in accordance with generally accepted accounting principles, and that receipts and expenditures of the company are being made only in accordance with authorizations of management and directors of the company; and (3) provide reasonable assurance regarding prevention or timely detection of unauthorized acquisition, use, or disposition of the company's assets that could have a material effect on the financial statements.

[Inherent limitations paragraph]

Because of its inherent limitations, internal control over financial reporting may not prevent or detect misstatements. Also, projections of any evaluation of effectiveness to future periods are subject to the risk that controls may become inadequate because of changes in conditions, or that the degree of compliance with the policies or procedures may deteriorate.

[Opinion paragraph]

In our opinion, except for the effect of matters we might have discovered had we been able to examine evidence about the effectiveness of the new cash receipts system, management's assessment that W Company maintained effective internal control over financial reporting as of December 31, 20X3, is fairly stated, in all material respects, based on *[Identify control criteria, for example, "criteria established in Internal Control—Integrated Framework issued by the Committee of Sponsoring Organizations of the Treadway Commission (COSO)."]*. Also, in our opinion, except for the effect of matters we might have discovered had we been able to examine evidence about the effectiveness of the new cash receipts system, W Company

---

1. If the auditor has identified a material weakness that is not included in management's assessment, add the following wording to the report: "In addition, we have identified the following material weakness that has not been identified as a material weakness in management's assessment."

---

maintained, in all material respects, effective internal control over financial reporting as of December 31, 20X3, based on [*Identify control criteria, for example, "criteria established in Internal Control—Integrated Framework issued by the Committee of Sponsoring Organizations of the Treadway Commission (COSO)."*].

[*Explanatory paragraph*]

We have also audited, in accordance with the standards of the Public Company Accounting Oversight Board (United States), the [*identify financial statements*] of W Company and our report dated [*date of report, which should be the same as the date of the report on the effectiveness of internal control over financial reporting*] expressed [*include nature of opinion*].

[*Signature*]

[*City and State or Country*]

[*Date*]

Example A-4

ILLUSTRATIVE REPORT DISCLAIMING AN OPINION ON MANAGEMENT'S AS-SESSMENT OF THE EFFECTIVENESS OF INTERNAL CONTROL OVER FINAN-CIAL REPORTING AND DISCLAIMING AN OPINION ON THE EFFECTIVENESS OF INTERNAL CONTROL OVER FINANCIAL REPORTING BECAUSE OF A LIM-ITATION ON THE SCOPE OF THE AUDIT

Report of Independent Registered Public Accounting Firm

[*Introductory paragraph*]

We were engaged to audit management's assessment included in the accompanying [*title of management's report*] that W Company maintained effective internal control over financial reporting as of December 31, 20X3 based on [*Identify control criteria, for example, "criteria established in Internal Control—Integrated Framework issued by the Committee of Sponsoring Organizations of the Treadway Commission (COSO)."*]. W Company's management is responsible for maintaining effective internal control over financial reporting and for its assessment of the effectiveness of internal control over financial reporting.

[*Omit scope paragraph*]

[*Explanatory paragraph that describes scope limitation*][1]

[*Definition paragraph*]

A company's internal control over financial reporting is a process designed to provide reasonable assurance regarding the reliability of financial reporting and the preparation of financial statements for external purposes in accordance with generally accepted accounting principles. A company's internal control over financial reporting includes those policies and procedures that (1) pertain to the maintenance of records that, in reasonable detail, accurately and fairly reflect the transactions and dispositions of the assets of the company; (2) provide reasonable assurance that transactions are recorded as necessary to permit preparation of financial statements in accordance with generally accepted accounting principles, and that re-

---

1. If, through the limited procedures performed, the auditor concludes that a material weakness exists, the auditor should add the definition of material weakness (as provided in paragraph 10) to the explanatory paragraph. In addition, the auditor should include a description of the material weakness and its effect on the achievement of the objectives of the control criteria.

---

ceipts and expenditures of the company are being made only in accordance with authorizations of management and directors of the company; and (3) provide reasonable assurance regarding prevention or timely detection of unauthorized acquisition, use, or disposition of the company's assets that could have a material effect on the financial statements.

[*Inherent limitations paragraph*]

Because of its inherent limitations, internal control over financial reporting may not prevent or detect misstatements. Also, projections of any evaluation of effectiveness to future periods are subject to the risk that controls may become inadequate because of changes in conditions, or that the degree of compliance with the policies or procedures may deteriorate.

[*Opinion paragraph*]

Since management [*describe scope restrictions*] and we were unable to apply other procedures to satisfy ourselves as to the effectiveness of the company's internal control over financial reporting, the scope of our work was not sufficient to enable us to express, and we do not express, an opinion either on management's assessment or on the effectiveness of the company's internal control over financial reporting.

[*Explanatory paragraph*]

We have also audited, in accordance with the standards of the Public Company Accounting Oversight Board (United States), the [*identify financial statements*] of W Company and our report dated [*date of report, which should be the same as the date of the report on the effectiveness of internal control over financial reporting*] expressed [*include nature of opinion*].

[*Signature*]

[*City and State or Country*]

[*Date*]

Example A-5

ILLUSTRATIVE REPORT EXPRESSING AN UNQUALIFIED OPINION ON MANAGEMENT'S ASSESSMENT OF THE EFFECTIVENESS OF INTERNAL CONTROL OVER FINANCIAL REPORTING THAT REFERS TO THE REPORT OF OTHER AUDITORS AS A BASIS, IN PART, FOR THE AUDITOR'S OPINION AND AN UNQUALIFIED OPINION ON THE EFFECTIVENESS OF INTERNAL CONTROL OVER FINANCIAL REPORTING

Report of Independent Registered Public Accounting Firm

[*Introductory paragraph*]

We have audited management's assessment, included in the accompanying [*title of management's report*], that W Company maintained effective internal control over financial reporting as of December 31, 20X3, based on [*Identify control criteria, for example, "criteria established in Internal Control—Integrated Framework issued by the Committee of Sponsoring Organizations of the Treadway Commission (COSO)."*]. W Company's management is responsible for maintaining effective internal control over financial reporting and for its assessment of the effectiveness of internal control over financial reporting. Our responsibility is to express an opinion on management's assessment and an opinion on the effectiveness of the company's internal control over financial reporting based on our audit. We did not examine the effectiveness of internal control over financial reporting of B Company, a wholly owned subsidiary, whose financial statements reflect total assets and revenues constituting 20 and 30 percent, respectively, of the related consolidated financial statement amounts as of and for the year ended December 31, 20X3. The effectiveness of B Company's internal control over financial reporting was audited by other auditors whose report has been furnished to us, and our opinion, insofar as it relates to the effectiveness of B Company's internal control over financial reporting, is based solely on the report of the other auditors.

[*Scope paragraph*]

We conducted our audit in accordance with the standards of the Public Company Accounting Oversight Board (United States). Those standards require that we plan and perform the audit to obtain reasonable assurance about whether effective internal control over financial reporting was maintained in all material respects. Our audit included obtaining an understanding of internal control over financial reporting, evaluating management's assessment, testing and evaluating the design and operating effectiveness of internal control, and performing such other procedures as we considered necessary in the circumstances. We believe that our audit and the report of the other auditors provide a reasonable basis for our opinion.

[*Definition paragraph*]

A company's internal control over financial reporting is a process designed to provide reasonable assurance regarding the reliability of financial reporting and the preparation of financial statements for external purposes in accordance with generally accepted accounting principles. A company's internal control over financial reporting includes those policies and procedures that (1) pertain to the maintenance of records that, in reasonable detail, accurately and fairly reflect the transactions and dispositions of the assets of the company; (2) provide reasonable assurance that transactions are recorded as necessary to permit preparation of financial statements in accordance with generally accepted accounting principles, and that receipts and expenditures of the company are being made only in accordance with authorizations of management and directors of the company; and (3) provide reasonable assurance regarding prevention or timely detection of unauthorized acquisition, use, or disposition of the company's assets that could have a material effect on the financial statements.

[*Inherent limitations paragraph*]

Because of its inherent limitations, internal control over financial reporting may not prevent or detect misstatements. Also, projections of any evaluation of effectiveness to future periods are subject to the risk that controls may become inadequate because of changes in conditions, or that the degree of compliance with the policies or procedures may deteriorate.

[*Opinion paragraph*]

In our opinion, based on our audit and the report of the other auditors, management's assessment that W Company maintained effective internal control over financial reporting as of December 31, 20X3, is fairly stated, in all material respects, based on [*Identify control criteria, for example, "criteria established in Internal Control—Integrated Framework issued by the Committee of Sponsoring Organizations of the Treadway Commission (COSO)."*]. Also, in our opinion, based on our audit and the report of the other auditors, W Company maintained, in all material respects, effective internal control over financial reporting as of December 31, 20X3, based on [*Identify control criteria, for example, "criteria established in Internal Control—Integrated Framework issued by the Committee of Sponsoring Organizations of the Treadway Commission (COSO)."*].

[*Explanatory paragraph*]

We have also audited, in accordance with the standards of the Public Company Accounting Oversight Board (United States), the [*identify financial statements*] of W Company and our report dated [*date of report, which should be the same as the date of the report on the effectiveness of internal control over financial reporting*] expressed [*include nature of opinion*].

[*Signature*]

[*City and State or Country*]

[*Date*]

Example A-6

ILLUSTRATIVE REPORT EXPRESSING AN ADVERSE OPINION ON MANAGEMENT'S ASSESSMENT OF THE EFFECTIVENESS OF INTERNAL CONTROL OVER FINANCIAL REPORTING AND AN ADVERSE OPINION ON THE EFFECTIVENESS OF INTERNAL CONTROL OVER FINANCIAL REPORTING BECAUSE OF THE EXISTENCE OF A MATERIAL WEAKNESS

Report of Independent Registered Public Accounting Firm

[*Introductory paragraph*]

We have audited management's assessment, included in the accompanying [*title of management's report*], that W Company maintained effective internal control over financial reporting as of December 31, 20X3, based on [*Identify control criteria, for example, "criteria established in Internal Control—Integrated Framework issued by the Committee of Sponsoring Organizations of the Treadway Commission (COSO)."*]. W Company's management is responsible for maintaining effective internal control over financial reporting and for its assessment of the effectiveness of internal control over financial reporting. Our responsibility is to express an opinion on management's assessment and an opinion on the effectiveness of the company's internal control over financial reporting based on our audit.

[*Scope paragraph*]

We conducted our audit in accordance with the standards of the Public Company Accounting Oversight Board (United States). Those standards require that we plan and perform the audit to obtain reasonable assurance about whether effective internal control over financial reporting was maintained in all material respects. Our audit included obtaining an understanding of internal control over financial reporting, evaluating management's assessment, testing and evaluating the design and operating effectiveness of internal control, and performing such other procedures as we considered necessary in the circumstances. We believe that our audit provides a reasonable basis for our opinion.

[*Definition paragraph*]

A company's internal control over financial reporting is a process designed to provide reasonable assurance regarding the reliability of financial reporting and the preparation of financial statements for external purposes in accordance with generally accepted accounting principles. A company's internal control over financial reporting includes those policies and procedures that (1) pertain to the maintenance of records that, in reasonable detail, accurately and fairly reflect the transactions and dispositions of the assets of the company; (2) provide reasonable assurance that transactions are recorded as necessary to permit preparation of financial statements in accordance with generally accepted accounting principles, and that receipts and expenditures of the company are being made only in accordance with authorizations of management and directors of the company; and (3) provide reasonable assurance regarding prevention or timely detection of unauthorized acquisition, use, or disposition of the company's assets that could have a material effect on the financial statements.

[Inherent limitations paragraph]

Because of its inherent limitations, internal control over financial reporting may not prevent or detect misstatements. Also, projections of any evaluation of effectiveness to future periods are subject to the risk that controls may become inadequate because of changes in conditions, or that the degree of compliance with the policies or procedures may deteriorate.

[Explanatory paragraph]

A material weakness is a control deficiency, or combination of control deficiencies, that results in more than a remote likelihood that a material misstatement of the annual or interim financial statements will not be prevented or detected. We have identified the following material weakness that has not been identified as a material weakness in management's assessment [*Include a description of the material weakness and its effect on the achievement of the objectives of the control criteria.*] This material weakness was considered in determining the nature, timing, and extent of audit tests applied in our audit of the 20X3 financial statements, and this report does not affect our report dated [*date of report, which should be the same as the date of this report on internal control*] on those financial statements.[1]

[Opinion paragraph]

In our opinion, because of the effect of the material weakness described above on the achievement of the objectives of the control criteria, management's assessment that W Company maintained effective internal control over financial reporting as of December 31, 20X3, is not fairly stated, in all material respects, based on [*Identify control criteria, for example, "criteria established in Internal Control—Integrated Framework issued by the Committee of Sponsoring Organizations of the Treadway Commission (COSO)."*]. Also, in our opinion, because of the effect of the material weakness described above on the achievement of the objectives of the control criteria, W Company has not maintained effective internal control over financial reporting as of December 31, 20X3, based on [*Identify control criteria, for example, "criteria established in Internal Control—Integrated Framework issued by the Committee of Sponsoring Organizations of the Treadway Commission (COSO)."*].

[*Signature*]

[*City and State or Country*]

[*Date*]

---

1. Modify this sentence when the auditor's opinion on the financial statements is affected by the adverse opinion on the effectiveness of internal control over financial reporting.

Example A-7

ILLUSTRATIVE COMBINED REPORT EXPRESSING AN UNQUALIFIED OPINION ON FINANCIAL STATEMENTS, AN UNQUALIFIED OPINION ON MANAGEMENT'S ASSESSMENT OF THE EFFECTIVENESS OF INTERNAL CONTROL OVER FINANCIAL REPORTING AND AN UNQUALIFIED OPINION ON THE EFFECTIVENESS OF INTERNAL CONTROL OVER FINANCIAL REPORTING

Report of Independent Registered Public Accounting Firm

[*Introductory paragraph*]

We have audited the accompanying balance sheets of W Company as of December 31, 20X3 and 20X2, and the related statements of income, stockholders' equity and comprehensive income, and cash flows for each of the years in the three-year period ended December 31, 20X3. We also have audited management's assessment, included in the accompanying [*title of management's report*], that W Company maintained effective internal control over financial reporting as of December 31, 20X3, based on [*Identify control criteria, for example, "criteria established in Internal Control—Integrated Framework issued by the Committee of Sponsoring Organizations of the Treadway Commission (COSO)."*]. W Company's management is responsible for these financial statements, for maintaining effective internal control over financial reporting, and for its assessment of the effectiveness of internal control over financial reporting. Our responsibility is to express an opinion on these financial statements, an opinion on management's assessment, and an opinion on the effectiveness of the company's internal control over financial reporting based on our audits.

[*Scope paragraph*]

We conducted our audits in accordance with the standards of the Public Company Accounting Oversight Board (United States). Those standards require that we plan and perform the audits to obtain reasonable assurance about whether the financial statements are free of material misstatement and whether effective internal control over financial reporting was maintained in all material respects. Our audit of financial statements included examining, on a test basis, evidence supporting the amounts and disclosures in the financial statements, assessing the accounting principles used and significant estimates made by management, and evaluating the overall financial statement presentation. Our audit of internal control over financial reporting included obtaining an understanding of internal control over financial reporting, evaluating management's assessment, testing and evaluating the design and operating effectiveness of internal control, and performing such other procedures as we considered necessary in the circumstances. We believe that our audits provide a reasonable basis for our opinions.

[*Definition paragraph*]

A company's internal control over financial reporting is a process designed to provide reasonable assurance regarding the reliability of financial reporting and the preparation of financial statements for external purposes in accordance with generally accepted accounting principles. A company's internal control over financial reporting includes those policies and procedures that (1) pertain to the maintenance of records that, in reasonable detail, accurately and fairly reflect the transactions and dispositions of the assets of the company; (2) provide reasonable assurance that transactions are recorded as necessary to permit preparation of financial statements in accordance with generally accepted accounting principles, and that receipts and expenditures of the company are being made only in accordance with authorizations of management and directors of the company; and (3) provide reasonable assurance regarding prevention or timely detection of unauthorized acquisition, use, or disposition of the company's assets that could have a material effect on the financial statements.

[*Inherent limitations paragraph*]

Because of its inherent limitations, internal control over financial reporting may not prevent or detect misstatements. Also, projections of any evaluation of effectiveness to future periods are subject to the risk that controls may become inadequate because of changes in conditions, or that the degree of compliance with the policies or procedures may deteriorate.

[*Opinion paragraph*]

In our opinion, the financial statements referred to above present fairly, in all material respects, the financial position of W Company as of December 31, 20X3 and 20X2, and the results of its operations and its cash flows for each of the years in the three-year period ended December 31, 20X3 in conformity with accounting principles generally accepted in the United States of America. Also in our opinion, management's assessment that W Company maintained effective internal control over financial reporting as of December 31, 20X3, is fairly stated, in all material respects, based on [*Identify control criteria, for example, "criteria established in Internal Control—Integrated Framework issued by the Committee of Sponsoring Organizations of the Treadway Commission (COSO)."*]. Furthermore, in our opinion, W Company maintained, in all material respects, effective internal control over financial reporting as of December 31, 20X3, based on [*Identify control criteria, for example, "criteria established in Internal Control—Integrated Framework issued by the Committee of Sponsoring Organizations of the Treadway Commission (COSO)."*].

[*Signature*]

[*City and State or Country*]

[*Date*]

APPENDIX B

Additional Performance Requirements and Directions; Extent-of-Testing Examples

Tests to be Performed When a Company Has Multiple Locations or Business Units

B1. To determine the locations or business units for performing audit procedures, the auditor should evaluate their relative financial significance and the risk of material misstatement arising from them. In making this evaluation, the auditor should identify the locations or business units that are individually important, evaluate their documentation of controls, and test controls over significant accounts and disclosures. For locations or business units that contain specific risks that, by themselves, could create a material misstatement, the auditor should evaluate their documentation of controls and test controls over the specific risks.

B2. The auditor should determine the other locations or business units that, when aggregated, represent a group with a level of financial significance that could create a material misstatement in the financial statements. For that group, the auditor should determine whether there are company-level controls in place. If so, the auditor should evaluate the documentation and test such company-level controls. If not, the auditor should perform tests of controls at some of the locations or business units.

B3. No further work is necessary on the remaining locations or businesses, provided that they are not able to create, either individually or in the aggregate, a material misstatement in the financial statements.

Locations or Business Units That Are Financially Significant

B4. Because of the importance of financially significant locations or business units, the auditor should evaluate management's documentation of and perform tests of controls over all relevant assertions related to significant accounts and disclosures at each financially significant location or business unit, as discussed in paragraphs 83 through 105. Generally, a relatively small number of locations or business units will encompass a large portion of a company's operations and financial position, making them financially significant.

B5. In determining the nature, timing, and extent of testing at the individual locations or business units, the auditor should evaluate each entity's involvement, if any, with a central processing or shared service environment.

Locations or Business Units That Involve Specific Risks

B6. Although a location or business unit might not be individually financially significant, it might present specific risks that, by themselves, could create a material misstatement in the company's financial statements. The auditor should test the controls over the specific risks that could create a material misstatement in the company's financial statements. The auditor need not test controls over all relevant assertions related to all significant accounts at these locations or business units. For example, a business unit responsible for foreign exchange trading could expose the company to the risk of material misstatement, even though the relative financial significance of such transactions is low.

Locations or Business Units That Are Significant Only When Aggregated with Other Locations and Business Units

B7. In determining the nature, timing, and extent of testing, the auditor should determine whether management has documented and placed in operation companylevel controls (See paragraph 53) over individually unimportant locations and business units that, when aggregated with other locations or business units, might have a high level of financial significance. A high level of financial significance could create a greater than remote risk of material misstatement of the financial statements.

B8. For the purposes of this evaluation, company-level controls are controls management has in place to provide assurance that appropriate controls exist throughout the organization, including at individual locations or business units.

B9. The auditor should perform tests of company-level controls to determine whether such controls are operating effectively. The auditor might conclude that he or she cannot evaluate the operating effectiveness of such controls without visiting some or all of the locations or business units.

B10. If management does not have company-level controls operating at these locations and business units, the auditor should determine the nature, timing, and extent of procedures to be performed at each location, business unit, or combination of locations and business units. When determining the locations or business units to visit and the controls to test, the auditor should evaluate the following factors:

- The relative financial significance of each location or business unit.
- The risk of material misstatement arising from each location or business unit.
- The similarity of business operations and internal control over financial reporting at the various locations or business units.
- The degree of centralization of processes and financial reporting applications.

- The effectiveness of the control environment, particularly management's direct control over the exercise of authority delegated to others and its ability to effectively supervise activities at the various locations or business units. An ineffective control environment over the locations or business units might constitute a material weakness.

- The nature and amount of transactions executed and related assets at the various locations or business units.

- The potential for material unrecognized obligations to exist at a location or business unit and the degree to which the location or business unit could create an obligation on the part of the company.

- Management's risk assessment process and analysis for excluding a location or business unit from its assessment of internal control over financial reporting.

B11. Testing company-level controls is not a substitute for the auditor's testing of controls over a large portion of the company's operations or financial position. If the auditor cannot test a large portion of the company's operations and financial position by selecting a relatively small number of locations or business units, he or she should expand the number of locations or business units selected to evaluate internal control over financial reporting.

> **Note:** The evaluation of whether controls over a large portion of the company's operations or financial position have been tested should be made at the overall level, not at the individual significant account level.

Locations and Business Units That Do Not Require Testing

B12. No testing is required for locations or business units that individually, and when aggregated with others, could not result in a material misstatement to the financial statements.

Multi-Location Testing Considerations Flowchart

B13. Illustration B-1 depicts how to apply the directions in this section to a hypothetical company with 150 locations or business units, along with the auditor's testing considerations for those locations or business units.

Illustration B-1

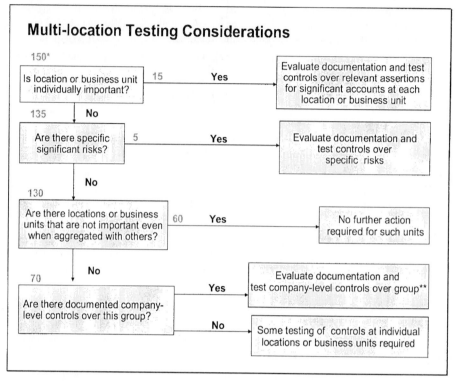

Multi-location Testing Considerations

150*

Is location or business unit individually important? — 15 — **Yes** → Evaluate documentation and test controls over relevant assertions for significant accounts at each location or business unit

135 **No**

Are there specific significant risks? — 5 — **Yes** → Evaluate documentation and test controls over specific risks

No

130

Are there locations or business units that are not important even when aggregated with others? — 60 — **Yes** → No further action required for such units

No

70

Are there documented company-level controls over this group? — **Yes** → Evaluate documentation and test company-level controls over group**

No → Some testing of controls at individual locations or business units required

* Numbers represent number of locations affected.
** See paragraph B7.

Special Situations

B14. The scope of the evaluation of the company's internal control over financial reporting should include entities that are acquired on or before the date of management's assessment and operations that are accounted for as discontinued operations on the date of management's assessment. The auditor should consider this multiple locations discussion in determining whether it will be necessary to test controls at these entities or operations.

B15. For equity method investments, the evaluation of the company's internal control over financial reporting should include controls over the reporting in accordance with generally accepted accounting principles, in the company's financial statements, of the company's portion of the investees' income or loss, the investment balance, adjustments to the income or loss and investment balance, and related disclosures. The evaluation ordinarily would not extend to controls at the equity method investee.

B16. In situations in which the SEC allows management to limit its assessment of internal control over financial reporting by excluding certain entities, the auditor may limit the audit in the same manner and report without reference to the limitation in scope. However, the auditor should evaluate the reasonableness of management's conclusion that the situation meets the criteria of the SEC's allowed exclusion and the appropriateness of any required disclosure related to such a limitation. If the auditor believes that management's disclosure about the limitation requires modification, the auditor should follow the same communication responsibilities as described in paragraphs 204 and 205. If management and the audit committee do not respond appropriately, in addition to fulfilling those responsibilities, the auditor should modify his or her report on the audit of internal control over financial reporting to include an explanatory paragraph describing the reasons why the auditor believes management's disclosure should be modified.

B17. For example, for entities that are consolidated or proportionately consolidated, the evaluation of the company's internal control over financial reporting should include controls over significant accounts and processes that exist at the consolidated or proportionately consolidated entity. In some instances, however, such as for some variable interest entities as defined in Financial Accounting Standards Board Interpretation No. 46, *Consolidation of Variable Interest Entities,* management might not be able to obtain the information necessary to make an assessment because it does not have the ability to control the entity. If management is allowed to limit its assessment by excluding such entities,[1] the auditor may limit the audit in the same manner and report without reference to the limitation in scope. In this case, the evaluation of the company's internal control over financial reporting should include evaluation of controls over the reporting in accordance with generally accepted accounting principles, in the company's financial statements, of the company's portion of the entity's income or loss, the investment balance, adjustments to the income or loss and investment balances, and related disclosures. However, the auditor should evaluate the reasonableness of management's conclusion that it does not have the ability to obtain the necessary information as well as the appropriateness of any required disclosure related to such a limitation.

Use of Service Organizations

B18. AU sec. 324, *Service Organizations,* applies to the audit of financial statements of a company that obtains services from another organization that are part of its information system. The auditor may apply the relevant concepts described in AU sec. 324 to the audit of internal control over financial reporting. Further, although AU sec. 324 was designed to address auditor-to-auditor communications as part of the audit of financial statements, it also is appropriate for management to apply the relevant concepts described in that standard to its assessment of internal control over financial reporting.

B19. Paragraph .03 of AU sec. 324 describes the situation in which a service organization's services are part of a company's information system. If the service organization's services are part of a company's information system, as described therein, then they are part of the information and communication component of the company's internal control over financial reporting. When the service organization's services are part of the company's internal control over financial reporting, management should consider the activities of the service organization in making its assessment of internal control over financial reporting, and the auditor should consider the activities of the service organization in determining the evidence required to support his or her opinion.

---

1. It is our understanding that the SEC Staff may conclude that management can limit the scope of its assessment if it does not have the authority to affect, and therefore cannot assess, the controls in place over certain amounts. This would relate to entities that are consolidated or proportionately consolidated when the issuer does not have sufficient control over the entity to assess and affect controls. If management's report on its assessment of the effectiveness of internal control over financial reporting is limited in that manner, the SEC staff may permit the company to disclose this fact as well as information about the magnitude of the amounts included in the financial statements from entities whose controls cannot be assessed. This disclosure would be required in each filing, but outside of management's report on its assessment of the effectiveness of internal control over financial reporting.

Note: The use of a service organization does not reduce management's responsibility to maintain effective internal control over financial reporting.

B20. Paragraphs .07 through .16 in AU sec. 324 describe the procedures that management and the auditor should perform with respect to the activities performed by the service organization. The procedures include:

a. Obtaining an understanding of the controls at the service organization that are relevant to the entity's internal control and the controls at the user organization over the activities of the service organization, and

b. Obtaining evidence that the controls that are relevant to management's assessment and the auditor's opinion are operating effectively.

B21. Evidence that the controls that are relevant to management's assessment and the auditor's opinion are operating effectively may be obtained by following the procedures described in paragraph .12 of AU sec. 324. These procedures include:

a. Performing tests of the user organization's controls over the activities of the service organization (for example, testing the user organization's independent reperformance of selected items processed by the service organization or testing the user organization's reconciliation of output reports with source documents).

b. Performing tests of controls at the service organization.

c. Obtaining a service auditor's report on controls placed in operation and tests of operating effectiveness, or a report on the application of agreed-upon procedures that describes relevant tests of controls.

Note: The service auditor's report referred to above means a report with the service auditor's opinion on the service organization's description of the design of its controls, the tests of controls, and results of those tests performed by the service auditor, and the service auditor's opinion on whether the controls tested were operating effectively during the specified period (in other words, "reports on controls placed in operation and tests of operating effectiveness" described in paragraph .24b of AU sec. 324). A service auditor's report that does not include tests of controls, results of the tests, and the service auditor's opinion on operating effectiveness (in other words, "reports on controls placed in operation" described in paragraph .24a of AU sec. 324) does not provide evidence of operating effectiveness. Furthermore, if the evidence regarding operating effectiveness of controls comes from an agreed-upon procedures report rather than a service auditor's report issued pursuant to AU sec. 324, management and the auditor should evaluate whether the agreed-upon procedures report provides sufficient evidence in the same manner described in the following paragraph.

B22. If a service auditor's report on controls placed in operation and tests of operating effectiveness is available, management and the auditor may evaluate whether this report provides sufficient evidence to support the assessment and opinion, respectively. In evaluating whether such a service auditor's report provides sufficient evidence, management and the auditor should consider the following factors:

- The time period covered by the tests of controls and its relation to the date of management's assessment,

- The scope of the examination and applications covered, the controls tested, and the way in which tested controls relate to the company's controls,

- The results of those tests of controls and the service auditor's opinion on the operating effectiveness of the controls.

Note: These factors are similar to factors the auditor would consider in determining whether the report provides sufficient evidence to support the auditor's assessed level of control risk in an audit of the financial statements as described in paragraph .16 of AU sec. 324.

B23. If the service auditor's report on controls placed in operation and tests of operating effectiveness contains a qualification that the stated control objectives might be achieved only if the company applies controls contemplated in the design of the system by the service organization, the auditor should evaluate whether the company is applying the necessary procedures. For example, completeness of processing payroll transactions might depend on the company's validation that all payroll records sent to the service organization were processed by checking a control total.

B24. In determining whether the service auditor's report provides sufficient evidence to support management's assessment and the auditor's opinion, management and the auditor should make inquiries concerning the service auditor's reputation, competence, and independence. Appropriate sources of information concerning the professional reputation of the service auditor are discussed in paragraph .10a of AU sec. 543, *Part of Audit Performed by Other Independent Auditors.*

B25. When a significant period of time has elapsed between the time period covered by the tests of controls in the service auditor's report and the date of management's assessment, additional procedures should be performed. The auditor should inquire of management to determine whether management has identified any changes in the service organization's controls subsequent to the period covered by the service auditor's report (such as changes communicated to management from the service organization, changes in personnel at the service organization with whom management interacts, changes in reports or other data received from the service organization, changes in contracts or service level agreements with the service organization, or errors identified in the service organization's processing). If management has identified such changes, the auditor should determine whether management has performed procedures to evaluate the effect of such changes on the effectiveness of the company's internal control over financial reporting. The auditor also should consider whether the results of other procedures he or she performed indicate that there have been changes in the controls at the service organization that management has not identified.

B26. The auditor should determine whether to obtain additional evidence about the operating effectiveness of controls at the service organization based on the procedures performed by management or the auditor and the results of those procedures and on an evaluation of the following factors. As these factors increase in significance, the need for the auditor to obtain additional evidence increases.

- The elapsed time between the time period covered by the tests of controls in the service auditor's report and the date of management's assessment,
- The significance of the activities of the service organization,
- Whether there are errors that have been identified in the service organization's processing, and
- The nature and significance of any changes in the service organization's controls identified by management or the auditor.

B27. If the auditor concludes that additional evidence about the operating effectiveness of controls at the service organization is required, the auditor's additional procedures may include:

- Evaluating the procedures performed by management and the results of those procedures.
- Contacting the service organization, through the user organization, to obtain specific information.
- Requesting that a service auditor be engaged to perform procedures that will supply the necessary information.
- Visiting the service organization and performing such procedures.

B28. Based on the evidence obtained, management and the auditor should determine whether they have obtained sufficient evidence to obtain the reasonable assurance necessary for their assessment and opinion, respectively.

B29. The auditor should not refer to the service auditor's report when expressing an opinion on internal control over financial reporting.

Examples of Extent-of-Testing Decisions

B30. As discussed throughout this standard, determining the effectiveness of a company's internal control over financial reporting includes evaluating the design and operating effectiveness of controls over all relevant assertions related to all significant accounts and disclosures in the financial statements. Paragraphs 88 through 107 provide the auditor with directions about the nature, timing, and extent of testing of the design and operating effectiveness of internal control over financial reporting.

B31. Examples B-1 through B-4 illustrate how to apply this information in various situations. These examples are for illustrative purposes only.

Example B-1 — Daily Programmed Application Control and Daily Information Technology-Dependent Manual Control

The auditor has determined that cash and accounts receivable are significant accounts to the audit of XYZ Company's internal control over financial reporting. Based on discussions with company personnel and review of company documentation, the auditor learned that the company had the following procedures in place to account for cash received in the lockbox:

a. The company receives a download of cash receipts from the banks.

b. The information technology system applies cash received in the lockbox to individual customer accounts.

c. Any cash received in the lockbox and not applied to a customer's account is listed on an exception report (Unapplied Cash Exception Report).

- Therefore, the application of cash to a customer's account is a programmed application control, while the review and follow-up of unapplied cash from the exception report is a manual control.

To determine whether misstatements in cash (existence assertion) and accounts receivable (existence, valuation, and completeness) would be prevented or detected on a timely basis, the auditor decided to test the controls provided by the system in the daily reconciliation of lock box receipts to customer accounts, as well as the control over reviewing and resolving unapplied cash in the Unapplied Cash Exception Report.

Nature, Timing, and Extent of Procedures. To test the programmed application control, the auditor:

- Identified, through discussion with company personnel, the software used to receive the download from the banks and to process the transactions and determined that the banks supply the download software.

  —The company uses accounting software acquired from a third-party supplier. The software consists of a number of modules. The client modifies the software only for upgrades supplied by the supplier.

- Determined, through further discussion with company personnel, that the cash module operates the lockbox functionality and the posting of cash to the general ledger. The accounts receivable module posts the cash to individual customer accounts and produces the Unapplied Cash Exception Report, a standard report supplied with the package. The auditor agreed this information to the supplier's documentation.

- Identified, through discussions with company personnel and review of the supplier's documentation, the names, file sizes (in bytes), and locations of the executable files (programs) that operate the functionality under review. The auditor then identified the compilation dates of these programs and agreed them to the original installation date of the application.

- Identified the objectives of the programs to be tested. The auditor wanted to determine whether only appropriate cash items are posted to customers' accounts and matched to customer number, invoice number, amount, etc., and that there is a listing of inappropriate cash items (that is, any of the above items not matching) on the exception report.

In addition, the auditor had evaluated and tested general computer controls, including program changes (for example, confirmation that no unauthorized changes are undertaken) and logical access (for example, data file access to the file downloaded from the banks and user access to the cash and accounts receivable modules) and concluded that they were operating effectively.

To determine whether such programmed controls were operating effectively, the auditor performed a walkthrough in the month of July. The computer controls operate in a systematic manner, therefore, the auditor concluded that it was sufficient to perform a walkthrough for only the one item. During the walkthrough, the auditor performed and documented the following items:

a. Selected one customer and agreed the amount billed to the customer to the cash received in the lockbox.

b. Agreed the total of the lockbox report to the posting of cash receipts in the general ledger.

c. Agreed the total of the cash receipt download from the bank to the lockbox report and supporting documentation.

d. Selected one customer's remittance and agreed amount posted to the customer's account in the accounts receivable subsidiary ledger.

To test the detective control of review and follow up on the Daily Unapplied Cash Exception Report, the auditor:

a. *Made inquiries of company personnel.* To understand the procedures in place to en-sure that all unapplied items are resolved, the time frame in which such resolution takes place, and whether unapplied items are handled properly within the system, the auditor discussed these matters with the employee responsible for reviewing and resolving the Daily Unapplied Cash Exception Reports. The auditor learned that, when items appear on the Daily-Unapplied Cash Exception Report, the employee must manually enter the correction into the system. The employee typically performs the resolution procedures the next business day. Items that typically appear on the Daily Unapplied Cash Excep-tion Report relate to payments made by a customer without reference to an invoice num-ber/purchase order number or to underpayments of an invoice due to quantity or pricing discrepancies.

b. *Observed personnel performing the control.* The auditor then observed the employee reviewing and resolving a Daily Unapplied Cash Exception Report. The day selected contained four exceptions three related to payments made by a customer without an in-voice number, and one related to an underpayment due to a pricing discrepancy.

- For the pricing discrepancy, the employee determined, through discussions with a sales person, that the customer had been billed an incorrect price; a price break that the sales person had granted to the customer was not reflected on the customer's in-voice. The employee resolved the pricing discrepancy, determined which invoices were being paid, and entered a correction into the system to properly apply cash to the customer's account and reduce accounts receivable and sales accounts for the amount of the price break.

c. *Reperformed the control.* Finally, the auditor selected 25 Daily Unapplied Cash Ex-ception Reports from the period January to September. For the reports selected, the audi-tor reperformed the follow-up procedures that the employee performed. For instance, the auditor inspected the documents and sources of information used in the follow-up and determined that the transaction was properly corrected in the system. The auditor also scanned other Daily Unapplied Cash Exception Reports to determine that the control was performed throughout the period of intended reliance.

Because the tests of controls were performed at an interim date, the auditor had to determine whether there were any significant changes in the controls from interim to year-end. There-fore, the auditor asked company personnel about the procedures in place at year-end. Such procedures had not changed from the interim period, therefore, the auditor observed that the controls were still in place by scanning Daily Unapplied Cash Exception Reports to deter-mine the control was performed on a timely basis during the period from September to year-end.

Based on the auditor's procedures, the auditor concluded that the employee was clearing ex-ceptions in a timely manner and that the control was operating effectively as of year-end.

Example B-2 — **Monthly Manual Reconciliation**

The auditor determined that accounts receivable is a significant account to the audit of XYZ Company's internal control over financial reporting. Through discussions with company per-sonnel and review of company documentation, the auditor learned that company personnel reconcile the accounts receivable subsidiary ledger to the general ledger on a monthly basis. To determine whether misstatements in accounts receivable (existence, valuation, and com-pleteness) would be detected on a timely basis, the auditor decided to test the control pro-vided by the monthly reconciliation process.

Nature, Timing, and Extent of Procedures. The auditor tested the company's reconciliation control by selecting a sample of reconciliations based upon the number of accounts, the dollar value of the accounts, and the volume of transactions affecting the account. Because the auditor considered all other receivable accounts immaterial, and because such accounts had only minimal transactions flowing through them, the auditor decided to test only the reconciliation for the trade accounts receivable account. The auditor elected to perform the tests of controls over the reconciliation process in conjunction with the auditor's substantive procedures over the accounts receivable confirmation procedures, which were performed in July.

To test the reconciliation process, the auditor:

a. *Made inquiries of personnel performing the control.* The auditor asked the employee performing the reconciliation a number of questions, including the following:

- What documentation describes the account reconciliation process?
- How long have you been performing the reconciliation work?
- What is the reconciliation process for resolving reconciling items?
- How often are the reconciliations formally reviewed and signed off?
- If significant issues or reconciliation problems are noticed, to whose attention do you bring them?
- On average, how many reconciling items are there?
- How are old reconciling items treated?
- If need be, how is the system corrected for reconciling items?
- What is the general nature of these reconciling items?

b. *Observed the employee performing the control.* The auditor observed the employee performing the reconciliation procedures. For nonrecurring reconciling items, the auditor observed whether each item included a clear explanation as to its nature, the action that had been taken to resolve it, and whether it had been resolved on a timely basis.

c. *Reperformed the control.* Finally, the auditor inspected the reconciliations and reperfomed the reconciliation procedures. For the May and July reconciliations, the auditor traced the reconciling amounts to the source documents on a test basis. The only reconciling item that appeared on these reconciliations was cash received in the lockbox the previous day that had not been applied yet to the customer's account. The auditor pursued the items in each month's reconciliation to determine that the reconciling item cleared the following business day. The auditor also scanned through the file of all reconciliations prepared during the year and noted that they had been performed on a timely basis. To determine that the company had not made significant changes in its reconciliation control procedures from interim to year-end, the auditor made inquiries of company personnel and determined that such procedures had not changed from interim to year-end. Therefore, the auditor verified that controls were still in place by scanning the monthly account reconciliations to determine that the control was performed on a timely basis during the interim to year-end period.

Based on the auditor's procedures, the auditor concluded that the reconciliation control was operating effectively as of year-end.

Example B-3 — *Daily Manual Preventive Control*

The auditor determined that cash and accounts payable were significant accounts to the audit of the company's internal control over financial reporting. Through discussions with company personnel, the auditor learned that company personnel make a cash disbursement only after they have matched the vendor invoice to the receiver and purchase order. To determine whether misstatements in cash (existence) and accounts payable (existence, valuation, and completeness) would be prevented on a timely basis, the auditor tested the control over making a cash disbursement only after matching the invoice with the receiver and purchase.

Nature, Timing, and Extent of Procedures. On a haphazard basis, the auditor selected 25 disbursements from the cash disbursement registers from January through September. In this example, the auditor deemed a test of 25 cash disbursement transactions an appropriate sample size because the auditor was testing a manual control performed as part of the routine processing of cash disbursement transactions through the system. Furthermore, the auditor expected no errors based on the results of company-level tests performed earlier. [If, however, the auditor had encountered a control exception, the auditor would have attempted to identify the root cause of the exception and tested an additional number of items. If another control exception had been noted, the auditor would have decided that this control was not effective. As a result, the auditor would have decided to increase the extent of substantive procedures to be performed in connection with the financial statement audit of the cash and accounts payable accounts.]

    a. After obtaining the related voucher package, the auditor examined the invoice to see if it included the signature or initials of the accounts payable clerk, evidencing the clerk's performance of the matching control. However, a signature on a voucher package to indicate signor approval does not necessarily mean that the person carefully reviewed it before signing. The voucher package may have been signed based on only a cursory review, or without any review.

    b. The auditor decided that the quality of the evidence regarding the effective operation of the control evidenced by a signature or initials was not sufficiently persuasive to ensure that the control operated effectively during the test period. In order to obtain additional evidence, the auditor reperformed the matching control corresponding to the signature, which included examining the invoice to determine that (a) its items matched to the receiver and purchase order and (b) it was mathematically accurate.

Because the auditor performed the tests of controls at an interim date, the auditor updated the testing through the end of the year (initial tests are through September to December) by asking the accounts payable clerk whether the control was still in place and operating effectively. The auditor confirmed that understanding by performing a walkthrough of one transaction in December.

Based on the auditor's procedures, the auditor concluded that the control over making a cash disbursement only after matching the invoice with the receiver and purchase was operating effectively as of year-end.

Example B-4 — *Programmed Prevent Control and Weekly Information Technology-Dependent Manual Detective Control*

The auditor determined that cash, accounts payable, and inventory were significant accounts to the audit of the company's internal control over financial reporting. Through discussions with company personnel, the auditor learned that the company's computer system performs a three-way match of the receiver, purchase order, and invoice. If there are any exceptions, the system produces a list of unmatched items that employees review and follow up on weekly.

In this case, the computer match is a programmed application control, and the review and follow-up of the unmatched items report is a detective control. To determine whether misstatements in cash (existence) and accounts payable/inventory (existence, valuation, and completeness) would be prevented or detected on a timely basis, the auditor decided to test the programmed application control of matching the receiver, purchase order, and invoice as well as the review and follow-up control over unmatched items.

Nature, Timing, and Extent of Procedures. To test the programmed application control, the auditor:

a. Identified, through discussion with company personnel, the software used to process receipts and purchase invoices. The software used was a third-party package consisting of a number of modules.

b. Determined, through further discussion with company personnel, that they do not modify the core functionality of the software, but sometimes make personalized changes to reports to meet the changing needs of the business. From previous experience with the company's information technology environment, the auditor believes that such changes are infrequent and that information technology process controls are well established.

c. Established, through further discussion, that the inventory module operated the receiving functionality, including the matching of receipts to open purchase orders. Purchase invoices were processed in the accounts payable module, which matched them to an approved purchase order against which a valid receipt has been made. That module also produced the Unmatched Items Report, a standard report supplied with the package to which the company has not made any modifications. That information was agreed to the supplier's documentation and to documentation within the information technology department.

d. Identified, through discussions with the client and review of the supplier's documentation, the names, file sizes (in bytes), and locations of the executable files (programs) that operate the functionality under review. The auditor then identified the compilation dates of the programs and agreed them to the original installation date of the application. The compilation date of the report code was agreed to documentation held within the information technology department relating to the last change made to that report (a change in formatting).

e. Identified the objectives of the programs to be tested. The auditor wanted to determine whether appropriate items are received (for example, match a valid purchase order), appropriate purchase invoices are posted (for example, match a valid receipt and purchase order, non-duplicate reference numbers) and unmatched items (for example, receipts, orders or invoices) are listed on the exception report. The auditor then reperformed all those variations in the packages on a test-of-one basis to determine that the programs operated as described.

In addition, the auditor had evaluated and tested general computer controls, including program changes (for example, confirmation that no unauthorized changes are undertaken to the functionality and that changes to reports are appropriately authorized, tested, and approved before being applied) and logical access (for example, user access to the inventory and accounts payable modules and access to the area on the system where report code is maintained), and concluded that they were operating effectively. (Since the computer is deemed to operate in a systematic manner, the auditor concluded that it was sufficient to perform a walkthrough for only the one item.)

To determine whether the programmed control was operating effectively, the auditor performed a walkthrough in the month of July. As a result of the walkthrough, the auditor performed and documented the following items:

a. Receiving cannot record the receipt of goods without matching the receipt to a purchase order on the system. The auditor tested that control by attempting to record the receipt of goods into the system without a purchase order. However, the system did not allow the auditor to do that. Rather, the system produced an error message stating that the goods could not be recorded as received without an active purchase order.

b. An invoice will not be paid unless the system can match the receipt and vendor invoice to an approved purchase order. The auditor tested that control by attempting to approve an invoice for payment in the system. The system did not allow the auditor to do that. Rather, it produced an error message indicating that invoices could not be paid without an active purchase order and receiver.

c. The system disallows the processing of invoices with identical vendor and identical invoice numbers. In addition, the system will not allow two invoices to be processed against the same purchase order unless the sum of the invoices is less than the amount approved on the purchase order. The auditor tested that control by attempting to process duplicate invoices. However, the system produced an error message indicating that the invoice had already been processed.

d. The system compares the invoice amounts to the purchase order. If there are differences in quantity/extended price, and such differences fall outside a preapproved tolerance, the system does not allow the invoice to be processed. The auditor tested that control by attempting to process an invoice that had quantity/price differences outside the tolerance level of 10 pieces, or $1,000. The system produced an error message indicating that the invoice could not be processed because of such differences.

e. The system processes payments only for vendors established in the vendor master file. The auditor tested that control by attempting to process an invoice for a vendor that was not established in the vendor master file. However, the system did not allow the payment to be processed.

f. The auditor tested user access to the vendor file and whether such users can make modifications to such file by attempting to access and make changes to the vendor tables. However, the system did not allow the auditor to perform that function and produced an error message stating that the user was not authorized to perform that function.

g. The auditor verified the completeness and accuracy of the Unmatched Items Report by verifying that one unmatched item was on the report and one matched item was not on the report.

Note: It is inadvisable for the auditor to have uncontrolled access to the company's systems in his or her attempts described above to record the receipt of goods without a purchase order, approve an invoice for payment, process duplicate invoices, etc. These procedures ordinarily are performed in the presence of appropriate company personnel so that they can be notified immediately of any breach to their systems.

To test the detect control of review and follow up on the Unmatched Items Report, the auditor performed the following procedures in the month of July for the period January to July:

a. *Made inquiries of company personnel.* To gain an understanding of the procedures in place to ensure that all unmatched items are followed-up properly and that corrections are made on a timely basis, the auditor made inquiries of the employee who follows up on the weekly-unmatched items reports. On a weekly basis, the control required the employee to review the Unmatched Items Report to determine why items appear on it. The employee's review includes proper followup on items, including determining whether:

- All open purchase orders are either closed or voided within an acceptable amount of time.
- The requesting party is notified periodically of the status of the purchase order and the reason for its current status.
- The reason the purchase order remains open is due to incomplete shipment of goods and, if so, whether the vendor has been notified.
- There are quantity problems that should be discussed with purchasing.

b. *Observed the performance of the control.* The auditor observed the employee performing the control for the Unmatched Items Reports generated during the first week in July.

c. *Reperformed the control.* The auditor selected five weekly Unmatched Items Reports, selected several items from each, and reperformed the procedures that the employee performed. The auditor also scanned other Unmatched Items Reports to determine that the control was performed throughout the period of intended reliance.

To determine that the company had not made significant changes in their controls from interim to year-end, the auditor discussed with company personnel the procedures in place for making such changes. Since the procedures had not changed from interim to year-end, the auditor observed that the controls were still in place by scanning the weekly Unmatched Items Reports to determine that the control was performed on a timely basis during the interim to year-end period.

Based on the auditor's procedures, the auditor concluded that the employee was clearing exceptions in a timely manner and that the control was operating effectively as of year-end.

APPENDIX C

Safeguarding of Assets

C1. *Safeguarding of assets* is defined in paragraph 7 as those policies and procedures that "provide reasonable assurance regarding prevention or timely detection of unauthorized acquisition, use or disposition of the company's assets that could have a material effect on the financial statements." This definition is consistent with the definition provided in the Committee of Sponsoring Organizations (COSO) of the Treadway Commission's Addendum, *Reporting to External Parties,* which provides the following definition of internal control over safeguarding of assets:

Internal control over safeguarding of assets against unauthorized acquisition, use or disposition is a process, effected by an entity's board of directors, management and other personnel, designed to provide reasonable assurance regarding prevention or timely detection of unauthorized acquisition, use, or disposition of the entity's assets that could have a material effect on the financial statements. Such internal control can be judged effective if the board of directors and management have reasonable assurance that unauthorized acquisition, use or disposition of the entity's assets that could have a material effect on the financial statements is being prevented or detected on a timely basis.

C2. For example, a company has safeguarding controls over inventory tags (preventive controls) and also performs periodic physical inventory counts (detective control) timely in relation to its quarterly and annual financial reporting dates. Although the physical inventory count does not safeguard the inventory from theft or loss, it prevents a material misstatement to the financial statements if performed effectively and timely.

C3. Therefore, given that the definitions of material weakness and significant deficiency relate to the likelihood of misstatement of the financial statements, the failure of a preventive control such as inventory tags will not result in a significant deficiency or material weakness if the detective control (physical inventory) prevents a misstatement of the financial statements. The COSO Addendum also indicates that to the extent that such losses might occur, controls over financial reporting are effective if they provide reasonable assurance that those losses are properly reflected in the financial statements, thereby alerting financial statement users to consider the need for action.

> **Note:** *Properly reflected* in the financial statements includes both correctly recording the loss and adequately disclosing the loss.

C4. Material weaknesses relating to controls over the safeguarding of assets would only exist when the company does not have effective controls (considering both safeguarding and other controls) to prevent or detect a material misstatement of the financial statements.

C5. Furthermore, management's plans that could potentially affect financial reporting in future periods are not controls. For example, a company's business continuity or contingency planning has no effect on the company's current abilities to initiate, authorize, record, process, or report financial data. Therefore, a company's business continuity or contingency planning is not part of internal control over financial reporting.

C6. The COSO Addendum provides further information about safeguarding of assets as it relates to internal control over financial reporting.

APPENDIX D

Examples of Significant Deficiencies and Material Weaknesses

D1. Paragraph 8 of this standard defines a control deficiency. Paragraphs 9 and 10 go on to define a significant deficiency and a material weakness, respectively.

D2. Paragraphs 22 through 23 of this standard discuss materiality in an audit of internal control over financial reporting, and paragraphs 130 through 140 provide additional direction on evaluating deficiencies in internal control over financial reporting.

D3. The following examples illustrate how to evaluate the significance of internal control deficiencies in various situations. These examples are for illustrative purposes only.

Example D-1 — *Reconciliations of Intercompany Accounts Are Not Performed on a Timely Basis*

Scenario A — Significant Deficiency. The company processes a significant number of routine intercompany transactions on a monthly basis. Individual intercompany transactions are not material and primarily relate to balance sheet activity, for example, cash transfers between business units to finance normal operations.

A formal management policy requires monthly reconciliation of intercompany accounts and confirmation of balances between business units. However, there is not a process in place to ensure performance of these procedures. As a result, detailed reconciliations of intercompany accounts are not performed on a timely basis. Management does perform monthly procedures to investigate selected large-dollar intercompany account differences. In addition, management prepares a detailed monthly variance analysis of operating expenses to assess their reasonableness.

Based only on these facts, the auditor should determine that this deficiency represents a significant deficiency for the following reasons: The magnitude of a financial statement misstatement resulting from this deficiency would reasonably be expected to be more than inconsequential, but less than material, because individual intercompany transactions are not material, and the compensating controls operating monthly should detect a material misstatement. Furthermore, the transactions are primarily restricted to balance sheet accounts. However, the compensating detective controls are designed only to detect material misstatements. The controls do not address the detection of misstatements that are more than inconsequential but less than material. Therefore, the likelihood that a misstatement that was more than inconsequential, but less than material, could occur is more than remote.

Scenario B — Material Weakness. The company processes a significant number of intercompany transactions on a monthly basis. Intercompany transactions relate to a wide range of activities, including transfers of inventory with intercompany profit between business units, allocation of research and development costs to business units and corporate charges. Individual intercompany transactions are frequently material.

A formal management policy requires monthly reconciliation of intercompany accounts and confirmation of balances between business units. However, there is not a process in place to ensure that these procedures are performed on a consistent basis. As a result, reconciliations of intercompany accounts are not performed on a timely basis, and differences in intercompany accounts are frequent and significant. Management does not perform any alternative controls to investigate significant intercompany account differences.

Based only on these facts, the auditor should determine that this deficiency represents a material weakness for the following reasons: The magnitude of a financial statement misstatement resulting from this deficiency would reasonably be expected to be material, because individual intercompany transactions are frequently material and relate to a wide range of activities. Additionally, actual unreconciled differences in intercompany accounts have been, and are, material. The likelihood of such a misstatement is more than remote because such misstatements have frequently occurred and compensating controls are not effective, either because they are not properly designed or not operating effectively. Taken together, the magnitude and likelihood of misstatement of the financial statements resulting from this internal control deficiency meet the definition of a material weakness.

Example D-2—*Modifications to Standard Sales Contract Terms Not Reviewed To Evaluate Impact on Timing and Amount of Revenue Recognition*

Scenario A — Significant Deficiency. The company uses a standard sales contract for most transactions. Individual sales transactions are not material to the entity. Sales personnel are allowed to modify sales contract terms. The company's accounting function reviews significant or unusual modifications to the sales contract terms, but does not review changes in the standard shipping terms. The changes in the standard shipping terms could require a delay in the timing of revenue recognition. Management reviews gross margins on a monthly basis and investigates any significant or unusual relationships. In addition, management reviews the reasonableness of inventory levels at the end of each accounting period. The entity has experienced limited situations in which revenue has been inappropriately recorded in advance of shipment, but amounts have not been material.

Based only on these facts, the auditor should determine that this deficiency represents a significant deficiency for the following reasons: The magnitude of a financial statement misstatement resulting from this deficiency would reasonably be expected to be more than inconsequential, but less than material, because individual sales transactions are not material and the compensating detective controls operating monthly and at the end of each financial reporting period should reduce the likelihood of a material misstatement going undetected. Furthermore, the risk of material misstatement is limited to revenue recognition errors related to shipping terms as opposed to broader sources of error in revenue recognition. However, the compensating detective controls are only designed to detect material misstatements. The controls do not effectively address the detection of misstatements that are more than inconsequential but less than material, as evidenced by situations in which transactions that were not material were improperly recorded. Therefore, there is a more than remote likelihood that a misstatement that is more than inconsequential but less than material could occur.

Scenario B — Material Weakness. The company has a standard sales contract, but sales personnel frequently modify the terms of the contract. The nature of the modifications can affect the timing and amount of revenue recognized. Individual sales transactions are frequently material to the entity, and the gross margin can vary significantly for each transaction.

The company does not have procedures in place for the accounting function to regularly review modifications to sales contract terms. Although management reviews gross margins on a monthly basis, the significant differences in gross margins on individual transactions make it difficult for management to identify potential misstatements. Improper revenue recognition has occurred, and the amounts have been material.

Based only on these facts, the auditor should determine that this deficiency represents a material weakness for the following reasons: The magnitude of a financial statement misstatement resulting from this deficiency would reasonably be expected to be material, because individual sales transactions are frequently material, and gross margin can vary significantly with each transaction (which would make compensating detective controls based on a reasonableness review ineffective). Additionally, improper revenue recognition has occurred, and the amounts have been material. Therefore, the likelihood of material misstatements occurring is more than remote. Taken together, the magnitude and likelihood of misstatement of the financial statements resulting from this internal control deficiency meet the definition of a material weakness.

Scenario C — Material Weakness. The company has a standard sales contract, but sales personnel frequently modify the terms of the contract. Sales personnel frequently grant unauthorized and unrecorded sales discounts to customers without the knowledge of the accounting department. These amounts are deducted by customers in paying their invoices and are recorded as outstanding balances on the accounts receivable aging. Although these amounts are individually insignificant, they are material in the aggregate and have occurred consistently over the past few years.

Based on only these facts, the auditor should determine that this deficiency represents a material weakness for the following reasons: The magnitude of a financial statement misstatement resulting from this deficiency would reasonably be expected to be material, because the frequency of occurrence allows insignificant amounts to become material in the aggregate. The likelihood of material misstatement of the financial statements resulting from this internal control deficiency is more than remote (even assuming that the amounts were fully reserved for in the company's allowance for uncollectible accounts) due to the likelihood of material misstatement of the gross accounts receivable balance. Therefore, this internal control deficiency meets the definition of a material weakness.

Example D-3—*Identification of Several Deficiencies*

Scenario A — Material Weakness. During its assessment of internal control over financial reporting, management identified the following deficiencies. Based on the context in which the deficiencies occur, management and the auditor agree that these deficiencies individually represent significant deficiencies:

- Inadequate segregation of duties over certain information system access controls.

- Several instances of transactions that were not properly recorded in subsidiary ledgers; transactions were not material, either individually or in the aggregate.

- A lack of timely reconciliations of the account balances affected by the improperly recorded transactions.

Based only on these facts, the auditor should determine that the combination of these significant deficiencies represents a material weakness for the following reasons: Individually, these deficiencies were evaluated as representing a more than remote likelihood that a misstatement that is more than inconsequential, but less than material, could occur. However, each of these significant deficiencies affects the same set of accounts. Taken together, these significant deficiencies represent a more than remote likelihood that a material misstatement could occur and not be prevented or detected. Therefore, in combination, these significant deficiencies represent a material weakness.

Scenario B — Material Weakness. During its assessment of internal control over financial reporting, management of a financial institution identifies deficiencies in: the design of controls over the estimation of credit losses (a critical accounting estimate); the operating effectiveness of controls for initiating, processing, and reviewing adjustments to the allowance for credit losses; and the operating effectiveness of controls designed to prevent and detect the improper recognition of interest income. Management and the auditor agree that, in their overall context, each of these deficiencies individually represent a significant deficiency.

In addition, during the past year, the company experienced a significant level of growth in the loan balances that were subjected to the controls governing credit loss estimation and revenue recognition, and further growth is expected in the upcoming year.

Based only on these facts, the auditor should determine that the combination of these significant deficiencies represents a material weakness for the following reasons:

- The balances of the loan accounts affected by these significant deficiencies have increased over the past year and are expected to increase in the future.

- This growth in loan balances, coupled with the combined effect of the significant deficiencies described, results in a more than remote likelihood that a material misstatement of the allowance for credit losses or interest income could occur.

Therefore, in combination, these deficiencies meet the definition of a material weakness.

APPENDIX E—BACKGROUND AND BASIS FOR CONCLUSIONS

Introduction

E1. This appendix summarizes factors that the Public Company Accounting Oversight Board (the "Board") deemed significant in reaching the conclusions in the standard. This appendix includes reasons for accepting certain views and rejecting others.

Background

E2. Section 404(a) of the Sarbanes-Oxley Act of 2002 (the "Act"), and the Securities and Exchange Commission's (SEC) related implementing rules, require the management of a public company to assess the effectiveness of the company's internal control over financial reporting, as of the end of the company's most recent fiscal year. Section 404(a) of the Act also requires management to include in the company's annual report to shareholders management's conclusion as a result of that assessment of whether the company's internal control over financial reporting is effective.

E3. Sections 103(a)(2)(A) and 404(b) of the Act direct the Board to establish professional standards governing the independent auditor's attestation and reporting on management's assessment of the effectiveness of internal control over financial reporting.

E4. The backdrop for the development of the Board's first major auditing standard was, of course, the spectacular audit failures and corporate malfeasance that led to the passage of the Act. Although all of the various components of the Act work together to help restore investor confidence and help prevent the types of financial reporting breakdowns that lead to the loss of investor confidence, Section 404 of the Act is certainly one of the most visible and tangible changes required by the Act.

E5. The Board believes that effective controls provide the foundation for reliable financial reporting. Congress believed this too, which is why the new reporting by management and the auditor on the effectiveness of internal control over financial reporting received such prominent attention in the Act. Internal control over financial reporting enhances a company's ability to produce fair and complete financial reports. Without reliable financial reports, making good judgments and decisions about a company becomes very difficult for anyone, including the board of directors, management, employees, investors, lenders, customers, and regulators. The auditor's reporting on management's assessment of the effectiveness of internal control over financial reporting provides users of that report with important assurance about the reliability of the company's financial reporting.

E6. The Board's efforts to develop this standard were an outward expression of the Board's mission, "to protect the interests of investors and further the public interest in the preparation of informative, fair, and independent audit reports." As part of fulfilling that mission as it relates to this standard, the Board considered the advice that respected groups had offered to other auditing standards setters in the past. For example, the Public Oversight Board's Panel on Audit Effectiveness recommended that "auditing standards need to provide clear, concise and definitive imperatives for auditors to follow."[1] As another example, the International Organization of Securities Commissioners advised the International Auditing and Assurance Standards Board "that the IAASB must take care to avoid language that could inadvertently encourage inappropriate shortcuts in audits, at a time when rigorous audits are needed more than ever to restore investor confidence."[2]

E7. The Board understood that, to effectively fulfill its mission and for this standard to achieve its ultimate goal of restoring investor confidence by increasing the reliability of public company financial reporting, the Board's standard must contain clear directions to the auditor consistent with investor's expectations that the reliability of financial reporting be significantly improved. Just as important, the Board recognized that this standard must appropriately balance the costs to implement the standard's directions with the benefits of achieving these important goals. As a result, all of the Board's decisions about this standard were guided by the additional objective of creating a rational relationship between costs and benefits.

E8. When the Board adopted its interim attestation standards in Rule 3300T on an initial, transitional basis, the Board adopted a pre-existing standard governing an auditor's attestation on internal control over financial reporting.[3] As part of the Board's process of evaluating that pre-existing standard, the Board convened a public roundtable discussion on July 29, 2003 to discuss issues and hear views related to reporting on internal control over financial reporting. The participants at the roundtable included representatives from public companies, accounting firms, investor groups, and regulatory organizations. Based on comments made at the roundtable, advice from the Board's staff, and other input the Board received, the Board determined that the preexisting standard governing an auditor's attestation on internal control over financial reporting was insufficient for effectively implementing the requirements of Section 404 of the Act and for the Board to appropriately discharge its standard-setting obligations under Section 103(a) of the Act. In response, the Board developed and issued, on October 7,

---

1. Panel on Audit Effectiveness, *Report and Recommendations*, sec. 2.228 (August 31, 2000).
2. April 8, 2003 comment letter from the International Organization of Securities Commissions to the International Auditing and Assurance Standards Board regarding the proposed international standards on audit risk (Amendment to ISA 200, "Objective and Principles Governing an Audit of Financial Statements;" proposed ISAs, "Understanding the Entity and Its Environment and Assessing the Risks of Material Misstatement;" "Auditor's Procedures in Response to Assessed Risks;" and "Audit Evidence").
3. The pre-existing standard is Chapter 5, "*Reporting on an Entity's Internal Control Over Financial Reporting*" of Statement on Standards for Attestation Engagements (SSAE) No. 10, *Attestation Standards: Revision and Recodification*(AICPA, *Professional Standards*, Vol. 1, AT sec. 501). SSAE No. 10 has been codified into AICPA Professional Standards, Volume 1, as AT sections 101 through 701.

2003, a proposed auditing standard titled, *An Audit of Internal Control Over Financial Reporting Performed in Conjunction with An Audit of Financial Statements.*

E9. The Board received 189 comment letters on a broad array of topics from a variety of commenters, including auditors, investors, internal auditors, issuers, regulators, and others. Those comments led to changes in the standard, intended to make the requirements of the standard clearer and more operational. This appendix summarizes significant views expressed in those comment letters and the Board's responses.

Fundamental Scope of the Auditor's Work in an Audit of Internal Control over Financial Reporting

E10. The proposed standard stated that the auditor's objective in an audit of internal control over financial reporting was to express an opinion on management's assessment of the effectiveness of the company's internal control over financial reporting. To render such an opinion, the proposed standard required the auditor to obtain reasonable assurance about whether the company maintained, in all material respects, effective internal control over financial reporting as of the date specified in management's report. To obtain reasonable assurance, the auditor was required to evaluate both management's process for making its assessment and the effectiveness of internal control over financial reporting.

E11. Virtually all investors and auditors who submitted comment letters expressed support for this approach. Other commenters, primarily issuers, expressed concerns that this approach was contrary to the intent of Congress and, therefore, beyond what was specifically required by Section 404 of the Act. Further, issuers stated their views that this approach would lead to unnecessary and excessive costs. Some commenters in this group suggested the auditor's work should be limited to evaluating management's assessment process and the testing performed by management and internal audit. Others acknowledged that the auditor would need to test at least some controls directly in addition to evaluating and testing management's assessment process. However, these commenters described various ways in which the auditor's own testing could be significantly reduced from the scope expressed in the proposed standard. For instance, they proposed that the auditor could be permitted to use the work of management and others to a much greater degree; that the auditor could use a "risk analysis" to identify only a few controls to be tested; and a variety of other methods to curtail the extent of the auditor's work. Of those opposed to the scope, most cited their belief that the scope of work embodied in the standard would lead to a duplication of effort between management and the auditor which would needlessly increase costs without adding significant value.

E12. After considering the comments, the Board retained the approach described in the proposed standard. The Board concluded that the approach taken in the standard is consistent with the intent of Congress. Also, to provide the type of report, at the level of assurance called for in Sections 103 and 404, the Board concluded that the auditor must evaluate both management's assessment process and the effectiveness of internal control over financial reporting. Finally, the Board noted the majority of the cost to be borne by companies (and ultimately investors) results directly from the work the company will have to perform to maintain effective internal control over financial reporting and to comply with Section 404(a) of the Act. The cost of the auditor's work as described in this standard ultimately will represent a smaller portion of the total cost to companies of implementing Section 404.

E13. The Board noted that large, federally insured financial institutions have had a similar internal control reporting requirement for over ten years. The Federal Deposit Insurance Corporation Improvement Act of 1991 (FDICIA) has required, since 1993, managements of large financial institutions to make an assessment of internal control over financial reporting effectiveness and the institution's independent auditor to issue an attestation report on management's assessment.

E14. The attestation standards under which FDICIA engagements are currently performed are clear that, when performing an examination of management's assertion on the effectiveness of internal control over financial reporting (management's report on the assessment required by Section 404(a) of the Act must include a statement as to whether the company's internal control over financial reporting is effective), the auditor may express an opinion either on management's assertion (that is, whether management's assessment about the effectiveness of the internal control over financial reporting is fairly stated) or directly on the subject matter (that is, whether the internal control over financial reporting is effective) because the level of work that must be performed is the same in either case.

E15. The Board observed that Congress indicated an intent to require an examination level of work in Section 103(a) of the Act, which states, in part, that each registered public accounting firm shall:

> describe in each audit report the scope of the auditor's testing of the internal control structure and procedures of the issuer, required by Section 404(b), and present (in such report or in a separate report)—

> (I) the findings of the auditor from such testing;

> **(II) an evaluation of whether such internal control structure and procedures—**

>> **(aa) include maintenance of records that in reasonable detail accurately reflect the transactions and dispositions of the assets of the issuer;**

>> **(bb) provide reasonable assurance that transactions are recorded as necessary to permit preparation of financial statements in accordance with generally accepted accounting principles, and that receipts and expenditures of the issuer are being made only in accordance with authorizations of management and directors of the issuer; and**

> (III) a description, at a minimum, of material weaknesses in such internal controls, and of any material noncompliance found on the basis of such testing. [emphasis added].

E16. The Board concluded that the auditor must test internal control over financial reporting directly, in the manner and extent described in the standard, to make the evaluation described in Section 103. The Board also interpreted Section 103 to provide further support that the intent of Congress was to require an opinion on the effectiveness of internal control over financial reporting.

E17. The Board concluded that the auditor must obtain a high level of assurance that the conclusion expressed in management's assessment is correct to provide an opinion on management's assessment. An auditing process restricted to evaluating what management has done would not provide the auditor with a sufficiently high level of assurance that management's conclusion is correct. Instead, it is necessary for the auditor to evaluate management's assessment process to be satisfied that management has an appropriate basis for its statement, or assertion, about the effectiveness of the company's internal control over financial reporting. It also is necessary for the auditor to directly test the effectiveness of internal control over financial reporting to be satisfied that management's conclusion is correct, and that management's assertion is fairly stated.

E18. This testing takes on added importance with the public nature of the internal control reporting. Because of the auditor's association with a statement by management that internal control over financial reporting is effective, it is reasonable for a user of the auditor's report to expect that the auditor tested the effectiveness of internal control over financial reporting. For the auditor to do otherwise would create an expectation gap, in which the assurance that the auditor obtained is less than what users reasonably expect.

E19. Auditors, investors, and the Federal bank regulators reaffirmed in their comment letters on the proposed auditing standard that the fundamental approach taken by the Board was appropriate and necessary. Investors were explicit in their expectation that the auditor must test the effectiveness of controls directly in addition to evaluating management's assessment process. Investors further recognized that this kind of assurance would come at a price and expressed their belief that the cost of the anticipated benefits was reasonable. The federal banking regulators, based on their experience examining financial institutions' internal control assessments and independent auditors' attestation reports under FDICIA, commented that the proposed auditing standard was a significant improvement over the existing attestation standard.

Reference to Audit vs. Attestation

E20. The proposed standard referred to the attestation required by Section 404(b) of the Act as the *audit* of internal control over financial reporting instead of an *attestation* of management's assessment. The proposed standard took that approach both because the auditor's objective is to express an opinion on management's assessment of the effectiveness of internal control over financial reporting, just as the auditor's objective in an audit of the financial statements is to express an opinion on the fair presentation of the financial statements, and because the level of assurance obtained by the auditor is the same in both cases. Furthermore, the proposed standard described an *integrated* audit of the financial statements and internal control over financial reporting and allowed the auditor to express his or her opinions on the financial statements and on the effectiveness of internal control in separate reports or in a single, combined report.

E21. Commenters' views on this matter frequently were related to their views on whether the proposed scope of the audit was appropriate. Those who agreed that the scope in the proposed standard was appropriate generally agreed that referring to the engagement as an *audit* was appropriate. On the other hand, commenters who objected to the scope of work described in the proposed standard often drew an important distinction between an *audit* and an *attestation.* Because Section 404 calls for an attestation, they believed it was inappropriate to call the engagement anything else (or to mandate a scope that called for a more extensive level of work).

E22. Based, in part, on the Board's decisions about the scope of the audit of internal control over financial reporting, the Board concluded that the engagement should continue to be referred to as an "audit." This term emphasizes the nature of the auditor's objective and communicates that objective most clearly to report users. Use of this term also is consistent with the integrated approach described in the standard and the requirement in Section 404 of the Act that this reporting not be subject to a separate engagement.

E23. Because the Board's standard on internal control is an auditing standard, it is preferable to use the term *audit* to describe the engagement rather than the term *examination,* which is used in the attestation standards to describe an engagement designed to provide a high level of assurance.

E24. Finally, the Board believes that using the term *audit* helps dispel the misconception that an audit of internal control over financial reporting is a different level of service than an attestation of management's assessment of internal control over financial reporting.

Form of the Auditor's Opinion

E25. The proposed auditing standard required that the auditor's opinion in his or her report state whether management's assessment of the effectiveness of the company's internal control over financial reporting as of the specified date is fairly stated, in all material respects, based on the control criteria. However, the proposed standard also stated that nothing precluded the auditor from auditing management's assessment and opining directly on the effectiveness of internal control over financial reporting. This is because the scope of the work, as defined by the proposed standard, was the same, regardless of whether the auditor reports on management's assessment or directly on the effectiveness of internal control over financial reporting. The form of the opinion was essentially interchangeable between the two.

E26. However, if the auditor planned to issue other than an unqualified opinion, the proposed standard required the auditor to report directly on the effectiveness of the company's internal control over financial reporting rather than on management's assessment. The Board initially concluded that expressing an opinion on management's assessment, in these circumstances, did not most effectively communicate the auditor's conclusion that internal control was not effective. For example, if management expresses an adverse assessment because a material weakness exists at the date of management's assessment ("...internal control over financial reporting is not effective...") and the auditor expresses his or her opinion on management's assessment ("...management's assessment that internal control over financial reporting is not effective is fairly stated, in all material respects..."), a reader might not be clear about the results of the auditor's testing and about the auditor's conclusions. The Board initially decided that reporting directly on the effectiveness of the company's internal control over financial reporting better communicates to report users the effect of such conditions, because direct reporting more clearly states the auditor's conclusions about the effectiveness of internal control over financial reporting ("In our opinion, because of the effect of the material weakness described..., the Company's internal control over financial reporting is not effective.").

E27. A number of commenters were supportive of the model described in the previous paragraph, as they agreed with the Board's reasoning. However, several commenters believed that report users would be confused as to why the form of the auditor's opinion would be different in various circumstances. These commenters thought that the auditor's opinion should be consistently expressed in all reports. Several auditors recommended that auditors always report directly on the effectiveness of the company's internal control over financial reporting. They reasoned that the scope of the audit— which always would require the auditor to obtain reasonable assurance about whether the internal control over financial reporting was effective—would be more clearly communicated, in all cases, by the auditor reporting directly on the effectiveness of internal control over financial reporting. Other commenters suggested that the auditor always should express two opinions: one on management's assessment and one directly on the effectiveness of internal control over financial reporting. They believed the Act called for two opinions: Section 404 calls for an opinion on management's assessment, while Section 103 calls for an opinion directly on the effectiveness of internal control over financial reporting.

E28. The Board believes that the reporting model in the proposed standard is appropriate. However, the Board concluded that the expression of two opinions — one on management's assessment and one on the effectiveness of internal control over financial reporting — in all reports is a superior approach that balances the concerns of many different interested parties. This approach is consistent with the scope of the audit, results in more consistent reporting in differing circumstances, and makes the reports more easily understood by report users. Therefore, the standard requires that the auditor express two opinions in all reports on internal control over financial reporting.

Use of the Work of Others

E29. After giving serious consideration to a rational relationship between costs and benefits, the Board decided to change the provisions in the proposed standard regarding using the work of others. The proposed standard required the auditor to evaluate whether to use the work of others, such as internal auditors and others working under the direction of management, and described an evaluation process focused on the competence and objectivity of the persons who performed the work that the auditor was required to use when determining the extent to which he or she could use the work of others.

E30. The proposed standard also described two principles that limited the auditor's ability to use of the work of others. First, the proposed standard defined three categories of controls and the extent to which the auditor could use the work of others in each of those categories:

- Controls for which the auditor should not rely on the work of others, such as controls in the control environment and controls specifically intended to prevent or detect fraud that is reasonably likely to have a material effect on the company's financial statements,

- Controls for which the auditor may rely on the work of others, but his or her reliance on the work of others should be limited, such as controls over nonroutine transactions that are considered high risk because they involve judgments and estimates, and

- Controls for which the auditor's reliance on the work of others is not specifically limited, such as controls over routine processing of significant accounts.

E31. Second, the proposed standard required that, on an overall basis, the auditor's own work must provide the principal evidence for the audit opinion (this is referred to as the *principal evidence provision*).

E32. In the proposed standard, these two principles provided the auditor with flexibility in using the work of others while preventing him or her from placing inappropriate overreliance on the work of others. Although the proposed standard required the auditor to reperform some of the tests performed by others to use their work, it did not establish specific requirements for the extent of the reperformance. Rather, it allowed the auditor to use his or her judgment and the directions provided by the two principles discussed in the previous two paragraphs to determine the appropriate extent of reperformance.

E33. The Board received a number of comments that agreed with the proposed three categories of controls and the principal evidence provision. However, most commenters expressed some level of concern with the categories, the principal evidence provision, or both.

E34. Comments opposing or criticizing the categories of controls varied from general to very specific. In general terms, many commenters (particularly issuers) expressed concern that the categories described in the proposed standard were too restrictive. They believed the auditor should be able to use his or her judgment to determine in which areas and to what extent to rely on the work of others. Other commenters indicated that the proposed standard did not place enough emphasis on the work of internal auditors whose competence and objectivity, as well as adherence to professional standards of internal auditing, should clearly set their work apart from the work performed by others in the organization (such as management or third parties working under management's direction). Further, these commenters believed that the standard should clarify that the auditor should be able to use work performed by internal auditors extensively. In that case, their concerns about excessive cost also would be partially alleviated.

E35. Other commenters expressed their belief that the proposed standard repudiated the approach established in AU sec. 322, *The Auditor's Consideration of the Internal Audit Function in an Audit of Financial Statements,* for the auditor's use of the work of internal auditors in a financial statement audit. Commenters also expressed very specific and pointed views on the three categories of controls. As defined in the proposed standard, the first category (in which the auditor should not use the work of others at all) included:

- Controls that are part of the control environment, including controls specifically established to prevent and detect fraud that is reasonably likely to result in material misstatement of the financial statements.

- Controls over the period-end financial reporting process, including controls over procedures used to enter transaction totals into the general ledger; to initiate, record, and process journal entries in the general ledger; and to record recurring and nonrecurring adjustments to the financial statements (for example, consolidating adjustments, report combinations, and reclassifications).

- Controls that have a pervasive effect on the financial statements, such as certain information technology general controls on which the operating effectiveness of other controls depend.

- Walkthroughs.

E36. Commenters expressed concern that the prohibition on using the work of others in these areas would (a) drive unnecessary and excessive costs, (b) not give appropriate recognition to those instances in which the auditor evaluated internal audit as having a high degree of competence and objectivity, and (c) be impractical due to resource constraints at audit firms. Although each individual area was mentioned, the strongest and most frequent objections were to the restrictions imposed over the inclusion in the first category of walkthroughs, controls over the period-end financial reporting process, and information technology general controls. Some commenters suggested the Board should consider moving these areas from the first category to the second category (in which using the work of others would be limited, rather than prohibited); others suggested removing any limitation on using the work of others in these areas altogether.

E37. Commenters also expressed other concerns with respect to the three control categories. Several commenters asked for clarification on what constituted *limited* use of the work of others for areas included in the second category. Some commenters asked for clarification about the extent of reperformance necessary for the auditor to use the work of others. Other commenters questioned the meaning of the term *without specific limitation* in the third category by asking, did this mean that the auditor could use the work of others in these areas without performing or reperforming any work in those areas?

E38. Although most commenters suggested that the principal evidence threshold for the auditor's own work be retained, some commenters objected to the principal evidence provision. Although many commenters identified the broad array of areas identified in the first category (in which the auditor should not use the work of others at all) as the key driver of excessive costs, others identified the principal evidence provision as the real source of their excessive cost concerns. Even if the categories were redefined in such a way as to permit the auditor to use the work of others in more areas, any associated decrease in audit cost would be limited by the principal evidence provision which, if retained, would still require significant original work on the part of the auditor. On the other hand, both investors and auditors generally supported retaining the principal evidence provision as playing an important role in ensuring the independence of the auditor's opinion and preventing inappropriate overreliance on the work of internal auditors and others.

E39. Commenters who both supported and opposed the principal evidence provision indicated that implementing it would be problematic because the nature of the work in an audit of internal control over financial reporting does not lend itself to a purely quantitative measurement. Thus, auditors would be forced to use judgment when determining whether the principal evidence provision has been satisfied.

E40. In response to the comments, the Board decided that some changes to the guidance on using the work of others were necessary. The Board did not intend to reject the concepts in AU sec. 322 and replace them with a different model. Although AU sec. 322 is designed to apply to an audit of financial statements, the Board concluded that the concepts contained in AU sec. 322 are sound and should be used in an audit of internal control over financial reporting, with appropriate modification to take into account the differences in the nature of the evidence necessary to support an opinion on financial statements and the evidence necessary to support an opinion on internal control effectiveness. The Board also wanted to make clear that the concepts in AU sec. 322 also may be applied, with appropriate auditor judgment, to the relevant work of others.

E41. The Board remained concerned, however, with the possibility that auditors might overrely on the work of internal auditors and others. Inappropriate overreliance can occur in a variety of ways. For example, an auditor might rely on the work of a highly competent and objective internal audit function for proportionately too much of the evidence that provided the basis for the auditor's opinion. Inappropriate overreliance also occurs when the auditor incorrectly concludes that internal auditors have a high degree of competence and objectivity when they do not, perhaps because the auditor did not exercise professional skepticism or due professional care when making his or her evaluation. In either case, the result is the same: unacceptable risk that the auditor's conclusion that internal control over financial reporting is effective is incorrect. For example, federal bank regulators commented that, in their experience with FDICIA, auditors have a tendency to rely too heavily on the work of management and others, further noting that this situation diminishes the independence of the auditor's opinion on control effectiveness.

E42. The Board decided to revise the categories of controls by focusing on the nature of the controls being tested, evaluating the competence and objectivity of the individuals performing the work, and testing the work of others. This allows the auditor to exercise substantial judgment based on the outcome of this work as to the extent to which he or she can make use of the work of internal auditors or others who are suitably qualified.

E43. This standard emphasizes the direct relationship between the assessed level of competence and objectivity and the extent to which the auditor may use the work of others. The Board included this clarification to highlight the special status that a highly competent and objective internal auditor has in the auditor's work as well as to caution against inappropriate overreliance on the work of management and others who would be expected to have lower degrees of competence and objectivity in assessing controls. Indeed, the Board noted that, with regard to internal control over financial reporting, internal auditors would normally be assessed as having a higher degree of competence and objectivity than management or others and that an auditor will be able to rely to a greater extent on the work of a highly competent and objective internal auditor than on work performed by others within the company.

E44. The Board concluded that the principal evidence provision is critical to preventing over-reliance on the work of others in an audit of internal control over financial reporting. The requirement for the auditor to perform enough of the control testing himself or herself so that the auditor's own work provides the principal evidence for the auditor's opinion is of paramount importance to the auditor's assurance providing the level of reliability that investors expect. However, the Board also decided that the final standard should articulate clearly that the auditor's judgment about whether he or she has obtained the principal evidence required is qualitative as well as quantitative. Therefore, the standard now states, "Because the amount of work related to obtaining sufficient evidence to support an opinion about the effectiveness of controls is not susceptible to precise measurement, the auditor's judgment about whether he or she has obtained the principal evidence for the opinion will be qualitative as well as quantitative. For example, the auditor might give more weight to work performed on pervasive controls and in areas such as the control environment than on other controls, such as controls over low-risk, routine transactions."

E45. The Board also concluded that a better balance could be achieved in the standard by instructing the auditor to factor into the determination of the extent to which to use the work of others an evaluation of the nature of the controls on which others performed their procedures.

E46. Paragraph 112 of the standard provides the following factors the auditor should consider when evaluating the nature of the controls subjected to the work of others:

- The materiality of the accounts and disclosures that the control addresses and the risk of material misstatement.
- The degree of judgment required to evaluate the operating effectiveness of the control (that is, the degree to which the evaluation of the effectiveness of the control requires evaluation of subjective factors rather than objective testing).
- The pervasiveness of the control.
- The level of judgment or estimation required in the account or disclosure.
- The potential for management override of the control.

E47. As these factors increase in significance, the need for the auditor to perform his or her own work on those controls increases. As these factors decrease in significance, the auditor may rely more on the work of others. Because of the nature of controls in the control environment, however, the standard does not allow the auditor to use the work of others to reduce the amount of work he or she performs on such controls. In addition, the standard also does not allow the auditor to use the work of others in connection with the performance of walkthroughs of major classes of transactions because of the high degree of judgment required when performing them (See separate discussion in paragraphs E51 through E57).

E48. The Board decided that this approach was responsive to those who believed that the auditor should be able to use his or her judgment in determining the extent to which to use the work of others. The Board designed the requirement that the auditor's own work must provide the principal evidence for the auditor's opinion as one of the boundaries within which the auditor determines the work he or she must perform himself or herself in the audit of internal control over financial reporting. The other instructions about using the work of others provide more specific direction about how the auditor makes this determination, but allow the auditor significant flexibility to use his or her judgment to determine the work necessary to obtain the principal evidence, and to determine when the auditor can use the work of others rather than perform the work himself or herself. Although some of the directions are specific and definitive, such as the directions for the auditor to perform tests of controls in the control environment and walkthroughs himself or herself, the Board decided that these areas were of such audit importance that the auditor should always perform this testing as part of obtaining the principal evidence for his or her opinion. The Board concluded that this approach appropriately balances the use of auditor judgment and the risk of inappropriate overreliance.

E49. The Board was particularly concerned by comments that issuers might choose to reduce their internal audit staff or the extent of internal audit testing in the absence of a significant change in the proposed standard that would significantly increase the extent to which the auditor may use the work of internal auditors. The Board believes the standard makes clear that an effective internal audit function does permit the auditor to reduce the work that otherwise would be necessary.

E50. Finally, as part of clarifying the linkage between the degree of competence and objectivity of the others and the ability to use their work, the Board decided that additional clarification should be provided on the extent of testing that should be required of the work of others. The Board noted that the interaction of the auditor performing walkthroughs of every significant process and the retention of the principal evidence provision precluded the need for the auditor to test the work of others in every significant account. However, testing the work of others is an important part of an ongoing assessment of their competence and objectivity. Therefore, as part of the emphasis on the direct relationship between the assessed level of competence and objectivity to the extent of the use of the work of others, additional provisions were added discussing how the results of the testing of the work of others might affect the auditor's assessment of competence and objectivity. The Board also concluded that testing the work of others should be clearly linked to an evaluation of the quality and effectiveness of their work.

Walkthroughs

E51. The proposed standard included a requirement that the auditor perform walkthroughs, stating that the auditor should perform a walkthrough for all of the company's significant processes. In the walkthrough, the auditor was to trace all types of transactions and events, both recurring and unusual, from origination through the company's information systems until they were included in the company's financial reports. As stated in the proposed standard, walkthroughs provide the auditor with evidence to:

- Confirm the auditor's understanding of the process flow of transactions;

- Confirm the auditor's understanding of the design of controls identified for all five components of internal control over financial reporting, including those related to the prevention or detection of fraud;

- Confirm that the auditor's understanding of the process is complete by determining whether all points in the process at which misstatements related to each relevant financial statement assertion that could occur have been identified;

- Evaluate the effectiveness of the design of controls; and

- Confirm whether controls have been placed in operation.

E52. A number of commenters expressed strong support for the requirement for the auditor to perform walkthroughs as described in the proposed standard. They agreed that auditors who did not already perform the type of walkthrough described in the proposed standard should perform them as a matter of good practice. These commenters further recognized that the first-hand understanding an auditor obtains from performing these walkthroughs puts the auditor in a much better position to design an effective audit and to evaluate the quality and effectiveness of the work of others. They considered the walkthrough requirement part of "getting back to basics," which they viewed as a positive development.

E53. Some commenters expressed general support for walkthroughs as required procedures, but had concerns about the scope of the work. A number of commenters suggested that requiring walkthroughs of *all* significant processes and *all* types of transactions would result in an overwhelming and unreasonable number of walkthroughs required. Commenters made various suggestions for alleviating this problem, including permitting the auditor to determine, using broad auditor judgment, which classes of transactions to walk through or refining the scope of "all types of transactions" to include some kind of consideration of risk and materiality.

E54. Other commenters believed that required walkthroughs would result in excessive cost if the auditor were prohibited from using the work of others. These commenters suggested that the only way that required walkthroughs would be a reasonable procedure is to permit the auditor to use the work of others. Although commenters varied on whether the auditor's use of the work of others for walkthroughs should be liberal or limited, and whether it should include management or be limited to internal auditors, a large number of commenters suggested that limiting walkthroughs to only the auditor himself or herself was impractical.

E55. The Board concluded that the objectives of the walkthroughs cannot be achieved second-hand. For the objectives to be effectively achieved, the auditor must perform the walkthroughs himself or herself. Several commenters who objected to the prohibition on using the work of internal auditors for walkthroughs described situations in which internal auditors would be better able to effectively perform walkthroughs because internal auditors understood the company's business and controls better than the external auditor and because the external auditor would struggle in performing walkthroughs due to a lack of understanding. The Board observed that these commenters' perspectives support the importance of requiring the external auditor to perform walkthroughs. If auditors struggle to initially perform walkthroughs because their knowledge of the company and its controls is weak, then that situation would only emphasize the necessity for the auditor to increase his or her level of understanding. After considering the nature and extent of the procedures that would be required to achieve these objectives, the Board concluded that performing walkthroughs would be the most efficient means of doing so. The first-hand understanding the auditor will obtain of the company's processes and its controls through the walkthroughs will translate into increased effectiveness and quality throughout the rest of the audit, in a way that cannot be achieved otherwise.

E56. The Board also decided that the scope of the transactions that should be subjected to walkthroughs should be more narrowly defined. To achieve the objectives the Board intended for walkthroughs to accomplish, the auditor should not be forced to perform walkthroughs on what many commenters reasoned was an unreasonably large population. The Board decided that the auditor should be able to use judgment in considering risk and materiality to determine which transactions and events within a given significant process to walk through. As a result, the directions in the standard on determining significant processes and major classes of transactions were expanded, and the population of transactions for which auditors will be required to walk through narrowed by replacing "all types of transactions" with "major classes of transactions."

E57. Although judgments of risk and materiality are inherent in identifying major classes of transactions, the Board decided to also remove from the standard the statement, "walkthroughs are required procedures" as a means of further clarifying that auditor judgment plays an important role in determining the major classes of transactions for which to perform a walkthrough. The Board observed that leading off the discussion of walkthroughs in the standard with such a sentence could be read as setting a tone that diminished the role of judgment in selecting the transactions to walk through. As a result, the directions in the standard on performing walkthroughs begin with, "The auditor should perform at least one walkthrough for each major class of transactions..." The Board's decision to eliminate the statement "walkthroughs are required procedures" should not be viewed as an indication that performing walkthroughs are optional under the standard's directions. The Board believes the auditor might be able to achieve the objectives of a walkthrough by performing a combination of procedures, including inquiry, inspection, observation, and reperformance; however, performing a walkthrough represents the most efficient and effective means of doing so. The auditor's work on the control environment and walkthroughs is an important part of the principal evidence that the auditor must obtain himself or herself.

Small Business Issues

E58. Appendix E of the proposed standard discussed small and medium-sized company considerations. Comments were widely distributed on this topic. A number of commenters indicated that the proposed standard gave adequate consideration to how internal control is implemented in, and how the audit of internal control over financial reporting should be conducted at, small and medium-sized companies. Other commenters, particularly smaller issuers and smaller audit firms, indicated that the proposed standard needed to provide much more detail on how internal control over financial reporting could be different at a small or medium-sized issuer and how the auditor's approach could differ. Some of these commenters indicated that the concepts articulated in the Board's proposing release concerning accommodations for small and medium-sized companies were not carried through to the proposed standard itself.

E59. On the other hand, other commenters, particularly large audit firms and investors, expressed views that the proposed standard went too far in creating too much of an accommodation for small and medium-sized issuers. In fact, many believed that the proposed standard permitted those issuers to have less effective internal control over financial reporting than larger issuers, while providing guidance to auditors permitting them to perform less extensive testing at those small and medium-sized issuers than they might have at larger issuers. These commenters stressed that effective internal control over financial reporting is equally important at small and medium-sized issuers. Some commenters also expressed concerns that the guidance in proposed Appendix E appeared to emphasize that the actions of senior management, if carried out with integrity, could offset deficiencies in internal control over financial reporting, such as the lack of written policies and procedures. Because the risk of management override of controls is higher in these types of environments, such commenters were concerned that the guidance in proposed Appendix E might result in an increased fraud risk at small and medium-sized issuers. At a minimum, they argued, the interpretation of Appendix E might result in a dangerous expectation gap for users of their internal control reports. Some commenters who were of this view suggested that Appendix E be deleted altogether or replaced with a reference to the report of the Committee of Sponsoring Organizations

(COSO) of the Treadway Commission, *Internal Control—Integrated Framework*, which they felt contained sufficient guidance on small and medium-sized company considerations.

E60. Striking an appropriate balance regarding the needs of smaller issuers is particularly challenging. The Board considered cautionary views about the difficulty in expressing accommodations for small and medium-sized companies without creating an inappropriate second class of internal control effectiveness and audit assurance. Further, the Board noted that the COSO framework currently provides management and the auditor with more guidance and flexibility regarding small and medium-sized companies than the Board had provided in the proposed Appendix E. As a result, the Board eliminated proposed Appendix E and replaced the appendix with a reference to COSO in paragraph 15 of the standard. The Board believes providing internal control criteria for small and medium-sized companies within the internal control framework is more appropriately within the purview of COSO. Furthermore, the COSO report was already tailored for special small and medium-sized company considerations. The Board decided that emphasizing the existing guidance within COSO was the best way of recognizing the special considerations that can and should be given to small and medium-sized companies without inappropriately weakening the standard to which these smaller entities should, nonetheless, be held. If additional tailored guidance on the internal control framework for small and medium-sized companies is needed, the Board encourages COSO, or some other appropriate body, to develop this guidance.

Evaluation of the Effectiveness of the Audit Committee

E61. The proposed standard identified a number of circumstances that, because of their likely significant negative effect on internal control over financial reporting, are significant deficiencies as well as *strong indicators* that a material weakness exists. A particularly notable significant deficiency and strong indicator of a material weakness was the ineffective oversight by the audit committee of the company's external financial reporting and internal control over financial reporting. In addition, the proposed standard required the auditor to evaluate factors related to the effectiveness of the audit committee's oversight of the external financial reporting process and the internal control over financial reporting.

E62. This provision related to evaluating the effectiveness of the audit committee was included in the proposed standard for two primary reasons. First, the Board initially decided that, because of the significant role that the audit committee has in the control environment and monitoring components of internal control over financial reporting, an ineffective audit committee is a gravely serious control weakness that is strongly indicative of a material weakness. Most auditors should have already been reaching this conclusion when confronted with an obviously ineffective audit committee. Second, highlighting the adverse consequences of an ineffective audit committee would, perhaps, further encourage weak audit committees to improve.

E63. Investors supported this provision. They expressed an expectation that the auditor would evaluate the audit committee's effectiveness and speak up if the audit committee was determined to be ineffective. Investors drew a link among restoring their confidence, audit committees having new and enhanced responsibilities, and the need for assurance that audit committees are, in fact, meeting their responsibilities.

E64. Auditors also were generally supportive of such an evaluation. However, many requested that the proposed standard be refined to clearly indicate that the auditor's responsibility to evaluate the effectiveness of the audit committee's oversight of the company's external financial reporting and internal control over financial reporting is not a separate and distinct evaluation. Rather, the evaluation is one element of the auditor's overall understanding and assessment of the company's control environment and monitoring components. Some commenters suggested that, in addition to needing clarification of the auditor's responsibility, the auditor would have difficulty in evaluating all of the factors listed in the proposed standard, because the auditor's normal interaction with the audit committee would not provide sufficient basis to conclude on some of those factors.

E65. Issuers and some others were opposed to the auditor evaluating the effectiveness of the audit committee on the fundamental grounds that such an evaluation would represent an unacceptable conflict of interest. Several commenters shared the view that this provision would reverse an important improvement in governance and audit quality. Whereas the auditor was formerly retained and compensated by management, the Act made clear that these responsibilities should now be those of the audit committee. In this way, commenters saw a conflict of interest being remedied. Requiring the auditor to evaluate the effectiveness of the audit committee led commenters to conclude that the same kind of conflict of interest was being reestablished. These commenters also believed that the auditor would not have a sufficient basis on which to evaluate the effectiveness of the audit committee because the auditor does not have complete and free access to the audit committee, does not have appropriate expertise to evaluate audit committee members (who frequently are more experienced businesspeople than the auditor), does not have the legal expertise to make determinations about some of the specific factors listed in the proposed standard, and other shortcomings. These commenters also emphasized that the board of directors' evaluation of the audit committee is important and that the proposed standard could be read to supplant this important evaluation with that of the auditor's.

E66. The Board concluded that this provision should be retained but decided that clarification was needed to emphasize that the auditor's evaluation of the audit committee was not a separate evaluation but, rather, was made as part of the auditor's evaluation of the control environment and monitoring components of internal control over financial reporting. The Board reasoned that clarifying both this context and limitation on the auditor's evaluation of the audit committee would also address, to some degree, the conflict-of-interest concerns raised by other commenters. The Board also observed, however, that conflict is, to some extent, inherent in the duties that society expects of auditors. Just as auditors were expected in the past to challenge management when the auditor believed a material misstatement of the financial statements or material weakness in internal control over financial reporting existed, the auditor similarly is expected to speak up when he or she believes the audit committee is ineffective in its oversight.

E67. The Board decided that when the auditor is evaluating the control environment and monitoring components, if the auditor concludes that the audit committee's oversight of the company's external financial reporting and internal control over financial reporting is ineffective, the auditor should be strongly encouraged to consider that situation a material weakness and, at a minimum, a significant deficiency. The objective of the evaluation is not to grade the effectiveness of the audit committee along a scale. Rather, in the course of performing procedures related to evaluating the effectiveness of the control environment and monitoring components, including evaluating factors related to the effectiveness of the audit committee's oversight, if the auditor concludes that the audit committee's oversight of the external financial reporting and internal control over financial reporting is ineffective, then the auditor should consider that a strong indicator of a material weakness.

E68. The Board concluded that several refinements should be made to this provision. As part of emphasizing that the auditor's evaluation of the audit committee is to be made as part of evaluating the control environment and not as a separate evaluation, the Board determined that the evaluation factors should be modified. The factors that addressed compliance with listing standards and sections of the Act were deleted, because those factors were specifically criticized in comment letters as being either outside the scope of the auditor's expertise or outside the scope of internal control over financial reporting. The Board also believed that those factors were not significant to the type of evaluation the auditor was expected to make of the audit committee. The Board decided to add the following factors, which are based closely on factors described in COSO, as relevant to evaluating those who govern, including the audit committee:

- Extent of direct and independent interaction with key members of financial management, including the chief financial officer and chief accounting officer.

- Degree to which difficult questions are raised and pursued with management and the auditor, including questions that indicate an understanding of the critical accounting policies and judgmental accounting estimates.

- Level of responsiveness to issues raised by the auditor, including those required to be communicated by the auditor to the audit committee.

E69. The Board also concluded that the standard should explicitly acknowledge that the board of directors is responsible for evaluating the effectiveness of the audit committee and that the auditor's evaluation of the control environment is not intended to supplant those evaluations. In addition, the Board concluded that, in the event the auditor determines that the audit committee's oversight is ineffective, the auditor should communicate that finding to the full board of directors. This communication should occur regardless of whether the auditor concludes that the condition represents a significant deficiency or a material weakness, and the communication should take place in addition to the normal communication requirements that attach to those deficiencies.

Definitions of Significant Deficiency and Material Weakness

E70. As part of developing the proposed standard, the Board evaluated the existing definitions of significant deficiency (which the SEC defined as being the same as a reportable condition) and material weakness to determine whether they would permit the most effective implementation of the internal control reporting requirements of the Act.

E71. AU sec. 325, *Communication of Internal Control Related Matters Noted in an Audit*, defined a material weakness as follows:

A *material weakness* in internal control is a reportable condition in which the design or operation of one or more of the internal control components does not reduce to a *relatively low level* the risk that misstatements caused by error or fraud in amounts that would be material in relation to the financial statements being audited may occur and not be detected within a timely period by employees in the normal course of performing their assigned functions.

E72. The framework that defined a material weakness focused on likelihood of and magnitude for evaluating a weakness. The Board decided that this framework would facilitate effective implementation of the Act's internal control reporting requirements; therefore, the Board's proposed definitions focused on likelihood and magnitude. However, as part of these deliberations, the Board decided that likelihood and magnitude needed to be defined in terms that would encourage more consistent application.

E73. Within the existing definition of material weakness, the magnitude of "material in relation to the financial statements" was well supported by the professional standards, SEC rules and guidance, and other literature. However, the Board decided that the definition of likelihood would be improved if it used "more than remote" instead of "relatively low level." FASB Statement No. 5, *Accounting for Contingencies* (FAS No. 5) defines "remote." The Board decided that, because auditors were familiar with the application of the likelihood definitions in FAS No. 5, using "more than remote" in the definition of material weakness would infuse the evaluation of whether a control deficiency was a material weakness with the additional consistency that the Board wanted to encourage.

E74. AU sec. 325 defined *reportable conditions* as follows:

> ...matters coming to the auditor's attention that, in his judgment, should be communicated to the audit committee because they represent significant deficiencies in the design or operation of internal control, which could adversely affect the organization's ability to initiate, record, process, and report financial data consistent with the assertions of management in the financial statements.

E75. The Board observed that this definition makes the determination of whether a condition is reportable solely a matter of the auditor's judgment. The Board believed that this definition was insufficient for purposes of the Act because management also needs a definition to determine whether a deficiency is significant and that the definition should be the same as the definition used by the auditor. Furthermore, using this existing definition, the auditor's judgment could never be questioned.

E76. The Board decided that the same framework that represented an appropriate framework for defining a material weakness also should be used for defining a significant deficiency. Although auditor judgment is integral and essential to the audit process (including in determining the severity of control weaknesses), auditors, nonetheless, must be accountable for their judgments. Increasing the accountability of auditors for their judgments about whether a condition represents a significant deficiency and increasing the consistency with which those judgments are made are interrelated. Hence, the same framework of likelihood and magnitude were applied in the Board's proposed definition of significant deficiency.

E77. In applying the likelihood and magnitude framework to defining a significant deficiency, the Board decided that the "more than remote" likelihood of occurrence used in the definition of material weakness was the best benchmark. In terms of magnitude, the Board decided that "more than inconsequential" should be the threshold for a significant deficiency.

E78. A number of commenters were supportive of the definitions in the proposed standard. These commenters believed the definitions were an improvement over the previous definitions, used terms familiar to auditors, and would promote increased consistency in evaluations.

E79. Most commenters, however, objected to these definitions. The primary, overarching objection was that these definitions set too low a threshold for the reporting of significant deficiencies. Some commenters focused on "more than remote" likelihood as the driver of an unreasonably low threshold, while others believed "more than inconsequential" in the definition of significant deficiency was the main culprit. While some commenters understood "more than inconsequential" well enough, others indicated significant concerns that this represented a new term of art that needed to be accompanied by a clear definition of "inconsequential" as well as supporting examples. Several commenters suggested retaining the likelihood and magnitude approach to a definition but suggested alternatives for likelihood (such as reasonably likely, reasonably possible, more likely than not, probable) and magnitude (such as material, significant, insignificant).

E80. Some commenters suggested that the auditing standard retain the existing definitions of material weakness and significant deficiency, consistent with the SEC's final rules implementing Section 404. In their final rules, the SEC tied management's assessment to the existing definitions of material weakness and significant deficiency (through the existing definition of a reportable condition) in AU sec. 325. These commenters suggested that, if the auditing standard used a different definition, a dangerous disconnect would result, whereby management would be using one set of definitions under the SEC's rules and auditors would be using another set under the Board's auditing standards. They further suggested that, absent rulemaking by the SEC to change its definitions, the Board should simply defer to the existing definitions.

E81. A number of other commenters questioned the reference to "a misstatement of the annual or interim financial statements" in the definitions, with the emphasis on why "interim" financial statements were included in the definition, since Section 404 required only an annual assessment of internal control over financial reporting effectiveness, made as of year-end. They questioned whether this definition implied that the auditor was required to identify deficiencies that could result in a misstatement in interim financial statements; they did not believe that the auditor should be required to plan his or her audit of internal control over financial reporting at a materiality level of the interim financial statements.

E82. The Board ultimately concluded that focusing the definitions of material weakness and significant deficiency on likelihood of misstatement and magnitude of misstatement provides the best framework for evaluating deficiencies. Defaulting to the existing definitions would not best serve the public interest nor facilitate meaningful and effective implementation of the auditing standard.

E83. The Board observed that the SEC's final rules requiring management to report on internal control over financial reporting define material weakness, for the purposes of the final rules, as having "the same meaning as the definition under GAAS and attestation standards." Those rules state:

> The term "significant deficiency" has the same meaning as the term "reportable condition" as used in AU § 325 and AT § 501. The terms "material weakness" and "significant deficiency" both represent deficiencies in the design or operation of internal control that could adversely affect a company's ability to record, process, summarize and report financial data consistent with the assertions of management in the company's financial statements, with a "material weakness" constituting a greater deficiency than a "significant deficiency." Because of this relationship, it is our judgment that an aggregation of significant deficiencies could constitute a material weakness in a company's internal control over financial reporting.[4]

E84. The Board considered the SEC's choice to cross-reference to generally accepted auditing standards (GAAS) and the attestation standards as the means of defining these terms, rather than defining them outright within the final rules, noteworthy as it relates to the question of whether any disconnect could result between auditors' and managements' evaluations if the Board changed the definitions in its standards. Because the standard changes the defini-

---

4. See footnote 73 to *Final Rule: Management's Reports on Internal Control Over Financial Reporting and Certification of Disclosure in Exchange Act Periodic Reports,* Securities and Exchange Commission Release No. 33-8238 (June 5, 2003) [68 FR 36636].

tion of these terms within the interim standards, the Board believes the definitions are, therefore, changed for both auditors' and managements' purposes.

E85. The Board noted that commenters who were concerned that the definitions in the proposed standard set too low of a threshold for significant deficiencies and material weaknesses believed that the proposed standard required that each control deficiency be evaluated in isolation. The intent of the proposed standard was that control deficiencies should first be evaluated individually; the determination as to whether they are significant deficiencies or material weaknesses should be made considering the effects of compensating controls. The effect of compensating controls should be taken into account when assessing the likelihood of a misstatement occurring and not being prevented or detected. The proposed standard illustrated this type of evaluation, including the effect of compensating controls when assessing likelihood, in the examples in Appendix D. Based on the comments received, however, the Board determined that additional clarification within the standard was necessary to emphasize the importance of considering compensating controls when evaluating the likelihood of a misstatement occurring. As a result, the note to paragraph 10 was added.

E86. The Board concluded that considering the effect of compensating controls on the likelihood of a misstatement occurring and not being prevented or detected sufficiently addressed the concerns that the definitions set too low a threshold. For example, several issuer commenters cited concerns that the proposed definitions precluded a rational cost-benefit analysis of whether to correct a deficiency. These issuers believed they would be compelled to correct deficiencies (because the deficiencies would be considered to be at least significant deficiencies) in situations in which management had made a previous conscious decision that the costs of correcting the deficiency outweighed the benefits. The Board observed that, in cases in which management has determined not to correct a known deficiency based on a cost-benefit analysis, effective compensating controls usually lie at the heart of management's decision. The standard's use of "likelihood" in the definition of a significant deficiency or material weakness accommodates such a consideration of compensating controls. If a deficiency is effectively mitigated by compensating controls, then the likelihood of a misstatement occurring and not being prevented or detected may very well be remote.

E87. The Board disagreed with comments that "more than inconsequential" was too low a threshold; however, the Board decided the term "inconsequential" needed additional clarity. The Board considered the term "inconsequential" in relation to the SEC's guidance on audit requirements and materiality. Section 10A(b)(1)(B)[5] describes the auditor's communication requirements when the auditor detects or otherwise becomes aware of information indicating that an illegal act has or may have occurred, "unless the illegal act is clearly inconsequential." Staff Accounting Bulletin (SAB) No. 99, *Materiality,* provides the most recent and definitive guidance on the concept of materiality as it relates to the financial reporting of a public company. SAB No. 99 uses the term "inconsequential" in several places to draw a distinction between amounts that are not material. SAB No. 99 provides the following guidance to assess the significance of a misstatement:

> Though the staff does not believe that registrants need to make finely calibrated determinations of significance with respect to immaterial items, plainly it is "reasonable" to treat misstatements whose effects are clearly inconsequential differently than more significant ones.

---

5. See Section 10A of the Securities Exchange Act of 1934, 15 U.S.C., 78j-1.

E88. The discussion in the previous paragraphs provided the Board's context for using "material" and "more than inconsequential" for the magnitude thresholds in the standard's definitions. "More than inconsequential" indicates an amount that is less than material yet has significance.

E89. The Board also considered the existing guidance in the Board's interim standards for evaluating materiality and accumulating audit differences in a financial statement audit. Paragraph .41 of AU sec. 312, *Audit Risk and Materiality in Conducting an Audit,* states:

> In aggregating likely misstatements that the entity has not corrected, pursuant to paragraphs .34 and .35, the auditor may designate an amount below which misstatements need not be accumulated. This amount should be set so that any such misstatements, either individually or when aggregated with other such misstatements, would not be material to the financial statements, after the possibility of further undetected misstatements is considered.

E90. The Board considered the discussion in AU sec. 312 that spoke specifically to evaluating differences individually *and in the aggregate,* as well as to considering the possibility of additional undetected misstatements, important distinguishing factors that should be carried through to the evaluation of whether a control deficiency represents a significant deficiency because the magnitude of the potential misstatement is more than inconsequential.

E91. The Board combined its understanding of the salient concepts in AU sec. 312 and the SEC guidance on materiality to develop the following definition of inconsequential:

> A misstatement is *inconsequential* if a reasonable person would conclude, after considering the possibility of further undetected misstatements, that the misstatement, either individually or when aggregated with other misstatements, would clearly be immaterial to the financial statements. If a reasonable person could not reach such a conclusion regarding a particular misstatement, that misstatement is *more than inconsequential.*

E92. Finally, the inclusion of *annual or interim financial statements* in the definitions rather than just "annual financial statements" was intentional and, in the Board's opinion, closely aligned with the spirit of what Section 404 seeks to accomplish. However, the Board decided that this choice needed clarification within the auditing standard. The Board did not intend the inclusion of the interim financial statements in the definition to require the auditor to perform *an audit of internal control over financial reporting* at each interim date. Rather, the Board believed that the SEC's definition of internal control over financial reporting included all financial reporting that a public company makes publicly available. In other words, internal control over financial reporting includes controls over the preparation of annual and quarterly financial statements. Thus, an evaluation of internal control over financial reporting as of yearend encompasses controls over the annual financial reporting and quarterly financial reporting as such controls exist at that point in time.

E93. Paragraphs 76 and 77 of the standard clarify this interpretation, as part of the discussion of the period-end financial reporting process. The period-end financial reporting process includes procedures to prepare both annual and quarterly financial statements.

Strong Indicators of Material Weaknesses and DeFacto Significant Deficiencies

E94. The proposed standard identified a number of circumstances that, because of their likely significant negative effect on internal control over financial reporting, are significant deficiencies as well as strong indicators that a material weakness exists. The Board developed this list to promote increased rigor and consistency in auditors' evaluations of weaknesses. For the implementation of Section 404 of the Act to achieve its objectives, the public must have confidence that all material weaknesses that exist as of the company's year-end will be publicly reported. Historically, relatively few material weaknesses have been reported by the auditor to management and the audit committee. That condition is partly due to the nature of a financial statement audit. In an audit of only the financial statements, the auditor does not have a detection responsibility for material weaknesses in internal control; such a detection responsibility is being newly introduced for all public companies through Sections 103 and 404 of the Act. However, the Board was concerned about instances in which auditors had identified a condition that should have been, but was not, communicated as a material weakness. The intention of including the list of strong indicators of material weaknesses in the proposed standard was to bring further clarity to conditions that were likely to be material weaknesses in internal control and to create more consistency in auditors' evaluations.

E95. Most commenters were generally supportive of a list of significant deficiencies and strong indicators of the existence of material weaknesses. They believed such a list provided instructive guidance to both management and the auditor. Some commenters, however, disagreed with the proposed approach of providing such a list. They believed that the determination of the significance of a deficiency should be left entirely to auditor judgment. A few commenters requested clarification of the term "strong indicator" and specific guidance on how and when a "strong indicator" could be overcome. A number of commenters expressed various concerns with individual circumstances included in the list.

- *Restatement of previously issued financial statements to reflect the correction of a misstatement.* Some commenters expressed concern about the kinds of restatements that would trigger this provision. A few mentioned the specific instance in which the restatement reflected the SEC's subsequent view of an accounting matter when the auditor, upon reevaluation, continued to believe that management had reasonable support for its original position. They believed this specific circumstance would not necessarily indicate a significant deficiency in internal control over financial reporting. Others commented that a restatement of previously issued financial statements would indicate a significant deficiency and strong indicator of a material weakness in the prior period but not necessarily in the current period.

- *Identification by the auditor of a material misstatement in financial statements in the current period that was not initially identified by the company's internal control over financial reporting (even if management subsequently corrects the misstatement).* Several commenters, issuers and auditors alike, expressed concern about including this circumstance on the list. They explained that, frequently, management is completing the preparation of the financial statements at the same time that the auditor is completing his or her auditing procedures. In the face of this "strong indicator" provision, a lively debate of "who found it first" would ensue whenever the auditor identifies a misstatement that management subsequently corrects. Another argument is that the company's controls would have detected a misstatement identified by the auditor if the controls had an opportunity to operate (that is, the auditor performed his or her testing before the company's controls had an opportunity to operate). Several issuers indicated that they would prevent this latter situation by delaying the auditor's work until the issuers had clearly completed their entire period-end financial reporting process — a delay they viewed as detrimental.

- *For larger, more complex entities, the internal audit function or the risk assessment function is ineffective.* Several commenters asked for specific factors the auditor was expected to use to assess the effectiveness of these functions.

- *For complex entities in highly regulated industries, an ineffective regulatory compliance function.* Several commenters, particularly issuers in highly regulated industries, objected to the inclusion of this circumstance because they believed this to be outside the scope of internal control over financial reporting. (They agreed that this would be an internal control-related matter, but one that falls into operating effectiveness and compliance with laws and regulations, not financial reporting.) Many of these commenters suggested that this circumstance be deleted from the list altogether. Fewer commenters suggested that this problem could be addressed by simply clarifying that this circumstance is limited to situations in which the ineffective regulatory function relates solely to those aspects for which related violations of laws and regulations could have a direct and material effect on the financial statements.

- *Identification of fraud of any magnitude on the part of senior management.* Several commenters expressed concern that the inclusion of this circumstance created a detection responsibility for the auditor such that the auditor would have to plan and perform procedures to detect fraud of *any magnitude* on the part of senior management. Others expressed concern that identification of fraud on the part of senior management by the company's system of internal control over financial reporting might indicate that controls were operating effectively rather than indicating a significant deficiency or material weakness. Still others requested clarification on how to determine who constituted "senior management."

E96. A couple of commenters also suggested that an ineffective control environment should be added to the list.

E97. The Board concluded that the list of significant deficiencies and strong indicators of material weakness should be retained. Such a list will promote consistency in auditors' and managements' evaluations of deficiencies consistent with the definitions of significant deficiency and material weakness. The Board also decided to retain the existing structure of the list. Although the standard leaves auditor judgment to determine whether those deficiencies are material weaknesses, the existence of one of the listed deficiencies is by definition a significant deficiency. Furthermore, the "strong indicator" construct allows the auditor to factor extenuating or unique circumstances into the evaluation and possibly to conclude that the situation does not represent a material weakness, rather, only a significant deficiency.

E98. The Board decided that further clarification was not necessary within the standard itself addressing specifically how and when a "strong indicator" can be overcome. The term "strong indicator" was selected as opposed to the stronger "presumption" or other such term precisely because the Board did not intend to provide detailed instruction on how to overcome such a presumption. It is, nevertheless, the Board's view that auditors should be biased toward considering the listed circumstances as material weaknesses.

E99. The Board decided to clarify several circumstances included in the list:

- *Restatement of previously issued financial statements to reflect the correction of a misstatement.* The Board observed that the circumstance in which a restatement reflected the SEC's subsequent view of an accounting matter, when the auditor concluded that management had reasonable support for its original position, might present a good example of only a significant deficiency and not a material weakness. However, the Board concluded that requiring this situation to, nonetheless, be considered by definition a significant deficiency is appropriate, especially considering that the primary result of the circumstance being considered a significant deficiency is the communication of the matter to the audit committee. Although the audit committee might already be well aware of the circumstances of any restatement, a restatement to reflect the SEC's view on an accounting matter at least has implications for the quality of the company's accounting principles, which is already a required communication to the audit committee.

With regard to a restatement being a strong indicator of a material weakness in the prior period but not necessarily the current period, the Board disagreed with these comments. By virtue of the restatement occurring during the current period, the Board views it as appropriate to consider that circumstance a strong indicator that a material weakness existed during the current period. Depending on the circumstances of the restatement, however, the material weakness may also have been corrected during the current period. The construct of the standard does not preclude management and the auditor from determining that the circumstance was corrected prior to year-end and, therefore, that a material weakness did not exist at year-end. The emphasis here is that the circumstance is a strong indicator that a material weakness exists; management and the auditor will separately need to determine whether it has been corrected. The Board decided that no further clarification was needed in this regard.

- *Identification by the auditor of a material misstatement in financial statements in the current period that was not initially identified by the company's internal control over financial reporting (even if management subsequently corrects the misstatement).* Regarding the "who-found-it-first" dilemma, the Board recognizes that this circumstance will present certain implementation challenges. However, the Board decided that none of those challenges were so significant as to require eliminating this circumstance from the list.

When the Board developed the list of strong indicators, the Board observed that it is not uncommon for the financial statement auditor to identify material misstatements in the course of the audit that are corrected by management prior to the issuance of the company's financial statements. In some cases, management has relied on the auditor to identify misstatements in certain financial statement items and to propose corrections in amount, classification, or disclosure. With the introduction of the requirement for management and the auditor to report on the effectiveness of internal control over financial reporting, it becomes obvious that this situation is unacceptable, unless management is willing to accept other than an unqualified report on the internal control effectiveness. (This situation also raises the question as to the extent management may rely on the annual audit to produce accurate and fair financial statements without impairing the auditor's independence.) This situation is included on the list of strong indicators because the Board believes it will encourage management and auditors to evaluate this situation with intellectual honesty and to recognize, first, that the company's internal control should provide reasonable assurance that the company's financial statements are presented fairly in accordance with generally accepted accounting principles.

Timing might be a concern for some issuers. However, to the extent that management takes additional steps to ensure that the financial information is correct prior to providing it to their auditors, this may, at times, result in an improved control environment. When companies and auditors work almost simultaneously on completing the preparation of the annual financial statements and the audit, respectively, the role of the auditor can blur with the responsibility of management. In the year-end rush to complete the annual report, some companies might have come to rely on their auditors as a "control" to further ensure no misstatements are accidentally reflected in the financial statements. The principal burden seems to be for management's work schedule and administration of their financial reporting deadlines to allow the auditor sufficient time to complete his or her procedures.

Further, if the auditor initially identified a material misstatement in the financial statements but, given the circumstances, determined that management ultimately would have found the misstatement, the auditor could determine that the circumstance was a significant deficiency but not a material weakness. The Board decided to retain the provision that this circumstance is at least a significant deficiency because reporting such a circumstance to the audit committee would always be appropriate.

- *For larger, more complex entities, the internal audit function or the risk assessment function is ineffective.* Relatively few commenters requested clarification on how to evaluate these functions. The Board expects that most auditors will not have trouble making this evaluation. Similar to the audit committee evaluation, this evaluation is not a separate evaluation of the internal audit or risk assessment functions but, rather, is a way of requiring the auditor to speak up if either of these functions is obviously ineffective at an entity that needs them to have an effective monitoring or risk assessment component. Unlike the audit committee discussion, most commenters seemed to have understood that this was the context for the internal audit and risk assessment function evaluation. Nonetheless, the Board decided to add a clarifying note to this circumstance emphasizing the context.

- *For complex entities in highly regulated industries, an ineffective regulatory compliance function.* The Board decided that this circumstance, as described in the proposed standard, would encompass aspects that are outside internal control over financial reporting (which would, of course, be inappropriate for purposes of this standard given its definition of internal control over financial reporting). The Board concluded that this circumstance should be retained, though clarified, to only apply to those aspects of an ineffective regulatory compliance function that could have a material effect on the financial statements.

- *Identification of fraud of any magnitude on the part of senior management.* The Board did not intend to create any additional detection responsibility for the auditor; rather, it intended that this circumstance apply to fraud on the part of senior management that came to the auditor's attention, regardless of amount. The Board decided to clarify the standard to make this clear. The Board noted that identification of fraud by the company's system of internal control over financial reporting might indicate that controls were operating effectively, except when that fraud involves senior management. Because of the critical role of tone-at-the-top in the overall effectiveness of the control environment and due to the significant negative evidence that fraud of any magnitude on the part of senior management reflects on the control environment, the Board decided that it is appropriate to include this circumstance in the list, regardless of whether the company's controls detected the fraud. The Board also decided to clarify who is included in "senior management" for this purpose.

E100. The Board agreed that an ineffective control environment was a significant deficiency and a strong indicator that a material weakness exists and decided to add it to the list.

Independence

E101. The proposed standard explicitly prohibited the auditor from accepting an engagement to provide an internal control-related service to an audit client that has not been specifically pre-approved by the audit committee. In other words, the audit committee would not be able to pre-approve internal control-related services as a category. The Board did not propose any specific guidance on permissible internal control-related services in the proposed standard but, rather, indicated its intent to conduct an in-depth evaluation of independence requirements in the future and highlighted its ability to amend the independence information included in the standard pending the outcome of that analysis.

E102. Comments were evenly split among investors, auditors, and issuers who believed the existing guidance was sufficient versus those who believed the Board should provide additional guidance. Commenters who believed existing guidance was sufficient indicated that the SEC's latest guidance on independence needed to be given more time to take effect given its recency and because existing guidance was clear enough. Commenters who believed more guidance was necessary suggested various additions, from more specificity about permitted and prohibited services to a sweeping ban on any internal control-related work for an audit client. Other issuers commented about auditors participating in the Section 404 implementation process at their audit clients in a manner that could be perceived as affecting their independence.

E103. Some commenters suggested that the SEC should change the pre-approval requirements on internal control-related services to specific pre-approval. Another commenter suggested that specific pre-approval of all internal control-related services would pose an unreasonable burden on the audit committee and suggested reverting to pre-approval by category.

E104. The Board clearly has the authority to set independence standards as it may deem necessary or appropriate in the public interest or for the protection of investors. Given ongoing concerns about the appropriateness of auditors providing these types of services to audit clients, the fact-specific nature of each engagement, and the critical importance of ongoing audit committee oversight of these types of services, the Board continues to believe that specific pre-approval of internal control-related services is a logical step that should not pose a burden on the audit committee beyond that which effective oversight of financial reporting already entails. Therefore, the standard retains this provision unchanged.

Requirement for Adverse Opinion When a Material Weakness Exists

E105. The existing attestation standard (AT sec. 501) provides that, when the auditor has identified a material weakness in internal control over financial reporting, depending on the significance of the material weakness and its effect on the achievement of the objectives of the control criteria, the auditor may qualify his or her opinion ("except for the effect of the material weakness, internal control over financial reporting was effective") or express an adverse opinion ("internal control over financial reporting was not effective").

E106. The SEC's final rules implementing Section 404 state that, "Management is not permitted to conclude that the registrant's internal control over financial reporting is effective if there are one or more material weaknesses in the registrant's internal control over financial reporting." In other words, in such a case, management must conclude that internal control over financial reporting is not effective (that is, a qualified or "except-for" conclusion is not acceptable).

E107. The Board initially decided that the reporting model for the auditor should follow the required reporting model for management. Therefore, because management is required to express an "adverse" conclusion in the event a material weakness exists, the auditor's opinion also must be adverse. The proposed standard did not permit a qualified audit opinion in the event of a material weakness.

E108. Comments received on requiring an adverse opinion when a material weakness exists were split. A large number affirmed that this seemed to be the only logical approach, based on a philosophical belief that if a material weakness exists, then internal control over financial reporting is ineffective. These commenters suggested that permitting a qualified opinion would be akin to creating another category of control deficiency material weaknesses that were really material (resulting in an adverse opinion) and material weaknesses that weren't so material (resulting in a qualified opinion).

E109. A number of commenters agreed that the auditor's report must follow the same model as management' reporting, but they believe strongly that the SEC's guidance for management accommodated either a qualified or adverse opinion when a material weakness existed.

E110. These commenters cited Section II.B.3.c of the SEC Final Rule and related footnote no. 72:

> The final rules therefore preclude management from determining that a company's internal control over financial reporting is effective if it identifies one or more material weaknesses in the company's internal control over financial reporting. This is consistent with interim attestation standards. See AT sec. 501.

E111. They believe this reference to the interim attestation standard in the SEC Final Rule is referring to paragraph .37 of AT sec. 501, which states, in part,

> Therefore, the presence of a material weakness will preclude the practitioner from concluding that the entity has effective internal control. However, depending on the significance of the material weakness and its effect on the achievement of the objectives of the control criteria, the practitioner may qualify his or her opinion (that is, express an opinion that internal control is effective "except for" the material weakness noted) or may express an adverse opinion.

E112. Their reading of the SEC Final Rule and the interim attestation standard led them to conclude that it would be appropriate for the auditor to express either an adverse opinion or a qualified "except-for" opinion about the effectiveness of the company's internal control over financial reporting depending on the circumstances.

E113. Some commenters responded that they thought a qualified opinion would be appropriate in certain cases, such as an acquisition close to year-end (too close to be able to assess controls at the acquiree).

E114. After additional consultation with the SEC staff about this issue, the Board decided to retain the proposed reporting model in the standard. The primary reason for that decision was the Board's continued understanding that the SEC staff would expect only an adverse conclusion from management (not a qualified conclusion) in the event a material weakness existed as of the date of management's report.

E115. The commenters who suggested that a qualified opinion should be permitted in certain circumstances, such as an acquisition close to year-end, were essentially describing scope limitations. The standard permits a qualified opinion, a disclaimer of opinion, or withdrawal from the engagement if there are restrictions on the scope of the engagement. As it relates specifically to acquisitions near year-end, this is another case in which the auditor's model needs to follow the model that the SEC sets for management. The standard added a new paragraph to Appendix B permitting the auditor to limit the scope of his or her work (without referring to a scope limitation in the auditor's report) in the same manner that the SEC permits management to limit its assessment. In other words, if the SEC permits management to exclude an entity acquired late in the year from a company's assessment of internal control over financial reporting, then the auditor could do the same.

Rotating Tests of Controls

E116. The proposed standard directed the auditor to perform tests of controls on "relevant assertions" rather than on "significant controls." To comply with those requirements, the auditor would be required to apply tests to those controls that are important to presenting each relevant assertion in the financial statements. The proposed standard emphasized controls that affect relevant assertions because those are the points at which misstatements could occur. However, it is neither necessary to test all controls nor to test redundant controls (unless redundancy is itself a control objective, as in the case of certain computer controls). Thus, the proposed standard encouraged the auditor to identify and test controls that addressed the primary areas in which misstatements could occur, yet limited the auditor's work to only the necessary controls.

E117. Expressing the extent of testing in this manner also simplified other issues involving extent of testing decisions from year to year (the so-called "rotating tests of controls" issue). The proposed standard stated that the auditor should vary testing from year to year, both to introduce unpredictability into the testing and to respond to changes at the company. However, the proposed standard maintained that each year's audit must stand on its own. Therefore, the auditor must obtain evidence of the effectiveness of controls over all relevant assertions related to all significant accounts and disclosures every year.

E118. Auditors and investors expressed support for these provisions as described in the proposed standard. In fact, some commenters compared the notion of rotating tests of control in an audit of internal control over financial reporting to an auditor testing accounts receivable only once every few years in a financial statement audit. Permitting so-called rotation of testing would compromise the auditor's ability to obtain reasonable assurance that his or her opinion was correct.

E119. Others, especially issuers concerned with limiting costs, strongly advocated some form of rotating tests of controls. Some commenters suggested that the auditor should have broad latitude to perform some cursory procedures to determine whether any changes had occurred in controls and, if not, to curtail any further testing in that area. Some suggested that testing as described in the proposed standard should be required in the first year of the audit (the "baseline" year) and that in subsequent years the auditor should be able to reduce the required testing. Others suggested progressively less aggressive strategies for reducing the amount of work the auditor should be required to perform. In fact, several commenters (primarily internal auditors) described "baselining" controls as an important strategy to retain. They argued, for example, that IT application controls, once tested, could be relied upon (without additional testing) in subsequent years as long as general controls over program changes and access controls were effective and continued to be tested.

E120. The Board concluded that each year's audit must stand on its own. Cumulative audit knowledge is not to be ignored; some natural efficiencies will emerge as the auditor repeats the audit process. For example, the auditor will frequently spend less time to obtain the requisite understanding of the company's internal control over financial reporting in subsequent years compared with the time necessary in the first year's audit of internal control over financial reporting. Also, to the extent that the auditor has previous knowledge of control weaknesses, his or her audit strategy should, of course, reflect that knowledge. For example, a pattern of mistakes in prior periods is usually a good indicator of the areas in which misstatements are likely to occur. However, the absence of fraud in prior periods is not a reasonable indicator of the likelihood of misstatement due to fraud.

E121. However, the auditor needs to test controls every year, regardless of whether controls have obviously changed. Even if nothing else changed about the company — no changes in the business model, employees, organization, etc. — controls that were effective last year may not be effective this year due to error, complacency, distraction, and other human conditions that result in the inherent limitations in internal control over financial reporting.

E122. What several commenters referred to as "baselining" (especially as it relates to IT controls) is more commonly referred to by auditors as "benchmarking." This type of testing strategy for application controls is not precluded by the standard. However, the Board believes that providing a description of this approach is beyond the scope of this standard. For these reasons, the standard does not address it.

Mandatory Integration with the Audit of the Financial Statements

E123. Section 404(b) of the Act provides that the auditor's attestation of management's assessment of internal control shall not be the subject of a separate engagement. Because the objectives of and work involved in performing both an attestation of management's assessment of internal control over financial reporting and an audit of the financial statements are closely interrelated, the proposed auditing standard introduced an integrated audit of internal control over financial reporting and audit of financial statements.

E124. However, the proposed standard went even further. Because of the potential significance of the information obtained during the audit of the financial statements to the auditor's conclusions about the effectiveness of internal control over financial reporting, the proposed standard stated that the auditor could not audit internal control over financial reporting without also auditing the financial statements. (However, the proposed standard retained the auditor's ability to audit *only* the financial statements, which might be necessary in the case of certain initial public offerings.)

E125. Although the Board solicited specific comment on whether the auditor should be prohibited from performing an audit of internal control over financial reporting without also performing an audit of the financial statements, few commenters focused on the significance of the potentially negative evidence that would be obtained during the audit of the financial statements or the implications of this prohibition. Most commenters focused on the wording of Section 404(b), which indicates that the auditor's attestation of management's assessment of internal control over financial reporting shall not be the subject of a separate engagement. Based on this information, most commenters saw the prohibition in the proposed standard as superfluous and benign.

E126. Several commenters recognized the importance of the potentially negative evidence that might be obtained as part of the audit of the financial statements and expressed strong support for requiring that an audit of financial statements be performed to audit internal control over financial reporting.

E127. Others recognized the implications of this prohibition and expressed concern: What if a company wanted or needed an opinion on the effectiveness of internal control over financial reporting as of an interim date? For the most part, these commenters (primarily issuers) objected to the implication that an auditor would have to audit a company's financial statements as of an interim date to enable him or her to audit and report on its internal control over financial reporting as of that same interim date. Other issuers expressed objections related to their desires to engage one auditor to provide an opinion on the effectiveness of internal control over financial reporting and another to audit the financial statements. Others requested clarification about which guidance would apply when other forms of internal control work were requested by companies.

E128. The Board concluded that an auditor should perform an audit of internal control over financial reporting only when he or she has also audited company's financial statements. The auditor *must* audit the financial statements to have a high level of assurance that his or her conclusion on the effectiveness of internal control over financial reporting is correct. Inherent in the reasonable assurance provided by the auditor's opinion on internal control over financial reporting is a responsibility for the auditor to plan and perform his or her work to obtain reasonable assurance that material weaknesses, if they exist, are detected. As previously discussed, this standard states that the identification by the auditor of a *material misstatement* in the financial statements that was not initially identified by the company's internal control over financial reporting, is a strong indicator of a material weakness. Without performing a financial statement audit, the auditor would not have reasonable assurance that he or she had detected all material misstatements. The Board believes that allowing the auditor to audit internal control over financial reporting without also auditing the financial statements would not provide the auditor with a high level of assurance and would mislead investors in terms of the level of assurance obtained.

E129. In response to other concerns, the Board noted that an auditor can report on the effectiveness of internal control over financial reporting using existing AT sec. 501 for purposes other than satisfying the requirements of Section 404. This standard supersedes AT sec. 501 only as it relates to complying with Section 404 of the Act.

E130. Although reporting under the remaining provisions of AT sec. 501 is currently permissible, the Board believes reports issued for public companies under the remaining provisions of AT sec. 501 will be infrequent. In any event, additional rulemaking might be necessary to prevent confusion that might arise from reporting on internal control engagements under two different standards. For example, explanatory language could be added to reports issued under AT sec. 501 to clarify that an audit of financial statements was not performed in conjunction with the attestation on internal control over financial reporting and that such a report is not the report resulting from an audit of internal control over financial reporting performed in conjunction with an audit of the financial statements under this standard. This report modification would alert report readers, particularly if such a report were to appear in an SEC filing or otherwise be made publicly available, that the assurance obtained by the auditor in that engagement is different from the assurance that would have been obtained by the auditor for Section 404 purposes. Another example of the type of change that might be necessary in separate rulemaking to AT sec. 501 would be to supplement the performance directions to be comparable to those in this standard. Auditors should remain alert for additional rulemaking by the Board that affects AT sec. 501.

¶ 500. PCAOB Release No. 2003-017: Proposed Auditing Standard—An Audit of Internal Control Over Financial Reporting Performed in Conjunction with an Audit of Financial Statements

Summary:

The Public Company Accounting Oversight Board (the "Board" or "PCAOB") has proposed an Auditing Standard, *An Audit of Internal Control Over Financial Reporting Performed in Conjunction With an Audit of Financial Statements.* If adopted, this standard would be the standard on attestation engagements referred to in Section 404(b) as well as Section 103(a)(2)(A) of the Sarbanes-Oxley Act of 2002.

Public Comment:

Interested persons may submit written comments to the Board. Such comments should be sent to the Office of the Secretary, PCAOB, 1666 K Street, N.W., Washington, D.C. 20006-2803. Comments may also be submitted by e-mail to comments@pcaobus.org or through the Board's Web site at www.pcaobus.org. All comments should refer to PCAOB Rulemaking Docket Matter No. 008 in the subject or reference line and should be received by the Board no later than 5:00 PM (EST) on November 21, 2003.

Board Contacts:

Thomas Ray, Deputy Chief Auditor (202/207-9112; rayt@pcaobus.org), Laura Phillips, Assistant Chief Auditor (202/207-9111; phillipsl@pcaobus.org).

Section 404(a) of the Sarbanes-Oxley Act of 2002 (the Act), and the Securities and Exchange Commission's ("SEC") related implementing rules,[1] require the management of a public company to assess the effectiveness of the company's internal control over financial reporting, as of the end of the company's most recent fiscal year. Section 404(a) of the Act also requires management to include in the company's annual report to shareholders management's conclusion as a result of that assessment about whether the company's internal control is effective. Companies considered accelerated filers (seasoned U.S. companies with public float exceeding $75 million) are required to comply with the internal control reporting and disclosure requirements of Section 404(a) of the Act for fiscal years ending on or after June 15, 2004. Other companies (including smaller companies, foreign private issuers and companies with only registered debt securities) have until fiscal years ending on or after April 15, 2005, to comply with these internal control reporting and disclosure requirements.

Sections 103(a)(2)(A) and 404(b) of the Act direct the Board to establish professional standards governing the independent auditor's attestation and reporting on management's assessment of the effectiveness of internal control over financial reporting.

An attestation, in a general sense, is an expert's communication of a conclusion about the reliability of someone else's assertion. For example, a financial statement audit is a form of attestation. In a financial statement audit, the auditor attests to the fairness of a company's financial statements, which are assertions by management regarding the financial performance and financial condition of the company. To accomplish this task, the auditor evaluates the process management uses to prepare the company's financial statements and gathers evidence to support or refute the assertions. Similarly, the auditor's attestation on management's as-

---

1. See Final Rule: Management's Reports on Internal Control Over Financial Reporting and Certification of Disclosure in Exchange Act Periodic Reports, Securities and Exchange Commission Release No. 33-8238 (June 5, 2003) [68 FR 36636].

---

sessment of the effectiveness of the company's internal control over financial reporting involves evaluating management's assessment process and gathering evidence regarding the design and operating effectiveness of the company's internal control, determining whether that evidence supports or refutes management's assessment, and opining as to whether management's assessment is fair.

When the Board adopted its interim attestation standards in Rule 3300T on a transitional basis, the Board adopted a pre-existing standard governing an auditor's attestation on internal control. As part of the Board's process of evaluating that preexisting standard, the Board convened a public roundtable discussion on July 29, 2003 to discuss issues and hear views related to reporting on internal control. The participants at the roundtable included representatives from public companies, accounting firms, investor groups and regulatory organizations. As a result of comments made at the roundtable, advice from the Board's staff, and other input the Board received, the Board determined that the pre-existing standard governing an auditor's attestation on internal control was insufficient for purposes of effectively implementing the requirements of Section 404 of the Act, and for the Board to appropriately discharge the Board's standard-setting obligations under Section 103(a) of the Act. In response, the Board developed this proposed auditing standard.

An Integrated Audit of the Financial Statements and Internal Control Over Financial Reporting

Section 404(b) of the Act provides that the auditor's attestation of management's assessment of internal control shall not be the subject of a separate engagement. Because the objectives of and work involved in performing both an attestation of management's assessment of internal control and an audit of the financial statements are closely interrelated, the proposed auditing standard introduces an integrated audit of internal control and financial statements. The proposed auditing standard is an integrated standard, addressing both the work that is required to audit internal control over financial reporting and the relationship of that audit to the audit of the financial statements. Nevertheless, the integrated audit results in two opinions: one on internal control over financial reporting and one on the financial statements, which may be expressed in a combined report or in separate reports. Throughout the proposed standard, the auditor's attestation of management's assessment of the effectiveness of internal control over financial reporting is referred to as the "audit of internal control over financial reporting."

To conduct and report on the results of an audit of internal control over financial reporting pursuant to the proposed standard, the auditor also would be required to audit the company's financial statements. That is because of the potential significance of the information that might be obtained during the audit of the financial statements to the auditor's conclusions about the effectiveness of internal control.

In evaluating the proposed standard, the Board seeks comments on 31 questions. The Board requests respondents to answer the questions and provide explanations as to why they agree or disagree with the positions the Board has taken in the proposed standard. The first three of these questions are presented below.

Questions regarding an integrated audit of the financial statements and internal control over financial reporting:

1. Is it appropriate to refer to the auditor's attestation of management's assessment of the effectiveness of internal control over financial reporting as the audit of internal control over financial reporting?

2. Should the auditor be prohibited from performing an audit of internal control over financial reporting without also performing an audit of the financial statements?

3. Rather than requiring the auditor to also complete an audit of the financial statements, would an appropriate alternative be to require the auditor to perform work with regard to the financial statements *comparable to* that required to complete the financial statement audit?

Internal Control Over Financial Reporting

Internal control is a process designed to provide reasonable assurance regarding the achievement of a company's objectives in the areas of financial reporting reliability, operating efficiency and effectiveness, and compliance with applicable laws and regulations. The SEC's rules implementing Section 404(a) of the Act, and the Board's proposed auditing standard, focus on those objectives exclusively related to the reliability of a company's external financial reporting. This subset of internal control is commonly referred to as *internal control over financial reporting*.

Internal control over financial reporting consists of company policies and procedures that are designed and operated to provide reasonable assurance — that is, a high but not absolute level of assurance — about the reliability of a company's financial reporting and its process for preparing and fairly presenting financial statements in accordance with generally accepted accounting principles. It includes policies and procedures that pertain to the maintenance of accounting records, the authorization of receipts and disbursements, and the safeguarding of assets.

Management is required to base its assessment of the effectiveness of the company's internal control over financial reporting on a suitable, recognized control framework established by a body of experts that followed due-process procedures to develop the framework. In the United States, the Committee of Sponsoring Organizations ("COSO") of the Treadway Commission has published *Internal Control—Integrated Framework*. Known as the "COSO Report," it provides a suitable framework for purposes of management's assessment. Because of the frequency with which management of public companies is expected to use COSO as the framework for the assessment, the directions in the proposed standard are based on the COSO framework. Other suitable frameworks have been published in other countries and likely will be published in the future. Although different frameworks may not contain exactly the same elements as COSO, they should have elements that encompass all of COSO's general themes. The auditor should therefore be able to apply the concepts and guidance in the proposed standard in a reasonable manner if management uses a framework other than COSO.

Regardless of how well any system of internal control over financial reporting is designed and operating, it cannot provide absolute assurance of achieving financial reporting objectives because of inherent limitations. These inherent limitations exist because internal control over financial reporting is a process that involves human diligence and compliance and, consequently, can be intentionally circumvented.

The Costs and Benefits of Internal Control

Effective internal control over financial reporting is essential for a company to effectively manage its affairs and to fulfill its obligation to its investors. A company's management and its owners — public investors — and others must be able to rely on the financial information reported by companies to make decisions.

Reliable financial reporting adds value and also can offset risks in a costbeneficial manner. Evaluating a company's internal control over financial reporting is sometimes costly, but there also are many far-reaching benefits. Some of the benefits of a company developing, maintaining, and improving its system of internal control include identifying cost-ineffective procedures, reducing costs of processing accounting information, increasing productivity of the company's financial function, and simplifying financial control systems. It also may result in fewer financial statement restatements and less litigation. The primary benefit, however, is to provide the company, its management, its board and audit committee, and its owners and other stakeholders with a reasonable basis to rely on the company's financial reporting. The integrity of financial reporting represents the foundation upon which this country's public markets are built.

As companies develop processes to assist management in its internal control assessment under Section 404 and in its quarterly certification under Section 302, the annual assessment process should result in a continuous strengthening of internal controls while simultaneously reducing the future time and costs of compliance with these requirements. The Board anticipates that most companies will experience the highest cost of complying with Section 404 during the first year of implementation.

The Board is sensitive to the possible effects of the proposed standard on small and medium-sized companies. Internal control is not "one-size-fits-all," and the nature and extent of controls that are necessary depend, to a great extent, on the size and complexity of the company. Large, complex, multi-national companies, for example, are likely to need extensive and sophisticated internal control systems. In smaller companies, or in companies with less complex operations, the ethical behavior and core values of a senior management group that is directly involved in daily interactions with both internal and external parties might reduce the need for elaborate internal control systems. For a smaller, less complex company, the Board expects that the auditor will exercise reasonable professional judgment in determining the extent of the audit of internal control and perform only those tests that are necessary to ascertain the effectiveness of the company's internal control.

> *Question regarding the costs and benefits of internal control:*
>
> 4. Does the Board's proposed standard give appropriate consideration to how internal control is implemented in, and how the audit of internal control over financial reporting should be conducted at, small and medium-sized issuers?

The Audit of Internal Control Over Financial Reporting

An audit of internal control over financial reporting is an extensive process involving several steps. It is integrated with the audit of the financial statements. Under the proposed auditing standard, these steps would include: planning the audit; evaluating the process management used to perform its assessment of internal control effectiveness; obtaining an understanding of the internal control; evaluating the effectiveness of both the design and operation of the internal control; and forming an opinion about whether internal control over financial reporting is effective.

The auditor's objective is to express an opinion about whether management's assessment, or conclusion, on the effectiveness of internal control over financial reporting is stated fairly, in all material respects. To support his or her opinion, the auditor must obtain evidence about whether internal control over financial reporting is effective. The auditor obtains this evidence in several ways, including evaluating and testing management's assessment process;

evaluating and testing work on internal control performed by others, such as internal auditors; and testing the effectiveness of the controls himself or herself.

Question regarding the audit of internal control over financial reporting:

5. Should the Board, generally or in this proposed standard, specify the level of competence and training of the audit personnel that is necessary to perform specified auditing procedures effectively? For example, it would be inappropriate for a new, inexperienced auditor to have primary responsibility for conducting interviews of a company's senior management about possible fraud.

Evaluating Management's Assessment

A natural starting place for the audit of a company's internal control over financial reporting is an evaluation of management's assessment. This evaluation provides the auditor with confidence that management has a basis for expressing its opinion on the effectiveness of internal control, provides information that will help the auditor understand the company's internal control, helps the auditor plan the work necessary to complete the audit, and provides some of the evidence the auditor will use to support his or her opinion.

The objective of an audit of internal control over financial reporting is to form an opinion "as to whether management's assessment of the effectiveness of the registrant's internal control over financial reporting is fairly stated in all material respects."[2] Further, Section 103(a)(2)(A)(iii) of the Act requires the auditor's report to present an evaluation of whether the internal control structure provides reasonable assurance that transactions are recorded as necessary, among other requirements. Importantly, the auditor's conclusion will pertain directly to whether the auditor can agree with management that internal control is effective, not just to the adequacy of management's process for determining whether internal control is effective. An auditing process restricted to evaluating what management has done would not provide the auditor with a sufficiently high level of assurance that management's conclusion is correct. The auditor needs to evaluate management's assessment process to be satisfied that management has an appropriate basis for its conclusion. The auditor, however, also needs to test the effectiveness of internal control to be satisfied that management's conclusion is correct and, therefore, fairly stated. Indeed, as the Board heard at the internal control roundtable, investors expect the independent auditor to test whether the company's internal control over financial reporting is effective, and the proposed auditing standard would require the auditor to do so.

Nevertheless, the work that management performs in connection with its assessment can have a significant effect on the nature, timing, and extent of the work the independent auditor will need to perform. The proposed auditing standard would allow the auditor to use, to a reasonable degree, the work performed by others, including management. Thus, the more extensive and reliable management's assessment is, the less extensive and costly the auditor's work will need to be.

As a part of evaluating management's assessment, the auditor must evaluate the adequacy of management's documentation of the design of the internal controls and their assessment of internal control effectiveness. The proposed standard would provide the auditor with criteria to use in evaluating the adequacy of management's documentation. Inadequate documentation would be considered an internal control deficiency, the severity of which the auditor would

---

2. See SEC Regulation S-X 2-02(f), 17 C.F.R. 210.2-02(f).

---

evaluate just as he or she would be required to evaluate the severity of other internal control deficiencies.

Questions regarding evaluation of management's assessment:

6. Is the scope of the audit appropriate in that it requires the auditor to both evaluate management's assessment and obtain, directly, evidence about whether internal control over financial reporting is effective?

7. Is it appropriate that the Board has provided criteria that auditors should use to evaluate the adequacy of management's documentation?

8. Is it appropriate to state that inadequate documentation is an internal control deficiency, the severity of which the auditor should evaluate? Or should inadequate documentation automatically rise to the level of significant deficiency or material weakness in internal control?

Planning the Audit

Planning the audit of internal control over financial reporting allows the auditor to develop an overall strategy for the audit. Many factors enter into audit planning, and the proposed auditing standard includes among them the auditor's knowledge of the company, matters affecting the company's industry, matters relating to the company's business, and the extent of recent changes in the company's operations or internal control over financial reporting. Armed with a good understanding of these types of factors, the auditor is in a position to effectively design the nature, timing, and scope of the audit.

Obtaining an Understanding of Internal Control Over Financial Reporting

The auditor should understand how internal control over financial reporting is designed and operates to evaluate and test its effectiveness. The auditor obtains a substantial amount of this understanding when evaluating management's assessment process.

The auditor also should be satisfied, however, that the controls *actually* have been implemented and are operating as they were designed to operate. Thus, while inquiry of company personnel and a review of management's assessment provide the auditor with an understanding of how the system of internal control is designed and operates, other procedures are necessary for the auditor to confirm his or her understanding.

The proposed auditing standard would have the auditor confirm his or her understanding by performing procedures that include making inquiries of and observing the personnel who actually perform the controls; reviewing documents that are used in, and that result from, the application of the controls; and comparing supporting documents (for example, sales invoices, contracts, and bills of lading) to the accounting records. The most effective means of accomplishing this objective is for the auditor to perform "walkthroughs" of the company's significant processes. For this reason, and because of the importance of several other objectives that walkthroughs accomplish, the proposed auditing standard would require the auditor to perform walkthroughs in each audit of internal control over financial reporting.

In a walkthrough, the auditor traces all types of company transactions and events — both those that are routine and recurring and those that are unusual — from origination, through the company's accounting and information systems and financial report preparation processes, to their being reported in the company's financial statements. Walkthroughs provide the auditor with audit evidence that supports or refutes his or her understanding of the process flow of transactions, the design of controls, and whether controls are in operation. Walkthroughs also help the auditor to determine whether his or her understanding is complete and provide information necessary for the auditor to evaluate the effectiveness of the design of the internal control over financial reporting.

Because of the judgment that a walkthrough requires and the significance of the objectives that walkthroughs allow the auditor to achieve, the proposed auditing standard would require the auditor to perform the walkthroughs himself or herself. In other words, the proposed auditing standard would not allow the auditor to use the work performed by management or others to satisfy the requirement to perform walkthroughs.

As a part of obtaining an understanding of internal control, the auditor also determines which controls should be tested, either by the auditor, management or others. The proposed standard would require that the auditor obtain evidence about the operating effectiveness of internal control over financial reporting for all relevant assertions for all significant accounts or disclosures. This requirement relies heavily on two concepts: significant account and relevant assertion.

The auditing standards implicitly recognize that some accounts are more significant than others. The proposed standard provides additional direction on how to determine significant accounts for purposes of the audit of internal control over financial reporting. In short, the auditor begins by performing a quantitative evaluation of accounts at the financial-statement caption or note-disclosure level. Then the auditor expands the evaluation to include qualitative factors, such as differing risks, company organization structure, and other factors, which would likely result in additional accounts being identified as significant.

Financial statement amounts and disclosures embody what are known as financial statement assertions. Does the asset exist, or did the transaction occur? Has the company included all loans outstanding in its loans payable account? Have marketable investments been properly valued? Does the company have the rights to the accounts receivable, and are the loans payable the proper obligation of the company? Are the amounts in the financial statements appropriately presented, and is there adequate disclosure about them? This process will allow the auditor to identify the relevant financial statement assertions for which the company should have controls.

Identifying "relevant" assertions is a familiar process for experienced auditors. Because of the importance relevant assertions play in the required extent of testing, the proposed standard provides additional direction.

Questions regarding obtaining an understanding of internal control over financial reporting:

9. Are the objectives to be achieved by performing walkthroughs sufficient to require the performance of walkthroughs?

10. Is it appropriate to require that the walkthrough be performed by the auditor himself or herself, rather than allowing the auditor to use walkthrough procedures performed by management, internal auditors, or others?

Testing and Evaluating the Effectiveness of the Design of Controls

To be effective, internal controls must be designed properly and all the controls necessary to provide reasonable assurance about the fairness of a company's financial statements should be in place and performed by appropriately qualified people who have the authority to implement them. At some point during the internal control audit, the auditor will need to make a determination as to whether the controls would be effective if they were operated as designed, and whether all the necessary controls are in place. This is known as *design effectiveness*.

The procedures the auditor performs to test and evaluate design effectiveness include inquiries of company personnel, observation of internal controls, walkthroughs, and a specific evaluation of whether the controls are likely to prevent or detect financial statement misstatements if they operate as designed. The proposed auditing standard would adopt these methods of testing and evaluating design effectiveness. The last step is especially important because it calls for the auditor to apply professional judgment and knowledge of and experience with internal control over financial reporting to his or her understanding of the company's controls.

Testing Operating Effectiveness

The proposed standard would require the auditor to obtain evidence about the design and operating effectiveness of controls related to all relevant financial statement assertions for all significant accounts and disclosures in the financial statements.

For this reason, in addition to being satisfied as to the effectiveness of the design of the internal controls, the auditor performs tests of controls to obtain evidence about the operating effectiveness of the controls. These tests include a mix of inquiries of appropriate company personnel, inspection of relevant documentation, such as sales orders and invoices, observation of the controls in operation, and reperformance of the application of the control.

The proposed standard directs required tests of controls to "relevant assertions" rather than to "significant controls." To comply with the requirements of the proposed standard, the auditor would apply tests to those controls that are important to fairly presenting each relevant assertion in the financial statements. It is neither necessary to test all controls nor is it necessary to test redundant controls (unless redundancy is itself a control objective, as in the case of certain computer controls). However, the emphasis is better placed on addressing relevant assertions (because those are the points where misstatements could occur) rather than significant controls. This emphasis encourages the auditor to identify and test controls that address the primary areas where misstatements could occur yet limits the auditor's work to only the necessary controls.

Expressing the extent of testing in this manner also resolves the issue of the extent of testing from year to year (the so-called "rotating tests of controls" issue). The proposed standard states that the auditor should vary testing from year to year, both to introduce unpredictability into the testing and to respond to changes at the company. However, each year's audit must stand on its own. Therefore, the auditor must obtain evidence of the effectiveness of controls for all relevant assertions for all significant accounts and disclosures every year.

The Act requires management's assessment and the auditor's opinion to address whether internal control was effective as of the end of the company's most recent fiscal year, in other words, as of a point-in-time. Performing all of the testing on December 31 is neither practical nor appropriate, however. To form a basis to express an opinion about whether internal control was effective as of a point in time requires the auditor to obtain evidence that the internal control operated effectively over an appropriate period of time. The proposed auditing standard recognizes this and allows the auditor to obtain evidence about operating effectiveness at different times throughout the year, provided that the auditor updates those tests or obtains other evidence that the controls still operated effectively at the end of the company's fiscal year.

Also at the Board's roundtable, public company representatives and auditors indicated that providing examples of extent of testing decisions would be helpful. In response, paragraph B41 of Appendix B of the proposed standard includes several examples.

Question regarding testing operating effectiveness:

11. Is it appropriate to require the auditor to obtain evidence of the effectiveness of controls for all relevant assertions for all significant accounts and disclosures every year or may the auditor use some of the audit evidence obtained in previous years to support his or her current opinion on management's assessment?

Using the Work of Management and Others

The auditor also should consider other relevant and available information about internal control when evaluating internal control effectiveness. In this regard, the proposed standard would require the auditor to understand the results of procedures performed by management and others, for example, internal auditors and third parties working under the direction of management, on internal control over financial reporting. At a minimum, the auditor should consider the results of those tests in designing the audit approach and ultimately in forming an opinion on the effectiveness of internal control over financial reporting. To this end, the proposed standard would require the auditor to review all reports issued during the year by internal audit (or similar functions, such as loan review in a financial institution) that address internal controls over financial reporting and evaluate any internal control deficiencies identified in those reports.

Additionally, the auditor may use the results of testing by others to alter the nature, timing, and extent of his or her tests of controls. At the Board's roundtable, public company representatives indicated their concern that at some point, the Board's standard could require an excessive amount of retesting by the auditor in order to use the work of others, especially internal auditors. Public company representatives were particularly sensitive to this issue because of its direct bearing on their total cost to comply with Section 404. On the other hand, the federal bank regulator representative indicated that experience with the Federal Deposit Insurance Corporation Improvement Act of 1991, which requires internal control reporting similar to Section 404 of the Act, revealed instances where the auditor used the work of internal auditors to an inappropriately high degree, where the auditor himself or herself did not perform sufficient work to provide a reasonable basis for his or her opinion.

The proposed standard describes an evaluation process, focusing on the competence and objectivity of the persons who performed the work, that the auditor should use in determining the extent to which he or she may use the work of others. The proposed standard also describes two principles that limit the auditor's use of the work of others. First, the proposed standard defines three categories of controls and the extent to which the auditor may use the work of others for each of these categories:

(1) controls for which the auditor should not rely on the work of others, such as controls in the control environment and controls specifically intended to prevent or detect fraud that is reasonably likely to have a material effect on the company's financial statements,

(2) controls for which the auditor may rely on the work of others but his or her reliance on the work of others should be limited, such as controls over nonroutine transactions that are considered high risk because they involve judgments and estimates, and

(3) controls for which the auditor's reliance on the work of others is not specifically limited, such as controls over routine processing of significant accounts.

Second, the proposed standard requires that, on an overall basis, the auditor's own work must provide the principal evidence for the audit opinion.

These two principles interact to provide the auditor with flexibility in using the work of others and also prevent inappropriate over-reliance on the work of others. Although the proposed standard requires that the auditor reperform some of the tests performed by others in order to use their work, it does not set any specific requirement on the extent of the reperformance. For example, the standard does not require that the auditor reperform tests of controls over all significant accounts for which the auditor uses the work of others. Rather, the proposed standard relies on the auditor's judgment and the interaction of the two principles discussed above to determine the appropriate extent of reperformance.

Questions regarding using the work of management and others:

12. To what extent should the auditor be permitted or required to use the work of management and others?

13. Are the three categories of controls and the extent to which the auditor may rely on the work of others appropriately defined?

14. Does the proposed standard give appropriate recognition to the work of internal auditors? If not, does the proposed standard place too much emphasis and preference on the work of internal auditors or not enough?

15. Is the flexibility in determining the extent of reperformance of the work of others appropriate, or should the auditor be specifically required to reperform a certain level of work (for example, reperform tests of all significant accounts or reperform every test performed by others that the auditor intends to use)?

16. Is the requirement for the auditor to obtain the principle evidence, on an overall basis, through his or her own work the appropriate benchmark for the amount of work that is required to be performed by the auditor?

Evaluating the Results

Both management and the auditor may identify deficiencies in internal control over financial reporting. An *internal control deficiency* exists when the design or operation of a control does not allow the company's management or employees, in the normal course of performing their assigned functions, to prevent or detect misstatements on a timely basis.

The proposed auditing standard would require the auditor to evaluate the severity of all identified internal control deficiencies because such deficiencies can have an effect on the auditor's overall conclusion about whether internal control is effective. The auditor also has a responsibility to make sure that certain parties, such as the audit committee, are aware of internal control deficiencies that rise to a certain level of severity.

Under the proposed auditing standard, an internal control deficiency (or a combination of internal control deficiencies) should be classified as a *significant deficiency* if, by itself or in combination with other internal control deficiencies, it results in more than a remote likelihood of a misstatement of the company's annual or interim financial statements that is more than inconsequential in amount will not be prevented or detected. A significant deficiency should be classified as a *material weakness* if, by itself or in combination with other internal control deficiencies, it results in more than a remote likelihood that a material misstatement in the company's annual or interim financial statements will not be prevented or detected.

At the Board's roundtable, issuers, investors and auditors all suggested that while the existing definitions of internal control deficiencies are familiar and not fundamentally flawed, additional guidance that provides additional specificity would be very helpful. However, the participants acknowledged that articulating such guidance is very difficult, particularly because the process of evaluating deficiencies and whether they constitute significant deficiencies or material weaknesses will necessarily always involve judgment. The Roundtable participants suggested that the Board provide additional guidance in the form of examples.

The proposed auditing standard's definitions of significant deficiency and material weakness focus on likelihood and magnitude as the framework for evaluating deficiencies. The Board anticipates that this framework will bring increased consistency to these evaluations yet preserve an appropriate degree of judgment. Additionally, the proposed standard includes examples in Appendix D of how these definitions would be applied in several different scenarios.

The proposed auditing standard requires the auditor to communicate in writing to the company's audit committee all significant deficiencies and material weaknesses of which the auditor is aware. The auditor also is required to communicate to the company's management, in writing, all internal control deficiencies of which he or she is aware and to notify the audit committee that such communication has been made.

The proposed standard identifies a number of circumstances that, because of their likely significant negative effect on internal control over financial reporting, are significant deficiencies as well as *strong indicators* that a material weakness exists, including—

- *Ineffective oversight of the company's external financial reporting and internal control over financial reporting by the company's audit committee.* Effective oversight by the company's board of directors, including its audit committee, is essential to the company's achievement of its objectives and is an integral part of a company's monitoring of internal control. In addition to requiring the audit committee to oversee the company's external financial reporting and internal control over financial reporting, the Act makes the audit committee directly responsible for the appointment, compensation, and oversight of the work of the auditor. Thus, an ineffective audit committee can have detrimental effects on the company and its internal control over financial reporting, as well as on the independent audit. The proposed auditing standard requires the auditor to evaluate factors related to the effectiveness of the audit committee's oversight of the external financial reporting process and internal control over financial reporting, including whether audit committee members act independently from management.

- *Material misstatement in the financial statements not initially identified by the company's internal controls.* The audit of internal control over financial reporting and the audit of the company's financial statements are an integrated activity and are required by the Act to be a single engagement. The results of the work performed in a financial statement audit provide evidence to support the auditor's conclusions on the effectiveness of internal control, and vice-versa. Therefore, if the auditor discovers a material misstatement in the financial statements as a part of the audit of the financial statements, the auditor should consider whether internal control over financial reporting is effective. That the company's internal controls did not first detect the misstatement is a strong indicator that the company's internal control over financial reporting is not effective.

• *Significant deficiencies that have been communicated to management and the audit committee, but that remain uncorrected after some reasonable period of time.* Significant deficiencies in internal control that are not also determined to be material weaknesses, as defined in the proposed auditing standard, are not so severe as to require the auditor to conclude that internal control is ineffective. However, these deficiencies are, nonetheless, significant, and the auditor should expect the company to correct them. If management fails to correct significant deficiencies within a reasonable period of time, that situation reflects poorly on tone-at-thetop as well as the control environment. Additionally, the significance of the deficiency can change over time (for example, increases in sales volume or added complexity in sales transaction structures would increase the severity of a significant deficiency affecting sales).

Questions regarding evaluating results:

17. Will the definitions in the proposed standard of significant deficiency and material weakness provide for increased consistency in the evaluation of deficiencies? How can the definitions be improved?

18. Do the examples in Appendix D of how to apply these definitions in various scenarios provide helpful guidance? Are there other specific examples that commenters could suggest that would provide further interpretive help?

19. Is it necessary for the auditor to evaluate the severity of all identified internal control deficiencies?

20. Is it appropriate to require the auditor to communicate all internal control deficiencies (not just material weaknesses and significant deficiencies) to management in writing?

21. Are the matters that the Board has classified as strong indicators that a material weakness in internal control exists appropriately classified as such?

22. Is it appropriate to require the auditors to evaluate the effectiveness of the audit committee's oversight of the company's external financial reporting and internal control over financial reporting?

23. Will auditors be able to effectively carry out their responsibility to evaluate the effectiveness of the audit committee's oversight?

24. If the auditor concludes that ineffective audit committee oversight is a material weakness, rather than require the auditor to issue an adverse opinion with regard to the effectiveness of the internal control over financial reporting, should the standard require the auditor to withdraw from the audit engagement?

Forming an Opinion and Reporting

If the auditor has identified no material weaknesses in internal control after having performed all of the procedures that the auditor considers necessary in the circumstances, then the proposed standard would permit the auditor to express an unqualified opinion that management's assessment of the effectiveness of internal control over financial reporting is fairly stated in all material respects. In the event that the auditor could not perform all of the procedures that the auditor considers necessary in the circumstances, then the proposed standard would permit the auditor to either qualify or disclaim an opinion. If an overall opinion cannot be expressed, the proposed auditing standard would require the auditor to explain why.[3]

No Disclosure of Significant Deficiencies

The auditor's report must follow the same disclosure model as management's assessment. The SEC's final rules implementing Section 404 only require management's assessment to disclose material weaknesses, not significant deficiencies. Therefore, because management's assessment will disclose only material weaknesses, the auditor's report should disclose only material weaknesses.[4]

Material Weaknesses Result in Adverse Opinion

The existing attestation standard provides that when the auditor has identified a material weakness in internal control, depending on the significance of the material weakness and its effect on the achievement of the objectives of the control criteria, the auditor may qualify his or her opinion ("except for the effect of the material weakness, internal control was effective") or may express an adverse opinion ("internal control over financial reporting was not effective").

The SEC's final rules implementing Section 404 state that "Management is not permitted to conclude that the registrant's internal control over financial reporting is effective if there are one or more material weaknesses in the registrant's internal control over financial reporting." In other words, in such a case, management must conclude that internal control is not effective (i.e., a qualified or "except for" conclusion is not acceptable).

Similar to the reporting of significant deficiencies, the reporting model for the auditor must follow the required reporting model for management. Therefore, because management is required to express an "adverse" conclusion in the event a material weakness exists, the auditor's opinion must also be adverse; the proposed standard does not permit a qualified audit opinion in the event of a material weakness.

Questions regarding forming an opinion and reporting:

25. Is it appropriate that the existence of a material weakness would require the auditor to express an adverse conclusion about the effectiveness of the company's internal control over financial reporting, consistent with the required reporting model for management?

26. Are there circumstances where a qualified "except for" conclusion would be appropriate?

27. Do you agree with the position that when the auditor issues a nonstandard opinion, such as an adverse opinion, that the auditor's opinion should speak directly to the effec-

---

3. See also SEC Regulation S-X 2-02(f), 17 C.F. R. § 212.2-02(f) ("The attestation report on management's assessment of internal control over financial reporting shall be dated, signed manually, identify the period covered by the report and clearly state the opinion of the accountant as to whether management's assessment of the effectiveness of the registrant's internal control over financial reporting is fairly stated in all material respects, or must include an opinion to the effect that an overall opinion cannot be expressed. If an overall opinion cannot be expressed, explain why.").

4. It should be noted, however, that the final rules indicated that an aggregation of significant deficiencies may constitute a material weakness in a company's internal control over financial reporting, in which case disclosure would be required. See Final Rule: Management's Reports in Internal Control Over Financial Reporting and Certification of Disclosure in Exchange Act Periodic Reports, Securities and Exchange Commission Release No. 33-8238, (June 5, 2003) [68 FR 36636].

tiveness of the internal control over financial reporting rather than to whether management's assessment is fairly stated?

Fraud Considerations in an Audit of Internal Control Over Financial Reporting

Strong internal controls provide better opportunities to detect and deter fraud. For example, many frauds resulting in financial statement restatement relied upon the ability of management to exploit weaknesses in internal control. To the extent that the internal control reporting required by Section 404 can help restore investor confidence by improving the effectiveness of internal controls (and reducing the incidence of fraud), the auditing standard on performing the audit of internal control over financial reporting should emphasize controls that prevent or detect errors as well as fraud. For this reason, the proposed standard specifically addresses and emphasizes the importance of controls over possible fraud and requires the auditor to test controls specifically intended to prevent or detect fraud that is reasonably likely to result in material misstatement of the financial statements.

Auditor Independence

The Act, and the SEC rules implementing Section 404 of the Act, require the auditor to be independent to perform an audit of internal control over financial reporting. Under the SEC's Rule 2-01 on auditor independence, an auditor impairs his or her independence if the auditor audits his or her own work, including any work on designing or implementing an audit client's internal control system. The proposed standard explicitly prohibits the auditor from accepting an engagement to provide an internal control-related non-audit service to an audit client that has not been specifically preapproved by the audit committee. In other words, the audit committee would not be able to pre-approve internal control-related non-audit services as a category. Rather, each specific engagement would be required to be specifically pre-approved.

While the Board has not proposed to provide specific guidance on permissible internal control-related non-audit services in the proposed standard on the audit of internal control, the Board intends to conduct an in-depth evaluation of independence requirements in the future. The Board may, as a result of its evaluation, amend the independence information included in the proposed auditing standard.

Questions regarding auditor independence:

28. Should the Board provide specific guidance on independence and internal control-related non-audit services in the context of this proposed standard?

29. Are there any specific internal control-related non-audit services the auditor should be prohibited from providing to an audit client?

Auditor's Responsibilities With Regard to Management's Certifications

The proposed standard also outlines the auditor's work related to management's quarterly and annual certifications required by Section 302 of the Act.

A company's principal executive and financial officers are responsible for internal control over financial reporting. Section 302 of the Act emphasizes this responsibility by requiring these parties to certify, quarterly and annually, their responsibility, among others, for establishing and maintaining internal control over financial reporting and for disclosing changes in the company's internal control over financial reporting that occurred during the most recent quarter (or the fourth quarter, for the annual certification) that have materially affected, or are likely to affect materially, the company's internal control over financial reporting.

The Board believes that the auditor's responsibility for management's disclosure of a material weakness corrected by the end of one of the first three quarters should be similar to the auditor's responsibility regarding material misstatements of interim financial statements. Under AU sec. 722, *Interim Financial Information*,[5] the auditor performs limited procedures on the interim financial information which are substantially less than an audit; however, if the auditor became aware that the financial statements are materially misstated, the auditor would be required to communicate the matter to management. If management fails to respond appropriately, the auditor would be required to communicate the matter to the audit committee. If the audit committee did not respond appropriately, the auditor would be required to evaluate whether or not to resign from the engagement. The auditor also has responsibilities under AU sec. 317, *Illegal Acts by Clients*, and Section 10A of the Securities Exchange Act of 1934. If the auditor became aware that a material weakness in internal control had been identified and corrected yet management had not appropriately disclosed the correction in its report as indicated in the quarterly certification, that situation would be closely analogous to the auditor's knowledge of a material financial statement misstatement. Therefore, the responsibilities should run a similar path.

The auditor has a different level of responsibility as it relates to changes in internal control made in the fourth quarter. While the auditor is not required to issue a report on his or her quarterly review procedures, the auditor is required to report on management's annual assessment based on his or her audit of internal control. If, as a result of the auditor's audit procedures, the auditor becomes aware that management's annual report fails to appropriately disclose a material weakness that was corrected during the fourth quarter, the auditor has the responsibility to modify his or her audit report on internal control. Assume, for example, that management identified and corrected a material weakness during the fourth quarter and that the material weakness was corrected in time for both management and the auditor to have a sufficient period of time to test the operating effectiveness of the correction. Management makes the conclusion in its report on its assessment of internal control over financial reporting that internal control over financial reporting is effective; the auditor's opinion is unqualified, stating that management's assessment is stated fairly. However, if the company's annual report fails to also disclose the material weakness that was identified and corrected in the fourth quarter, and the auditor concludes that the disclosure is material information, the auditor would have to include an explanatory paragraph in his or her report describing the material weakness that was identified and corrected in the fourth quarter and note it was omitted from the company's annual report.

Questions regarding auditor's responsibilities with regard to management's certifications:

30. Are the auditor's differing levels of responsibility as they relate to management's quarterly certifications versus the annual (fourth quarter) certification, appropriate?

31. Is the scope of the auditor's responsibility for quarterly disclosures about the internal control over financial reporting appropriate?

---

5. The Board adopted the generally accepted auditing standards, as described in the American Institute of Certified Public Accountants' ("AICPA") Auditing Standards Board's ("ASB") Statement on Auditing Standards No. 95, *Generally Accepted Auditing Standards*, as in existence on April 16, 2003, on an initial, transitional basis. The Statements on Auditing Standards promulgated by the ASB have been codified into the AICPA *Professional Standards*, Volume 1, as AU sections 100 through 900. References in this Release to AU sections refer to those generally accepted auditing standards, as adopted on an interim basis in PCAOB Rule 3200T.

Effective Date of the Proposed Standard

Companies considered accelerated filers (seasoned U.S. companies with public float exceeding $75 million) are required to comply with the internal control reporting and disclosure requirements of Section 404 of the Act for fiscal years ending on or after June 15, 2004. Accordingly, auditors engaged to audit the financial statements of such companies for fiscal years ending on or after June 15, 2004, also are required to audit and report on the company's internal control over financial reporting as of the end of such fiscal year. Other companies (including smaller companies, foreign private issuers and companies with only registered debt securities) have until fiscal years ending on or after April 15, 2005, to comply with these internal control reporting and disclosure requirements and the requirement for audit reporting on internal control is similarly delayed. The proposed standard would be effective at the same time as these requirements. Early implementation of the proposed standard would be permitted.

Opportunity for Public Comment

The Board will seek comment on the proposed standard for a 45-day period. Interested persons are encouraged to submit their views to the Board. Written comments should be sent to Office of the Secretary, PCAOB, 1666 K Street, N.W., Washington, D.C. 20006-2803. Comments may also be submitted by e-mail to comments@pcaobus.org or through the Board's Web site at www.pcaobus.org. All comments should refer to PCAOB Rulemaking Docket Matter No. 008 in the subject or reference line and should be received by the Board no later than 5:00 PM (EST) on November 21, 2003.

The Board will carefully consider all comments received. Following the close of the comment period, the Board will determine whether to adopt a final standard, with or without amendments. Any final standard adopted will be submitted to the Securities and Exchange Commission for approval. Pursuant to Section 107 of the Act, proposed rules of the Board do not take effect unless approved by the Commission. Standards are deemed to be rules under the Act.

*   *   *

On the 7th day of October, in the year 2003, the foregoing was, in accordance with the by-laws of the Public Company Accounting Oversight Board,

ADOPTED BY THE BOARD.

/s/ J. Gordon Seymour

J. Gordon Seymour

Acting Secretary

October 7, 2003

Proposed Auditing Standard—An Audit of Internal Control Over Financial Reporting Performed in Conjunction with An Audit of Financial Statements

STATEMENT OF AUTHORITY

The Public Company Accounting Oversight Board (the "Board") is a private-sector, non-profit corporation, created by the Sarbanes-Oxley Act of 2002 (the "Act") to oversee the audits of public companies in order to protect the interests of investors and further the public interest in the preparation of informative, fair, and independent audit reports.

The Board has adopted Rule 3100 to require all registered public accounting firms to adhere to the Board's auditing and related professional practice standards (including interim professional standards) in the audits of public companies. Any registered public accounting firm that fails to adhere to the Board's standards is subject to disciplinary proceedings in accordance with Section 105 of the Act and the Board's rules.

Reference in the Board's standards to "the auditor" means a registered public accounting firm or an associated person of such a firm as defined in the Act and the Board's rules, unless specifically stated otherwise.

Reference in the Board's standards to the AICPA Professional Standards refers to those professional standards as they existed on April 16, 2003, the date the Board adopted them as interim standards.

The Board has proposed Rule 3101 regarding the use of certain terms in the Board's standards.* The Board's standards use the words "must," "shall," or "is required" to indicate unconditional obligations. The auditor's performance of these obligations is necessary to the accomplishment of the audit. The standards use the word "should" to indicate obligations that are presumptively mandatory. The auditor must comply with the requirements of this nature specified in the Board's standards unless the auditor can demonstrate, by verifiable objective and documented evidence, that alternative actions he or she followed in the circumstances were sufficient to achieve the objectives of the standard and serve adequately to protect the interests of investors and further the preparation of informative, fair, and independent audit reports. The Board uses the words "may," "might," "could," or other terms and phrases to describe actions and procedures that the auditor has a professional obligation to consider. Matters described in this fashion require the auditor's attention and understanding; how and whether they are implemented in the audit will depend on the exercise of professional judgment in the circumstances. Additionally, appendices to the Board's standards are an integral part of the standard and carry the same authoritative weight as the body of the standard.

This Statement of Authority is an integral part of the Board's auditing and related professional practice standards.

*. See PCAOB Release No. 2003-019, *Proposed Rule Regarding Certain Terms Used in Auditing and Related Professional Practice Standards.*

Appendix A—   Illustrative Reports on Internal Control Over Financial Reporting
Appendix B—   Additional Performance Requirements and Guidance; Extent of Testing Examples
Appendix C—   Safeguarding of Assets
Appendix D—   Examples of Material Weaknesses and Significant Deficiencies
Appendix E—   Special Internal Control Over Financial Reporting Considerations for Small and Mid-
               Sized Companies

1. This standard establishes requirements that apply when an auditor is engaged to audit both a company's financial statements and management's assessment of the effectiveness of internal control over financial reporting.[1]

2. A company subject to the reporting requirements of the Securities Exchange Act of 1934 is required to include in its annual report a report of management on the company's internal control over financial reporting. Registered investment companies, issuers of asset-backed securities, and nonpublic companies are not subject to the reporting requirements mandated by Section 404 of the Sarbanes-Oxley Act (the Act) of 2002 (PL 107-204). The report of management is required to contain management's assessment of the effectiveness of the company's internal control over financial reporting as of the end of the company's most recent fiscal year, including a statement as to whether the company's internal control over financial reporting is effective. The auditor that audits the company's financial statements included in the annual report is required to attest to and report on management's assessment. The company is required to file the auditor's attestation report as part of the annual report.

3. This standard is the standard on attestation engagements referred to in Section 404(b) of the Act.[2] Throughout this standard, the auditor's attestation of management's assessment of

---

1. This standard supersedes Chapter 5, "Reporting on an Entity's Internal Control Over Financial Reporting" of *Statement on Standards for Attestation Engagements No. 10, Attestation Standards: Revision and Recodification* (AICPA, *Professional Standards*, Vol. 1, AT sec. 501), as it relates to performing an audit (referred to in AT sec. 501 as an "examination") of the design and operating effectiveness of internal control over financial reporting. This standard also supersedes *Statement on Auditing Standards No. 60, Communication of Internal Control Related Matters Noted in an Audit* (AICPA, *Professional Standards*, Vol. 1, AU sec. 325). This standard requires that, for public companies, the auditor cannot audit internal control over financial reporting without also auditing the financial statements. However, the auditor may audit the financial statements without also auditing internal control over financial reporting. When an auditor is engaged to audit only the financial statements of a public company, this standard does not apply. However, in that situation, the auditor should follow this standard as it relates to the definition of a deficiency in internal control over financial reporting, a significant deficiency, and a material weakness, as well as the required communications of these matters described herein.

2. This standard is also the standard referred to in Section 103(a)(2)(A)(iii).

---

the effectiveness of internal control over financial reporting required by Section 404(b) of the Act is referred to as the *audit of internal control over financial reporting.*[3]

Auditor's Objective in an Audit of Internal Control Over Financial Reporting

4. The auditor's objective in an audit of internal control over financial reporting is to express an opinion on management's assessment of the effectiveness of the company's internal control over financial reporting. To form a basis for expressing such an opinion, the auditor must plan and perform the audit to obtain reasonable assurance about whether the company maintained, in all material respects, effective internal control over financial reporting as of the date specified in management's assessment.

5. To obtain reasonable assurance, the auditor evaluates the assessment performed by management and obtains and evaluates evidence about whether the internal control over financial reporting is designed and operated effectively. The auditor obtains this evidence from a number of sources, including using the work performed by management in making its assessment, internal auditors and others under the direction of management, and performing auditing procedures himself or herself.

Definitions Related to Internal Control Over Financial Reporting

6. For purposes of management's assessment and the audit of internal control over financial reporting in this standard, *internal control over financial reporting* is defined as follows:[4]

> A process designed by, or under the supervision of, the company's principal executive and principal financial officers, or persons performing similar functions, and effected by the company's board of directors, management, and other personnel, to provide reasonable assurance regarding the reliability of financial reporting and the preparation of financial statements for external purposes in accordance with generally accepted accounting principles and includes those policies and procedures that:
>
> (1) Pertain to the maintenance of records that, in reasonable detail, accurately and fairly reflect the transactions and dispositions of the assets of the company;
>
> (2) Provide reasonable assurance that transactions are recorded as necessary to permit preparation of financial statements in accordance with generally accepted accounting principles, and that receipts and expenditures of the company are being made only in accordance with authorizations of management and directors of the company; and
>
> (3) Provide reasonable assurance regarding prevention or timely detection of unauthorized acquisition, use or disposition of the company's assets that could have a material effect on the financial statements.

7. An *internal control deficiency* exists when the design or operation of a control does not allow management or employees, in the normal course of performing their assigned functions, to prevent or detect misstatements on a timely basis.

---

3. The two terms "audit of internal control over financial reporting" and "attestation of management's assessment of the effectiveness of internal control over financial reporting" refer to the same professional service. The first refers to the process, and the second refers to the result of that process.

4. This definition is the same one used by the SEC in its rules requiring management to report on internal control over financial reporting, except the word "registrant" has been changed to "company" to conform to the wording in this standard. (See Final Rule: Management's Reports on Internal Control Over Financial Reporting and Certification of Disclosure in Exchange Act Periodic Reports, Securities and Exchange Commission Release No. 33-8238 (June 5, 2003) [68 FR 36636].)

- A deficiency in *design* exists when (a) a control necessary to meet the control objective is missing or (b) an existing control is not properly designed so that even if the control operates as designed, the control objective is not always met.

- A deficiency in *operation* exists when a properly designed control does not operate as designed, or when the person performing the control does not possess the necessary authority or qualifications to perform the control effectively.

8. A *significant deficiency* is an internal control deficiency that adversely affects the company's ability to initiate, record, process, or report external financial data reliably in accordance with generally accepted accounting principles. A significant deficiency could be a single deficiency, or a combination of deficiencies, that results in more than a remote likelihood[5] that a misstatement of the annual or interim financial statements that is more than inconsequential in amount will not be prevented or detected.

9. A *material weakness* is a significant deficiency that, by itself, or in combination with other significant deficiencies, results in more than a remote likelihood that a material misstatement of the annual or interim financial statements will not be prevented or detected.

10. Internal controls over financial reporting may be *preventive controls* or *detective controls*.

- Preventive controls have the objective of preventing a misstatement from occurring in the first place.

- Detective controls have the objective of detecting a misstatement that has already occurred.

11. Even well-designed internal controls might not prevent a misstatement from occurring. However, this possibility is countered by detective controls. Therefore, effective internal control over financial reporting often includes a combination of preventive and detective controls to achieve a specific control objective. The auditor's procedures as part of either the audit of internal control over financial reporting or the audit of the financial statements are not part of a company's internal controls over financial reporting.

Framework Used by Management to Conduct Its Assessment

12. Management is required to base its assessment of the effectiveness of the company's internal control over financial reporting on a suitable, recognized control framework established by a body of experts that followed due-process procedures, including the broad distribution of the framework for public comment. In addition to being available to users of management's reports, a framework is suitable only when it:

- Is free from bias;

- Permits reasonably consistent qualitative and quantitative measurements of a company's internal control over financial reporting;

---

5. The term "remote likelihood" as used in the definition of *significant deficiency* and *material weakness* has the same meaning as the term "remote" as used in Financial Accounting Standards Board Statement No. 5, *Accounting for Contingencies* (FAS No. 5). Paragraph 3 of FAS No. 5 states:

When a loss contingency exists, the likelihood that the future event or events will confirm the loss or impairment of an asset or the incurrence of a liability can range from probable to remote. This Statement uses the terms *probable, reasonably possible,* and *remote* to identify three areas within that range, as follows:

a. *Probable.* The future event or events are likely to occur.

b. *Reasonably possible.* The chance of the future event or events occurring is more than remote but less than likely.

c. *Remote.* The chance of the future events or events occurring is slight.

- Is sufficiently complete so that those relevant factors that would alter a conclusion about the effectiveness of a company's internal controls over financial reporting are not omitted; and

- Is relevant to an evaluation of internal control over financial reporting.

Committee of Sponsoring Organizations Framework

13. In the United States, the Committee of Sponsoring Organizations (COSO) of the Treadway Commission has published *Internal Control—Integrated Framework.* Known as the COSO report, it provides a suitable and available framework for purposes of management's assessment. For that reason, the performance and reporting directions in this standard are based on the COSO framework. Other suitable frameworks have been published in other countries and may be developed in the future. Such other suitable frameworks may be used in an audit of internal control over financial reporting. Although different frameworks may not contain exactly the same elements as COSO, they should have elements that encompass, in general, all the themes in COSO. The auditor should therefore be able to apply the concepts and guidance in this standard in a reasonable manner.

14. The COSO perspective on internal control over financial reporting does not ordinarily encompass elements related to the effectiveness and efficiency of operations or compliance with laws and regulations. However, operations and compliance with laws and regulations directly related to the presentation of and required disclosures in financial statements are encompassed in internal control over financial reporting. Additionally, not all controls relevant to financial reporting are accounting controls. The auditor should identify all controls that could materially affect financial reporting, including controls that focus primarily on the effectiveness and efficiency of operations or compliance with laws and regulations and which also have a material effect on the reliability of financial reporting. More information about the COSO framework is included in AU sec. 319, *Consideration of Internal Control in a Financial Statement Audit.*[6] Appendix E discusses special internal control over financial reporting considerations for small and medium-sized companies.

Inherent Limitations in Internal Control Over Financial Reporting

15. Internal control over financial reporting cannot provide absolute assurance of achieving financial reporting objectives because of its inherent limitations. Internal control over financial reporting is a process that involves human diligence and compliance and is subject to lapses in judgment and breakdowns resulting from human failures. Internal control over financial reporting also can be circumvented by collusion or improper management override. Because of such limitations, there is a risk that material misstatements may not be prevented or detected on a timely basis by internal control over financial reporting. However, these inherent limitations are known features of the financial reporting process. Therefore, it is possible to design into the process safeguards to reduce, though not eliminate, this risk.

Reasonable Assurance

16. Management's assessment of the effectiveness of internal control over financial reporting is expressed at the level of *reasonable assurance.* The concept of reasonable assurance is built

---

6. The Board adopted the generally accepted auditing standards, as described in the AICPA Auditing Standards Board's (ASB) Statement on Auditing Standards No. 95, *Generally Accepted Auditing Standards,* as in existence on April 16, 2003, on an initial, transitional basis. The Statements on Auditing Standards promulgated by the ASB have been codified into the AICPA *Professional Standards, Volume 1,* as AU sections 100 through 900. References in this standard to AU sections refer to those generally accepted auditing standards, as adopted on an interim basis in PCAOB Rule 3200T.

into the definition of internal control over financial reporting and also is integral to the auditor's opinion.[7] Reasonable assurance includes the understanding that there is a relatively low risk that material misstatements will not be prevented or detected on a timely basis. Although not absolute assurance, reasonable assurance is, nevertheless, a high level of assurance.

17. Just as there are inherent limitations on the assurance that can be provided by effective internal control over financial reporting, as discussed in paragraph 15, there are limitations on the amount of assurance the auditor can obtain as a result of performing his or her audit of internal control over financial reporting. Limitations arise because an audit is conducted on a test basis and requires the exercise of professional judgment. Nevertheless, the audit of internal control over financial reporting includes obtaining an understanding of internal control over financial reporting, testing and evaluating the design and operating effectiveness of internal control over financial reporting, and performing such other procedures as the auditor considers necessary to obtain reasonable assurance about whether internal control over financial reporting is effective.

18. Users of the reports from management and the auditor are entitled to receive the same level of assurance from both management and the auditor. This means that users should expect reasonable assurance that internal control over financial reporting is effective. There is no difference in the level of work or assurance given by the auditor when expressing an opinion on management's assessment of effectiveness or when expressing an opinion directly on the effectiveness of internal control over financial reporting. In either case, the auditor must obtain sufficient evidence in order to provide a reasonable basis for his or her opinion and the use and evaluation of management's assessment is inherent in expressing either opinion. The auditor provides the same level of assurance, though not the same assurance, as management. However, the auditor's assurance does not relieve management of its responsibility for assuring users of its financial reports about the effectiveness of internal control over financial reporting.

Management's Responsibilities in an Audit of Internal Control Over Financial Reporting

19. For the auditor to satisfactorily complete an audit of internal control over financial reporting, management must do the following:[8]

a. Accept responsibility for the effectiveness of the company's internal control over financial reporting,

b. Evaluate the effectiveness of the company's internal control over financial reporting using suitable control criteria,

c. Support its evaluation with sufficient evidence, including documentation, and

d. Present a written assessment about the effectiveness of the company's internal control over financial reporting as of the end of the company's most recent fiscal year.

20. If the auditor concludes that management has not fulfilled the responsibilities enumerated in the preceding paragraph, the auditor should communicate, in writing, to management and the audit committee that the audit of internal control over financial reporting cannot be satis-

---

7. See Final Rule: Management's Reports on Internal Control Over Financial Reporting and Certification of Disclosure in Exchange Act Periodic Reports, Securities and Exchange Commission Release No. 33-8238 (June 5, 2003) [68 FR 36636] for further discussion of reasonable assurance.

8. Management is required to fulfill these responsibilities. See Final Rule: Management's Reports on Internal Control Over Financial Reporting and Certification of Disclosure in Exchange Act Periodic Reports, Securities and Exchange Commission Release No. 33-8238 (June 5, 2003) [68 FR 36636].

---

factorily completed and that he or she is required to disclaim an opinion. Paragraphs 41 through 47 provide information for the auditor on understanding management's process for evaluating and reporting on internal control over financial reporting.

Materiality Considerations in an Audit of Internal Control Over Financial Reporting

21. The auditor should apply the concept of materiality in an audit of internal control over financial reporting at both the financial-statements level and at the individual account-balance level. The auditor uses materiality at the financial-statements level in deciding whether a significant deficiency, or combination of significant deficiencies, in controls is a material weakness. Materiality at the individual account-balance level is relevant to deciding whether a deficiency represents a significant deficiency; accordingly, it is lower than materiality at the financial-statements level.

22. The same conceptual definition of materiality that applies to financial reporting applies to information on internal control over financial reporting, including the relevance of both quantitative and qualitative considerations.[9]

- The quantitative considerations are essentially the same as in an audit of financial statements, and relate to whether misstatements that would not be prevented or detected by internal control over financial reporting, individually or collectively, have a quantitatively material effect on the financial statements.

- The qualitative considerations apply to evaluating materiality with respect to the financial statements and to additional factors that relate to the perceived needs of reasonable persons who will rely on the information.

23. The auditor should be aware that persons who rely on the information concerning internal control over financial reporting include investors, creditors, the board of directors and audit committee, and regulators in specialized industries, such as banking or insurance. Information on internal control over financial reporting is intended to provide an early warning to those inside and outside the company who are in a position to insist on improvements in internal control over financial reporting, such as the audit committee and regulators in specialized industries. The auditor should also be aware that external users are also interested in information on internal control over financial reporting because it enhances the quality of financial reporting and increases their confidence in financial information, particularly financial information issued between annual reports, such as quarterly information.

Fraud Considerations in an Audit of Internal Control Over Financial Reporting

24. The auditor should evaluate all controls specifically intended to address the risks of fraud that are reasonably likely to have a material effect on the company's financial statements, which may be a part of any of the five components of internal control over financial reporting, as discussed in paragraph 50. However, the auditor should place a special emphasis on the evaluation of such controls in the control environment. Controls related to the prevention, identification, and detection of fraud in the control environment often have a pervasive effect on the risk of fraud. Such controls include, but are not limited to, the:

- Controls restraining the inappropriate use of company assets,
- Company's risk assessment processes,

---

9. AU sec. 312, *Audit Risk and Materiality in Conducting an Audit,* provides additional explanation of materiality.

- Code of ethics/conduct provisions, especially those related to conflicts of interest, related party transactions, illegal acts, and the monitoring of the code by management and the audit committee or board,

- Adequacy of the internal audit activity and whether it reports functionally to the audit committee, and

- Adequacy of the company's procedures for handling complaints and for accepting confidential submissions of concerns about questionable accounting or auditing matters.

25. Part of management's responsibility when designing a company's internal control over financial reporting is to design and implement programs and controls to prevent, deter, and detect fraud. Management, along with those who have responsibility for oversight of the financial reporting process (such as the audit committee), should set the proper tone; create and maintain a culture of honesty and high ethical standards; and establish appropriate controls to prevent, deter, and detect fraud. When management and those responsible for the oversight of the financial reporting process fulfill those responsibilities, the opportunities to commit fraud can be reduced significantly.

26. In an audit of internal control over financial reporting, the auditor's evaluation of controls is interrelated with the auditor's evaluation of controls in a financial statement audit, as required by AU sec. 316, *Consideration of Fraud in a Financial Statement Audit.* Often, controls identified and evaluated by the auditor during the audit of internal control over financial reporting also address or mitigate fraud risks, which the auditor is required to consider in a financial statement audit. If an auditor identifies deficiencies in controls related to the prevention, identification, and detection of fraud during the audit of internal control over financial reporting, the auditor should alter the nature, timing and extent of procedures to be performed during the financial statement audit to be responsive to such deficiencies, as provided in AU sec. 316.

Performing an Audit of Internal Control Over Financial Reporting

27. In an audit of internal control over financial reporting, the auditor must obtain sufficient competent evidence about the design and operating effectiveness of controls related to all relevant financial statement assertions for all significant accounts and disclosures in the financial statements. Because of the potential significance of the information obtained during the audit of the financial statements to the auditor's conclusions about the effectiveness of internal control over financial reporting, the auditor cannot audit internal control over financial reporting without also auditing the financial statements.[10]

28. The auditor must adhere to the general and applicable fieldwork and reporting standards in performing an audit of a company's internal control over financial reporting. This involves the following:

a. Planning the engagement,

b. Evaluating management's assessment process,

c. Obtaining an understanding of internal control over financial reporting,

---

10. However, the auditor may audit the financial statements without also auditing internal control over financial reporting, as might be necessary, for example, in the case of certain initial public offerings by a company. See the discussion beginning at paragraph 131 for more information about the importance of auditing both internal control over financial reporting as well as the financial statements when the auditor is engaged to audit internal control over financial reporting.

d. Testing and evaluating design effectiveness of internal control over financial reporting,

e. Testing and evaluating operating effectiveness of internal control over financial reporting, and

f. Forming an opinion on the effectiveness of internal control over financial reporting.

29. Even though some requirements of this standard are set forth in a manner that suggests a sequential process, auditing internal control over financial reporting involves a process of gathering, updating, and analyzing information. Accordingly, the auditor may perform some of the procedures and evaluations described in this section on "Performing an Audit of Internal Control Over Financial Reporting" concurrently.

General and Applicable Fieldwork and Reporting Standards

30. The general standards (see AU sec. 150, *Generally Accepted Auditing Standards*) are applicable to an audit of internal control over financial reporting. These standards require technical training and proficiency as an auditor, independence in fact and appearance, and the exercise of due professional care, including professional skepticism.

31. *Technical Training and Proficiency.* To perform an audit of internal control over financial reporting, the auditor should have competence in the subject matter of internal control over financial reporting.

32. *Independence.* The applicable basic principles of independence are that, to remain independent, the auditor must not function in the role of management and must not audit his or her own work. If the auditor were to design or implement controls, that situation would place the auditor in a management role and result in auditing the auditor's own work. This does not necessarily preclude the auditor from making substantive recommendations as to how management may improve the design or operation of the company's internal controls.

33. For any internal control services the auditor provides, management must be actively involved and cannot delegate responsibility for these matters to the auditor. Management's involvement must be substantive and extensive. Management's acceptance of responsibility for documentation and testing performed by the auditor is not enough to satisfy the independence requirements. Additionally, the auditor must not accept an engagement to provide internal control-related services to an issuer audit client that has not been specifically pre-approved by the audit committee.

34. Maintaining independence, in fact and appearance, requires more than ordinary attention in an audit of internal control over financial reporting due to its complexity. Unless the auditor and the audit committee are diligent in evaluating the nature and extent of services provided, the services might violate basic principles of independence and cause an impairment of independence in fact or appearance.

35. The independent auditor and the audit committee have significant and distinct responsibilities for evaluating whether the auditor's services impair independence in fact or appearance. The test for independence in fact is whether the activities would impede the ability of anyone on the engagement team or in a position to influence the engagement team from exercising objective judgment in the audits of the financial statements or internal control over financial reporting. The test for independence in appearance is whether a reasonable investor, knowing all relevant facts and circumstances, would perceive an auditor as having interests which could jeopardize the exercise of objective and impartial judgments on all issues brought to the auditor's attention.

36. *Due Professional Care.* The auditor must exercise due professional care in an audit of internal control over financial reporting. One important tenet of due professional care is exercising professional skepticism. In an audit of internal control over financial reporting, exercising professional skepticism involves essentially the same considerations as in an audit of financial statements. It includes a critical assessment of the work that management has performed in evaluating and testing controls. Inquiry of management and employees is the beginning point for obtaining an understanding of internal control over financial reporting, but inquiry alone is not adequate for reaching a conclusion on any aspect of internal control over financial reporting effectiveness.

37. *Fieldwork and Reporting Standards.* This standard establishes the fieldwork and reporting standards applicable to an audit of internal control over financial reporting.

38. The concept of materiality, as discussed in paragraphs 21 through 23, underlies the application of the general and fieldwork standards.

Planning the Engagement

39. The audit of internal control over financial reporting should be properly planned and assistants, if any, are to be properly supervised. When planning the audit of internal control over financial reporting, the auditor should evaluate how the following matters will affect the auditor's procedures:

- Knowledge of the company's internal control over financial reporting obtained during other engagements.

- Matters affecting the industry in which the company operates, such as financial reporting practices, economic conditions, laws and regulations, and technological changes.

- Matters relating to the company's business, including its organization, operating characteristics, capital structure, and distribution methods.

- The extent of recent changes, if any, in the company, its operations, or its internal control over financial reporting.

- Management's process for assessing the effectiveness of the company's internal control over financial reporting based upon control criteria.

- Preliminary judgments about materiality, risk, and other factors relating to the determination of material weaknesses.

- Internal control deficiencies previously communicated to the audit committee or management.

- Legal or regulatory matters of which the company is aware.

- The type and extent of available evidence related to the effectiveness of the company's internal control over financial reporting.

- Preliminary judgments about the effectiveness of internal control over financial reporting.

- The number of significant business locations or units, including management's documentation and monitoring of controls over such locations or business units. (Appendix B, paragraphs B1 through B16, discusses factors the auditor should evaluate to determine the locations at which to perform auditing procedures.)

40. The auditor could also evaluate additional relevant factors when planning the audit of internal control over financial reporting.

Evaluating Management's Assessment Process

41. The auditor must obtain an understanding of, and evaluate, management's process for assessing the effectiveness of the company's internal control over financial reporting. When obtaining the understanding, the auditor should determine whether management has addressed the following elements:

- Determining which controls should be tested, including controls over relevant assertions related to all significant accounts and disclosures in the financial statements. Generally, such controls include:

    —Controls over initiating, recording, processing, and reporting significant accounts and disclosures and related assertions embodied in the financial statements.

    —Controls over the selection and application of accounting policies that are in conformity with generally accepted accounting principles.

    —Antifraud programs and controls.

    —Controls, including information technology general controls, on which other controls are dependent.

    —Controls over significant nonroutine and nonsystematic transactions, such as accounts involving judgments and estimates.

    —Controls over the period-end financial reporting process, including controls over procedures used to enter transaction totals into the general ledger; to initiate, record, and process journal entries in the general ledger; and to record recurring and non-recurring adjustments to the financial statements (for example, consolidating adjustments, report combinations, and reclassifications).

- Evaluating the likelihood that failure of the control could result in a misstatement and the degree to which other controls, if effective, achieve the same control objectives.

- Determining the locations or business units to include in the evaluation for a company with multiple locations or business units (see paragraphs B1 through B16).

- Evaluating the design effectiveness of controls.

- Evaluating the operating effectiveness of controls based on procedures sufficient to assess their operating effectiveness. Examples of such procedures include testing of the controls by internal audit, testing of controls by others under the direction of management, using a service organization's reports (see paragraphs B24 through B39), or testing by means of a self-assessment process. Inquiry alone is not adequate to complete this evaluation. To evaluate the effectiveness of the company's internal control over financial reporting, management must have evaluated controls over all relevant assertions related to all significant accounts and disclosures.

- Determining the deficiencies in internal control over financial reporting that are of such a magnitude and likelihood of occurrence that they constitute significant deficiencies or material weaknesses.

- Communicating findings to the auditor and to others, if applicable.

- Evaluating whether findings are reasonable and support management's assessment.

42. As part of the understanding and evaluation of management's process, the auditor should obtain an understanding of the results of procedures performed by others. Others include internal audit and third parties working under the direction of management, including other auditors and accounting professionals engaged to perform procedures as a basis for management's assessment.

43. *Documentation.* When determining whether management's documentation provides reasonable support for its assessment, the auditor should evaluate whether such documentation includes the following:

- The design of controls over relevant assertions related to all significant accounts and disclosures in the financial statements. The documentation should include the five components of internal control over financial reporting as discussed in paragraph 50,

- Information about how significant transactions are initiated, recorded, processed and reported,

- Enough information about the flow of transactions to identify where material misstatements due to error or fraud could occur,

- Controls designed to prevent or detect fraud, including who performs the controls and the related segregation of duties,

- Controls over the period-end financial reporting process,

- Controls over safeguarding of assets (see paragraphs C1 through C3), and

- The results of management's testing and evaluation.

44. Documentation might take many forms of presentation and can include a variety of information, including policy manuals, process models, flowcharts, job descriptions, documents, and forms. No one form of documentation is required, and the extent of documentation will vary depending on the size, nature, and complexity of the company.

45. Documentation of the design of controls over relevant assertions related to significant accounts and disclosures is evidence that controls related to management's assessment about the effectiveness of internal control over financial reporting, including changes to those controls, have been identified, are capable of being communicated to those responsible for their performance, and are capable of being monitored by the company. Such documentation also provides the foundation for appropriate communication concerning responsibilities for performing controls and for the company's evaluation of and monitoring of the effective operation of controls.

46. Inadequate documentation of the design of controls over relevant assertions related to significant accounts and disclosures is a deficiency in the company's internal control over financial reporting. As discussed in paragraph 125, the auditor should evaluate this documentation deficiency. The auditor might conclude that the deficiency is only a deficiency, or that the deficiency represents a significant deficiency or a material weakness. In evaluating the deficiency as to its significance, the auditor should determine whether management can demonstrate the monitoring component of internal control over financial reporting in the absence of documentation.

47. Inadequate documentation also could cause the auditor to conclude that there is a limitation on the scope of the engagement.

Obtaining an Understanding of Internal Control Over Financial Reporting[11]

48. The auditor should obtain an understanding of the *design* of specific controls by applying procedures that include:

- Making inquiries of appropriate management, supervisory, and staff personnel,
- Inspecting company documents,
- Observing the application of specific controls, and
- Tracing transactions through the information system relevant to financial reporting.

49. The auditor could also apply additional procedures to obtain an understanding of the design of specific controls.

50. The auditor must obtain an understanding of the design of controls related to each component of internal control over financial reporting, as discussed below.

- *Control Environment.* Because of the pervasive effect of the control environment on the reliability of financial reporting, the auditor's preliminary judgment about its effectiveness often influences the nature, timing, and extent of the tests of operating effectiveness considered necessary. Weaknesses in the control environment should cause the auditor to alter the nature, timing, or extent of tests of operating effectiveness that otherwise would have been performed.

- *Risk Assessment.* When obtaining an understanding of the company's risk assessment process, the auditor should evaluate whether management has identified the risks of material misstatement in the significant accounts and disclosures and related assertions of the financial statements and has implemented controls to prevent or detect material misstatements. For example, the risk assessment process should address how management considers the possibility of unrecorded transactions or identifies and analyzes significant estimates recorded in the financial statements. Risks relevant to reliable financial reporting also relate to specific events or transactions.

- *Control Activities.* The auditor's understanding of control activities relates to the controls that management has implemented to prevent or detect material misstatement in the accounts and disclosures and related assertions of the financial statements. For the purposes of evaluating the effectiveness of internal control over financial reporting, the auditor's understanding of control activities encompasses a broader range of accounts and disclosures than what is normally obtained for the financial statement audit.

- *Information and Communication.* The auditor's understanding of management's information and communication involves understanding the same systems and processes that he or she addresses in an audit of financial statements. In addition, this understanding includes a greater emphasis on comprehending the safeguarding controls and the processes for authorization of transactions and the maintenance of records, as well as the period-end financial reporting process (discussed further beginning at paragraph 71).

- *Monitoring.* The auditor's understanding of management's monitoring of controls extends to and includes its monitoring of all controls, including control activities, which management has identified and designed to prevent or detect material misstatement in the accounts and disclosures and related assertions of the financial statements.

---

11. For additional information with regard to special internal control considerations for small and medium-sized companies, see Appendix E.

---

51. Some controls (such as company-level controls, described in paragraph 53) might have a pervasive effect on achieving many overall objectives of the control criteria. For example, information technology general controls over program development, program changes, computer operations, and access to programs and data help ensure that specific controls over the processing of transactions are operating effectively. In contrast, other controls are designed to achieve specific objectives of the control criteria. For example, management generally establishes specific controls, such as accounting for all shipping documents, to ensure that all valid sales are recorded.

52. The auditor should focus on combinations of controls, in addition to specific controls in isolation, in assessing whether the objectives of the control criteria have been achieved. The absence or inadequacy of a specific control designed to achieve the objectives of a specific criterion might not be a deficiency if other controls specifically address the same criterion. Further, when one or more controls achieve the objectives of a specific criterion, the auditor might not have to evaluate other controls designed to achieve those same objectives.

53. *Identifying Company-Level Controls.* Company-level controls are controls such as the following:

- Control environment, including tone at the top, the assignment of authority and responsibility, consistent policies and procedures, and company-wide programs, such as codes of conduct and fraud prevention, that apply to all locations and business units,

- Management's risk assessment process,

- Centralized processing and controls, including shared service environments,

- Monitoring results of operations,

- Monitoring of controls, including activities of the internal audit function, the audit committee, and self-assessment programs,

- The period-end financial reporting process, and

- Board-approved policies that address significant business control and risk management practices.

54. Controls that exist at the company-level often have a pervasive impact on controls at the process, transaction, or application level. For that reason, as a practical consideration, it may be appropriate for the auditor to test and evaluate the design effectiveness of company-level controls first, because the results of that work might affect the way the auditor evaluates the other aspects of internal control over financial reporting.

55. Testing company-level controls alone is not sufficient for the purpose of expressing an opinion on the effectiveness of a company's internal control over financial reporting.

56. *Evaluating the Effectiveness of the Audit Committee's Oversight of the Company's External Financial Reporting and Internal Control Over Financial Reporting.*[12] The company's audit committee plays an important role within the control environment and monitoring components of internal control over financial reporting. Within the control environment, the existence of an effective audit committee is essential to setting a positive tone at the top. Within the monitoring component, an effective audit committee is crucial to challenging the company's activities in the financial arena.

---

12. If no such committee exists with respect to the company, all references to the audit committee in this standard apply to the entire board of directors of the company.

---

57. The auditor should evaluate factors related to the effectiveness of the audit committee's oversight of the company's external financial reporting and internal control over financial reporting, including:

- Independence of the audit committee members from management (see paragraph 58),

- Clarity with which the audit committee's responsibilities are articulated and how well the audit committee and management understand those responsibilities,

- Level of involvement and interaction with the independent auditor, including the committee's role in the appointment, retention, and compensation of the independent auditor,

- Level of involvement and interaction with internal audit, including the committee's line of authority and role in appointing and compensating employees in the internal audit function,

- Committee's compliance with applicable listing standards adopted pursuant to Section 301 of the Act,

- Whether the committee includes one or more financial experts as described in Section 407 of the Act, and

- Amount of time that the audit committee devotes to control issues, as well as the amount of time that audit committee members are able to devote to committee activity.

58. As part of evaluating the independence of committee members, the auditor should evaluate how audit committee members are nominated and selected and whether they act independently from management.[13] Generally, the more independence that is built into the process of nominating members of the audit committee to the board, the more the auditor can be assured of committee independence. For example, are qualified candidates identified by outsiders, such as an outside search firm or a nominating committee composed of outside directors, or does management pick "friends?" Are board candidates for the audit committee selected based upon desired skill sets?

59. Ineffective oversight by the audit committee of the company's external financial reporting and internal control over financial reporting should be regarded as at least a significant deficiency and is a strong indicator that a material weakness in internal control over financial reporting exists.

60. *Identifying Significant Accounts.* The auditor should identify significant accounts and disclosures, first at the financial statement level and then at the account or disclosure component level. Determining specific controls to test begins by identifying significant accounts and disclosures within the financial statements. When identifying significant accounts, the auditor should evaluate both quantitative and qualitative factors.

61. An account is significant if there is more than a remote likelihood that the account could contain misstatements that individually or when aggregated with others could have a material effect on the financial statements. Other accounts may be significant on a qualitative basis based on the expectations of a reasonable user. For example, investors might be interested in a particular financial statement account even though it is not quantitatively large because it represents an important performance measure in a specialized industry.

---

13. The auditor should be aware that elections to the board of directors may be governed by state law, SRO listing standards, and the SEC's Regulation 14A.

---

62. Components of an account balance subject to differing risks (inherent and control) or different controls should be considered separately as potential significant accounts. For instance, inventory accounts often consist of raw materials (purchasing process), work in process (manufacturing process), finished goods (distribution process), and an allowance for obsolescence.

63. In some cases, separate components of an account may also need to be considered a significant account because of the company's organizational structure. For example, for a company that has a number of separate business units, each with unique management and accounting processes, the accounts at each separate business unit are considered individually as potential significant accounts.

64. An account may also be considered significant because of the exposure to unrecognized obligations represented by the account. For example, loss reserves related to a captive insurance entity or self-insurance program may have historically been insignificant in amount yet might represent a more than remote likelihood of material misstatement due to the existence of material unrecorded claims.

65. Appendix B, paragraphs B17 through B19, contains additional requirements about determining which accounts and disclosures are significant.

66. *Identifying Relevant Financial Statement Assertions.* For each significant account, the auditor should determine the relevance of each of these financial statement assertions:[14]

- Existence or occurrence,
- Completeness,
- Valuation or allocation,
- Rights and obligations, and
- Presentation and disclosure.

67. To identify relevant assertions, the auditor should determine the source of likely potential misstatements in each significant account. In determining whether a particular assertion is relevant to a significant account balance or disclosure, the auditor should evaluate:

- The nature of the assertion,
- The volume of transactions or data related to the assertion, and
- The nature and complexity of the systems, including the use of information technology by which the company processes and controls information supporting the assertion.

68. *Relevant assertions* are assertions that have a meaningful bearing on whether the account is fairly stated. For example, valuation may not be relevant to the cash account unless currency translation is involved; however, existence and completeness are always relevant. Similarly, valuation may not be relevant to the gross amount of the accounts receivable balance, but is relevant to the related allowance accounts. Additionally, the auditor may focus on the *presentation and disclosure* assertion separately in connection with the period-end financial reporting process.

69. *Identifying Significant Processes.* The auditor should identify each significant process over each major class of transactions affecting significant accounts or groups of accounts. For each significant process, the auditor should:

---

14. See AU sec. 326, *Evidential Matter,* which provides additional information on financial statement assertions.

- Understand the flow of transactions, including how transactions are initiated, recorded, processed, and reported.

- Identify the points within the process where a misstatement — including a misstatement due to fraud — related to each relevant financial statement assertion could arise.

- Identify the controls that management has implemented to address these potential misstatements.

- Identify the controls that management has implemented over the prevention or timely detection of unauthorized acquisition, use, or disposition of the company's assets.

70. The nature and characteristics of a company's use of information technology in its information system affect the company's internal control over financial reporting. Paragraphs 16 through 20 of AU sec. 319, *Consideration of Internal Control in a Financial Statement Audit,* discusses the effect of information technology on internal control over financial reporting.

71. *Understanding the Period-end Financial Reporting Process.* The period-end financial reporting process includes the following:

- The procedures used to enter transaction totals into the general ledger;

- The procedures used to initiate, record, and process journal entries in the general ledger;

- Other procedures used to record recurring and nonrecurring adjustments to the financial statements, such as consolidating adjustments, report combinations, and classifications; and

- Procedures for drafting financial statements and related disclosures.

72. As part of understanding and evaluating the period-end financial reporting process, the auditor should evaluate:

- The inputs, procedures performed, and outputs of the processes the company uses to produce its financial statements,

- The extent of information technology involvement in each period-end financial reporting process element,

- Who participates from management,

- The number of locations involved,

- Types of adjusting entries (for example, standard, nonstandard, eliminating, and consolidating), and

- The nature and extent of the audit committee's involvement in the process.

73. The period-end financial reporting process is always a significant process because of its importance to financial reporting and to the auditor's opinions on internal control over financial reporting and the financial statements. The auditor's understanding of the company's period-end financial reporting process and how it interrelates with the company's other significant processes assists the auditor in identifying and testing controls that are the most relevant to financial statement risks.

74. *Identifying Controls to Test.* The auditor should obtain evidence about the effectiveness of controls (either by performing tests of controls himself or herself, or by using the work of others)[15] for all relevant assertions related to all significant accounts and disclosures in the fi-

---

15. See paragraphs 103-110 for additional direction on using the work of others.

---

nancial statements. After identifying significant accounts, relevant assertions, and significant processes, the auditor should evaluate the following to identify the controls to be tested:

- Where errors or fraud could occur,
- The nature of the controls implemented by management,
- The significance of each control in achieving the objectives of the control criteria and whether more than one control achieves a particular objective,
- The nature and extent of tests of the operating effectiveness of the controls performed by the company, if any, and
- The risk that the controls might not be operating effectively. Factors that affect whether the control might not be operating effectively include the following:

  —Whether there have been changes in the volume or nature of transactions that might adversely affect control design or operating effectiveness,

  —Whether there have been changes in the design of controls,

  —The degree to which the control relies on the effectiveness of other controls (for example, the control environment or information technology general controls),

  —Whether there have been changes in key personnel who perform the control or monitor its performance,

  —Whether the control relies on performance by an individual or is automated, and

  —The complexity of the control.

75. The auditor should clearly link individual controls with the significant accounts and assertions to which they relate.

76. The auditor should evaluate whether to test preventive controls, detective controls, or a combination of both for individual relevant assertions for individual significant accounts. For instance, when performing tests of preventive and detective controls, the auditor might conclude that a deficient preventive control could be compensated for by an effective detective control and, therefore, not result in a significant deficiency or material weakness. For example, a monthly reconciliation control procedure, which is a detective control, might detect an out-of-balance situation resulting from an unauthorized transaction being initiated due to an ineffective authorization procedure, which is a preventive control. When determining whether the detective control is effective, the auditor should evaluate whether the detective control is sufficient to achieve the control objective to which the preventive control relates.

77. Because effective internal control over financial reporting often includes a combination of preventive and detective controls, the auditor ordinarily will test a combination of both.

78. The auditor should apply tests of controls to those controls that are important to achieving each control objective. It is neither necessary to test all controls nor is it necessary to test redundant controls (that is, controls that duplicate other controls that achieve the same objective and already have been tested), unless redundancy is itself a control objective, as in the case of certain computer controls.

79. *Performing Walkthroughs.* Walkthroughs are required procedures. The auditor should perform a walkthrough for all of the company's significant processes. In a walkthrough, the auditor should trace all types of transactions and events, both recurring and unusual, from origination through the company's information systems until they are reflected in the company's financial reports. Walkthroughs provide the auditor with evidence to:

- Confirm the auditor's understanding of the process flow of transactions,

- Confirm the auditor's understanding of the design of controls identified for all five components of internal control over financial reporting, including those related to the prevention or detection of fraud,

- Confirm that the auditor's understanding of the process is complete by determining whether all points in the process where misstatements related to each relevant financial statement assertion that could occur have been identified,

- Evaluate the effectiveness of the design of controls, and

- Confirm whether controls have been placed in operation.

80. The auditor's walkthroughs should encompass the entire process of initiating, recording, processing, and reporting individual transactions, and controls for all five internal control components and fraud, not just control activities. During the walkthrough, at each point where important processing procedures or controls occur, the auditor should question the company's personnel about their understanding of what is required by the company's pre-scribed procedures and controls and determine whether the processing procedures are per-formed as originally understood and on a timely basis. (Controls might not be performed reg-ularly but still be timely.) During the walkthrough, the auditor should be alert for exceptions to the company's prescribed procedures and controls.

81. While performing a walkthrough, the auditor should evaluate the quality of the evidence obtained and perform walkthrough procedures that produce a level of evidence consistent with the objectives listed in paragraph 79. Rather than reviewing copies of documents and making inquiries of a single person at the company, the auditor should follow the process flow using the same documents and information technology that company personnel use and make inquiries of relevant personnel involved in significant aspects of the process or controls. To corroborate information at various points in the walkthrough, the auditor might ask per-sonnel to describe their understanding of the previous and succeeding processing or control activities and to demonstrate what they do. In addition, inquiries should include follow-up questions that could help identify the abuse of controls or indicators of fraud. Examples of follow-up inquiries include asking personnel:

- What they do when they find an error or what they are looking for to determine if there is an error (rather than simply asking them if they perform listed procedures and controls); what kind of errors they have found; what happened as a result of finding the errors, and how the errors were resolved. If the person being interviewed has never found an error, the auditor should evaluate whether that is due to good preventive con-trols or whether the individual performing the control lacks the necessary skills.

- Whether they have ever been asked to override the process or controls, and if so, to describe the situation, why it occurred, and what happened.

82. During the period under audit, when there have been significant changes in the process flow of transactions, including the supporting computer applications, the auditor should eval-uate the nature of the change(s) and the effect on related accounts to determine whether to walkthrough transactions that were processed both before and after the change.

83. For non-routine and estimation processes, the auditor can often gain an understanding of the transaction flow, identify and understand controls, and conduct the walkthrough simulta-neously.

Testing and Evaluating Design Effectiveness

84. Internal control over financial reporting is effectively designed when the controls complied with would be expected to prevent or detect material misstatements in the financial statements. The auditor should determine whether the company has controls to meet the objectives of the control criteria by:

- Identifying the company's control objectives in each area,
- Identifying the controls that satisfy each objective, and
- Determining whether the controls, if operating properly, can effectively prevent or detect material misstatements in the financial statements.

85. Procedures the auditor performs to test and evaluate design effectiveness include inquiry, observation, walkthroughs, and a specific evaluation of whether the controls are likely to prevent or detect misstatements if they are operated as prescribed by appropriately qualified persons.

86. The procedures that the auditor performs in evaluating management's assessment process and obtaining an understanding of internal control over financial reporting also provide the auditor with evidence about the design effectiveness of internal control over financial reporting.

87. The procedures the auditor performs to test and evaluate design effectiveness also might provide evidence about operating effectiveness.

Testing and Evaluating Operating Effectiveness

88. An auditor should evaluate the operating effectiveness of a control by determining whether the control is operating as designed and whether the person performing the control possesses the necessary authority and qualifications to perform the control effectively.

89. *Nature of Tests of Controls.* Tests of controls over operating effectiveness should include a mix of inquiries of appropriate personnel, inspection of relevant documentation, observation of the company's operations, and reperformance of the application of the control. For example, the auditor might observe the procedures for opening the mail and processing cash receipts to test the operating effectiveness of controls over cash receipts. Because an observation is pertinent only at the point in time at which it is made, the auditor should supplement the observation with inquiries of company personnel and inspection of documentation about the operation of such controls at other times.

90. Inquiry is a procedure that is used extensively throughout the audit and often is complementary to performing other procedures. Inquiry consists of seeking information, both financial and nonfinancial, of knowledgeable persons throughout the company. Inquiries may range from formal written inquiries to informal oral inquiries.

91. Evaluating responses to inquiries is an integral part of the inquiry procedure. Responses to inquiries might provide the auditor with information not previously possessed or with corroborative evidence. Alternatively, responses might provide information that differs significantly from other information the auditor obtains (for example, information regarding the possibility of management override of controls). In some cases, responses to inquiries provide a basis for the auditor to modify or perform additional procedures.

92. Because inquiry alone does not provide sufficient evidence to support the operating effectiveness of a control, the auditor should perform additional tests of controls. For example, if the company implements a control activity whereby its sales manager reviews and investigates a report of invoices with unusually high or low gross margins, inquiry of the sales manager as to whether he or she investigates discrepancies would be inadequate. To obtain sufficient evidence about the operating effectiveness of the control, the auditor should corroborate the sales manager's responses by performing other procedures, such as inspecting reports or other documentation used in or generated by the performance of the control, and evaluate whether appropriate actions were taken regarding discrepancies.

93. The nature of the control also influences the nature of the tests of controls the auditor can perform. For example, the auditor might examine documents regarding controls for which documentary evidence exists. However, documentary evidence regarding some aspects of the control environment, such as management's philosophy and operating style, might not exist. In circumstances in which documentary evidence of controls or the performance of controls does not exist and is not expected to exist, the auditor's tests of controls would consist of inquiries of appropriate personnel and observation of company activities. As another example, a signature on a voucher package to indicate that the signer approved it does not necessarily mean that the person carefully reviewed the package before signing. The package may have been signed based on only a cursory review (or without any review). As a result, the quality of the evidence regarding the effective operation of the control might not be sufficiently persuasive. If that is the case, the auditor should reperform the control (for example, checking prices, extensions, and additions) as part of the test of the control.

94. *Timing of Tests of Controls.* The auditor must perform tests of controls over a period of time that is adequate to determine whether, as of the date specified in management's report, the controls necessary for achieving the objectives of the control criteria are operating effectively. The period of time over which the auditor performs tests of controls varies with the nature of the controls being tested and with the frequency with which specific controls operate and specific policies are applied. Some controls operate continuously (for example, controls over sales), while others operate only at certain times (for example, controls over the preparation of monthly or quarterly financial statements and controls over physical inventory counts).

95. The auditor's testing of the operating effectiveness of such controls should occur at the time the controls are operating. Controls "as of" a specific date encompass controls that are relevant to the company's internal control over financial reporting "as of" that specific date, even though such controls might not operate until after that specific date. For example, some controls over the period-end financial reporting process normally operate only after the "as of" date. Therefore, if controls over the December 31, 20X4 period-end financial reporting process operate in January 20X5, the auditor tests the control operating in January 20X5 to have sufficient evidence of operating effectiveness "as of" December 31, 20X4.

96. When the auditor reports on the effectiveness of controls "as of" a specific date and obtains evidence about the operating effectiveness of controls at an interim date, he or she should determine what additional evidence to obtain concerning the operation of the control for the remaining period. In making that determination, the auditor should evaluate:

- The specific controls tested prior to the "as of" date and the results of those tests,
- The degree to which evidence about the operating effectiveness of those controls was obtained,
- The length of the remaining period, and
- The possibility that there have been any significant changes in internal control over financial reporting subsequent to the interim date.

97. The auditor could also evaluate additional factors when determining what additional evidence to obtain.

98. For controls over significant nonroutine transactions, controls over accounts or processes with a high degree of subjectivity or judgment in measurement, or controls over the recording of period-end adjustments, the auditor should perform tests of controls closer to or at the "as of" date rather than at an interim date. However, the auditor should balance performing the tests of controls closer to the "as of" date with the need to obtain sufficient evidence of operating effectiveness.

99. Prior to the date specified in management's report, management might implement changes to the company's controls to make them more effective or efficient or to address control deficiencies. In that case, the auditor might not need to evaluate controls that have been superseded. For example, if the auditor determines that the new controls achieve the related objectives of the control criteria and have been in effect for a sufficient period to permit the auditor to assess their design and operating effectiveness by performing tests of controls,[16] he or she will not need to evaluate the design and operating effectiveness of the superseded controls for purposes of expressing an opinion on internal control over financial reporting.

100. As discussed in paragraph 190, however, the auditor must communicate any identified significant deficiencies and material weaknesses in controls to the audit committee in writing. In addition, the auditor should evaluate how the design and operating effectiveness of the superseded controls relates to the auditor's reliance on controls for financial statement audit purposes.

101. *Extent of Tests of Controls.* Each year the auditor must obtain sufficient evidence about whether the company's internal control over financial reporting, including the controls for all internal control components, is operating effectively. The auditor also should vary from year to year the nature, timing, and extent of testing of controls to introduce unpredictability into the testing and respond to changes in circumstances. For example, each year the auditor might test the controls at a different interim period; increase or reduce the number and types of tests performed; or change the combination of procedures used.

102. In determining the extent of procedures to perform, the auditor should design the procedures to provide a high level of assurance that the control being tested is operating effectively. In making this determination, the auditor should consider the following factors:

- *Nature of the control.* Manual controls should be subjected to more extensive testing than automated controls. In some circumstances, testing a single operation of an automated control may be sufficient to obtain a high level of assurance that the control operated effectively, provided that information technology general controls also are operating effectively. For manual controls, sufficient evidence about the operating effectiveness of the controls is obtained by evaluating multiple operations of the control and the results of each operation. The auditor also should consider the complexity of the controls, the significance of the judgments that must be made in connection with their operation, and the level of competence of the person performing the controls that is necessary for the control to operate effectively. As the complexity and level of judgment increase or the level of competence of the person performing the control decreases, the extent of the auditor's testing should increase.

---

16. Paragraph 166 provides reporting directions in circumstances when the auditor has not been able to obtain evidence that the new controls were appropriately designed or have been operating effectively for a sufficient period of time.

- *Frequency of operation.* The more frequently a manual control operates, the more operations of the control the auditor should test. For example, for a manual control that operates in connection with each transaction, the auditor tests multiple operations of the control over a sufficient period of time to obtain a high level of assurance that the control operated effectively. For controls that operate less frequently, such as monthly account reconciliations and controls over the period-end financial reporting process, the auditor may test significantly fewer operations of the control. However, the auditor's evaluation of each operation of controls operating less frequently is likely to be more extensive. For example, when evaluating the operation of a monthly exception report, the auditor should evaluate whether the judgments made with regard to the disposition of the exceptions were appropriate and adequately supported.

- *Importance of the control.* Controls that are relatively more important should be tested more extensively. For example, some controls may address multiple financial statement assertions, and certain period-end detective controls might be considered more important than related preventive controls. The auditor should test more operations of such controls or, if such controls operate infrequently, the auditor should evaluate each operation of the control more extensively.

103. *Use of the Work of Management and Others.* The auditor should evaluate whether to use the work performed by management and others. When evaluating whether to use the results of procedures performed by others, the auditor should evaluate the following factors:

- The materiality or the risk of misstatement of the accounts and disclosures that the controls address.

- The degree of judgement required to evaluate the operating effectiveness of the control.

- The degree the control can be subjected to objective testing vs. a subjective evaluation.

- The pervasiveness of the control.

- The level of judgment or estimation that is required in the account or disclosure.

104. There are a number of areas in which the auditor should not use the results of testing performed by management and others, including:

- Controls that are part of the control environment, including controls specifically established to prevent and detect fraud that is reasonably likely to result in material misstatement of the financial statements.

- Controls over the period-end financial reporting process, including controls over procedures used to enter transaction totals into the general ledger; to initiate, record, and process journal entries in the general ledger; and to record recurring and nonrecurring adjustments to the financial statements (for example, consolidating adjustments, report combinations, and reclassifications).

- Controls that have a pervasive effect on the financial statements, such as certain information technology general controls on which the operating effectiveness of other controls depend.

- Walkthroughs, as discussed beginning at paragraph 79.

105. The auditor's use of the results of procedures performed by management and others should be limited in the following areas:

- Controls over significant nonroutine and nonsystematic transactions (such as accounts involving *significant* judgments and estimates).

- Controls over significant accounts, processes, or disclosures where the auditor has assessed the risk of failure of the controls to operate effectively as high.

106. The auditor might decide to use the results of tests performed by management and others within the company in other areas, such as controls over routine processing of significant accounts and disclosures, without specific limitation.

107. If the auditor intends to use the results of tests performed by others to alter the nature, timing, and extent of the tests of controls that the auditor performs, he or she should assess the degree of objectivity and competence of the individuals performing the tests of controls. In addition to assessing the objectivity and competence of those performing the tests, the auditor should reperform some of the tests of controls originally performed by others.

108. Internal auditors would normally be expected to have greater competence with regard to internal control over financial reporting and objectivity than other company personnel. Therefore, the auditor may be able to use the results of their procedures to a greater extent than the results of procedures performed by others. This is particularly true in the case of internal auditors who follow the *International Standards for the Professional Practice of Internal Auditing* issued by the Institute of Internal Auditors. At companies where the importance of the internal audit function results in a high degree of competence and objectivity and their work is extensive, the auditor could use their work to the greatest extent an auditor could use the work of others. On the other hand, if, for example, internal audit reports solely to management, which would reduce internal audit's objectivity, or if limited resources allocated to internal audit result in very limited testing procedures on its part, the auditor would need to perform more testing himself or herself.

109. In addition to following the directions in paragraphs 103-108, the auditor must perform enough of the testing himself or herself so that the auditor's own work provides the principal evidence for the auditor's opinion.

110. Appendix B, paragraphs B20 through B23, provides additional guidance as well as an application example on using the work of others.

111. *Use of Professional Skepticism when Evaluating the Results of Testing.* The auditor must conduct the audit of internal control over financial reporting and the audit of the financial statements with professional skepticism, which is an attitude that includes a questioning mind and a critical assessment of audit evidence. For example, even though a control is performed by the same employee whom the auditor believes performed the control effectively in prior periods, the control may not be operating effectively during the current period because the employee could have become complacent, distracted, or otherwise not effectively carry out his or her responsibilities. Also, regardless of any past experience with the entity or the auditor's beliefs about management's honesty and integrity, the auditor should recognize the possibility that a material misstatement due to fraud could be present. Furthermore, professional skepticism requires the auditor to consider whether evidence obtained suggests that a material misstatement due to fraud has occurred. In exercising professional skepticism in gathering and evaluating evidence, the auditor must not be satisfied with less-thanpersuasive evidence because of a belief that management is honest.

112. When the auditor identifies exceptions to the company's prescribed control procedures, he or she should determine, using professional skepticism, the effect of the exception on the nature and extent of additional testing that may be appropriate or necessary and on the operating effectiveness of the control being tested. A conclusion that an identified exception does not represent an internal control deficiency is appropriate only if evidence beyond what the auditor had initially planned and beyond inquiry supports that conclusion.

Forming an Opinion on the Effectiveness of Internal Control Over Financial Reporting

113. When forming an opinion on internal control over financial reporting, the auditor should evaluate all evidence obtained from all sources, including:

- The results of tests of controls,
- The results of substantive procedures performed during the financial statement audit, and
- Any identified internal control deficiencies.

114. As part of this evaluation, the auditor should review all reports issued during the year by internal audit (or similar functions, such as loan review in a financial institution) that address controls related to internal control over financial reporting and evaluate any internal control deficiencies identified in those reports. This review should include reports issued by internal audit as a result of operational audits or specific reviews of key processes if those reports address controls related to internal control over financial reporting.

115. *Circumstances for Issuance of Unqualified Opinion.* The auditor may issue an unqualified opinion only when there are no identified material weaknesses and when there have been no restrictions on the scope of the auditor's work. The existence of a material weakness in internal control over financial reporting requires the auditor to express an adverse opinion (see paragraph 162), while a scope limitation requires the auditor to express a qualified opinion or a disclaimer of opinion, depending on the significance of the limitation in scope (see paragraph 165). The following paragraphs provide directions on evaluating internal control deficiencies noted during the audit.

116. *Evaluating Deficiencies in Internal Control Over Financial Reporting.* The auditor must evaluate identified internal control deficiencies and determine whether the deficiencies, individually or in combination, are significant deficiencies or material weaknesses.

117. The auditor should evaluate the significance of a deficiency in internal control over financial reporting initially by determining the following:

- The likelihood that a deficiency, or a combination of deficiencies, could result in a misstatement of an account balance or disclosure, and
- The magnitude of the potential misstatement resulting from the deficiency or deficiencies.

118. The significance of a deficiency in internal control over financial reporting depends on the *potential* for a misstatement, not on whether a misstatement actually has occurred.

119. Several factors affect the *likelihood* that a deficiency, or a combination of deficiencies, could result in a misstatement of an account balance or disclosure. The factors include, but are not limited to, the following:

- The susceptibility of the related assets or liability to loss or fraud; that is, greater susceptibility increases risk.
- The subjectivity, complexity, or extent of judgment required to determine the amount involved; that is, greater subjectivity, complexity, or judgment, like that related to an accounting estimate, increases risk.

- The nature of the accounts, processes, or disclosures; for example, suspense accounts and related party transactions involve greater risk.

- The cause and frequency of known or detected exceptions for the operating effectiveness of a control; for example, a control with an observed non-negligible deviation rate is a deficiency.

- The interaction or relationship of the control with other controls; that is, the interdependence or redundancy of the control.

120. When evaluating the likelihood that a deficiency or combination of deficiencies could result in a misstatement, the auditor should evaluate how the controls interact with other controls. There are controls, such as information technology general controls, on which other controls depend. Some controls function together as a group of controls. Other controls overlap, in the sense that these other controls achieve the same objective.

121. Several factors affect the magnitude of the misstatement that could result from a deficiency or deficiencies in controls. The factors include, but are not limited to, the following:

- The financial statement amounts or total of transactions that are exposed to the deficiency.

- The volume of activity in the account balance or class of transactions exposed to the deficiency that has occurred in the current period, or that is expected in future periods.

122. In evaluating the magnitude of the potential misstatement, the auditor should recognize that the maximum amount that an account balance or total of transactions can be overstated is generally the recorded amount. However, the recorded amount is not a limitation on the amount of potential understatement. The auditor also should recognize that the risk of misstatement might be different for the maximum possible misstatement than for lesser possible amounts.

123. The interaction of qualitative considerations that affect internal control over financial reporting with quantitative considerations ordinarily results in deficiencies in the following areas being at least significant deficiencies in internal control over financial reporting:

- Controls over the selection and application of accounting policies that are in conformity with generally accepted accounting principles,

- Antifraud programs and controls,

- Controls over non-routine and nonsystematic transactions, and

- Controls over the period-end financial reporting process, including controls over procedures used to enter transaction totals into the general ledger; initiate, record, and process journal entries into the general ledger; and record recurring and nonrecurring adjustments to the financial statements.

124. When evaluating the significance of a deficiency in internal control over financial reporting, the auditor also should determine the level of detail and degree of assurance that would satisfy prudent officials in the conduct of their own affairs that they have reasonable assurance that transactions are recorded as necessary to permit the preparation of financial statements in conformity with generally accepted accounting principles. If the auditor determines that the deficiency would prevent prudent officials in the conduct of their own affairs from concluding that they have reasonable assurance,[17] then the auditor should consider the deficiency to be at least a significant deficiency. Having determined in this manner that a deficiency represents a significant deficiency, the auditor must further evaluate the deficiency to determine whether individually, or in combination with other deficiencies, the deficiency is a material weakness.

125. Inadequate documentation of the design of controls and the absence of sufficient documented evidence to support management's assessment of the operating effectiveness of internal control over financial reporting also are internal control deficiencies. As with other internal control deficiencies, the auditor should evaluate these deficiencies as to their significance.

126. Each of the following circumstances should be regarded as at least a significant deficiency and is a strong indicator that a material weakness in internal control over financial reporting exists:

- Restatement of previously issued financial statements to reflect the correction of a misstatement.

- Identification by the auditor of a material misstatement in financial statements in the current period that was not initially identified by the company's internal control over financial reporting. (This is still a strong indicator of a material weakness even if management subsequently corrects the misstatement.)

- Oversight of the company's external financial reporting and internal control over financial reporting by the company's audit committee is ineffective. (Paragraphs 56 through 59 present factors to evaluate when determining whether the audit committee is ineffective.)

- For larger, more complex entities, the internal audit function or the risk assessment function is ineffective.

- For complex entities in highly regulated industries, an ineffective regulatory compliance function.

- Identification of fraud of any magnitude on the part of senior management.

- Significant deficiencies that have been communicated to management and the audit committee remain uncorrected after some reasonable period of time.

127. In addition, Appendix D provides examples of significant deficiencies and material weaknesses.

Requirement for Written Representations

128. In an audit of internal control over financial reporting, the auditor should obtain written representations from management:

a. Acknowledging management's responsibility for establishing and maintaining effective internal control over financial reporting,

b. Stating that management has performed an evaluation of the effectiveness of the company's internal control over financial reporting and specifying the control criteria,

c. Stating management's conclusion about the effectiveness of the company's internal control over financial reporting based on the control criteria as of a specified date,

---

17. See SEC Staff Accounting Bulletin Topic 1M2, *Immaterial Misstatements That Are Intentional,* for further discussion about the level of detail and degree of assurance that would satisfy prudent officials in the conduct of their own affairs.

d. Stating that management has disclosed to the auditor all significant deficiencies in the design or operation of internal control over financial reporting that it believes to be material weaknesses in internal control over financial reporting,

e. Describing any material fraud and any other fraud that, although not material, involves senior management or management or other employees who have a significant role in the company's internal control over financial reporting,

f. Stating whether internal control deficiencies identified and communicated to the audit committee during previous engagements pursuant to paragraph 190 have been resolved, and specifically identifying any that have not, and

g. Stating whether there were, subsequent to the date being reported on, any changes in internal control over financial reporting or other factors that might significantly affect internal control over financial reporting, including any corrective actions taken by management with regard to significant deficiencies and material weaknesses.

129. The failure to obtain written representations from management, including management's refusal to furnish them, constitutes a limitation on the scope of the audit sufficient to preclude an unqualified opinion. As discussed further in paragraph 165, when management limits the scope of the audit, the auditor should either withdraw from the engagement or disclaim an opinion. Further, the auditor should evaluate the effects of management's refusal on his or her ability to rely on other representations, including, if applicable, representations obtained in an audit of the company's financial statements.

130. AU sec. 333, *Management Representations*, explains matters such as who should sign the letter, the period to be covered by the letter, and when to obtain an updating letter.

Relationship of an Audit of Internal Control over Financial Reporting to an Audit of Financial Statements

131. The audit of internal control over financial reporting should be integrated with the audit of the financial statements. The objectives of the procedures for the audits are not identical, however, and the auditor must plan and perform the work to achieve the objectives of both audits.

132. The understanding of internal control over financial reporting the auditor obtains and the procedures the auditor performs for purposes of expressing an opinion on management's assessment are interrelated with the internal control over financial reporting understanding the auditor obtains and procedures the auditor performs to assess control risk for purposes of expressing an opinion on the financial statements. As a result, it is efficient for the auditor to coordinate obtaining the understanding and performing the procedures.

Tests of Controls in an Audit of Internal Control Over Financial Reporting

133. The objective of the tests of controls in an audit of internal control over financial reporting is to obtain evidence about the effectiveness of internal controls to support the auditor's opinion on whether management's assessment of the effectiveness of the company's internal control over financial reporting is fairly stated. The auditor's opinion relates to the effectiveness of the company's internal control over financial reporting as of a *point in time* and *taken as a whole.*

134. To express an opinion on internal control over financial reporting effectiveness as of a *point in time*, the auditor should obtain evidence that internal control over financial reporting has operated effectively for a sufficient period of time, which may be less than the entire period (ordinarily one year) covered by the company's financial statements. To express an opinion on internal control over financial reporting effectiveness *taken as a whole*, the auditor must obtain evidence about the effectiveness of controls related to all relevant assertions for all significant accounts and disclosures in the financial statements. This requires the auditor to test the design and operating effectiveness of controls he or she ordinarily would not test if expressing an opinion only on the financial statements.

135. When concluding on the effectiveness of internal control over financial reporting for purposes of expressing an opinion on management's assessment, the auditor should incorporate the results of any additional tests of control performed to achieve the objective related to expressing an opinion on the financial statements, as discussed in the following section.

Tests of Controls in an Audit of Financial Statements

136. To express an opinion on the financial statements, the auditor ordinarily performs tests of controls and substantive procedures. The objective of the tests of controls the auditor performs for this purpose is to assess control risk. To assess control risk for specific financial statement assertions at less than the maximum, the auditor is required to obtain evidence that the relevant controls operated effectively during the *entire period* covered by the company's financial statements. However, the auditor is not required to assess control risk at less than the maximum for *all* relevant assertions for the entire period covered by the financial statements, and, for a variety of reasons, the auditor may choose not to do so.[18]

137. When concluding on the effectiveness of controls for the purpose of assessing control risk, the auditor also should consider the results of any additional tests of controls performed to achieve the objective related to expressing an opinion on management's assessment, as discussed in paragraphs 133 through 135. Consideration of these results may require the auditor to alter the nature, timing, and extent of substantive procedures and to plan and perform further tests of controls, particularly in response to identified internal control deficiencies.

Effect of Tests of Controls on Substantive Procedures

138. Regardless of the assessed level of control risk or the assessed risk of material misstatement in connection with the audit of the financial statements, the auditor should perform substantive procedures for all relevant assertions for all significant accounts and disclosures. Performing procedures to express an opinion on internal control over financial reporting does not diminish this requirement.

139. The substantive procedures that the auditor should perform consist of tests of details of transactions and balances and analytical procedures. Before using the results obtained from substantive analytical procedures, the auditor should either test the design and operating effectiveness of controls over financial information used in the substantive analytical procedures or perform other procedures to support the completeness and accuracy of the underlying information. For significant risks of material misstatement, it is unlikely that audit evidence obtained from substantive analytical procedures alone will be sufficient.

140. When designing substantive analytical procedures, the auditor also should evaluate the risk of management override of controls. As part of this process, the auditor should evaluate whether such an override might have allowed adjustments outside of the normal period-end financial reporting process to have been made to the financial statements. Such adjustments might have resulted in artificial changes to the financial statement relationships being ana-

---

18. See paragraph 146 for additional documentation requirements when the auditor assesses control risk as other than low.

---

lyzed, causing the auditor to draw erroneous conclusions. For this reason, substantive analytical procedures are not well suited to detecting fraud.

141. The auditor's substantive procedures must include reconciling the financial statements to the accounting records and examining material adjustments made during the course of preparing the financial statements. Also, other auditing standards require auditors to perform specific tests of details in the financial statement audit. For instance, AU sec. 316, *Consideration of Fraud in a Financial Statement Audit*, requires the auditor to perform certain tests of details to further address the risk of management override, whether or not a specific risk of fraud has been identified. AU sec. 330.34, *The Confirmation Process*, states that there is a presumption that the auditor will request the confirmation of accounts receivable. Similarly, AU sec. 331.01, *Inventories*, states that observation of inventories is a generally accepted auditing procedure and that the auditor who issues an opinion without this procedure "has the burden of justifying the opinion expressed."

142. If, during the audit of internal control over financial reporting, the auditor identifies an internal control deficiency, he or she should determine the effect on the nature, timing, and extent of substantive procedures to be performed to reduce the risk of material misstatement of the financial statements to an appropriately low level.

Effect of Substantive Procedures on the Auditor's Conclusions About the Operating Effectiveness of Controls

143. In an audit of internal control over financial reporting, the auditor should evaluate the effect of the findings of all substantive auditing procedures performed in the audit of financial statements on the effectiveness of internal control over financial reporting. This evaluation should include, but not be limited to:

- The auditor's risk evaluations in connection with the selection and application of substantive procedures, especially those related to fraud (see paragraph 26),
- Findings with respect to illegal acts and related party transactions,
- Indications of management bias in making accounting estimates and in selecting accounting principles, and
- Misstatements detected by substantive procedures. The extent of such misstatements might alter the auditor's judgment about the effectiveness of controls.

144. However, the absence of misstatements detected by substantive procedures does not provide evidence that controls related to the assertion being tested are effective.

Documentation Requirements

145. In addition to the documentation requirements in AU sec. 339, *Audit Documentation*, the auditor should document:

- The understanding obtained and the evaluation of the design of each of the five components of the company's internal control over financial reporting,
- The process used to determine significant accounts, classes of transactions, and disclosures, including the determination of the locations or business units at which to perform testing,
- The identification of where misstatements related to relevant financial statement assertions could occur within significant accounts, assertions, and processes,
- The extent to which the auditor relied upon work performed by management or others,

- The evaluation of any deficiencies noted as a result of the auditor's testing, and

- Other findings that could result in a modification to the auditor's report.

146. For a company that has effective internal control over financial reporting, the auditor ordinarily will be able to perform sufficient testing of controls to be able to assess control risk related to relevant assertions for significant accounts and disclosures at a low level. If, however, the auditor assesses control risk as other than low for certain assertions or significant accounts, the auditor should document the reasons for that conclusion. Examples of when it is appropriate to not assess control risk as low include:

- When a control over a relevant assertion related to a significant account or disclosure was superseded late in the year and only the new control was tested for operating effectiveness.

- When a material weakness existed during the period under audit and was corrected by the end of the period.

147. The auditor also should document the effect of a conclusion that control risk is other than low for any relevant assertions for any significant accounts on his or her opinion on the audit of internal control over financial reporting.

Reporting on Internal Control Over Financial Reporting

Management's Report

148. Management is required to include in its annual report its assessment of the effectiveness of the company's internal control over financial reporting in addition to its audited financial statements as of the end of the most recent fiscal year. Management's report on internal control over financial reporting is required to include the following:[19]

- A statement of management's responsibility for establishing and maintaining adequate internal control over financial reporting for the company,

- A statement identifying the framework used by management to conduct the required evaluation of the effectiveness of the company's internal control over financial reporting,

- An assessment of the effectiveness of the company's internal control over financial reporting as of the end of the company's most recent fiscal year, including an explicit statement as to whether that internal control over financial reporting is effective, and

- A statement that the registered public accounting firm that audited the financial statements included in the annual report has issued an attestation report on management's assessment of the company's internal control over financial reporting.

149. Management should provide, both in its report on internal control over financial reporting and in its representation letter to the auditor, a written conclusion about the effectiveness of the company's internal control over financial reporting. The conclusion about the effectiveness of a company's internal control over financial reporting can take many forms, however, management is required to state a direct conclusion about whether the company's internal control over financial reporting is effective. This standard, for example, includes the phrase "management's assessment that W Company maintained effective internal control over finan-

---

19. Management is required to include these matters in their report. See Final Rule: Management's Reports on Internal Control Over Financial Reporting and Certification of Disclosure in Exchange Act Periodic Reports, Securities and Exchange Commission Release No. 33-8238 (June 5, 2003) [68 FR 36636].

cial reporting as of [*date*]" to illustrate such a conclusion. Other phrases, such as "management's assessment that W Company's internal control over financial reporting as of [*date*] is sufficient to meet the stated objectives," also might be used. However, the conclusion should not be so subjective (for example, "very effective internal control") that people having competence in and using the same or similar criteria would not ordinarily be able to arrive at similar conclusions.

150. Management is precluded from concluding that the company's internal control over financial reporting is effective if there are one or more material weaknesses. In addition, management is required to disclose all material weaknesses that exist as of the end of the most recent fiscal year.

151. Management might be able to accurately represent that internal control over financial reporting, as of the end of the company's most recent fiscal year, is effective even if one or more material weaknesses existed during the period. To make this representation, management must have changed the internal control over financial reporting to eliminate the material weaknesses sufficiently in advance of the "as of" date and have satisfactorily tested the effectiveness over a period of time that is adequate for it to determine whether, as of the end of the fiscal year, the design and operation of internal control over financial reporting is effective.[20]

Auditor's Evaluation of Management's Report

152. With respect to management's report on its assessment, the auditor should evaluate the following matters:

a. Whether management has properly stated its responsibility for establishing and maintaining adequate internal control over financial reporting.

b. Whether the framework used by management to conduct the evaluation is suitable. (As discussed in paragraph 13, the framework described in COSO constitutes a suitable and available framework.)

c. Whether management's assessment of the effectiveness of internal control over financial reporting, as of the end of the company's most recent fiscal year, is free of material misstatement.

d. Whether management has expressed its assessment in an acceptable form.

—Management is required to state whether the company's internal control over financial reporting is effective.

—A negative assurance statement indicating that, "Nothing has come to management's attention to suggest that the company's internal control over financial reporting is not effective," is not acceptable.

—Management is not permitted to conclude that the company's internal control over financial reporting is effective if there are one or more material weaknesses in the company's internal control over financial reporting.

---

20. However, when the reason for a change in internal control over financial reporting is the correction of a material weakness, management and the auditor need to evaluate whether the reason for the change and the circumstances surrounding the change are material information necessary to make the disclosure about the change not misleading in a filing subject to certification under Section 302. See discussion beginning at paragraph 183 for further direction.

---

e. Whether material weaknesses identified in the company's internal control over financial reporting, if any, have been properly disclosed, including those corrected during the period.[21]

Auditor's Report on Management's Assessment of Internal Control Over Financial Reporting

153. The auditor's report on management's assessment of the effectiveness of internal control over financial reporting must include the following elements:

a. A title that includes the word *independent,*

b. An identification of management's conclusion about the effectiveness of the company's internal control over financial reporting as of a specified date based on the control criteria [for example, criteria established in *Internal Control—Integrated Framework* issued by the Committee of Sponsoring Organizations of the Treadway Commission (COSO)],

c. An identification of the title of the management report that includes management's assessment (the auditor should use the same description of the company's internal control over financial reporting as management uses in its report),

d. A statement that the assessment is the responsibility of management,

e. A statement that the auditor's responsibility is to express an opinion on the-written assessment based on his or her audit,

f. A definition of internal control over financial reporting as stated in paragraph 4,

g. A statement that the audit was conducted in accordance with auditing and related professional practice standards established by the Public Company Accounting Oversight Board (PCAOB),

h. A statement that the PCAOB standards require that the auditor plan and perform the audit to obtain reasonable assurance about whether effective internal control over financial reporting was maintained in all material respects,

i. A statement that an audit includes obtaining an understanding of internal control over financial reporting, testing and evaluating the design and operating effectiveness of internal control, and performing such other procedures as the auditor considered necessary in the circumstances,

j. A statement that the auditor believes the audit provides a reasonable basis for his or her opinion,

k. A paragraph stating that, because of inherent limitations, internal control over financial reporting may not prevent or detect misstatements and that projections of any evaluation of effectiveness to future periods are subject to the risk that controls may become inadequate because of changes in conditions, or that the degree of compliance with the policies or procedures may deteriorate,

l. The auditor's opinion on whether management's assessment of the effectiveness of the company's internal control over financial reporting as of the specified date is fairly

---

21. See paragraph 189 for direction when a material weakness was corrected during the fourth quarter and the auditor believes that modification to the disclosures about changes in internal control over financial reporting are necessary for the annual certifications to be accurate and to comply with the requirements of Section 302.

stated, in all material respects, based on the control criteria (see discussion beginning at paragraph 148),[22]

m. The manual or printed signature of the auditor's firm,

n. The date of the audit report.

154. Example A-1 in Appendix A is an illustrative auditor's report — an unqualified opinion — on management's assessment of the effectiveness of the company's internal control over financial reporting.

155. *Separate or Combined Reports.* The auditor may choose to issue a combined report (that is, one report containing both an opinion on the financial statements and an opinion on internal control over financial reporting) or separate reports on the company's financial statements and on internal control over financial reporting. Appendix A includes an illustrative combined audit report on internal control over financial reporting and examples of separate reports on internal control over financial reporting.

156. If the auditor chooses to issue a separate report on internal control over financial reporting, he or she should add the following paragraph to the auditor's report on the financial statements:

> We also have audited, in accordance with auditing and related professional practice standards established by the Public Company Accounting Oversight Board, the effectiveness of W Company's internal control over financial reporting as of December 31, 20X3, based on [*identify criteria*] and our report dated [*date of report, which should be the same as the date of the report on the financial statements*] expressed [*include nature of opinion*].

157. *Report Date.* As stated previously, the auditor cannot audit internal control over financial reporting without also auditing the financial statements. Therefore, the reports should be dated the same.

158. When the auditor elects to issue a combined report on the audit of the financial statements and the audit of internal control over financial reporting, the audit opinion will address multiple reporting periods for the financial statements presented but only the end of the most recent fiscal year for management's assessment of the effectiveness of internal control over financial reporting. See a combined report in Example A-6 in Appendix A.

159. *Report Modifications.* The auditor should modify the standard report if any of the following conditions exist.

a. Management's assessment is inadequate or management's report is inappropriate. (See paragraph 161.)

b. There is a material weakness in the company's internal control over financial reporting. (See paragraphs 162 through 164.)

c. There is a restriction on the scope of the engagement. (See paragraphs 165 through 167.)

d. The auditor decides to refer to the report of other auditors as the basis, in part, for the auditor's own report. (See paragraphs 168 and 169.)

---

22. Nothing precludes the auditor from auditing management's assessment but opining directly on the effectiveness of internal control over financial reporting.

---

e. A significant subsequent event has occurred since the date being reported on. (See paragraphs 170 through 173.)

f. There is other information contained in management's report on internal control over financial reporting. (See paragraphs 174 through 176.)

160. If, for any of the situations listed in the paragraph above, the auditor plans to issue other than an unqualified opinion, the auditor should report directly on the effectiveness of the company's internal control over financial reporting rather than on management's assessment. Expressing an opinion on management's assessment in these circumstances could result in confusion. For example, if management makes an adverse assessment because a material weakness has been identified and not corrected ("...internal control over financial reporting is not effective...") and the auditor expressed his or her opinion on management's assessment ("...management's assessment that internal control over financial reporting is not effective is fairly stated, in all material respects..."), a reader might not be clear about the results of the auditor's testing and about the auditor's conclusions. Reporting directly on the effectiveness of the company's internal control over financial reporting better communicates to report users the effect of such conditions, because direct reporting more clearly states the auditor's conclusions about the effectiveness of internal control over financial reporting ("In our opinion, because of the effect of the material weakness described..., the Company's internal control over financial reporting is not effective.").

161. *Management's Assessment Inadequate or Report Inappropriate.* If the auditor determines that management's process for assessing internal control over financial reporting is inadequate, the auditor should modify his or her opinion for a scope limitation (discussed further beginning at paragraph 165). If the auditor determines that management's report is inappropriate, the auditor should modify his or her report to include, at a minimum, an explanatory paragraph describing the reasons for this conclusion.

162. *Material Weaknesses.* Paragraphs 116 through 127 describe significant deficiencies and material weaknesses. If there are significant deficiencies that, individually or in combination, result in one or more material weaknesses, management is precluded from concluding that internal control over financial reporting is effective. In these circumstances, the auditor must express an adverse opinion on the company's internal control over financial reporting.

163. When expressing an adverse opinion because of a material weakness, the auditor's report must include:

• The definition of a material weakness and a significant deficiency, as provided in paragraphs 8 and 9.

• A statement that a material weakness has been identified and included in management's assessment. (If the material weakness has not been included in management's assessment, this sentence should be modified to state that the material weakness has been identified but not included in management's assessment. In this case, the auditor also is required to communicate to the audit committee that the material weakness was not disclosed or identified as a material weakness in management's report, as discussed in paragraph 190.)

• A description of any material weaknesses identified in a company's internal control over financial reporting. This description should provide the users of the audit report with specific information about the nature of any material weakness, and its actual and potential effect on the presentation of the company's financial statements issued during the existence of the weakness. This description also should address requirements described in paragraph 178.

164. In addition, the auditor should modify the opinion paragraph to express an adverse opinion directly on the effectiveness of the company's internal control over financial reporting. Example A-2 in Appendix A illustrates the form of the report that is appropriate in this situation.

165. *Scope Limitations.* The auditor can express an unqualified opinion on internal control over financial reporting only if the auditor has been able to apply all the procedures necessary under the circumstances. If there are restrictions on the scope of the engagement imposed by the circumstances, the auditor should withdraw from the engagement, disclaim an opinion, or express a qualified opinion. The auditor's decision depends on his or her assessment of the importance of the omitted procedure(s) to his or her ability to form an opinion on the effectiveness of the company's internal control over financial reporting. However, when the restrictions are imposed by management, the auditor should withdraw from the engagement or disclaim an opinion on the effectiveness of internal control over financial reporting.

166. For example, management might have identified a material weakness in its internal control over financial reporting prior to the date specified in its report and implemented controls to correct it. If management believes that the new controls have been operating for a sufficient period of time to determine that they are both effectively designed and operating, management would be able to include in its assessment its conclusion that internal control over financial reporting is effective as of the date specified. However, if the auditor disagrees with the sufficiency of the time period, he or she would be unable to obtain sufficient evidence that the new controls have been operating effectively for a sufficient period. In that case, the auditor should modify the opinion because of a scope limitation.

167. When the auditor plans either to issue a qualified opinion or to disclaim an opinion because of a scope limitation, the auditor should report directly on the effectiveness of internal control over financial reporting (rather than on management's assessment) to best communicate the effect of such factors on his or her opinion. Example A-3 in Appendix A illustrates the form of report when there is a limitation on the scope of the audit causing the auditor to issue a qualified opinion. Example A-4 illustrates the form of report when restrictions on the scope of the audit cause the auditor to disclaim an opinion.

168. *Opinion Based in Part on the Report of Another Auditor.* When another auditor has audited internal control over financial reporting of one or more subsidiaries, divisions, branches, or components of the company, the auditor should determine whether he or she may serve as the principal auditor and use the work and reports of another auditor as a basis, in part, for his or her opinion on internal control over financial reporting. If the auditor decides it is appropriate to serve as the principal auditor, he or she should decide whether to make reference in the report to the audit performed by the other auditor. In these circumstances, the auditor's criteria are similar to those of the independent auditor who uses the work and reports of other independent auditors when reporting on a company's financial statements. AU sec. 543, *Part of Audit Performed by Other Independent Auditors*, provides direction on the auditor's decision of whether to serve as the principal auditor and, if so, whether to make reference to the audit performed by the other auditor.

169. When the auditor decides to make reference to the report of the other auditor as a basis, in part, for his or her opinion, the auditor should disclose this when describing the scope of the audit and should refer to the report of the other auditor when expressing the opinion. Whether the other auditor's opinion is expressed on management's assessment or on the effectiveness of internal control over financial reporting does not affect the determination of whether the principal auditor's opinion is expressed on the assessment or on the subject matter itself.

170. *Subsequent Events.* Changes in internal control over financial reporting or other factors that might significantly affect internal control over financial reporting might occur subsequent to the date as of which internal control over financial reporting is being audited but before the date of the auditor's report. As described in paragraph 128, the auditor should obtain written representations from management relating to such matters. Additionally, to obtain information about whether changes have occurred that might affect the effectiveness of the company's internal control over financial reporting and, therefore, the auditor's report, the auditor should inquire about and examine, for this subsequent period, the following:

- Relevant internal audit reports (or similar functions, such as loan review in a financial institution) issued during the subsequent period,
- Independent auditor reports (if other than the auditor's) of significant deficiencies or material weaknesses,
- Regulatory agency reports on the company's internal control over financial reporting, and
- Information about the effectiveness of the company's internal control over financial reporting obtained through other engagements.

171. The auditor could inquire about and examine other documents for the subsequent period. Paragraphs .01 through .09 of AU sec. 560, *Subsequent Events,* provides direction on subsequent events for a financial statement audit that may also be helpful to the auditor performing an audit of internal control over financial reporting.

172. If the auditor obtains knowledge about subsequent events that materially and adversely affect the effectiveness of the company's internal control over financial reporting as of the date specified in the assessment the auditor should issue an adverse opinion. If the auditor is unable to determine the effect of the subsequent event on the effectiveness of the company's internal control over financial reporting, the auditor should disclaim an opinion. As described in paragraph 175, the auditor should disclaim an opinion on management's disclosures about corrective actions taken by the company after the date of management's assessment, if any.

173. The auditor may obtain knowledge about subsequent events with respect to conditions that did not exist at the date specified in the assessment but arose subsequent to that date. If a subsequent event of this type has a material effect on the company, the auditor should include in his or her report an explanatory paragraph describing the event and its effects or directing the reader's attention to the event and its effects as disclosed in management's report. Management's consideration of such events to be disclosed in its report should be limited to a change that has materially affected, or is reasonably likely to materially affect, the company's internal control over financial reporting.

174. *Management's Report Containing Additional Information.* Management's report on internal control over financial reporting may contain information in addition to management's assessment of the effectiveness of its internal control over financial reporting. Such information might include, for example:

- Disclosures about corrective actions taken by the company after the date of management's assessment,
- The company's plans to implement new controls, and

- A statement that management believes the cost of correcting a material weakness would exceed the benefits to be derived from implementing new controls.

175. If management's assessment includes such additional information, the auditor should disclaim an opinion on the information. For example, the auditor should use the following language as the last paragraph of the report to disclaim an opinion on management's cost-benefit statement:

> We do not express an opinion or any other form of assurance on management's statement referring to the costs and related benefits of implementing new controls.

176. If the auditor believes that management's additional information contains a material misstatement of fact, he or she should discuss the matter with management. If the auditor concludes that there is a valid basis for concern, he or she should propose that management consult with some other party whose advice might be useful, such as the company's legal counsel. If, after discussing the matter with management and those management has consulted, the auditor concludes that a material misstatement of fact remains, the auditor should notify management and the audit committee, in writing, of the auditor's views concerning the information. The auditor also should consider consulting the auditor's legal counsel about further actions to be taken, including the auditor's responsibility under Section 10A of the Securities Exchange Act of 1934.

177. *Effect of Auditor's Adverse Opinion on Internal Control Over Financial Reporting on the Opinion on Financial Statements.* In some cases, the auditor's report on internal control over financial reporting might describe a material weakness that resulted in an adverse opinion on the effectiveness of internal control over financial reporting while the audit report on the financial statements remains unqualified. Consequently, during the audit of the financial statements, the auditor did not rely on that control. However, he or she performed additional substantive procedures to determine whether there was a material misstatement in the account related to the control. If, as a result of these procedures, the auditor determines that there was not a material misstatement in the account, he or she would be able to express an unqualified opinion on the financial statements.

178. When the auditor's opinion on the financial statements is unaffected by the adverse opinion on the effectiveness of internal control over financial reporting, the report on internal control over financial reporting (or the combined report, if a combined report is issued) should include the following or similar language in the paragraph that describes the material weakness:

> This material weakness was considered in determining the nature, timing, and extent of audit tests applied in our audit of the 20X3 financial statements, and this report does not affect our report dated [*date of report*] on those financial statements. [*Revise this wording appropriately for use in a combined report.*]

179. Such disclosure is important to ensure that users of the auditor's report on the financial statements understand why the auditor issued an unqualified opinion on those statements.

180. *Subsequent Discovery of Information Existing at the Date of the Auditor's Report on Internal Control Over Financial Reporting.* After the issuance of the report on internal control over financial reporting, the auditor may become aware of conditions that existed at the report date that might have affected the auditor's opinion had he or she been aware of them. The auditor's evaluation of such subsequent information is similar to the auditor's evaluation of information discovered subsequent to the date of the report on an audit of financial statements, as described in AU sec. 561, *Subsequent Discovery of Facts Existing at the Date of the Auditor's Report*. That standard requires the auditor to determine whether the information is reliable and whether the facts existed at the date of his or her report. If so, the auditor should determine (1) whether the facts would have changed the report if he or she had been aware of them and (2) whether there are persons currently relying on or likely to rely on the auditor's report. For instance, if previously issued financial statements and the auditor's report have been recalled and reissued to reflect the correction of an error, the auditor should presume that his or her report on the company's internal control over financial reporting as of same specified date also should be recalled and reissued to reflect the material weakness that existed at that date. Based on these considerations, AU sec. 561.06 provides detailed requirements for the auditor.

181. *Filings Under Federal Securities Statutes.* AU sec. 711, *Filings Under Federal Securities Statutes*, describes the auditor's responsibilities when an auditor's report is included in registration statements, proxy statements, or periodic reports filed under the federal securities statutes. The auditor should also apply AU sec. 711 with respect to the auditor's report on management's assessment of the effectiveness of internal control over financial reporting included in such filings. In addition, the direction in AU sec. 711.10 to inquire of and obtain written representations from officers and other executives responsible for financial and accounting matters about whether any events have occurred that have a material effect on the audited financial statements should be extended to matters that could have a material effect on management's assessment of internal control over financial reporting.

182. When the auditor has fulfilled these responsibilities and intends to consent to the inclusion of his or her report on management's assessment of the effectiveness of internal control over financial reporting in the securities filing, the auditor's consent should clearly indicate that both the audit report on financial statements and the audit report on management's assessment of the effectiveness of internal control over financial reporting (or both opinions if a combined report is issued) are included in his or her consent.

Auditor's Responsibilities for Evaluating Management's Certification Disclosures About Internal Control Over Financial Reporting

Required Management Certifications

183. Section 302 of the Act, as amended, requires a company's management, with the participation of the principal executive and financial officers (the certifying officers), to make the following quarterly and annual certifications with respect to the company's internal control over financial reporting:

- A statement that the certifying officers are responsible for establishing and maintaining internal control over financial reporting,

- A statement that the certifying officers have designed such internal control over financial reporting, or caused such internal control over financial reporting to be designed under their supervision, to provide reasonable assurance regarding the reliability of financial reporting and the preparation of financial statements for external purposes in accordance with generally accepted accounting principles, and

- A statement that the report discloses any changes in the company's internal control over financial reporting that occurred during the most recent fiscal quarter (the company's fourth fiscal quarter in the case of an annual report) that have materially affected, or are reasonably likely to materially affect, the company's internal control over financial reporting.

184. When the reason for a change in internal control over financial reporting is the correction of a material weakness, management and the auditor need to evaluate whether the reason for the change and the circumstances surrounding that change are material information necessary to make the disclosure about the change not misleading.[23]

Auditor Evaluation Responsibilities

185. The auditor's responsibility as it relates to management's quarterly certifications on internal control over financial reporting is different from the auditor's responsibility as it relates to management's annual assessment of internal control over financial reporting. The auditor should perform limited procedures quarterly to provide a basis for determining whether he or she has become aware of any material modifications that, in the auditor's judgment, should be made to the disclosures about changes in internal control over financial reporting in order for the certifications to be accurate and to comply with the requirements of Section 302.

186. To fulfill this responsibility, the auditor should perform, on a quarterly basis, the following procedures:

- Inquire of management about significant changes in the design or operation of internal control over financial reporting as it relates to the preparation of annual as well as interim financial information that could have occurred subsequent to the preceding annual audit or prior review of interim financial information, and

- Determine, through a combination of observation and inquiry, whether significant changes in internal control over financial reporting may introduce significant deficiencies or material weaknesses in the design of internal control over financial reporting.

187. When matters come to auditor's attention that lead him or her to believe that modification to the disclosures about changes in internal control over financial reporting are necessary for the certifications to be accurate and to comply with the requirements of Section 302, the auditor should communicate the matter(s) to the appropriate level of management as soon as practicable.

188. If, in the auditor's judgment, management does not respond appropriately to the auditor's communication within a reasonable period of time, the auditor should inform the audit committee. If, in the auditor's judgment, the audit committee does not respond appropriately to the auditor's communication within a reasonable period of time, the auditor should evaluate whether to resign from the engagement. The auditor should evaluate whether to consult with his or her attorney when making these evaluations. In these circumstances, the auditor also has responsibilities under AU sec. 317, *Illegal Acts by Clients*, and Section 10A of the Securities Exchange Act of 1934. The auditor's responsibilities for evaluating the disclosures about changes in internal control over financial reporting do not diminish in any way management's responsibility for ensuring that their certifications comply with the requirements of Section 302.

189. If matters come to the auditor's attention as a result of the audit of internal control over financial reporting that lead him or her to believe that modification to the disclosures about

---

23. The SEC's Final Rule: Management's Reports on Internal Control Over Financial Reporting and Certification of Disclosure in Exchange Act Periodic Reports, Securities and Exchange Commission Release No. 33-8238 (June 5, 2003) [68 FR 36636], states: "Although the final rules do not explicitly require the company to disclose the reasons for any change that occurred during a fiscal quarter, or to otherwise elaborate about the change, a company will have to determine, on a facts and circumstances basis, whether the reasons for the change, or other information about the circumstances surrounding the change, constitute material information necessary to make the disclosure about the change not misleading."

---

changes in internal control over financial reporting (addressing changes in internal control over financial reporting occurring during the fourth quarter) are necessary for the annual certifications to be accurate and to comply with the requirements of Section 302, the auditor should follow the same communication responsibilities as described in paragraphs 187 and 188. However, if management and the audit committee do not respond appropriately, in addition to the responsibilities described in the preceding two paragraphs, the auditor should modify his or her report on the audit of internal control over financial reporting to include an explanatory paragraph describing the reasons the auditor believes management's certification should be modified.

Required Communications in An Audit of Internal Control Over Financial Reporting

190. The auditor must communicate in writing to the audit committee all significant deficiencies and material weaknesses identified during the audit. The written communication should be made prior to the issuance of the auditor's report on internal control over financial reporting. The auditor's communication should distinguish clearly between those matters considered significant deficiencies and those considered material weaknesses, as defined beginning in paragraph 8.

191. In addition, the auditor should communicate to management, in writing, all deficiencies in internal control over financial reporting (that is, those deficiencies in internal control over financial reporting that are of a lesser magnitude than significant deficiencies) identified during the audit and inform the audit committee when such a communication has been made. When making this communication, it is not necessary for the auditor to repeat information about such deficiencies that have been included in previously issued written communications, whether those communications were made by the auditor, internal auditors, or others within the organization. Rather, the auditor may incorporate those deficiencies by referring to the title and date of such reports. Furthermore, the auditor is not required to perform procedures sufficient to identify all internal control deficiencies; rather, the auditor should communicate deficiencies in internal control over financial reporting of which he or she is aware.

192. When auditing internal control over financial reporting, the auditor may become aware of fraud or possible illegal acts. If the matter involves fraud, it must be brought to the attention of the appropriate level of management. If the fraud involves senior management, the auditor must communicate the matter directly to the audit committee as described in AU sec. 316, *Consideration of Fraud in a Financial Statement Audit*. If the matter involves possible illegal acts, the auditor must assure himself or herself that the audit committee is adequately informed, unless the matter is clearly inconsequential, in accordance with AU sec. 317, *Illegal Acts by Clients*. The auditor also must determine his or her responsibilities under Section 10A of the Securities Exchange Act of 1934.

193. When timely communication is important, the auditor should communicate the preceding matters during the course of the audit rather than at the end of the engagement. The decision about whether an interim communication should be issued should be determined based on the relative significance of the matters noted and the urgency of corrective follow-up action required.

Effective Date

194. Companies considered *accelerated filers* under Exchange Act Rule 12b-2 are required to comply with the internal control reporting and disclosure requirements of Section 404 of the Act *for fiscal years ending on or after June 15, 2004.* (Other companies have until fiscal years ending on or after April 15, 2005, to comply with these internal control reporting and disclosure requirements.) Accordingly, independent auditors engaged to audit the financial statements of accelerated filers for fiscal years ending on or after June 15, 2004, also are required to audit and report on the company's internal control over financial reporting as of the end of such fiscal year. This standard is required to be complied with for such engagements.

195. Early compliance with this standard is permitted.

APPENDIX A

Illustrative Reports on Internal Control Over Financial Reporting

A.1 Paragraphs 152 through 179 of this standard provide direction on the auditor's report on management's assessment of internal control over financial reporting. The following examples illustrate how to apply that guidance in several different situations.

ILLUSTRATIVE REPORT

Example A-1—*Expressing an Unqualified Opinion on Management's Assessment of the Effectiveness of Internal Control Over Financial Reporting (Separate Report)*

Example A-2—*Expressing an Adverse Opinion on the Effectiveness of Internal Control Over Financial Reporting Because of the Existence of a Material Weakness*

Example A-3—*Expressing a Qualified Opinion on the Effectiveness of Internal Control Over Financial Reporting Because of a Limitation on the Scope of the Audit*

Example A-4—*Disclaiming an Opinion on the Effectiveness of Internal Control Over Financial Reporting Because of a Limitation on the Scope of the Audit*

Example A-5—*Expressing an Unqualified Opinion on Management's Assessment of the Effectiveness of Internal Control Over Financial Reporting That Refers to the Report of Other Auditors As a Basis, in Part, for the Auditor's Opinion*

Example A-6— *Expressing an Unqualified Opinion on Financial Statements and an Unqualified Opinion on Management's Assessment of the Effectiveness of Internal Control Over Financial Reporting (Combined Report)*

Example A-1

ILLUSTRATIVE REPORT EXPRESSING AN UNQUALIFIED OPINION ON MANAGEMENT'S ASSESSMENT OF THE EFFECTIVENESS OF INTERNAL CONTROL OVER FINANCIAL REPORTING (SEPARATE REPORT)[1]

Independent Auditor's Report

[Introductory paragraph]

We have audited management's assessment, included in the accompanying [*title of management's report*], that W Company maintained effective internal control over financial reporting as of December 31, 20X3, based on [*Identify criteria, for example, "criteria established in Internal Control—Integrated Framework issued by the Committee of Sponsoring Organizations of the Treadway Commission (COSO)."*]. W Company's management is responsible for its assessment about the effectiveness of internal control over financial reporting. Our responsibility is to express an opinion on management's assessment based on our audit.

---

1. If the auditor issues separate reports on the audit of internal control and the audit of the financial statements, both reports should include a statement that the audit was conducted in accordance with auditing and related professional practice standards established by the Public Company Accounting Oversight Board.

[Definition paragraph]

A company's internal control over financial reporting is a process designed to provide reasonable assurance regarding the reliability of financial reporting and the preparation of financial statements for external purposes in accordance with generally accepted accounting principles. A company's internal control over financial reporting includes those policies and procedures that (1) pertain to the maintenance of records that in reasonable detail accurately and fairly reflect the transactions and dispositions of the assets of the company; (2) provide reasonable assurance that transactions are recorded as necessary to permit preparation of financial statements in accordance with generally accepted accounting principles, and that receipts and expenditures of the company are being made only in accordance with authorizations of management and directors of the company; and (3) provide reasonable assurance regarding prevention or timely detection of unauthorized acquisition, use, or disposition of the company's assets that could have a material effect on the financial statements.

[Scope paragraph]

We conducted our audit in accordance with auditing and related professional practice standards established by the Public Company Accounting Oversight Board. Those standards require that we plan and perform our audit to obtain reasonable assurance about whether effective internal control over financial reporting was maintained in all material respects. Our audit included obtaining an understanding of internal control over financial reporting, testing and evaluating the design and operating effectiveness of internal control, and performing such other procedures as we considered necessary in the circumstances. We believe that our audit provides a reasonable basis for our opinion.

[Inherent limitations paragraph]

Because of its inherent limitations, internal control over financial reporting may not prevent or detect misstatements. Also, projections of any evaluation of effectiveness to future periods are subject to the risk that controls may become inadequate because of changes in conditions, or that the degree of compliance with the policies or procedures may deteriorate.

[Opinion paragraph]

In our opinion, management's assessment that W Company maintained effective internal control over financial reporting as of December 31, 20X3, is fairly stated, in all material respects, based on [*Identify criteria, for example, "criteria established in Internal Control—Integrated Framework issued by the Committee of Sponsoring Organizations of the Treadway Commission (COSO)."*].

[Signature]

[Date]

Example A-2

ILLUSTRATIVE REPORT EXPRESSING AN ADVERSE OPINION ON THE EFFECTIVENESS OF INTERNAL CONTROL OVER FINANCIAL REPORTING BECAUSE OF THE EXISTENCE OF A MATERIAL WEAKNESS

Independent Auditor's Report

[Introductory paragraph]

We have audited management's assessment included in the accompanying [*title of management's report*] that W Company did not maintain effective internal control over financial reporting as of December 31, 20X3, because of the effect of [*material weakness identified in management's assessment*], based on [*Identify criteria, for example, "criteria established in Internal Control—Integrated Framework issued by the Committee of Sponsoring Organizations of the Treadway Commission (COSO)."*]. W Company's management is responsible for its assessment about the effectiveness of internal control over financial reporting. Our responsibility is to express an opinion on management's assessment based on our audit.

[Definition paragraph]

A company's internal control over financial reporting is a process designed to provide reasonable assurance regarding the reliability of financial reporting and the preparation of financial statements for external purposes in accordance with generally accepted accounting principles. A company's internal control over financial reporting includes those policies and procedures that (1) pertain to the maintenance of records that in reasonable detail accurately and fairly reflect the transactions and dispositions of the assets of the company; (2) provide reasonable assurance that transactions are recorded as necessary to permit preparation of financial statements in accordance with generally accepted accounting principles, and that receipts and expenditures of the company are being made only in accordance with authorizations of management and directors of the company; and (3) provide reasonable assurance regarding prevention or timely detection of unauthorized acquisition, use, or disposition of the company's assets that could have a material effect on the financial statements.

[Scope paragraph]

We conducted our audit in accordance with auditing and related professional practice standards established by the Public Company Accounting Oversight Board. Those standards require that we plan and perform our audit to obtain reasonable assurance about whether effective internal control over financial reporting was maintained in all material respects. Our audit included obtaining an understanding of internal control over financial reporting, testing and evaluating the design and operating effectiveness of internal control, and performing such other procedures as we considered necessary in the circumstances. We believe that our audit provides a reasonable basis for our opinion.

[Inherent limitations paragraph]

Because of its inherent limitations, internal control over financial reporting may not prevent or detect misstatments. Also, projections of any evaluation of effectiveness to future periods are subject to the risk that controls may become inadequate because of changes in conditions, or that the degree of compliance with the policies of procedures may deteriorate.

[Explanatory paragraph]

A *material weakness* is a significant deficiency that, by itself, or in combination with other significant deficiencies, results in more than a remote likelihood of a material misstatement of the annual or interim financial statements. A significant deficiency is an internal control deficiency that adversely affects the company's ability to initiate, record, process, and report external financial data reliably in accordance with generally accepted accounting principles. The following material weakness has been identified and included in management's assessment.[1] [*Include a description of the material weakness and its effect on the achievement of the*

---

1. If the auditor has identified a material weakness that is not included in management's assessment, add the following wording to the report: "In addition, we have identified the following material weakness that has not been identified as a material weakness in management's assessment. [*Include a description of the material weakness and its effect on the achievement of the objectives of the control criteria.*"]

objectives of the control criteria.] This material weakness was considered in determining the nature, timing, and extent of audit tests applied in our audit of the 20X3 financial statements, and this report does not affect our report dated [*date of report, which should be the same as the date of this report on internal control*] on those financial statements.

[Opinion paragraph]

In our opinion, because of the effect of the material weakness described above on the achievement of the objectives of the control criteria, W Company has not maintained effective internal control over financial reporting as of December 31, 20X3, based on [*Identify criteria, for example, "criteria established in Internal Control—Integrated Framework issued by the Committee of Sponsoring Organizations of the Treadway Commission (COSO)."*].

[*Signature*]

[*Date*]

Example A-3

ILLUSTRATIVE REPORT EXPRESSING A QUALIFIED OPINION ON THE EFFECTIVENESS OF INTERNAL CONTROL OVER FINANCIAL REPORTING BECAUSE OF A LIMITATION ON THE SCOPE OF THE AUDIT

Independent Auditor's Report

[Introductory paragraph]

We have audited management's assessment included in the accompanying [*title of management's report*] that W Company maintained effective internal control over financial reporting as of December 31, 20X3, based on [*Identify criteria, for example, "criteria established in Internal Control—Integrated Framework issued by the Committee of Sponsoring Organizations of the Treadway Commission (COSO)."*]. W Company's management is responsible for its assessment about the effectiveness of internal control over financial reporting. Our responsibility is to express an opinion on management's assessment based on our audit.

[Definition paragraph]

A company's internal control over financial reporting is a process designed to provide reasonable assurance regarding the reliability of financial reporting and the preparation of financial statements for external purposes in accordance with generally accepted accounting principles. A company's internal control over financial reporting includes those policies and procedures that (1) pertain to the maintenance of records that in reasonable detail accurately and fairly reflect the transactions and dispositions of the assets of the company; (2) provide reasonable assurance that transactions are recorded as necessary to permit preparation of financial statements in accordance with generally accepted accounting principles, and that receipts and expenditures of the company are being made only in accordance with authorizations of management and directors of the company; and (3) provide reasonable assurance regarding prevention or timely detection of unauthorized acquisition, use, or disposition of the company's assets that could have a material effect on the financial statements.

[Scope paragraph]

Except as described below, we conducted our audit in accordance with auditing and related professional practice standards established by the Public Company Accounting Oversight Board. Those standards require that we plan and perform our audit to obtain reasonable assurance about whether effective internal control over financial reporting was maintained in all material respects. Our audit included obtaining an understanding of internal control over financial reporting, testing and evaluating the design and operating effectiveness of internal control, and performing such other procedures as we considered necessary in the circumstances. We believe that our audit provides a reasonable basis for our opinion.

[Explanatory paragraph that describes scope limitation]

A *material weakness* is a significant deficiency that, by itself, or in combination with other significant deficiencies, results in more than a remote likelihood of a material misstatement of the annual or interim financial statements. A *significant deficiency* is an internal control deficiency that adversely affects the company's ability to initiate, record, process, and report external financial data reliably in accordance with generally accepted accounting principles. The following material weakness has been identified and included in management's assessment.[1] Prior to December 20, 20X3, W Company had an inadequate system for recording cash receipts, which could have prevented the Company from recording cash receipts on accounts receivable completely and properly. Therefore, cash received could have been diverted for unauthorized use, lost, or otherwise not properly recorded to accounts receivable. We believe this condition was a material weakness in the design or operation of the internal control of W Company in effect prior to December 20, 20X3. Although the Company implemented a new cash receipts system on December 20, 20X3, the system has not been in operation for a sufficient period of time to enable us to obtain sufficient evidence about its operating effectiveness.

[Inherent limitations paragraph]

Because of its inherent limitations, internal control over financial reporting may not prevent or detect misstatements. Also, projections of any evaluation of effectiveness to future periods are subject to the risk that controls may become inadequate because of changes in conditions, or that the degree of compliance with the policies or procedures may deteriorate.

[Opinion paragraph]

In our opinion, except for the effect of matters we might have discovered had we been able to examine evidence about the effectiveness of the new cash receipts system, W Company maintained, in all material respects, effective internal control over financial reporting as of December 31, 20X3, based on [*Identify criteria, for example, "criteria established in Internal Control—Integrated Framework issued by the Committee of Sponsoring Organizations of the Treadway Commission (COSO)."*].

[*Signature*]

[*Date*]

---

1. If the auditor has identified a material weakness that is not included in management's assessment, add the following wording to the report: "In addition, we have identified the following material weakness that has not been identified as a material weakness in management's assessment. [*Include a description of the material weakness and its effect on the achievement of the objectives of the control criteria.*"]

Example A-4

ILLUSTRATIVE REPORT DISCLAIMING AN OPINION ON THE EFFECTIVE-NESS OF INTERNAL CONTROL OVER FINANCIAL REPORTING BECAUSE OF A LIMITATION ON THE SCOPE OF THE AUDIT

Independent Auditor's Report

[Introductory paragraph]

We were engaged to audit management's assessment included in the accompanying [*title of management's report*] that W Company maintained effective internal control over financial reporting as of December 31, 20X3 based on [*Identify criteria, for example, "criteria established in Internal Control—Integrated Framework issued by the Committee of Sponsoring Organizations of the Treadway Commission (COSO)."*]. W Company's management is responsible for maintaining effective internal control over financial reporting.

[Definition paragraph]

A company's internal control over financial reporting is a process designed to provide reasonable assurance regarding the reliability of financial reporting and the preparation of financial statements for external purposes in accordance with generally accepted accounting principles. A company's internal control over financial reporting includes those policies and procedures that (1) pertain to the maintenance of records that in reasonable detail accurately and fairly reflect the transactions and dispositions of the assets of the company; (2) provide reasonable assurance that transactions are recorded as necessary to permit preparation of financial statements in accordance with generally accepted accounting principles, and that receipts and expenditures of the company are being made only in accordance with authorizations of management and directors of the company; and (3) provide reasonable assurance regarding prevention or timely detection of unauthorized acquisition, use, or disposition of the company's assets that could have a material effect on the financial statements.

[Omit scope paragraph]

[Explanatory paragraph that describes scope limitation]

[Inherent limitations paragraph]

Because of its inherent limitations, internal control over financial reporting may not prevent or detect misstatements. Also, projections of any evaluation of effectiveness to future periods are subject to the risk that controls may become inadequate because of changes in conditions, or that the degree of compliance with the policies or procedures may deteriorate.

[Opinion paragraph]

Since management [*describe scope restrictions*] and we were unable to apply other procedures to satisfy ourselves as to the company's internal control over financial reporting, the scope of our work was not sufficient to enable us to express, and we do not express, an opinion on the effectiveness of the company's internal control over financial reporting.

[*Signature*]

[*Date*]

Example A-5

ILLUSTRATIVE REPORT EXPRESSING AN UNQUALIFIED OPINION ON MAN-
AGEMENT'S ASSESSMENT OF THE EFFECTIVENESS OF INTERNAL CONTROL
OVER FINANCIAL REPORTING THAT REFERS TO THE REPORT OF OTHER
AUDITORS AS A BASIS, IN PART, FOR THE AUDITOR'S OPINION

Independent Auditor's Report

[Introductory paragraph]

We have audited management's assessment that W Company maintained, in all material respects, effective internal control over financial reporting as of December 31, 20X3, based on
[*Identify criteria, for example, "criteria established in Internal Control—Integrated Frame-*
work issued by the Committee of Sponsoring Organizations of the Treadway Commission
(COSO)."]. W Company's management is responsible for maintaining effective internal control over financial reporting. Our responsibility is to express an opinion on management's assessment based on our audit. We did not examine the effectiveness of internal control over financial reporting of B Company, a wholly owned subsidiary, whose financial statements
reflect total assets and revenues constituting 20 and 30 percent, respectively of the related
consolidated financial statement amounts as of and for the year ended December 31, 20XX.
The effectiveness of B Company's internal control over financial reporting was audited by
other auditors whose report has been furnished to us, and our opinion, insofar as it relates to
the effectiveness of B Company's internal control over financial reporting, is based solely on
the report of the other auditors.

[Definition paragraph]

A company's internal control over financial reporting is a process designed to provide reasonable assurance regarding the reliability of financial reporting and the preparation of financial statements for external purposes in accordance with generally accepted accounting principles. A company's internal control over financial reporting includes those policies and
procedures that (1) pertain to the maintenance of records that in reasonable detail accurately
and fairly reflect the transactions and dispositions of the assets of the company; (2) provide
reasonable assurance that transactions are recorded as necessary to permit preparation of financial statements in accordance with generally accepted accounting principles, and that receipts and expenditures of the company are being made only in accordance with authorizations of management and directors of the company; and (3) provide reasonable assurance
regarding prevention or timely detection of unauthorized acquisition, use, or disposition of
the company's assets that could have a material effect on the financial statements.

[Scope paragraph]

We conducted our audit in accordance with auditing and related professional practice standards established by the Public Company Accounting Oversight Board. Those standards require that we plan and perform our audit to obtain reasonable assurance about whether effective internal control over financial reporting was maintained in all material respects. Our
audit included obtaining an understanding of internal control over financial reporting, testing
and evaluating the design and operating effectiveness of internal control, and performing such
other procedures as we considered necessary in the circumstances. We believe that our audit
and the report of the other auditors provide a reasonable basis for our opinion.

[Inherent limitations paragraph]

Because of its inherent limitations, internal control over financial reporting may not prevent or detect misstatements. Also, projections of any evaluation of effectiveness to future periods are subject to the risk that controls may become inadequate because of changes in conditions, or that the degree of compliance with the policies or procedures may deteriorate.

[Opinion paragraph]

In our opinion, based on our audit and the report of the other auditors, W Company maintained, in all material respects, effective internal control over financial reporting as of December 31, 20X3, based on *[Identify criteria, for example, "criteria established in Internal Control—Integrated Framework issued by the Committee of Sponsoring Organizations of the Treadway Commission (COSO)."]*.

[Signature]

[Date]

Example A-6

ILLUSTRATIVE COMBINED REPORT EXPRESSING AN UNQUALIFIED OPINION ON FINANCIAL STATEMENTS AND AN UNQUALIFIED OPINION ON MANAGEMENT'S ASSESSMENT OF THE EFFECTIVENESS OF INTERNAL CONTROL OVER FINANCIAL REPORTING

Independent Auditor's Report

[Introductory paragraph]

We have audited the accompanying balance sheets of W Company as of December 31, 20X3 and 20X2, and the related statements of income, stockholders' equity and comprehensive income, and cash flows for each of the years in the three-year period ended December 31, 20X3. We also have audited management's assessment, included in the accompanying *[identify title of management's report]*, that W Company maintained effective internal control over financial reporting as of December 31, 20X3, based on *[Identify criteria, for example, "criteria established in Internal Control—Integrated Framework issued by the Committee of Sponsoring Organizations of the Treadway Commission (COSO)."]*. W Company's management is responsible for these financial statements and for the assessment about the effectiveness of internal control over financial reporting. Our responsibility is to express an opinion on these financial statements and on management's assessment based on our audits.

[Definition paragraph]

A company's internal control over financial reporting is a process designed to provide reasonable assurance regarding the reliability of financial reporting and the preparation of financial statements for external purposes in accordance with generally accepted accounting principles. A company's internal control over financial reporting includes those policies and procedures that (1) pertain to the maintenance of records that in reasonable detail accurately and fairly reflect the transactions and dispositions of the assets of the company; (2) provide reasonable assurance that transactions are recorded as necessary to permit preparation of financial statements in accordance with generally accepted accounting principles, and that receipts and expenditures of the company are being made only in accordance with authorizations of management and directors of the company; and (3) provide reasonable assurance regarding prevention or timely detection of unauthorized acquisition, use, or disposition of the company's assets that could have a material effect on the financial statements.

[Scope paragraph]

We conducted our audits in accordance with auditing and related professional practice standards established by the Public Company Accounting Oversight Board. Those standards require that we plan and perform the audits to obtain reasonable assurance about whether the financial statements are free of material misstatement and whether effective internal control over financial reporting was maintained in all material respects. An audit of financial statements includes examining, on a test basis, evidence supporting the amounts and disclosures in the financial statements, assessing the accounting principles used and significant estimates made by management, and evaluating the overall financial statement presentation. An audit of internal control includes obtaining an understanding of internal control over financial reporting, testing and evaluating the design and operating effectiveness of internal control, and performing such other procedures as we considered necessary in the circumstances. We believe that our audits provide a reasonable basis for our opinions.

[Inherent limitations paragraph]

Because of its inherent limitations, internal control over financial reporting may not prevent or detect misstatements. Also, projections of any evaluation of effectiveness to future periods are subject to the risk that controls may become inadequate because of changes in conditions, or that the degree of compliance with the policies or procedures may deteriorate.

[Opinion paragraph]

In our opinion, the financial statements referred to above present fairly, in all material respects, the financial position of W Company as of December 31, 20X3 and 20X2, and the results of its operations and its cash flows for each of the years in the three-year period ended December 31, 20X3 in conformity with accounting principles generally accepted in the United States of America. Also in our opinion, management's assessment that W Company maintained effective internal control over financial reporting as of December 31, 20X3, is fairly stated, in all material respects, based on [*Identify criteria, for example, "criteria established in Internal Control—Integrated Framework issued by the Committee of Sponsoring Organizations of the Treadway Commission (COSO)."*].

[Signature]

[Date]

APPENDIX B

Additional Performance Requirements and Guidance; Extent of Testing Examples

Tests to be Performed When a Company Has Multiple Locations or Business Units

B1. To determine the locations or business units for performing audit procedures, the auditor should evaluate their relative financial significance and the risk of material misstatement arising from them. In making this evaluation, the auditor should identify the locations or business units that are individually important, evaluate their documentation of controls, and test controls over significant accounts and disclosures. For locations or business units that contain specific risks that, by themselves, could create a material misstatement, the auditor should evaluate the documentation of controls and test controls over the specific risks.

B2. The auditor should determine which other locations or business units, when aggregated, represent a group with a level of financial significance that could create a material misstatement in the financial statements. For that group, the auditor should determine whether there are company-level controls in place. If so, the auditor should evaluate the documentation and test such company-level controls. If not, the auditor should perform tests of controls at some of the locations or business units.

B3. No further work is necessary on the remaining locations and businesses, provided that they are not able to create, either individually or in the aggregate, a material misstatement in the financial statements.

Locations or Business Units That are Financially Significant

B4. Because of the importance of financially significant locations, the auditor should evaluate management's documentation of and perform tests of controls over all relevant assertions related to significant accounts and disclosures at each financially significant location or business unit, as discussed in paragraphs 84 through 110. Generally, a relatively small number of locations or business units will encompass a large portion of a company's operations and financial position, making them financially significant.

B5. In determining the nature, timing, and extent of testing at the individual locations or business units, the auditor should evaluate each entity's involvement, if any, with a central processing or shared service environment.

Locations or Business Units That Involve Specific Risks

B6. Although a location or business unit might not be individually financially significant, it might present specific risks that, by themselves, could create a material misstatement in the company's financial statements. The auditor should test the controls over the specific risks that could create a material misstatement in the company's financial statements. The auditor need not test controls over all relevant assertions for all significant accounts at these locations or business units. For example, a business unit responsible for foreign exchange trading could expose the company to the risk of material misstatement, even though the relative financial significance of such transactions is low.

Locations or Business Units That are Significant Only When Aggregated with Other Locations and Business Units

B7. In determining the nature, timing, and extent of testing, the auditor should determine whether management has documented and placed in operation companylevel controls (see paragraph 53) over individually unimportant locations and business units that, when aggregated with other locations or business units, might have a high level of financial significance. Such a level of financial significance could create a greater than remote risk of material misstatement of the financial statements.

B8. For the purposes of this evaluation, company-level controls are controls management has in place to monitor the operations and to oversee the control environment and risk assessment process at these locations or business units.

B9. The auditor should perform tests of company-level controls to determine whether such controls are operating effectively. The auditor might conclude that he or she cannot evaluate the operating effectiveness of such controls without visiting some or all of the locations or business units.

B10. If management does not have company-level controls operating at these locations and business units, the auditor should determine the nature, timing, and extent of procedures to be performed at each location, business unit, or combination of locations and business units. When determining the locations or business units to visit and the controls to test, the auditor should evaluate the following factors:

- The relative financial significance of each location or business unit.

- The risk of material misstatement arising from each location or business unit.
- The similarity of business operations and internal control over financial reporting at the various locations or business units.
- The degree of centralization of processes and financial reporting applications.
- The effectiveness of the control environment, particularly management's direct control over the exercise of authority delegated to others and its ability to effectively supervise activities at the various locations or business units. An ineffective control environment over the locations or business units might constitute a material weakness.
- The nature and amount of transactions executed and related assets at the various locations or business units.
- The potential for material unrecognized obligations to exist at a location or business unit and to what degree the location or business unit could create an obligation on the part of the company.
- Management's risk assessment process and analysis for excluding a location or business unit from its assessment of internal control over financial reporting.

B11. Testing company-level controls is not a substitute for the auditor's testing of controls over a large portion of the company's operations or financial position. If the auditor cannot test a large portion of the company's operations and financial position by selecting a relatively small number of locations or business units, he or she should expand the number of locations or business units selected to evaluate internal control over financial reporting.

Locations and Business Units That Do Not Require Testing

B12. No testing is required with respect to locations or business units that individually, and when aggregated with others, could not result in a material misstatement to the financial statements.

Multi-Location Testing Considerations Flowchart

B13. Illustration B-1 depicts how to apply the directions in this section to a hypothetical company with 150 locations or business units, along with the auditor's testing considerations for those locations or business units.

Illustration B-1

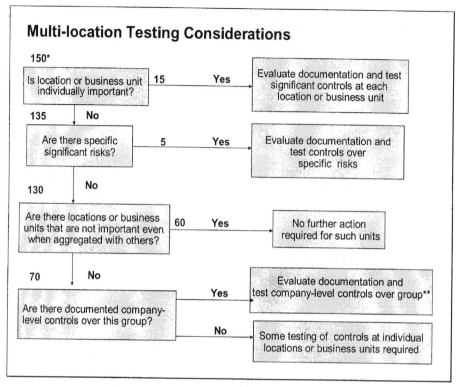

Multi-location Testing Considerations

* Numbers represent number of locations affected.
** See paragraph B7.

Special Situations

B14. The scope of the evaluation of the company's internal control over financial reporting should include entities that are acquired on or before the date of management's assessment and operations that are accounted for as discontinued operations on the date of management's assessment. The auditor should consider this multiple locations discussion in determining whether it will be necessary to test controls at these entities or operations.

B15. For equity method investments, the evaluation of the company's internal control over financial reporting should include controls over the reporting in accordance with generally accepted accounting principles, in the company's financial statements, of the company's portion of the investees' income or loss, the investment balance, adjustments to the income or loss and investment balance, and related disclosures. The evaluation ordinarily would not extend to controls at the equity method investee.

B16. For entities that are consolidated or proportionately consolidated, the evaluation of the company's internal control over financial reporting should include controls over significant accounts and processes that exist at the consolidated or proportionately consolidated entity. In some instances, however, such as for some variable interest entities as defined in Financial Accounting Standards Board Interpretation No. 46, *Consolidation of Variable Interest Entities*, management might not have the ability to obtain the information necessary to make an assessment because it does not have the ability to control the entity. If management is allowed to limit its assessment by excluding such entities,[1] the auditor may limit the audit in the same manner, and report without reference to the limitation in scope. However, the auditor should evaluate the reasonableness of management's conclusion that they do not have the ability to obtain the necessary information as well as the appropriateness of any required disclosure related to such a limitation. If the auditor believes that management's disclosure about the limitation requires modification, the auditor should follow the same communication responsibilities as described in paragraphs 187 and 188. If management and the audit committee do not respond appropriately, in addition to fulfilling those responsibilities, the auditor should modify his or her report on the audit of internal control over financial reporting to include an explanatory paragraph describing the reasons the auditor believes management's disclosure should be modified.

Identifying Significant Accounts

B17. When deciding whether an account is significant, it is important for the auditor to evaluate both quantitative and qualitative factors, including the:

- Size and composition of the account,
- Susceptibility of loss due to errors or fraud,
- Volume of activity, complexity, and homogeneity of the individual transactions processed through the account,
- Nature of the account (for example, suspense accounts generally warrant greater attention),
- Accounting and reporting complexities associated with the account,
- Exposure to losses represented by the account (for example, loss reserves related to a consolidated captive insurance company),
- Likelihood (or possibility) of significant contingent liabilities arising from the activities represented by the account,
- Existence of related party transactions in the account, and
- Changes from the prior period in account characteristics (for example, new complexities or subjectivity or new types of transactions).

B18. For example, in a financial statement audit, the auditor might not consider the fixed asset accounts significant when there is a low volume of transactions and inherent risk is assessed as low, even though the balances are material to the financial statements. Accordingly, he or she might decide to perform only substantive tests on such balances. In an audit of internal control over financial reporting, however, such accounts are significant accounts because of their materiality to the financial statements.

B19. As another example, the auditor of the financial statements of a financial institution might not consider trust accounts significant to the institution's financial statements because

---

1. It is our understanding that the SEC Staff may conclude that management can limit the scope of its assessment if it does not have the authority to affect, and therefore cannot assess, the controls in place over certain amounts. This would relate to entities that are consolidated or proportionately consolidated when the issuer does not have sufficient control over the entity to assess and affect controls. If management's report on its assessment of the effectiveness of internal control over financial reporting is limited in that manner, the SEC staff may permit the company to disclose this fact as well as information about the magnitude of the amounts included in the financial statements from entities whose controls cannot be assessed. This disclosure would be required in each filing, but outside of management's report on its assessment of the effectiveness of internal control over financial reporting.

such accounts are not included in the institution's balance sheet and the associated fee income generated by trust activities is not material. However, in determining whether trust accounts are a significant account for purposes of the audit of internal control over financial reporting, the auditor should assess whether the activities of the trust department are significant to the institution's financial reporting, which also would include considering the contingent liabilities that could arise if a trust department failed to fulfill its fiduciary responsibilities (for example, if investments were made that were not in accordance with stated investment policies). When assessing the significance of possible contingent liabilities, consideration of the amount of assets under the trust department's control may be useful. For this reason, an auditor who has not previously considered trust accounts significant accounts for purposes of the financial statement audit might determine that they are significant for purposes of the audit of internal control over financial reporting.

Using the Work of Others

Other Standards to Consider

B20. The auditor might find the directions in AU sec. 322, *The Auditor's Consideration of the Internal Audit Function in an Audit of Financial Statements*, useful in assessing the competence and objectivity of internal auditors and others who have performed procedures as a basis for management's assessment.

Application Example

B21. The example included in the following paragraphs demonstrates how to apply the directions discussed in this section.

B22. In evaluating controls over the recording of revenue, the auditor needs to look at a variety of factors including, among other things, information technology general controls and controls over (1) determining the appropriate methods of revenue recognition under generally accepted accounting principles as it relates to the company's operations, (2) evaluating nonroutine sales transactions and contracts to determine the appropriate accounting and (3) the routine processing of daily sales through the company's accounting system.

- Because of the pervasive impact of the controls in (1) and the material impact those controls ordinarily have on the financial statements, the auditor should not use the results of testing by management and others within the company, as discussed in paragraph 104.

- The auditor should limit use of the results of testing performed by others within the company for the controls identified in (2), since the nonroutine nature of these transactions and contracts involve controls over decisions requiring considerable judgment.

- On the other hand, the auditor could increase the use of the results of testing by management and others relating to the controls in (3), which relate to the routine processing of daily sales transactions and accounts receivable. In that case, the auditor should follow the directions in paragraphs 106 through 109.

B23. In the situations described in (1) through (3) above, when evaluating whether sufficient evidence has been obtained, the auditor should understand that evidence obtained through his or her direct personal knowledge, observation, reperformance, and inspection is more persuasive than information obtained indirectly from others, such as from management, internal auditors, or other personnel. Furthermore, judgments about the sufficiency of evidence obtained and other factors affecting the auditor's opinion, such as the materiality of identified control deficiencies, should be those of the auditor.

Use of Service Auditor's Report

B24. When the company uses a service organization, the auditor, when planning the audit, should obtain an understanding of the portion of the company's internal control over financial reporting (that is, the initiating, recording, processing, and reporting of its transactions) performed at the service organization and the interaction of controls at the service organization with controls at the company.

B25. The use of a service organization does not reduce management's responsibility to maintain effective internal control over financial reporting. Rather, management should evaluate controls at the service organization, as well as related controls at the company, when making its assessment about internal control over financial reporting.

B26. The auditor should determine whether management has evaluated the activities of the service organization when making its assessment about internal control over financial reporting. For instance, a service organization is considered part of the company's internal control over financial reporting when it provides services that affect—

- How the company initiates its transactions,
- How the company's transactions are processed and reported in its accounting records, supporting information, and specific financial statement accounts,
- How the company's transactions are processed from the initiation of the transaction to its inclusion in the financial statements, or
- How the financial reporting process is used to prepare the client's financial statements.

B27. In addition, the auditor should evaluate the activities of the service organization in determining the nature, timing, and extent of evidence required to support his or her opinion on internal control over financial reporting. Paragraph .07 of AU sec. 324, *Service Organizations*, describes the procedures that management and the auditor should perform with respect to the activities performed by the service organization, which include:

- Obtaining an understanding of the controls at the service organization that are relevant to the company's internal control over financial reporting, and
- Obtaining evidence that the controls that are relevant to management's assessment and the auditor's opinion are operating effectively.

B28. A service organization might do several things to assist the auditor. For example, the service organization might:

- Engage its own auditor (service auditor) to review and report on the systems it uses to process the company's transactions.
- Engage a service auditor to test the effectiveness of the controls applied to the company's transactions to enable the auditor to evaluate controls at the service organization in an audit of internal control over financial reporting.

Auditor's Use of Service Auditor's Report

B29. Whenever the company uses a service organization to provide services that are part of the company's information system, the auditor should inquire whether management has received a service auditor's report. If so, the auditor should read the report for information that might be useful in planning the audit.

B30. A service auditor's *report on controls placed in operation*, as described in Paragraph .24a of AU sec. 324, expresses an opinion on a description of the controls at the service organization as of a specified date. The opinion indicates whether the controls described (a) were presented fairly in all material respects and (b) were suitably designed to provide reasonable assurance that the control objectives specified in the description would be achieved if complied with satisfactorily.

B31. A report on controls placed in operation might be helpful when planning the audit; however, it provides assurance only with respect to the control objectives specified in the description. Accordingly, there is no assurance that the specified objectives include all those that would be relevant to the company's internal control over financial reporting. Furthermore, if such a report contains a caveat that the stated control objectives might be achieved only if the company applies controls contemplated in the design of the system by the service organization, the auditor should evaluate whether the company is applying the necessary procedures. For example, completeness of processing payroll transactions might depend on the company's validation that all payroll records sent to the service center were processed by checking a control total. Finally, this type of report does not provide any evidence of the operating effectiveness of controls.

B32. If the auditor uses a service auditor's report when planning the audit, he or she should make inquiries concerning the service auditor's reputation, competence, and independence. In making those inquiries, the auditor should evaluate the relevance of the information in AU sec. 543, *Part of Audit Performed by Other Independent Auditors of Financial Statements.* The auditor also should read the report to determine whether it provides information the auditor needs, for example, by addressing the service organization's controls relevant to the assertions the auditor is testing. If the service auditor's report is not sufficient to meet the auditor's objectives, the auditor should gather the desired information from other sources, such as those discussed in the next section.

Unavailable Service Auditor's Report

B33. If a service auditor's report on controls placed in operation is unavailable, the auditor might obtain information about the service organization's controls needed to plan the audit from a variety of sources, such as—

- User manuals.
- System overviews.
- Technical manuals.
- The contract between the client and the service organization.
- Reports by internal auditors or regulatory authorities on the information system and other controls placed in operation by the service organization.
- Inquiries or observations of personnel at the company or at the service organization.

B34. In addition, the auditor's prior experience with the specific service organization might be helpful in planning the audit.

Report on Operating Effectiveness

B35. If the auditor believes that he or she also must obtain evidence about the operating effectiveness of service center controls, one way an auditor can obtain such evidence is by obtaining a service auditor's *report on controls placed in operation and tests of operating effectiveness,* as described in Paragraph .24b of AU sec. 324. This report provides a description of the tests of controls and results of those tests performed by the service auditor, as well as the service auditor's opinion on whether the controls that were tested were operating effectively during the specified period. If a service auditor's report on controls placed in operation and tests of operating effectiveness is available, management and the auditor should evaluate whether the report provides sufficient evidence to support their assessment and opinion, respectively. The evaluation should include the following factors:

- The time period covered by the service auditor's tests of controls in relationship to the date of management's assessment of internal control over financial reporting,

- The controls tested by the service auditor and how they relate to the company's controls,

- The results of the tests of controls performed by the service auditor, and

- The service auditor's opinion on the operating effectiveness of the controls.

B36. Such evaluations are similar to those the auditor would make when determining whether the service auditor's report provides sufficient evidence to support the auditor's assessed level of control risk in an audit of the financial statements, as described in Paragraph .16 of AU sec. 324. However, the auditor is responsible for evaluating the evidence provided by the service auditor's report and for determining its effect on the audit of internal control over financial reporting.

Inquiries About Changes in Controls

B37. When a significant period of time has elapsed between the time period covered by the service auditor's tests of controls and the date of management's assessment, the auditor should inquire of management about whether there have been changes in the service organization's controls subsequent to the period covered by the service auditor's report. Such changes might include:

- Changes communicated to management from the service organization,

- Changes in personnel, with whom management interacts, at the service organization,

- Changes in reports or other data received from the service organization,

- Changes in contracts or service level agreements with the service organization, or

- Errors indentified in the service organization's processing.

B38. If management has informed the auditor of the types of changes noted in the preceding paragraph, the auditor should determine whether management has performed procedures to evaluate the effect of the changes on the effectiveness of the company's internal control over financial reporting. The auditor also should evaluate whether management was aware of changes in the service organization's controls that the auditor discovered while performing other procedures during the audit of internal control over financial reporting. In light of such evaluations, the auditor should determine whether there is a need for obtaining additional evidence about the operating effectiveness of controls at the service organization. If additional evidence is necessary, the auditor should:

- Reperform tests performed by management or others within the company,

- Contact the service organization, through the client, to obtain specific information,

- Request that a service auditor be engaged to perform procedures that will supply the necessary information, or

- Visit the service organization and perform procedures that will supply the necessary evidence.

B39. Because the auditor is responsible for obtaining sufficient evidence to support the opinion on internal control over financial reporting, he or she should not refer to the service auditor's report when expressing such an opinion.

Examples of Extent of Testing Decisions

B40. As discussed throughout this standard, determining the effectiveness of a company's internal control over financial reporting includes evaluating the design and operating effectiveness of controls over all relevant assertions related to all significant accounts and disclosures in the financial statements. Paragraphs 88 through 110 provide the auditor with directions about the nature, timing, and extent of testing of the operating effectiveness of internal control over financial reporting.

B41. Examples B-1 through B-4 illustrate how to apply this information in various situations. These examples are for illustrative purposes only.

Example B-1—*Daily Programmed Application Control and Daily Information Technology-Dependent Manual Control*

The auditor has determined that cash and accounts receivable are significant accounts to the audit of XYZ Company's internal control over financial reporting. Based on discussions with company personnel and review of company documentation, the auditor learned that the company had the following procedures in place to account for cash received in the lockbox:

a. The company receives a download of cash receipts from the banks.

b. The information technology system applies cash received in the lockbox to individual customer accounts.

c. Any cash received in the lockbox and not applied to a customer's account is listed on an exception report (Unapplied Cash Exception Report).

—Therefore, the application of cash to a customer's account is a programmed application control, while the review and follow-up of unapplied cash from the exception report is a detective control.

To determine whether misstatements in cash (existence assertion) and accounts receivable (existence, valuation, and completeness) would be prevented or detected on a timely basis, the auditor decided to test the controls provided by the system in the daily reconciliation of lock box receipts to customer accounts, as well as the control over reviewing and resolving unapplied cash in the Unapplied Cash Exception Report.

Nature, Timing, and Extent of Procedures. To test the programmed application control, the auditor:

- Identified, through discussion with company personnel, the software used to receive the download from the banks and to process the transactions and determined that the banks supply the download software.

  —The company uses accounting software used from a third-party supplier. The software consists of a number of modules. The client modifies the software only for upgrades supplied by the supplier.

- Determined, through further discussion with company personnel, that the cash module operates the lockbox functionality and the posting of cash to the general ledger. The accounts receivable module posts the cash to individual customer accounts and produces the Unapplied Cash Exception Report, a standard report supplied with the package. The auditor agreed this information to the supplier's documentation.

- Identified, through discussions with company personnel and review of the supplier's documentation, the names, file sizes (in bytes), and locations of the executable files (programs) that operate the functionality under review. The auditor then found the compilation dates of these programs and agreed them to the original installation date of the application.

- Identified the objectives of the programs to be tested. The auditor wanted to determine whether only appropriate cash items are posted to customers' accounts and matched to customer number, invoice number, amount, etc., and that there is a listing of inappropriate cash items (that is, any of the above items not matching) on the exception report.

In addition, the auditor had evaluated and tested general computer controls, including program changes (for example, confirmation that no unauthorized changes are undertaken) and logical access (for example, data file access to the file downloaded from the banks and user access to the cash and accounts receivable modules) and concluded that they were operating effectively.

To determine whether such programmed controls were operating effectively, the auditor performed a walkthrough in the month of July. The computer controls operate in a systematic manner, therefore, the auditor concluded that it was sufficient to walkthrough only the one item. During the walkthrough, the auditor performed and documented the following items:

a. Selected one customer and agreed the amount billed to the customer to the cash received in the lockbox.

b. Agreed the total of the lockbox report to the posting of cash receipts in the general ledger.

c. Agreed the total of the cash receipt download from the bank to the lockbox report and supporting documentation.

d. Selected one customer's remittance and agreed amount posted to the customer's account in the accounts receivable subsidiary ledger.

To test the detect control of review and follow up on the Daily Unapplied Cash Exception Report, the auditor:

a. *Made Inquiries of Company Personnel.* To understand the procedures in place to ensure that all unapplied items are resolved, the time frame in which such resolution takes place, and whether unapplied items are handled properly within the system, the auditor discussed these matters with the employee responsible for reviewing and resolving the Daily Unapplied Cash Exception Reports. The auditor learned that when items appear on the Daily-Unapplied Cash Exception Report, the employee must manually enter the correction into the system. The employee typically performs the resolution procedures the next business day. Items that typically appear on the Daily Unapplied Cash Exception Report relate to payments made by a customer without reference to an invoice number/ purchase order number or underpayments of an invoice due to quantity or pricing discrepancies.

b. *Observed Personnel Performing the Control.* The auditor then observed the employee reviewing and resolving a Daily Unapplied Cash Exception Report. The day selected contained four exceptions—three related to payments made by a customer without an invoice number, and one related to an underpayment due to a pricing discrepancy.

—For the pricing discrepancy, the employee determined, through discussions with a sales person, that the customer had been billed an incorrect price; a price break that the sales person had granted to the customer was not reflected on the customer's invoice. The employee resolved the pricing discrepancy, determined which invoices were being paid, and entered a correction into the system to properly apply cash to the customer's account and reduce accounts receivable and sales accounts for the amount of the price break.

c. *Reperformed the Control.* Finally, the auditor selected 25 Daily Unapplied Cash Exception Reports from the period January to September. For the reports selected, the auditor reperformed the follow-up procedures that the employee performed. For instance, the auditor inspected the documents and sources of information used in the follow-up and determined that the transaction was properly corrected in the system. The auditor also scanned other Daily Unapplied Cash Exception Reports to determine that the control was performed throughout the period of intended reliance.

Because the tests of controls were performed at an interim date, the auditor had to determine whether there were any significant changes in the controls from interim to year-end. Therefore, the auditor asked company personnel about the procedures in place at year-end. Such procedures had not changed from the interim period, therefore, the auditor observed that the controls were still in place by scanning Daily Unapplied Cash Exception Reports to determine the control was performed on a timely basis during September to year-end.

Based on the auditor's procedures, the auditor concluded that the employee was clearing exceptions in a timely manner and that the control was operating effectively as of year-end.

Example B-2—*Monthly Manual Reconciliation*

The auditor determined that accounts receivable is a significant account to the audit of XYZ Company's internal control over financial reporting. Through discussions with company personnel and review of company documentation, the auditor learned that company personnel reconcile the accounts receivable subsidiary ledger to the general ledger on a monthly basis. To determine whether misstatements in accounts receivable (existence, valuation, and completeness) would be detected on a timely basis, the auditor decided to test the control provided by monthly reconciliation process.

Nature, Timing, and Extent of Procedures. The auditor tested the company's reconciliation control by selecting a sample of reconciliations based upon the number of accounts, the dollar value of the accounts, and the volume of transactions affecting the account. Because the auditor considered all other receivable accounts immaterial, and because such accounts had only minimal transactions flowing through them, the auditor decided to test only the reconciliation for the trade accounts receivable account. The auditor elected to perform the tests of controls over the reconciliation process in conjunction with the auditor's substantive tests over the accounts receivable confirmation procedures, which were performed in July.

To test the reconciliation process, the auditor:

- *Made Inquiries of Personnel Performing the Control.* The auditor asked the employee performing the reconciliation a number of questions, including the following:

  —What documentation describes the account reconciliation process?

—How long have you been performing the reconciliation work?

—What is the reconciliation process for resolving reconciling items?

—How often are the reconciliations formally reviewed and signed off?

—If significant issues or reconciliation problems are noticed, to whose attention do you bring them?

—On average, how many reconciling items are there?

—How are old reconciling items treated?

—If need be, how is the system corrected for reconciling items?

—What is the general nature of these reconciling items?

- *Observed the Employee Performing the Control.* The auditor observed the employee performing the reconciliation procedures. For nonrecurring reconciling items, the auditor observed whether each item included a clear explanation as to its nature, the action that had been taken to resolve it, and whether it had been resolved on a timely basis.

- *Reperformed the Control.* Finally, the auditor inspected the reconciliations and reperfomed the reconciliation procedures. For the May and July reconciliations, the auditor traced the reconciling amounts to the source documents on a test basis. The only reconciling item that appeared on these reconciliations was cash received in the lockbox the previous day that had not been applied yet to the customer's account. The auditor pursued the items in each month's reconciliation to determine that the reconciling item cleared the following business day. The auditor also scanned through the file of all reconciliations prepared during the year and noted that they had been performed on a timely basis. To determine that the company had not made significant changes in its reconciliation control procedures from interim to year-end, the auditor made inquiries of company personnel and determined that such procedures had not changed from interim to year-end. Therefore, the auditor verified that controls were still in place by scanning the monthly account reconciliations to determine that the control was performed on a timely basis during the interim to year-end period.

Based on the auditor's procedures, the auditor concluded that the reconciliation control was operating effectively as of year-end.

Example B-3 — *Daily Manual Prevent Control*

The auditor determined that cash and accounts payable were significant accounts to the audit of the company's internal control over financial reporting. Through discussions with company personnel, the auditor learned that company personnel make a cash disbursement only after they have matched the vendor invoice to the receiver and purchase order. To determine whether misstatements in cash (existence) and accounts payable (existence, valuation, and completeness) would be prevented on a timely basis, the auditor tested the control over making a cash disbursement only after matching the invoice with the receiver and purchase.

Nature, Timing, and Extent of Procedures. On a haphazard basis, the auditor selected 25 disbursements from the cash disbursement registers from January through September. In this example, the auditor deemed a test of 25 cash disbursement transactions an appropriate sample size because the auditor was testing a manual control performed as part of the routine processing of cash disbursement transactions through the system. Furthermore, the auditor expected no errors based on the results of company-level tests performed earlier. [If, however, the auditor had encountered a control exception, the auditor would have tested an additional number of items. If another control exception had been noted, the auditor would have decided (a) that this control was not effective and (b) to increase the extent of substantive tests to be performed in connection with the financial statement audit of the cash and accounts payable accounts.]

After obtaining the related voucher package, the auditor examined the invoice to see if it included the signature or initials of the accounts payable clerk, evidencing the clerk's performance of the matching control. However, a signature on a voucher package to indicate signor approval does not necessarily mean that the person carefully reviewed it before signing. The voucher package may have been signed based on only a cursory review (or without any review).

The auditor decided that the quality of the evidence regarding the effective operation of the control evidenced by a signature or initials was not sufficiently persuasive to ensure that the control operated effectively during the test period. In order to obtain additional evidence, the auditor reperformed the matching control corresponding to the signature, which included examining the invoice to determine that (a) its items matched to the receiver and purchase order and (b) it was mathematically accurate.

Because the auditor performed the tests of controls at an interim date, the auditor updated the testing through the end of the year (initial tests are through September to December) by asking the accounts payable clerk whether the control was still in place and operating effectively. The auditor confirmed that understanding by performing a walkthrough of one transaction in December.

Based on the auditor's procedures, the auditor concluded that the control over making a cash disbursement only after matching the invoice with the receiver and purchase was operating effectively as of year-end.

Example B-4—*Programmed Prevent Control and Weekly Information Technology-Dependent Manual Detect Control*

The auditor determined that cash, accounts payable, and inventory were significant accounts to the audit of the company's internal control over financial reporting. Through discussions with company personnel, the auditor learned that the company's computer system performs a three-way match of the receiver, purchase order, and invoice. If there are any exceptions, the system produces a list of unmatched items that is reviewed and followed up by employees on a weekly basis.

In this case, the computer match is a programmed application control, and the review and follow-up of the unmatched items report is a detect control. To determine whether misstatements in cash (existence) and accounts payable/inventory (existence, valuation, and completeness) would be prevented or detected on a timely basis, the auditor decided to test the programmed application control of matching the receiver, purchase order, and invoice as well as the review and follow-up control over unmatched items.

Nature, Timing, and Extent of Procedures. To test the programmed application control, the auditor:

- Identified, through discussion with company personnel, the software used to process receipts and purchase invoices. The software used was a third party package consisting of a number of modules.

- The auditor established through further discussion with company personnel that they do not modify the core functionality of the software, but sometimes make personalized changes to reports to meet the changing needs of the business. From previous experience with the company's information technology environment, the auditor believes that such changes are infrequent and that information technology process controls are well established.

- Established, through further discussion, that the inventory module operated the receiving functionality, including the matching of receipts to open purchase orders. Purchase invoices were processed in the accounts payable module, which matched them to an approved purchase order against which a valid receipt has been made. That module also produced the Unmatched Items Report, a standard report supplied with the package to which the company has not made any modifications. That information was agreed to the supplier's documentation and to documentation within the information technology department.

- Identified, through discussions with the client and review of the supplier's documentation, the names, file sizes (in bytes), and locations of the executable files (programs) that operate the functionality under review. The auditor then identified the compilation dates of the programs and agreed them to the original installation date of the application. The compilation date of the report code was agreed to documentation held within the information technology department relating to the last change made to that report (a change in formatting).

- Identified the objectives of the programs to be tested. The auditor wanted to determine whether appropriate items are received (for example, match a valid purchase order), appropriate purchase invoices are posted (for example, match a valid receipt and purchase order, non-duplicate reference numbers) and unmatched items (for example, receipts, orders or invoices) are listed on the exception report. The auditor then reperformed all those variations in the packages on a test-of-one basis to determine that the programs operated as described.

In addition, the auditor had evaluated and tested general computer controls, including program changes (for example, confirmation that no unauthorized changes are undertaken to the functionality and that changes to reports are appropriately authorized, tested, and approved before being applied) and logical access (for example, user access to the inventory and accounts payable modules and access to the area on the system where report code is maintained), and concluded that they were operating effectively. (Since the computer is deemed to operate in a systematic manner, the auditor concluded that it was sufficient to walkthrough only the one item.)

- To determine whether the programmed control was operating effectively, the auditor performed a walkthrough in the month of July. As a result of the walkthrough, the auditor performed and documented the following items:

  —Receiving cannot record the receipt of goods without matching the receipt to a purchase order on the system. The auditor tested that control by attempting to record the receipt of goods into the system without a purchase order. However, the system did not allow the auditor to do that. Rather, the system produced an error message stating that the goods could not be recorded as received without an active purchase order.

  —An invoice will not be paid unless the system can match the receipt and vendor invoice to an approved purchase order. The auditor tested that control by attempting to approve an invoice for payment in the system. The system did not allow the auditor to do that. Rather, it produced an error message indicating that invoices could not be paid without an active purchase order and receiver.

—The system disallows the processing of invoices with identical vendor and identical invoice numbers. In addition, the system will not allow two invoices to be processed against the same purchase order unless the sum of the invoices is less than the amount approved on the purchase order. The auditor tested that control by attempting to process duplicate invoices. However, the system produced an error message indicating that the invoice had already been processed.

—The system compares the invoice amounts to the purchase order. If there are differences in quantity/extended price, and such differences fall outside a preapproved tolerance, the system does not allow the invoice to be processed. The auditor tested that control by attempting to process an invoice that had quantity/price differences outside the tolerance level of 10 pieces, or $1,000. The system produced an error message indicating that the invoice could not be processed because of such differences.

—The system processes payments only for vendors established in the vendor master file. The auditor tested that control by attempting to process an invoice for a vendor that was not established in the vendor master file. However, the system did not allow the payment to be processed.

—The auditor tested user access to the vendor file and whether such users can make modifications to such file by attempting to access and make changes to the vendor tables. However, the system did not allow the auditor to perform that function and produced an error message stating that the user was not authorized to perform that function.

—The auditor verified the completeness and accuracy of the Unmatched Items Report by verifying that one unmatched item was on the report and one matched item was not on the report.

To test the detect control of review and follow up on the Unmatched Items Report, the auditor performed the following procedures in the month of July for the period January to July:

- *Made Inquiries of company personnel.* To gain an understanding of the procedures in place to ensure that all unmatched items are followed-up properly and that corrections are made on a timely basis, the auditor made inquiries of the employee who follows up on the weekly-unmatched items reports. On a weekly basis, the control required the employee to review the Unmatched Items Report to determine why items appear on it. The employee's review includes proper follow-up on items, including determining whether:

  —All open purchase orders are either closed or voided within an acceptable amount of time.

  —The requesting party is notified periodically of the status of the purchase order and the reason for its current status.

  —The reason the purchase order remains open is due to incomplete shipment of goods and, if so, whether the vendor has been notified.

  —There are quantity problems that should be discussed with purchasing.

 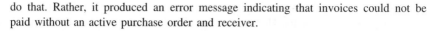

- *Observed the Performance of the Control.* The auditor observed the employee performing the control for the Unmatched Items Reports generated during the first week in July.
- *Reperformance of the Control.* The auditor selected five weekly Unmatched Items Reports, selected several items from each, and reperformed the procedures that the employee performed. The auditor also scanned other Unmatched Items Reports to determine that the control was performed throughout the period of intended reliance.

To determine that the company had not made significant changes in their controls from interim to year-end, the auditor discussed with company personnel the procedures in place for making such changes. Since the procedures had not changed from interim to year-end, the auditor observed that the controls were still in place by scanning the weekly Unmatched Items Reports to determine that the control was performed on a timely basis during the interim to year-end period.

Based on the auditor's procedures, the auditor concluded that the employee was clearing exceptions in a timely manner and that the control was operating effectively as of year-end.

APPENDIX C

Safeguarding of Assets

C1. *Safeguarding of assets* in a financial reporting context includes protection only against losses arising from intentional and unintentional misstatements in processing transactions and handling the related assets. Examples of unintentional misstatements include:

- Understatement of sales through failure to prepare invoices or through incorrect pricing or computation;
- Overpayments to vendors or employees arising from inaccuracies in quantities of materials or services, prices or rates, or computations;
- Physical loss or misappropriation of assets such as cash, securities, or inventory; and
- Improper allocation of certain costs, which would result in failure to recover these costs from customers.

C2. Examples of intentional misstatements include falsification of records for the purpose of causing improper computation of commissions, profit-sharing bonuses, royalties, and similar payments based on the recording of other transactions. Consequently, safeguarding controls over the use of a lockbox system for collecting cash and over access controls, such as passwords, that limit access to data and programs that process cash disbursements might both be relevant to an audit of internal control over financial reporting.

C3. The definition of *safeguarding of assets* used in this standard does not encompass the concept that one of management's primary functions is to protect the company's existing assets and acquire new ones. Thus, when evaluating whether the company's internal control over financial reporting is effective, the auditor is not required to understand and test controls over management's decision-making process for all sales and acquisitions. For example, management's decision to sell a product at a price that proves to be unprofitable might be regarded as a failure to protect existing assets. However, because that decision is outside the financial reporting process, it is not considered to be a deficiency in internal control over financial reporting. Likewise, decisions to incur expenditures for equipment that prove to be unnecessary or inefficient, for materials that prove to be unsatisfactory in production, for merchandise that proves to be unsaleable, for research that proves to be unproductive, for advertising that proves to be ineffective, and for similar management decisions are not deficiencies in a company's internal control over financial reporting because they are outside the scope of internal control over financial reporting.

APPENDIX D

Examples of Material Weaknesses and Significant Deficiencies

D1. Paragraph 7 of this standard defines an *internal control deficiency*. Paragraphs 8 and 9 go on to define a *significant deficiency* and a *material weakness*.

D2. Materiality in an audit of internal control over financial reporting is discussed in paragraphs 21-23, and paragraphs 116-126 provide additional direction on evaluating deficiencies in internal control over financial reporting.

D3. The following examples illustrate how to evaluate the significance of internal control deficiencies in various situations. These examples are for illustrative purposes only.

Example D-1—*Reconciliations of Intercompany Accounts Are Not Performed on a Timely Basis*

Scenario A—Significant Deficiency. The company processes a significant number of routine intercompany transactions on a monthly basis. Individual intercompany transactions are not material and primarily relate to balance sheet activity, for example, cash transfers between business units to finance normal operations.

A formal management policy requires monthly reconciliation of intercompany accounts and confirmation of balances between business units. However, there is not a process in place to ensure performance of these procedures. As a result, detailed reconciliations of intercompany accounts are not performed on a timely basis. Management does perform monthly procedures to investigate selected large-dollar intercompany account differences. In addition, management prepares a detailed monthly variance analysis of operating expenses to assess their reasonableness.

Based only on these facts, the auditor should determine that this deficiency represents a significant deficiency for the following reasons: The magnitude of a financial statement misstatement resulting from this deficiency would reasonably be expected to be more than inconsequential, but less than material, because individual intercompany transactions are not material and the compensating controls operating monthly should detect a material misstatement. Furthermore, the transactions are primarily restricted to balance sheet accounts. However, the compensating detective controls are designed only to detect material misstatements. The controls do not address the detection of misstatements that are more than inconsequential but less than material. Therefore, the likelihood that a misstatement that was more than inconsequential, but less than material, could occur is more than remote.

Scenario B—Material Weakness. The company processes a significant number of intercompany transactions on a monthly basis. Intercompany transactions relate to a wide range of activities, including transfers of inventory with intercompany profit between business units, allocation of research and development costs to business units and corporate charges. Individual intercompany transactions are frequently material.

A formal management policy requires monthly reconciliation of intercompany accounts and confirmation of balances between business units. However, there is not a process in place to ensure that these procedures are performed on a consistent basis. As a result, reconciliations of intercompany accounts are not performed on a timely basis, and differences in intercompany accounts are frequent and significant. Management does not perform any alternative controls to investigate significant intercompany account differences.

Based only on these facts, the auditor should determine that this deficiency represents a material weakness for the following reasons: The magnitude of a financial statement misstatement resulting from this deficiency would reasonably be expected to be material, because individual intercompany transactions are frequently material and relate to a wide range of activities. Additionally, actual unreconciled differences in intercompany accounts have been, and are, material. The likelihood of such a misstatement is more than remote because such misstatements have frequently occurred and compensating controls are not effective, either because they are not properly designed or not operating effectively. Taken together, the magnitude and likelihood of misstatement of the financial statements resulting from this internal control deficiency meet the definition of a material weakness.

Example D-2—*Modifications to Standard Sales Contract Terms Not Reviewed To Evaluate Impact on Timing and Amount of Revenue Recognition*

Scenario A—Significant Deficiency. The company uses a standard sales contract for most transactions. Individual sales transactions are not material to the entity. Sales personnel are allowed to modify sales contract terms. The company's accounting function reviews significant or unusual modifications to the sales contract terms, but does not review changes in the standard shipping terms. The changes in the standard shipping terms could require a delay in the timing of revenue recognition. Management reviews gross margins on a monthly basis and investigates any significant or unusual relationships. In addition, management reviews the reasonableness of inventory levels at the end of each accounting period. The entity has experienced limited situations in which revenue has been inappropriately recorded in advance of shipment, but amounts have not been material.

Based only on these facts, the auditor should determine that this deficiency represents a significant deficiency for the following reasons: The magnitude of a financial statement misstatement resulting from this deficiency would reasonably be expected to be more than inconsequential, but less than material, because individual sales transactions are not material and the compensating detective controls operating monthly and at the end of each financial reporting period should reduce the likelihood of a material misstatement going undetected. Furthermore, the risk of material misstatement is limited to revenue recognition errors related to shipping terms as opposed to broader sources of error in revenue recognition. However, the compensating detective controls are only designed to detect material misstatements. The controls do not effectively address the detection of misstatements that are more than inconsequential but less than material, as evidenced by situations where transactions that were not material were improperly recorded. Therefore, there is a more than remote likelihood that a misstatement that is more than inconsequential but less than material could occur.

Scenario B—Material Weakness. The company has a standard sales contract, but sales personnel frequently modify the terms of the contract. The nature of the modifications can affect the timing and amount of revenue recognized. Individual sales transactions are frequently material to the entity and the gross margin can vary significantly for each transaction.

The company does not have procedures in place for the accounting function to regularly review modifications in sales contract terms. Although management reviews gross margins on a monthly basis, the significant differences in gross margin on individual transaction make it difficult for management to identify potential misstatements. Improper revenue recognition has occurred, and the amounts have been material.

Based only on these facts, the auditor should determine that this deficiency represents a material weakness for the following reasons: The magnitude of a financial statement misstatement resulting from this deficiency would reasonably be expected to be material, because individual sales transactions are frequently material, and gross margin can vary significantly with each transaction (which would make compensating detective controls based on a reasonableness review ineffective). Additionally, improper revenue recognition has occurred, and the amounts have been material. Therefore, the likelihood of material misstatements occurring is more than remote. Taken together, the magnitude and likelihood of misstatement of the financial statements resulting from this internal control deficiency meet the definition of a material weakness.

Scenario C—Material Weakness. The company has a standard sales contract, but sales personnel frequently modify the terms of the contract. Sales personnel frequently grant unauthorized and unrecorded sales discounts to customers without the knowledge of the accounting department. These amounts are deducted by customers in paying their invoices and are recorded as outstanding balances on the accounts receivable aging. Although these amounts are individually insignificant, they are material in the aggregate and have occurred consistently over the past few years.

Based on only these facts, the auditor should determine that this deficiency represents a material weakness for the following reasons: The magnitude of a financial statement misstatement resulting from this deficiency would reasonably be expected to be material, because the frequency of occurrence allows insignificant amounts to become material in the aggregate. The likelihood of material misstatement of the financial statements resulting from this internal control deficiency is more than remote (even assuming that the amounts were fully reserved for in the company's allowance for uncollectible accounts) due to the likelihood of material misstatement of the gross accounts receivable balance. Therefore, this internal control deficiency meets the definition of a material weakness.

Example D-3—*Identification of Several Deficiencies*

Scenario A—Material Weakness. During its assessment of internal control over financial reporting, management identified the following deficiencies. Based on the context in which the deficiencies occur, management and the auditor agree that these deficiencies individually represent significant deficiencies:

- Inadequate segregation of duties over certain information system access controls.

- Several instances of transactions that were not properly recorded in subsidiary ledgers; transactions were not material, either individually or in the aggregate.

- A lack of timely reconciliations of the account balances affected by the improperly recorded transactions.

Based only on these facts, the auditor should determine that the combination of these significant deficiencies represents a material weakness for the following reasons: Individually, these deficiencies were evaluated as representing a more than remote likelihood that a misstatement that is more than inconsequential, but less than material, could occur. However, each of these significant deficiencies affects the same set of accounts. Taken together, these significant deficiencies represent a more than remote likelihood that a material misstatement could occur and not be prevented or detected. Therefore, in combination, these significant deficiencies represent a material weakness.

Scenario B—Material Weakness. During its assessment of internal control over financial reporting, management of a financial institution identifies deficiencies in: the design of controls over the estimation of credit losses (a critical accounting estimate); the operating effectiveness of controls for initiating, processing, and reviewing adjustments to the allowance for credit losses; and the operating effectiveness of controls designed to prevent and detect the improper recognition of interest income. Management and the auditor agree that, in their overall context, each of these deficiencies individually represent a significant deficiency.

In addition, during the past year, the company experienced a significant level of growth in the loan balances that were subjected to the controls governing credit loss estimation and revenue recognition and further growth is expected in the upcoming year.

Based only on these facts, the auditor should determine that the combination of these significant deficiencies represents a material weakness for the following reasons:

- The balances of the loan accounts affected by these significant deficiencies have increased over the past year and are expected to increase in the future.
- This growth in loan balances, coupled with the combined effect of the significant deficiencies described, results in a more than remote likelihood that a material misstatement of the allowance for credit losses or interest income could occur.

Therefore, in combination, these deficiencies meet the definition of a material weakness.

APPENDIX E

Special Internal Control Over Financial Reporting Considerations for Small and Medium-Sized Companies

E1. Although the five components of internal control over financial reporting apply to every company, regardless of its size, the manner in which each component applies depends on a number of factors, including the:

- Nature and size of the business,
- Diversity and complexity of operations,
- Methods for processing financial information, and
- Applicable legal and regulatory requirements.

E2. The following paragraphs discuss how the five components of internal control over financial reporting might be applied in a typical small or medium-sized company (referred to as a *small company* throughout this section).

E3. *Control Environment.* The integrity of senior management often plays a critical role in establishing a strong control environment in a small company. Because written policies and procedures at such companies often are less complete or less formal than at large companies, the behavior and interaction of senior managers is critical to an effective control environment. For instance, a small company might not monitor developments in corporate governance best practices or maintain codes of conduct that reflect current best practice except for senior financial officers. However, ethical behavior and core values can still exist and be supported by the senior management through their daily interaction with employees.

E4. In a small company, the actions of senior management play an important role in the control environment. Sometimes, senior management interacts directly with external parties such as critical suppliers, vendors, customers, independent auditors, and regulators. For that reason, their integrity and ethical values are critical.

E5. Another component of the control environment is the organizational structure. A company's size, complexity, and operations determine the proper organizational structure for that company. Generally, larger organizations that have several operating divisions with prescribed responsibilities and reporting protocols are structured more formally than small companies that focus on accomplishing business objectives with only a few employees. The challenge in a small company is to ensure that the organizational structure does not hinder the company's ability to produce reliable financial reports and to safeguard assets.

E6. If a company has not formed an audit committee, Section 301 of the Act states that the entire board of directors will be designated as the audit committee.

E7. *Risk Assessment.* Small companies generally have a less formal risk assessment process than larger ones. Fewer layers of management in a small company often results in more timely and direct communication of risks with senior management. Furthermore, senior managers who are directly involved in business operations often have a more in-depth understanding of the company's processes and, thus, are in a much better position to identify problems with them than are senior managers in a larger organization. For instance, managers involved in the company's day-to-day operations are more likely to be aware of risks posed by the following—

- Variances between actual and expected results.
- Problems with operational or financial data.
- Issues and concerns about operational issues, such as production processes, inventory shortages.
- Complaints and other communications received from customers or vendors.
- Communications received from regulators and other third parties.

E8. Also, once risks are identified, a small company might be able to more quickly develop and implement action plans.

E9. *Control Activities.* As with the risk assessment process, although the concept of control activities in a small company is the same as in a larger one, the formality with which the activities operate might be different. Furthermore, because of the active involvement of senior managers, certain control activities might not be necessary. For example, the CFO's careful review of daily sales and key ratios might be just as effective in a small company as lower level control activities that might be found in a larger business. In fact, the CFO's day-to-day involvement in the company goes a long way in identifying and preventing material errors in the financial statements.

E10. Because of the limited number of employees in a small company, segregation of duties is not always possible. However, even small companies with few employees might be able to achieve adequate segregation of duties by assigning responsibilities wisely. If that is not possible, the president or other senior manager usually can provide the necessary control through his or her direct oversight. For example, procedures performed directly by the CFO (such as signing all checks and reviewing all bank statements and reconciliations) might mitigate the lack of segregation of duties in the cash area.

E11. *Information and Communication.* Although it might be less formal, the process of communication in a small company can be both effective and efficient. Effective communication often is easier to achieve in small companies since they usually have fewer layers of management. In fact, communication often takes place through daily discussions with senior management. Such communication usually is not only more frequent but more effective. Nevertheless, even with frequent and effective communications, smaller public companies need effective accounting systems and most will benefit greatly from modest investments in information technology. Indeed, completely manual accounting systems have almost completely disappeared.

E12. *Monitoring.* Similar to many of the other components previously discussed, the monitoring component in a small company is likely to be informal. Generally, a small company does not have an internal audit department or other group that evaluates internal controls throughout the company. Rather, senior managers often perform monitoring procedures as part of their normal, routine tasks. Sometimes, while performing such procedures, they identify a deficiency in internal control over financial reporting. When other employees identify a deficiency, the few layers of management usually simplify determining to whom communication of the deficiency should be made.

¶ 600. Selected Public Comments on the Proposed Standard

¶ 600. Introduction to the Selected Public Comments on the Proposed Standard

After the PCAOB proposed its much-anticipated auditing standard, *An Audit of Internal Control Over Financial Reporting Performed in Conjunction with an Audit of Financial Statements*, on October 7, 2003, the Board received an unprecedented 193 public comment letters. Companies, associations, consultants, audit firms, government agencies, and individuals from around the globe responded to the proposed standard with their opinions and feedback. The level of interest generated by the proposed standard reflects the lasting impact of the Sarbanes-Oxley Act of 2002 and its internal control reporting requirements.

A representative sample of the public comments received by the PCAOB is provided here in order to give the reader an idea of the context in which the PCAOB revised the proposed standard and created a final version. The PCAOB addressed many, but not all, of the issues raised by the interested parties. In Appendix E of the final standard, the PCAOB provides a summary of the reasoning behind some of the changes—or lack of changes.

The 40 public comment letters included here represent the insights and concerns of:

- associations (¶ 601 through ¶ 619);
- public companies (¶ 620 through ¶ 628);
- private companies (¶ 629 and ¶ 630);
- public accounting and consulting firms (¶ 631 through ¶ 637); and
- government agencies (¶ 638 through ¶ 640).

The wide ranges of opinions expressed and subject matter covered demonstrate the complexity of internal control over financial reporting. It remains to be seen how the issuance of the PCAOB's final standard will affect how U.S. and foreign issuers incorporate internal controls in their organizations.

¶ 601. American Bankers Association

1120 Connecticut Avenue, NW
Washington, DC 20036

1-800-BANKERS
www.aba.com

*World-Class Solutions,
Leadership & Advocacy
Since 1875*

Donna Fisher
Director of Tax and
Accounting

Tel: 202-663-5318
Fax: 202-828-4548
dfisher@aba.com

December 10, 2003

Mr. Thomas Ray
Deputy Chief Auditor
Office of the Secretary
Public Company Accounting Oversight Board
1666 K Street, N.W.
Washington, DC 20006-2803

Re: Release No. 2003-17, Rulemaking Docket Matter No. 008 Proposed Auditing
Standard – An Audit of Internal Control Over Financial Reporting Performed in
Conjunction with an Audit of Financial Statements

Dear Mr. Ray,

The American Bankers Association (ABA) is pleased to have this opportunity to
comment on the proposed auditing standard issued by the Public Company
Accounting Oversight Board (PCAOB), "An Audit of Internal Control Over
Financial Reporting Performed in Conjunction with an Audit of Financial
Statements" (the proposal). ABA brings together all categories of banking
institutions to best represent the interests of the rapidly changing industry. Its
membership – which includes community, regional, and money center banks and
holding companies, as well as savings associations, trust companies and savings
banks – makes ABA the largest banking trade association in the country.

The ABA commends the PCAOB on its efforts to establish standards for the audit
of internal controls over financial reporting in conjunction with the audit of the
financial statements as directed under the Sarbanes-Oxley Act of 2002. The banking
industry is unique compared with other industries, as it has been required to follow
rules to maintain strong internal control environments for many years under the
Federal Deposit Insurance Corporation Improvement Act of 1991 (FDICIA).
Strong internal controls are critical, not only to provide users of financial statements
with reasonable assurance about the integrity of financial statements, but also to
provide management with a foundation for appropriately managing the company's
risks.

We are concerned the proposal goes beyond the requirements set forth under the
Sarbanes-Oxley Act and what is prudent at this time. The proposal requires an audit
of internal controls over financial reporting rather than the attestation regarding
management's assessment of internal controls that is required under the Sarbanes-
Oxley Act. We agree with the definition of an attestation in the introduction to the
proposal, which states that: "An attestation, in a general sense, is an expert's
communication of a conclusion about the reliability of someone else's assertion."

This is what was intended in the Sarbanes-Oxley Act, and we believe that the PCAOB should require attestations rather than audits.

During the development of FDICIA, the accounting profession lobbied members of Congress to require that financial institutions provide certifications and accounting firms provide attestations on management assertions. Banking institutions are responsible for maintaining strong internal control environments. Banks document internal control responsibilities of employees, document the functions of internal controls and flow of processes, and test the reliance on internal controls. Since 1991, banks have been required to produce annual reports on internal controls, and external audit firms have assessed the effectiveness of bank internal controls and have attested to these reports. Many hours have been spent among bankers, banking regulators, and representatives from the accounting profession to specifically determine how such attestations were to be achieved. The Sarbanes-Oxley Act used the FDICIA attestation as its model.

The PCAOB's requirement to go beyond an attestation, to require a full audit, significantly alters the requirements under the Sarbanes-Oxley Act and will significantly increase the costs to companies. Audit firms are already quoting exorbitant fees to bankers under the assumption that the PCAOB will require audits rather than attestations. (In fact, audit firms are telling their banking clients that they must follow the PCAOB proposal for 2003 reporting – even though the rule is not final.) The accounting firms have not been able to sufficiently justify to bankers how their procedures will differ, how they are more valuable to shareholders, or specifically why the costs are so excessive.

We strongly suggest that the PCAOB require attestations rather than audits. Many industries, other than banking institutions, will have an enormous amount of work to do to document their internal control systems so that management will have a foundation on which to certify to its internal controls. Piling on the huge additional fees that are being quoted by the accounting firms for audits, as opposed to attestations, is simply unnecessary at this time. We believe that it would be much better for the PCAOB to require attestations, as contemplated during the development of and required by the Sarbanes-Oxely Act. We believe that the quality of attestations will likely improve dramatically even if the PCAOB does not require audits, simply because of the focus that has recently been placed on the accounting profession. Additionally, we respectfully encourage the PCAOB to reconsider the following areas in the proposal:

- External auditors should be permitted to rely on work performed by internal audit when appropriate.
- The walkthrough requirements are excessive and unnecessary.
- The requirement for external auditors to evaluate the effectiveness of audit committee should be removed from the proposal.
- The definitions of "significant deficiency" and "material weakness" are too broad and should be modified.
- "Except for opinions" should be permitted for circumstances involving business combinations or operating system changes.

External auditors can rely on work of others.

The proposal requires certain procedures to be followed by the external auditor to complete an audit of the internal controls over financial reporting. Because of the vast number of tests and extent of the audit, we believe that external auditors will need to be and should be permitted to exercise discretion on the extent to which the external auditor can rely on information provided by internal auditors.

We are concerned that the proposal creates unnecessary work for external auditors, and, frankly, unnecessary costs. Many functions performed by internal auditors within a company are recurring and routine in nature, and to require the external audit firm to prepare its own original documentation is duplicative. Further, if the quality of the internal audit function within a company is deemed to be reliable, there is no reason why the external auditor must duplicate such work. In fact, we would argue that if the external auditor relies on the work of a sound internal audit process, it frees up the auditing firm to focus on the important issue: areas of risk. We believe that the external audit firm, the company, and investors would benefit more by permitting the external audit firm to identify which tests should be performed and exercise professional judgment regarding the completion of the attestation. External auditors should not be prohibited from relying on the work of internal auditors, and should be permitted to use their work when it is prudent to do so.

Walkthroughs are excessive.

The proposal requires external audit firms to perform walkthroughs of all significant processes of a company each year as part of the audit firm's attestation on the effectiveness of internal controls. Banking institutions are required to maintain a reliable internal control environment. Instead of automatically requiring walkthroughs, external audit firms should use professional judgment to determine what additional evidence is needed each year regarding accounts, disclosures, or processes for the audit firm to gather sufficient, competent evidence to attest to management's assertion on internal controls.

External auditors should not assess audit committee.

The proposal requires that the external audit firm assess the effectiveness and independence of the audit committee. This should be eliminated from the proposal. External audit firms are not necessarily equipped to make such an assessment, they are not trained in making these types of evaluations, and there are no rules or guidelines against which firms would make such assessments. Further, this requirement creates a conflict of interest between auditors and audit committees with respect to independence. Under rules issued by the SEC and stock exchanges, the external audit firm reports to the audit committee. The audit committee also has the sole authority to hire and remove the external audit firm and establishes the compensation for the external audit firm. Independence of the accounting firm is also disclosed to shareholders by the Board of Directors for shareholders to evaluate. We believe that the proposal, as drafted, is not workable and should be removed from the proposal.

Definitions of "significant deficiency" and "material weakness" are too prescriptive.

The terms "significant deficiency" and "material weakness" in the proposal are too narrowly defined and could cause unwarranted concern over a company's internal control structure. Defining a material weakness as having a "more than remote likelihood of occurrence" is broad and too low a threshold to assist in evaluating internal control deficiencies.

The American Institute of Certified Public Accountants (AICPA) identified thresholds for evaluating reportable conditions regarding material weaknesses in its Professional Standard AU Section 325 and Standard AT Section 501. Rules issued by the Securities and Exchange Commission pursuant to Section 404 of the Sarbanes-Oxley Act reference the AICPA's Section 325 and Section 501 as the standards that should be used in determining whether a significant deficiency or material weakness exists within a company. We believe that those particular AICPA Standards contain a more clear definition of a reportable material weakness than the definition provided in the PCAOB proposal. We encourage the PCAOB to modify the definitions of "significant deficiency" and "material weakness" to be based on the reasonably likelihood that an internal control would cause a significant or material misstatement of the annual or interim financial statements. In this way, disclosures would be based on a reasonable level and would provide investors with more important and useful information about failures in internal controls. It is important that the definitions be based on reasonable thresholds that would provide reasonable assurance that a failure in internal controls exists.

"Except for opinions" should be permitted.

External audit firms should be permitted to issue "except for" opinions in situations that involve mergers, acquisitions, or systems changes that affect the internal control environment of the bank. During the time when companies engage in mergers or acquisitions, it often takes time for the acquiring company to learn the internal functions of the acquired company, integrate operating systems, and convert internal control processes to the acquiring company. Often, legacy systems are maintained for a brief period of time until systems can be transitioned to the surviving company. There can also be situations near the end of the reporting cycle that would make it difficult for the acquiring company to consolidate, evaluate, and certify the internal control environment of the combined company. In these situations, it may not be possible for the audit firm to conduct a comprehensive evaluation of the combined company's internal controls, and external audit firms should be given permission to issue "except for" opinions on the attestation on the combined company's internal control environment.

In conclusion, we believe that the PCAOB should require attestations rather than audits. We believe that external auditors should be permitted to rely on work performed by internal audit when appropriate and that external auditors should evaluate processes in order to determine whether walkthroughs on all processes are needed. The requirement for external auditors to evaluate the effectiveness of audit committees should be removed from the proposal. The definitions of "significant deficiency" and "material weakness" are too narrow and should be modified to provide users of financial statements with useful and meaningful information. Last, we believe that "except for opinions" should be permitted for circumstances involving business combinations or operating system changes.

Thank you for the opportunity to comment on this proposal and for your consideration. If you would like to discuss this letter in more detail, please contact me at 202-663-5318.

Sincerely,

Donna Fisher

¶ 602. American Bar Association

AMERICAN BAR ASSOCIATION
Section of Business Law
750 North Lake Shore Drive
Chicago, IL 60611

December 2, 2003

Office of the Secretary
Public Company Accounting Oversight Board
1666 K Street, N.W.
Washington, D.C. 20006-2803

Re: PCAOB Rulemaking Docket Matter No. 008

Dear Board Members:

On behalf of the Committee on Law and Accounting and the Committee on Federal Regulation of Securities, Section of Business Law of the American Bar Association (jointly, the "Committees"), we are pleased to have the opportunity to comment on the Public Company Accounting Oversight Board's (the "PCAOB") proposed auditing standards relating to audits of internal control over financial reporting (the "Proposed Standards").

The comments expressed in this letter represent the views of the Committees only and have not been approved by the American Bar Association's House of Delegates or Board of Governors and therefore do not represent the official position of the ABA. In addition, they do not represent the official position of the ABA Section of Business Law, nor do they necessarily reflect the views of all members of the Committees.

The Committees recognize the PCAOB's obligation to implement the legislative mandate of Sections 103(a)(2)(iii) and 404(b) of the Sarbanes-Oxley Act of 2002 ("Sarbanes-Oxley") and support the PCAOB's overall approach in the Proposed Standards. While the Committees believe that the Proposed Standards should achieve the goal of ensuring the confidence of the investing public in the integrity of public companies' internal control over financial reporting, highlighted below are certain aspects of the PCAOB's proposals with which the Committees do not agree and our suggestions that are intended to clarify the Proposed Standards.

Office of the Secretary
Public Company Accounting Oversight Board
December 2, 2003
Page 2

I.   Audit Committee Proposals.

The Committees acknowledge the central role of the audit committee in the oversight of a company's financial reporting process. However, we believe that the proposed attestation standards relating to the audit committee are not consistent with the requirement that the audit committee appoint and oversee the outside auditors.

Under Section 301 of Sarbanes-Oxley and the rules and regulations promulgated thereunder by the Securities and Exchange Commission (the "SEC"), the New York Stock Exchange and The Nasdaq Stock Market (the "SROs"), a listed company's audit committee is directly responsible for the appointment, compensation and oversight of the work of the company's outside auditors. Because of the direct supervision obligations that have been imposed on such audit committees by Congress, the Proposed Standards appear flawed and circular in their requirement that the very body that is directly responsible for appointing and determining compensation of the outside auditors, as well as directly overseeing their work, would be subject, in turn, to that outside auditors' scrutiny as part of its audit of internal control over financial reporting.

In addition, we believe that a weakness in the oversight by the audit committee of the financial reporting process may suggest a deficiency in the way the outside auditors manage their relationship with the audit committee. Such a deficiency should be addressed by the outside auditors through better communication with the audit committee. If such dialogue does not improve the effectiveness of the audit committee, the outside auditors should consider resigning.

We disagree with the identification in Paragraph 53 of the activities of the audit committee as an example of the activities that the outside auditors should evaluate as a part of the "monitoring of controls." The audit committee's oversight role is not comparable to the monitoring role of the internal audit function, the CEO and CFO certification process or any other process that a company follows to ensure the adequacy of its financial disclosures, including as a result of the certifications required by Sections 302 and 906 of Sarbanes-Oxley. In our opinion, it is more appropriate for any evaluation of the audit committee's oversight role to be considered in connection with a general review of a company's control environment.

In our view, not only are the proposed attestation procedures relating to the audit committee not contemplated by Sarbanes-Oxley, they may be duplicative of the responsibilities imposed and enforced by the SEC, the SROs, state law and stockholders on boards of directors and audit committees. Moreover, some of these proposed procedures would require that the outside auditors make legal judgments and therefore not judgments within their expertise. We specifically recommend deleting, or revising, if not deleting, the following proposed procedures:

Office of the Secretary
Public Company Accounting Oversight Board
December 2, 2003
Page 3

- Paragraph 57 of the Proposed Standards would require the outside auditors to evaluate the independence of the audit committee as one of the factors related to the effectiveness of the audit committee's oversight of external financial reporting and internal control over financial reporting. In evaluating the audit committee's independence, Paragraph 58 of the Proposed Standards would require the outside auditors to evaluate how audit committee members are nominated and selected and whether they act independently from management. We do not agree with, and are troubled by, the conclusion in Paragraph 58 that audit committee members are more likely to be independent if they are nominated through an independent process. More importantly, the evaluation of independence is more properly a corporate governance matter, which is governed by the mandates of Section 301 of Sarbanes-Oxley, state law, SEC regulations and listing standards (as acknowledged by the PCAOB in Footnote 13 to the Proposed Standards), than a matter for the outside auditors in the context of their evaluation of internal control. Boards of directors are required by applicable listing standards to make an affirmative determination of independence for each outside director. Furthermore, a recently-adopted SEC rule that addresses, in part, disclosure relating to nominating committee functions, will result in significant public disclosure of the details surrounding a company's nomination process. See SEC Release No. 33-8340 (November 24, 2003). Therefore, the Committees find it an unnecessarily duplicative and costly requirement, and one with respect to which the outside auditors lack expertise, for the outside auditors to evaluate matters of director independence. Moreover, because the audit committee is established by the board of directors, which has the ability and responsibility to replace committee members and alter the audit committee charter as necessary or appropriate, the board of directors is the proper body to evaluate the audit committee's performance.

- Paragraph 57 would require the outside auditors to evaluate the clarity with which the audit committee's responsibilities are articulated and how well the audit committee and management understand those responsibilities. We assume that this factor would require a review of the audit committee charter, which is a publicly-filed document available to stockholders. We believe that the review of the charter by the outside auditors and evaluation of whether the audit committee and management understand those responsibilities are matters more appropriately covered by the board self-assessment process and are not matters within the expertise of the outside auditors.

- Paragraph 57 would require the outside auditors to evaluate the level of involvement and interaction of the audit committee with the outside auditors, including the audit committee's role in their appointment, retention and compensation. This circular requirement could create conflicts of interest for the audit committee. As noted above, audit committees of listed committees will be required by law to perform these duties.

- Paragraph 57 would require the outside auditors to evaluate the level of involvement and interaction of the audit committee with the internal audit department, including

Office of the Secretary
Public Company Accounting Oversight Board
December 2, 2003
Page 4

the audit committee's line of authority and role in appointing and compensating employees in the internal audit function. In addition, Paragraph 24 identifies the internal audit activity as a control intended to address the risks of fraud. These Paragraphs assume, incorrectly, that all companies have an internal audit function. While NYSE-listed companies are required by the new corporate governance listing standards to have an internal auditor function, NYSE-listed companies are permitted to outsource the internal auditor function and Nasdaq-listed companies and other companies are not so required. Therefore, this requirement, if retained, should be revised to acknowledge that some companies may not have employees performing internal audit functions or may not have, and may not need to have, an internal audit function at all.

- Paragraph 57 would require the outside auditors to evaluate the audit committee's compliance with applicable listing standards adopted pursuant to Section 301 of Sarbanes-Oxley. As noted above, this is a circular requirement and one that would be inconsistent with Rule 10A-3 promulgated under the Securities Exchange Act of 1934, as amended, under which audit committees must comply with applicable listing standards or face delisting.

- Paragraph 57 would require the outside auditors to evaluate whether the audit committee has an audit committee financial expert. Besides the fact that this information is required to be disclosed in a company's public filings, we question whether the existence of an audit committee financial expert is probative of whether an audit committee is functioning appropriately.

- Paragraph 57 would require the outside auditors to evaluate the amount of time the audit committee devotes to control issues and other committee activities. An evaluation of the time spent would be incomplete absent discussions with the members of the audit committee to determine the time that each member spends preparing for audit committee meetings. Interviewing audit committee members to determine this accurately does not seem like a good use of auditor time. In addition, the time spent by the audit committee is of far less importance to the evaluation of the oversight role played by the audit committee than the way in which that time was used. Intense analytical discussions about accounting or internal control issues during a four-hour period among fully prepared audit committee members will result in far more effective oversight than unfocused discussions between audit committee members who are not prepared to discuss the issues. We believe this proposal should be deleted. If it is retained, we request that the PCAOB consider revising the language to focus on the audit committee's quality of participation in committee activities rather than the amount of time the members devote to those activities.

- Paragraph 72 would require the outside auditors to evaluate the nature and extent of the audit committee's involvement in the period-end financial reporting process. This evaluation would appear to require, with respect to NYSE-listed companies, an

Office of the Secretary
Public Company Accounting Oversight Board
December 2, 2003
Page 5

evaluation of compliance with listing standards, a legal judgment. Furthermore, because the audit committee's period-end evaluation process significantly depends upon input from and interaction with the outside auditors, we are not certain what is contemplated by the inclusion of this factor as an auditing standard.

Finally, we believe that the Proposed Standards inappropriately broaden or characterize the scope of audit committee duties. In some cases, the Proposed Standards go beyond what the law requires. For example, Paragraph 24 of the Proposed Standards suggests that the audit committee is responsible for monitoring the code of conduct. Although the audit committee often has this responsibility, it is not required under applicable listing standards and regulations or any state or federal law. In addition, the reference in Paragraphs 34 and 35 of the Proposed Standards to the audit committee's responsibilities with respect to the outside auditors' independence could be understood to suggest a shift to the audit committee of some of the outside auditors' independent burden to determine its own independence.

II.   <u>Issues Related to the Scope of the Audit.</u>

The Committees agree that the process of auditing internal control over financial reporting should be done in connection with audit of the financial statements and will require more than just merely acknowledging that auditor agrees with management's assessment. Audit fees appear to have increased significantly since 2002, and costs associated with an audit of internal controls will surely result in substantial additional increases in audit fees. We urge the PCAOB to consider ways to reduce the scope of the procedures required by the Proposed Standards, and thereby reduce the attendant costs to reporting companies, to more closely tailor the procedures to those required by Sarbanes-Oxley without adversely affecting the quality of the internal control audit.

Mindful of mounting compliance costs, the Committees submit that certain of the approaches contemplated by the Proposed Standards appear to be duplicative of other procedures and, therefore, unnecessary. In addition, the Proposed Standards require a great deal of origination of supporting evidence by the outside auditors. For those procedures that are necessary in the audit process, we generally support, where appropriate, greater permissibility of the outside auditors' use of professional judgment in determining the extent to which reliance on the work performed by the internal auditors is appropriate.

The PCAOB states on page eight of the Summary of the Proposed Standards that: "the more extensive and reliable management's assessment is, the less extensive and costly the auditor's work will need to be." We agree with the appropriateness of this approach but, as drafted, the outside auditors do not appear to be permitted to rely very much on management's work at all. Therefore, we question the conclusion that the Proposed Standards will permit the outside auditor's work to be less extensive if management's assessment is relatively more complete. Given that management's

Office of the Secretary
Public Company Accounting Oversight Board
December 2, 2003
Page 6

assessment is at a level of "reasonable assurance," which "includes the understanding that there is a relatively low risk that material misstatements will not be prevented or detected on a timely basis" (as contemplated by Paragraph 16 of the Proposed Standards), we also recommend that the Proposed Standards permit a reasonableness evaluation by the outside auditors in determining what procedures are required in the audit.

As noted above, the Proposed Standards require that a great deal of the supporting evidence for the outside auditors' opinion originate with the outside auditor. However, Paragraph 109 of the Proposed Standards is unclear as to whether all "principal evidence" must originate with the outside auditors.

We also question whether the procedures called for by the Proposed Standards ought to be required to be performed on an annual basis and whether the same level of testing each year is really necessary to justify the additional expense of such testing. It may be more appropriate to permit the outside auditors to use the previous year's audit evidence in some cases. However, with increased reliance on internal auditors, as discussed below, annual testing may be more acceptable.

Where appropriate, the PCAOB should consider permitting more reliance on the internal auditors' work once the outside auditors confirm their understanding of internal control over financial reporting and test the internal auditors' tests. We note that Statements on Auditing Standards Number 65, *The Auditor's Consideration of the Internal Audit Function in an Audit of Financial Statements*, provides well-established guidance to outside auditors in determining the nature, timing and extent of auditing procedures to be performed in an audit of an entity's financial statements. We would suggest that the PCAOB consider allowing outside auditors to use the same or similar criteria in assessing the appropriateness of reliance on the work of the internal auditors in connection with an internal control audit, even with respect to matters covered in Paragraphs 104 and 105 of the Proposed Standards. To do otherwise could result in unnecessary re-testing of controls. If an internal auditor follows applicable professional standards, reports to the audit committee, is deemed independent of management and is considered by the outside auditors to do reliable work, reliance ought to be permitted consistent with current practice.

One of the procedures called for by the Proposed Standards with respect to which the outside auditors would be precluded from relying on others is the proposed requirement that the outside auditors perform "walkthroughs" in the audit process. To the extent that it is reasonable for the outside auditors to rely upon the work of the internal auditors, the outside auditors should be permitted to rely, to a significant extent, on walkthroughs that have already been completed. That said, if a walkthrough is required as part of the final standards, the PCAOB should consider whether it is necessary and cost-effective to extend that procedure to all of the company's significant processes and include all types of company transactions and events, both routine and unusual, as is currently required by Paragraph 79 of the Proposed Standards.

Office of the Secretary
Public Company Accounting Oversight Board
December 2, 2003
Page 7

In our opinion, additional reliance could also be placed on management's work or the work of third parties where the outside auditors appropriately test the work to evaluate the extent to which the outside auditors could reasonably rely upon it. We encourage the PCAOB to consider whether that approach could be permitted in the following specific areas:

- The identification of significant accounts as contemplated by Paragraph 60.
- The identification of relevant financial statement assertions as contemplated by Paragraph 66.
- The identification of significant processes as contemplated by Paragraph 69.
- The identification of controls to test as contemplated by Paragraph 74.
- The evaluation of the use of work performed by management and others as contemplated by Paragraph 103.

We also question the proposal to broaden the responsibilities of the outside auditors to include disclosures outside the financial statements. Paragraph 184 would require the outside auditors to "evaluate" with management appropriate disclosure about a change in internal control over financial reporting resulting from the need to correct a material weakness. It may be more appropriate to require a "review" rather than an "evaluation," as the latter would appear to come very close to requiring the outside auditors to act in a managerial capacity.

We recommend that the Proposed Standards address the attestation and reporting requirements when a company's internal control over financial reporting has not been fully reviewed and appropriately modified after a merger, acquisition or corporate restructuring that took place too close to the end of the fiscal year for such a review to have been completed. For example, the requirement in Paragraph 128 for management representations should acknowledge and provide guidance as to how to respond when management may be unable to make the necessary representations as to the internal controls. In addition, in such circumstances, a qualified opinion or "except for" opinion should be acceptable rather than an adverse opinion, which is what the Proposed Standards would require.

A qualified opinion can be useful to convey information to stockholders that would otherwise not be conveyed by a blanket adverse opinion. In addition to a qualified opinion providing more meaningful information about the impact of a recent acquisition or restructuring on a company than an adverse opinion, a qualified opinion may be preferable to an adverse opinion in other contexts. For example, it could highlight that a deficiency is confined to one business segment.

Finally, we question the requirement in Paragraph 145 of the Proposed Standards that the outside auditors' documentation of their attestation work include an evaluation of

Office of the Secretary
Public Company Accounting Oversight Board
December 2, 2003
Page 8

all deficiencies. We encourage the PCAOB to consider whether the documentation needs to include an evaluation of deficiencies other than "significant deficiencies."

III.   Clarification of Definitions.

We are concerned about the clarity and potential consequences of the proposed definitions of "significant deficiency" and "material weakness." Not only has the PCAOB not used the definitions in existing generally accepted auditing standards ("GAAS") (AU Sections 325 and 501) of "reportable condition" and "material weakness," but the PCAOB has also not explained how the proposed definitions would differ from the existing terms under GAAS. Moreover, the PCAOB's use of the term "more than a remote likelihood" in the proposed definitions would appear to be a lower standard than existing GAAS and would require many more deficiencies in internal control to be identified as "significant" or as "material weaknesses" than under current GAAS.

In view of the severe consequences to a company if its internal control over financial reporting is considered to have significant deficiencies or material weaknesses, we recommend that the definitions be clarified to be consistent with existing GAAS. In addition, we recommend that the PCAOB provide further examples of significant deficiencies and material weaknesses to enhance the likelihood of more consistent conclusions by outside auditors as to the types of deficiencies in internal control that should be considered to be significant deficiencies or material weaknesses. Such guidance would be particularly important with respect to the independence and effectiveness of the audit committee if the PCAOB retains the attestation procedures related to the independence and effectiveness of the audit committee.

Thank you for your consideration of our comments on this important matter. Please do not hesitate to contact the undersigned with any questions you may have.

Cordially,

/s/ Thomas L. Riesenberg

Thomas L. Riesenberg,
Chair of the Committee on Law and Accounting of the American Bar Association, Section of Business Law

/s/ Dixie L. Johnson

Dixie L. Johnson,
Chair of the Committee on Federal Regulation of Securities of the American Bar Association, Section of Business Law

Office of the Secretary
Public Company Accounting Oversight Board
December 2, 2003
Page 9

cc: Drafting Committee:
           Linda L. Griggs, Chair
           Susan Blount
           John T. Bostelman
           Richard E. Gutman
           Stanley Keller
           Sam Scott Miller
           John F. Olson
           Richard H. Rowe

¶ 603. American Institute of Certified Public Accountants

November 21, 2003

Office of the Secretary
Public Company Accounting Oversight Board
1666 K Street, N.W.
Washington, D.C. 20006-2803

RE: **PCAOB Rulemaking Docket Matter No. 008**

        Proposed Auditing Standard, *An Audit of Internal Control Over Financial Reporting Performed in Conjunction With an Audit of Financial Statements*

Dear Mr. Secretary:

The American Institute of Certified Public Accountants ("AICPA") respectfully submits the following written comments on the Public Company Accounting Oversight Board's ("PCAOB" or "Board") proposed auditing standard (the proposed standard) governing the independent auditor's attestation and reporting on management's assessment of the effectiveness of internal control over financial reporting pursuant to Section 103(a)(2)(A) of the Sarbanes-Oxley Act of 2002 ("the Act"). Our comments reflect our views as they pertain to audits of issuers subject to the Act and do not necessarily reflect our viewpoint for audits of nonissuers. The AICPA is the largest professional association of Certified Public Accountants in the United States, with more than 330,000 members in public practice, business, industry, government, and education.

Executive Summary

The AICPA has long supported reporting on the effectiveness of internal control over financial reporting by public companies accompanied by auditor attestation because effective internal control is a critical component of reliable financial reporting. We believe that this practice will lead to increased quality in the preparation of financial statements.

The AICPA recognizes the enormous effort put forth by the PCAOB members and staff to implement the provisions of the Act. Initially, a significant responsibility of the PCAOB will be to help restore public confidence in audited financial statements of public companies. The establishment and maintenance of high quality auditing and other professional standards is critical to that goal. The AICPA is committed to working cooperatively with the PCAOB in the continuous improvement of high quality audit standards.

We believe that incorporating our recommendations into the final standard will enhance auditors' reports for users and also will significantly improve implementation of the requirements of the Act both by auditors and issuers. The following are among our more significant recommendations:

- **Retain the auditor's option to express either a qualified opinion or an adverse opinion when there is a material weakness in internal control over financial reporting.** Reporting options provide better, more flexible disclosure and thus are more informative for users of the report. We believe reporting alternatives also are consistent with the Securities and Exchange Commission's ("SEC") reporting guidance for management.

- **Identify and communicate to the profession and to the public *all* areas where proposed requirements diverge from existing requirements in the Board's interim standards.** Some significant changes have been made that relate to audit areas other than internal control over

American Institute of Certified Public Accountants
1211 Avenue of the Americas, New York, NY 10036-8775 • (212) 596-6200 • fax (212) 596-6213 • www.aicpa.org
ISO 9001 Certified

financial reporting. These modifications are not discussed in the introductory material to the proposed standard and easily could be overlooked by auditors.

- **Require the auditor to assess the effectiveness of the audit committee within the consideration of the overall control environment instead of as a separate evaluation.** The audit committee is only one element of the control environment and its effectiveness should be assessed as part of the overall control environment. In addition, the criteria to assess this element of the control environment should be clarified and strengthened.

- **Change the requirement that the auditor, in performing walkthroughs, should trace *all* types of transactions and events, both recurring and unusual, from origination to reflection in the financial reports.** This requirement excludes any consideration of materiality, removes auditor judgment, and will be costly to implement with little incremental benefit. We believe that the auditor should perform independent walkthroughs for all the company's significant processes and for *significant* events and transactions.

- **Work in conjunction with the SEC to develop more definitive guidance about management's extent of testing.** Issuers appear to hold widely differing views about the extent of tests of controls that is appropriate to provide sufficient evidence to support management's assessment. We urge the PCAOB to coordinate with the SEC on the issuance of guidance on management's extent of testing.

Specific Recommendations

Forming an Opinion and Reporting

We strongly believe that the auditor should be permitted to express either a qualified opinion or an adverse opinion when there is a material weakness in internal control because these different reporting options are more informative for users of the auditor's report. We also believe that permitting these reporting options is consistent with the SEC's reporting guidance for management.

The SEC's release on the final rules implementing section 404 "preclude management from determining that a company's internal control over financial reporting is effective if it identifies one or more material weaknesses in the company's internal control over financial reporting." Footnote 72 at this sentence states that "this is consistent with interim attestation standards. See AT § 501."We agree with the above conclusion and with paragraph 37 of AT section 501 in the Board's interim standards which states:

> . . . the presence of a material weakness will preclude the practitioner from concluding that the entity has effective internal control. However, depending on the significance of the material weakness and its effect on the achievement of the objectives of the control criteria, the practitioner may qualify his or her opinion (that is, express an opinion that internal control is effective "except for" the material weakness noted) or may express an adverse opinion.

Accordingly, we believe that the SEC's final rule does not preclude management's expression of a qualified "except for" conclusion about the effectiveness of its internal control over financial reporting, depending on the significance of the material weakness, consistent with the above guidance.

Alternative reporting options that are based on the significance of the material weakness and its effect on the achievement of the objectives of the control criteria provide better, more flexible disclosure that is more informative for users of the report. In some circumstances, the auditor may conclude that the effect of one or more material weaknesses on the achievement of the objectives of the control criteria is pervasive enough that it renders internal control, taken as a whole, ineffective. An example of such a material weakness might be the existence of multiple material weaknesses in several different applications. In such circumstances, an adverse opinion that "internal control over financial reporting is not effective in all material respects" is appropriate and communicates to users of the report the gravity of the effect of the material weakness on achieving the entity's overall internal control objectives.

In other circumstances, the auditor may conclude that the effect of the material weakness on the achievement of the objectives of the control criteria is more isolated and does not result in ineffective internal control taken as a whole. An example of such a material weakness might be inadequate controls at a subsidiary that the company acquired in the last week of the year. In such circumstances, the auditor may determine that an adverse opinion is not appropriate, and perhaps potentially misleading, because the significance of the material weakness is not pervasive enough to warrant a conclusion that internal control, taken as a whole, is ineffective. In such circumstances, the auditor may determine that a qualified, "except for," opinion, such as the following from paragraph 55 of AT section 501 in the Board's interim standards, is more appropriate, and also more informative for users of the report, than a conclusion that "internal control is not effective":

> In our opinion, except for the effect of the material weakness described in the preceding paragraph on the achievement of the objectives of the control criteria, W Company has maintained, in all material respects, effective internal control over financial reporting as of December 31, 20X3, based on [identify criteria].

In addition, we believe that the requirement always to express an adverse opinion when there is a material weakness places smaller companies at a disadvantage since smaller companies may be more predisposed to have specific material weaknesses that are not pervasive. In such circumstances we believe that a qualified "except for" report is more informative for investors.

We agree that when the auditor issues a non-standard opinion, such as a qualified or adverse opinion, the auditor's opinion should speak directly to the effectiveness of the internal control rather than to whether management's assertion about the effectiveness of internal control is fairly stated.

Process for Identifying and Communicating Changes to Various Interim Standards

We note areas where guidance in the Board's interim standards has been modified in subtle but significant ways, particularly with regard to substantive procedures. For example, paragraph 138 states that "the auditor should perform substantive procedures *for all relevant assertions* [italics added] for all significant accounts and disclosures." As additional examples, paragraph 141 states that "the auditor's substantive procedures must include reconciling the financial statements to the accounting records;" and paragraph 140 states that "for significant risks of material misstatement, it is unlikely that audit evidence obtained from substantive analytical procedures alone will be sufficient."

Our comment does not relate to the substance of the proposed changes, but to the process by which these proposed changes have been identified and communicated. We believe that proposed standards should identify and communicate to the profession and to the public how requirements diverge from existing requirements and how issuance of the standard would affect existing standards. The introductory discussion of the proposed standard appropriately focuses on reporting on internal control. However, it fails to mention other changes in auditing requirements, some of which auditors would consider to be significant. Furthermore, since some of these changes are only a sentence or two in a document that is over 100 pages in length, they easily could be overlooked.

Accordingly, we strongly urge the PCAOB to highlight in the final standard all such changes to existing requirements and describe how the issuance of this proposed standard affects the Board's existing interim standards.

Evaluating the Effectiveness of the Audit Committee's Oversight

Office of the Secretary
November 21, 2003
Page 4 of 17

We agree that the audit committee, which along with the board of directors comprises one of the factors of the control environment in the Committee of Sponsoring Organizations of the Treadway Commission's report, *Internal Control—Integrated Framework* (the COSO report), plays a significant role in the oversight of a company's internal control over financial reporting and in creating a positive "tone at the top." Accordingly, we believe that the auditor's responsibility to evaluate the control environment encompasses consideration of factors about the board of directors and the audit committee such as those outlined on pages 26 and 27 of the COSO report. Even though the auditor evaluates the control environment in its totality and does not separately conclude on any single element of the control environment, we do agree that the importance of those who govern is such that their overall ineffectiveness generally would lead to a conclusion that the control environment is ineffective. Therefore, we recommend that the proposed standard be revised to require the auditor to assess the audit committee's effectiveness as part of evaluating the company's overall control environment which includes those who govern. We also believe that it is the responsibility of the board of directors to evaluate the effectiveness of the overall board including the audit committee.

In order to achieve more consistent and effective assessment of the audit committee as part of the auditor's evaluation of the overall control environment, we also believe that the PCAOB should clarify and strengthen the guidance in paragraph 57. For example, some of the factors that the auditor would be required to assess in paragraph 57 of the proposed standard could be subject to inconsistent interpretation. Since the auditor does not have unfettered access to the audit committee, the auditor's ability to assess the committee's commitment of time to its activities or to internal control and to evaluate the involvement and interaction with external and internal auditors would be difficult and additionally may not be a meaningful measure of the audit committee's effectiveness. It presumes that levels of time and interaction are measurable when in reality each situation will call for different efforts and degrees of involvement. Therefore, to assess effectiveness against levels of time, effort, and interaction is neither appropriate nor effective.

In addition, in the first bullet of paragraph 57 or in paragraph 58, "independence" should be specifically defined so that everyone is using the same criteria to assess it. The second bullet of paragraph 57 should be clarified to identify potential written sources (for example, the charter) that would be expected to enumerate the audit committee's responsibilities. Finally, we believe that the audit committee's "compliance with applicable listing standards adopted pursuant to Section 301 of the Act" and "whether the committee includes one or more financial experts as described in Section 407 of the Act" (the fifth and sixth bullets) are matters for legal determination and outside the scope of the auditor's responsibility.

As discussed above, the auditor does not have unlimited access to the audit committee. Therefore, if the PCAOB retains the requirement that the auditor make a separate evaluation of the audit committee, we recommend that the PCAOB require the auditor to obtain a written representation from the audit committee in order to facilitate the auditor's obtaining the additional evidence necessary to support this evaluation. At a minimum, such a letter must be signed by the chair of the audit committee. An audit committee's refusal to furnish written representations constitutes a scope limitation.

Because we agree that an effective audit committee is an important element of the control environment, we also believe that management should be required to assess the audit committee as part of its assessment of the overall control environment. Accordingly, the PCAOB should require that the auditor obtain from management its assessment of the audit committee and consider that assessment in forming the auditor's opinion.

Finally, in response to question 24, we strongly believe it would be a disservice to investors and to the public to require the auditor to withdraw from an audit engagement because the auditor has concluded that the audit committee is ineffective. The auditor always has the option to withdraw from an engagement. Requiring that action, however, does not appear to be in anyone's interest. The auditor could still express an unqualified opinion on the financial statements. Furthermore, the communication of the material weakness(es) that resulted in the adverse opinion is useful information to the public.

Office of the Secretary
November 21, 2003
Page 5 of 17

Walkthroughs

We believe walkthroughs have always been an important part of the auditor's evaluation of internal control. We therefore support the PCAOB's requirement that the auditor perform walkthroughs "for all of the company's significant processes."

However, the requirement that the auditor "should trace *all* types of transactions and events, both recurring and unusual, from origination through the company's information systems until they are reflected in the company's financial reports" appears to be an additional requirement which is separate from the discussion of significant processes and which is unnecessarily onerous given that it potentially encompasses hundreds of immaterial types of transactions and events. As stated later in this letter in the discussion of the use of the term "all," a requirement related to all of a population by its nature excludes any consideration of materiality, removes auditor judgment, and will be costly to implement with little incremental benefit. We do not believe the auditor needs to walk through every immaterial or insignificant event and transaction within a significant process in order to identify risks that could create a material misstatement of the financial statements.

Furthermore, we do not believe the concept of significant processes that appears in paragraph 79 is consistent with that in paragraph 69. Paragraph 69 states that "the auditor should identify each significant process over each major class of transactions affecting significant accounts or groups of accounts." This suggests that the processes that are of concern to the auditor are those that are both significant and also are related to major classes of transactions affecting significant accounts or groups of accounts. We believe that this guidance is appropriate. The discussion of significant processes in paragraph 79, however, seems to have lost the notion of relatedness to major classes of transactions affecting significant accounts or groups of accounts. We believe that the guidance in paragraph 79 should be clarified and made consistent with that in paragraph 69.

In order to achieve the objectives described in paragraph 79, we believe that the auditor should perform independent walkthroughs for all the company's significant processes and for *significant* events and transactions. We do not believe the auditor should be required to perform independent walkthroughs for insignificant events and transactions.

Consideration of Management's Extent of Testing

There is considerable confusion among issuers about the extent of testing that management must perform in order to obtain sufficient evidence to support management's assessment. There appears to be a wide range of views among issuers as to what the appropriate levels of testing should be, including how monitoring controls and other aspects of the control environment affect the extent of testing. We believe that the PCAOB should work with the SEC to develop some definitive guidance for preparers. Furthermore, such guidance needs to make it clear that the auditor's testing cannot be used as the basis for management's assertion about the effectiveness of internal control.

In general, and as it relates to control activities in particular, we believe that management's extent of testing needs to be, *at a minimum*, at the same level as the auditor's in order for management to have sufficient evidence to provide a basis for its assessment. This concept needs to be applied on an overall basis. It should recognize that the controls tested and the nature of tests might differ, however, management's testing needs to provide the same level of reasonable assurance that is required of the auditor, and therefore the level of evidence to support management's assessment should be at least equal to the level of evidence obtained by the auditor.

Paragraph 125 of the proposed standard states:

> Inadequate documentation of the design of controls *and the absence of sufficient documented evidence to support management's assessment of the operating effectiveness of internal*

> *control over financial reporting* [italics added] also are internal control deficiencies. As with other internal control deficiencies, the auditor should evaluate these deficiencies as to their significance.

We believe that the above guidance should be expanded to address the extent of testing. We also believe that the proposed standard should require that the absence of sufficient evidence to support the responsible party's evaluation of the operating effectiveness of internal control constitutes either a significant deficiency or a material weakness because the monitoring component of internal control cannot be demonstrated in the absence of sufficient evidence to support management's assertion. Accordingly, we believe that the absence of sufficient evidence to support management's assessment should be added to the list of circumstances in paragraph 126 that is a strong indicator of a material weakness.

Considerations for Small and Medium-Sized Issuers

Page 6 of the introductory discussion in the proposed standard states:

> The Board is sensitive to the possible effects of the proposed standard on small and medium-sized companies . . . For a smaller, less complex company, the Board expects that the auditor will exercise reasonable professional judgment in determining the extent of the audit of internal control and perform only those tests that are necessary to ascertain the effectiveness of the company's internal control.

We agree with this statement because we believe that, *regardless of entity size and complexity*, the auditor should exercise reasonable professional judgment in determining the extent of the audit of internal control and perform only those tests that are necessary to ascertain the effectiveness of the entity's internal control. We are concerned, however, that the PCAOB's statement above will create an expectation among smaller issuers that the auditor should apply to audits of smaller entities a lower standard concerning sufficiency of evidence. Appendix E also appears to create a lower standard of internal control for smaller issuers that may be inappropriately interpreted by some as a justification for giving inadequate attention to their assessment of internal control.

Appendix E focuses primarily on the lack of formality in implementing various components of internal control at smaller companies. While this may be valid, the examples that are given fail to describe sufficiently what kinds of controls are likely to be different in smaller issuers, and importantly, what kinds of compensating controls can smaller issuers implement to overcome potential control deficiencies. For example, paragraph E9 suggests that a "CFO's careful review of daily sales and key ratios might be just as effective in a small company as lower level control activities that might be found in a larger business." We do not believe that such a review is an adequate compensating control that would appropriately address all relevant financial statement assertions. Additionally, we believe the discussion throughout Appendix E substantially overemphasizes the benefits of direct interaction by senior management with employees in smaller entities as a compensating control.

Paragraph 27 states that:

> . . . the auditor must obtain sufficient competent evidence about the design and operating effectiveness of controls related to all relevant financial statement assertions for all significant accounts and disclosures in the financial statements.

We believe that the above requirement or objective applies to small, medium-sized, and large issuers. It is important for the auditor to understand the difference of auditing internal control over financial reporting in a smaller less formal setting than a highly complex large organization. However, we believe the proposed guidance does not adequately emphasize that the auditor of small entities is still required to meet the objective of paragraph 27 and to evaluate design and operating effectiveness for all relevant assertions for all significant accounts and disclosures.

Office of the Secretary
November 21, 2003
Page 7 of 17

Finally, Appendix E provides *no* guidance on how the auditor might tailor his or her procedures for smaller issuers. Some examples of how this may be done and still meet the objective set forth in paragraph 27 would be helpful.

Safeguarding of Assets

The guidance in Appendix C of the proposed standard should be significantly enhanced. As currently written, it is not sufficient to answer the questions that are arising in practice about which controls over safeguarding of assets are within the scope of internal control over financial reporting, and which are not. Following are several examples where it would be difficult to conclude, using the guidance provided in Appendix C, that management or the auditor should be concerned about the effectiveness of the controls related to safeguarding the selected assets.

Retail Inventory Shrinkage. A retail client has made a cost-benefit decision not to install theft prevention techniques (for example, tagged clothing and security devices at entrances) in their retail stores. Actual shrinkage in each store ranges from 5-10 percent of inventory on a monthly basis. Are the controls related to theft prevention part of internal control over financial reporting? If so, does the lack of controls over inventory shrinkage represent a significant deficiency or a material weakness if management takes a quarterly physical inventory and properly records the shrinkage?

Music Piracy. The auditor has a client that produces music for sale on CDs. Customers copy the CDs and make them available over Internet sites that allow for file swapping. Technology exists that allows the CDs to be encrypted in such a way that they cannot be copied. Management makes a decision not to encrypt the CDs because they do not want to alienate their customers.

Does management's decision not to encrypt the CDs (and thus not protect the related asset – music) fall within internal control over financial reporting? If so, does it represent a significant deficiency or a material weakness?

Disaster Recovery. A client has made a cost-benefit decision not to provide controls for adequate disaster recovery. Is management's decision not to provide disaster recovery controls part of internal control over financial reporting? If so, does it represent a significant deficiency or a material weakness? If it is an internal control over financial reporting, how would management and the auditor test disaster recovery?

Insurance Underwriting. Do the controls over accepting risk and pricing an insurance policy fall into controls related to financial reporting? These controls affect the level of risk and therefore the balance sheet reserves required, however, the company has strong controls over setting loss reserves and those controls take into account the level of controls that exist over the underwriting process. Does the lack of such controls represent a significant deficiency or a material weakness?

We believe that none of the examples would be a significant deficiency or a material weakness. The definitions of both significant deficiency and material weakness require there be more than a remote likelihood that a misstatement of the annual or interim financial statements will not be prevented. In the retail and insurance underwriting examples, the company has a detective control (quarterly physical inventories, controls over setting loss reserves, and monthly bank reconciliations) to ensure that the financial statements are not misstated. The music piracy issue and the lack of a formal disaster recovery policy do not result in a misstatement of the financial statements.

Based on the proposed definitions, we do not believe an ineffectiveness issue could be raised in any of the above scenarios since an ineffective system of internal control results only when a material weakness exists, and in these cases no deficiency exists that could cause the financial statements to be misstated. If the PCAOB concludes that these types of controls *do* fall within the definition of internal control over financial reporting, and the lack of such controls results in an ineffective system of internal control over financial reporting, we believe the PCAOB should modify its proposed definitions of internal control deficiency, significant deficiency, and material weakness to be consistent with that conclusion.

Service Organizations

We believe the PCAOB should revise the guidance on service organizations that appears in Appendix B of the proposed standard to clarify how it relates to the Board's existing interim standard, *Service Organizations*. Some of the guidance from the interim standard has been paraphrased or described using different wording. As a result, it is not clear whether the Board intended to change the interim standard and just omitted any mention of such changes from the introduction to the proposed rule (see our comment above entitled "Process for Identifying and Communicating Changes to Various Interim Standards"). In addition, we believe the Board should significantly enhance the guidance on what the auditor should do, and what management should do, when the company uses a service organization as part of its internal control.

Use of "All"

The proposed auditing standard significantly increases various requirements for auditors to perform a procedure for "all" of a specific item. By its nature, a requirement related to all of a population excludes any consideration of materiality, removes auditor judgment, and will be costly to implement. Consideration must be given to whether the benefits to be achieved outweigh the cost of such requirements. In addition, we are concerned that in some instances the proposed guidance is establishing a threshold for the auditor that may be unachievable because the auditor's testing is generally selective. Requiring the auditor to perform a procedure for "all" of a population also inappropriately removes the auditor's ability to apply his or her professional judgment to the unique facts and circumstances of an audit engagement. The following are examples of paragraphs where we believe the word "all" (identified in boldface italics) needs to be reconsidered to ensure the requirements do not exceed the benefits obtained and result in the auditor performing procedures that would not result in discovery of material weakness in internal control over financial reporting.

79. In a walkthrough, the auditor should trace *all* types of transactions and events, both recurring and unusual, from origination through the company's information systems until they are reflected in the company's financial reports. (Also see the discussion of walkthroughs earlier in this letter)

114. As part of this evaluation, the auditor should review *all* reports issued during the year by internal audit (or similar functions, such as loan review in a financial institution) that address controls related to internal control over financial reporting and evaluate any internal control deficiencies identified in those reports.

191. In addition, the auditor should communicate to management, in writing, *all* deficiencies in internal control over financial reporting (that is, those deficiencies in internal control over financial reporting that are of a lesser magnitude than significant deficiencies) identified during the audit and inform the audit committee when such a communication has been made. (Also see our response to question number 20)

Indicators of Material Weakness

We agree with the guidance in paragraph 126 of the proposed standard that a restatement of previously issued financial statements to reflect the correction of a misstatement is at least a significant deficiency and is a strong indicator that a material weakness in internal control over financial reporting existed at that time. However, the subsequent discovery of a material misstatement of the financial statements, or of a material weakness in internal control, is not, in and of itself, evidence of (a) failure to obtain reasonable assurance; (b) inadequate planning, performance, or judgment; (c) the absence of due professional care; or (d) a failure to comply with PCAOB standards. Given the inherent limitation of an audit as described in

Office of the Secretary
November 21, 2003
Page 9 of 17

paragraph 15 of the proposed standard, absolute assurance is not possible. Therefore, we believe the proposed standard should include the following statement: "Since the practitioner's opinion on internal control is based on the concept of obtaining reasonable assurance, the practitioner is not an insurer and his or her report does not constitute a guarantee."

Effective Date

We understand that the PCAOB's effective date for the proposed standard is based on the date established by the Securities and Exchange Commission for implementation by registrants of its final 404 rule.

Nonetheless, we do not believe it is realistic to require implementation by accelerated filers of the internal control reporting and disclosure requirements of Section 404 of the Act for fiscal years ending in June, July, or August of 2004. Under the best of circumstances, we do not believe this proposed standard can be issued as a final document before early 2004. Since management as well as auditors are looking to this guidance to undertake what is a significant new approach to the audits of public companies, we do not believe that a time frame that is less than six months is sufficient to implement these requirements. In addition to the lack of final guidance, many implementation questions will need to be addressed by both management and the auditor. Time will be required to surface, resolve, and provide guidance on these issues. Accordingly, we believe that the effective date should be extended to audits of financial statements for fiscal years ending on or after September 15, 2004.

Authoritative Appendices

The Statement of Authority at the beginning of the proposed standard states that "appendices to the Board's standards are an integral part of the standard and carry the same authoritative weight as the body of the standard." We believe that the PCAOB should clarify whether this statement applies to the appendices in the Board's interim transitional standards.

We also recommend that the PCAOB clarify whether examples in the appendices are intended to establish requirements, or to provide illustrative guidance to be used by the auditor in making judgments about similar circumstances. For example, paragraph D3 states: "The following examples illustrate how to evaluate the significance of internal control deficiencies in various situations. These examples are for illustrative purposes only." However, each of the scenarios in Appendix D has a conclusion that states, "based only on these facts, the auditor *should determine* that this deficiency represents a significant deficiency [material weakness] for the following reasons" (italics added). The "should determine" language is inconsistent with the statement in paragraph D3 that the examples are for illustrative purposes only.

Responses to Questions

Questions regarding an integrated audit of the financial statements and internal control over financial reporting:

1. **Is it appropriate to refer to the auditor's attestation of management's assessment of the effectiveness of internal control over financial reporting as the audit of internal control over financial reporting?**

   It is appropriate to refer to the auditor's attestation as an audit. The auditor's objective is to express an opinion on management's assertion about the effectiveness of internal control over financial reporting, just as the auditor's objective in an audit of the financial statements is to express an opinion on the financial statements. The level of assurance provided by the auditor's opinion is the same for either engagement. The requirement to obtain sufficient competent audit evidence to support the opinion is the same for either engagement. Only the subject matter on which the opinion is expressed is different.

Office of the Secretary
November 21, 2003
Page 10 of 17

2. Should the auditor be prohibited from performing an audit of internal control over financial reporting without also performing an audit of the financial statements?

We agree that for public company audits, the auditor should be prohibited from performing an audit of internal control over financial reporting without also performing an audit of the financial statements.

The applicability of the proposed standard and the continuing applicability of AT section 501 needs to be clarified. The first sentence of paragraph 2, on its own, does not appear to be correct since not all companies subject to the reporting requirements of the Securities Exchange Act of 1934 are required to report on internal control over financial reporting. Furthermore, footnote 1 states that "this standard supersedes AT section 501 as it relates to performing an audit of the design and operating effectiveness of internal control over financial reporting." Does that mean that AT section 501 is superseded, or that it is superseded only with respect to some guidance? Should public companies not subject to section 404 of the Sarbanes-Oxley Act but that voluntarily wish to obtain an auditor attestation of internal control use the proposed standard or AT section 501?

3. Rather than requiring the auditor to also complete an audit of the financial statements, would an appropriate alternative be to require the auditor to perform work with regard to the financial statements comparable to that required to complete the financial statement audit?

No. Requiring something less would be difficult to define and would result in significant inconsistencies in practice for public company audits. We also agree that the audit of internal control and the audit of financial statements should be completed as of the same date.

Question regarding the costs and benefits of internal control:

4. Does the Board's proposed standard give appropriate consideration to how internal control is implemented in, and how the audit of internal control over financial reporting should be conducted at, small and medium-sized issuers?

See comment above entitled "Considerations for Small and Medium-Sized Issuers."

Question regarding the audit of internal control over financial reporting:

5. Should the Board, generally or in this proposed standard, specify the level of competence and training of the audit personnel that is necessary to perform specified auditing procedures effectively? For example, it would be inappropriate for a new, inexperienced auditor to have primary responsibility for conducting interviews of a company's senior management about possible fraud.

The PCAOB's interim standards require that the person or persons performing the engagement have adequate technical training and proficiency as an auditor (or in the attest function) and adequate knowledge of the subject matter, and that work is to be properly supervised. SAS No. 47, *Audit Risk and Materiality in Conducting an Audit* (AICPA, *Professional Standards*, vol. 1, AU sec. 312.17), further states:

> Whenever the auditor has concluded that there is significant risk of material misstatement of the financial statements, the auditor should consider this conclusion in determining the nature, timing, or extent of procedures; assigning staff; or requiring appropriate levels of supervision. The knowledge, skill, and ability of personnel assigned significant engagement responsibilities should be commensurate with the auditor's assessment of the level of risk for the engagement. Ordinarily, higher risk requires more experienced personnel or more extensive supervision by the auditor with final responsibility for the engagement during both the planning and the conduct of the engagement.

We believe the existing interim standards are adequate. We do not believe that it is realistic to mandate levels of experience for the performance of specific procedures because development of personnel does not progress on a uniform timetable. We believe appropriate judgment needs to be made around staffing assignments and it would be inappropriate to specify the level of staff for specific audit procedures.

Questions regarding evaluation of management's assessment:

6. **Is the scope of the audit appropriate in that it requires the auditor to both evaluate management's assessment and obtain, directly, evidence about whether internal control over financial reporting is effective?**

Yes, we believe that for public companies it is appropriate that the scope of the audit requires the auditor to both evaluate management's assessment and obtain, directly, evidence about whether internal control over financial reporting is designed and operating effectively, as stated in paragraph 5 of the proposed standard.

We also believe that the auditor's opinion in report Examples A-1 and A-6 should run directly to the effectiveness of internal control over financial reporting rather than to management's assessment both to be consistent with the scope paragraph in those reports and to eliminate any confusion that the auditor is expressing an opinion on the effectiveness of internal control over financial reporting. Accordingly, we believe that report element "l" in paragraph 153 should be changed to read "the auditor's opinion on whether the company maintained, in all material respects, effective internal control over financial reporting as of the specified date based on the control criteria" so that it is consistent with report element "h."

7. **Is it appropriate that the Board has provided criteria that auditors should use to evaluate the adequacy of management's documentation?**

Yes. It is appropriate to provide criteria. However, we believe the Board needs to clarify paragraph B-3 of the proposed standard. Does the guidance in B-3 mean that management would not be required to have controls documented at locations or business units that are not able to create, either individually or in the aggregate, a material misstatement? We believe that management should have at least a minimum level of documentation of controls at these locations or business units consistent with the requirement that registrants must maintain adequate books and records.

We also believe more guidance is needed in the area of documentation of locations or business units that individually are insignificant but when aggregated could result in a material misstatement. We believe management should be required to document all significant controls at these locations as it relates to the significant accounts at the consolidated financial levels. Without appropriate documentation, we do not believe management can demonstrate adequate company wide controls since documentation of controls is a foundation of company wide controls.

Further, as part of providing criteria that auditors should use to evaluate the adequacy of management's documentation, we believe that the Board, in conjunction with the SEC, should address the matter of management's level of documentation and retention of documentation as well as the auditor's documentation of the entity's systems and controls.

8. **Is it appropriate to state that inadequate documentation is an internal control deficiency, the severity of which the auditor should evaluate? Or should inadequate documentation automatically rise to the level of significant deficiency or material weakness in internal control?**

We do not believe inadequate documentation should automatically rise to the level of a significant deficiency or a material weakness. The effect of inadequate documentation is a judgmental matter to be considered in the auditor's evaluation of internal control over financial reporting.

Paragraph 46 states that "in evaluating the deficiency as to its significance, the auditor should determine whether management can demonstrate the monitoring component of internal control over financial reporting in the absence of documentation." This language suggests that there are ways in which management can demonstrate the monitoring component in the absence of documentation of controls. We believe there needs to be clarification around this statement and if this statement is retained, examples of how management would do this should be provided. We believe that documentation provides the foundation for the entity's evaluation of and monitoring of the effective operation of controls.

Questions regarding obtaining an understanding of internal control over financial reporting:

9. **Are the objectives to be achieved by performing walkthroughs sufficient to require the performance of walkthroughs?**

10. **Is it appropriate to require that the walkthrough be performed by the auditor himself or herself, rather than allowing the auditor to use walkthrough procedures performed by management, internal auditors, or others?**

See comment above entitled "Walkthroughs."

Question regarding testing operating effectiveness:

11. **Is it appropriate to require the auditor to obtain evidence of the effectiveness of controls for all relevant assertions for all significant accounts and disclosures every year or may the auditor use some of the audit evidence obtained in previous years to support his or her current opinion on management's assessment?**

We believe that the auditor needs to obtain evidence of the effectiveness of controls for all relevant assertions for all significant accounts and disclosures every year. Reliance on prior year work is inappropriate.

We do not, however, believe that this requirement is clearly stated in the proposed standard. Paragraph 101 of the proposed standard states:

Each year the auditor must obtain sufficient evidence about whether the company's internal control over financial reporting, including the controls for all internal control components, is operating effectively. The auditor also should vary from year to year the nature, timing, and extent of testing of controls to introduce unpredictability into the testing and respond to changes in circumstances. For example, each year the auditor might test the controls at a different interim period; increase or reduce the number and types of tests performed; or change the combination of procedures used.

We believe that the guidance in the above paragraph does not make it clear that the auditor is required to obtain evidence of the effectiveness of controls for all relevant assertions for all significant accounts and disclosures every year, without using some of the audit evidence obtained in previous years to support his or her current opinion on management's assessment. The guidance in the proposed standard should be stated as explicitly as question 11 so that it is clear to auditors.

Questions regarding using the work of management and others:

12. **To what extent should the auditor be permitted or required to use the work of management and others?**

Office of the Secretary
November 21, 2003
Page 13 of 17

Allowing the auditor to rely on certain testing performed by management should be permitted but not required. It should be based on the auditor's judgment of the competence and objectivity of those performing the work, and subject to the overall requirement that the auditor should obtain the principal evidence for the opinion.

13. **Are the three categories of controls and the extent to which the auditor may rely on the work of others appropriately defined?**

Paragraph 104 of the proposed standard states that areas in which the auditor should not use the work of others includes "controls that have a pervasive effect on the financial statements, such as certain information technology general controls on which the operating effectiveness of other controls depend." Internal auditors in many companies possess both the skills and the objectivity to perform tests of IT general controls very effectively. We believe that to prohibit using the work of such professionals altogether would result in a costly redundancy of work effort between the company and the auditor that provides no benefit. Accordingly, we strongly believe that controls that have a pervasive effect on the financial statements, such as IT general controls, should be included among the areas of controls discussed in paragraph 105 where the auditor's use of the results of procedures performed by others should be limited, but not prohibited.

With regard to the areas in which the work of others should be limited (paragraph 105), we believe the PCAOB should provide additional guidance to clarify the meaning of "limited."

In paragraph 106, the phrase "without specific limitation" does not clearly communicate what level of auditor involvement is appropriate in areas such as controls over routine processing of significant accounts and disclosures. Does this imply the auditor would not necessarily be required to do some testing of each control in this category? We believe that the auditor needs to perform some tests in the areas described in paragraph 106 because it is inappropriate to rely exclusively on the results of tests performed by others. See also our response to question 15.

14. **Does the proposed standard give appropriate recognition to the work of internal auditors? If not, does the proposed standard place too much emphasis and preference on the work of internal auditors or not enough?**

We do believe that the proposed standard gives appropriate recognition to the work of internal auditors in paragraph 108. The guidance in paragraph 108 supports our response to question 13 as it relates to using the results of tests of IT general controls performed by internal auditors.

15. **Is the flexibility in determining the extent of reperformance of the work of others appropriate, or should the auditor be specifically required to reperform a certain level of work (for example, reperform tests of all significant accounts or reperform every test performed by others that the auditor intends to use)?**

Paragraph 107 states that if the auditor intends to use the work of others, "the auditor should reperform some of the tests of controls originally performed by others." We believe more guidance is needed here to indicate if reperformance must be done at each individual control level, the account balance level, or just on an overall basis.

In addition, it is not clear whether the guidance in paragraph 107 is intended to apply to both paragraphs 105 and 106 or only to paragraph 105.

16. **Is the requirement for the auditor to obtain the principal evidence, on an overall basis, through his or her own work the appropriate benchmark for the amount of work that is required to be performed by the auditor?**

Yes, the requirement in paragraph 109 that "the auditor must perform enough of the testing himself or herself so that the auditor's own work provides the principal evidence for the auditor's opinion" is an appropriate benchmark for the amount of work that is required to be performed by the auditor. However, we believe the following guidance should be added to paragraph 109: "Because controls over certain areas are not always susceptible to mathematical measurement, the auditor will need to apply judgment to determine that he or she has obtained the principal evidence from his or her own testing."

Questions regarding evaluating results:

17. Will the definitions in the proposed standard of significant deficiency and material weakness provide for increased consistency in the evaluation of deficiencies? How can the definitions be improved?

We recognize how difficult it is to develop a meaningful definition of internal control deficiency that can be understood and applied consistently. The AICPA's Auditing Standards Board task force spent significant time in its own deliberations on this subject. We believe the definitions included in the proposed standard provide a reasonable level of clarity that would provide a more consistent application. However, we believe by including the probability concept of "remote" in the definition of significant deficiency, the PCAOB has lowered the threshold and as a result will increase the number of deficiencies that will be classified as significant deficiencies. Although the number of deficiencies is not of major concern to us, what does concern us is that the number may ultimately dilute the importance of significant deficiencies and, as a result, cause management, audit committees, boards of directors, and others to view this category as irrelevant or unimportant. At the same time, requiring unresolved significant deficiencies to be strong indicators of a material weakness would capture significant deficiencies when the likelihood of a misstatement is slightly more than remote (for example, a 5-8 percent likelihood) and the amount of misstatement is slightly more than inconsequential (for example, more than 1 percent). Doing so seems inappropriate and could result in adopting controls that far exceed the benefit. We believe the Board needs to evaluate if it intended to have these consequences when applying the proposed definitions and consider removing the concept of "remote" from the definition.

We also note that in the report Examples A-2 and A-3, the definition of significant deficiency in the explanatory paragraphs includes only the part of the definition that states that "a significant deficiency is an internal control deficiency that adversely affects the company's ability to initiate, record, process, and report external financial data reliably in accordance with generally accepted accounting principles." We do not believe that this definition will be meaningful to users of the report since it does not communicate anything about the materiality or the likelihood of the deficiency, in contrast to the definition of material weakness.

In addition, we think the Board should change the definition of significant deficiency to read "A significant deficiency *is*" rather than "A significant deficiency *could be*" so that the construction is parallel to the definition of material weakness. Finally, we believe the Board should drop the words "in amount" following "more than inconsequential," since we believe the determination of what is "more than inconsequential," just as well as what is "material," could involve qualitative as well as quantitative considerations.

18. Do the examples in Appendix D of how to apply these definitions in various scenarios provide helpful guidance? Are there other specific examples that commenters could suggest that would provide further interpretive help?

We believe the examples are helpful in providing some clarity around the application of the definition. However, they are reasonably straightforward (black and white) situations. The difficulty will come in the gray areas. Additional examples should be provided where deficiencies would not meet the threshold of "more than remote" and less obvious examples and conclusions are needed.

Office of the Secretary
November 21, 2003
Page 15 of 17

19. **Is it necessary for the auditor to evaluate the severity of all identified internal control deficiencies?**

    Yes. Once the auditor becomes aware of an internal control deficiency, the auditor needs to evaluate whether it is a significant deficiency or a material weakness.

20. **Is it appropriate to require the auditor to communicate all internal control deficiencies (not just material weaknesses and significant deficiencies) to management in writing?**

    We believe it is appropriate to require the auditor to communicate to management all deficiencies in internal control (that is, those deficiencies that are of a lesser magnitude than significant deficiencies) that were identified by the auditor during the audit.

    However, paragraph 191 goes beyond communication of deficiencies identified by the auditor and includes all deficiencies identified by management, internal auditors, or others. In large multi-national companies this could amount to hundreds, even thousands, of comments that do not reach the level of significant deficiency and would create a level of effort that would far exceed the benefits. We believe that management should be expected to be responsible for accumulating these comments as part of its overall monitoring function. It is inappropriate for the auditor to play this role.

21. **Are the matters that the Board has classified as strong indicators that a material weakness in internal control exists appropriately classified as such?**

    As stated earlier, we believe that the absence of sufficient evidence to support the responsible party's evaluation of the operating effectiveness of internal control would result in a strong indicator of material weakness. We believe that this matter should be added to the list in paragraph 126 and deleted from paragraph 125.

    While we agree that an ineffective regulatory compliance function may result in a material misstatement in the financial statements, there are many aspects of the function that by themselves may be ineffective without affecting the financial statements. Singling out the entire function will lead to confusion regarding whether the regulatory process falls within the definition of internal control over financial reporting. We believe each deficiency within the regulatory function first needs to be evaluated to determine if it applies to internal control over financial reporting. If it does, then it should be evaluated to determine whether it is a significant deficiency or a material weakness.

    We agree fraud on the part of senior management is a serious issue, however, we do not believe it is the responsibility of the auditor to identify fraud of any magnitude. We also do not believe that fraud of any magnitude would necessarily constitute a significant deficiency or a material weakness, particularly in situations where the company's controls uncovered the issue. We also do not believe that the auditor should be required to consider issues that occur outside the company's environment such as filing a false tax return.

22. **Is it appropriate to require the auditors to evaluate the effectiveness of the audit committee's oversight of the company's external financial reporting and internal control over financial reporting?**

23. **Will auditors be able to effectively carry out their responsibility to evaluate the effectiveness of the audit committee's oversight?**

24. **If the auditor concludes that ineffective audit committee oversight is a material weakness, rather than require the auditor to issue an adverse opinion with regard to the effectiveness of the internal control over financial reporting, should the standard require the auditor to withdraw from the audit engagement?**

See comment above entitled "Evaluating the Effectiveness of the Audit Committee's Oversight."

Questions regarding forming an opinion and reporting:

25. Is it appropriate that the existence of a material weakness would require the auditor to express an adverse conclusion about the effectiveness of the company's internal control over financial reporting, consistent with the required reporting model for management?

26. Are there circumstances where a qualified "except for" conclusion would be appropriate?

27. Do you agree with the position that when the auditor issues a non-standard opinion, such as an adverse opinion, that the auditor's opinion should speak directly to the effectiveness of the internal control over financial reporting rather than to whether management's assessment is fairly stated?

   See comment above entitled "Forming an Opinion and Reporting."

Questions regarding auditor independence:

28. Should the Board provide specific guidance on independence and internal control-related non-audit services in the context of this proposed standard?

   No. We do not believe that this proposed standard is the appropriate place for guidance on independence and internal control-related non-audit services.

29. Are there any specific internal control-related non-audit services the auditor should be prohibited from providing to an audit client?

   We believe that the non-audit services currently prohibited for audits of issuers are appropriate and that no additional rules are necessary.

Questions regarding auditor's responsibilities with regard to management's certifications:

30. Are the auditor's differing levels of responsibility as they relate to management's quarterly certifications versus the annual (fourth quarter) certification, appropriate?

31. Is the scope of the auditor's responsibility for quarterly disclosures about the internal control over financial reporting appropriate?

   As in financial statement reporting, we believe differing levels of responsibility are appropriate.

   We believe paragraphs 8 and 9 of the proposed standard may imply that the auditor is obligated to identify deficiencies that could result in a misstatement to interim financial statements. We do not believe that an auditor should be required to plan his or her annual audit of internal control to consider materiality or tolerable errors at the materiality level of the interim financial statement. Therefore, we believe the PCAOB needs to be explicit that this is not required or state what they believe is required relative to the existing model (that is, SAS 100).

   In addition, we believe that the language in the second bullet of paragraph 186 should be changed from "whether significant changes in internal control over financial reporting may introduce significant deficiencies or material weaknesses in the design of internal control over financial reporting" to "whether any change in internal control over financial reporting has materially affected, or is reasonably likely to materially affect, the company's internal control over financial reporting" to conform to wording in the SEC's final 404 rule. We do not believe that the auditor's responsibility should be extended beyond that required for management.

Finally, we believe the auditor evaluation responsibilities described in paragraphs 185 through 189 should not be required until the first quarter after the company's issuance of its first annual 404 report.

Additional/Editorial Comments

1. The proposed standard should include guidance on the work that is required of the auditor to determine whether an identified deficiency in one interim period has been corrected in a subsequent interim period. Since the auditor has no responsibility to do testing on a quarterly basis, what would be the basis for the auditor to conclude that the control is now designed and operating effectively?

2. In regard to paragraph B15 of the proposed standard, we believe that the internal control of all equity investees should be excluded from the company's evaluation of internal control over financial reporting, except with regard to controls over accounting for these investments in accordance with generally accepted accounting principles. Therefore, we believe the word "ordinarily" should be eliminated from the statement that "the evaluation *ordinarily* [italics added] would not extend to controls at the equity method investee." However, if it is not eliminated, we believe an example should be provided of a situation where the evaluation of the company's internal control would extend to controls at an equity method investee.

3. In paragraph 2, change the beginning of the fourth sentence to either "the audit firm that audits" or "the auditor who audits."

4. Although we agree with the statement, the last sentence of paragraph 11 seems misplaced.

5. Although we agree with the statement, the last sentence of paragraph 36 seems off point in that it doesn't tie back to the discussion of professional skepticism.

Thank you for the opportunity to comment on this proposed standard. We would be pleased to meet with PCAOB members and staff to discuss our comments.

Sincerely,

S. Scott Voynich, CPA
Chairman of the Board

Barry C. Melancon, CPA
President and CEO

¶ 604. American Society of Corporate Secretaries

American Society of Corporate Secretaries

November 21, 2003

Office of the Secretary
Public Company Accounting Oversight Board
1666 K Street, N.W.
Washington, D.C. 20006-2803

Re: PCAOB Rulemaking Docket Matter No. 008

Dear Board Members:

The American Society of Corporate Secretaries, Inc. ("Society") is a professional association founded in 1946, serving more than 4,000 corporate attorneys and other business executives who represent over 3,000 companies. The members' major duties include working with corporate boards of directors to improve corporate governance; assuring company compliance with securities regulations; coordinating activities of stockholders, including proxy voting for the annual meeting of shareholders; and administering other activities handled by the Corporate Secretary's Office. The majority of the Society's members are attorneys.

We appreciate the opportunity to comment on the Public Company Accounting Oversight Board's Proposed Auditing Standard – An Audit of Internal Control Over Financial Reporting Performed in Conjunction with an Audit of Financial Statements (the "Proposed Standard"). The Proposed Standard covers attestation engagements under Sections 404(b) and 103(a)(2)(A) of the Sarbanes-Oxley Act of 2002 (the "Act").

First, the Society would like to make general comments about its perception of the approach that the Proposed Standard seems to be taking. Then we would like to address selected topics of particular interest to our members: External auditors' oversight of the effectiveness of audit committees; communications among external auditors, management and the audit committee; the ability of external auditors to rely on the work of others, especially internal audit; the introduction of new terminology; and the characterization of the external auditors' attestation opinion.

* * * * *

General

We applaud the PCAOB for being sensitive to the fact that internal control over financial reporting cannot be "one-size-fits-all." However, as a general comment, we would like to note that the Proposed Standard takes away much of the professional judgment and expertise that external auditors could bring to the assessment of internal controls over financial reporting in a given factual situation. We recommend that the Board allow external auditors to exercise their judgment to a greater extent than currently contemplated under the Proposed Standard.

Oversight of Effectiveness of Audit Committees

Section 301 of the Act states that "[t]he audit committee . . . shall be directly responsible for the appointment, compensation, and oversight of the work of any registered public accounting firm employed by the issuer . . . and each such registered public accounting firm shall report directly to the audit committee . . . ." Paragraphs 56-59 of the Proposed Standard require the external auditors to evaluate the effectiveness of the audit committee's oversight of the company's external financial reporting and internal control over financial reporting.

Conflict of Interest. We believe that Paragraphs 56 – 59 create an unworkable conflict of interest for the external auditors. Paragraph 59 of the Proposed Standard states that "[i]neffective oversight by the audit committee of the company's external financial reporting and internal control over financial reporting should be regarded as at least a significant deficiency and is a strong indicator that a material weakness in internal control over financial reporting exists." Paragraph 57 states that the external auditor should evaluate the "Committee's compliance with applicable listing standards adopted pursuant to Section 301 of the Act." Major new laws, rules and standards have arisen from numerous regulatory fronts affecting both issuers and their external auditors. One of the audit committee's primary responsibilities is to retain, terminate and determine the compensation paid to external auditors. In its final listing standards' discussion on the role of audit committees, the New York Stock Exchange ("NYSE") states that one of the committee's purposes is to "assist board oversight of... the independent auditor's qualifications and independence. We believe this critical responsibility and oversight function of the audit committee is incompatible with, and would be compromised by, an evaluation of the audit committee by the external auditors under the Proposed Standard.

Scope of External Auditors' Evaluation. The Proposed Standard gives as examples seven factors that the external auditor should consider in evaluating the effectiveness of the audit committee's oversight of the company's external financial reporting and internal control over financial reporting. With due deference to the professionalism and expertise of external auditors, some of the proposed factors venture into the realm of what the Securities and Exchange Commission (the "SEC") and the stock exchanges are addressing, not matters inherently within the expertise of external auditors. For instance, paragraph 58 of the Proposed Standard states that "[a]s part of evaluating the independence of committee members, the auditor should evaluate how audit committee members are nominated and selected and whether they act independently from management . . . For example, are qualified candidates identified by outsiders, such as an outside search firm or a nominating committee composed of outside directors, . . . ?"

We strongly recommend that the PCAOB defer to Section 303A.4(b) of the NYSE's final listing standards as approved by the SEC on November 4, 2003, which states that the nominating committee's purpose and responsibilities at a minimum must be to "identify individuals qualified to become board members, consistent with criteria approved by the board, and to select, or to recommend that the board select, the director nominees for the next annual meeting of shareholders . . . ." There are mechanisms to monitor and enforce the listing standards.

We note that, as a result of the Proposed Standard, external auditors are now planning significant audit procedures including lengthy surveys and interviews with audit committee members to fulfill this evaluation requirement. Given the existence of the NYSE listing standards addressing board and committee nominees and their independence, we believe that any added benefit of the external auditors also reviewing directors' independence would be immaterial and unnecessary, particularly when balanced against the significant added burden of the extra audit procedures.

Communications

Paragraph 191 of the Proposed Standard requires the external auditor to communicate "to management, in writing, *all* [emphasis supplied] deficiencies in internal control over financial reporting (that is, those deficiencies in internal control over financial reporting that are of a lesser magnitude than significant deficiencies) identified during the audit . . . ." In addition, the external auditor must "inform the audit committee when such a communication has been made." This provision would require a change from external auditors' current practice of communicating significant deficiencies (reportable conditions) and material weaknesses in writing to the audit committee to an approach that would require communication to management of **all** deficiencies in internal controls over financial reporting identified during the audit and to inform the audit committee when a communication has been made.

The probable result is that most audit committees will feel that they cannot simply take on its face the fact that the external auditor reported deficiencies to management without exploring further. Instead, audit committees are likely to feel compelled to ask about the substance of all the deficiencies. What may then happen is that the committee will become bogged down in reviewing insignificant matters rather than focusing on topics of greater importance to the company and its owners. Accordingly, we recommend that the PCAOB retain the current reporting structure.

Reliance on Work of Others, Especially Internal Audit

The Society appreciates the PCAOB's recognition of the expense and work incurred by companies: "[t]he more extensive and reliable management's assessment is, the less extensive and costly the auditor's work will need to be." It seems to recognize that the external auditor can rely on the work of internal audit in certain areas: "The proposed auditing standard . . . would allow the auditor to incorporate into the audit . . . some of the work performed by others, such as internal auditors or third parties . . . ."

However, other provisions limit the circumstances in which internal audit may be used. The draft proposes that internal audit *cannot* be used for the following areas:

- Control environment, including fraud controls.
- Controls over period-end financial reporting process.
- Controls that have a pervasive effect on the financial statements, such as certain IT general controls on which the operating effectiveness of other controls depend.

- Walkthroughs.

These prohibited functions are some of the key areas in which an internal audit group can provide significant insight and audit evidence based on its experience with the company. Public companies do not expect external auditors to rely solely on internal audit for 100% of testing. Eliminating internal audit from these critical areas, however, is a dramatic change from present accepted practices. In addition, this proposed point does not allow the external auditors latitude to use their own professional judgment. For example, in the new "walkthrough" concept that the Proposed Standard introduces, it is not clear if all processes in all locations (significant or otherwise) must have a walkthrough. Multinationals with complex global operations could have hundreds of processes located in numerous geographies involving multiple sites. We believe that external auditors should be allowed to use their judgment, taking into account the specific circumstances of the company, to determine the operating effectiveness of controls for all relevant assertions for all significant accounts and disclosures.

The proposed auditing standard also would require that, overall, the external auditor obtain directly the "principal evidence" about the effectiveness of internal control over financial reporting. It is our understanding that many external auditors are interpreting the Proposed Standard to mean that only they can provide the principal evidence. The result is significant increased costs to companies, without necessarily any more benefits going to the investing public. For all companies, small, mid-sized and large, the additional costs are likely to be very high. Anecdotally, our members report that their external auditors have told them to expect 25-100% fee hikes to cover internal control work.

Unfortunately, one unintended consequence if the Proposed Standard is adopted in this area will be to diminish or eliminate the role of internal audit. In its final listing standards, the NYSE reaffirmed the importance of internal audit by requiring that all listed companies have an internal audit function, a stance we urge the PCAOB to support. Effectively decimating strong internal audit functions will diminish, not enhance, the ability of corporations to maintain a strong control environment from which management can produce transparent financial statements with integrity that will inspire investor confidence.

Introduction of New and Broad Terminology

While we appreciate the Board's efforts to clarify the definition of "significant deficiency," which is not currently well defined in the auditing literature, we believe the Board's proposed definitions of both "significant deficiency" and "material weakness" capture an unnecessarily low and insignificant level of control deficiencies which were not within the intent of Congress when it adopted the Act. These new definitions also introduce significant ambiguities that make it difficult for companies or external auditors to interpret and apply the definitions. As an alternative to the Board's approach, we recommend the Proposed Standard give companies and the external auditors latitude to exercise judgment in determining those deficiencies that are significant enough to be elevated to management and the audit committee, or disclosed in public filings, while using more well-established terminology to provide definitional guidance. Rather than introducing the term "inconsequential" in the significant deficiency definition, we recommend that the Board use the well-understood concept of materiality in addressing the magnitude of both a significant deficiency and a material weakness, and use different degrees of likelihood to distinguish between the two. Specifically, we recommend that the definitions hinge on whether there is a reasonable possibility that individual or aggregated deficiencies would lead to a material adjustment in the financial statements, in the case of significant deficiencies, and on whether it is reasonably likely the deficiencies would lead to a material adjustment in the financial statements, in the case of material weaknesses. Using terminology that is already well interpreted in the auditing literature, SEC guidance and judicial decisions will give companies and auditors greater ability to apply the definitions in exercising their judgment.

In addition, we ask that the Board avoid using terminology that appears to extend beyond the financial reporting controls scope of the SEC's rules. For instance, ineffective internal audit, risk assessment, and regulatory compliance functions are listed as examples of significant deficiencies. Yet in many companies, these functions extend beyond the realm of internal controls over financial reporting.

Characterization of Qualified Attestation

The Proposed Standard, in Paragraphs 177-179 discusses situations where there is an adverse opinion on the effectiveness of internal controls over financial reporting due to a material weakness but the auditor's opinion on the financial statements is unqualified because they were able to perform substantive procedures to satisfy themselves that there was no material misstatement in the financial statements. Paragraph 178 proposes the inclusion of qualifying language in the report on internal control over financial reporting explaining that the material weakness does not impact the audit report on financial statements. We are concerned that the appearance of an unqualified opinion on the financial statements alongside an *adverse* opinion on the effectiveness of internal control over financial reporting due to a material weakness that did not result in a material misstatement in the financial statements will create the perception to the investing public that the financial reports are unreliable despite the inclusion of the qualifying language in the report on internal control over financial reporting. We recommend that the external auditor be allowed to exercise judgment as to whether the opinion on the effectiveness of internal control over financial reporting should be regarded as a *qualified* opinion rather than an *adverse* opinion based upon the materiality of the weakness and scope limitations if any.

* * * * *

The Society's members vigorously support the accountability of management for establishing and maintaining adequate internal controls over financial reporting. We hope that the Proposed Standard will permit companies and their owners to take full advantage of the professional and thorough work and expertise of management and internal audit. We also hope that external auditors are permitted to exercise their considerable professional expertise and judgment. If not, we risk violating the PCAOB's sensitivity that "internal control is not 'one-size-fits-all,' and the nature and extent of controls that are necessary depend, to a great extent, on the size and complexity of the company."

We appreciate your consideration of these comments. If you have any questions, please call me at 650-752-5339.

Cordially,

American Society of Corporate Secretaries

By: Marie Oh Huber
         Chair, PCAOB Subcommittee
         of the ASCS Securities Law Committee

cc: Alan Beller
       Peggy Foran
       Kathy Gibson
       David Smith
       Susan Wolf

¶ 605. America's Community Bankers

November 21, 2003

Office of the Secretary
Public Company Accounting Oversight Board
1666 K Street, NW
Washington, DC 20006-2803

Re: PCAOB Rulemaking Docket Matter No. 008
Proposed Auditing Standard – An Audit of Internal Control Over Financial Reporting
Performed in Conjunction With an Audit of Financial Statements

Dear Sir or Madam:

America's Community Bankers ("ACB")[1] is pleased to comment on the proposed auditing standard for attestation engagements required by Section 404(b) and Section 103(a)(2)(A) of the Sarbanes-Oxley Act of 2002 ("Sarbanes-Oxley") issued by the Public Company Accounting Oversight Board "PCAOB".[2]

Sarbanes-Oxley was passed to strengthen public company corporate governance and financial disclosure in an effort to restore investor confidence in the public markets. To further the public interest in the preparation of complete and accurate public company audit reports, Sarbanes-Oxley mandated the creation of the ("PCAOB") to oversee and regulate the public company auditing profession. The proposed standard would establish professional guidelines to govern the independent auditor's attestation of and reporting on management's assessment of the effectiveness of internal control over financial reporting.

---

[1] America's Community Bankers represents the nation's community banks. ACB members, whose aggregate assets total more than $1 trillion, pursue progressive, entrepreneurial and service-oriented strategies in providing financial services to benefit their customers and communities.
[2] Pub. L. 107-204 (2002).

Public Company Accounting Oversight Board
November 21, 2003
Page 2

ACB Position

The PCAOB's proposed auditing standard would add burdensome, conflicting, and overlapping requirements on community banks. ACB believes that section 404 was meant to mirror the similar requirements imposed on financial institutions by the Federal Deposit Insurance Corporation Improvement Act of 1991 ("FDICIA").[3] FDICIA, which has been in place for 12

years, requires management of depository institutions with $500 million or more in assets to assess the effectiveness of the institution's internal control structure.[4] The institution's independent public accountant must examine, attest to, and report separately on, management's assessment. The federal banking regulators have never interpreted this legislative language to require an independent audit of the effectiveness of the internal control structure, as is being proposed by the PCAOB. Congress was aware of the process used to comply with FDICIA, but still adopted almost identical language in section 404(b) of Sarbanes-Oxley to describe the responsibility of the public auditor.

We believe that the PCAOB should conform the standard to the requirement mandated by Congress by requiring an attestation only of management's assessment of the internal control structure to avoid duplication of work and unnecessary expense. If the PCAOB adopts the proposal to require an audit of internal control over financial reporting, the PCAOB should exempt from that requirement insured depository institutions that are regularly examined and subject to continuing supervision by federal banking regulators. The PCAOB should recognize the significant and substantial protections afforded to depositors and investors by the banking laws and establish a standard for depository institutions that mirrors the standard in FDICIA that only requires an attestation of management's evaluation of internal control over financial reporting.

ACB also has concerns with the following provisions of the proposal:

- The requirement that the auditor conduct evaluations of the internal control structure over financial reporting be conducted on a *quarterly* basis.
- The requirement that the external auditor evaluate the effectiveness of the audit committee's oversight of the company's financial reporting and internal control structure.
- The requirement that the external auditor limit the use of testing performed by management and others in a number of areas.
- The lack of adequate guidance regarding attestation procedures for small and medium-size businesses.

Attestation of Management's Assessment of Internal Control

In its proposed auditing standard, the PCAOB proposes to adopt an unnecessary and significantly expanded interpretation of the Sarbanes-Oxley requirements. Two sections of Sarbanes-Oxley

---

[3] Pub. L. 102-242 (1991).
[4] 12 U.S.C. § 1831m and 12 C.F.R. Part 363.

WG
                    &L Warren, Gorham & Lamont

Public Company Accounting Oversight Board
November 21, 2003
Page 3

address the attestation of management's assessment of the internal control structure. Section 103(a)(2)(A) stipulates that the PCAOB develop an auditing standard that would require the external auditor to "*describe in each audit report the scope of the auditor's testing of the internal control structure and procedures of the issuer, required by section 404(b)....*" Following this wording, Section 404(b) of Sarbanes-Oxley directs public company auditors to "*attest to, and report on, the assessment made by management.*" However, the PCAOB is proposing that the auditor perform a detailed integrated audit of internal control and financial statements and opine directly on the effectiveness of internal controls.

An attestation traditionally refers to a process in which the auditor provides a conclusion about the reliability of management's written assertion, while an audit traditionally involves examination of the financial statements. There is a very distinct difference between the two that was recognized by Congress. Requiring an independent audit of internal control over financial reporting will be duplicative of work performed by a company's internal audit function and senior management and will ultimately be very costly and burdensome. Public company auditors will interpret their responsibilities under the standard quite broadly and, in an effort to avoid future liability, will err on the side of doing too much, rather than not doing enough. This would be understandable in light of recent corporate scandals and the collapse of Arthur Andersen. However, the public auditors will be adequately compensated for this work at a significant cost to public companies and their shareholders.

We urge the PCAOB to reconsider whether a separate audit of internal controls is really necessary and scale back these standards to a reasonable level of inquiry that allows an auditor to opine on the conclusions reached by management. There are other requirements recently put in place that will protect the investing public and that make a more burdensome standard inappropriate. For instance, the chief executive officer and chief financial officer must certify each quarter as to the accuracy of the company's financial statements and their responsibility for establishing and maintaining internal controls.[5] They also must certify that the internal controls have been designed to provide reasonable assurance about the reliability of the financial statements and that they have evaluated the effectiveness of the internal controls. The certifications with regard to the compliance of the periodic filing with the Securities Exchange Act of 1934 are made under the threat of criminal liability if the officer knowingly makes a false certification.

ACB believes that the standard adopted by the banking regulators under FDICIA of requiring an attestation of management's assessment of internal controls, as provided for in section 36 of the Federal Deposit Insurance Act and implemented by Part 363 of the Federal Deposit Insurance Corporation,[6] should be adopted as the standard under the plain language of section 404(b) of Sarbanes-Oxley. If the PCAOB does not believe that this standard is appropriate for all public companies, it should at least acknowledge the comprehensive scheme of regulation and examination that governs depository institutions and their holding companies and exempt these institutions and holding companies from the more burdensome requirement of an independent internal control audit. Insured depository institutions are required to have internal controls,

---

[5] Sections 302 and 906 of Sarbanes-Oxley; Final Rule: Certification of Disclosure in Companies' Quarterly and Annual Reports, 67 Fed. Reg. 57276 (Sept. 9, 2003).
[6] 12 U.S.C. § 1831m and 12 C.F.R. Part 363.

Public Company Accounting Oversight Board
November 21, 2003
Page 4

information systems and an internal audit function adequate and appropriate for the institution's size and the nature and scope of its activities.[7] An institution's compliance with these safety and soundness requirements is subject to regular examinations by the federal bank regulators.[8]

Quarterly Reviews

The proposed standard outlines some responsibilities that the auditor would have for evaluating management's section 302 disclosures about internal control over financial reporting. ACB opposes the requirement that the auditor perform limited procedures on a quarterly basis to confirm that management's disclosures are complete. Quarterly evaluations are not mandated by Sarbanes-Oxley. Section 404 of Sarbanes-Oxley requires that annual reports include an internal control report and that the independent auditor attest to, and report on, this annual assessment. ACB believes that quarterly evaluations would be impractical, time-consuming, and costly. The experience of the banking industry under FDICIA has shown that an annual auditor review of management's evaluation of internal controls is quite adequate.

Evaluation of the Audit Committee

The proposed standard would require the independent auditor to evaluate the effectiveness of the audit committee's oversight of the company's financial reporting and internal control over financial reporting. This would create serious conflict of interest issues for the auditor and the audit committee. Among the most important goals of Sarbanes-Oxley was to strengthen the role of the audit committee in overseeing the auditor. The audit committee is now specifically responsible for hiring and compensating the external auditor. The proposed requirement will, in effect, dilute the power of the audit committee and may lead to inadequate oversight in an effort to ensure a satisfactory evaluation. The auditor, on the other hand, may be reluctant to issue a harsh evaluation of the committee that is responsible for his or her hiring and compensation. Furthermore, there are no objective criteria or adequate guidelines for the auditor to use to evaluate the audit committee. The evaluation would be completely subjective and based on each auditor's opinions and beliefs on how an audit committee should function. We believe that the review of the effectiveness of the audit committee, at least for regulated financial institutions, is more properly left to the federal banking agencies.

Reliance on the Work of Others

The proposed standard addresses the auditor's use of testing performed by management and others and limits this use in a number of areas, including controls over the period-end financial reporting process and certain information technology general controls. The inability to use the testing performed by management to the fullest extent possible, together with requiring the auditor to conduct walkthroughs of the company's significant processes, would result in unnecessary cost and burden. The external auditor's responsibility should be to obtain a thorough understanding of the processes in place and evaluate if, and to what extent, he or she

---

[7] 12 U.S.C. § 1831p-1; 12 C.F.R. Parts 30, 364, and 570, and Appendix D-1 to Part 208.
[8] *See*, for example, section 355 of the Office of Thrift Supervision's *Thrift Activities Handbook*, available at www.ots.treas.gov

Public Company Accounting Oversight Board
November 21, 2003
Page 5

can rely on the work performed by management and others by considering the factors discussed in paragraph 103 of the standard. The company's professional and independent audit staff, especially in the highly technical areas like IT controls, may be better suited than the external auditor to understand the internal accounting controls and how they perform. The external auditor's task should be to determine whether he or she can rely on the work performed by the company's professional staff.

If a walkthrough has been sufficiently performed and documented by the company's internal auditors, there is no reason for duplicating their work. This is particularly true in the case of financial institutions, which are required by banking law and regulation to have an internal audit function and that function is evaluated during safety and soundness examinations. The PCAOB itself acknowledges the importance of internal audit by indicating in paragraph 108 of the standard that the auditor may be able to use the results of procedures conducted by internal auditors to a greater extent than the results of procedures performed by others.

Guidance for Small and Medium-Size Companies

ACB is particularly concerned about the effect of the proposed auditing standard on small and medium-sized community banks. The PCAOB states that it is sensitive to the possible effects of the auditing standard on small and medium-size businesses. However, the PCAOB does not offer any specific examples that might serve as guidelines for reviewing internal controls for these companies. The external auditor is left to decide what constitutes an acceptable review and will most likely take a conservative approach. The PCAOB also does not indicate what constitutes a small or medium-size company.

The PCAOB should provide more specific guidance to auditors in evaluating internal controls at small and medium-size companies. As a preliminary matter, the PCAOB should define these companies. An approach would be to define these companies as those that are not considered "accelerated filers" under the rules of the Securities and Exchange Commission ("SEC"). The SEC defines an accelerated filer as a company that (i) has a common equity public float of at least $75 million; (ii) has been subject to the reporting requirements of the Securities Exchange Act for a period of at least 12 months; and (iii) has filed at least one annual report as a public company.[9]

Small and medium-sized businesses will find the extensive walkthroughs, quarterly evaluations, and other requirements in the proposed standard to be prohibitively burdensome and costly. This is especially true for small community banks, which, in addition to the lack of resources that larger banks possess, might not have ready access to auditors experienced in attestation procedures. The requirements would only add to already increasing costs and would likely decrease the competitiveness of these institutions. The PCAOB should provide specific examples of how the external auditor should address the issues particular to small and medium-size businesses and how the attestation process for those companies would differ from that used for larger companies. For example, the requirements for the walkthroughs could be scaled back and the auditor could be given more leeway to rely on the testing performed by management.

---

[9] 17 C.F.R. § 240.12b-2.

Public Company Accounting Oversight Board
November 21, 2003
Page 6

Also, the PCAOB could provide guidance on the review that is expected when there cannot be complete segregation of duties because of the limited staff resources at many smaller companies. While we appreciate the PCAOB's efforts to recognize the special circumstances of small and medium-size companies, more specific guidance in this area is needed to limit the cost and burden of the attestation for community banks.

Conclusion

ACB believes that many aspects of the proposed standard would be unnecessarily costly and burdensome. The standard goes beyond what is required by Sarbanes-Oxley by requiring an integrated audit of internal control and financial statements. Quarterly evaluations and limits on the use of testing performed by others will multiply the cost of the audit and the requirement to evaluate the audit committee will create conflicts of interest. If the PCAOB adopts the standard as proposed, exceptions should be made for depository institutions in light of the existing substantial oversight of those institutions by federal banking agencies.

ACB appreciates the invitation to comment on this issue. If you have any questions about our comments, please do not hesitate to contact me. You can also contact ACB's Senior Regulatory Counsel, Diane Koonjy, at (202) 857-3144 or via e-mail at dkoonjy@acbankers.org, and Accounting and Financial Management Specialist, Dusan Jovanovic at (202) 857-3158, or via e-mail at djovanovic@acbankers.org.

Sincerely,

Charlotte M. Bahin

Charlotte M. Bahin
Senior Vice President, Regulatory Affairs

¶ 606. Association for Investment Management and Research

ASSOCIATION FOR
INVESTMENT MANAGEMENT
AND RESEARCH®

CHARLOTTESVILLE • HONG KONG • LONDON

560 Ray C. Hunt Drive • P.O. Box 3668
Charlottesville, VA 22903-0668 USA
Tel: 434-951-5499 • Fax: 434-951-5262
Email: info@aimr.org • Internet: www.aimr.org

24 November 2003

Judith Primus
Office of the Secretary
Public Company Accounting Oversight Board
1666 K Street, NW
Washington, DC 20006-2803

Email: **comments@pcaobus.org**

File Reference: **PCAOB Rulemaking Docket Matter No. 008—Proposed Auditing Standard:** *An Audit of Internal Control Over Financial Reporting Performed in Conjunction With an Audit of Financial Statements*

Dear Ms. Primus:

The Association for Investment Management and Research® (AIMR) is pleased to comment on the Public Company Accounting Oversight Board's (PCAOB) Proposed Auditing Standard, *An Audit of Internal Control Over Financial Reporting Performed in Conjunction With an Audit of Financial Statements.* With headquarters in Charlottesville, VA, and regional offices in Hong Kong and London, AIMR is a non-profit professional organization of 67,000 financial analysts, portfolio managers, and other investment professionals in 115 countries of which 55,800 are holders of the Chartered Financial Analyst® (CFA®) designation. AIMR's membership also includes 127 affiliated societies and chapters in 46 countries. AIMR is internationally renowned for its rigorous CFA curriculum and examination program. More than 102,000 candidates worldwide enrolled for the June 2003 CFA Examination.

General Comments

We commend the efforts of the Public Company Accounting Oversight Board (PCAOB) to strengthen the financial reporting system for companies that are publicly traded in the United States, increase the reliability and validity of financial reports, and provide greater oversight and transparency of both the attest function and the evaluation of systems of internal controls. Reliable financial information is the life blood of the financial markets. Participants in these markets must have complete, reliable, and transparent information in order to make appropriate financial decisions, including valuation and investment decisions, and to properly allocate capital.

Setting a Higher Standard for Investment Professionals Worldwide ™

AIMR Letter to the PCAOB Office of the Secretary
Re: PCAOB Rulemaking Docket Matter No. 008—Proposed Auditing Standard: *An Audit of Internal Control Over Financial Reporting Performed in Conjunction With an Audit of Financial Statements*
24 November 2003
Page 2 of 4

In recent years, when it became apparent to investors and other users of financial statements that they might no longer be able to rely upon the reliability of companies' financial disclosures, their trust and confidence in the markets collapsed. The loss of investor confidence has harmed everyone who participates in the financial markets, including the issuers of securities themselves. Consequently, we support strongly the PCAOB's initiatives which we believe will contribute in a fundamental way to restoring the essential trust and confidence of investors and other users of financial statements.

In particular, we support the Board's proposal to:

    1.   Require auditors to evaluate management's process for determining whether its standards are effective; and

    2.   Require auditors to gather evidence through testing to determine whether the

        a.   Controls are effective, and

        b.   Management's assertion to that effect is fairly stated.

The critical core of any audit of financial statements is the evaluation of the effectiveness of the company's system of internal controls. If material failures occur in the internal control systems, as we have seen in a number of the recent corporate collapses, then the reporting system cannot be relied upon to produce reliable financial statements. It is not sufficient that auditors merely review internal control system documentation and management's assertions as to the effectiveness of the system. Attestation as to the effectiveness of the system requires direct tests to evaluate the:

- Control environment;

- Control and other business and operational risks;

- Control activities;

- Information and communication system; and

- Monitoring of the control and reporting systems.

Auditors must test each of the critical components of internal control systems, and provide sufficient independent and competent evidence to be able to provide an opinion that can be relied upon by investors and other users of the statements. In the absence of such tests and evidence, there is no basis for reliance on the system, or for auditors to formulate an opinion on the

AIMR Letter to the PCAOB Office of the Secretary
Re: PCAOB Rulemaking Docket Matter No. 008—Proposed Auditing Standard: *An Audit of Internal Control Over Financial Reporting Performed in Conjunction With an Audit of Financial Statements*
24 November 2003
Page 3 of 4

financial statements, or for users (whether they are internal or external to the company) to rely on system outputs. Consequently, the risk premium that investors and other providers of capital will demand if they are to provide their capital to issuers of such financial statements will place a great burden on the operations of companies. We believe that failure to ensure the reliability of these systems will ultimately be more costly for everyone.

We realize and expect that the costs of audits will likely increase with the increased audit activities and that these costs will ultimately be borne by shareholders. We would observe, however, as been widely reported, that the average cost of audits has been artificially low in the past because of the effective subsidization of audit fees by revenues generated from additional services auditors provided to their audit clients. Indeed, one of the chief objections raised by the audit profession to the prohibition under the Sarbanes-Oxley Act of 2002 of auditors' providing non-audit consulting services to their audit clients was that without those services, the audit firms would have to increase their audit fees significantly. Shareholders were already bearing the costs of *both* the audits and the additional consulting services.

There is a clear economic tradeoff between the cost of audits and the cost of capital. That is, if, in order to reduce or contain audit costs, the scope of audit activities is restricted, then the resulting decrease in the confidence that users have in audited financial reports will be reflected directly in higher costs of capital demanded by investors. Moreover, because of the greater uncertainty resulting from reduced reliability, we believe the increased risk premium is likely to be greater than the cost savings realized by the reduced audit activities. Such a circumstance would ill-serve issuers and their existing shareholders as well as other investors.

We also concur with the Board's proposal that auditors should identify circumstances that constitute a significant deficiency and which are a strong indicator of material weakness. In particular, the proposal states that the auditor should evaluate the effectiveness of the audit committee's oversight of the company's internal control and external financial reporting systems. A cornerstone of effective as well as efficient internal control systems is a strong and continuous internal monitoring and audit function.

The Sarbanes-Oxley Act mandated that US registrants must have an effective and independent audit subcommittee within their boards of directors. This committee would serve as the apex of the internal audit and financial reporting functions. However, it is not sufficient that such a committee be formed. Rather, in order to fulfill the intent of the Sarbanes-Oxley legislation, the effectiveness with which the committee performs its fiduciary responsibilities to oversee the internal control system and financial reporting process must be assessed as well. Again, in a number of the recent corporate collapses, it was clear that the directors failed in their responsibility to monitor and evaluate such systems, and, in some cases, had even acquiesced in management's overriding of the control systems.

AIMR Letter to the PCAOB Office of the Secretary
Re: PCAOB Rulemaking Docket Matter No. 008—Proposed Auditing Standard: *An Audit of Internal Control Over Financial Reporting Performed in Conjunction With an Audit of Financial Statements*
24 November 2003
Page 4 of 4

Consequently, we concur with the provision to expand the auditor's current responsibilities to evaluate the effectiveness of the oversight function, particularly with regard to the audit committee's responsibilities. We do not believe that this will involve a significant increase in the costs of audits because auditors are currently required to communicate with the audit committee and discuss with them both the results of their audits and any concerns or material deficiencies revealed by their tests. Indeed, this increased responsibility could lead to greater cooperation between auditors and the committee. We believe that improving this relationship could make a very constructive contribution to both the auditor's work and the audit committee's efforts and effectiveness.

Concluding Remarks

In conclusion we support the Board's efforts to improve the quality and effectiveness of audits of companies that are publicly traded in the United States and believe these proposals will lead to greater reliability and transparency of the financial reports that are essential to investors and other participants in the financial markets. We strongly encourage the Board to continue with such improvements.

AIMR appreciates the opportunity to express its views on the Proposed Auditing Standard, *An Audit of Internal Control over Financial Reporting Performed in Conjunction with an Audit of Financial Statements.* If the Board or staff have questions or seek amplification of our views, please contact Rebecca McEnally at 1-434-951-5319 or at rebecca.mcenally@aimr.org. We would be pleased to answer any questions or provide additional information you might request.

Respectfully yours,

/s/ Patricia Doran Walters   /s/ Rebecca Todd McEnally

Patricia Doran Walters, Ph.D., CFA   Rebecca McEnally, Ph.D., CFA
Senior Vice President, Professional Standards   Vice-President, Advocacy, AIMR
     And Advocacy

cc: Advocacy Distribution List

¶ 607. Association of Chartered Certified Accountants

Consultation Response

PROPOSED AUDITING STANDARD

AN AUDIT OF INTERNAL CONTROL OVER FINANCIAL REPORTING PERFORMED IN CONJUNCTION WITH AN AUDIT OF FINANCIAL STATEMENTS

PCAOB Rulemaking Docket Matter No. 008

Comments from ACCA

November 2003

Page 1

ACCA is the largest and fastest-growing international accountancy body. Over 300,000 students and members in 160 countries are served by more than 70 staffed offices and other centres.

ACCA's mission is to work in the public interest to provide quality professional opportunities to people of ability and application, to promote the highest ethical and governance standards and to be a leader in the development of the accountancy profession.

Further information on ACCA is available on ACCA's website, www.accaglobal.com

Page 2

General Comments

ACCA is please to provide comments on PCAOB Rulemaking Docket Matter No. 008 – Proposed Auditing Standard – *An Audit of Internal Control over Financial Reporting Performed in Conjunction with an Audit of Financial Statements* (the Proposed Standard).

PCAOB is currently issuing new standards while having established Interim Professional Auditing Standards in respect of auditing, attestation, quality control, ethics, and independence. These Interim Professional Auditing Standards are essentially those that were established by the American Institute of Certified Public Accountants (AICPA). ACCA considers that, to further its objectives over the longer term, it is vital that PCAOB develops new standards that promote consistent, high quality auditing around the world. To achieve this, we strongly encourage PCAOB to ensure that, wherever possible, it develops standards that are consistent with those of the International Auditing and Assurance Standards Board of the International Federation of Accountants. Global harmonisation of auditing standards of the highest quality is essential to the integrity and efficiency of capital markets and we encourage PCAOB to work closely with IAASB to achieve that end.

Page 3

Our primary concern with the Proposed Standard is that its emphasis on requiring auditors to obtain direct evidence of the effectiveness of internal control, taken together with the extent of detailed requirements and guidance, may cause auditors to adopt a 'bottom up' rather than a 'top down' approach to their work. The 'bottom up' approach is neither effective nor efficient.

Corporate failures, such as Enron and WorldCom can be attributed to weaknesses in the control environment. The risk is that a 'bottom up' approach may mean that auditors pay insufficient attention to the control environment, which COSO rightly recognises as *'the foundation for all other components of internal control'*.

Companies already face cost increases relating to their own compliance with the Act. There is a risk that they will also experience both direct and indirect costs of auditor inefficiency that are greatly disproportionate to the benefit to their investors.

ACCA has a wide experience of auditing in many jurisdictions and we are aware of the fact that many will heed the words in the Proposed Standard that: *'the Board expects that the auditor will exercise reasonable professional judgment in determining the extent of the audit of internal control and perform only those tests that are necessary to ascertain the effectiveness of the company's internal control.'* Nevertheless, we perceive a significant risk that, particularly for larger enterprises, auditors will do too much work. If this happens, there is a risk that PCAOB standards themselves will be devalued. We urge PCAOB to address this perception problem aggressively to ensure that standards are seen as proportionate and cost effective as well as being of the highest quality.

Page 4

Response to the Questions in the PCAOB's Request for Comments

1   Is it appropriate to refer to the auditor's attestation of management's assessment of the effectiveness of internal control over financial reporting as the audit of internal control over financial reporting?

No. It would be better to retain the term 'audit' for the financial statement audit and to refer to the attestation as an attestation.

2   Should the auditor be prohibited from performing an audit of internal control over financial reporting without also performing an audit of the financial statements?

Yes. The Act does not anticipate that these engagements will be separate.

3   Rather than requiring the auditor to also complete an audit of the financial statements, would an appropriate alternative be to require the auditor to perform work with regard to the financial statements comparable to that required to complete the financial statement audit?

We see no value in requiring equivalent work without actually reporting as the financial statement auditor.

Page 5

4   Does the Board's proposed standard give appropriate consideration to how internal control is implemented in, and how the audit of internal control over financial reporting should be conducted at, small and medium-sized issuers?

Yes. Much of the guidance is, however, given in Appendix E rather than in the main body of the Proposed Standard.

5   Should the Board, generally or in this proposed standard, specify the level of competence and training of the audit personnel that is necessary to perform specified auditing procedures effectively? For example, it would be inappropriate for a new, inexperienced auditor to have primary responsibility for conducting interviews of a company's senior management about possible fraud.

Yes - generally. This is an area where the PCAOB should consider harmonisation with the IFAC standards on education and quality control.

6   Is the scope of the audit appropriate in that it requires the auditor to both evaluate management's assessment and obtain, directly, evidence about whether internal control over financial reporting is effective?

Yes. It is important that the auditor does not simply rely on others throughout. In our general comments we have, however, drawn attention to the risk of auditors doing too much work because they perceive that obtaining direct evidence is emphasised.

Page 6

7   Is it appropriate that the Board has provided criteria that auditors should use to evaluate the adequacy of management's documentation?

Yes. Criteria are necessary and the provision of consistent criteria beneficial. We suggest, however, that the criteria in paragraphs 43 to 47 may be perceived as inflexible and that auditors might concentrate too much on documentation.

8   (a) Is it appropriate to state that inadequate documentation is an internal control deficiency, the severity of which the auditor should evaluate? (b) Or should inadequate documentation automatically rise to the level of significant deficiency or material weakness in internal control?

(a) Yes. This allows for the use of professional judgement.
(b) No.

9   Are the objectives to be achieved by performing walkthroughs sufficient to require the performance of walkthroughs?

No. Walkthroughs may be useful in some systems but provide little evidence of effectiveness. The 'controls' identified by walkthroughs are often no more than aspects of the accounting system which provide little mitigation of business risks.

10   Is it appropriate to require that the walkthrough be performed by the auditor himself or herself, rather than allowing the auditor to use walkthrough procedures performed by management, internal auditors, or others?

No. The auditor should use professional judgement to determine the extent to which he or she performs walkthroughs.

11   (a) Is it appropriate to require the auditor to obtain evidence of the effectiveness of controls for all relevant assertions for all significant accounts and disclosures (b) every year or (c) may the auditor use some of the audit evidence obtained in previous years to support his or her current opinion on management's assessment?

(a) Yes. We are concerned however that this will be perceived as requiring all low level controls to be tested.
(b) & (c) Although audit evidence may be obtained from work carried out in previous periods, the migration of that evidence to the current period is a complex matter of audit methodology which is rightly left to the judgement of the auditor.

12   To what extent should the auditor be permitted or required to use the work of management and others?

This should be permitted as a matter for the judgement of the auditor.

Page 8

13 Are the three categories of controls and the extent to which the auditor may rely on the work of others appropriately defined?

No. We suggest that such material would be better presented as guidance and the decisions on reliance on the work of others left to the auditor.

14 Does the proposed standard give appropriate recognition to the work of the internal auditors? If not, does the proposed standard place too much emphasis and preference on the work of internal auditors or not enough?

Yes. Internal auditors play a vital role in many companies and it is appropriate that the independent auditor has the capacity to rely on their work.

15 (a) Is the flexibility in determining the extent of reperformance of the work of others appropriate, or (b) should the auditor be specifically required to reperform a certain level of work (for example, reperform tests of all significant accounts or reperform every test performed by others that the auditor intends to use)?

(a) Yes.
(b) No. This should be a matter of professional judgement.

Page 9

16 Is the requirement for the auditor to obtain the principal
    evidence, on an overall basis, through his or her own work the
    appropriate benchmark for the amount of work that is required to
    be performed by the auditor?

    No. This should be a matter of professional judgement. A
    requirement in this regard would add substantially to the perception
    that the Proposed Standard is not cost effective.

17 Will the definitions in the proposed standard of significant
    deficiency and material weakness provide for increased
    consistency in the evaluation of deficiencies? How can the
    definitions be improved?

    Yes. Auditors need to focus on matters of significance and
    materiality. The definitions are one area where PCAOB should avoid
    issuing a Standard that is not easily reconcilable to the output of
    IAASB.

18 (a) Do the examples in Appendix D of how to apply these
    definitions in various scenarios provide helpful guidance? (b) Are
    there other specific examples that commenters could suggest that
    would provide further interpretive help?

    (a) Yes.
    (b) We do not suggest any further examples.

Page 10

19 Is it necessary for the auditor to evaluate the severity of all identified internal control deficiencies?

Yes. The evaluation need not be extensive except where there is a potentially significant deficiency.

20 Is it appropriate to require the auditor to communicate all internal control deficiencies (not just material weaknesses and significant deficiencies) to management in writing?

Yes. Trivial matters should, however, be excluded from such a requirement.

21 Are the matters that the Board has classified as strong indicators that a material weakness in internal control exists appropriately classified as such?

Yes.

Page 11

22   Is it appropriate to require the auditors to evaluate the effectiveness of the audit committee's oversight of the company's external financial reporting and internal control over financial reporting?

This is a difficult question. Theoretically the auditor's relationship with the audit committee may preclude such an evaluation. Nevertheless, oversight exercised by the audit committee may in itself be important to internal control. On balance we suggest that there be no requirement to evaluate the effectiveness of oversight as a separate matter but that the impact of the work of the audit committee can be a factor that the auditor considers as part of his or her evaluation of the internal control environment at the highest levels.

23   Will auditors be able to effectively carry out their responsibility to evaluate the effectiveness of the audit committee's oversight?

See our answer above.

24   If the auditor concludes that ineffective audit committee oversight is a material weakness, rather than require the auditor to issue an adverse opinion with regard to the effectiveness of the internal control over financial reporting, should the standard require the auditor to withdraw from the audit engagement?

See our answer above.

Page 12

25   Is it appropriate that the existence of a material weakness would require the auditor to express an adverse conclusion about the effectiveness of the company's internal control over financial reporting, consistent with the required reporting model for management?

No. The auditor should use professional judgement to determine whether an adverse conclusion is appropriate (see answer below).

26   Are there circumstances where a qualified "except for" conclusion would be appropriate?

Yes. In some circumstances, such an opinion will provide better information to users and this should, therefore, be a matter of professional judgement.

27   Do you agree with the position that when the auditor issues a non-standard opinion, such as an adverse opinion, that the auditor's opinion should speak directly to the effectiveness of internal control over financial reporting rather than to whether management's assessment is fairly stated?

No. The Act is concerned with management's assessment. PCAOB should consider research of user understanding before moving towards a direct report.

Page 13

28 Should the Board provide specific guidance on independence and
    internal control-related non-audit services in the context of this
    proposed standard?

    No. Independence should be addressed in other pronouncements.

29 Are there any specific internal control-related non-audit services
    the auditor should be prohibited from providing to an audit client? .

    It would be appropriate to refer to the SEC independence rules.

30 Are the auditor's differing levels of responsibility as they relate to
    management's quarterly certifications versus the annual (fourth
    quarter) certification, appropriate?

    Yes. In the case where a rule requires quarterly certifications of a
    different nature to annual certifications it is appropriate for the
    responsibility of the auditor also to differ.

31 Is the scope of the auditor's responsibility for quarterly disclosures
    about the internal control over financial reporting appropriate?

    Yes. Given the limited nature of quarterly certification we do not
    believe that more should be required.

TECH-CDR-349

The Association of Chartered Certified Accountants
29 Lincoln's Inn Fields London WC2A 3EE United Kingdom
tel: +44 (0)20 7396 7000 fax: +44 (0)20 7396 7070 www.accaglobal.com

$^{WG}_{&L}$ Warren, Gorham & Lamont

¶ 608. Association of the Bar of the City of New York

THE ASSOCIATION OF THE BAR
OF THE CITY OF NEW YORK
42 WEST 44TH STREET
NEW YORK, NY 10036-6689

FINANCIAL REPORTING COMMITTEE

November 21, 2003

Via email: comments@pcaobus.org
Public Company Accounting Oversight Board
1666 K Street, N.W.
Washington, D.C. 20006-2803

Attention: Office of the Secretary

Re: PCAOB Release No. 2003-17; Rulemaking Docket Matter No. 008
Proposed Auditing Standard – An Audit of Internal Control Over
Financial Reporting Performed in Conjunction with an Audit of Financial
Statements

Ladies and Gentlemen:

This letter is submitted on behalf of the Financial Reporting Committee of The
Association of the Bar of the City of New York (the "Committee") in response to Release
No. 2003-17, October 7, 2003 (the "Release"), in which the Public Company Accounting
Oversight Board (the "PCAOB") announced a proposed auditing standard for Internal
Control Over Financial Reporting (the "proposed standard" or "proposal"). Our
Committee is composed of lawyers with diverse perspectives on securities issues,
including members of law firms, counsel to major corporations, investment banks, and
institutional investors.

Introduction

The Committee supports the PCAOB's objective of creating an integrated
standard for the purpose of performing an audit of internal control over financial
reporting in conjunction with an audit of the financial statements. The recommendations
that follow are offered with the intention of revising definitions which could lead to
unintended outcomes with costs to companies and shareholders that far exceed the
benefits to investors and to make suggestions that further support the goal of an efficient,
effective, and integrated audit through principles-based rulemaking as opposed to overly

Public Company Accounting Oversight Board
November 21, 2003
Page 2

rigid, technical rules. While our responses refer to specific question numbers, we have organized our responses not by the sequential numbering of the PCAOB's questions, but rather by the importance we believe each topic deserves.

1. <u>Overview.</u>

We request that the PCAOB consider four main themes:

- Certain of the key definitions have thresholds that are too low.
- Certain of the rules, particularly those related to the identification of fraud, should be more principles-based and less rigid to allow external auditors to assess the facts and circumstances of each individual situation and to exercise their professional judgment in light of these facts and circumstances.
- Certain of the required activities of auditors are inappropriate, beyond their expertise and impose inherent conflicts of interest that will impede the relationship between the audit committee and the auditor and undermine the enhanced authority of the audit committee granted by Sarbanes-Oxley.
- Auditors should be given greater ability to rely on internal audits where, in their professional judgment, such reliance is appropriate.

A. <u>Certain Definitions Should Have Higher Thresholds.</u>

Although the PCAOB may not be able to perform a cost impact analysis as to the new requirements to be implemented in the proposed standard, we believe the PCAOB should consider the impact of definitions that we believe include excessively low thresholds by which to measure deficiencies. A complete discussion of our proposed revisions to the thresholds definitions is included below. We request that the PCAOB keep in mind while reviewing our comments that the proposed requirements will be broadly applied and will not be limited to issuers and auditors with unlimited resources.

B. <u>Rules, Particularly Those Related to the Identification of Fraud, Should Be Less Prescriptive and Rigid and More Principles-Based to Allow External Auditors to Exercise Professional Judgment.</u>

We believe the general preference of the Securities and Exchange Commission ("SEC") for principles-based accounting over rules-based accounting should extend to some of the new PCAOB proposals identified below. In our opinion, certain proposed standards are too prescriptive and rigid and we respectfully suggest that those technical, rigid rules be replaced with more principles-based rules under which certain facts and circumstances would be identified as factors to be considered by the external auditor rather than as items mandating certain findings. The proposal states repeatedly that external auditors must be able to exercise judgment so that their procedures adapt to the size and complexity of each public company. We respectfully submit, however, that the

Public Company Accounting Oversight Board
November 21, 2003
Page 3

proposal in certain areas does not adequately allow exercise of that professional judgment because in many instances the rules are too mechanical in that they mandate certain findings and are more "check-the-box" in approach rather than allowing the external auditor to give appropriate consideration and weight to the items specified in the proposed rules.

For example, the proposal specifies a rigid list of circumstances in which an external auditor must find at least a significant deficiency and provides that an auditor should consider those circumstances as a strong indicator of a material weakness. We believe such a rigid list would detract from the ability of external auditors to exercise their professional judgment in a meaningful manner.

We believe mandating annual walkthroughs of **all** of the company's significant processes for **all** types of transactions and events, both recurring and unusual, is excessively prescriptive. Also, the extent to which external auditors must review management's documentation should be determined in part by the external auditors using the PCAOB's principles on how to make that determination, not by rigid rules that dictate the degree of review required.

The SEC Fortune 500 review resulted in a substantial number of financial restatements by corporations to reflect the current SEC policy on identification and aggregation of segments. Applying the proposal, the external auditor may be required to automatically label a company as having a significant deficiency or material weakness in financial reporting even though the segment reporting was not intentionally misleading or fraudulent, but instead improperly aggregated in light of guidance released after the publication of the financial statements in question. We believe such a result would be inappropriate and perhaps even unfair. External auditors should be guided by the principle that the factors surrounding the need for a restatement should be considered in determining whether a significant deficiency or material weakness exists. There should not be an arbitrary rule that all restatements must fall into one of those categories without having the external auditors exercise their professional judgment in considering the circumstances surrounding the restatement. A restatement reflects an issue in a prior reporting period; it should not automatically result in a significant deficiency or material weakness in subsequent periods.

Similarly, we respectfully submit that the identification of fraud *of any magnitude* as an automatic significant deficiency and a strong indicator of a material weakness is too rigid and arbitrary. The magnitude of the fraud, the length of time over which the fraud was committed and the method of its discovery are all factors that should be considered by external auditors in determining whether a significant deficiency exists. If fraud is detected through existing internal control procedures and it is determined that the fraud in question was isolated, not material to the company and was not committed over a lengthy period of time, that may in fact evidence proper internal controls. As stated in the proposed standard, there are both preventive and detective controls, and the discovery of

Public Company Accounting Oversight Board
November 21, 2003
Page 4

fraud is an accomplishment of the detective control system. Accordingly, we submit that the external auditors should be able to consider discovery of the fraud by the internal control system as a mitigating factor.

In our opinion, the appropriate principle should be that circumstances surrounding a finding of fraud should be examined by external auditors and they should use their professional judgment about the circumstances surrounding and the seriousness of each fraud. Using that judgment, the external auditors will likely determine that a fraudulent act committed by a senior member of a multinational retail chain's internal accounting staff indicates a greater likelihood of a serious problem than a single double billing fraudulent act related to an airline ticket reimbursement committed by a senior marketing manager. The latter does not indicate a significant deficiency and possibly a material weakness, whereas the former may very well so indicate.

Proposed Rule: Paragraph 126 -- "Each of the following circumstances should be regarded as at least a significant deficiency and is a strong indicator that a material weakness in internal control over financial reporting exists," and continues to list said circumstances.

Suggested Revised Rule: "In each of the following circumstances, *the external auditor should conduct appropriate inquiries and procedures to determine whether a significant deficiency, and possibly a material weakness, exists.*"

2. Definitions.

Questions 17-18: Will the definitions in the proposed standard of significant deficiency and material weakness provide for increased consistency in the evaluation of deficiencies? How can the definitions be improved? Do the examples in Appendix D of how to apply these definitions in various scenarios provide helpful guidance? Are there other specific examples that commenters could suggest that would provide further interpretive help?

Considering that the proposal revolves around identifying significant deficiencies and ultimately material weaknesses in the internal control of financial reporting, we feel most strongly about implementing definitions with realistic thresholds that are principles-based and act as proper filters for identifying internal deficiencies.

First, both terms center on the standard of "remote likelihood," and refer to the definition of "remote" in SFAS No. 5. SFAS No. 5 defines "remote" as the "chance of the future event or events occurring is slight." It is our belief that such a threshold is far too low, and not only differs from the "reasonable assurance" standard required by management that was adopted by the SEC in Release No. 33-8238 and reflected under COSO and Codification of Statement on Auditing Standards AU §319.18, but would also

Public Company Accounting Oversight Board
November 21, 2003
Page 5

make for a condition in which every auditor would be forced to create a laundry list of deficiencies, no matter how small or insignificant.

This lies in stark contrast to the AICPA standard of a "reportable condition," which allows the auditor to use professional judgment in determining whether a significant deficiency exists. Under the current state of the proposal, the PCAOB would essentially be tying the AICPA auditing standards to the lowest threshold of probability for a material misstatement under SFAS No. 5. Creating such a definition for "significant deficiency" would have consequences that lower the bar across all auditing procedures.

The possibility of human error or inadvertent misjudgment at every level of preventive or detective control would make it difficult, and nearly impossible, to categorize even the most stringent internal control system as reducing possibility to "slight." We believe that even in corporations with the most effective internal oversight, the chances of a material misstatement can be reduced only to "probably not," a definition that follows most closely the "reasonably possible" standard of SFAS No. 5, which is defined to mean "the chance that a future event or events occurring is more than remote but less than likely." Even at this level, however, we believe that many of the significant deficiencies identified will not be material, but nevertheless may cause auditors to issue unwarranted adverse opinions or refuse to issue an opinion at all. Investor confidence will not be restored in financial reporting of public companies if well-managed companies with robust internal controls are not able to meet unnecessarily strict and inadequately differentiated standards.

Probable	The future event or events are likely to occur.
Reasonably possible	The chance of the future event or events occurring is more than remote but less than likely.
Remote	The chance of the future event or events occurring is slight.

The term "inconsequential" in the definition of significant deficiency is not defined and confuses the definition of the threshold at which auditors must declare that such a problem exists.

Proposed Rule:
- Paragraph 8 -- A *significant deficiency* is an internal control deficiency that adversely affects the company's ability to initiate, record, process, or report external financial data reliably in accordance with generally accepted accounting principles. A significant deficiency could be a single deficiency, or a combination of deficiencies, that results in more than a remote likelihood that a misstatement of the annual or

Public Company Accounting Oversight Board
November 21, 2003
Page 6

interim financial statements that is more than inconsequential in amount will not be prevented or detected.

- Paragraph 9 -- A *material weakness* is a significant deficiency that, by itself, or in combination with other significant deficiencies, results in more than a remote likelihood that a material misstatement of the annual or interim financial statements will not be prevented or detected.

Suggested Revised Rule:

- "Significant deficiency" *is a single deficiency, or a combination of deficiencies in the same or closely related reporting area, that results in a reasonable possibility that a misstatement of the annual or interim financial statements* in an amount that is *more than de minimis but less than material will not be prevented or detected."* **OR** the term as currently used by the AICPA.

- "Material weakness" *is a significant deficiency that, by itself, or in combination with other significant deficiencies in the same or a closely related reporting area, results in a reasonable possibility that a material misstatement of the annual or interim financial statements will not be prevented or detected."*

These revised definitions have higher thresholds using terms with which accountants already have experience and extensive accounting literature and guidance. We believe the higher thresholds are more likely to provide practical warning flags rather than extensive laundry lists of false negatives.

3. <u>External Auditors Should Be Able to Use the Work of Others At the External Auditors' Discretion.</u>

Question 12-15: To what extent should the auditor be permitted or required to use the work of management and others? Are the three categories of controls and the extent to which the auditor may rely on the work of others appropriately defined? Does the proposed standard give appropriate recognition to the work of internal auditors? If not, does the proposed standard place too much emphasis and preference on the work of internal auditors or not enough? Is the flexibility in determining the extent of reperformance of the work of others appropriate, or should the auditor be specifically required to reperform a certain level of work (for example, reperform tests of all significant accounts or reperform every test performed by others that the auditor intends to use)?

The proposal specifies certain procedures that must be performed by the auditor such as mandatory requirements for the external auditor to retest internal controls over other controls as well as those over fraud. We believe this rule should be rewritten to allow the auditors to exercise discretion on the extent of review required and the frequency with which these reviews must occur (for example, if a review was done in a

Public Company Accounting Oversight Board
November 21, 2003
Page 7

prior year, we do not believe it necessarily, under all circumstances and for all issuers, needs to be completely redone in subsequent years). We believe the PCAOB should also recognize that unnecessary retesting by auditors can result in interruption of the operations and financial reporting processes of companies.

In being so prescriptive, the PCAOB proposal risks undermining the role of an internal audit entirely, or, in the case of a smaller company, creating a financially unsupportable situation for the simultaneous presence of both internal and external oversight structures. The rules should make clear that the auditors should be free to exercise their reasonable professional judgment on the appropriate reliance level on internal work, including the work of internal auditors.

If the testing of the controls listed in Paragraph 104 of the proposal becomes mandatory for an outside auditor, management's incentives could shift from ensuring that their own internal auditors properly test the design and operation of these controls, at a high cost, to limiting the internal audit function involvement in such testing, thereby encouraging companies to cut costs in areas which will be retested by external auditors rather than paying twice for the same services. This will have the effect of undermining the role of the internal auditors.

We believe the three-tiered categorization of where to retest certain internal controls is too rigid and precludes auditors from exercising professional judgment. Why is it more important for an outside auditor to retest internal controls designed to prevent fraud on nonroutine transaction errors instead of testing those controls over routine transactions? We do not believe in a blanket rule that implies the existence of a hierarchy between transactions within a system of internal controls. The professional judgment of auditors should not be hindered or superceded in this rigid manner.

Proposed Rule:
- Paragraph 104 -- "There are a number of areas in which the auditor should not use the results of testing performed by management and others, including: (list of certain tests)"

- Paragraph 105 -- "The auditor's use of the results of procedures performed by management and others should be limited in the following areas: (list of certain tests)"

- Paragraph 106 -- "The auditor might decide to use the results of tests performed by management and others within the company in other areas, such as controls over routine processing of significant accounts and disclosures, without specific limitations."

Suggested Revised Rule: We respectfully submit that Paragraphs 104-106 be omitted and that the PCAOB rely solely on Paragraph 103 as proposed:

Public Company Accounting Oversight Board
November 21, 2003
Page 8

"The auditor should evaluate whether to rely on the work performed by management and others. When evaluating whether to use the results of procedures performed by others, the auditor should evaluate the following factors:

- The materiality or the risk of misstatement of the accounts and disclosures that the controls address.
- The degree of judgment required to evaluate the operating effectiveness of the control.
- The degree the control can be subjected to objective testing vs. a subjective evaluation.
- The pervasiveness of the control.
- The level of judgment or estimation that is required in the account or disclosure."

4. Evaluating Audit Committee Oversight Should be Significantly Reduced and the Proposal Requiring the Auditors to Evaluate Audit Committees Should be Dropped.

Questions 22-23: Is it appropriate to require the auditors to evaluate the effectiveness of the audit committee's oversight of the company's external financial reporting and internal control over financial reporting? Will auditors be able to effectively carry out their responsibility to evaluate the effectiveness of the audit committee's oversight?

Audit committees retain, supervise, compensate and fire auditors, as directed by Sarbanes-Oxley and the rules of securities exchanges and self-regulatory organizations. We respectfully believe, therefore, that the auditors should not be required to test the "effectiveness" of the audit committee. Effectiveness is not defined - does it mean failure to recognize issues, ability to recognize issues but failure to adequately address them, or something entirely different?

The proposal would require the auditor to evaluate the effectiveness of the audit committee's oversight of external financial reporting and internal control. Included in this evaluation are factors such as independence from management, clarity of the committee's responsibilities, level of involvement and interaction with the auditor and internal audit, including the committee's role in appointment and compensation of the auditor and internal audit, presence of an audit committee financial expert, compliance with applicable listing standards, the amount of time the committee devotes to control issues, and the amount of time committee members are able to devote to committee activities. This would require a much greater degree of involvement by the auditors in the internal operation of the audit committee and require observation of the work of the audit committee and the individual members as well as their interaction with third parties, such as internal audit. This would require skills that are beyond the expertise of auditors (such as knowledge of listing standards and interpretations). It would also interfere with

Public Company Accounting Oversight Board
November 21, 2003
Page 9

the allocation of responsibility to the audit committee by state corporation law and by Sarbanes-Oxley.

In particular, the proposed standard requires the auditor to determine independence in the selection of candidates for the audit committee. This raises many issues of whether an auditor is qualified and able to make the subjective and perhaps legal determinations required by the proposal. It also presents conflicts since the auditors are to report to and be compensated by the audit committee. Can they be realistically requested to objectively make the enumerated determinations? Or does this present such a fundamental conflict of interest that it should not be required? We believe auditors currently view the audit committee as an important part of the financial integrity of a company and its internal control, but the key consideration for them is whether they have adequate access to and reaction from the audit committee rather than whether the audit committee is acting as a monitor.

Proposed Rule: Paragraph 58 -- "As part of evaluating the independence of committee members, the auditor should evaluate how audit committee members are nominated and selected and whether they act independently from management. Generally, the more independence that is built into the process of nominating members of the audit committee to the board, the more the auditor can be assured of committee independence. For example, are qualified candidates identified by outsiders, such as an outside search firm or a nominating committee composed of outside directors, or does management pick 'friends?' Are board candidates for the audit committee selected based upon desired skill sets?"

Suggested Revised Rule: Delete the requirement.

In addition, auditors should not be in a position of undermining the current requirement that boards determine the qualifications of the audit committee Financial Expert ("ACFE"). Sarbanes-Oxley made this decision the responsibility of the Board of Directors; the PCAOB should not change that responsibility. The standards for determining an ACFE are prescribed by the SEC pursuant to statutory direction, as implemented by the SEC's rule, and the Board's determination of satisfying that standard, which is likely a legal interpretation, should not be challenged by the auditor if the Board has based its decision on the SEC's implementing regulation. Sarbanes-Oxley also made the audit committee financial expert not a requirement, but a disclosure item. The Board of a reporting company could conclude that finding a person meeting the rather restrictive qualifications of the SEC's rule was unnecessary because it has confidence in the expertise of the members of its audit committee. The PCAOB would change this dynamic with its proposal.

Public Company Accounting Oversight Board
November 21, 2003
Page 10

5. Qualified Opinions Should be Allowed.

Questions 25-26: Is it appropriate that the existence of a material weakness would require the auditor to express an adverse conclusion about the effectiveness of the company's internal control over financial reporting, consistent with the required reporting model for management? Are there circumstances where a qualified "except for" conclusion would be appropriate?

Under the proposal, if there are one or more material weaknesses, management would be precluded from concluding that internal control over financial reporting is effective. In these circumstances, the auditor is required to express an adverse opinion on the company's internal control over financial reporting in connection with the annual attestation report and would not be permitted to issue a qualified "except for" opinion. For the reasons specified below, we respectfully submit that qualified "except for" opinions might be appropriate under certain circumstances.

We believe that during any given year, a significant number of public companies have outstanding "material weakness" designations, and we believe that it almost invariably takes more than one quarter to rectify them. Because it is in everyone's interest, particularly investors', to have problems identified and remedied, detecting a material weakness should not so significantly penalize a company that no opinion can be issued, resulting in consequences far beyond the magnitude of the material weakness, such as limiting the company's access to the capital markets. This result would have an enormous chilling effect on identifying problems in the first place and on capital markets transactions.

Proposed Rule: Paragraph 162 -- "If there are significant deficiencies that, individually or in combination, result in one or more material weaknesses, management is precluded from concluding that internal control over financial reporting is effective. In these circumstances, the auditor must express an adverse opinion on the company's internal control over financial reporting."

Suggested Revised Rule: Paragraph 162 -- "If there are significant deficiencies that, individually or in combination, result in one or more material weaknesses, management *must consider the extent of one or more material weaknesses in* concluding that internal control over financial reporting is effective, *and must disclose the nature of the material weaknesses and the actions being taken to correct them, in all earnings releases and 1934 Act filings.* In these circumstances, the auditors *should exercise professional judgment in deciding whether the nature of the material weakness requires them to issue* an adverse opinion on the company's internal control over financial reporting."

We respectfully propose that the PCAOB alter the requirement to allow for judgment on the part of auditors in identifying material weaknesses and determining

Public Company Accounting Oversight Board
November 21, 2003
Page 11

whether the material weaknesses are being corrected as quickly as possible before issuing an adverse opinion.

6. Small and Medium-Sized Issuers

Question 4: Does the Board's proposed standard give appropriate consideration to how internal control is implemented in, and how the audit of internal control over financial reporting should be conducted at, small and medium-sized issuers?

We applaud the PCAOB for not having prescribed a single method for compliance by all types of companies. Particularly, we agree with the PCAOB's view that "the nature and extent of controls that are necessary depend, to a great extent, on the size and complexity of the company." We respectfully urge the PCAOB to extend this acceptance of subjective decision-making by the auditors to the overall proposal as we have outlined in this letter.

7. Effective Date Question and Degree of Quarterly Auditor Involvement

The proposed standard would require the auditor to make inquiries of management on a quarterly basis about significant changes in the design or operation of internal control over financial reporting as it relates to the preparation of annual as well as interim financial information and to assess whether significant changes in internal control over financial reporting may have resulted in significant deficiencies or material weaknesses. Depending upon management's response, the auditor would be required to take additional action, ranging from communicating with the audit committee to reach an appropriate resolution to considering resigning from the engagement. Any communications of significant deficiencies or material weaknesses by the auditor may have an impact on and will need to be considered by management in making its Section 302 certifications and the company's disclosures under Item 308 of Regulation S-K. The effective date of the proposal, however, looks only to the 404 audit. We believe that the effective date of the proposal should be clarified to indicate that the 302 certification process with respect to matters covered in the proposal will not become effective until the respective 404 effective date.

The proposed standard would require an auditor to make certain determinations, "through a combination of observation and inquiry" as to whether significant changes in internal control over financial reporting have occurred during the quarter. We request the PCAOB to clarify that these determinations can be accomplished in connection with the current usual level of quarterly auditor involvement and will not require continuous observation by the auditor during the quarter.

Public Company Accounting Oversight Board
November 21, 2003
Page 12

Conclusion

    We commend the PCAOB for proposing new standards of audits for internal controls over financial reporting. It is the belief of the Committee that the public would be well served if the PCAOB gave additional consideration to specific elements of the proposed rule, as set forth in this letter.

    Please note that Committee member Wayne Carlin of the United States Securities and Exchange Commission did not participate in the preparation of this letter or the vote by the Committee to submit this letter to the PCAOB. In addition, this letter does not necessarily reflect the individual views of members of the Committee.

    Members of the Committee would be pleased to answer any questions you might have regarding our comments, and to meet with the Staff if that would assist the PCAOB's efforts.

Respectfully Submitted,

/s/ N. Adele Hogan
N. Adele Hogan, Chair of Committee on
Financial Reporting

Drafting Subcommittee*

N. Adele Hogan
Raymond Lin
Michael E. Lubowitz
Rise B. Norman
Neila B. Radin
Knute Salhus
Kathleen E. Shannon
Norman D. Slonaker
Gavin Solotar
Michael Zuckert

*The drafting subcommittee gratefully acknowledges the assistance of Eliot Bencuya in the preparation of this letter.

¶ 609. Council of Institutional Investors

COUNCIL OF INSTITUTIONAL INVESTORS

Suite 512 • 1730 Rhode Island Avenue, N.W. • Washington, D.C. 20036 • (202) 822-0800 • Fax (202) 822-0801

November 24, 2003

Office of the Secretary
PCAOB
1666 K Street NW
Washington, DC 20006-2803

Re: PCAOB Release 2003-017
       Audit of Internal Control Over Financial Reporting Performed in Conjunction
       With an Audit of Financial Statements

Dear Secretary:

The Council of Institutional Investors, an association of more than 140 corporate, public and union pension funds collectively holding more than $3 trillion in pension assets, is writing in support of the PCAOB's proposed auditing standard, "An Audit of Internal Control Over Financial Reporting Performed in Conjunction With an Audit of Financial Statements."

Audited financial statements are one of the primary sources of information available to guide and monitor Council members' investment decisions. The integrity of these statements is critical to Council members and their millions of pension system participants and beneficiaries. Since effective internal controls are a cornerstone of reliable financial information, Council members are interested in ensuring that internal controls are as effective as possible.

The Council agrees that outside auditors should be responsible for more than simply evaluating the adequacy of management's process for determining whether internal controls are effective. The investing public expects the outside auditor to not simply audit the financial numbers but also to test the effectiveness of a company's internal controls.

The Council wholeheartedly supports the PCAOB's provisions requiring outside auditors to evaluate management's process for determining the effectiveness of internal controls and to test whether the controls are effective and management's determination is appropriate.

Massive accounting scandals in recent years—at large and small companies—have shined a spotlight on outside auditors, audit committees and their critical role in assuring high-quality financial reporting. The Council has supported legislative and regulatory efforts to enhance the independence of audit committees and to ensure greater audit committee and outside auditor accountability to shareholders.

November 24, 2003
Office of the Secretary
Page 2

As a result, the Council strongly supports the proposal requiring the outside auditor to evaluate the effectiveness of the audit committee's oversight of the external financial reporting process and internal control over financial reporting, including whether audit committee members act independently from management.

The Council commends the PCAOB for the thoughtful and comprehensive approach taken in this proposed rulemaking. Please contact me with any questions.

Sincerely,

Sarah A.B. Teslik
Executive Director

¶610. Edison Electric Institute

United States of America

Public Company Accounting Oversight Board

	)
	)
Proposed Auditing Standard	) PCAOB Release No. 2003-017
An Audit of Internal Control Over	) PCAOB Rulemaking Docket Matter No. 8
Financial Reporting Performed in	)
Conjunction with an Audit of	)
Financial Statements	)

Comments of the Edison Electric Institute

I.   **Introduction and Executive Summary**

The Edison Electric Institute (EEI) appreciates the opportunity to comment on the Public Company Accounting Oversight Board's ("PCAOB's") Proposed Rulemaking[1] on Auditing Standard – An Audit of Internal Control Over Financial Reporting Performed in Conjunction with An Audit of Financial Statements.

EEI is the association of United States shareholder-owned electric companies, and international affiliates and industry associates worldwide. In 2001, our U.S. members served more than 90 percent of the ultimate customers in the shareholder-owned segment of the industry, and nearly 70 percent of all electric utility ultimate customers in the nation. They generated almost 70 percent of the electricity generated by U.S. electric utilities.

While EEI is supportive of much of the PCAOB's proposal, we have several concerns as outlined in these comments. The approach taken in our comments is to respond to questions posed by the PCAOB in the proposed auditing standard. In several instances, we have commented on two questions

---

[1] Public Company Accounting Oversight Board, Proposed Rulemaking; Release No. 2003-017, Docket Matter No. 008, October 7, 2003.

together with one response. EEI commends the PCAOB for the thorough and detailed proposal submitted for public comment and is generally in agreement with many of the proposed rules. However, EEI is concerned that the proposed auditing standard represents a rules-based approach rather than providing a standards/principles-based document for consideration. Additionally, EEI believes there are several areas where the proposed auditing standard could be improved including:

- Extent and form of documentation required by management;

- The restrictive nature of certain key terms and definitions, such as "significant deficiency;"

- Reliance on the work of management and internal auditors by the independent auditors;

- Real or perceived conflicts of interest in evaluating the effectiveness of the Audit Committee; and

- The inability to issue a qualified "except for" opinion.

As a result, EEI would like to comment on the questions addressing these and other issues as put forth by the PCAOB in its proposal.

II. The PCAOB's Proposed Standard

a. Is it appropriate that the Board has provided criteria that auditors should use to evaluate the adequacy of management's documentation? (Question 7)

Paragraph 43 of the proposed auditing standard sets forth guidelines auditors should use to evaluate management's documentation of internal controls over financial reporting. EEI believes that the guidelines are overly prescriptive.

As properly noted in paragraph 44, management's documentation may take many forms and can include a variety of information. Management utilizes many different methods to document its internal controls; examples include policy and procedure manuals, flowcharts, etc. Management may also utilize formal and informal training courses to instruct employees on how to use systems or process transactions. The methods used to document controls are as varied as the controls themselves.

Paragraph 43 specifies, among other things, that management's documentation should include:

- The design of controls over relevant assertions related to significant accounts and disclosures;

- Information about how transactions are initiated, recorded, processed and reported;

- Enough information about the flow of transactions to identify where material misstatements due to error or fraud could occur.

Based on this guidance, existing internal control documentation in many companies may have to be substantially revised to meet the proposed requirements. Generally, documentation of internal control policies and procedures discusses what "must be done right" as compared to what "could go wrong." Documentation often does not include or refer to the five financial statement assertions. Management views controls in its policies and procedures as actions taken to achieve some general or specific objective. It is rare to encounter a description of a control and its relationship to the relevant financial statement assertions. The documentation linking a control to an assertion and to a significant account is also a rare occurrence.

To accomplish what the proposed guidelines require, would require that each financial reporting control be linked to its relevant assertions as well as to a significant account. While this linkage could be accomplished, the effort to do so would require a significant amount of work and resources because, in a large company, there are likely several thousand controls over financial reporting.

Alternatively, on an overall basis, management could determine that the relevant assertions for each financial statement line item are adequately covered by controls. If the financial statement line items are linked to specific assertions and each line item is mapped to various financial statement cycles and controls, this documentation would serve as the link between financial statement assertions and the underlying controls supporting them. This approach would require a more reasonable effort to comply with the standard and would accomplish the same objective.

Further, the documentation requirement will necessitate a very large up-front effort and may be impractical to implement in a timely and meaningful manner for certain events, such as acquisitions of non-public companies, new system implementations and significant changes to business procedures. The impact is magnified for those events that occur at or near end. The focus for these types of events has always been on controls that provide reasonable assurance that financial statements are reliable.

b. **Is it appropriate to state that inadequate documentation is an internal control deficiency, the severity of which the auditor should evaluate? Or should inadequate documentation automatically rise to the level of significant deficiency or material weakness in internal control? (Question 8)**

EEI believes that the guidance in paragraph 46 is adequate. The auditor should evaluate the documentation deficiency, which should take into consideration the significance of the deficiency. All facts and circumstances should be considered along with any mitigating controls the company may utilize to monitor information in the absence of clear and available documentation. Therefore, EEI believes that it is not appropriate to automatically raise inadequate documentation issues to the level of a significant deficiency or material weakness.

c. **Is it appropriate to require that the walkthrough be performed by the auditor himself or herself, rather than allowing the auditor to use walkthrough procedures performed by management, internal auditors, or others? (Question 10)**

EEI believes that it is not necessary to require that the walkthrough be performed solely by the auditor. Rather, the auditor should be permitted to use procedures performed by management. If management, internal auditors or others have sufficiently documented the company's processes to provide the same information that would be captured via a walkthrough, then the auditor should only be required to review this documentation and apply professional judgment as to whether it is necessary to perform any independent walkthroughs.

The procedures performed by the auditor should be intended to be an audit of management's process to assess the design and operating effectiveness of controls. EEI believes that procedures, as required by the proposed auditing standard, are intended to "validate" work rather than repeat or replicate work previously performed by management of the company.

d. Is it appropriate to require the auditor to obtain evidence of the effectiveness of controls for all relevant assertions for all significant accounts and disclosures every year or may the auditor use some of the audit evidence obtained in previous years to support his or her current opinion on management's assertions? (Question 11)

Paragraph 74 states that "the auditor should obtain evidence about the effectiveness of controls (either by performing tests of controls himself or herself or by using the work of others) for all relevant assertions related to all significant accounts and disclosures in the financial statements." Paragraph 101 further states that "the auditor should vary from year to year the nature, timing, and extent of testing of controls to introduce unpredictability into the testing and respond to changes in circumstances."

EEI believes the auditor should be allowed to use some degree of the audit evidence obtained in the previous years to support the nature and extent of his or her testing for the current year's opinion on management's assessment. In a subsequent year, the auditor should be allowed to incorporate the results of his or her testing in a previous year into the planning for the current year audit.

A requirement that the auditor perform its own testing of effectiveness of all controls over significant accounts and disclosures each year will eliminate some level of judgment in the auditor's planning process and make it more difficult to introduce variability in the auditor's plan from year-to-year, as is discussed in paragraph 101 of the PCAOB's proposed rules. Additionally, paragraph 101 seems to indicate that not all controls would be tested independently by the auditor each year. This requirement has the potential to focus a significant amount of testing in the same areas each year rather than appropriately identifying areas which should require more attention, such as those that are affected by other changes in the organization (*e.g.,* employee turnover, increases in volume/nature of transactions, etc.).

EEI believes the draft auditing standard should allow the auditor to incorporate the results of its testing in previous years, along with the review of both management's and internal audit's (when applicable) testing of internal controls in the current year, in supporting his or her opinion on the effectiveness of internal control over financial reporting. Further, EEI believes the current guidance included in the draft auditing standard will result in an independent controls assessment by the auditor which, in essence, duplicates management's assessment rather than resulting in an audit to express an opinion on management's assessment of the effectiveness of the company's internal control over financial reporting as required by paragraph 4 of the proposed rules.

e. To what extent should the auditor be permitted or required to use the work of management and others? (Question 12)

EEI believes that auditors should be permitted to use the work performed by management, internal auditors or by other professionals on behalf of management, based on the auditor's assessment of management's control environment and the competence and objectivity of the people performing the work. For most companies, substantial time and effort has been and will be devoted to documentation and testing of controls by management and internal audit.

The proposed restrictions on the auditor's use of the work of others for evaluating controls regarding (a) the control environment; (b) the period-end financial reporting process; (c) those with a pervasive effect on the financial statements; (d) those over significant non-routine and nonsystematic transactions; and (e) those over significant accounts are too restrictive. Tests of controls by other than external auditors can be documented to the extent that the auditor can review the documentation and then use professional judgment as to the extent of re-testing. As discussed throughout this letter, EEI does not believe that the final auditing standard should impose absolute requirements upon the auditor to replicate and re-perform significant amounts of work previously performed by management. Rather, the requirements should provide the auditor sufficient latitude to exercise professional judgment regarding the nature and extent of testing necessary to audit management's assessment of the design and operating effectiveness of internal controls over financial reporting. Such latitude is permitted in conducting the audit of financial statements and is also appropriate for an audit of internal controls over the preparation of those financial statements.

f. Does the proposed standard give appropriate recognition to the work of internal auditors? If not, does the proposed standard place too much emphasis and preference on the work of internal auditors or not enough? (Question 14)

The discussion in paragraph 108 regarding using the work of internal auditors provides an appropriate level of recognition to the necessity of evaluating the competence and objectivity of internal auditors. The emphasis that reliance can be greater when those functions adhere to the Institute of Internal Auditor's Association's (IIA) Standards is appropriate.

However, EEI believes that the provisions of paragraphs 103 – 106 inappropriately fail to distinguish internal audit from the broad category of operating management and are likely to restrict the level of reliance that can be placed on the work of internal auditors, even those who exhibit the highest levels of independence, competence and objectivity.

In companies with a strong internal audit function, extensive work will be done by internal audit to evaluate and test (a) processes to prevent and detect fraud; (b) controls over the period-end financial reporting process; and (c) controls that have a pervasive effect on the financial statements, such as information technology general and application controls.

In most cases, the work of internal audit may be even more robust than that performed by the external auditors. Prohibiting reliance on the work of internal auditors in these areas will result in a failure to take advantage of significant on-point evaluations of internal control effectiveness.

Additionally, independent auditors currently evaluate and place some reliance on the work of internal auditors in order to perform an audit of a company's financial statements. Establishing a standard for auditing internal controls over the preparation of financial statements that is more restrictive than the current standards governing audits of financial statements is inconsistent and would confuse financial statement users. EEI agrees that the reliance on the work of internal auditors related to controls discussed in paragraphs 104 and 105 should be more limited than reliance on controls over routine processing as discussed in paragraph 106. However, the independent auditor should be given the flexibility to rely on the work of internal auditors in all areas deemed appropriate in the exercise of his or her professional judgment.

The proposed standard's limitation on using the work of internal audit is also internally inconsistent with other aspects of its provisions. Specifically, paragraph 126 of the proposed standard indicates that an ineffective internal audit function should be a "strong indicator that a material weakness in internal control over financial reporting exists." As a result, most companies will determine that an effective internal audit function is necessary, and it seems appropriate that the independent auditor should be able to rely on the internal auditor's work to a significant degree.

Finally, EEI believes that those provisions of the proposed standard are at variance with existing Statement on Auditing Standards (SAS) No. 65, *The Auditor's Consideration of the Internal Audit Function in an Audit of Financial Statements.* SAS 65 permits the auditor to request direct assistance from the internal auditors. Direct assistance relates to work the auditor specifically requests the internal auditors to perform to complete some aspect of the auditor's work. It typically includes assisting the auditor in gaining an understanding of internal control, performing tests of controls and other substantive audit procedures. Internal auditors work under the direct supervision of the auditor and apply auditing procedures as prescribed by the auditor. The work is supervised and reviewed by the auditor. This direct assistance is used as a means to leverage the skills and knowledge of the resident internal audit function and reduce the total cost of the audit.

Internal auditors historically have fulfilled an independent role in assisting the external auditors in connection with an audit of financial statements. Considering the implementation of the proposed internal control standard is expected to require substantial effort and significant cost. EEI believes the final standard should recognize explicitly that the internal auditors are permitted to assist the auditor in such examinations consistent with the direct assistance provisions in SAS 65. The position in the proposed standard is not consistent with the role internal auditors play in connection with an audit of financial statements.

g. **Is the flexibility in determining the extent of re-performance of the work of others appropriate, or should the auditor be specifically required to re-perform a certain level of work (for example, re-perform tests of all significant accounts or re-perform every test performed by others that the auditor intends to use)? (Question 15)**

Paragraph 103 states that "the auditor should evaluate whether to use the work performed by management and others." However, paragraph 104 lists four major areas where the auditor should not use the results of testing performed by others and paragraph 105 lists two major areas where the auditor's use of work performed by others is limited. The net result is to require the auditor to re-perform the majority of all tests of controls. Therefore, EEI believes that the final standard should provide greater flexibility to the independent auditors in determining the extent of re-performance work required.

h. Is the requirement for the auditor to obtain the principle evidence, on an overall basis, through his or her own work the appropriate benchmark for the amount of work that is required to be performed by the auditor? (Question 16)

The key to this limitation is centered on the interpretation of the auditor's "own work." This term could be interpreted to mean that the auditor's documented review of the work of others would be sufficient; or, "own work" could be interpreted to mean that the auditor must either perform or re-perform all tests of controls. EEI believes the former would be the best interpretation.

i. Will the definitions in the proposed standard of significant deficiency and material weakness provide for increased consistency in the evaluation of deficiencies? How can the definitions be improved? (Question 17)

EEI has serious concerns regarding the definition of "significant deficiency" and "material weakness" centered on the use of the terms "more than a remote likelihood" and "more than inconsequential in amount." These phrases are likely to be interpreted to go beyond the "reasonable assurance" intent of COSO and the Securities & Exchange Commission ("SEC").

The COSO framework indicated the following regarding what internal controls cannot do: "An internal control system, no matter how well conceived and operated, can provide only reasonable – not absolute – assurance to management and the board regarding achievement of an entity's objectives. The likelihood of achievement is affected by the limitations inherent in all internal control systems. These include the realities that judgments in decision-making can be faulty, and that breakdowns can occur because of simple error or mistake." EEI believes that controls designed and operated to meet the standards in COSO's "Internal Control – Integrated Framework" will not be adequate given the definitions of significant deficiency and material weakness in the proposed standard. Specifically, the phrases "more than a remote likelihood" and "more than inconsequential in amount" are too restrictive for most internal controls over financial reporting.

EEI believes it is critical that clear definitions are established - considering standards already in place such as those provided in the COSO framework – that describes the terms (a) deficiency; (b) significant deficiency; and (c) material weakness.

The definitions used in the final standard are critical to an investor's understanding of a company's internal controls over financial reporting and the related audit opinion. For example, with non-routine and non-systematic transactions, an evaluation of "likelihood" is not appropriate because, in this instance, the auditor must be concerned with the qualitative nature of the deficiency. One "remote" non-standard journal entry can materially affect the financial statements. While the chance of this event occurring may be "remote," when it does occur, the consequences can be significant. Therefore, for non-recurring and non-standard transactions, EEI believes the evaluation of the significance of a control deficiency must take into account the qualitative aspects of the deficiency as opposed to its likelihood of occurrence.

EEI believes the term "more than inconsequential in amount" establishes a very low threshold of significance. Although it is not defined explicitly in the proposed standard, EEI interprets this term to mean an amount that is substantially less than that which would be considered "immaterial" to the financial statements. Consequently, a deficiency that could misstate the financial statements by an immaterial amount would still be considered significant in quantitative terms. As a result, EEI believes that using this definition will elevate, unnecessarily, many control deficiencies to the "significant" category and result in many unnecessary discussions between auditors, management and the Audit Committee on the resulting categorizations. Using overly restrictive criteria has the potential to take the focus away from those areas that are truly material to the company.

j. Is it appropriate to require the auditors to evaluate the effectiveness of the audit committee's oversight of the company's external financial reporting and internal control over financial reporting? (Question 22) Will auditors be able to effectively carry out their responsibility to evaluate the effectiveness of the audit committee's oversight? (Question 23)

EEI does not believe that it is appropriate to have the auditors evaluate the effectiveness of the Audit Committee's oversight of a company's external financial reporting and internal control over financial reporting.

This requirement presents a conflict of interest for the auditors due to the Audit Committee's responsibilities as defined in Section 301 of the Act which requires the Audit Committee to be directly responsible for the appointment, compensation, and oversight of the work of any registered public accounting firm employed by the company for the purpose of preparing or issuing an audit report or related work; the registered public accounting firm shall report directly to the Audit Committee.

Paragraph 57 of the proposed auditing standard requires the auditor to evaluate the Audit Committee's level of involvement and interaction with the auditors, including the Audit Committee's role in the appointment, retention and compensation of the auditor. EEI believes this conflict of interest will inhibit the auditor's ability to successfully evaluate the effectiveness of the Audit Committee's oversight.

Additionally, the auditor is currently required to evaluate the role of the Audit Committee as part of understanding the control environment to appropriately plan the financial statement audit in accordance with SAS No. 55, *Internal Control in a Financial Statement Audit*. This evaluation is appropriate because it is for the auditor's own use in planning its work, rather than for reporting to the body responsible for engaging its services. EEI believes that the proposed rules should not impose a separate and more prescriptive requirement of an auditor's evaluation of the Audit Committee than is already established by the American Institute of Certified Public Accountant's generally accepted auditing standards.

k. Is it appropriate that the existence of a material weakness would require the auditor to express an adverse conclusion about the effectiveness of the company's internal control over financial reporting, consistent with the required reporting model for management? (Question 25)Are there circumstances where a qualified "except for" conclusion would be appropriate? (Question 26)

EEI does not believe it is appropriate that the existence of one material weakness would require management and the auditor to express an adverse conclusion about the effectiveness of the company's internal control over financial reporting.

By only allowing one type of audit opinion - an adverse audit opinion – there is no ability to differentiate the impact and/or severity of material weaknesses among various companies. As an example, a company that has one isolated material weakness, the effects of which are limited and can be compensated for by substantive testing, will have the same opinion as a company that has one material weakness that is pervasive in its effect over financial reporting. EEI believes that such differentiation is critical to a financial statement user's understanding of a company's internal control over financial reporting and is necessary to provide a meaningful conclusion on the reliability and effectiveness of internal controls.

Given the proposed standard's definition of a material weakness in internal control and the broad spectrum of potential impacts of a material weakness in internal control, significant judgment is required for management's conclusion on the effectiveness of internal control and the independent audit opinion to be meaningful. EEI believes there are many circumstances where a qualified "except for" opinion would more accurately communicate relevant information about the existence and effectiveness of the entity's internal controls and would be more useful for investors and other users of the financial statements.

Investors and other users of financial statements are familiar with the types of audit opinions expressed for a financial statement audit. Most investors and other users of financial statements have a clear understanding of the potential ramifications of an adverse opinion and also understand the circumstances where a qualified "except for" opinion may be required. Consistent with that understanding, financial statement users view an adverse audit opinion as one where the effects of deviations from generally accepted accounting principles ("GAAP") are so material and pervasive that they overshadow the fairness of the financial statements. Users also understand that a qualified "except for" opinion is issued when the financial statements are presented in accordance with GAAP, except for the matters to which the qualification relates.

With this understanding, the absolute requirement that a single material weakness requires management to conclude that internal controls over financial reporting are not effective and for the auditor to express an adverse opinion about the effectiveness of the company's internal control over financial reporting, without provision for exercising judgment, has the potential to have significant negative implications in financial markets; it would create confusion and would be misleading to investors and other financial statement users and would potentially reduce investor confidence.

As mentioned previously, considerable professional judgment is required to effectively evaluate the significance of a material weakness and its impact on the opinion to be issued. By requiring management to conclude that controls are not effective and for the auditor to issue an adverse opinion for one material weakness, regardless of other circumstances surrounding the weakness, does not provide the ability to adequately communicate to the investing pubic the actual impact of the weakness to the company. EEI believes that the proposed rule should be modified to eliminate this absolute requirement to issue an adverse opinion on the audit of internal control over financial reporting and to provide examples of circumstances in which management and the auditor should evaluate the impact of a material weakness. Some considerations which may result in a qualified "except for" opinion rather than an adverse opinion should include:

- A material control weakness that is isolated to one system or area;

- The significance and impact on the financial statements;

- The type of material control weakness and compensating controls;

- The nature of assets at risk;

- The presence of other control weaknesses;

- The extent, nature and timing of recent changes in the company's accounting process or procedures, business practices, or regulatory requirements;

- Past experience with the entity.

An adverse opinion should be limited to those situations where control weaknesses are material and pervasive, where little or no reliance may be placed on the internal control structure, or where there is fraud committed by management or employees with a significant role in internal control over financial reporting.

In addition, under the proposed rules, it is possible for a company to obtain a clean audit opinion on the financial statements, yet obtain an adverse audit opinion on its internal controls over financial reporting. This will certainly confuse investors as they believe that internal controls are designed to provide reasonable assurance regarding the reliability of financial statements.

I. Should the Board provide specific guidance on independence and internal control-related non-audit services in the context of this proposed standard? (Question 28)

EEI believes that the three broad principles as set forth by the SEC on auditor independence provide adequate, complete guidance regarding auditor independence.[2] These principles state that the auditor cannot function in the role of management, cannot audit his or her own work, and cannot serve as an advocate for management. These principles, when combined with the SEC's rules governing Audit Committee pre-approval of all services to be provided by the independent auditor constitute appropriate guidance in this area and no additional guidance is necessary.

III. Conclusion

EEI understands and acknowledges that, in order to restore broad investor confidence, most public companies will be required to make new investments to comply with many provisions of the Act, particularly to strengthen and report on internal control in accordance with section 404. EEI supports the spirit of the requirements of the Act and generally concurs with the provisions of the proposed rule on auditing internal controls. However, EEI also believes that the final standard should not impose any more requirements than are necessary in order to achieve the

---

[2] Securities & Exchange Commission, Regulation SX Rule 2-01.

objectives of the Act. Thus, many of the comments in this letter focus on ensuring that the final standard does not mandate duplicative procedures that add little value and will place excessive burdens on companies working to comply with the Act. In particular, EEI recognizes the value of independent review and testing by the independent auditors; however, excessive duplication of efforts already performed by management and internal auditors will not enhance the value of the attestation process.

EEI appreciates the opportunity to provide comments on this proposal and respectfully requests that the PCAOB consider our concerns and recommendations.

Sincerely,

David K. Owens
Executive Vice President – Business Operations Group

¶ 611. Federation des Experts Comptables Europeens—European Federation of Accountants

Date	Secrétariat Général	Fédération des Experts	Rue de la Loi 83 1040 Bruxelles
21 November 2003		Comptables Européens AISBL	Tél. 32 (0) 2 285 40 85 Fax : 32 (0) 2 231 11 12 E-mail : secretariat@fee.be

Office of the Secretary
Public Company Accounting Oversight Board (PCAOB)
1666 K Street, NW
USA - Washington D.C. 20006-2803

Dear Sirs,

Re: PCAOB Rulemaking Docket Matter No. 008 – "Proposed Auditing Standard – An Audit of Internal Control over Financial Reporting Performed in Conjunction with an Audit of Financial Statements"

FEE (Fédération des Experts Comptables Européens – European Federation of Accountants) is pleased, as the representative organisation of the European accountancy profession, to comment on the exposure draft released by the PCAOB on 7 October 2003 on "Proposed Auditing Standard – An Audit of Internal Control over Financial Reporting Performed in Conjunction with an Audit of Financial Statements" (referred to as "the proposed standard").

Because of the importance of the issues raised by the proposed standard we are sending a copy of our response to the International Auditing and Assurance Standards Board (IAASB) and the European Commission. In summary, we believe that the PCAOB's rulemaking on the subject of internal control over financial reporting would be enhanced by:

- taking account of global developments in auditing standards designed to serve the interests of investors;
- considering whether the practical application of the proposed standard will encourage management to identify and resolve financial reporting issues in a timely and appropriate manner;
- ensuring that the work performed by auditors to report on financial statements is not duplicated or made less effective;
- reflecting and encouraging the adoption by management of best practices in internal control that are cost-effective and widely accepted;
- emphasising the need for auditors to take responsibility for exercising professional judgement; and
- explaining how auditors' reports on internal control over financial reporting (and adverse opinions in particular) are expected to restore confidence in capital markets.

In addition to our response to the questions set out in the request for comments to the proposed standard, this letter includes our overall comments on matters of principle. Some of our overall comments are reflected on a stand-alone basis in the next section. Other areas of significant concern have been addressed in our responses to the questions. They have been referenced separately hereafter and are all of equal importance.

Overall comments

(a)   Worldwide repercussions of proposed standard

The proposed standard will have a very wide impact not only on US-based auditors, but also on auditors throughout the world serving:
(1)   SEC foreign registrant companies who choose to be listed in the US; and
(2)   the relevant subsidiaries of US domestic SEC registrants which fall under the same requirements as the US domestic portion of the entity.
Both types of registrants will require management and auditors to obtain the required coverage for management's assessment of and the auditor's attestation of the effectiveness of internal control over financial reporting.

The pervasive impact of the proposed standard on global audit practice and, potentially, on the platform used by global audit firms for their audit methodologies places a significant responsibility on the PCAOB in finalising the proposed standard.   We believe there are significant potential shortcomings in the process.

We respectfully suggest that, with a 45 day consultation period for such an important and far reaching standard, the PCAOB is operating to inappropriate deadlines for due process and consultation that are inferior to those followed by the IAASB.

When discharging its onerous responsibility for this standard, we request the PCAOB to give due consideration to the impact its proposals will have on the IAASB's global audit standards. In particular, we strongly encourage the PCAOB to consider how the proposed standard fits in with International Standards on Auditing (ISAs).   For example, there appear to be inconsistencies with the new risk ISAs which have recently been issued and agreed by the IAASB after an extensive joint project with the American Institute of Certified Public Accountants (AICPA). These ISAs should be carefully taken into account and integrated in the proposed standard.

(b)   Conflict over who finds the adjustments

The proposed standard requires the auditor to issue an adverse opinion regarding the effectiveness of internal control over financial reporting should one or more material weaknesses arise.

Circumstances presumed to be at least a significant deficiency and a "strong indicator" of a material weakness include identification by the auditor of a material misstatement in the year-end financial statements that was not identified by the company's internal controls, even if management subsequently corrects the misstatement prior to issuance of the financial statements.

As a consequence, we would hope that management raises and discusses any likely issues at an early stage with its auditors to reach an agreement on the most suitable resolution for any issues.

Unfortunately, in practice, we are afraid that this increased likelihood for an adverse auditor's opinion might lead to quite the opposite result. Typically, the auditor commences his audit long before management has approved the financial statements and management will provide the auditor with a draft. While the auditor performs his audit work on this draft, management continues their checks and controls of processes and systems to ensure the draft financial statements are fairly presented. During this time of progressing the preparation and the audit of the financial statements simultaneously, either management or the auditor might uncover material adjustments.

Where there is the need for an adjustment there will be a strong incentive for management to claim that they "found it first" or would have done, had they had time to complete there own checks.   The proposed standard is also likely to increase management resistance to auditor proposed adjustments because under the proposed standard, each such adjustment recorded by management would result in an adverse auditor's opinion regarding the effectiveness of internal control over financial reporting.

It even may make it impossible for the auditor to perform his work as management may try to defer the audit as long as possible until management is fully ready with the preparation of the financial statements in order to ensure that the auditor is not the first in identifying adjustments. We do not believe that this will contribute to restoring confidence in the capital markets.

(c)   Two audits

The guidance provided in the new risk ISAs whereby significant risks are identified to determine which internal controls should be the subject of further audit work is not reflected in the proposed standard which requires auditors to perform audit work on all internal controls regardless of their risk profile.

The guidance in paragraphs 133 to 144 is meant to interrelate the two audits, i.e. the attestation on management's assessment of the effectiveness of internal control over financial reporting and the audit of the financial statements. However, the integration of both audits and their purpose should be enhanced. The objective of an audit of internal controls should be to form a judgement on the control risks which are part of the financial statement audit. The concepts of materiality and complexity should be introduced whereby the testing of internal control systems should only be performed for material and complex assertions, transactions, account balances and disclosures. Substantive procedures may suffice for other transactions and balances. The proposed standard currently appears to require both tests of controls and substantive procedures for all assertions, accounts and disclosures.

(d)   Reasonable assurance is not high assurance

Paragraph 16 implies that "reasonable assurance" is a high level of assurance. We disagree with the PCAOB's point of view which is also at odds with the IAASB's latest thinking. There is a range of levels of assurance in relation to different aspects of financial reporting, each of which is "reasonable" when considered in context, as certain aspects are inherently more risky than others.

The level of assurance that the auditor can obtain depends on the circumstances. For example, the assurance that can be obtained by the auditor in relation to the absence of material misstatements caused by management fraud involving collusion with external parties will be considerably less than if the misstatement results from human error in routine processes.

FEE has considered these matters in detail in its April 2003 Issues Paper "Principles of Assurance: Fundamental Theoretical Issues with Respect to Assurance in Assurance Engagements".

(e)   Assertions too prominent

Financial statements are meant to report on the status and progress of the business of an entity for the benefit of stakeholders including investors and are not an end in themselves. An audit of internal control over financial reporting should not be based on a bottom-up approach starting with financial statement assertions, but should rather commence by determining risks of material misstatements, followed by considering systems and controls to finally result in the accounts and disclosures included in the financial statements of the entity.

In more general terms, the proposed standard should make it clear that careful consideration of the control environment is essential in developing an audit approach. More emphasis should be put on the behavioural types of controls, such as integrity of management, rather than on detailed processes and systems.

The references to financial statement assertions on page 4 in the second paragraph under the section 'Internal Control Over Financial Reporting', in paragraphs 66 to 70 and in Appendix A, Example A-1 in the second part of the scope paragraph on page A-66 are too prominent and misconceived. The guidance related to financial statement assertions in the paragraphs indicated above is also inconsistent with the guidance provided in the first paragraph on page 12 which commences with the design and operating effectiveness of controls.

Moreover, the prominence given to detailed financial statement assertions in the proposed standard and the assertions themselves are not in line with the ISAs which large and medium size audit firms in Europe are committed to follow. Such inconsistency has considerable practical consequences for the adoption of global standards. It also has a profound effect on the audit methodology to be developed by audit firms which will become extremely complex and require considerable investment to redevelop software and retrain staff. Therefore, we urge the Board to revisit the guidance provided in the proposed standard in respect of the prominence given to detailed financial statement assertions.

(f)   Controls which do not naturally give rise to documentary evidence

Many important controls over financial reporting do not routinely give rise to documentary evidence. For instance, day to day supervision, coaching and reviewing of staff and their work in the accounting department are sound preventive controls but are ordinarily not documented on a continuing basis.

We fully agree that management should prepare documentary evidence for all significant processes and controls on which the auditor should be able to rely to perform his work in relation to his attestation of management's assessment of the effectiveness of internal control over financial reporting. However, auditors can also, by a process of enquiry and proper evidential corroboration, gain reasonable assurance that other controls exist and work effectively.

Management's responsibilities related to documentation in paragraph 19 are minimal as compared to the detailed requirements for documentation by the auditor in paragraphs 145 to 147. These requirements should be comparable and equally enforceable, as further discussed in our overall comment under (g) below.

The proposed standard indirectly plays down the importance of controls which do not naturally give rise to documentary evidence and incentivises companies to prepare documentation that may not previously have been necessary from a commercial point of view. In contrast, the Sarbanes-Oxley Act does not necessarily require documentation of the effectiveness and operation of controls. We question whether these additional documentation requirements of the proposed standard will provide an increased level of protection for investors commensurate with the increased cost of compliance.

(g)   Management acceptance of the PCAOB rules

The Board should not lose sight of the fact that the proposed standard is an auditing standard, compliance with which cannot necessarily be forced upon management of an entity.

Especially where the proposed standard goes further than the Sarbanes-Oxley Act, as highlighted in our response to question 6 and in our overall comment under (f) above, management adherence might be extremely difficult to enforce. In our view the Board has a duty to investors to ensure that its proposed standards for auditors are not made less effective by a lack of corresponding obligations for management.

(h)   Divided responsibility

Example A-5 on page A-75 implies that the proposed standard allows for divided responsibility (as distinct from joint responsibility) for auditors in the case of a group audit of consolidated financial statements. While FEE recognises that there are often good reasons to appoint different audit firms to perform the audits of a group of entities, FEE believes that this should not result in divided responsibility for the group auditor. FEE is a long standing opponent of divided responsibility for financial statement audits and strongly favours the auditor of the consolidated financial statements having sole responsibility for his report. The public has to understand who is ultimately responsible for the audit of group financial statements. The same logic applies to opinions on internal control over financial reporting.

(i) Need to reflect IT reality and service organisation auditor guidance

Internal control systems are largely IT driven and are developed not only in-house but also by third parties including service providers.

The guidance in the proposed standard frequently fails to take this IT reality into account and instead provides guidance which appears to be geared toward manual internal control systems. The proposed standard should acknowledge and provide additional guidance reflecting present day reality.

Where an IT driven internal control system is developed by a service provider, this may result in situations where the auditor will not be able to obtain sufficient comfort for his attestation on management's assessment of the effectiveness of internal control over financial reporting because the extensive US guidance on this issue cannot be forced on non US service providers and their auditors. The Board should address such practicalities.

(j) Major concerns about missing guidance for small and medium-sized issuers

The proposed standard indicates that inadequate management documentation of the design of controls and the absence of sufficient documented evidence to support management's assessment of the operating effectiveness of internal control may be a significant deficiency or material weakness or could lead to a scope limitation. This results in additional risks for management and the auditor.

Larger entities might be able to bear and absorb the bureaucratic cost of having documentary evidence for all controls and their effective operation in order for management and the auditor to manage such risks.

Smaller entities typically have a high degree of hands-on, direct management controls which cannot easily be documented. They will also have considerable difficulties to absorb costs of documentation which does not serve a commercial purpose. In these circumstances, management and in particular the auditor will be exposed to greater risk related to the attestation of management's assessment of the effectiveness of internal control over financial reporting.

Therefore, we are in favour of principle-based standards which allow the auditor to use professional judgement. The proposed standard should in this respect include express acknowledgement of small and medium-sized entities by incorporation of the guidance provided in Appendix E within the main text of the proposed standard.

Other overall areas of concern arising from our responses to questions in the PCAOB's Request for Comments

Limited reliance on management and internal control testing: see our response to question 6.

Prohibition on use of periodical testing: see our response to question 11.

Under-emphasis on materiality: see our response to questions 11 and 19.

Problems with definitions: see our response to question 17.

Direct reporting by auditors: see our response to question 26.

Independence issues: see our response to question 29.

Impact of quarterly reporting requirements: see our response to question 30.

Use of professional judgement: see our response to questions 4, 7, 8, 10, 11, 12, 14, 15, 16, 19, 25 and 26.

Response to the questions in the PCAOB's Request for Comments

1. **Is it appropriate to refer to the auditor's attestation of management's assessment of the effectiveness of internal control over financial reporting as the audit of internal control over financial reporting?**

   No. It is not appropriate as it is inconsistent with the practice of the IAASB which uses the term 'audit' to refer to the audit of financial statements only. The auditor's attestation of management's assessment of the effectiveness of internal control over financial reporting is an assurance engagement leading to reasonable assurance and not an audit.

2. **Should the auditor be prohibited from performing an audit of internal control over financial reporting without also performing an audit of the financial statements?**

   No. Although it is more efficient for the auditor of the financial statements to perform the attestation of internal control over financial reporting, we favour principle-based standards which require the use of professional judgement and do not include unnecessary prohibitions.

3. **Rather than requiring the auditor to also complete an audit of the financial statements, would an appropriate alternative be to require the auditor to perform work with regard to the financial statements comparable to that required to complete the financial statement audit?**

   Not applicable in view of our response to Question 2.

4. **Does the Board's proposed standard give appropriate consideration to how internal control is implemented in, and how the audit of internal control over financial reporting should be conducted at, small and medium-sized issuers?**

   Yes, provided that the guidance provided in Appendix E is incorporated within the main text.
   As already noted, we are in favour of principle-based standards which allow the auditor to use professional judgement. Therefore, we believe that the guidance provided in Appendix E is also useful in relation to the work to be performed in a larger entity when it is managed in a similar way to that described in Appendix E.

5. **Should the Board, generally or in this proposed standard, specify the level of competence and training of the audit personnel that is necessary to perform specified auditing procedures effectively? For example, it would be inappropriate for a new, inexperienced auditor to have primary responsibility for conducting interviews of a company's senior management about possible fraud.**

   No. Auditing standards should not specify levels of competence and training for specified procedures.

6. **Is the scope of the audit appropriate in that it requires the auditor to both evaluate management's assessment and obtain, directly, evidence about whether internal control over financial reporting is effective?**

   Qualified yes. We do not disagree with the proposition that the auditor needs to obtain evidence directly. However, we believe that the proposed requirements for the performance of such procedures by the auditor are excessive.

   Restricting the reliance on management assertions is not acceptable under a principle-based approach. We also believe that some requirements in paragraphs 104 and 105 of the proposed standard are too restrictive and diverge from the requirements of the Sarbanes-Oxley Act.

   More generally, the proposed standard requires the auditor both to evaluate management's assessment and obtain direct evidence about whether the internal control over financial reporting is effective. This goes further than the Sarbanes-Oxley Act, which requires the auditor to report on the assessment made by management.

The proposed standard addresses at length how the auditor should obtain direct evidence of control effectiveness. In contrast, the guidance on evaluating management's assessment process is covered in just seven paragraphs.

We are not convinced that the requirement to obtain direct evidence of effectiveness in all areas of internal controls over financial reporting represents a reasonable use of resources from the point of view of investors, particularly in respect of the testing of control activities. The issuer is already required to carry out its own testing in this regard and those tests should yield the same results as external audit testing.

7. **Is it appropriate that the Board has provided criteria that auditors should use to evaluate the adequacy of management's documentation?**

No. Although the suggestions included in paragraphs 43 to 47 might be helpful, the auditor should be allowed to apply professional judgement. It would be helpful to introduce the terms 'might', 'may' and 'could' in the first sentence of paragraph 43.

We also recommend that additional guidance is included to address documentation requirements in the context of the size of the entity and its management structure.

8. **(a) Is it appropriate to state that inadequate documentation is an internal control deficiency, the severity of which the auditor should evaluate? (b) Or should inadequate documentation automatically rise to the level of significant deficiency or material weakness in internal control?**

(a): Yes as it allows for the use of professional judgement by the auditor.
(b): No.

9. **Are the objectives to be achieved by performing walkthroughs sufficient to require the performance of walkthroughs?**

Qualified yes. Walkthroughs are useful to document an understanding of processes and systems, but are not a comprehensive way of testing the effectiveness of controls. We strongly recommend application of the concept of materiality in the context of deciding which systems and processes should be subject to walkthroughs.

10. **Is it appropriate to require that the walkthrough be performed by the auditor himself or herself, rather than allowing the auditor to use walkthrough procedures performed by management, internal auditors, or others?**

No. In the light of using his professional judgement in a principle-based approach, the auditor should be allowed to rely on walkthroughs performed by internal auditors and others, as long as they have been performed using the same high standard as when the auditor would have performed them. We would advise caution before using walkthroughs performed by management, but would not support a prohibition on their use.

11. **(a) Is it appropriate to require the auditor to obtain evidence of the effectiveness of controls for all relevant assertions for all significant accounts and disclosures (b) every year or (c) may the auditor use some of the audit evidence obtained in previous years to support his or her current opinion on management's assessment?**

(a): Qualified yes, see detailed comments hereafter.
(b): Qualified yes, see detailed comments hereafter.
(c): Yes.

The basic principle that the auditor should rely on prior knowledge and experience is applicable for every audit and should also be adopted for this type of engagement, under the condition that the auditor only relies on past experience having first satisfactorily updated his prior experience and knowledge by corroborating evidence on the current design and current operation of the controls. In this manner, the auditor can identify where changes have occurred on which he needs to focus.

A requirement to obtain evidence on the effectiveness of controls for every control assertion, for every significant account balance and disclosure, every year is impractical for the auditor and represents a disproportionate use of resources from the point of view of investors as well as disproportionate costs in comparison to the limited benefit for stakeholders.

Again, the auditor should be allowed to use his professional judgement and make materiality judgements.

12. To what extent should the auditor be permitted or required to use the work of management and others?

The auditor should never be required to use the work of management and others, but should be permitted to do so using his good professional judgement. The extent to which the auditor should be allowed to do so is further detailed in the response to Question 13 below.

13. Are the three categories of controls and the extent to which the auditor may rely on the work of others appropriately defined?

No. We are sceptical about the practical application of such a rule-based approach to categorisation of controls. We prefer a principle based approach whereby a range from high level, management driven controls to low level routine controls is used to determine the acceptable level of reliance for the auditor. Control categorisation is not required as the determining factor is the integrity and good faith of management, internal audit and others upon whom the auditors may rely.

14. Does the proposed standard give appropriate recognition to the work of the internal auditors? If not, does the proposed standard place too much emphasis and preference on the work of internal auditors or not enough?

Qualified yes. The guidance provided in paragraph 108 is acceptable if the categorisation as described in Question 13 is abolished. Internal auditors should be able to perform work classified as (1) in the categories referred to in Question 13 and external auditors should be able to rely on such work based on their professional judgement.

15. (a) Is the flexibility in determining the extent of reperformance of the work of others appropriate, or (b) should the auditor be specifically required to reperform a certain level of work (for example, reperform tests of all significant accounts or reperform every test performed by others that the auditor intends to use)?

(a): Yes.
(b): No.

The auditor should use his professional judgement to determine whether it is appropriate to rely on the work of others.

We refer to our response to Question 6 for further details.

16. **Is the requirement for the auditor to obtain the principal evidence, on an overall basis, through his or her own work the appropriate benchmark for the amount of work that is required to be performed by the auditor?**

No. Again, the auditor should have the overall responsibility to decide which sources of evidence to rely on by using his professional judgement to determine whether it is appropriate to rely on the work of others or whether there is a need to obtain evidence through his or her own work.

17. **Will the definitions in the proposed standard of significant deficiency and material weakness provide for increased consistency in the evaluation of deficiencies? How can the definitions be improved?**

The answer is 'no', although it is not clear what the basis for comparison is supposed to be. The definitions of 'material', 'significant', 'remote' and 'inconsequential' are not in line with the definitions included in the ISAs or are not included in the ISAs which will be adopted in the European Union from 2005. Additionally, the meaning of the term 'remote likelihood' as used in the definitions of 'significant deficiency' and 'material weakness" will mean that very little will not need to be reported as a finding in the auditor' attestation of management's assessment of the effectiveness of internal control over financial reporting. Therefore, we prefer the continued use of the definitions included in Statement on Auditing Standards ('SAS') No. 60.

18. **(a) Do the examples in Appendix D of how to apply these definitions in various scenarios provide helpful guidance? (b) Are there other specific examples that commenters could suggest that would provide further interpretive help?**

(a): No, taking into account our response to Question 17;
(b): No.

19. **Is it necessary for the auditor to evaluate the severity of all identified internal control deficiencies?**

Yes. However, it would be helpful to define the term 'evaluate'; we understand it to mean that the auditor is allowed to use his professional judgement and make materiality judgements, including judgments on the documentation of the 'evaluation'.

20. **Is it appropriate to require the auditor to communicate all internal control deficiencies (not just material weaknesses and significant deficiencies) to management in writing?**

Yes. However, one would expect that, as a result of the audit of the financial statements, all internal control deficiencies would already have been communicated to management in writing under the form of a 'management letter' in accordance with existing professional standards. Such a process should not be duplicated and there is no need for a new standard on this topic.

We also refer to our overall comment on 'two audits' detailed under item (c).

21. **Are the matters that the Board has classified as strong indicators that a material weakness in internal control exists appropriately classified as such?**

Yes, they are acceptable as risk indicators.

22. **Is it appropriate to require the auditors to evaluate the effectiveness of the audit committee's oversight of the company's external financial reporting and internal control over financial reporting?**

Yes, but some issues resulting from the inherent "conflict of interest" between the audit committee and the auditor need to be addressed as the audit committee is expected to supervise the work performed by the external auditor. In accordance with the principle-based "threats and safeguards"

approach reflected in the IFAC Ethics Code, the auditor could for example request an independent colleague ("review partner") to assist him.

23. Will auditors be able to effectively carry out their responsibility to evaluate the effectiveness of the audit committee's oversight?

Yes, taking into account the considerations indicated in our response to question 22.

24. If the auditor concludes that ineffective audit committee oversight is a material weakness, rather than require the auditor to issue an adverse opinion with regard to the effectiveness of the internal control over financial reporting, should the standard require the auditor to withdraw from the audit engagement?

No the auditor should be allowed to use his professional judgment. Also, this would not be possible in certain European countries where a statutory auditor is appointed for a certain period of time.

25. Is it appropriate that the existence of a material weakness would require the auditor to express an adverse conclusion about the effectiveness of the company's internal control over financial reporting, consistent with the required reporting model for management?

No. We do not believe that a material weakness should automatically result in an adverse opinion from the auditor. The auditor should be allowed to use his professional judgement to determine whether a material weakness merits a qualified rather than an adverse opinion.

26. Are there circumstances where a qualified "except for" conclusion would be appropriate?

Yes. Consistent with the possibility for the auditor to decide to issue a qualified rather than an adverse audit opinion on financial statements, the auditor should be able to use his or her professional judgement to determine the type of opinion to issue in respect of the auditor's attestation of management's assessment of the effectiveness of internal control over financial reporting.

More generally, we note that the proposed unqualified opinion refers to management's assessment process, and offers no view on the effectiveness of internal controls. However, an adverse opinion requires the auditor to opine on the (in)effectiveness of internal control without mention of management's assessment process. We would have expected these two opposite types of auditor's opinion to be a mirror image of each other. Unfortunately this is not the case. Direct reporting by the auditor in respect of ineffective internal controls will not assist the reader in understanding the auditor's attestation.

Further confusion arises in Example A-6 where the auditor issues an unqualified opinion that refers to the report of other auditors. There the example opinion provides a view on the effectiveness of controls, but not on management's assessment process.

27. Do you agree with the position that when the auditor issues a non-standard opinion, such as an adverse opinion, that the auditor's opinion should speak directly to the effectiveness of internal control over financial reporting rather than to whether management's assessment is fairly stated?

No. We refer to our response to Question 26.

28. Should the Board provide specific guidance on independence and internal control-related non-audit services in the context of this proposed standard?

No, other existing standards address such issues at length. See our response to Question 29 below.

29. **Are there any specific internal control-related non-audit services the auditor should be prohibited from providing to an audit client?**

    Yes. Although we favour principle-based standards which rarely include prohibitions, we believe that it is appropriate to limit the performance of certain internal control-related non-audit services by the auditor of the financial statements. No additional guidance is required in this respect as the SEC independence rules deal with this topic in sufficient detail.

30. **Are the auditor's differing levels of responsibility as they relate to management's quarterly certifications versus the annual (fourth quarter) certification, appropriate?**

    Yes, but not applicable in the European Union. There is no SEC requirement for foreign registrants to have the auditor perform and report on quarterly work, whether related to the financial statement audit or to the attestation of management's assessment of the effectiveness of internal control over financial reporting. The Sarbanes-Oxley Act (Section 302) requires management to report quarterly on internal control. However, no auditor's attestation is required on a quarterly basis.

    Where quarterly work is performed by the auditor, the auditor should have a different level of responsibility for management's quarterly interim certifications.

31. **Is the scope of the auditor's responsibility for quarterly disclosures about the internal control over financial reporting appropriate?**

    Yes, but not applicable for foreign registrants in the European Union. We refer to our response to Question 30 above.

If you have any further questions about our views on these matters, do not hesitate to contact us.

Yours sincerely,

David Devlin
President

¶ 612. Financial Executives International

fei

financial executives
international

November 20, 2003

Office of the Secretary
Public Company Accounting Oversight Board
1666 K Street, N.W.
Washington, D.C. 20006-2803

Re: PCAOB Rulemaking Docket Matter No. 008

Ladies and Gentlemen:

The Committee on Corporate Reporting ("CCR") of Financial Executives International ("FEI") would like to thank you for this opportunity to comment on the Public Company Accounting Oversight Board's ("the Board") proposed auditing standard, *An Audit of Internal Control Over Financial Reporting Performed in Conjunction with an Audit of Financial Statements* ("the proposed standard"). FEI is a leading international organization of 15,000 members, including Chief Financial Officers, Controllers, Treasurers, Tax Executives and other senior financial executives. CCR is a technical committee of FEI, which reviews and responds to research studies, statements, pronouncements, pending legislation, proposals and other documents issued by domestic and international agencies and organizations. This document represents the views of CCR and not necessarily those of FEI.

CCR would like to recognize the Board members and staff for their diligent work in preparing this proposal. FEI has long been a supporter of management's responsibility for creating and maintaining an effective control environment. We take this responsibility seriously and believe that the management certification process alone will significantly improve the strength of internal control. While we acknowledge that an external review of management's assessment will provide additional assurances, we believe the proposed standard requires the auditor to perform attestation procedures that are not only beyond the scope of Sections 103 and 404 of the Sarbanes-Oxley Act ("the Act"), but will provide questionable additional benefit to financial statement users at a high financial and time-consuming cost.

In summary, we are pleased that the proposed standard appears to have incorporated some of the views previously expressed by CCR. Additionally, we would agree that from a high level, the proposed standard seems to represent a balanced approach. However, we have significant concerns on several sections of the proposed standard and we believe that if it is implemented in its current state, the level of duplicative testing and the resulting impact on business operations will result in unnecessary costs to investors in public companies that are far beyond the benefits expected.

Specific responses to the Board's questions on the proposed standard are included in Attachment A. In addition to these responses, we respectfully submit the following general observations for the Board's consideration:

- We believe that the standard as currently drafted creates a situation where the costs far outweigh the benefits of implementation. Given the limited level of reliance that the external auditor can place on the work of others (as discussed further below), the resultant level of duplicative testing will cause numerous interruptions to the operations of our businesses. These interruptions alone are very costly; however, when coupled with the cost of internal and external resources to support management's assertion and the fees associated with the increased work to be performed by the external auditor, the costs are far beyond the benefits attained. Most CCR companies estimate an increase of approximately 30% to 50% in audit fees as a direct result of the required audit of internal control over financial reporting. Most would not mind the cost if we believed that the work being done would really improve controls or prevent future corporate scandals similar to those experienced over the past few years. We believe the work required by the final standard should be focused on the significant issues such as business risk and fraud prevention and detection.

- We believe that management's assertion of internal control effectiveness must be thoroughly supported by annual testing. However, we do not agree that the auditor's review must be equally thorough, annually. Given that the Act requires the auditor to evaluate management's process and assertion, we do not believe the auditor must independently evaluate all controls annually, but rather should rotate its efforts in assessing management's process. This rotation will prove cost efficient and support user's interests.

- We also believe that the proposed standard does not allow the auditor to exercise sufficient judgment and in particular, use as a basis, prior audit experience with their clients. The proposed standard is prescriptive, causing auditors to perform the same level of testing at companies with strong control structures as would be performed at those with weak control structures. For example, in the area of appropriate levels of testing, we believe that the proposed standard should grant the auditor more latitude on testing strategies and rotating tests of controls, dependent upon the auditor's evaluation of the overall control environment of the organization. Specifically, in situations where the control environment is very strong, the level of detail testing of the controls over routine data processing should be permitted to be minimal, or in such situations where processes remain unchanged, the auditor should be able to use his or her judgment in determining what level of testing would be appropriate (e.g., rotation or obtain an update of their understanding followed by a walkthrough of the process). Further, we are concerned that the proposed standard has been too prescriptive in requiring the auditor to evaluate ***all*** controls addressing the risk of fraud. The auditor should be able to exercise judgment in this area as well.

- The Board's three-tiered approach to reliance on the work of others, while intending to be helpful, has the effect of allowing very little reliance on the work of others or restricting such reliance to only routine transaction processing. Specifically, we do not believe the Board has adequately supported its proposed requirements with respect to the auditor's required evaluation of IT general controls and the financial statement closing process with no reliance upon internal audit or management's procedures. These are pervasive areas that will lead to significant levels of repetitive, detailed testing by numerous parties if the proposed standard is adopted.

- As stated above, we believe that the proposed standard places very little value on the work of a company's management and its internal auditors. In doing so, the standard requires that the external auditors reperform a significant level of testing for which the results of identical testing are easily obtainable from management. We would like the Board to recognize that many management groups have significant financial reporting controls expertise and operate within strong internal control structures. High quality management work should limit the scope of required testing by both internal and external audit. Further, we would like the Board to be more flexible in terms of how much reliance the external auditor can place on the work of both management and the internal audit function. As drafted, the proposed standard seems to equate management testing with that of internal auditors. A properly functioning internal audit function is competent, objective and independent from management. As such, the proposed standard should allow for a significant amount of reliance on the work performed by internal auditors, especially in areas beyond routine transaction processing. Moreover, the work of an internal audit function adds accountability to a company's control structure, which in turns causes the control execution to be more consistent.

The relationship of the internal audit function to the external audit of financial statements is already addressed in detail within the Statement of Auditing Standards. No. 65, *The Auditor's Consideration of the Internal Audit Function in an Audit of Financial Statements* ("SAS 65"). CCR believes that the relationship defined in SAS 65 is appropriate and does not need to be redefined. Rather, the Board's standard should utilize the provisions of SAS 65 to determine the minimal additional audit steps to evaluate internal control over financial reporting. Further, CCR is concerned that if unchanged, the apparent diminished recognition of internal audit's vital role could eventually lead to decreased reliance on the internal audit function as it relates to the audit of the financial statements. We believe this diminished recognition of the internal audit function is not intended by, and is contrary to, the SEC's ruling under Section 404 of the Act.

- We believe that the proposed standard should expand on the requirements for the auditor to execute a walkthrough. In doing so, the standard should explicitly state when and where a walkthrough is needed. We believe walkthroughs are only one method in which to achieve audit evidence and, therefore, should not be mandated for every significant process. Further, most routine processes lend themselves easily to walkthroughs, whereas other processes that are non-routine and involve a significant amount of judgment do not. To that end, a more detailed explanation of what constitutes a walkthrough in such circumstances would be helpful. Again, this is an area where the auditor should be able to exercise significant judgment.

- We agree philosophically that effective oversight by the audit committee is an important component of the control environment. However, we do not believe that the auditor is in an objective position to evaluate the audit committee. Considering that the audit committee makes the decisions regarding hiring and firing of the external auditors, such an evaluation would put the auditor in an awkward position. This position could cause the auditor to be unwilling to conclude that the committee is ineffective. Further, and perhaps more importantly, we believe that a properly functioning audit committee is comprised of individuals with a much broader expertise than that held by the professional auditor. Accordingly, we do not respectfully believe that most external auditors carry the level of expertise necessary to effectively evaluate an audit committee.

- We would like to commend the Board for their conclusions that only material weaknesses be reported publicly. However, the proposed standard should be more explicit in defining how a deficiency elevates to a significant deficiency and a significant deficiency to a material weakness. We believe the Board should further define or clarify what the term "inconsequential" means as it relates to the definition of a significant deficiency. Further, we believe that internal control over financial reporting is a network of controls with multiple levels. To this point, the standard should require the auditor to evaluate the presence of other compensating controls that would prevent a misstatement of the financial information. We are concerned that the examples outlined in Appendix D of the proposed standard are too narrow and do not appropriately consider materiality. These examples only focus on the first layer of controls, rather than considering the entire structure as a whole. We believe that in most organizations, there would likely be other mitigating or compensating controls in place to detect material misstatements. We believe that examples of compensating controls that keep a deficiency from elevating would be helpful.

We truly appreciate the opportunity to comment on the Board's proposed standard and the Board's consideration of our concerns. Moreover, we welcome the opportunity to discuss these issues at your convenience. Finally, we would like to encourage the Board to issue the final standard as expeditiously as possible, especially considering the significant time constraints for our June 30, 2004 filers. If you have questions regarding this letter, please feel free to contact Frank Brod at (989) 636-1541 or Kate Asbeck at (607) 974-8242.

Sincerely,

Frank Brod
Chair, Committee on Corporate Reporting
Financial Executives International

Kate Asbeck
Chair, PCAOB Subcommittee
Committee on Corporate Reporting
Financial Executives International

Attachment A
Responses to Specific Questions

Questions regarding an integrated audit of the financial statements and internal control over financial reporting:

1. *Is it appropriate to refer to the auditor's attestation of management's assessment of the effectiveness of internal control over financial reporting as the audit of internal control over financial reporting?*

    Yes, we believe it is appropriate to refer to the auditor's attestation as the audit of internal control over financial reporting.

2. *Should the auditor be prohibited from performing an audit of internal control over financial reporting without also performing an audit of the financial statements?*

    Yes, we believe an audit of internal control over financial reporting should be integrated with an audit of the financial statements and therefore, the same auditor should perform both audits.

3. *Rather than requiring the auditor to also complete an audit of the financial statements, would an appropriate alternative be to require the auditor to perform work with regard to the financial statements comparable to that required to complete the financial statement audit?*

    As stated in the response to question two above, we believe that the same auditor should perform both the audit of the financial statements as well as the audit of internal control over financial reporting.

Question regarding the costs and benefits of internal control:

4. *Does the Board's proposed standard give appropriate consideration to how internal control is implemented in, and how the audit of internal control over financial reporting should be conducted at, small and medium-sized issuers?*

    We believe the standard should further explain the importance of the control environment (i.e., financial leadership with a high level of integrity, etc.) as it relates to the impact of the testing and documentation requirements of the proposed standard. In small to medium sized companies, the senior financial leadership is much closer to the operations of the entity and, as such, various levels of control are not as necessary.

Question regarding the audit of internal control over financial reporting:

5. *Should the Board, generally or in this proposed standard, specify the level of competence and training of the audit personnel that is necessary to perform specified auditing procedures effectively? For example, it would be inappropriate for a new, inexperienced auditor to have primary responsibility for conducting interviews of a company's senior management about possible fraud.*

> No, we believe the Board should leave it to the audit firm to determine the professional competencies and training necessary to execute the attestation in accordance with the Standard's framework. The Board, however, should encourage audit firms to include COSO and other internal controls training in their curriculums. Similar to an audit of financial statements, it is important for the auditors to have the business context and industry perspective for that particular engagement in order to perform an internal controls evaluation effectively.

Questions regarding evaluation of management's assessment:

6. *Is the scope of the audit appropriate in that it requires the auditor to both evaluate management's assessment and obtain, directly, evidence about whether internal control over financial reporting is effective?*

> CCR would like to reiterate its position that the auditor should be evaluating management's process in arriving at management's assertion, rather than performing a duplicative level of testing to support the auditor's own conclusions. We respectfully disagree with the Board's interpretation of Section 103 (a) (2) (A) (iii) of the Act, that the auditor must be able to agree that internal controls are operating effectively, rather that they are designed effectively. Therefore, we do not believe the scope of the audit of internal control over financial reporting is appropriate.

7. *Is it appropriate that the Board has provided criteria that auditors should use to evaluate the adequacy of management's documentation?*

> We believe that guidance for the auditor is appropriate; however, we also believe that the standard should leave room for the auditor's professional judgment in evaluating the adequacy of the documentation.

8. *Is it appropriate to state that inadequate documentation is an internal control deficiency, the severity of which the auditor should evaluate? Or should inadequate documentation automatically rise to the level of significant deficiency or material weakness in internal control?*

> We believe that the standard should allow for the auditor to exercise judgment around the appropriate level of documentation of internal control over financial reporting. We do not believe that a "one size fits all" approach is appropriate in this case. Many different factors, such as size and complexity of the organization,

compensating controls and senior management tone over the control environment should influence the level of documentation necessary. Furthermore, we believe that inadequate documentation is *at most* a deficiency, as a lack of documentation alone will not lead to any misstatement of financial information. It is the lack of actual controls, not the documentation of the controls, which may lead to misstatements.

Questions regarding obtaining an understanding of internal control over financial reporting:

9. *Are the objectives to be achieved by performing walkthroughs sufficient to require the performance of walkthroughs?*

    We believe that, for routine processes with high transaction volumes, a walkthrough of the process is an important procedure. However, as mentioned in the body of our letter, there are numerous processes that will not lend themselves easily to walkthroughs. Accordingly, a blanket requirement for walkthroughs of all significant processes may not achieve the desired objectives. Again, we believe the auditor should have the flexibility to exercise judgment about the appropriate procedures to be performed for specific accounts and assertions. Review of management's policies and procedures, interviews with personnel and transaction reviews are other methods that can be used to meet this same objective.

10. *Is it appropriate to require that the walkthrough be performed by the auditor himself or herself, rather than allowing the auditor to use walkthrough procedures performed by management, internal auditors or others?*

    We believe the Proposed Standard should allow for more auditor judgment in determining what types of work the auditor can rely upon to support their attestation report. It is not clear why the Board believes such procedures can only be performed by the auditors in all cases and challenge whether work performed (and documented) by others would not meet the same objective.

Question regarding testing operating effectiveness:

11. *Is it appropriate to require the auditor to obtain evidence of the effectiveness of controls for all relevant assertions for all significant accounts and disclosures every year or may the auditor use some of the audit evidence obtained in previous years to support his or her current opinion on management's assessment?*

    We believe that in many organizations, the controls are substantially unchanged from year to year. In such circumstances, the auditor should be able to utilize his or her cumulative audit knowledge and judgment in determining the appropriate level of testing. In a well-controlled environment, an update of the auditor's understanding along with minimal testing should be appropriate.

Questions regarding using the work of management and others:

12. To what extent should the auditor be permitted or required to use the work of management and others?

As outlined in the body of our letter and in response to question 10 above, we believe that the Board has not fully recognized the competence and objectivity of most internal audit functions. The practice of utilizing the work of the internal auditor should be permitted to a much greater extent than currently considered in the proposed standard. Furthermore, in certain routine processing, the auditor should be able to use the work of management, obviously to a lesser degree than that of an internal auditor, but still to a substantial degree.

13. Are the three categories of controls and the extent to which the auditor may rely on the work of others appropriately defined?

We believe that the categories of controls are appropriate. However, we would argue that the examples of what is categorized into each section are too restrictive. For instance, the auditor should be able to rely heavily on the walkthroughs performed by others, the work of an internal audit specialist and, in some cases, management, on IT general controls, and the work of others on the routine portions of the financial statement close process.

14. Does the proposed standard give appropriate recognition to the work of internal auditors? If not, does the proposed standard place too much emphasis and preference on the work of internal auditors or not enough?

As previously stated in the body of the letter and in response to question numbers 10 and 12 above, the standard does not give appropriate recognition to the work of the internal auditors. Further, the Board has seemed to equate the work of management and the work of the internal auditor. As stated before, in a properly functioning internal audit system, the internal audit function is both independent and objective. The determination as to what level of reliance the auditor can place on the work of the internal auditor is already addressed in SAS 65 for audits of financial statements and should be no different in the audit of internal control over financial reporting. To reiterate, this standard *does not place enough emphasis* on relying on the work of the internal auditor.

15. Is the flexibility in determining the extent of reperformance of the work of others appropriate, or should the auditor be specifically required to reperform a certain level of work (for example, reperform tests of all significant accounts or reperform every test performed by others that the auditor intends to use)?

We believe that the standard should allow for auditor judgment in determining the extent of reperformance necessary.

16. Is the requirement for the auditor to obtain the principle evidence, on an overall basis, through his or her own work the appropriate benchmark for the amount of work that is required to be performed by the auditor?

We do not believe this requirement is appropriate. We caveat this response by reiterating our previous point that we believe the auditor's responsibility under Section 404 of the Act is to evaluate management's process in arriving at their conclusions as to the effectiveness of internal control over financial reporting. If this requirement remains in the final standard, we encourage the Board to provide a more robust explanation of what is meant by "principal evidence".

Questions regarding evaluating results:

17. Will the definitions in the proposed standard of significant deficiency and material weakness provide for increased consistency in the evaluation of deficiencies? How can the definitions be improved?

We believe that the definitions in the proposed standard are appropriate. However, we also believe that the standard should outline the considerations of other controls within the control structure that could prevent a deficiency from becoming a significant deficiency, and a significant deficiency from becoming a material weakness. Additionally, we believe the introduction of the new term "inconsequential" in the description of a significant deficiency has created unnecessary ambiguity. Instead, the auditor should have the responsibility to exercise his or her professional judgment in determining those deficiencies to be reported to the audit committee.

18. Do the examples in Appendix D of how to apply these definitions in various scenarios provide helpful guidance? Are there other specific examples that commenters could suggest that would provide further interpretive help?

As discussed in the body of our letter, we believe that the examples in Appendix D should be expanded to further explain situations where controls in place would keep a deficiency from elevating to the next level. Furthermore, the examples of significant deficiencies include an ineffective risk assessment and regulatory compliance functions. These appear to extend beyond the scope of financial reporting.

19. Is it necessary for the auditor to evaluate the severity of all identified internal control deficiencies?

We agree that it is important for the auditor to evaluate all identified deficiencies.

20. Is it appropriate to require the auditor to communicate all internal control deficiencies (not just material weaknesses and significant deficiencies) to management in writing?

We believe that the standard should allow for auditor judgment in determining which deficiencies should be reported to management. The auditor does not report all findings in a financial statement audit, especially findings of insignificant value. Accordingly, using the same logic, the auditor should not be required to report *all* deficiencies to management. Such required reporting would likely carry a cost that is beyond the benefits gained.

21. *Are the matters that the Board has classified as strong indicators that a material weakness in internal control exists appropriately classified as such?*

We do not disagree with most of the indicators mentioned in the proposed standard. However, considering that both Section 404 of the Act and the proposed standard focus on the internal control over financial reporting and not on the controls related to compliance with laws and regulations and controls related to efficiency of operations, the indicator related to ineffective regulatory compliance seems out of scope with the Act.

22. *Is it appropriate to require the auditors to evaluate the effectiveness of the audit committee's oversight of the company's external financial reporting and internal control over financial reporting?*

We do not disagree philosophically with the notion that effective oversight by the audit committee is an important component of the control environment. However, we do not believe that the auditor is in an objective position to evaluate the audit committee. This is primarily due to the fact that the audit committee has the responsibility for hiring and firing the external auditor.

23. *Will auditors be able to effectively carry out their responsibility to evaluate the effectiveness of the audit committee's oversight?*

As discussed in our response to question number 22, we do not believe that the auditor is in an objective position to evaluate the audit committee as a result of the fact that the audit committee has the responsibility for hiring and firing the external auditor.

24. *If the auditor concludes that ineffective audit committee oversight is a material weakness, rather than require the auditor to issue an adverse opinion with regard to the effectiveness of the internal control over financial reporting, should the standard require the auditor to withdraw from the audit engagement?*

We do not believe that this would be an appropriate response.

Questions regarding forming an opinion and reporting:

25. *Is it appropriate that the existence of a material weakness would require the auditor to express an adverse conclusion about the effectiveness of the company's internal control over financial reporting, consistent with the required reporting model for management?*

> We believe that this requirement is appropriate only if the material weakness has not been corrected prior to the "as of" date in management's assessment.

26. *Are there circumstances where a qualified "except for" conclusion would be appropriate?*

> We believe that, in certain circumstances, an "except for" conclusion may be appropriate. Such circumstances may include an acquisition completed within a short timeframe of a fiscal year end.

27. *Do you agree with the position that when the auditor issues a non-standard opinion, such as an adverse opinion, that the auditor's opinion should speak directly to the effectiveness of the internal control over financial reporting rather than to whether management's assessment is fairly stated?*

> We believe that the standard should require the reports to be consistently directed either at management's assessment of internal control over financial reporting or the internal control over financial reporting itself.

Questions regarding auditor independence:

28. *Should the Board provide specific guidance on independence and internal control-related non-audit services in the context of this proposed standard?*

> We believe that all parties would benefit from additional guidance in this area.

29. *Are there any specific internal control-related non-audit services the auditor should be prohibited from providing to an audit client?*

> We believe that the external auditor should be prohibited from performing any significant work that assists management in arriving at its assessment of the internal control over financial reporting.

Questions regarding auditor's responsibilities with regard to management's certifications:

30. *Are the auditor's differing levels of responsibility as they relate to management's quarterly certifications versus the annual (fourth quarter) certification, appropriate?*

We believe that the differing levels of responsibility are appropriate in this case. The auditor's quarterly requirements should be limited to inquiry only and focused very heavily on negative assurance.

31. Is the scope of the auditor's responsibility for quarterly disclosures about the internal control over financial reporting appropriate?

We agree with the scope of the auditor's responsibility for quarterly disclosures about the internal control over financial reporting.

¶ 613. Financial Management Division of the Securities Industry Association

FINANCIAL MANAGEMENT DIVISION
SECURITIES INDUSTRY ASSOCIATION

OFFICERS:

Marshall J. Levinson, President
Bear, Stearns & Co. Inc.

Dan McIsaac, Vice President
UBS Warburg LLC

Jeffrey Kottkamp, Treasurer
Deloitte & Touche LLP

MAIL ADDRESS:

Anthony Anzevino, Secretary
KPMG LLP
757 Third Avenue - 10th Floor
New York, NY 10017

November 21, 2003

VIA E-MAIL – comments@pcaobus.org

Office of the Secretary
Public Company Accounting Oversight Board
1666 K Street, N.W.
Washington, D.C. 20006-2803

   Re: PCAOB Rulemaking Docket Matter No. 008—Audit of Internal Control Over
      Financial Reporting

Ladies and Gentlemen:

The Financial Management Division of the Securities Industry Association[1] appreciates the
opportunity to comment on the Public Company Accounting Oversight Board's (the "Board's")

---

[1] The Securities Industry Association, established in 1972 through the merger of the
Association of Stock Exchange Firms and the Investment Banker's Association, brings
together the shared interests of more than 600 securities firms to accomplish common
goals. SIA member-firms (including investment banks, broker-dealers, and mutual fund
companies) are active in all U.S. and foreign markets and in all phases of corporate and

Office of the Secretary
Public Company Accounting Oversight Board
Page 2

Proposed Auditing Standard, "An Audit of Internal Control Over Financial Reporting Performed in Conjunction With an Audit of Financial Statements" (the "Proposed Standard").[2]

We support the Proposed Standard, and share the Board's view that effective internal control over financial reporting is necessary to ensure that investors and others may rely on a company's financial reporting. We do have comments on specific areas covered by the Proposed Standard. We are concerned that in most of these areas, the Proposed Standard, without revision, will require significant work and resources to be expended by auditors and companies without producing a commensurate benefit for investors and others relying upon the integrity of a company's financial statements.

Our comments and requests for clarification relate to the following aspects of the Proposed Standard:

- The Board should clarify that regulatory compliance unrelated to financial reporting is outside the scope of the proposal (Board Question 21);

- The Board should clarify the requirements with respect to evaluations of service organizations;

- Outside auditors should be permitted to use the work of others to a greater degree when appropriate (Board Question 12);

- Discretion should be permitted as to the extent of control testing (Board Questions 10 and 11);

- The definitions of significant deficiency and material weakness should be consistent with the definitions of reportable condition and material weakness set forth in current generally accepted auditing standards (Board Questions 17 and 18);

- The Board should consider whether outside auditors are in the best position to evaluate the effectiveness of audit committees given the inherent conflict of interest in such an evaluation (Board Questions 22 and 23); and

---

public finance. According to the Bureau of Labor Statistics, the U.S. securities industry employs nearly 800,000 individuals. Industry personnel manage the accounts of nearly 93 million investors directly and indirectly through corporate, thrift, and pension plans. In 2002, the industry generated $222 billion in domestic revenue and $356 billion in global revenues. (More information about SIA is available on its home page: www.sia.com.)

[2] This letter does not necessarily represent the views of each member of the Securities Industry Association or its Financial Management Division.

Office of the Secretary
Public Company Accounting Oversight Board
Page 3

- We support the Board's proposed integration of the audit of financial statements with the audit of internal control over financial reporting and the Board's proposal that directs auditors to use their professional judgment to determine whether inadequate documentation constitutes a significant deficiency (Board Questions 2 and 8).

1. The Board Should Clarify that Regulatory Compliance Unrelated to Financial Reporting is Outside the Scope of the Proposal.

Paragraph 126 of the Proposed Standard would provide that for complex entities in highly regulated industries, an ineffective regulatory compliance function should be regarded as at least a significant deficiency and is a strong indicator of a material weakness in internal control over financial reporting. In paragraph 14 of the Proposed Standard, the Board indicates that compliance with laws and regulations directly related to the presentation of and required disclosures in financial statements are encompassed in internal control over financial reporting.

As the Board is aware, the securities industry is highly regulated. Although certain areas in which the industry is regulated, such as trade authorizations, regulatory capital requirements, margin requirements and codes of conduct, may relate to financial reporting, many other areas, such as sales practices, continuing education requirements, trading surveillance and certain recordkeeping requirements, do not directly relate to the financial statements. Requiring independent auditors to assess compliance in all of these areas would not only result in a great deal of effort on the part of auditors due to the wide range of regulations covered, but would also yield little benefit to investors given the lack of relationship between many of these regulations and the financial statements. In that regard, we suggest that the Board clarify that only regulatory compliance directly related to the presentation of and required disclosures in financial statements would be covered by this aspect of the auditing standard. We believe that this approach is consistent with the provisions of the Sarbanes-Oxley Act of 2002 and related rules relating to management's assessment of the effectiveness of internal control over financial reporting. We note that in the adopting release relating to the Securities and Exchange Commission's rules in this area, the SEC states that the definition of internal control over financial reporting does not encompass the elements of the definition set forth in the "Internal Control—Integrated Framework" Report of the Committee of Sponsoring Organizations of the Treadway Commission that relate to regulatory compliance, except where applicable laws and regulations directly relate to the preparation of financial statements.[3]

---

[3] The SEC also notes that its definition of internal control over financial reporting is consistent with the definition of internal accounting controls set forth in Section 13(b)(2)(B) of the Securities Exchange Act of 1934.

Office of the Secretary
Public Company Accounting Oversight Board
Page 4

2. The Board Should Clarify the Requirements with Respect to Evaluations of Service Organizations.

Paragraph 41 of the Proposed Standard would direct an auditor to determine whether management has evaluated the operating effectiveness of controls based on procedures sufficient to assess their operating effectiveness. Examples of such procedures include using a service auditor's report. Paragraph B29 of the Proposed Standard would provide that whenever the company uses a service organization to provide services that are part of the company's information system, the auditor should inquire whether management has received a service auditor's report. According to paragraph B33 of the Proposed Standard, if a service auditor's report on controls placed in operation is unavailable, the auditor might obtain information about the service organization's controls needed to plan the audit from a variety of sources such as user manuals, system overviews, technical manuals and inquiries or observations of personnel at the company or at the service organization, among others. As discussed below, we respectfully request that the Board clarify these requirements.

In particular, we believe the Board should clarify the extent to which service auditors' reports are required and how often the reports must be obtained. Statement on Auditing Standards No. 70, *Service Organizations* ("SAS 70"), provides some guidance as to the level of review and the types of service organizations that should be reviewed during an audit of financial statements. In addition, SAS 70 states that the significance of the controls of the service organization to those of the user organization depends on the nature of the services provided by the service organization, the nature and materiality of the transactions it processes for the user organization and the degree of interaction between the service organization's activities and those of the user organization. We encourage the Board to provide guidance similar to that set forth in SAS 70, as we believe that concepts of materiality of controls of service organizations and "facts and circumstances" determinations are appropriate in order to foster efficient and effective audits of internal control over financial reporting. In particular, we believe that auditors should be permitted to limit their review to those service organizations providing services most likely to have a material impact on the financial statements and similarly should be able to apply a materiality standard in determining the level of testing for a particular service organization.

We also recommend that the Board clarify the procedures to be performed by an auditor once a service auditor's report is obtained. In particular, we suggest that the Board clarify that once the auditor has evaluated the service auditor's reputation, competence and independence and once the auditor has reviewed the report and made the appropriate inquiries of management, if the report provides the information that the auditor needs about the operation of a particular control and if the auditor has tested the user organization's input and output controls relating to the particular organization, no further testing of the control may be necessary.

Office of the Secretary
Public Company Accounting Oversight Board
Page 5

Finally, we recommend that the Board clarify the procedures to be performed when a service auditor's report is unavailable. For example, in the case of service organizations in non-U.S. jurisdictions, where the SAS 70 standard would not apply and SAS 70 reports are therefore not available, we believe the Board should permit the use of comparable reports under non-U.S. generally accepted auditing standards. In other situations in which reports are unavailable altogether, but only in appropriate circumstances as determined by the auditor, we believe that it should be sufficient that the auditor review the user organization controls over information that is "input" to and "output" from service organizations. In addition, in instances in which management has conducted due diligence to determine whether to use a particular vendor, management has performed ongoing monitoring of that vendor to ensure a high quality of service and an outside auditor has difficulty obtaining technical manuals or directly observing personnel at the service organization, the outside auditor should be permitted to use the information obtained by management in the course of its due diligence and monitoring.

3. Outside Auditors Should Be Permitted to Use the Work of Others to a Greater Degree When Appropriate.

Paragraph 103 of the Proposed Standard would direct auditors to evaluate a number of factors in determining whether to use the results of procedures performed by others. These factors include the materiality or the risk of misstatement of the accounts and disclosures that the controls address and the degree of judgment required to evaluate the operating effectiveness of the controls. We agree with the Board's approach of permitting outside auditors to use the work of others while also cautioning against inappropriate over-reliance on that work. However, as discussed below, we question the appropriateness of the Board's proposal for a blanket prohibition on the use of the work of others in certain areas, including controls that have a pervasive effect on the financial statements, such as certain information technology general controls on which the operating effectiveness of other controls depend.

We understand the Board's concern that there are certain areas in which use of the work of others may be inappropriate. However, taking into account (1) the guidelines already set forth in paragraphs 103 through 110 and Appendix B of the Proposed Standard regarding use of the work of others (including directing outside auditors to evaluate the independence of the internal audit function from management and requiring auditors to perform enough of the testing themselves so that the auditors' own work provides the principal evidence for the audit opinion), (2) the increased focus (through listing standards, among others) on having an internal audit function that reports to the audit committee and (3) the fact that in instances in which an issuer has an internal audit function, the requirements of the Sarbanes-Oxley Act and related rules could result in three levels of review of controls (outside auditors, management and internal auditors), we believe that absolute prohibitions on using the work of others, especially internal auditors, are not necessary to protect investors and are inefficient.

Office of the Secretary
Public Company Accounting Oversight Board
Page 6

As discussed above, we believe that in keeping with the spirit of the Sarbanes-Oxley Act, the auditing standards under that Act should focus on adding value, in an efficient manner, to investors and other users of financial statements. Investors are harmed not only by ineffective internal controls and misleading financial statements, but also by inefficient use of resources and unnecessary increases in fees paid to service providers resulting from redundant efforts. Therefore, we urge the Board to impose only those requirements that are necessary to protect investors and the integrity of financial reporting.

We encourage the Board to follow the approach set forth in Statement on Auditing Standards No. 65, *The Auditor's Consideration of the Internal Audit Function in an Audit of Financial Statements* ("SAS 65"). SAS 65 provides that if the auditor decides that it would be efficient to consider how the internal auditors' work might affect the nature, timing and extent of audit procedures, the auditor should assess the competence and objectivity of the internal audit function in light of the intended effect of the internal auditors' work on the audit. SAS 65 notes that in making judgments about the extent of the effect of the internal auditors' work on the auditor's procedures, the auditor must consider the materiality of the financial statement amounts, the risk of material misstatement of the assertions related to these financial statement amounts and the degree of subjectivity involved in the evaluation of the audit evidence gathered in support of the assertions. SAS 65 also notes that the degree of reliance on the work of others should be on a sliding scale — as the materiality of the financial statement amounts increases and either the risk of material misstatement or the degree of subjectivity increases, the need for the auditor to perform his or her own tests of the assertions increases; the converse of this statement would also be true. Rather than setting forth blanket prohibitions on the use of the work of internal auditors, SAS 65 allows the auditors to use their professional judgment in determining when and how much reliance should be given to the use of the internal audit function.

We encourage the Board to adopt a similar standard and to permit outside auditors, in appropriate circumstances and as outlined in paragraph 103 of the Proposed Standard, to use the work of others in forming their opinion on the effectiveness of all controls, including information technology general controls.

4.   Discretion Should Be Permitted as to the Extent of Control Testing.

Paragraph 27 of the Proposed Standard would require auditors to obtain sufficient competent evidence about the design and operating effectiveness of controls related to *all* relevant financial statement assertions for *all* significant accounts and disclosures in the financial statements. The Board's proposing release setting forth the Proposed Standard (the "Proposing Release") notes that although auditors should vary testing from year to year, each year's audit must stand on its own and therefore, auditors must obtain evidence of the effectiveness of controls for all relevant assertions for all significant accounts and disclosures every year.

Office of the Secretary
Public Company Accounting Oversight Board
Page 7

Rather than mandating that evidence be gathered each year for all assertions for all significant accounts and disclosures, auditors should be directed to use their professional judgment to determine not only what accounts and disclosures are "significant" (paragraphs 60-65 of the Proposed Standard) but also to determine when it is appropriate to gather new evidence and when it is appropriate to leverage prior years' evidence. We recommend that the Proposed Standard set forth guidelines in this area. For example, the Proposed Standard could direct auditors to inquire of management as to whether there has been a significant change from the prior year in a control related to a particular financial statement assertion for a particular account. If after performing testing procedures, the extent of which would be determined by the auditor's professional judgment, to validate management's determination, the auditor is satisfied that there has been no such change, and if the auditor otherwise deems it appropriate, the auditor could reasonably rely on prior years' evidence for that particular assertion. We believe that in appropriate circumstances, comprehensive testing of controls can be accomplished without re-testing each particular control on an annual basis; auditors should be permitted to use their professional judgment to determine when re-testing is and is not necessary.

Paragraph 79 of the Proposed Standard would require an auditor to perform a walkthrough for all of the company's significant processes. The Proposed Standard appears to require these walkthroughs to be performed each year. We believe that it is neither efficient nor beneficial to investors to require walkthroughs of *all* significant processes each year. Rather, we believe that the Proposed Standard should permit auditors to use their professional judgment to determine, on an annual basis, the significant processes for which walkthroughs should be performed. We anticipate that by using their professional judgment, auditors will still perform walkthroughs for a substantial portion of a company's significant processes, but that in certain instances, auditors may be able to rotate those significant processes for which walkthroughs are performed. This approach is consistent with the goal of having auditing standards that protect investors while at the same time being efficient and cost-effective. We do not believe that the benefit, if any, to investors of having auditors test *all* financial statement assertions warrants the added costs to companies and investors. Instead, we believe that investors will be benefited most by testing of controls that the auditor determines is sufficient to permit the auditor to reach an opinion on the effectiveness of a company's internal control over financial reporting.

5. The Definitions of Significant Deficiency and Material Weakness Should Be Consistent with the Definitions of Reportable Condition and Material Weakness Set Forth in Current Generally Accepted Auditing Standards.

We believe that the changes made by the Proposed Standard to the definitions of "significant deficiency" and "material weakness" are inadvisable, for the reasons discussed below. Instead, the existing definitions in generally accepted auditing standards should be retained.

Office of the Secretary
Public Company Accounting Oversight Board
Page 8

The proposed definitions of material weakness and significant deficiency would depart from the definitions set forth in generally accepted auditing standards – AU Section 325, *Communication of Internal Control Related Matters Noted in an Audit* ("AU 325"), and AT Section 501, *Reporting on an Entity's Internal Control Over Financial Reporting* ("AT 501") (incorporating the AU 325 definitions) – and appear generally to lower the threshold for identifying significant deficiencies and material weaknesses.

A significant deficiency under the Proposed Standard would be triggered by any deficiency that results in *more than a remote likelihood* of misstatements of *inconsequential amounts*,[4] whereas under AU 325 it is triggered by any *significant* deficiency that *could adversely affect* reported financial data.[5] Furthermore, the proposed definition would change the threshold for a material weakness to *more than a remote likelihood*, rather than a *relatively low level of risk*.

We have a number of concerns regarding the proposed changes to these definitions. First, the SEC's rules issued in June 2003 relating to management's assessment of internal controls, and conforming changes to management's certifications, appear to incorporate the definitions included in AU 325 and AT 501.[6] If this is the case, we believe that there will be many instances in which

---

[4]   Paragraph 9 of the Proposed Standard would define "material weakness" to be a significant deficiency that, by itself, or in combination with other significant deficiencies, results in **more than a remote likelihood** that a material misstatement of the annual or interim financial statements will not be prevented or detected. "Significant deficiency" would be defined to be an internal control deficiency that **adversely affects** the company's ability to initiate, record, process or report external financial data reliably in accordance with generally accepted accounting principles. Under the Proposed Standard, a significant deficiency could be a single deficiency, or a combination of deficiencies, that results in **more than a remote likelihood** that a misstatement of the annual or interim financial statements that is **more than inconsequential in amount** will not be prevented or detected.

[5]   AU 325 currently defines "material weakness" to be a reportable condition in which the design or operation of one or more of the internal control components **does not reduce to a relatively low level** the risk that misstatements caused by error or fraud in amounts that would be material in relation to the financial statements being audited may occur and not be detected within a timely period by employees in the normal course of performing their assigned functions. A "reportable condition" (significant deficiency) under AU 325 is triggered by **significant** deficiencies that **could adversely affect** the entity's ability to initiate, record, process and report financial data consistent with the assertions of management in the financial statements.

[6]   Although the SEC's June 2003 adopting release (No. 33-8238) provides that the definitions of material weakness and significant deficiency would have the same meanings as under

---

Office of the Secretary
Public Company Accounting Oversight Board
Page 9

management's assessment may not identify a material weakness under the SEC's rules but where the auditors would identify a material weakness under the auditing standards applicable to the auditor's assessment. In this instance, auditors would be required to issue a qualified opinion even though management's assessment complied with the SEC's rules.

Second, even if the SEC were to clarify that its rules incorporate any new definitions of material weakness and significant deficiency, we are more generally concerned with the change in the threshold for identifying material weaknesses and significant deficiencies. We believe that the lower threshold set forth in the Proposed Standard would result in nearly every company having significant deficiencies even though their reporting processes may be functioning in such a manner as would protect investors. We are particularly concerned about the lack of a difference between an internal control deficiency and a significant deficiency and believe that given the low threshold presented by the Proposed Standard, there will be few internal control deficiencies as to which auditors feel confident do not rise to the level of a significant deficiency. Our concern is compounded by the fact that under paragraph 126 of the Proposed Standard, significant deficiencies that have been communicated to management and the audit committee and that remain uncorrected after some reasonable period of time would be regarded as at least a significant deficiency and would be a strong indicator of a material weakness. In addition, under the Proposed Standard, if auditors identify multiple significant deficiencies, none of which are significantly above the threshold, they may believe that they are required to report material weaknesses, even though the probability of one or more of any of these significant deficiencies actually resulting in a material misstatement is very low. We believe that the change in the threshold could have the unintended effect of harming the quality of financial reporting by distracting outside auditors, internal auditors, management and the audit committee into focusing on the deficiencies that have only slightly more than a remote likelihood of failing to detect non-material (but more than "inconsequential" of amount) misstatements of financial statements rather than focusing on more serious deficiencies that, if not corrected, would have a harmful effect on the quality of financial reporting.

Although we recommend that the Board retain the language used in AU 325 and AT 501, if the Board decides to adopt different definitions than those set forth in AU 325 and AT 501, we respectfully request that the Board adopt a "reasonably possible" standard rather than a "more than remote likelihood" standard for both the material weakness and significant deficiency definitions, as those terms are used in Financial Accounting Standards Board Statement No. 5, *Accounting for Contingencies*, or at least clarify that the two phrases establish the same threshold for disclosure to management and the audit committee. We also request that the "inconsequential amount"

---

generally accepted auditing standards, the release specifically references AU 325 and AT 501, which may indicate that the SEC intended to incorporate the definitions as in effect at the time of the release.

Office of the Secretary
Public Company Accounting Oversight Board
Page 10

threshold in the proposed definition of significant deficiency be replaced with a threshold requiring a "significant" misstatement. We believe that an "inconsequential amount" threshold will in practice eliminate the difference between *any* internal control deficiency and a *significant* deficiency. By setting forth a significance test, the standard would clarify the difference between a significant deficiency and an internal control deficiency, while at the same time retaining the distinction between the concepts of material weakness and significant deficiency. Finally, we suggest that the Board clarify that the companies in the examples set forth in Appendix D of the Proposed Standard have no mitigating controls to correct the effect of the identified internal control deficiency, and that that is why the situations lead to conclusions of significant deficiency and material weakness. We believe that in appropriate circumstances, other effective internal controls over financial reporting should be able to compensate for an internal control that is identified to be deficient.

6.   The Board Should Consider Whether Outside Auditors Are in the Best Position to Evaluate the Effectiveness of Audit Committees Given the Inherent Conflict of Interest in Such an Evaluation.

Under paragraph 57 of the Proposed Standard, an auditor would be required to evaluate factors relating to the effectiveness of the audit committee's oversight of the company's external financial reporting and internal control over financial reporting. The factors that an auditor would be directed to evaluate would include the independence of the audit committee members from management, the level of involvement and interaction with the independent auditor (including the audit committee's role in the appointment, retention and compensation of the auditor), the audit committee's compliance with applicable listing standards and whether the audit committee includes one or more "audit committee financial experts" as defined by SEC rules under the Sarbanes-Oxley Act. The auditor would also be directed to evaluate how audit committee members are nominated and selected and whether they are selected based upon "desired skill sets".

As provided in the Sarbanes-Oxley Act and as noted in the Proposing Release, that Act makes the audit committee directly responsible for the appointment, compensation and oversight of the work of the auditor. By directing outside auditors to evaluate the committee that has the power to hire and fire the audit firm and the responsibility to oversee and direct their work, the Proposed Standard would create an inherent irreconcilable conflict for the outside auditors which is likely to affect their ability to conduct effectively such a review.

Although we understand the Board's concern about the relationship of the audit committee to the internal control structure, given the inherent conflict discussed above and considering the numerous regulatory requirements imposed on audit committees (*e.g.*, rules promulgated by the SEC, disclosure requirements, applicable listing standards and state law concepts of fiduciary duty), as well as pressure from investors, we believe that mandating auditor review of the audit committee in this manner is neither necessary nor appropriate.

Office of the Secretary
Public Company Accounting Oversight Board
Page 11

In addition to creating an inherent conflict, many of the determinations that the auditors would be required to make under the Proposed Standard (*e.g.*, whether an audit committee member qualifies as an "audit committee financial expert" and whether the audit committee and its members are in compliance with applicable listing standards) are determinations more appropriately made by the company, usually with the advice of counsel.

We believe that as a matter of general corporate governance, it is the board of directors that is responsible for establishing and maintaining an audit committee that is effective and complies with the relevant rules, including Section 301 of the Sarbanes-Oxley Act. We believe that a separate requirement for evaluation of the audit committee should not be established or implied in the context of Section 404 of the Sarbanes-Oxley Act or the rules and auditing standards related to that part of the Act.

If the Board does retain this concept of auditor evaluation of the audit committee in the final standard, we respectfully request that the Board clarify the qualifications necessary for an auditor to perform this evaluation, including the extent to which the auditor should be familiar with the Sarbanes-Oxley Act and applicable SEC rules and stock exchange listing standards related to audit committees, as well as the manner in which the auditor should gather information required for this evaluation. We also urge that the Board clarify the procedures to be followed in the event that the auditors disagree with a board of directors as to whether a particular audit committee member, or the entire committee, is in compliance with the applicable requirements.

Finally, we recommend that the Board clarify that the required evaluation would apply only to the auditor's evaluation of the audit committee and would not result in management having to conduct a similar evaluation. We believe that, absent clarification, confusion may arise based on the current wording of the Proposed Standard due to the fact that ineffective oversight of external financial reporting and internal control over financial reporting by the audit committee would be considered at least a significant deficiency and would be a strong indicator that a material weakness in internal control over financial reporting exists. If, in light of this provision, auditors take the position that *any* factor that could lead to a significant deficiency should be evaluated by management in order for management's assessment to be adequate, the Proposed Standard could result in auditors expecting management to evaluate the effectiveness of the audit committee in order to receive a "clean" opinion from the auditors. We believe the Proposed Standard should state that such a management evaluation is not required.

Office of the Secretary
Public Company Accounting Oversight Board
Page 12

7. We Support the Board's Proposed Integration of the Audit of Financial Statements with the Audit of Internal Control Over Financial Reporting and the Board's Proposal that Directs Auditors to Use Their Professional Judgment to Determine Whether Inadequate Documentation Constitutes a Significant Deficiency.

As discussed in the Proposing Release, the Proposed Standard integrates the audit of internal control over financial reporting with the audit of the financial statements. In particular, paragraph 27 of the Proposed Standard states that in order to perform an audit of internal control over financial reporting, the auditor must also audit the financial statements. We agree with the Board that information gathered in the audit of financial statements may be significant to an assessment of internal control. In addition, having the same outside auditors perform both audits will create efficiencies as the auditors will already be knowledgeable about the company's internal control structure through their work on the audit of the financial statements. We support the Board's integrated approach and efforts to create auditing standards that seek to provide guidance to auditors in determining how to use information gathered in an audit of financial statements in an audit of internal control over financial reporting.

We also support the Board's proposal that inadequate documentation of internal control over financial reporting by management should be evaluated to determine whether it rises to the level of a significant deficiency. We believe that auditors are in a position to determine whether inadequate documentation of the design of internal control over financial reporting is so severe as to constitute a significant deficiency. In many instances, inadequate documentation of the design of internal control, by itself, will not rise to the level of a significant deficiency. Rather than setting forth a firm standard, we believe that this determination is better made by auditors who can consider the significance of this deficiency in light of other aspects of a company's internal control over financial reporting.

We would be glad to discuss this letter with representatives of the Board's staff. If you have any questions or require additional information, please call me at 212-272-2000.

Yours truly,

/s/ Marshall J Levinson

Marshall J Levinson
President
Financial Management Division
Securities Industry Association

¶ 614. Information Systems Audit and Control Association and IT Governance Institute

November 21, 2003

Office of the Secretary
Public Company Accounting Oversight Board
1666 K Street, NW
Washington, DC 20006-2803

Via E-mail to comments@pcaobus.org

RE: PCAOB Rulemaking Docket Matter No. 008
       PCAOB Release No. 2003-017, October 7, 2003
       (Proposed Auditing Standard – An Audit of Internal Control over Financial Reporting Performed
       in Conjunction with an Audit of Financial Statements)

Dear Board Members:

We very much appreciate the opportunity to provide comments to the Public Company
Accounting Oversight Board's ("Board" or "PCAOB") proposed auditing standard.
These comments are offered on behalf of the Information Systems Audit and Control
Association (ISACA) and IT Governance Institute (ITGI), in my capacity as the
International President of both of these organizations.

ISACA is an international professional, technical and educational organization dedicated
to being a recognized global leader in IT governance, security, control and assurance.
With members in more than 100 countries, ISACA is uniquely positioned to fulfill the
role of a central, harmonizing source of IT control practice standards the world over. Its
strategic alliances with other organizations in the financial, accounting, auditing and IT
professions ensure an unparalleled level of integration and commitment by business
process owners.

ITGI strives to assist enterprise leaders in their responsibility to make IT successful in
supporting the enterprise's mission and goals. Its goals are to raise awareness and
understanding among, and provide guidance and tools to, boards of directors, executive
management and chief information officers (CIOs). The ultimate goal is to ensure that IT
meets and exceeds expectations, and its risks are mitigated.

Taken as a whole, we support the draft standard and what it sets out to accomplish. We
list below our comments on some of the areas covered in the draft standard. We have
made comments in 4 areas:

- IT Controls—We suggest clarification of some of the IT control-related terminology
  used in the standard.

The recognized global leader in IT governance, security, control and assurance.

Office of the Secretary PCAOB   Page 2   November 21, 2003

- IT Control Framework—We suggest an alternative view of IT controls using the *Control Objectives for Information and related Technology* (COBIT) as a formal guidance framework.
- Reliance on IT Internal Audit—We suggest revisiting this area and allowing public accounting firms to rely on the work of IT internal audit.
- Audit Committee Effectiveness—We suggest that additional definition regarding the role of the audit committee in the IT governance area be provided, and that the IT Governance Institute be used as a resource for this.

IT Controls

We note that "IT general controls" are referred to throughout the proposed standard. However, the scope of the IT general controls is not defined. We are concerned that organizations and auditors may focus on only the control activities component of general controls defined in COSO, i.e., "General controls commonly include controls over data center operations, system software acquisition and maintenance, access security, and application system development and maintenance." We explain below what we feel is a more comprehensive view of IT controls.

We also noted an inconsistency and lack of clarity in the references to application controls within the draft standard. We feel that this should be addressed as well, and provide below a view on how this could be accomplished.

If the scope of IT general and application controls is not further clarified, then there is an increased risk that organizations and their auditors will not consider the entire IT governance framework in their evaluation of the effectiveness of the financial reporting control framework. We believe that further clarification and definition of the term "certain information technology general controls" used within the document should be considered. Once again, we offer the alternative detailed below to cover this concern.

As noted in our recent publication, *IT Control Objectives for Sarbanes-Oxley,* which we have attached to this submission, IT controls apply to all COSO components, not just the control activities component. We believe that the Board may want to consider referencing COBIT within the final guidance, as a framework for the IT control environment, much as COSO has been recommended as the internal control framework (see the Framework section below for further clarification).

COSO identifies five essential components of effective internal control. Below, we highlight, in each of the five COSO component areas, our rationale for requesting further clarification be provided within the standard, by referring to COBIT as the IT control framework. A description of the relationship of IT to all five COSO components follows.

1. Control Environment

   The control environment primarily addresses the company level. However, IT frequently has characteristics that may require additional emphasis on business alignment, roles and responsibilities, policies and procedures, and technical competence. The following list describes some considerations related to the control environment and IT:

- IT is often mistakenly regarded as a separate organization of the business and thus a separate control environment.
- IT is complex, not only with regard to its technical components but also in how those components integrate into the company's overall system of internal control.
- IT can introduce additional or increased risks that require new or enhanced control activities to mitigate successfully.
- IT requires specialized skills that may be in short supply.
- IT may require reliance on third parties where significant processes or IT components are outsourced.
- The ownership of IT controls may be unclear.

2. Risk Assessment

   It is likely that internal control risks could be more pervasive in the IT organization than in other areas of the company. Risk assessment may occur at the company level (for the overall organization) or at the activity level (for a specific process or business unit). At the company level, the following may be expected:
   - An IT strategy subcommittee of the company's overall Sarbanes-Oxley steering committee, with the following responsibilities:
     - Oversight of the development of the IT internal control strategic plan, its effective and timely execution/implementation, and its integration with the overall Sarbanes-Oxley compliance plan
     - Assessment of IT risks, e.g., data integrity, security, confidentiality and availability

   At the activity level, the following may be expected:
   - Risk assessments built throughout the systems development methodology
   - Risk assessments built into the infrastructure operation and change process
   - Risk assessments built into the program change process

3. Control Activities

   Control activities primarily address the activity level. Without reliable information systems and effective IT control activities, public companies would not be able to generate accurate financial reports. As general and application controls increasingly replace manual controls, IT general and application controls are becoming more important.

4. Information and Communication

   COSO states that information is needed at all levels of an organization to run the business and achieve the entity's control objectives. However, the identification, management and communication of relevant information represent an ever-increasing challenge to the IT department. Supporting the other four components of the COSO framework, are the determination of which information is required to achieve control objectives and the communication of this information in a form and time frame that allow people to carry out their duties. The IT organization processes most financial reporting information. However, its scope is usually much broader. For example, the

IT department may also assist in implementing mechanisms to identify and communicate significant information or events, such as regulatory reporting or accounting disclosures.

5. Monitoring

Monitoring, which covers the oversight of internal control by management through continuous and point-in-time assessment processes, is becoming increasingly important to IT management. There are two types of monitoring activities: continuous monitoring and separate evaluations. IT performance and effectiveness are increasingly monitored using performance measures that indicate if an underlying control is operating effectively. Consider the following examples:

- Defect identification and management—Establishing metrics and analyzing the trends of actual results against metrics can provide a basis for understanding the underlying reasons for processing failures. Correcting these causes can improve system accuracy, completeness of processing and system availability.
- Security monitoring—Building an effective IT security infrastructure reduces the risk of unauthorized access. Improving security can reduce the risk of processing unauthorized transactions and generating inaccurate reports, and can ensure a reduction of the availability of key systems if applications and IT infrastructure components have been compromised.

At the company level, the following may be expected:

- Centralized continuous monitoring of computer operations
- Centralized monitoring of security
- IT internal audit reviews. (While the audit may occur at the activity level, the reporting of audit results to the audit committee will be at the company level.)

At the activity level, the following may be expected:

- Defect identification and management
- Local monitoring of computer operations or security
- Supervision of local IT personnel

IT Control Framework

We believe that, where IT is significant to the financial reporting of business enterprises, these enterprises need to use an IT control framework to supplement the overall COSO framework, as illustrated in the attached publication *IT Control Objectives for Sarbanes-Oxley*.

COBIT, originally introduced in 1996, is an open, *de facto* IT governance and control framework, now in its third edition. The framework, which is entirely compliant with COSO, is referred to and used globally by assurance and control professionals, and by business process owners and IT management. Again, we applaud the PCAOB for taking on the issues, especially as they apply to IT controls.

We would like to recommend that the Board adopt COBIT as the IT control framework. While the importance of IT control is embedded in the COSO internal control framework, IT management requires more examples to help document and evaluate controls. COBIT is an IT governance model, which provides both company-level and activity-level objectives and associated controls. Using the COBIT framework, a company can design a system of IT controls to comply with S404 of the Sarbanes-Oxley Act. The following depicts the COSO–COBIT relationship within the requirements of Sarbanes-Oxley.

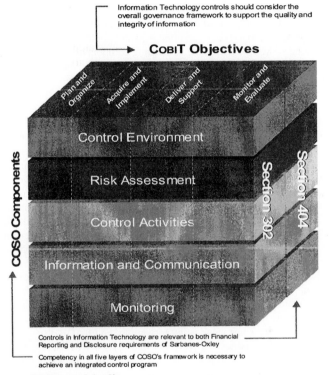

Reliance on IT Internal Audit

While we agree that a public accounting firm should independently review IT controls within the IT control environment, we do have reservations about the inference that the public accountant cannot use the results of testing performed by management and others within other COSO components. IT audit professionals normally perform this testing. Many of those hold the Certified Information Systems Auditor (CISA) certification, offered by ISACA since 1978 and earned by more than 30,000 professionals worldwide. We suggest that the public accounting firm could determine the adequacy and appropriateness of such testing, based on the competence of the internal auditor and the auditor's positioning and independence, with additional testing being performed as necessary in the circumstances. If reliance cannot be placed on IT general controls testing then no credit can be given to the work that internal audit professionals are carrying out every day. We recommend that the Board consider revising this rule to provide further clarification on the reliance public accounting firms can place on the work of IT internal auditors.

Audit Committee Effectiveness
Reference paragraph 56:
"Evaluating the Effectiveness of the Audit Committee's Oversight of the Company's External Financial Reporting and Internal Control Over Financial Reporting"

The company's audit committee plays an important role within the control environment, including the monitoring components of internal control over financial reporting. Within the control environment, the existence of an effective audit committee is essential to setting a positive tone at the top. Within the monitoring component, an effective audit committee is crucial to challenging the company's activities in the financial arena.

However we do have the following comments:
- We suggest that the main issue is the effectiveness of the audit committee in overseeing corporate governance over financial reporting, which includes governance over the IT function. Additional emphasis on the spirit of the controls over IT governance should be considered.
- IT governance is such an integral part of corporate governance, including internal control, which we believe boards and the audit committee need to extend governance to IT. Doing so will in turn provide the leadership, organizational structures and processes that ensure that the enterprise's IT sustains and extends the enterprises strategies and objectives. The current environment, which encompasses the new standard and other issues the PCAOB is addressing, calls for increasing emphasis on a broader corporate governance role for audit committees. The audit committee must deal effectively with IT governance and its implications if it is to deal effectively with processes to monitor risk and ensure that the system of internal control is effective in reducing those risks to an acceptable level.
- The ITGI was created for such reasons, and has been focusing on creating and delivering seminal research to assist in the provision of solutions to deal with these issues. We feel that the ITGI can provide some value going forward to the PCAOB, especially as it deals with the overarching issues of governance and IT. Much of the research and thought-provoking work the ITGI has created is closely linked back to COBIT—the framework for IT governance and control.

Again, we appreciate the opportunity to comment on the proposed standard. Thank you for considering our views. We would be happy to discuss them with you in further detail.

Respectfully submitted,

Marios Damianides, CISA, CISM, CA, CPA
2003-2004 International President
ISACA (info@isaca.org) ITGI (info@itgi.org)

Enc. *IT Control Objectives for Sarbanes Oxley*

¶ 615. Institute of Chartered Accountants in England and Wales

21 November 2003

Office of the Secretary
Public Company Accounting Oversight Board
1666 K Street NW
Washington DC 20006-2083
USA

Dear Sirs

PCAOB Rulemaking Docket Matter No. 008

Proposed Auditing Standard – An Audit of Internal Control over Financial Reporting Performed in Conjunction with an Audit of Financial Statements

The Institute of Chartered Accountants in England & Wales is pleased to provide a letter of comment in response to the PCAOB's proposed standard entitled "An Audit of Internal Control over Financial Reporting Performed in Conjunction with an Audit of Financial Statements".

The Institute is the largest individual body of professionally qualified accountants in Europe with over 125,000 members. Individual members work in many sectors in business, the public sector as well as practising accountants and auditors. We operate under a Royal Charter that reflects our commitment to the public interest.

The proposed standard will have a significant impact on the work not only of US-based auditors and registrants, but also on the UK profession and those individuals throughout the world serving:
- foreign private issuers listed in the US; and
- foreign subsidiaries of US domestic SEC registrants which are bound by the same requirements as the US domestic entity as well as joint ventures with SEC registrant companies.

Consequently, we are sending a copy of this letter to the UK Auditing Practices Board and the International Auditing and Assurances Standards Board.

Introductory remarks

We are aware of the challenges faced by the PCAOB in preparing this exposure draft. Internal control is not a straightforward concept and the measurement of its effectiveness is not easy. Balancing the requirements of the Sarbanes-Oxley Act and the needs and views of investors, regulators, auditors and cost benefit considerations for businesses requires very careful consideration. Upon the Board's decisions on the future of the proposed standard appears to hang issues of expectations, the costs of implementation and future interpretation in the US courts. The pervasive impact of the proposed standard on global audit practice and, potentially, on the platforms used by global audit firms for their audit methodologies, imposes additional significant responsibilities on the PCAOB in finalising the proposed standard.

We are also aware of the debate in the US as to whether or not the Board's proposed standard extends the boundaries of Section 404(b) of the Sarbanes-Oxley Act from 'attestation' to 'audit'. Not all 'attestations' are 'audits'. Whatever the technical arguments for or against this proposed extension, it is a fundamental issue upon which there is a need for clarity from all those involved. We strongly urge the Board to be certain that the many outcomes that are likely to result from the proposed standard, including the costs and benefits to both investors and companies, as well as the liability to external auditors, the level of regulation, the consequent impact on external auditor judgement and the extensive additional work that is required for all SEC registrants, is what was intended by Congress when it passed the Sarbanes-Oxley Act and is also their current view (taking into account the other requirements and sanctions in the Act).

Finally, we hope that the PCAOB will give due consideration to the impact of its proposals on the IAASB's global audit standards and recognise the significance of those standards in discharging its responsibilities.

Key Comments

In addition to our introductory remarks, this letter contains key comments on adverse audit opinions, external auditor reliance on the work of management and others, reporting of control weaknesses and audit committee evaluations. Other general comments are also provided on significant issues. Our answers to the PCAOB's thirty one questions are included in the Appendix to this letter.

1　　Adverse audit opinions and definitions

The proposed standard indicates that (under defined circumstances) a material weakness automatically gives rise to an adverse opinion. The proposed standard gives no apparent scope for an 'except for' opinion. Automatic adverse, rather than qualified, audit opinions leave external auditors with nothing left in their armoury as a last resort for situations in which things have gone very seriously wrong in many respects. An adverse opinion is almost universally understood by standard setters to mean that a pervasive, fundamental problem has arisen. Suggesting that such an opinion should be issued where this is not the case is likely to spread confusion.

The proposed definition of a material weakness in paragraph 9 states that a "…material weakness is a significant deficiency that…..results in more than a remote likelihood that a material misstatement of the annual or interim financial statements will not be detected".

The phrase 'more than a remote likelihood' is derived from FAS 5 and is more tightly defined than the corresponding phrase in the existing AT 501 auditing standard, "does not reduce to a relatively low level". The use of the proposed phrase in connection with the definition of significant deficiencies is likely to result in very few material weaknesses being excluded. This will significantly affect the amount of work to be undertaken by both external auditors and management. We suggest that PCAOB considers whether the definition used in AT 501 is in fact preferable.

Overall, the proposed standard gives the impression of trying to achieve, and having an overall expectation of, 'perfection'. This somewhat over-enthusiastic approach may not be cost-effective, particularly for smaller and medium sized companies. An appropriate balance of cost, benefit and regulation to improve investor protection is necessary but businesses should not be subjected to unnecessary, costly and stifling bureaucracy. We fear that the combined effect of these proposals would be to:

- inflate the scope of work that external auditors (and presumably, management) will be obliged to carry out;
- lead to scope changes to Section 404 readiness projects already underway at companies; and
- inflate the number of adverse opinions, thereby devaluing their impact which will not enhance investor confidence.

We therefore believe that a material weakness should *not automatically* result in an adverse opinion, and that external auditors should be allowed to use their professional judgement to determine whether a material weakness merits a qualified rather than an adverse opinion. Guidance might be provided on situations in which an adverse, rather than a qualified opinion would be appropriate. Such guidance might be aligned with the IAASB's standards and guidance on auditors' reports.

The specific requirements of section 404 (as interpreted by the SEC rules) relate to internal controls over financial reporting. The proposed standard sometimes refers to 'internal control' and sometimes to 'internal control over financial reporting'. The latter is a much narrower term than the former. It is not always clear as to whether references to internal control in the text should be read as references to internal control over financial reporting. We suggest that the matter should be clarified at the beginning of the standard.

In example A-5 the auditor issues an unqualified opinion that refers to the report of the other auditors. We do not understand why a direct report on internal control effectiveness is given here rather than a report on management's assessment, as with other unqualified opinions.

2   Reliance on internal audit and management testing

The proposed standard appears to restrict unnecessarily the use of judgement by external auditors when deciding whether, and to what extent, to rely on the work of others.

The wording in the proposed standard also appears contradictory. Wording in the introduction to the document seems encouraging about less work being required for companies that have good controls, but paragraphs in the main text of the proposed standard seem to negate this. For example, the second paragraph on page 8 of the introduction states that the work that management performs in connection with its assessment can have a "…significant effect on the nature, timing, and extent of the work the independent auditor will need to perform". It goes on to state that the proposed auditing standard would allow the auditor to use, to a reasonable degree, the work performed by others, including management and that the more extensive and reliable management's assessment is, the less extensive and costly the auditor's work will need to be. Contrast this with paragraphs 104 and 105 of the proposed standard which detail areas where the external auditors should not, or are limited in their ability to, place reliance on the work of others. Paragraph 109 goes on to state that the external auditor must perform enough of the testing himself/herself such that that the external auditors' own work forms the "principal evidence".

Paragraphs 104 and 105 are unnecessarily restrictive. We believe that external auditors should be able use their judgement as to when they can rely upon the work of internal audit, provided that they are satisfied that the internal audit department's work is objective and performed by competent people who adhere to relevant professional standards.

We believe that the proposed standard builds in wasteful inefficiencies by insisting that the external auditor re-performs a substantial amount of testing. Management might reasonably ask (inhibited only by the fear of a qualified or adverse report) why internal audit or management should bother to perform tests if the external auditors are specifically required by the standard to do them again.

In practice, it is a possibility that CEOs will now ask for substantial help from their internal audit functions in complying with the requirements of the proposed standard; either by reviewing the processes and output of the testing on internal financial controls undertaken by management, or even by undertaking much of the detailed testing work on behalf of management. These scenarios, particularly the latter, may not be a welcome development where the remit of internal audit is directed to the provision of assurance to the audit committee and the board on the wider aspects of all an organisation's controls rather than just internal control over financial reporting.

Paragraph 108 of the proposed standard states that internal auditors "…would normally be expected to have greater competence with regard to internal control over financial reporting and objectivity than other company personnel". Whilst internal auditors would normally be expected to have greater *objectivity* than others in this and other areas, they may not have greater competence in financial reporting than financial reporting specialists.

3   Reporting of control weaknesses

We suggest that the requirement for the external auditor to communicate *all* deficiencies to the audit committee will lead to information overload for audit committees. It is likely that audit committees will receive the same or similar lists of issues from both internal and external auditors in the light of the fact that external auditors will have reviewed internal audit reports and must therefore re-communicate all the deficiencies already reported by internal auditors.

Paragraph 126 of the proposed standard states that a significant deficiency that remains uncorrected after some reasonable period of time is a strong indicator of a material weakness. This judgement as to what is 'reasonable' could be problematic, for example where the costs of a suggested control solution outweigh the benefits. Recognition should also be given to situations in which a company has several significant deficiencies but in completely unrelated areas. Does the aggregation principle apply in this case? If so, adverse audit opinions may become commonplace and will their significance be debased in the eyes of investors.

Furthermore, where errors are found, testing would usually be extended to determine whether this is a one-off insignificant error or evidence of a systematic breakdown in a control. Is the standard intended to be read such that one-off errors should be reported even when the auditor was prepared to stand by the judgement that they were not significant?

4   **Audit committee evaluation**

Paragraph 57 of the proposed standard requires the external auditors to form a view on the effectiveness of the audit committee.

These requirements introduce some circularity in that the audit committee which appoints, removes, approves the remuneration of, and evaluates the external auditor will itself be evaluated by the external auditor. This requirement may place the external auditor in conflict with the audit committee.

Whilst we believe that an assessment of the audit committee is appropriate because the audit committee is an important part of the internal control framework, there is no need for a separate stand-alone requirement. We believe that assessment of the audit committee by the external auditor will be effective provided that safeguards are implemented. These safeguards might involve a requirement for particular attention to be paid to the assessment by a partner or other senior person within the audit firm who is not directly involved with the audit (such as the independent review partner).

We disagree with paragraph 59 which requires that where the external audit evaluates the audit committee as being ineffective, this "…should be regarded as at least a significant deficiency and a strong indicator that a material weakness in internal control over financial reporting exists". A material weakness would automatically lead to an adverse audit opinion. We believe that the external auditor should be allowed to exercise professional judgement and consider other relevant factors, such as the role played by the board of directors. Furthermore, we also believe that reference to the use of judgement should also be made in paragraph 126 which describes other situations which should be regarded as at least a significant deficiency and a strong indicator that a material weakness exits.

In the UK, following the revised Combined Code on Corporate Governance issued in July 2003, from now on boards of directors will have to conduct a performance evaluation of the audit committee (Code provision A.6.1).

Other General Comments

5   **Level of controls testing**

Appendix B provides four examples of control testing procedures. All are low-level examples that relate to only one of the five COSO components, the 'control activities'. Whilst important, 'control activities' are not the principle areas of concern in cases of fraudulent manipulation of financial reporting.

It was frequently senior management's manipulation of earnings that was a major issue in recent scandals. Issues related to senior management and their ethics are part of the control environment and if examples are to be given at all, then some examples relating to the control environment would be particularly helpful. This is especially the case in the light of paragraph 104 which prohibits reliance by external auditors on the testing of internal audit or management.

The four examples illustrate that a very substantial amount of audit work is expected of external auditors at this basic level. The issuer is already required to carry out its own testing in this regard and those tests should yield the same results as external audit testing. We are not convinced that the requirement to test so much at this low level is necessary to protect investors.

Whilst we would expect basic low level controls to form an important element of the overall comfort obtained by CEOs and CFOs when making their certification, we would expect that they would represent a relatively low proportion. For example, high-level detective controls are typically a very significant element of overall comfort but they are not addressed in the examples.

6   Controls which do not naturally give rise to documentary evidence

Many companies are likely to have effectively designed controls, but it is not always easy to demonstrate or document their operational effectiveness.

For example, day to day supervision, coaching and reviewing of staff and their work in the accounting department are sound preventative controls but are ordinarily not documented on a continuing basis. Despite this, external auditors can often, by a process of enquiry and proper evidential corroboration, gain reasonable assurance that such controls exist and work effectively.

The proposed standard indirectly plays down the importance of such controls and may encourage companies to prepare documentation that would not otherwise be necessary from a business point of view.

We envisage that even routine meetings of management that act as a form of control, such as credit control meetings, will now have to be documented in detail to satisfy the perceived requirements of the standard. This will add additional cost and bureaucracy. The operation of some IT controls may also not be easy to document to the level that may be perceived as necessary under the proposed standard.

We question whether all this additional work on documentation will provide an increased level of protection for investors commensurate with the increased cost of compliance. We also question whether the proposals go further than the intentions of the Sarbanes-Oxley Act.

7   Reasonable assurance is not high assurance

Paragraph 16 states that reasonable assurance is a high level of assurance and that it includes the understanding that there is a relatively low risk that material misstatements will not be prevented or detected. This is a misleading over-simplification of current thinking on this subject that will encourage investors to take much greater comfort from the work performed by external auditors than is warranted.

It is generally accepted that reasonable assurance represents a range of different levels of assurance, depending in part on the qualities inherent in the subject matter. Paragraph 15 of ISA 200 *Objectives and general principles governing an audit of financial statements* issued by IAASB in November 2003 states that reasonable assurance is obtained when the auditor has reduced risk to an acceptably low level. We respectfully suggest that PCAOB aligns its description of reasonable assurance with current thinking in order to prevent false expectations, confusion and misunderstanding in an important area.

8   Need to reflect IT reality and service organisation auditor guidance

Major parts of many internal control systems are IT driven and have been developed either in-house, by a third party, or by a service provider. The guidance in the proposed standard often does not take this reality into account and instead provides guidance which is geared toward manual internal control systems. The proposed standard should acknowledge this reality and provide additional guidance reflecting it.

International and European guidance on the use by external auditors of service provider auditors is very limited and guidance for the service auditors themselves is non-existent. This will undoubtedly result in situations where external auditors will not be able to obtain sufficient comfort for their attestation on management's assessment because the use of the extensive US guidance on this issue cannot be forced on non US service providers and their auditors.

9   Management and auditor imbalances

The PCAOB should not lose sight of the fact that the proposed standard is a standard for external auditors, compliance with which cannot necessarily be forced upon the management of a company. The proposed standard introduces examples of new and specific requirements for companies that exceed those described in the relevant SEC rules on matters including the documentation and testing of controls by management.

Whilst the external auditor may qualify his report on internal controls or issue an adverse opinion if management fails to prepare documentation or test controls to the required standard, the external auditor effectively becomes an agent to prompt management action. Taking a worst case view, the external auditor could be held liable for failure to enforce the requirements of the proposed standards which relate to management, with no corresponding liability for management itself.

It may be appropriate for the SEC to consider the specific responsibilities of issuers in this regard.

10   Conflict over who finds adjustments

The proposed standard requires the auditor to issue an adverse opinion regarding the effectiveness of internal control over financial reporting in case of one or more material weaknesses.

Circumstances presumed to be at least a significant deficiency and a 'strong indicator' of a material weakness include identification by the external auditor of a material misstatement in the year-end financial statements that was not identified by the company's internal controls, even if management subsequently corrects the misstatement prior to issuance of the financial statements.

This change will have a profound effect on the relationship between an entity's management and its external auditors. It does not foster co-operation between management and the external auditor and will increase resistance to adjustments proposed by external auditors. Where the need for an adjustment is agreed there will be a strong incentive for management to claim that they 'found it first' or would have done if they had delayed providing information to auditors until they had completed their own checks. In extreme circumstances, it even may make it difficult for external auditors to perform their work because management may try to keep them out until the preparation of the financial statements is at an advanced stage, thus ensuring that the auditor is not the first to identify adjustments.

11   Assertions too prominent

Several references to financial statement assertions are too prominent and misconceived (penultimate paragraph page 4, paragraphs 66 to 70, Appendix A Example A-1 first paragraph). An audit of internal control over financial reporting should not be based on a 'bottom-up' approach starting with financial statement assertions, but should rather commence by determining the risks of material misstatement, followed by considering controls, and finally considering the financial statements of the entity. Financial statements are designed to report on the status and progress of the business of an entity and are not an end in themselves.

The prominence given to financial statement assertions in the proposed standard is not in line with IAASB standards and guidance on risk assertions. Large and medium size audit firms in Europe are committed to follow IAASB standards as of 2005. This inconsistency would have significant consequences for the move towards global standards. It would also have a profound effect on the audit methodologies to be developed by audit firms. These will become hugely complex and require considerable investment to redevelop software and retrain staff. Therefore, we urge the PCAOB to reconsider the prominence given to financial statement assertions in the proposed standard.

The guidance related to financial statement assertions in the paragraphs indicated above is also inconsistent with the guidance provided in the first paragraph on page 12 which commences with the design and operating effectiveness of controls.

12   Two audits

IAASB standards and guidance on risk require external auditors to identify significant risks to determine which internal controls should be audited further. This is not reflected in the Board's proposed standard which requires auditors to perform audit work on *all* internal controls, regardless of their risk profile.

The guidance in paragraphs 133 to 144 is meant to integrate the two audits (attestation on management's assessment and the audit of financial statements). The level of integration should be deepened such that the two audits serve the same purpose. The objective of an audit of internal controls over financial reporting should be to form a judgement on the control risks; this is part of the financial statement audit. The concepts of materiality and complexity should be introduced whereby internal controls should only be tested for material and complex control assertions, transactions, account balances and disclosures; substantive procedures may suffice for other transactions and balances. The proposed standard currently appears to require both tests of controls and substantive procedures for all assertions, accounts and disclosures.

13   The external auditor's responsibility with respect to fraud

The proposed standard is unclear as to the precise level of responsibility the external auditor assumes in connection with the prevention and detection of fraud.

The auditor is required in paragraph 24 to evaluate *all* controls specifically intended to address the risks of fraud that are reasonably likely to have a material effect on the company's financial statements, which presumably means controls falling under all five COSO components. Does this mean that external auditors are required to confirm that fraud controls are designed to prevent 'more than a remote likelihood of a financial reporting misstatement' arising from fraud and that these controls have operated effectively?

Collusion by more than one member of management to overcome existing controls and thereby perpetrate fraud is often more than a remote likelihood. But collusion is an inherent limitation in any control system and it is very difficult (and expensive) at best for management to implement controls to prevent it; careful consideration by management of the cost-effectiveness of a control must take place before implementation. Similarly, external auditors considering making control recommendations must also take account of cost-benefit considerations.

We fear that failure by external auditors to detect a control weakness in either design or operation which subsequently facilitates a fraudulent act at the issuer may, under the proposals, substantially alter the risk profile of the audit profession.

These requirements are potentially wide in scope and have substantial implications for the amount of work to be undertaken and the associated costs.

If you require any further information, please do contact me.

Yours faithfully

Robert Hodgkinson

Robert Hodgkinson
Director, Technical
Direct line:+44 20 7920 8492
e-mail: robert.hodgkinson@icaew.co.uk

APPENDIX

Response to the questions in the PCAOB's Request for Comments

1. **Is it appropriate to refer to the auditor's attestation of management's assessment of the effectiveness of internal control over financial reporting as the audit of internal control over financial reporting?**

No. Firstly, it is not appropriate because it is inconsistent with the practice of the IAASB which uses the term 'audit' to refer to the audit of financial statements only. The auditor's attestation of management's assessment is an assurance engagement leading to reasonable assurance and not an audit. Second, whilst we understand that the US accounting profession understands the word 'attestation' to cover audit, attest and other engagements, not all 'attestations' are audits. Is an audit of internal control what Congress intended when it used the words 'attestation and report' in section 404(b) of the Act?

2. **Should the auditor be prohibited from performing an audit of internal control over financial reporting without also performing an audit of the financial statements?**

Qualified yes. Whilst we do not like restrictive prohibitions, we understand that legislation requires the two audits should be done together.

3. **Rather than requiring the auditor to also complete an audit of the financial statements, would an appropriate alternative be to require the auditor to perform work with regard to the financial statements comparable to that required to complete the financial statement audit?**

In view of the answer to question 2, no.

4. **Does the Board's proposed standard give appropriate consideration to how internal control is implemented in, and how the audit of internal control over financial reporting should be conducted at, small and medium-sized issuers?**

Qualified yes. Whilst we recognise that the PCAOB is sensitive to the needs of the many small and medium sized issuers, time will tell if the consideration was 'appropriate'. We are particularly concerned about the additional burdens on the small and medium sized registrants and hope that Appendix E will assist them and that its thinking will be incorporated into the proposed standard.

5. **Should the Board, generally or in this proposed standard, specify the level of competence and training of the audit personnel that is necessary to perform specified auditing procedures effectively? For example, it would be inappropriate for a new, inexperienced auditor to have primary responsibility for conducting interviews of a company's senior management about possible fraud.**

No. Auditing standards should not specify levels of competence and training for audit specified procedures. These matters are already found in the national and international guidance on ethics.

6.   **Is the scope of the audit appropriate in that it requires the auditor to both evaluate management's assessment and obtain, directly, evidence about whether internal control over financial reporting is effective?**

Qualified yes. We believe that the standard's proposed requirements for the performance of procedures to obtain evidence directly are at the same time excessive and unnecessarily restrictive, particularly insofar as auditors are not permitted to use their judgement in determining the extent to which they may use the results of testing by management and others (paragraphs 104 and 105).

We are not convinced that the requirement to obtain direct evidence of effectiveness in all areas of internal controls over financial reporting represents a reasonable use of resources from the point of view of investors, particularly in respect of the testing of control activities. The issuer is already required to carry out its own testing in this regard and those tests should yield the same results as external audit testing.

7.   **Is it appropriate that the Board has provided criteria that auditors should use to evaluate the adequacy of management's documentation?**

No. Although the suggestions included in paragraphs 43 to 47 on documentation might be helpful, the auditor should be allowed to apply professional judgement. We suggest that additional guidance is included on documentation requirements in line with the size of the entity.

Paragraph 43 refers indirectly to the COSO framework. Where a company is using a different framework for evaluation internal controls, the documentation may use different but equivalent components. Paragraph 43 should be amended to make this clear.

8.   **(a) Is it appropriate to state that inadequate documentation is an internal control deficiency, the severity of which the auditor should evaluate? (b) Or should inadequate documentation automatically rise to the level of significant deficiency or material weakness in internal control?**

(a) Yes, as it allows for the use of professional judgement by the auditor.
(b) No.

9.   **Are the objectives to be achieved by performing walkthroughs sufficient to require the performance of walkthroughs?**

Qualified yes. Walkthroughs are useful to document an understanding of processes and systems, but are not a comprehensive way of testing the effectiveness of controls. Materiality should be used by the external auditor in his judgement when deciding which systems and processes should be subject to walkthroughs.

10.   **Is it appropriate to require that the walkthrough be performed by the auditor himself or herself, rather than allowing the auditor to use walkthrough procedures performed by management, internal auditors, or others?**

No. The external auditors using their professional judgement should be allowed to rely on walkthroughs performed by internal auditors and others after evaluating the objectivity and competence of the internal audit function. We refer to key comment 2 in our covering letter.

11.   **(a) Is it appropriate to require the auditor to obtain evidence of the effectiveness of controls for all relevant assertions for all significant accounts and disclosures (b) every year or (c) may the auditor use some of the audit evidence obtained in previous years to support his or her current opinion on management's assessment?**

(a) No.
(b) No.
(c) Yes.

The basic principle that external auditors should be able to use their prior knowledge and experience is applicable to every audit and should also be adopted for this type of engagement. Use of such knowledge is of course subject to the proviso that external auditors only rely on past experience after having satisfactorily updated their knowledge of the business in order to identify and focus on changes. This approach is reflected in IAASB's recently revised standards and guidance on risk assessment and internal controls

A requirement to obtain evidence on the effectiveness of controls for every control assertion, for every account balance and disclosure every year is impractical for the auditor and represents a disproportionate use of resources from the point of view of investors. External auditors who undertake high quality audit work should be permitted to use their professional judgement.

12.   **To what extent should the auditor be permitted or required to use the work of management and others?**

External auditors should never be required to *use* the work of management and others, but should be permitted to do so using their good professional judgement where appropriate. External auditors should only be able to *rely* on the work of others once they have satisfied themselves that it appropriate so to do.

The extent to which external auditors should be permitted to do so is further detailed in the response to question 13 below. We refer to key comment 2 in our covering letter.

13.   **Are the three categories of controls and the extent to which the auditor may rely on the work of others appropriately defined?**

No. We refer to key comment 2 in our covering letter.

We are sceptical about the practical application of such a rule-based approach to categorisation of controls, as described in paragraphs 104 and 105. We prefer a more principle-based approach whereby a range of controls from high level, management driven controls to low level routine controls is used to determine the acceptable level of reliance for the auditor. Control categorisation is not required because the important determining factors are the integrity and good faith of management, internal audit and others upon whom the external auditors may rely.

14. **Does the proposed standard give appropriate recognition to the work of the internal auditors? If not, does the proposed standard place too much emphasis and preference on the work of internal auditors or not enough?**

Qualified yes. The guidance provided in paragraph 108 is acceptable if the categorisation as described in question 13 is abolished and external auditors are be able to rely on internal audit work in the areas described in paragraph 104, when they consider it appropriate.

15. **(a) Is the flexibility in determining the extent of reperformance of the work of others appropriate, or (b) should the auditor be specifically required to reperform a certain level of work (for example, reperform tests of all significant accounts or reperform every test performed by others that the auditor intends to use)?**

(a) Yes.
(b) No.

External auditors should use their professional judgement to determine whether it is appropriate to rely on the work of others.

We refer to key comment 2 in our covering letter.

16. **Is the requirement for the auditor to obtain the principal evidence, on an overall basis, through his or her own work the appropriate benchmark for the amount of work that is required to be performed by the auditor?**

No. External auditors should use their professional judgement to decide on which sources of evidence to rely, to determine whether it is appropriate to rely on the work of others, and to determine whether there is a need to obtain the principal evidence through their own work.

We refer to key comment 2 in our covering letter.

17. **Will the definitions in the proposed standard of significant deficiency and material weakness provide for increased consistency in the evaluation of deficiencies? How can the definitions be improved?**

No. We refer to key comment 1 in our covering letter for our views.

18. **(a) Do the examples in Appendix D of how to apply these definitions in various scenarios provide helpful guidance? (b) Are there other specific examples that commenters could suggest that would provide further interpretive help?**

(a)   Yes.
(b)   No.

19. **Is it necessary for the auditor to evaluate the severity of all identified internal control deficiencies?**

Yes.

20.   **Is it appropriate to require the auditor to communicate all internal control deficiencies (not just material weaknesses and significant deficiencies) to management in writing?**

Qualified no. We refer to key comment 3 in our covering letter, particularly in respect of reporting to the audit committee.

21.   **Are the matters that the Board has classified as strong indicators that a material weakness in internal control exists appropriately classified as such?**

Qualified yes. The issues identified are appropriate but external auditors should be permitted to use their judgement in this area.

22.   **Is it appropriate to require the auditors to evaluate the effectiveness of the audit committee's oversight of the company's external financial reporting and internal control over financial reporting?**

Qualified yes. The assessment should not be a separate requirement. We refer to key comment 4 in our covering letter.

23.   **Will auditors be able to effectively carry out their responsibility to evaluate the effectiveness of the audit committee's oversight?**

Qualified yes. We refer to key comment 4 in our covering letter.

24.   **If the auditor concludes that ineffective audit committee oversight is a material weakness, rather than require the auditor to issue an adverse opinion with regard to the effectiveness of the internal control over financial reporting, should the standard require the auditor to withdraw from the audit engagement?**

No. We consider that requiring an auditor to resign is not something that should be encouraged in anything other than extreme circumstances. Such a general requirement is unlikely to help investor confidence. External auditors should be allowed to use their professional judgement, depending on the circumstances of the situation.

25.   **Is it appropriate that the existence of a material weakness would require the auditor to express an adverse conclusion about the effectiveness of the company's internal control over financial reporting, consistent with the required reporting model for management?**

No. We refer to key comment 1 in our covering letter.

26.   **Are there circumstances where a qualified "except for" conclusion would be appropriate?**

Yes. We refer to key comment 1 in our covering letter.

27.   **Do you agree with the position that when the auditor issues a non-standard opinion, such as an adverse opinion, that the auditor's opinion should speak directly to the effectiveness of internal control over financial reporting rather than to whether management's assessment is fairly stated?**

No.

28. Should the Board provide specific guidance on independence and internal control-related non-audit services in the context of this proposed standard?

No. Other existing standards address such issues at length. We refer to our response to question 29.

29. Are there any specific internal control-related non-audit services the auditor should be prohibited from providing to an audit client?

Yes. Although we favour principle-based standards which rarely include prohibitions, we believe that it is appropriate to limit the performance of certain internal control-related non-audit services by the financial statement auditor. No additional guidance is required in this respect as the SEC independence rules deal with this topic in sufficient detail.

30. Are the auditor's differing levels of responsibility as they relate to management's quarterly certifications versus the annual (fourth quarter) certification, appropriate?

Yes. However we note that section 302 of the Sarbanes-Oxley Act and the related SEC rules do not require quarterly reporting for foreign registrants.

31. Is the scope of the auditor's responsibility for quarterly disclosures about the internal control over financial reporting appropriate?

See answer to question 30.

¶ 616. Institute of Internal Auditors

**The Institute of
Internal Auditors**

William G. Bishop III, CIA
President

Tel: +1 407 937 1200
wbishop@theiia.org

November 21, 2003

Office of the Secretary
Public Company Accounting Oversight Board
1666 K Street, N.W.
Washington, D.C. 20006-2803

Re: PCAOB Rulemaking Docket No. 008

Dear Sir/Madam:

The Institute of Internal Auditors (IIA) commends the efforts of the Public Company
Accounting Oversight Board (PCAOB) to promote effective corporate governance. The
IIA has long advocated that good governance and accurate financial reporting emanate
from the balanced interaction of board members, executives, internal auditors, and external
auditors.

Established in 1941, The IIA is an international professional organization with world
headquarters in Altamonte Springs, Florida. We have over 87,500 members worldwide in
internal auditing, governance, internal control, IT audit, education, and security; many of
whom are also members of professional accountancy bodies. The IIA, with representation
in more than 100 countries, is the acknowledged global leader in standards, certification,
education, research, and technological guidance for the internal auditing profession. The
IIA maintains the *International Standards for the Professional Practice of Internal
Auditing (Standards)*, which are recognized around the world and support the internal
auditing profession.

The IIA represents over 37,700 members in 133 chapters across the United States and is the
principal voice of the internal auditing profession. The IIA is well positioned to offer
unique insights into issues related to improving corporate governance, risk management,
and control processes. In December 1999, The IIA adopted the following definition of
internal auditing that acknowledges the role of internal auditing in corporate governance:

*"Internal auditing is an independent, objective assurance and consulting activity designed
to add value and improve an organization's operations. It helps an organization
accomplish its objectives by bringing a systematic, disciplined approach to evaluate and
improve the effectiveness of risk management, control, and governance processes."*

Since the adoption of this definition, The IIA has intensified its efforts to contribute to the
reform of governance practices of public companies around the world. The IIA is pleased
to provide our views regarding your proposed rules, released October 7, 2003, for public
comment. Leading IIA members, including prominent chief audit executives from various
industries, have contributed to developing our response. We also gathered information from
a survey of our chief audit executive members, and received comments from over 370 of
them.

Global Headquarters
247 Maitland Avenue
Altamonte Springs, FL
32701-4201 U.S.A.
Tel: +1-407-937-1100
Fax: +1-407-937-1101
www.theiia.org

Overall, we found the proposed standard's approach to be very detailed and prescriptive. This seems to contradict the move towards principles-based standards, which most oversight and regulatory bodies are striving to achieve. We also believe that too much emphasis is placed on explicit procedures as opposed to the auditor's use of judgment, risk assessment, and analyses. Finally, we found that the prescriptive directives contained in the detailed standard contradict general comments in the introduction that discuss the ability of the auditor to rely on management and internal audit's work.

From the internal auditor's unique perspective as both a key contributor to corporate governance and as an objective observer of that process, The IIA offers the following comments:

1. We think that the auditor should be able to place much more reliance on a competent and objective internal audit function than the proposed standard indicates. There should also be "limited" and "full" reliance categories instead of the "non-reliance" category within the proposed standard. It should be left up to the professional judgment of the auditor as to the level of reliance to be placed on the work of others in the "limited" category. The proposed standard should express strong reservations about, but not prohibitions against, work related to pervasive or sensitive key controls that fall into the new "limited" category, e.g., fraud and information technology controls. As part of the understanding and evaluation of management's process used as a basis for management's assessment, the auditor should assess the competence and objectivity of the parties performing the procedures to determine the level of reliance that can be placed on the procedures performed by others.

2. Audit committees are assigned primary responsibilities for assessing and monitoring governance practices, so they must have sufficient resources to fulfill them. We continue to recommend that all publicly held companies should be expected to establish and maintain an objective, adequately resourced, and competently staffed internal audit function to provide management and the audit committee with ongoing assessments of the organization's risk management processes and the accompanying system of internal control. Lack of an effective internal audit function is an indicator of weak monitoring of controls and the control environment. If an internal audit function is not present, the board of directors should disclose in the company's annual report why the function is not in place and the auditor should consider such disclosure in reporting significant deficiencies. Recently, the U.S. Securities and Exchange Commission (SEC) approved the New York Stock Exchange's requirement that listed companies have an internal audit function, at our recommendation, and we urge the PCAOB to support this initiative more broadly. In addition, we recommend that the internal audit function practice in accordance with The IIA's Standards, and we are pleased that this is recognized in the proposed standard.

3. The standard should be consistent with the requirement that the auditor examine management's assertion of the efficiency and effectiveness of internal controls over financial reporting and evaluate whether it is fairly stated in all material respects. The proposed standard should not establish a new requirement beyond that of the SEC's rules that the auditor must obtain the same level of assurance as is expected of management. The proposed standard should reduce the overly prescriptive nature of the audit testing to be performed, (e.g., walkthroughs and IT general controls), and require the auditor to perform those procedures necessary to obtain a reasonable level of assurance as to management's assertion regarding the effectiveness of the controls. The guidance should focus on how to properly evaluate management's assertion, not establish a new requirement to complete a separate audit of internal controls over financial reporting.

Office of the Secretary
November 21, 2003
Page Three

4. The requirement in the proposed standard that recommends the auditor evaluate audit committee oversight should be deleted. The evaluation of the audit committee by the auditor presents a conflict of interest because the audit committee is normally charged with the oversight (hiring, compensation, termination) of the public accountant; therefore, a lack of independence on the part of the auditor would exist. Governance evaluation of the performance of the various board committees is and should remain a board of directors' responsibility.

5. The proposed standard expands the definition of significant deficiency to include more matters than reflected in the SEC rules. Significant deficiency should be defined as any item requiring the attention of the audit committee. The determination of the deficiency as significant should be based on a consideration of a number of factors and circumstances, not simply the interpretation of two words (remote and inconsequential).

6. With regard to the extent of testing of controls, the auditor should use judgment in determining whether partial reliance on the results of testing from prior years is acceptable. Such reliance will more likely be possible when the design and operations of the controls have not changed significantly from the prior year. The auditor would need to confirm that the risk of an unnoticed change in controls is low when planning on partial reliance on evidence gathered in the prior year.

The enclosed document provides additional details and further recommendations in the areas where we believe the PCAOB can enhance its final rules to further improve governance processes.

We have enclosed copies of two of our recent publications on governance, *Corporate Governance and the Board: What Works Best* and *Audit Committee Effectiveness: What Works Best*, both of these books discuss corporate governance models and the effective interaction of key governance stakeholders. This information may be useful in developing future audit guidance. We also have numerous other publications that promote good governance practices, including the periodical *Tone at the Top*, which is specifically designed to provide useful information for directors who serve on audit committees. These other publications are available for review at our Web site, www.theiia.org.

We appreciate the opportunity to express our views on these important matters and welcome the opportunity to discuss any and all issues with your organization at any time.

Best regards,

William G. Bishop III

Attachment
      A - Detailed Comments on the Proposal
      B - Reconciliation of PCAOB Questions to IIA Response
Enclosures
      1. *Corporate Governance and the Board: What Works Best* – An Institute of Internal Auditors Research Foundation report.
      2. *Audit Committee Effectiveness: What Works Best* – An Institute of Internal Auditors Research Foundation report.

THE INSTITUTE OF INTERNAL AUDITORS (IIA)
Attachment A
Detailed Comments on the Proposed Standard - November 21, 2003

The Institute of Internal Auditors (IIA) is supportive of the PCAOB proposal; however, opportunities exist for changes and additions to greatly enhance the proposal. The proposed standard will help those charged with governance responsibilities and increase the confidence of stakeholders. A strong and comprehensive plan of action for implementing the final rules will be vital in obtaining buy-in from the business community.

Our suggestions and answers to many of the questions posed in the *Request for Comment*, with reference to the appropriate sections of the document, are provided below. Our comments are presented according to the 11 key issues identified by our response team. In Attachment B we have included a cross-reference to the proposed PCAOB standard and/or questions involved for each issue. We have also referenced each question below.

IIA Issue #1 – Reliance on Internal Audit Efforts

Relevant Sections of the PCAOB Proposed Standard:
Paragraphs 108 and 114

Question 14 - Does the proposed standard give appropriate recognition to the work of internal auditors? If not, does the proposed standard place too much emphasis and preference on the work of internal auditors or not enough?

Issues

1. We commend the efforts of PCAOB to recognize the important unique role of internal auditors. Paragraph 108 is very helpful and is accurate in differentiating the work of internal auditors from others who may not have the competence and objectivity internal audit uniquely possesses. It is very important that the PCAOB set a strong tone supporting internal auditing in organizations.

2. The proposed standard does not place enough emphasis on the work of internal auditors. This can be seen in areas discussed further in this attachment, such as where the external auditors could rely on a competent and objective internal audit function's work in the areas of:

    a. Walkthroughs.
    b. Control environment documentation and testing.
    c. Audits of financial reporting and information technology.
    d. Detection of fraud and pervasive areas such as information technology controls.

3. In the auditor's retesting of internal audit's work in forming a basis for external auditor reliance, we believe that greater specificity is required. There have been many comments regarding implementation of the Sarbanes-Oxley Act (Act) on how to achieve the intent of the Act in a way that is cost effective and sustainable for companies. Reliance on a competent and objective internal audit function's work is important for the PCAOB to emphasize — to demonstrate cost effective and sound ways for auditors to achieve the required level of assurance.

4. In the current standard, a reader could erroneously assume that the auditor must retest some transactions underlying every control that internal auditors test. We suggest that the auditors assess internal audit's work overall and perform valid overall retesting of internal audit's work, but that this does not require retesting of every control that internal audit tests. Not specifying this may risk confusion. The approach and level of retesting should be based on the reliability of internal audit's work overall, not the retesting of every control tested by internal audit.

5. We concur with paragraph 114 in its requirement that the auditor should review all reports issued during the year by internal audit that address controls related to internal control over financial reporting.

Recommendations

1. The auditor should be allowed to rely on a competent and objective internal audit function's work in the areas such as: a) walkthroughs, b) control environment documentation and testing, c) audits of financial reporting and information technology, and d) detection of fraud.

2. We continue to recommend that all publicly held companies should be expected to establish and maintain an objective, adequately resourced, and competently staffed internal audit function to provide management and the audit committee with ongoing assessments of the organization's risk management processes and the accompanying system of internal control. Lack of an effective internal audit function is an indicator of weak monitoring controls and control environment. If an internal audit function is not present, the board of directors should disclose in the company's annual report why the function is not in place and the auditor should consider such disclosure in reporting significant deficiencies. Recently, the U.S. Securities and Exchange Commission (SEC) approved the New York Stock Exchange's requirement for listed companies to have an internal audit function, at our recommendation, and we urge the PCAOB to support this proposal.

IIA Issue #2 – Walkthroughs

Relevant Sections of the PCAOB Proposed Standard:
Paragraphs 79-83 and 104

Question 9 - Are the objectives to be achieved by performing the walkthroughs sufficient to require performance of the walkthroughs?

Question 10 - Is it appropriate to require that the walkthrough be performed by the auditor himself or herself, rather than allowing the auditor to use walkthrough procedures performed by management, internal auditors, or others?

Issues

1. The proposed standard goes well beyond the intent of Sarbanes-Oxley, which requires that the auditors attest to and report on the assessments made by management (Section 404(b)):

> *"(b) Internal Control Evaluation and Reporting — with respect to the internal control assessment required by subsection (a), each registered public accounting firm that prepares or issues the*

audit report for the issuer shall attest to, and report on, the assessment made by management of the issuer."

and not that they conduct an extensive audit of internal controls through walkthroughs of "all the company's significant processes" from

"Initiating, recording processing, and reporting individual transactions, and controls for all five internal control components and fraud and not just control activities. " (paragraph 80, page A-31 – of Proposed Standard)

This would also include field visits and interviews of personnel "involved in significant aspects of the process or controls" (paragraph 81, page A-32). The proposed standard then specifies potential questions the auditors should ask.

The focus should be on testing how management made its assessments, and performing tests as required to gain assurance regarding management's assessment process and conclusion. These tests may or may not require the extensive walkthroughs currently specified in the proposed standard. Requiring walkthroughs of all significant processes is a very comprehensive scope depending on the definition of "significant".

2. Requiring the auditors to perform all walkthroughs (page 9 and paragraph 104, page A-38) without the ability to rely on the work of others is excessive and cost prohibitive. This is especially true, considering paragraph 82 (page A-32) which requires that auditors assess whether significant changes in a process flow require them to perform "before" and "after" walkthroughs including changes to computer systems.

    Instead, the auditors should be allowed to rely on walkthroughs performed by others, especially those completed by internal auditors. The focus of the standard should be on the criteria required to rely on the work of others, especially with regard to computer system changes. This would be consistent with other sections of the standard.

In addition to the above two issues, the proposed standard provides too much detail delineating how walkthroughs should be done and examples of questions to ask – almost providing the audit steps – especially in paragraph 81 (page A-32). This should be eliminated to keep the standard crisp. While the procedures and questions are good, a standard is not the place for a "how to." This information should be in appendix material, similar to the sample reports.

Recommendations

1. For the reasons given above, eliminate walkthroughs from paragraph 104, which specifies that the auditor must complete them.

2. Paragraph 79: Change "walkthroughs are required" to "walkthroughs are a recommended technique based on risk and the availability of reliable work done by others." Precisely define or give guidelines regarding "significant."

3. Paragraphs 80 and 81: Recommend keeping these to the lead sentences and moving the detail on "suggested means to do the work" to an appendix on walkthroughs.

4. Paragraph 82 and 83: No changes, if the work of others can be relied upon.

> ### IIA Issue #3 – Reliance on the Work of Others

Relevant Sections of the PCAOB Proposed Standard:
Paragraphs 41,42, 103-110, 145, B8, B9, and B22

Questions 12 - To what extent should the auditor be permitted or required to use the work of management and others?

Question 13 - Are the three categories of controls and the extent to which the auditor may rely on the work of others appropriately defined?

Question 15 - Is the flexibility in determining the extent of reperformance of the work of others appropriate, or should the auditor be specifically required to reperform a certain level of work (e.g. reperform tests of all significant accounts or reperform every test performed by others that the auditor intents to use)?

Issues

1. The proposed rules greatly limit the auditor's ability to rely on the work of others.

2. Sampling the work of others should be allowed – particularly when performed in conjunction with the financial audit efforts.

3. Auditors should emphasize judgment based on the competence and objectivity of other resources as to the level of reliance that can be placed on them.

Recommendations

1. The auditor must obtain an understanding of internal controls over financial reporting. The auditor should assess the competence and objectivity of management, internal audit, and others to determine the level of reliance that can be placed on procedures performed by them. As part of the understanding and evaluation of management's process(s) used as a basis for management's assessment the auditor should assess the competence and objectivity of the parties performing the procedures to determine the level of reliance that can be placed on the procedures performed by them.

2. Paragraph 103 – Use of the Work of Management and Others. . . [ADD THE FOLLOWING BULLET]

   - The competence and objectivity of those performing the work.

3. Paragraph 104 – There are many areas where the auditor should not use the testing performed by management and others, including: [MODIFY THE THIRD BULLET – adding bolded section]

   - Controls that have a pervasive effect on the financial statements, such as certain information technology general controls on which the operating effectiveness of other controls depend, **unless the auditor determines that the competence and objectivity of internal audit or others performing the work is sufficient to allow for reliance on the results by the auditor.**

> **IIA Issue #4 - Principal Evidence Requirements for Auditors**

Relevant Sections of the PCAOB Proposed Standard:
Paragraphs 103-109

Question 6 - Is the scope of the audit appropriate in that it requires the auditor to both evaluate management's assessment and obtain, directly, evidence about whether internal control over financial reporting is effective?

Issues

1. The proposed rules require the auditor to directly perform the procedures that form the principal evidence in expressing their opinion.

2. Allowing internal audit to gather, test, audit, and document principal evidence of the existence and effectiveness of internal controls is not supported by the proposed rules.

3. Allowing external auditors to place partial reliance on the tests performed by internal audit would be more efficient.

Recommendations

1. Paragraphs 103-109 - [MODIFY Paragraph 109 – adding bolded content] In addition to following the directions in paragraphs 103-108, the auditor must compile enough of the testing evidence himself or herself so that the auditor's work provides the principal evidence for the auditor's opinion. **The auditor may rely on internal audit testing results to supplement principal evidence based on the auditor's assessment of the competence and objectivity of the internal audit function.**

2. Paragraph B22 - In evaluating controls over . . . through the company's accounting system. [MODIFY BULLET #1 – adding bolded content]

- Because of the pervasive impact of the controls in (1) and the material impact those controls ordinarily have on the financial statements, the auditor should not use the results of testing by management and others within the company, as discussed in paragraph 104, **unless the auditor determines that the competence and objectivity of internal audit or others performing the work is sufficient to allow for reliance on the results by the auditor.**

> **IIA Issue # 5 – Should the Auditor's Assurance Levels be the Same as Management's?**

Relevant Sections of the PCAOB Proposed Standard:
Paragraph 18

Issues

We do not believe, as is stated in the proposed standard (page A-13, paragraph 18) that "Users of the reports ....are entitled to receive the same level of assurance from both management and the auditor..."

We reach this conclusion based on the following points:

1. It is well accepted, and included in the COSO definition of internal control, that management is responsible for internal control. The SEC stated in Final Rule 33-8238: "Management cannot delegate its responsibility to assess its internal controls over financial reporting to the independent accountant." Also, the proposed standard's statement of "Management's responsibilities in an audit of internal control over financial reporting" says that management must accept responsibility for the effectiveness of the company's internal control and for evaluating the effectiveness of internal control."

2. In addition to the assertions required by Section 404, management is required under Section 302 to take responsibility for disclosure controls and to certify conclusions as to their effectiveness.

3. Under Section 906, there are criminal penalties attached to management's knowingly false certifications.

4. The many companies impacted by the Act are implementing more rigorous processes and systems to document and evaluate internal controls. In many cases, this effort has included implementing new systems to support 404 compliance, new evaluation processes, extensive documentation efforts, and related work. These efforts are in addition to the many control assessment activities that management has been performing all along.

Requiring the auditor to provide this very high level of assurance that management provides will be nearly impossible to fulfill and is inconsistent with the concept of auditors needing to obtain "reasonable assurance." Management must take more responsibility for internal controls than the auditor.

Recommendation

We recommend that the standard require the auditor to examine management's assertion of the effectiveness of internal control and to evaluate whether it is fairly stated in all material respects, and not require the same level of assurance by the auditor as required by management.

IIA Issue #6 - Audit Assurance Levels

Relevant Sections of the PCAOB Proposed Standard:
Question 6 – Is the scope of the audit appropriate in that it requires the auditor to both evaluate management's assessment and obtain directly, evidence about whether internal control over financial reporting is effective?

Issues

We believe that it is not appropriate for the PCAOB to require that the auditor conduct an audit of internal controls and provide an opinion on their effectiveness.

Supporting this position are the following points.

1. If Congress intended such an audit and opinion by the auditor, it would have included such requirements in the Sarbanes-Oxley Act. Instead, the Act requires the external auditor to attest to and – report on the assessments made by management (Section 404(b)): "(b) Internal Control Evaluation and Reporting — with respect to the internal control assessment required by subsection (a), each

registered public accounting firm that prepares or issues the audit report for the issuer shall attest to, and report on, the assessment made by management of the issuer."

2. The many companies impacted by the Act are implementing more rigorous processes and systems to document and evaluate internal controls. The internal audit staffs of these companies are also playing key roles in the compliance effort. These new systems, processes, and testing activities are costing significant time and resources. The proposed standard indicates that "the work that management performs in connection with its assessment can have a significant effect on the nature, timing, and extent of the work of the independent auditor" and that "the more extensive and reliable management's assessment is, the less extensive and costly the auditor's work will need to be." However, the detailed provisions of the proposed standard related to the requirement of the auditor to "obtain evidence about whether internal control over financial reporting is effective", will significantly reduce this reliance and result in significant and duplicative work on the part of the auditor. The most significant of these provisions are as follows:

    - On page A-39, paragraph 109, the proposed standard states that "In addition to following the directions in paragraphs 103-108, the auditor must perform enough of the testing himself or herself so that the auditor's own work provides the principal evidence for the auditor's opinion."
    - The proposed standard requires the auditor to perform "walkthroughs" of significant processes. (page 10 & page A-38, paragraph 104)
    - The proposed standard lists a large number of areas "in which the auditor should not use the results of testing performed by management and others…" These include:
        o Controls specifically intended to prevent or detect fraud (that could have a material impact on the financial statements). (page 14)
        o Controls over period-end financial reporting. (page A-38, paragraph 104)
        o Controls that have a pervasive effect on the financial statements, such as certain IT general controls on which the operating effectiveness of other controls depend. (page A-38, paragraph 104)
    - The proposed standard limits the use of the results of procedures performed by management in the following areas:
        o Controls over non-routine transactions that are considered high-risk. (page 14 and page A-38, paragraph 105)
        o Controls over significant accounts, processes, or disclosures where the auditor as assessed the risk of failure of the controls to operate effectively as high. (page A-38, paragraph 105)
    - The proposed standard (page A-13, paragraph 18) states that "Users of the reports ….are entitled to receive the same level of assurance from both management and the auditor…" and goes on to say that "There is no difference in the level of work or assurance given by the auditor when expressing an opinion on management's assessment of effectiveness or when expressing an opinion directly on the effectiveness of internal control over financial reporting." Requiring the same level of assurance would require significant and duplicative activities on the part of the auditor and is likely very difficult to achieve.
    - The proposed standard (page A-28, paragraph 69) requires the auditor to "Identify each significant process for each major class of transactions affecting significant accounts…" and to perform significant work related to each process.

3. There is a traditional distinction between the auditors directly expressing an opinion on the effectiveness of internal control as compared to determining whether or not management's assessment of their effectiveness is fairly stated.

4. An "attest engagement" concerning matters other than financial statements has traditionally been distinguished from an "audit" of the financial statements. The SEC has also made distinction, and in its recent release adopting rules for management's report on internal controls required by Section

404(a) of the Sarbanes-Oxley Act, the SEC refers to the auditor's report on management's assessment required by Section 404(b) as an "attestation report" which is to be made in accordance with standards for "attestation engagements."

Recommendations

1. The proposed standard should not establish a new requirement beyond that of the SEC's rules that the auditor must obtain the same level of assurance as is expected of management. The proposed standard should reduce the overly prescriptive nature of the audit testing to be performed, e.g., walkthroughs, IT general controls, and require the auditor to perform those procedures necessary to obtain a reasonable level of assurance as to management's assertion regarding the effectiveness of the controls. The guidance should focus on how to properly evaluate management's assertion, not establish a new requirement to complete a separate audit of internal controls over financial reporting.

2. The auditor should be required to test and to gather only enough evidence to corroborate or refute management's assertion. The IIA recommends using SAS 65 as a guide in assessing reliance on the work of others.

3. The IIA recommends that the auditor's report should be called an "attestation report" on management's assessment of internal controls rather than referring to it as an "audit" of internal controls over financial reporting which results in an "audit report."

IIA Issue # 7 – Evaluating Audit Committee Governance

Relevant Sections of the PCAOB Proposed Standard:
Paragraphs 56-58

Question 22 - Is it appropriate to require the auditors to evaluate the effectiveness of the audit committee's oversight of the company's external financial reporting and internal control over financial reporting?

Issues

The proposed standard directs the auditor to evaluate the oversight effectiveness of the audit committee. This adds an additional level of oversight and scrutiny to the audit committee and its activities and actions already implemented by listed company audit committee standards, SEC rules, and auditor independence rules. While the audit committee is one major element in the control environment, this proposed standard weakens the recently strengthened role and responsibility of the audit committee by placing the auditor in the role as oversight over the audit committee. This has the effect of introducing the perception of weakened independence as the audit committee has the given authority to evaluate the performance, qualifications, and independence of the auditor. The audit committee also hires, pays, and dismisses the auditor (Rule 10A-3 of the Exchange Act). Currently the board of directors has a responsibility for receiving committee reports and evaluating performance. The proposed standard in effect removes this responsibility from the board of directors and places it in the hands of the auditors. Both the board of directors' and the audit committee's power and authority and responsibility to the shareholders could become diluted. Governance evaluation of the performance of the various board committees is and should remain a board of directors' responsibility.

Relevant Sections of the PCAOB Proposed Standard:
Question 23 - Will auditors be able to effectively carry out their responsibility to evaluate the effectiveness of the audit committee's oversight?

Issues

The proposed standard would require the auditor to be independent in fact and appearance. A reasonable investor could perceive an auditor as having interests that could impair objectivity and impartial judgment when they are responsible to the audit committee for their appointment, evaluation, and fees. In addition, the auditor may not be in a position to factually reach an informed judgment/evaluation on the oversight effectiveness of the audit committee, e.g., the auditors may not be present for the entire audit committee meeting.

Under current rules the audit committee is to establish an audit charter inclusive of all SEC and listed company rules, publicly communicate this all-inclusive charter, evaluate itself and affirm compliance to the charter, and report all of the above to the board of directors and the listing stock exchange. The auditors should not dilute these responsibilities and accountabilities.

Recommendations

1. The requirement in the proposed standard that recommends the auditor evaluate the audit committee should be deleted. The evaluation of the audit committee by the auditor presents a conflict of interest as the audit committee is normally charged with the oversight (hiring, compensation, termination) of the public accountant, therefore a lack of independence on the part of the auditor would exist. Governance evaluation of the performance of the various board committees is and should remain a board of directors' responsibility.

2. As the effectiveness of the audit committee is important in ensuring an effective control environment, the standard should include guidance that the absence of effective evaluation of the audit committee's performance by the board with the appropriate objectivity and competence to perform this task is a strong indicator of a weak control environment.

IIA Issue # 8 – Review of Information Technology Controls

Relevant Sections of the PCAOB Proposed Standard:
Paragraphs 51, 53-55, 104, and B22

Question 13 - Are the three categories of controls and the extent to which the auditor may rely on the work of others appropriately defined?

Issues

1. Reliance on internal audit's evaluation of controls should be in all areas, unless the auditor's evaluations of the competence and/or objectivity of internal audit are unsatisfactory.

2. The auditor should be able to rely on the tests performed by the internal auditor in all respects, provided that the internal auditor satisfies the level and type of testing required by the standard.

3. There should not be any "-no reliance-" areas; they should be moved into a "limited reliance" category.

4. PCAOB is taking the position that the auditor must directly test all IT general controls.

5. Internal audit should be viewed as independent from management and as such the auditor should be able to rely on internal audit's work.

<u>Recommendations</u>

1. Paragraph 104 – There are many areas where the auditor should not use the testing performed by management ands others, including: [MODIFY THIRD BULLET – adding bolded content]

   - Controls that have a pervasive effect on the financial statements, such as certain information technology general controls on which the operating effectiveness of other controls depend, **unless the auditor determines that the competence and objectivity of internal audit or others performing the work is sufficient to allow for reliance on the results by the auditor.**

2. Paragraph B22 – In evaluating controls over . . . through the company's accounting system. [MODIFY BULLET 1 – adding bolded content]

   - Because of the pervasive impact of the controls in (1) and the material impact those controls ordinarily have on the financial statements, the auditor should not use the results of testing by management and others within the company, as discussed in paragraph 104, **unless the auditor determines that the competence and objectivity of internal audit or others performing the work is sufficient to allow for reliance on the results by the auditor.**

3. There should be "limited" and "full" reliance categories, i.e., there should not be a "non-reliance" category within the standard. It should be left up to the professional judgment of the auditor as to the level of reliance to be placed on the work of others in the "limited" category. The standard should express strong reservations, but not prohibitions, for work related to pervasive or sensitive key controls that fall into this new "limited" category.

IIA Issue # 9 – Fraud Requirements

<u>Relevant Sections of the PCAOB Proposed Standard:</u>
Paragraphs 24-26

<u>Issues</u>

1. Similar to our issues on the review of information technology controls, reliance on the testing of others should be allowed, unless the auditor's evaluations of the competence and/or objectivity of internal audit are unsatisfactory. The same logic applies here as to other areas of reliance on testing of others.

2. The only difference in the consideration of the risks of fraud as compared to other areas is that there are certain levels of expertise in assessing fraud that go beyond the normal professional levels of competency of external auditors and internal auditors. For instance, The IIA's *Standards* state: "The internal auditor should have sufficient knowledge for identifying the indicators of fraud but is not expected to have the expertise of a person whose primary responsibility is detecting and investigating fraud." When appropriate, external auditors and management should involve persons whose primary responsibility is detecting and investigating fraud. PCAOB should consider whether to make reference to this.

Recommendations

The proposed standard should express reservations, but not prohibitions, for work related to pervasive or sensitive key controls for fraud prevention and detection. As part of the understanding and evaluation of management's process used as a basis for management's assessment, the auditor should assess the competence and objectivity of the parties performing the procedures to determine the level of reliance that can be placed on the procedures performed by others.

IIA Issue # 10 – Definition of Significant Deficiencies

Relevant Sections of the PCAOB Proposed Standard:

Question 17 - Will the definitions in the proposed standard of significant deficiency and material weakness provide for increased consistency in the evaluation of deficiencies? How can the definitions be improved?

Question 18 - Do the examples in Appendix D of how to apply these definitions in various scenarios provide helpful guidance? Are there other specific examples that commenters could suggest that would provide further interpretive help?

Issues

1. The definition proposed for a *significant deficiency* is stated too broadly. GAAS and Attestation Standards issued by the AICPA define *material weaknesses* and *reportable conditions*. The final rules issued by the SEC related to the requirements of §404 of the Sarbanes-Oxley Act of 2002 state that the term *significant deficiency* has the same meaning as the term *reportable condition* (footnote 73). The PCAOB proposed standard has expanded the meaning of significant deficiency/reportable condition beyond the original meaning of a reportable condition.

2. There is a large difference between a small error and an error that would result in a material misstatement of financial statements. With the current proposal, any control weakness that could allow an error that is not inconsequential will be considered a significant deficiency. Inconsequential is difficult to define and will likely result in minor weaknesses considered as significant deficiencies. The term significant deficiencies should be reserved for those deficiencies where errors of some importance could occur. In addition, reportable conditions were not precisely defined and were left to auditor judgment as to which issues were of enough importance to report to the audit committee. The proposed definition of significant deficiency has been defined to include essentially all weaknesses that could result in any observable error, as anything that is not irrelevant (defined as inconsequential per Webster's Dictionary) is now "significant." This category should only include those weaknesses with enough importance to warrant the attention of the audit committee.

3. An example of the potential result of the current proposed definition is included in example D1 of Appendix D. In this example, a weakness would allow errors in the financial statements, but would not allow errors that would result in a material misstatement due to adequate compensating controls. However, this weakness is considered a significant deficiency because it could allow errors that are more than inconsequential. The inherent risk in this example of a material misstatement, coupled with the presence of effective high-level compensating controls, should not result in a weakness in internal controls rising to the level of attention by the audit committee. This weakness should not result in a material misstatement nor "grow into" such a weaknesses.

4. The definition of significant deficiency should not rely on two key words (i.e., remote and inconsequential) but should be explained through a discussion of the concepts. This is a difficult concept to define and brevity of words is not possible. The standard should describe the attributes of a weakness which would cause it to be considered a significant deficiency. These attributes would likely include: potential to become a material weaknesses, pervasiveness in longevity and occurrence, involving amounts that are important and normally warrant management's immediate attention when identified, occurrence in areas with high inherent risk of errors, lack of compensating controls, and ability of management to manipulate financial statements as a result of the weakness.

Recommendations

1. The proposed standard has expanded the definition of significant deficiency to include more matters than are reflected in the SEC rules. Significant deficiency should be defined as any item requiring the attention of the audit committee. The determination of the deficiency as significant should be based on a consideration of a number of factors and circumstances, not simply the interpretation of two words (remote and inconsequential).

2. The examples in Appendix D could be improved by removing the immediate classification of the deficiencies as significant primarily because of the potential errors being more than inconsequential. The determination of the deficiency as significant should be based on a consideration of more factors and circumstances, which would then need to be added to the examples.

IIA Issue # 11 – Rotation of Audit Work

Relevant Sections of the PCAOB Proposed Standard:
Paragraph 101

Question 11 - Is it appropriate to require the auditor to obtain evidence of the effectiveness of controls for all relevant assertions for all significant accounts and disclosures every year, or may the auditor use some of the audit evidence obtained in previous years to support his or her current opinion on management's assertion?

Issues

1. It is appropriate to require an auditor to obtain evidence of the effectiveness of controls for relevant assertions for all significant accounts and disclosures every year, but not with a prohibition of using some of the audit evidence obtained in previous years to support his or her current opinion on management's assertion. Requiring evidence of effectiveness every year does not preclude relying, in part, on evidence obtained in prior years.

2. The prohibition against auditors relying on evidence obtained in prior years (i.e., using a rotational audit plan) may reduce the effectiveness and efficiency of the audit. The proposed standard requires the auditor to obtain sufficient evidence each year, which is interpreted as prohibiting rotational areas of emphasis in audit testing from year to year. Rotating audit emphasis from year to year is a well-established technique. Many processes and control systems do not change significantly from one year to the next. This can be validated through sufficient evidence gathering during the planning stage of an audit. Requiring an auditor to test an area at the same level each year ignores this common situation, reducing the efficiency of the audit. In addition, rotational testing allows an auditor to focus

deeply on some areas in a given year. This deep level of testing brings a different perspective than the auditor would get from a "minimum" level of testing required to be performed each year.

3. Rotating the depth of audit testing over a series of years does not preclude an auditor from obtaining sufficient audit evidence to support an opinion each year. Professional judgment should be allowed for the auditor to choose when he or she can rely on extensive audit work in a prior year, having confirmed the lack of significant changes in the design or operating effectiveness of controls.

4. The wording of the current proposed standard is confusing as to the acceptability of rotational testing. The introduction explanation on page 12 states that the new rules – "Resolves the issue of the extent of testing from year to year (the 'rotating tests of controls' issue)." However, paragraph 101 of the proposed rules directs the auditor to change the extent of testing from year to year and increase or decrease the number of tests each year. These directives imply either a rotational testing approach, or interjecting extraneous tests each year.

Recommendations

Paragraph 101 – *Extent of Tests of Controls*. [MODIFY – adding bolded content].

Each year the auditor must obtain sufficient evidence about whether the company's internal control over financial reporting, including the controls for all internal control components, is operating effectively. The auditor also should vary from year to year the nature, timing, and extent of testing of controls to introduce unpredictability into the testing and respond to changes in circumstances. For example, each year the auditor might test the controls at a different interim period; increase or reduce the number and types of tests performed; or change the combination of procedures used. **The auditor should use judgment to determine whether partial reliance on the results of testing from prior years is acceptable. Such reliance will more likely be possible when the design and operations of the controls have not changed significantly from the prior year. The auditor would need to confirm that the risk of an unnoticed change in controls is low when planning on partial reliance on evidence gathered in the prior year.**

THE INSTITUTE OF INTERNAL AUDITORS (IIA)

Attachment B - Reconciliation of Questions to IIA Response

Question	Relevant Reference in IIA Response
1. Is it appropriate to refer to the auditor's attestation of management's assessment of the effectiveness of internal control over financial reporting as the audit of internal control over financial reporting?	Issues #5, #6
2. Should the auditor be prohibited from performing an audit of internal control over financial reporting without also performing an audit of the financial statements?	Issues #5, #6
3. Rather than requiring the auditor to also complete an audit of the financial statements, would an appropriate alternative be to require the auditor to perform the work with regard to the financial statements comparable to that required to complete the financial statement audit?	--
4. Does the Board's proposed standard give appropriate consideration to how internal control is implemented in, and how the audit of internal control over financial reporting should be conducted at, small and medium sized firms?	--
5. Should the Board, generally or in this proposed standards, specify the level of competence and training of the audit personnel that is necessary to perform specified auditing procedures effectively?	--
6. Is the scope of the audit appropriate in that it requires the auditor to both evaluate management's assessment and obtain, directly, evidence about whether internal control over financial reporting is effective?	Issues #4, #6
7. Is it appropriate that the Board has provided criteria that auditors should use to evaluate the adequacy of management's documentation?	--
8. Is it appropriate to state that inadequate documentation is an internal control deficiency, the severity of which the auditor should evaluate? Or should inadequate documentation automatically rise to the level of significant deficiency or material weakness in internal control?	--
9. Are the objectives to be achieved by performing walkthrough sufficient to require the performance of walkthroughs?	Issue #2
10. Is it appropriate to require that the walkthrough be performed by the auditor himself or herself, rather than allowing the auditor to use walkthrough procedures performed by management, internal auditors, or others?	Issues #1, #2, #3
11. Is it appropriate to require the auditor to obtain evidence of the effectiveness of controls for all relevant assertions for all significant accounts and disclosures every year or may the auditor use some of the audit evidence obtained in previous years to support his or her current opinion on management's assessment?	Issue #11
12. To what extent should the auditor be permitted or required to use the work of management and others?	Issues #1, #3, #9
13. Are the three categories of controls and the extent to which the auditor may rely on the work of others appropriately defined?	Issues #3, #8, #9

Question	Relevant Reference in IIA Response
14. Does the proposed standard give appropriate recognition to the work of internal auditors? If not, does the proposed standard place too much emphasis and preference on the work of internal auditors or not enough?	Issue #1
15. Is the flexibility in determining the extent of reperformance of the work of others appropriate, or should the auditor be specifically required to reperform a certain level of work (e.g. reperform tests of all significant accounts or reperform every test performed by others that the auditor intents to use)?	Issue #3, #8, #9
16. Is the requirement for the auditor to obtain the principle evidence, on an overall basis, through his or her own work the appropriate benchmark for the amount of work that is required to be performed by the auditor?	Issue #4
17. Will the definitions in the proposed standard of significant deficiency and material weakness provide for increased consistency in the evaluation of deficiencies? How can the definitions be improved?	Issue #10
18. Do the examples in Appendix D of how to apply these definitions in various scenarios provide helpful guidance? Are there other specific examples that commenters could suggest that would provide further interpretive help?	Issue #10
19. Is it necessary for the auditor to evaluate the severity of all identified internal control deficiencies?	--
20. Is it appropriate to require the auditor to communicate all internal control deficiencies (not just material weaknesses and significant deficiencies) to management in writing?	--
21. Are the matters that the Board has classified as strong indicators that a material weakness in internal control exists appropriately classified as such?	Issues #7, #10
22. Is it appropriate to require the auditors to evaluate the effectiveness of the audit committee's oversight of the company's external financial reporting and internal control over financial reporting?	Issue #7
23. Will auditors be able to effectively carry out their responsibility to evaluate the effectiveness of the audit committee's oversight?	Issue #7
24. If the auditor concludes that ineffective audit committee oversight is a material weakness, rather than require the auditor to issue an adverse opinion with regard to the effectiveness of the internal control over financial reporting, should the standard require the auditor to withdraw from the engagement?	Issue #7
25. Is it appropriate that the existence of a material weakness would require the auditor to express an adverse conclusion about the effectiveness of the company's internal control over financial reporting, consistent with the required reporting model for management?	--
26. Are there circumstances where a qualified "except for" conclusion would be appropriate?	--
27. Do you agree with the position that when the auditor issues a non-standard opinion, such as an adverse opinion, that the auditor's opinion should speak directly to the effectiveness of the internal control over financial reporting rather than to whether management's assessment is fairly stated?	Issue #6

Question	Relevant Reference in IIA Response
28. Should the Board provide specific guidance on independence and internal control-related non-audit services in the context of this proposed standard?	--
29. Are there any specific internal control-related non-audit services the auditor should be prohibited from providing to an audit client?	--
30. Are the auditor's differing levels of responsibility as they relate to management's quarterly certifications versus the annual (fourth quarter) certification, appropriate?	--
31. Is the scope of the auditor's responsibility for quarterly disclosures about the internal control over financial reporting appropriate?	--

¶ 617. National Association of Black Accountants

"Lifting As We Climb"

National Association of Black Accountants, Inc.
7249-A Hanover Parkway
Greenbelt, Maryland 20770
Phone: (301) 474-NABA
Fax: (301) 220-0172
www.nabainc.org

Office of the Executive Director

November 21, 2003

Mr. William J. McDonough,
Chairman
Public Company Accounting Oversight Board
Washington Office
1666 K Street, NW
Washington, DC 20006-2803

Re: PCAOB rulemaking Docket Matter No. 008
Comments on Proposed Auditing Standard

Dear Mr. McDonough:

A careful review of the Proposed Auditing Standard on auditing internal control of a financial statement audit makes one thing patently clear. The standard requires reliance on the underlying internal control, and on the financial statements. The auditor would be required to understand the systems in place. Then design and test the system, and provide an analysis on the efficacy of that system.

It is fair to state that this is a major initiative for each firm executing this plan. Moreover, it is a major initiative for any Organization that might be subject to the standard. Implementation would create a greater staffing need for both the accounting firm and the Organization to meet the need of adherence to this standard. Consequently, greater costs increase will be passed to the Organization. This will impact management planning initiatives and strategies.

Therefore, we suggest that the standard also require the large public accounting firms to hire smaller minority firms to assist in their performance of the requirements. NABA is convinced that the access to greater markets and the lower cost structure would be very beneficial to all involved. It would also do more toward gaining access to the market place for those Firms that never had the opportunity before. The larger Firms could provide leadership and guidance through oversight review of the work. This is supported by the standard which provides guidance on this issue. Under the section "Using the work of Management and Others" it clearly stipulates that such a practice is acceptable.

The current PCAOB proposed auditing standards will effectively "bundle" Sarbanes-Oxley Section 404 (b) work within the "Big 4" firms. Under contract bundling, large contract awards go to large firms due to the size and complexity of the work requirements. This violates the White House strategy for increasing opportunities for Small Business.
It is only logical to conclude that there is a serious legal problem if "Big 4" firms continue to monopolize the auditing of publicly held companies while being the sole service providers for required

"Change = Opportunity"

National Association of Black Accountants, Inc.
7249-A Hanover Parkway
Greenbelt, Maryland 20770
Phone: (301) 474-NABA
Fax: (301) 220-0172
www.nabainc.org

"Lifting As We Climb"

Office of the Executive Director

assessments of internal control systems. Under Sarbanes Oxley, this action is characterized as self dealing amongst firms. Not to mention that the actions would further weaken the public confidence in financial reporting. The independence and competitive strength of CPA firms performing auditing services for public corporations will be strengthened if Sarbanes Oxley legislation on auditing standards is implemented. Therefore all CPA firms in America must be encouraged to participate in implementing compliance with Sarbanes Oxley.

The current Administration is committed to unbundling procurements that have excluded Small Businesses like minority CPA firms from succeeding in today's market economy. NABA is of the firm belief that concentration of public company audits and related compliance with Sarbanes Oxley within the 4 largest CPA firms in America is detrimental to the strengthening of capital markets. It also a restraint on trade and it creates a false perception of auditor independence.

The Division of Firms of the National Association of Black Accountants has over 50 Member firms that have the experience and expertise to significantly participate in getting America's public companies to comply with the Sarbanes-Oxley Act.

Sincerely,

Darryl R. Matthews, Sr.

Darryl R. Matthews, Sr.
Executive Director and COO

"Change = Opportunity"

¶ 618. National Venture Capital Association

January 9, 2004

FILED ELECTRONICALLY

Public Company Accounting Oversight Board
Attention: Office of the Secretary
1666 K Street, NW
Washington, DC 20006-2803
comments@pcaobus.org

> *RE: PCAOB Release No. 2003-017, PCAOB Rulemaking Docket Matter No. 008,*
> *Proposed Auditing Standard – An Audit of the Internal Controls over Financial*
> *Reporting Performed in Conjunction with an Audit of Financial Statements*

Introduction

The National Venture Capital Association (NVCA)[1] represents the vast majority of American venture capital under management. NVCA member firms and the funds they manage provide the start-up and development funding for innovative entrepreneurial businesses.[2]

VC firms form and manage the funds that invest in start-up and early-stage businesses, commonly referred to as "portfolio companies." Venture capital investing relies on exit strategies whereby venture capital positions in portfolio companies are exited, with the proceeds being distributed to investors. Regardless of the likely exit strategy, portfolio companies operate with minimal staff and a necessarily narrow focus on achieving business objectives – research, market definition, product development, manufacture and sales. Though very few of these venture-backed companies are subject to the Sarbanes-Oxley Act ("SOXA" or "the Act"), as a practical matter, the Public Company Accounting Oversight Board (PCAOB) Rules on auditing internal controls will have a significant impact on them.

---

[1] The National Venture Capital Association (NVCA) represents more than 430 venture capital and private equity firms. NVCA's mission is to foster the understanding of the importance of venture capital to the vitality of the U.S. and global economies, to stimulate the flow of equity capital to emerging growth companies by representing the public policy interests of the venture capital and private equity communities at all levels of government, to maintain high professional standards, and to provide research data and professional development for its members.

[2] In 2002, venture capital (VC) funds invested $21.2 billion in 2500 companies, the fourth largest amount ever in the history of venture capital. Eighty-five percent of these companies were in information technology, medical/health or life sciences. The success of venture investing is encouraging greater capital flow to these types of companies. At the end of 2002, VC firms had an estimated $253 billion under management, up from $32 billion in 1990.

Comment of NVCA on Release No. 2003-017   January 9, 2004
Page 2

Impact of PCAOB on venture capital and entrepreneurship

Successful exits of venture capital investments occur either through an initial public offering ("IPO") or through acquisition by another company, often a public company. A company in a pre-IPO, or a pre-acquisition, situation needs to prepare its financial statements on the assumption that it will soon be subject to SOXA. Therefore, management must implement policies and procedures to enable them to prepare Section 404 reports.

Because of the uncertain timing of either exit event, many venture-backed private companies have concluded that they must be SOXA-compliant, even if an acquisition or an IPO is not imminent. Therefore, Section 404 compliance is a fact for companies that are clearly outside the intended reach of SOXA.

General comment

Our comments relate primarily to the impact of PCAOB rules on private companies that are not SOXA "issuers" and the need for PCAOB rules to allow auditors to exercise appropriate judgment in performing an audit of internal control over financial reporting. However, these comments are generally applicable to small publicly traded companies also.[3]

With regard to both types of companies, our main concern is that Section 404 be implemented in a cost effective manner. The Proposing Release states a similar view:

> "For a smaller, less complex company, the Board expects that the auditor will exercise reasonable professional judgment in determining the extent of the audit of internal control and perform only those tests that are necessary to ascertain the effectiveness of the company's internal controls."

PCAOB Release No. 2003-17 ("Proposing Release"), page 6. We believe that this statement sets up a test that should be applied to every aspect of PCAOB Rules: <u>does the standard provide sufficient flexibility for the auditor to exercise judgment in the extent of testing and, as to use of the work of others, including the work of management?</u>

Specific comment on Proposed Audit Standard, Appendix A to Proposing Release, ("Proposed Rules") pertaining to private and smaller publicly traded companies

One of the basic tenets of auditing is that auditors must exercise their professional judgment and expertise in determining the scope of the specific audit procedures to be performed. The Proposed Rules acknowledge that the auditor should apply the concept of materiality at both the financial-statement and the individual account-balance level. However, the Proposed Rules specifically limit the auditor's flexibility to exercise its professional

---

[3] As we read the Act and PCAOB Rule 3100, we do not believe that audit firms, including PCAOB-registered audit firms, will be required *by law or regulation* to apply the proposed PCAOB rules to the audits of private companies.

judgment and expertise by requiring audit evidence to be obtained for "all" items in several situations. For example, the Proposed Rules state:

> "The auditor should perform a walkthrough for *all* of the company's significant processes." *Proposing Release,* page A-31, paragraph 79 [emphasis added].

> "The auditor should obtain evidence about the effectiveness of controls (either by performing tests of controls himself or herself (or by using the work of others) for *all* relevant assertions related to *all* significant accounts, relevant assertions, and significant processes…" *Id.,* page A-29, paragraph 74 [emphasis added].

> "The auditor should evaluate *all* controls specifically intended to address the risks of fraud that are reasonably likely to have a material effect on the company's financial statements, which may be a part of any of the five components of internal control over financial reporting, as discussed in paragraph 50." *Id.,* page A-15, paragraph 24 [emphasis added].

> "Monitoring – The auditor's understanding of management's monitoring of controls extends to and includes it monitoring of *all* controls, including control activities, which management has identified and designed to prevent or detect material misstatement in the accounts and disclosures and related assertions of the financial statements." *Id.,* page A-23, paragraph 50 [emphasis added].

> "As part of this evaluation, the auditor should review *all* reports issued during the year by internal audit (or similar functions, such as loan review in a financial institution) that address controls relating to internal control over financial reporting and evaluate any internal control deficiencies identified in those reports." *Id.,* page A-40, paragraph 114 [emphasis added].

The Proposed Rules further limit the ability of auditors to exercise their professional judgment and expertise by limiting the extent to which auditors may use the work of others, including management and internal audit. Auditing standards historically have allowed the independent auditor to consider the work of internal audit when determining the nature and extent of their audit procedures. The Proposed Rules embrace this concept, but, also, limit the areas where reliance can be placed upon the work of internal audit. For example, work of internal auditors cannot be used for assessing: (1) the controls that are part of the control environment; (2) controls over the period-end financial reporting process; (3) controls that have a pervasive effect on the financial statements, such as information technology general controls; or (4) walkthroughs. This is overly restrictive, especially in the small company or private company context. If the auditor has determined in its professional opinion that the internal audit is sufficiently competent and objective, there should not be such limitations.

Under current auditing standards, auditors are able to use their assessment of the effectiveness of senior management controls and monthly boards of directors' oversight of company operations in their audits of smaller companies to limit the nature and extent of their work in a <u>financial statement</u> audit. Similarly, the Proposed Rules appear to acknowledge that the integrity and actions of senior management in small and medium-size organizations are key components of establishing strong <u>internal controls</u> in those companies. *Proposing Release, Appendix E.* For the same reasons, auditors of small and medium-size companies should be allowed, if warranted based upon their professional judgment and expertise, to use the work of management in their audit of internal controls over financial reporting, especially in performing walkthroughs.

We believe that by limiting the auditor's ability to exercise their professional judgment in each of the above situations, the Proposed Rules will impede the PCAOB's goal of implementing Section 404 in a cost effective manner. Indeed, many aspects of the Proposed Rules would have the opposite effect. They would require the auditor to unnecessarily increase the amount of work to be performed, which will result in higher costs with little added benefits to financial reporting.

We have an additional concern regarding the Proposed Rules – the requirement that the auditor evaluate the effectiveness of the audit committee's oversight of the company's external financial reporting and internal control over financial reporting. *Proposing Release*, page A-25, paragraphs 56-59. Many of NVCA members serve on boards of directors and audit committees for their portfolio companies. These boards of directors and audit committees are responsible for the appointment and oversight of the external auditors. The Proposed Rule's requirement that auditors evaluate the effectiveness of the audit committee's oversight of internal control over financial reporting creates an unnecessary ambiguity in the relationship between the audit committee and the external auditor.

Comments on Proposed Rules related to venture-backed private companies, in particular

The "COSO Report" titled, *Internal Control – Integrated Framework[4]*, provides the basis for the current proposed rules. *Proposing Release*, page 5. The COSO Framework explains that internal control in smaller companies can be less formal and structured. COSO, *Internal Control – Integrated Framework, Executive Summary, page 1.* This is an especially important consideration for developing auditing rules that will be applied to private, venture-backed companies.

In venture-backed companies, internal controls, systems and periodic testing of internal controls by management are commensurate to the risk that management and private investors, who sit on the board, find acceptable. There is no standard approach to these very subjective cost-benefit determinations.

In this private company context, the following statement has particular meaning. "The primary benefit [of internal controls over financial reporting] is to provide the company, its management, *its board and audit committee, and its owners* and other stakeholders with a reasonable basis to rely on the company's financial reporting." *Proposing Release*, page 5 [*emphasis supplied*]. In a venture-backed company, the current owners are members of the board and the audit committee. While we recognize that an auditor's 404 report will necessarily

---

[4] Committee of Sponsoring Organizations of the Treadway Report, *Internal Controls -- Integrated Framework* (1992).

assume that the company will become a public company, or part of a public company, during the coming fiscal year, the PCAOB's 404 Rules must allow the auditor to accommodate the fact that costs and benefits are weighed differently for a private company than for even the smallest publicly traded company.

For example, the COSO framework notes that the control environment is "the foundation for all other components of internal control, providing discipline and structure," *Internal Control – Integrated Framework, Executive Summary, page. 2*. Accordingly, an auditor should be able to weight aspects of the control environment in determining how much they need to test other aspects of internal control in a private company.

In many small companies, a key control consists of the fact that financial management and authority is centralized at the CEO or CFO level. If this is the case in a given company, the auditor should be permitted to assign significant weight to those facts alone in determining whether to test other functions. If, in addition, the board meets monthly to review the company's finances in detail – a common practice in portfolio companies -- the auditor should have the latitude to find it unnecessary to do additional extensive testing to determine whether the owners (board members) have "a reasonable basis to rely on the company's financial reporting," *Proposing Release*, page 5. Internal control costs, and the cost of evaluating internal controls should be weighed against their benefits to financial reporting. If there is no real benefit, a particular review or test should not be required.

The COSO Framework's emphasis on control environment has particular application in the private company context. The board of directors' cost-benefit choices should, by themselves, carry significant weight absent some indication of special financial reporting risks. Just as the Proposed Rules should provide auditors with the flexibility to make appropriate cost-benefit judgments for smaller public companies, they must be still more flexible for the appropriate balance to be struck in a private company 404 report.

Conclusion

NVCA encourages the PCAOB to expand the scope of special internal control considerations for small and medium-sized companies in the Proposed Rules. We also request that the Rule note that different considerations apply in preparing a report for a private company. Without such special considerations, the audits of internal control over financial reporting for these companies will be unnecessarily costly, both in external auditor fees and management and board time that will be devoted towards Section 404 compliance. We would be pleased to discuss these and any related matters with Board members or staff. Please feel free to contact NVCA's Vice President Jennifer Connell Dowling, our outside SEC counsel, Brian Borders (202 822 9306), or me to discuss these matters.

Sincerely yours,

Mark G. Heesen
President

¶ 619. New York Clearing House Association

Jeffrey P. Neubert
President and CEO

100 Broad Street
New York, NY 10004
te.c 212 612 9203

jeffrey.neubert@thec ear nghouse.org

November 21, 2003

Office of the Secretary
Public Company Accounting Oversight Board
1666 K Street, N.W.
Washington, D.C. 20006-2803

          Re: PCAOB Rulemaking Docket Matter No. 008 – Audit of Internal
                 Control Over Financial Reporting

Ladies and Gentlemen:

          The New York Clearing House Association L.L.C., an association of major
commercial banks[1], appreciates the opportunity to comment on the proposed auditing standard
("Proposed Standard"), recently published by the Public Company Accounting Oversight Board
(the "Board"), for conducting an audit of internal control over financial reporting pursuant to
Section 404 of the Sarbanes-Oxley Act of 2002 (the "Act").

          As financial institutions, we have long recognized that an effective system of
internal controls is the essential foundation for sound banking practices, including those relating
to financial disclosure and reporting. We believe that requiring independent accountants to play
a bigger role in evaluating the effectiveness of internal control over financial reporting can
strengthen controls in this area and improve the quality and integrity of financial reporting by
public companies. Consequently, we generally support the Proposed Standard.

          We have serious reservations, however, about several specific aspects of the
proposal that are likely to prove impractical and in some cases unworkable in operation. We
believe that the proposal needs to be modified in the ways we describe below. We do not believe
that these modifications will weaken the effectiveness of the proposal; on the contrary, by

---

[1]   The members of The Clearing House are Bank of America, National Association, The Bank of New York,
      Bank One, National Association, Citibank, N.A., Deutsche Bank Trust Company Americas, Fleet National
      Bank, HSBC Bank USA, JPMorgan Chase Bank, LaSalle Bank National Association, Wachovia Bank,
      National Association, and Wells Fargo Bank, National Association.

Office of the Secretary   2   November 21, 2003
Public Company Accounting Oversight Board

eliminating those aspects of the Proposed Standard that are likely to create significant practical problems for public companies, we think our suggested changes will promote compliance with the standard and advance the broad purposes of Section 404 of the Act.

(1)   **The Final Rule Should Permit Auditors Greater Flexibility in Relying on the Work of Others and in Conducting Control Testing and Walkthroughs**

By requiring an audit of internal control over financial reporting, rather than merely an attestation regarding management's assessment of those controls, the Proposed Standard goes well beyond the requirements of Section 404 of the Act. If auditors will be required to conduct an audit of those controls, they should be given considerable flexibility in determining the appropriate scope of the audit, just as they are with regard to an audit of financial statements. Given the breadth and complexity of the work that may be required to conduct an audit of those controls in any particular case, we believe it is critical that auditors be permitted to exercise their professional judgment, based on their knowledge of the relevant facts and circumstances, in planning and conducting the audit and, in particular, in determining the extent to which they may rely on the work of others and the extent to which they must conduct control testing and walkthroughs.

We think this flexibility is especially appropriate in light of the significant new reforms enacted this past year with regard to public company financial reporting and disclosure. The SEC's new rules under Section 404 of the Act will require management to dedicate significant resources to periodic assessments of internal control over financial reporting. In addition, new SEC and stock market rules encourage both audit committees and internal auditors to play bigger roles in monitoring the effectiveness of internal control over financial reporting. Prohibiting auditors from relying on broad categories of work performed by management and internal auditors in all cases, without allowing auditors to exercise their professional judgment about the extent to which they should duplicate this work in light of the specific facts and circumstances, is excessive and is likely to result in needless and costly duplication of effort, especially in light of these new regulations. We have similar concerns about requiring auditors to conduct control testing and walkthroughs without being able to use their discretion in determining the appropriate scope and frequency of these procedures.

Relying on Work of Others. We do not believe the Proposed Standard should prohibit auditors from relying on the work of others in the areas identified in Paragraph 104 of the proposal in all cases. A blanket prohibition with respect to these areas would be inappropriate for the reasons discussed above. Auditors should instead be permitted to exercise their professional judgment — as contemplated in Paragraph 103 of the Proposed Standard — in determining whether to rely on another party's work with respect to each control that must be audited.

Requiring auditors to duplicate the efforts of management and internal audit across the board for all companies is especially unwarranted with regard to insured depository

Office of the Secretary   3   November 21, 2003
Public Company Accounting Oversight Board

institutions and bank holding companies, such as our members. These companies are required under the Federal Deposit Insurance Corporation Improvement Act of 1991 to produce annual internal control reports, attested by independent auditors, assessing the effectiveness of internal controls. In response to this requirement, insured depository institutions and many bank holding companies have developed sophisticated and reliable internal systems for monitoring the effectiveness of internal controls. We believe that prohibiting auditors from using their discretion to determine whether and to what extent reliance on these existing systems may be appropriate, at least in some areas, will subject these institutions to significant additional expense that is likely to yield little or no improvement in the reliability of these controls.

We believe the Board should follow the approach set forth in SAS 65[2], which permits the auditor take into account the work of internal auditors in certain circumstances. SAS 65 allows the auditor to make judgments about the degree to which it may rely on internal auditors' work, provided that the auditor makes an assessment of the competence and objectivity of the internal audit function, and of the materiality and degree of subjectivity relating to the particular financial amounts in issue. Rather than imposing a blanket prohibition on the use of internal auditors' work, SAS 65 allows auditors to use their professional judgment in determining when and to what extent they should rely on the internal audit function. Reliance on the work of others may be inappropriate in some areas but not necessarily in all areas for all companies. In addition, by limiting an auditor's ability to rely on work performed by the internal audit function, the Proposed Standard could have the unintended effect of reducing the importance of the internal audit function, a result that would be contrary to Act's goal of promoting strong and effective internal control over financial reporting.

Principal Evidence for Audit Opinion. Closely related to the issue of auditors' reliance on the work of others is the requirement in Paragraph 109 of the Proposed Standard that the auditor's own work provide the "principal evidence" for the audit opinion. This requirement is both difficult to apply and potentially very burdensome. Without further clarification, it is unclear by what metric – such as hours worked, number of controls reviewed or importance of controls – auditors should determine whether their own work constitutes principal evidence. Regardless of the metric used to measure the relative amount of work performed by the auditor, it would be time consuming and expensive to require auditors to perform a majority of the work required for an audit. This is particularly true for large, multinational financial institutions that maintain extensive systems of internal controls. While we agree that there should be *qualitative* restrictions on an auditor's ability to rely on others' work, we do not think there should be a *quantitative* test that would require the independent auditor to perform a specified volume of work.

---

[2]   Statement on Auditing Standards No. 65, *The Auditor's Consideration of the Internal Audit Functions in an Audit of Financial Statements.*

Control Testing and Walkthroughs. For the reasons set forth above, we believe that Paragraphs 27 and 74 of the Proposed Standard, relating to control testing, and Paragraph 79, relating to walkthroughs, should be modified to allow auditors to use their professional judgment in determining the extent and frequency of their testing and walkthrough activity. Paragraphs 27 and 74 requires an auditor to gather sufficient competent evidence for *all* assertions for *all* significant accounts and disclosures in the financial statements, presumably *every* year. We think auditors should be directed to use their professional judgment to determine not only what accounts and disclosures are significant but when it is appropriate to gather new evidence or use the prior year's evidence. Similarly, we do not think it is necessary or helpful to investors to require an auditor to perform a walkthrough of *all* significant processes of a company *every* year, as Paragraph 79 appears to require. We think the Proposed Standard should be revised to make it clear that an auditor must conduct control testing and walkthroughs to the extent that it determines is sufficient to enable it to form an opinion about the effectiveness of a company's internal control over financial reporting.

(2)   **The Definition of "Material Weakness" Should not Be Broader than the Definition Recognized by the SEC, and "Significant Deficiency" Should Be Limited in a Consistent Manner**

The Proposed Standard would preclude an auditor from giving an unqualified opinion if it identified a "material weakness," which would be defined as any significant deficiency that results in *more than a remote likelihood*[3] that a material misstatement of the annual or interim financial statements will not be prevented or detected. We believe this definition sets far too low a threshold for what constitutes a material weakness. The concept of "remote" is extreme, and we are concerned that it may be interpreted as referring to any event whose likelihood of occurring is only slightly more than non-existent. Given the serious consequences for auditors who are judged in hindsight as having taken too lax an approach in this area, we think auditors will naturally choose to err on the side of caution when applying this concept, leading them to regard as a material weakness many conditions whose likely impact on the financial statements is little more than theoretical. We agree that the threshold for material weakness should be lower than "probable" or "more likely than not." However, the range of probabilities between this threshold and the "remote" threshold is simply too wide. We think the appropriate threshold lies somewhere in the middle of this range.

The new SEC rules under Section 404 of the Act prohibit management from concluding in its annual internal control report that internal control over financial reporting is effective when one or more material weaknesses exist. In its adopting release for these rules, the SEC defined material weakness by reference to current accounting literature, as a "reportable

---

[3]   "Remote likelihood" would have the same meaning as the term "remote" used in Financial Accounting Standards Board No. 5, *Accounting for Contingencies*, which states that "remote" means the chance of a certain future event or events occurring is slight.

Office of the Secretary   5   November 21, 2003
Public Company Accounting Oversight Board

condition" in which the design or operation of one or more internal control components does not reduce the risk of misstatement to a *relatively low level.*[4] We think the SEC's interpretation appropriately targets the middle ground between "remote" and "probable." We urge the Board to take a similar approach, and to define material weakness as a significant deficiency that is *reasonably likely* to result in a material misstatement. We do not think that the definition of material weakness will be workable unless the Board makes clear that there must be some reasonable likelihood that a material misstatement may occur.

The proposed definition of "significant deficiency" raises similar problems. "Significant deficiency" would be defined as an internal control deficiency or a combination of such deficiencies that results in *more than a remote likelihood* that a financial misstatement of *more than an inconsequential amount* will not be prevented or detected. For the reasons described above, we think the concept of "remote" sets far too low a threshold. We think the concept of "more than an inconsequential amount" does so as well. With these low thresholds, there would be no meaningful distinction between a deficiency that is significant and one that is not. In defining "significant deficiency," we believe the Board should replace "remote" with "reasonably likely" and should replace "inconsequential" with a "significance" standard. In other words, a "significant deficiency" should be defined as an internal control deficiency or a combination of such deficiencies that is reasonably likely to result in a significant financial misstatement not being prevented or detected.

(3)   **The Proposed Standard Should Clarify the Scope of an Auditor's Duty to Evaluate the Effectiveness and Independence of the Audit Committee**

Paragraphs 57 and 58 of the Proposed Standard would require an auditor to evaluate the effectiveness and independence of the audit committee, which under the new SEC and stock market rules is responsible for hiring the auditor, fixing its compensation and overseeing its work. Requiring an auditor to pass judgment on its overseers creates a significant conflict of interest for the auditor (and perhaps for the audit committee). While we agree that an effective audit committee is an important element of internal control over financial reporting and that some level of review of this element by an auditor is appropriate, we think the scope of that review needs to be clearly delineated to ensure that the inherent conflict of interest remains

---

[4]   See *Final Rule: Management's Reports on Internal Control Over Financial Reporting and Certification of Disclosure in Exchange Act Periodic Reports*, Release No. 34-47986 (June 5, 2003), 68 Fed. Reg. 36,636 (June 18, 2003), available at http://www.sec.gov/rules/final/33-8238.htm. The adopting release references AU Section 325 and AT Section 501, which define "material weakness" to be a reportable condition in which the design or operation of one or more of the internal control components does not reduce to a *relatively low level* the risk that misstatements caused by error or fraud in amounts that would be material in relation to the financial statements being audited may occur and not be detected within a timely period by employees in the normal course of performing their assigned functions. While AU Section 325 and AT Section 501 may be superseded by the Board's Proposed Standard, we think the SEC's approach in this area is persuasive.

manageable for an auditor and does not undermine the audit committee's auditor-oversight role. The Proposed Standard should clarify that an auditor's review of the audit committee's functions should focus on its structural and procedural aspects and not on the personal qualifications of the audit committee members.

We think it is appropriate to require an auditor to review the structural and procedural aspects of the audit committee function – that is, to determine whether the audit committee has appropriate access to and interaction with the internal auditors and those members of management responsible for financial reporting, is given enough information about the company's internal control over financial reporting so as to understand how it operates and what its strengths and weaknesses are and generally is provided adequate administrative and professional support. However, requiring the auditor to evaluate the personal qualifications of individual audit committee members –their independence and financial expertise – has the potential to create a serious and unmanageable conflict of interest.

In particular, the audit committee should not be required to make an affirmative, de novo determination of whether an audit committee member meets the independence standards under SEC and stock market rules. Applying these standards requires a significant degree of business judgment and legal analysis, and the responsibility for applying them is properly reserved for the company and its board of directors in consultation with its attorneys. Requiring an auditor to make its own determination about the independence of an audit committee could lead to highly disruptive second guessing of the company and its board, would require the auditor to make judgments beyond its expertise and could bring the auditor into direct conflict with the audit committee.[5] For the same reasons, we do not think an auditor should be required to evaluate the financial expertise of audit committee members, including any member identified by the company as a financial expert.

In sum, we urge the Board to provide clear guidance about which aspects of the audit committee function an auditor is and is not expected to evaluate. The Proposed Standard should make clear that this evaluation is to focus on structural and procedural aspects of the kind described above and not on the personal qualifications, including the independence and financial expertise, of the audit committee members.

---

[5]   If an auditor learns about a relationship between an audit committee member and the company that could significantly impair the member's independence and has not been publicly disclosed, it may be appropriate to require the auditor to discuss the relationship with the company and the audit committee. Requiring an auditor to raise questions about material facts relating to independence that may come to its attention is very different, however, from requiring it to make a de novo determination about whether the audit committee member is independent.

(4)   **The Proposed Standard Should Provide Guidance About
Bring-Down Procedures for Audit Report and Consent Filings**

       Paragraph 181 of the Proposed Standard would require auditors to perform bring-down procedures in accordance with AU Section 711 with respect to the filing of an audit report on management's assessment of internal controls. The Proposed Standard would direct auditors to inquire of and obtain written representations from executives responsible for financial accounting matters about whether any events have occurred that have a material effect on management's assessment of internal control over financial reporting. We are concerned that this provision could be interpreted to require management and auditors to perform costly and time-consuming evaluations of changes in internal control that take place at any time *after* the close of the relevant reporting period and up to the relevant filing date. This could require management and the auditor to review every change in internal control over financial reporting since the report period to determine whether any of them have had or could have a material effect on those controls. We urge the Board to clarify that the required bring-down procedures apply only to developments that are relevant to the effectiveness of those controls as in existence during the report period. Alternatively, if these procedures are to apply to developments relevant to these controls as in effect after the report period, then procedures should apply only to those developments having a material *adverse* effect on these controls. Clarifying the scope of the required bring-down procedures is particularly important with regard to the filing of auditor consents (*e.g.*, relating to registration statements), which can occur many times throughout the fiscal year and on relatively short notice. We believe that clarification of this kind is especially necessary for large, multinational financial institutions that maintain extensive systems of internal controls and must modify and update those systems on a regular basis.

(5)   **The Circumstances Listed in Paragraph 126 Should Not Be Presumed to
Reflect Significant Deficiencies or to Be Strong Indicators of Material
Weaknesses in All Cases**

       Paragraph 126 of the Proposed Standard would require auditors to regard a number of different circumstances listed in that paragraph as significant deficiencies and "strong indicators" that a material weakness may exist. While any one of these circumstances might be attributable to a significant deficiency or material weakness in internal control over financial reporting in some cases, mandating a presumption that all of them are so attributable in all cases would be inappropriate. For example, the Proposed Standard would require auditors to regard any material misstatement in a current period not initially identified by a company's internal control over financial reporting as a significant deficiency and "a strong indicator" that a material weakness may exist. While some current-period audit adjustments may in fact be attributable to significant deficiencies or material weaknesses in internal control over financial reporting, a presumption that all such adjustments are likely to be is overly broad. Audit adjustments are often made to items requiring a significant degree of judgment about factors that are not known or measurable and thus arise because of differences of opinion between management and the

Office of the Secretary   8   November 21, 2003
Public Company Accounting Oversight Board

auditor, not because of a breakdown in internal control. This is particularly true for valuation of financial instruments and other assets for which no ready market exists, as well as for assessments about the probability and potential magnitude of contingent liabilities such as those arising from pending litigation or complex contractual arrangements.

The other items listed in Paragraph 126 may also, in some cases, be attributable to significant deficiencies or material weaknesses. In other cases, however, auditors may be able to determine that one or more of these items are unrelated to any significant deficiency or material weakness in internal control. In addition, the vagueness of some of the items – such as the existence of an "ineffective regulatory compliance function" – could lead to overly broad application of the presumption. Rather than imposing an across-the-board presumption, the Proposed Standard should permit auditors to use their professional judgment in determining whether any of these items is attributable to a significant deficiency or material weakness in internal control over financial reporting in any particular case.

For the reasons set forth above, we do not think it is appropriate to include a list of any specific circumstances that should be presumed to reflect a significant deficiency or considered a strong indicator that a material weakness exists. We believe the list of circumstances in Paragraph 126 should be deleted.

(6)   Audit Committees Should Not Be Required to Pre-Approve All Non-Audit Services Relating to Internal Controls

The SEC's new auditor independence rules require that any non-audit service provided by an auditor to an issuer or its subsidiaries either be specifically pre-approved by the issuer's audit committee or fall within a clearly defined category of services that has been pre-approved by the audit committee. While the SEC staff has cautioned against pre-approval of broad, vaguely defined categories of services, it recognizes that categorical pre-approval is permitted if the categories are sufficiently well defined and appropriately limited in scope.[6] Under the Proposed Standard, in contrast, audit committees would not be able to pre-approve any non-audit services relating to internal controls on a categorical basis and instead would have to specifically pre-approve each of those services.

We believe the SEC's approval policy strikes an appropriate balance between the need to give management sufficient flexibility to address internal control issues as they arise and the need to ensure adequate auditor oversight by the audit committee. Striking a balance between these two needs is especially important for large, multinational financial institutions,

---

[6]   See *Office of the Chief Accountant: Application of the January 2003 Rules on Auditor Independence Frequently Asked Questions*, available at http://www.sec.gov/info/accountants/ ocafaqaudind080703.htm (August 13, 2003).

Office of the Secretary   9   November 21, 2003
Public Company Accounting Oversight Board

which maintain extensive, complex systems of internal control that must be continuously monitored and frequently updated to reflect changes in the many different business practices they are designed to control. We do not think the Board should impose a pre-approval rule for internal control-related services that differs from the SEC's rule for non-audit services generally. We think the Proposed Standard should be revised to allow categorical pre-approval of audit services relating to internal control, consistent with the SEC's auditor independence rules. In particular, the Board should make it clear that an audit committee may pre-approve services to be rendered in connection with the annual audit of internal control over financial reporting on a categorical basis, and should not have to specifically pre-approve each aspect of these services that might be rendered throughout the annual audit cycle.

(7)   **The Proposed Standard Should Provide Guidance Regarding Business Combinations Consummated Late in the Audit Cycle**

Companies that combine by merger, acquisition or other transactions may have very different systems of internal control over financial reporting. Often, these systems must be integrated into a single, comprehensive system through a lengthy process involving modification of technology and operating systems, retraining of personnel and documenting the changes. If a combination occurs late in the surviving company's annual audit cycle, its management and auditors may not have enough time to become familiar with the different internal control systems used by the acquired company, much less with any comprehensive system to be formed through the integration process, before an audit of the annual financial statements for the combined company is required to be completed. In these circumstances, it may not be possible to evaluate internal control for the combined company without relying on the work of management and the auditor for the acquired company. It may not even be possible to provide a single, comprehensive evaluation for the combined company as a whole; separate evaluations of the constituent companies by their respective management teams and auditors may be the only feasible approach. Accordingly, we urge the Board to provide guidance to management and auditors of surviving companies of business combinations consummated late in an audit cycle, indicating the extent to which they may rely on work performed by management and auditors of the constituent companies, including separate evaluations of the effectiveness of those companies' controls. An example of constructive guidance in this area would be to permit auditors to issue "except for" opinions in connection with business combinations effected late in the audit cycle. In these situations, an auditor simply may not have time to complete the necessary work regarding all relevant aspects of an acquired company's internal controls. We believe that the auditor should have the latitude to issue an "except for" opinion in these situations with regard to all or part of the internal controls of the acquired company.

Office of the Secretary   10   November 21, 2003
Public Company Accounting Oversight Board

(8)   **The Proposed Standard Should Provide Guidance Regarding**
               Evaluations of Service Organizations

      The Proposed Standard directs auditors to obtain information regarding the
controls maintained by service organizations with regard to the services they provide to a
company as part of the company's information system. Auditors may obtain information from a
service auditor's "report on controls placed in operation" pursuant to AU Section 324; if a
service auditor's report is not available, the auditor may obtain information from other sources,
including user manuals and the contract between the company and the service organization. We
urge the Board to clarify these requirements, particularly the extent to which and how often
service auditors' reports will have to be obtained, the extent of procedures that must be
performed when a service auditor's report is unavailable and the extent to which auditors may
rely on service auditors' reports. We think SAS 70[7] provides useful guidance on these matters
with regard to audits of financial statements. Among other things, SAS 70 states that the
significance of the controls of the service organization to those of the user organization depends
on the nature of the services provided by the service organization, the nature and materiality of
the transactions it processes for the user organization and the degree of interaction between the
service organization's activities and those of the user organization. We believe that guidance
similar to that contained in SAS 70, which has been in effect for many years and is already
familiar to those in the financial services industry, would be appropriate in the context of audits
of internal control over financial reporting. We think that SAS 70's reliance on concepts of
materiality and the auditor's exercise of professional judgment based on particular facts and
circumstances are especially appropriate in this context.

               *   *   *

      We recognize that the Board faces a number of difficult challenges in developing
the Proposed Standard and in fulfilling its overall mandate to the investing public. We welcome
the opportunity to comment on the proposal, and we would be pleased to meet with the Board or
its staff to discuss our comments if that would be helpful. If you have any questions about our
comments or would like to discuss them with us, please contact Norman R. Nelson, General
Counsel of The Clearing House, at 212-612-9205.

                                  Sincerely yours,

---

[7]   Statement on Auditing Standards No. 70, *Service Organizations* ("SAS 70").

¶ 620. Allstate Corporation

November 21, 2003

Office of the Secretary
Public Company Accounting Oversight Board
1666 K Street, N.W.
Washington, D.C. 20006-2803

Re: PCAOB Rulemaking Docket No. 008
        Proposed Auditing Standard – An Audit of Internal Control Over Financial
        Reporting Performed in Conjunction with an Audit of Financial Statements

Dear Secretary:

Thank you for the opportunity to comment on the above referenced Proposed Auditing
Standard (Proposed AS) which we believe represents an important step in promoting
investor confidence through the effective assessment and reporting on internal controls over
financial reporting. While we support your overall efforts concerning this very complex
subject, we also appreciate the opportunity to comment on several important areas
addressed in the Proposed AS. These areas include certain inconsistencies between the
general framework and the Proposed AS, the testing of operational effectiveness, use of the
work of management and others, and the definition of a significant deficiency. We urge the
Board to carefully consider our comments, which we believe will promote a more efficient,
cost-effective, and balanced evaluation of internal controls over financial reporting.

Inconsistencies between the Framework and Proposed AS

The general framework of the Proposed AS appropriately identifies a number of key
concepts common to audits and evaluations of internal controls including the following:

- **Auditor's Objective in an Audit of Internal Control Over Financial Reporting**

  - *The auditor's objective in an audit of internal control over financial reporting is to form a
    basis for expressing such an opinion, the auditor must plan and perform the audit to obtain
    <u>reasonable assurance</u> about whether the company maintained, in all material respects,
    effective internal control over financial reporting.....*

  - *To obtain <u>reasonable assurance</u>, the auditor evaluates the assessment performed by
    management and obtains and evaluates evidence about whether the internal control over
    financial reporting is designed and operated effectively......*

- **Inherent Limitations in Internal Control Over Financial Reporting**

  - *Internal control over financial reporting <u>cannot provide absolute assurance</u> of achieving
    financial reporting objectives because of its inherent limitations.....*

- **Reasonable Assurance**

  - *Management's assessment of <u>the effectiveness of internal control over financial reporting is
    expressed at the level of reasonable assurance</u>. The concept of reasonable assurance is built
    into the definition of internal control over financial reporting and also is integral to the*

---

auditor's opinion. Reasonable assurance includes the understanding that there is a relatively low risk that material misstatements will not be prevented or detected on a timely basis. Although not absolute assurance, reasonable assurance is, nevertheless, a high level of assurance.

- **Materiality Considerations in an Audit of Internal Control Over Financial Reporting**

  - *The auditor should apply the concept of materiality in an audit of internal control over financial reporting at both the financial-statements level and at the individual account-balance level......*

  - *The same conceptual definition of materiality that applies to financial reporting applies to information on internal control over financial reporting, including the relevance of both quantitative and qualitative considerations.*

Despite recognition of the key concepts of reasonable assurance, inherent limitations, and materiality in the general framework of the Proposed AS, the Proposed Standard itself abandons these critical concepts through the inappropriate use of words such as "all", "each," and "entire". We believe that through the use of these "all inclusive" words the Proposed AS directly contradicts the basic notion of reasonable assurance, inherent limitations, and materiality and in so doing sets an unattainable standard for both the registrant and the independent auditors in carrying out their responsibilities under the Proposed AS. More specifically, we do not believe it would be either cost-beneficial or possible to document, test, and attest to the effectiveness of "all" or "each" control within the "entire" internal control over financial reporting system as could reasonably be construed by the language in the Proposed AS. It is our assumption that the use of words such as "all", "each", and "entire" was unintended as it is inconsistent with the PCAOB's recognition in it's general framework that there are inherent limitations in any internal control system such that obtaining "absolute assurance" of its effectiveness cannot be obtained. Moreover, we believe the PCAOB recognized that fact when it suggested that when testing internal controls over financial reporting the tests should be designed to obtain "reasonable assurance" that the controls are operating effectively. Although the term "reasonable assurance" is not adequately defined in either the Proposed AS or related literature, it is our understanding that it has historically incorporated judgment and an assessment of materiality in designing tests to meet the "reasonable assurance" threshold which is definitively different than the "absolute assurance" threshold implied by the use of words such as "all", "each," and "entire". Accordingly, we strongly suggest eliminating words such as "all", "each," and "entire" in the Proposed AS as they suggest the imposition of a level of review and testing that is neither cost-beneficial or possible.

Testing Operating Effectiveness

Question 11:

Is it appropriate to require the auditor to obtain evidence of the effectiveness of controls for all relevant assertions for all significant accounts and disclosures every year or may the auditor use some of the audit evidence obtained in previous years to support his or her current opinion on management's assessment?

We believe the independent auditor should apply their judgment and place appropriate reliance on their previous experience within the industry and with the registrant when determining the evidence necessary to support their opinion on management's assessment of internal controls over financial reporting. We believe the independent auditor's knowledge and understanding of a registrant's internal control structure is enhanced with experience as many components within a company's internal control structure do not change significantly from year to year. Accordingly, the independent auditor should be permitted to appropriately leverage this experience and modify the timing and extent of internal control testing aimed at determining whether controls over financial reporting are appropriately designed and operating effectively. Assuming the preceding, the independent auditor would appropriately focus their substantive tests on areas within the registrant's internal control structure that have changed.

Use of the Work of Management and Others

The Proposed AS summary suggests that the work performed by management in connection with its assessment of internal controls over financial reporting can have a significant effect on the nature, timing and extent of the work performed by the independent auditor, however, the Proposed AS does not appear to support this statement given its restrictions on the use of the work of management and internal auditors.

Question 13:

Are the three categories of controls and the extent to which the auditor may rely on the work of others appropriately defined?

We believe the complete restriction placed on the use of the results of testing performed by management and internal auditors is inappropriate and severely limits the independent auditor's ability to appropriately alter the nature, timing and extent of their substantive tests. While we generally understand the Board's attempt to identify more critical areas for the independent auditors in the current business environment, we believe the work of management and internal auditors should not be ignored when determining the nature, extent and timing of substantive audit procedures. We believe that to the extent the independent auditor's consideration of work completed by internal auditors expressly considers their independence, approach, and competence there is no reason their work should not be relied on. The same approach should be applied to the work of management, not withstanding their lack of independence.

Question 9:

Are the objectives to be achieved by performing walkthroughs sufficient to require the performance of walkthroughs?

We believe walkthroughs would be very time-consuming and costly for the independent auditors to complete for each of the registrant's significant processes. Moreover, the independent auditor's primary focus should be on evaluating the design and operational effectiveness of internal controls over financial reporting. In contrast, documenting internal controls over financial reporting is typically completed by management and internal auditors. Furthermore, as noted above in our response to question 11, requiring auditors to perform walkthroughs each year does not appropriately consider the independent auditors previous experience and knowledge of the industry or the registrant. Assuming documentation supporting the control environment already exists, we believe the independent auditor should only perform walkthroughs of significant processes on a limited test basis applying their judgment by taking into account their previous experience with the industry and with the registrant to validate their understanding of the process as documented by management and the internal auditors.

Question 14:

Does the proposed standard give appropriate recognition to the work of internal auditors? If not, does the proposed standard place too much emphasis and preference on the work of internal auditors or not enough?

We believe the Proposed AS does not appropriately leverage the work completed by internal auditors. The Proposed AS would require significant duplication of work and inefficiencies resulting in a higher cost of performing substantive tests by the independent auditors. Accordingly, we believe the Proposed AS should consider the outcome of the required assessment of the competence and objectivity of the internal auditors as outlined in AU § 322 and allow the independent auditors to apply an appropriate level of reliance on the work of internal auditors. AU § 322 requires the independent auditor to obtain information on the educational level and professional experience of internal auditors (including professional certifications and continuing education), audit policies, audit programs and procedures, practices regarding assignment of internal auditors, supervision and review of internal auditors' activities, quality of working-paper documentation, reports and recommendations, an evaluation of internal auditors' performance, and consideration of the organizational status of the internal auditors. We believe that, depending on the outcome of this comprehensive review, the independent auditors should be allowed to rely on the work of internal auditors.

Significant Deficiency Definition

Question 17:

Will the definitions in the proposed standard of a significant deficiency and material weakness provide for increased consistency in the evaluation of deficiencies? How can the definitions be improved?

We believe the definition of a significant deficiency in the Proposed AS is ambiguous, would be difficult to apply, and therefore would not provide for increased consistency in the evaluation of deficiencies (both individually and collectively). To improve upon the definition in the Proposed AS we believe the PCAOB should incorporate specific evaluative criteria into the definition against which reporting entities could easily and consistently evaluate deficiencies in internal controls over financial reporting. Moreover, we believe the evaluation criteria should give due consideration to both the nature and the actual (or potential) materiality of the item in relation to the annual or interim financial statements to which they (it) relate(s).

The definition in the Proposed AS of a significant deficiency in internal controls over financial reporting is as follows:

> *A significant deficiency is an internal control deficiency that adversely affects a reporting entity's ability to initiate, record, process, or report external financial data reliably in accordance with generally accepted accounting principles. A significant deficiency is a deficiency that, by itself or a combination of deficiencies, results in more than a remote likelihood of a misstatement of the annual or interim financial statements that is more than inconsequential in amount and would not be prevented or detected.*

We do not believe the term "more than a remote likelihood of a misstatement of the annual or interim financial statements that is more than inconsequential" provides clear, objective criteria against which one can easily and consistently evaluate deficiencies in internal control over financial reporting. More specifically, we believe that without evaluative criteria against which to evaluate deficiencies, reporting entities will interpret and apply the terms "more than a remote likelihood" and "more than inconsequential" in an inconsistent manner. Moreover, when developing the evaluative criteria we suggest that certain concepts be incorporated to eliminate the potential that minor deficiencies, that exist in even the most well-controlled business environments, are not inappropriately designated as significant deficiencies as that could have the unintended consequence of de-sensitizing relevant parties (i.e. financial statement preparers, users, and independent auditors) to the importance of significant deficiencies.

To ensure that deficiencies (both individually and collectively) are consistently evaluated against a set of objective criteria designed to identify only those individual and collective deficiencies that warrant designation as a significant deficiency we propose the following definition and set of evaluative criteria:

Proposed Definition – Significant Deficiency

> *A significant deficiency is a deficiency in internal controls over financial reporting that adversely affects a reporting entity's ability to initiate, record, process, or report external financial data reliably in accordance with generally accepted accounting principles. A significant deficiency is a deficiency that, by itself or in combination with other deficiencies, results in the reasonable possibility of a misstatement of the annual or interim financial statements that would not be prevented or detected and that by its nature or amount, represents a misstatement that would affect the judgments of a reasonable investor or creditor.*

Proposed Evaluative Criteria – Nature of the Deficiency

When evaluating the nature of a deficiency (or combination of deficiencies) in internal controls over financial reporting the following factors should be considered:

- Whether the related actual (or potential) misstatement arises from an item capable of precise measurement or whether it arises from an estimate and, if so, the degree of imprecision inherent in the estimate;
- Whether the related actual (or potential) misstatement masks a change in earnings or other trends;
- Whether the related actual (or potential) misstatement changes a loss into income or vice versa; and
- Whether the related actual (or potential) misstatement involves concealment of an unlawful transaction.

Proposed Evaluative Criteria – Actual or Potential Significance of the Deficiency

When evaluating the significance of a deficiency (or combination of deficiencies) the following criteria should be used as a guide to determine whether the deficiency (or combination of deficiencies) is significant (or has the potential to become significant) as it relates to the annual or interim financial statements of the relevant registrant:

- Does the deficiency (or combination of deficiencies) concern information related to the registrant that would cause a reasonable investor to make a different decision with regard to the purchase of the registrant's securities (either debt or equity)?
  - Does the deficiency (or combination of deficiencies) significantly affect the reported earnings or financial strength ratings of the registrant? A deficiency affecting reported earnings but not the financial strength of the registrant may not affect the investing decisions of a holder of the registrant's debt securities.

- Are the financial statements filed by the registrant for a specific purpose (e.g. are they required to support the issuance of certain products – e.g. variable insurance policies)?
  - If so consider how the purchasers of those products would view the deficiency in light of what information they consider important to their investment decision.

- Determine whether the deficiency (or combination of deficiencies) could significantly affect the registrant's financial strength ratings.
  - Does the deficiency significantly affect the registrant's regulatory capital ratios, if any?
  - Does the deficiency significantly affect the registrant's asset/liability management, asset quality, liability duration, or key financial strength measures?
  - Does the deficiency (or combination of deficiencies) significantly affect the run-rate of the registrant's business operations?

I can be reached at (847) 402-2213 if you would like to discuss the contents of this letter.

Sincerely,

Samuel H. Pilch
Controller
The Allstate Corporation

¶ 621. American Airlines

November 21, 2003

Office of the Secretary
Public Company Accounting Oversight Board
1666 K Street NW
Washington, D.C. 20006-2803

Re: PCAOB Rulemaking Docket Matter No. 008- An Audit of Internal Control over Financial Reporting Performed in Conjunction with an Audit of Financial Statements

Members and Staff of the Public Company Accounting Oversight Board:

I appreciate the opportunity to comment on the above-referenced docket matter.

I am both surprised and concerned about the language in the draft relating to reliance on the work of internal audit.

I am surprised because there has been an enormous amount of work put into developing a very thorough framework for the auditor's consideration of the internal audit function in an audit. The framework can be found in the AICPA professional standards/U.S. Auditing Standards (AU)/Section 322. This standard is based on Statement of Auditing Standard (SAS) 65. SAS 78 also further strengthens the framework by requiring a focus on corporate controls.

These current auditing standards already require a high degree of consideration before an external auditor can rely on the work of internal audit. The external auditor, among many other things, has to obtain an understanding of the internal audit function, assess their competence as well as their objectivity, consider the extent of the effect of the audit work, evaluate and test the quality and effectiveness of the internal auditors' work, assess the risk of a misstatement, and obtain evidence of management's assertions. The standard also specifically states that the external auditor has the ultimate responsibility to express an opinion and that responsibility can not be shared with the internal auditors.

I believe the auditing standards referenced (AU Section 322) should be incorporated into the language of the audit of internal control over financial reporting. Paragraph 104 in the current draft in particularl should be eliminated. This paragraph would prevent the external auditor from relying on the work of internal audit in a number of areas. Specifically, certain general controls such as physical environment, disaster recovery, business continuity, change management, network security, back-up procedures, database security, operating system security, and operations are possible areas where external audit might want to rely on the work of internal audit. Unfortunately, if the broadest interpretation of the limitation on information technology control testing is adopted, the external auditors will not be able to choose to rely on the work of internal audit. Consequently, the external auditors will perform much redundant work – in many cases with less competent staff – resulting in a lower quality of work at an unnecessarily high expense.

Many registrants have dedicated significant resources and achieved a high level of expertise in their internal audit departments. Particularly in the area of information technology, organizational expertise becomes more of a necessity as an organization's technology infrastructure gets larger and more complex. I believe most investors would prefer to place reliance on a seasoned group of information technology professionals with deep company-specific knowledge rather than a third party with less experience and more limited company-specific knowledge. Particularly if the work was performed in an objective manner and reperformed on a test-basis by the third party.

Another problem with paragraph 104 is that it is very ambiguous and appears to be contrary to the relevant auditing standards discussed above. Consequently, there appears to be a conflict regarding the reliance of internal audit for a financial statement audit versus the audit of internal control. Since these are for all intents and purposes performed in the same annual audit, I would recommend using the same audit standards.

I agree that under any number of scenarios a decision in which the auditor should not use the results of others, including external audit, might be the right decision. However, I believe current auditing standards already provide adequate guidance about how an external auditor should make that assessment.

Thank you for your consideration.

Charlie T. Wright, CIA, CISA
General Auditor, American Airlines

¶ 622. Caterpillar Inc.

CATERPILLAR

Caterpillar Inc.

100 N. E. Adams Street
Peoria, Illinois 61629

November 21, 2003

Office of the Secretary
Public Company Accounting Oversight Board
1666 K Street, N.W.
Washington, D.C. 20006-2803

Re: PCAOB Rulemaking Docket Matter No. 008

Ladies and Gentlemen:

Caterpillar Inc. commends the Public Company Accounting Oversight Board ("the Board") and its staff for the thorough and expeditious manner in which you have discharged your responsibilities. Caterpillar would like to thank you for the opportunity to comment on your proposed auditing standard, *An Audit of Internal Control Over Financial Reporting Performed in Conjunction with an Audit of Financial Statements* ("the proposed standard").

For more than 75 years, Caterpillar Inc. has been building the world's infrastructure, and in partnership with Caterpillar dealers, is driving positive and sustainable change on every continent. A Fortune 100 company, Caterpillar is the world's leading manufacturer of construction and mining equipment, diesel and natural gas engines and industrial gas turbines. The company is a technology leader in construction, transportation, mining, forestry, energy, logistics, electronics, financing and electric power generation.

Over the years, Caterpillar has built a solid reputation as a highly ethical company. We recognize and take seriously our role in restoring public confidence in Corporate America, including our responsibility to maintain an effective system of internal controls. We also acknowledge that the external auditor's independent oversight role is critically important to this restoration. Accordingly, we support, in principle, the Board's goal of enhancing the effectiveness of internal control over financial reporting. However, we believe the proposed standard exceeds the intended requirements of Section 404 of the Sarbanes-Oxley Act ("the Act") and is insensitive to the cost of compliance for U.S. companies and audit firms. We believe the proposed standard, as written, sets forth requirements that create a cost disadvantage and operational disruptions for U.S. companies versus foreign competitors. In our opinion, the disadvantages to implementing the proposed standard will far outweigh the benefits to investors in public companies.

Please accept our comments to the Board's specific questions in Attachment I in the constructive manner in which they are intended. The following summarizes our key observations and concerns:

- *Adverse consequences and costs of implementation and on-going compliance with the proposed standard*

We believe the following provisions of the standard will impose significant, unintended consequences and costs to implement and comply on a continuing basis:

Restricting the auditor's reliance on the work of management and others -- In our opinion, paragraphs 103-110 represent the most onerous provisions of the standard and will cause significant and unnecessary duplication of effort by the external auditor, internal auditors, and management. **We strongly object to the limitations placed on the external auditor in relying on the work of others.** We agree that the work of others cannot replace the work of the external auditor. However, we believe the auditor should be allowed to rely on competent, objective internal auditors, and to a large extent management, similar to the reliance permitted under Statement of Auditing Standards No. 65 (SAS 65), *The Auditor's Consideration of the Internal Audit Function in an Audit of Financial Statements.* This reliance should not be limited to the internal auditor's tests of routine transactions and processes.

We understand the importance of auditor independence from management. **However, the collaborative relationship that often exists between the external and internal auditors is extremely effective and cost-efficient in providing the broadest audit coverage and greatest level of assurance to investors.** This collaborative assurance is greatly reduced under the proposed standard.

Furthermore, we believe the scope of the auditor's work under the proposed standard exceeds the scope intended in Section 404 of the Act. In our opinion, the scope of the auditor's work was intended to be an attestation of management's assertion of the process used to evaluate the effectiveness of internal controls; not an audit of internal controls. Requiring the same level of assurance from both management and the auditor will unnecessarily require significant and duplicative work.

Prescriptive audit procedures -- We do not believe the proposed standard sufficiently permits the external auditor to use professional judgment in designing and executing audit strategies and procedures. For the same reasons the Board concluded internal control is not "one-size-fits-all," audit procedures should not be "one-size-fits-all." It is our belief the auditor should be allowed the latitude to apply audit strategies and procedures based on the auditor's trained and professional judgment, the size and complexity of the organization, and the competence and objectivity of management.

We agree that walkthroughs of significant processes, limited rotation of audit procedures, and year-to-year unpredictability of testing can all be effective audit procedures and strategies. However, we believe the application of these strategies and procedures should be the discretion of the auditor based on the numerous and varied factors affecting management's assertion regarding the effectiveness of its internal controls.

Appropriate consideration of well-controlled companies -- We agree with the Board that an effectively designed internal control framework, must have the five components of internal control. However, we believe the proposed standard focuses too narrowly on the auditor's responsibilities with respect to only two of those components -- *Control Activities* and *Monitoring*. We do not believe the proposed standard's restricted use of others' work and the prescriptive nature of the audit procedures enable the auditor to consider the *Control Environment, Risk Assessment, and Information and Communication* components of the framework in determining the nature, timing and extent of his/her work.

A strong internal control framework, including proper interaction of the five components, should enable the auditor to rely on the work of others, rotate audit focus, and design audit strategies and procedures that are commensurate with the internal control risk environment.

- *Evaluating the effectiveness of the audit committee's oversight of the company's external financial reporting and internal control over financial reporting*

We agree that an effective audit committee is an important monitoring control and is essential in maintaining an effective control environment. Accordingly, effective audit committee oversight is yet another control expected in the overall internal control framework. Therefore, in our opinion, the specific requirement that the external auditor evaluate the effectiveness of the audit committee's oversight of the company's external financial reporting and internal control over financial reporting is unnecessary. Furthermore, because the audit committee is charged with oversight of the auditor, including their appointment, compensation, and dismissal, this relationship could preclude the auditor from making an unbiased evaluation.

Additionally, we do not believe it is appropriate for the auditor to evaluate aspects of the audit committee where there is no measurable criteria (e.g., amount of time the audit committee devotes to control issues), or require the auditor to evaluate aspects of the audit committee for which the board of directors has already performed (e.g., independence of audit committee members from management, committee's compliance with listing standards, whether the committee includes a financial expert).

We believe the audit committee is best evaluated by the board of directors.

- *Definitions and reporting of significant deficiency and material weakness in internal control over financial reporting*

  Under the proposed standard, a significant deficiency or material weakness can exist as either a single deficiency or a combination of deficiencies. In our opinion, the definitions as worded, could guide the auditor to evaluate a single internal control deficiency as a significant deficiency or material weakness without regard to the entire internal control framework or other mitigating controls. We urge the Board to recognize that an effective internal control framework consists of numerous, interrelated control activities and processes and that a single control is seldom effective on a standalone basis. Rather, the effectiveness of controls depends on all five components of the control framework.

  Furthermore, we believe the terms *"more than inconsequential"* and *"more than remote"* unreasonably lower the bar, vis-à-vis FAS No. 5, in evaluating whether control deficiencies represent reportable conditions. In our opinion, terms used in the definitions in paragraphs 7 through 9 of the standard should be more closely aligned with FAS No. 5.

*   *   *   *   *

We welcome the opportunity to discuss these issues at your convenience. If you have questions regarding this letter, please contact Mr. Ali Bahaj at (309) 675-4212.

Sincerely,

Ali M. Bahaj
Vice President
Auditing & Compliance Division
Caterpillar Inc.

Attachment I
Responses to Specific Questions

Questions regarding an integrated audit of the financial statements and internal control over financial reporting:

1. *Is it appropriate to refer to the auditor's attestation of management's assessment of the effectiveness of internal control over financial reporting as the audit of internal control over financial reporting?*

   No, we believe that if Congress intended for the external auditor to perform an "audit" of internal controls, Section 404(b) of the Sarbanes-Oxley Act ("the Act") would have been so written. In our opinion, the scope of the auditor's work was intended to be an attestation of management's assertion of the process used to evaluate the effectiveness of internal controls; not an audit of internal controls. Requiring the same level of assurance from both management and the auditor will unnecessarily require significant and duplicative work.

   In its report (Report 107-205) of major provisions of the Act, The Committee on Banking, Housing and Urban Affairs states that, "In requiring the registered public accounting firm preparing the audit report to attest to and report on management's assessment of internal controls, the Committee does not intend that the auditor's evaluation be the subject of a separate engagement or the basis for increased charges or fees." Prior to the Board's issuance of the proposed audit standard, Financial Executives International reported that, "In this new regulatory environment, companies will have to add financial staff and pay significantly higher auditing fees - projected at 20 percent to 200 percent over pre-Enron/Andersen fees."

2. *Should the auditor be prohibited from performing an audit of internal control over financial reporting without also performing an audit of the financial statements?*

   We believe the auditor should perform both an attestation of management's assertions regarding internal control and perform the audit of the financial statements.

3. *Rather than requiring the auditor to also complete an audit of the financial statements, would an appropriate alternative be to require the auditor to perform work with regard to the financial statements comparable to that required to complete the financial statement audit?*

   As stated in the response to question two above, we believe the same auditor should perform both an attestation of management's assertions regarding internal control and perform an audit of the financial statements.

Question regarding the costs and benefits of internal control:

4. *Does the Board's proposed standard give appropriate consideration to how internal control is implemented in, and how the audit of internal control over financial reporting should be conducted at, small and medium-sized issuers?*

> We appreciate that the Board acknowledges internal control is not "one-size-fits-all," and, to a great extent, depends on the size and complexity of the company. However, as evidenced by proposed restrictions placed on the external auditor's reliance on management, we do not believe the standard gives appropriate consideration or importance to a strong control environment ("tone-at-the-top") and sophistication and competence of management, including internal audit, which may be present in larger companies.

Question regarding the audit of internal control over financial reporting:

5. *Should the Board, generally or in this proposed standard, specify the level of competence and training of the audit personnel that is necessary to perform specified auditing procedures effectively? For example, it would be inappropriate for a new, inexperienced auditor to have primary responsibility for conducting interviews of a company's senior management about possible fraud.*

> No, we believe that existing attestation and audit standards provide sufficient guidance in the supervision of audit personnel. We believe that penalties to audit firms provide sufficient incentive to ensure their personnel possess the necessary professional competencies and training to conduct attestation engagements.

Questions regarding evaluation of management's assessment:

6. *Is the scope of the audit appropriate in that it requires the auditor to both evaluate management's assessment and obtain, directly, evidence about whether internal control over financial reporting is effective?*

> No. Please refer to our response to question 1. We do not believe that the auditor should provide the same level of assurance as management. We believe the collaborative effort of the external auditor, internal auditor and management provides investor the broadest, most cost-efficient assurance regarding a company's system of internal accounting controls.

7. *Is it appropriate that the Board has provided criteria that auditors should use to evaluate the adequacy of management's documentation?*

> We believe the Board has provided an appropriate level of criteria to enable the auditor to exercise judgment in evaluating the adequacy of management's documentation.

8. *Is it appropriate to state that inadequate documentation is an internal control deficiency, the severity of which the auditor should evaluate? Or should inadequate documentation automatically rise to the level of significant deficiency or material weakness in internal control?*

> We believe the auditor should be permitted to evaluate whether the absence of documentation represents an internal control deficiency. The absence of internal control procedural documentation does not alone represent a deficiency that would lead to misstated financial statements. However, the absence of management's evidential documentation that controls are operating effectively, could call into question the validity of management's assertion. In our opinion, neither the absence of procedural documentation nor the absence of evidential documentation represent de facto evidence those internal controls are non-existent or ineffective.

> We believe the absence of documentation represents a <u>potential</u> internal control deficiency that the auditor should evaluate to determine whether the severity warrants elevation to significant deficiency or material weakness.

Questions regarding obtaining an understanding of internal control over financial reporting:

9. *Are the objectives to be achieved by performing walkthroughs sufficient to require the performance of walkthroughs?*

> We agree that walkthroughs are an extremely effective and necessary procedure in identifying and understanding the operation of internal controls in complex transaction systems. However, we believe the auditor should be permitted to exercise professional judgment in selecting and designing audit procedures and testing strategies.

10. *Is it appropriate to require that the walkthrough be performed by the auditor himself or herself, rather than allowing the auditor to use walkthrough procedures performed by management, internal auditors or others?*

> We do not believe the external auditor should be precluded from relying on the results of walkthrough procedures conducted by others, such as a competent internal audit function or even management. In addition, paragraph 101 of the standard appears to preclude the year-to-year rotation of audit procedures. We do not agree that full, detailed walkthrough procedures be conducted annually, if the auditor is satisfied, through inquiry and validation, that process change controls and IT general controls over processes and systems are operating effectively.

Question regarding testing operating effectiveness:

11. Is it appropriate to require the auditor to obtain evidence of the effectiveness of controls for all relevant assertions for all significant accounts and disclosures every year or may the auditor use some of the audit evidence obtained in previous years to support his or her current opinion on management's assessment?

> Again, we believe the auditor should be permitted to exercise professional judgment in determining the nature, timing and extent of audit procedures. One factor used by the auditor is the cumulative knowledge and evidence obtained in previous years.
>
> In addition, we believe an effective internal control framework should include process change controls. Therefore, we believe evidence of the effectiveness of controls can be efficiently obtained every year if the auditor is satisfied, through inquiry and validation testing, that process change controls and IT general controls over processes and systems are operating effectively.

Questions regarding using the work of management and others:

12. To what extent should the auditor be permitted or required to use the work of management and others?

> We are sensitive to the need for the external auditor to maintain an "arms-length" relationship with management. However, we believe the Auditor Independence provisions of Title II of the Act will achieve the desired relationship. We believe restrictions placed on the external auditor in paragraphs 103–110 are not sensitive to the public company representative's concerns voiced at the Board's July 29 roundtable discussions. In our opinion, paragraphs 103-110 represent the most onerous provisions of the standard and will cause a significant and unnecessary duplication of effort.
>
> We understand the work of others should not replace the work of the external auditor, in whole or in part. Rather, we believe that the external auditor should be able to attest to management's assertion on the effectiveness of internal controls by understanding management's evaluation process through auditor testing on a sample basis and through re-performing work conducted by management and internal auditors on a sample basis.
>
> Furthermore, internal auditors performing their work in accordance with the Institute of Internal Auditors' Standards for the Professional Practice of Internal Auditing should be relied upon, by the external auditor, to conduct their work with competence and objectivity. Of course, we recognize the external auditor will be required to re-perform certain work of internal audit to develop a basis on which to judge the internal auditors' competence and objectivity.

13. Are the three categories of controls and the extent to which the auditor may rely on the work of others appropriately defined?

> We believe the three categories outlined by the Board are appropriate. However, as stated in our cover letter and in our response to question 12 above, we believe paragraphs 104-106 of the Standard unnecessarily restrict the external auditor's use of others' work.

> We believe the external auditor, subject to his/her professional judgment and direction, should be able to use the results of controls testing performed by internal auditors, and to a large extent, by management. For example, we believe internal audit can competently and objectively carry out audit tests of those areas specifically restricted by the standard including: fraud controls, controls over period-end financial reporting, IT general controls, walkthroughs, significant non-routine and non-systematic transactions, and controls over significant accounts where the external auditor has assessed the risk of failure as high.

14. Does the proposed standard give appropriate recognition to the work of internal auditors? If not, does the proposed standard place too much emphasis and preference on the work of internal auditors or not enough?

> As stated in our cover letter and in responses to questions 12 and 13 above, we do not believe the standard permits enough reliance on the work performed by internal auditors and creates unnecessary duplication of work between the internal and external auditors.

> Furthermore, the monitoring component of an effective internal framework should include an internal audit function. If, through adequate re-performance of a sample of their work, the external auditor has judged the internal auditors to be competent and objective, then the external auditor should be permitted to use the work of internal auditors.

15. Is the flexibility in determining the extent of reperformance of the work of others appropriate, or should the auditor be specifically required to reperform a certain level of work (for example, reperform tests of all significant accounts or reperform every test performed by others that the auditor intends to use)?

> We agree the auditor should have the flexibility in determining the extent of reperformance of the work of others. However, consistent with our responses to questions 10-14, we believe the Standard does not permit the auditor enough latitude in applying professional judgment to the design and execution of audit procedures. We believe Congress did not intend for compliance with the Act to increase audit fees. Therefore, we believe the Standard should allow for more flexibility in reperformance.

16. *Is the requirement for the auditor to obtain the principle evidence, on an overall basis, through his or her own work the appropriate benchmark for the amount of work that is required to be performed by the auditor?*

Again, the auditor should be permitted to exercise professional judgment in determining the evidence necessary to attest to management's assertion on the effectiveness of internal controls. It is the auditor's responsibility to evaluate the credibility of the evidence obtained. If this concept remains in the final standard, "principle evidence" should be better defined.

Questions regarding evaluating results:

17. *Will the definitions in the proposed standard of significant deficiency and material weakness provide for increased consistency in the evaluation of deficiencies? How can the definitions be improved?*

We believe that definitions are necessary. However, we believe the terms "more than remote likelihood" and "more than inconsequential in amount" significantly lower the bar for determining when and internal control deficiency is considered significant vis-à-vis existing authoritative literature – FAS 5. We see no reason for the proposed standard definitions to differ from FAS 5. Again, we believe the auditor should use professional judgment in determining whether an internal control deficiency is a reportable condition.

18. *Do the examples in Appendix D of how to apply these definitions in various scenarios provide helpful guidance? Are there other specific examples that commenters could suggest that would provide further interpretive help?*

We agree the examples in Appendix D are helpful in applying the definitions of material weakness and significant deficiency. However, the examples do not demonstrate how other components of the internal control framework could help to mitigate weaknesses in control activities or minimize the likelihood of significant deficiencies or material weaknesses.

19. *Is it necessary for the auditor to evaluate the severity of all identified internal control deficiencies?*

Yes, it is essential the auditor evaluate the severity of all identified internal control deficiencies. However, deficiencies should not be evaluated as a standalone control but rather in the context of all five components of the control framework and in relation to company-level controls and mitigating controls.

20. Is it appropriate to require the auditor to communicate all internal control deficiencies (not just material weaknesses and significant deficiencies) to management in writing?

> Currently, our external auditor reports internal control weaknesses noted while conducting the financial statement audit. We believe it is appropriate for the auditor to report internal control deficiencies that warrant the attention of management. However, we believe it is unnecessary for the auditor to report internal control deficiencies that management is already aware of or is addressing via remedial actions.

21. Are the matters that the Board has classified as strong indicators that a material weakness in internal control exists appropriately classified as such?

> We agree that most of the matters identified by the Board represent strong indicators, but not represent de facto evidence, that a potential material weakness in internal control may exist.

22. Is it appropriate to require the auditors to evaluate the effectiveness of the audit committee's oversight of the company's external financial reporting and internal control over financial reporting?

> We agree that an effective audit committee is an important monitoring control and is essential in maintaining an effective control environment. Accordingly, effective audit committee oversight is yet another control expected in the overall internal control framework. Therefore, in our opinion, the <u>specific requirement</u> that the external auditor evaluate the effectiveness of the audit committee's oversight of the company's external financial reporting and internal control over financial reporting is unnecessary.

> In addition, we believe this provision could be construed a conflict of interest for the auditor. Because the audit committee is charged with oversight of the auditor, including appointment, dismissal and compensation, this conflicting interest could bias the external auditor's evaluation of the audit committee.

> In addition, we believe the criteria, outlined in paragraph 57 of the standard, against which the external auditor is expected to evaluate the audit committee, are either immeasurable or already performed by the board of directors.

> We believe the audit committee is best evaluated by the board of directors.

23. Will auditors be able to effectively carry out their responsibility to evaluate the effectiveness of the audit committee's oversight?

> No. Please refer to our response to question 22. In addition, audit committee members' expertise and background is varied and broad generally well exceeding that of the auditor. Accordingly, the auditor would only be able to evaluate the audit committee on an incomplete set of criteria.

24. If the auditor concludes that ineffective audit committee oversight is a material weakness, rather than require the auditor to issue an adverse opinion with regard to the effectiveness of the internal control over financial reporting, should the standard require the auditor to withdraw from the audit engagement?

> No. Please refer to our response to question 23. We do not believe the auditor is in a position to objectively evaluate the audit committee.
>
> If the requirement of the auditor to evaluate the effectiveness of the audit committee survives the final standard, we believe the decision whether to withdrawal from the engagement should be at the auditor's discretion. Furthermore, we believe it is inappropriate to presuppose the severity of ineffective audit committee oversight as warranting withdrawal from an engagement vis-à-vis other material weaknesses.

Questions regarding forming an opinion and reporting:

25. Is it appropriate that the existence of a material weakness would require the auditor to express an adverse conclusion about the effectiveness of the company's internal control over financial reporting, consistent with the required reporting model for management?

> Yes, we believe it is appropriate for the auditor to express an adverse opinion on the effectiveness of the company's internal controls if a material weakness exists. However, this conclusion is only appropriate if the auditor is not satisfied that other controls within the five components of the control framework have not effectively mitigated the weakness. In addition, an adverse opinion is inappropriate if management remedies the weakness before the date of management's assertion.

26. *Are there circumstances where a qualified "except for" conclusion would be appropriate?*

> Yes. For example, we believe that outsourcing a significant service or a material acquisition, particularly a non-U.S. company, in the fourth quarter would not allow sufficient time for management to assess, and the auditor to attest, as to the internal controls of the acquired company. In these examples, a qualified opinion would be appropriate.

27. *Do you agree with the position that when the auditor issues a non-standard opinion, such as an adverse opinion, that the auditor's opinion should speak directly to the effectiveness of the internal control over financial reporting rather than to whether management's assessment is fairly stated?*

> If the auditor concurs with management, we believe the auditor's report should refer to whether management's assessment is fairly stated. If however, the auditor does not concur with management, then the auditor's opinion should speak directly to the effectiveness of internal control over financial reporting.

Questions regarding auditor independence:

28. *Should the Board provide specific guidance on independence and internal control-related non-audit services in the context of this proposed standard?*

> Yes, additional guidance may be helpful.

29. *Are there any specific internal control-related non-audit services the auditor should be prohibited from providing to an audit client?*

> We believe the external auditor should be prohibited from designing and implementing internal controls that have a significant impact over financial reporting.

Questions regarding auditor's responsibilities with regard to management's certifications:

30. *Are the auditor's differing levels of responsibility as they relate to management's quarterly certifications versus the annual (fourth quarter) certification, appropriate?*

> Yes, we believe the limited scope the auditor's responsibility related to management's quarterly certifications are appropriate. However, we believe the scope of the auditor's work should be limited to inquiry of management and review of internal audit reports. We do not believe it is practicable for the auditor to observe whether significant changes in internal control have occurred over significant accounts each quarter.

31. Is the scope of the auditor's responsibility for quarterly disclosures about the internal control over financial reporting appropriate?

> Please refer to our response to question 30 above. We believe the scope of the auditor's quarterly procedures should be limited to inquiry.

¶ 623. Citigroup

citigroup

William P. Hannon   Citigroup Inc.
Controller   399 Park Avenue
                             New York, NY 10022

                             Tel. 212 793 4514
                             Fax 212 793 4508

William P. Hannon
Controller
Citigroup Inc.
399 Park Avenue - 3rd Floor
New York, NY 10043

November 21, 2003

Office of the Secretary
Public Company Accounting Oversight Board
1666 K Street N.W.
Washington, D.C. 20006-2803

Re: PCAOB Rulemaking Docket Matter No. 008 – Proposed Auditing Standard – An Audit of Internal Control Over Financial Reporting Performed in Conjunction with an Audit of Financial Statements

Ladies and Gentlemen:

Citigroup Inc. appreciates the opportunity to comment on the Public Company Accounting Oversight Board's (the "Board" or "PCAOB") Proposed Auditing Standard – An Audit of Internal Control Over Financial Reporting Performed in Conjunction with an Audit of Financial Statements. Citigroup is supportive of the Board's efforts to establish professional standards governing the independent auditor's attestation and reporting on management's assessment of the effectiveness of internal control.

We agree with the overall objective of the proposed standard, and believe that a new auditing standard will assist a company's independent auditors in reporting on management's assessment of the effectiveness of internal control. However, as explained more fully below, we believe that certain aspects of the proposed standard should be reconsidered. In general, we believe that the standard is too prescriptive and that independent auditors must have significantly more flexibility to determine the nature and scope of their testing, including the extent of their reliance on the work of others, in order to form an opinion on the effectiveness of a company's internal controls. We are particularly troubled that the proposed standard does not adequately recognize the benefits of a strong internal audit function.

The accounting abuses which led to the Sarbanes-Oxley Act and this proposed auditing standard resulted from the breakdown of key controls over high-risk areas of financial reporting. By prescribing limits on the extent to which the auditor can use the work of management and others, the proposed standard draws the auditor's attention and resources away from areas of high audit risk to areas that, for many companies with sophisticated systems, would otherwise be deemed to represent low audit risks (e.g., internal controls related to certain routine and recurring period-end financial reporting processes).

Using the Work of Management and Others

The proposed standard prescribes certain circumstances where the independent auditor would be precluded from using the results of testing performed by management and others. These prohibitions include:

(1) Controls that are part of the control environment, including controls specifically established to prevent and detect fraud that is reasonably likely to result in material misstatement of the financial statements;

(2) Controls over the period-end financial reporting process, including controls over procedures used to enter transaction totals into the general ledger; to initiate, record, and process journal entries in the general ledger; and to record recurring and nonrecurring adjustments to the financial statements (for example, consolidating adjustments, report combinations, and reclassifications);

(3) Controls that have a pervasive effect on the financial statements, such as certain information technology general controls on which the operating effectiveness of other controls depend; and,

(4) The proposed auditing standard would not allow the auditor to use the work performed by management or others to satisfy the requirement to perform walkthroughs.

Additionally, the proposed standard prescribes two areas where the independent auditor's use of the results of procedures performed by management and others should be limited:

(1) Controls over significant non-routine and nonsystematic transactions (such as accounts involving significant judgments and estimates); and,

(2) Controls over significant accounts, processes or disclosures where the auditor has assessed the risk of failure of the controls to operate effectively as high.

The specific internal controls in place, the inherent risks underlying those controls, and the competency of management, internal audit and others in reviewing and testing those controls, may vary greatly from company to company. The limitations and prohibitions the proposed standard places on the use of the work of management, internal audit and others, are unduly focused on specific types of controls without regard to the risks inherent in those controls. As a result, the proposed standard requires excessive independent testing by the auditor where the inherent audit risk might be deemed low. The standard should place more emphasis on the identification of those controls that represent the greatest audit risk and focus on the independent auditor's exercise of professional judgment in assessing those controls. The proposed standard should be amended to permit the independent auditor to use the work of management and others based on their assessment of the risks being reviewed, their understanding of the control environment, and the competency of the party performing the primary work. Furthermore, the auditor should be permitted to reduce the scope of their testing in favor of the work of others in recurring audits of those controls, especially where those controls are deemed to have low inherent risk. This will promote a more effective and efficient audit, particularly for large and complex organizations.

Limitations related to routine processes

We believe that the limitations related to the period-end financial reporting process, including controls over procedures used to enter transaction totals into the general ledger; to initiate, record, and process journal entries in the general ledger; and to record recurring and nonrecurring adjustments to the financial statements, are unduly restrictive. In paragraph 106, the proposed standard supports the independent auditor's use of the work of management and others to assess controls over the routine processing of significant accounts and disclosures, without specific limitation. For a company with sophisticated systems, the controls over the period-end financial reporting process are basic and routine and we believe that the limitations on the independent auditor's use of the work of management and others are contradictory to the guidance in paragraph 106. These controls are extensively reviewed, monitored and tested by management and internal audit. The blanket limitations related to the routine processes noted above will result in an excessive amount of work for the independent auditor in areas where it would be more sensible and efficient to use the work of others. We believe that the independent auditor should have full discretion in terms of their use of the work of others in these areas, particularly where the inherent audit risks are deemed low.

Limitations related to non-routine and non-systematic transactions

We believe that the limitation related to significant non-routine and nonsystematic transactions (such as accounts involving significant judgments and estimates) is too restrictive. Such controls could encompass a broad spectrum of activities with varying levels of audit risk. Certainly, the audit risks inherent in many such controls require that the auditor perform the primary work, but the assessment of other controls with lower audit risk should be subject to the auditor's discretion. The proposed standard indicates that the reliance on the work of management and others in such circumstances should be "limited", but there is no explanation of what "limited" means. We believe that the independent auditor should evaluate each type of transaction and, using their professional judgment, determine the scope of their work and the extent of their testing based on their knowledge of related internal controls, documentation of processes, the competence of company personnel involved and the auditor's overall familiarity with these non-routine and non-systematic transactions.

Limitation related to walkthroughs

While Citigroup supports the notion that walkthroughs are important, their extent and timing should be left to the judgment of the auditor. The proposed standard does not allow the independent auditor to use the work performed by management or others to satisfy the requirement to perform walkthroughs. Walkthroughs are described as encompassing the entire process of initiating, recording, processing and reporting individual transactions, and controls for all five internal control components and fraud. We believe that this limitation is too broad in scope and that it will lead to the independent auditor's duplicating the work of internal audit in many cases. The limitation also fails to recognize that where certain processes are static it is not efficient or cost effective to prohibit using the work of management and others. In a large and complex organization, this limitation will place an overwhelming burden on the auditor that will draw their resources away from addressing more substantive issues where the audit risk is greater. We believe that the independent auditor should be permitted to use their professional judgment in determining where it is appropriate to use the work of internal audit and others to complete a walkthrough of controls. At the very least, the standard should permit the auditor to rotate its walkthrough testing, alternating with the internal auditor, so that the auditor can focus on areas of change and higher risk.

Limitations related to the work of internal audit

We are particularly troubled that the proposed standard does not adequately recognize the benefits of a strong internal audit function. The independent auditor should be able to place considerable reliance on the work of internal auditors if internal audit is sufficiently independent of management, has a strong reporting relationship directly with the audit committee and performs appropriate tests of controls. In a large and complex multi-national company such as Citigroup, the internal audit function performs a critical role in assessing the company's internal controls. At Citigroup, the internal audit group includes more than 700 professional audit staff who perform an independent and objective review of the Company's operations and procedures and report their findings to management and the audit committee. Their work includes a rigorous assessment of the Company's risk and control environment through the evaluation of financial, operational, and administrative controls; risk management practices; and adherence with laws, regulations and company policies. During 2003, Citigroup's internal audit group is expected to spend approximately 1,000,000 hours performing their work, including approximately 175,000 hours reviewing and testing technology operations with the majority covering information technology general controls. The internal audit function is independent of management and reports directly to the audit committee. Internal audit has no authority or responsibility for the activities it audits. Additionally, they neither develop nor install systems or procedures, prepare records, or engage in any other activity that would normally be audited.

As noted above, the independent auditors are limited from using the work of internal audit with respect to walkthroughs and in the assessment of certain important processes including the assessment of controls over the period-end financial reporting process, over procedures used to enter transaction totals into the general ledger; to initiate, record, and process journal entries in the general ledger; and to record recurring and nonrecurring adjustments to the financial statements. These functions are generally not where audit risk lies. The proposed standard also prohibits the use of the work of internal auditors in the testing of certain information technology general controls on which the operating effectiveness of other controls depends. However, in paragraph 108, the proposed standard acknowledges that, "Internal auditors would normally be expected to have greater competence with regard to internal control over financial reporting and objectivity than other company personnel. Therefore, the auditor may be able to use the results of their procedures to a greater extent than the results of procedures performed by others. This is particularly true in the case of internal auditors who follow the International Standards for the Professional Practice of Internal Auditing issued by the Institute of Internal Auditors. At companies where the importance of the internal audit function results in a high degree of competence and objectivity and their work is extensive, the auditor could use their work to the greatest extent an auditor could use the work of others."

We are very concerned that the limitations imposed by the proposed standard do not recognize the competency and objectivity of the internal audit function and the significant amount of effort this group puts forth in performing their duties. It seems irrational that our internal audit group will perform approximately 175,000 hours auditing technology operations including IT general controls, and the proposed standard would preclude the independent auditor from using that work. These limitations will only serve to marginalize the efforts of the internal audit function to the detriment of the overall control environment. In determining the extent to which they will use the work of internal audit, the independent auditor should determine whether the internal audit function is independent of management, if they are qualified to do the work and whether the scope of their testing is adequate. Regardless of the work done by the independent auditor, management will continue to require internal audit's attention to these areas. This will result in a duplication of effort and significant additional cost with no real benefit. In order for management to complete its assessment of internal controls, management and internal audit are necessarily involved in the review and testing of critical areas, and we feel strongly that the independent auditors should have the flexibility to consider those efforts when determining the scope of their testing.

Requirement for the Auditor's Work to Provide the Principal Evidence for the Audit Opinion

In addition to the limitations described above, the proposed standard requires that, on an overall basis, the auditor's own work must provide the principal evidence for the audit opinion (paragraph 109). It is unclear what is meant by "principal evidence". Since internal controls may affect many individual account balances and related financial statement disclosures, it is difficult to relate the testing of a particular internal control to the either the size of an individual account balance, a particular disclosure or the financial statements taken as a whole. Moreover, when any level of reliance is placed on the work of others it may be impossible to assert that the independent auditor has met the "principal evidence" threshold. Should "principal evidence" be measured in terms of hours worked, the number of individual transactions tested, or the size of individual items tested? Should it be measured in terms of individual account balances at a point in time affected by a particular control or is it somehow measured by the risk inherent in a particular control?

We believe that it will not be possible to measure in a meaningful way the testing performed by the independent auditor against the work performed by management and others to determine whether the independent auditor's own work has provided the principal evidence for the audit opinion. This is particularly true since the independent auditor, management, internal audit and others will be assessing internal controls with varying levels of inherent risk that affect the same individual account balances. For a large, complex company such as Citigroup, we believe that achieving the level of "principal evidence" that is required by the proposed standard (regardless of how that is measured), will necessitate that the independent auditor perform an unreasonable amount of testing in light of the extensive work performed by the internal audit group and management. At a high level, the concept of "principal evidence" may be relevant to the question of whether to base the opinion in part on the report of another auditor, but is not operable in respect of the interrelated controls that may be tested by both the auditor and others. We believe that the requirement that the independent auditor's own work provide the principal evidence for the audit opinion should be removed from the standard as it is inoperable and is likely to cause considerable confusion. The primary consideration should be whether the overall scope and nature of the work performed supports the audit opinion, and we believe the standard provides sufficient guidance for the independent auditor to plan and perform the audit to obtain reasonable assurance about the effectiveness of internal control without the "principal evidence" requirement.

Use of a Service Auditor's Report

The proposed standard directs an auditor to determine whether management has evaluated the operating effectiveness of controls based on procedures sufficient to assess their operating effectiveness. Such procedures include the use of a service auditor's report. However, the proposed standard does not provide adequate guidance with respect to which service auditor reports are required and how often the reports should be obtained. With respect to financial statement audit reports, SAS 70 provides guidance as to the level of review and the types of service organizations that should be reviewed during an audit of financial statements. SAS 70 states that the significance of the controls of the service organization to those of the user organization depends on the nature of the services provided by the service organization, the nature and materiality of the transactions it processes for the user organization and the degree of interaction between the service organization's activities and those of the user organization. We encourage the Board to adopt similar guidance, as we believe that concepts of materiality of the controls related to service organizations and "facts and circumstances" determinations are appropriate to promote efficient and effective audits of internal control. We believe that an auditor should be permitted to limit his or her review to those service organizations providing services likely to have a material impact on the financial statements.

Furthermore, in the case of service organizations located where U.S. auditing standards are not applied, SAS 70 reports may not be available. We believe the Board should permit the use of comparable reports under non-U.S. generally accepted auditing standards.

Definitions of "Significant Deficiency" and "Material Weakness"

The Board is likely to receive many comments on the proposed standard's definitions of "significant deficiency" and "material weakness" because these definitions represent a lower threshold for reporting internal control deficiencies than the current definitions established in AU §325. These definitions are critical not only because of the reporting requirements they carry, but also because of the resources a company must employ to implement corrective action. As discussed in more detail below, we believe the proposed thresholds for identifying a significant deficiency and a material weakness are too low and this will cause management and the audit committee to focus limited company resources on issues that represent lower risks to financial reporting and may otherwise be sufficiently mitigated by compensating controls.

The proposed standard states that an internal control deficiency exists when the design or operation of a control does not allow management or employees, in the normal course of performing their assigned functions, to prevent or detect misstatements on a timely basis. A "significant deficiency" is defined as an internal control deficiency (or a combination of internal control deficiencies) that, by itself or in combination with other internal control deficiencies, results in **more than a remote likelihood** that a misstatement of the company's annual or interim financial statements that is **more than inconsequential in amount** will not be prevented or detected. We believe that the threshold for identifying a significant deficiency is too low. Clearly the Board did not intend that every internal control deficiency should be considered a significant deficiency, however, we see very little space between the two. In practical terms, it will be very difficult to assert that any internal control deficiency does not meet the "more than a remote likelihood" and "more than inconsequential in amount" thresholds.

We would agree that management should address all internal control deficiencies. However, we are concerned the definitions as proposed present such a low threshold that management and the auditor may report items to the audit committee that are not indicators of "significant deficiencies", but are more recommendations of best practices or deficiencies that are otherwise sufficiently mitigated by compensating controls. In a large and complex organization with worldwide operations and multiple product offerings, certain internal control deficiencies that in the opinion of management and the auditors do not present a significant risk to the consolidated company will nonetheless be reported as "significant deficiencies". We believe that it will be more effective to provide a greater distinction between internal control deficiencies and significant deficiencies so that senior management and the audit committee can focus resources on those issues that warrant more attention. With this in mind, we suggest the Board consider adopting a threshold for identifying significant deficiencies that is at least "reasonably possible" as described in FAS 5.

The PCAOB has introduced the term "more than inconsequential" in the definition of a significant deficiency. We believe this is a new term in accounting literature and, as such, the proposed standard should provide guidance on how to determine if an amount is "more than inconsequential". In order to ensure that the audit committee's attention and company resources are focused on the most important internal control issues, we suggest that the Board adopt a definition such as "significant, but less than material".

We are also concerned that the definition of a "material weakness" is inconsistent with the definition of that term under the SEC's final rules relating to management's assessment of the effectiveness of internal control over financial reporting. The SEC's Section 404 Release refers to SAS 60 when defining a "material weakness". The SEC's Release states, "a "material weakness" is defined in Statement on Auditing Standards No. 60 (codified in Codification of Statements on Auditing Standards AU §325) as a reportable condition in which the design or operation of one or more of the internal control components does not reduce to a **relatively low level** the risk that misstatements caused by errors or fraud in amounts that would be material in relation to the financial statements being audited may occur and not be detected within a timely period by employees in the normal course of performing their assigned functions." In contrast, the proposed standard defines a "material weakness" as "a significant deficiency that, by itself, or in combination with other significant deficiencies, results in a more than a **remote likelihood** that a material misstatement of the annual or interim financial statements will not be prevented or detected." The difference between a "remote likelihood" and a "relatively low level" creates the possibility that there could be a difference in the application of the final auditing standard and the SEC's Release. We believe that the definition in the proposed standard will be difficult to reconcile with the definition in the SEC's Release. Accordingly, we believe that the proposed standard should adopt the existing AU §325 definitions of a material weakness and a significant deficiency (reportable weakness).

Identifying Significant Deficiencies

The proposed standard provides a list of certain circumstances that should be regarded as at least a significant deficiency in internal control and strong indicators that a material weakness in internal control exists. As indicated in paragraph 126 of the proposed standard, such circumstances include:

- Restatement of previously issued financial statements to reflect the correction of a misstatement.

- Identification by the auditor of a material misstatement in financial statements in the current period that was not initially identified by the company's internal control over financial reporting. (This is still a strong indicator of a material weakness even if management subsequently corrects the misstatement.)

- Oversight of the company's external financial reporting and internal control over financial reporting by the company's audit committee is ineffective. (Paragraphs 56 through 59 present factors to evaluate when determining whether the audit committee is ineffective.)

- For larger, more complex entities, the internal audit function or the risk assessment function is ineffective.

- For complex entities in highly regulated industries, an ineffective regulatory compliance function.

- Identification of fraud of any magnitude on the part of senior management.

- Significant deficiencies that have been communicated to management and the audit committee remain uncorrected after some reasonable period of time.

We believe that it is not appropriate to include such a list in the final standard. This list may be intended to create a bright-line standard for identifying significant deficiencies, but, in practice, we believe it will force the reporting of certain issues that do not rise to the level of a significant deficiency in the opinion of management and the independent auditor. Certain items on the list are vague and could be subject to a broad interpretation. For example, several of the items use the term "ineffective" which is not adequately defined in the proposed standard. We agree that the items on this list could easily rise to the level of a significant deficiency and even a material weakness. However, since the circumstances surrounding any of the items on this list and the potential impact on the internal control environment will vary for every company, we believe it is not appropriate to create such a bright-line for reporting significant deficiencies. We feel that the final standard should not include any specific list of deficiencies, significant deficiencies or material weaknesses.

Consideration of Regulatory Compliance in the Assessment of Internal Control

The proposed standard states that the operations and compliance with laws and regulations directly related to the presentation of and required disclosures in financial statements are encompassed in internal control over financial reporting. Where a company operates in highly regulated industries as Citigroup does, the consideration of compliance includes many areas that are directly related to financial reporting and many areas that are not. For example, sales practices, privacy standards, staff licensing requirements, and trade supervision are important areas of regulatory compliance, but they are not directly related to financial reporting. While such areas may be subject to review under other laws and regulations, we believe that these areas of regulatory compliance that are not directly related to financial reporting should be outside the scope of the proposed standard. Paragraph 126 of the proposed standard is written very broadly, indicating that for complex entities in highly regulated industries, an ineffective regulatory compliance function would be regarded as at least a significant internal control deficiency. We are concerned that this paragraph does not distinguish those areas of regulatory compliance that relate to financial reporting from the areas that do not. As written, this paragraph seems to imply that the independent auditor is required to perform an assessment of controls that are not directly related to financial reporting. There is no such requirement under the SEC's Release or this proposed standard and the auditor might not be in a position to determine if controls unrelated to financial reporting are effective. Notwithstanding our comment above regarding the list of significant deficiencies in paragraph 126, we recommend that the standard be amended to clarify that only regulatory compliance directly related to financial reporting is within the scope of the standard.

Reporting of "Except For" Conclusions

The Board has asked whether there are circumstances where a qualified "except for" conclusion would be appropriate. As the Board noted, the SEC's final rules implementing Section 404 state, "Management is not permitted to conclude that the registrant's internal control over financial

---

reporting is effective if there are one or more material weaknesses in the registrant's internal control over financial reporting." We do not believe this precludes an "except for" conclusion.

There are certain circumstances where management and the independent auditor will not have an opportunity to assess the internal controls of a part of a company, particularly with respect to acquisitions that take place close to the reporting date. This will be a particular issue in acquisitions of certain non-public US companies and foreign companies that have not been subject to the requirements of Section 404. We believe that the inability to assess the internal control environment of a recently acquired business is not, by itself, indicative of a significant deficiency or a material weakness in internal control. In such circumstances, management should be permitted a reasonable amount of time, given the size and complexity of the acquired business, to assess the internal controls of the acquired company and the independent auditor should be permitted to issue an opinion that is "except for" the acquired business.

Audit Committee Pre-Approval of Internal Control-Related Services

The proposed standard expands the SEC's auditor independence rules related to pre-approval of non-audit services by requiring that any non-audit service related to internal control be specifically pre-approved by the audit committee, rather than being pre-approved as part of a category of non-audit services related to internal control.

The audits of internal control, in many cases, are required by regulators in the U.S. and overseas. In a large complex organization, there can be hundreds of such reviews required each year. The audits are normally part of the financial statement audit, or a separate engagement specifically for the purpose of issuing an opinion on the effectiveness of the internal control environment (FDICIA or SAS 70 reviews are two examples). To require the pre-approval of the audit committee for each and every internal control review would place undue burden on the audit committee. A specifically pre-approved limit for these type of reviews delegated to senior management would be more appropriate.

Documentation Standards

The proposed standard in paragraph 43 defines the standards for the external auditor to determine whether management's documentation provides reasonable support for its assessment of internal control effectiveness. The standard would dictate the exact items that the auditor would look for including:

- Design of controls over relevant assertions related to all significant accounts and disclosures in the financial statements, including all five components in paragraph 50.

- Information about how significant transactions are initiated, recorded, processed, and reported.

- Enough information about the flow of transactions to identify where material misstatements due to error or fraud could occur.

- Controls designed to prevent or detect fraud, including who performs the controls and the related segregation of duties.

- Controls over the safeguarding of assets.

- The results of management's testing and evaluation.

We believe that the requirement to include all five components of internal control as part of the individual documentation related to "all significant accounts and disclosures" is unduly prescriptive and will add tremendous burden to management's assessment. While we support the need to document the five components of internal control as stated in paragraph 50, this can be done at a business level, or company level, and should not be required at an individual control level. We believe that paragraph 44, which allows for many forms of documentation and requires no one specific form of documentation, is the right standard that the PCAOB should adopt. Any list in paragraph 43 should include language stating that the items on the list are examples, and are not required at the individual control level. Alternatively, the list should be deleted and included as an appendix of examples. We are also concerned with the use of language such as "enough information" leaves this open to interpretation and should be deleted.

Overall, the level of documentation should be a matter of judgment depending on the level of complexity of the organization, size, systems etc., and no one approach to documentation should be prescribed.

Report Date

The proposed standard indicates that the independent auditor cannot audit internal control without also auditing the financial statements. As a technical matter, we do not believe that this requirement should preclude the independent auditor from issuing their report on internal controls at a date subsequent to the financial statement audit report date.

The proposed standard indicates that an auditor could issue an updated report on internal controls in response to the subsequent discovery of information existing at the date of their original report on internal controls if such information would have affected their internal control opinion (see paragraph 180). If the information leading to an updated internal control report does not impact the original financial statement audit opinion, this could create a situation where the revised internal control report and the audit report would have different dates. While we expect that the internal control report and the financial statement report will have the same date because the work on both will coincide, we believe it is more appropriate to tie the date of the internal control report to the completion of the fieldwork related to the assessment internal controls. Ultimately the dates on both reports will be driven by the underlying requirement for the reports (e.g., the requirement to file a certification with the SEC or the issuance of the financial statements). As a technical matter, we believe that the proposed standard should be amended to remove the requirement that the two opinions share the same date.

Conclusion

Citigroup is appreciative of the opportunity to comment on the proposed auditing standard and we thank you for considering our comments. If you have any questions regarding this letter, please contact me at your convenience.

Sincerely,

William P. Hannon
Controller

¶ 624. Goldman Sachs

November 21, 2003

Office of the Secretary
Public Company Accounting Oversight Board
1666 K Street, N.W.
Washington, DC 20006-2803

Re: PCAOB Rulemaking Docket Matter No. 008
Proposed Auditing Standard – An Audit of Internal Control Over Financial Reporting Performed in Conjunction with an Audit of Financial Statements

Goldman, Sachs & Co. strongly supports the Public Company Accounting Oversight Board ("the Board") in its mission to oversee the auditing of public companies and to protect the interests of investors, specifically in the preparation of informative, accurate, and independent audit reports. Therefore, we appreciate the opportunity to comment on the above-referenced standard.

In general, we support the Board's proposal and believe that it will significantly enhance the value of an auditor's opinion on financial statements. And, while we are concerned about the additional costs and burden of work that will be placed on issuers, we acknowledge the need for a more meaningful and effective process for overseeing internal controls and we recognize that this cannot be achieved without additional expense. We do, however, have some comments and concerns that we hope will be helpful to the Board; they are noted in the attachment to this letter.

Once again, we appreciate the opportunity to offer our views and we would be happy to meet with you to discuss them.

Sincerely,

/s/ Sarah E. Smith

Sarah E. Smith
Chief Accounting Officer
(212) 902-5675

ATTACHMENT: Comments and Concerns

Creation of an Appropriate Environment

Paragraph 150 precludes management from concluding that a company's internal controls over financial reporting are effective if a single instance of a material weakness is identified, material weakness defined as *more than remote likelihood* that a *material misstatement* will not be prevented. Our concern is that the proposal sets too low a trigger event for an outcome that could have very serious financial and reputational consequences for an issuer. And, when the "sufficiently in advance of the as of date" remediation requirement is considered, we believe there is substantial risk that an open and communicative environment for the purposes of identifying and deliberating internal control issues may not be fully realized.

Further, the auditor is required to report in writing all "significant deficiencies" to the audit committee. A "significant deficiency" is defined as a single deficiency or a combination of deficiencies, that results in a *more than remote likelihood* that a misstatement of the annual or interim financial statements *that is more than inconsequential* in amount would not be prevented or detected. We believe that for a large, complex, global organization, to set the levels at "more than remote" and "more than inconsequential" is likely to generate a multitude of marginal items, diluting the audit committee's ability to focus on issues material to the financial statements.

Accordingly, we would offer the following comments and suggestions:

Definition of "Significant Deficiency" and "Material Weakness"

A significant deficiency should be defined as a deficiency that results in a *reasonable possibility* that a *material* misstatement in the financial statements would not be prevented. Under this definition, the audit committee would be alerted to critical control issues requiring their immediate focus and attention. Material weakness should be re-defined as a deficiency that results in a *probable* likelihood that a *material* misstatement in the financial statements would not be prevented. We believe this would ensure that both management and the auditor would properly and quickly focus on those issues that could lead to a material misstatement of the financial statements.

Remediation Period

Paragraph 151 would prohibit management from concluding that controls were free of material weakness if a material weakness was identified in the fourth quarter and yet was not remediated "sufficiently in advance of the as of date." Further, this situation would trigger an adverse (or scope limitation) opinion by the auditor. We believe this requirement does not credit management with best efforts where a material weakness is discovered and acted upon immediately, including execution of an appropriate remediation plan. Under the proposal, in that situation the opinion would still be adverse, simply because remediation wasn't completed "sufficiently in advance of the as of date."   We have similar concerns over the subsequent event period. Management during the period-end close may detect an issue, adjust the financial statements accordingly, implement and complete a remediation plan, all prior to the release of the year-end financial statements, yet still receive an adverse opinion because of the "sufficiently in advance of the as of date" requirement.

At the same time, the Board refers to the audit of internal controls and the audit of the financial statements as an integrated audit resulting in two opinions. During a financial statement audit, the auditor may propose adjustments to the financial statements, and management is accorded the opportunity to adjust the financial statements, and receive an unqualified opinion. If the audit of internal controls over financial reporting performed in conjunction with an audit of financial statements is structured as a single engagement, and we agree with the Board that it should be, we would propose that management have the same opportunity to correct any internal control weaknesses, and still receive an unqualified opinion. In paragraph 95, the Board acknowledges that certain controls are performed after the "as of date," and it requires the auditor to test those controls and include them in the "as of date" opinion. We propose that actions taken by management during this period should be treated identically, with the ability to remediate any weaknesses discovered during the period-end close, up to and including the date on which the audit opinion is rendered. We believe this will foster an open and communicative environment in which management and the auditor are eager to both identify problems and remediate them whenever they are identified.

Material Misstatements Identified by Auditors

Paragraph 126 lists examples that would be regarded as significant deficiencies and strong indicators of material weaknesses. One such example is a material misstatement in the financial statements in the current period identified *by the auditor* prior to the company's internal control structure identifying the issue. We believe there are situations where a breakdown in an internal control that could lead to a potential misstatement in the financial statements would be effectively detected and resolved by management's period-end control procedures. Yet, under the proposal, if the auditor were to identify the issue first[1], it would trigger a strong indicator that a material weakness exists. In this situation, it seems to us unduly harsh that management not receive credit for the full range of controls in place that would have identified the error, simply because the auditor identified the issue prior to management. Accordingly, we would suggest that when a material misstatement is found by the auditor, the auditor should conduct an immediate assessment of the downstream controls, and only in the event that the auditor were to determine these to be ineffective would a material weakness be deemed to exist.

In summary, we believe the suggestions outlined above would significantly improve the likelihood that an appropriate environment would be created by which the Board would achieve

---

[1] Typically the auditor would begin their fieldwork simultaneously with the period-end close.

its objective of enhancing the quality of audits and of ensuring the swift identification and remediation of control issues.

Reliance on the Work of Others

Paragraphs 103 through 110 limit the extent to which the auditor can rely on work performed by others. The proposal states that (i) an auditor cannot place any reliance on work performed by others in the areas of fraud controls, period-end financial reporting controls, certain general information technology controls, or walkthroughs; (ii) limited reliance can be placed in the area of non-routine, judgmental transactions or areas where the risk of failure of the control to operate effectively is deemed to be high; and (iii) wider reliance may be placed by the auditor on work performed by others involving routine transactions.

While we fully agree that the auditor must gather the "principal evidence" to support the audit opinion, and that reliance by the auditor on the company for the review of required period-end financial reporting controls or for performing walkthroughs should be prohibited, we think that giving prescriptive rules to the auditor in the other areas referenced would not be optimal. In these other areas, an auditor should be allowed to exercise judgment as to the level of reliance that can be placed on management and its control structure for the purposes of testing operational effectiveness of internal controls, as we believe this will provide incentive to companies to establish and maintain a robust system of internal controls.

Accordingly, we would propose that the auditor perform a full assessment of the control environment and "tone at the top" before determining the scope of the audit work. This assessment would include the audit committee, internal audit and other control areas such as controllers, which compose the organization's financial reporting oversight. If such an assessment revealed a relatively weak control environment, we would expect auditors to question even the extent to which they could rely on the company's work involving routine transactions. Conversely, a strong control environment would indicate that more reliance could be placed on work performed by others.

Assessment of the Audit Committee

Paragraphs 56 through 59 and Paragraph 126 discuss the inclusion of the audit committee in the scope of the audit opinion. While we agree that an ineffective audit committee represents a deficiency in the control environment, we are troubled by the inherent conflict of interest present in requiring the auditor to give an opinion on the committee that is directly responsible for his or her appointment, retention and compensation. Further, if such a review is included in the audit opinion, management would be required formally to evaluate the audit committee, notwithstanding its own reporting relationship to the committee. Alternatively, we would propose that the auditor perform a review of the effectiveness of the audit committee, not as part of the audit opinion, but rather as an integral part of the overall assessment of the company's financial reporting oversight when determining the scope of the audit work to be performed and the extent to which the auditor may rely on the work of others. Accordingly, we believe that this assessment should replace the specific inclusion of the audit committee in the scope of the audit opinion.

Assessment of the Compliance Department

Paragraph 126 of the proposal states an ineffective compliance department in a highly regulated industry would be considered a significant deficiency, which implies that the compliance department would be included within the scope of the audit opinion. While we agree that such ineffectiveness would be at least a significant deficiency, the specific inclusion of compliance seems to us inconsistent with the direction provided by Final Rule: Management's Reports on Internal Control Over Financial Reporting and Certification of Disclosure in Exchange Act Periodic Reports, which specifically limited scope to internal controls over financial reporting (and not to regulatory or compliance issues)[2]. Furthermore, the expanded scope appears to establish a higher standard for particular industries, and we do not believe industry specific requirements were intended by the proposal.

In contrast, we would again propose that the compliance department, and other areas within a company that are an integral part of the control infrastructure, should be considered in a broad assessment of the control environment. Ineffectiveness of such areas should be considered by the auditor in determining the scope of work and the extent to which reliance can be placed on the work of others. Accordingly, we believe that this assessment should replace the specific inclusion of the compliance department in the scope of the audit opinion.

Walkthroughs

Paragraphs 79 through 83 require the auditor to perform "walkthroughs." In a walkthrough of significant business processes, the auditor traces all types of transactions and events, both recurring and unusual, from origination through the company's information systems until they are reflected in the company's financial reports. We believe this is an excellent proposal, and that walkthroughs confirm an auditor's understanding of the flow of transactions, the nature of the business, the design of internal controls, and the interrelationship of controls to processes. We believe this is a welcome return to basic audit techniques and that the auditor should be required to perform the walkthrough directly rather than rely on the work of others.

*   *   *   *

---

[2] Section 404 scope has been consistently bounded with a focus on financial reporting; e.g., the proposal defines safeguarding of assets in Appendix C within the context of financial reporting.

¶ 625. Intel Corporation

INTEL CORPORATION
5350 N.E. Elam Young Parkway
Hillsboro, OR 97124

November 19, 2003

Office of the Secretary
Public Company Accounting Oversight Board
1666 K Street, N.W.
Washington, D.C. 20006-2803

Re: PCAOB Rulemaking Docket Matter No. 008

Ladies and Gentlemen:

Thank you for the opportunity to comment on the Proposed Auditing Standard, *An Audit of Internal Control Over Financial Reporting Performed in Conjunction With an Audit of the Financial Statements* (the "Proposed Standard"). This Proposed Standard concerns attestation engagements pursuant to Sections 103(a)(2)(A)(iii) and 404(b) of the Sarbanes-Oxley Act of 2002 (the "Act"). On behalf of Intel Corporation, we offer the following comments with regard to the Proposed Standard.

EXECUTIVE SUMMARY

General Comment.
We believe it is important to retain focus on the Act's original objective of reinforcing "the responsibility of management for establishing and maintaining an adequate internal control structure and procedures for financial reporting."[1] Unfortunately, the prescriptive nature of the Proposed Standard could undermine the Act's objective by seemingly placing much of the burden of providing reasonable assurance on the shoulders of external auditors. Instead, we recommend the Proposed Standard be modified to reinforce management's role in assessing internal controls over financial reporting.

Reliance on the work of others.
We applaud the Public Company Accounting Oversight Board's ("PCAOB") sensitivity to cost-benefit considerations in its statement: "[t]he more extensive and reliable management's assessment is, the less extensive and costly the auditor's work will need to be."[2] However, we believe the totality of the Proposed Standard unnecessarily restricts the auditor's ability to rely on competent management and internal audit work. Specifically, the Proposed Standard states: "the auditor's own work must provide the principal evidence for the audit opinion."[3] The Proposed Standard then proceeds to bar the use of management and internal audit testing in the broad areas of: (1) "controls that are part of the control environment"; (2) "controls over the

---

[1] Sarbanes-Oxley Act of 2002 §404(a)(1), Pub. L. No. 107-204, 116 Stat. 745.
[2] PCAOB Release No. 2003-017, Proposed Auditing Standard, *An Audit of Internal Control Over Financial Reporting Performed in Conjunction With an Audit of Financial Statements* 8 (Oct. 7, 2003).
[3] *Id.* at 14.

period-end financial reporting process"; and (3) "controls that have a pervasive effect on the financial statements, such as certain information technology general controls . . . ."[4] Finally, the Proposed Standard limits the use of management and internal audit testing of "controls over significant nonroutine and nonsystematic transactions."[5]

The Proposed Standard should allow both internal and external audit to modulate the scope of required testing consistent with the quality of management's work as determined in the auditor's judgment. If management's work is sufficiently planned and executed, then duplicative testing imposes substantial costs on companies with questionable benefit for investors. Additionally, as discussed further below, while we do not support the PCAOB's proposal to characterize the internal control attestation as an audit, the concept of integrating the financial statement audit and internal controls attestation should be reinforced throughout the Proposed Standard. We expect there will be ample opportunity to leverage the financial statement audit to satisfy internal controls validation requirements.

Moreover, the Proposed Standard should allow broad reliance on internal audit's work where external audit determines internal audit is competent, objective, and sufficiently independent. As drafted, the Proposed Standard is even more restrictive than the current model used for financial statement audits under Statement on Auditing Standards No. 65.[6] For example, when conducting the financial statement audit, external audit routinely relies on internal audit to test IT general controls. The Proposed Standard should carry such reliance forward to the attestation work.

Introduction of new and broad terminology.
While we appreciate the PCAOB's efforts to clarify the definition of "significant deficiency," which is not currently well defined in the auditing literature, we believe the PCAOB's proposed definitions of both "significant deficiency" and "material weakness" capture an unnecessarily low and insignificant level of control deficiencies which were not within the intent of Congress when the Act was adopted, and also introduce significant ambiguities which will make it difficult for companies or external auditors to interpret and apply the definitions. This lowering of the reporting threshold, with its effect of inundating management and the audit committee with an overwhelming volume of low-level deficiencies, could unintentionally dilute management and audit committee focus on those deficiencies truly warranting their attention. Furthermore, we are concerned by language that indicates an accumulation of significant deficiencies, in and of itself, could lead to a material weakness. If the significant deficiency threshold is lowered and significant deficiencies are then accumulated to lead to a material weakness conclusion, the unintended result may be investor confusion, not insight, on the actual severity of internal controls deficiencies.

As an alternative to the PCAOB's approach, we recommend the Proposed Standard give companies and the external auditors latitude to exercise judgment in determining those deficiencies that are significant enough to be elevated to management and the audit committee, or disclosed in public filings, while using more well-established terminology to provide

---

[4] *Id.* at A-38.
[5] *Id.*
[6] *The Auditor's Consideration of the Internal Audit Function in an Audit of Financial Statements* (AICPA, *Professional Standards*, vol. 1, AU § 322).

definitional guidance. Rather than introducing the term "inconsequential" in the significant deficiency definition, we recommend that the PCAOB use the well-understood concept of materiality in addressing the magnitude of both a significant deficiency and a material weakness, and use different degrees of likelihood to distinguish between the two. Specifically, we recommend that the definitions hinge on whether there is a reasonable possibility individual or aggregated deficiencies would lead to a material adjustment in the financial statements, in the case of significant deficiencies, and on whether it is reasonably likely the deficiencies would lead to a material adjustment in the financial statements, in the case of material weaknesses. Using terminology that is already well-interpreted in the auditing literature, Securities and Exchange Commission ("SEC") guidance and judicial decisions will give companies and auditors greater ability to apply the definitions in exercising their judgment.

In addition, we request the PCAOB avoid using terminology that appears to extend beyond the financial reporting controls scope of the SEC's rules. For instance, ineffective internal audit, risk assessment, and regulatory compliance functions are listed as examples of significant deficiencies.[7] Yet in many companies, these functions extend beyond the realm of internal controls over financial reporting.

Role of the audit committee.
We recognize and fully support the audit committee's critical role in corporate governance. The audit committee should ensure proper tone at the top and act as an escalation point, but because it is difficult for the committee to truly understand the detailed operation of the company, it should not be expected to engage in the lower levels of internal control. The audit committee should not be inundated with reports of mundane and immaterial deficiencies. Thus, the Proposed Standard should not require the auditor to report *all* deficiencies to the audit committee, but should instead require the auditor to exercise judgment to determine which issues are sufficiently significant to warrant audit committee notification. In exercising this professional judgment, the auditor should evaluate whether there are effective measures and escalation channels in place to provide appropriate management and audit committee visibility to significant deficiencies and material weaknesses. In summary, we believe the Proposed Standard should focus on proper reporting processes and escalation procedures as opposed to requiring the escalation of all deficiencies.

Furthermore, under Section 301 of the Act, "[t]he audit committee . . . shall be directly responsible for the appointment, compensation, and oversight of the work of any registered public accounting firm employed by that issuer . . . ."[8] Therefore, there is an inherent conflict of interest with the external auditor evaluating the effectiveness of the audit committee.

Consistency with the COSO Framework.
The Proposed Standard aptly recognizes many of the inherent limitations of internal control over financial reporting; however, the Proposed Standard fails to include the critical cost-benefit limitation called out in the COSO Framework. The COSO Framework states: "Another limiting factor is that the design of an internal control system must reflect the fact that there are resource

---

[7] *Id.* at A-43.
[8] Sarbanes-Oxley Act of 2002, Pub. L. No. 107-204, 116 Stat. 745.

constraints, and the benefits of controls must be considered relative to their costs."[9] We request this, or similar, language be added to the inherent limitations section of the Proposed Standard.

In closing, we would like to reinforce that Intel fully supports management accountability for maintaining effective internal controls over financial reporting. The Proposed Standard should build on that ownership model and allow greater reliance on the thorough and competent work of both management and internal audit. Otherwise, costs are likely to escalate well beyond any benefits to be achieved.

We thank you for consideration of our views. We have also attached our responses to the PCAOB's 31 questions in Exhibit A. Please contact Jim Campbell at (503) 696-7931 if you would like any further information in connection with our comments.

Regards,

Jim Campbell
Corporate Controller
Intel Corporation

EXHIBIT A
RESPONSES TO PCAOB QUESTIONS

<u>Questions regarding an integrated audit of the financial statements and internal control over financial reporting:</u>

1. Is it appropriate to refer to the auditor's attestation of management's assessment of the effectiveness of internal control over financial reporting as the audit of internal control over financial reporting?

No. Pursuant to Section 404(b) of the Act, "each registered public accounting firm . . . shall attest to, and report on, the assessment made by the management of the issuer."[10] In doing so, the auditor is expressing a conclusion about the reliability of management's written assertion. To conclude on management's assertion, the auditor will need to perform sufficient attest procedures to reduce to a low level the probability of not discovering materially misstated assertions. But the level of testing would not be as extensive as that required in an "audit" of internal control over financial reporting, where it would be necessary for the auditor to opine on the effectiveness of the design and operation of controls.

We are concerned that the PCAOB's use of the term audit in place of attestation conveys an inordinate emphasis on independent testing. While we acknowledge the benefits of selective independent testing to validate management's assessment, non-value-added, duplicative testing needlessly increases costs to companies and investors. Additionally, calling this the audit of internal control over financial reporting makes it appear this is a stand-alone audit. Instead, we recommend the PCAOB select language that reinforces the concept of integrating the financial statement audit and internal controls attestation.

2. Should the auditor be prohibited from performing an audit of internal control over financial reporting without also performing an audit of the financial statements?

While an absolute bar on separate engagements is theoretically unnecessary, in practice, separate engagements would be costly and inefficient. We therefore expect to use the same auditing firm for both the internal control attestation and the financial statements audit.

3. Rather than requiring the auditor to also complete an audit of the financial statements, would an appropriate alternative be to require the auditor to perform work with regard to the financial statements comparable to that required to complete the financial statement audit?

Some companies may feel it is important to have this flexibility. This would not be a cost-effective approach for us, and we therefore have no issue with requiring that the same auditing firm conduct both engagements.

---

[10] Sarbanes-Oxley Act of 2002, Pub. L. No. 107-204, 116 Stat. 745.

Question regarding the costs and benefits of internal control:

4. Does the Board's proposed standard give appropriate consideration to how internal control is implemented in, and how the audit of internal control over financial reporting should be conducted at, small and medium-sized issuers?

As this question does not pertain to Intel, we have no comment on this matter. However, it should be noted that COSO's study of fraudulent financial reporting found:

> Relative to public registrants, companies committing financial statement fraud were relatively small. The typical size of the sample companies ranged well below $100 million in total assets in the year preceding the fraud period. Most companies (78 percent of the sample) were not listed on the New York or American Stock Exchanges.[11]

Question regarding the audit of internal control over financial reporting:

5. Should the Board, generally or in this proposed standard, specify the level of competence and training of the audit personnel that is necessary to perform specified auditing procedures effectively? For example, it would be inappropriate for a new, inexperienced auditor to have primary responsibility for conducting interviews of a company's senior management about possible fraud.

No. The PCAOB should leave it to the audit firm to determine the professional competencies and training necessary to execute the attestation in accordance with the Proposed Standard's framework. The PCAOB, however, should encourage audit firms to include COSO and other internal controls training in their curriculums. Additionally, it is important for the auditors to have the business context for the particular engagement in order to perform an internal controls evaluation effectively.

Questions regarding evaluation of management's assessment:

6. Is the scope of the audit appropriate in that it requires the auditor to both evaluate management's assessment and obtain, directly, evidence about whether internal control over financial reporting is effective?

While the auditor should leverage competent management work and the integrated financial statement audit to minimize redundant testing, we do support selective independent testing. This cost-sensitive approach will allow the auditor to satisfy his or her obligation to validate management's assessment and will encourage management to develop quality documentation and test procedures.

---

[11] COSO, *Fraudulent Financial Reporting: 1987-1997 - An Analysis of U.S. Public Companies, available at* http://www.coso.org.

7. Is it appropriate that the Board has provided criteria that auditors should use to evaluate the adequacy of management's documentation?

We also support the flexibility to tailor the form of the documentation to the individual company circumstances and to allow auditor judgment in evaluating the adequacy of the documentation.

8. Is it appropriate to state that inadequate documentation is an internal control deficiency, the severity of which the auditor should evaluate? Or should inadequate documentation automatically rise to the level of significant deficiency or material weakness in internal control?

The auditor should evaluate the impact of inadequate documentation on internal control. As documentation is only one indication of good internal control, inadequate documentation should not automatically rise to the level of a significant deficiency, material weakness, or for that matter, a deficiency. Per the COSO Framework: "Many controls are informal and undocumented, yet are regularly performed and highly effective. . . . The fact that controls are not documented does not mean that an internal control system is not effective, or that it cannot be evaluated."[12]

Questions regarding obtaining an understanding of internal control over financial reporting:

9. Are the objectives to be achieved by performing walkthroughs sufficient to require the performance of walkthroughs?

First, we believe the Proposed Standard should give the auditor latitude to determine the appropriate scope of walkthroughs. Additionally, the Proposed Standard should reinforce the concept of integration. Wherever possible, walkthroughs should be conducted in a manner that simultaneously achieves the objectives of both the financial statement audit and internal controls attestation. Furthermore, as discussed in our answer to Question 10, the auditor need not personally conduct *all* walkthroughs but should instead be able to rely on walkthroughs performed by management and internal audit. Finally, certain processes do not lend themselves to walkthroughs so auditor judgment would be required to determine the appropriate test procedures.

10. Is it appropriate to require that the walkthrough be performed by the auditor himself or herself, rather than allowing the auditor to use walkthrough procedures performed by management, internal auditors, or others?

No, it would not be appropriate to require the auditor to personally conduct *all* walkthroughs. We believe the auditor should have the flexibility to vary the number and scope of the required walkthroughs based on the quality and completeness of management's documentation and internal audit's test procedures. In addition, the walkthrough strategy should capitalize on the integration of the financial statement audit and internal controls attestation.

---

[12] COSO, *Internal Control-Integrated Framework* 73 (1994).

Question regarding testing operating effectiveness:

11. Is it appropriate to require the auditor to obtain evidence of the effectiveness of controls for all relevant assertions for all significant accounts and disclosures every year or may the auditor use some of the audit evidence obtained in previous years to support his or her current opinion on management's assessment?

While it is reasonable for the auditor to obtain annual *evidence* of the effectiveness of controls for significant accounts, the Proposed Standard should not require the auditor to obtain *direct evidence* on *all* accounts every year. Instead, the auditor should have the flexibility to rely on management's work and the ability to leverage accumulated learning from prior years. A more restrictive approach would increase costs with questionable benefit for investors.

In addition, the test plan should carefully consider the quality of management's assessment to determine the scope of testing required. Similarly, based on the independence and proficiency of the internal audit function, greater reliance could be placed on internal audit's testing.

Questions regarding using the work of management and others:

12. To what extent should the auditor be permitted or required to use the work of management and others?

The Proposed Standard should allow both internal and external audit to modulate the scope of the required testing based on the quality of management's assessment. Moreover, the Proposed Standard should allow greater reliance on independent, competent testing by internal audit. If management's work and internal audit's testing are sufficiently planned and executed, duplicative efforts needlessly increase costs to companies and investors.

13. Are the three categories of controls and the extent to which the auditor may rely on the work of others appropriately defined?

The categories are overly restrictive. To avoid non-value-added rework, the Proposed Standard should reinforce integration of the financial statement audit and internal controls attestation and should allow the auditor to flex the reliance level based on the competence and completeness of management's and internal audit's work.

14. Does the proposed standard give appropriate recognition to the work of internal auditors? If not, does the proposed standard place too much emphasis and preference on the work of internal auditors or not enough?

No. As stated in our cover letter, the independent testing guidelines unduly restrict the use of internal audit's work. The Proposed Standard should allow broad reliance on internal audit's work where external audit determines internal audit is competent, objective, and sufficiently independent.

15. Is the flexibility in determining the extent of reperformance of the work of others appropriate, or should the auditor be specifically required to reperform a certain level of work (for example, reperform tests of all significant accounts or reperform every test performed by others that the auditor intends to use)?

Additional restrictions are not necessary. The auditor should be able to use his or her professional judgment to determine the extent of reperformance.

16. Is the requirement for the auditor to obtain the principal evidence, on an overall basis, through his or her own work the appropriate benchmark for the amount of work that is required to be performed by the auditor?

No. First, we would ask for a more robust definition of what would constitute principal evidence. This definition should recognize that principal evidence is composed of both quantitative and qualitative elements. Additionally, we note that an inflexible principal evidence benchmark would fail to recognize fact-specific circumstances. The auditor should utilize his or her professional judgment to vary reliance consistent with the quality of management's work and internal audit's testing. Where management has performed a quality assessment and internal audit has performed competent testing, the auditor should have the flexibility to rely more heavily on their work.

Questions regarding evaluating results:

17. Will the definitions in the proposed standard of significant deficiency and material weakness provide for increased consistency in the evaluation of deficiencies? How can the definitions be improved?

As stated in our cover letter, we recommend the Proposed Standard give companies and external auditors latitude to exercise judgment in determining those deficiencies that are significant enough to be elevated to management and the audit committee, or disclosed in SEC filings. It is important though, to promote consistency in exercising this judgment, that the rules provide adequate definitional guidance using terminology that is already well-interpreted in the auditing literature, SEC rules and interpretations, and judicial decisions. We believe that Congress intended the Act's reporting and disclosure requirements related to significant deficiencies and material weaknesses to apply to serious control issues that run real risks of causing significant financial reporting issues, and the definitions set forth in the Proposed Standard instead reach immaterial and insignificant control issues. Consequently, if these definitions are adopted, we believe audit committees and investors will be inundated with irrelevant information, increasing the risks that audit committees will fail to fully appreciate and follow up on the truly serious issues and investors will simply be confused. We do not believe the "more than remote" and "more than inconsequential" terminology used in these definitions will promote increased consistency, because we believe that the lines between "slight" and "more than slight", and between "inconsequential" and "more than inconsequential" are very difficult to draw and even reasonable issuers acting with the best of intentions will inevitably interpret those terms differently in similar fact situations.

As an initial matter, by introducing the term "more than inconsequential" in the description of a significant deficiency, the PCAOB has created unnecessary ambiguity. It is not at all clear what this term means, or where the line is between something that is completely inconsequential and something that is slightly less, or in the PCAOB's terminology, "more than" inconsequential. Both definitions should hinge on whether the deficiencies at issue could lead to a material adjustment in the financial statements, and the distinction between a significant deficiency and a material weakness should be determined by reference to the degree of likelihood that a material financial reporting issue will result.

The use of "more than remote" as the degree of likelihood in the significant deficiency and material weakness definitions establishes an unnecessarily low bar for control deficiencies that would require reporting to the audit committee or a conclusion that the company's controls are ineffective.[13] We believe the PCAOB's definitions are inconsistent with the definitions of material weakness and reportable condition (from which the term "significant deficiency" appears to have been derived) that existed in the audit literature at the time the Act was passed and therefore must be afforded due consideration in determining Congressional intent. The definition of material weakness is a "reportable condition in which the design or operation of one or more of the internal control components **does not reduce to a relatively low level** the risk that misstatements caused by error or fraud in amounts that would be material in relation to the financial statements being audited may occur and not be detected within a timely period by employees in the normal course of performing their assigned functions."[14] Reportable conditions are "matters coming to the auditor's attention that, in his (or her) judgment, should be communicated to the audit committee because they represent significant deficiencies in the design or operation of the internal control, which **could** adversely effect the organization's ability to initiate, record, process, and report financial data consistent with the assertions of management in the financial statements."[15] The auditing literature already contains substantial guidance on the factors that should be considered in determining whether there is a reportable condition or a material weakness and we do not believe the PCAOB should supplant that guidance in these rules.

We believe it would be more appropriate for the PCAOB rules to use the existing terms "reasonably possible" and "reasonably likely" in these definitions. The FAS 5 definition of "reasonably possible" is more than remote but less than likely, and the SEC's definition of "reasonably likely" is more than merely possible but not necessarily more likely than not.[16] By using a range, these definitions provide better guidance for the exercise of judgment when evaluating the seriousness of control deficiencies.

---

[13] We have the same concern with the "more than remote" threshold as used in other parts of the Proposed Standard, such as paragraph 61 addressing the definition of a significant account. We strongly urge the PCAOB to address the difficulties of determining when the chances of an event occurring are more than slight, and to revise these references throughout the Proposed Standard to, at minimum, a "reasonably possible" standard.

[14] Statement on Auditing Standards No. 60, *Communication of Internal Control Structure Related Matters Noted in an Audit* (AICPA, *Professional Standards*, vol. 1, AU § 325) (emphasis added).

[15] *Id.* (emphasis added).

[16] See SEC Release No. 33-8182; 34-47264 - Disclosure in Management's Discussion and Analysis ("MD&A") about Off-Balance Sheet Arrangements and Aggregate Contractual Obligations, note 99 and related text; SEC Release Nos. 33-8185; 34-47276 - Implementation of Standards of Professional Conduct for Attorneys, note 50 and related text.

We note that in SEC Release No. 33-8182; 34-47264 - Disclosure in Management's Discussion and Analysis ("MD&A") about Off-Balance Sheet Arrangements and Aggregate Contractual Obligations, the SEC decided to adopt a "reasonably likely" standard for disclosure of off-balance sheet arrangements in MD&A, after first considering an earlier proposed "higher than remote" standard. The "higher than remote" standard was initially proposed by the SEC because Section 401(a) of the Act refers to disclosure of off-balance sheet arrangements that "may" have a material future effect on the registrant. In its commentary on why it chose to adopt the "reasonably likely" threshold, the SEC noted that this standard reached the information most relevant to investors, noted the difficulties issuer would have in applying the "higher than remote" threshold, and concluded: "We believe that the 'reasonably likely' threshold best promotes the utility of the disclosure requirements by reducing the possibility that investors will be overwhelmed by voluminous disclosure of insignificant and possibly unnecessarily speculative information." We note the use of the word "could" in the reportable condition definition and Section 401(a)'s use of the word "may," and the SEC's adoption of a "reasonably likely" threshold in the Section 401(a) context.

In light of the SEC's interpretation of Section 401(a), it is possible to conclude that the term "could" in the reportable condition definition translates into a "reasonably likely" threshold for significant deficiencies, and the threshold for material weaknesses should be even higher, such as a "more likely than not" or "probable" standard. However, we believe that the term "does not reduce to a relatively low level" from the existing material weakness definition is inconsistent with the use of a threshold higher than reasonable likelihood. Therefore, we think thresholds of "reasonable likelihood" for material weaknesses, and "reasonable possibility" for significant deficiencies are the most consistent with existing literature and interpretations, and we also believe these thresholds will promote greater certainty and reduced compliance burdens for issuers, while avoiding the risk of inundating audit committees and investors with voluminous and irrelevant information.

In conclusion, we recommend that the definitions hinge on whether there is a reasonable possibility individual or aggregated deficiencies would lead to a material adjustment in the financial statements, in the case of significant deficiencies, and on whether it is reasonably likely the deficiencies would lead to a material adjustment in the financial statements, in the case of material weaknesses.

18. Do the examples in Appendix D of how to apply these definitions in various scenarios provide helpful guidance? Are there other specific examples that commenters could suggest that would provide further interpretive help?

Providing examples in the Proposed Standard would perhaps be useful, but the examples in the Proposed Standard are limited in their usefulness. First, in the two examples of a significant deficiency, the PCAOB indicates compensating controls may prevent a significant deficiency from rising to the level of a material weakness. We agree with that premise but would also note that such controls could keep a deficiency from becoming a significant deficiency. Additionally, it is difficult to understand why Example D-1 (Reconciliations of Intercompany Accounts Are

Not Performed on a Timely Basis) would rise to the level of a significant deficiency or material weakness. Such intercompany accounts are eliminated in consolidation.

19. Is it necessary for the auditor to evaluate the severity of all identified internal control deficiencies?

The auditor should only elevate internal control deficiencies where the significance and materiality are at an appropriately high level. There should be a threshold of significance below which the auditor relies on management

20. Is it appropriate to require the auditor to communicate all internal control deficiencies (not just material weaknesses and significant deficiencies) to management in writing?

No, refer to our response to Question 19.

Furthermore, as discussed in our cover letter, the Proposed Standard sets up an unwarranted escalation of non-significant and non-material items to the audit committee. "The auditor . . . is required to communicate to the company's management, in writing, *all* internal control deficiencies of which he or she is aware and to *notify* the audit committee that such communication has been made."[17]

21. Are the matters that the Board has classified as strong indicators that a material weakness in internal control exists appropriately classified as such?

We agree with the majority of the examples provided they are merely illustrative and do not impede the auditor's ability to take the facts and circumstances of each case into account. However, in some cases, the examples of ineffective internal audit, risk assessment, and regulatory compliance functions would extend beyond the Act's scope of financial reporting controls. In addition, in accordance with our response to Question 22, we would strike the example of ineffective audit committee oversight as the external auditor could have difficulty objectively evaluating the audit committee.

22. Is it appropriate to require the auditors to evaluate the effectiveness of the audit committee's oversight of the company's external financial reporting and internal control over financial reporting?

No. There is the potential for compromised independence with the proposed evaluation process. An auditor cannot be expected to objectively evaluate the effectiveness of the committee that carries the responsibility for its continued employment and compensation.

23. Will auditors be able to effectively carry out their responsibility to evaluate the effectiveness of the audit committee's oversight?

No. Refer to our answer to Question 22.

---

[17] PCAOB Release No. 2003-017, Proposed Auditing Standard, *An Audit of Internal Control Over Financial Reporting Performed in Conjunction With an Audit of Financial Statements* 16 (Oct. 7, 2003) (emphasis added).

24. If the auditor concludes that ineffective audit committee oversight is a material weakness, rather than require the auditor to issue an adverse opinion with regard to the effectiveness of the internal control over financial reporting, should the standard require the auditor to withdraw from the audit engagement?

No. We do not believe this would be an appropriate response.

<u>Questions regarding forming an opinion and reporting:</u>

25. Is it appropriate that the existence of a material weakness would require the auditor to express an adverse conclusion about the effectiveness of the company's internal control over financial reporting, consistent with the required reporting model for management?

In answering this question, we are assuming the PCAOB is referring to a situation where a material weakness exists as of the end of the period. In that circumstance, the SEC's rules make it clear that: "[m]anagement is not permitted to conclude that the [company's] internal control over financial reporting is effective . . . ."[18] To avoid confusing investors, the auditor should also express an adverse conclusion about the effectiveness of the company's internal control over financial reporting.

If, however, the material weakness has been identified and *corrected* prior to the end of the period, both management and the auditor could conclude the company's internal control over financial reporting is effective.

26. Are there circumstances where a qualified "except for" conclusion would be appropriate?

Yes. We believe qualified "except for" conclusions would actually allow for more meaningful public disclosure in certain cases. For instance, mergers and acquisitions occurring close to year end could warrant an "except for" conclusion. An adverse opinion in that circumstance could mislead the public to believe internal controls are not effective, when in fact, this is just a case of having inadequate time to fully assess the internal controls. Another example might be a case where a subsidiary representing an insignificant percentage of the parent's equity has a material weakness. As the Proposed Standard is drafted, the auditor would be required to issue an adverse opinion. However, this adverse opinion would do little to inform investors of the true nature of the deficiency or its effect on the overall control environment of the parent corporation.

---

[18] Final Rule: Management's Report on Internal Control Over Financial Reporting and Certification of Disclosure in Exchange Act Periodic Reports, Securities and Exchange Commission Release Nos. 33-8238, 34-47986, IC-26068, 68 Fed. Reg. 36663 (June 18, 2003).

27. Do you agree with the position that when the auditor issues a nonstandard opinion, such as an adverse opinion, that the auditor's opinion should speak directly to the effectiveness of the internal control over financial reporting rather than to whether management's assessment is fairly stated?

Consistent with our answer to Question 1, we believe the auditor should conclude on management's written assertion, not opine on the effectiveness of the internal controls over financial reporting. The opinion would speak to management's assessment and the basis of disagreeing with management's assessment would be the auditor's concern about the internal controls.

Questions regarding auditor independence:

28. Should the Board provide specific guidance on independence and internal control-related non-audit services in the context of this proposed standard?

No. It should be left to the discretion of individual boards of directors, based on the existing SEC guidance. Many boards, including Intel's, already supply such guidance.

29. Are there any specific internal control-related non-audit services the auditor should be prohibited from providing to an audit client?

Yes, but we believe the existing SEC guidance is sufficient.[19]

Questions regarding auditor's responsibilities with regard to management's certifications:

30. Are the auditor's differing levels of responsibility as they relate to management's quarterly certifications versus the annual (fourth quarter) certification, appropriate?

In general, yes. However, the written representation requirements in paragraph 128 on page A-44 largely replicate the signed 302 certifications. The notarized 302 certifications should be sufficient representation.

31. Is the scope of the auditor's responsibility for quarterly disclosures about the internal control over financial reporting appropriate?

Our answer to this question depends on the PCAOB's interpretation of "limited procedures."[20] If observation is broadly construed to include walkthroughs, it is an unnecessary change.

---

[19] *See* Final Rule: Strengthening the Commission's Requirements Regarding Auditor Independence, Securities and Exchange Commission Release Nos. 33-8183, 34-47265, 35-27642, IC-25915, IA-2103, 68 Fed. Reg. 6010-17 (February 5, 2003).
[20] PCAOB Release No. 2003-017, Proposed Auditing Standard, *An Audit of Internal Control Over Financial Reporting Performed in Conjunction With an Audit of Financial Statements* A-61 (Oct. 7, 2003).

Additionally, given there is no audit of the quarterly financial statements, walkthroughs would be inconsistent with the integration concept.

¶ 626. Irwin Financial Corporation

November 21, 2003

Office of the Secretary
Public Company Accounting Oversight Board
1666 K Street, N.W.
Washington, DC 20006-2803

Re: Proposed Auditing Standards Concerning the Audit of Internal Control
    (PCAOB Rulemaking Docket Matter No. 008)

The purpose of this letter is to respond on behalf of Irwin Financial Corporation to the proposed auditing standards for the audit of internal control over financial reporting performed in conjunction with an audit of financial statements. Irwin Financial Corporation is a diversified financial services company with $5 billion in assets that provides a broad range of consumer and commercial financial services in selected markets.

We believe, in general, that the Board's proposals to require greater oversight of internal controls by the external auditor will continue to enhance corporate governance practices and public confidence that registered companies in the United States have implemented and maintain appropriate control environments and systems of internal controls. However, we have some concerns regarding certain requirements in the proposal that we believe will result in substantial duplication of control testing and cost, and which will substantially exceed the benefits derived. Accordingly, our comments below address those specific issues in the proposal that are of greatest concern on our part.

The proposed standards equate the work performed by internal auditors with procedures and testing performed by management. The current proposal also places significant limitations on the ability of the external auditor to rely on the work of internal auditors. For example, the external auditor is required to perform all "walkthroughs" in each annual audit, all testing of information technology general controls, all work concerning evaluation of the control environment, including controls intended to prevent or detect fraud, and all testing of controls over the period-end financial reporting process. The standards also require that the external auditor's work must provide the "principal" evidence for their opinion.

We believe that the proposed standards are overly prescriptive and rigid. Based on our discussion with external auditors, these requirements will result in significant duplication of the work already performed by our internal auditors, significant increases in external audit costs, and significant disruptions to our operations as multiple parties review and test the same controls every year. We do not believe that such duplication and increased cost is necessary or warranted in most cases.

Office of the Secretary
Public Company Accounting Oversight Board
November 21, 2003
Page 2

It appears that the prescriptive nature of the standards is based on a lack of comfort with the work performed by internal audit functions. In fact, the proposal does not distinguish between the work performed by internal audit and management. Most internal audit functions report directly to the audit committee of the Board of Directors, with the engagement, termination, and compensation of the Chief Audit Executive being determined by the Audit Committee, the same as in the case of the external auditor. Many internal audit functions are also highly professional, with staffs whose experience often exceed those of the external auditors participating in the examination of the company. On the other hand, control self-assessments or other control verification performed by management is not independent and may not be objective or completed by individuals with the appropriate level of expertise. Therefore, we believe that the standards should reflect these differences, and accordingly, the level of external auditor reliance that is appropriate based on the work of these groups should be differentiated.

We believe that the external auditor should have significant discretion in placing reliance on the work of internal audit and be able to rely on that work extensively, if deemed appropriate based on the quality of the internal audit function. Rather than placing significant restrictions on the use of internal audit work, we believe that it would be more appropriate to place standards that the internal auditor must satisfy in order for the external auditor to rely on their work. Standards established by the *Institute of Internal Auditors* or other professional organizations may be appropriate. Clearly, the external auditor must assess the independence, objectivity, competence and quality of the work performed by internal audit and their compliance with agreed-upon standards before they could conclude on their ability to rely on internal audit's work. Standards for such an assessment of the internal audit function are already addressed in SAS No. 65, *The Auditor's Consideration of the Internal Audit Function in an Audit of Financial Statements*, and could also be applied to the audit of controls over financial reporting. Based on the results of this assessment, the external auditor should then be able to place extensive reliance on the work of the internal auditor if it determines that it is appropriate based on the assessment of the internal audit function.

We believe this approach will also have positive side-benefits. Since weaknesses in internal audit functions will require greater external auditor validation of internal controls, and consequently greater cost, this will provide a significant incentive for board of directors and audit committees to raise the quality of their internal audit functions. Conversely, the currently proposed standards are likely to result in unintended consequences. Given the Board's responsibility to balance the expectations of various stakeholders, including shareholders, board of directors may conclude that the testing of internal audit functions is duplicative and unnecessary in those areas where the external auditor is not permitted to place reliance on internal audit work. This could result in situations where management certifications are solely based on management self-assessments, which may not be objective or verified by individuals who have expertise in risk and control analysis, with the independent validation left to the testing that the external auditor is required to perform. Therefore, we believe that the current proposals could result in decreased reliance in internal auditors and overall weakening of these

Office of the Secretary
Public Company Accounting Oversight Board
November 21, 2003
Page 3

independent risk and control oversight functions. Such an occurrence will actually result in reduced assurance on the quality of internal controls over financial reporting.

For example, although we currently have a small audit function consisting of 11 employees, the staff consists of professional auditors with an average of 11 years of audit experience and 19 years of financial services experience (including experience in senior financial reporting positions, such as controller, senior accounting managers, etc.). All of our internal auditors have at a minimum a bachelors' degree (primarily finance or accounting majors) with 36% having obtained a masters degree; 64% have obtained audit related professional certifications (CPA, CBA, CISA, etc.); and 36% of our staff have earned their CPA. We believe that continued investment in such an internal audit function will be difficult if the proposed standards limit the external auditor's ability to rely on their work, including reliance on the walkthroughs and I.T. general controls audits which are an integral part of our Corporation's internal audit processes.

The requirement that "the auditor must obtain evidence of the effectiveness of controls for all relevant assertions for all significant accounts and disclosures every year" also appears excessive. We believe that the external auditor should have the discretion to use their judgment and risk assessment to determine the extent of testing necessary to support the opinion concerning the effectiveness of controls over financial reporting. The current proposal could result in significant testing in areas where no changes have occurred from prior audits and does not adequately differentiate for different levels of risk at different organizations. For example, the level of control testing necessary should be much different in an organization with a history of poor controls, negative surprises, and significant changes than in an organization that has a strong control environment and stable operations that have proven effective for many years, and where changes from previous years have been minimal. However, this requirement does not permit the external auditor to differentiate the level of testing necessary based on such risk assessments.

We also believe that it is inappropriate to require the external auditor to assess the effectiveness of audit committees. This is not practical and will place the external auditor in a significant conflict of interest since the audit committee is responsible for the engagement or termination of the audit firm, as well as approval of any non-audit services that the external auditor performs and the level of compensation for such services. This will again place the external auditor in a conflict of interest situation when the intent of various reforms in recent year has been to reduce or eliminate such conflicts.

We also do not believe that the external auditor is in a position to assess the effectiveness of the audit committee. Audit committee members generally include individuals with significant experience and expertise in a broad number of areas. In addition to the external auditor's interaction with the audit committee, the committee has substantial interaction with members of management, corporate risk management, the internal auditor, and others without the external auditor's participation. Such interaction is necessary and appropriate for the committee to ensure that it is receiving information that

Office of the Secretary
Public Company Accounting Oversight Board
November 21, 2003
Page 4

is unbiased. Accordingly, we believe that the external auditor is not in the best position, in terms of breadth of knowledge or involvement in all committee activities, to assess the effectiveness of the committee. Furthermore, audit committees are required to be constituted entirely of independent directors, at least one of whom is acknowledged to be a financial expert, and to conduct annual self-assessments. We believe that the board of directors of the company is responsible for the oversight of the self-assessment process and the overall evaluation of the effectiveness of the audit committee.

In conclusion, we believe that the proposed standards will result in significant duplication of internal control testing and unnecessary cost. We believe that the external auditor should have the ability to use significant discretion and judgment in determining the level of testing necessary to support their internal control opinion. We also believe that the proposed standards should eliminate any restrictions on the use of internal audit work and the current requirements that the external auditor's own testing must provide the principal basis for their opinion. Instead, internal audit work should be used extensively if the internal audit function meets specified requirements and the external auditor validates that those standards have been met. Finally, we do not believe that the external auditor is in an appropriate position to evaluate the effectiveness of the audit committee.

We thank you for the opportunity to comment on the proposed auditing standard.

Sincerely,

Will Miller

Will Miller
Chairman & CEO

cc: Audit & Risk Management Committee, Irwin Financial Corporation

¶ 627. J.P. Morgan Chase & Co.

Joseph L. Sclafani
Executive Vice President and Controller

November 21, 2003

Via email: comments@pcaob.org
Public Company Accounting Oversight Board
1666 K Street, N.W.
Washington, D.C. 20006-2803

Attention: Office of the Secretary

> Re: PCAOB Rulemaking Docket Matter No. 008
> PCAOB Release No. 2003-017

Ladies and Gentlemen:

J.P. Morgan Chase & Co. ("JPMorgan Chase") is pleased for this opportunity to comment on the auditing standard, *An Audit of Internal Control Over Financial Reporting Performed in Conjunction with an Audit of Financial Statements (the "proposed standard")*, proposed by the Public Company Accounting Oversight Board ("PCAOB").

JPMorgan Chase is a leading global financial services firm with assets of more than $750 billion and operations in more than 50 countries. JPMorgan Chase agrees with the basic principle enunciated by the PCAOB as to the importance of internal controls. Internal controls add value and mitigate risks, thereby enabling a company's management, board and shareholders to rely, with more reasonable assurance, upon the integrity of a company's financial reports. As a financial institution that has been, for over a decade, applying the framework recommended by the Committee of Sponsoring Organizations of the Treadway Commission ("COSO") to satisfy the requirements of the Federal Deposit Insurance Corporation Improvement Act of 1991 ("FDICIA"), JPMorgan Chase understands the importance of a strong internal control environment and supports the PCAOB's objective of creating an integrated audit of both financial statements and internal controls over financial reporting.

J.P. Morgan Chase & Co. ● 270 Park Avenue, Floor 28, New York, NY 10017-2070

Telephone: 212 270 7559 ● Facsimile: 212 270 9589
joseph.sclafani@chase.com

The comments which follow highlight four areas of the proposed standard that JPMorgan Chase believes require additional consideration by the PCAOB:

- The definitions of "significant deficiency" and "material weakness" should be modified
- The external auditor should be permitted to use the work of others, particularly that of the internal auditors, to a greater extent
- The external auditor should be given more latitude to determine the level and extent of the procedures and testing to be performed
- The proposed standard should permit the issuance of audit reports with "except for" opinions

1.   <u>Definitions of Significant Deficiency and Material Weakness</u>

We agree with the PCAOB that material weaknesses be reported to the public, as we believe it is important to provide investors transparency about a company's internal controls. However, we do not believe that disclosure of such information should be based on a "more than remote likelihood" of occurrence.

We believe that the "more than remote likelihood" standard is too low a threshold by which to evaluate internal control deficiencies. In addition, it is a threshold that is lower than the threshold related to "reportable condition" and "material weakness" articulated under current auditing standards, particularly AICPA Professional Standards AU Section 325 and AICPA Attestation Standards AT Section 501. We believe that since the rules promulgated by the Securities and Exchange Commission pursuant to Section 404 of the Sarbanes-Oxley Act ("SOX 404") refer to AU Section 325 and AT Section 501, those standards should be applied in determining whether a significant deficiency or material weakness exists. Those standards are more appropriate than the "remote likelihood" threshold which is based on the concept of "remote" defined in Statement of Financial Accounting Standards No. 5.

The appropriate threshold for the definitions of "significant deficiency" and "material weakness" is a critical issue. Use of an inappropriately low standard will make the scope of work to be performed by management, the internal auditor and the external auditor too expansive without providing any meaningful benefit. The level of significance drives, among other things, the accounts and processes to be evaluated, the controls to be tested, the level of detail of the tests to be performed and the number of walkthroughs to be conducted. A too-low threshold has the potential of creating a vast range of work to evaluate and test processes and controls that may not be the key drivers of an effective internal control system, resulting in assessments and testing that are not value-added nor cost effective.

In addition, we are concerned a too-low threshold could potentially encompass deficiencies that will not have a significant effect on the financial statements. Disclosure of such deficiencies may actually mislead investors about the integrity of a company's internal controls. Even the most effective internal controls may not be able to prevent the occurrence of a control deficiency to a level that is "remote. " In any complex organization, control deficiencies may periodically arise in the normal course of business; most are detected and corrected in a timely fashion without the company incurring any material loss and without materially affecting the financial statements. While we strongly believe it is important to provide transparency about a company's internal controls, we also believe that setting an appropriate threshold for disclosure is necessary to ensure that investors are not provided information at such a level of insignificance that the disclosure becomes, in effect, a litany of "false alarms."

We therefore respectfully propose that the PCAOB, in defining the terms "significant deficiency" and "material weakness," use a *reasonably likely* threshold, a threshold which the PCAOB itself refers to in paragraph 183 of the proposed standard. We believe the "reasonably likely" standard is consistent with the concept of management providing (and auditors obtaining) reasonable assurance in an audit of internal controls. We also believe this term is more consistent with the term "reduce to a relatively low level" used in AU Section 325 and AT Section 501. In addition, we are concerned that the threshold of "more than inconsequential" in connection with "significant deficiency" will not clearly delineate a non-significant internal control deficiency from a significant deficiency. We therefore propose a threshold of "significant" misstatement, which will be clearer and also retain a distinction from material weakness.

We therefore propose that the PCAOB modify the definitions of "significant deficiency" and "material weakness" as follows:

- a "significant deficiency" is a "single deficiency, or a combination of deficiencies in the same or closely related reporting areas, that is *reasonably likely* to result in a *significant* misstatement of the annual or interim financial statements; and

- a "material weakness" is a "significant deficiency that, by itself, or in combination with other significant deficiencies, is *reasonably likely* to result in a *material* misstatement of the annual or interim financial statements."

In this way, control deficiencies that would pose a reasonable risk of material misstatement would be appropriately reported to investors and the public, while ensuring that significant deficiencies continue to be reported to management and the audit committee.

We further believe the list referred to in paragraph 126 is too prescriptive, as these items do not necessarily indicate, in all cases, the existence of a significant deficiency. We believe no specific list of circumstances should be presumptively regarded as "significant deficiencies"; rather, a significant deficiency must be evaluated based on all relevant facts and circumstances. For example, the evaluation needs to consider how the control deficiency was discovered, how long the deficiency had occurred before being discovered, and the magnitude of loss, if any, resulting from the deficiency. In addition, the proposed list does not take into consideration the fact that the deficiency was discovered, demonstrating that internal controls were functioning properly, nor does it take into consideration the existence of other controls that might exist that would prevent the identified deficiency from elevating to the level of a significant deficiency or material weakness. In our view, the examples do not permit sufficient exercise of the external auditor's professional judgment.

For the above reasons, we believe the definitions of significant deficiency and material weakness used in the standard should be more judgment-based and contain more realistic thresholds. In this way, the disclosure of the existence of material weaknesses will provide investors with information that is meaningful and material.

2.   The Extent to which the External Auditor Should be Permitted to Use the Work of Others, Particularly the Work of the Internal Auditors

As currently proposed, the standard defines three categories of controls and sets forth, for each category, the extent to which the external auditor may – or may not – rely upon the work of others.

We believe that these categories are too rigid. Certain controls defined to belong in one category may more appropriately be included in another. For example, we believe there are controls, such as those that are related to period-end financial reporting (including controls over initiating, recording and processing general ledger entries), that relate to activities that are primarily routine and recurring. Accordingly, these controls should be ones where the external auditor be permitted to rely upon the work of others. In addition, with respect to "controls that are part of the control environment" and "information technology general controls" (controls which the PCAOB acknowledges are pervasive and upon which the effectiveness of so many other controls depends), it is important to recognize that these controls are generally subject to extensive reviews by internal auditors. Therefore, it may not be practicable for the external auditor not to rely upon the work of others; the blanket prohibition in the proposed standard on the use of the work of others with respect to these controls is, simply, not realistic and too costly. Finally, with respect to controls over significant non-routine and non-systematic transactions, the proposed standard does not provide the external auditor with sufficient flexibility in appropriately relying on the testing performed by internal auditors. We therefore believe the limitations imposed by the proposed standard as to how the external auditor must perform its own assessment are too inflexible.

In this regard, we believe the proposed standard does not give appropriate recognition to the work of internal auditors. The competency and objectivity of a company's internal audit function should be evaluated in light of the circumstances of each company, as each organization will differ; therefore, where appropriate, the proposed standard should permit more reliance by the external auditor on the work of internal auditors. For example, where internal audit reports directly to the audit committee, is independent of management, is highly trained and competent, is a significant element of the firm's control environment, is appropriately staffed with the necessary resources, is experienced in detecting control weaknesses, and where the results of internal audits are transparent to both the audit committee and the external auditor, requiring the external auditor to reperform significant amounts of testing done by the internal auditors is duplicative and inefficient.

By limiting and restricting the extent of reliance by the external auditor on the work of the internal audit function, the proposed standard may adversely affect the importance placed on the internal auditors; over time, the standard as currently proposed may have the unintended effect of diminishing the importance of the internal audit function within the organization and, particularly, as it relates to the audit of financial statements and controls over financial statements. This result would be counter to the intent of SOX 404 to improve the internal control environment of companies.

We therefore respectfully propose the PCAOB incorporate in the proposed standard an approach similar to that set forth in Statement on Auditing Standards No. 65, *The Auditor's Consideration of the Internal Audit Function in an Audit of Financial Statements* ("SAS 65"). SAS 65 permits the external auditor to rely upon the internal auditor's work in light of, among other things, the external auditor's assessment of the competency and objectivity of the internal auditors.

For the above reasons, we believe there should not be any rigid, tiered categorizations of areas defining the extent to which the external auditor may or may not use the work of others; rather, we believe the external auditor should be permitted to exercise its professional judgment as to the appropriate level of its reliance on the work of others, particularly the use of the work of the internal auditors.

3. The Extent to which the Proposed Standard Should Permit More Latitude to the External Auditor to Use its Judgment to Determine the Level and Extent of the Procedures and Testing to be Performed

We believe the external auditor should be permitted more flexibility with respect to the procedures and testing strategies employed. The nature, timing and extent of the procedures and testing should be based on the specific circumstances of the company. Factors to be considered should include the external auditor's evaluation of the entity's internal control processes, the effectiveness of the entity's internal audit function, the complexity of the transactions or processes being evaluated and whether there have been changes in the control environment.

With regard to testing, the external auditor should be given the latitude to determine whether it is necessary to perform testing each year with respect to each significant control function. If, for example, there has not been a significant change from the prior year in the process flow of transactions with respect to a routine control function, the proposed standard should permit the external auditor to determine if it would be appropriate to rely upon the prior year's evidence, in full or in part, with respect to the particular assertion being tested.

Likewise, more discretion should be permitted to the external auditor to determine the nature and extent of procedures to be performed in order to gain an understanding of process flows and the design and effectiveness of controls. In this regard, walkthroughs should not be mandated for every significant process. While walkthroughs are valuable tools, they are only one method of providing important audit evidence for external auditors; alternate audit procedures that meet the audit objectives should also be acceptable if deemed appropriate by the external auditor.

The prescriptive nature of the proposed standard will increase audit fees in a way that will not add value nor be cost effective to the control environment. Redundant work and burdensome procedures will not help companies or their investors. We believe the proposed standard should permit the external auditor to focus on the areas where, given its professional judgment and its knowledge of the company and its processes, there is the greatest potential for risk and where the costs to be incurred in connection with the audit have the greatest likelihood of identifying internal control deficiencies. The proposed standard should grant the external auditor the necessary latitude to use its professional skepticism in designing and executing the audit.

4.   <u>The Proposed Standard Should Permit the Issuance of an "Except For" Opinion in the Auditor's Report</u>

The proposed standard should permit the issuance of a qualified, "except for" opinion, in the audit report. We recognize that a company's management, in its Section 404 certification, may not provide a qualified certification; that is, if a material weakness in internal controls exists, management must conclude that the company's internal controls are not effective. In that situation, however, management would have the opportunity within the Management's Discussion and Analysis section of its SEC filings to fully discuss the material weakness and management's assessment of its impact.

We therefore believe that the external auditor should have the latitude, when the material weakness is not deemed to be so severe and pervasive as to warrant an adverse opinion, to issue an "except for" opinion. For example, if the material weakness is limited to a specific account or disclosure that does not taint the entire internal control environment, an "except for" opinion may be appropriate. Similarly, if the material weakness were discovered in the latter part of the fiscal year, there had been a prompt response by the company to develop corrective action, and good progress had been made to remedy the weakness, the external auditor might deem it appropriate to issue a report with an "except for" opinion. Additionally, an "except for" opinion may be the only viable opinion that an external auditor can deliver when an entity was recently acquired by the company.

For the reasons set forth above, we believe an "except for" opinion may provide a more appropriate assessment of a company's internal control environment. It allows the external auditors to describe any material weakness and its likely consequences to the financial statements, as well as the steps being taken by the company to correct the weakness. Disclosure of more information in this regard would be more helpful to investors than a "blanket" adverse opinion.

*****

JPMorgan Chase appreciates the opportunity to provide our views on this important matter. We believe our proposed modifications would improve the ability of companies to comply with the proposed standard, without weakening its effectiveness. We would be pleased to discuss our comments or answer any questions you may have.

Very truly yours,

¶ 628. UBS AG

αβ

UBS AG
Financial Services Group
P.O. Box, 8098 Zurich
Tel. +41-1-234 11 11

Group Chief Risk Officer
Member of the Group Managing Board

Walter H. Stuerzinger
GCCR-STR FH507
Pelikanstrasse 6/8, 8001 Zurich
Tel. +41-1-234 40 11
Fax +41-1-234- 48 99
Walter.stuerzinger@ubs.com

19 November 2003

Office of the Secretary
Public Company Accounting Oversight Board
1666 K Street, N.W.
Washington, D.C. 20006-2803
USA

Via E-Mail: comments@pcaobus.org

Re: PCAOB Rulemaking Docket Matter No. 008

Dear PCAOB Members:

The Sarbanes-Oxley Section 404 ("SOX 404") requirements on internal control over financial reporting are a key initiative in the effort to restore investor confidence and to ensure integrity in financial reporting. As an SEC registrant, UBS welcomes the opportunity to provide comments on the PCAOB proposed auditing standard, *An Audit of Internal Control Over Financial Reporting Performed in Conjunction with an Audit of Financial Statements,* (the "Proposed Standard"). The following letter will provide some general comments followed by specific responses to some of the questions on which the PCAOB seeks feedback.

General Comments

As you may be aware, UBS is the world's leading provider of wealth management services, one of the largest asset managers globally, and among the major global investment banking and securities houses. Although it is headquartered in Zurich, UBS is listed on the NYSE and has nearly 40% of its workforce (over 25,000 individuals) located in the U.S. UBS is committed to meeting the leading corporate governance standards worldwide and will comply with SOX 404 for its 2005 financial reports.

UBS believes that it is important that foreign registrants (and particularly financial institutions) have a recognized voice in the comment process related to Sarbanes-Oxley requirements because of the different perspectives (and often different legal requirements) under which such companies operate.
UBS strongly supports the Sarbanes-Oxley legislation and the associated rules that have been developed as they are helping create a level playing field for corporate governance standards globally. In addition, UBS sees a strong connection between SOX 404 requirements and the qualitative aspects of the operational risk requirements within the Basel Accord reform proposals.

Indeed, UBS has combined its efforts to comply with these two regulatory requirements under a broader operational risk management framework and therefore values alignment of these requirements to the extent possible. UBS appreciates the recognition

α β

the PCAOB and SEC have provided to the linkage between SOX 404 and the FDICIA process and hopes that the Basel Committee will recognize the linkages between their own efforts on operational risk and SOX 404.

In general, UBS supports the general framework outlined by the Proposed Standard as it will ensure that auditors contribute to the development of sound internal controls over financial reporting. In particular, UBS believes that the approach of requiring a link from financial statement assertions and preventive/detective controls to financial accounts provides an appropriate basis for ensuring that a company's internal controls have been appropriately designed and are operating effectively. The following will provide specific comments in response to the PCAOB questions.

Specific Comments

Question 6: Is the scope of the audit appropriate in that it requires the auditor to both evaluate management's assessment and obtain, directly, evidence about whether internal control over financial reporting is effective?

UBS agrees with the PCAOB's proposed scope for the audit because it believes that this will be the only way in which the spirit and intent of SOX 404 can be met. A simple audit of the management assessment process, and not the controls themselves, would be insufficient as it would emphasize form over substance. UBS notes here that the proposed scope appears to go further than what is typically required in other current auditing standards on internal controls (e.g., SAS 70 in the U.S. and FRAG 21/94 in England and Wales).

Therefore, UBS believes it would be helpful for the PCAOB to note explicitly the relationship of the Proposed Standard to SAS 70 to ensure that it is clearly recognized that the Proposed Standard imposes a stronger requirement (i.e., by requiring the auditor to not only evaluate whether management has met its stated control goals but also whether those goals are effective enough to ensure effective internal control over financial reporting) than a SAS 70 certification. This will help ensure clarity between different internal control audit processes and ensure that the SOX 404 audit does lead to greater confidence in financial reporting.

Question 5: Should the Board, generally or in this proposed standard, specify the level of competence and training of the audit personnel that is necessary to perform specified auditing procedures effectively? For example, would it be inappropriate for a new, inexperienced auditor to have primary responsibility for conducting interviews of a company's senior management about possible fraud.

Question 7: Is it appropriate that the Board has provided criteria that auditors should use to evaluate the adequacy of management's documentation?

UBS sees a linkage between these two questions in that they are related to the ability of auditors to form an independent judgment on the internal management documentation and testing. UBS believes it is appropriate for Proposed Standard paragraph 43 to provide suggested criteria that auditors should look for from management in planning their audit. However, UBS notes that these suggestions need to be considered carefully and clearly labeled as examples only in order to ensure that they do not become a mandatory list of items that auditors require of companies. As such, UBS appreciates the

αβ

PCAOB RuleMaking
Docket Matter No. 008
Page 3 of 9

statement in Proposed Standard paragraph 44 that "no one form of documentation is required." UBS believes that this concept should be emphasized even further.

Within the list contained in paragraph 43, UBS has some concerns about the suggestion for documentation of "information about how significant transactions are initiated, recorded, processed, and reported" and "enough information about the flow of transactions to identify where material misstatements due to error or fraud could occur." In particular, UBS is concerned that these suggestions may lead to an auditor expectation for management to have process or transaction flowcharts available for review.

In order to ensure effective internal control, UBS believes that management should identify the key control related responsibilities of the functions that make up the organization. Implicit in this is an understanding of key process flows. However, documented process analysis is less important than having clearly identified and documented functional roles and responsibilities, key control objectives, and related control standards that ensure the objectives are met. While flowcharts may be useful training devices in certain cases, they are not necessary tools for ensuring internal control. In addition, flowcharts also may quickly become outdated as processes adapt to changing organizational or market circumstances. Thus, a requirement by auditors for companies to maintain flowcharts merely for the purposes of their audit would be unduly burdensome.

UBS notes by way of contrast that Proposed Standard paragraph 69 would require the auditors themselves to identify significant processes and to "understand the flow of transactions, including how transactions are initiated, recorded, processed, and reported" and to "identify the points within the process where a misstatement – including a misstatement due to fraud – related to each relevant financial statement assertion could arise." UBS believes that this is an appropriate expectation to place on auditors as they must be able to understand where the key control points are in a process. However, auditors should not necessarily expect management to maintain detailed flowcharts (as might occur given the current drafting of paragraph 43) to assist in this.

This is where UBS sees a connection with PCAOB Question 5. UBS believes that auditors engaged in the SOX 404 audits should be required to be sufficiently experienced in the industry that they are auditing to have an understanding not only of the processes of the company that they are auditing but also where the key control points are likely to be located within those processes. This will ensure that the SOX 404 audit, which is expected to be burdensome enough, is as efficient as possible. It will also ensure that auditors are focused on evaluating the effectiveness of the controls themselves and not the efficiency of the processes within which the controls are embedded. An emphasis on flowcharts could result in a focus on documentation of what currently exists as opposed to what controls should exist in order to ensure effective internal control.

Question 9: Are the objectives to be achieved by performing walkthroughs sufficient to require the performance of walkthroughs?

Question 10: Is it appropriate to require that the walkthrough be performed by the auditor himself or herself, rather than allowing the auditor to use walkthrough procedures performed by management, internal auditors, or others?

Proposed Standard paragraph 48 states that auditors should obtain an understanding of the design of controls via procedures that may include inquiry, inspection, observation, and tracing transactions. In addition, Proposed Standard paragraph 74 states that auditors should obtain evidence of the effectiveness of controls either by performing tests or by using the work of others. However, Proposed Standard paragraphs 79 and 104 both state that walkthroughs should be a mandatory procedure for auditors both as part of the effort to understand and test both the design and operating effectiveness of controls.

UBS does not object to a requirement for walkthroughs per se, but does believe that the currently proposed walkthrough requirements may be overly burdensome and misdirected. Under Proposed Standard paragraph 80, an auditor would be required to conduct a walkthrough that encompasses "the entire process of initiating, recording, processing, and reporting individual transactions, and controls for all five internal control components and fraud, not just control activities." UBS believes that a walkthrough that examines every link in a process chain is more than what is actually necessary to evaluate internal control. In addition, UBS also believes that such a walkthrough may focus on the efficiency of the process and thereby might lose sight of the internal control aspects, which should be the primary focus for SOX 404.

Given this, UBS appreciates the statements in proposed paragraph 79 that the walkthrough should be intended to provide the auditor with evidence to "confirm the auditor's understanding of the design of controls", to "evaluate the effectiveness of the design of controls" and to "confirm whether controls have been placed in operation." However, UBS does not believe that paragraph 79 (and by implication the related statements in paragraphs 80-83) should state that the walkthrough is intended to provide the auditor with evidence to "confirm the auditor's understanding of the process flow of transactions" and to "confirm that the auditor's understanding of the process is complete."

As noted in its comments on Questions 5 and 7, UBS believes that the auditors performing the SOX 404 audits should be sufficiently experienced to understand the process flows within the company that they are auditing without detailed flowcharts or walkthrough procedures. Instead, the SOX 404 audit should focus solely on an evaluation of the key control points that must be designed and operating effectively to ensure the reliability of financial reporting.

Question 11: Is it appropriate to require the auditor to obtain evidence of the effectiveness of controls for all relevant assertions for all significant accounts and disclosures every year or may the auditor use some of the audit evidence obtained in previous years to support his or her current opinion on management's assessment?

UBS does not believe that auditors should be required to obtain evidence of the effectiveness of controls over all significant accounts and disclosures via relevant financial statement assertions on a yearly basis. All controls, accounts, and disclosures will not necessarily change on a yearly basis. Thus, there may be many cases where a full re-audit would be redundant. In addition, the requirement for a full audit each year would preclude the adoption of a risk-based audit approach.

UBS also has concern with two proposed aspects of the auditor requirements for evaluating operating effectiveness. First, Proposed Standard paragraph 88 states that an auditor should not only evaluate whether the control is operating as designed but

αβ

PCAOB RuleMaking
Docket Matter No. 008
Page 5 of 9

also "whether the person performing the control possesses the necessary authority and qualifications to perform the control effectively." UBS is concerned that this is a highly subjective evaluation that could be interpreted as a requirement for a company to justify the qualifications of its staff. UBS does not believe that this is necessarily the intention of the PCAOB and suggests that this merely be clarified.

Second, UBS notes that Proposed Standard paragraph 102 makes a distinction between manual and automatic controls with respect to auditor testing. In particular, the Proposed Standard states that "manual controls should be subjected to more extensive testing than automated controls" and that "the more frequently a manual control operates, the more operations of the control the auditor should test." UBS does not believe that these distinctions are meaningful or useful. When evaluating internal controls, management and auditors should be concerned with whether the control objectives were met. Whether this is done through a manually applied or an automatically applied control is not relevant to the determination of whether the control is operating effectively. The extensiveness and frequency of testing should be determined by the nature of the control itself (i.e., how important it is to meeting the objective) and not the form of the control. UBS believes that the proposed distinctions between manual and automatic controls would only result in additional burdens (from the need to distinguish those controls that are manually applied from those that are automatically applied) without substantial additional benefits.

Question 12: *To what extent should the auditor be permitted or required to use the work of management and others?*

Question 13: *Are the three categories of controls and the extent to which the auditor may rely on the work of others appropriately defined?*

UBS agrees with the goal of the PCAOB to draft the Proposed Standard in such a way that auditors are provided with flexibility in using the work of others while at the same time preventing inappropriate reliance on the work of others. This requires a fine balancing of interests and a clear specification of guidelines for when auditors should and should not rely on the work of others. In general, UBS agrees with the concept of having three categories of controls (i.e., those where the auditor cannot rely on the work of others when performing the evaluation; those where reliance should be limited because they pose a high risk due to judgmental decisions; and those where reliance is not limited in any manner).

UBS believes that the list of items where reliance is prohibited in Proposed Standard paragraph 104 may be too broad in the following two areas:
- Controls that are part of the control environment, including controls specifically established to prevent and detect fraud that is reasonably likely to result in material misstatement of the financial statements
- Walkthroughs, as discussed beginning at paragraph 74.

With respect to the first item, it may be appropriate to ask auditors to separately evaluate the general control environment separately from management. However, this is an area where it is often difficult to perform specific "tests" of controls as many of the controls relate to corporate culture and other intangible aspects of a company. UBS also is not clear about the significance of the separation of the fraud concerns both in this paragraph and in other paragraphs in the Proposed Standard (e.g., 24-26, 43, 53, 69) when these are part of the Control Environment component of internal control

WG
&L Warren, Gorham & Lamont

αβ

PCAOB RuleMaking
Docket Matter No. 008
Page 6 of 9

frameworks such as COSO. UBS strongly believes that segregation of duties and the development of key control objectives is part of the process of addressing the risk of fraud. An attempt to separate fraud prevention as another activity appears artificial. Of course, material misstatements that could arise from fraud must be addressed. However, the identification of fraud controls in several paragraphs of the Proposed Standard may lead to the assumption that a separate control process is necessary specifically for fraud issues.

With respect to walkthroughs, please see the comments on Questions 9 and 10.

UBS also notes that Proposed Standard paragraph 53 defines a new term "company level controls" to include the following items:

- Control environment, including tone at the top, the assignment of authority and responsibility, consistent policies and procedures, and company-wide programs, such as codes of conduct and fraud prevention, that apply to all locations and business units.
- Management's risk assessment process.
- Centralized processing and controls, including shared service environments.
- Monitoring results of operations.
- Monitoring of controls, including activities of the internal audit function, the audit committee, and self-assessment programs.
- The period-end financial reporting process.
- Board-approved policies that address significant business control and risk management practices

Proposed Standard paragraph 54 then suggests that auditors may wish to test and evaluate these controls first while paragraph 55 states that this testing is not sufficient for opining on the effectiveness of a company's internal control. UBS does not object to this definition and believes it is generally aligned with the term "entity level controls" that has been used by a number of auditors. In general, when following the COSO or other internal control frameworks, it is sensible to start with a comprehensive evaluation of the internal controls. UBS merely seeks clarification around the use of the terms "company level controls" and "entity level controls" and the limitations imposed under paragraph 104.

Question 14: Does the proposed standard give appropriate recognition to the work of internal auditors? If not, does the proposed standard place too much emphasis and preference on the work of internal auditors or not enough?

UBS sees a clear need to give appropriate recognition to the work done by internal audit and other internal independent control functions regarding assessment of the effectiveness of the design of the control framework and its operation. A global financial institution of the size of UBS has a high number of significant processes across many legal entities and geographical locations that impact the significant accounts and disclosures. A validation of these activities is achieved through a large number of control activities carefully located in the front-to-back process chain. Internal audit is particularly well suited to ensure the integrity and the overall effectiveness of the processes and the reliability of the financial information flow.

UBS has an internal audit function that is fully independent, has unrestricted audit rights, and reports significant results to the Board of Directors and the Audit Committee. The head of internal audit reports to the Chairman of the Board of Directors and has regular

αβ

PCAOB RuleMaking
Docket Matter No. 008
Page 7 of 9

meetings with the Audit Committee. The methodologies and the quality of work of internal audit are assessed by the Audit Committee and by external auditors and regulators (e.g. UK FSA, FED).

UBS agrees with the concept of having three categories of controls that differentiate the extent to which the external auditors may rely on the work of others when evaluating internal control in any individual instance. UBS also uses different categories for the definition of the internal review processes (e.g., the highest level requires an assessment by a control function independent of the business which is the owner of the control). The internal audits conducted over time are risk-based and include an assessment of the overall design of the control framework in the audited area, its documentation and its effective operation.

The recognition of the work performed by internal audit and other internal independent control functions would not only provide clear benefits from an efficiency point of view, but also increase the overall effectiveness of the evaluation of the internal controls in the front-to-back processes across geographical locations. While UBS understands the rationale for imposing high standards on the external auditor to obtain independently an unbiased opinion, UBS believes that the work performed by its internal audit function - highly independent from business management - reflects to a high degree the aims of the walkthroughs described in paragraph 79 through 83. Therefore, the recognition of the testing performed by internal audit should be better reflected in the relevant sections of the Proposed Standard where reference is made to the use of the work performed by management and others (including internal audit).

Question 17: Will the definitions in the proposed standard of significant deficiency and material weakness provide for increased consistency in the evaluation of deficiencies? How can the definitions be improved?

UBS appreciates the effort by the PCAOB to provide definitions of key terms such as deficiency, significant deficiency, and material weakness (Proposed Standard paragraphs 7-9 and Appendix D Examples D1-D3) and to provide guidance on significant locations and accounts (Proposed Standard Appendix B paragraphs B4-B19 and examples B1- B4) and materiality considerations (Proposed Standard paragraphs 21-23). UBS takes note of the fact that the participants at the PCAOB roundtable did not express concerns with the existing understanding regarding these definitions in the U.S. accounting profession.

However, UBS finds the proposed terms confusing and their use within the Proposed Standard difficult to reconcile. It is logical to distinguish between those control failures that pose only a slight risk of misstatement in the financial statements and therefore should be reported to a company's internal management and audit committee and those control failures that are deemed so material that they pose a severe risk of misstatement and therefore should be disclosed to investors and other third parties. It is unclear, however, why a simple materiality concept cannot be used to distinguish these two types of control failures and why there needs to be three levels of control failures plus additional guidance regarding materiality. UBS would prefer a simple materiality standard that is used to distinguish those control failures that merely indicate some questions regarding the financial statement reporting process from those control failures that call into question the reliability and validity of the financial reporting process.

WG
&L Warren, Gorham & Lamont

$\alpha\beta$

PCAOB RuleMaking
Docket Matter No. 008
Page 8 of 9

No matter what definitions are adopted, UBS agrees that the guidance provided in Appendix B and D of the Proposed Standard are vital to understanding the concepts that should be applied. As far as UBS is aware, this is the first concrete examples of the appropriate scope and nature for the SOX 404 evaluations by management and/or auditors. Therefore, UBS believes that this guidance should be reviewed carefully as it will likely become the leading reference source for those seeking practical examples when designing SOX 404 compliance and auditing programs.

Question 22: Is it appropriate to require the auditors to evaluate the effectiveness of the audit committee's oversight of the company's external financial reporting and internal control over financial reporting?

UBS believes that the Proposed Standard should encourage companies to have strong internal audit functions. UBS believes that companies should be motivated to have internal audit functions that are well-staffed with qualified individuals that have demonstrable independence from management and who comply with best practice standards. For example, UBS has a clear separation between its Executive Board, which has management responsibilities, and its Board of Directors, which has oversight responsibilities. The independent internal audit function reports to the Board of Directors only. This has provided a sound structure for ensuring the quality of internal auditing practices. To the extent possible, the Proposed Standard should encourage companies to develop sound governance structures around internal audit functions as this will help strengthen the internal controls over financial reporting generally.

$\alpha\beta$

PCAOB RuleMaking
Docket Matter No. 008
Page 9 of 9

UBS appreciates the opportunity to comment on the Proposed Standard. If you have any questions on the matters we have raised in this letter or would like to discuss any of them further, please contact:

Nick Bolton, Group Head of Operational Risk
+41 1 234 90 30, nick.bolton@ubs.com

Peter Thurneysen, Group Controlling and Accounting
+ 41 1 236 87 96, peter.thurneysen@ubs.com

Yours sincerely,

UBS AG

Walter Stuerzinger
Group Chief Risk Officer

Hugo Schaub
Group Controller

¶ 629. Guidance Software

 The Leader in Computer Forensics and Incident Response Solutions

November 14, 2003

VIA EMAIL

Office of the Secretary
PCAOB
1666 K Street, N.W.
Washington, DC 20006-2803

Re: **PCAOB Rulemaking Docket Matter No. 8**

Dear Sirs or Madams:

These comments are submitted on behalf of Guidance Software, Inc. in response to the Proposed Auditing Standard, *An Audit of Internal Control Over Financial Reporting Performed in Conjunction With an Audit of Financial Statements* (the "Proposed Standard") contained in PCAOB Release No. 2003-017 (the "Release") (PCAOB Rulemaking Docket Matter No. 008). The Proposed Standard, if adopted, would be the standard on attestation engagements referred to in Section 404(b) and Section 103(a)(2)(A) of the Sarbanes-Oxley Act of 2002 ("Sarbanes-Oxley").

Guidance Software applauds the PCAOB as it continues its efforts to re-establish the independence of the auditing profession and improve the quality of audits, and thus their utility to investors. The Proposed Standard, however, falls short in addressing the auditor's role in preventing, detecting, and responding to fraud. Since a lack of effective internal controls enables fraud, and the result of fraud is often an improper use or disposition of assets (and is thus covered by the definition of "internal control over financial reporting"), the audit of internal control over financial reporting should address a company's policies and practices aimed at discouraging and responding to fraud.

Although the Release sets forth thirty-one specific questions, on topics ranging from an integrated audit to auditor's independence, the PCAOB has not set forth any question concerning the issue of fraud. The entirety of the PCAOB's commentary concerning fraud, in a twenty-five-page letter, consists of one paragraph, which is set forth below:

> **Fraud Considerations in an Audit of Internal Control Over Financial Reporting**
>
> Strong internal controls provide better opportunities to detect and deter fraud. For example, many frauds resulting in financial statement restatement relied upon the ability of management to exploit weaknesses in internal control. To the extent that the internal control reporting required by Section 404 can help restore investor confidence by improving

The Leader in Computer Forensics and Incident Response Solutions

PCAOB
November 14, 2003
Page 2 of 6

> the effectiveness of internal controls (and reducing the incidence of fraud), the auditing standard on performing the audit of internal control over financial reporting should emphasize controls that prevent or detect errors as well as fraud. For this reason, the proposed standard specifically addresses and emphasizes the importance of controls over possible fraud and requires the auditor to test controls specifically intended to prevent or detect fraud that is reasonably likely to result in material misstatement of the financial statements.[1]

The PCAOB has glossed over the central point of Sarbanes-Oxley: that public companies must engage in effective self-policing to combat internal corporate fraud. Sarbanes-Oxley represented the Congressional response to "the shenanigans . . .that ha[d] been going on in corporate America"[2] such as the Enron debacle.[3] Thus, Sarbanes-Oxley was enacted to protect investors by combating corporate crime and improving corporate governance.[4] One of the central themes underlying Sarbanes-Oxley is that public companies need to institute and maintain adequate internal controls, which must include "controls related to the **prevention, identification and detection of fraud**."[5] (Emphasis added). As many commentators have noted, Sarbanes-Oxley requires companies to implement extensive corporate governance policies to prevent and to respond timely to fraudulent activity within the company.[6] For example, Sarbanes-Oxley expressly requires publicly traded companies to create anonymous hotlines for the reporting of fraud, it requires executives to certify that their financial statements are accurate, and it provides additional protections for employees of public companies who report fraud. The inclusion of a requirement for an internal control audit was an effort to have the auditing profession, instead of shredding evidence as in the Andersen case, directly involved in the effort to prevent, identify, and discover fraud. Clearly, the requirement that a financial statement audit encompass controls that address or mitigate fraud risk, as required by AU sec. 316, *Consideration of Fraud in Financial Statement Audit*, proved ineffective prior to Sarbanes-Oxley, at least in the eyes of Congress. Thus, a new audit requirement was instituted to have auditors conduct a separate audit of a company's internal controls.

The Section 404 requirement of effective internal controls encompasses more than mere accounting practices. In June 2003 the SEC issued its final rules under Section 404 of Sarbanes-Oxley. The SEC noted that "internal control is a broad concept that extends beyond the accounting functions of a company."[7] Under the SEC's definition of "internal control over financial reporting," a definition which the Release purportedly adopts,[8] the internal controls process must include policies and procedures that:

> Provide reasonable assurance regarding prevention or timely detection of unauthorized acquisition, use or disposition of the [company's] assets that **could have** a material effect on the financial statements.[9]

215 North Marengo Avenue, Second Floor • Pasadena, California 91101 | tel. 626 229 9191 | fax. 626 229 9199 | www.guidancesoftware.com

The Leader in Computer Forensics and Incident Response Solutions

PCAOB
November 14, 2003
Page 3 of 6

The definition is crystal clear: internal controls over financial reporting must include those controls designed to prevent or detect activities such as insider trading and other internal financial fraud, theft of intellectual property, large-scale misappropriation of customer information, or other similar losses that "could have" a material effect on the financial statements. The Proposed Standard, however, narrows the "safeguarding of assets" function of internal controls to "protection only against losses arising from intentional and unintentional misstatements in processing transactions and handling the related assets."[10] As noted above, however, safeguarding of assets is intimately linked to the prevention and detection of fraud; the occurrence of fraud often leads directly to the misappropriation or destruction of a company's assets. Note that the COSO Framework recognizes that one of the "temptations" for employee fraud is "nonexistent or ineffective controls," as well as "high decentralization that . . . reduces the chances of getting caught."[11] Thus, in order to prevent employee fraud, or unauthorized acquisition, use or disposition of a company's assets, the company should have in place effective controls that increase the likelihood of getting caught. In discussing fraud, however, the Proposed Standard restricts the review of controls "intended to address the risks of fraud that are **reasonably likely** to have a material affect on the company's financial statements."[12] As a result, a failure of controls against fraud that "could have," but is not "reasonably likely to have," a material affect on the company's financial statements is written out of the Proposed Standard. There is no justification for this narrow focus. Rather, the Proposed Standard should focus on controls to fight fraud (which leads to unauthorized acquisition, use or disposition of the company's assets) that **could have** a material effect on the financial statements.

A pair of hypotheticals highlights the shortcomings of the Proposed Standard:

> 1)   Assume a company in which a senior executive who has access to material, nonpublic information is facilitating a friend's trading in the company's stock based on that information, in violation of the company's internal policies and the securities laws, by using an instant messaging service. Assume further that the company has failed to implement available technology that would allow it to capture the relevant evidence concerning the rogue employee's activities, and thereby enforce its policies, and refer the case to law enforcement.[13] Finally, assume that public knowledge of this executive's activities would materially harm the company by causing it to defend itself from regulatory investigations and shareholder suits. In an audit under the Proposed Standard, the Company's "nonexistent or ineffective controls," to use the COSO language, would be unlikely to be unmasked, since the controls in question would not govern "intentional and unintentional misstatements in processing transactions." Certainly, if the auditors uncovered the executive's fraud, it would result in at least a significant deficiency under Section 126 of the Proposed Standard. However, the auditing profession's track record in uncovering executive fraud is not comforting. It would be far better for auditors to focus on looking for and demanding effective controls that increase the

215 North Marengo Avenue, Second Floor • Pasadena, California 91101 | tel. 626 229 9191 | fax. 626 229 9199 | www.guidancesoftware.com

The Leader in Computer Forensics and Incident Response Solutions

PCAOB
November 14, 2003
Page 4 of 6

likelihood of catching employee malfeasance, thereby helping prevent employee fraud in the first place.

2)   Assume an entertainment company that has valuable intellectual property, both in already released films, and in films currently being produced. Assume further that if one of the pre-released films were to transmitted by a rogue employee to a file-sharing website prior to the scheduled launch of the film, that the company would suffer material financial harm. Finally, assume that the company has failed to install readily available controls to detect the rogue employee's unauthorized disposition of this important company asset. Under the definition of "internal control over financial reporting," the hypothetical entertainment company has a problem (whether defined as an internal control deficiency, a significant deficiency, or a material weakness) – its internal controls do not "provide reasonable assurance regarding prevention or timely detection of unauthorized . . . disposition of . . . assets that could have a material effect on the financial statements." Under the Proposed Standard, however, the auditors would have nothing to say about this hypothetical company's grievous lack of internal controls, because the controls in question would not govern "intentional and unintentional misstatements in processing transactions."

COSO specifically recognizes the risks of internal wrongdoing: "Former or disgruntled employees can be more of a threat to a system than hackers."[14] Indeed, "the assessment of risks not only influences the control activities, but may also highlight a need to reconsider information and communication needs."[15] The Proposed Standard does nod towards the broader COSO approach by noting that "[t]he auditor should identify all controls that could materially affect financial reporting, including controls that focus primarily on the effectiveness and efficiency of operations or compliance with laws and regulations and which also have a material effect on the reliability of financial reporting."[16] The Proposed Standard, however, should focus more on those controls that can safeguard the company's assets from fraud or other unauthorized use or disposition. For example, Section 126 of the Proposed Standard sets forth specific circumstances that "should be regarded as at least a significant deficiency and [are] a strong indicator that a material weakness in internal control over financial reporting exists."[17] In addition to the items listed, there should be added:

- Fraud prevention, detection and/or response programs and controls are ineffective.[18]
- Controls to protect the company's assets from unauthorized acquisition, use or disposition are ineffective.

As noted above, Section 126 of the Proposed Standard lists "[i]dentification of fraud of any magnitude on the part of senior management." Certainly, if fraud is identified, that is indicative

215 North Marengo Avenue, Second Floor • Pasadena, California 91101 | tel. 626 229 9191 | fax. 626 229 9199 | www.guidancesoftware.com

The Leader in Computer Forensics and Incident Response Solutions

PCAOB
November 14, 2003
Page 5 of 6

of a serious control issue. The more fundamental point, however, is that the lack of effective controls to prevent, detect, and respond to fraud is a serious control issue, whether or not any fraud is identified at the time of the audit. Moreover, it is a control issue that ultimately impacts the accuracy and quality of the company's financial reporting.

In sum, internal fraud and insider malfeasance in corporate America caused widespread harm to investors and the overall economy, leading directly to the passage of Sarbanes-Oxley. Because the lack of adequate controls to deter, prevent, and respond to such fraud creates an unreasonable risk of such fraud occurring, which very well could impact the financial statements, the standard ultimately adopted by the PCAOB should, at a minimum, require auditors to address a company's internal controls for fighting fraud.

Sincerely,

Guidance Software, Inc. by:

/s/ Victor T. Limongelli

Victor T. Limongelli
General Counsel

---

[1] Release, at 20-21.
[2] Representative Bentsen, 148 Cong. Rec. H5462-02, at *H5467.
[3] Congress acted "in response to Enron, Global Crossing and other bankruptcies." Representative Oxley, 148 Cong. Rec. H5462-02, at *H5462. *See also* "The events of the past months have underscored the importance of transparency in corporate governance. While many believed that Enron was an isolated occurrence, the failures of Tyco, Global Crossing, and WorldCom have eroded confidence in the markets, both here and overseas" Representative Jones, 148 Cong. Rec. H5462-02, at *H5469.
[4] According to Senator Sarbanes, "[t]he bill sets significantly higher standards for corporate responsibility governance. . . . There are also extensive criminal penalties contained in this legislation . . . These provisions, among other things, require the CEOs and CFOs to certify their company's financial statements under penalty of potentially severe punishments." Senator Sarbanes, 148 Cong. Rec. S7350-04, at *S7351.
[5] 68 FR 36636, 36643, June 18, 2003.
[6] Another galvanizing factor was the rampant destruction of computer evidence that occurred in the Arthur Andersen/Enron case. *See* the Arthur Andersen indictment, which alleges that "an unparalleled initiative was undertaken to . . . delete computer files" available at:
http://news.findlaw.com/hdocs/docs/enron/usandersen030702ind.pdf
[7] 68 FR 36636, 36638, June 18, 2003.
[8] Release, § 6.
[9] 68 FR 36636, 36640, June 18, 2003 (Emphasis added).
[10] Release, Appendix C, ¶ C1.
[11] COSO Framework, at 25.
[12] Release, § 24.

215 North Marengo Avenue, Second Floor • Pasadena, California 91101 | tel. 626 229 9191 | fax. 626 229 9199 | www.guidancesoftware.com

---

The Leader in Computer Forensics and Incident Response Solutions

PCAOB
November 14, 2003
Page 6 of 6

---

[13] Even before the passage of Sarbanes-Oxley, the SEC's official position regarding internal investigations was that effective self-policing and cooperation with law enforcement could reduce or even eliminate a corporation's liability for violation of the federal securities laws. For instance, the SEC's investigation into Seaboard Corporation found that the controller of one of Seaboard's divisions had caused Seaboard's books and records to overstate assets and understate expenses, and had subsequently actively concealed such misstatements. *See In the Matter of Gisela de Leon-Meredith*, Exchange Act Release No. 44970 (October 23, 2001). Although the SEC ordered relief against the controller, it took no enforcement action against Seaboard, due to the company's prompt and thorough response to the incident, as well as its cooperation with the SEC. *See* Exchange Act Release No. 44969 (October 23, 2001). The SEC noted that the public at large benefits when "businesses seek out, self-report and rectify illegal conduct." Id. The SEC, in deciding "whether, and how much, to credit self-policing, self-reporting, remediation and cooperation," (Exchange Act Release No. 44969 (October 23, 2001)) established four broad measures for it to assess:

- Self-policing prior to the discovery of the misconduct . . .
- Self-reporting of misconduct when it is discovered, including conducting a thorough review of the nature, extent, origins and consequences of the misconduct . . .
- Remediation . . . modifying and improving internal controls . . .
- Cooperation with law enforcement authorities, including providing the [SEC] staff with all information relevant to the underlying violations . . .

SEC Release 2001-117 (October 23, 2001). Indeed, in order to cooperate effectively with the SEC and law enforcement, a company must be able to "identify . . . evidence with sufficient precision to facilitate prompt enforcement actions against those who violated the law." Exchange Act Release No. 44969 (October 23, 2001).

[14] COSO Framework, at 53.

[15] COSO Framework, at 18.

[16] Release, § 14.

[17] Release § 126.

[18] Although Section 123 of the Release mentions "antifraud programs and controls," it does so in the context of discussing the interaction of qualitative and quantitative considerations. It would be better addressed in Section 126.

215 North Marengo Avenue, Second Floor • Pasadena, California 91101 | tel. 626 229 9191 | fax. 626 229 9199 | www.guidancesoftware.com

---

¶ 630. Health Insurance Plan of Greater New York

November 20, 2003

Office of the Secretary
Public Company Accounting Oversight Board
1666 K Street, N.W.
Washington, D.C. 20006-2803

Re: PCAOB Rulemaking Docket Matter No. 008 – Proposed Auditing Standard – An Audit of Internal Control Over Financial Reporting Performed in Conjunction with an Audit of Financial Statements

Dear Board Members:

As Executive Vice President and Chief Financial Officer of the Health Insurance Plan of Greater New York ("HIP"), I am pleased to be able to respond to the request for comments from the Public Company Accounting Oversight Board regarding *Proposed Auditing Standard – An Audit of Internal Control Over Financial Reporting Performed in Conjunction with an Audit of Financial Statement (PCAOB Rulemaking Docket Matter No. 008).*

HIP is a managed care company with revenues in excess of $3 billion. Even though HIP is a not a public company, HIP began the process in February 2003 of building the infrastructure necessary to comply with the provisions of Sections 302 and 404 of the Sarbanes Oxley Act of 2002. HIP chose COSO as its framework for management's assessment of internal controls over financial reporting. As of November 2003, it is projected that the cost to complete the company's initial assessment, document all policies and procedures and perform the initial test work of internal controls will approximate $5 million in consulting hours alone (approximately 30,000 man hours of consulting time). Staffing costs to ensure ongoing compliance are estimated at $2.0 - 3.0 million annually. The company also estimates that annual audit costs may triple from current levels by fiscal 2005 due to the required internal control attestation. As with most managed care companies, HIP faces significant pressures from employer groups to hold premium increases to a minimum, in an environment of rapidly rising

Office of the Secretary
Public Company Accounting Oversight Board
November 20, 2003
Page 2

medical costs. These additional audit and operational costs, if not recovered in additional savings from internal control improvements, will regrettably have to be passed along to HIP's subscribers, many of whom are small and medium size businesses.

The Sarbanes Oxley legislation specifically states that a public accounting firm that prepares and issues the audit report should attest to, and report on, the assessment of internal controls made by the issuer of the financial statements. The proposed auditing standard requires the external auditor not only to report on and attest to management's assessment, but also to perform a detailed audit of internal controls. If management has properly assessed the effectiveness of the company's internal controls, why is it necessary for the external auditor to duplicate this effort? Current auditing standards allow for an auditor to issue an attestation report on management's assertion over internal controls as opposed to auditing internal controls. Consideration must be given to the additional audit costs incurred and the serious disruptions to the company's operations caused by the duplicate testing and evaluation of internal controls required by the proposed standard.

If the auditor must evaluate and audit the effectiveness of internal controls in addition to attesting to the assessment made by management, why shouldn't they be able to follow current auditing standards related to the use of testing performed by the company's internal audit department? Under current auditing standards if a company has an effective, competent internal audit function that has performed relevant tests, an auditor may rely on such work. Relief should be given in the final standard to allow the auditor to place greater reliance, if appropriate, on management or internal audit's testing of internal controls.

The proposed standard also indicates that each year's audit of internal control must stand alone. If there have been no changes to a particular set of internal control activities, why shouldn't the external auditor be allowed to rotate the activities tested from year to year? The external auditor should be allowed to use some of the audit evidence obtained in previous years to support the current opinion on management's assessment.

We are also concerned that the Board has changed the definition of material weakness in internal controls from what currently exists in auditing standards. Current auditing standards define material weakness as a "reportable condition in which the design or operation of one or more of the internal control components does not reduce to a <u>relatively low level</u> the risk that misstatement caused by error or fraud in amounts that would be material in relation to the financial statements..... may occur and not be detected within a timely period...". The

Office of the Secretary
Public Company Accounting Oversight Board
November 20, 2003
Page 3

proposed standard defines material weakness as "a significant deficiency that, by itself, or in combination with other significant deficiencies, results in <u>more than</u> <u>a</u> <u>remote likelihood</u> that a material misstatement of the annual or interim financial statements will not be prevented or detected." We believe that the gap that exists between "low level of risk" of material misstatement and "more than remote likelihood" of material misstatement is significant. Based on the proposed standards, the auditor's attestation of management's assessment of internal control and the effectiveness of those controls is tantamount to a guarantee or warranty that the company's internal controls over financial reporting are effective and result in financial statements that are free of material misstatement. This is an invitation to the plaintiff's bar to bring yet more litigation in our already highly litigious society. The increased risk to auditing firms that will result from such a warranty can only result in greatly increased costs upon those firms and in due course upon public companies.

The requirement in the proposed standard that the external auditor evaluate the effectiveness of the audit committee's oversight is impracticable and untenable. A significant conflict of interest exists in having the external auditor assess the effectiveness of the audit committee, since the audit committee is responsible for hiring, compensating, and supervising the external auditor. The responsibility for hiring and managing the relationship with the external auditor has been placed with the audit committee, as opposed to management, in part to prevent a conflict of interest between management and the external auditor. Requiring the external auditor to evaluate the effectiveness of the audit committee merely re-establishes this conflict of interest at the audit committee level. The suggestion in the proposed standard that the external auditor can provide an honest evaluation of the effectiveness of the committee that determines its tenure to a full Board of Directors is fundamentally flawed. We believe that this process will not result in meaningful evaluations of the effectiveness of audit committees and, therefore, does not serve the public interest. It places unacceptable political burden on the external auditor and does not enhance, but rather complicates, good corporate governance. This aspect of the proposed standard should be dropped entirely.

HIP asks the Board to establish a set of standards that are reasonable, without creating unnecessary costs that are essentially impairing the productivity of public companies. It should be noted that none of the accounting scandals that gave rise to Sarbanes Oxley resulted from breakdowns of systematic operational and accounting controls. Instead, they resulted largely from improper, non-systematic transactions driven by a lack of integrity on the part of management and the Boards of those companies. The proposed standard requires significant focus, and therefore significant cost, be devoted to evaluating internal controls

Office of the Secretary
Public Company Accounting Oversight Board
November 20, 2003
Page 4

operating within systematic processes.   While significant focus should appropriately be directed at material non-systematic transactions, the requirement to expend significant resources evaluating systematic transactions does not appear to be cost-justified. There is no amount of money that can be spent, or control testing that can take place, to prevent unscrupulous, complicit individuals from committing a fraud if said individuals are determined to do so. We strongly urge the Board to consider ways to reduce the burden of the proposed standard, while still achieving the objectives of enhanced financial reporting and protection of the public interest.

Sincerely,

Michael D. Fullwood
Executive Vice President
Chief Financial Officer
Secretary and General Counsel
Health Insurance Plan of Greater New York

¶ 631. BDO Seidman

BDO Seidman, LLP

330 Madison
New York, NY 10017-5001
Phone 212-885-8000
Fax   212-885-1299

November 21, 2003

Office of the Secretary
Public Company Accounting Oversight Board
1666 K Street, N.W.
Washington, D.C. 20006-2803

RE: **PCAOB Rulemaking Docket Matter No. 008**
       Proposed Auditing Standard, *An Audit of Internal Control Over Financial Reporting*
       Performed in Conjunction With an Audit of Financial Statements

Dear Mr. Secretary:

BDO Seidman, LLP respectfully submits the following comments on the Public Company Accounting Oversight Board's ("PCAOB" or "Board") proposed auditing standard ("the proposed standard") governing the independent auditor's attestation and reporting on management's assessment of the effectiveness of internal control over financial reporting referred to in Sections 103(a)(2)(A) and 404(b) of the Sarbanes-Oxley Act of 2002 ("the Act"). BDO Seidman, LLP is pleased to serve on the Task Force of the PCAOB considering implementation issues and the AICPA Task Forces that developed draft standards prior to the effective certification date of the PCAOB, and since that date has been discussing practical implementation issues.

We recognize the importance of establishing and enforcing standards that will restore confidence in our financial reporting environment and are anxious to participate further in the initiatives of the PCAOB and other regulatory bodies to advance the quality of our professional standards. We appreciate the dedicated effort necessary to develop quality standards.

In addition to the direct questions posed by the Exposure Draft, there are several overarching points related to the proposed standard we would like to communicate, as follows:

Lack of Preparer Guidance

We have previously communicated to the PCAOB (Letter dated August 6, 2003 to Douglas R. Carmichael, Chief Auditor) our concern that the preparer community lacks effective guidance relating to the extent of documentation and testing required to meet its responsibilities under Section 404 of the Act and the related SEC rules. In the absence of such guidance, the auditor must apply judgment on a case-by-case basis when assessing the adequacy of the documentation and testing performed by the preparer to support its assertion. We find it unreasonable to require the expression of an audit opinion covering a subject matter that is effectively "undefined."

Preparers are anxiously seeking guidance from their auditors as to their documentation and testing responsibilities under the Act and SEC rules. It is possible that auditors providing this guidance might be misconstrued as providing legal advice, or impairing the independence of the auditor. We understand that the PCAOB may not be able to mandate preparer responsibilities. We do acknowledge the criteria for auditor evaluation of preparer documentation in the proposed standard, which we believe are very helpful. However, we urge the PCAOB to work with the SEC to provide the necessary implementation standards and guidance to the preparer community.

BDO Seidman, LLP

330 Madison
New York, NY 10017-5001
Phone 212-885-8000
Fax   212-885-1299

Lack of Preparer Document Retention Guidance - The final standard should be expanded to include guidance relating to the retention of internal controls documentation and testing by the preparer. This is especially important in this standard, as auditors have not previously performed audits of internal controls as now envisioned.

An issue related to both audit documentation and the lack of current preparer guidance, is the lack of any specific documentation retention requirements for preparers. For example, some preparers are currently documenting and testing their internal controls using web-based tools. These systems may be set up so that documentation can be updated on a contemporaneous basis as elements of the systems change. In addition, preparers may use a proprietary software product to document their activities and software-licensing issues could make it difficult for the auditor to obtain or utilize the assessment. We believe that preparers should maintain an archived copy of the controls documentation that relate to each year's management assertion. We also believe that any software, licenses or tools needed for the auditor to review the documentation of the entity should be made available by the entity. In the absence of assurances that such documentation will be retained, the auditor may need to obtain copies of the preparer's documentation to include in the auditor workpapers and retain such documentation as evidence of the documents reviewed. In that regard, we believe it is inappropriate and inefficient for auditors to become the repository of corporate records.

This issue is broader than audits of internal controls, but has arisen as particularly troublesome in this context. Many preparers in our marketplace that have begun their 404 projects related to the internal controls documentation and testing had not initially considered this issue in their plans.

Some may believe that such an archived, indexed record may already be required under regulations requiring the retention of documentation supporting matters contained in SEC filings or under the existing "books and records" provision of the 1934 Exchange Act (13(b)). We do not think these provisions are currently worded broadly enough to clearly require the retention of management's support for its 404 assertion. Nevertheless, we have observed that the need to retain such documentation has not been universally recognized as a requirement by all preparers. Therefore, the final standard should include "the adequate retention of documentation of controls, evaluation of design effectiveness, and testing and monitoring of operating effectiveness" as an expected attribute that could, if absent, be a presumptive indicator of a material weakness.

Overall Efficiency of the Standard

While we believe the auditor's attestation regarding the effectiveness of internal control should contribute to better financial reporting, the underlying standard should recognize that there are a number of elements of existing auditing requirements and recent regulatory actions that already provide a significant measure of cost-effective public protection and risk reduction. Notably:
- The Implementation of Corporate Anti-Fraud Programs (recommended in Statement of Auditing Standards No. 99 "Consideration of Fraud in a Financial Statement Audit " and a component of an effective corporate control environment under the COSO framework)
- The implementation of the required auditing procedures and inquiries outlined in SAS 99, which are being applied for the first time this year.
- Improvements in the investigatory and legal processes wherein corporate executives will be investigated and prosecuted for fraud.
- Improvements in corporate governance to ensure independent and competent directors and effective audit committees

BDO Seidman, LLP

330 Madison
New York, NY 10017-5001
Phone 212-885-8000
Fax   212-885-1299

- A more effective industry-wide inspection program to ensure firm compliance with the form and substance of the standards, and to ensure the firms' focus on the proper "tone at the top" in their organizations.

In that context, we are concerned that the current proposed standard requires redundant and excessive procedures to be performed by the auditor during an audit of internal controls. While we acknowledge the importance of significant auditor involvement in testing the work of management, in many places the auditor is required to go well beyond the traditional audit concept of testing and examining evidence. For example, the auditor is required in all significant processes to perform all the walkthrough procedures, and to perform all the procedures necessary to assess general controls and the control environment. We believe these requirements will not significantly contribute to more effective internal controls audits, and will unnecessarily raise the related auditing costs. We recommend the final standard better reflect the concept of testing by the auditor. Of course, this is subject to evaluating the objectivity and competence of internal auditors, contracted service providers, management or employees performing the documentation, testing and monitoring required of companies by the Act.

We have provided specific suggestions regarding this matter in our responses to questions 10, 14, 15 and 20.

The Proposed Auditing Standard Does Not Create a Cohesive and Comprehensive Body of Auditing Literature

In addition to addressing the issues related to the reporting and performance of audits of internal controls, the proposed standard modifies existing literature not directly related to the audit of internal controls.

For example, paragraph 138 states that "the auditor should perform substantive procedures for all relevant assertions for all significant accounts and disclosures" (emphasis added). Also, paragraph 141 states that "the auditor's substantive procedures must include reconciling the financial statements to the accounting records." These new audit requirements are not related to the audit of internal controls. While we believe these requirements are appropriate, and believe they are consistent with the "risk assessment" Exposure Draft of the AICPA, we are concerned about their subtle placement in this document.

These issues are neither highlighted in the text nor discussed in the briefing paper. Thus readers might not identify these changes in the literature. Additionally, if the existing AICPA standards adopted by the PCAOB as interim standards are not marked for conforming changes, the body of auditing literature applicable to audits of public companies may become confusing and contradictory. We strongly recommend the PCAOB clearly indicate any and all changes to its adopted interim standards as part of its exposure process.

It is our understanding that the body of AICPA standards applicable to private company audits conducted under AICPA standards will continue to grow and evolve. We assume the interim standards adopted by the PCAOB would not reflect changes in the AICPA standards after their adoption date as interim standards, and therefore that literature would be static for public company audits unless modified by the PCAOB. Therefore, it is likely that the two bodies of standards will diverge over time. Accordingly, to make the auditing literature relating to public companies clear and to maintain quality auditing in public company audits, we strongly recommend a "marked for changes" version of any paragraph or section edits of the adopted

BDO Seidman, LLP

330 Madison
New York, NY 10017-5001
Phone 212-885-8000
Fax   212-885-1299

interim standards necessary as conforming changes be released with the new adopted standards of the PCAOB.

While we support the PCAOB's development of quality control standards, we recommend that they be presented in the appropriate section of the PCAOB Professional Literature. If there are very narrow implementation issues relating to a subject matter of a standard, we do not object to including that narrow guidance in a section of the auditing standard, but encourage such guidance to also be repeated in the PCAOB Quality Control Literature, where it otherwise would be expected to appear.

Effective Date

It is our understanding that after approval of a final standard by the PCAOB, an additional exposure period by the SEC is required. Therefore, a final "published" rule is unlikely until well into 2004. We believe this will not provide time for issuers to complete their documentation, evaluate and test controls, and correct any deficiencies identified, nor an opportunity for the auditing firms to ensure the requisite trained personnel are in place to perform the procedures required by the final standard. Most firms will find it impossible to provide timely training on the final standard during the "busy season," even though many auditors already have orientation and training in the subject matter.

Under these time constraints we see a risk that the implementation of the final standard for accelerated filers that must begin reporting on internal controls for years ending after June 15, 2004 will raise the potential for mistakes and misunderstandings that could undermine the intention of this requirement to restore investor confidence.

In that regard, we urge the PCAOB to make a recommendation to the SEC to delay the effective implementation of the final standard for accelerated filers. We believe it appropriate, assuming no further delays in issuing the standard, to require the audit of internal controls to accompany the financial statements of entities whose fiscal years end on or after October 15, 2004, but no earlier than six months after the final standard is published.

PCAOB Comment Letter – Draft Responses to Questions

Questions regarding an integrated audit of the financial statements and internal control over financial reporting:

1. **Is it appropriate to refer to the auditor's attestation of management's assessment of the effectiveness of internal control over financial reporting as the audit of internal control over financial reporting?**

Yes. We believe the "audit" terminology clearly communicates the service being performed to users of financial statements and distinguishes the service from an attestation service performed under the standards of the AICPA which we believe should still be available to public entities for internal or other purposes.

2. **Should the auditor be prohibited from performing an audit of internal control over financial reporting without also performing an audit of the financial statements?**

Yes. We believe that the auditor performing an audit of internal controls under the PCAOB auditing and related standards must also audit the financial statements. This is a clear requirement of Rule

330 Madison
New York, NY 10017-5001
Phone 212-885-8000
Fax   212-885-1299

BDO Seidman, LLP

2-02 of Regulation S-X and is mandated by Section 404 of the Sarbanes-Oxley Act.

It is our understanding that the final standard will replace the current AICPA AT Section 501 guidance in the PCAOB standards literature. In that circumstance, there would be no public company auditing literature guiding an attest service relating to internal controls unless performed in conjunction with an audit of the financial statements. However, we can envision a circumstance where such an attest service might be requested without requiring a full financial statement audit, such as a pre-merger attestation to evaluate to the effectiveness of controls of that entity as of a specific date or an attestation engagement for an interim financial period. In our view, an attestation service can be performed under AICPA AT 501 standards in such circumstances.

3. **Rather than requiring the auditor to also complete an audit of the financial statements, would an appropriate alternative be to require the auditor to perform work with regard to the financial statements comparable to that required to complete the financial statement audit?**

With respect to the required audit of internal controls accompanying the annual audit of the financial statements, we believe the rules are clear that a division of auditor responsibility is not permitted, and thus the concept of "comparable" work is not relevant in that context.

Questions regarding the costs and benefits of internal control:

4. **Does the Board's proposed standard give appropriate consideration to how internal control is implemented in, and how the audit of internal control over financial reporting should be conducted at, small and medium-sized issuers?**

No. We believe the proposed standard does not give adequate guidance on how internal control audits differ when conducted for small and medium size businesses. While we do not believe there should be a lower standard for evaluating or reporting on the effectiveness of internal controls in smaller enterprises, we acknowledge the techniques of auditing the internal controls of such smaller issuers will likely differ.

We believe the example in the Appendix, suggesting that management oversight might compensate for a missing or ineffective control, improperly implies that management supervision is an acceptable alternative to controls. We believe such an implication may be used by many entities to excuse missing or ineffective controls. However, recent history is replete with examples where management is the problem, and not the control.

We also think it inappropriate that the responsibility for defining the different small company environment and the associated audit responsibilities in these environments rests with the auditor. We are not aware of any guidance that would aid in achieving a consistent approach across companies and among firms on this issue. Absent guidance tailored to the small and medium sized issuers or changes in the reporting options, the proposed standard will likely result in a large proportion of smaller issuers receiving adverse opinions.

We do not feel a remedy for this is to weaken the value of an unqualified opinion on internal controls for smaller entities. The public will be unable to identify when an unqualified audit report may mean something different because the entity's controls were evaluated according to a small entity standard. We would rather see a deferral of the implementation date for smaller entities (perhaps using a non-accelerated filer definition) pending further research and experimentation in providing and reporting on this service.

BDO Seidman, LLP

330 Madison
New York, NY 10017-5001
Phone 212-885-8000
Fax   212-885-1299

Question regarding the audit of internal control over financial reporting:

5. **Should the Board, generally or in this proposed standard, specify the level of competence and training of the audit personnel that is necessary to perform specified auditing procedures effectively? For example, it would be inappropriate for a new, inexperienced auditor to have primary responsibility for conducting interviews of a company's senior management about possible fraud.**

No, we believe this level of guidance in the public company auditing standards is unnecessary and not a response to an identified issue. We believe the interim AICPA standards adopted by the PCAOB adequately address this issue in the existing general and field work standards for auditing and attestation engagements.

Questions regarding evaluation of management's assessment:

6. **Is the scope of the audit appropriate in that it requires the auditor to both evaluate management's assessment and obtain, directly, evidence about whether internal control over financial reporting is effective?**

Yes, both management's assessment and the underlying effectiveness of internal controls are important for the auditor to consider when rendering an opinion on internal controls. Management's assessment is a public communication that has great flexibility permitted in its form and content. That document should not be misleading by commission or significant omission or a presentation that obscures important information from the reader. To render an audit report on internal controls, the auditor must accumulate sufficient evidence of controls effectiveness.

7. **Is it appropriate that the Board has provided criteria that auditors should use to evaluate the adequacy of management's documentation?**

Yes, we believe that providing examples of such criteria are appropriate. As we stated earlier, we suggest the final standard also list the preparer's failure to plan for and retain (archive) its documentation of its controls and its evaluation, testing and monitoring to support its assessment as a potential material weakness.

8. **Is it appropriate to state that inadequate documentation is an internal control deficiency, the severity of which the auditor should evaluate? Or should inadequate documentation automatically rise to the level of significant deficiency or material weakness in internal control?**

Yes, we believe it appropriate to require the auditor to assess the significance of the deficiency on a case-by-case basis. At this time, as commented previously, law or regulation does not specify the level and format of documentation required of preparers. In the absence of such guidance or a benchmark, we do not believe that an imposition of an automatic categorization of an undefined condition as a significant deficiency or material weakness will have any value in user reporting. We do encourage a re-visitation of this point if either by practical experience in applying the requirements or legislation, a more objective definition of what constitutes "inadequate documentation" can be developed.

Paragraph 46 says: "In evaluating the deficiency as to its significance, the auditor should determine whether management can demonstrate the monitoring component of internal control over financial

330 Madison
New York, NY 10017-5001
Phone 212-885-8000
Fax 212-885-1299

BDO Seidman, LLP

reporting in the absence of documentation." We do not understand how, if an objective and clear definition of a documentation deficiency can be agreed, obvious documentation deficiencies can be overcome in such cases, and in the absence of any such rationale, recommend this guidance be changed to state affirmatively that documentation deficiencies ordinarily cannot be overcome.

Questions regarding obtaining an understanding of internal control over financial reporting:

9. Are the objectives to be achieved by performing walkthroughs sufficient to require the performance of walkthroughs?

Yes. Walkthroughs to confirm the auditor's understanding of the design and implementation of controls are well established in auditing practice, and we believe would be performed in many circumstances, even if not required. We concur that such procedures are important to perform, but also caution that they do not provide sufficient evidence of manual control operations. They are simply a "sample of one."

10. Is it appropriate to require that the walkthrough be performed by the auditor himself or herself, rather than allowing the auditor to use walkthrough procedures performed by management, internal auditors, or others?

We believe it important that auditors perform many of the critical walkthroughs for significant systems and accounts. However, we believe that walkthroughs performed by others (assessed as competent and objective) on all controls and to a greater extent on less critical control operations, could be tested by the auditor to still achieve a high degree of audit assurance, in lieu of requiring that they be redundantly performed 100% by the auditor. Following this approach would represent a significant cost saving to businesses over the proposed approach. We believe a properly implemented testing approach would accomplish the desired protection for the pubic at a lower cost.

Additionally, we believe that the current wording of the standard would require that, say, if revenue were identified as a significant account, then walkthroughs of all revenue processes, regardless of their significance or materiality are required. Paragraph 79 of the draft states the requirement that the auditor "should trace all types of transactions and events, both recurring and unusual, from origination through the company's information systems until they are reflected in the company's financial reports." The extent of work required by setting the scope to "all" could be extraordinary for a large, distributed enterprise, and is inefficient.

We believe the concept of a "significant process" in this proposed standard when used as a basis for assessing which controls require walkthroughs, for example, has a profound impact on how management and the auditor view the controls for an entity. We believe it worthwhile to provide examples of what the proposed standard intended by the use of this term. This is fundamental to a common understanding between the auditor and preparer.

A remedy that should be considered is the requirement to consider measures of significance or materiality when identifying the necessity of performing walkthroughs, and whether the auditor in all circumstances must perform such walkthroughs.

Currently, we believe the guidance in paragraph 79 of the proposed standard requiring auditor walkthroughs is in conflict with the guidance in Appendix B 13. Under B13, "locations or business units that are not important, even when aggregated with others" do not require any auditor action. Yet, the provisions of paragraph 79 might require a walkthough of a transaction type at these

BDO Seidman, LLP

330 Madison
New York, NY 10017-5001
Phone 212-885-8000
Fax 212-885-1299

locations. Furthermore, if the location was not previously documented and tested by management, then the walkthrough of a transaction to "confirm" the documented control makes no sense. We therefore support the documentation, assessment and selective testing of all locations by management if the auditor might have some responsibility to perform procedures at those locations

We support the broad performance of walkthroughs by management in more instances than required of the auditor as an element of their procedures to support their assertion.

Question regarding testing operating effectiveness:

11. Is it appropriate to require the auditor to obtain evidence of the effectiveness of controls for all relevant assertions for all significant accounts and disclosures every year or may the auditor use some of the audit evidence obtained in previous years to support his or her current opinion on management's assessment?

We believe that evidence needs to be accumulated annually that controls are effective in order to issue an audit report on internal controls. In our view, management needs to fully test these important elements to the extent necessary to provide a high degree of assurance annually as part of their monitoring function. However, from an audit perspective, once it is established that a control is effective, and a system as well as the environment in which it operates has not changed, the passing of a calendar date alone should not change that basic conclusion.

With respect to the most critical controls over all relevant assertions for all significant accounts, we believe that at a minimum the auditor devote some attention each year to each of those controls. However, we believe it would be more efficient, with no loss of effectiveness, to encourage the rotation of testing <u>emphasis</u> on controls (not the rotation of controls testing). While some controls might, based on a risk assessment and entity testing findings, warrant extensive testing annually by the auditor, we believe a more effective audit could be performed when the auditor would be encouraged to focus on certain controls on a periodic basis, extending the analysis and testing of some of these controls   As reflected in SAS 99, varying the nature and extent of procedures performed from year to year is an effective strategy to achieve a high degree of assurance on the subject matter and prevent/detect fraud. On balance, the increased depth of testing in some areas should compensate for the lesser level of testing in others.

We believe this concept is already reflected in paragraph 101 of the proposed standard. However, if this was not intended, then the proposed standard should be clarified.

Questions regarding using the work of management and others:

12. To what extent should the auditor be permitted or required to use the work of management and others?

The auditor should be permitted to use the work of management and others within or engaged by the company to the extent supported by the auditor's assessment of their objectivity and competence. Generally, management would not be considered to be as objective as those outside the entity or of internal auditors, and their work might not be relied on, or relied on significantly less than if an outsourced competent service provider or objective internal audit function performed the same work.

BDO Seidman, LLP

330 Madison
New York, NY 10017-5001
Phone 212-885-8000
Fax   212-885-1299

We cannot identify any circumstances where the auditor should be <u>required</u> to use the work of management or others within or engaged by the company. Since the independent auditor has the professional responsibility for his or her opinion, such a requirement would be inappropriate.

However, we acknowledge that the engagement of specialists by auditors may be more frequently encountered than before under this standard due to the specialized nature of many topics in, for example, information technology based controls. Where an engagement team does not possess the requisite skills and knowledge to evaluate the design of or perform tests of a complex, technology based control, for example, a resource should be engaged to assist the auditor. In these cases we would expect that the auditor would continue to follow the provisions of SAS 73.

We also ask the Board to clarify whether its guidance in the proposed standard (Appendix B) on the use of service organizations is intended to modify the exiting SAS 70 literature, and if so, how. One area of likely significant implementation questions will include the role of service organizations and SAS 70 reports as they relate to the required audit of internal controls.

13. Are the three categories of controls and the extent to which the auditor may rely on the work of others appropriately defined?

We believe the categories are appropriate and helpful as a conceptual aid for auditors to understand the requirements of the proposed standard. However, as noted in several of the following responses, we have concerns that the proposed auditor requirements related to these three categories require adjustment in the final standard.

14. Does the proposed standard give appropriate recognition to the work of internal auditors? If not, does the proposed standard place too much emphasis and preference on the work of internal auditors or not enough?

Yes to the first question. Appropriate recognition is given to the value internal audit can bring to the organization and the overall audit process.

But the answer to the second question is more complicated, as we feel the mix of procedures required in the proposed standard is inefficient and ineffective.

We do not agree with the proposed standard's requirement that all the assurance the auditor receives with respect to general controls and IT controls need come solely from the auditor's procedures. In circumstances where the objectivity and competence of the internal auditor or others is assessed as high, we believe it appropriate and cost effective to permit some assurance be taken for work performed by others in these areas. We concur with the assessment of the importance of these areas overall, but believe the objectives can be achieved by requiring that most, but not necessarily all, assurance come from the independent auditor's procedures.

We also do not agree with the proposed standard's requirement that the auditor can rely "without limitation" on the work of others with regards to controls over routine processing. This can be interpreted as permitting the auditor to rely solely on others for this work. We believe it inappropriate to permit such limited involvement in controls over transactions that constitute a large portion of the transactions processed by most entities. We support the requirement in paragraph 107 that the auditor reperform some procedures as a basis for reliance <u>and</u> conduct some independent tests of the controls over routine processing. We believe that most of the assurance in this area could come from work performed by others who are assessed as objective and competent. However, we are mindful that many of the unfortunate incidents leading to corporate failures took place in

BDO Seidman, LLP

330 Madison
New York, NY 10017-5001
Phone 212-885-8000
Fax   212-885-1299

organizations that had internal audit staffs that were assessed as objective and competent. Thus, we believe in all circumstances the auditor should perform some procedures in each category of classification of controls.

15. Is the flexibility in determining the extent of reperformance of the work of others appropriate, or should the auditor be specifically required to reperform a certain level of work (for example, reperform tests of all significant accounts or reperform every test performed by others that the auditor intends to use)?

We believe that it is appropriate in this standard to provide flexibility in the extent of reperformance required in a particular circumstance. Paragraph 107 states that if the auditor intends to use the work of others, "the auditor should reperform some of the tests of controls originally performed by others." This level of guidance seems appropriate.

We believe it would be inefficient, and without an associated reduction in risk, to require the reperformance of each test performed by others on which the auditor intends to place some reliance. When work is performed by individuals or separate organizations (whose objectivity and competence is separately assessed) we believe it would be appropriate in the application of reperformance guidance to confirm the assessment of the competence of the work of that person by reperforming a sufficient level of that work to corroborate the competence with which the work was performed. Thus, a strong Firm-wide organization of internal auditors could require fewer reperformance tests to achieve the auditor's objectives than a loose organization of independent contractors performing the same procedures at different locations. In general, we believe the objectives embodied in the word "all" can in many instances be achieved at a lower cost and without a loss in quality if careful consideration is given to the principles of testing.

16. Is the requirement for the auditor to obtain the principle (sic. principal) evidence, on an overall basis, through his or her own work the appropriate benchmark for the amount of work that is required to be performed by the auditor?

Yes. However, it needs to be explicitly recognized in the standard that this is an auditor judgment, and not subject to an exact mathematical measurement.

Questions regarding evaluating results:

17. Will the definitions in the proposed standard of significant deficiency and material weakness provide for increased consistency in the evaluation of deficiencies? How can the definitions be improved?

In our view the use of the concept "remote likelihood" in the definition of a significant deficiency will needlessly and inappropriately sweep many issues into this category. We would favor a tolerance threshold that is considerably higher than remote (e.g., reasonably possible).

We urge the PCAOB to continue to gather practical examples and further develop this guidance as professional experience grows in this area.

18. Do the examples in Appendix D of how to apply these definitions in various scenarios provide helpful guidance? Are there other specific examples that commenters could suggest that would provide further interpretive help?

BDO Seidman, LLP

330 Madison
New York, NY 10017-5001
Phone 212-885-8000
Fax   212-885-1299

Yes. We encourage the PCAOB to consider an outlet such as a "Q&A" publication that can help create more consistent applications. The examples seem rather clear cut, but the more difficult decisions will be in the gray areas.

Our comments in other sections of this letter extend to the examples provided.

19. Is it necessary for the auditor to evaluate the severity of all identified internal control deficiencies?

Yes. It is necessary to make judgments of the significance and severity of all identified deficiencies We do not believe the profession yet has the requisite experience in these areas to set narrow guidelines requiring a specific treatment for specific identified deficiencies that are less than significant.

20. Is it appropriate to require the auditor to communicate all internal control deficiencies (not just material weaknesses and significant deficiencies) to management in writing?

No. Paragraph 191 refers to deficiencies from all sources such as regulators, internal auditor reports, etc. We believe that for a large and complex organization this is an unreasonable requirement that will be very costly. We believe that isolated and insignificant deficiencies may need only be communicated to local management. Deficiencies identified by internal audit or regulatory auditors or others that have already been communicated to management should not have to be repeated by the auditor. The requirement to prepare a written report should be limited to deficiencies that, in combination with other deficiencies, raise the risk of a potential significant deficiency in an account, assertion or location, plus all significant deficiencies and material weaknesses found. We note that an audit committee may request a written report of all deficiencies of any nature and significance. However we do not feel such a report should be mandated.

21. Are the matters that the Board has classified as strong indicators that a material weakness in internal control exists appropriately classified as such?

Yes. However, see our response to question 22 with respect to the proposed separate evaluation of the audit committee. We believe that the indicators listed in paragraph 126 should also include "the absence of sufficient evidence to support the responsible party's evaluation of the operating effectiveness of internal control constitutes a material weakness," as suggested in the AICPA draft standard forwarded to the PCAOB.

22. Is it appropriate to require the auditors to evaluate the effectiveness of the audit committee's oversight of the company's external financial reporting and internal control over financial reporting? And
23. Will auditors be able to effectively carry out their responsibility to evaluate the effectiveness of the audit committee's oversight?

Corporate governance is a critical component of the control environment. The audit committee, as that role has been strengthened recently by the rules of the stock exchanges, is an increasingly important element of the governance process. However, we disagree with the requirement in the proposed standard for the auditor to assess the effectiveness of the audit committee as a separate element of the internal control environment in order to determine whether a weak audit committee might be indicative of a material weakness in internal controls. COSO acknowledges the importance of the audit committee function, but does not single out this function. Rather, it considers it within the context of the board of directors and other Control Environment elements.

BDO Seidman, LLP

330 Madison
New York, NY 10017-5001
Phone 212-885-8000
Fax 212-885-1299

We believe it is not possible for the auditor to provide implicit assurance on the effectiveness of the audit committee. In our view, the auditor is not in a position to observe all the meetings, communications and actions of the audit committee as a basis for making such an assessment. We have difficulty envisioning the evidence and procedures that would support this assessment. While an auditor may be able to distinguish some weaker from stronger audit committees, and may observe an act or condition calling into question the effectiveness of the committee, an overall assessment of effectiveness is still a very subjective assessment.

Moreover, since the auditor is hired and retained by the audit committee, the requirement that the auditor conclude separately on the effectiveness of the audit committee creates a clear conflict. The imposition of such a requirement will likely hinder effective and open communication between the audit committee and the auditor at a time when better communication should be encouraged.

We also ask that regulators and the PCAOB understand that smaller entities have been responding to the requirements that audit committees improve in quality, but this is an ongoing process. The imposition of a requirement at this time to separately assess the audit committee may not have the desired effects on communication and continued improvement.

We urge that the final standard not require a specific assessment of the audit committee, but acknowledge its place within the governance structure and control environment.

If the final standard continues to require a separate assessment of the audit committee, we suggest the standard also make clear that management must also make a separate assessment of the audit committee as a basis for management's assertion

23. Will auditors be able to effectively carry out their responsibility to evaluate the effectiveness of the audit committee's oversight?

See response to question 22 above.

24. If the auditor concludes that ineffective audit committee oversight is a material weakness, rather than require the auditor to issue an adverse opinion with regard to the effectiveness of the internal control over financial reporting, should the standard require the auditor to withdraw from the audit engagement?

No. We see no basis for requiring the auditor's withdrawal from the engagement nor any benefit to the investing public or the business community from leaving the entity without an auditor based solely on this one issue. We believe that communicating this weakness provides better information for investors than the lack of an auditor's report resulting from the auditor's withdrawal. We believe that regulatory action would be more effective than auditing standards as a way to correct such deficiencies.

Questions regarding forming an opinion and reporting:

25. Is it appropriate that the existence of a material weakness would require the auditor to express an adverse conclusion about the effectiveness of the company's internal control over financial reporting, consistent with the required reporting model for management?

No. We believe there are circumstances where the issuance of an "except for" opinion by the auditor is appropriate. While Item 308 of Regulation S-K precludes an unqualified opinion where

BDO Seidman, LLP

330 Madison
New York, NY 10017-5001
Phone 212-885-8000
Fax 212-885-1299

there are material weaknesses, we believe that a qualified opinion is not precluded. Furthermore, the adopted interim standard AT 501, which the SEC specifically cites in its conclusions, precludes an unqualified opinion in the presence of a material weakness, but permits a qualified opinion.

26. Are there circumstances where a qualified "except for" conclusion would be appropriate?

Yes. For example, if a merger occurs at or near year-end, it may not be practicable to identify or correct any material weaknesses in internal controls of such entity in the short time between acquisition date and the year-end. In those circumstances, it seems unnecessarily harsh to require an adverse opinion unless the acquired business is highly significant to the consolidated entity. This may be common in the acquisition of a private entity where an opinion on internal control has not previously been rendered. To require an adverse opinion would present the issuer in an inappropriately bad light and could even chill the market for acquisitions made late in the year. In those cases, it would be appear more informative for the user to issue a qualified opinion.

In many smaller entities it will be impossible to create an effective segregation of duties over some functions to avoid a material weakness. Similarly a qualified opinion is more useful to readers than an adverse opinion when other compensating controls have been established and are operating effectively.

We are also concerned that the excessive use of the adverse opinion resulting from the guidance in the proposed standard will lessen the potential message to readers when such a conclusion is truly warranted. We believe that adverse opinions should provide a signal of the magnitude of a pervasive weakness such as when there is severely inadequate documentation or testing or an inattention to internal controls in general.

27. Do you agree with the position that when the auditor issues a non-standard opinion, such as an adverse opinion, that the auditor's opinion should speak directly to the effectiveness of the internal control over financial reporting rather than to whether management's assessment is fairly stated?

We believe the auditor's report should be clear that it covers the effectiveness of internal controls in all cases. We do not believe the extent of work required to attest to management's assertion rather than to issue an audit opinion on internal controls should differ.

It is our view that the issue of the auditor's attesting to management's assessment has already led to significant confusion in the business community as to the auditor's role and extent of procedures that auditors are required to perform to issue such a report. We believe the user community will better understand the nature and extent of auditor involvement when an auditor issues an opinion on internal control.

Questions regarding auditor independence

28. Should the Board provide specific guidance on independence and internal control-related non-audit services in the context of this proposed standard?

If the PCAOB intends to include narrow, subject focused guidance on the subjects in this standard, that guidance should also be repeated in the Independence and Quality Control sections of the PCAOB literature. We think that the SEC independence guidance and the guidance in this standard are sufficient at this time.

330 Madison
New York, NY 10017-5001
Phone 212-885-8000
Fax 212-885-1299

BDO Seidman, LLP

We acknowledge the PCAOB's authority to write the auditing standards for public companies in whatever format it wishes, but think that to the extent that its proposed structure for its literature will be organized somewhat along the lines of the existing literature will be more useful. Accordingly we believe it should not commingle general independence, attest and general quality control standards guidance with auditing performance and reporting standards.

29. Are there any specific internal control-related non-audit services the auditor should be prohibited from providing to an audit client?

Yes. We believe the SEC has provided significant guidance in this area, and those examples need not be repeated here.

Questions regarding auditor's responsibilities with regard to management's certifications:

30. Are the auditor's differing levels of responsibility as they relate to management's quarterly certifications versus the annual (fourth quarter) certification, appropriate?

Yes, we believe that differing levels are appropriate, but urge the Board to not expand the Section 404 requirement to cover or appear to cover quarterly procedures regarding internal controls. See our response to question 31.

31. Is the scope of the auditor's responsibility for quarterly disclosures about the internal control over financial reporting appropriate?

Paragraph 186, in referring to quarterly procedures states "Determine, through a combination of observation and inquiry, whether significant changes in internal control over financial reporting may introduce significant deficiencies or material weaknesses in the design of internal control over financial reporting". We believe that in using the terms "observation" and "Determine," this requirement goes beyond the nature of procedures required for reviewing financial reporting information required under SAS 100, and is an expansion of scope we do not support.

In that regard, we believe the auditor's procedures regarding controls at the interim period should be limited to inquiries, and in the case of inconclusive or contradictory information, the auditor should apply whatever procedures considered necessary to resolve the issue.

In addition, review procedures are not determinative, but rather are a basis for creating an awareness of any material modifications necessary in the circumstances.

We also have not been able to conclude whether quarterly closing and related controls are intended to be swept-in under the Section 404 audit standard. However, we find no legislative, regulatory or other support to expand the 404 requirements to cover controls over interim reporting. We encourage the PCAOB to clarify its intention. We do not support including such procedures at this time.

If quarterly internal control procedures are required by the PCAOB, it would be most logical that they be required to be performed contemporaneously with the quarterly filing and the nature and extent of procedures be defined to promote consistency in application. While a retrospective evaluation of the quarterly closing and reporting controls may be possible, the risk of a weakness being identified in a subsequent procedure, after management has certified to the period, is an

330 Madison
New York, NY 10017-5001
Phone 212-885-8000
Fax   212-885-1299

BDO Seidman, LLP

undesirable result. We note the quarterly reporting timeframe is currently significantly constrained due to shortened filing times for accelerated filers, and increased involvement by the auditors in the review of financial information under SAS 100.

Any requirement that Section 404 engagements include interim controls tests should also be communicated to preparers, as some preparers are not currently including quarterly procedures in the scope of their Section 404 projects.

If quarterly responsibilities related to internal controls (beyond inquiries) are imposed, we believe that they should only become effective for the first quarter following the first annual reporting period for which a Section 404 audit opinion is rendered. Prior to this date, management's documentation, testing and monitoring over these quarterly controls may not be in place, and the auditor might not have an adequate basis for making an assessment. Moreover, such timing would be consistent with the SEC's transition approach for Exchange Act Rules 13a-15(d) and 15d-15(d), which require issuers to begin evaluating changes in internal control over financial reporting on a quarterly basis. Issuers are not required to comply with these rules until the first periodic report due after the first annual report that must include a management report on internal control over financial reporting.

Other Matters

Sampling

We believe the first sentence in the second bullet in paragraph 102 is incorrect as stated. In general, sample sizes for tests of controls do not increase as the number of control procedures increase. The exception to the rule is that for very small populations (say, less than a couple of hundred items), fewer items need to be examined. The example given is a small population of controls operating infrequently, and small populations such as this do require fewer items to test. However, the general statement in the first sentence is not supported by sampling theory or the guidance in the Audit Sampling Guide. Since attribute samples are seeking comfort that exceptions do not exceed some tolerable <u>rate</u>, increasing population size (once a threshold population size is reached) does not increase the required sample size.

The sentence referred to is generally true in all cases where substantive tests based on dollar values is performed. In a substantive test, the precision of the substantive test is linked to materiality (which is a specific amount), so, as the population grows, the sample size necessary to test for misstatement grows. We do not believe that the proposed standard intended that tests of controls be designed as substantive tests, using materiality thresholds to drive the sample size. Therefore, we believe the sentence should be corrected or clarified.

The Relationship Between Preparer and Auditor Test Levels

A common question asked by preparers is how much testing are they required to perform. As we mentioned earlier in this comment letter, this is a result of the lack of guidance for preparers. This often brings into question the relationship between the extent of testing of auditors and that of preparers. It is our view that the final standard should reflect that when auditors have assessed the documentation and testing by management and concluded that management has achieved a high level of assurance that their assertion concerning internal control is supported, that auditor test levels can often be expected to be <u>less</u> than those used by management. This is because the auditors have a significant and important piece of evidence the preparer did not have prior to their testing – management's analysis and test results. Thus, the levels of tests by management to

BDO Seidman, LLP

330 Madison
New York, NY 10017-5001
Phone 212-885-8000
Fax   212-885-1299

achieve a high assurance of effective operation should be greater than the levels required of auditors in their tests of internal control.

The Use of the "All" Requirement in the Proposed Standard

When the term "all" is used it provides no room for judgment for application of procedures that are effective and efficient. We believe the term "all" applies more appropriately to management's need to be very thorough in identifying, documenting and testing controls. It has been a long-standing practice that the auditor could practically and economically limit his or her procedures by testing. While we can envision circumstances where "all" might be the right scope, in many cases it will cause the performance of unproductive and expensive procedures. Examples from the proposed standard include:

> 114   As part of this evaluation, the auditor should review *all* reports issued during the year by internal audit (or similar functions, such as loan review in a financial institution) that address controls related to internal control over financial reporting and evaluate any internal control deficiencies identified in those reports.

> 191   In addition, the auditor should communicate to management, in writing, *all* deficiencies in internal control over financial reporting (that is, those deficiencies in internal control over financial reporting that are of a lesser magnitude than significant deficiencies) identified during the audit and inform the audit committee when such a communication has been made.

We recommend that the final standard reconsider the use or concept of "all" throughout the document. In our view, if the preparer has done a good job in documentation, testing and monitoring, and has demonstrated an adequate basis for its assessment, "all" will rarely be the correct requirement for the independent auditor.

Safeguarding of Assets

We believe that there will be a considerable number of implementation questions on the auditor's responsibility for identifying and testing controls related to the safeguarding of assets. We believe a mechanism, such as a PCAOB staff Q&A document, can help provide consistent and timely answers to questions about which controls should be included in the controls assessment and how they should be tested.

For example, in a retail operation, is the failure to use security cameras or merchandise theft tags a weakness? Does the auditor need to test or have a security expert test such controls if they are represented to be in use? Are poor pricing policies a control weakness? Is inefficiency a control weakness? Should controls be established to prevent the loss of customer lists and intellectual property and to what degree of security must these controls operate to be considered effective?

We believe this subject area can quickly mushroom into something unintended such that every business problem might be articulated in terms of it being evidence of an absence or failure of controls.

Additional Specific Comments

BDO Seidman, LLP

330 Madison
New York, NY 10017-5001
Phone 212-885-8000
Fax   212-885-1299

1. Paragraph 2 should be modified to directly address benefit plans that file Form 11-K. The SEC staff has recently informally stated that such issuers are not subject to the reporting requirements of Section 404.

2. Paragraph 33 introduces a level of audit committee pre-approval for "internal control-related services" that appears to exceed the pre-approval requirements in the SEC rule, since they must be "specifically" pre-approved.

    The SEC set the requirements for the pre-approval of services after due process. In our view, if modifications of those requirements are considered necessary, we would expect those modifications to come from the SEC.

3. Paragraph 34 says internal control auditing requires more than ordinary attention to maintaining independence. This implies that auditors can give only "ordinary" attention in "ordinary" engagements, which presumably include audits of financial statements. We don't understand the rationale for this statement or what extraordinary measures the auditor needs to take. We also do not agree that this requires any more diligence regarding independence than other attest engagements.

4. Paragraph 57 – The fifth bullet refers to complying with listing standards. We do not understand the reason for this. First, not all issuers are subject to the listing standards (because not all are listed). Second, the listing standards deal with the composition and activities of the audit committee and thus only deal indirectly with reliable financial reporting.

5. Paragraph 94 focuses on timing from the standpoint of work at an interim date vs. work at the "as of" date. The final standard should also provide guidance on what to do when the auditor is hired after the "as of" date.

6. Paragraph 126 – The first sentence should say that the following "should *usually* be regarded …" There are often cases where a restatement of financial statements is not due to any weakness in internal control (e.g., cases where accounting or disclosure is responsibly reviewed at all levels of the company and at the highest levels of the auditing firm, but a restatement is still required due to the insistence of the SEC staff based upon differing judgment).

7. Paragraph 134 states: "the auditor should obtain evidence that internal control over financial reporting has operated effectively for a sufficient period of time, which may be less than the entire period (ordinarily one year) covered by the company's financial statements." We believe the term "sufficient" in this case is unclear. We assume the Board means that they must operate for a long enough time to allow for testing of their effectiveness (e.g., a few weeks or a month for frequent controls), and not over an extended time during the year.

8. Paragraph 156 says that when separate reports are issued on the audits of the internal control over financial reporting and the financial statements, an auditor needs to add to the report on the financial statements audit a reference to the audit of the internal control over financial reporting. Shouldn't the auditor also add a comment to the report on the internal control audit referring to the financial statements audit?

BDO Seidman, LLP

330 Madison
New York, NY 10017-5001
Phone 212-885-8000
Fax   212-885-1299

9. Paragraph 173 seems to presume that management would disclose in its report on internal control over financial reporting a subsequent event that materially affects the effectiveness of the controls. We do not believe there is currently any specific SEC requirement for management to make such disclosure until the subsequent quarter, in which the change occurred. Therefore, we believe the PCAOB should clarify its view on management's disclosure requirement in the final standard. If the PCAOB believes that disclosure is implicitly required, the PCAOB should add a footnote or use some other means to fully explain the rationale for this conclusion. This will ensure that auditors and issuers focus on this point

10. Paragraph 181 presumes that reports on internal control are "part" of a registration statement and subject to Securities Act liability. We question whether this is the case, as such reports are required in Securities Act filings only when the issuer *elects* to use a short-form registration statement that requires the issuer to incorporate the most recent annual report by reference.

11. B15 states: "the evaluation ordinarily would not extend to controls at the equity method investee..." We cannot envision a circumstance where it should, and unless one can be identified we suggest the word "ordinarily" be struck.

*   *   *   *   *

We appreciate your consideration of our comments and suggestions, and would be pleased to communicate or meet with the PCAOB and its staff to clarify any of our comments.

Please direct comments to Wayne Kolins National Director of Assurance at 212-885-8595 Wkolins@bdo.com or Lynford Graham, National Director of Auditing at 212-885-8551 Lgraham@bdo.com.

Sincerely,

BDO Seidman, LLP

BDO Seidman, LLP

¶ 632. Deloitte & Touche

Deloitte & Touche LLP
10 Westport Road
PO Box 820
Wilton, CT 06897-0820

Tel: 203-761-3000
Fax: 203-834-2200

Deloitte
& Touche

November 21, 2003

Office of the Secretary
Public Company Accounting Oversight Board
1666 K Street, N.W.
Washington, D.C. 20006-2803

Re: **PCAOB Rulemaking Docket Matter No. 008**
Proposed Auditing Standard: An Audit of Internal Control over Financial Reporting
Performed in Conjunction with an Audit of Financial Statements

Deloitte & Touche LLP is pleased to respond to the request for comments from the Public Company Accounting Oversight Board (the "PCAOB" or the "Board") on its Proposed Auditing Standard, *An Audit of Internal Control Over Financial Reporting Performed in Conjunction with an Audit of Financial Statements*, PCAOB Rulemaking Docket Matter No. 008 (the "Proposed Standard") (October 7, 2003), to implement Sections 103(a)(2)(A) and 404 of the Sarbanes-Oxley Act of 2002 (the "Act"). Overall, we are very supportive of the Proposed Standard, and we recognize the efforts of the PCAOB in its development and commend many aspects of it.

While we agree with the overall approach of the Proposed Standard, we also believe there are many issues that must be addressed to permit the standard to be applied and implemented consistently and in a manner that meets the objectives of the Board and the Act.

We strongly agree with the position of the Board with respect to the need for the auditor to audit the effectiveness of internal control rather than solely evaluate management's assessment process. Overall, we believe the scope of the work described for the auditor generally is appropriate but will be subject to wide variations in interpretation, especially in relation to the extent of the walkthroughs, the degree of reliance that can be placed on the work of others, and the implications of company-level controls. We have concerns about the extent to which the requirements in the standard also apply to management's assessment, in particular with respect to the extent of management's documentation and testing.

We have organized our comments into three sections as follows: (I) Overall Comments, (II) Comments Related to Certain Paragraphs, and (III) Responses to Specific Questions.

I. OVERALL COMMENTS

1. Decision Mandating the Auditor to Audit the Underlying Controls as Well as Management's Assessment Process

We believe the aspect most critical to the achieving the purpose of the Act is the decision by the Board to require the auditor to test the effectiveness of internal control over financial reporting as well as evaluate management's assessment process to meet the objective of expressing an opinion about whether management's assessment is fairly stated. This decision, in our view, is in the best interests of investors, who will expect the independent auditor to obtain independent evidence as to whether the public company's internal control over financial reporting is effective, rather than solely evaluating management's process and evidence.

2. Increase the Focus on Areas With the Highest Risk of Material Weaknesses in Internal Control Over Financial Reporting

A study released by the GAO in 2002[1] indicates that the majority of financial restatements of companies relate to nonroutine, complex areas such as revenue recognition, corporate restructurings, and accounting for acquisitions. The risks of material misstatement associated with these areas are not easily mitigated by process-level control activities. The Proposed Standard appears to focus more on the control activities component of the COSO framework, including process-level control activities, than the more judgmental and high-risk areas, such as the control environment, risk assessment, and monitoring. For example the Proposed Standard provides very detailed guidance for identifying and considering the controls related to the significant accounts and processes, many of which, while significant, are typically routine in nature. This focus also is illustrated by the examples provided in Appendix D of the Proposed Standard.

We recognize the Board's attempt to address the more judgmental areas, such as the control environment, as illustrated by guidance on the evaluation of the effectiveness of the audit committee's oversight role. However, we believe that, overall, the Proposed Standard should provide more guidance on the key risk areas such as the control environment; the significant nonroutine, nonsystematic, and period-end financial reporting processes; and the company's risk assessment and monitoring processes to help focus both management's and the auditor's evaluation of internal control over financial reporting on areas of greatest potential risk of material misstatement of the financial statements. For example, the Board's current discussion of risk assessment focuses solely on the transactional level and does not specifically address the entity-level risk assessment process. Such an assessment should specifically consider, for example, the evaluation of the risk of fraud, including the risk of management override, and the company's antifraud programs and controls, including the company's need to identify and review unusual and significant journal entries—areas where most companies have not traditionally focused their efforts.

---

1   U.S. General Accounting Office. *Financial Statement Restatements—Trends, Market Impacts, Regulatory Responses, and Remaining Challenges* 03-138. Washington, D.C., October 4, 2002.

Also, given the increasing importance of fair disclosures, the Board should consider providing guidance relating to the identification and evaluation of control deficiencies that have an adverse effect on the presentation and disclosures assertions.

3. Management's Responsibilities

The Proposed Standard, while establishing requirements of the auditor, also establishes requirements of management (e.g., paragraphs 41-47 in the Proposed Standard). However, throughout the Proposed Standard there are numerous specific requirements established for the auditor that are not explicit for management to consider in paragraphs 41-47. An example is paragraph 57, related to the evaluation of the effectiveness of the audit committee. Additionally there are a number of places within the Proposed Standard where it is unclear whether the guidance applies only to the auditor or to management's assessment as well. For example, in paragraph 55, are company-level controls alone not sufficient for the purpose of management supporting their assessment? In paragraph 126, is it the Board's intent that if the company's internal control identified a fraud of any magnitude on the part of senior management, that would be a strong indicator of a material weakness for management's assessment purposes or does this apply only if the auditor identifies the fraud? Another example is paragraph 144. These are all indicators that a framework, requirements, and guidance should be sufficiently established to describe management's assessment process before auditing standards can be appropriately implemented.

While we agree with the Board that management's assessment must meet the various requirements currently embedded in various sections of the Board's Proposed Standard, including paragraphs 41 through 47, we do not believe the Proposed Standard is the best medium to establish the requirements that management must follow. We encourage the Board to work with the SEC to improve the appropriate evaluation framework, requirements, and guidelines that management should follow in preparing its assessment of internal control over financial reporting. We believe that paragraphs 41-47 of the Proposed Standard represent a good starting point that should be expanded to provide an adequate base for management's evaluation process that will be consistent with the auditor's process. In the course of establishing such guidelines, the Board and the SEC should consider harmonizing differences that currently exist between the definitions of significant deficiency and material weakness in the Proposed Standard and the definitions in the SEC's final rule on Section 404 of the Act. Otherwise, auditors and management might use different definitions to evaluate control deficiencies identified in the audit and assessment, respectively.

Nevertheless, we believe the Board should clarify its guidance relating to the management's responsibilities in the following areas.

a. Management's Assessment Process

The Proposed Standard focuses on procedures that the auditor should follow with respect to significant accounts, major classes of transactions, and other items of importance. It does not provide similar guidance for management in terms of their documentation requirements and assessment process. Nor is it clear what should be considered with respect to the insignificant accounts, minor classes of transactions, and other items, which are of lesser importance but are important when considered in the aggregate. We recommend that the Board provide such clarification in paragraphs 41-47 regarding management's responsibilities, including guidance with respect to identifying significant accounts, processes, locations, and those accounts that remain after the significant and important ones have been addressed.

We also strongly urge the Board to provide guidance relating to the testing by management to promote consistency and to clarify the confusion that exists between evidence that may be derived from a self-assessment process as opposed to independent testing. Companies are seeking specific guidance in terms of: (1) the appropriateness of evidence, including nature, extent and format, from a self-assessment process and (2) the nature, extent, and timing of independent testing by internal audit or by others under the direction of management, presumably to verify that the self-assessment process has integrity.

b. Extent of Documentation

The Board's Proposed Standard discusses two aspects of documentation. One relates to management's documentation of its assessment of the effectiveness of internal control over financial reporting ("documentation of management's assessment"), and the other relates to the documentation of the underlying control procedures and responsibilities for internal control within the company ("documentation of the design of internal control"). As established in paragraph 45, the documentation of the design of internal control is important for purposes of communicating responsibilities and providing a foundation for monitoring the effectiveness of internal control (e.g., to apply company-level controls).

There is confusion over management's responsibilities and the resulting implications on management's and the auditor's reports. For example, some companies are interpreting the Proposed Standard as suggesting that they do not need to document the design of internal control at locations that are insignificant individually or in the aggregate because they are documenting and testing company-level controls. However, without adequate documentation, monitoring activities, such as company-level controls, are unlikely to be effective, as the control will not be consistently understood and accountability will not have been clearly established. Additionally, in paragraph 46, the Proposed Standard adds further confusion by providing that "in evaluating the deficiency as to its significance, the auditor should determine whether management can demonstrate the monitoring component of internal control over financial reporting in the absence of documentation." Accordingly we believe the last sentence in paragraph 46 should be deleted. Further, we recommend that the Board clearly establish management's responsibility with respect to maintaining company-wide internal control documentation.

We agree that the lack of adequate documentation of the design of internal control is a deficiency in internal control over financial reporting, the significance of which should be determined first by management in preparing its assessment and then by the auditor in performing their evaluation.

However, if the auditor concludes that there is insufficient documentation of management's assessment, paragraph 20 requires the auditor to disclaim an opinion, with which we agree. The auditor also should consider whether the insufficient documentation also identifies a deficiency in the documentation of the design of internal control that is judged to constitute a material weakness, in which case the auditor should be directed to issue a report with an adverse opinion as opposed to a disclaimer (please refer to our separate comment in Section 2 regarding paragraph 20).

Accordingly we recommend the following to replace Paragraph 47 (assuming the guidance in paragraph 20 is modified).

> If the auditor concludes that the documentation of management's assessment is insufficient to support management's evaluation of the operating effectiveness of internal control, the auditor should also consider whether there is inadequate documentation of the design of internal control that constitutes a material weakness and follow the guidance in paragraph 20.

c. *Consideration of Extended Relationships*

Aside from consolidated entities and other financial interests accounted for as investments, companies engage in an increasing number of relationships, which have a direct impact on their financial reporting. These range from the outsourcing of software applications, application hosting, and in some cases, a portion to all of the financial transaction processing and financial reporting processes. It is unclear whether the guidance in Appendix B of the Proposed Standard with respect to SAS 70 and the use of service organizations also applies to management. We strongly recommend that paragraphs 41-47 be expanded to indicate explicitly the other paragraphs that management also should incorporate in its assessment, such as the guidance in Appendix B related to service organizations.

4. Issues Regarding the Scope of an Audit of Internal Control Over Financial Reporting

a. *Significant Accounts*

The Proposed Standard provides that a significant account may be identified at a number of different levels including (1) the financial statement line item level, (2) the account or account balance, which is not defined but is referred to in paragraphs 61 and 62, and (3) the account component level, which suggests it is a subset of an account balance in paragraph 62. Identifying significant accounts at multiple levels is likely to create confusion and, thus, we suggest that the identification of a significant account occur only at the account balance level.

To simplify this structure, we suggest that the standard begin by identifying all "significant" financial statement line items and disclosures. A line item or disclosure should be considered significant if there is a more than a remote likelihood that the financial statement line item or disclosure could contain misstatements that could result in a material effect on the financial statements, considering the risk of both overstatement and understatement. The assessment of a more than remote likelihood should be made without giving any consideration to the effectiveness of internal control. We would expect that virtually all financial statement line items and disclosures will be considered significant.

Next, within those financial statement line items and disclosures, account balances should be determined by aggregating general ledger accounts that have similar risks and share common processes and controls and by disaggregating those general ledger balances that have differing risks and controls. The account balances should be evaluated to identify significant accounts based on materiality and a more than remote likelihood the account balance could contain misstatements that could result in a material misstatement to the financial statements including both understatement and overstatement considerations. Additionally, accounts that are not material may also be identified as a significant account taking into consideration qualitative factors such as those listed in Paragraph B17 and the expectations of a reasonable user as presented in Paragraph 61. Again, the assessment of a more than remote likelihood should be made without giving any consideration to the effectiveness of internal control.

The intent of paragraph 61 of the Proposed Standard is unclear to us in terms of the aggregation consideration. Is it intended to aggregate virtually all the accounts and disclosures that do not meet the definition of a significant account? This results in a scope that, in our view, is too broad and impractical. Accordingly, clarification is needed. The accounts and disclosures that were not identified as a significant account should be aggregated. If material in the aggregate, the key control(s) over this group of account balances (e.g., an effective monitoring control such as reconciling the account on a monthly basis) should be identified and documented. The rationale for focusing on the monitoring control is that the processing-related controls in these individually insignificant accounts generally are not the important controls. The detective and general controls, such as the monitoring, segregation of duty, and financial reporting controls, generally are the important controls to focus on for these individually insignificant accounts. The tests of design and operating effectiveness should focus on determining that the key control(s) had been placed in operation and is operating effectively by sampling from the group of such account balances and disclosures on a test basis.

Paragraph 63 of the Proposed Standard implies that the identification of potential significant accounts is performed on a location-by-location basis. However, it is not clear how this should be applied when considered in conjunction with the multiple location guidance in Appendix B. Further guidance and an example will enhance consistency in application of this guidance.

b. Performance of Walkthroughs

We agree that the performance of walkthroughs should be required for all of the company's significant processes as indicated in the Proposed Standard. We also agree that it is appropriate to require that the auditor perform the walkthroughs to ensure that the auditor has a sufficient understanding to plan their work. However, we have six concerns with regard to certain aspects of the proposed requirements.

First, the standard should clarify the following with regard to the walkthroughs:

- Whether the term "significant process" referred to in paragraph 79 is the same as the "significant processes" referred to in paragraph 69.

- The relationship between "types of transactions" in paragraph 79 and "major classes of transactions" in paragraph 69. Also, providing examples of "types of transactions" and "major classes of transactions" would be helpful.

Second, depending on the clarifications of the terms above, the scope of the walkthroughs as proposed in paragraphs 79 and 80 may be interpreted by some as overly broad and expansive. Paragraph 79 states the following:

> The auditor should perform a walkthrough for **all** of the company's **significant processes**. In a walkthrough, the auditor should trace **all types** of transactions and events, both recurring and unusual, from origination through the company's information systems until they are reflected in the company's financial reports. Walkthroughs provide the auditor with evidence to . . . confirm that the auditor's understanding of the process is complete by determining whether **all points** in the process where misstatements related to each relevant financial statement assertion that could occur have been identified.

We agree with the desire of the Board for the auditor to identify and consider the unusual and infrequent types of transactions that may occur within a "significant process." However, the concept of tracing all types of transactions is inconsistent with the guidance the Board provides in paragraphs B12 and B13 of Appendix B relating to locations, which allows for consideration of materiality and risk. We agree with the guidance contained in Appendix B, and we recommend that paragraph 79 be modified to incorporate a similar concept.

Third, paragraph 80 also states that the walkthrough should "encompass the **entire process** of initiating, recording, processing, and reporting individual transactions, and controls for all five internal control components and fraud, not just control activities." Based on this language, it is not clear which processes and transactions are required to be covered by the walkthrough. Paragraph 80 should be clarified such that the walkthrough relates only to those processes identified in paragraph 69, not all processes within the company. Further, the combining of the five internal control components may cause confusion, because many of them are pervasive in nature and do not relate directly to transactional processing. Accordingly, we recommend revising the first sentence in paragraph 80 to read as follows:

> The auditor's walkthroughs should encompass the entire process of initiating, recording, processing, and reporting individual transactions, and controls for each of the significant processes identified. Additionally, the auditor should gain an understanding of the Company's internal control related to the control environment, risk assessment, monitoring, and information and communication components.

Furthermore, the extent of walkthroughs should vary depending upon a number of factors including the nature of the transaction, complexity, and exposure to loss, particularly relating to the more insignificant types of transactions. We believe these factors should be set forth in the standard.

Fourth, also in paragraph 80, the phrase "controls for all five internal control components and fraud" implies that fraud controls are something separate and distinct from controls for the five internal control components. In our view, fraud is an important consideration with respect to each of the five internal control components and, thus, the word "and" should be replaced with "including."

Fifth, paragraph 82 states that "when there have been significant changes in the process flow of transactions, including the supporting computer applications, the auditor should evaluate the nature of the change(s) and the effect on related accounts to determine whether to walkthrough transactions that were processed both before and after the change." This language seems to indicate that it is optional as to whether the auditor should understand the changes that have occurred. For any significant changes to the significant processes that impact controls over financial reporting, we believe that the auditor should walkthrough transactions that were processed after the change. Additionally, if there has been a significant change, we do not believe it is necessary to perform procedures prior to the change. Moreover, the auditor may not be aware of the change until after it has occurred. Therefore, paragraph 82 should be modified to state that "when there have been significant changes in the process flow of transactions, including the supporting computer applications, the auditor should evaluate the nature of the change(s) and the effect on related accounts and transactions. Additionally, for significant changes in the significant processes that impact controls over financial reporting, the auditor should walkthrough transactions that were processed after the change."

Sixth, in paragraph 83, the guidance only refers to nonroutine and estimation processes. We believe this is guidance is applicable for <u>all</u> processes for which a walkthrough is performed and that the Proposed Standard should so state.

c. Company-Level Controls

We agree with the Board's position in paragraph 54 of the Proposed Standard that company-level controls have a pervasive effect on controls at the process, transaction, or application level. However, we believe further clarification is needed pertaining to certain elements of company-level controls.

First, we believe that further discussion is warranted to clarify that the purpose for evaluating company-level controls is to understand, evaluate, and test the effectiveness with which these controls are applied across locations or business units. The separation of company-level controls as discussed in paragraphs 53-55 from the multiple location guidance contained in paragraphs B4, B8, and B9 of Appendix B creates confusion. Accordingly, the Proposed Standard should clarify that company-level controls are important to consider when determining the locations that management and the auditor should include in its scope. Further clarification also is needed to indicate that the controls presented are illustrative and are not intended to be a complete list of company-level controls nor is a company required to have all the controls in the list to support its assessment of effective company-level controls. However, ineffective company-level controls may be a serious deficiency that will affect the scope of the work performed at the locations.

Second, we suggest clarifying in paragraph 53 that the listing of company-level controls presented are not suggesting that only these controls need to be considered to address the components of the COSO framework but that these controls represent part of one or more of the five components of the COSO framework.

Third, to support that company-level controls are effective at multiple locations, there should be evidence that the relevant controls had been documented and communicated at these locations.

Accordingly the Proposed Standard should state:

> A foundation for the entity-wide controls is the significant controls at the location or business unit. Therefore, these significant controls also should be documented by [management].

Fourth, paragraph B9 of Appendix B states, "The auditor should perform tests of company-level controls to determine whether such controls are operating effectively. The auditor might conclude that he or she cannot evaluate the operating effectiveness of such controls without visiting some or all of the locations or business units." We believe that the term "might conclude" does not adequately state that the auditor (and management) has a responsibility to test company-level controls at some locations. We believe that the Board should be specific in Appendix B regarding performing company-level controls at multiple locations.

d. The Auditor's Use of the Work Performed by Management and Others

We agree with the Board that the auditor should be permitted, but not required, to use the work of management or others. Nowhere else in professional literature is the auditor required to use the work of management or others. We believe that the scope of the auditor's work should be determined by the auditor. However, we also believe that further guidance is needed with respect to certain items in paragraphs 103-109 of the Proposed Standard pertaining to the auditor's use of the work performed by management and others.

First, the Proposed Standard separates work performed by management into three categories. However, it is not clear how the auditor's ability to use the work of management and others reconciles with the requirement that the auditor obtain the "principal evidence" to support its opinion. The Board should clarify how these two concepts work together.

Second, we believe that some may interpret the language in paragraphs 103-109 as a means to inappropriately minimize the level of effort on the part of the external auditor to test the effectiveness of internal control. That is, auditors may conclude that they only need to independently test those areas in which the auditor is not permitted to use management's procedures (paragraph 104) and those areas in which the auditor's use of management's procedures should be limited (paragraph 105). We believe the unintended consequence is that auditors will not perform any of their own tests in regard to the largest category of controls – controls over routine processing of significant accounts and disclosures (paragraph 106). This will result in over-reliance on work performed by management and internal audit. We recommend that in addition to performing tests in those areas designated in paragraphs 104 and 105, the auditor also be required to perform some independent tests of controls over routine processing of significant accounts and disclosures (paragraph 106).

Third, as proposed, auditors are required to reperform "some" of the tests of controls performed by others. We recommend that additional guidance be provided with respect to the meaning of "some" in the context of the areas where the auditor's reliance on the work of management and others should be limited (paragraph 105) and where there is no specific limitation (paragraph 106). We suggest that the Board develop examples for illustration in the appendix.

Fourth, we are concerned that auditors may use the work performed by management not only to satisfy the audit of internal control over financial reporting but also to reduce the level of substantive testing related to the financial statement audit. We do not believe this is the intention of the Board. For financial statement audit purposes, we believe that the auditor should continue to follow the guidance of SAS No. 65, *The Auditor's Consideration of the Internal Audit Function in an Audit of Financial Statements*. However, the Proposed Standard does not set any limitations with respect to the auditor's ability to reduce substantive testing. Therefore, how the Proposed Standard and SAS 65 interrelate should be clarified.

Fifth, paragraph 104 of the Proposed Standard states that the areas in which the auditor should not use the work of others include "controls that have a pervasive effect on the financial statements, such as certain information technology general controls on which the operating effectiveness of other controls depend." Many companies have an internal staff that is well qualified to perform IT general control work. We believe that testing of IT controls should be moved from the category where the auditor should not use the work of others to the category where the use of the work of others should be limited.

e. *General Computer Controls*

We suggest that the Board provide more explicit guidance on the types of general computer controls that fall within the definition of internal control over financial reporting versus operational effectiveness and efficiency. For example, we believe that business continuity and disaster recovery, while an important operational control, is not a component of internal control over financial reporting, except to the extent that they relate to the recovery of data to achieve the objective to maintain records.

f. *Safeguarding of Assets*

While we agree that additional guidance on what is meant by safeguarding of assets is helpful and important, we believe that Appendix C of the Proposed Standard should be significantly enhanced. Appendix C should be specifically linked to the definition of safeguarding of assets set forth in paragraph 6 of the Proposed Standard. It also is not clear how the guidance in Appendix C relates to the COSO Addendum, *Reporting to External Parties*, which is referred to in the SEC's Final Rule for Section 404. The guidance in paragraph C1 also should be specifically linked to the definition in the COSO Addendum.

As proposed, Appendix C does not sufficiently answer which controls over safeguarding of assets are within the scope of internal control over financial reporting and which are not. For example, assume that a company has safeguarding controls over inventory such as inventory tags (preventative controls) and that the company also performs periodic physical inventory counts (detective control) timely in relation to their interim and annual financial reporting dates. Although the physical inventory count does not safeguard the inventory from theft or loss, it prevents a material misstatement to the financial statements if performed effectively and timely. Therefore, given that the definitions of material weaknesses and significant deficiencies relate to the likelihood of misstatement of the financial statements, the failure of a preventive control such as inventory tags will not result in a significant deficiency or material weakness because the detective control (physical inventory) prevents a misstatement of the financial statements.

The COSO Addendum also indicates that a company does not have to consider preventive controls over inventory shrinkage if it has sufficient detective controls to measure and record any shrinkage on a timely basis. If the Board intended to extend safeguarding of assets beyond financial reporting (e.g., the ineffectiveness of the inventory tags to prevent inventory theft or loss illustrated above), then the Proposed Standard should indicate areas that management and the auditor should include in safeguarding of assets, and the definitions of significant deficiencies and material weaknesses will need to be modified to address safeguarding controls.

Also, the first two examples and, perhaps, the fourth example in paragraph C1 of the Proposed Standard arguably may not result in a misstatement of the financial statements and, therefore, seem problematic from a definitional perspective. The intent of the fourth bullet is not clear, because ultimately all costs impact pricing decisions, which seems to sweep in improper allocation as a consideration for all cost categories. We suggest clarifying that this relates only to programs whereby costs are directly recovered from customers. Examples would be helpful to ensure proper application.

Finally, Appendix C categorizes all of the bulleted items as "unintentional misstatement." While some situations may be unintentional, the misappropriation of assets generally is intentional.

5. Reporting

a. Requirement to Issue an Adverse Opinion in Certain Circumstances

The Proposed Standard requires the auditor to render an adverse opinion when a material weakness is identified. An adverse opinion concludes with the opinion that due to the effect of the material weakness on the achievement of the objectives of the control criteria, the company has not maintained effective internal control over financial reporting. We strongly disagree with this approach. We believe that the auditor should render the appropriate type of opinion based on the circumstances that caused the material weakness. This approach would provide better information about the nature and impact of the material weakness identified.

While we agree that material weaknesses that are pervasive to the company should result in an adverse opinion, we also believe that an adverse opinion is not appropriate if the material weakness is not pervasive. For example, a company with effective internal control might make an acquisition of a business that has a material weakness. Users of the report should be permitted to understand whether the material weakness relates only to the acquisition or has a more pervasive impact. A qualified opinion best communicates this situation. The Proposed Standard should be modified to provide for flexibility in evaluating the material weakness based on significance to the entire company and should permit the auditor to issue either an adverse or a qualified "except for" opinion, depending on the circumstances.

In addition, we are concerned that a scope limitation will not adequately inform the public in situations where a material weakness has been identified and corrective action has been taken but insufficient time has passed to determine whether the material weakness has been corrected. In such cases, the auditor should conclude that management's assessment is inadequate, leading to a modification of the auditor's report due to the existence of a material weakness. If the Board decides that such cases should result in a scope limitation, then the standard should require descriptive language of the scope limitation that includes a description of the material weakness and a statement that if such weakness were not corrected, the auditor could not conclude that internal control is effective.

This scenario further supports the need for clear guidance as to what constitutes a "sufficient period" in paragraph 166 of the Proposed Standard. The relevance of evidence subsequent to the "as of" date should be explicitly addressed. In our view, in the case of a deficiency in the design of internal control, there must be substantive evidence that the control had been implemented prior to the "as of" date sufficient to correct the deficiency. Accordingly, failure to implement adequate controls at the "as of" date is a deficiency without regard to any corrective action that may have been taken after the "as of" date. However when there is not a sufficient period of time to obtain adequate evidence about the operating effectiveness of the new control prior to the "as of" date, then we believe that management and the auditor may consider evidence subsequent to the "as of" date, but before the date of the auditor's report as to whether the control was operating effectively. If such sufficient evidence cannot be obtained, then the condition results in a deficiency as opposed to a scope limitation.

We recommend providing examples of illustrative language disclaiming an opinion on disclosures about corrective actions taken by the company and the company's plans to implement new controls (the first two bullet points of paragraph 174).

b. Explanatory Footnotes to Management's and the Auditor's Reports

Similar to the preparation and audit of the financial statements, an assessment and audit of the effectiveness of internal control involve a number of important considerations. When reading the financial statements, an understanding of the important aspects, which can range from critical accounting policies to segment and other disclosures, is crucial in providing the reader with the proper context to evaluate the financial statements presented. Similarly, we believe information relevant to assisting users to better understand management's assessment and the auditor's evaluation of the effectiveness of internal control over financial reporting should be disclosed in management's report on internal control. We believe that relevant information includes (1) disclosure of what management included in safeguarding of assets, (2) the entities excluded from the scope of management's evaluation (whether or not consolidated) such as provided in paragraphs in B15 and B16, and (3) the nature and extent of the use of service auditor reports as the basis for its assessment relating to outsourcing and other service relationships.

Currently, when relying on the work of other auditors the auditor is able to apportion responsibility in their report. Yet under SAS 70, neither management nor the auditor makes reference in their report to the use of the service auditor's report. SAS 70 was designed for an audit of the financial statement whereby the auditor is also required to perform his or her own substantive tests and, thus was not relying exclusively on the service auditor's report. However, for purposes of the audit of internal control, neither management nor the auditor is required to perform any additional procedures. Therefore, the only evidence with respect to the service organization's controls comes from the evaluation and testing performed by the service auditor. Accordingly we believe that the reliance on a service auditor should be clearly disclosed in management's and the auditor's report to provide transparency as to the source of the evidence.

We believe it is important for users of management's report and the auditor's report to understand the boundaries of the internal control being reported on, in terms of entities covered and not covered. We do not believe that a narrowing of the boundaries should be discussed as a limitation in scope but rather as a means to clarify the boundaries of the company's internal control over financial reporting that their respective reports cover.

6. Evaluating the Effectiveness of the Audit Committee's Oversight

a. *Effectiveness of the Audit Committee as an Element of the Control Environment*

We agree with the Board's emphasis on the importance of the effectiveness of the audit committee. The audit committee plays an important role in setting the "tone at the top" and providing an important oversight function with respect to financial reporting. Although some may take the view that the effectiveness of the audit committee is outside the scope of the company's internal control over financial reporting, the COSO framework has long recognized the effectiveness of the audit committee as one of the elements of the control environment. However, we expect that the Proposed Standard's requirement will be controversial and difficult to implement. Accordingly, the Proposed Standard should be changed to reflect the effectiveness of the audit committee as an important aspect of the control environment, rather than what appears to be a separate evaluation. In addition, we believe this requirement contains elements that should be significantly changed.

First, the Proposed Standard does not make clear whether management's assessment is required to also include an evaluation of the effectiveness of the audit committee's oversight. Keeping with the construct of the audit of internal control (i.e., management first makes its assessment and then the auditor evaluates and tests that assessment), we believe that management (in conjunction with the Board or the audit committee itself) also should be required to evaluate the performance and effectiveness of the audit committee's oversight considering the requirements set forth for auditors in the Proposed Standard. This requirement is consistent with Section 407 of the Act, whereby boards of directors are required to determine whether members of the audit committee are financial experts. Additionally, newly adopted listing exchange standards require that an annual assessment of the audit committee be performed.

Second, ordinarily the auditor does not have full and complete access to the audit committee. Without full and complete access, the auditor will be unable to identify all of audit committee's activities, interactions with other parties, and conclusions reached. Therefore, we do not believe that the auditor will have available all of the information needed to effectively perform its evaluation and will be unable to adequately assess the effectiveness of the audit committee against the specific requirements of paragraph 57 of the Proposed Standard unless it has full and complete access to the audit committee. We believe that the Board needs to provide guidance as to how this issue should be addressed.

b. *Factors Related to the Evaluation of the Audit Committee's Oversight*

The Board has provided a list of factors in paragraph 57 of the Proposed Standard for auditors to consider related to the evaluation of the effectiveness of the audit committee's oversight. For the auditor to carry out this responsibility effectively, we believe certain of the listed factors need to be more specific while others should not be included in the list.

First, testing for compliance with laws and regulations, such as applicable listing standards implemented as a result of Section 301 of the Act, is outside the scope of internal control over financial reporting. The SEC rule, *Management's Reports on Internal Control Over Financial Reporting and Certification of Disclosure in Exchange Act Periodic Reports,* defines internal control over financial reporting, and this definition, as stated in the SEC's rule, "does not encompass the elements of the COSO definition that relate to the effectiveness and efficiency of a company's operations and a company's compliance with applicable laws and regulations, with the exception of compliance with the applicable laws and regulations directly related to the preparation of financial statements, such as the Commission's financial reporting requirements."[2] We do not believe compliance with applicable listing standards adopted pursuant to Section 301 of the Act is directly related to the preparation of the financial statements. Therefore, we do not believe this aspect of evaluating the audit committee should be encompassed with the audit of internal control over financial reporting.

Second, the definition of "independence" should be specifically identified so that the same criteria are applied for all evaluations of audit committees. Moreover, it is unclear how an auditor can reasonably evaluate whether the nominating process for the audit committee is appropriately independent or whether management picks "friends."

In response to Question 24 of the Board's request for comments on specific questions, we do not believe that it is in the interest of investors or the public to require the auditor to withdraw from the audit engagement because the auditor has concluded that the audit committee is ineffective. If the auditor is able to form a conclusion regarding the effectiveness of internal control over financial reporting, which includes the assessment of the audit committee, then the auditor should issue the appropriate report. Ineffective audit committees will likely result in adverse opinions based on the guidance in paragraph 126 of the Proposed Standard. The communication of the material weakness that resulted in the adverse opinion is useful information to the public. Furthermore, the auditor always has the option to withdraw from the engagement when the company and the audit committee do not respond appropriately to the situation.

7. Effective Date

We are fully committed to successfully implementing and performing the audits of internal control over financial reporting, and we understand the need to timely implement the new standard to meet the objectives of the Act. We also understand that the SEC has set the implementation date for Section 404 of the Act as the first fiscal year ending on or after June 15, 2004 for accelerated filers and for fiscal years ending on or after April 15, 2005 for non-accelerated filers and foreign companies. We recognize that the PCAOB is striving to meet that time frame under challenging circumstances.

However, this Proposed Standard is extremely significant due to both its complexity and its impact on companies and the auditors. While companies and auditors are preparing for implementation based on the knowledge and understanding to date, we are concerned that this Proposed Standard will not be finalized by the Board and approved by the SEC within a time frame that allows for successful implementation of the final standard for companies with June 2004 fiscal year ends. Indeed, companies with June 2004 fiscal year ends will likely be well into the third quarter of their fiscal year before this standard is finalized. Accordingly, it will be very difficult for companies and auditors to apply the provisions of the Proposed Standard to a fiscal year that is almost completed before the standard is final, especially considering that some

---

2 SEC final rule, page 10.

internal controls over financial reporting may operate only on a quarterly basis. When the standard is finalized, companies and auditors will require a reasonable amount of time to understand the requirements, train staff, and implement changes. We urge the Board to work with the SEC and consider delaying the effective date for accelerated filers to fiscal years ending on or after September 15, 2004. This slight delay in the effective date contributes to a more successful implementation of the Proposed Standard and still results in the implementation in 2004 by the vast majority of public companies.

Additionally, if the Board decides to modify the auditor's interim responsibilities through this standard, we believe the effective date for any required changes to procedures performed for reviews of interim financial information should be effective starting the first quarter after the initial audit of internal control over financial reporting is performed.

8. Implementation Guidance

Because of the complexity and importance of properly implementing the Proposed Standard, we believe that a substantial amount of interpretation will be necessary as implementation occurs. Therefore, we believe that the Board should establish a formal process for responding to implementation questions from auditors and companies that will undoubtedly be forthcoming.

9. Impact of the Proposed Standard on Interim Standards

We are concerned with the impacts of the Proposed Standard on the Board's current interim standards, especially in relation to the procedures performed in connection with the financial statement audit, as well as for interim reviews of quarterly financial information. Throughout the Proposed Standard, the Board has incorporated changes that also have a significant impact on the Board's interim standards, creating inconsistencies between the Proposed Standard and the interim standards. However, this is not clearly evident. For instance, paragraph 138 of the Proposed Standard states that "the auditor should perform substantive procedures for all relevant assertions for all significant accounts and disclosures." However, the AICPA Statement on Auditing Standards that have been adopted by the Board as interim standards only require the auditor to perform substantive tests at the account balance or class of transactions level.[3] Another example relates to language in paragraph 141 of the Proposed Standard, which states that the auditor's substantive procedures must include "examining material adjustments made during the course of preparing the financial statements." This statement could be interpreted to mean that auditors are required to test every material journal entry made throughout the year and in the closing process, since they all relate to preparing the financial statements. Currently, auditors are not required to test every material journal entry during a financial statement audit.

It also is not clear how the Proposed Standard impacts the auditor's responsibilities with respect to interim financial information and the requirements under AICPA Statement on Auditing Standards No. 100, *Interim Financial Information.*

---

[3]   AICPA Statements on Auditing Standards, *Internal Control in a Financial Statement Audit* (AU 119.81).

We suggest that each proposed auditing standard issued by the Board should clearly identify how the proposed changes will impact current standards, and what conforming changes will need to be made to existing interim standards. This will assist the auditor and the public in understanding the intentions of the Board and help to maintain consistency in the application of standards. An appendix with such changes might be a way to communicate the information.

10. Consideration of Small and Medium-Sized Companies

While the nature of controls at large companies may differ from the nature of controls at small and medium companies due to the size of the entity, management's responsibility with regard to assessment, evidence, and documentation should not be different. As indicated in paragraph E9 of the Proposed Standard, "the concept of control activities in a small company is the same as in a larger one."

However, Appendix E of the Proposed Standard does not articulate clearly that management's responsibilities remain the same regardless of the size of the entity and seems to imply that for small or medium-sized companies, management's assessment process, evidence, and documentation may differ from those for large companies. As such, Appendix E may allow interpretation by small and medium-sized entities that their assessment and documentation does not need to cover all significant accounts and all relevant assertions and may have the unintended consequence of the forcing the auditor to rely on inquiries of management regarding higher level monitoring practices rather than on reliable evidential matter.

Accordingly, we believe Appendix E should be modified to indicate that small and medium-sized companies are responsible for supporting the evaluation of internal control with sufficient evidence, including documentation (as indicated in paragraph 19 of the Proposed Standard) and that inadequate documentation of the design of controls and the absence of sufficient documented evidence to support management's assessment of the operating effectiveness of internal control over financial reporting are internal control deficiencies that may rise to the level of a significant deficiency or material weakness based on the auditor's judgment.

II. COMMENTS RELATED TO CERTAIN PARAGRAPHS

1. Specific Comments

Paragraph 14—Committee of Sponsoring Organizations Framework

The reference for more information about the Committee of Sponsoring Organizations (COSO) framework should be to the COSO document itself and not to AU 319.

Paragraph 15—Inherent Limitations in Internal Control Over Financial Reporting

In addition to the inherent limitation of internal control, we believe that the Proposed Standard should discuss the inherent limitations of management's assessment and the audit of internal control over financial reporting. We suggest the following language:

> The practitioner should plan and perform the engagement to obtain reasonable assurance about whether effective internal control over financial reporting was maintained in all material respects. Absolute assurance is not attainable because of the nature of attestation evidence and the inherent limitations of internal control. Therefore, an examination of internal control conducted in accordance with attestation standards may not detect a material weakness. The subsequent discovery that a material weakness exists is not, in and of itself, evidence of (1) failure to obtain reasonable assurance; (2) inadequate planning, performance, or judgment; (3) the absence of due professional care; or (4) a failure to comply with attestation standards. Since the practitioner's opinion on internal control is based on the concept of obtaining reasonable assurance, the practitioner is not an insurer, and his or her report does not constitute a guarantee.

Paragraph 20—Management's Responsibilities and Disclaimer of Opinion

Paragraph 20 contains an unconditional requirement (under proposed Rule 3101) that the auditor disclaims an opinion if management has not fulfilled the four responsibilities enumerated in paragraph 19. We do not believe that a disclaimer is an appropriate form of report in all situations. For example, if management fails to support its evaluation with sufficient evidence but the auditor is otherwise able to conclude that effective internal control has *not* been maintained, we believe that a report expressing an adverse opinion is a more appropriate response. In situations in which fraud is detected, the auditor may be unwilling to continue with the engagement, depending on the magnitude. While we agree that a communication to management and the audit committee is warranted, issuing a report disclaiming an opinion does not seem adequate in such situations.

Paragraph 21—Materiality Considerations

The Board has proposed that the auditor should apply the concept of materiality at both (1) the financial-statement level in deciding whether a significant deficiency, or a combination thereof, represents a material weakness, and (2) the individual account-balance level in deciding whether a control deficiency, or combination thereof, represents a significant deficiency. We believe that management and the auditor have the responsibility to plan the evaluation to detect a material weakness, which is based on the threshold of a material misstatement, not at the individual-account-balance level. Accordingly we suggest that paragraph 21 of the Proposed Standard be clarified to clearly distinguish that materiality at the financial-statements level is relevant for the purpose of planning the scope of the audit of internal control, not materiality at the individual-account-balance level. We also suggest that the Board clarify materiality at the individual-account-balance level as it relates to the term "more than inconsequential," which is included in the definition of a significant deficiency of in paragraph 8.

Paragraphs 24-26—Fraud Considerations

We agree that both management and the auditor should consider the risk of fraud, as defined by existing auditing standards. However the requirement to evaluate "all controls specifically intended" to address the risks of fraud could be too broad or at least result in inconsistent application in practice. We do not believe it is possible for the auditor to determine which controls were intended by management to address the risks of fraud, nor can one distinguish between some controls to determine whether they are for just fraud or for fraud and error. We recommend that this be highlighted as a key consideration in the risk assessment component.

We believe the requirements set out in paragraphs 24-26, while laudable, do not provide adequate specificity against which the design and operating effectiveness of a company's fraud program and controls can be properly evaluated. Lacking such specificity, there will be wide variation in practice across companies and auditors. We recommend that the Board clarify what the auditor should consider in addition to the requirements in Statement of Auditing Standards No. 99. For example, the auditor must test the design and operating effectiveness of the company's antifraud programs and controls in response to the risks of fraud identified in the audit of the financial statements.

Paragraph 41—Evaluating Management's Assessment Process

We recommend inserting the word "all" in front of "relevant assertions."

Paragraph 43—Evaluating Management's Assessment Process

We recommend inserting the word "all" in front of "relevant assertions" in the first bullet point. Also it appears that bullet points four through six are a subset of bullet point one.

Paragraph 66—Assertions

The term "meaningful bearing" may confuse people in terms of deciding what a relevant assertion is and may result in inappropriate rationalization to exclude assertions that may be applicable but judged not to have an elevated risk associated with it. We believe the term should be replaced with "applicable."

Paragraph 69—Identifying Significant Processes

The concept of a significant process and major class of transactions are not defined, nor is it clear how one should go about identifying a significant process. Also the phrase "groups of accounts" is introduced here for the first time, but it is unclear as to what is a group of accounts and how it relates to a significant account. This step is important because the designation of a process as significant in paragraph 69 determines the scope of the auditor's walkthrough in paragraph 79. An example demonstrating the intent of these terms would be helpful.

Paragraphs 74-78—Identifying Controls to Test

We believe that the heading for this section of the Proposed Standard may be misleading as the section also addresses the linkage of the assertions and controls. Accordingly we suggest dividing this section into a section to describe the consideration of the linkage of the assertions, control objectives, risks and control activities and a section to provide guidance relating to identifying and planning the tests of controls. Recognizing that the audit process is seldom performed in a finite sequence, nonetheless it appears more logical to place the walkthrough before the identification of controls to test.

Additionally paragraph 75 notes that the auditor should "link individual controls with the significant accounts and assertions." Separately, in paragraph 78, the concept of control objectives is introduced but is it is not clear how this interrelates with paragraph 75. We suggest further clarification as to how the relevant assertions relate to control objectives and the intersection with the identification of risks and the related control activities.

Paragraph 84—Testing and Evaluating Design Effectiveness

Similar to the previous comment related to paragraph 74-78, there is no linkage of the control objectives to the relevant assertions mentioned, nor is there any mention of risks and the linkage to control objectives and control activities.

Paragraphs 94-99—Timing of Tests of Controls

More guidance on the period of time needed to conclude controls are effective at the "as-of" date is necessary, particularly for those control activities that are performed infrequently (e.g., controls performed monthly or quarterly). We also believe that it is important to provide more explicit guidance related to the term "sufficient period of time" in paragraph 99 as it relates to the auditor's responsibility and in paragraph 151 as it relates to management's responsibility. Unless the Board provides guidance on "sufficient period" and the appropriate time frame for obtaining sufficient evidence, there will be inconsistency in evaluating controls, particularly those implemented late in the year to correct significant deficiencies or material weaknesses.

Paragraphs 113-127—Forming an Opinion on the Effectiveness of Internal Control Over Financial Reporting

The first bullet point in paragraph 113 refers only to "the results of tests of controls." To avoid possible confusion, we recommend that the wording be expanded to read "the adequacy of the assessment performed by management and the results of the auditor's evaluation of the design and tests of operating effectiveness."

Paragraph 114 states that the auditor should review "all" review reports issued during the year by internal audit that address internal control over financial reporting and that such review should include reports issued by internal audit as a result of operational audits or specific reviews if those reports address controls related to internal control over financial reporting. We believe that in certain circumstances it may not be practical or reasonable for the auditor to review "all" reports. For example, a retailer with 1000 stores might perform 50 corporate audits and 400 store audits during a year. Additionally as part of the review of the internal audit function, the auditor should evaluate whether internal audit properly reports its findings to management and the audit committee and whether the company has in place an appropriate monitoring process to ensure that deficiencies identified are accumulated, monitored, and corrected on a timely basis. Accordingly if these processes are judged to be reliable, then we do not believe that the auditor should be required to read each internal audit report.

Paragraph 123 and 126—Examples of Significant Deficiencies and Strong Indicators of a Material Weakness

We believe it important to clarify that the listings contained in paragraphs 123 and 126 are not intended to be all-inclusive (e.g., if a type of deficiency is not listed, then it is not appropriate to presume that the deficiency is not a significant deficiency or material weakness). Furthermore, we believe clarification with respect to the reference in paragraph 126 to the identification of "fraud of any magnitude on the part of senior management" is necessary. The Board should clarify that the type of fraud referred to in paragraph 126 is consistent with the definition of fraud in Statement of Auditing Standards 99.

Additionally, the Board should clarify that the auditor is not required to assess a company's regulatory compliance function. The Proposed Standard requires the auditor to consider "an ineffective regulatory compliance function" as a strong indicator of a material weakness. However, we do not believe it is the auditor's responsibility to assess the effectiveness of a company's regulatory compliance function. COSO, as well as the SEC, recognizes that compliance with laws and regulations is a separate area from internal control over financial reporting. As such, we believe that if the auditor becomes aware of events and circumstances leading him or her to believe company's regulatory compliance function to be ineffective, then the auditor should assess the impact of such ineffectiveness on the auditor's own conclusions about the effectiveness of internal control over financial reporting. However, the auditor should not be required to perform procedures to directly or indirectly assess the effectiveness of a company's regulatory compliance.

Paragraph 128-129—Requirement for Management Representations

We recommend that representations from management also include representations related to the requirements under Section 302 of the Act, including that management has disclosed all significant deficiencies, not just material weaknesses in item d. In addition, similar to the construct for the financial statement audit, we suggest that the auditor be required to include as an appendix to the representations letter a listing of those deficiencies identified by the auditor, which had not been identified by management and, accordingly, include in the letter a representation that, in management's opinion, the deficiencies identified by the auditor when considered with all other deficiencies do or do not rise to the level of a material weakness and that deficiencies identified by management and the auditors do not result in a material weakness for any of the three interim periods.

We also suggest that a representation be included in the letter that confirms that management has communicated the findings of their assessment, including all deficiencies identified by management, to the auditors, as required by paragraph 41.

If management refuses to provide a representation letter, the auditor should not have the option of issuing a report disclaiming an opinion; rather, no report should be issued and the auditor should withdraw from the engagement. The language used in paragraph 129 appears similar to that in the AICPA Attestation Standards; however, it omits one word that significantly alters the concept of reporting. The AICPA Attestation Standards provides for disclaiming an opinion or withdrawing from the engagement only when management fails to furnish *all* appropriate written representations. If management fails to provide any written representations, we believe the auditor is precluded from issuing a report. Further, the presumptively mandatory requirement in paragraph 128 should be changed to an unconditional obligation (e.g., "must") but specifically linked to the reporting ramifications in paragraph 129 of the Proposed Standard.

Paragraph 138-142—Effect of Tests of Control on Substantive Procedures

The requirement, in paragraph 139 of the Proposed Standard to test the controls over financial information used in substantive analytical procedures appears to prohibit the use of information obtained from an external source (e.g., external indices or ratios). Since substantial analytical procedures are often useful in detecting fraud, we suggest modifying the last sentence in paragraph 140 to read, "the use of analytics alone are generally not sufficient for detecting fraud." Furthermore, the last sentence in paragraph 139 makes reference to the significant risks of material misstatements. We believe the Board should clarify its definition of significant risks by providing a few examples of such risks. For instance, does the Board consider fraud or areas involving estimates and management judgment to represent significant risks of material misstatement?

In paragraph 141, the auditor is charged with the responsibility to examine material adjustments made during the course of preparing the financial statements. As discussed previously, we believe that this provision needs additional clarification. Additionally, we believe that similar requirements should be explicitly included in paragraph 41 relative to the Company's responsibility to identify and review material adjustments, in particular to address the risk of fraud related to management override.

We believe that any changes to the interim standards related to substantive procedures need to be highlighted in the Proposed Standard because they may not be obvious to the reader and may create inconsistencies with the Board's interim standards.

Paragraph 145-146—Documentation Requirements

The third bullet point in paragraph 145 of the Proposed Standard seems to require documentation of every possible risk, which is too far reaching. As stated previously, we believe that the Proposed Standard should more explicitly address the extent of consideration and documentation of risk in terms of both management (e.g., paragraph 41) and the auditor (e.g., paragraphs 74-78).

Paragraph 149—Management's Report

We strongly believe that the guidance provided that "other phrases" of an acceptable management conclusion may be appropriate is *not* appropriate for reporting under Section 404 of the Act and should be deleted.

Paragraph 152—Management's Report

The requirement in item e, "including those corrected during the period" is not required to be included in management's annual report as set forth in paragraph 148. This is a requirement of Section 302 of the Act and is addressed in paragraphs 183-189. Accordingly we believe this provision should be deleted.

Paragraph 161—Management's Report Inappropriate

Paragraph 161 states, "The auditor should modify his or her report to include, at a minimum, an explanatory paragraph describing the reasons for this conclusion" and fails to address whether the auditor should modify his or her opinion.

Paragraph 163 – Material Weakness

Paragraph 163 includes a list of elements required to be included in the auditor's report when a material weakness exists; however, the example in Appendix A does not appear to be consistent with these requirements. Additionally, the last bullet point states that the description of the material weakness should also address the requirements in paragraph 178; however, paragraph 178 requires the auditor to make a determination of whether the auditor's *opinion* on the financial statements was affected, but only requires language when it is *not* affected. We believe that the language illustrated in paragraph 178 should be included in all reports where there are material weaknesses, because it merely puts the reader on notice that the issued auditor's report has considered such matters and is appropriate. Accordingly, we recommend that a separate bullet point be added to paragraph 163. Further, we recommend that the Proposed Standard provide illustrative wording in paragraph 178 for a combined report rather than the current instructions to "revise this wording appropriately for use in a combined report."

The third bullet point requires the auditor to provide specific disclosure regarding any material weaknesses identified. We believe, that consistent with existing reporting models, such disclosure should be the responsibility of management in their report and that the auditor will provide supplemental disclosures only if management's disclosures were concluded to be deficient.

Paragraph 180—Subsequent Discovery of Information

Paragraph 180 "presumes" that if the financial statements are restated, the report on internal control should also be restated. This seems inconsistent with paragraph 126, which establishes a restatement as a "strong indicator," not a presumption. Further the wording "based on these considerations" appears irrelevant, as there are no considerations; it is a presumption.

Paragraphs 188-189—Auditor Evaluation Responsibilities

An inconsistency exists between paragraphs 188 and 189. Paragraph 189 requires the auditor to modify his or her report (a presumptively mandatory obligation), whereas paragraph 188 permits the auditor to resign from the engagement, in which case no report will be issued. An auditor concluding that withdrawal is necessary will not be able to comply with paragraph 189.

Appendices—General Comment

The Board has stated in its Statement of Authority that appendices to the Board's standards are an integral part of the auditing standards and carry the same authoritative weight as the body of the standard.[4] However, the status of appendices in AICPA Professional Standards, which the Board has adopted as interim standards, is different. AICPA Statement on Auditing Standards No. 95, *Generally Accepted Auditing Standards* (AU 150), which is incorporated into the Board's interim standards, includes appendices as interpretive publications that the auditor should be aware of and consider but are not required to apply. Under Statement of Auditing Standards 95 (AU 150.6), if the auditor does not apply the auditing guidance in an applicable interpretive publication, the auditor should be prepared to explain how he or she complied with the SAS provisions addressed by such guidance. As such, while the auditor is responsible for following the interim standards themselves, the auditor has a lower level of responsibility for following the guidance in the appendices. Therefore, we believe the Board should clarify that the Board did not elevate the appendices as they exist today in the interim standards adopted by the Board to the same authoritative level as their related interim standards.

Appendix A—Illustrative Reports on Internal Control Over Financial Reporting

We have the following comments with respect to the illustrative report examples in Appendix A:

- We recommend that the definition paragraph be placed immediately preceding the inherent limitations paragraph. Such placement will significantly improve the readability of the reports, particularly when material weaknesses are reported or the report is a combined report on both the audit of the financial statements and the audit of internal control.

- The statement about management's responsibility is inconsistent. Some examples include a very narrow responsibility statement (e.g., that management is responsible for its assessment about the effectiveness), while other examples use a broader responsibility statement (e.g., that management is responsible for maintaining effective internal control). We believe that the latter should be used in all report examples.

- Paragraph 153e requires the report to include "a statement that the auditor's responsibility is to express an opinion on the *written* assessment based on his

---

[4]   Proposed Standard, "Statement of Authority," Page A-2.

or her audit" [emphasis added]; however, the illustrated examples lack the word "written."

- We believe that the definition paragraph should refer to "accounting principles generally accepted in the [identify the country]". Additionally, the second sentence of the definition paragraph is misleading, as it implies that any internal control provides reasonable assurance, including those with material weaknesses. We believe such language should read as follows: "Effective internal control over financial reporting includes those policies and procedures. . . ."

- The inherent limitations paragraph does not address the unauthorized acquisition, use, or disposition of assets discussed in the definition paragraph. Accordingly, we believe that users of the report will inappropriately assume that there are no inherent limitations with respect to such matters.

- The auditor cannot opine on the management's assessment (process), which includes additional details that are not included in the company's report. We believe that the opinion paragraph should refer to "management's *written* assessment" [emphasis added] or "management's conclusion."

- We believe the following revisions should be made to the explanatory paragraph in Example A-2: (1) "will not be prevented or detected" should be added to the end of the first sentence, (2) the reference to management's assessment should be to "management's written assessment," and (3) the elements required by paragraph 163 should be described or illustrated. Further, the references in footnote 1 should be to management's *written* assessment.

- We noted the following additional inconsistencies in Example A-3: (1) "will not be prevented or detected" was omitted from the end of the definition of a material weakness in the explanatory paragraph, (2) the definition of a significant deficiency does not conform to the definition proposed by the Board in paragraph 8, (3) the reference to management's assertion in the introductory paragraph fails to recognize the material weakness referred to in the explanatory paragraph, and (4) footnote 1 provides an illustration as to how to modify the explanatory paragraph when the auditor detects additional material weaknesses; however, the opinion paragraph illustrated in the report appears to be the wrong opinion for such situation (i.e., the auditor should express an adverse opinion and not a qualified opinion).

- We believe that the introductory paragraph of Example A-4 should refer to the PCAOB's standards, given that there will be two different standards for auditing internal control (e.g., "We were engaged to audit, *in accordance with auditing and related professional practice standards established by the Public Company Accounting Oversight Board,* management's assessment. . . ."). Further, we believe that the opinion paragraph should read "we were unable to apply other procedures to satisfy ourselves as to *the effectiveness* of the company's internal control"; we believe the phrase "the effectiveness" was inadvertently omitted from the AICPA illustration for such situation.

- In Example A-6, we believe that the last sentence should refer to "opinion" singularly, consistent with reporting when the auditor reports on both the financial statements and financial statement schedules in a combined report.

Appendix B—Paragraphs B1-B16

While we agree with the framework set forth herein, it is not clear how this guidance intersects with the identification of significant accounts, significant processes and requirements to perform walkthroughs and tests of controls in the main body of the standard. We believe that, in multi-location situations, the locations or units will be selected first based on the guidance in Appendix B and then the guidance for identification of significant accounts, significant processes, and performing of walkthroughs, and tests will then be applied to each location, as applicable. An example of how the Board intends for this guidance to be applied is necessary; distinguishing between scenarios in which a common process/system is utilized for more than one location versus a scenario in which each location utilizes a different process/system.

We recommend that the Board provide guidance as to their view of "some" in paragraph B2 and "large portion" in paragraph B11. In addition, the terminology in Illustration B-1 should be conformed to the terminology used elsewhere in the Proposed Standard (e.g., "significant controls," "specific significant risks," and "specific risks").

Paragraph B10, which states that "if management does not have company-level controls" should be clarified to address whether the absence of common company-level controls is indicative of a deficiency. Additionally we suggest adding to the end of the first sentence "considering each of the 5 control components." We also suggest that additional guidance be added that although company-level controls may not exist at the overall company-level, they may exist, and therefore can be separately evaluated, at a level below the overall company-level (e.g., for one or more of the segments or line of businesses, etc).

We recommend that the Board clarify what is meant by the term "ordinarily" in paragraph B15 and "sufficient control" in footnote 1 to paragraph B16. Due to the lead times needed for coordination with third parties, it is important that companies and auditors clearly understand what is included in the public company's assessment and what is not. We believe that the scope for two companies with the same investees should not have different conclusions, just because one of them has access to evaluate the controls of the investee (e.g., via a contractual provision). Accordingly we support the determining factor as whether the Company has voting control, which is the lowest threshold at which companies are reasonably be expected to have access and the ability to evaluate the investee's controls.

Similar to the concept in paragraph B15, paragraph B16 should provide that for those entities not included in management's assessment, the Company and the auditor should include the controls over the reporting in accordance with generally accepted accounting principles of the company's portion of the income or loss, the investment balance, adjustments to the income or loss and investment balance, and related disclosures.

Appendix B—Paragraphs B24-B39

The criteria set forth in paragraph B26 list factors (the bullets in paragraph B26) for determining whether a service organization is considered part of the company's internal control over financial reporting. However there are no criteria for establishing what is a service organization, which is a very important decision for purposes of determining the scope of management's assertion. Additionally it is unclear how these factors relate to the similar items in AU324.03 of the Board's interim auditing standards.

Given the pervasiveness of the "extended enterprise" whereby outsourcing of processes and systems is commonplace, we suggest that clear guidance and examples of service organizations be provided including addressing the following types of relationships that are common today:

- Application systems

- Computing environments

- Transaction oriented processes (e.g., customer service, collections, manufacturing, warranty claims, coupons)

- Other back-office processes or support functions (e.g., legal, internal audit, taxes, environmental, actuarial, financial reporting).

The guidance does not establish any limitations of an auditor's use of service auditor reports. For example, if a company outsourced their entire accounting function including systems, processes, and financial reporting and the service organization makes an appropriate service auditor's report available, is it appropriate for management or the auditor to conclude on the effectiveness of the company's internal control solely on the basis of the service auditor's report? Our view is that guidance should be provided that establishes when it is appropriate to obtain and use a service auditor's report versus when it is not.

The second bullet point of paragraph B27 should refer to controls that are relevant to the company's internal control and not to controls that are relevant to management's assessment and the auditor's opinion. Additionally, paragraph B27 refers to AU Sec. 324.07, which describes procedures that auditors should perform, not management. The Board should separately provide guidance (e.g., paragraph 41 as to the procedures management should perform with respect to service organizations).

Paragraph B28 inappropriately refers to a service auditor performing a "review" of systems; however, the term "review" is reserved under the AICPA *Professional Standards* for services that are permitted when analytical procedures can be performed. As analytics cannot be applied to systems, we recommend that the word "review" be replaced with "apply procedures" or "examine."

The first sentence in paragraph B35 states, "If the auditor believes that he or she also *must* obtain evidence about the operating effectiveness of service center controls, one way an auditor can obtain such evidence is by obtaining a service auditor's report on controls placed in operation and tests of the operating effectiveness, as described in paragraph .245b of AU sec. 324." The use of the term "must" does not appear appropriate in this sentence given that this sentence implicitly requires auditor judgment (hence, the reference to "if the auditor believes") and, therefore, it cannot be considered an unconditional obligation as the PCAOB has described the meaning of the term "must."

The description of a report on operating effectiveness in paragraph B35 fails to recognize that such report also provides an opinion on the suitability of design of the controls.

Paragraphs B37-B38 discusses the procedures that the auditor should perform with respect to changes in controls at the service organization and presumes that management is aware of any and all changes. We believe that inquiries should include such matters as inquiring of management what they have done to ascertain whether there have been any changes in the service organization's controls. Paragraph B37 also incorrectly categorizes errors identified in the service organization's processing as a change in controls; this situation is better presented as an indicator that a change may have occurred. Accordingly, we expect the auditor to focus on how management investigated such matters, including the cause of the errors, and then evaluate the implications on management's assessment and the auditor's evidence.

For purposes of performing an audit of internal control over financial reporting, it is not clear whether the considerations of a service organization's controls include only control activities or the other control components as they relate to the service organization as well. We also suggest the Proposed Standard provide guidance as to the impact on management's and the auditor's report, if management and the auditor are unable to obtain sufficient evidence as to controls at a service organization.

Appendix B—Paragraphs B40 and B41

We suggest that the Board clarify whether the examples included in the appendices, which are deemed to be authoritative, are also authoritative or only illustrative in terms of the nature, extent, or timing of the procedures. For example, has the Board established that a sample size of 25 items for a manual control and one item for a programmed control, in conjunction with inquiry and observation, is the minimum scope?

The following comments relate to Example B-1:

- Page A-91, first paragraph, item c, distinguishes between a programmed control and a detective control. We believe the distinction is a programmed control versus a manual control.

- Page A-93, item a, carried over from previous page states that "items that typically appear on the Daily Unapplied Cash Exception Report" suggests that the auditor's focus is only on the "typical" items, not the unusual and infrequent.

- Page A-93, since the Daily Unapplied Cash Exception Report is a cumulative listing, we believe that it is necessary to observe it only once to update the tests to year-end, which could be done as a dual-purpose test for both the audit of internal control and the audit of the financial statements.

The following comments relate to Example B-2:

- Page A-94 it appears that the example, in the second paragraph, carves out other receivables from testing. It is not clear what the basis for that decision is based on the guidance provided in the standard.

- Page A-95, the first bullet point describes observing the control being performed. While observation is helpful for controls performed infrequently such as reconciliations, it is unlikely, within practical limits, that the auditor will be able to observe the employee performing the reconciliation.

- It is unclear why it is necessary for the auditor to scan the file of all reconciliations prepared during the year for the audit of internal control, since the auditor's report is "as of" a point of time, unless the intent is to portray this as a dual-purpose test for the benefit of the audit of the financial statements. Otherwise the auditor's responsibility is to determine whether the control has been operating for a sufficient period of time, the whole year seems to be too far reaching. We support testing the control for two months, once at interim and once at year-end.

The following comments relate to Example B-3:

- In Example B-3, it suggests that if "the auditor had encountered a control exception, the auditor would have tested an additional number of items." We suggest that testing more items is not necessarily the best response, particularly if the exception relates to a very large population. We suggest that a better response is to identify the root cause of the exception and then design tests to specifically search for additional exceptions.

- On page A-96, the first paragraph states, "the auditor expected no errors based on the results of company-level tests performed earlier." It is not clear how company-level controls in this example may impact the auditor's scope. Is this implying that there is a common process/system across multiple locations? Why does that impact the sample size? Further, the example goes on to say, "If the auditor had encountered a control exception, the auditor would have tested an additional number of items." It is unclear what control exception is being referred to—does this mean that if company-level controls were not adequate, the auditor should increase the sample size for testing cash disbursements?

The following comment relate to Example B-4:

- Page A-98 implies that the auditor has uncontrolled access to the company's systems in its description of the auditor's attempts to record the receipt of goods without a purchase order, to approve an invoice for payment, to process duplicate invoices, etc. We recommend that such procedures be described as being performed in the presence of appropriate individuals of the company. Had the auditor's attempts been successful, the auditor could be at risk for having altered the client's records; accordingly, such attempts should only be made in the client's presence so that the client can be immediately notified of any breach to their systems.

2. Pervasive Comments

Use of Consistent Terminology

We noted the following items, which we believe are examples of inconsistencies that should be addressed by the Board:

    a. Management's assessment, management's written assessment and management's conclusion

Throughout the Proposed Standard these phrases are used. We believe that the phrase ***management's assessment*** encompasses various phases of management analyzing the design of its controls, testing and evaluating their operating effectiveness, forming its conclusion, documenting its work and preparing its written report. We also believe that the report that management prepares might be referred to as ***management's written assessment*** that contains, among other things, ***management's conclusion*** on the effectiveness of its internal control. The Proposed Standard, however, appears to use management's assessment interchangeably for both the process and the written report, resulting in confusion or factually inaccurate statements.

For example, management's assessment is much more than what is contained in the report of management. Paragraph 2 states that "The report of management is required to contain management's assessment . . . including a statement as to whether the company's internal control . . . is effective" while paragraph 5 states "the auditor evaluates the assessment performed by management." While only a description of the process (activities) can be included in the report, the auditor should be evaluating the process rather than the report. Accordingly, we recommend that the phrase "management's report" or "management's written assessment" be used when referring to the written communication of management required under Section 404.

Another inconsistency appears in paragraph 128b, which uses "evaluation" instead of "assessment" (i.e., the auditor should obtain written representations "stating that management has performed an evaluation of the effectiveness"). Evaluation is also used in paragraph 148.

    b. Internal control over financial reporting, internal controls over financial reporting, controls, and internal controls

The Committee of Sponsoring Organizations of the Treadway Commission ("COSO") refers to internal control (singular) as a process; systems and controls make up the process. Individual controls or subsets of controls are referred to by COSO without the term "internal." The Proposed Standard will create confusion by using inconsistent terminology. For example, "internal controls [plural] over financial reporting" are used in paragraph 10-12 (although such paragraphs also contain the appropriate singular usage of "internal control over financial reporting"); "internal controls" is used in paragraph 11, 32, and 133.

c.   Specific risks and significant risks

The term "specific risks" in used in paragraph B1, "significant risks" in paragraph 139, and "high risks" are referred to in the explanatory material and existing interim standards. We recommend consistently using "significant risk" throughout.

Compliance With Proposed Rule 3101

The Board's proposed Rule 3101 sets forth certain terms to describe the degree to which the Board expects auditors to comply with professional obligations included in the Board's Auditing and Related Professional Practice Standards. This Proposed Standard uses terminology that is inconsistent with the proposed Rule 3101 or describes procedures in a manner in which it is unclear as to the level of obligation. Paragraph 79 of the Proposed Standard discusses performing walkthroughs and states both "walkthroughs are required procedures" (a possible unconditional obligation) and "the auditor should perform a walkthrough for all of the company's significant processes" (a presumptively mandatory obligation). Other examples where it is unclear as to the auditor's obligation and that should be clarified include the following:

- Paragraph 85, "procedures the auditor performs to test and evaluate design effectiveness"

- Footnote 20 and paragraph 184, "need to evaluate"

- Paragraph 52, "should focus on combinations of controls"

- Paragraph 98, "should balance performing the tests"

- Paragraph 101, "should vary" the nature, timing and extent of tests

- Paragraph 180, "should presume that his or her report on the company's internal control over financial reporting . . . should be recalled"

- Paragraph 181, "the direction of AU sec. 711.10 to inquire of and obtain written representations . . . should be extended to matters that could have a material effect on management's assessment."

For presumptively mandatory obligations, the procedures "should inquire about and examine, for this subsequent period," various types of reports and "information about the effectiveness of the company's internal control over financial reporting obtained through other engagements" are far too vague.[5] Whom should the auditor inquire of—management, internal auditors, regulators? Is it some or all? And to what is "obtained through other engagements" making reference? It will be difficult for the auditor to comply with something that is not clear and subject to extensive interpretation.

---

[5] Proposed Standard, paragraph 171.

Although consulting the auditor's legal counsel about further actions to be taken when the auditor is addressing problematic situations is always advisable, we do not believe that the standard should create any presumptively mandatory obligations for the auditor to do so. We believe that documentation to demonstrate that the auditor considered consulting (as is currently be required under paragraph 176) and evaluated whether to consult (as is currently be required under paragraph 188) serves no useful purpose.

Paragraph 176 contains various other presumptively mandatory obligations that are again lacking in specificity, including such phrases as the auditor "should propose that management consult with some other party whose advice might be useful" and imply that the auditor should also discuss the matter with "those management has consulted." Further, we believe this paragraph should address whether the auditor should refrain from issuing a report.

We recommend that the Board analyze the use of the above phrases within the Proposed Standard and conform the terminology used so that it is clear which procedures the auditor is obligated to perform, presumptively required to perform, and required to consider.

References to Auditing Standards Issued by the AICPA

We question the extensive references to the AICPA *Professional Standards* throughout the Proposed Standard, as the PCAOB has only adopted the standards as in effect at a certain date. We recommend that references be made to the codification of the Board's interim standards, because the AICPA may subsequently amend its standards and, if so, the amended AICPA standards will differ from those adopted by the PCAOB.

III. RESPONSES TO SPECIFIC QUESTIONS

Questions Regarding an Integrated Audit of the Financial Statements and Internal Control Over Financial Reporting:

1. Is it appropriate to refer to the auditor's attestation of management's assessment of the effectiveness of internal control over financial reporting as the audit of internal control over financial reporting?

Yes. It is appropriate to refer to the auditor's attestation of management's assessment of the effectiveness of internal control over financial reporting as the audit of internal control over financial reporting.

2. Should the auditor be prohibited from performing an audit of internal control over financial reporting without also performing an audit of the financial statements?

Yes. Section 404(b) of the Act and the related SEC rule require that the attestation on management's assessment of internal control over financial reporting be performed by the registered public accounting firm that prepares or issues the audit report. We do not believe it is appropriate for an auditor to report on internal control over financial reporting of a public company unless the auditor performs the financial statement audit for the same period.

3. Rather than requiring the auditor to also complete an audit of the financial statements, would an appropriate alternative be to require the auditor to perform work with regard to the financial statements comparable to that required to complete the financial statement audit?

No. As stated above, the auditor that performs the audit of internal control over financial reporting should also be the auditor that performs the financial statement audit. In addition, we see no practical basis to define "work comparable to that required to complete the financial statement audit."

Question Regarding the Costs and Benefits of Internal Control:

4. Does the Board's proposed standard give appropriate consideration to how internal control is implemented in, and how the audit of internal control over financial reporting should be conducted at, small and medium-sized companies?

No. Please refer to our comments in Section I, Overall Comments, Item 10, "Consideration of Small and Medium-Sized Entities."

Question Regarding the Audit of Internal Control Over Financial Reporting:

5. Should the Board, generally or in this proposed standard, specify the level of competence and training of the audit personnel that is necessary to perform specified auditing procedures effectively? For example, it would be inappropriate for a new, inexperienced auditor to have primary responsibility for conducting interviews of a company's senior management about possible fraud.

Interim auditing standards as adopted by the PCAOB require that, through the first general standard, the audit be performed by a person or persons having adequate technical training and proficiency as an auditor, and, through the first standard of field work, assistants to be properly supervised. The decision to allocate tasks to assistants involved in an engagement is a professional judgment made by the auditor, after taking into account various factors including the level of experience of the staff involved and their knowledge of the company's operations. Supervision of assistants includes instructing assistants, keeping informed of significant problems encountered, and reviewing the work performed. Therefore, we do not believe it is necessary to specify the levels of competence and training necessary to perform certain auditing or attest procedures, as existing standards already require appropriate assignment and supervision of auditors.

Questions Regarding Evaluation of Management's Assessment:

6. Is the scope of the audit appropriate in that it requires the auditor to both evaluate management's assessment and obtain directly evidence about whether internal control over financial reporting is effective?

Yes. Please refer to our comment under Section I, Overall Comments, Item 1, "Decision Mandating the Auditor to Audit the Underlying Controls as Well as Management's Assessment Process."

7. Is it appropriate that the Board has provided criteria that auditors should use to evaluate the adequacy of management's documentation?

Yes. The auditor is responsible for determining whether management's documentation provides reasonable support for its assessment. Because the auditor is required to evaluate the sufficiency of management's process and documentation, we believe it is appropriate to provide the auditor with guidelines for performing such evaluation. However, the Board should provide more extensive and detailed criteria on this subject. Please refer to our comment under Section I, Overall Comments, Item 2.

8. Is it appropriate to state that inadequate documentation is an internal control deficiency, the severity of which the auditor should evaluate? Or should inadequate documentation automatically rise to the level of significant deficiency or material weakness in internal control?

Please refer to our specific comment in Section 1, Overall Comments, Item 3b, "Management's Responsibilities: Extent of Documentation."

Questions Regarding Obtaining an Understanding of Internal Control Over Financial Reporting:

9. Are the objectives to be achieved by performing walkthroughs sufficient to require the performance of walkthroughs?

10. *Is it appropriate to require that the walkthrough be performed by the auditor himself or herself, rather than allowing the auditor to use walkthrough procedures performed by management, internal auditors, or others?*

For questions 9 and 10, please refer to our specific comments in Section I, Overall Comments, Item 4b, "Issues Regarding the Scope of an Audit of Internal Control Over Financial Reporting: Performance of Walkthroughs."

<u>*Question Regarding Testing Operating Effectiveness:*</u>

11. *Is it appropriate to require the auditor to obtain evidence of the effectiveness of controls for all relevant assertions for all significant accounts and disclosures every year or may the auditor use some of the audit evidence obtained in previous years to support his or her current opinion on management's assessment?*

With regard to performing an audit of internal control over financial reporting, we believe it is necessary for management and the auditor to obtain sufficient evidence each year to form conclusions about the effectiveness of the design and operating effectiveness of internal control over financial reporting. In general, we do not believe it is appropriate to rely principally on audit evidence obtained in previous years in order to support a subsequent opinion. However, we do think the locations that are not individually significant could be tested by the auditor through the annual testing of company-level controls combined with testing at the location on a cyclical basis. This concept is consistent with the views expressed in Appendix B of the Proposed Standard. As such, we believe paragraph 101 of the Proposed Standard should be modified accordingly.

<u>*Questions Regarding Using the Work of Management and Others:*</u>

12. *To what extent should the auditor be permitted or required to use the work of management and others?*

13. *Are the three categories of controls and the extent to which the auditor may rely on the work of others appropriately defined?*

14. *Does the proposed standard give appropriate recognition to the work of internal auditors? If not, does the proposed standard place too much emphasis and preference on the work of internal auditors or not enough?*

15. *Is the flexibility in determining the extent of reperformance of the work of others appropriate, or should the auditor be specifically required to reperform a certain level of work (for example, reperform tests of all significant accounts or reperform every test performed by others that the auditor intends to use)?*

16. *Is the requirement for the auditor to obtain the principle evidence, on an overall basis, through his or her own work the appropriate benchmark for the amount of work that is required to be performed by the auditor?*

For questions 12-16, please refer to our specific comments in Section I, Overall Comments, Item 4d, "Issues Regarding the Scope of an Audit of Internal Control Over Financial Reporting: The Auditor's Use of the Work Performed by Management and Others."

Questions Regarding Evaluating Results:

17. Will the definitions in the proposed standard of significant deficiency and material weakness provide for increased consistency in the evaluation of deficiencies? How can the definitions be improved?

It is unclear to us whether the proposed definitions will provide for increased consistency. However, we do believe that the proposed definitions will result in more significant deficiencies and material weaknesses than the existing definitions. We believe the Board should clarify certain aspects of the proposed definitions.

First, the concept of immaterial is familiar to most users of financial statements; however, the concept of inconsequential is not as widely used or understood. Therefore, the Board should define inconsequential, clarify the relationship between inconsequential and immaterial, and explain how inconsequential relates to materiality at the account-balance level.

Second, the definitions of a significant deficiency and material weakness both refer to annual as well as interim financial statements. We agree that deficiencies identified in the audit of internal control should be evaluated for both the annual and interim impacts. However, some may read this to also imply that the auditor should plan and perform the annual audit of internal control, as well as evaluate any control deficiencies found, in the context of a materiality related to interim periods rather than the annual materiality. This appears to be inconsistent with the auditor's responsibilities with regard to management's certifications. Accordingly, we suggest the Board clarify that the auditor is not required to plan the audit of internal control to identify material weaknesses or significant deficiencies relating to interim periods; the annual or interim financial statements language applies only to the evaluation of deficiencies identified.

18. Do the examples in Appendix D of how to apply these definitions in various scenarios provide helpful guidance? Are there other specific examples that commenters could suggest that would provide further interpretive help?

In general, the examples provided in Appendix D of the Proposed Standard provide helpful guidance in the application of the definitions of various levels of control deficiencies to particular fact patterns. However, we believe the Board should clarify several issues.

First, while the Board specified that the examples in Appendix D are only for illustrative purposes, the Board also separately stated that appendices to the Board's standards are an "integral part of the standard and carry the same authoritative weight as the body of the standard."[6] It is unclear as to whether an auditor will be in violation of the Proposed Standard if he or she failed to arrive at the same conclusion as in the Board's examples, given similar fact

---

[6] Proposed Standard, "Statement of Authority."

patterns. Additionally, Appendix D uses the terminology "should" in several places; the word "should" signifies a presumptive obligation. Given the above, the Board should clarify the authoritative level of the illustrative examples included in Appendix D.

Second, the Board specified in paragraph 118 of the Proposed Standard that the significance of a deficiency in internal control over financial reporting does not depend on whether a misstatement actually has occurred however, the Board's examples D-1 and D-2 (Scenario B in both cases) includes within the fact patterns that a history of actual misstatements played a significant role in elevating a significant deficiency to the level of a material weakness in each case. To support the guidance in paragraph 118, we suggest that the fact patterns in one or more of the examples be revised to result in a material weakness when a misstatement has not occurred.

Third, the definition of internal control over financial reporting adopted by the SEC in its final rule contains considerations that expand beyond the reliability of financial reporting to include, among other considerations, the maintenance of records, as well as safeguards against unauthorized acquisition, use, and disposition of company assets. The Board should consider providing examples of control deficiencies in those areas, as well as the process and considerations for evaluating such deficiencies within the framework of the definitions of significant deficiency and material weakness proposed by the Board.

19. Is it necessary for the auditor to evaluate the severity of all identified internal control deficiencies?

Because any one control deficiency could be a material weakness and a material weakness causes the auditor to issue an adverse opinion, the auditor must evaluate the significance of all internal control deficiencies identified as well as those internal control deficiencies identified by management. Otherwise, the auditor may fail to appropriately modify his or her report on management's assessment of the company's internal control over financial reporting. Furthermore, because an audit is conducted on a test basis, control deficiencies identified have actual as well as indicative significance. The actual significance of a control deficiency should be evaluated in terms of likelihood and magnitude, and its indicative significance should be evaluated to determine whether the existence of such deficiencies implies, points to, or raises the likelihood that other control deficiencies exist.

20. Is it appropriate to require the auditor to communicate all internal control deficiencies (not just material weaknesses and significant deficiencies) to management in writing?

Yes. We believe it is appropriate to communicate all internal control deficiencies found in the course of the attestation engagement to management in writing. Communicating all deficiencies identified (and not just material weaknesses and significant deficiencies) in writing to management assists the company in improving its internal control over financial reporting. Management's propensity to correct all identified control deficiencies is also an indicator of the tone at the top and the control environment.

In terms of communicating with the audit committee, the Proposed Standard requires that the auditor communicate in writing all significant deficiencies and material weaknesses identified during the audit. We agree with this approach; however, we are not clear as to how this reconciles with the SEC's rule, *Strengthening the Commission's Requirements Regarding*

Auditor Independence, as it relates to required communications with the audit committee. The SEC's rule requires that the auditor provide the audit committee with copies of all material communications with management; therefore, it seems that the auditor will be required to provide the audit committee with a copy of the letter to management describing all deficiencies in internal control over financial reporting. The Board should reconcile the guidance in paragraph 190 with the requirements under the SEC's rule regarding audit committee communications.

21. Are the matters that the Board has classified as strong indicators that a material weakness in internal control exists appropriately classified as such?

In general, the Board should consider clarifying the meaning of the phrase "strong indicator" by providing examples or additional factors to consider for determining when a deficiency represents no more than a significant deficiency despite the existence of the strong indicator that a material weakness exists. For example, when might a restatement of a prior period or a material misstatement in the current period not be considered a material weakness? Further, the Board should clarify that the list of strong indicators of a material weakness is not meant to be an exhaustive list and that other issues that may not be on the list may be determined to be material weaknesses. With respect to individual strong indicators, we believe that a restatement of prior period financials should be a strong indicator that a material weakness existed *in the prior period,* but not necessarily in the current period.

22. Is it appropriate to require the auditors to evaluate the effectiveness of the audit committee's oversight of the company's external financial reporting and internal control over financial reporting?

23. Will auditors be able to effectively carry out their responsibility to evaluate the effectiveness of the audit committee's oversight?

24. If the auditor concludes that ineffective audit committee oversight is a material weakness, rather than require the auditor to issue an adverse opinion with regard to the effectiveness of the internal control over financial reporting, should the standard require the auditor to withdraw from the audit engagement?

For questions 22-24, please refer to our specific comments in Section I, Overall Comments, Item 6, "Evaluating the Effectiveness of the Audit Committee's Oversight."

Questions Regarding Forming an Opinion and Reporting:

25. Is it appropriate that the existence of a material weakness would require the auditor to express an adverse conclusion about the effectiveness of the company's internal control over financial reporting, consistent with the required reporting model for management?

26. Are there circumstances where a qualified "except for" conclusion would be appropriate?

For questions 25 and 26, please refer to our comments in Section 1, Item 5a, "Reporting: Requirement to Issue an Adverse Opinion in Certain Circumstances. "

27. Do you agree with the position that when the auditor issues a nonstandard opinion, such as an adverse opinion, that the auditor's opinion should speak directly to the effectiveness of the internal control over financial reporting rather than to whether management's assessment is fairly stated?

Yes. We believe the auditor's opinion should speak directly to the effectiveness of the internal control over financial reporting in all situations. It can be confusing to users if the auditors issue a "clean" opinion on management's report that contained a material weakness. Indeed, the AICPA Statements on Standards for Attestation Engagements were modified by the Auditing Standards Board to require that the auditor's opinion speak directly to the effectiveness of internal control in order to address practices that developed among users who were not reading management's assertions but were only reading the auditor's report, and because initially the auditor's report only referred to management's assertion, users were not aware of the existence of material weaknesses in management's assertions. Accordingly, due to prior experience in practice, we believe it is important for the auditor to also disclose the material weakness by reporting directly on the effectiveness of the internal control rather than on management's process.

Questions Regarding Auditor Independence:

28. Should the Board provide specific guidance on independence and internal control-related nonaudit services in the context of this proposed standard?

29. Are there any specific internal control-related nonaudit services the auditor should be prohibited from providing to an audit client?

Strengthening the Commission's Requirements Regarding Auditor Independence, recently adopted by the SEC, modified rules with respect to auditor independence and set forth new limitations regarding the provision of nonaudit services by auditors. We do not believe further guidance is necessary.

Questions Regarding Auditor's Responsibilities with Regard to Management's Certifications:

30. Are the auditor's differing levels of responsibility as they relate to management's quarterly certifications versus the annual (fourth quarter) certification, appropriate?

We believe there is a general inconsistency in requiring the modification of the auditor's report on the effectiveness of internal control over financial reporting as of the company's fiscal year end (a point in time) based on procedures performed to determine changes to internal control over financial reporting during the fourth quarter (a time period.) The Board should consider separating the auditor's responsibilities with respect to quarterly certifications from the auditor's responsibilities with respect to the annual assertion by management. We suggest that the Board devise a reporting mechanism for the auditor to follow for any quarter in which the auditor believes material modifications should be made to management's quarterly certification.

31. Is the scope of the auditor's responsibility for quarterly disclosures about the internal control over financial reporting appropriate?

The extent of work to be performed by the auditor in regard to quarterly disclosures about internal control is not clear in the Proposed Standard. Paragraph 186 requires the auditor to *determine* through "a combination of observation and inquiry" whether significant changes in internal control over financial reporting may introduce significant deficiencies or material weaknesses in the design of internal control over financial reporting.

Under current standards, procedures performed by auditors with regard to an interim review of financial information do not require the auditor to "determine" whether there are misstatements; rather, only to consider, based on the procedures performed, whether material modifications are necessary to the financial information as presented. The term "determine" implies that the auditor has a duty to identify all significant changes in internal control over financial reporting, which is likely to significantly increase the scope of the auditor's work. Furthermore, "observation" is a substantive procedure that is not currently part of the auditor's responsibility in the context of an interim review of financial information.

Further it is unclear what responsibility, if any, the auditor has with respect to management's conclusion at an interim period that a material weakness or significant deficiency previously identified and reported has been corrected. Does the auditor perform sufficient procedures to satisfy themselves that the deficiency has been corrected, or is inquiry and observation sufficient? Furthermore, what are the auditor's (and management's) responsibilities with respect to deficiencies that both arise and are corrected in the same period?

Additionally, some practical issues should be addressed including (1) some controls may not be observable either due to timing or because the controls are automated; it is not clear how the auditor should proceed with respect to those that can not be observed, and (2) it is not clear whether such procedures must be performed within the quarter as opposed to after the quarter-end when reviews of quarterly financial information typically occur.

We appreciate the opportunity to comment, and would be pleased to discuss these issues with you further. If you have any questions or would like to discuss these issues further, please contact Robert J. Kueppers at (203) 761-3579.

Very truly yours,

/s/ Deloitte & Touche LLP

cc: William J. McDonough, Chairman of the PCAOB
Kayla J. Gillan, Member
Daniel L. Goelzer, Member
Willis D. Gradison, Jr., Member
Charles D. Niemeier, Member

¶ 633. Ernst & Young

≡ ERNST & YOUNG

■ Ernst & Young LLP
Suite 1300
925 Euclid Avenue
Cleveland, OH 44115-1476

■ Phone: (216) 861-5000
www.ey.com

November 21, 2003

Mr. J. Gordon Seymour
Acting Secretary
Public Company Accounting Oversight Board
1666 K Street, NW
Washington, D.C. 20006-2803

PCAOB Rulemaking Docket Matter No. 008
Proposed Auditing Standard—An Audit of Internal Control Over Financial Reporting
Performed in Conjunction With an Audit of Financial Statements

Dear Mr. Seymour:

We are pleased to comment on the PCAOB's proposed auditing standard (the "Proposed Standard") related to an audit of internal control over financial reporting in conjunction with an audit of financial statements (an "audit of internal control over financial reporting"). Overall, we support the Proposed Standard because we believe it would provide improved guidance for auditors in the execution of audits of internal control over financial reporting. The performance and reporting guidance in the Proposed Standard is consistent with the level of assurance an audit of internal control over financial reporting is expected to provide, and the PCAOB has appropriately recognized the responsibilities of management to assess and report on internal control over financial reporting, as described in the final rule issued by the Securities and Exchange Commission (the "SEC Final Rule").

While we commend the Board for its thorough Proposed Standard, we believe the Board should modify some aspects of the Proposed Standard to address a number of key matters, including the following:

Use of the Work of Management and Others (Paragraphs 103-110)
Provide the auditor more flexibility in using the work of internal auditors, especially where "the importance of the internal audit function results in a high degree of competence and objectivity." We believe paragraph 104 unnecessarily prohibits the use of the work of management and others, particularly internal audit, in three areas—walkthroughs, controls over the period-end financial reporting process, and controls that have a pervasive effect on the financial statements, such as certain information technology general controls. We believe the auditor should be permitted to use, on a "limited basis," the work of internal audit in these areas based on the auditor's assessment of the competence and objectivity of those performing the work.

Evaluating the Effectiveness of the Audit Committee's Oversight (Paragraphs 56-59)
Clarify that the auditor's responsibility to evaluate the effectiveness of the audit committee's oversight of the company's external financial reporting and internal control over financial reporting is not a separate and distinct evaluation. Rather, it is

one element of the auditor's overall understanding and assessment of the company's control environment and monitoring components.

Evaluating the Results (Paragraphs 8 and 21 and Appendix D)
Reconsider whether "more than inconsequential" is the appropriate threshold for identifying significant deficiencies, and the effect of this threshold on other aspects of the Proposed Standard dealing with materiality and evaluating the results of the audit of internal control over financial reporting.

Auditor's Responsibility Relating to Management's Quarterly Certifications (Paragraphs 185-189)
We believe it is inappropriate to include additional responsibilities with regard to management's quarterly certifications in this Proposed Standard, which addresses "an audit of internal control over financial reporting performed in conjunction with an audit of financial statements." We do not believe the auditor's responsibility for management's quarterly certifications and related disclosures extends beyond the responsibility to inform the audit committee of matters coming to his or her attention.

Considerations for Small and Medium-Sized Companies (Appendix E)
Further clarify how an audit of internal control over financial reporting should be conducted for small and medium-sized issuers. We believe the COSO framework currently provides management and the auditor with sufficient guidance and flexibility with regard to small and medium-sized companies. We suggest the Board modify Appendix E to refer to the COSO guidance or provide more specific examples based on the COSO guidance.

Effect of Material Weaknesses on Reporting (Paragraphs 162-164)
Permit a qualified (e.g., "except for") management assessment and audit opinion in certain cases based on an evaluation of the significance of a material weakness. As further described in our response to question 25 in a later section, we believe this reporting alternative would more clearly communicate to users of the reports the effect of a material weakness and would be consistent with the SEC Final Rule.

We also urge the Board to clearly identify the changes being made to the Board's interim professional standards as a result of the Proposed Standard, including the substantive procedures with respect to audits of financial statements described in paragraphs 138-142.

We have organized our comment letter to first respond to the 31 questions on which the Board seeks public comment and then to provide additional comments that do not relate to a particular question. Our responses and additional comments include specific observations on those matters we have highlighted above.

We believe our comments and suggestions are in the spirit of the Board's broad objectives of promoting strong corporate governance and the communication of appropriate information on internal control over financial reporting.

An Integrated Audit of the Financial Statements and Internal Control Over Financial Reporting

1. Is it appropriate to refer to the auditor's attestation of management's assessment of the effectiveness of internal control over financial reporting as the audit of internal control over financial reporting?

Yes. The term "audit" appropriately denotes the level of assurance that the auditor's attestation report provides.

2. Should the auditor be prohibited from performing an audit of internal control over financial reporting without also performing an audit of the financial statements?

For purposes of reporting on internal control over financial reporting under Section 404 as described in the Proposed Standard, we believe the accounting firm should be prohibited from performing an audit of internal control over financial reporting without also performing an audit of the company's financial statements as of the same date. We recognize this requirement would mean (1) the same accounting firm would have to perform both audits, (2) the audit of internal control would necessarily coincide with the entity's fiscal year end, and (3) the auditor's report on the effectiveness of internal control over financial reporting, under these circumstances, would be as of a point in time. We agree with the Board's view that the audits are closely interrelated and the auditor needs to consider the potential significance of the information that might be obtained during the audit of the financial statements to his or her conclusions about the effectiveness of internal control over financial reporting.

However, we believe there may be other situations that require an audit of internal control over financial reporting of a public company, but do not also require an audit of financial statements. For example, a regulatory agency or a potential buyer might require an audit of internal control over financial reporting of a public company or one or more of its subsidiaries as of a point in time that does not coincide with the entity's fiscal year end. Under these circumstances, the audit of internal control over financial reporting need not be performed in conjunction with an audit of the financial statements. To address these circumstances, we suggest the Board not supersede Chapter 5, "Reporting on an Entity's Internal Control Over Financial Reporting" of Statement on Standards for Attestation Engagements No. 10 *Attestation Standards: Revision and Recodification* (AICPA, Professional Standards, Vol. 1, AT sec 501). We recommend this chapter be updated or otherwise amended as necessary for use in situations other than an audit of internal control over financial reporting in conjunction with an audit of financial statements.

3. Rather than requiring the auditor to also complete an audit of the financial statements, would an appropriate alternative be to require the auditor to perform work with regard to the financial statements comparable to that required to complete the financial statement audit?

No. For purposes of reporting on internal control over financial reporting under Section 404 as described in the Proposed Standard, we believe the audit of the financial statements necessarily must be completed at the same time as the audit of internal control over financial reporting. We agree with the Board's view that the audits are closely interrelated and that the two audit reports should be dated the same (paragraph 157).

The Costs and Benefits of Internal Control

4.   Does the Board's proposed standard give appropriate consideration to how internal control is implemented in, and how the audit of internal control over financial reporting should be conducted at, small and medium-sized issuers?

We believe the COSO framework currently provides management and the auditor with sufficient guidance and flexibility with regard to how the internal control components relate to small and medium-sized companies.

While we understand the Board is sensitive to the possible effects of the Proposed Standard on small and medium-sized companies, we believe Appendix E implies that, due to the involvement and interaction of senior management, there is a lower threshold for the design of effective internal control over financial reporting and a lower threshold for evidence of operating effectiveness for small and medium-sized companies. We agree the behavior and interaction of senior management is critical to an effective control environment. However, we do not agree that it is necessarily more so for smaller or medium-sized companies and, in any event, the owner-manager should not be viewed as a replacement for necessary controls that address the relevant assertions related to significant accounts and disclosures.

While it has been our experience with audits of smaller or medium-sized companies that systems and processes often are less complex and thus generally require fewer, less formal controls, the true measure of the overall effectiveness of internal control is the consistent execution of these controls and their sensitivity to identifying potential misstatements, whether caused by error or fraud.

The Audit of Internal Control Over Financial Reporting

5.   Should the Board, generally or in this proposed standard, specify the level of competence and training of the audit personnel that is necessary to perform specified auditing procedures effectively? For example, it would be inappropriate for a new, inexperienced auditor to have primary responsibility for conducting interviews of a company's senior management about possible fraud.

No. We believe interim professional standards adopted by the Board provide sufficient guidance regarding the level of competence, training and professional skepticism of audit personnel, and it is not necessary to reiterate the information from these standards as has been done in paragraphs 30-38 and paragraph 111 of the Proposed Standard. We believe it would be redundant to specify in the Proposed Standard the level of competence, training, and professional skepticism of audit personnel performing specific procedures for audits of internal control over financial reporting, while similar guidance on training, professional skepticism, and supervision relating to audits of financial statements is already included in the interim general and field work standards.

Mr. J. Gordon Seymour

Evaluating Management's Assessment

6. Is the scope of the audit appropriate in that it requires the auditor to both evaluate management's assessment and obtain, directly, evidence about whether internal control over financial reporting is effective?

Yes. We agree with the Board that "an auditing process restricted to evaluating what management has done would not provide the auditor with a sufficiently high level of assurance that management's conclusion is correct." To conclude that internal control over financial reporting is effective, the auditor necessarily will need to perform sufficient procedures to determine whether he or she agrees with management that internal control is effective.

7. Is it appropriate that the Board has provided criteria auditors should use to evaluate the adequacy of management's documentation?

Yes. We believe providing criteria auditors should use to evaluate the adequacy of management's documentation will more clearly define the documentation requirements under management's responsibilities, align the approaches used by management and the auditor to evaluate internal control over financial reporting, and drive consistency in practice. For example, requiring documentation about how significant transactions are initiated, recorded, processed, and reported helps to clarify that, as part of its assessment, management is expected to identify and evaluate controls over processes or activities at the transaction level. In the absence of this requirement, management might conclude that they need only identify higher-level management controls. Such higher-level controls might not be sufficiently sensitive to prevent or detect errors relating to one or more relevant assertions.

We also agree with the Board's statement in paragraph 45 that "documentation . . . is evidence that controls related to management's assessment . . . have been identified, are capable of being communicated to those responsible for their performance, and are capable of being monitored by the company."

8. Is it appropriate to state that inadequate documentation is an internal control deficiency, the severity of which the auditor should evaluate? Or should inadequate documentation automatically rise to the level of significant deficiency or material weakness in internal control?

If documentation is indeed inadequate, we agree it would be an internal control deficiency, the severity of which the auditor should evaluate. Documentation affects both the information and communication and monitoring components of internal control, providing the foundation for appropriate communication of responsibilities for performing controls and the entity's evaluation and monitoring of the effective operation of controls. Because the auditor should consider the facts and circumstances of any documentation deficiency, we believe the effect of inadequate documentation should be evaluated similar to other deficiencies in internal control and not automatically rise to the level of a significant deficiency or material weakness.

Obtaining and Understanding of Internal Control Over Financial Reporting

9.   Are the objectives to be achieved by performing walkthroughs sufficient to require the performance of walkthroughs?

Yes. However, we believe the requirement to "trace all types of transactions and events, both recurring and unusual" is too broad.

We believe the word "all" would require the auditor to perform extensive procedures to search for, and walk through, an extensive number of transactions regardless of their risk. Additionally, notwithstanding that tracing "all types of transactions and events, both recurring and unusual" is not feasible, we do not believe the additional procedures will aid the auditor in further understanding how a process functions and the design of the related controls. We recommend the Board include qualifying language to denote that the auditor should walk through significant classes of transactions and related controls within significant processes, and possibly offer an example to clearly demonstrate the Board's intent with this requirement.

We also suggest the Board alter the second phrase in the first sentence of paragraph 80, i.e., "controls for all five internal control components and fraud." While we agree the auditor should perform procedures to confirm his or her understanding of the design of controls and that the controls have been placed in operation, we do not believe it feasible to "walk through" controls for all five internal control components or controls intended to address the risks of fraud.

We also suggest the Board revise paragraph 82 to make it clear that, for an audit of internal control over financial reporting as of the end of the year, the auditor should, when applicable, walk through transactions that were processed <u>after</u> there have been significant changes in the related processes and controls during the year.

10. Is it appropriate to require that the walkthrough be performed by the auditor himself or herself, rather than allowing the auditor to use walkthrough procedures performed by management, internal auditors, or others?

No. We believe there will be many situations where internal audit will perform walkthroughs as part of management's assessment process. The auditor should consider the nature and extent of those walkthroughs in determining his or her own walkthrough procedures. For example, the auditor should be able to use walkthrough procedures related to routine processes when internal auditors who possess a high degree of competence and objectivity perform those procedures.

Mr. J. Gordon Seymour

Testing Operating Effectiveness

11. Is it appropriate to require the auditor to obtain evidence of the effectiveness of controls for all relevant assertions for all significant accounts and disclosures every year or may the auditor use some of the audit evidence obtained in previous years to support his or her current opinion on management's assessment?

We believe it is appropriate to require the auditor to obtain such evidence every year, because each annual audit of internal control over financial reporting needs to stand on its own.

Using the Work of Management and Others

12. To what extent should the auditor be permitted or required to use the work of management and others?

We agree with the statement in paragraph 103, "The auditor should evaluate whether to use the work performed by management or others."

We believe the auditor should be permitted, but never required, to use the work of management or others based on the auditor's assessment of the competence and objectivity of those performing the work, and the relative importance of that work to the overall audit of internal control over financial reporting. However, as further discussed in our responses to questions 13 through 15 and elsewhere in this letter, when the auditor's evaluation indicates that the individuals performing the work have a high degree of competence and objectivity (e.g., internal audit), we believe the auditor should be permitted to use this work more extensively. Similarly, the auditor should be permitted to use the work of "others" more extensively, but only when such individuals perform roles similar to internal auditors and have a high degree of competence and objectivity (e.g., a loan review function in a financial institution). This also is conditioned on the auditor re-performing a sufficient amount of the work to be satisfied as to the sufficiency of the procedures performed and accuracy of the results.

13. Are the three categories of controls and the extent to which the auditor may rely on the work of others appropriately defined?

No. In the first category of controls, we believe paragraph 104 unnecessarily prohibits the use of the work of management and others in three areas—walkthroughs, controls over the period-end financial reporting process, and controls that have a pervasive effect on the financial statements, such as certain information technology general controls. We believe these three areas should be moved to paragraph 105, which describes procedures performed by management and others where the auditor's use of such work "should be limited." Our rationale for walkthroughs is described in our response to question 10 in this section.

We agree that certain IT general controls have a pervasive effect on other controls, and further agree that controls over the period-end financial reporting process are important to the auditor's assessment of the effectiveness of internal control over financial reporting and the detection of fraud. However, we are not convinced that the criteria in paragraph 103 should preclude the auditor from using the work of competent and objective internal auditors in these areas. The internal audit departments of public companies often include professionals with specialized skills (e.g., information technology), and who appropriately follow established professional standards in the conduct of their work. We believe the auditor's inability to use the work of these professionals potentially would detract from, rather than enhance, the quality of audits of internal control over financial reporting and, at a minimum, would unnecessarily add to the cost borne by public companies.

In the second category of controls, where the use of the results of procedures performed by management and others should be "limited," we suggest the Board clarify the extent of the use of the work of management and others it considers acceptable in these situations. In our view, it is inconsistent to conclude that internal audit is competent and objective, but then discount their training and experience when planning to use their work. While we agree that certain accounts involve significant judgments and estimates that affect the account balance or disclosure as noted in the fifth bullet in paragraph 103, it does not necessarily follow that the evaluation of all of the related processes and controls also is subjective.

In the third category of controls, the description in paragraph 106 ("other areas, such as controls over routine processing of significant accounts and disclosures") indicates the auditor might decide to use the work of "management and others *within the company*" (emphasis added). This differs from the reference to "management and others" used elsewhere in the Proposed Standard. The term "others" is defined in paragraph 42 to "include internal audit and third parties working under the direction of management, including other auditors and accounting professionals engaged to perform procedures as a basis for management's assessment." We recommend the words "within the company" be deleted.

14. Does the proposed standard give appropriate recognition to the work of internal auditors? If not, does the proposed standard place too much emphasis and preference on the work of internal auditors or not enough?

Paragraph 108 appears to give appropriate recognition to the work of internal auditors. However, we do not believe this recognition has been reflected in paragraphs 103-107. Where the auditor's evaluation indicates that the internal audit function has a high degree of competence and objectivity, we suggest the auditor be permitted to use the work of internal audit more extensively, including some areas of the audit of internal control over financial reporting where the auditor is otherwise prohibited from using the work of management (see response to question 13 above). Similarly, the auditor should be permitted to use the work of "others" more extensively, but only when such individuals perform roles similar to internal auditors and have a high degree of competence and objectivity (e.g., a loan review function in a financial institution).

15. Is the flexibility in determining the extent of re-performance of the work of others appropriate, or should the auditor be specifically required to re-perform a certain level of work (for example, re-perform tests of all significant accounts or re-perform every test performed by others that the auditor intends to use)?

We believe the flexibility in determining the extent of re-performance of the work of others is appropriate. The auditor should use professional judgment in determining the extent of re-performance based on the type of control and the assessment of the competence and objectivity of those performing the tests.

16. Is the requirement for the auditor to obtain the principal evidence, on an overall basis, through his or her own work the appropriate benchmark for the amount of work that is required to be performed by the auditor?

We agree that a benchmark is appropriate; however, we suggest the Proposed Standard be revised to explicitly state that meeting the "principal evidence" requirement is based on qualitative, not just quantitative, factors.

Evaluating the Results

17. Will the definitions in the proposed standard of significant deficiency and material weakness provide for increased consistency in the evaluation of deficiencies? How can the definitions be improved?

We acknowledge the Board's effort to improve the definition of a significant deficiency and material weakness. We believe the focus in the definitions on the magnitude of the potential misstatement and the likelihood of their occurrence, along with the examples provided in Appendix D, have the potential for increasing consistency in the evaluation of internal control deficiencies. While we believe the auditor's consideration of the likelihood of occurrence is clear, we believe the auditor's consideration of magnitude requires further clarification.

We believe the examples in Appendix D generally are consistent with the definition of a significant deficiency in paragraph 8—that is, "a misstatement of the annual or interim financial statements that is more than inconsequential." However, the definition in paragraph 8 appears to conflict with the materiality discussion in paragraph 21, which indicates that materiality at the individual account-balance level is relevant to deciding whether a deficiency represents a significant deficiency. While the term "inconsequential" in paragraph 8 is not defined, we believe it implies a lower threshold than individual account-balance materiality. We suggest the Board define the term "inconsequential" in paragraph 8 and otherwise provide clarification on the interrelationship of these two materiality concepts. We believe auditors will continue to need to use significant professional judgment in determining whether a deficiency represents a significant deficiency and suggest that the Proposed Standard acknowledge this.

We believe the inclusion of the phrase "annual or interim" in paragraphs 8 and 9 causes confusion as to the intended scope of an audit of internal control over financial reporting. The phrase is not defined elsewhere in the Proposed Standard, and it is unclear how the phrase "period-end financial reporting process" as used in paragraphs 41 and 43 relates to "annual or interim financial statements" in paragraphs 8 and 9.

If it is the Board's intention that the scope of management's assessment process and the auditor's audit procedures address controls over both the preparation of interim financial statements and year-end financial statements, we suggest that it be made clear in paragraph 41 describing the scope of controls that are to be evaluated. We also recommend the Board clarify the relationship of the auditor's responsibilities for evaluating internal control over interim financial statements with the auditor's responsibilities with respect to interim financial statements described in SAS No. 100, *Interim Financial Statements*.

Further, we believe the Proposed Standard is not clear regarding whether the phrase "annual or interim" is intended to change the concept of materiality, because this phrase suggests that materiality needs to be determined based on quarterly as well as annual financial results. Materiality in an annual audit of financial statements generally is based upon the annual financial results. In an integrated audit, we believe it is both inappropriate and inconsistent to require materiality at a much lower level (i.e., interim financial results) for purposes of the audit of internal control.

18. Do the examples in Appendix D of how to apply these definitions in various scenarios provide helpful guidance? Are there other specific examples that commenters could suggest that would provide further interpretive help?

Yes. The examples demonstrate a consistent thought process the auditor should employ in determining whether control deficiencies are either a significant deficiency or material weakness.

We suggest the Board consider also providing one or more examples where the likelihood of material misstatement is remote, resulting in the conclusion that a significant deficiency does not represent a material weakness even when the magnitude of potential misstatement is material. We believe these additional examples would help auditors better understand how to apply the concepts of likelihood and magnitude together when evaluating deficiencies in internal control.

19. Is it necessary for the auditor to evaluate the severity of all identified internal control deficiencies?

Yes.

20. Is it appropriate to require the auditor to communicate all internal control deficiencies (not just material weaknesses and significant deficiencies) to management in writing?

We do not believe the auditor should be required to communicate all internal control deficiencies to management in writing, and therefore suggest this requirement be eliminated.

We believe it is appropriate that all internal control deficiencies that are identified by the auditor and of which management is unaware should be communicated to management. In our view, however, requiring the auditor to communicate deficiencies regardless of who first identified them would create confusion when the deficiencies already have been reported to management internally (e.g., by internal audit). Management has the primary responsibility for implementing an effective system of internal control over financial reporting and for assessing its effectiveness at the end of the most recent year. Accordingly, we believe the auditor should first determine whether the company has implemented a process that provides for the communication of internal control deficiencies to appropriate levels of management on a timely basis.

Under the COSO framework, internal control should be self-monitoring and self-correcting. There should be an expectation that internal control deficiencies identified through ongoing monitoring activities (as well as the annual assessment of internal control over financial reporting required by the Act) are raised to appropriate levels of management. We believe it would be more appropriate for the auditor, as part of his or her evaluation of internal control over financial reporting, to determine that internal control deficiencies identified by the company through its monitoring activities and annual assessment are reported to appropriate levels of management in a timely manner. We also suggest the Board acknowledge that the lack of an internal process to report deficiencies in internal control to management on a timely basis represents an internal control deficiency that should be evaluated for severity by the auditor.

Requiring the auditor to report all deficiencies to management in an environment where control deficiencies are already routinely raised to management potentially detracts from the relevance of the auditor's work and management's monitoring activities and undermines the Board's promotion of strong corporate governance through effective systems of internal control.

21.   Are the matters that the Board has classified as strong indicators that a material weakness in internal control exists appropriately classified as such?

We do not agree that all the matters listed are necessarily strong indicators that a material weakness in internal control exists. We believe the auditor needs to first gain an understanding of the facts and circumstances of the matter. In this regard, we suggest that the Board clarify whether the evaluation would be different if the matters discussed in paragraph 126 were detected by the company's system of internal control or by the auditors in the performance of their procedures. For example, the identification of fraud on the part of senior management by the company's system of internal control might indicate that internal control is operating effectively rather than indicating a significant deficiency or material weakness. Moreover, a presumption that the identification of fraud of any magnitude on the part of senior management is at least a significant deficiency fails to adequately consider the inherent limitations of internal control.

We suggest the Board clarify or provide examples of the instances when restatement of previously issued financial statements to reflect the correction of a misstatement should be regarded as at least a significant deficiency in internal control over financial reporting. For example, we believe a restatement to reflect the SEC's subsequent view of an accounting matter when the auditor concluded that management has reasonable support for its original position would not necessarily be a significant deficiency in internal control over financial reporting. Also, we believe a restatement relating to a nonrecurring transaction in a prior year would not necessarily reflect a material weakness in internal control over financial reporting in the current year.

Mr. J. Gordon Seymour

Page 12
November 21, 2003

We also suggest the Board clarify that identification by an auditor of a material misstatement in the current period before all of management's controls had an opportunity to function would not necessarily result in a conclusion that a significant deficiency exists in internal control over financial reporting. For example, it is normal for the auditor to perform his or her review and other procedures relating to year-end financial statement information at about the same time that management performs its review and other procedures. In this situation, the auditor might identify a material misstatement in draft financial statements while the corporate controller, chief financial officer, and other members of executive management are still completing their respective reviews and other procedures. Therefore, we believe the second bullet in paragraph 126 is impractical as stated, in that it would require the auditor to consider whether the reviews and other procedures performed by the company's executives (i.e., a higher-level detect control) would have identified the material misstatement. In effect this would require the auditor to predict the future functioning of the company's controls.

While some controls that focus primarily on compliance with laws and regulations also might have a material effect on the reliability of financial reporting, we do not believe assessing the effectiveness of a company's regulatory compliance function is within the scope of an audit of internal control over financial reporting. As noted in the SEC Final Rule, the definition of internal control "does not encompass the elements of the COSO Report definition that relate to . . . a company's compliance with applicable laws and regulations, with the exception of compliance with the applicable laws and regulations directly related to the preparation of financial statements, such as the Commission's financial reporting requirements."

We suggest the auditor's consideration of the effectiveness of the internal audit function for larger, more complex entities also consider the focus of the internal audit function. We observe that some internal audit functions, while effective, primarily focus on internal control objectives other than financial reporting and thus do not necessarily contribute as much to effective internal control over financial reporting.

22.   Is it appropriate to require the auditors to evaluate the effectiveness of the audit committee's oversight of the company's external financial reporting and internal control over financial reporting?

We believe the audit committee plays a critical role. Like the independent auditor, the audit committee is independent of management. However, the audit committee is not a separate component of the company's system internal control. The system of internal control should function without the direct involvement of the audit committee. The audit committee's role, like the independent auditor's, is an evaluative one.

We agree that the auditor's assessment of the control environment and monitoring components should consider the effectiveness of the audit committee's oversight role, but only as it relates to the audit committee's assessment of *management's* approach to designing, implementing and monitoring internal control over financial reporting. For example, as part of the assessment of the control environment, the auditor generally would consider whether the audit committee appropriately reacts when management fails to respond appropriately to control deficiencies or other matters.

Mr. J. Gordon Seymour

23. Will auditors be able to effectively carry out their responsibility to evaluate the effectiveness of the audit committee's oversight?

We believe the auditor can evaluate aspects of the audit committee's oversight role as part of the company's control environment and monitoring components of the system of internal control over financial reporting. However, the Proposed Standard would require the auditor to evaluate certain aspects of the audit committee's oversight for which objective and measurable criteria are not provided in the Proposed Standard (e.g., clarity with which the audit committee's responsibilities are articulated and how well the audit committee and management understand those responsibilities). In addition, when assessing the effectiveness of the audit committee's oversight, the quality of the time and effort put forth by the committee members, and the way they react to and interact with management and the independent auditors in dealing with critical issues, is arguably more important than the amount of time spent on various activities. Finally, there are other aspects of the audit committee's oversight that involve legal determination (e.g., independence of audit committee members from management, compliance with applicable listing standards).

24. If the auditor concludes that ineffective audit committee oversight is a material weakness, rather than require the auditor to issue an adverse opinion with regard to the effectiveness of the internal control over financial reporting, should the standard require the auditor to withdraw from the audit engagement?

No. While the auditor always has the option to withdraw from an engagement, we do not believe it would be appropriate for the standard to require the auditor to withdraw in this situation. Requiring the auditor to withdraw without first providing the company's board of directors the opportunity to react to the matter could cause irreparable harm to the company and its shareholders.

Forming an Opinion and Reporting

25. Is it appropriate that the existence of a material weakness would require the auditor to express an adverse conclusion about the effectiveness of the company's internal control over financial reporting, consistent with the required reporting model for management?

We believe it would be consistent with the SEC Final Rule for management and the auditor, in certain circumstances, to issue a qualified assessment and opinion about the effectiveness of the company's internal control over financial reporting (i.e., internal control is effective "except for" an identified material weakness).

Section II.B.3.c of the SEC Final Rule and related footnote no. 72 states,

> "The final rules therefore preclude management from determining that a company's internal control over financial reporting is effective if it identifies one or more material weaknesses in the company's internal control over financial reporting. This is consistent with interim attestation standards. See AT sec. 501."

We believe this reference to the interim attestation standard in the SEC Final Rule is referring to AT sec. 501, par. 37, which states in part,

> "Therefore, the presence of a material weakness will preclude the practitioner from concluding that the entity has effective internal control. However, depending on the significance of the material weakness and its effect on the achievement of the objectives of the control criteria, the practitioner may qualify his or her opinion (that is, express an opinion that internal control is effective "except for" the material weakness noted) or may express an adverse opinion."

Our reading of the SEC Final Rule and the interim attestation standard leads us to conclude that it would be appropriate for the auditor to express either an adverse opinion or a qualified "except for" opinion about the effectiveness of the company's internal control over financial reporting depending on the circumstances. See our response to question 26 for an example of where a qualified opinion might be appropriate.

26. Are there circumstances where a qualified "except for" conclusion would be appropriate?

Yes. We believe that management and auditors might encounter situations in practice where a qualified "except for" conclusion would be appropriate, as it would provide more meaningful information to investors. For example, a company may have adopted a new accounting principle in the current year, which required a material audit adjustment. The auditor concluded that this adjustment resulted from a material weakness, but the material weakness was confined to one significant account. The company otherwise has effective internal control over financial reporting. We believe an auditor's report with a qualification explaining the material weakness, rather than an adverse opinion on the effectiveness of internal control over financial reporting as a whole, would provide more meaningful information to investors.

27. Do you agree with the position that when the auditor issues a nonstandard opinion, such as an adverse opinion, that the auditor's opinion should speak directly to the effectiveness of the internal control over financial reporting rather than to whether management's assessment is fairly stated?

Yes. We also suggest the Board require in all cases that the auditor's opinion speak directly to the effectiveness of the internal control over financial reporting. We believe such a requirement would help to address potential misconceptions as to the scope and objective of an audit of internal control over financial reporting.

Page 15
November 21, 2003

Mr. J. Gordon Seymour

Auditor Independence

28.   Should the Board provide specific guidance on independence and internal control-related non-audit services in the context of this proposed standard?

29.   Are there any specific internal control-related non-audit services the auditor should be prohibited from providing to an audit client?

No. We do not believe it is appropriate to include specific independence guidance in the Proposed Standard. We believe all independence guidance should be located in a discrete section of the professional standards and it would be helpful to refer to this guidance where appropriate in the Proposed Standard. We also believe current SEC independence rules and related SEC interpretations (e.g., Frequently Asked Questions) are sufficient in the context of this Proposed Standard, and potential changes to or further interpretation of such rules and interpretations should be subject to separate notice and comment rulemaking.

Auditor's Responsibilities With Regard to Management's Certifications

30.   Are the auditor's differing levels of responsibility as they relate to management's quarterly certifications versus the annual (fourth quarter) certification, appropriate?

31.   Is the scope of the auditor's responsibility for quarterly disclosures about the internal control over financial reporting appropriate?

We believe it is inappropriate to include additional responsibilities with regard to management's quarterly certifications in this Proposed Standard, which addresses "an audit of internal control over financial reporting performed in conjunction with an audit of financial statements." Additional requirements relating to the auditor's quarterly review responsibilities should be separately proposed and exposed for public comment.

We do not believe the auditor's responsibility for management's quarterly certifications and related disclosures extends beyond the responsibility to inform the audit committee of matters coming to his or her attention. We believe a requirement for the auditor to describe in his or her report the reasons the auditor believes management's certification should be modified would create an inappropriate dual-reporting responsibility and imply the auditor's responsibility extends beyond the scope of his or her audit report on internal control over financial reporting.

Additional Comments

Our additional comments are organized by corresponding paragraph number of the Proposed Standard.

Par. 10—The definitions of preventive and detective controls state these controls have the objective of either preventing or detecting a misstatement. We suggest that preventive and detective controls have the objective of preventing or detecting errors or fraud that could result in a misstatement of the financial statements. We believe there are many types of controls that are relevant to the overall effectiveness of internal control over financial reporting for which it may be difficult to identify a direct relationship to potential misstatements in the financial statements. For example, edit or range checks over the input of transaction data that help assure that transaction files are accurate are fundamental controls in an effective system of internal control over financial reporting, but do not have a direct bearing on preventing misstatements in the financial statements. The definitions of preventive and detective controls in the Proposed Standard may cause management or the auditor to exclude controls important to assessing the overall effectiveness of internal control over financial reporting.

Par. 14—We suggest clarifying the wording of this paragraph to state: (1) the COSO framework identifies three primary objectives of internal control (i.e., efficiency and effectiveness of operations, financial reporting, and compliance with laws and regulations) and an audit of internal control over financial reporting is concerned with only the financial reporting objective, and (2) the controls that management designs and implements may achieve more than one objective.

Par. 16—We suggest practitioners and other parties might find the correlation of reasonable assurance to "a high level of assurance" confusing and it may be appropriate to further clarify this concept in the Proposed Standard. We suggest the Board analogize the audit of internal control to the audit of financial statements where traditionally an "audit" of financial statements provides a high level of assurance while a "review" of financial statements provides a moderate level of assurance.

Par. 24—This paragraph states "the auditor should review all controls specifically intended to address the risks of fraud that are reasonably likely to have a material effect on the company's financial statements." We believe the word "all" is too broad and potentially would require the auditor to review controls that are not relevant to the audit of internal control over financial reporting. Further, the requirement to review "all" controls potentially conflicts with the requirement to place "special emphasis on the evaluation of such controls in the control environment," which implies that some of the controls management may have implemented to specifically address the risks of fraud are more relevant than other controls.

We suggest the Board remove the second bullet, "Company's risk assessment processes," as it is not part of the control environment. We also suggest changing the wording in the fourth bullet point to change the focus from functional reporting, which is not defined, to a focus on direct reporting to the audit committee and the audit committee's involvement and interaction with internal audit. We believe the wording in this bullet point should be consistent with the description in the fourth bullet point in paragraph 57 relating to audit committee oversight of the internal audit function. Finally, we suggest the Board clarify the terminology in the first bullet point, "controls restraining the inappropriate use of company assets."

Par. 41—We believe the examples of procedures management may use to evaluate the operating effectiveness of controls in the fifth bullet point of this paragraph do not reflect the full range of procedures management may employ. For example, the COSO framework indicates management might be able to determine that controls operate effectively through direct and ongoing monitoring of the functioning of controls. This might be accomplished through regular management and supervisory activities, monitoring adherence to policies and procedures, and other routine actions. While we agree with the Board's statement in paragraph 18 that "users of the reports from management and the auditor are entitled to receive the same level of assurance from management and the auditor," we believe management's daily interaction with the system of internal control provides it with a broader array of procedures to achieve that level of assurance.

Par. 50—The word "should" in the last sentence of the bullet point discussing the control environment creates a presumptively mandatory obligation (based on the terminology in the Board's Proposed Rule 3101, *Certain Terms Used in Auditing and Related Professional Practice Standards*) on the part of the auditor to alter the nature, timing, or extent of tests of operating effectiveness without first considering the effects, if any, of the weakness noted in the control environment on the effectiveness of other controls. This presumptively mandatory obligation to alter the nature, timing, and extent of tests of controls also may be inappropriate if the auditor already had designed tests sufficient to detect such effects, if any.

Par. 51-52—We agree that the objective of an audit of internal control over financial reporting is to evaluate the overall effectiveness of internal control over financial reporting and not to evaluate individual controls in isolation. Accordingly, the auditor also has to consider that certain internal controls (e.g., higher-level monitoring controls) often are dependent on the functioning of other controls or work in combination to achieve the objectives of effective internal control. However, it is not clear how the concepts discussed in paragraphs 51 and 52 are consistent with the requirement stated in paragraph 27, and other places throughout the Proposed Standard, that the auditor "must obtain sufficient competent evidence about the design and operating effectiveness of controls related to all relevant financial statement assertions for all significant accounts and disclosures in the financial statements."

We suggest the Board clarify how the auditor should apply the concepts in paragraphs 51 and 52 in light of the focus on assertions in paragraph 27.

Par. 53-54—We suggest the Board reverse the order of these paragraphs to better set up the discussion of company-level controls.

Par. 62-63—We suggest the Board clarify the use of the term "component" in these two paragraphs. Paragraph 62 refers to a component as a portion of an account balance (for example, the allowance for doubtful accounts and trade receivables are components of the net trade receivables account balance). Paragraph 63 refers to a component as the corresponding account balance of a business unit. We suggest the Board not refer to corresponding account balances of individual business units as significant accounts as this implies that the determination of significant accounts should be based on individual locations or business units, rather than at the financial-statement level.

Par. 72—We suggest the Board clarify in the last bullet point under this paragraph, or elsewhere in the Proposed Standard, the contemplated nature and extent of involvement of the audit committee in the period-end financial reporting process. Is the Board suggesting that the audit committee's involvement extend beyond its oversight role for the external financial reporting process to include some level of involvement or oversight in the aspects of the financial reporting process discussed in paragraph 51 of AU319?

Mr. J. Gordon Seymour   November 21, 2003

Par. 91—We recommend the Board provide additional examples of information that inquiries might provide, including 1) the skill and competency of those performing the control, 2) the relative sensitivity of the control to prevent or detect errors, and 3) the frequency with which the control operates to prevent and detect errors.

Par. 92—We suggest the Board incorporate a similar discussion in paragraph 41 to indicate that in performing its assessment, management also should not rely solely on inquiry and should obtain sufficient evidence through other procedures, including inspection and re-performance.

Par. 97—We do not find this paragraph helpful and suggest the Board consider combining it with another paragraph.

Par. 102—See comment on paragraph 16 in this section. We suggest the phrase "high level of assurance" may be confusing to practitioners in that the concept is being used in a different context in this paragraph than used elsewhere in the Proposed Standard. The phrase "high level of assurance" applies to the auditor's overall opinion on internal control in paragraph 16 and we do not believe the concept is relevant to the individual tests of operating effectiveness of controls.

Par. 103, 107-108—We suggest the Board move the discussion of the competence and objectivity of "individuals performing tests of controls" in paragraph 107 and "internal auditors who follow the *International Standards for the Professional Practice of Internal Auditing* issued by the Institute of Internal Auditors" in paragraph 108 so that it follows the general discussion of evaluating whether to use the work of management and others in paragraph 103, and precedes the discussion of the three categories for using the work of management and others discussed in paragraphs 104-106. We believe this positioning will better demonstrate that the auditor should consider, regardless of the category of controls, both the subject matter of the work of management and others and the competence and objectivity of those performing the work in evaluating whether to use the results of procedures performed by others.

Please see our other comments related to these paragraphs in our responses to questions 12-14 in the previous section.

Par. 113—We suggest the Board change the second bullet point to denote that only negative results derived from substantive procedures (for example, recorded and unrecorded adjustments resulting from performing these procedures) provides evidence relevant to the audit of internal control over financial reporting. This change would be consistent with paragraph 144 that states, "The absence of misstatements detected by substantive procedures does not provide evidence that controls related to the assertion being tested are effective."

Par. 124—We believe the requirement that auditors, when evaluating the significance of a deficiency in internal control over financial reporting, "also should determine the level of detail and degree of assurance that would satisfy prudent officials in the conduct of their own affairs," applies a different definition of a significant deficiency than provided in paragraph 8. Paragraph 8 sets the threshold as a matter "that adversely affects the company's ability to initiate, record, process, or report external financial data." We believe the difference in the definitions in paragraphs 8 and 124 is more than subtle and recommend the Board address this difference in the final standard.

Par. 136-137—We do not believe it is likely that the auditor would perform further tests of controls in the audit of the financial statements in response to identified control deficiencies as a result of tests performed in the audit of internal control. Additionally, we question the necessity of these two paragraphs.

Par. 138-142—We believe the discussion in these paragraphs regarding substantive procedures performed in the conduct of an audit of financial statements is not relevant to an audit of internal control over financial reporting. We also believe certain elements of the discussion in these paragraphs suggest requirements for the audit of financial statements that exceed current requirements under interim auditing standards, and should not be introduced in a standard devoted to auditing internal control over financial reporting. For example, in paragraph 138, the Board states, "the auditor should perform substantive procedures for all relevant assertions for all significant accounts and disclosures." Under existing interim auditing standards (AU 319.107), the auditor should perform substantive procedures for "significant account balances and transaction classes" (but not necessarily for all relevant assertions).

We suggest the Board revise paragraph 141 to indicate that the auditor's substantive procedures should include testing management's process for reconciling the financial statements to the accounting records. In addition, paragraph 139 refers to the term "significant risks" but does not define it.

We urge the Board to clearly identify all the changes being made to the Board's interim professional standards as a result of the Proposed Standard. Inclusion in the Proposed Standard of important performance requirements for auditors that relate to, or differ from, interim professional standards without clearly identifying such changes and their applicability increases the risk that such changes might not be fully understood. We also urge the Board to consider whether certain of these matters should be exposed for public comment separately rather than making "conforming" changes to interim professional standards that have not been previously identified in the Proposed Standard.

Par. 145—We suggest the Board include a discussion in the Proposed Standard as to the types of documentation of the entity's systems and controls the auditor should retain in the working papers to support his or her assessment of the design and operating effectiveness of internal control over financial reporting. We believe this is particularly important in light of the extensive documentation that management will prepare to support its assessment of the design and operating effectiveness of internal control over financial reporting. For example, will it be appropriate for the auditor to refer to management's documentation or should the auditor include copies of all items of management documentation relevant to his or her evaluation of internal control over financial reporting? If the auditor can refer in his or her working papers to management's documentation, should the auditor obtain management's agreement that it will retain such documentation in its current form for a period of no less than seven years? If the auditor intends to use the results of testing performed by management and others, does he or she need to retain copies of the original working papers documenting the performance of and conclusions from these tests?

Par. 168—We believe the premise for this paragraph is incorrect, because an audit of internal control over financial reporting performed under this Proposed Standard will be in conjunction with an audit of the financial statements. The decision as to principal auditor would be made based on an analysis of the facts and circumstances relating to the audit of the financial statements.

We also suggest this paragraph discuss the situation where the decision whether to make reference to another auditor in the report on the audit of internal control over financial reporting might differ from the corresponding decision as it relates to the audit of the financial statements. For example, the audit report on the financial statements may make reference to the audit of a significant equity investment, but the report on internal control over financial reporting would not make a similar reference because management's evaluation ordinarily would not extend to controls at the equity method investee.

Par. 181-182—We suggest the Board provide additional guidance on the specific procedures to perform when the auditor is consenting to the inclusion of his or her report on internal control over financial reporting in a securities filing.

Par. 186—We suggest the Board state in paragraph 186 that foreign private issuers filing Forms 20-F and 40-F are not subject to quarterly reporting requirements and therefore the auditor's responsibilities would only extend to the certifications in the annual report.

Par. 194—The discussion of the effective date of the Proposed Standard does not make clear when the responsibilities for evaluating management's certification disclosures described in paragraphs 183-189 are first applicable. For instance, for a calendar-year issuer that is required to include its first report on internal control in its annual report for the year ended December 31, 2004, would these responsibilities commence in the first quarter of fiscal 2004 or the first quarter of fiscal 2005?

Appendix B—We suggest the Board clarify that the performance requirements and guidance in Appendix B only apply to an audit of internal control over financial reporting and do not apply to an audit of financial statements.

Appendix B, Par. B11—We understand this paragraph is meant to require that the auditor first identify, evaluate, and test controls at individually important locations and business units, including those business units or locations where there are specific risks. However, the paragraph states if this approach does not result in the auditor testing a *large portion* of the company's operations and financial position, he or she should expand the number of business units and locations evaluated in this manner. We suggest the Board clarify the term "a large portion" in this paragraph to better define what is considered an appropriate threshold.

Appendix B, Par. B13—We recommend the Board clarify whether "company-level" controls in the table refer to the same controls described in paragraph 53, or a narrower subset of those controls. If they are a subset, we recommend changing the terminology in the table to reflect the difference.

Appendix B, Par. B14-16—We suggest the Board provide guidance indicating that certain entities that are not service organizations as defined in AU324 but which provide information affecting the financial statements of the issuer (e.g., amounts covered by reinsurance contracts, information provided by actuaries) are not within the scope of the company's assessment of internal control over financial reporting.

Appendix B, Par. B15—We suggest the Board clarify in the last sentence of this paragraph those situations where management's evaluation of internal control over financial reporting would extend to controls at an equity method investee. Otherwise, we suggest the Board delete the word "ordinarily."

Appendix B, Par. B18—We believe the example is inappropriate. If an account is material to the financial statements, the account should be significant to both the audit of the financial statements and the audit of internal control over financial reporting.

Appendix B, Par. B24-39—We have the following observations and recommendations regarding the section titled *Use of Service Auditor's Report*.

The title of this section should be changed from *Use of Service Auditor's Report* to something such as *Use of Service Organizations*. The use of a service auditor's report is only one way of obtaining the required information when the company uses a service organization. This section should address (1) when a service organization is important to the audit of internal control over financial reporting and (2) what management and the auditor should do for purposes of the audit of internal control over financial reporting when a service organization is used.

It is not clear how this section relates to the existing guidance in AU324. For example, these paragraphs summarize certain (but not all) material in AU324 and, in doing so they alter the current content of AU324. For example, paragraph B27 states:

"Paragraph .07 of AU324, Service Organizations, describes the procedures that management and the auditor should perform with respect to the activities performed by the service organization, which include:
- Obtaining an understanding of the controls at the service organization that are relevant to the company's internal control over financial reporting, and
- Obtaining evidence that the controls that are relevant to management's assessment and the auditor's opinion are operating effectively."

However, AU324.07 does not contain this guidance, but instead includes guidance on how a service organization affects the understanding needed by the auditor in planning the audit. In the context of AU324, this clearly means the procedures to obtain evidence to support the opinion on the financial statements, not to express an opinion on internal control, because AU324 was never intended to address the "audit of internal control." Further, there are several references to the "audit" in this section (e.g., paragraphs B29, B31, B32, B33), without clarifying whether this guidance replaces or merely changes the existing (and more complete) guidance in AU324 regarding the procedures to obtain evidence to support the opinion on the financial statements. Finally, this section appears to modify the opening paragraphs of AU324 that define when a service organization is part of the company's information system (e.g., B26 and AU324.03).

We believe the proposed rules should (1) refer to AU324 for definitions of terms and guidance on the procedures the auditor should perform in obtaining evidence to support the

Mr. J. Gordon Seymour

opinion on the financial statements, and (2) include only additional considerations and additional (or changed) procedures required to support an opinion on internal control.

Additional specific comments on this section are:

1. Paragraph B26—Should the word "reported" in the second bullet be "recorded?"

2. Paragraph B27—In addition to misstating the material in AU324.07 as described above, the phrase "nature, timing and extent of evidence" is unclear. We believe this should be changed to something such as "nature, timing and extent of procedures to obtain evidence."

3. Paragraph B28—This paragraph does not recognize the fact that the service organization has a relationship with the "user organization," not the "user auditor" (which are defined terms in AU324.02.) We believe one of the fundamental changes in the relationship between the service organization, its users, and auditors resulting from Section 404 reporting is that the user organization—that is, the company making the assessment on internal control—now has a vital interest and need to obtain information about the controls at a service organization to support its assessment. We believe this paragraph misses this point. The service organization may do things to assist both its user—the company—and the auditor.

4. Paragraph B30—The summary of the SAS 70 opinion is incomplete. It omits the very important portion of the opinion that the controls described have been placed in operation.

5. Paragraph B31—The statement, "this report does not provide any evidence of the operating effectiveness of controls," changes the guidance in AU324.12 that states, "Such a report is not intended to provide any evidence of the operating effectiveness of the relevant controls." This is an example of the difficulty of paraphrasing or summarizing the material in existing standards. We believe it would be better to simply refer to existing AU324 than to restate it in different words that will inevitably have different meanings. However, if this standard does summarize or restate existing guidance in the interim standards, we believe it is imperative that those standards be amended to reflect the conforming changes being made through the new standard being adopted by the Board.

6. Paragraph B32—The first half of this paragraph summarizes the existing guidance in AU324.18-19; however, it does not contain all of the guidance. Again, we believe the Proposed Standard should clearly indicate how existing guidance is being changed. Further, this paragraph does not refer to management. As noted above, we believe one of the fundamental changes resulting from Section 404 reporting is that management also has a need for information about the service organization's controls to support its assessment. The last half of B32 is flawed in that it refers only to the auditor's needs.

7. Appendix B, Paragraph B33—We suggest the list of sources of information for the auditor described in this paragraph include the documentation and evaluation of controls at the service organization that management obtains as part of its required assessment of internal control over financial reporting as described in paragraph B25.

Page 23
November 21, 2003

Mr. J. Gordon Seymour

Appendix C—We believe the material in Appendix C raises many questions as to the scope of controls over the safeguarding of assets that are to be included in the assessment of internal control over financial reporting. We recommend the Board clarify that material weaknesses relating to controls over the safeguarding of assets would exist only when the company does not have effective controls (considering both safeguarding and other controls) to prevent or detect a material misstatement of the financial statements.

****

We would be pleased to discuss our comments with members of the Public Company Accounting Oversight Board or its staff.

Very truly yours,

Ernst & Young LLP

¶ 634. KPMG

280 Park Avenue   Telephone 212-909-5600
New York, N.Y. 10017   Fax 212-909-5699
8ᵗʰ Floor

November 21, 2003

Office of the Secretary
Public Company Accounting Oversight Board
1666 K Street, N.W.
Washington, D.C. 20006-2803

PCAOB Rulemaking Docket Matter No. 008
Proposed Auditing Standard, *An Audit of Internal Control Over Financial Reporting Performed in Conjunction with An Audit of Financial Statements*

Dear Mr. Secretary:

KPMG appreciates this opportunity to comment on the Public Company Accounting Oversight Board's (PCAOB or Board) Proposed Auditing Standard, *An Audit of Internal Control Over Financial Reporting Performed in Conjunction with An Audit of Financial Statements* (Proposed Standard). KPMG also recognizes and acknowledges the significant efforts of the PCAOB staff as evidenced by the comprehensive nature of the Proposed Standard.

We agree with the Board that the existing Interim Standards pertaining to the conduct and reporting of an auditor's attestation on internal control over financial reporting (ICOFR) is not sufficient to effectively implement the requirements of the Securities and Exchange Commission's (SEC) rule implementing Section 404 of Sarbanes-Oxley. We believe that the Board's Proposed Standard represents a significant improvement over the relevant Interim Standards and hope that the comments and observations included in this letter will assist the Board in finalizing a standard on audits of internal control. KPMG fully supports the Board's efforts to improve financial reporting, corporate governance and audit quality with the objective of furthering the public interest and restoring confidence in our capital markets system.

This letter is organized by first providing a number of general observations and comments on the Proposed Standard followed by responses to the specific questions posed in PCAOB Release No. 2003-17 that includes the Proposed Standard as an appendix. Less significant and editorial comments and suggestions are included in Appendix A to this letter.

KPMG, LLP. KPMG, LLP a U.S. limited liability partnership, is
a member of KPMG International, a Swiss association.

KPMG

Office of the Secretary
Public Company Accounting Oversight Board
November 21, 2003
Page 2

General Observations and Comments

Use of the term "all." Auditing standards historically have not included the term "all" as audit evidence generally is obtained on a test basis and test item selection and sample sizes are principally a matter of auditor judgment. In addition, it may not be possible for an auditor to evidence compliance with a standard that requires an evaluation or assessment of "all" of a particular item. We suggest that the Board reconsider the propriety of using the term "all" in its final standard, principally due to the belief that use of such term may establish an unachievable threshold. For example, we believe the Board should reconsider use of the term "all" in the following paragraphs:

- In paragraph 24, "The auditor should evaluate **all** controls specifically intended to address the risks of fraud…"

- In the monitoring section of paragraph 50, "The auditor's understanding of management's monitoring of controls extends to and includes its monitoring of **all** controls, including control activities..."

- In paragraph 79, in reference to walkthroughs, "…the auditor should trace **all** types of transactions and events, both recurring and unusual…"

- In paragraph 114, in reference to the auditor's evaluation of evidence, "…the auditor should review **all** reports issued during the year by internal audit…that address internal control over financial reporting and evaluate any deficiencies identified in those reports."

- In paragraph 191, "…the auditor should communicate to management, in writing, **all** deficiencies in internal control over financial reporting…" (Also see response to Question 20 below)

Changes to other standards. We note that, in several instances, provisions of the Proposed Standard modify existing Interim Standards adopted by the Board. For example:

- Paragraphs 139 and 140 of the Proposed Standard provide conditions that should be met and factors that should be evaluated before performing substantive analytical procedures. (Modifies AU Section 329)

- Paragraph 141 refers to a substantive procedure requiring reconciling the financial statements to the accounting records and examining material adjustments made during the course of preparing the financial statements. (Modifies AU Section 316)

2534 €

Office of the Secretary
Public Company Accounting Oversight Board
November 21, 2003
Page 3

- Paragraphs 190 to 193 refer to requirements for communication of internal control matters to audit committees. (Modifies AU Section 380)

We encourage the Board, in its final standard, to identify each instance in which the final standard modifies the Interim Standards to help ensure consistent application of the provisions of the modified Interim Standards by auditors.

Authoritative appendices. We note in the Board's Statement of Authority that, "...appendices to the Board's standards are an integral part of the standard and carry the same authoritative weight as the body of the standard." We believe that appendices generally should be used for informational or illustrative purposes and should not carry the same authoritative weight as an auditing standard. In addition, we note that the Board's Interim Standards include a number of appendices that historically have not been viewed as carrying the same authoritative weight as the respective standards. In Appendix D to the Proposed Standard, we note that, while the information is intended to be illustrative, use of phrases such as "the auditor should determine" may be interpreted to establish imperatives in similar fact patterns.

Considerations for small and medium-sized issuers. The fundamental tenets of internal control apply equally to entities of all sizes and complexity. While the level of formality embedded in ICOFR may vary between entities of different size, paragraph 27 of the Proposed Standard indicates that, "...the auditor must obtain sufficient competent evidence about the design and operating effectiveness of controls related to all relevant financial statement assertions for all significant accounts and disclosures in the financial statements." We believe the information provided in Appendix E of the Proposed Standard may inadvertently serve to create a separate, and lower, standard of internal control for smaller issuers. We believe that the Committee of Sponsoring Organizations of the Treadway Commission's (COSO) report, *Internal Control – Integrated Framework,* adequately addresses smaller entity considerations and recommend that Appendix E be eliminated from the final standard.

Safeguarding of assets. Appendix C of the Proposed Standard provides examples of intentional and unintentional misstatements arising from deficiencies in controls over safeguarding of assets. We believe the information included in Appendix C and the provisions of the Proposed Standard addressing safeguarding of assets, while helpful, do not sufficiently address the question of which safeguarding controls should be considered within the scope of ICOFR. For instance, determination of an acceptable inventory shrinkage level due to theft is a management decision related to safeguarding of assets, but has financial reporting implications in the form of establishing an adequate reserve for such shrinkage. We suggest the final standard provide additional guidance on matters for the auditor to consider when identifying those safeguarding controls that directly affect ICOFR.

Office of the Secretary
Public Company Accounting Oversight Board
November 21, 2003
Page 4

Inadequate documentation. Paragraphs 46 and 47 of the Proposed Standard indicate that inadequate documentation of the design of controls over relevant assertions related to significant accounts and disclosures represents a deficiency in ICOFR. We believe that inadequate documentation is an internal control deficiency, the severity of which should be evaluated by the auditor. The evaluation of inadequate documentation should be based on the individual facts and circumstances of the particular entity and such inadequacy should not automatically rise to the level of a significant deficiency or material weakness in internal control. This notion is consistent with our expectation that deficiencies in documentation may encompass a wide range of severity and are not necessarily subject to a predetermined assessment.

Information technology. Paragraph 70 of the Proposed Standard references paragraphs 16 through 20 of AU Section 319, *Consideration of Internal Control in a Financial Statement Audit,* regarding the nature and characteristics of the use of information technology in an entity's ICOFR. AU Section 319.19 indicates that one of the specific risks of information technology (IT) is, "Reliance on systems or programs that are inaccurately processing data..." This risk may arise when an entity relies on a program or system to perform a function (e.g., calculate, accumulate, etc.) that has no specific application controls (either within the program or manual controls) to ensure that it is appropriately processing information.

The lack of an application control may be mitigated by an IT general control, such as the review and testing of the system during development or implementation. However, to the extent that the application has been in place for a substantial period of time, the auditor may not be able to ascertain that the appropriate extent of testing was performed during system development. Further, many companies do not extensively test the processing accuracy when implementing a third party application.

The Board should consider further discussion in its final standard of the effect of IT on the auditor's consideration of internal control, and provide guidance in those situations where there is little, or no, direct control over the processing of information within an IT application.

Reporting. The reporting guidance provided in paragraph B16 of the Proposed Standard indicates that, should management and the audit committee not respond appropriately to auditor communications regarding certain consolidation matters, the auditor's report should include an explanatory paragraph describing the reasons why management's disclosure should be modified. In these instances, we believe that the auditor's report should disclose a scope limitation, rather than include an explanatory paragraph.

We note that the Proposed Standard contemplates a situation where the auditor reaches a conclusion that a material weakness has been identified; yet management has not disclosed the same matter in its report (paragraph 163). In this situation, it would appear

Office of the Secretary
Public Company Accounting Oversight Board
November 21, 2003
Page 5

that the Proposed Standard contemplates the auditor issuing an adverse opinion and
management reaching a conclusion that its ICOFR is effective. We also note that the
SEC does not accept auditor's reports on financial statements that are qualified as to
scope or accounting principle (refer to Codification of Staff Accounting Bulletins, Topic
1E). We encourage the Board to coordinate efforts with the SEC staff to provide
guidance to issuers and auditors on the SEC staff's willingness to accept the different
forms of reporting and situations contemplated in the Proposed Standard.

Responses to Individual Questions

Our responses to the questions outlined in PCAOB Release No. 2003-17 that includes the
Proposed Standard as an appendix follow:

Questions regarding an integrated audit of the financial statements and internal
control over financial reporting:

1. **Is it appropriate to refer to the auditor's attestation of management's
   assessment of the effectiveness of internal control over financial reporting as
   the audit of internal control over financial reporting?**

   Yes. We believe such reference reinforces the notion of an integrated financial
   statement and internal control audit.

2. **Should the auditor be prohibited from performing an audit of internal
   control over financial reporting without also performing an audit of the
   financial statements?**

   No. We believe that an auditor can perform an audit of ICOFR without also
   auditing the entity's financial statements as of that date. While not commonplace,
   an entity may request, pursuant to contractual or regulatory requirements, an audit
   of ICOFR as of a date other than its financial reporting year-end. We recommend
   that the final standard not limit an audit of an entity's ICOFR to those instances
   when the auditor also is conducting and reporting on an audit of the entity's
   financial statements. We do believe, however, that an audit of an entity's ICOFR
   as of a date other than its financial reporting year-end is appropriate only if the
   entity's most recent year-end financial statements have been audited.

3. **Rather than requiring the auditor to also complete an audit of the financial
   statements, would an appropriate alternative be to require the auditor to
   perform work with regard to the financial statements *comparable* to that
   required to complete the financial statement audit?**

KPMG

Office of the Secretary
Public Company Accounting Oversight Board
November 21, 2003
Page 6

As stated in response to Question 2 above, we believe that an auditor can conduct and report on an audit of ICOFR without also performing an audit of the related financial statements, assuming that the entity's most recent year-end financial statements have been audited. We do not believe that it is necessary to perform procedures *comparable* to that required to complete a financial statement audit in order to conduct and report on ICOFR. In addition, the term "comparable" is subject to wide interpretation and does not adequately define the extent of procedures that might be necessary in such circumstances.

Question regarding the cost and benefits of internal control:

4. Does the Board's proposed standard give appropriate consideration to how internal control is implemented in, and how the audit of internal control over financial reporting should be conducted at, small and medium-sized issuers?

We believe that the underlying concepts regarding ICOFR do not discriminate based on the size of any particular entity. The application of auditing standards in general is subject to auditor judgment and is dependent on a number of factors, including the size and complexity of the particular entity. We believe that the Proposed Standard provides a framework for the audit of ICOFR for all entities, regardless of size. In addition, we believe that the guidance provided in Appendix E is incomplete and does not address a number of issues applicable to the audit of ICOFR for small and medium-sized entities. Accordingly we recommend the elimination of Appendix E in the final standard adopted by the Board. As an alternative, the Board may consider referring to existing guidance on internal control for small and medium-sized companies provided in the COSO report, *Internal Control – Integrated Framework.*

Question regarding the audit of internal control over financial reporting:

5. Should the Board, generally or in this proposed standard, specify the level of competence and training of the audit personnel that is necessary to perform specified auditing procedures effectively? For example, it would be inappropriate for a new, inexperienced auditor to have primary responsibility for conducting interviews of a company's senior management about possible fraud.

No. Existing Interim Standards (AU Sections 210, *Training and Proficiency of the Independent Auditor,* and 311, *Planning and Supervision*) provide guidance for professional competence, training and supervision of audit staff. We do not believe it is appropriate for an individual auditing standard to prescribe the level of competency and training of personnel required to conduct auditing procedures. This is a matter of judgment by the auditor with final responsibility for the audit.

KPMG

Office of the Secretary
Public Company Accounting Oversight Board
November 21, 2003
Page 7

Any such prescribed requirements would be, by their very nature, arbitrary, not applicable in all circumstances, and incomplete.

Questions regarding evaluation of management's assessment:

6. **Is the scope of the audit appropriate in that it requires the auditor to both evaluate management's assessment and obtain, directly, evidence about whether internal control over financial reporting is effective?**

    Yes. We believe the scope of the audit of ICOFR articulated in the Proposed Standard is appropriate. In addition, we believe that the scope of the audit would be better understood by all interested parties if the auditor's report spoke directly the effectiveness of ICOFR, rather than management's assessment. Accordingly, we suggest that the Board consider requiring that the auditor report directly on the effectiveness of ICOFR in all situations.

7. **Is it appropriate that the Board has provided criteria that auditors should use to evaluate the adequacy of management's documentation?**

    Yes. We believe that the guidance provided in the Proposed Standard would serve to enhance the consistency of documentation prepared and maintained by management in supporting its assessment of ICOFR. However, we believe that management should maintain sufficient documentation for locations and businesses that are not considered significant, either individually or in the aggregate, to evidence compliance with existing books and records requirements under the securities laws.

8. **Is it appropriate to state that inadequate documentation is an internal control deficiency, the severity of which the auditor should evaluate? Or should inadequate documentation automatically rise to the level of significant deficiency or material weakness in internal control?**

    We believe that inadequate documentation is an internal control deficiency, the severity of which should be evaluated by the auditor. The evaluation of inadequate documentation should be based on the individual facts and circumstances of the particular entity and such inadequacy should not automatically rise to the level of a significant deficiency or material weakness in internal control. This notion is consistent with our expectation that deficiencies in documentation may encompass a wide range of severity and are not necessarily subject to a predetermined assessment.

KPMG

Office of the Secretary
Public Company Accounting Oversight Board
November 21, 2003
Page 8

Questions regarding obtaining an understanding of internal control over financial reporting:

9. Are the objectives to be achieved by performing walkthroughs sufficient to require the performance of walkthroughs?

We believe that walkthroughs represent an effective means of obtaining an understanding of an entity's ICOFR and an important component of an auditor's related evaluation. We support the requirement outlined in the Proposed Standard for the performance of walkthroughs for the entity's significant processes.

10. Is it appropriate to require that the walkthrough be performed by the auditor himself or herself, rather than allowing the auditor to use walkthrough procedures performed by management, internal auditors, or others?

While we agree that, in obtaining an understanding of an entity's ICOFR, walkthroughs should be performed, we do not believe that auditors should be prohibited from using the documented work of others in conducting walkthroughs. We suggest that the Board consider limiting the extent to which the auditor may use the work of others in the performance of walkthroughs, consistent with guidance outlined in paragraph 105 of the Proposed Standard.

Question regarding testing operating effectiveness:

11. Is it appropriate to require the auditor to obtain evidence of the effectiveness of controls for all relevant assertions for all significant accounts and disclosures every year or may the auditor use some of the audit evidence obtained in previous years to support his or her current opinion on management's assessment?

We believe that the auditor should obtain evidence of effectiveness of controls for relevant assertions for significant accounts and disclosures each year. However, we also believe that the nature, timing and extent of test work directed toward relevant assertions can, and should, vary from year to year based on prior years' findings, changes in a company's internal control, or changes in management. We recommend that the Board consider including language in its final standard clearly stating that the auditor may not rely on specific audit evidence obtained from specific audit tests performed in prior years to support his or her current opinion on ICOFR.

KPMG

Office of the Secretary
Public Company Accounting Oversight Board
November 21, 2003
Page 9

Questions regarding using the work of management and others:

12. To what extent should the auditor be permitted or required to use the work of management and others?

Auditors should not be required to use the work of management or others in evidencing compliance with the performance provisions of an auditing standard. An auditor's conclusions regarding using the work of management and others are based solely on the auditor's judgment. The factors outlined in paragraph 103 of the Proposed Standard represent appropriate matters for the auditor to consider when evaluating whether to use the work of management and others. However, we recommend that the Board consider emphasizing the level of competency and objectivity of management and others currently addressed in paragraph 107 of the Proposed Standard as a factor for the auditor to consider when evaluating whether to use the work performed by management or others.

13. Are the three categories of controls and the extent to which the auditor may rely on the work of others appropriately defined?

In general, we agree with the three-category approach outlined in the Proposed Standard for determining the extent to which the auditor may use the work of others. However, we have several comments regarding specific control types and control activities identified in the individual categories:

- The second bullet point in paragraph 104 of the Proposed Standard requires auditors to independently test controls over the period-end financial reporting process. We believe the nature of these controls are more appropriately categorized as a control over a significant process identified in paragraph 105 of the Proposed Standard and, as such, should allow for limited use of the work of others.

- Under the third bullet point in paragraph 104, "Controls that have a pervasive effect on the financial statements, such as certain information technology general controls," are required to be tested by the auditor. Internal audit personnel in many entities possess the skills and objectivity to effectively perform tests of information technology general controls. We believe that these controls should be considered in the same light as controls over significant non-routine and nonsystematic transactions and, accordingly, are more appropriately categorized as controls for which the auditor's use of the work of others should be limited as discussed in paragraph 105 of the Proposed Standard.

- Paragraph 106 of the Proposed Standard indicates that the auditor has the ability to use the testing results of management and others "without specific

Office of the Secretary
Public Company Accounting Oversight Board
November 21, 2003
Page 10

limitation" for controls over routine processing of significant accounts and disclosures. One could interpret "without specific limitation" to indicate that the auditor may rely solely on the work of others in certain instances. We recommend that the Board provide additional guidance in its final standard regarding the meaning of "without specific limitation." In that regard, we believe that the auditor should not rely solely on the work of others in the areas identified in paragraph 106 of the Proposed Standard.

14. Does the proposed standard give appropriate recognition to the work of internal auditors? If not, does the proposed standard place too much emphasis and preference on the work of internal auditors or not enough?

Yes. We believe the Proposed Standard, in paragraph 108, provides appropriate recognition to the work of internal auditors.

15. Is the flexibility in determining the extent of reperformance of the work of others appropriate, or should the auditor be specifically required to reperform a certain level of work (for example, reperform tests of all significant accounts or reperform every test performed by others that the auditor intends to use)?

We believe that flexibility in determining the extent of reperformance of the work of others is appropriate as auditor judgment is required in assessing the level of auditor reperformance. For example, the auditor's evaluation of the competency and objectivity of an entity's internal audit function may influence the extent of auditor reperformance of internal audit's work.

16. Is the requirement for the auditor to obtain the principal evidence, on an overall basis, through his or her own work the appropriate benchmark for the amount of work that is required to be performed by the auditor?

Yes. We believe that the auditor should obtain, through his or her own work, the principal evidence for conducting an audit of and reporting on ICOFR. We believe that this notion is necessarily based on a number of subjective determinations and is not susceptible to objective measurement. Accordingly, we believe that the final standard should specifically make reference to the fact that, because controls over certain areas are not always susceptible to mathematical measurement, the auditor will need to apply judgment to determine whether he or she has obtained the principal evidence in support of the auditor's opinion.

KPMG

Office of the Secretary
Public Company Accounting Oversight Board
November 21, 2003
Page 11

Questions regarding evaluating results:

17. Will the definitions in the proposed standard of significant deficiency and material weakness provide for increased consistency in the evaluation of deficiencies? How can the definitions be improved?

Evaluating the severity of an internal control deficiency requires a high degree of judgment and, accordingly, is not conducive to a high degree of consistency in application. The Proposed Standard identifies several instances of internal control deficiencies that ordinarily would be considered significant deficiencies or, potentially, material weaknesses, thereby enhancing the level of consistency in practice relative to those particular matters.

We believe the definition of the term "significant deficiency" in the Proposed Standard is too broad and represents a significant departure from the current definition of a reportable condition in AU Section 325. Included in the definition of a significant deficiency in the Proposed Standard is "…a single deficiency, or a combination of deficiencies, that results in more than a remote likelihood that a misstatement of the annual or interim financial statements that is more than inconsequential in amount will not be prevented or detected." In reference to this definition, we believe there will be few internal control deficiencies identified where the likelihood of a potential misstatement is "remote" and the magnitude of such a potential misstatement is "inconsequential." In fact, this definition could lead to literally every misstatement identified during the course of a financial statement audit resulting in at least a significant deficiency.

The varying magnitude of potential financial statement misstatements between those considered inconsequential and those considered material represents a wide range of possibilities. We believe that the Board should consider revising the definition of a significant deficiency to more clearly reflect those matters coming to the auditor's attention that adversely affect the entity's ability to initiate, record, process and report reliable external financial data (consistent with the definition of a significant deficiency in report examples A-2 and A-3 in Appendix A of the Proposed Standard). To that end, we suggest that the following replace the second sentence of paragraph 8 of the Proposed Standard: "A significant deficiency is an internal control deficiency or an aggregation of such deficiencies that could result in a misstatement of the financial statements that is more than inconsequential." We believe that the definition of a significant deficiency in the Proposed Standard will ultimately and inadvertently dilute the importance of significant deficiencies and the related responses by management, the audit committee, the board of directors, and others to such deficiencies.

KPMG

Office of the Secretary
Public Company Accounting Oversight Board
November 21, 2003
Page 12

18. Do the examples in Appendix D of how to apply these definitions in various scenarios provide helpful guidance? Are there other specific examples that commenters could suggest that would provide further interpretive help?

Use of examples to demonstrate the application of concepts in the Proposed Standard to an individual fact pattern may be useful to auditors. However, we note the following in the Board's Statement of Authority: "Additionally, appendices to the Board's standards are an integral part of the standard and carry the same authoritative weight as the body of the standard." We do not believe it is appropriate to include examples such as those evidenced in Appendix D in an auditing standard, but rather believe such examples are more appropriately included in non-authoritative implementation guidance. The possibility exists that practitioners may draw analogies to alternative fact patterns, resulting in inappropriate conclusions. In addition, examples have a tendency to take on definitional status over time and, accordingly, result in a dilution of judgment influencing an auditor's ultimate evaluation.

19. Is it necessary for the auditor to evaluate the severity of all identified internal control deficiencies?

Upon becoming aware of internal control deficiencies, we believe that the auditor should evaluate the severity of such deficiencies, in much the same manner as the auditor evaluates identified misstatements to the entity's financial statements.

20. Is it appropriate to require the auditor to communicate all internal control deficiencies (not just material weaknesses and significant deficiencies) to management in writing?

We believe it is appropriate for the auditor to communicate to management in writing all internal control deficiencies identified by the auditor during the audit. We recommend that paragraph 191 of the Proposed Standard be revised to clarify that the auditor is responsible for communication to management only those internal control deficiencies *identified* by the auditor.

21. Are the matters that the Board has classified as strong indicators that a material weakness in internal control exists appropriately classified as such?

We have a number of comments on this subject:

- With regard to the first bullet point in paragraph 126 of the Proposed Standard, we agree that a restatement of previously issued financial statements is a strong indicator of a material weakness, but suggest the Board provide

КРМС

Office of the Secretary
Public Company Accounting Oversight Board
November 21, 2003
Page 13

guidance regarding how to treat a material weakness identified in a subsequent period yet pertaining to a prior period. For example, it appears that if a financial statement restatement occurs, there is a strong indicator of a material weakness in the period that is restated, but not necessarily as of the latest balance sheet date.

- With regard to the fourth bullet point in paragraph 126, we believe that an ineffective internal audit function has implications for all entities that support such a function. In addition, this bullet point infers that all larger, more complex entities should support an internal audit function, effectively mandating the same for such entities. We recommend the Board clarify its intentions with regard to the application of this provision to larger entities that do not support an internal audit function and smaller entities that support an internal audit function that is found to be ineffective.

- With regard to the fifth bullet point in paragraph 126, we believe further clarification of the auditor's responsibility with regard to the entity's regulatory compliance function is necessary in order to effectively interpret the scope of this provision. In other words, is the auditor responsible for evaluating the effectiveness of the entity's controls that do not have a direct impact on the entity's financial statements and disclosures? Many entities operating in highly regulated industries maintain extensive regulatory compliance functions addressing, for example, product development, environmental matters, workplace safety, and employment opportunities. Many of the activities of these compliance functions do not directly impact the entity's financial statements and disclosures.

  We note that paragraph 14 of the Proposed Standard refers to "…operations and compliance with laws and regulations directly related to the presentation of and required disclosures in financial statements" as being encompassed in ICOFR. We recommend the Board clarify in the final standard that the reference to an entity's regulatory compliance function in paragraph 126 is consistent with the notion of compliance activities directly related to the presentation of and required disclosures in financial statements addressed in paragraph 14 of the Proposed Standard.

- With regard to the sixth bullet point in paragraph 126, it appears that the Proposed Standard establishes an obligation on the part of the auditor to determine whether senior management has been party to any fraud. AU Section 317.08 indicates that, "Normally, an audit in accordance with generally accepted auditing standards does not include audit procedures specifically designed to detect illegal acts". However, instances of management fraud that come to the auditor's attention may require some action on the part of the auditor.

КРМС

Office of the Secretary
Public Company Accounting Oversight Board
November 21, 2003
Page 14

> We believe that the auditor should consider compliance with laws and regulations that are generally recognized by auditors to have a direct and material effect on the determination of financial statement amounts. In addition, the auditor should be aware of compliance matters that may have a material, but indirect, effect on the entity's financial statements. If the auditor becomes aware of compliance matters that could have a material, indirect effect on financial statements, action on the part of the auditor should be required. We recommend that the Board consider revising the sixth bullet point in paragraph 126 to clarify that the auditor is responsible for considering those illegal acts that may be significant to the entity's financial reporting process.

- We believe that instances of an ineffective control environment should be considered at least a significant deficiency, and a strong indicator of a material weakness, in ICOFR.

22. Is it appropriate to require the auditors to evaluate the effectiveness of the audit committee's oversight of the company's external financial reporting and internal control over financial reporting?

We believe that the auditor's consideration of the effectiveness of the audit committee's oversight of the entity's external reporting and ICOFR is contemplated in his or her responsibility to obtain an understanding of and test the design and operating effectiveness of controls related to the control environment in its entirety. In addition, we believe that an effective audit committee plays a significant role in setting a positive "tone at the top." However, we do not believe that the auditor should be required to separately conclude on the effectiveness of the audit committee's oversight.

Ultimately, we believe that an entity's board of directors, not its independent auditor, is responsible to evaluate the effectiveness of the audit committee's oversight of the entity's external financial reporting process and ICOFR.

23. Will auditors be able to effectively carry out their responsibility to evaluate the effectiveness of the audit committee's oversight?

We believe that an auditor's ability to effectively evaluate the effectiveness of the audit committee's oversight is negatively affected by a number of factors. Auditors generally do not have unfettered access to audit committee members, may not attend all audit committee meetings, and do not have access to all information considered by audit committee members in the performance of their stated duties.

KPMG

Office of the Secretary
Public Company Accounting Oversight Board
November 21, 2003
Page 15

In addition, it is not clear to us how the auditor determines how well the audit committee understands its responsibilities, the amount of time that the audit committee devotes to control issues or the amount of time audit committee members are able to devote to committee activity. Further, the determination of whether the audit committee complies with the applicable listing standards adopted pursuant to Section 301 of Sarbanes-Oxley and includes one or more financial experts as described in the SEC's rule implementing Section 407 of Sarbanes-Oxley appear to be matters of legal interpretation and regulatory compliance that generally fall outside the scope of reliable financial reporting.

If this requirement is retained in the final standard, we recommend that:

- The criteria referenced in the auditor's evaluation be clarified to facilitate consistent application;
- Management be required to evidence its evaluation of the audit committee as part of its assessment of ICOFR; and
- The auditor be required to obtain written representation from the audit committee as evidence in performing his or her evaluation.

Refusal by an audit committee to furnish the aforementioned written representation should constitute a scope limitation.

24. If the auditor concludes that ineffective audit committee oversight is a material weakness, rather than require the auditor to issue an adverse opinion with regard to the effectiveness of the internal control over financial reporting, should the standard require the auditor to withdraw from the audit engagement?

No. We do not believe that resignation by the auditor necessarily serves the public interest. In addition, we do not believe that an auditing standard should dictate client retention conclusions to the auditor. While an auditor may decide to withdraw from an audit engagement in these instances, such decision is a professional matter for the auditor to consider based on available facts and circumstances.

Questions regarding forming an opinion and reporting:

25. Is it appropriate that the existence of a material weakness would require the auditor to express an adverse conclusion about the effectiveness of the company's internal control over financial reporting, consistent with the required reporting model for management?

Yes. We believe that, by definition, identification of a material weakness in ICOFR should result in the auditor expressing an adverse opinion. The SEC final rule implementing the provisions of Section 404 of Sarbanes-Oxley states that, "Management is not permitted to conclude that the registrant's internal control

▟▛▀▛

Office of the Secretary
Public Company Accounting Oversight Board
November 21, 2003
Page 16

over financial reporting is effective if there are one or more material weaknesses in the registrant's internal control over financial reporting." We believe that the SEC's rule implementing the provisions of Section 404 requires management, upon determining the existence of a material weakness, to conclude and report that the entity's ICOFR is not operating effectively. Accordingly, we believe that the auditor's reporting should be consistent with the required reporting model for management.

26. Are there circumstances where a qualified "except for" conclusion would be appropriate?

As illustrated in example A-3 in the Proposed Statement, we believe that examples of scope limitations beyond management's control may exist where the auditor's issuance of a qualified "except for" conclusion is an appropriate alternative. However, as noted in the response to question 25 above, we do not believe that a qualified "except for" conclusion is appropriate in those instances where a material weakness exists.

27. Do you agree with the position that when the auditor issues a non-standard opinion, such as an adverse opinion, that the auditor's opinion should speak directly to the effectiveness of the internal control over financial reporting rather than to whether management's assessment is fairly stated?

Yes. Further, in order to definitively conclude on the engagement scope contemplated by the Proposed Standard and eliminate potential confusion regarding the meaning of "management's assessment" as referred to in the auditors' report, we recommend that the Board consider requiring that the auditors' report speak directly to the effectiveness of internal control over financial reporting. We believe that, despite the clarifications as to scope included in the Proposed Standard, continued use of the "management's assessment" terminology in the auditors' report serves to detract from a consistent understanding of the scope of an audit of ICOFR.

Questions regarding auditor independence:

28. Should the Board provide specific guidance on independence and internal control-related non-audit services in the context of this proposed standard?

No. We believe that the SEC rules on independence are sufficiently comprehensive. Additionally, we do not believe that the Proposed Standard is the appropriate forum for providing guidance on independence and internal control related non-audit services.

Office of the Secretary
Public Company Accounting Oversight Board
November 21, 2003
Page 17

29. Are there any specific internal control-related non-audit services the auditor should be prohibited from providing to an audit client?

We believe that the independence matters relating to the provision of non-audit services by an entity's independent auditor are sufficiently addressed in the aforementioned SEC rules. We do not believe that additional guidance in this area is necessary at this time.

Questions regarding auditor's responsibilities with regard to management's certifications:

30. Are the auditor's differing levels of responsibility as they relate to management's quarterly certifications versus the annual (fourth quarter) certification, appropriate?

We do not believe the auditor has, or should have, a different level of responsibility in reference to management's disclosures responsive to the requirements of the quarterly and annual certifications, other than as outlined in the Interim Standards. We believe that existing guidance outlined in the Interim Standards addressing the auditor's responsibility for other information in documents containing audited financial statements (AU Section 550) or interim financial information (AU Section 722), and illegal acts by clients (AU Section 317), is sufficiently comprehensive and well understood in practice.

Clearly, an auditor's responsibility in the conduct of a review of interim financial information is different from that in an audit of financial statements or ICOFR. AU Section 550, the provisions of which also apply to reviews of interim financial information pursuant to AU Section 722, states that, "The auditor's responsibility with respect to information in a document does not extend beyond the financial information identified in his report, and the auditor has no obligation to perform any procedures to corroborate other information contained in a document. However, he should read the other information and consider whether such information, or the manner of its presentation, is materially inconsistent with information, or the manner of its presentation appearing in the financial statements."

AU Section 317, also referenced in AU Section 722, addresses the auditor's consideration of the possibility of illegal acts and the auditor's response to detected illegal acts. Accordingly, we believe that those instances where an auditor encounters inaccurate or omitted disclosures by management are clearly and sufficiently addressed in the Board's Interim Standards, and further analysis is unnecessarily duplicative in a final standard on auditing ICOFR.

KPMG

Office of the Secretary
Public Company Accounting Oversight Board
November 21, 2003
Page 18

31. Is the scope of the auditor's responsibility for quarterly disclosures about the internal control over financial reporting appropriate?

We do not believe the auditor's responsibilities relative to management's quarterly disclosures regarding ICOFR should go beyond those outlined in AU Sections 722, 550 and 317 (including Section 10A of the Securities Exchange Act of 1934). In fulfilling this responsibility, we believe that it is appropriate for the auditor to perform, on a quarterly basis, the procedures outlined in paragraph 186 of the Proposed Standard. See response to Question 30 above.

* * * * * *

If you have questions regarding the information included in this letter, please contact Sam Ranzilla, (212) 909-5837, sranzilla@kpmg.com or Craig W. Crawford, (212) 909-5536, ccrawford@kpmg.com.

Very truly yours,

KPMG LLP

The following editorial and other comments and suggestions are presented for your consideration:

1. Paragraph 8 – the definition of significant deficiency includes "interim financial statements." As the Proposed Standard provides for an "as of" date audit, which is generally assumed to be the audited balance sheet date, clarification should be provided regarding the inclusion of the term "interim financial statements" and the related implications for test work and reporting.

2. In paragraph 33, the auditor can provide certain permissible internal control-related services if *specifically* pre-approved by the audit committee.   On the surface, this requirement appears to be a modification of the SEC's rules relative to pre-approval of auditor services included in the SEC's final rules on independence (Release No. 33-8183). In order for audit committees to understand their obligations regarding pre-approval of auditor services, we believe that the SEC should provide similar guidance in the securities laws governing audit committee pre-approval requirements.

3. Paragraph 61 - the definition of a significant account appears too broad. Literally, all accounts, when aggregated with other accounts, could contain more than a remote likelihood of a significant misstatement. We encourage the Board to clarify the intent of this paragraph in the final standard.

4. Paragraph 82 infers that walkthroughs of transactions both before and after a significant change in the process flow of transactions may be necessary in some circumstances. We believe that this concept is confusing in light of the auditor's requirement to report on ICOFR as of the audited balance sheet date. We suggest that this paragraph be deleted from the final standard.

5. In paragraph 102, the term "high level of assurance" is used (this term also is used elsewhere in the document). The use of different terms to refer to the concept of "reasonable assurance" is confusing. We believe that the term "reasonable assurance" should be used in those instances where the auditor's level of assurance is referenced.

6. In paragraph 126, the existence of significant deficiencies that have been communicated to management and the audit committee and remain uncorrected after some reasonable period of time is considered a strong indicator of a material weakness. We believe the Board should consider defining a "reasonable period" in the final standard as no later than the entity's next "as of" reporting date.

7. Paragraph 145 states that, "the auditor should document the identification of where misstatements related to relevant financial statement assertions could occur within significant accounts, assertions, and processes." The term "where" generally refers to a location. We recommend that the term "how" be used in place of the term "where" in the final standard.

8. Paragraphs 146 and 147 appear to be out of place in the Proposed Standard. We suggest that information included in these two paragraphs be reflected in a section addressing the interaction of the audit of ICOFR and the financial statement audit.

9. In paragraph 179, we believe that the term "how" should be used in place of the term "why" in the final standard.

10. Paragraph 189 refers to an auditor's reporting obligation in instances when the "...auditor believes management's certifications should be modified." The term "certification" should be replaced with the term "disclosure" to appropriately describe the auditor's responsibility in these instances. Refer to responses to Questions 30 and 31.

11. Paragraph 194 should be revised to clarify that the final standard also will apply to audits of financial statements of entities other than accelerated filers for years ending on or after April 15, 2005. This paragraph currently appears to refer only to the auditor's obligation for audits of ICOFR for accelerated filers.

12. The footnote to example A-3 should note that, in the event the auditor identifies a material weakness that is not included in management's assessment, the auditor expresses an adverse opinion on the entity's ICOFR.

13. All example reports in Appendix A should be revised to include reference to City and State above the date line. In addition, these example reports should indicate by footnote that the ICOFR audit report date should be the same as the financial statement audit report date.

* * * * * *

¶ 635. Grant Thornton

Grant Thornton LLP
The US Member Firm of
Grant Thornton International

175 West Jackson
Chicago, Il 60604
312 602-8000

Grant Thornton 🐦

November 21, 2003

Office of the Secretary
Public Company Accounting Oversight Board
1666 K Street, N.W.
Washington, DC 20006-2803

Via e-mail: comments@pcaobus.org

Re: PCAOB Rulemaking Docket Matter No. 008, *Proposed Auditing Standard – An Audit of Internal Control Over Financial Reporting Performed in Conjunction with an Audit of Financial Statements*

Dear Board Members and Staff,

We appreciate the opportunity to comment and commend the Public Company Accounting Oversight Board's ("Board" or "PCAOB") efforts on the proposed auditing standard, *An Audit of Internal Control Over Financial Reporting Performed in Conjunction with an Audit of Financial Statements.* Our concerns with respect to the proposal are expressed below and in Appendix A, which contains our responses to the questions put forward by the Board. Additional paragraph-level comments are presented in Appendix B. Other recommendations are included in Appendix C.

Management's Assessment of Effectiveness

Management is required to present a written assessment of the effectiveness of internal control over financial reporting. The auditor's attestation of management's assessment is referred to as the audit of internal control over financial reporting ("audit of internal control"). There is a clear distinction, however, between management's **assessment** and their **assertion** and the auditor's responsibilities with respect to such. We believe that an audit of internal control is an attestation of management's **assertion**, rather than their **assessment**, of internal control effectiveness.

Management makes an assertion as to whether internal control is effective, just as management makes assertions that are embodied in the financial statements. Management's assessment is their process of determining whether internal control over financial reporting is effective. Accordingly, management's assessment process supports their assertion. When performing an audit of internal control over financial reporting, the auditor evaluates management's assessment process and management's assertion of effectiveness. Further, the auditor is not prohibited from opining directly on internal control over financial reporting. It is more evident that when opining directly, the auditor is opining on management's assertions regarding internal control effectiveness and not management's assessment. Accordingly, we object to the use of the term assessment to describe the auditor's attestation. Management's report should also contain their assertion regarding the effectiveness of internal control over financial reporting and not their assessment or evaluation of such effectiveness.

Safeguarding of Assets

We suggest that the Board enhance Appendix C to provide additional guidance on safeguarding controls that fall within the scope of internal control over financial reporting. In addition, as indicated in our response to question number 18, it would be very useful to provide examples that illustrate internal control deficiencies relating to safeguarding of assets that are financial reporting in nature, deficiencies that relate to the assertions about safeguarding that management is required to make under Section 404 of the Sarbanes-Oxley Act of 2002, and deficiencies in safeguarding that are not within the scope of financial reporting and Section 404 assertions.

Revisions to Existing Interim Standards

The Board appears to be using this proposed standard to revise, summarize, and/or supplement existing interim standards, including independence, fraud, the work of internal audit, the work of other auditors, analytical procedures, interim reviews, and filings under federal securities statutes. The Board has also revised the requirement related to the performance of substantive procedures on material account balances and has provided significant guidance with respect to the company's use of a service organization.

With respect to service organizations, we do not clearly understand how this relates or may even supersede existing interim standards (AU Section 324, *Service Organizations*). While summarizing some of the content in the existing standards, the proposed standard changes the content of the interim standards. For example, the proposed standard, among other things, appears to change the requirements for when a service organization is part of the company's information system (paragraph B26) and omits the fact that an auditor's report on controls placed in operation also provides evidence as to whether the controls have been placed in operation (paragraph B30).

We urge the Board not to use this proposed standard as a vehicle for revising, summarizing, and/or supplementing the interim standards. When summarizing existing literature or restating it using different words, the intent, meaning, and requirements may be inadvertently altered. Further, when revising, summarizing, and/or supplementing the interim standards, the requirements for an audit of internal control versus an audit of the financial statements may be undistinguishable. Accordingly, we suggest that the Board amend existing interim standards to reflect newly adopted requirements. We prefer that requirements and guidance relating to the same subject matter be kept intact to promote compliance with the standards, rules and regulations. The Board may choose to only include additional considerations or requirements necessary for the opinion on internal control over financial reporting in the proposed standard, while referencing the existing interim standard for the fundamental definitions, requirements, and guidance. The Board should, at a minimum, delete the requirements and guidance from the interim standards that are no longer applicable.

Authoritative Status of Appendices

The Board has indicated that the appendices carry the "same authoritative weight" as the standards. We recommend that the Board clarify whether the examples are being used to establish requirements, including whether they are setting a standard for documentation. In addition, we suggest clarifying whether the Board's statement also applies to the interim standards. The Board should perform a standard-by-standard review of the interim standards prior to adopting the "same authoritative weight" requirement for such standards.

We would be pleased to discuss any of our comments with you. If you have any questions, please contact Mr.. John L. Archambault, Managing Partner of Professional Standards, at (312) 602-8701.

Very truly yours,

Grant Thornton LLP

Appendix A – Responses to Questions

Questions Regarding an Integrated Audit of the Financial Statements and Internal Control Over Financial Reporting

1. **Is it appropriate to refer to the auditor's attestation of management's assessment of the effectiveness of internal control over financial reporting as the audit of internal control over financial reporting?**

    As discussed in our cover letter, we object to the use of the term "assessment" to describe the auditor's attestation. Accordingly, it is not appropriate to refer to the auditor's attestation of management's "assessment" of the effectiveness of internal control over financial reporting as an audit of internal control over financial reporting ("an audit of internal control"), but it is appropriate to refer to the auditor's attestation of management's "assertion" as to effectiveness as an audit of internal control. An "audit" is an attest engagement that is designed to provide a high level of assurance. In an audit of internal control, a high level of assurance is obtained to provide a basis for expressing an opinion on management's assertion.

    In the past, the American Institute of Certified Public Accountants used the terms "audit" and "examination" synonymously. The term audit was restricted to the audit of the financial statements, while the term examination referred to the same level of assurance given on other management assertions. Whether the auditor's attestation of management's assertion is referred to as an audit or an examination is not very important, as very few people ever grasped the distinction.

2. **Should the auditor be prohibited from performing an audit of internal control over financial reporting without also performing an audit of the financial statements?**

    An audit of internal control over financial reporting and an audit of the financial statements are two types of attest engagements that provide a high level of assurance on different subject matter. Although the auditor may gain efficiencies by performing both the audit of internal control and the audit of the financial statements, the auditor's procedures for each engagement should be sufficient to reduce attestation risk to an appropriately low level. We believe that each engagement can be performed without the performance of the other, and that it is important to preserve attestation standards that support audits of internal control as a separate service.

    An audit of internal control provides reasonable assurance about whether the company maintained, in all material respects, effective internal control over financial reporting. The identification of a material weakness or a significant deficiency, however, does not necessarily imply that a material misstatement in the financial statements exists. Nor does the lack of the identification of a material misstatement in a financial statement audit imply that internal control is effective. Accordingly, an audit of the financial statements is not necessary to opine on the effectiveness of internal control over financial reporting. Further, due to the performance of substantive procedures, an audit of internal control is not necessary to perform a financial statement audit.

    In addition, there may be situations where a separate attestation standard that supports audits of internal control, without the performance of a financial statement audit, may be necessary. For example, an auditor may be asked to opine on the effectiveness of an entity's internal control as of an interim date where an audit of the financial statements has not been performed. The auditor may also be involved in a re-audit situation, where the auditor that performed the audit of internal control is not the auditor that re-audited the financial statements. An auditor may also be asked to perform an audit of internal control for registered investment companies or issuers of asset-back securities that are not subject to the Section 404 requirements but may be subject to the PCAOB's Auditing and Related Professional Practice Standards.

Therefore, while we believe the auditor can perform an audit of internal control over financial reporting without also performing an audit of the financial statements (and vice versa), we cannot offer a specific situation where such a request would arise for companies required to include in their annual report a management report on internal control over financial reporting. For such companies, it is appropriate to require that the same auditor perform both the financial statement audit and the audit of internal control over financial reporting, as we believe this is the intent of the Act and in the public interest.

Our response to question three discusses the auditor's procedures in an audit of internal control over financial reporting when an audit of the financial statements has not been performed.

3. **Rather than requiring the auditor to also complete an audit of the financial statements, would an appropriate alternative be to require the auditor to perform work with regard to the financial statements *comparable* to that required to complete the financial statement audit?**

It is not an appropriate alternative to require the auditor to perform work with regard to the financial statements comparable to that required to complete the financial statement audit. As described in our response to question number two, an audit of the financial statements need not be performed in order to execute an audit of internal control. However, it is appropriate to consider the evidence obtained in a financial statement audit in light of the auditor's conclusions regarding the effectiveness of an entity's internal control over financial reporting.

Where a financial statement audit is not performed, however, certain procedures with respect to obtaining an understanding of the entity and its environment and communicating with the auditor of the financial statements may need to be more extensive. For instance, the auditor should perform sufficient procedures to ensure that they appropriately identify controls related to relevant financial statement assertions for significant accounts and disclosures in the financial statements. Where the auditor has not performed the financial statement audit, the auditor may need to perform additional inquiries and/or other procedures to enhance their understanding of such processes and controls. The auditor may also need to communicate with the current auditor as to their internal control findings, any material misstatements noted, and any disagreements with respect to such matters. Such information, however, may be obtained through discussions with management and/or those charged with governance.

Conversely, the performance of substantive procedures is not necessary for an audit of internal control over financial reporting. However, while performing an audit of internal control, the auditor may review source documents (such as sales invoices) through tests of controls.

Question Regarding the Costs and Benefits of Internal Control

4. **Does the Board's proposed standard give appropriate consideration to how internal control is implemented in, and how the audit of internal control over financial reporting should be conducted at, small and medium-sized issuers?**

As stated by the board in the introductory discussion to the proposed standard, "Internal control is not a "one-size-fits-all," and the nature and extent of controls that are necessary depend, to a great extent, on the size and complexity of the company." Although we concur that internal control may be implemented differently at smaller, mid-sized entities and are pleased that the proposed standard allows professional judgment in evaluating effectiveness, we have concerns with respect to the guidance provided by the Board on how internal control is implemented and on how the audit of internal control over financial reporting should be conducted at such entities.

The Board states (on page 6 of the introductory discussion to the proposed standard), "For a smaller, less complex company, the Board expects that the auditor will exercise reasonable professional judgment in determining the extent of the audit of internal control and perform only those tests that are necessary to ascertain the effectiveness of the company's internal control." We concur that an auditor should exercise professional judgment to perform only those procedures necessary. However, we believe that such judgment must be exercised on each engagement to audit internal control over financial reporting, regardless of the size and complexity of the entity. Small and medium-sized companies may have complex operations, while large, complex, multi-national companies may also have some simple operations. Accordingly, each company must establish and maintain necessary internal controls to prevent and detect misstatements on a timely basis, and the proposed standard imposes the minimum procedures that must be performed on all audits to evaluate the effectiveness of such controls.

The statement made above in conjunction with the guidance in Appendix E may be interpreted to infer that smaller, mid-sized companies can take a casual approach in implementing the necessary controls and in evaluating their effectiveness. Further, the auditor's standards for performance and evaluation appear to be lowered for such entities. The proposed standard requires the auditor to obtain sufficient competent evidence about the design and operating effectiveness of controls related to all relevant financial statement assertions for all significant accounts and disclosures in the financial statements. However, Appendix E discusses matters such as informal processes, monitoring controls performed by senior management, and the lack of documentation. This indirectly implies that there are certain internal control matters that the auditor can overlook when evaluating effectiveness for small and mid-sized companies.

In addition, Appendix E is currently being used as a supplement to the framework used by management to conduct its assessment, rather than as a guide on how the audit of internal control should be conducted for small and mid-sized companies. As the Committee of Sponsoring Organizations of the Treadway Commission's *Internal Control – Integrated Framework* already provides guidance on the application of the five internal control components to small and midsized entities, the proposed standard should not be used to modify or supplement such framework.

We recognize the PCAOB's well-intended efforts to provide guidance specifically related to smaller, mid-sized entities and to allow for professional judgment. However, due to the concerns expressed above, we believe that Appendix E should be deleted. Auditors of such entities would be able to apply the proposed standard in the absence of such guidance.

Question Regarding the Audit of Internal Control Over Financial Reporting

5. Should the Board, generally or in this proposed standard, specify the level of competence and training of the audit personnel that is necessary to perform specified auditing procedures effectively? For example, it would be inappropriate for a new, inexperienced auditor to have primary responsibility for conducting interviews of a company's senior management about possible fraud.

It is not necessary to specify the level of competence and training needed to perform a specific audit procedure, generally or in the proposed standard. The interim standards (see AU Section

210, *Technical Training and Proficiency of the Independent Auditor*) appropriately describe the auditor's training, education, experience, supervision, review, and judgment with respect to performing an audit. As discussed in the interim standards, "The auditor charged with final responsibility for the engagement must exercise a seasoned judgment in the varying degrees of his supervision and review of the work done and judgment exercised by his subordinates, who in turn must meet the responsibility attaching to the varying gradations and functions of their work."

The proposed standard requires (in paragraph 31) the auditor to have competence in the subject matter of internal control over financial reporting in order to perform an audit of such. We believe this guidance is sufficient and appropriate. However, we suggest providing a reference to AU Section 210, which governs the technical training and proficiency of the auditor.

Questions Regarding Evaluation of Management's Assessment

6. **Is the scope of the audit appropriate in that it requires the auditor to both evaluate management's assessment and obtain, directly, evidence about whether internal control over financial reporting is effective?**

It is appropriate to require the auditor to evaluate the process management used to support its certifications and assertion to the auditor about the effectiveness of internal control over financial reporting. Although this arrangement places the auditor in the difficult position of having to make a judgment about the adequacy of management's efforts, we believe this is appropriate. We also believe it is important for the auditor to obtain his or her own evidence in order to provide an independent and objective opinion on management's assertion.

On the other hand, it may not be appropriate to require the auditor to disclaim an opinion where management has not fulfilled their responsibilities, as described in paragraphs 19 and 20. As previously discussed, the auditor's attestation is on management's assertion of the effectiveness of internal control over financial reporting. Even though management may not have performed adequate procedures to support their assertion, the auditor may be able to perform procedures to determine whether internal control over financial reporting is effective.

7. **Is it appropriate that the Board has provided criteria that auditors should use to evaluate the adequacy of management's documentation?**

It is appropriate that the Board has provided criteria against which auditors can evaluate the adequacy of management's documentation to determine whether such documentation provides reasonable support for management's assessment. Not only does this criteria assist the auditor in determining whether management's documentation is adequate, it also assists management in determining the nature and extent of documentation that is necessary to support their assessment. Without such guidance, the auditor has no basis in evaluating the significance of the deficiency or the nature of the potential scope limitation.

When evaluating the adequacy of management's documentation, however, we believe that the auditor should also evaluate whether such documentation includes (a) the identification of where misstatements due to fraud or error could occur, (b) the specific controls that have been implemented to prevent or detect such misstatements, (c) the nature, timing and extent of the testing performed, and (d) the identification of the specific controls that were tested for operating effectiveness.

8. **Is it appropriate to state that inadequate documentation is an internal control deficiency, the severity of which the auditor should evaluate?   Or should inadequate documentation automatically rise to the level of significant deficiency or material weakness in internal control?**

It is appropriate to allow auditor judgment in evaluating whether management's inadequate documentation represents an internal control deficiency, a significant deficiency, or a material weakness in internal control. Because documentation may take many forms, can include a variety of information, and can vary depending on the size, nature, and complexity of the company, the severity of the deficiency is a matter of professional judgment, as is the evaluation of the adequacy of management's documentation.

We recommend, however, that the Board clarify and revise the last sentence in paragraph 46, which states, "In evaluating the deficiency as to its significance, the auditor should determine whether management can demonstrate the monitoring component of internal control over financial reporting in the absence of documentation." This statement may have unintended consequences and could lead to arguments between management and the auditor as to the adequacy of management's efforts. It provides management a reason not to support their assessment through adequate documentation.

We further recommend a cross-reference to paragraph 20, which discusses the issuance of a disclaimer when management has not fulfilled its responsibilities.

Questions Regarding Obtaining an Understanding of Internal Control Over Financial Reporting

9. **Are the objectives to be achieved by performing walkthroughs sufficient to require the performance of walkthroughs?**

As stated in paragraph 79, the objectives of a walkthrough are to:

1. Confirm the auditor's understanding of the process flow of transactions.
2. Confirm the auditor's understanding of the design of controls identified for all five components of internal control over financial reporting, including those related to the prevention or detection of fraud.
3. Confirm that the auditor's understanding of the process is complete by determining whether all points in the process where misstatements related to each relevant financial statement assertion that could occur have been identified.
4. Evaluate the effectiveness of the design of controls.
5. Confirm whether controls have been placed in operation.

We believe that all of the items listed above constitute what can be achieved through the performance of a walkthrough and other audit procedures, but does not necessarily represent the objectives of a walkthrough itself. We further believe that numbers 1 and 5 above constitute the objectives of a walkthrough, but numbers 2, 3 and 4 do not.

Walkthroughs are performed to confirm or obtain an understanding of the process flow of transactions and the related controls and whether the documentation is accurate. While performing a walkthrough, the auditor can also determine whether such controls are placed in operation. Walkthroughs are not performed to evaluate the design of such controls. The auditor uses his or her professional judgment to evaluate design effectiveness based on all of the evidence obtained. Although a walkthrough may assist with obtaining information to perform such evaluation, it would rarely in itself be sufficient to conclude on design effectiveness.

Further, walkthroughs do not assist the auditor to confirm or obtain an understanding of the design of controls identified for <u>all five internal control components</u>. For example, the control environment does not relate to a specific transaction or event that can be traced through the information system. Finally, a walkthrough does not determine whether all points in the process where misstatements related to each relevant financial statement assertion that could occur have been identified.

Accordingly, we do not believe that it is necessary for the auditor to perform a walkthrough for <u>all</u> of the company's significant processes, including <u>all</u> types of transactions and events, whether they are recurring or unusual, on <u>each</u> audit of internal control over financial reporting. However, we do believe that there are certain circumstances where a walkthrough should be required to be performed by the auditor, as discussed in our response to question number 10.

We advise the Board not to overstate the benefits of a walkthrough. The "objectives" identified in the proposed standard can be achieved through the performance of other procedures, including inquiry, observation, and other tests of controls where the auditor reviews and compares supporting documents to the accounting records. We suspect such procedures are equally applicable to other processes also. So, while we agree that walkthroughs provide valuable evidence to the auditor, other procedures are sometimes available, which is why we urge that some judgment be afforded the auditor to choose the appropriate procedure to apply in the circumstances. For example, where the auditor performs tests of controls directly, he or she may not need to perform a walkthrough. However, where the auditor plans to rely on tests performed by others, the auditor may need to perform a walkthrough to obtain and/or confirm his or her understanding of the process flow of transactions.

Additionally, walkthrough procedures may differ for each audit. For example, in an initial audit, the auditor may need to perform more walkthrough procedures than in a continuing engagement. In a continuing engagement, the auditor may perform other procedures to achieve the objectives of the walkthrough and to update his or her understanding of the entity's processes and controls. In continuing engagements, the auditor may also alter the nature, timing, and extent of walkthrough procedures performed directly (or the use of walkthrough procedures performed by management and others) to introduce an element of unpredictability.

Finally, we recommend that the Board adequately define the term "significant process." We note that it always includes the period-end financial reporting process, which we agree with.

10. **Is it appropriate to require that the walkthrough be performed by the auditor himself or herself, rather than allowing the auditor to use walkthrough procedures performed by management, internal auditors, or others?**

Hopefully, the Board will agree with our response to question number 9. If so, we believe that it is appropriate to require the auditor to perform the walkthrough.

However, to achieve the objectives, as stated in the proposed standard, we believe the guidance provided by paragraphs 103 through 110 regarding the use of the work performed by management and others applies equally to walkthrough procedures and any other procedures performed by management and others. Accordingly, the auditor should be allowed to use his or her professional judgment in determining whether to use walkthrough procedures performed by management and others to alter the nature, timing, and extent of the tests of controls performed directly by the auditor to achieve the objectives of the walkthrough procedures. That said, however, the restrictions and limitations on the work performed by management and others should also be adhered to.

Question Regarding Testing Operating Effectiveness

11. **Is it appropriate to require the auditor to obtain evidence of the effectiveness of controls for all relevant assertions for all significant accounts and disclosures every year or may the auditor use some of the audit evidence obtained in previous years to support his or her current opinion on management's assessment?**

It is appropriate to require the auditor to obtain sufficient competent evidence about the design and operating effectiveness of controls related to all relevant financial statement assertions for all significant accounts and disclosures in the financial statements. The auditor should obtain such evidence each year to support his or her opinion on management's assertion of the effectiveness of internal control over financial reporting. However, the sufficiency of the evidence obtained is a matter of professional judgment. Additionally, such evidence may differ from year to year, as the auditor alters the nature, timing, and extent of his or her procedures.

As stated in paragraph 101, "The auditor also should vary from year to year the nature, timing, and extent of testing of controls to introduce unpredictability into the testing and respond to changes in circumstances. For example, each year the auditor might test the controls at a different interim period; increase or reduce the number and types of tests performed; or change the combination of procedures used." A particular area where testing may vary significantly is over information technology systems. As technology operates in a systematic manner, the auditor may evaluate and test general computer controls, including program changes and security access, while performing only limited procedures over the specific program controls.

We acknowledge, however, that auditing is a continuous process. While the auditor uses his or her experience and knowledge of effectiveness from previous years to alter the nature, timing and extent of test of controls, he or she does not necessarily rely on the audit evidence obtained from such prior periods as the sole evidence for the current year's opinion. Further, the auditor may be placed in a unique situation where the period between opinions is less than a year. For example, the auditor may be asked to provide an opinion on the effectiveness of internal control over financial reporting as of an interim date or the company may decide to change its year-end for reporting purposes. We view such circumstances as tests performed at an interim date, where the opinion on the previous period constitutes the interim testing date. Accordingly, the auditor determines what additional evidence to obtain concerning the design and operation of the controls for the remaining period and considers significant changes in controls from the "interim" date to the "as-of" date. The auditor also considers controls that may only operate during or apply to the interim or annual periods. Where a change in the company's year-end occurs, the auditor should only be required to perform an audit of internal control when audited financial statements are required to be presented.

Questions Regarding Using the Work of Management and Others

12. **To what extent should the auditor be permitted or required to use the work of management and others?**

As the auditor is ultimately responsible for his or her opinion, he or she should be allowed to apply professional judgment in determining whether to use the work of management and others to alter the nature, timing and extent of his or her procedures to obtain sufficient competent evidence to render the report. The auditor should never be "required" to use the work of management and others, as the independence and objectivity of the individuals that performed such work may have been impaired. Additionally, such individuals may not be deemed competent with respect to internal control.

Our responses to questions 13 through 16 provide additional comments on the extent the auditor should be permitted to use the work of management and others.

13. Are the three categories of controls and the extent to which the auditor may rely on the work of others appropriately defined?

The three categories of controls and the extent to which the auditor may rely on the work performed by management and others need some clarification. We believe that it is appropriate to prohibit the use of the work performed by management and others when evaluating controls that are part of the control environment, controls over the period-end financial reporting process, and controls that have a pervasive effect on the financial statements, due to the extensive judgment involved with such evaluation and the impact on the nature, timing and extent of the auditor's procedures. It also is appropriate to limit the use of the work of management and others in the areas addressed by paragraph 105. Such matters also involve a significant amount of judgment, but do not ordinarily have a pervasive effect on the auditor's procedures.

With respect to the third category, controls over routine processing of significant accounts and disclosures, we suggest that the Board clarify the phrase "without specific limitation." As written, it may be misinterpreted to mean that the auditor does not have any responsibilities and can rely on the work of others without performing any additional procedures. Although the auditor can use the results of tests performed by management and others, we believe that the auditor must still reperform some of the tests performed by others and use such tests to alter the nature, timing and extent of procedures he or she performs directly. However, reperforming more of the procedures performed by management and others may significantly reduce such direct procedures.

In regards to the first category where the use of the work performed by management and others is prohibited, we recommend that the Board view information technology general controls as those where the auditor's use of the work of management and others is limited. Such controls do not ordinarily involve extensive judgment.

14. Does the proposed standard give appropriate recognition to the work of internal auditors? If not, does the proposed standard place too much emphasis and preference on the work of internal auditors or not enough?

The proposed standard gives appropriate and adequate recognition to the work of internal auditors. It is also consistent with existing interim standards (AU Section 322, *The Auditor's Consideration of the Internal Audit Function in an Audit of Financial Statements*) with respect to evaluating internal audit's competence and objectivity in determining how internal audit's work may affect the audit of internal control over financial reporting. Such existing literature provides guidance to the auditor on evaluating internal audit's competence and objectivity and in evaluating the relevancy of their work. As such, we believe that it would be appropriate and necessary to include a reference to AU Section 322 within paragraph 108, even though the proposed standard provides a reference to such existing literature in Appendix B.

The proposed standard should not, however, add additional emphasis on the use of internal audit's work. Although the auditor may be able to use their work to a greater extent than the work performed by other personnel, internal audit is a part of the company's monitoring component of internal control. Accordingly, to place more emphasis on the use of internal audit's work may inappropriately reduce the work directly performed by the auditor.

15. **Is the flexibility in determining the extent of reperformance of the work of others appropriate, or should the auditor be specifically required to reperform a certain level of work (for example, reperform tests of all significant accounts or reperform every test performed by others that the auditor intends to use)?**

The auditor uses the work performed by management and others to alter the nature, timing and extent of his or her procedures. When using the work of management and others, the auditor should perform tests to evaluate the quality and effectiveness of the work performed. The tests performed by the auditor to make this evaluation depend on the extent of the effect of the work of management and others on the procedures performed directly by the auditor. When performing such tests, the auditor may either (a) reperform some of the work performed by management or others, or (b) examine the work performed, perform similar tests, and compare such tests to the results of the work performed by management and others.

The combination of the procedures performed to test the work performed by management and others and the tests performed directly by the auditor are a matter of professional judgment and together should provide sufficient competent evidence to support the auditor's opinion. Accordingly, it is appropriate to allow flexibility in determining both the extent of reperformance of the work of management and others and the nature, timing and extent of procedures performed directly by the auditor. The proposed standard should not mandate that the auditor reperform a certain level of work, including reperforming tests of all significant accounts or reperforming every test performed by others that the auditor intends to use.

16. **Is the requirement for the auditor to obtain the principle evidence, on an overall basis, through his or her own work the appropriate benchmark for the amount of work that is required to be performed by the auditor?**

As stated previously, the auditor is ultimately responsible for the opinion expressed. As such, it would be inappropriate for the auditor to obtain most of his or her evidence by using the work performed by management and others. On an overall basis, the auditor should perform enough procedures directly to be able to make his or her own conclusions. That said, however, the benchmark for the amount of work that is required to be performed directly by the auditor is a matter of professional judgment.

We believe that the Board intends the principal evidence requirement to apply on an overall basis, rather than on a relevant assertion or significant account basis. Accordingly, we suggest that the Board clarify its intents in the proposed standard.

Questions Regarding Evaluating Results

17. **Will the definitions in the proposed standard of significant deficiency and material weakness provide for increased consistency in the evaluation of deficiencies? How can the definitions be improved?**

We acknowledge the Board's efforts to clarify and narrow the definitions of a significant deficiency and a material weakness, to provide detailed examples on the application of such definitions, and to list the matters that are strong indicators that a material weakness exists. Altogether, this guidance should promote consistency in evaluating whether an internal control deficiency is a significant deficiency or a material weakness. Nevertheless, such evaluations involve extensive judgment, and each individual may conclude differently as to the severity of a deficiency.

With respect to the definitions of a significant deficiency and a material weakness, however, the discussion of "likelihood" should be enhanced and clarified. The proposed discussion of likelihood could be read to allow a conclusion that a deficiency is not a material weakness because it has never been a problem in the past. For instance, management can argue that there is a "remote likelihood" that a material misstatement will not be prevented or detected in the future because a material misstatement as it relates to a particular deficiency has never occurred. As such, language should be added to state that the absence of a past material error in financial reporting due to a deficiency does not mean that likelihood is low enough to keep a deficiency from being a material weakness. The definition of material weakness is focused on what could happen and is not limited to what has happened.

18. **Do the examples in Appendix D of how to apply these definitions in various scenarios provide helpful guidance? Are there other specific examples that commenters could suggest that would provide further interpretive help?**

As stated in our response to question number 17 above, the examples in Appendix D are useful and should assist in promoting the consistency with which internal control deficiencies are evaluated. It would be helpful, however, if one or more examples were added dealing with deficiencies relating to information technology systems or deficiencies dealing with controls over operations or compliance with laws and regulations that could materially affect financial reporting. Also, with respect to the safeguarding of assets, it would be very useful to have examples that illustrate deficiencies that are financial reporting in nature, deficiencies that relate to the assertions about safeguarding that management is required to make under Section 404, and deficiencies in safeguarding that are not within the scope of financial reporting and Section 404 assertions.

19. **Is it necessary for the auditor to evaluate the severity of all identified internal control deficiencies?**

The auditor's objective in an audit of internal control over financial reporting is to express an opinion on management's "assessment" of effectiveness. Where significant deficiencies, either individually or in the aggregate, constitute a material weakness in internal control, management is precluded from concluding that internal control over financial reporting is effective and the auditor must express an adverse opinion. Consequently, in order for the auditor to achieve his or her objectives, he or she should be required to evaluate the severity of all identified internal control deficiencies. Otherwise, the auditor may inappropriately conclude that internal control over financial reporting is effective.

20. **Is it appropriate to require the auditor to communicate all internal control deficiencies (not just material weaknesses and significant deficiencies) to management in writing?**

We believe that the auditor should communicate all identified significant deficiencies and material weakness in writing. We do not believe it is appropriate to require the auditor to communicate in writing internal control deficiencies that are below the level of a significant deficiency. Any oral or written communications of such matters should be made at the discretion of the auditor. For example, the auditor may choose to communicate deficiencies that management may not be aware of. As with the reporting of misstatements that come to the auditor's attention during an audit of financial statement, there is no need to require the reporting of every minor internal control deficiency that comes to the auditor's attention. However, the auditor may report all deficiencies noted if requested to do so by management or the audit committee.

21. Are the matters that the Board has classified as strong indicators that a material weakness in internal control exists appropriately classified as such?

The matters that the Board has classified as strong indicators that a material weakness exists are appropriately classified as such. These matters clearly fall within the definition of a significant deficiency, where there is more than a remote likelihood that a misstatement that is more than inconsequential in amount will not be prevented or detected. Such misstatements may be material to the financial statements and therefore, these matters could also constitute a material weakness.

There may be circumstances where the auditor identifies a material weakness in internal control over financial reporting in the current period that was not initially identified by the company's internal control evaluation and testing process. We believe that this is, at a minimum, a significant deficiency and also a strong indicator that a material weakness exists, even if management subsequently corrects the weakness. As such, we suggest that the Board add this matter to paragraph 126 as a strong indicator of a material weakness.

22. Is it appropriate to require the auditors to evaluate the effectiveness of the audit committee's oversight of the company's external financial reporting and internal control over financial reporting?

The proposed standard states, "The company's audit committee plays an important role within the control environment and monitoring components of internal control over financial reporting." We agree with this statement. Thus, the audit committee falls within the bounds of internal control over financial reporting, and the auditor has a responsibility to evaluate the effectiveness of the audit committee's oversight. Therefore, it is appropriate to require the auditor to evaluate the effectiveness of the audit committee's oversight of the company's external financial reporting and internal control over financial reporting as a component of internal control, but not separate from its effectiveness as it relates to the overall internal control. There are certain factors that the Board proposes to require the auditor to evaluate for which the auditor does not possess the appropriate qualifications. Such factors may not be necessary for the auditor's evaluation of the company's internal control over financial reporting.

For example, we believe that the auditor's training and experience provide a basis for evaluating the clarity with which the audit committee's responsibilities are articulated and understood by the audit committee and management and the audit committee's involvement and interaction with the external and internal auditor. However, such training and experience is insufficient to evaluate the audit committee's independence and their compliance with applicable listing standards. We believe such matters involve legal determinations that are beyond the auditor's professional competence and are not necessary to evaluate the company's internal control over financial reporting.

In the context of an audit of internal control over financial reporting, we also question the emphasis placed on the evaluation of the effectiveness of the audit committee's oversight. Effective oversight does not necessarily imply that internal control over financial reporting is effective. We believe that the audit committee's oversight is one element of the control environment (a very important one) and monitoring components of the company's internal control. Accordingly, the standard should indicate that as with any other control where a deficiency exists, the auditor evaluates the severity of the deficiency and the impact on the conclusions reached.

– 15 –   November 21, 2003

23. **Will auditors be able to effectively carry out their responsibility to evaluate the effectiveness of the audit committee's oversight?**

As auditors, we generally are not privy to the entire conduct of the audit committee. Further, the evaluation of the effectiveness of the audit committee's capabilities, competence, and oversight processes requires extensive judgment on the part of the auditor and, as described in our response to question number 22, certain matters related to those considerations are beyond the realm of the auditor's expertise and also may not be relevant to the auditor's consideration of the effectiveness of the company's internal control over financial reporting.

The auditor should, however, be able to effectively carry out his or her responsibility to evaluate the effectiveness of the audit committee's oversight as it relates to the evaluation of the company's internal control over financial reporting, even though the auditor may not be able to separately evaluate the effectiveness of their oversight as a whole. The auditor evaluates the effectiveness of the audit committee's oversight primarily through the appropriate use of inquiry and observation techniques focused on the audit committee's involvement with financial reporting matters. For example, the auditor focuses on metrics such as how often the audit committee meets, the audit committee's expectations, and their involvement with the risk management process, rather than evaluating their independence and compliance with external requirements.

24. **If the auditor concludes that ineffective audit committee oversight is a material weakness, rather than require the auditor to issue an adverse opinion with regard to the effectiveness of the internal control over financial reporting, should the standard require the auditor to withdraw from the audit engagement?**

The auditor should not be required to withdraw from the audit engagement in response to <u>any</u> identified material weakness. The presence of a material weakness, including a material weakness where the audit committee's oversight is ineffective, does not necessarily impose a limitation on the scope of the engagement. Accordingly, whether to withdraw should remain a judgment made by the auditor. Further, it would not be in the public interest to require the auditor to withdraw from the engagement due to ineffective audit committee oversight.

Questions Regarding Forming an Opinion and Reporting

25. **Is it appropriate that the existence of a material weakness would require the auditor to express an adverse conclusion about the effectiveness of the company's internal control over financial reporting, consistent with the required reporting model for management?**

When one or more material weaknesses in internal control over financial reporting exist, management is not permitted to conclude that internal control over financial reporting is effective. In such circumstances, we concur with the Board's conclusions that (a) management must report that internal control is not effective, (b) the auditor's reporting model must be consistent with managements reporting model, and (c) the issuance of a qualified "except for" conclusion by management or the auditor is not acceptable. As such, it is appropriate that the existence of a material weakness would require the auditor to express an adverse opinion about the effectiveness of the company's internal control over financial reporting.

26. **Are there circumstances where a qualified "except for" conclusion would be appropriate?**

We do not believe there are any circumstances where a qualified "except for" opinion would be appropriate. This would require the auditor to evaluate the severity of a material weakness, in essence creating another category of deficiencies.

27. **Do you agree with the position that when the auditor issues a non-standard opinion, such as an adverse opinion, that the auditor's opinion should speak directly to the effectiveness of the internal control over financial reporting rather than to whether management's assessment is fairly stated?**

With the public interest in mind, we agree with the Board's position to require the auditor to opine directly on internal control effectiveness when a non-standard report is to be issued. Although both opinions would be appropriate, we believe that this approach will eliminate potential confusion relating to the auditor's opinion on the effectiveness of internal control over financial reporting.

We have concerns, however, with respect to the overall reporting model, specifically relating to the identification of the financial statements to which the opinion applies. The introductory paragraph of the independent auditor's report states the following:

> "We have audited management's assessment, included in the accompanying [*title of management's report*], that W Company maintained effective internal control over financial reporting as of December 31, 20X3, based on [*Identify criteria, for example "criteria established in Internal Control – Integrated Framework issued by the Committee of Sponsoring Organization of the Treadway Commission (COSO)."*]. W company's management is responsible for its assessment about the effectiveness of internal control over financial reporting. Our responsibility is to express an opinion on management's assessment based on our audit."

From a user perspective, we suggest that the scope of the term "financial reporting" be clearly delineated in management's assertion and the auditor's report. We believe that this generic term could be interpreted to extend to all financial reporting that occurs on the "as of" date. For example, management's assertion on internal control effectiveness over financial reporting of a consolidated entity could be interpreted by the user community to include: financial statements issued by each of the subsidiaries in accordance with generally accepted accounting principles or another comprehensive basis of accounting, and reporting of financial information at a consolidated and subsidiary level to government agencies, such as the Internal Revenue Service. Accordingly, we suggest that the Board clearly define the term "internal control over financial reporting" and limit it to the specific financial statements covered by the report, for example, the financial statements required to be filed in accordance with generally accepted accounting principles and SEC rules and regulations under the Securities Exchange Act of 1934. For example, the introductory paragraph may be worded as follows:

> We have audited management's assertion, included in the accompanying [*title of management's report*], that W Company maintained effective internal control over financial reporting as of December 31, 20X3 in the Company's financial statements filed with the Securities and Exchange Commission, based on [*Identify criteria, for example "criteria established in Internal Control – Integrated Framework issued by the Committee of Sponsoring Organization of the Treadway Commission (COSO)."*].

Questions Regarding Auditor Independence

28. **Should the Board provide specific guidance on independence and internal control-related services in the context of this proposed standard?**

Although we believe the Board should provide specific guidance and adopt certain rules on independence and internal control-related matters, as indicated in our response to question number 29, the Board should not provide them within this standard. We suggest that independence matters not reside directly in the auditing and other attest standards. Such matters should exist independently, through separate independence standards or the SEC's rules and regulations.

An auditor is required to adhere to all requirements imposed by the PCAOB's Auditing and Related Professional Practice Standards and those imposed directly by the SEC. Accordingly, it is not necessary to repeat such requirements in multiple locations (and can even be burdensome for the regulators to maintain). A reference to the relevant standards, rules and regulations is sufficient and does not alter the auditor's responsibilities. Additionally, it promotes compliance with the standards, rules and regulations, as such information is contained within the related subject matter.

29. Are there any specific internal control-related non-audit services the auditor should be prohibited from providing to an audit client?

We believe that the Board should adopt Grant Thornton's position on independence in regards to internal control-related services by the external auditor. Our position is expressed in the following excerpt from a testimony given by Ed Nusbaum, Grant Thornton's Chief Executive Officer, on September 23, 2003, before a full committee hearing of the U.S. Senate Committee on Banking, Housing and Urban Affairs, the subject: "The Implementation of the Sarbanes-Oxley Act and Restoring Investor Confidence."

> "...The degree of an auditor's independence is driven by the separation between management (which produces the financial information) and the users of the information provided by management. The standard for independence is heightened as that separation increases. We firmly believe that the auditors of publicly held companies must hold themselves to the highest possible standard of independence.

> For this reason, Grant Thornton will not accept engagements to document, evaluate or design our public audit clients' internal controls, including engagements to document existing controls, or to perform evaluations of existing controls that management uses to support their conclusions regarding the effective design of those controls. To do so, we feel, is a conflict of interest. Instead, as auditors, we will audit the internal controls as designed, documented and evaluated by management, in accordance with the provisions of the Act."

Questions Regarding Auditor's Responsibilities with Regard to Management's Certifications

30. Are the auditor's differing levels of responsibility as they relate to management's quarterly certifications versus the annual (fourth quarter) certification, appropriate?

The differing levels of responsibility as they relate to management's quarterly and annual certifications are appropriate and are consistent with the current reporting model. For example, the accountant performs a review of the company's interim financial information and management's quarterly 302 certifications (as it relates to the disclosure of any material change in internal control over financial reporting during the period), while he or she performs an audit of the company's annual financial statements and management's assertion of the effectiveness of internal control over financial reporting. However, we do believe that the responsibility for the accountant to determine whether significant changes in internal control over financial reporting may introduce significant deficiencies or material weaknesses in the design of internal control over financial reporting discussed in paragraph 186 is inconsistent with the objective of a review of interim financial information.

The objective of a review of interim financial information pursuant to AU Section 722, *Interim Financial Information*, is to provide the accountant with a basis for communicating whether he or she is aware of any material modifications that should be made to the interim financial information for it to conform with generally accepted accounting principles. A review consists principally of performing analytical procedures and making inquiries of persons responsible for financial and accounting matters, and does not contemplate tests of accounting records through inspection, observation or confirmation. We believe that paragraph 186, as currently written, creates a responsibility that is inconsistent with the objective of a review of interim financial information. We suggest the following language as an alternative:

> "If there have been significant changes in the design or operation of internal control over financial reporting, perform procedures to obtain sufficient knowledge to understand the effect of such changes on internal control as it relates to the preparation of interim financial information and inquire of management whether such changes may introduce significant deficiencies or material weaknesses in the design of internal control over financial reporting."

AU Section 722 addresses the matters discussed in paragraphs 185 through 188. We urge the Board to consider revising this section in light of AU Section 722, and in lieu of providing such guidance in the proposed standard, amend AU Section 722 for the requirements of Section 302 and make reference to the guidance in AU Section 722 in the proposed standard. We also urge the Board to use "accountant" rather than "auditor" when discussing interim reviews in paragraphs 185 through 188 to be consistent with AU Section 722.

31. Is the scope of the auditor's responsibility for quarterly disclosures about the internal control over financial reporting appropriate?

Please see our response to question number 30. The scope of the accountant's responsibility for quarterly disclosures should be consistent with the accountant's responsibility for material misstatements of interim financial statements under AU Section 722.

Appendix B – Specific Paragraph-Level Comments

The following describes additional concerns and offers other substantive comments and/or suggestions relating to specific paragraphs.

- **Footnote 1** – Where the PCAOB believes that there will be any need or request for an audit of internal control over financial reporting other than those mandated by Section 404 of the Sarbanes-Oxley Act, they should maintain a standalone standard for such attestation engagement. Please see our response to question number two.

- **Paragraph 7** - A deficiency in operation is described, among other things, as one where a person performing the control does not possess the necessary authority or qualifications to perform the control effectively. This is an element of design, as well as operation. For example, assigning the appropriate individual to perform a control (e.g., segregation of duties) relates to design. Whether the assigned individual performed the control and how well that person performed the control relates to operation. We suggest that the Board revise the definitions of a design deficiency and an operating deficiency, accordingly.

- **Paragraphs 21 and 22** – We believe that the concepts in these paragraphs need clarification. These paragraphs should clearly state that materiality, as it is described herein, relates to evaluating the severity of internal control deficiencies to determine whether they are significant deficiencies and material weaknesses, rather than used for purposes of performing the audit of internal control over financial reporting. In addition, the proposed standard should not suggest that we conduct the audit at a lower level of materiality at the individual account-balance level. Paragraph 61 describes that an account is significant if there is more than a remote likelihood that the account could have a material effect on the financial statements. Accordingly, the audit would be planned in consideration of materiality at the financial statement level.

- **Paragraph 36** - The last sentence of this paragraph states "Inquiry of management and employees is the beginning point for obtaining an understanding of internal control over financial reporting, but inquiry alone is not adequate for reaching a conclusion on any aspect of internal control over financial reporting effectiveness." We believe that the word "any" should be deleted. In many instances, inquiry may be the only procedure that can be performed to support the effectiveness of a "single" control. Inquiry alone is not sufficient to support our opinion on management's assertion, but may be sufficient to support a conclusion that certain controls are operating effectively.

- **Paragraph 61** - The definition of a significant account would seem to allow the auditor some latitude in determining which accounts will require testing, for example limiting work to those where a material misstatement could exist rather than requiring testing for either quantitative or qualitative materiality. This approach, however, seems to be at odds with the example in B18. For instance, if the auditor were to conclude that the likelihood of a misstatement of the property, plant and equipment account is remote in the example presented, we would argue that we do not need to test controls over that account solely on the basis of the materiality of the balance to the financial statements.

- **Paragraph 74** – This paragraph lists items that should be evaluated by the auditor when identifying controls to test. With respect to the third bullet, we recommend replacing the phrase "whether more than one control achieves a particular objective" with the phrase "whether more than one control is necessary to achieve a particular objective." In regards to the fourth bullet, the auditor should not consider the nature and extent of tests performed by management and others when determining which controls to test. The auditor should make his or her own judgment as to which controls should be tested and then determine the nature, timing and extent of the tests to be performed directly (or tests to reperform the work of management and others). With respect to the very last item, we do not believe that the complexity of the control is a consideration. Processes and systems may be complex; however, individual controls are quite simple.

- **Paragraph 88** – Please refer to our comments for paragraph7 regarding the definitions of a design deficiency and an operating deficiency.

- **Paragraph 92** – This paragraph states, "Because inquiry alone does not provide sufficient evidence to support the operating effectiveness of a control, the auditor should perform additional tests of controls." Please see our comments relating to paragraph 36. Inquiry may be a sufficient procedure for evaluating "a" single control.

- **Paragraph 136** – This paragraph states, "To assess control risk for specific financial statement assertions at less than maximum, the auditor is required to obtain evidence that the relevant controls operated effectively during the entire period covered by the company's financial statements." We disagree with this statement. The auditor should test controls over the period in which the controls are being relied upon, which may not be the entire period covered by the financial statements. Other substantive procedures can be performed to cover the "stub-period." Together, such procedures would be sufficient to reduce audit risk to an appropriately low level.

- **Paragraph 139** – We suggest defining the term "significant risk," as it is not currently defined in the interim standards.

- **Paragraph 140** – We suggest the following revision: "For this reason, substantive analytical procedures **alone** are not well suited to detecting fraud." Perhaps there are situations where substantive analytical procedures alone may not be effective; however, we disagree that they are never effective as the statement implies. For example, the performance of disaggregated analytical procedures over revenue may assist in detecting fraud or potential fraud.

- **Paragraph 143** – This paragraph requires the auditor to evaluate his or her findings from substantive procedures performed in the audit of the financial statements and their effect on the effectiveness of internal control over financial reporting. It also lists matters the auditor should include when performing such an evaluation. We believe the requirement to evaluate **all** findings is unnecessary and improperly excludes the auditor's professional judgment and consideration of materiality and the significance of the finding. In addition, certain matters listed do not represent findings from substantive procedures (e.g., risk evaluations), and the impact on internal control effectiveness is not necessarily apparent from some of the items presented (e.g., findings with respect to related party transactions). Accordingly, we urge the Board clarify its intents with respect to this paragraph and eliminate the requirement to evaluate **all** findings.

- **Paragraph 145** – The proposed standard requires the auditor to document "the process used to determine significant accounts, classes of transactions, and disclosures, including the determination of the locations or business units at which to perform testing." We suggest that the Board clarify what is meant by this documentation requirement, including what the Board expects to be documented. For example, could the process be a firm's methodology?

- **Paragraphs 146 & 147** – This paragraph states "The auditor also should document the effect of a conclusion that control risk is other than low for any relevant assertions for any significant accounts on his or her opinion on the audit of internal control over financial reporting." We suggest that the Board clarify the documentation requirements and the auditor's control risk assessments. For example, the matters described in paragraph 146 may alter the control risk assessment for the audit of the financial statements. By definition, control risk is the risk that a material misstatement in an assertion will not be prevented or detected on a timely basis by internal control policies or procedures. Accordingly, with respect to the audit of internal control, we believe that only a material weakness precludes the auditor from assessing control risk at low. As such, the items in paragraph 146 would preclude the issuance of an unqualified opinion on the effectiveness of internal control over financial reporting.

- **Paragraph 163** – As indicated in our response to question number 21, where the auditor identified a material weakness that was not identified by management, this in itself may be a material weakness. Accordingly, clarification of the second bullet point may be necessary.

- **Paragraph B15** – The last sentence of this paragraph states "The evaluation ordinarily would not extend to controls at the equity method investee." We suggest that the PCAOB delete the word "ordinarily," as it extends beyond the scope of the auditor's responsibilities.

- **Example B-1** – The extent of the expected information technology testing is a concern; it would appear that an information technology expert will need to be involved on all audits for all information technology processes that the auditor relies on to independently verify that there were no changes made in the system, or that the system was put in operation on the date the client maintained. Inquiry of the company's information technology manager will be insufficient in and of itself to audit the changes to the system. Nor would we be able to rely on a change log kept by the information technology manager, as it would be subject to alteration/manipulation.

November 21, 2003

Appendix C – Other Recommendations

The following represent other recommendations.

- **Footnote 1** – We suggest that in lieu of stating the "standard does not apply," stating that the "standard applies to a limited extent," when an auditor audits the financial statements but does not audit a company's internal control over financial reporting.

- **Paragraph 5** – In the first sentence, we recommend replacing the word "operated" with the word "operating" or replacing the word "is" with the word "was."

- **Footnote 9** – The Board may also choose to add a reference to Staff Accounting Bulletin No. 99, *Materiality*.

- **Paragraph 18** – We suggest that the Board clarify the level of assurance provided by management versus that provided by the auditor. Specifically, an explanation as to why the auditor does not provide the "same assurance" as management would be helpful.

- **Paragraph 24** – With respect to the controls that address the risk of fraud, we agree that the auditor should pay particular attention to the control environment; however, given this requirement is presumptively mandatory, we suggest the Board clarify their intent with respect to the term "special emphasis."

- **Paragraph 27** – We suggest adding a cross-reference to where the phrases "relevant financial statement assertions" and "significant accounts and disclosures" are defined.

- **Paragraph 39** – This paragraph describes certain matters the auditor should evaluate when planning the audit to determine the affect on his or her procedures. We suggest adding a cross-reference to paragraph 101, which discusses altering the nature, timing and extent of testing to introduce an element of unpredictability and to respond to changes in circumstances.

- **Paragraphs 48-50** – We recommend linking the term "specific controls" to the requirement to evaluate controls over "relevant assertions and significant account balances."

- **Paragraph 113** – The schedule of passed adjustments and the adjustments recorded by management are an important element to consider when forming an opinion on internal control over financial reporting. Accordingly, a specific mention of such is appropriate within this paragraph.

- **Paragraph 157** – This paragraph discusses that the date of the auditor's report on the financial statements and the date of the auditor's report on the audit of internal control should be the same. We suggest the Board consider the impact of dual-dating for subsequent events. We believe that a dual-date for a subsequent event relating to either opinion should not impact the date of the other report.

- **Paragraph 168** – The SEC staff has provided certain guidance with respect to meeting the requirements of a principal auditor for a financial statement audit. We suggest the Board clarify such requirements and their applicability to an audit of internal control over financial reporting.

¶ 636. PricewaterhouseCoopers

PRICEWATERHOUSECOOPERS ⬚

PricewaterhouseCoopers LLP
500 Campus Dr.
Florham Park NJ 07932
Telephone (973) 236 7000
Facsimile (973) 236 7200

November 21, 2003

Office of the Secretary
Public Company Accounting Oversight Board
1666 K Street, N.W.
Washington, D.C. 20006-2803

Re: **PCAOB Rulemaking Docket Matter No. 008, Proposed Auditing Standard – An Audit of
Internal Control Over Financial Reporting Performed in Conjunction With an Audit of
Financial Statements (PCAOB Release No. 2003-017, October 7, 2003)**

Dear Mr. Secretary:

PricewaterhouseCoopers LLP appreciates the opportunity to comment on the proposed auditing
standard, *An Audit of Internal Control Over Financial Reporting Performed in Conjunction With an
Audit of Financial Statements* ("the proposed standard"), that has been prepared by the Public
Company Accounting Oversight Board (the "Board").

We fully support the Board's efforts to further define and clarify management's and the auditor's
respective responsibilities under Section 404 of the Sarbanes-Oxley Act (the "Act"). We believe the
proposed standard strikes the proper balance between management's responsibility for the company's
controls and their effectiveness, and the auditor's need to perform an independent audit while making
appropriate use of the work performed by management and others to support management's assertion.
It provides a logical framework and generally allows for the necessary exercise of the auditor's
professional judgment. Specifically, we point to the following areas where we strongly support the
proposed standard's conclusions:

- The proposed standard operationalizes the concept of one integrated audit process meeting two
  distinct objectives and resulting in two opinions—one on internal control over financial
  reporting and one on the financial statements. We believe this integration is key to meeting the
  public's expectations.

- The proposed standard properly recognizes that the auditor can make appropriate use of work
  done by management as part of its Section 404 assessment process. The standard's framework
  relating to the auditor's use of work performed by management and others generally provides a
  sound basis for auditors to make appropriate professional judgments, while still requiring that
  the auditor's own work must, at the end of the day, provide the "principal" basis for his or her
  opinion.

- We believe the Board's recognition of the importance of financial statement assertions as a key underpinning of an audit of internal control will significantly help auditors in performing effective audits of internal control. This will also emphasize the proper "linkage" between the audit of internal control and the additional procedures the auditor performs to complete the financial statement audit.

We have provided our answers to the Board's specific questions as well as more detailed comments in the attachment to this letter. However, we have several recommendations that we respectfully submit to the Board on how the goals of the proposed standard may be better achieved. These address the following:

- Reporting by the auditor
- Reasonable assurance
- Internal control deficiencies
- Evaluation of the audit committee's effectiveness
- Safeguarding of assets
- Multi-location testing considerations
- Walkthroughs
- Use of the work of others
- Extent of management's testing
- Evaluation of internal control for small and medium-sized companies
- Evaluation of management's assessment

Reporting by the Auditor

The proposed standard requires the auditor to issue an adverse opinion when one or more material weaknesses exist in the company's internal control over financial reporting. In our view, this requirement is too restrictive. We believe that the existence of one or more material weaknesses should not automatically result in an adverse opinion. In situations where a material weakness has an isolated impact on the overall effectiveness of internal control over financial reporting, we believe that the auditor should be allowed to apply professional judgment and issue a qualified or "except for" opinion. Examples of such situations might be a material weakness related to the preparation of timely account reconciliations at an individual business unit or location, or other instances where the impact is not so pervasive as to affect the overall integrity of the company's internal control. In these situations, a qualified or "except for" opinion provides more useful information to readers of the auditor's report as it allows the auditor to communicate a meaningful distinction between material weaknesses that have an isolated impact as opposed to a pervasive impact. This reporting alternative is particularly important considering the number of material weaknesses potentially being reported in the initial year. We believe auditors need flexibility to address situations where an adverse opinion resulting from an isolated material weakness could result in a disproportionately negative impression on users of a company's financial statements.

If the auditor is able to issue a qualified or "except for" opinion, management should also have that reporting alternative. The SEC's final rules implementing Section 404 state, "Management is not permitted to conclude that the registrant's internal control over financial reporting is effective if there are one or more material weaknesses in the registrant's internal control over financial reporting." This does not appear to preclude management from making a qualified or "except for" assertion when there are one or more material weaknesses. Alternatively, if it is concluded that the existing 404 rules would not permit a qualified report by management, we believe the SEC should modify its Section 404 rules to allow management to make a qualified or "except for" assertion. This will provide the necessary symmetry between the rules governing management's assertion and those governing the auditor's opinion. We would be pleased to participate in discussions with staff of the PCAOB and the SEC to further explain our views in this regard.

<u>Reasonable Assurance</u>

We believe the following sentences in paragraph 18 of the proposed standard may create confusion as to the responsibilities of management and of the auditor with respect to the effectiveness of internal control over financial reporting:

"Users of the reports from management and the auditor are entitled to receive the same level of assurance from both management and the auditor. This means that users should expect reasonable assurance that internal control over financial reporting is effective."

"The auditor provides the same level of assurance, though not the same assurance, as management."

The responsibilities of management and the auditor are very different. As noted in Section 404 of the Act and in the SEC's final Section 404 rules, management is responsible for establishing and maintaining adequate internal controls and procedures for financial reporting and for evaluating the effectiveness of the company's internal control over financial reporting. The auditor is responsible for performing an audit and expressing an opinion on management's assessment of effectiveness or directly on the effectiveness of internal control over financial reporting. The auditor is not responsible for the effectiveness of the company's internal control over financial reporting.

Reasonable assurance for the auditor relates to performing an audit to evaluate whether effective internal control over financial reporting was maintained in all material respects. Reasonable assurance for management relates to management's assessment of internal control over financial reporting, not to management's responsibility for the effectiveness of the company's internal control over financial reporting.

We believe these sentences should be deleted from paragraph 18. In addition, we believe the following should be added to paragraph 18:

"The subsequent discovery of a material weakness in internal control existing at the date of the auditor's report on internal control over financial reporting is not, in and of itself, evidence of (a) failure to obtain reasonable assurance; (b) inadequate planning, performance, or judgment; (c) the absence of due professional care; or (d) a failure to comply with PCAOB standards. Since the auditor's opinion on internal control is based on the concept of obtaining reasonable assurance, the auditor is not an insurer and his or her report does not constitute a guarantee."

Internal Control Deficiencies

We believe the definitions of a significant deficiency and a material weakness included in the proposed standard provide greater clarity and permit more consistent application than the definitions in existing auditing literature. The new definitions better reflect a continuum from an internal control deficiency to a significant deficiency to a material weakness. However, we believe that by using the concept of "remote likelihood" in the standard's definition of significant deficiency, the Board has significantly, and in our view inappropriately, increased the number of internal control deficiencies that will be classified as significant deficiencies. As a result, auditors, management, and audit committees may spend excessive time reviewing deficiencies that are unlikely to ever rise to the level of a material weakness, while perhaps not giving enough attention to more significant items presenting greater risk. Also, the requirement that unresolved significant deficiencies be regarded as strong indicators of a material weakness, when combined with the proposed definition, could result in companies adopting controls that are not justified from a cost–benefit perspective.

We recommend that the Board reconsider its definition of significant deficiency in light of these potential consequences. We acknowledge the significant efforts of the Board and others in developing a workable definition of significant deficiency. We suggest that the Board engage interested parties—including the SEC, the preparer community, and auditors—in a coordinated effort to resolve this issue.

The examples of significant deficiencies and material weaknesses in Appendix D are helpful. We believe management and auditors would benefit from additional guidance and examples at the lower part of the continuum (i.e., examples of internal control deficiencies that would not be deemed to be significant deficiencies). Additional guidance and examples on distinguishing between testing exceptions that do not rise to the level of an internal control deficiency versus those that do also would be helpful.

Evaluation of the Audit Committee's Effectiveness

We agree that the auditor should evaluate the effectiveness of the audit committee's oversight, recognizing its role within the critically important control environment and monitoring components of internal control over financial reporting. Consistent with the framework established by the Committee of Sponsoring Organizations of the Treadway Commission's (COSO) report, *Internal Control – Integrated Framework*, the auditor has a responsibility to evaluate the "participation by those who govern," including the audit committee, the board of directors, and management. However, we believe the evaluation of the audit committee's effectiveness should be in the context of the auditor's evaluation of the overall control environment. Singling out audit committee effectiveness for individual assessment overemphasizes one element of the control environment to the exclusion of others. As such, we believe that the auditor's responsibility to evaluate the effectiveness of those who govern, including the audit committee, does not extend beyond the auditor's evaluation of the company's control environment in the context of internal control over financial reporting. We also believe that it is the board of directors' role to determine the overall effectiveness of the audit committee.

We believe the auditor's evaluation of the effectiveness of those who govern—as part of the control environment—should be a qualitative assessment. We believe the list of factors in paragraph 57 for evaluating the effectiveness of the audit committee in the context of the overall control environment should be revised as they are not necessarily the most relevant for this purpose. For example, the amount of time that the audit committee devotes to control issues, and that audit committee members devote to committee activity, may not be directly relevant to the effectiveness of the audit committee. In addition, including the audit committee's compliance with the applicable listing standards adopted pursuant to Section 301 of the Act may be viewed as inappropriately extending the auditor's evaluation outside the scope of internal control over financial reporting and into areas of regulatory compliance, which are matters for legal determination and are outside the scope of the auditor's responsibility.

We recommend that the Board consider adding factors outlined on pages 26 and 27 of the COSO report as factors relevant to evaluating the effectiveness of those who govern, including the audit committee. Specifically, we believe factors such as the following should be considered for inclusion:

- Courage, willingness and ability to raise, scrutinize, and pursue difficult questions with both management and the auditor;
- Focus on areas of higher business or corporate governance risk;
- Understanding of critical accounting policies and highly subjective and judgmental accounting estimates; and
- Direct and independent interaction with key members of financial management, including the chief financial officer and the chief accounting officer.

However, by suggesting these factors, our intent is not to create a "checklist" approach for evaluating the effectiveness of those who govern. In this regard, we recommend that the standard clearly indicate that the auditor, while required to consider these factors, is not required to separately conclude on the audit committee's effectiveness with regard to each and every factor.

Safeguarding of Assets

We appreciate the Board's efforts in Appendix C of the proposed standard to clarify which controls are covered by the definition of safeguarding of assets. However, we do not believe the guidance in Appendix C is sufficient to answer the many questions that we see in practice regarding which controls relate to safeguarding of assets in a financial reporting context. For example, it is not clear what the Board's views are with respect to whether controls related to disaster recovery procedures, or controls designed to prevent unauthorized use of intellectual property (software, music, etc.), would be considered safeguarding of assets in a financial reporting context and therefore would require management and the auditor to evaluate their design and operating effectiveness. Such controls typically would have no direct impact on whether the historical financial statements are fairly stated. Accordingly, we do not believe that such controls should be included in the definition of safeguarding of assets for purposes of the proposed standard.

We believe Appendix C should be expanded to address these and other situations in order to avoid confusion as to what is intended by the definition of safeguarding of assets. This is particularly important because the effort to test many of the controls that might possibly be considered as relating to safeguarding of assets would be significant. Furthermore, depending on the final definition of safeguarding, such testing might require skill sets different from those normally encompassed by auditors' professional training and experience.

We also believe the existing definitions of internal control deficiencies, significant deficiencies, and material weaknesses may need to be revisited, once the scope of safeguarding of assets is better defined. These definitions are currently in the context of a potential "misstatement" in the financial statements. Deficiencies in areas such as those mentioned above, however, would not typically result in the risk of "misstatement" of the financial statements.

Multi-location Testing Considerations

We believe the guidance in Appendix B on multi-location testing considerations provides the auditor with a useful framework for exercising the considerable judgment needed to effectively plan an audit of internal control involving multiple locations or business units. We believe that auditors will require implementation guidance for situations where a company has many locations or business units (e.g., hundreds of retail stores or hotels) that are of approximately the same size, no one of which is relatively more financially significant than another. For example, guidance permitting the auditor to use some form of sampling in this type of situation may be appropriate.

Walkthroughs

We believe independent walkthroughs are an important part of the auditor's evaluation of the design effectiveness of controls and we support the PCAOB's requirement that the auditor perform walkthroughs of significant processes. We also believe that the objectives of walkthroughs set forth in paragraph 79 of the proposed standard are sufficient to make walkthroughs required procedures. Further, we believe the auditor should perform walkthroughs himself or herself rather than using walkthrough procedures performed by management, internal auditors, or others. To conclude on design effectiveness, it is essential for the auditor to develop his or her own point of view about risks and controls within significant processes. This is effectively accomplished by performing walkthroughs.

In our view, the requirement that the auditor "should trace *all* types of transactions and events, both recurring and unusual, from origination through the company's information systems until they are reflected in the company's financial reports" is excessive and inappropriately constrains the auditor's use of professional judgment. For example, a literal reading of this sentence could result in an auditor of a large multinational company performing hundreds of walkthroughs encompassing immaterial transactions and events at business units or locations that are immaterial individually and in the aggregate. We believe such a requirement is also inconsistent with the proposed standard's thrust—which we strongly support—of driving the auditor's efforts to those areas that the auditor judges to be important (e.g., significant accounts and disclosures, significant processes, important locations, etc.).

We do not believe the concept of significant processes that appears in paragraph 79 is consistent with that in paragraph 69. Paragraph 69 states that "the auditor should identify each significant process over each major class of transactions affecting significant accounts or groups of accounts." We recommend that this important point be incorporated in paragraph 79 to emphasize that the auditor's consideration of significant processes is solely in the context of major classes of transactions affecting significant accounts or groups of accounts and disclosures.

Use of the Work of Others

We believe that it is appropriate to consider the work of others in certain circumstances. We agree that the auditor's use of others' work must be subject to the auditor's overall conclusion, using professional judgment, that his or her own work provides the "principal" evidence for the auditor's opinion. We believe the proposed standard should clearly state that the auditor's judgment with regard to "principal evidence" is qualitative and not subject to quantitative measurements. For example, the auditor's determination of principal evidence might appropriately give greater weight to some areas of work performed by the auditor (e.g., the control environment) than to other areas (e.g., controls over routine processing of significant accounts and disclosures).

We agree generally with the three categories that the Board has outlined. However, we believe that the auditor should not be automatically precluded from using the results of testing performed by management and others of information technology general computer controls. Companies generally recognize the importance of information technology general computer controls and many (particularly in the financial services industry) have large and sophisticated internal audit functions that perform extensive testing of such controls. We believe the auditor's ability to obtain the principal evidence to support the opinion on internal control will not be adversely affected by permitting the auditor to use some of the testing performed by management. Accordingly, we recommend these controls be regarded as an area where auditors may make limited use of work performed by management and others, where appropriate.

We believe it would be highly unusual for the auditor's own work to provide the principal evidence required for the auditor's opinion without the auditor performing at least some independent testing of controls over routine processing of significant accounts and disclosures included in the third category.

Extent of Management's Testing

We believe the proposed standard provides useful guidance to the auditor in determining the nature, timing, and extent of testing to perform in evaluating design and operating effectiveness. However, similar guidance does not exist with respect to the required testing by management. As a result, many registrants do not have a consistent view of the extent of testing that is required for management to have sufficient evidence to provide a basis for its assertion. As a general rule, we believe that management's testing should be at a level that is at least equivalent to the level of testing generally expected of the auditor. We recommend that the PCAOB work with the SEC to provide management with appropriate guidance to ensure that management's testing is adequate and at least at a level reasonably consistent with that performed by the auditor.

We also believe that paragraph 126 of the proposed standard should be revised to add the following to the list of circumstances that are considered significant deficiencies and strong indicators of a material weakness: "The lack of sufficient evidence to support the management assertion regarding the operating effectiveness of internal control."

Evaluation of Internal Control for Small and Medium-Sized Companies

We believe that there should be no significant difference in the standard's requirements for small companies, other than to acknowledge the potential for a less formal internal control structure. While we agree that a small company will likely have less complex processes and, therefore, less complex controls, the same basic internal control tenets apply equally to all companies. The standard can provide only general guidance that auditors must then apply—using their professional judgment—to the facts and circumstances of a specific audit, only one of which is the company's size. While such facts and circumstances differ from company to company and affect the auditor's approach to gaining evidence, the auditor's need to obtain sufficient evidence to support his or her opinion is unchanged. Accordingly, we believe it is inappropriate for auditing standards to set forth different expectations for auditor performance based on the entity's size. Rather, standards should be written so that auditors can apply them in a flexible manner that appropriately recognizes each entity as unique.

Evaluation of Management's Assessment

We recognize that one of the issues faced by the Board in developing the proposed standard was whether the auditor's conclusion should relate to the effectiveness of a company's internal control over financial reporting or, alternatively, relate solely to the company's assessment process under Section 404. Both in the United States and globally, many organizations, companies, and auditors (including one of our territorial firms) have differing views on this subject. Some believe that Congress' intent in Section 404 was to have the auditor report on the effectiveness of internal control rather than on management's assessment process. Others believe—for various environmental, legal, and commercial reasons—that the auditor should report only on management's assessment process. While recognizing this honest divergence of opinions, we nevertheless strongly support the proposed standard's conclusion that, to best serve the public interest, the auditor's opinion must run directly to the effectiveness of internal control over financial reporting. We believe the auditor's independent audit of internal control effectiveness meets the intent of the Act.

To ensure clarity around this point and to eliminate confusion on the part of users, we believe the auditor should report in all cases directly on the effectiveness of the company's internal control over financial reporting rather than on management's assertion. Accordingly, the auditor's unqualified opinions in Report Examples A-1 and A-6 should run directly to the effectiveness of internal control. Consistent with these views, we agree with the proposed standard's requirement that the auditor report directly on effectiveness rather than on management's assertion when the auditor issues other than an unqualified opinion.

* * * * *

We appreciate the opportunity to express our views and would be pleased to discuss our comments or answer any questions the staff may have. Please do not hesitate to contact Ray Bromark (973-236-7781), Gary Stauffer (973-236-5419), or Jim Lee (973-236-4478) regarding our submission.

Sincerely,

PricewaterhouseCoopers LLP

This attachment includes:

- Comments on the impact of the proposed standard on other auditing standards,
- Responses to the specific questions presented in the proposed standard, and
- Other comments related to specific paragraphs in the proposed standard.

Comments on the Impact of the Proposed Standard on Other Auditing Standards

The proposed standard modifies guidance in the PCAOB's interim standards in several areas beyond AT Section 501. For example, paragraph 141 states that "the auditor's substantive procedures must include reconciling the financial statements to the accounting records." While we support this requirement, it and others, particularly in the section, "Effect of Tests of Controls on Substantive Procedures," would appear to go beyond existing auditing standards.

In such cases, we believe the PCAOB should identify and communicate how requirements in a proposed standard diverge from existing requirements and how issuance of the standard would affect existing standards.

As the PCAOB issues new standards or modifies its interim standards, we believe a formal process should be put in place to communicate in a clear and direct manner any changes to existing standards.

We also note the "Statement of Authority" preceding the proposed standard as it relates to the Board's proposed Rule 3101 regarding the use of certain terms in the Board's standards. We interpret the discussion as requiring adherence to the Board's proposed rule on use of certain terms, including its additional documentation requirements, in connection with the audit of internal control under this proposed standard. We believe this is inappropriate and suggest that its application to this standard await issuance of the final standard on use of terms.

Responses to Specific Questions Presented in the Proposed Standard

Questions regarding an integrated audit of the financial statements and internal control over financial reporting:

1. Is it appropriate to refer to the auditor's attestation of management's assessment of the effectiveness of internal control over financial reporting as the audit of internal control over financial reporting?

Yes, we believe it is appropriate to refer to the auditor's attestation of management's assertion on the effectiveness of internal control over financial reporting as the audit of internal control over financial reporting.

2. Should the auditor be prohibited from performing an audit of internal control over financial reporting without also performing an audit of the financial statements?

Yes, the auditor should be prohibited from performing an audit of internal control over financial reporting, as required by Section 404 of the Act, without also performing an audit of the financial statements. In our view, only an integrated audit performed by the company's independent auditor can achieve the desired improvement in financial reporting effectively and efficiently.

3. Rather than requiring the auditor to also complete an audit of the financial statements, would an appropriate alternative be to require the auditor to perform work with regard to the financial statements *comparable* to that required to complete the financial statement audit?

No. Requiring the auditor to perform work with regard to the financial statements comparable to that required to complete the financial statement audit is not an appropriate alternative to performing a financial statement audit.

Question regarding the costs and benefits of internal control:

4. Does the Board's proposed standard give appropriate consideration to how internal control is implemented in, and how the audit of internal control over financial reporting should be conducted at, small and medium-sized issuers?

See our separate comments on the evaluation of internal control for small and medium-sized companies in our comment letter.

Question regarding the audit of internal control over financial reporting:

5. Should the Board, generally or in this proposed standard, specify the level of competence and training of the audit personnel that is necessary to perform specified auditing procedures effectively? For example, it would be inappropriate for a new, inexperienced auditor to have primary responsibility for conducting interviews of a company's senior management about possible fraud.

We agree that competence and proper training of audit personnel are essential for the performance of effective audits. However, we believe the existing auditing standards (*PCAOB Interim Professional Standards*, AU Section 150) provide sufficient general guidance and the Board should not in this standard attempt to specify the level of competence and training of the audit personnel necessary to perform specific auditing procedures effectively. Any general consideration of auditor competence and training should be done as part of the Board's review of its interim standards. While such review could encompass this issue, we believe that auditors—at an engagement level—require flexibility in determining the appropriate staff to perform different aspects of the audit work.

Questions regarding evaluation of management's assessment:

6. Is the scope of the audit appropriate in that it requires the auditor to both evaluate management's assessment and obtain, directly, evidence about whether internal control over financial reporting is effective?

See our separate comments on evaluation of management's assessment in our comment letter.

7. Is it appropriate that the Board has provided criteria that auditors should use to evaluate the adequacy of management's documentation?

Yes, it is appropriate for the Board to provide criteria that auditors should use to evaluate the adequacy of management's documentation. Comparable to the auditor's documentation, management's documentation is the principal record of the assessment procedures applied, evidence obtained, and conclusions reached by management as to the effectiveness of the company's internal control. Criteria for evaluating the adequacy of management's documentation provide a useful frame of reference, benefiting both auditors and management.

We believe the Board needs to clarify paragraph B-3 of the proposed standard with regard to documentation of controls where the company has multiple locations or business units. For example, does the guidance in paragraph B-3 mean that management would not be required to have controls documented at locations or business units that are not able to create, either individually or in the aggregate, a material misstatement? We believe management should have at least a minimum level of documentation of controls at these locations consistent with the requirement that registrants must maintain adequate books and records.

We believe more guidance is needed also in the area of documentation of locations or business units that individually are insignificant but when aggregated could result in a material misstatement. For these locations, we believe management should be required to document controls over relevant assertions relating to significant accounts at the consolidated financial statement level. Without appropriate documentation, we do not believe management could demonstrate adequate company-level controls since documentation of controls is a foundation of company-level controls.

Further, as part of providing criteria that auditors should use to evaluate the adequacy of management's documentation, we believe that the Board and the SEC should provide guidance on management's retention of documentation as well as the auditor's retention of management's documentation of the entity's systems and controls.

8. Is it appropriate to state that inadequate documentation is an internal control deficiency, the severity of which the auditor should evaluate? Or should inadequate documentation automatically rise to the level of significant deficiency or material weakness in internal control?

It is appropriate to state that inadequate documentation is an internal control deficiency, the severity of which the auditor should evaluate. We do not believe that inadequate documentation would automatically rise to the level of a significant deficiency or material weakness in internal control.

We believe the severity of the inadequate documentation should be evaluated by the auditor and, based on his or her professional judgment, appropriately categorized as an internal control deficiency, a significant deficiency, or a material weakness. Every situation will be different and will require its own evaluation and conclusion.

We recommend that the last sentence in paragraph 46 be revised to more clearly communicate what we believe to be the intended meaning—that the monitoring component of internal control cannot be demonstrated in the absence of sufficient evidence to support management's assertion. Alternatively, if the Board believes that there are ways in which management can demonstrate the monitoring component in the absence of documentation of controls, we believe there needs to be clarification around this statement and examples of how management would do this.

9. Are the objectives to be achieved by performing walkthroughs sufficient to require the performance of walkthroughs?

See separate discussion of walkthroughs in our comment letter.

10. Is it appropriate to require that the walkthrough be performed by the auditor himself or herself, rather than allowing the auditor to use walkthrough procedures performed by management, internal auditors, or others?

See separate discussion of walkthroughs in our comment letter.

Question regarding testing operating effectiveness:

11. Is it appropriate to require the auditor to obtain evidence of the effectiveness of controls for all relevant assertions for all significant accounts and disclosures every year or may the auditor use some of the audit evidence obtained in previous years to support his or her current opinion on management's assessment?

We believe that it is appropriate to require the auditor to obtain evidence of the effectiveness of controls for all relevant assertions for significant accounts and disclosures every year. Reliance on prior year work is inappropriate. However, we believe the source of the evidence (direct or indirect) and the nature, timing, and extent can vary from year to year.

In the case of automated application controls, where the auditor believes that controls are unchanged, evidence of the lack of change and the continued operating effectiveness can come from annual walkthroughs of major transactions within significant processes, along with testing of IT general computer controls annually.

We believe that paragraph 101 of the proposed standard should be revised to clarify that each year's audit of internal control must stand on its own and encompass not just all internal control components but all relevant assertions for all significant accounts and disclosures.

Questions regarding using the work of management and others:

12. To what extent should the auditor be permitted or required to use the work of management and others?

The auditor should be permitted—but not required—to use the work of management and others. The auditor should evaluate the competence and objectivity of those performing the work and apply professional judgment to determine how the work of management and others affects the nature, timing, and extent of the auditor's own procedures, underpinned by the requirement that the auditor's opinion be based principally on evidence that the auditor has independently obtained.

13. Are the three categories of controls and the extent to which the auditor may rely on the work of others appropriately defined?

See separate discussion on use of the work of others in our comment letter.

14. Does the proposed standard give appropriate recognition to the work of internal auditors? If not, does the proposed standard place too much emphasis and preference on the work of internal auditors or not enough?

We believe the proposed standard gives appropriate recognition to the work of internal auditors. As outlined in the proposed standard, the auditor should assess internal audit's objectivity and competence using the same criteria as for the objectivity and competence of management and others when determining the level of use of their work.

15. Is the flexibility in determining the extent of reperformance of the work of others appropriate, or should the auditor be specifically required to reperform a certain level of work (for example, reperform tests of all significant accounts or reperform every test performed by others that the auditor intends to use)?

We believe that the judgment contemplated in the proposed standard with regard to the level of reperformance when using the work of others is appropriate.

16. Is the requirement for the auditor to obtain the principal evidence, on an overall basis, through his or her own work the appropriate benchmark for the amount of work that is required to be performed by the auditor?

Yes. Recognizing that this determination must necessarily be based on the auditor's qualitative judgments and not quantitative measures, we believe that the standard of principal evidence is the appropriate benchmark for the amount of work required to be performed by the auditor.

Questions regarding evaluating results:

17. Will the definitions in the proposed standard of significant deficiency and material weakness provide for increased consistency in the evaluation of deficiencies? How can the definitions be improved?

See our separate comments on internal control deficiencies in our comment letter.

18. Do the examples in Appendix D of how to apply these definitions in various scenarios provide helpful guidance? Are there other specific examples that commenters could suggest that would provide further interpretive help?

See our separate comments on internal control deficiencies in our comment letter.

19. Is it necessary for the auditor to evaluate the severity of all identified internal control deficiencies?

Yes.   We believe that it is necessary for the auditor to evaluate the significance of all identified internal control deficiencies. Without performing an evaluation, auditors would have no basis for determining whether an item was of "inconsequential" magnitude or "remote likelihood," or alternatively rose to the level of a significant deficiency or material weakness. We also believe that it is essential for management to develop a similar process to evaluate all identified internal control deficiencies. In our view, management and auditors would benefit from additional guidance and examples, as discussed in our comment letter.

20. Is it appropriate to require the auditor to communicate all internal control deficiencies (not just material weaknesses and significant deficiencies) to management in writing?

Yes. We believe it is appropriate for the auditor to communicate to management all internal control deficiencies he or she has identified. Documentation and communication of this identification and evaluation process are necessary and will contribute to consistency on engagements and also provide a formal mechanism for management to address and respond to identified deficiencies. However, we believe the requirement in paragraph 191 of the proposed standard for the auditor's communication to also include or refer to deficiencies identified by internal audit and others is inappropriate. We believe it is management's responsibility to ensure they receive such communications.

21. Are the matters that the Board has classified as strong indicators that a material weakness in internal control exists appropriately classified as such?

We believe the guidance in paragraph 126 regarding circumstances that are strong indicators of a material weakness in internal control over financial reporting is useful to both management and the auditor. We do, however, have several points on the specific circumstances cited:

- We believe that the absence of sufficient evidence to support the responsible party's evaluation of the operating effectiveness of internal control is a strong indicator of a material weakness and should be added to the list in paragraph 126 and deleted from paragraph 125.

- Consistent with our views expressed in our comment letter, we believe that an ineffective control environment should be added to paragraph 126.

- As stated in the Board's interim standard, AU Section 317, auditors are responsible to consider laws and regulations that have a *direct and material* effect on the determination of financial statement amounts. While we agree an ineffective regulatory compliance function may result in a direct and material misstatement in the financial statements (e.g., noncompliance with tax laws affecting the determination of financial statement amounts) and therefore be encompassed within internal control over financial reporting, there are many aspects of regulatory compliance that by themselves may be ineffective but would not affect the financial statements, or would affect them only indirectly (e.g., contingent liabilities for violations of environmental laws and regulations). Accordingly, we believe it is inappropriate to specify the entire regulatory compliance function. This gives the erroneous impression that regulatory compliance (encompassing laws and regulations related to areas such as securities trading, occupational safety and health, food and drug administration, environmental protection, equal employment, price fixing, and antitrust) is entirely within the definition of internal control over financial reporting and within the auditor's expertise to evaluate. We believe the fifth bullet in paragraph 126 should be deleted or, at a minimum, modified to make it clear that it is limited to situations where the ineffective regulatory function relates solely to those aspects where related violations of laws and regulations could have a direct and material effect on the financial statements.

- While we agree fraud on the part of senior management is a serious issue, we do not believe it is the responsibility of the auditor to identify fraud of any magnitude. We also do not believe that fraud of any magnitude would necessarily constitute a significant deficiency or a material weakness, particularly in situations where the company's controls uncovered the issue. Further, we do not believe that the auditor should be required to identify issues that occur outside the company's environment, such as an individual's filing a false tax return.

22. Is it appropriate to require the auditors to evaluate the effectiveness of the audit committee's oversight of the company's external financial reporting and internal control over financial reporting?

See our separate comments on the evaluation of the effectiveness of the audit committee in our comment letter.

We note that the proposed standard would require the auditor to evaluate factors related to the effectiveness of the audit committee's oversight of the company's external financial reporting and internal control over financial reporting, including, among other factors, the independence of the audit committee members from management. Paragraph 58 of the proposed standard states that as part of evaluating the independence of audit committee members, the auditor should evaluate how audit committee members are nominated and selected and whether they act independently from management. The SEC release implementing Section 301 of the Act contains certain exemptions with respect to independence requirements for foreign private issuers. Accordingly, to be consistent with the provisions of the SEC rules implementing Section 301 of the Act, we believe that the exemptions granted to foreign private issuers should be considered in the auditor's evaluation of the independence of committee members.

23. Will auditors be able to effectively carry out their responsibility to evaluate the effectiveness of the audit committee's oversight?

See our separate comments on the evaluation of the effectiveness of the audit committee in our comment letter.

24. If the auditor concludes that ineffective audit committee oversight is a material weakness, rather than require the auditor to issue an adverse opinion with regard to the effectiveness of the internal control over financial reporting, should the standard require the auditor to withdraw from the audit engagement?

We believe the existence of a specific material weakness should not automatically result in the auditor's resignation. The existence of an ineffective audit committee, coupled with a mandate for auditor resignation, clearly would not be in the public's interest. Rather, auditors should be able to make this decision, as they do now, based on all the facts and circumstances of the engagement.

Questions regarding forming an opinion and reporting:

25. Is it appropriate that the existence of a material weakness would require the auditor to express an adverse conclusion about the effectiveness of the company's internal control over financial reporting, consistent with the required reporting model for management?

See our separate comments on reporting by the auditor in our comment letter.

26. Are there circumstances where a qualified "except for" conclusion would be appropriate?

See our separate comments on reporting by the auditor in our comment letter.

27. Do you agree with the position that when the auditor issues a nonstandard opinion, such as an adverse opinion, that the auditor's opinion should speak directly to the effectiveness of the internal control over financial reporting rather than to whether management's assessment is fairly stated?

See our separate comments on reporting by the auditor in our comment letter.

Questions regarding auditor independence:

28. Should the Board provide specific guidance on independence and internal control-related non-audit services in the context of this proposed standard?

We believe that adequate guidance is contained within the independence rules issued by the SEC.

29. Are there any specific internal control-related non-audit services the auditor should be prohibited from providing to an audit client?

We believe the existing independence requirements that were adopted by the SEC in February 2003 are appropriate and should be given sufficient time to operate.

Questions regarding auditor's responsibilities with regard to management's certifications:

30. Are the auditor's differing levels of responsibility as they relate to management's quarterly certifications versus the annual (fourth quarter) certification, appropriate?

We believe it is appropriate to have a differing level of responsibility as it relates to the fourth quarter certification.

31. Is the scope of the auditor's responsibility for quarterly disclosures about the internal control over financial reporting appropriate?

We agree that inquiry coupled with observation are the appropriate procedures to perform for internal control over financial reporting for quarterly disclosures. We also believe that the Board should clarify that these procedures are not an adequate basis for reporting and that it was not envisioned that the auditor would be permitted to report on internal control over financial reporting on a quarterly basis.

We are concerned that paragraphs 8 and 9 of the proposed standard may imply that the auditor is required to identify deficiencies that could result in a misstatement in interim financial statements. We do not believe that the auditor should be required to plan his or her audit of internal control at a materiality level of the interim financial statements.

To conform the wording to that relating to management in the SEC's final 404 rule, we recommend that the existing language in the second bullet of paragraph 186 be changed to: "Determine, through a combination of observation and inquiry, whether any change in internal control over financial reporting has materially affected, or is reasonably likely to materially affect, the company's internal control over financial reporting."

We believe the auditor evaluation responsibilities described in paragraphs 185 through 189 should not be required until the first quarter after the company's issuance of its first annual 404 report.

Other Comments Relating to Specific Paragraphs in the Proposed Standard

Paragraph 21 – In our view, this paragraph intermingles—and is likely to cause confusion with regard to—several important concepts: planning materiality vs. materiality in evaluating internal control deficiencies; materiality at a financial statement level vs. materiality at an account-balance level; and significant deficiencies vs. material weaknesses. Specifically:

- We believe the concept of materiality at an account-balance level is more relevant to planning materiality than to an evaluation of deficiencies, as the paragraph seems to imply. The auditor must plan the audit to obtain reasonable assurance that deficiencies that, individually or in the aggregate, would represent material weaknesses are identified. In doing so, the auditor must appropriately plan his or her other work at an account-balance level.

- The auditor evaluates deficiencies at the overall financial statement level, not at the account-balance level, as the paragraph seems to imply. Deficiencies at an overall financial statement level, e.g., deficiencies in a particular facet of the control environment, may be significant deficiencies or rise to the level of material weaknesses. Similarly, an internal control deficiency present at an account-balance level may be a significant deficiency or rise to a material weakness, again when evaluated at the financial statement level, not at the account-balance level, as the proposed standard presently implies.

We recommend that the Board re-examine and clarify the important concepts in this paragraph.

Paragraph 24 – We recommend that the first bullet be changed from "controls restraining the inappropriate use of company assets" to "controls restraining misappropriation of assets that could result in a material misstatement." This would tie the statement to the definitions and guidance in the existing standard on fraud as well as eliminate overly subjective judgments as to what might be considered "inappropriate."

Paragraph 41 – We believe the second bullet should address magnitude as well as likelihood.

Paragraph 78 – We recommend including additional guidance on the extent to which redundant controls need to be tested, along with specific examples of those controls that the auditor would be expected to test because "redundancy is itself a control objective, as in the case of certain computer controls."

Paragraph 112 – The last sentence states, "A conclusion that an identified exception does not represent an internal control deficiency is appropriate only if evidence beyond what the auditor had initially planned and beyond inquiry supports that conclusion." We believe that auditors would benefit from additional guidance. We agree that the auditor should obtain evidence regarding the underlying reason for and implications of any exception. However, we do not believe that the existence of one or more exceptions would necessarily require the auditor to increase the number of items tested if the number of exceptions was within an acceptable range that would allow the auditor to conclude that the control was operating effectively.

Paragraph 114 – In our view, this paragraph is also overly prescriptive in requiring that the auditor review all reports issued during the year by internal audit. This inappropriately restricts the auditor's use of professional judgment and will potentially lead to inefficiencies. For example, in a multilocation audit this would require auditors to review internal audit reports for numerous locations that—even when aggregated—could not be material. Also, companies should have controls in place to assess all deficiencies identified by internal auditors, and the auditor should be allowed to make appropriate use of such work, without being required to directly review all reports.

Paragraph 128 – As presently written, item d. requires management in its representation letter to state only that it has disclosed to the auditor "all significant deficiencies … that it believes to be material weaknesses." We believe management's communication responsibilities to the auditor should be comparable to those of the auditor to management. Accordingly, in addition to material weaknesses, management's required communications should encompass inconsequential deficiencies as well as significant deficiencies that, in management's judgment, do not rise to the level of material weaknesses.

¶ 637. Protiviti

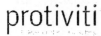

November 21, 2003

Office of the Secretary
PCAOB
1666 K Street, N.W.
Washington, D.C. 20006-2803

Dear Mr. Secretary:

Re: <u>PCAOB Rulemaking Docket Matter No. 008</u>: Comments on
     **Proposed Auditing Standard – An Audit of Internal Control
     Over Financial Reporting Performed in Conjunction with an
     Audit of Financial Statements**

We respectfully submit our comments on the PCAOB's proposed standard on auditing
internal control over financial reporting as part of an integrated audit. We have focused our
comments on several, rather than all, of the PCAOB's questions below. We have numbered
the questions according to the numbering scheme in the PCAOB's Release No. 2003-017
dated October 7, 2003.

**10. Is it appropriate to require that the auditor perform a walkthrough himself or
     herself, rather than allowing the auditor to use walkthrough procedures performed
     by management, internal auditors, or others?**

No. The auditor should be allowed to rely on competent and objective internal auditors
(or other similar parties, such as a separate process or risk control group which does not
have the responsibility for executing processes) in the performance of walkthroughs that
are effectively documented, provided the auditor is able to satisfy himself or herself
about the adequacy of this work through appropriate procedures.

If the PCAOB (hereinafter sometimes referred to as the "Board") does not concur with
this view, then at a minimum the Board should clarify that, for purposes of performing a
walkthrough, the auditor may rely on documentation (process maps, process narratives,
etc.) prepared by the audit client. As a practical matter, the Section 404 compliance
teams for many companies, as well as their internal auditors, are documenting
walkthroughs as a basis for understanding internal control over financial reporting,
including the process flow of transactions, the completeness of the design of controls
within the processes and whether and how the controls really operate – the same
objective as that of the external auditor. The external auditor should be able to rely on
this documentation and use it when reviewing documents that are used in, and that
result from, the application of the controls, and comparing supporting documents to the
accounting records.

protiviti

Office of the Secretary
PCAOB
1666 K Street, N.W.
Washington, D.C. 20006-2803

13. Are the three categories of controls and the extent to which the auditor may rely on the work of others appropriately defined?

Generally, if the intent is to prescribe the nature and extent of auditor reliance, the three categories of controls provide an effective framework for articulating the extent of reliance (however, please see our comment on Question 14 regarding the commingling of internal audit into the definition of "others"). Within the "no reliance" category, however, the proposed standard includes such pervasive controls as "certain information technology general controls on which the operating effectiveness of other controls depend." We do not understand the rationale for this conclusion. We recommend that the Board clarify the nature of these "certain" controls and reconsider specifically which controls should be included in the "no reliance" category.

General IT processes are expansive in scope. They include, among other things: security administration, application change controls and data management and disaster recovery. We recommend the Board clarify the nature of the "certain information technology general controls" to which it refers in the proposed standard.

We suggest the Board also reconsider its position on general IT controls and include general IT controls in the second category of reliance, i.e., "controls for which there may be limited reliance." IT general controls are not "soft controls" subject to a significant amount of judgment in evaluation. While the Board is correct that they are pervasive in scope and can impact the effectiveness of other controls, general IT controls are effected through processes that function just like revenue, purchasing and other routine processes, and are subject to similar kinds of testing. For example, general IT controls ordinarily address the critical IT processes within each entity or for each key location that supports significant financial applications. In certain circumstances, the same general controls area must be reviewed more than once. If there are multiple processes impacting each priority financial reporting area that are not subject to similar policies, process activities and control procedures, these multiple processes may need to be separately reviewed. Many of these control areas consist of controls that are subject to reperformance by the external auditor. Thus we recommend that general IT controls be included in the second category of reliance.

14. Does the proposed standard give appropriate recognition to the work of internal auditors? If not, does the proposed standard place too much emphasis and preference on the work of internal auditors or not enough?

We do not believe that the proposed standard gives sufficient recognition to or enough emphasis on the work of internal auditors in applying the Board's proposed "three categories" construct. The Board should consider differentiating between the work of competent and objective internal auditors (or other similar parties) and the work of process or control owners who execute the processes and document management's assertion in the internal control report. As companies experiment with ways to structure their organizations

protiviti

Office of the Secretary
PCAOB
1666 K Street, N.W.
Washington, D.C. 20006-2803

to accomplish the Sarbanes-Oxley certification objectives, the Board's standards should be flexible enough to recognize that internal audit or similar parties, such as a separate process or risk control group, may be capable of providing a reliable basis for conclusions.

We recommend that the Board separately evaluate the three categories of reliance against two groups – (i) management and others, excluding internal audit (or other similar parties), and (ii) internal audit (or other similar parties). We believe that there are some areas within the three categories that might be viewed differently between these two groups. For example, if competent and objective internal auditors (or other similar parties) test the general IT controls, as discussed above under Question 13, the auditor should be able to place at least limited reliance on that work.

16. Is the requirement for the auditor to obtain the principle evidence, on an overall basis, through his or her own work the appropriate benchmark for the amount of work that is required to be performed by the auditor?

No. This requirement has the potential to severely limit the extent of the auditor's reliance, regardless of the Board's guidance with respect to the "three categories", the effectiveness of the internal control structure and the nature, extent and timing of management's work and documentation supporting the conclusion expressed in the internal control report. Because the "three categories" already place a limit on the extent of reliance, the Board should evaluate whether this statement is really needed. If the PCAOB concludes the statement should be retained in the final standard, the Board should clarify how the statement is applied in view of the guidance it already provides with respect to the "three categories".

21. Are the matters that the Board has classified as strong indicators that a material weakness in internal control exists appropriately classified as such?

In the list of circumstances that should be regarded as at least a significant deficiency and as a strong indicator of a material weakness, the proposed standard included a reference to "an ineffective regulatory compliance function" in highly regulated industries. We agree that this type of deficiency can be troublesome. However, does the reference to this type of deficiency suggest that documentary evidence is required to support an assertion that such a deficiency does not exist? We cannot find any guidance in the proposed standard where this question is addressed. Because this is a potentially broad audit area, we recommend that the Board clarify the nature, extent and timing of work needed to address it.

If the standard is intended to require additional work, the question arises as to whether such a requirement extends beyond the coverage intended by the SEC's final rule on Section 404. Note that in its final rule, the SEC states "our definition [of internal control over financial reporting] does not encompass the elements of the COSO Report definition that relate to effectiveness and efficiency of a company's operations and a company's compliance with applicable laws and regulations, with the exception of

protiviti

Office of the Secretary
PCAOB
1666 K Street, N.W.
Washington, D.C. 20006-2803

compliance with the applicable laws and regulations directly related to the preparation of financial statements, such as the Commission's financial reporting requirements."

We suggest that the Board clarify its intentions on this point.

22. Is it appropriate to require the auditors to evaluate the effectiveness of the audit committee's oversight of the company's external financial reporting and internal control over financial reporting?

We believe that the board of directors is ultimately responsible for evaluating audit committee effectiveness using the criteria set forth in the proposed standard. The external auditor, who is hired by the audit committee, is not in the best position to make the call as to the committee's effectiveness and would have a difficult (if not impossible) challenge to do so while retaining a position of independence both in fact and appearance. We agree that an ineffective audit committee adversely affects an evaluation of internal control over financial reporting. However, under Section 301 of The Sarbanes-Oxley Act, an audit committee has direct responsibility to hire, fire, compensate and evaluate the auditors. In addition, the auditor is not always present during committee meetings and deliberations.

If the PCAOB decides to retain this requirement, the question arises as to how auditors are required to satisfy themselves that a company's audit committee is providing effective oversight of external financial reporting and internal control over financial reporting? Are the criteria provided by the proposed standard of certain legal and regulatory requirements and certain qualitative factors adequate? What procedures will the auditor need to perform? What are the implications of those procedures in terms of requiring auditor access to audit committee deliberations and interfaces with management and others in situations in which the auditor is not always present? What is an appropriate level of involvement and interaction by the Committee? How does the auditor determine whether audit committee members "act independently from management?" Clarity is needed for these questions not only for auditors but also for audit committees and management so they will better understand what to expect from the audit process.

28. Should the Board provide specific guidance on independence and internal control-related non-audit services in the context of this proposed standard?

Yes. We recommend that the Board provide specific guidance on independence in the context of this proposed standard. In our experience, there continues to be divergent views between public companies and between and within the accounting firms themselves as to the nature and scope of internal control-related services a company's external auditors can provide. For example, we see different approaches being taken in similar circumstances where, on the one hand, companies hire their external auditors to document their internal controls and, on the other hand, companies decide not to engage their auditors to do this work on the basis that such action could present independence in appearance issues. We also see instances where some external audit

protiviti

Office of the Secretary
PCAOB
1666 K Street, N.W.
Washington, D.C. 20006-2803

firms have taken similar public positions to not engage in this work for the same reasons. It is therefore an issue where reasonable men and women can differ. While specificity exists regarding the prohibited services associated with financial statement audits, no such list has been addressed with respect to reporting on internal controls since the issuance of the new Section 404 reporting requirement. Some degree of granularity, similar to the list of ten prohibited non-audit services in conjunction with the audit of financial statements, would enable boards and audit committees to better comply and avoid public misconceptions regarding auditor independence.

We have attached to this letter an excerpt from our frequently asked questions publication, released in August, which includes a question on the internal controls documentation matter. We also point out to the Board that there are other issues besides documentation that the Board should provide guidance on with respect to independence and internal control-related non-audit services in the context of the proposed standard.

We appreciate the opportunity to submit our comments. We hope they are helpful to the staff. If the staff would like to discuss any of the points made in this letter, please contact Jim DeLoach at (713) 314-4981.

Very truly yours,

PROTIVITI INC.

James DeLoach

By: James W. DeLoach, Jr.
      Managing Director

ATTACHMENT

protiviti

Office of the Secretary
PCAOB
1666 K Street, N.W.
Washington, D.C. 20006-2803

ATTACHMENT

**Excerpt from *Guide to the Sarbanes-Oxley Act: Internal
Control Reporting Requirements* -- QUESTION 150**

**Can the company engage the independent public accountant to create original
documentation of its internal control over financial reporting without impairing
independence?**

The safe answer in today's environment is probably not. According to Rule 2.01 of
Regulation S-X of the SEC, the external auditor must be independent both in fact and in
appearance. While the standards have not been promulgated by which the external
auditor will be required to attest, significant involvement in the documentation of a
company's internal control structure, followed by an attestation process in which the
same documentation is reviewed, would be tantamount to keeping the books and
auditing the books. The SEC's position is that the auditor cannot perform in the role of
management or audit his or her own work.

During its open meeting in May 2003, the SEC made statements to the effect that the
documentation of controls and the evaluation of their effectiveness is indeed a
management function. Therefore, if the auditor has been asked to perform that role
instead of or on behalf of management that would involve the auditor taking on a
management role. Thus the SEC staff pointed out that companies and their auditors
need to be mindful of the independence requirements and determine how involved the
auditor needs to be to understand adequately the controls and what management has
done without having to actually "step into a management role."

The final rules released on June 6, 2003, do not reconcile clearly to the discussion
during the open meeting in May. Specifically, in the open meeting, an absolute
restriction was articulated as a "red light" to prohibit the independent accountant from
documenting internal control over financial reporting for audit clients. The final rules,
however, do not prohibit this practice but instead place limits around this activity and
remind issuers and their auditors to adhere to the independence restrictions.

This development is not a surprise. The SEC has a long-standing practice of allowing
issuers to formulate their own policies with respect to compliance matters. Subsequent
to the open meeting, the SEC staff pointed out to us that nothing said in the open
meeting or included in the final release on Section 404 is intended to change the
independence release or rules, or the appropriate interpretation of those rules. When
formulating company policies in this regard, management and audit committees must
take into account the SEC's oral comments in the open meeting as well as its written
rules. Thus the burden is on management and the audit committee to evaluate the
desirability of engaging the independent accountant in documenting internal control over
financial reporting on behalf of management. In effect, the final rules constitute a "yellow
light" of caution signaling to companies that it would be wise to monitor further SEC and

protiviti

Office of the Secretary
PCAOB
1666 K Street, N.W.
Washington, D.C. 20006-2803

PCAOB developments for additional clarification in what could very well be an evolving area.

In the final rules, the SEC states it understands the need for management and the company's independent auditors to coordinate their respective activities relating to documenting and testing internal control over financial reporting. In stating that understanding, the SEC also issued two reminders to companies and their auditors:

- First, the Commission's rules on auditor independence prohibit an auditor from providing certain nonaudit services to an audit client.

- Second, management cannot delegate its responsibility to assess its internal control over financial reporting to the auditor.

The SEC also made two other points on independence:

- If the auditor is engaged to assist management in documenting internal controls, management must be actively involved in the process.

- Management's acceptance of responsibility for the documentation and testing performed by the auditor does not satisfy the auditor independence rules.

The above views expressed by the SEC raises several points.

- First, documentation of internal control over financial reporting by the independent accountant is implied to constitute a nonaudit service.

- Second, if the auditor performs documentation and testing of internal controls, management cannot simply accept responsibility for that work. This would be tantamount to management accepting responsibility for the results of bookkeeping or other services provided by the auditor related to the company's significant accounting records or financial reporting areas. Management must be actively involved in the documentation process.

- Third, the auditor must exercise care to ensure that he or she does not end up auditing his or her own work or provide a service acting in a management capacity.

- Finally, while there is some ambiguity in the final rules that didn't exist during the SEC's open meeting in May 2003, it appears the overriding message is for management, and the audit committee, to proceed with care when engaging independent accountants to document internal control over financial reporting.

One practical approach to addressing the ambiguity of this issue is to focus on the magnitude of the documentation required to bring a company into compliance. This approach, which has been embraced by one major accounting firm, would prescribe that any situation in which "significant" documentation was necessary should avoid engagement of the external auditor other than in an advisory role. On the other hand, those environments in which minimal additional documentation was necessary might

protiviti

Office of the Secretary
PCAOB
1666 K Street, N.W.
Washington, D.C. 20006-2803

utilize the external auditor to help management identify and finalize the Section 404 documentation.

Sarbanes-Oxley requires management to establish and maintain controls and procedures to ensure all material information is presented to the public in accordance with the SEC's rules and forms, i.e., management is required to design the internal control structure. The documentation issue represents a minefield for boards and management teams because it will forever remain difficult to delineate the difference between documenting the internal control structure and designing the internal control structure. Documenting an internal control structure is similar to "blazing a trail." It requires a decision-tree type approach in which someone must decide each path to achieve an appropriate control structure. The selection of the primary path is a function of the risks that management perceives the company faces. Subsequent decision points will revolve around questions such as:

- What is the proper combination of preventive controls or detective controls?

- Do transaction volume and velocity permit manual controls or must computerized system controls be utilized?

- Within a process, how much segregation of duties is required?

- Are there pervasive controls affecting multiple processes and, if so, what is their impact?

- What is the impact of a centralized versus decentralized organization?

Each of these and other decisions require significant professional judgment. They represent trail markers about which management must make the ultimate determination. If the independent public accountant is asked to blaze and mark the trail and subsequently also determine if the markings are correct, then management, the board and the auditor could be exposed to allegations that independence was impaired. While independence in fact may have been preserved, the appearance of independence would be difficult if not impossible to explain in the public arena. If explanations are subsequently required, the accounting firm could be placed in the position of an advocate for management, a position the SEC rules do not permit. Given today's hypersensitive environment, this issue does not appear to be one in which it is in anyone's interest to test.

¶ 638. Defense Contract Audit Agency (Department of Defense)

DEFENSE CONTRACT AUDIT AGENCY
DEPARTMENT OF DEFENSE
8725 JOHN J. KINGMAN ROAD, SUITE 2135
FORT BELVOIR, VA 22060-6219

OFFICE OF THE DIRECTOR

PAS 730.3.B.2.4   November 21, 2003

Office of the Secretary
Public Company Accounting Oversight Board
1666 K Street, N.W.
Washington, D.C. 20006-2803

SUBJECT: PCAOB Rulemaking Docket No. 008 Proposed Auditing Standard - An Audit
of Internal Control Over Financial Reporting

Members and Staff of the Public Company Accounting Oversight Board (PCAOB):

The Defense Contract Audit Agency (DCAA), under the authority, direction, and control of the Under Secretary of Defense (Comptroller) is responsible for performing all contract audits for the Department of Defense (DoD), and for providing accounting and financial advisory services regarding contracts and subcontracts to all DoD Components responsible for procurement and contract administration. DCAA provides a wide variety of products and services to contracting officers including independent attestation audits of defense contractors' internal control systems. Many of the largest DoD contractors that DCAA audits are publicly traded and therefore would be required to implement the standards issued by the PCAOB.

DCAA audits are conducted in accordance with Generally Accepted Government Auditing Standards (GAGAS) which incorporate American Institute of Certified Public Accountants (AICPA) standards. The GAGAS also prescribe additional field work and reporting standards. DCAA makes every effort to exceed the minimum requirements of the standard setting bodies in providing timely and responsive audits, reports, and financial advisory services to DoD contracting officers and other customers. In addition, a significant percentage of DCAA auditors are certified public accountants.

With regard to the proposed standard on internal control audits, in many areas, DCAA auditing procedures mirror the proposed standard. At the largest DoD contractors, DCAA performs attestation engagements of the 10 internal control systems that most affect Government contracts (for example, billing systems). We believe that audit work performed by DCAA is a quality product, distinguished by the Agency's independence, integrity, and objectivity. As such, we are providing comments on the Board's question number 12 regarding using the work of management and others.

PAS 730.3.B.2.4   November 21, 2003
SUBJECT: PCAOB Rulemaking Docket No. 008 Proposed Auditing Standard - An Audit
           of Internal Control Over Financial Reporting

12. *To what extent should the auditor be permitted or required to use the work of management and others?*

Paragraph 5 of the proposed standard states that auditors obtain reasonable assurance by evaluating the assessment performed by management and *others under the direction of management* (emphasis added). Paragraph 41 further directs the auditor to evaluate management's process for assessing the effectiveness of the company's internal controls including determining which controls in the process should be tested. The controls and evaluation criteria listed under paragraph 41 of the proposed PCAOB standard are an integral part of DCAA's fundamental requirements and responsibilities for obtaining and documenting an understanding of a contractor's internal controls, assessing control risk, and determining which controls should be tested.

If the extensive and independent testing of internal controls performed by DCAA is any guide, we believe that it is possible that other governmental audit organizations at the Federal or state levels may also produce audit work that meets the standards necessary to warrant reliance by the independent public accountants that are reporting on companies' internal controls over financial reporting.

Consequently, we recommend that the proposed standard be revised to allow audits of internal controls performed by government audit agencies to be included among management's potential sources of reliance. We believe strongly that if CPAs can consider the work of management and management-directed organizations in assessing the firm's internal controls, the CPAs can also consider audit work performed by independent third parties such as government auditors who have no potential conflicts of interest. Limiting the sources of reliance to only those internal to the firm potentially ignores a considerable body of relevant work performed by independent third parties, and could result in duplication of effort and increased audit costs.

Using the Defense Contract Audit Agency (DCAA) as an example, we find that:

- DCAA performs its audit for third party requestors, is not paid by or under the control of management, and is therefore unquestionably independent.
- DCAA's audit guidance for examining internal controls is based on the guidance published by the Committee of Sponsoring Organizations of the Treadway Commission (COSO). The proposed standard is also based on the COSO framework.
- It is DCAA's policy that each relevant accounting or management system that has a significant impact on Government contract cost be audited on a cyclical basis.
- DCAA audits examine relevant assertions, express an opinion, and report on all significant deficiencies.
- All DCAA audits include consideration of the assessment of the risk of material misstatement due to fraud.

PAS 730.3.B.2.4   November 21, 2003

SUBJECT: PCAOB Rulemaking Docket No. 008 Proposed Auditing Standard - An Audit
of Internal Control Over Financial Reporting

- Defense contractors routinely place reliance on DCAA accounting and management system
(internal control) reports as a means of verifying and validating that controls in place are
functioning as intended, and of implementing corrective actions, when controls are not
functioning or could be improved.

Finally, we noted that the Board's summary discussion and the proposed standard's text
in paragraph 5 and paragraph 104 regarding "Using the Work of Management and Others" is
inconsistent. Paragraph 5 specifically refers to the work of "others under the direction of
management", while Paragraph 104 states "others" with no reference to management. Are
"Others" in the context of paragraph 104 limited to those groups under the control of
management as indicated by paragraph 5 or does it also encompass others that are outside of the
scope of management's control, such as government agencies, as we recommend?

We appreciate the opportunity to provide comments on the proposed auditing standard on
an audit of internal control over financial reporting performed in conjunction with an audit of a
financial statement. Questions or comments regarding this commentary should be addressed to
Ms. Deaune C. Volk, Program Manager, Auditing Standards Division, at (703)767-3233 or
Ms. Mary L. Silva, Chief, Auditing Standards Division, at (703)767-3220.

/Signed/
Robert DiMucci
Assistant Director
Policy and Plans

¶ 639. GAO

G A O
Accountability • Integrity • Reliability

United States General Accounting Office
Washington, DC 20548

Comptroller General
of the United States

December 9, 2003

Office of the Secretary
Public Company Accounting Oversight Board
1666 K Street, NW
Washington, DC 20006-2803

Subject: *PCAOB Rulemaking Docket Matter No.008—Proposed Auditing Standard—An Audit of Internal Control over Financial Reporting Performed in Conjunction with an Audit of Financial Statements*

This letter provides the U.S. General Accounting Office's (GAO) comments on the Public Company Accounting Oversight Board's (PCAOB) October 7, 2003, proposed standard for the audit of internal control over financial reporting performed in conjunction with the audit of financial statements.

We commend the PCAOB for giving this important issue high priority and on the release of the proposed auditing standard. Overall, we support the proposed standard and believe that it is on track. We especially support the requirements for

- obtaining direct evidence about the design and operating effectiveness of internal control as well as evaluating management's assessment; and
- requiring tests of controls for "relevant assertions" rather than "significant controls" in order to link the internal control engagement to the entity's financial reporting.

GAO strongly believes that management's assessment of the effectiveness of internal control, along with the auditor's attestation on that assessment, are critical components of monitoring the effectiveness of an organization's risk management and accountability systems. Auditors will better serve their clients and other financial statement users and will better protect the public interest by providing assurances about the effectiveness of internal control. In this regard, GAO seeks to lead by example in establishing an appropriate level of auditor reporting on internal control for federal agencies and programs, and for entities receiving significant amounts of federal funding. We already provide opinions on internal control for all our major federal audit clients, including the consolidated financial statements of the U.S. government.

Attached are GAO's responses to selected questions in PCAOB Release No 2003-017, along with our additional comments regarding the following:

- nonroutine transactions and processes,
- testing IT controls,
- materiality considerations,
- illustrative auditor's reports, and
- other clarifications.

We thank you for considering our comments on this very important issue.

Sincerely yours,

David M. Walker
Comptroller General
of the United States

Enclosures

cc: The Honorable William H. Donaldson, Chairman
         Securities and Exchange Commission

         The Honorable William J. McDonough, Chairman
         Public Company Accounting Oversight Board

GAO'S RESPONSE TO SELECTED QUESTIONS IN
PCAOB RELEASE NO. 2003-017
AND OTHER RELATED COMMENTS

Integrated audit of financial statements and internal control over financial reporting

Question 1. Is it appropriate to refer to the auditor's attestation of management's assessment of the effectiveness of internal control over financial reporting as the audit of internal control over financial reporting?

We believe it is appropriate to refer to an auditor's attestation of management's assessment of the effectiveness of internal control over financial reporting as an "audit of **the effectiveness** of internal control over financial reporting." (We suggest adding "the effectiveness," as shown in bold.) As stated throughout the standard, the auditor will perform procedures and testing that go beyond evaluating management's assessment in order to determine whether management's assessment of the effectiveness of internal control is fairly stated. This will result in an audit of the effectiveness of internal controls, which we support.

Question 2. Should the auditor be prohibited from performing an audit of internal control over financial reporting without also performing an audit of the financial statements?

Question 3. Rather than requiring the auditor to also complete an audit of the financial statements, would an appropriate alternative be to require the auditor to perform work with regard to the financial statements comparable to that required to complete the financial statement audit?

We believe that it is most efficient for the audit of the effectiveness of internal control over financial reporting to be performed in conjunction with the financial statement audit. However, we believe that there should be flexibility should the auditor wish to perform this work apart from the financial statement audit, and we do not support a prohibition against doing so.

Audit of internal control over financial reporting

Question 5. Should the Board, generally or in this proposed standard, specify the level of competence and training of the audit personnel that is necessary to perform specified auditing procedures effectively? For example, it would be inappropriate for a new, inexperienced auditor to have primary

responsibility for conducting interviews of a company's senior management about possible fraud.

We agree with the criterion set forth in paragraph 31 of the proposed standard "that the auditor should have competence in the subject matter of internal control over financial reporting." We also agree with the additional general guidance in the proposed standard such as the example cited in question 5, "for example, it would be inappropriate for a new, inexperienced auditor to have primary responsibility for conducting interviews of a company's senior management about possible fraud." At the same time, we believe that any additional guidance added to the standard should avoid becoming overly prescriptive. An alternative would be for the Board to issue implementing guidance on this issue to supplement the standard if it further specified the level of competence and training.

Evaluation of management's assessment

Question 6. Is the scope of the audit appropriate in that it requires the auditor to both evaluate management's assessment and obtain, directly, evidence about whether internal control over financial reporting is effective?

To provide an opinion on management's assessment of the effectiveness of internal control, it is necessary for the auditor to both evaluate management's assessment and obtain direct evidence about whether internal control is effective.

Question 8. Is it appropriate to state that inadequate documentation is an internal control deficiency, the severity of which the auditor should evaluate? Or should inadequate documentation automatically rise to the level of significant deficiency or material weakness in internal control?

Inadequate documentation of management's assessment, by itself, does not meet the definition of material weakness or significant deficiency. We agree with the guidance provided in paragraphs 43-47 of the proposed standard, that inadequate documentation is a deficiency that the auditor should evaluate to determine whether management can demonstrate adequate monitoring of internal control over financial reporting by other means.

Obtaining an understanding of internal control over financial reporting

Question 9. Are the objectives to be achieved by performing walkthroughs sufficient to require the performance of walkthroughs?

We agree that performing walkthroughs can provide the auditor with helpful information about internal control design and operations. At the same time, we believe that walkthrough procedures are not always necessary or appropriate. For instance, performing walkthroughs of highly automated processes or certain unusual nonroutine transactions could be extremely difficult or even impossible. Therefore, we suggest that the Board encourage auditors to use such procedures for relevant assertions for all significant accounts and disclosures but, at the same time, allow auditors to use other means for obtaining an understanding of internal control and determining the nature and extent of testing where appropriate. When alternative procedures are used, those procedures should provide the auditor with a similar level of evidence as walkthrough procedures would provide for understanding internal control and determining the appropriate level of testing.

Question 10. Is it appropriate to require that the walkthrough be performed by the auditor himself or herself, rather than allowing the auditor to use walkthrough procedures performed by management, internal auditors, or others?

Under certain conditions it is appropriate for the auditor to use walkthrough procedures performed by internal auditors. Internal auditors can play an important role in concluding about the effectiveness of internal control. In some cases, the internal auditors may be assisting management with its assessment of internal control. In other cases, internal auditors may be testing controls and testing management's assessment. In either scenario, there are contributions that the internal auditor can make to the external auditor's understanding of internal control—including the results of procedures such as walkthroughs—as input to the auditor's determination of the nature and extent of testing to be conducted as part of the audit of internal control. However, the work of the internal auditor should not be used as the principal evidence, and the external auditor will need to determine the level of reliance to place on that work. Such a determination should be made on a case-by-case basis, based on facts, circumstances, and risk. We believe that the guidance in paragraph 108 for relying on the work of internal auditors is appropriate for making this determination.

If the auditor uses walkthrough procedures performed by management or a consultant hired by management, the auditor should test the walkthrough for validity and completeness, as the auditor would test any information provided by management.

Requirement for the auditor to obtain evidence of the effectiveness of controls for all relevant assertions for all significant accounts and disclosures every year

Question 11. Is it appropriate to require the auditor to obtain evidence of the effectiveness of controls for all relevant assertions for all significant accounts and disclosures every year or may the auditor use some of the audit evidence obtained in previous years to support his or her current opinion on management's assessment?

We support a requirement for the auditor to obtain evidence every year of the effectiveness of internal control for assertions for **material** accounts and disclosures **that present moderate or high risk,** as opposed to a requirement for the auditor to obtain evidence of the effectiveness for **all relevant** assertions for **all significant** accounts and disclosures every year.

We also believe that rotational testing of controls would be acceptable under the following conditions: (1) control risk is evaluated as low, the control environment is strong, and inherent and fraud risk factors are low, (2) the auditor possesses from past and current work a foundation of audit evidence on which to develop current audit conclusions; (3) financial reporting controls over all significant cycles or applications have been evaluated and tested during a fairly recent period (no more than 3 years); and (4) no specific reporting or risk issues preclude the use of rotation.

A requirement for evaluating the effectiveness of controls for all relevant assertions for **material** accounts and disclosures **presenting moderate or high risk** every year would not only guide the auditor in the audit of effectiveness of internal control, but would also contribute to the quality of the financial statement audit. This is a powerful means for linking the financial statement audit and the audit of the effectiveness of internal control and gaining synergy and overall improved audit quality.

Extent of reliance on the work of management and others

Question 12. To what extent should the auditor be permitted or required to use the work of management and others?

Question 13. Are the three categories of controls and the extent to which the auditor may rely on the work of others appropriately defined?

Question 14. Does the proposed standard give appropriate recognition to the work of internal auditors? If not, does the proposed standard place too much emphasis and preference on the work of internal auditors or not enough?

This section of the standard should be made more specific to indicate that this section does not deal with the auditor's reliance on the work of other external auditors. Our answers are based on the assumption that the board will provide separate guidance for relying on the work of another external auditor.

We agree with the concept of delineating controls and procedures for which it is not appropriate that the auditor rely on the work of management and consultants hired by management. We would suggest, however, that the terminology "use the work of others" be changed to "**rely** on the work of others." Certainly, the auditor would want to use any information or evidence provided by management or consultants hired by management about control problems. The key point is that the auditor would not **rely** on that work, but use it as part of the process of gaining an understanding of controls to determine the nature, timing, and extent of the auditor's tests.

We agree with the category of controls and with the degree of reliance set forth in paragraph 106; specifically, that the auditor might decide to use the results of tests performed by management and others within the company in areas such as controls over routine processing of significant accounts and disclosures without specific limitation.

We disagree, however, with the classification of controls and procedures listed in paragraphs 104 and 105. For instance, in paragraph 105, the proposed standard states that the auditor's use of the results of procedures performed by management and others should be limited for (1) controls over significant nonroutine and nonsystematic transactions, and (2) controls over significant accounts, processes, or disclosures where the auditor has assessed as high the risk of failure of the controls to operate effectively. We believe that these are significant controls and that the auditor should not rely on procedures performed by management or consultants hired by management for these controls. However, the auditor could, based on the auditor's assessment of the internal audit function in accordance with criteria set forth in paragraph 108, determine the appropriate reliance to place on the internal audit function for the controls and procedures listed in both paragraphs 104 and 105.

Finally, as stated in our answers to questions 9 and 10, we believe that the auditor could place some reliance on walkthrough procedures performed by internal auditors. If the auditor uses a walkthrough provided by management or another party (such as a consultant hired by management), the auditor should test the walkthrough for such factors as validity and completeness, as the auditor would in testing any information received by management.

Therefore, we suggest restructuring and rewording paragraphs 104 and 105 to read as follows:

The following are controls for which the auditor should not **rely** on the results of testing performed **by management or by consultants hired by management**:

- controls that are part of the control environment, including controls specifically established to prevent and detect fraud that is reasonably likely to result in material misstatement of the financial statements;

- controls over the period-end financial reporting process, including controls over procedures used to enter transaction totals into the general ledger; to initiate, record, and process journal entries in the general ledger; and to record recurring and nonrecurring adjustments to the financial statements (for example, consolidating adjustments, report combinations, and reclassifications);

- controls that have a pervasive effect on the financial statements, such as certain information technology general controls on which the operating effectiveness of other controls depend;

- controls over significant nonroutine and nonsystematic transactions (such as accounts involving significant judgments and estimates); and

- controls over significant accounts, processes, or disclosures where the auditor has assessed as high the risk that the controls will fail to operate effectively.

In some cases, it may be appropriate for the auditor to place some reliance on work performed by the internal auditor related to the above controls. Based on risk and the auditor's assessment of the internal audit function in accordance with criteria in paragraph 108, the external auditor should determine the appropriate level of reliance to place on the internal audit function.

Question 16. Is the requirement for the auditor to obtain the principle evidence, on an overall basis, through his or her own work the appropriate benchmark for the amount of work that is required to be performed by the auditor?

As we commented in our response to question 14, this section of the standard should be made more specific to indicate that it does not deal with the auditor's reliance on the work of other external auditors. Therefore, our answer to question 16 also is based on the assumption that the board will provide separate guidance for relying on the work of another external auditor.

We agree that requiring auditors overall to obtain the principal evidence through their own work (when relying on the work of internal auditors, management, or consultants hired by management) is an appropriate benchmark for the amount of work that is required to be performed by the auditor. We also agree with the criteria set forth in paragraph 103 for determining whether to use work performed by management and others. We further agree with the recognition given to the unique position of internal auditors in this process as set forth in paragraph 108.

Evaluating results

Question 17. Will the definitions in the proposed standard of significant deficiency and material weakness provide for increased consistency in the evaluation of deficiencies? How can the definitions be improved?

We support the revised definitions of significant deficiency and material weakness as set forth in paragraphs 8-9 of the proposed standard. The revised definitions are more specific and provide clearer guidance to the auditor than the previous definitions from AU section 325 and AT section 501.

Question 19. Is it necessary for the auditor to evaluate the severity of all identified internal control deficiencies?

Unless clearly inconsequential, the auditor should evaluate the severity of all identified internal control weaknesses in order to determine whether the deficiencies, individually or in combination, are significant deficiencies or material weaknesses.

Question 20. Is it appropriate to require the auditor to communicate all internal control deficiencies (not just material weaknesses and significant deficiencies) to management in writing?

With regard to communicating results that are not significant deficiencies, we recommend that the Board adopt requirements similar to *Government Audit Standards*, which state "When auditors detect deficiencies in internal control that are not reportable conditions, they should communicate those deficiencies separately in a management letter to officials of the audited entity unless the deficiencies are clearly inconsequential considering both quantitative and qualitative factors. Auditors should use their professional judgment in deciding whether or how to communicate to officials of the audited entity deficiencies in internal control that are clearly inconsequential. Auditors should include in their audit documentation evidence of all communications to officials of the audited entity about deficiencies in internal control found during the audit."[1]

Forming an opinion and reporting

Question 25. Is it appropriate that the existence of a material weakness would require the auditor to express an adverse conclusion about the effectiveness of the company's internal control over financial reporting, consistent with the required reporting model for management?

Question 26. Are there circumstances where a qualified "except for" conclusion would be appropriate?

We agree that it is only appropriate for the auditor to issue an unqualified opinion on internal control when there are no identified material weaknesses and when there have been no restrictions on the scope of the auditor's work.

When there is one or more material weaknesses, we believe that it is appropriate for the auditor to express an adverse or qualified opinion about the effectiveness of the company's internal control over financial reporting, depending on the facts and circumstances. In certain circumstances, qualified or "except for" reports could be

---

[1] *Government Auditing Standards* (GAO-03-673G, June 2003), paragraph 5.16.

appropriate for localized deficiencies, deficiencies involving one control cycle, or material weaknesses that are detected and corrected by management. Therefore, we do not support a requirement that would direct the auditor to issue an adverse opinion on internal control in the event of one or more material weaknesses. Instead, we believe the auditor would need to consider issuing an adverse opinion based on the facts and circumstances surrounding the weaknesses identified.

Auditor independence

28. Should the Board provide specific guidance on independence and internal control-related non-audit services in the context of this proposed standard?

29. Are there any specific internal control-related non-audit services the auditor should be prohibited from providing to an audit client?

We believe that the proposed standard, as written, provides an appropriate level of guidance on auditor independence. In particular, we are pleased that paragraphs 32-35 of the proposed standard incorporate GAO's two overarching principles for auditor independence. The GAO independence standard emphasizes a substance-over-form approach. We recommend that any additional requirements in the standards should take this approach, as follows:

> In making judgments on independence, audit organizations and audit committees should take a substance-over-form approach and consider the nature and significance of the services provided to the audited entity and the facts and circumstances surrounding those services. Before an audit committee approves and before an audit organization agrees to perform nonaudit services, careful consideration should be given to avoid situations that could lead reasonable third parties with knowledge of the relevant facts and circumstances to conclude that the auditor is not able to maintain independence in conducting the audits. It is imperative that auditors always be viewed as independent in fact and appearance.[2]

GAO issued its independence standard in January 2002,[3] and due to the many inquiries we received and the standard's significant effect on auditors of federal entities and programs, we subsequently provided additional guidance in the form of questions and answers to assist in implementing the standard.[4]

---

[2] Adapted from *Government Auditing Standards: Answers to Independence Standard Questions* (GAO-02-870G, July 2002).
[3] *Government Auditing Standards Amendment No. 3: Independence* (GAO-02-388G, January 2002).
[4] *Government Auditing Standards: Answers to Independence Standard Questions* (GAO-02-870G, July 2002).

Additional GAO Comments

Nonroutine Transactions and Processes

Controls over nonroutine transactions and processes may be less well developed and more susceptible to management override and therefore have increased risk of being ineffective. In paragraphs 74-78 on identifying controls to test, we suggest that the standard provide a more explicit requirement on testing controls over nonroutine transactions and indicate that normally the auditor should expand testing of these controls. We also suggest that the discussion of fraud considerations in paragraphs 24-26 emphasize controls over nonroutine transactions.

Testing IT controls

Paragraph 41 of the proposed standard states that, when obtaining an understanding of the entity's internal control over financial reporting, the auditor should determine whether management has addressed the need to test controls "including information technology general controls, on which other controls are dependent." In addition, paragraphs 53 and 61 seem to make reference to IT controls as company-level controls, but they are not specific. We suggest that the standard be expanded to include general controls, application controls, and controls over IT security. We also suggest that the standard incorporate guidance as to what is needed to evaluate management's assessment process of these IT controls and for the auditor's testing of IT controls.

Paragraph 70 is unclear about how the requirements of AU 319 relate to this standard. Instead of referring to Paragraphs 16-20 of AU section 319, *Consideration of Internal Control in a Financial Statement Audit,* in paragraph 70 of the proposed standard, we suggest that the PCAOB update and expand the guidance of this AU section and include it in this proposed standard. In today's environment, auditors normally would not be able to attest to the effectiveness of an entity's internal control without understanding and testing relevant IT controls.

Materiality Considerations

We believe that the concepts in the second and third sentences of paragraph 21 of the proposed standard could more clearly convey that, depending on the facts and circumstances, the auditor should consider materiality at the financial-statement level and/or at the individual account-balance level in determining whether a deficiency represents a significant deficiency or a material weakness.

Materiality considerations for internal control over financial reporting would logically follow the materiality considerations for the financial statement audit. However, this is one area where we believe the financial audit standards need to be strengthened.

For instance, we suggest that financial auditing standards require the auditor to document (1) the planning materiality selected, (2) the method of determining planning materiality, (3) the auditor's consideration of materiality in designing the nature, timing, and extent of audit procedures, and (4) the auditor's consideration of materiality in evaluating the results of audit procedures. We encourage the PCAOB to give high priority to revising the interim standards on materiality, which are in AU section 312, *Audit Risk and Materiality in Conducting an Audit.* We believe that additional guidance on applying the concept of materiality is needed in areas such as estimating materiality, determining an appropriate materiality base, and applying materiality concepts in audit planning and reporting. We also believe that the standard should require auditors to quantify and document their consideration of materiality.

Illustrative Auditor Reports

- Unqualified Opinion, Example A-1

In the illustrative report expressing an unqualified opinion, we believe that the opinion paragraph should be revised to clearly state the following: (1) management's assessment of internal control over financial reporting, (2) whether the auditor agrees with management's assessment, and (3) the auditor's opinion on the effectiveness of internal control.

> Management has assessed the internal control over financial reporting of W Company, and has concluded that internal control over financial reporting was effective as of December 31, 20x3. We agree with management's assessment. In our opinion, ~~management's assessment that~~ W Company maintained, in all material respects, effective internal control over financial reporting as of December 31, 20x3~~, is fairly stated, in all material respects,~~ based on [identify criteria…]

- Adverse Opinion, Example A-2

In the illustrative report expressing an adverse opinion, we suggest that the last sentence of the explanatory paragraph should be revised as indicated below:

> …We considered this material weakness in determining the nature, timing, and extent of the audit procedures applied in our audit of the 20x3 financial statements. As a result of performing these revised audit procedures, we were able to express an opinion on W Company's 20x3 financial statements. However, information that management uses in making decisions during the year, as well as information presented in its quarterly reports, could be misstated as a result of the material weakness. ~~This material weakness was considered in determining the nature, timing, and extent of audit tests applied in our audit of the 20x3 financial statements, and this report does not affect our report dated [date of report…] on those financial staztements.~~

- Disclaiming An Opinion, Example A-4

In the illustrative report disclaiming an opinion, we believe that guidance is needed for an auditor's explanation of how the disclaimer on the effectiveness of internal control over financial reporting affects the auditor's opinion on the entity's financial statements.

- Report That Refers to the Report of Other Auditors, Exhibit A-5

In the illustrative report that refers to the report of other auditors as a basis, in part, for the auditor's opinion, we believe that the introductory and opinion paragraphs are unclear and suggest revision to clarify that the opinion and the responsibility belong to the auditor of the consolidated entity. Even when a wholly owned subsidiary is autonomous of its parent, the parent establishes the subsidiary's overall control environment and the "tone at the top." We suggest that the last sentence of the introductory paragraph be revised as follows:

> The effectiveness of B Company's internal control over financial reporting was audited by other auditors whose report has been furnished to us, and <u>we considered their report and evidence obtained during our audit in order to form our opinion on the effectiveness of W Company's internal control over financial reporting.</u> ~~our opinion, insofar as it relates to the effectiveness of B Company's internal control over financial reporting, is based solely on the report of the other auditors~~

- Combined Report, Example A-6

In the illustrative combined report expressing an unqualified opinion on financial statements and an unqualified opinion on management's assessment of the effectiveness of internal control over financial reporting, we suggest revising the opinion paragraph to state: (1) management's assessment of internal control over financial reporting, (2) whether the auditor agrees with management's assessment, and (3) the auditor's opinion on the effectiveness of internal control. This parallels our recommendation for revising the opinion of the illustrative report expressing an unqualified opinion in Example A-1.

> <u>Management has assessed the internal control over financial reporting of W Company effective as of December 31, 20x3. We agree with management's assessment.</u> Also in our opinion, ~~management's assessment that~~ W Company maintained, <u>in all material respects,</u> effective internal control over financial reporting as of December 31, 20x3,<u>.</u>~~, is fairly stated, in all material respects,~~ based on [identify criteria…]

<u>Other Clarifications</u>

- <u>Clarify example of evaluating the operating effectiveness of internal control</u>

In the second example provided in the last sentence of paragraph 93 of the proposed standard, reperforming the control is recommended as a procedure for testing the control. We do not believe that this procedure provides the auditor with evidence of the effectiveness of the control. We suggest that instead, the auditor should be advised to ask the person responsible for signing the voucher what he or she looks for when approving packages and how many errors have been found on vouchers. We also suggest that the auditor be advised to ask others with knowledge of the procedure about their understanding of the number of errors found. The auditor could also ask whether management has knowledge of any errors that the person responsible for signing the vouchers failed to detect.

- Reconsider requirement regarding subsequent discovery of information existing at the date of the auditor's report on internal control over financial reporting

The PCAOB should reconsider the requirement that the auditor determine "whether there are persons currently relying on or likely to rely on the auditor's report" as discussed in paragraph 180 of the proposed standard in the context of AU section 561, *Subsequent Discovery of Facts Existing at the Date of the Auditor's Report.* Specifically, the requirement for the auditor to determine "whether there are persons currently relying on or likely to rely on the auditor's report" is not always possible in light of today's technology. The auditor cannot reasonably determine who may rely on an auditor's report when these reports are readily available on the Internet, often from the Web site of the Securities and Exchange Commission.

WG
&L Warren, Gorham & Lamont

¶ 640. OCC/FRB/FDIC/OTS

Office of the Comptroller of the Currency
Board of Governors of the Federal Reserve System
Federal Deposit Insurance Corporation
Office of Thrift Supervision

December 1, 2003

Office of the Secretary
Public Company Accounting Oversight Board
1666 K Street, N.W.
Washington, D.C. 20006-2803

      Re: PCAOB Rulemaking Docket Matter No. 008

Dear Board Members:

We appreciate the significant efforts of the Public Company Accounting Oversight Board (PCAOB) to propose and implement enhanced standards for the auditing of and reporting on the internal controls over financial reporting of public companies. In addition, we found the roundtable discussion on July 29, 2003, to be a useful and important aspect of the due process in the development of this proposal and we appreciated the opportunity to have participated in that discussion. Effective auditing, strong internal controls, and reliable financial reporting are critical to the safety and soundness of the organizations we regulate and, thus, we recognize the importance of an open and productive dialogue on these matters of mutual interest.

Since 1993, the Office of the Comptroller of the Currency, the Federal Reserve Board, the Federal Deposit Insurance Corporation and the Office of Thrift Supervision (collectively, the Agencies) have been responsible for evaluating insured depository institutions' implementation of Section 112 of the Federal Deposit Insurance Corporation Improvement Act (FDICIA 112). As you know, FDICIA 112 requires management of insured depository institutions with total assets of $500 million or more to annually assess and report on whether their internal controls over financial reporting are effective, and requires an independent accountant's attestation report on management's assertion. Thus, our collective experience examining depository institutions' internal control assessments and independent accountants' attestation reports provides unique insight into the practice of auditing and reporting on internal controls over financial reporting.

Overall, the PCAOB's proposed auditing standard, "An Audit of Internal Control Over Financial Reporting Performed in Conjunction with an Audit of Financial Statements," is a significant improvement over the existing attestation standard, "Reporting on an Entity's Internal Control Over Financial Reporting." The proposed standard presents improvements in the areas of (1) identifying management's responsibilities in an internal control audit, (2) explaining the relationship between audits of internal controls and of financial statements, (3) describing the effect of internal control deficiencies on the auditor's conclusion, and (4) specifying appropriate reporting approaches.

Office of the Secretary
PCAOB
November 26, 2003
Page 2 of 2

Based upon our review of the proposed standard, we are providing you with specific answers to certain questions in the release, as well as additional comments that we recommend to further improve the standard. The attachments to this letter provide our detailed comments. Please feel free to contact us if you wish to discuss our comments further.

Sincerely,

Zane D. Blackburn   Gerald A. Edwards, Jr.
Chief Accountant   Associate Director and
Office of the Comptroller of the Currency Chief Accountant – Supervision
                                          Federal Reserve Board

Robert F. Storch   Timothy J. Stier
Chief Accountant   Chief Accountant
Federal Deposit Insurance Corporation   Office of Thrift Supervision

Attachment 1 – Response to Specific Request for Comments - PCAOB Rulemaking Docket No. 008
Attachment 2 – Comments on Proposed Auditing Standard – PCAOB Rulemaking Docket No. 008

cc   Donald T. Nicolaisen, Chief Accountant, Securities and Exchange Commission
     Scott A. Taub, Deputy Chief Accountant, Securities and Exchange Commission
     Eric J. Schuppenhauer, Professional Accounting Fellow, Securities and Exchange Commission

Attachment 1
Response to Specific Request for Comments
PCAOB Rulemaking Docket No. 008

General Responses

The federal banking agencies support the position outlined in the PCAOB's proposal with regard to the issues raised in questions 1 – 7, 9 – 10, 13 – 15, 17 – 18, 21 – 22, and 30 – 31. We have, therefore, not provided specific responses to these questions. However, we are providing responses to questions 8, 11 – 12, 16, 19 – 20, and 23 – 29, because we believe the PCAOB will find it useful to consider the agencies' experience with similar matters in the attestation process for internal controls at insured depository institutions.

Specific Responses

Questions regarding evaluation of management's assessment:

8   Is it appropriate to state that inadequate documentation is an internal control deficiency, the severity of which the auditor should evaluate? Or should inadequate documentation automatically rise to the level of significant deficiency or material weakness in internal control?

  Response: In our experience, management's inability to adequately document its internal controls or its assessment of internal controls can be an indicator of a significant control deficiency within an organization. Thus, the standard should require the auditor to evaluate whether documentation deficiencies rise to the level of a significant deficiency or a material weakness as indicated in paragraphs 46, 47, and 125.

Question regarding testing operating effectiveness:

  Is it appropriate to require the auditor to obtain evidence of the effectiveness of controls for all relevant assertions for all significant accounts and disclosures every year or may the auditor use some of the audit evidence obtained in previous years to support his or her current opinion on management's assessment?

  Response: Paragraphs 94 – 100 indicate the timing of the auditor's tests should be adequate to determine whether the controls are effective as of the date specified in management's report. The clear implication of these paragraphs is to require the auditor to obtain evidence of the effectiveness of controls for all relevant assertions for all significant accounts and disclosures every year. Prior evidence would not be sufficient, particularly when business practices and internal controls have changed.

Questions regarding using the work of management and others:

12. To what extent should the auditor be permitted or required to use the work of management and others?

Attachment 1
Response to Specific Request for Comments
PCAOB Rulemaking Docket No. 008

Response: Paragraphs 104 – 105 provide guidance on instances where the auditor is either prohibited or limited from relying on the results of procedures performed by others when rendering an opinion on internal controls. In our experience, auditors have a tendency to rely too heavily on the work of management and others when performing internal control attestations. The inherent risk of such over-reliance diminishes the independence and objectivity of the auditor's opinion on control effectiveness. The requirement that the auditor obtain the principal evidence for the audit opinion would seem to preclude the auditor from relying on the work of management and others for most of the relevant assertions on significant accounts and disclosures. Thus, we recommend that the PCAOB clarify the meaning of the term "use the work of management or others" in the context of paragraphs 104-106. In addition, the standard should better explain the extent to which the results of tests performed by others, such as internal auditors, may or may not be relied upon by the auditor.

16. Is the requirement for the auditor to obtain the principal evidence, on an overall basis, through his or her own work the appropriate benchmark for the amount of work that is required to be performed by the auditor?

    Response: Our expectation is that the principal evidence standard would preclude the auditor from relying primarily on the work of management and others. Thus, the proposed approach appears to be an appropriate benchmark.

Questions regarding evaluating results:

19. Is it necessary for the auditor to evaluate the severity of all identified internal control deficiencies?

    Response: Yes. It appears that an auditor would need to evaluate the severity of all deficiencies to appropriately determine whether the deficiencies collectively or individually rise to the level of a significant deficiency or material weakness. In our experience, auditors routinely make such judgments in the normal course of an audit. As a result, the requirement to assess the severity of deficiencies should not significantly increase the amount of work performed by an auditor.

20. Is it appropriate to require the auditor to communicate all internal control deficiencies (not just material weaknesses and significant deficiencies) to management in writing?

    Response: Yes. Paragraphs 190 – 192 require auditors to communicate all control deficiencies and fraud to management and the audit committee. This type of communication is consistent with the objective of Section 404 of the Sarbanes-Oxley Act of 2002, which is intended to ensure that the organization maintains an effective system of internal control. Since auditors routinely become aware of deficiencies of lesser magnitude than a material weakness in the course of an audit, there should be little added burden associated with communicating these deficiencies in writing. In addition, written communication provides a

Attachment 1
Response to Specific Request for Comments
PCAOB Rulemaking Docket No. 008

clear audit trail for the audit committee, management, auditors and regulators. In our experience, written communication of all identified deficiencies to management and the audit committee facilitates prompt resolution of the deficiencies.

23. Will auditors be able to effectively carry out their responsibility to evaluate the effectiveness of the audit committee's oversight?

Response: Yes. Despite the inherent difficulties in evaluating the body directly responsible for appointing and compensating the auditor, it is quite appropriate for the auditor to evaluate the effectiveness of the audit committee. Paragraphs 57 – 58 enumerate factors that the auditor should evaluate related to the effectiveness of the audit committee's oversight of the company's external financial reporting and internal control over financial reporting. We believe that auditors have the professional qualifications, experience and knowledge to effectively carry out this responsibility.

24. If the auditor concludes that ineffective audit committee oversight is a material weakness, rather than require the auditor to issue an adverse opinion with regard to the effectiveness of the internal control over financial reporting, should the standard require the auditor to withdraw from the audit engagement?

Response: No. Paragraph 59 appropriately indicates that an auditor's determination that an audit committee is ineffective should, at least, be regarded as a significant deficiency. If the auditor concludes that the deficiencies in audit committee oversight rise to the level of a material weakness, the auditor should be required to issue an adverse opinion on the effectiveness of controls. It would seem to be inconsistent with the objective of the standard to suggest that an auditor should withdraw from an engagement rather than issue an adverse opinion on internal control effectiveness.

Questions regarding forming an opinion and reporting:

25. Is it appropriate that the existence of a material weakness would require the auditor to express an adverse conclusion about the effectiveness of the company's internal control over financial reporting, consistent with the required reporting model for management?

Response: Yes. It is appropriate for the existence of a material weakness to result in an adverse audit opinion. Paragraphs 162 – 164 and Appendix A provide appropriate guidance on adverse opinions resulting from the existence of material weaknesses. Based on this guidance, users of internal control reports would reasonably expect the existence of a material weakness to result in an adverse conclusion by both management and the auditor. The only logical outcome of the existence of a material weakness would be that internal control is not effective.

26. Are there circumstances where a qualified "except for" conclusion would be appropriate?

Attachment 1
Response to Specific Request for Comments
PCAOB Rulemaking Docket No. 008

Response: No. Paragraphs 15 – 18 explain the inherent limitations of internal control and the level of assurance users expect from reports on internal control. The use of "except for" opinions to explain the impact of deficiencies of a lesser magnitude than a material weakness would not send a clear message to users of internal control reports. Users expect the auditor's report to render an opinion on internal control taken as a whole. Qualified (i.e., "Except for") opinions diminish the usefulness of these reports.

27. Do you agree with the position that when the auditor issues a nonstandard opinion, such as an adverse opinion, that the auditor's opinion should speak directly to the effectiveness of the internal control over financial reporting rather than to whether management's assessment is fairly stated?

    Response: Yes. Consistent with our responses to questions 25 and 26, users expect audit opinions on internal control to be meaningful. As such, it would be more beneficial to users for the opinion to speak directly to the effectiveness of internal control rather than opine on management's assertion.

Questions regarding auditor independence:

28. Should the Board provide specific guidance on independence and internal control-related non-audit services in the context of this proposed standard?

    Response: No. The Securities and Exchange Commission (SEC) adequately addressed auditor independence in its final rule release *Strengthening the Commission's Requirements Regarding Auditor Independence*. The PCAOB should work with the SEC to develop questions and answers and other implementation guidance on auditor independence.

29. Are there any specific internal control-related non-audit services the auditor should be prohibited from providing to an audit client?

    Response: Consistent with our response to question 28, we recommend the PCAOB work with the SEC to develop consistent guidance on any prohibition of specific internal control-related non-auditor services.

Attachment 2
Comments on Proposed Auditing Standard
PCAOB Rulemaking Docket No. 008
An Audit of Internal Control Over Financial Reporting Performed in
Conjunction with an Audit of Financial Statements

Requirements for Written Representations

Paragraph 128(g) directs the auditor to obtain written representation from management stating whether, subsequent to the date being reported on, there were "any changes in internal control or other factors that might significantly affect internal control." Since the determination of what constitutes a significant change in internal control is subjective, we recommend requiring the auditor to review the documentation management used to make its written representation regarding changes in internal control. This would enable the auditor to make an independent determination as to whether management had a reasonable basis to support its written representation regarding the significance of any changes in internal control.

Appendix A

2.   The illustrative reports on the effectiveness of internal control over financial reporting expressing a qualified opinion and disclaiming an opinion, Examples A-3 and A-4 respectively, do not indicate the effect of such opinions on the financial statement audit. We recommend that language similar to that in the last sentence of the "Explanatory Paragraph" of Example A-2, which is an adverse opinion, be included in the illustrative reports for Examples A-3 and A-4.

Appendix B

3.   Paragraphs B3, B12, and B13, and Illustration B-1 indicate that it is not necessary to test any controls at locations and business units that "...individually, and when aggregated with others, could not result in a material misstatement to the financial statements." Since controls exist for designated purposes, we do not consider it appropriate or constructive to simply exclude groups of locations and units from potential testing. For the hypothetical company depicted in Illustration B-1, 40% (60 of 150) of the company's locations would never be tested. In our opinion, this process could result in a scope limitation on management's assertion because it, by design, restricts the locations or business units that are actually evaluated by management. While individual locations or business units may not be significant and may not result in a material misstatement to the financial statements as of a point in time, the nature of the activities and transactions at ostensibly "insignificant" locations or business units, together with a lack of managerial oversight and internal control testing, could be conducive to and result in material internal control weaknesses, improper transactions, or fraud. Removing any location or business unit from the population of locations or business units to be considered in the review of internal control or audit of the financial statements could create a wrong impression or create a climate whereby management or other employees may take advantage of the lack of review of internal controls at these so-called "insignificant" locations or business units. We suggest the aforementioned paragraphs and illustration

Attachment 2
Comments on Proposed Auditing Standard
PCAOB Rulemaking Docket No. 008
An Audit of Internal Control Over Financial Reporting Performed in
Conjunction with an Audit of Financial Statements

be revised to require management and the auditor to include testing of at least a sample of the controls over financial reporting at "insignificant" locations or business units to allow management and the auditor to assert that all controls are operating effectively. We believe no business unit or location should be permanently excluded from testing. We recommend paragraphs B3, B12, and B13, and Illustration B-1 be revised to read as follows:

> "Management and auditors should periodically test controls at a sample of locations and business units regardless of whether they are individually significant or, when aggregated, may result in a material misstatement to the financial statements."

¶ 700. PCAOB Briefing Paper for the Roundtable on Reporting on Internal Control

JULY 10, 2003

On July 29, 2003, the Public Company Accounting Oversight Board (the "Board") will convene a roundtable to discuss issues relating to the independent auditor's report on an issuer's internal control over financial reporting. The roundtable will start at 9:30 a.m. and conclude at 4:00 p.m., with a brief break for lunch. Specifically, the Board seeks the views of interested persons on the responsibilities of registered public accounting firms to report on the assessment of internal controls by issuers. This paper contains the agenda of roundtable issues.

The Board has invited representatives of public companies and accounting firms, as well as U.S. investor groups, to participate in the roundtable. Following the roundtable, the Board will also accept written public comment concerning the issues on the agenda.

Overview

Section 103(a)(2)(A)(iii) of the Sarbanes-Oxley Act of 2002 (the "Act") directs the Board to establish auditing standards that require registered public accounting firms to describe in audit reports the scope of testing of internal control that has been performed and report on the evaluation of internal control. Section 404(a) requires issuers to file with the SEC an annual report assessing internal controls and Section 404(b) provides that the issuer's auditor must attest to, and report on, the assessment made by management of the issuer. On June 5, 2003, the Securities and Exchange Commission ("SEC") adopted final rules implementing the requirements of Section 404(a). With some exceptions, public companies and their auditors must begin complying with the SEC rule in annual reports for fiscal years ending on or after June 15, 2004.

The Board has a related responsibility to issue or adopt standards for the auditor's attestation required by Section 404(b). The Board has adopted Interim Auditing and Related Professional Practice Standards that include the pre-existing standard on engagements to issue an examination report on either the effectiveness of an entity's internal control over financial reporting or on management's written assertion concerning internal control effectiveness.[1]

On March 18, 2003, the Auditing Standards Board of the American Institute of Certified Public Accountants ("AICPA") issued exposure drafts ("EDs") of several related pronouncements on internal control reporting that included the following—

- a proposed SSAE, *Reporting on an Entity's Internal Control Over Financial Reporting*, intended to replace Chapter 5 of SSAE No. 10 with an expanded set of requirements on attestation engagements on the effectiveness of internal control over financial reporting; and

- a proposed new Statement on Auditing Standards ("SAS"), *Auditing an Entity's Internal Control Over Financial Reporting in Conjunction with a Financial Statement Audit*.

The proposed SAS directs auditors of public companies to follow the guidance in the proposed SSAE when performing an audit of internal control and explains the difference between the auditor's attention to internal control in an audit of financial statements and the work necessary to provide a separate opinion on the effectiveness of internal control.

The Act gives the Board the exclusive authority to establish and amend auditing and related professional standards that must be adhered to by all registered public accounting firms in audits of public companies. Because the AICPA no longer has this authority, the AICPA has made a recommendation to the Board, based on the EDs and the comments received by the AICPA during the exposure period.

---

1. The pre-existing standard is Statement on Standards for Attestation Engagements ("SSAE") No. 10, *Attestation Standards: Revision and Recodification,* Chapter 1, *Attest Engagements,* and Chapter 5, *Reporting on an Entity's Internal Control Over Financial Reporting.* This standard is included in PCAOB Rule 3300T.

Roundtable Agenda

A. Objectives of the Engagement and Standards on Internal Control

Section 404(a) of the Sarbanes-Oxley Act of 2002 requires that annual reports filed with the SEC must be accompanied by a statement by management of the issuer declaring that management is responsible for creating and maintaining adequate internal controls, and presenting management's assessment of the effectiveness of the company's (issuer's) internal control. Section 404(b) requires that the public company's auditor must report on, and attest to, management's assessment. The Act provides that the attestation report on management's assertion is not to be the subject of a separate engagement. In other words, an issuer's financial statement auditor must also perform the internal control attestation.

Standards on considering internal control in a financial statement audit and for reporting on internal control effectiveness have existed for many years. In all financial statement audits, generally accepted auditing standards ("GAAS") require the auditor to obtain an understanding of internal control sufficient to plan the audit by performing procedures to understand the design of controls relevant to an audit of financial statements, and to determine whether they have been implemented. Existing GAAS also provides guidance on how the auditor may perform tests of controls to obtain evidence about their operating effectiveness and use such evidence to alter the nature, timing, and extent of procedures that the auditor would otherwise perform. However, except for certain financial institutions, auditors have rarely been engaged to separately report on the effectiveness of internal control.

Discussion Questions—

1. Are new standards or additional guidance needed for auditors to comply with the requirements of Section 404?

2. What should be the overall objective of an engagement to attest to management's assertion on internal control?

- Under existing standards, the auditor performs procedures that are sufficient to restrict the risk of issuing an inappropriate opinion on internal control to *an appropriately low level.* The appropriateness of the level of risk necessary to support the auditor's opinion is dependent solely on the auditor's judgment. A *low level of risk* also may be equated with a *high level of assurance.*

- Is there a more objective benchmark for the level of risk (or the level of assurance) that would be preferable?

3. Is reporting on management's assessment about the effectiveness of internal control over financial reporting a substantively different engagement, that would involve considerably less effort, than reporting directly on internal control effectiveness?

- Does the requirement to attest to and report on management's assessment of internal control mean that the auditor's work should be restricted to evaluating management's assessment process and reviewing documentation prepared by management in its assessment process?

- Is the amount of work to give an opinion on management's assessment roughly equivalent of the amount of work that would be necessary to give an opinion directly on the effectiveness of internal control?

4. Under the existing standards framework, auditors would need to refer to two different bodies of standards — auditing standards and attestation standards — to satisfy the requirements of the Act. Should the Board retain this approach and issue a separate attestation standard for the auditor's internal control attestation, which likely will require an additional auditing standard to reconcile the work related to the internal control attestation and the financial statement audit, or should there be one, integrated auditing standard to address the internal control attestation?

- Which approach will provide the most effective guidance for meeting the requirements of Section 404?

B. Documentation of Internal Control by Management

The SEC's final rules state that "a company must maintain evidential matter, including documentation, to provide reasonable support for management's assessment of the effectiveness of the company's internal control over financial reporting." The SEC's final rules include an instruction to remind registrants of the need to maintain such evidential matter.

Discussion Questions—

5. What is the understanding of issuers about the nature and extent of documentation that will be required to support their assessment of the effectiveness of internal control?

6. What are auditors' expectations about the nature and extent of documentation that will be essential to provide an unmodified report on management's assertion about internal control?

  • Do issuers have similar expectations about the nature and extent of required documentation?

7. Should the Board provide specific and detailed criteria that auditors should use to evaluate the sufficiency of management's documentation?

  • Should the Board provide documentation criteria for auditors similar to those applicable to management in the SEC's final rules?

8. Should inadequate documentation of significant controls be a basis for a significant deficiency or a material weakness in internal control?

  • Could it be a basis for a limitation on the scope of the independent auditor's examination?

C. Framework for Evaluation

The SEC's final rules specified that management must base its evaluation of the effectiveness of the company's internal control over financial reporting on a suitable, recognized control framework that is established by a body or group that has followed due-process procedures, including the broad distribution of the framework for public comment. The SEC's final rules do not mandate use of a particular framework, but the Committee of Sponsoring Organizations of the Treadway Commission's (commonly referred to and known as "COSO")[2] framework is explicitly identified as satisfying the SEC's criteria. The SEC recognizes that other evaluation standards exist outside of the United States, and identifies the *Guidance on Assessing Control,* published by the Canadian Institute of Chartered Accountants, and the *Turnbull Report,* published by the Institute of Chartered Accountants in England and Wales, as examples of suitable criteria. Management's report must identify the evaluation framework used to assess the effectiveness of internal control.

Discussion Questions—

9. What guidance should be provided on the framework for evaluating internal control?

10. Is a requirement that the evaluation framework must be issued by a group of experts that follow due process procedures sufficient?

11. Should particular frameworks be identified as meeting the requirement?

12. Should particular frameworks be mandated?

D. Significant Deficiencies and Material Weaknesses in Internal Control

In existing standards, the term "reportable condition" was used to describe the level of deficiency in internal control that had to be communicated to the audit committee. Reportable conditions were defined as matters coming to an auditor's attention that, in the auditor's judgment, represent significant deficiencies in the design or operation of internal control, that could adversely affect the entity's ability to initiate, record, process, and report financial data consistent with the

---

2. In 1985, the National Commission on Fraudulent Financial Reporting, also known as the Treadway Commission, was formed to study the financial reporting system in the United States. In 1987, the Treadway Commission issued a report recommending that its sponsoring organizations work together to integrate the various internal control concepts and definitions. Thus, in 1992, COSO published its study of internal control to establish a common definition that would serve the needs of issuers, private companies, independent auditors, and regulatory agencies.

assertions of management in the financial statements. Moreover, a material weakness in internal control was defined as a reportable condition in which the design or operation of a component(s) of internal control does not reduce to a relatively low level the risk that a material misstatement may be contained in the issuer's financial statements. The Act used the term "significant deficiency" and established certain communication requirements concerning them. The term "significant deficiency" is currently understood as substantially the same as "reportable condition." The definitions of "material weakness" and "significant deficiency" are important because the existence of a material weakness precludes an unqualified opinion that internal control is effective, and the existence of a significant deficiency must be communicated by management to the auditor and to the audit committee.

Discussion Questions—

13. What definitions of significant deficiency and material weakness in internal control should be adopted?

14. For a deficiency to be significant, what should be the likelihood of misstatements not being prevented or detected, and what should be the magnitude of those misstatements?

15. For a weakness to be material, what should be the likelihood of misstatements not being prevented or detected, and what should be the magnitude of those misstatements?

16. What other improvements, if any, should be made in the specificity of the definitions, or the guidance on factors to consider in determining them?

17. If an audit committee is not in compliance with the new security listing requirements under the Securities Exchange Act of 1934 Rule 10A-3,[3] should there be a presumption of a material weakness in internal control over financial reporting?

E. Material Weaknesses Corrected During the Period

The Act clearly mandates point-in-time reporting on internal control, but the benefits expected from this reporting are not limited to effectiveness on only one day of the year. The benefits, as with other provisions of the Act, were expected to enhance the quality of financial reporting and increase investor confidence. The SEC's final rules on internal control reporting are not limited to an annual report by management. Management is required to evaluate any change in the company's internal control over financial reporting that occurred during a fiscal quarter that has materially affected, or is reasonably likely to materially affect, the company's internal control over financial reporting. Management is required to disclose in its quarterly certification any such change in its internal control that occurred during the fiscal quarter covered by the quarterly report, or the last fiscal quarter, in the case of an annual report.

Discussion Questions—

18. What, if any, should the auditor's responsibility be with respect to management's disclosure of material weaknesses that existed during the period, but were corrected before the *as of* date of management's annual representation on internal control?

19. What, if any, should the auditor's responsibility be for—

- advising management on the need to make disclosure of a material weakness existing during a quarter, but corrected by the end of the quarter;

- advising the audit committee if management fails to make appropriate disclosure;

- making disclosure outside the company if the audit committee fails to persuade management to make appropriate disclosure; and

- disclosing in the auditor's annual report on internal control the existence of a material weakness that existed during the period, but was corrected by the *as of* date of management's representation on internal control?

---

3. Under this rule, the national securities exchanges and national securities associations are to prohibit the listing of any security of an issuer that is not in compliance with specific standards regarding issuer audit committees (*e.g.*, audit committee members must be independent according to certain criteria).

F. Using the Work of Others, Including Internal Auditors

In many organizations, the internal audit function monitors the effectiveness of internal control. Indeed, an important responsibility of the internal audit function is to monitor the operation of controls. In evaluating whether the monitoring component of internal control is effective, the auditor considers the work performed by internal audit.

Discussion Questions—

20. To what extent, and under what circumstances, may the auditor use the work of others, particularly internal auditors, as the principal evidence of the operating effectiveness of controls over significant account balances, classes of transactions, and disclosures?

- What is the extent of testing the independent auditor should perform on the work of others in order to rely upon that work?
- Does the extent of testing differ with respect to assessing the work of internal auditors?

21. Should there be a presumption that internal auditors cannot be considered to be objective if they report to management?

- For the independent auditor to consider the work of internal auditors, should internal auditors report to the audit committee?
- If the internal audit function is outsourced, are these internal auditors considered to be more objective than those that are employees of the issuer?

G. Scope of Testing Controls

Section 103(a)(2)(A)(iii) provides that the Board shall include in the auditing standards it adopts a requirement that the auditor "describe in each audit report the scope of the auditor's testing of the internal control structure and procedures of the issuer, required by section 404(b)." In the audit of a public company, the nature and extent of testing of internal control might still vary considerably because of differences in judgment about the extent of testing that is necessary to report *as of* a point in time, and because some auditors might decide to rely on internal control to a greater extent in connection with the auditor's tests of the financial statement amounts and disclosures. In other words, some auditors might decide to do the minimum testing necessary to give an opinion on effectiveness at a point in time, while other auditors will do considerably more testing because they intend to rely much more on internal control in order to reduce substantive procedures during the course of the audit.

Discussion Questions—

22. Should the Board's pronouncement include specific guidance on the nature, timing and extent of tests of controls?

- For example, should the auditor perform tests of internal control in effect during one or more interim periods covered by the annual financial statements?

23. Should the Board specifically address the issue of rotation of the testing of internal controls? (That is, can the auditor test certain internal controls every three years?)

- If so, should the rotation of testing be endorsed or prohibited?

24. Does a generic description of work on internal control satisfy the requirement of Section 103 of the Act? (Example of generic description: "Our examination included obtaining an understanding of internal control over financial reporting, testing and evaluating the design and operating effectiveness of internal control, and performing such other procedures as we considered necessary in the circumstances.")

25. Should there be a more extensive explanation of the nature and extent of testing performed?

26. Should the description of testing vary depending on the actual scope of work in the combined engagement, so that a user would know whether the auditor was relying on internal control

to reduce the extent of detailed testing of financial statement amounts and disclosures in a particular area?

- If so, how might this information be disclosed in the auditor's report?

H. Reporting

The auditor's report on internal control might be a separate report or a combined report on the audited financial statements and the examination of management's assertion on internal control over financial reporting. The audit report on financial statements has not included any warning that misstatements due to error or fraud may occur and not be detected. The auditor is supposed to take into consideration the inherent limitations of internal control, including the possibility of management override, when planning and performing the audit. In contrast, the existing reporting standards for an examination report on internal control contain such warnings.

Discussion Questions—

27. Should auditors be free to choose between a combined report and separate reports or should there be no option?

- If there should be no option, should separate reports or a combined report be required?
- Or, should this decision be made by the audit committee?

28. Is an inherent-limitations-of-internal-control paragraph still necessary for reporting on internal control?

- Should it be required even if management's report on internal control also describes inherent limitations?
- In a combined report, should it be clarified that the inherent limitations paragraph applies only to the report on internal control?

I. Auditor Independence

Management might request the auditor to provide a variety of nonaudit services related to its representation on internal control, including making recommendations on improvement to the entity's internal control, or assisting management in preparing or gathering documentation of controls. The Act specifically prohibits registered public accounting firms from providing certain nonaudit services, including bookkeeping services, financial information systems design and implementation, and internal audit outsourcing services, to their audit clients. The Act prohibits these services on the basis that they constitute a fundamental conflict of interest for the auditor because they involve auditing the auditor's own work, functioning as management or an employee, or acting as an advocate for the client.

Discussion Questions—

29. If existing independence requirements are insufficient, what additional requirements should the Board impose?

- Should the auditor be prohibited from providing documentation and testing services to management to assist management in making its assessment of internal control?
- If an outright prohibition is not warranted, can more explicit guidance than the admonition to avoid performing management functions, or making management decisions be established?
- Should a distinction be made between the auditor assisting in documenting existing internal control procedures versus recommending changes or enhancing internal control?

30. Are there nonaudit services that an auditor might be requested to provide management to assist in management's making the required representations on internal control that should be prohibited because they would impair independence?

31. Do existing independence requirements provide sufficient guidance on the nature of nonaudit services that can be provided to audit clients concerning documentation and testing of internal control?

* * *

The PCAOB is a private-sector, non-profit corporation, created by the Sarbanes-Oxley Act of 2002, to oversee the audits of public companies in order to protect the interests of investors and further the public interest in the preparation of informative, fair, and independent audit reports.

¶ 800. PCAOB Briefing Paper for the Public Meeting of the Board Regarding Proposed Auditing Standard—An Audit of Internal Control Over Financial Reporting Performed in Conjunction With An Audit of Financial Statements

OCTOBER 7, 2003

At its public meeting on October 7, 2003, the Public Company Accounting Oversight Board voted unanimously to propose, and seek comment on, an auditing standard, *An Audit of Internal Control Over Financial Reporting Performed in Conjunction with An Audit of Financial Statements*. This briefing paper describes the significant requirements in the proposed auditing standard as well as important, related concepts.

Introduction

Section 404(a) of the Sarbanes-Oxley Act of 2002, and the Securities and Exchange Commission's related implementing rules,[1] require the management of a public company to assess the effectiveness of the company's internal control over financial reporting, as of the end of the company's most recent fiscal year. Section 404 of the Act also requires management to include in the company's annual report to shareholders, management's conclusion as a result of that assessment about whether the company's internal control is effective. Section 404 of the Act, as well as Section 103, direct the PCAOB to establish professional standards governing the independent auditor's attestation, and reporting on, management's assessment of the effectiveness of internal control.

An attestation, in a general sense, is an expert's communication of a conclusion about the reliability of someone else's assertion. For example, a financial statement audit is a form of attestation. Specifically, the auditor attests to the fairness of a company's financial statements, which are assertions by management regarding the financial performance and condition of the company. To accomplish this task, the auditor evaluates the process management uses to prepare the company's financial statements and gathers evidence either supporting or refuting the assertions. Similarly, an auditor's attestation on management's assessment of the effectiveness of the company's internal control involves evaluating management's assessment process and gathering evidence regarding the design and operating effectiveness of the company's internal control, determining whether that evidence supports or refutes management's assessment, and opining as to whether management's assessment is fair.

Section 404(b) of the Act states that the auditor's attestation of management's assessment of internal control shall not be the subject of a separate engagement. Because the objectives of and work involved in performing both an audit of internal control and an audit of the financial statements are closely interrelated, the proposed auditing standard introduces an integrated audit of internal control and financial statements. The proposed auditing standard is an integrated standard, addressing both the work that is required to audit internal control over financial reporting and the relationship of that audit to the audit of the financial statements. The integrated audit results in two audit opinions: one on internal control over financial reporting and one on the financial statements.

Internal Control Over Financial Reporting

Internal control is a process designed to provide reasonable assurance regarding the achievement of a company's objectives in the areas of financial reporting reliability, operating efficiency and effectiveness, and compliance with laws and regulations. The SEC's rules implementing Section 404(a) of the Act, and the proposed auditing standard, focus on those objectives related to the reliability of a company's external financial reporting. This subset of internal control is commonly referred to as *internal control over financial reporting*.

Internal control over financial reporting consists of company policies and procedures that are designed and operated to provide reasonable assurance — a high, but not absolute, level of assurance — about the reliability of a company's financial reporting and its process for preparing financial statements in accordance with generally accepted accounting principles. It also includes

---

1. See *Final Rule: Management's Reports on Internal Control Over Financial Reporting and Certification of Disclosure in Exchange Act Periodic Reports* (Securities and Exchange Commission Release No. 33-8238, June 5, 2003).

policies and procedures that pertain to the maintenance of accounting records, the authorization of receipts and disbursements, and the safeguarding of assets.

Regardless of how well any system of internal control over financial reporting is designed and operating, it cannot provide absolute assurance of achieving financial reporting objectives because of inherent limitations. These inherent limitations exist because internal control over financial reporting is a process that involves human diligence and compliance and can be intentionally circumvented.

The Costs and Benefits of Internal Control

Effective internal control over financial reporting is essential for a company to effectively manage its affairs to fulfill its obligation to its investors. A company's management and its owners — public investors — and others must be able to rely on the financial information reported by companies to make decisions.

Reliable financial reporting adds value and also can offset risks in a manner that is cost-beneficial to a company. Evaluating a company's internal control over financial reporting is sometimes costly, but also has many far-reaching benefits. Some of the benefits of a company developing, maintaining, and improving its system of internal control include identifying cost-ineffective procedures, reducing costs of processing accounting information, increasing productivity of the company's financial function, and simplifying financial control systems. The primary benefit, however, is to provide the company, its management, its board and audit committee, and its owners, and other stakeholders with a reasonable basis to rely on the company's financial reporting.

The Board is sensitive to the possible effects of the proposed standard on small and medium-sized companies. Internal control is not "one-size-fits-all," and the nature and extent of controls that are necessary depend, to a great extent, on the size and complexity of the company. Large, complex, multi-national companies are likely to need extensive and sophisticated systems of internal control. In smaller companies, or in companies with less complex operations, the ethical behavior and core values of a senior management group that is directly involved in daily interactions with both internal and external parties might reduce the need for elaborate internal control systems. For a smaller, less complex company, the Board expects that the auditor will exercise reasonable judgment in determining the extent of the audit of internal control and perform only those tests that are necessary to ascertain the effectiveness of the company's internal control.

The Audit of Internal Control Over Financial Reporting

An audit of internal control over financial reporting is an extensive process, integrated with the audit of the financial statements. It involves several steps. In the proposed auditing standard, these steps would include planning the audit, evaluating the process management used to perform its assessment of internal control effectiveness, obtaining an understanding of the internal control, evaluating the effectiveness of both the design and operation of the internal control, and forming an opinion about whether internal control over financial reporting is effective.

Evaluating Management's Assessment

A natural starting place for the audit of a company's internal control over financial reporting is an evaluation of management's assessment. This evaluation provides the auditor with confidence that management has a basis for expressing its opinion on the effectiveness of internal control, provides information that will help the auditor understand the company's internal control, helps the auditor plan the work necessary to complete the audit, and provides some of the evidence the auditor will use to support his or her opinion.

The objective of an audit of internal control is to form an opinion "as to whether management's assessment of the effectiveness of the registrant's internal control over financial reporting is fairly stated in all material respects."[2] In addition, Section 103 of the Act requires the auditor's report to present an evaluation of whether the internal control structure provides reasonable assurance that transactions are recorded as necessary, among other requirements. Importantly, the auditor's conclusion will pertain directly to whether the auditor can agree with management that internal control

---

2. *Final Rule: Management's Reports on Internal Control Over Financial Reporting and Certification of Disclosure in Exchange Act Periodic Reports* (Securities and Exchange Commission Release No. 33-8238, § 210.2-02(f), June 5, 2003).

is effective, not just to the adequacy of management's process for determining whether internal control is effective. Indeed, investors expect the independent auditor to test whether the company's internal control over financial reporting is effective. The proposed auditing standard would require the auditor to do so.

Nevertheless, the work that management performs in connection with its assessment can have a significant effect on the nature, timing, and extent of the work the independent auditor will need to perform. The proposed auditing standard would allow the auditor to use, to a reasonable degree, the work performed by others, including management. Thus, the more extensive and reliable management's assessment is, the less extensive and costly the auditor's work will need to be.

The proposed auditing standard also would allow the auditor to incorporate into the audit of internal control over financial reporting some of the work performed by others, such as internal auditors or third parties who have performed work under the direction of management. To use that work, however, the auditor would need to assess the competence and objectivity of the persons who have performed it. The proposed auditing standard also would limit the auditor's ability to rely on the work of others in some key respects. That is, the standard would establish certain categories of work that the auditor must perform, such as work related to company-wide anti-fraud programs and controls and work related to other controls that have a pervasive effect on the company, such as general controls over the company's electronic data processing. The proposed auditing standard also would require that, overall, the auditor obtain directly the "principal evidence" about the effectiveness of internal control over financial reporting.

Planning the Audit

Planning the audit of internal control over financial reporting allows the auditor to develop an overall strategy for the audit. Many factors enter into audit planning, and the proposed auditing standard includes among them the auditor's knowledge of the company obtained during other engagements, matters affecting the company's industry, matters relating to the company's business, and the extent of recent changes in the company's operations or internal control over financial reporting. Armed with a good understanding of these types of factors, the auditor is in a position to effectively design the nature, timing, and scope of the planned audit.

Obtaining an Understanding of Internal Control Over Financial Reporting

To evaluate and test its effectiveness, the auditor must understand how the internal control over financial reporting is designed and operates. The auditor obtains a substantial amount of this understanding when evaluating management's assessment process.

The auditor also must be satisfied, however, that the controls *actually* have been implemented and are operating as they were designed to operate. Thus, while inquiry of company personnel and a review of management's assessment provide the auditor with an understanding of how the system of internal control is designed and operates, other procedures are necessary for the auditor to confirm his or her understanding.

The proposed auditing standard would have the auditor to confirm his or her understanding by performing procedures that include making inquiries of and observing the personnel that actually perform the controls; reviewing documents that are used in, and that result from, the application of the controls; and comparing supporting documents (for example, sales invoices, contracts, and bills of lading) to the accounting records. The most effective means of accomplishing this objective is for the auditor to perform "walkthroughs" of the company's significant processes. For this reason, and because of the importance of several other objectives that walkthroughs accomplish, the proposed auditing standard would require the auditor to perform walkthroughs.

In a walkthrough, the auditor traces all types of company transactions and events — both those that are routine and recurring and those that are unusual — from origination, through the company's accounting and information systems and financial report preparation processes, to their being reported in the company's financial statements. Walkthroughs provide the auditor with evidence that confirms his or her understanding of the process flow of transactions, the design of controls, and whether controls actually have been placed in operation. Walkthroughs also confirm that the auditor's understanding is complete and provide information necessary for the auditor to evaluate the effectiveness of the design of the internal control over financial reporting.

Because of the judgment that walkthroughs require and the significance of the objectives that walkthroughs allow the auditor to achieve, the proposed auditing standard would require the auditor to perform the walkthroughs himself or herself. In other words, the proposed auditing standard would not allow the auditor to use the work performed by management or others to satisfy the requirement to perform walkthroughs.

As a part of obtaining an understanding of internal control, the auditor also determines which controls should be tested, either by the auditor or by management or others. The proposed auditing standard, therefore, would require the auditor to identify those financial statement accounts and company processes that are significant.

The proposed standard would also require the auditor to identify relevant assertions. Does the asset exist, or did the transaction occur? Has the company included all loans outstanding in its loans payable account? Have marketable investments been properly valued? Does the company have the rights to the accounts receivable, and are the loans payable the proper obligation of the company? Are the amounts in the financial statements appropriately presented, and is there adequate disclosure about them? This process will allow the auditor to identify financial statement assertions that are relevant and for which the company should have controls.

Evaluating the Effectiveness of the Design of Controls

To be effective, internal controls must be designed properly and all the controls necessary to provide reasonable assurance about the fairness of a company's financial statements should be in place and performed by qualified people who have the authority to implement them. At some point during the internal control audit, the auditor will need to determine whether the controls would be effective if they are operated as designed, and whether all the necessary controls are in place. This is known as *design effectiveness*.

The procedures the auditor performs to test and evaluate design effectiveness include inquiry of company personnel, observation of internal controls, walkthroughs, and a specific evaluation of whether the controls are likely to prevent or detect financial statement misstatements if they are operated as designed. The proposed auditing standard would adopt these methods of testing and evaluating design effectiveness. The last step is particularly important. This evaluation calls for the auditor to apply his or her professional judgment and knowledge of and experience with internal control over financial reporting to his or her understanding of the company's controls.

Testing Operating Effectiveness

To express an opinion on internal control, the auditor must obtain evidence about whether the controls actually operate effectively. This is distinct and apart from design effectiveness.

The Act requires management's assessment and the auditor's opinion to address whether internal control was effective as of the end of the company's most recent fiscal year, in other words, as of a point-in-time. Performing all of the testing on December 31, however, is neither practical nor appropriate. To form a basis for expressing an opinion about whether internal control was effective as of a point in time requires the auditor to obtain evidence that the internal control operated effectively over an appropriate period of time. The proposed auditing standard recognizes this and allows the auditor to obtain evidence about operating effectiveness at different times throughout the year, provided that the auditor updates those tests or obtains other evidence that the controls continued to operate effectively at the end of the company's fiscal year.

The auditor should perform tests of controls to obtain evidence about the operating effectiveness of the controls. These tests include a mix of inquiries of appropriate company personnel, inspection of relevant documentation, such as sales orders and invoices, observation of the controls in operation, and reperformance of the application of the control. As indicated earlier, the auditor may use the results of tests performed by management and others, including internal auditors and third parties working under the supervision of management, provided that the auditor is satisfied that these persons are competent and performed their work in an objective manner. Therefore, the more testing management and others perform, and the better that work is, the less work will be necessary for the auditor to perform.

Tests of the effectiveness of internal control performed by management, internal auditors, or others are very important to the continued effective functioning of internal control over financial reporting and are a part of monitoring any effective system of internal control. The proposed auditing standard requires the auditor to read reports of internal auditors and others (such as the loan review function in a financial institution) that address internal control over financial reporting.

Evaluating the Results and Forming an Opinion

Both management and the auditor may identify deficiencies in the internal control over financial reporting. An internal control deficiency exists when the design or operation of a control does not allow the company's management or employees, in the normal course of performing their assigned functions, to prevent or detect misstatements on a timely basis.

The proposed auditing standard would require the auditor to evaluate the severity of all identified internal control deficiencies because such deficiencies can have an effect on his or her overall conclusion about whether internal control is effective. The auditor also has a responsibility to make sure that certain parties, such as the audit committee, are aware of internal control deficiencies that rise to a certain level of severity.

In the proposed auditing standard, an internal control deficiency (or a combination of internal control deficiencies) should be classified as a *significant deficiency* if it results in more than a remote likelihood of a misstatement of the company's annual or interim financial statements that is more than inconsequential in amount. A significant deficiency should be classified as a *material weakness* if, by itself or in combination with other internal control deficiencies, it results in more than a remote likelihood of a material misstatement in the company's annual or interim financial statements.

Most importantly, if a material weakness exists as of the end of the company's most recent fiscal year, management and the auditor must conclude that the internal control is ineffective.

The proposed auditing standard requires the auditor to communicate in writing to the company's audit committee all significant deficiencies and material weaknesses of which the auditor is aware. The auditor also is required to communicate in writing to the company's management all internal control deficiencies of which he or she is aware and to notify the audit committee that such communication has been made.

Inadequate documentation by management is a deficiency in internal control over financial reporting. The documentation that management prepares is important to the effective functioning of the internal control over financial reporting and to the auditor's internal control audit. This includes documentation about the design of the controls, including how the controls are supposed to operate; the objectives they are designed to achieve; and the necessary qualifications of the people performing the control for the control to function effectively. This documentation also includes information about the process management used to assess the effectiveness of the internal control over financial reporting, including the nature and results of the tests performed and management's evaluation. As with other internal control deficiencies, the auditor should evaluate the severity of documentation deficiencies and determine whether they rise to the level of a significant deficiency or material weakness.

The proposed auditing standard identifies a number of circumstances that would be, by definition, significant deficiencies and that also would be a strong indicator that a material weakness exists. The following paragraphs describe several of these circumstances.

- *Ineffective oversight of the company's external financial reporting and internal control over financial reporting by the company's audit committee.* The proposed auditing standard requires the auditor to evaluate factors related to whether the audit committee is effective, including whether audit committee members act independently from management. Effective oversight by the company's board of directors, including its audit committee, is essential to the company's achievement of its objectives and is an integral part of a company's monitoring of internal control. In addition to requiring the audit committee to oversee the company's external financial reporting and internal control over financial reporting, the Act makes the audit committee directly responsible for the appointment, compensation, and oversight of the work of the auditor. Thus, an ineffective audit committee can have serious detrimental effects on the company and its internal control over financial reporting as well as on the independent audit.

- *Material misstatement in the financial statements not initially identified by the company's internal controls.* The audit of internal control over financial reporting and the audit of the company's financial statements are an integrated activity and are required by the Act to be a single engagement. The results of the work performed in a financial statement audit provide evidence to support the auditor's conclusions on the effectiveness of internal control, and vice-versa. Therefore, if the auditor discovers a material misstatement in the financial statements as a part of his or her audit of the financial statements, the auditor should consider whether internal control over financial reporting is effective. That the company's internal controls did not first detect the misstatement is a strong indicator that the company's internal control over financial reporting is not effective.

- *Significant deficiencies that have been communicated to management and the audit committee but that remain uncorrected after a reasonable period of time.* Significant deficiencies in internal control that are not also determined to be material weaknesses, as defined in the proposed auditing standard, are not so severe as to require the auditor to conclude that internal control is ineffective. However, these deficiencies are significant, and the company should correct them. If management does not correct significant deficiencies within a reasonable period of time, that reflects poorly on tone-at-the-top and the control environment. Additionally, the significance of the deficiency can change over time (for example, increases in sales volume or added complexity in sales transaction structures would increase the severity of a significant deficiency affecting sales).

If, after having performed all of the procedures that the auditor considers necessary in the circumstances, the auditor has not identified any material weaknesses in internal control, then the proposed standard would permit the auditor to express an unqualified opinion that management's assessment of the effectiveness of internal control over financial reporting is fairly stated in all material respects. In the event that the auditor could not perform all of the procedures that the auditor considers necessary in the circumstances, then the proposed standard would permit the auditor to either qualify the opinion or disclaim an opinion. If an overall opinion cannot be expressed, the proposed auditing standard would require the auditor to explain why.[3]

Auditor's Responsibilities for Quarterly Reporting

Along with the auditor's work related to the annual audit of internal control over financial reporting, he or she has quarterly and annual responsibilities related to the certifications required by Section 302 of the Act.

A company's principal executive and financial officers are responsible for internal control over financial reporting. Section 302 of the Act emphasizes this responsibility by requiring these parties to certify, quarterly and annually, their responsibility, among others, for establishing and maintaining internal control over financial reporting and for disclosing changes in the company's internal control over financial reporting that occurred during the most recent quarter that have materially affected, or are likely to materially affect, the company's internal control over financial reporting.

The proposed standard also requires the auditor to play a role related to management's certifications. The auditor performs limited procedures, quarterly and annually, to identify any matters requiring modifications to management's certifications. Based on the procedures performed, if the auditor becomes aware of any matters leading to the belief that modifications to the quarterly certifications or associated disclosures about material changes in internal controls are necessary, then the proposed auditing standard would require the auditor to communicate the matters to management.

---

3. See also *Final Rule: Management's Reports on Internal Control Over Financial Reporting and Certification of Disclosure in Exchange Act Periodic Reports* (Securities and Exchange Commission Release No. 33-8328, § 210.2-02 (f), June 5, 2003) that indicates, "The attestation report on management's assessment of internal control over financial reporting shall be dated, signed manually, identify the period covered by the report and clearly state the opinion of the accountant as to whether management's assessment of the effectiveness of the registrant's internal control over financial reporting is fairly stated in all material respects, or must include an opinion to the effect that an overall opinion cannot be expressed. If an overall opinion cannot be expressed, explain why."

The proposed auditing standard would require certain additional actions of the auditor, depending on management's response. These actions range from communicating with the audit committee to reach an appropriate resolution to considering resigning from the engagement.

Effective Date of the Proposed Standard

Companies considered accelerated filers (seasoned U.S. companies with public float exceeding $75 million) are required to comply with the internal control reporting and disclosure requirements of Section 404 of the Act for fiscal years ending on or after June 15, 2004. Accordingly, auditors engaged to audit the financial statements of such companies for fiscal years ending on or after June 15, 2004, also are required to audit and report on the company's internal control over financial reporting as of the end of such fiscal year. Other companies (including smaller companies, foreign private issuers and companies with only registered debt securities) have until fiscal years ending on or after April 15, 2005, to comply with these internal control reporting and disclosure requirements and the requirement for audit reporting on internal control is similarly delayed.

Public Comment

If the Board issues the proposed standard, it will seek comment on the proposed standard for a 45-day period. Interested persons are encouraged to submit their views to the Board. Written comments should be sent to Office of the Secretary, PCAOB, 1666 K Street, N.W., Washington, D.C. 20006-2803. Comments may also be submitted by e-mail to comments@pcaobus.org or through the Board's Web site at www.pcaobus.org. All comments should refer to PCAOB Rulemaking Docket Matter No. 008 in the subject or reference line and should be received by the Board no later than 5:00 p.m. (EST) on November 21, 2003.

The Board will carefully consider all comments received. Following the close of the comment period, the Board will determine whether to adopt a final standard, with or without amendments. Any final standard adopted will be submitted to the Securities and Exchange Commission for approval. Pursuant to Section 107 of the Act, proposed rules of the Board do not take effect unless approved by the Commission. Standards are deemed to be rules under the Act.

* * *

The PCAOB is a private-sector, non-profit corporation, created by the Sarbanes-Oxley Act of 2002, to oversee the auditors of public companies in order to protect the interests of investors and further the public interest in the preparation of informative, fair, and independent audit reports.

¶ 900. PCAOB Briefing Paper for the Public Meeting of the Board: Board Considers Adopting Standard for Audits of Internal Control Over Financial Reporting

MARCH 9, 2004

Introduction

The series of business failures that began with Enron in late 2001 exposed serious weaknesses in the system of checks and balances that were intended to protect the interests of shareholders, pension beneficiaries and employees of public companies — and to protect the confidence of the American public in the stability and fairness of U.S. capital markets.

From the boardroom to the executive suite, to the offices of accountants and lawyers, the historic gatekeepers of this confidence were found missing or, worse, complicit in the breaches of the public trust.

Congress responded to the corporate failures with the Sarbanes-Oxley Act of 2002, creating a broad, new oversight regime for auditors of public companies while prescribing specific steps to address specific failures and codifying the responsibilities of corporate executives, corporate directors, lawyers and accountants.

The merits, benefits, cost and wisdom of each of the prescriptions can and will fuel debate. But the context for the passage of the Sarbanes-Oxley Act, and the President's signing it into law on July 30, 2002, cannot be ignored: Corporate leaders and advisors failed. People lost their livelihoods and their life savings. The faith of America and the world in U.S. markets was shaken to the core.

In that context, the Public Company Accounting Oversight Board is prepared to adopt the standard for auditors to use when assessing whether managers of a public company have accurately reported on companies' internal controls over financial reporting.

Failures in internal control, particularly over financial reporting, were among the specific concerns addressed by Congress in the Sarbanes-Oxley Act. Congress required not just that management report on a company's internal control over financial reporting, but that auditors attest to the accuracy of management's report.

The bottom line for Congress, and for the PCAOB, is the reliability of the company's financial statements — statements relied on by shareholders, management, directors, regulators, lenders, investors and the market at large.

To achieve reliable financial statements, internal controls must be in place to see that records accurately and fairly reflect transactions in and dispositions of a company's assets; to provide assurance that the records of transactions are sufficient to prepare financial statements in accordance with generally accepted accounting principles, and that receipts and expenditures are made only as authorized by management and directors; and to make sure that steps are in place to prevent or detect theft, unauthorized use or disposition of the company's assets of a value that could have a material effect on the financial statements.

In the simplest terms, investors can have much more confidence in the reliability of a corporate financial statement if corporate management demonstrates that it exercises adequate internal control over bookkeeping, the sufficiency of books and records for the preparation of accurate financial statements, adherence to rules about the use of company assets and the possibility of misappropriation of company assets.

The Sarbanes-Oxley Act, in Section 404, requires company management to assess and report on the company's internal control. It also requires a company's independent, outside auditors to issue an "attestation" to management's assessment — in other words, to provide shareholders and the public at large with an independent reason to rely on management's description of the company's internal control over financial reporting.

Reliable financial reporting is too important to relegate an auditor's attestation to a rubber-stamped endorsement of management's report on internal controls. As a result, the PCAOB is prepared to require that auditors perform an audit of internal control over financial reporting and to perform that audit in conjunction with the audit of a company's financial statements.

The one audit cannot be separated from the other. The information the auditor learns as a result of auditing the company's financial statements has a direct and important bearing on the auditor's conclusion about the effectiveness of the company's internal control over financial reporting.

Section 404 and the Board's requirements will entail extra work and, for companies, extra expense, particularly in the first year of implementation. The PCAOB will be vigilant in its inspections of accounting firms and conversations with issuers, particularly small and medium-sized companies, to see that expense isn't increased for its own sake.

The Board does not underestimate the demands this auditing standard will impose on auditors and public companies. But in the end, the Board, public companies and the accounting profession answer to the higher demand of accuracy, reliability and fairness in the financial statements that provide the basis for trust in our financial markets.

The Benefits of Effective Internal Control Over Financial Reporting

Companies use internal controls as checks on a variety of processes, including financial reporting, operating efficiency and effectiveness, and compliance with applicable laws and regulations. The Sarbanes-Oxley Act of 2002 focuses on companies' internal control over financial reporting.

Internal control over financial reporting consists of company policies and procedures that are designed and operated to provide reasonable assurance about the reliability of a company's financial reporting and its process for preparing and fairly presenting financial statements in accordance with generally accepted accounting principles. It includes policies and procedures for maintaining accounting records, authorizing receipts and disbursements, and the safeguarding of assets.

Effective internal control over financial reporting is essential for a company to effectively manage its affairs and to fulfill its obligation to its investors. A company's management, its owners — public investors — and others must be able to rely on the financial information reported by companies to make decisions.

Strong internal controls also provide better opportunities to detect and deter fraud. For example, many frauds resulting in financial statement restatement relied upon the ability of management to exploit weaknesses in internal control. To the extent that internal control reporting can help restore investor confidence by improving the effectiveness of internal controls (and reducing the incidence of fraud), assessments of internal controls over financial reporting should emphasize controls that prevent or detect errors as well as fraud.

Evaluating a company's internal control over financial reporting is not without cost, but it provides many far-reaching benefits. Regular assessments, and reporting on those assessments, can help management develop, maintain and improve existing internal control. Assessments can identify cost-ineffective procedures, reduce costs of processing accounting information, increase productivity of the company's financial function, and simplify financial control systems. It also may result in fewer financial statement restatements and less litigation.

The primary benefit of evaluations, however, is to provide the company, its management, its board and audit committee, and its owners and other stakeholders with a reasonable basis on which to rely on the company's financial reporting. The integrity of financial reporting represents the foundation upon which this country's public markets are built.

As with many endeavors, internal control over financial reporting is a process that involves human diligence and compliance and, consequently, can be intentionally circumvented. As a result, no system of internal control over financial reporting, regardless of how well it is designed and operating, can provide absolute assurance that a company's financial statements are accurate.

Nevertheless, as companies develop processes to assist management in assessing internal control and as auditors perform their evaluations, the assessment process should result in a continuous strengthening of internal control over financial reporting.

Basis for Internal Control Reporting and the Board's Standard

Section 404(a) of the Sarbanes-Oxley Act of 2002 requires the management of a public company to assess the effectiveness of the company's internal control over financial reporting as of the end of the company's most recent fiscal year and to include in the company's annual report to shareholders management's conclusion, as a result of that assessment, about whether the company's internal control is effective. The Securities and Exchange Commission implemented Section 404(a) in a rule on June 5, 2003.[1]

Section 404(b) of the Act requires the company's auditor to attest to and report on the assessment made by the company's management. Sections 103(a)(2)(A) and 404(b) of the Act direct the Public Company Accounting Oversight Board to establish professional standards governing the independent auditor's attestation.

In April 2003, the Board adopted pre-existing professional standards as the Board's interim standards, including a standard governing an auditor's attestation on internal control. Mindful of the requirements of the Sarbanes-Oxley Act and the need to evaluate the pre-existing standard, the Board convened a public roundtable discussion on July 29, 2003, to discuss issues and hear views related to reporting on internal control. The participants included representatives from public companies, accounting firms, investor groups, and regulatory organizations.

As a result of comments made at the roundtable, advice from the Board's staff, and other input, the Board determined that the pre-existing standard governing an auditor's attestation on internal control was insufficient for purposes of effectively implementing the requirements of Section 404(b) of the Act and for the Board to appropriately discharge the Board's standard-setting obligations under Section 103 of the Act. In response, the Board developed and issued, on October 7, 2003, a proposed auditing standard titled "An Audit of Internal Control over Financial Reporting in Conjunction with An Audit of Financial Statements."

The Board received 193 comment letters from a variety of interested parties, including auditors, investors, internal auditors, issuers, regulators, and others on a broad array of topics. Those comments led to changes in the proposed standard, intended to make the requirements of the standard clearer and more operational.

The Board is now prepared to approve PCAOB Auditing Standard No. 2, implementing the requirements of the Sarbanes-Oxley Act and incorporating comments received.

This document summarizes some of the significant considerations of the Board when it initially proposed this standard and when it evaluated the comments it received. The Board intends to release a more detailed analysis of the comments received and the Board's responses.

The Audit of Internal Control Over Financial Reporting

In preparing PCAOB Auditing Standard No. 2, the Board was guided by a number of broad considerations that have effect throughout the standard. Those broad considerations included: that "attestation" is insufficient to describe the process of assessing management's report on internal controls; that an audit of internal control over financial reporting must be integrated with an audit of the company's financial statements; and that the costs of the internal control audit be appropriate in consideration of the expected benefits to investors of improved internal control over financial reporting.

Attestation vs. Audit

Throughout Auditing Standard No. 2, the auditor's attestation of management's assessment of the effectiveness of internal control is referred to as the audit of internal control over financial reporting. The Board has noted, in comment letters and in other communications, that some people have drawn a distinction between an "audit" and an "attestation," suggesting that an attestation is a different type of engagement that involves a lesser amount of work than an audit. This idea is erroneous. An attestation engagement to examine management's assessment of internal control requires the same level of work as an audit of internal control over financial reporting.

---

1. See Management's Reports on Internal Control Over Financial Reporting and Certification of Disclosure in Exchange Act Periodic Reports, Securities and Exchange Commission Release No. 33-8238 (June 5, 2003) [68 FR 36636].

The objective of an audit of internal control over financial reporting is to form an opinion "as to whether management's assessment of the effectiveness of the registrant's internal control over financial reporting is fairly stated in all material respects."[2] Further, Section 103(a)(2)(A)(iii) of the Act requires the auditor's report to present an evaluation of whether the internal control structure provides reasonable assurance that transactions are recorded as necessary, among other requirements.

Importantly, the auditor's conclusion will pertain directly to whether the auditor can agree with management that internal control is effective, not just to the adequacy of management's process for determining whether internal control is effective.

An auditing process restricted to evaluating what management has done would not provide the auditor with a sufficiently high level of assurance that management's conclusion is correct. The auditor needs to evaluate management's assessment process to be satisfied that management has an appropriate basis for its conclusion. The auditor, however, also needs to test the effectiveness of internal control to be satisfied that management's conclusion is correct and, therefore, fairly stated. Indeed, as the Board heard at the internal control roundtable and in comment letters, investors expect the independent auditor to test whether the company's internal control over financial reporting is effective, and Auditing Standard No. 2 requires the auditor to do so.

Integrated Audit

PCAOB Auditing Standard No. 2 describes an *integrated audit* of the financial statements and internal control over financial reporting. Accordingly, it is an integrated standard that (1) addresses both the work that is required to audit internal control over financial reporting and the relationship of that audit to the audit of the financial statements and (2) refers to the attestation of management's assessment of the effectiveness of the internal control as the audit of internal control over financial reporting.

The Board decided that these audits should be integrated because the objectives of, and work involved in performing, an audit of internal control over financial reporting and an audit of the financial statements are closely related. Furthermore, Section 404(b) of the Sarbanes-Oxley Act provides that the auditor's attestation of management's assessment of internal control shall not be the subject of a separate engagement.

Each audit provides the auditor with information relevant to the auditor's evaluation of the results of the other audit. For example, the auditor's discovery of misstatements in the financial statements while performing financial statement auditing procedures indicates that there may be weaknesses in the company's internal control over financial reporting. Because of the significance of this interrelationship, the Board has made it clear that, to conduct and report on the results of an audit of internal control over financial reporting pursuant to Auditing Standard No. 2, the auditor also must audit the company's financial statements.

Notwithstanding the fact that the two audits are interrelated, the integrated audit results in two separate objectives: to express an opinion on management's assessment of the effectiveness of the company's internal control over financial reporting and to express an opinion on whether the financial statements are fairly stated.

Cost

The Board is sensitive to the costs Section 404 and Auditing Standard No. 2 may impose on all companies, particularly some small and medium-sized companies. The Board anticipates that most companies of all sizes will experience the highest cost of complying with Section 404 during the first year of implementation.

Internal control is not "one-size-fits-all," and the nature and extent of controls that are necessary depend, to a great extent, on the size and complexity of the company. Large, complex, multi-national companies, for example, are likely to need extensive and sophisticated internal control systems.

---

2. See SEC Regulation S-X 2-02(f), 17 C.F.R. 210.2-02(f).

In smaller companies, or in companies with less complex operations, the ethical behavior and core values of a senior management group that is directly involved in daily interactions with both internal and external parties might reduce the need for elaborate internal control systems. The Board expects that the auditor will exercise reasonable professional judgment in determining the extent of the audit of internal control and perform only those tests that are necessary to ascertain the effectiveness of the company's internal control.

Management is required to base its assessment of the effectiveness of the company's internal control over financial reporting on a suitable, recognized control framework established by a body of experts that followed due-process procedures to develop the framework. In the United States, the Committee of Sponsoring Organizations ("COSO") of the Treadway Commission has published *Internal Control —Integrated Framework*. COSO's publication (also referred to simply as COSO) provides a suitable framework for purposes of management's assessment.

The directions in Auditing Standard No. 2 are based on the internal control framework established by COSO because of the frequency with which management of public companies are expected to use that framework for their assessments. Other suitable frameworks have been published in other countries and likely will be published in the future. Although different frameworks may not contain exactly the same elements as COSO, they should have elements that encompass all of COSO's general themes. The auditor should therefore be able to apply the concepts and guidance in Auditing Standard No. 2 in a reasonable manner if management uses a suitable framework other than COSO.

The Board believes that the special considerations for small and medium-sized companies included within COSO provide well for the auditor's use of such judgment, more so than the appendix that the Board's proposed standard originally included. For this reason, the proposed appendix was removed from Auditing Standard No. 2 and replaced with a direct reference to the special considerations within COSO.

The Board also was cognizant of audit costs in its consideration of the appropriate extent to which the auditor may use the work of internal auditors and others to support the auditor's opinion on internal control effectiveness. Auditing Standard No. 2 provides the auditor with significant flexibility in using the relevant work of highly competent and objective personnel, while also requiring the auditor to obtain through his or her own auditing procedures a meaningful portion of the evidence that supports the auditor's opinion. The Board believes it has achieved an appropriate balance of work between the auditor and others that will ensure a high quality audit of internal control and that have the complementary benefit of encouraging companies to invest in competent and objective internal audit functions.

The Audit Process

An audit of internal control over financial reporting is an extensive process involving several steps, including planning the audit, evaluating the process management used to perform its assessment of internal control effectiveness, obtaining an understanding of the internal control, evaluating the effectiveness of both the design and operation of the internal control, and forming an opinion about whether internal control over financial reporting is effective.

The auditor's objective is to express an opinion about whether management's assessment, or conclusion, on the effectiveness of internal control over financial reporting is stated fairly, in all material respects. To support his or her opinion, the auditor must obtain evidence about whether internal control over financial reporting is effective. The auditor obtains this evidence in several ways, including evaluating and testing management's assessment process; evaluating and testing work on internal control performed by others, such as internal auditors; and testing the effectiveness of the controls himself or herself.

Auditor Independence

The Sarbanes-Oxley Act, and the SEC rules implementing Section 404(a) of the Act, require the auditor to be independent to perform an audit of internal control over financial reporting. Under the SEC's Rule 2-01 on auditor independence, an auditor impairs his or her independence if the auditor audits his or her own work, including any work on designing or implementing an audit client's internal control system. PCAOB Auditing Standard No. 2 explicitly prohibits the auditor from accepting an engagement to provide an audit client with an internal control-related service that has not been specifically pre-approved by the audit committee. That is, the audit committee cannot pre-approve internal control-related services as a category, but must approve each service.

* * *

The PCAOB is a private-sector, non-profit corporation, created by the Sarbanes-Oxley Act of 2002, to oversee the auditors of public companies in order to protect the interests of investors and further the public interest in the preparation of informative, fair, and independent audit reports.

¶ 1000. Management's Report on Internal Control Over Financial Reporting and Certification of Disclosure in Exchange Act Periodic Reports; Final Rule

SECURITIES AND EXCHANGE COMMISSION

17 CFR Parts 210, 228, 229, 240, 249, 270 and 274

[Release Nos. 33-8238; 34-47986; IC-26068; File Nos. S7-40-02; S7-06-03]

RIN 3235-AI66 and 3235-AI79

Management's Report on Internal Control Over Financial Reporting and Certification of Disclosure in Exchange Act Periodic Reports

AGENCY: Securities and Exchange Commission.

ACTION: Final rule.

SUMMARY: As directed by Section 404 of the Sarbanes-Oxley Act of 2002, we are adopting rules requiring companies subject to the reporting requirements of the Securities Exchange Act of 1934, other than registered investment companies, to include in their annual reports a report of management on the company's internal control over financial reporting. The internal control report must include: a statement of management's responsibility for establishing and maintaining adequate internal control over financial reporting for the company; management's assessment of the effectiveness of the company's internal control over financial reporting as of the end of the company's most recent fiscal year; a statement identifying the framework used by management to evaluate the effectiveness of the company's internal control over financial reporting; and a statement that the registered public accounting firm that audited the company's financial statements included in the annual report has issued an attestation report on management's assessment of the company's internal control over financial reporting. Under the new rules, a company is required to file the registered public accounting firm's attestation report as part of the annual report. Furthermore, we are adding a requirement that management evaluate any change in the company's internal control over financial reporting that occurred during a fiscal quarter that has materially affected, or is reasonably likely to materially affect, the company's internal control over financial reporting. Finally, we are adopting amendments to our rules and forms under the Securities Exchange Act of 1934 and the Investment Company Act of 1940 to revise the Section 302 certification requirements and to require issuers to provide the certifications required by Sections 302 and 906 of the Sarbanes-Oxley Act of 2002 as exhibits to certain periodic reports.

DATES: *Effective Date:* August 14, 2003.

Compliance Dates: The following compliance dates apply to companies other than registered investment companies. A company that is an "accelerated filer," as defined in Exchange Act Rule 12b-2, as of the end of its first fiscal year ending on or after June 15, 2004, must begin to comply with the management report on internal control over financial reporting disclosure requirements in its annual report for that fiscal year. A company that is not an accelerated filer as of the end of its first fiscal year ending on or after June 15, 2004, including a foreign private issuer, must begin to comply with the annual internal control report for its first fiscal year ending on or after April 15, 2005. A company must begin to comply with the requirements regarding evaluation of any material change to its internal control over financial reporting in its first periodic report due after the first annual report required to include a management report on internal control over financial reporting. Companies may voluntarily comply with the new disclosure requirements before the compliance dates. A company must comply with the new exhibit requirements for the certifications required by Sections 302 and 906 of the Sarbanes-Oxley Act of 2002 and changes to the Section 302 certification requirements in its quarterly, semi-annual or annual report due on or after August 14, 2003. To account for the differences between the compliance date of the rules relating to internal control over financial reporting and the effective date of changes to the language of the Section 302 certification, a company's certifying officers may temporarily modify the content of their Section 302 certifications to eliminate certain references to internal control over financial reporting until the compliance date, as further explained in Section III.E. below.

Registered investment companies must comply with the rule and form amendments applicable to them on and after August 14, 2003, except as follows. Registered investment companies must comply with the amendments to Exchange Act Rules 13a-15(a) and 15d-15(a) and Investment Company Act Rule 30a-3(a) that require them to maintain internal control over financial reporting with respect to fiscal years ending on or after June 15, 2004. In addition, a registered investment company's certifying officers may temporarily modify the content of their Section 302 certifications to eliminate certain references to internal control over financial reporting, as further explained in Section II.I. below. Registered investment companies may voluntarily comply with the rule and form amendments before the compliance dates.

FOR FURTHER INFORMATION CONTACT: N. Sean Harrison, Special Counsel, or Andrew D. Thorpe, Special Counsel, Division of Corporation Finance, at (202) 942-2910, or with respect to registered investment companies, Christian Broadbent, Senior Counsel, Division of Investment Management, at (202) 942-0721, or with respect to attestation and auditing issues, Edmund Bailey, Assistant Chief Accountant, Randolph P. Green, Professional Accounting Fellow, or Paul Munter, Academic Accounting Fellow, Office of the Chief Accountant, at (202) 942-4400, U.S. Securities and Exchange Commission, 450 Fifth Street, NW., Washington, DC 20549.

SUPPLEMENTARY INFORMATION: We are revising Items 307, 401 and 601 of Regulations S-B[1] and S-K;[2] adding new Item 308 to Regulations S-B and S-K; amending Form 10-K,[3] Form 10-KSB,[4] Form 10-Q,[5] Form 10-QSB,[6] Form 20-F,[7] Form 40-F,[8] Rule 12b-15,[9] Rule 13a-14,[10] Rule 13a-15,[11] Rule 15d-14[12] and Rule 15d-15[13] under the Securities Exchange Act of 1934 (the "Exchange Act");[14] amending Rules 1-02 and 2-02[15] of Regulation S-X;[16] amending Rules 8b-15,[17] 30a-2[18] and 30a-3[19] under the Investment Company Act of 1940 ("Investment Company Act");[20] and amending Forms N-CSR[21] and N-SAR[22] under the Exchange Act and the Investment Company Act.

Table of Contents

I. Background

A. Management's Report on Internal Control over Financial Reporting

B. Certifications

II. Discussion of Amendments Implementing Section 404

A. Definition of Internal Control

1. Proposed Rule

2. Comments on the Proposal

3. Final Rules

---

1. 17 CFR 228.10 *et seq.*
2. 17 CFR 229.10 *et seq.*
3. 17 CFR 249.310.
4. 17 CFR 249.310b.
5. 17 CFR 249.308a.
6. 17 CFR 249.308b.
7. 17 CFR 249.220f.
8. 17 CFR 249.240f.
9. 17 CFR 240.12b-15.
10. 17 CFR 240.13a-14.
11. 17 CFR 240.13a-15.
12. 17 CFR 140.15d-14.
13. 17 CFR 240.15d-15.
14. 15 U.S.C. 78a *et seq.*
15. 17 CFR 210.1-02 and 2-02.
16. 17 CFR 210.1-01 *et seq.*
17. 17 CFR 270.8b-15.
18. 17 CFR 270.30a-2.
19. 17 CFR 270.30a-3.
20. 15 U.S.C. 80a-1 *et seq.*
21. 17 CFR 249.331; 17 CFR 274.128.
22. 17 CFR 249.330; 17 CFR 274.101.

V. Cost-Benefit Analysis

VI. Effect on Efficiency, Competition and Capital Formation

VII. Final Regulatory Flexibility Analysis

VIII. Statutory Authority and Text of Rule Amendments

I. Background

A. *Management's Report on Internal Control Over Financial Reporting*

In this release, we implement Section 404 of the Sarbanes-Oxley Act of 2002 (the "Sarbanes-Oxley Act"),[23] which requires us to prescribe rules requiring each annual report that a company, other than a registered investment company,[24] files pursuant to Section 13(a) or 15(d) of the Exchange Act to contain an internal control report: (1) Stating management's responsibility for establishing and maintaining an adequate internal control structure and procedures for financial reporting; and (2) containing an assessment, as of the end of the company's most recent fiscal year, of the effectiveness of the company's internal control structure and procedures for financial reporting. Section 404 also requires every registered public accounting firm that prepares or issues an audit report on a company's annual financial statements to attest to, and report on, the assessment made by management. The attestation must be made in accordance with standards for attestation engagements issued or adopted by the Public Company Accounting Oversight Board ("PCAOB").[25] Section 404 further stipulates that the attestation cannot be the subject of a separate engagement of the registered public accounting firm.

We received over 200 comment letters in response to our release proposing requirements to implement Sections 404, 406 and 407 of the Sarbanes-Oxley Act.[26] Of these, 61 respondents commented on the Section 404 proposals.[27] These comment letters came from corporations, professional associations, accountants, law firms, consultants, academics, investors and others. In general, the commenters supported the objectives of the proposed new requirements. Investors supported the manner in which we proposed to achieve these objectives and, in some cases, urged us to require additional disclosure from companies. Other commenters, however, thought that we were requiring more disclosure than necessary to fulfill the mandates of the Sarbanes-Oxley Act and suggested modifications to the proposals.

We have reviewed and considered all of the comments that we received on the proposals. The adopted rules reflect many of these comments—we discuss our conclusions with respect to each topic and related comments in more detail throughout the release.

B. *Certifications*

We also are adopting amendments to require companies to file the certifications mandated by Sections 302 and 906 of the Sarbanes-Oxley Act as exhibits to annual, semi-annual and quarterly

---

23. Pub. L. 107-204, 116 Stat. 745 (2002).
24. Section 404 of the Sarbanes-Oxley Act does not apply to any registered investment company due to an exemption in Section 405 of the Sarbanes-Oxley Act. See sec. 405 of Pub. L. 107-204, 116 Stat. 745 (2002).
25. On April 25, 2003, the Commission approved the PCAOB's adoption of the auditing and attestation standards in existence as of April 16, 2003 as interim auditing and attestation standards. See Release No. 33-8222 (Apr. 25, 2003) [68 FR 23335].
26. Release No. 33-8138 (Oct. 22, 2002) [67 FR 66208] ("Proposing Release"). The public comments we received can be viewed in our Public Reference Room at 450 Fifth Street, NW, Washington, DC 20549, in File No. S7-40-02. Public comments submitted by electronic mail are available on our Web site, *http://www.sec.gov.*
27. The commenters on File No. S7-40-02 are as follows: *Academics* Paul Walker, Ph.D., CPA; *Accounting Firms* BDO Seidman, LLP; Deloitte & Touche LLP; Ernst & Young LLP; KPMG LLP; PricewaterhouseCoopers LLP; *Associations* America's Community Bankers; American Bankers Association; American Bar Association; American Corporate Counsel Association; American Institute of Certified Public Accountants; Association for Financial Professionals; the Association of the Bar of the City of New York; Association for Investment Management and Research; the Business Roundtable; Community Bankers Association of New York State; Edison Electric Institute; Financial Executives International; Independent Community Bankers of America; the Institute of Internal Auditors; Maine Bankers Association; Manufacturers Alliance/MAPI Inc.; Massachusetts Bankers Association; National Association of Real Estate Investment Trusts; New York Bankers Association; New York County Lawyers' Association; New York State Bar Association; Software & Information Industry Association; Software Finance and Tax Executives Council; Wisconsin Bankers Association; *Corporations* Cardinal Health, Inc.; Compass Bancshares, Inc.; Computer Sciences Corporation; Eastman Kodak Company; Eli Lilly and Company; Emerson Electric Co.; Executive Responsibility Advisors, LLC; Greif Bros.; Intel Corporation; International Paper Company; Protiviti; *Government Entities* Federal Reserve Bank of Atlanta; Small Business Administration; *Law Firms* Dykema Gossett PLLC; Karr Tuttle Campbell; Fried, Frank, Harris, Shriver and Jacobson; Sutherland, Asbill & Brennan LLP; *Individuals* Thomas Damman; D. Scott Huggins; Tim J. Leech; Simon Lorne; Ralph Saul; Lee Squire; Robert J. Stuckey; Foreign Companies Siemens Aktiengesellcraft; *International Entities* British Bankers Association; British Embassy; Canadian Bankers Association; Confederation of British Industry; European Commission; Institute of Chartered Accountants of England and Wales.

---

reports. Section 302 required the Commission to adopt final rules that were to be effective by August 29, 2002, under which the principal executive and principal financial officers, or persons performing similar functions, of a company filing periodic reports under Section 13(a) or 15(d) of the Exchange Act[28] must provide a certification in each quarterly and annual report filed with the Commission. Section 906 of the Sarbanes-Oxley Act added new Section 1350 to Title 18 of the United States Code,[29] which contains a certification requirement subject to specific federal criminal provisions and that is separate and distinct from the certification requirement mandated by Section 302.[30] On August 28, 2002, we adopted Exchange Act Rules 13a-14 and 15d-14 and Investment Company Act Rule 30a-2 and amended our periodic report forms to implement the statutory directive in Section 302.[31] These rules and amendments became effective on August 29, 2002. On January 27, 2003, we adopted Form N-CSR to be used by registered management investment companies to file certified shareholder reports with the Commission.[32] The provisions added to Title 18 by Section 906 were by their terms effective on enactment of the Sarbanes-Oxley Act.

To enhance the ability of interested parties to effectively access the certifications through our Electronic Data Gathering, Analysis and Retrieval ("EDGAR") system and thereby enhance compliance with the certification requirements, we proposed to amend our rules and forms to require a company to file the certifications as an exhibit to the periodic reports to which they relate.[33] The proposals addressed both Section 302 and 906 certifications. After discussions with the Department of Justice, we concluded that, in light of the inconsistent methods that companies have been employing to fulfill their obligations under Section 906,[34] an exhibit requirement would consistently enable investors and the Commission staff, as well as the Department of Justice, to more effectively monitor compliance with this certification requirement.

II. Discussion of Amendments Implementing Section 404

A. Definition of Internal Control

1. Proposed Rule

The proposed rules would have defined the term "internal controls and procedures for financial reporting"[35] to mean controls that pertain to the preparation of financial statements for external purposes that are fairly presented in conformity with generally accepted accounting principles as addressed by the Codification of Statements on Auditing Standards Sec. 319 or any superseding definition or other literature that is issued or adopted by the Public Company Accounting Oversight Board.

As noted in the Proposing Release, there has been some confusion over the exact meaning and scope of the term "internal control," because the definition of the term has evolved over time. Historically, the term "internal control" was applied almost exclusively within the accounting profession.[36] As the auditing of financial statements evolved from a process of detailed testing of transactions and account balances towards a process of sampling and testing, greater consideration of a

---

28. 15 U.S.C. 78m(a) or 78o(d). Section 13(a) of the Exchange Act requires every issuer of a security registered pursuant to Section 12 of the Exchange Act [15 U.S.C. 78l] to file with the Commission such annual reports and such quarterly reports as the Commission may prescribe. Section 15(d) of the Exchange Act requires each issuer that has filed a registration statement that has become effective pursuant to the Securities Act of 1933 [15 U.S.C. 77a *et seq.*] (the "Securities Act") to file such supplementary and periodic information, documents and reports as may be required pursuant to Section 13 in respect of a security registered pursuant to Section 12, unless the duty to file under Section 15(d) has been suspended for any fiscal year. See Exchange Act Rule 12h-3 [17 CFR 240.12h-3].

29. 29 18 U.S.C. 1350.

30. See Release No. 34-46300 (Aug. 2, 2002) [67 FR 51508] at n. 11, containing supplemental information on the Commission's original certification proposal in light of the enactment of the Sarbanes-Oxley Act of 2002.

31. See Release No. 33-8124 (Aug. 28, 2002) [67 FR 57276].

32. See Release No. IC-25914 (Jan. 27, 2003) [68 FR 5348].

33. See Release No. 33-8212 (Mar. 21, 2003) [68 FR 15600].

34. These methods have included: (1) Submitting the statement as non-public paper correspondence; (2) submitting the statement as non-public electronic correspondence with the EDGAR filing of the periodic report; (3) submitting the statement under (1) or (2) above supplemented by an Item 9 Form 8-K report so that the statement is publicly available; (4) submitting the statement as an exhibit to the periodic report; and (5) submitting the statement in the text of the periodic report (typically, below the signature block for the report).

35. We proposed to use this term throughout the rules implementing the annual internal control report requirements of Section 404 of the Sarbanes-Oxley Act, as well as the revised Sarbanes-Oxley Section 302 certification requirements, to complement the defined term "disclosure controls and procedures" referred to in the Section 302 requirements. Congress used the term "internal controls" in Section 302 and "internal control structure and procedures for financial reporting" in Section 404.

36. For a history of the development of internal control standards, see Steven J. Root, *Beyond COSO—Internal Control to Enhance Corporate Governance* (1998).

---

company's internal controls became necessary in planning an audit.[37] If an internal control component had been adequately designed, then the auditor could limit further consideration of that control to procedures to determine whether the control had been placed in operation. Accordingly, the auditor could rely on the control to serve as a basis to reduce the amount, timing or extent of substantive testing in the execution of an audit. Conversely, if an auditor determined that an internal control component was inadequate in its design or operation, then the auditor could not rely upon that control. In this instance, the auditor would conduct tests of transactions and perform additional analyses in order to accumulate sufficient, competent audit evidence to support its opinion on the financial statements.

From the outset, it was recognized that internal control is a broad concept that extends beyond the accounting functions of a company. Early attempts to define the term focused primarily on clarifying the portion of a company's internal control that an auditor should consider when planning and performing an audit of a company's financial statements.[38] However, this did not improve the level of understanding of the term, nor satisfactorily provide the guidance sought by auditors. Successive definitions and formal studies of the concept of internal control followed.

In 1977, based on recommendations of the Commission, Congress enacted the Foreign Corrupt Practices Act ("FCPA").[39] The FCPA codified the accounting control provisions contained in Statement of Auditing Standards No. 1 (codified as AU § 320 in the Codification of Statements on Auditing Standards). Under the FCPA, companies that have a class of securities registered under Section 12 of the Exchange Act, or that are required to file reports under Section 15(d) of the Exchange Act, are required to devise and maintain a system of internal accounting controls sufficient to provide reasonable assurances that:

- transactions are executed in accordance with management's general or specific authorization;

- transactions are recorded as necessary (1) to permit preparation of financial statements in conformity with generally accepted accounting principles or any other criteria applicable to such statements, and (2) to maintain accountability for assets;

- access to assets is permitted only in accordance with management's general or specific authorization; and

- the recorded accountability for assets is compared with the existing assets at reasonable intervals and appropriate action is taken with respect to any differences.[40]

In 1985, a private-sector initiative known as the National Commission on Fraudulent Financial Reporting, also known as the Treadway Commission, was formed to study the financial reporting system in the United States. In 1987, the Treadway Commission issued a report recommending that its sponsoring organizations work together to integrate the various internal control concepts and definitions and to develop a common reference point.

---

37. In 1941, the Commission adopted amendments to Rules 2-02 and 3-07 of Regulation S-X that formally codified this practice. See Accounting Series Release No. 21 (Feb. 5, 1941) [11 FR 10921].
38. An early definition for the term appeared in *Internal Control — Elements Of a Coordinated System and Its Importance to Management and the Independent Public Accountant*, a report published in 1949 by the American Institute of Accountants, the predecessor to the American Institute of Certified Public Accountants ("AICPA"). The report defined internal control to mean "the plan of organization and all of the coordinate methods and measures adopted within a business to safeguard its assets, check the accuracy and reliability of its accounting data, promote operational efficiency, and encourage adherence to prescribed managerial policies." Subsequent definitions of the term attempted to clarify the distinction by labeling the controls relevant to an audit as "internal accounting controls" and the non-accounting controls as "administrative controls." The AICPA officially dropped these distinctions in 1988. See Root, at p. 76.
39. Title I of Pub. L. 95-213 (1977). Beginning in 1973, as a result of the work of the Office of the Watergate Special Prosecutor, the Commission became aware of a pattern of conduct involving the use of corporate funds for illegal domestic political contributions. A subsequent Commission investigation revealed that instances of undisclosed questionable or illegal corporate payments — both domestic and foreign — were widespread. On May 12, 1976, the Commission submitted to the Senate Banking, Housing and Urban Affairs Committee a report entitled *Report on Questionable and Illegal Corporate Payments and Practices*. The report described and analyzed the Commission's investigation concerning improper corporate payments and outlined legislative and other responses that the Commission recommended to remedy these problems. One of the Commission's recommendations was that Congress enact legislation aimed expressly at enhancing the accuracy of the corporate books and records and the reliability of the audit process.
40. See Exchange Act Section 13(b)(2) [15 U.S.C. 78m(b)(2)].

In response, the Committee of Sponsoring Organizations of the Treadway Commission ("COSO")[41] undertook an extensive study of internal control to establish a common definition that would serve the needs of companies, independent public accountants, legislators and regulatory agencies, and to provide a broad framework of criteria against which companies could evaluate the effectiveness of their internal control systems. In 1992, COSO published its *Internal Control—Integrated Framework*.[42] The COSO Framework defined internal control as "a process, effected by an entity's board of directors, management and other personnel, designed to provide reasonable assurance regarding the achievement of objectives" in three categories—effectiveness and efficiency of operations; reliability of financial reporting; and compliance with applicable laws and regulations. COSO further stated that internal control consists of: the control environment, risk assessment, control activities, information and communication, and monitoring. The scope of internal control therefore extends to policies, plans, procedures, processes, systems, activities, functions, projects, initiatives, and endeavors of all types at all levels of a company.

In 1995, the AICPA incorporated the definition of internal control set forth in the COSO Report in Statement on Auditing Standards No. 78 (codified as AU § 319 in the Codification of Statements on Auditing Standards).[43] Although we recognized that the AU § 319 definition was derived from the COSO definition, our proposal referred to AU § 319 because we thought that the former constituted a more formal and widely-accessible version of the definition than the latter.

2. Comments on the Proposal

We received comments from 25 commenters on the proposed definition of "internal control and procedures for financial reporting." Eleven commenters stated that the proposed definition of internal control was appropriate or generally agreed with the proposal.[44] Two of these noted that the definition in AU § 319 had been adopted by the bank regulatory agencies for use by banking institutions.[45] Fourteen of the 25 commenters opposed the proposed definition. Two of these asserted that the proposed definition was too complex and would not resolve the confusion that existed over the meaning or scope of the term.

Several of the commenters that were opposed to the proposed definition thought that we should refer to COSO for the definition of internal control, rather than AU § 319.[46] Some of these commenters noted that the objective of AU § 319 is to provide guidance to auditors regarding their consideration of internal control in planning and performing an audit of financial statements. The common concern of these commenters was that AU § 319 does not provide any measure or standard by which a company's management can determine that internal control is effective, nor does it define what constitutes effective internal control. One commenter believed that absent such evaluative criteria or definition of effectiveness, the proposed rules could not be implemented effectively.[47] In addition, several of the commenters opposed to the proposed definition suggested that we use the term "internal control over financial reporting" rather than the term "internal controls and procedures for financial reporting,"[48] on the ground that the former is more consistent with the terminology currently used within the auditing literature.

---

41. The Treadway Commission was sponsored by the AICPA, the American Accounting Association, the Financial Executives International (formerly Financial Executives Institute), the Institute of Internal Auditors and the Institute of Management Accountants (formerly the National Association of Accountants). The Treadway Commission's report, the Report of the National Commission on Fraudulent Financial Reporting (Oct. 1987), is available at *www.coso.org*.

42. See COSO, *Internal Control—Integrated Framework* (1992) ("COSO Report"). In 1994, COSO published an addendum to the *Reporting to External Parties* volume of the COSO Report. The addendum discusses the issue of, and provides a vehicle for, expanding the scope of a public management report on internal control to address additional controls pertaining to safeguarding of assets. In 1996, COSO issued a supplement to its original framework to address the application of internal control over financial derivative activities.

43. Auditing Standards Board, AICPA, Statement on Auditing Standards No. 78, *Consideration of Internal Control in a Financial Statement Audit: An Amendment to Statement on Auditing Standards No. 55* (1995).

44. See letters regarding File No. S7-40-02 of: America's Community Bankers ("ACB"); American Corporate Counsel Association ("ACCA"); American Institute of Certified Public Accountants ("AICPA"); Compass Bancshares, Inc. ("Compass"); Computer Sciences Corporation ("CSC"); the Edison Electric Institute ("EEI"); the Independent Community Bankers of America ("ICBA"); the Institute of Internal Auditors ("IIA"); the Association of the Bar of the City of New York, Committee on Corporate Law ("NYCB-CCL"); Protiviti; and Siemens AG.

45. See letters regarding File No. S7-40-02 of ACB and ICBA.

46. See letters regarding File No. S7-40-02 of: the American Bar Association, Committee on the Federal Regulation of Securities and the Committee on Law and Accounting ("ABA"); the Federal Reserve Bank of Atlanta ("FED"); IIA; Simon Lorne ("Lorne"); and Pricewaterhouse Coopers LLP ("PwC").

47. See ABA letter regarding File No. S7-40-02.

48. See letters regarding File No. S7-40-02 of: AICPA; Compass; Deloitte & Touche LLP ("D&T"); IIA; KPMG LLP ("KPMG"); and PwC.

A few of the commenters urged us to adopt a considerably broader definition of internal control that would focus not only on internal control over financial reporting, but also on internal control objectives associated with enterprise risk management and corporate governance. While we agree that these are important objectives, the definition that we are adopting retains a focus on financial reporting, consistent with our position articulated in the Proposing Release. We are not adopting a more expansive definition of internal control for a variety of reasons. Most important, we believe that Section 404 focuses on the element of internal control that relates to financial reporting. In addition, many commenters indicated that even the more limited definition related to financial reporting that we proposed will impose substantial reporting and cost burdens on companies. Finally, independent accountants traditionally have not been responsible for reviewing and testing, or attesting to an assessment by management of, internal controls that are outside the boundary of financial reporting.

3. Final Rules

After consideration of the comments, we have decided to make several modifications to the proposed amendments. We agree that we should use the term "internal control over financial reporting" in our amendments to implement Section 404, as well as our revisions to the Section 302 certification requirements and forms of certification.[49] Rapidly changing terminology has been one obstacle in the development of an accepted understanding of internal control. The term "internal control over financial reporting" is the predominant term used by companies and auditors and best encompasses the objectives of the Sarbanes-Oxley Act. In addition, by using this term, we avoid having to familiarize investors, companies and auditors with new terminology, which should lessen any confusion that may exist about the meaning and scope of internal control.

The final rules define "internal control over financial reporting" as:

> A process designed by, or under the supervision of, the registrant's principal executive and principal financial officers, or persons performing similar functions, and effected by the registrant's board of directors,[50] management and other personnel, to provide reasonable assurance regarding the reliability of financial reporting and the preparation of financial statements for external purposes in accordance with generally accepted accounting principles and includes those policies and procedures that:
>
> (1) Pertain to the maintenance of records that in reasonable detail accurately and fairly reflect the transactions and dispositions of the assets of the registrant;
>
> (2) Provide reasonable assurance that transactions are recorded as necessary to permit preparation of financial statements in accordance with generally accepted accounting principles, and that receipts and expenditures of the registrant are being made only in accordance with authorizations of management and directors of the registrant; and
>
> (3) Provide reasonable assurance regarding prevention or timely detection of unauthorized acquisition, use or disposition of the registrant's assets that could have a material effect on the financial statements.[51]

We recognize that our definition of the term "internal control over financial reporting" reflected in the final rules encompasses the subset of internal controls addressed in the COSO Report that pertains to financial reporting objectives. Our definition does not encompass the elements of the COSO Report definition that relate to effectiveness and efficiency of a company's operations and a

---

49. See new Item 308 of Regulations S-K and S-B, amended Items 1-02 and 2-02 of Regulation S-X; amended Items 307and 401 of Regulations S-K and S-B; amended Exchange Act Rules 13a-14, 13a-15, 15d-14 and 15d-15; and amended Forms 20-F and 40-F.

50. The COSO Report states that the composition of a company's board and audit committee, and how the directors fulfill their responsibilities related to the financial reporting process, are key aspects of the company's control environment. An important element of the company's internal control over financial reporting "* * * is the involvement of the board or audit committee in overseeing the financial reporting process, including assessing the reasonableness of management's accounting judgments and estimates and reviewing key filings with regulatory agencies." See COSO Report at 130. The Commission similarly has stated in the past that both a company's management and board have important roles to play in establishing a supportive control environment. In its 1981 Statement of Policy regarding the FCPA, the Commission stated, "In the last analysis, the key to an adequate 'control environment' is an approach on the part of the board and top management which makes clear what is expected and that conformity to these expectations will be rewarded while breaches will be punished." See Release No. 34-17500 (Jan. 29, 1981) [46 FR 11544].

51. See amended Exchange Act Rules 13a-14(d) and 15d-14(d). The scope of the term "preparation of financial statements in accordance with generally accepted accounting principles" in the definition encompasses financial statements prepared for regulatory reporting purposes.

---

company's compliance with applicable laws and regulations, with the exception of compliance with the applicable laws and regulations directly related to the preparation of financial statements, such as the Commission's financial reporting requirements.[52] Our definition is consistent with the description of internal accounting controls in Exchange Act Section 13(b)(2)(B).[53]

Following the general language defining internal control over financial reporting, clauses (1) and (2) include the internal control matters described in Section 103 of the Sarbanes-Oxley Act that the company's registered public accounting firm is required to evaluate in its audit or attestation report.[54] This language is included to make clear that the assessment of management in its internal control report as to which the company's registered public accounting firm will be required to attest and report specifically covers the matters referenced in Section 103. A few commenters believed that it would cause confusion if the definition of internal control did not acknowledge the objectives set forth in Section 103 of the Sarbanes-Oxley Act. As discussed in Section II.G below, the PCAOB is responsible for establishing the Section 103 standards.

Our definition also includes, in clause (3), explicit reference to assurances regarding use or disposition of the company's assets. This provision is specifically included to make clear that, for purposes of our definition, the safeguarding of assets is one of the elements of internal control over financial reporting and it addresses the supplementation of the COSO Framework after it was originally promulgated. In the absence of our change to the definition, the determination of whether control regarding the safeguarding of assets falls within a company's internal control over financial reporting currently could be subject to varying interpretation.

Safeguarding of assets had been a primary objective of internal accounting control in SAS No. 1. In 1988, the ASB issued Statement of Auditing Standards No. 55 (codified as AU § 319 in the Codification of Statements on Auditing Standards), which replaced AU § 320. SAS No. 55 revised the definition of "internal control" and expanded auditors' responsibilities for considering internal control in a financial statement audit. The prior classification of internal control into the two categories of "internal accounting control" and "administrative control" was replaced with the single term "internal control structure," which consisted of three interrelated components — control environment, the accounting system and control procedures. Under this new definition, the safeguarding of assets was no longer a primary objective, but a subset of the control procedures component.[55] The COSO Report followed this shift in the iteration of safeguarding of assets. The COSO Report states that operations objectives "pertain to effectiveness and efficiency of the entity's operations, including performance and profitability goals and safeguarding resources against loss."[56]

---

52. Codification of Statements on Auditing Standards Section 317 requires auditors to consider a company's compliance with laws and regulations that have a direct and material effect on the financial statements.

53. 15 U.S.C. 78m(b)(2)(B).

54. Section 103 of the Sarbanes-Oxley Act requires the PCAOB to establish by rule standards to be used by registered public accounting firms in the preparation and issuance of audit reports. In carrying out this responsibility, the PCAOB must include in the auditing standards that it adopts, among other things: a requirement that each registered public accounting firm describe in each audit report the scope of its testing of the company's internal control structure and procedures performed in fulfilling its internal control evaluation and reporting required by Section 404(b) of the Sarbanes-Oxley Act; present in the audit report (or attestation report) its findings from such testing; and an evaluation of whether the company's internal control structure and procedures: (1) Include maintenance of records that in reasonable detail accurately and fairly reflect the transactions and dispositions of the company's assets; and (2) provide reasonable assurance that transactions are recorded as necessary to permit preparation of financial statements in accordance with generally accepted accounting principles, and that receipts and expenditures of the company are being made only in accordance with the authorization of management and directors of the company. In the audit report (or attestation report), the registered public accounting firm also must describe, at a minimum, material weaknesses in such internal controls and any material noncompliance found on the basis of such testing. See Sections 103(a)(2)(A)(iii)(I), (II) and (III) of the Sarbanes-Oxley Act. See also, Interim Professional Attestation Standards Rule 3300T, adopted in PCAOB Release No. 2003-006 (Apr. 18, 2003), and approved by the Commission on April 25, 2003.

55. Control procedures were described as policies and procedures in addition to the control environment and accounting system that management established to provide reasonable assurance that specific entity objectives will be achieved. SAS 55 also states that control procedures may generally be categorized as procedures that include, among other things, "adequate safeguards over access to and use of assets and records, such as secured facilities and authorization for access to computer programs and data files." See Statement on Auditing Standards No. 55, paragraph no. 11.

56. See COSO "Addendum to Reporting to External Parties," *Internal Control — Integrated Framework*, (1994) ("1994 Addendum") at p. 154.

However, the report also clarifies that safeguarding of assets can fall within other categories of internal control.[57]

In 1994, COSO published an addendum to the *Reporting to External Parties* volume of the COSO Report. The addendum was issued in response to a concern expressed by some parties, including the U.S. General Accounting Office, that the management reports contemplated by the COSO Report did not adequately address controls relating to safeguarding of assets and therefore would not fully respond to the requirements of the FCPA.[58] In the addendum, COSO concluded that while it believed its definition of internal control in its 1992 report remained appropriate, it recognized that the FCPA encompasses certain controls related to safeguarding of assets and that there is a reasonable expectation on the part of some readers of management's internal control reports that the reports will cover such controls. The addendum therefore sets forth the following definition of the term "internal control over safeguarding of assets against unauthorized acquisition, use or disposition":

> Internal control over safeguarding of assets against unauthorized acquisition, use or disposition is a process, effected by an entity's board of directors, management and other personnel, designed to provide reasonable assurance regarding prevention or timely detection of unauthorized acquisition, use or disposition of the entity's assets that could have a material effect on the financial statements.

As indicated above, to achieve the desired result and to provide consistency with COSO's 1994 addendum, we have incorporated this definition into our definition of "internal control over financial reporting." We are persuaded that this is appropriate given the fact that our definition will be used for purposes of public management reporting, and that the companies that will be subject to the Section 404 requirements also are subject to the FCPA requirements. So, under the final rules, safeguarding of assets as provided is specifically included in our definition of "internal control over financial reporting."

B. Management's Annual Assessment of, and Report on, the Company's Internal Control Over Financial Reporting

1. Proposed Rule

We proposed to amend Item 307 of Regulations S-K and S-B, as well as Forms 20-F and 40-F, to require a company's annual report to include an internal control report of management containing:

- A statement of management's responsibility for establishing and maintaining adequate internal controls and procedures for financial reporting;

- The conclusions of management about the effectiveness of the company's internal controls and procedures for financial reporting based on management's evaluation of those controls and procedures; and

- A statement that the registered public accounting firm that prepared or issued the company's audit report relating to the financial statements included in the company's annual report has attested to, and reported on, management's evaluation of the company's internal controls and procedures for financial reporting.

---

57. The COSO Report states: "Although these [objectives relating to safeguarding of resources] are primarily operations objectives, certain aspects of safeguarding can fall under other categories * * * [T]he goal of ensuring that any such asset losses are properly reflected in the entity's financial statements represents a financial reporting objective." The category in which an objective falls can sometimes depend on the circumstances. Continuing the discussion of safeguarding of assets, controls to prevent theft of assets—such as maintaining a fence around inventory and a gatekeeper verifying proper authorization of requests for movement of goods—fall under the operations category. These controls normally would not be relevant to the reliability of financial statement preparation, because any inventory losses would be detected pursuant to periodic physical inspection and recorded in the financial statements. However, if for financial reporting purposes management relies solely on perpetual inventory records, as may be the case for interim reporting, the physical security controls would then also fall within the financial reporting category. This is because these physical security controls, along with other controls over the perpetual inventory records, would be needed to ensure reliable financial reporting. Id. at 37.

58. As stated in n. 1 to the 1994 Addendum, the FCPA requires companies, among other things, to "devise and maintain a system of internal accounting controls sufficient to provide reasonable assurances that (i) transactions are executed in accordance with management's general or specific authorization; (ii) transactions are recorded as necessary * * * to maintain accountability for assets; (iii) access to assets is permitted only in accordance with management's general or specific authorization; and (iv) the recorded accountability for assets is compared with the existing assets at reasonable intervals and appropriate action is taken with respect to any differences."

The proposed amendments did not list any additional disclosure requirements for the management report, but rather would have afforded management the flexibility to tailor the report to fit its company's particular circumstances.

2. Comments on the Proposal

We received comments from 17 commenters on our proposed annual internal control report requirements. All of these commenters believed, in varying degrees, that we should set forth additional disclosure criteria or standards for the management report. Nine commenters stated that we should provide guidance as to the topics to be addressed in the management report, or specify standards or a common set of internal control objectives to be considered by management when assessing the effectiveness of its company's internal control over financial reporting to ensure that control objectives are addressed in a consistent fashion.[59] These commenters believed that consistent standards for management's report on internal control would help investors to understand and compare the quality of various management internal control reports.

Several commenters also thought that we should require management's internal control report to include certain recitations that would parallel recitations that the registered public accounting firm would have to make in its report attesting to management's assessment.[60] Additional commenters believed that the management report on internal control should specifically reference the objectives contained in Section 103 of the Sarbanes-Oxley Act.[61] Furthermore, although Section 404(b) of the Sarbanes-Oxley Act does not explicitly direct us to require companies to file the registered public accounting firms' attestation reports as part of the companies' annual report filings, we proposed a filing requirement that most of those commenting on this aspect of the proposal supported.

3. Final Rules

After evaluating the comments received, we are adopting the proposals with several modifications. The final rules require a company's annual report to include an internal control report of management that contains:

- A statement of management's responsibility for establishing and maintaining adequate internal control over financial reporting for the company;

- A statement identifying the framework used by management to conduct the required evaluation of the effectiveness of the company's internal control over financial reporting;

- Management's assessment of the effectiveness of the company's internal control over financial reporting as of the end of the company's most recent fiscal year, including a statement as to whether or not the company's internal control over financial reporting is effective.[62] The assessment must include disclosure of any "material weaknesses"[63] in the company's internal control over financial reporting identified by management. Management is not permitted to conclude that the company's internal control over financial reporting is effective if there are one or more material weaknesses in the company's internal control over financial reporting; and

- A statement that the registered public accounting firm that audited the financial statements included in the annual report has issued an attestation report on management's assessment of the registrant's internal control over financial reporting.[64]

---

59. See letters regarding File No. S7-40-02 of: ABA; CSC; EEI; FED; Eastman Kodak Co. ("Kodak"); KPMG; Protiviti; and PwC.
60. See letters regarding File No. S7-40-02 of: ACCA and Financial Executives Institute ("FEI").
61. See letters regarding File No. S7-40-02 of: AICPA; BDO Seidman, LLP ("BDO"); D&T; Ernst & Young LLP ("E&Y"); KPMG; and PwC.
62. Management must state whether or not the company's internal control over financial reporting is effective. A negative assurance statement indicating that nothing has come to management's attention to suggest that the company's internal control over financial reporting is not effective will not be acceptable.
63. A "material weakness" is defined in Statement on Auditing Standards No. 60 (codified in Codification of Statements on Auditing Standards AU § 325) as a reportable condition in which the design or operation of one or more of the internal control components does not reduce to a relatively low level the risk that misstatements caused by errors or fraud in amounts that would be material in relation to the financial statements being audited may occur and not be detected within a timely period by employees in the normal course of performing their assigned functions. See discussion in Section II.B.3.b. below.
64. See new Item 308 of Regulations S-B and S-K, Item 15 of Form 20-F and General Instruction B(6) of Form 40-F.

As proposed, our final rules also require a company to file, as part of the company's annual report, the attestation report of the registered public accounting firm that audited the company's financial statements.

a. Evaluation of Internal Control Over Financial Reporting

In the Proposing Release, we requested comment on whether we should establish specific evaluative criteria for management's report on internal control. All of the commenters responding to this request supported the establishment of such evaluative criteria in order to improve comparability among the standards used by companies to conduct their annual internal control evaluations.[65] Several commenters believed that we either should adopt the COSO Framework as the means by which management must evaluate its company's internal control over financial reporting or, alternatively, simply acknowledge the COSO Framework as being suitable for purposes of management's evaluation. Other commenters suggested that we require management to evaluate the effectiveness of a company's internal control over financial reporting using suitable control criteria established by a group that follows due process procedures.

After consideration of the comments, we have modified the final requirements to specify that management must base its evaluation of the effectiveness of the company's internal control over financial reporting on a suitable, recognized control framework that is established by a body or group that has followed due-process procedures, including the broad distribution of the framework for public comment.[66]

The COSO Framework satisfies our criteria and may be used as an evaluation framework for purposes of management's annual internal control evaluation and disclosure requirements. However, the final rules do not mandate use of a particular framework, such as the COSO Framework, in recognition of the fact that other evaluation standards exist outside of the United States,[67] and that frameworks other than COSO may be developed within the United States in the future, that satisfy the intent of the statute without diminishing the benefits to investors. The use of standard measures that are publicly available will enhance the quality of the internal control report and will promote comparability of the internal control reports of different companies. The final rules require management's report to identify the evaluation framework used by management to assess the effectiveness of the company's internal control over financial reporting.[68]

Specifically, a suitable framework must: be free from bias; permit reasonably consistent qualitative and quantitative measurements of a company's internal control; be sufficiently complete so that those relevant factors that would alter a conclusion about the effectiveness of a company's internal controls are not omitted; and be relevant to an evaluation of internal control over financial reporting.[69]

b. Auditor Independence Issues

Because the auditor is required to attest to management's assessment of internal control over financial reporting, management and the company's independent auditors will need to coordinate their processes of documenting and testing the internal controls over financial reporting. However, we remind companies and their auditors that the Commission's rules on auditor independence prohibit an auditor from providing certain nonaudit services to an audit client.[70] As the Commission stated in its auditor independence release, auditors may assist management in documenting internal controls. When the auditor is engaged to assist management in documenting internal controls, management must be actively involved in the process. We understand the need for coordination between management and the auditor, however, we remind companies and auditors that management

---

65. Many commenters cited the absence of evaluative criteria in AU § 319 in their arguments against the reference to AU § 319 in our proposed definition of "internal controls and procedures for financial reporting."
66. See amended Exchange Act Rule 13a-15(c) or 15d-15(c), amended Item 15 of Form 20-F and amended General Instruction (B) to Form 40-F.
67. The *Guidance on Assessing Control* published by the Canadian Institute of Chartered Accountants and the *Turnbull Report* published by the Institute of Chartered Accountants in England & Wales are examples of other suitable frameworks.
68. We are aware that some of the evaluation frameworks used to assess a foreign company's internal controls in its home country do not require a statement regarding whether the company's system of internal control has been effective. Under our final rules, management of a foreign reporting company who relies on such an evaluation framework used in its home country is nevertheless under an obligation to state affirmatively whether its company's internal controls are, or are not, effective.
69. See AT § 101, paragraph 24.
70. *See* Release No. 33-8183 (Jan. 28, 2003) [68 FR 6006].

cannot delegate its responsibility to assess its internal controls over financial reporting to the auditor.[71] The rules adopted today do not amend the Commission's rules on auditor independence.

c. Material Weaknesses in Internal Control Over Financial Reporting

In the Proposing Release, we did not propose any specific standard on which management would base its conclusion that the company's internal control over financial reporting is effective. We requested comment on whether we should prescribe specific standards upon which an effectiveness determination would be based, and also what standards we should consider. Several commenters agreed that the final rules should specify standards, and all believed that the existence of a material weakness in internal control over financial eporting should preclude a conclusion by management that a registrant's internal control over financial reporting is effective. We have considered these comments, and agree that the rules should set forth this threshold for concluding that a company's internal control over financial reporting is effective.

The final rules therefore preclude management from determining that a company's internal control over financial reporting is effective if it identifies one or more material weaknesses in the company's internal control over financial reporting.[72] For purposes of the final rules, the term "material weakness" has the same meaning as in the definition under GAAS and attestation standards.[73] The final rules also specify that management's report must include disclosure of any "material weakness" in the company's internal control over financial reporting identified by management in the course of its evaluation.[74]

d. Method of Evaluating

Many commenters addressed the method of evaluating internal control over financial reporting, and some sought additional precision or guidance regarding the extent of evaluation, including the documentation required.[75] The methods of conducting evaluations of internal control over financial reporting will, and should, vary from company to company. Therefore, the final rules do not specify the method or procedures to be performed in an evaluation. However, in conducting such an evaluation and developing its assessment of the effectiveness of internal control over financial reporting, a company must maintain evidential matter, including documentation, to provide reasonable support for management's assessment of the effectiveness of the company's internal control over financial reporting. Developing and maintaining such evidential matter is an inherent element of effective internal controls.[76] An instruction to new Item 308 of Regulations S-K and S-B and Forms 20-F and 40-F reminds registrants to maintain such evidential matter.[77]

The assessment of a company's internal control over financial reporting must be based on procedures sufficient both to evaluate its design and to test its operating effectiveness. Controls subject to such assessment include, but are not limited to: controls over initiating, recording, processing and reconciling account balances, classes of transactions and disclosure and related assertions included in the financial statements; controls related to the initiation and processing of non-routine and non-systematic transactions; controls related to the selection and application of appropriate ac-

---

71. Management's acceptance of responsibility for the documentation and testing performed by the auditor does not satisfy the auditor independence rules.

72. This is consistent with interim attestation standards. *See* AT § 501.

73. The term "significant deficiency" has the same meaning as the term "reportable condition" as used in AU § 325 and AT Sec. 501. The terms "material weakness" and "significant deficiency" both represent deficiencies in the design or operation of internal control that could adversely affect a company's ability to record, process, summarize and report financial data consistent with the assertions of management in the company's financial statements, with a "material weakness" constituting a greater deficiency than a "significant deficiency." Because of this relationship, it is our judgment that an aggregation of significant deficiencies could constitute a material weakness in a company's internal control over financial reporting.

74. *See* new Item 308(d) of Regulations S-B and S-K.

75. *See,* for example, letters re: File No. S7-40-02 of: ABA; AICPA; BDO; Intel; and Eli Lilly and Company.

76. Section 13(b)(2)(A) of the Exchange Act [15 U.S.C. 78m(b)(2)(A)] requires companies to "make and keep books, records, and accounts, which in reasonable detail, accurately and fairly reflect the transactions and dispositions of the assets of the issuer." *See* also Section 13(b)(2)(B) of the Exchange Act [15 U.S.C. 78m(b)(2)(B)] and *In re Microsoft Corp.*, Administrative Proceeding File No. 3-10789 (June 3, 2002). In the *Microsoft* order, the Commission stated that such books and records include not only general ledgers and accounting entries, but also memoranda and internal corporate reports. We have previously stated, as a matter of policy, that under Section 13(b)(2) "every public company needs to establish and maintain records of sufficient accuracy to meet adequately four interrelated objectives: appropriate reflection of corporate transactions and the disposition of assets; effective administration of other facets of the issuer's internal control system; preparation of its financial statements in accordance with generally accepted accounting principles; and proper auditing." Statement of Policy Regarding the Foreign Corrupt Practices Act of 1977, Release No. 34-17500 (Jan. 29, 1981) [46 FR 11544].

77. *See* Instruction 1 to new Item 308 of Regulations S-K and S-B, Instruction 1 to Item 15 of Form 20-F and Instruction 1 to paragraphs (b), (c), (d) and (e) of General Instruction B.6 to Form 40-F.

---

counting policies; and controls related to the prevention, identification, and detection of fraud. The nature of a company's testing activities will largely depend on the circumstances of the company and the significance of the control. However, inquiry alone generally will not provide an adequate basis for management's assessment.[78]

An assessment of the effectiveness of internal control over financial reporting must be supported by evidential matter, including documentation, regarding both the design of internal controls and the testing processes. This evidential matter should provide reasonable support: for the evaluation of whether the control is designed to prevent or detect material misstatements or omissions; for the conclusion that the tests were appropriately planned and performed; and that the results of the tests were appropriately considered. The public accounting firm that is required to attest to, and report on, management's assessment of the effectiveness of the company's internal control over financial reporting also will require that the company develop and maintain such evidential matter to support management's assessment.[79]

e. Location of Management's Report

Although the final rules do not specify where management's internal control report must appear in the company's annual report, we think it is important for management's report to be in close proximity to the corresponding attestation report issued by the company's registered public accounting firm. We expect that many companies will choose to place the internal control report and attestation report near the companies' MD&A disclosure or in a portion of the document immediately preceding the companies' financial statements.

C. Quarterly Evaluations of Internal Control Over Financial Reporting

1. Proposed Rule

We proposed to require a company's certifying officers to evaluate the effectiveness of the company's internal controls and procedures for financial reporting as of the end of the period covered by each annual and quarterly report that the company is required to file under the Exchange Act. The company's certifying officers already are required to evaluate the effectiveness of the company's disclosure controls and procedures on a quarterly basis.[80] We noted that a quarterly evaluation requirement with respect to internal controls would create symmetry between our requirements for periodic evaluations of both the company's disclosure controls and procedures and its internal controls and procedures for financial reporting, and give effect to the language in the Section 302 certification requirements regarding quarterly internal control evaluations.

2. Comments on the Proposal

We received responses from 25 commenters on the proposed amendments. Of the 25 commenters, four supported the proposal to require quarterly evaluations of internal controls and procedures for financial reporting.[81] One commenter specifically concurred with our objective of creating symmetry between the requirements to conduct periodic evaluations of both the company's disclosure controls and procedures and its internal controls and procedures for financial reporting.[82]

Twenty-one commenters opposed quarterly evaluations of internal controls.[83] Many of these believed that quarterly evaluations would impose substantial additional costs on companies without producing any incremental benefit to investors. One individual stated that the proper evaluation of a company's system of internal controls is a weighty and time-consuming process.[84] Twelve of the

---

78. This statement should not be interpreted to mean that management personally must conduct the necessary activities to evaluate the design and test the operating effectiveness of the company's internal control over financial reporting. Activities, including those necessary to provide management with the information on which it bases its assessment, may be conducted by non-management personnel acting under the supervision of management.
79. *See* Statements on Standards for Attestation Engagements No. 10.
80. *See* Exchange Act Rules 13a-15(b) and 15d-15(b) [17 CFR 240.13a-15(b) and 240.15d-15(b)].
81. *See* letters regarding File No. S7-40-02 of: AICPA; Executive Responsibility; FED; and Protiviti.
82. *See* Protiviti letter regarding File No. S7-40-02.
83. *See* letters regarding File No. S7-40-02 of: ABA; ACB; ACCA; Association for Financial Professionals ("AFP"); Am. Bankers Assoc.; BDO; Business Roundtable ("BRT"); Computer Sciences Corporation ("CSC"); Compass; Thomas Damman ("Damman"); EEI; Emerson Electric Co. ("Emerson"); FEI; Fried, Frank, Harris, Shriver and Jacobson ("Fried Frank"); International Paper Company ("IPC"); ICBA; NYCB-CCL; New York State Bar Association ("NYSBA"); Siemens AG ("Siemens"); Software & Information Industry Association ("SIIA"); and Software Finance and Tax Executives Council ("SOFTEC").
84. *See* Damman letter regarding File No. S7-40-02.

commenters opposed to quarterly evaluations indicated that quarterly evaluations of all aspects of internal controls and procedures would be extremely burdensome, expensive and difficult to perform under the time constraints of quarterly reporting, particularly as the accelerated filing deadlines for quarterly reports take effect.[85] Several other commenters argued that we should not go beyond the requirements of Section 404 of the Sarbanes-Oxley Act with respect to the frequency of internal control reporting without an adequate basis for doing so.[86] These commenters remarked that such a decision would be better made after we have had sufficient experience with the Section 302 certification requirements adopted in August of 2002.

Several commenters suggested alternatives to quarterly evaluations. Five commenters stated that it would be more appropriate and desirable if companies were required to make quarterly disclosure only of material changes to their internal control that occurred subsequent to management's most recent annual internal control evaluation.[87] Two other commenters similarly recommended that the quarterly evaluation be less rigorous than the annual evaluation.[88] One commenter stated that we should instead adopt an approach that requires less effort and assurance for purposes of quarterly reports, such as permitting companies to test compliance with controls relating to major applications on a rotating basis throughout the year.[89] This commenter further stated that the objective of the quarterly evaluation should be to identify changes in controls during the quarter and evaluate whether they would change the certifying officers' conclusions about disclosure controls and internal controls as stated in the most recent annual report. The other commenter, although opposed to any quarterly evaluation requirement, believed that if we did require it, the quarterly evaluation should be viewed as an update of the annual evaluation, just as the quarterly report on Form 10-Q is an update of the annual report on Form 10-K.[90] One commenter stated that if we require some form of quarterly certification, it should be limited to negative assurance that nothing has come to the certifying officers' attention since the prior year's evaluation to suggest that the controls are no longer effective.[91]

3. Final Rules

After consideration of the comments received, we have decided not to require quarterly evaluations of internal control over financial reporting that are as extensive as the annual evaluation. We recognize that some controls operate continuously while others operate only at certain times, such as the end of the fiscal year. We believe that each company should be afforded the flexibility to design its system of internal control over financial reporting to fit its particular circumstances. The management of each company should perform evaluations of the design and operation of the company's entire system of internal control over financial reporting over a period of time that is adequate for it to determine whether, as of the end of the company's fiscal year, the design and operation of the company's internal control over financial reporting are effective.

Accordingly, we are adopting amendments that require a company's management, with the participation of the principal executive and financial officers, to evaluate any change in the company's internal control over financial reporting that occurred during a fiscal quarter that has materially affected, or is reasonably likely to materially affect, the company's internal control over financial reporting. We also have adopted a modification to the Section 302 certification requirement and our disclosure requirements to adopt this approach, as discussed below.

The management of a foreign private issuer that has Exchange Act reporting obligations must also, like its domestic counterparts, report any material changes to the issuer's internal control over financial reporting. However, because foreign private issuers are not required to file quarterly reports under Section 13(a) or 15(d) of the Exchange Act, the final rules clarify that a foreign private issuer's management need only disclose in the issuer's annual report the material changes to its in-

---

85. *See* letters regarding File No. S7-40-02 of: ABA; ACB; ACCA; BRT; CSC; Emerson; Fried Frank; ICBA; IPC; NYCB-CCL; SIIA; and SOFTEC.
86. *See* letters regarding File No. S7-40-02 of: Am. Bankers Assoc.; CSC; Fried Frank.
87. *See* letters regarding File No. S7-40-02 of: Damman; Compass; EEI; Executive Responsibility Advisors, LLC ("Executive Responsibility"); and Siemens.
88. *See* letters regarding File No. S7-40-02 of: ABA and BDO.
89. *See* BDO letter regarding File No. S7-40-02.
90. *See* ABA letter regarding File No. S7-40-02.
91. *See* Emerson letter regarding File No. S7-40-02.

ternal control over financial reporting that have occurred in the period covered by the annual report.[92]

D. Differences Between Internal Control Over Financial Reporting and Disclosure Controls and Procedures

Many of the commenters on the Proposing Release indicated that they were confused as to the differences between a company's disclosure controls and procedures and a company's internal control over financial reporting. Exchange Act Rule 13a-15(d) defines "disclosure controls and procedures" to mean controls and procedures of a company that are designed to ensure that information required to be disclosed by the company in the reports that it files or submits under the Exchange Act is recorded, processed, summarized and reported, within the time periods specified in the Commission's rules and forms. The definition further states that disclosure controls and procedures include, without limitation, controls and procedures designed to ensure that the information required to be disclosed by a company in the reports that it files or submits under the Exchange Act is accumulated and communicated to the company's management, including its principal executive and principal financial officers, or persons performing similar functions, as appropriate to allow timely decisions regarding required disclosure.

While there is substantial overlap between a company's disclosure controls and procedures and its internal control over financial reporting, there are both some elements of disclosure controls and procedures that are not subsumed by internal control over financial reporting and some elements of internal control that are not subsumed by the definition of disclosure controls and procedures.

With respect to the latter point, clearly, the broad COSO description of internal control, which includes the efficiency and effectiveness of a company's operations and the company's compliance with laws and regulations (not restricted to the federal securities laws), would not be wholly subsumed within the definition of disclosure controls and procedures. A number of commenters suggested that the narrower concept of internal control, involving internal control over financial reporting, is a subset of a company's disclosure controls and procedures, given that the maintenance of reliable financial reporting is a prerequisite to a company's ability to submit or file complete disclosure in its Exchange Act reports on a timely basis. This suggestion focuses on the fact that the elements of internal control over financial reporting requiring a company to have a process designed to provide reasonable assurance regarding the reliability of financial reporting and the preparation of financial statements for external purposes in accordance with generally accepted accounting principles can be viewed as a subset of disclosure controls and procedures.

We agree that some components of internal control over financial reporting will be included in disclosure controls and procedures for all companies. In particular, disclosure controls and procedures will include those components of internal control over financial reporting that provide reasonable assurances that transactions are recorded as necessary to permit preparation of financial statements in accordance with generally accepted accounting principles. However, in designing their disclosure controls and procedures, companies can be expected to make judgments regarding the processes on which they will rely to meet applicable requirements. In doing so, some companies might design their disclosure controls and procedures so that certain components of internal control over financial reporting pertaining to the accurate recording of transactions and disposition of assets or to the safeguarding of assets are not included. For example, a company might have developed internal control over financial reporting that includes as a component of safeguarding of assets dual signature requirements or limitations on signature authority on checks. That company could nonetheless determine that this component is not part of disclosure controls and procedures. We therefore believe that while there is substantial overlap between internal control over financial reporting and disclosure controls and procedures, many companies will design their disclosure controls and procedures so that they do not include all components of internal control over financial reporting.

E. Evaluation of Disclosure Controls and Procedures

The rules in place starting in August 2002 requiring quarterly evaluations of disclosure controls and procedures and disclosure of the conclusions regarding effectiveness of disclosure controls and

---

92. See Exchange Act Rules 13a-15(d) and 15d-15(d) [17 CFR 240.13a-15(d) and 240.15d-15(d)].

procedures have not been substantively changed since their adoption, including in the rules that we adopt today. These evaluation and disclosure requirements will continue to apply to disclosure controls and procedures, including the elements of internal control over financial reporting that are subsumed within disclosure controls and procedures.

With respect to evaluations of disclosure controls and procedures, companies must, under our rules and consistent with the Sarbanes-Oxley Act, evaluate the effectiveness of those controls and procedures on a quarterly basis. While the evaluation is of effectiveness overall, a company's management has the ability to make judgments (and it is responsible for its judgments) that evaluations, particularly quarterly evaluations, should focus on developments since the most recent evaluation, areas of weakness or continuing concern or other aspects of disclosure controls and procedures that merit attention. Finally, the nature of the quarterly evaluations of those components of internal control over financial reporting that are subsumed within disclosure controls and procedures should be informed by the purposes of disclosure controls and procedures.[93]

The rules adopted in August 2002 required the management of an Exchange Act reporting foreign private issuer to evaluate and disclose conclusions regarding the effectiveness of the issuer's disclosure controls and procedures only in its annual report and not on a quarterly basis. The primary reason for this treatment is because foreign private issuers are not subject to mandated quarterly reporting requirements under the Exchange Act. The rules adopted today continue this treatment.[94]

F. Periodic Disclosure About the Certifying Officers' Evaluation of the Company's Disclosure Controls and Procedures and Disclosure About Changes to its Internal Control Over Financial Reporting

1. Existing Disclosure Requirements

The rules that we adopted in August 2002 to implement the certification requirements of Section 302 of the Sarbanes-Oxley Act included new Item 307 of Regulations S-B and S-K. Paragraph (a) of Item 307 requires companies, in their quarterly and annual reports, to disclose the conclusions of the company's principal executive and financial officers (or persons performing similar functions) about the effectiveness of the company's disclosure controls and procedures as of a date within 90 days of the filing date of the quarterly or annual report. This disclosure enables the certifying officers to satisfy the representation made in their certifications that they have "presented in the quarterly or annual report their conclusions about the effectiveness of the disclosure controls and procedures based on their evaluation."

Paragraph (b) of Item 307 requires the company to disclose in each quarterly and annual report whether or not there were significant changes in the company's internal controls or in other factors that could significantly affect these controls subsequent to the date of their evaluation, including any corrective actions with regard to significant deficiencies and material weaknesses. This disclosure enables the certifying officers to satisfy the representation made in their certifications that they have "indicated in the quarterly or annual report whether or not there were significant changes in internal controls or in other factors that could significantly affect internal controls subsequent to the date of their most recent evaluation, including any corrective actions with regard to significant deficiencies and material weaknesses."

2. Proposed Amendments to the Disclosure Requirements

In the Proposing Release, we proposed several revisions to the existing disclosure requirements regarding: (1) The certifying officers' evaluation of the company's disclosure controls and procedures; and (2) changes to the company's internal control over financial reporting. We also proposed to require quarterly disclosure regarding the conclusions of the certifying officers about the effectiveness of the company's internal control over financial reporting.

---

93. For example, where a component of internal control over financial reporting is subsumed within disclosure controls and procedures, even where systems testing of that component would clearly be required as part of the annual evaluation of internal control over financial reporting, management could make a different determination of the appropriate nature of the evaluation of that component for purposes of a quarterly evaluation of disclosure controls and procedures.
94. See Exchange Act Rules 13a-15(b) and 15d-15(b).

Moreover, we proposed to require evaluations of both types of controls as of the end of the period covered by the quarterly or annual report, rather than "as of a date within 90 days of the filing date" of the quarterly or annual report, as currently required with respect to disclosure controls. With respect to the disclosure about changes to the company's internal control over financial reporting, we proposed to require a company to disclose "any significant changes made during the period covered by the quarterly or annual report" rather than "whether or not there were significant changes in the company's internal control over financial reporting that could significantly affect these controls subsequent to the date of their evaluation."

The commenters were mixed in their reaction to these proposed changes. A couple of the commenters remarking on the point at which a company must undertake an evaluation of its controls "strongly agreed" with the proposed change to require evaluations as of the end of the period. Several other commenters preferred the existing "90 days within the filing date" evaluation point, noting that it provides more flexibility than the fixed point. Some of these commenters expressed concern that it would be hard to conduct evaluations on the last day of the period. One of the commenters suggested that the proposed requirement that a company disclose changes to its internal control over financial reporting that occurred at any time during a fiscal quarter was inconsistent with the proposed requirement that management evaluate such changes "as of the end of each fiscal quarter."[95] An additional commenter asserted that it was critical that we offer companies some guidance as to the types of changes that constitute "significant changes."[96] Finally, a few commenters noted that while we had proposed to delete the words "or other factors" from Exchange Act Rules 13a-14(b)(6) and 15d-14(b)(6) regarding disclosure of "significant changes in internal controls or in other factors that could significantly affect internal controls, * * * " we had not likewise proposed to delete those words from the actual certification language.

3. Final Disclosure Requirements

After consideration of the comments, we are adopting the proposals with several modifications. We are adopting as proposed the change of the evaluation date for disclosure controls to "as of the end of the period" covered by the quarterly or annual report. We are not specifying the point at which management must evaluate changes to the company's internal control over financial reporting. Given that the final rules do not require a company to state the conclusions of the certifying officers regarding the effectiveness of the company's internal control over financial reporting as of a particular date on a quarterly basis as proposed, as the company must with respect to disclosure controls and procedures, it is unnecessary to specify a date for the quarterly evaluation of changes in internal control over financial reporting. We believe that this change is consistent with the new accelerated reporting deadlines.[97]

We are amending the proposal that would have required companies to disclose any significant changes in its internal controls. Under the final rules, a company must disclose any change in its internal control over financial reporting that occurred during the fiscal quarter covered by the quarterly report, or the last fiscal quarter in the case of an annual report, that has materially affected, or is reasonably likely to materially affect, the company's internal control over financial reporting.[98] Furthermore, we have deleted the phrase "or in other factors" from Exchange Act Rules 13a-14 and 15d-15 and the form of certification. Although the final rules do not explicitly require the company to disclose the reasons for any change that occurred during a fiscal quarter, or to otherwise elaborate about the change, a company will have to determine, on a facts and circumstances basis, whether the reasons for the change, or other information about the circumstances surrounding the change, constitute material information necessary to make the disclosure about the change not misleading.[99]

---

95. See ABA letter regarding File No. S7-40-02.
96. See Intel letter regarding File No. S7-40-02.
97. See Release No. 33-8128 (Sept. 16, 2002) [67 FR 58480]. The final rule amendments do not require that the evaluation take place on the last day of the period, but that the statement of effectiveness of the issuer's disclosure controls and internal control over financial reporting be as of the end of the period.
98. We have also made conforming changes to Forms 20-F and 40-F to clarify that the management of a foreign private issuer must disclose in the issuer's annual report filed on Form 20-F or 40-F any change in the issuer's internal control over financial reporting that occurred during the period covered by the annual report and that materially affected, or is reasonably likely to affect, this internal control. See Item 15(d) of Form 20-F and General Instruction B(6)(e) of Form 40-F.
99. See Exchange Act Rules 10b-5 and 12b-20 [17 CFR 240.10b-5 and 17 CFR [sic]

While an evaluation of the effectiveness of disclosure controls and procedures must be undertaken on a quarterly basis, we expect that for purposes of disclosure by domestic companies, the traditional relationship between disclosure in annual reports on Form 10-K and intervening quarterly reports on Form 10-Q will continue. Disclosure in an annual report that continues to be accurate need not be repeated. Rather, disclosure in quarterly reports may make appropriate reference to disclosures in the most recent annual report (and, where appropriate, intervening quarterly reports) and disclose subsequent developments required to be disclosed in the quarterly report.

We note that, as required by the Sarbanes-Oxley Act, the quarterly certification regarding disclosure that the certifying officers must make to the company's auditors and audit committee provides:[100]

> The company's other certifying officer(s) and I have disclosed, based on our most recent evaluation of internal control over financial reporting, to the company's auditors and the audit committee of the company's board of directors (or persons performing the equivalent functions):
>
> (a) All significant deficiencies and material weaknesses in the design or operation of internal control over financial reporting which are reasonably likely to adversely affect the company's ability to record, process, summarize and report financial information; and
>
> (b) Any fraud, whether or not material, that involves management or other employees who have a significant role in the company's internal control over financial reporting.

We expect that if a certifying officer becomes aware of a significant deficiency, material weakness or fraud requiring disclosure outside of the formal evaluation process or after the management's most recent evaluation of internal control over financial reporting, he or she will disclose it to the company's auditors and audit committee.

4. Conclusions Regarding Effectiveness of Disclosure Controls and Procedures

In disclosures required under current Item 307 of Regulations S-K and S-B, Item 15 of Form 20-F and General Instruction B(6) to Form 40-F, some companies have indicated that disclosure controls and procedures are designed only to provide "reasonable assurance" that the controls and procedures will meet their objectives. In reviewing those disclosures, the Commission staff generally has not objected to that type of disclosure. The staff has, however, requested companies including that type of disclosure to set forth, if true, the conclusions of the principal executive and principal financial officer that the disclosure controls and procedures are, in fact, effective at the "reasonable assurance" level. Other companies have included disclosure that there is "no assurance" that the disclosure controls and procedures will operate effectively under all circumstances. In these instances, the staff has requested companies to clarify that the disclosure controls and procedures are designed to provide reasonable assurance of achieving their objectives and to set forth, if true, the conclusions of the principal executive and principal financial officers that the controls and procedures are, in fact, effective at the "reasonable assurance" level.

The concept of reasonable assurance is built into the definition of internal control over financial reporting that we are adopting. This conforms to the standard contained in the internal accounting control provisions of Section 13(b)(2) of the Exchange Act[101] and current auditing literature.[102] If management decides to include a discussion of reasonable assurance in the internal control report, the discussion must be presented in a manner that neither makes the disclosure in the report confusing nor renders management's assessment concerning the effectiveness of the company's internal control over financial reporting unclear.

G. *Attestation to Management's Internal Control Report by the Company's Registered Public Accounting Firm*

In the Proposing Release, we proposed to amend Rules 210.1-02 and 210.2-02 of Regulation S-X to make conforming revisions to Regulation S-X to reflect the registered public accounting firm attestation requirements mandated by Section 404(b) of the Sarbanes-Oxley Act. Under the propos-

---

100. This is the disclosure required by paragraph 5 of the certification form.
101. 15 U.S.C. 78m(b)(2).
102. *See* Codification of Statement on Auditing Standards AU Sec. 319.18.

als, we set forth a definition for the new term "attestation report on management's evaluation of internal control over financial reporting" and certain requirements for the accountant's attestation report. We are adopting the proposals substantially as proposed. However, the final rules define the expanded term "attestation report on management's evaluation of internal control over financial reporting." Several commenters suggested that we use this more specific term, noting that auditors currently perform attestation engagements on a broad variety of subjects. Amended Rule 2-02 requires every registered public accounting firm that issues an audit report on the company's financial statements that are included in its annual report required by Section 13(a) or 15(d) of the Exchange Act containing an assessment by management of the effectiveness of the registrant's internal control over financial reporting must attest to, and report on, such assessment.

At the time of the enactment of the Sarbanes-Oxley Act, the applicable standard for attestation by auditors of internal control over financial reporting was set forth in Statements on Standards for Attestation Engagements No. 10 ("SSAE No. 10"). That standard was used by auditors providing attestations on a voluntary basis to companies, as well as by auditors whose financial institution clients are required to obtain attestations under Federal Deposit Insurance Corporation Improvement Act of 1991,[103] as discussed below. Under the Sarbanes-Oxley Act, the PCAOB has become the body that sets auditing and attestation standards generally for registered public accounting firms to use in the preparation and issuance of audit reports on the financial statements of issuers, and under Section 404(b) of the Sarbanes-Oxley Act, the PCAOB is required to set standards for the registered public accounting firms' attestations to, and reports on, management's assessment regarding its internal control over financial reporting.

On April 16, 2003, the PCAOB designated Statements on Standards for Attestation Engagements as existed on April 16 as the standard for attestations of management's assessment of the effectiveness of internal control over financial reporting pending further PCAOB standard-setting in the area (and subject to our approval of the PCAOB's actions), and on April 25, we approved the PCAOB's action. SSAE No. 10 is thus the standard applicable on a transition basis for attestations required under Section 404 of the Act and the rules we are adopting today, again pending further PCAOB standard-setting (and our approval). We expect that the PCAOB will assess the appropriateness of those standards and modify them as needed, and any future standards adopted by the PCAOB will apply to registered public accounting firms in connection with the preparation and issuance of attestation reports on management's assessment of the effectiveness of internal control over financial reporting.

H. Types of Companies Affected

Section 404 of the Sarbanes-Oxley Act states that the Commission must prescribe rules that require each annual report required by Section 13(a) or 15(d) of the Exchange Act to contain an internal control report. The Act exempts registered investment companies from this requirement.[104]

1. Foreign Private Issuers

Section 404 of the Sarbanes-Oxley Act makes no distinction between domestic and foreign issuers and, by its terms, clearly applies to foreign private issuers. These amendments, therefore, apply the management report on internal control over financial reporting requirement to foreign private issuers that file reports under Section 13(a) or 15(d) of the Exchange Act. We have, however, adopted a later compliance date for foreign private issuers than for accelerated filers.

2. Asset-Backed Issuers

In the Proposing Release, we proposed to exclude issuers of asset-backed securities from the proposed rules implementing Section 404 of the Act. We noted that because of the unique nature of asset-backed issuers, such issuers are subject to substantially different reporting requirements. Most significantly, asset-backed issuers are generally not required to file the types of financial statements that other companies must file. Also, such entities typically are passive pools of assets, without a board of directors or persons acting in a similar capacity. We did not receive any comments on the proposed exclusion of asset-backed issuers from the internal control reporting re-

---

103. Pub. L. 102-242, 105 Stat. 2242 (1991).
104. *See* Section 405 of the Sarbanes-Oxley Act.

quirements, and we are excluding asset-backed issuers from the new disclosure requirements as proposed.

3. Small Business Issuers

Our proposed rules implementing Section 404 of the Act did not distinguish between large and small issuers. Similarly, Section 404 of the Act directs that the management report on internal control over financial reporting apply to any company filing periodic reports under Section 13(a) or 15(d) of the Exchange Act. Accordingly, these amendments apply to all issuers that file Exchange Act periodic reports, except registered investment companies, regardless of their size. However, we are sensitive that many small business issuers may experience difficulty in evaluating their internal control over financial reporting because these issuers may not have as formal or well-structured a system of internal control over financial reporting as larger companies. Accordingly, we are providing an extended compliance period for small business issuers and other companies that are not accelerated filers.[105] In addition, our approach of not mandating specific criteria to be used by management to evaluate a company's internal control over financial reporting should provide small issuers some flexibility in meeting these disclosure requirements.

4. Bank and Thrift Holding Companies

In the Proposing Release, we stated that we were coordinating with the Federal Deposit Insurance Corporation (the "FDIC") and the other federal banking regulators to eliminate, to the extent possible, any unnecessary duplication between our proposed internal control report and the FDIC's internal control report requirements. Under regulations adopted by the FDIC implementing Section 36 of the Federal Deposit Insurance Act,[106] a federally insured depository institution with total assets of $500 million or more ("institution"), is required, among other things, to prepare an annual management report that contains:

- A statement of management's responsibility for preparing the institution's annual financial statements, for establishing and maintaining an adequate internal control structure and procedures for financial reporting, and for complying with designated laws and regulations relating to safety and soundness;[107] and

- Management's assessment of the effectiveness of the institution's internal control structure and procedures for financial reporting as of the end of the fiscal year and the institution's compliance with the designated safety and soundness laws and regulations during the fiscal year.[108]

The FDIC's regulations additionally require the institution's independent accountant to examine, and attest to, management's assertions concerning the effectiveness of the institution's internal control structure and procedures for financial reporting.[109] The institution's management report and the accountant's attestation report must be filed with the FDIC, the institution's primary federal regulator (if other than the FDIC), and any appropriate state depository institution supervisor and must be available for public inspection.[110]

Although bank and thrift holding companies are not required under the FDIC's regulations to prepare these internal control reports, many of these holding companies do so under a provision of Part 363 of the FDIC's regulations[111] that permits an insured depository institution that is the sub-

---

105. *See* Section II. J. below.
106. 12 U.S.C. 1831m.
107. The designated laws and regulations are federal laws and regulations concerning loans to insiders and federal and state laws and regulations concerning dividend restrictions. See 12 CFR part 363, Appendix A, Guideline 12.
108. See 12 CFR 363.2, adopted in 58 FR 31332. These requirements only apply to an insured depository institution with total assets of $500 million or more. We recognize that the FDIC's regulations use the term "internal control structure and procedures for financial reporting" rather than the term "internal control over financial reporting" used in our rules. We think the differences in the meaning of the two terms are insignificant because both Section 36(b)(2) of the Federal Deposit Insurance Act and Section 404(a) of the Sarbanes-Oxley Act refer to "internal control structure and procedures for financial reporting." Nevertheless, the FDIC has defined the term "financial reporting" to include financial statements prepared in accordance with generally accepted accounting principles ("GAAP") and those prepared for regulatory reporting purposes (see FDIC Financial Institution Letter FIL-86-94, dated December 23, 1994).
109. 12 CFR 363.3.
110. 12 CFR 363.4(a) and (b).
111. 12 CFR Part 363.

---

sidiary of a holding company to satisfy its internal control report requirements with an internal control report of the consolidated holding company's management if:

- Services and functions comparable to those required of the subsidiary by Part 363 are provided at the holding company level;[112] and

- The subsidiary has, as of the beginning of its fiscal year, (i) total assets of less than $5 billion or (ii) total assets of $5 billion or more and a composite rating of 1 or 2 under the Uniform Financial Institutions Rating System.[113]

Section 404 of the Sarbanes-Oxley Act does not contain an exemption for insured depository institutions that are both subject to the FDIC's internal control report requirements and required to file Exchange Act reports. In fact, it makes no distinction whatsoever between institutions subject to the FDIC's requirements and other types of Exchange Act filers. Accordingly, regardless of whether an insured depository institution is subject to the FDIC's requirements, insured depository institutions or holding companies that are required to file periodic reports under Section 13(a) or 15(d) of the Exchange Act are subject to the internal control reporting requirements that we are adopting today.

Although our final rules are similar to the FDIC's internal control report requirements, the rules differ in a few significant respects. Most notably, our final rules do not require a statement of compliance with designated laws and regulations relating to safety and soundness. Conversely, the following provisions in our rules are not included in the FDIC's regulations:

- The requirement that the report include a statement identifying the framework used by management to evaluate the effectiveness of the company's internal control over financial reporting;[114]

- The requirement that management disclose any material weakness that it has identified in the company's internal control over financial reporting (and related stipulation that management is not permitted to conclude that the company's internal control over financial reporting is effective if there are one or more material weaknesses);

- The requirement that the company state that the registered public accounting firm that audited the financial statements included in the annual report has issued an attestation report on management's assessment of the company's internal control over financial reporting; and

- The requirement that the company must provide the registered public accounting firm's attestation report on management's assessment of internal control over financial reporting in the company's annual report filed under the Exchange Act.[115]

Several commenters generally supported our goal to eliminate or reduce duplicative reporting requirements. Some of these commenters asserted that we should recognize the substantial protections to depositors and investors provided by the federal laws that govern depository institutions and their holding companies. They suggested that our final rules should state that compliance with the FDIC's internal control report requirements satisfies the internal control report requirements that we are adopting under Section 404. A number of these commenters also thought that if we did not exempt insured depository institutions already filing internal control reports under the FDIC's

---

112. Services and functions are considered "comparable" if the holding company prepares and submits the management assessment of the effectiveness of the internal control structure and procedures for financial reporting and compliance with the designated safety and soundness laws and regulations based on information concerning the relevant activities and operations of those subsidiary institutions subject to Part 363. See 12 CFR Part 363, Appendix A, Guideline 4.

113. This rating is more commonly known as the CAMELS rating, which addresses Capital adequacy, Asset quality, Management, Earnings, Liquidity and Sensitivity to market risk. See 12 CFR 363.1(b)(2). The appropriate federal banking agency may determine that an insured depository institution with total assets in excess of $9 billion that is a subsidiary of a holding company may not satisfy its FDIC internal control report requirement with an internal control report of the consolidated holding company's management if the agency determines that there could be a significant risk to the affected deposit insurance fund if the institution were allowed to satisfy its requirements in this manner. See 12 CFR 363.1(b)(3).

114. The FDIC's regulations do not specifically require that management identify the control framework used to evaluate the effectiveness of the institution's internal control over financial reporting. However, given the requirements of Sections 101 and 501 of the American Institute of Certified Public Accountants' attestation standards, the FDIC believes that the framework used must be disclosed or otherwise publicly available to all users of reports that institutions file with the FDIC pursuant to Part 363 of the FDIC's regulations.

115. The FDIC's regulations do require an independent public accountant to examine, attest to, and report separately on, the assertion of management concerning the institution's internal control structure and procedures for financial reporting, but these regulations do not require the accountant to be a registered public accounting firm. See 12 CFR 363.3(b).

---

requirements, we should provide an exemption in our rules mirroring the FDIC's exemption that excludes insured depository institutions or their holding companies with less than $500 million in assets from the internal control report requirements.

After consultation with the staffs of the FDIC, the Federal Reserve Board, the Office of Thrift Supervision and the Office of the Comptroller of Currency, we have determined that insured depository institutions that are subject to Part 363 of the FDIC's regulations (as well as holding companies permitted to file an internal control report on behalf of their insured depository institution subsidiaries in satisfaction of these regulations) and also subject to our new rules implementing Section 404 of the Sarbanes-Oxley Act[116] should be afforded considerable flexibility in determining how best to satisfy both sets of requirements. Therefore, they can choose either of the following two options:

- They can prepare two separate management reports to satisfy the FDIC's and our new requirements; or

- They can prepare a single management report that satisfies both the FDIC's requirements and our new requirements.

If an insured depository institution or its holding company chooses to prepare a single report to satisfy both sets of requirements, the report of management on the institution's or holding company's internal control over financial reporting (as defined in Exchange Act Rule 13a-15(f) or 15d-15(f)) will have to contain the following:[117]

- A statement of management's responsibility for preparing the registrant's annual financial statements, for establishing and maintaining adequate internal control over financial reporting for the registrant, and for the institution's compliance with laws and regulations relating to safety and soundness designated by the FDIC and the appropriate federal banking agencies;

- A statement identifying the framework used by management to evaluate the effectiveness of the registrant's internal control over financial reporting as required by Exchange Act Rule 13a-15 or 15d-15;

- Management's assessment of the effectiveness of the registrant's internal control over financial reporting as of the end of the registrant's most recent fiscal year, including a statement as to whether or not management has concluded that the registrant's internal control over financial reporting is effective, and of the institution's compliance with the designated safety and soundness laws and regulations during the fiscal year. This discussion must include disclosure of any material weakness in the registrant's internal control over financial reporting identified by management;[118] and

- A statement that the registered public accounting firm that audited the financial statements included in the registrant's annual report has issued an attestation report on management's assessment of the registrant's internal control over financial reporting.

Additionally, the institution or holding company will have to provide the registered public accounting firm's attestation report on management's assessment in its annual report filed under the

---

116. Our rules do not provide an exemption that parallels the FDIC's exemption for insured depository institutions with less than $500 million in assets. It would be incongruous to provide an exemption in our rules for small depository institutions and not other small, non-depository Exchange Act reporting companies.

117. An insured depository institution subject to both the FDIC's requirements and our new requirements choosing to file a single report to satisfy both sets of requirements will file the report with its primary federal regulator under the Exchange Act and the FDIC, its primary federal regulator (if other than the FDIC), and any appropriate state depository institution supervisor under Part 363 of the FDIC's regulations. A holding company choosing to prepare a single report to satisfy both sets of requirements will file the report with the Commission under the Exchange Act and the FDIC, the primary federal regulator of the insured depository institution subsidiary subject to the FDIC's requirements, and any appropriate state depository institution supervisor under Part 363.

118. Management will not be permitted to conclude that the registrant's internal control over financial reporting is effective if there are one or more material weaknesses in the registrant's internal control over financial reporting.

Exchange Act.[119] For purposes of the report of management and the attestation report, financial reporting must encompass both financial statements prepared in accordance with GAAP and those prepared for regulatory reporting purposes.

I. Registered Investment Companies

Section 404 of the Sarbanes-Oxley Act does not apply to registered investment companies, and we are not extending any of the requirements that would implement section 404 to registered investment companies.[120] Several commenters objected to the proposed requirement that the Section 302 certification include a statement of the officers' responsibility for internal controls.[121] These commenters argued that this requirement would contradict Section 405 of the Sarbanes-Oxley Act and represent a "back-door" application of Section 404, from which registered investment companies are exempt.[122] We disagree. The certification requirements implement Section 302 of the Sarbanes-Oxley Act, from which registered investment companies are not exempt.[123] We are not subjecting registered investment companies to the requirements implementing Section 404 of the Sarbanes-Oxley Act, including the annual and quarterly evaluation requirements with respect to internal control over financial reporting and the requirements for an annual report by management on internal control over financial reporting and an attestation report on management's assessment.

We are adopting the following technical changes to our rules and forms implementing Section 302 of the Sarbanes-Oxley Act for registered investment companies in order to conform to the changes that we are adopting for operating companies.[124]

- *Paragraph (d) of Investment Company Act Rule 30a-3.* The amendments use the same term "internal control over financial reporting" that we are using in the rules for operating companies and include the same definition of "internal control over financial reporting" that we are adopting in Exchange Act Rules 13a-15(f) and 15d-15(f).

- *Paragraph (a) of Investment Company Act Rule 30a-3.* The amendments require every registered management investment company, other than a small business investment company, to maintain internal control over financial reporting. These amendments parallel those that we are adopting for operating companies in Exchange Act Rules 13a-15(a) and 15d-15(a).

- *Introductory text and sub-paragraph (b) of paragraph 4 of the certification in Item 10(a)(2) of Form N-CSR.* The amendments require the signing officers to state that they are responsible for establishing and maintaining internal control over financial reporting, and that they have designed such internal control over financial reporting, or caused such internal control over financial reporting to be designed under their supervision, to provide reasonable assurance regarding the reliability of financial reporting and the preparation of financial statements for external purposes in accordance with generally accepted accounting principles.

---

119. An insured depository institution subject to both the FDIC's requirements and our new requirements choosing to file a single management report to satisfy both sets of requirements will file the attestation report with its primary federal regulator under the Exchange Act and the FDIC, its primary federal regulator (if other than the FDIC), and any appropriate state depository institution supervisor under Part 363 of the FDIC's regulations. A holding company choosing to prepare a single management report to satisfy both sets of requirements will file the attestation report with the Commission under the Exchange Act and the FDIC, the primary federal regulator of the insured depository institution subsidiary subject to the FDIC's requirements, and any appropriate state depository institution supervisor under Part 363.

120. *See* Section 405 of the Sarbanes-Oxley Act ("Nothing in section 401, 402, or 404, the amendments made by those sections, or the rules of the Commission under those sections shall apply to any investment company registered under section 8 of the Investment Company Act of 1940 (15 U.S.C. 80a-8)."). The provisions that would not extend to registered investment companies include amendments to Exchange Act rules 13a-15(c) and 15d-15(c) (requiring annual evaluation of the effectiveness of internal control over financial reporting); Exchange Act rules 13a-15(d) and 15d-15(d) (requiring quarterly evaluation of any change in internal control over financial reporting that has materially affected, or is reasonably likely to materially affect, internal control over financial reporting); and Items 308(a) and (b) of Regulations S-K and S-B (requiring annual report by management on internal control over financial reporting and attestation report on management's evaluation of internal control over financial reporting).

121. Proposed paragraph 4 of the certification section of proposed Form N-CSR. Proposing Release, note 26 above, 67 FR at 66250. We received 7 comment letters on the proposed changes to the certification rules with respect to investment companies in the Proposing Release. See letters regarding File No. S7-40-02 of: the Investment Company Institute ("ICI"); Protiviti; OppenheimerFunds, Inc. ("Oppenheimer"); The Association of the Bar of the City of New York; Leslie Ogg of Board Services Corporation ("Ogg"); Federated Funds; and D&T.

122. *See* letters regarding File No. S7-40-02 of: Association of the Bar of the City of New York; ICI; and Oppenheimer.

123. *See* Section 302(a)(4)(A) and (B) of the Sarbanes-Oxley Act (requiring signing officers to certify that they are responsible for establishing and maintaining internal controls and have designed the internal controls to ensure that material information relating to the issuer is made known to the signing officers).

124. For a discussion of changes to the form of the Section 302 certification for operating companies, *see* Section III.D. below.

- *Paragraph (4)(d) of the certification of Item 10(a)(2), and Item 9(b) of Form N-CSR.* The amendments require disclosure of any change in the investment company's internal control over financial reporting that occurred during the most recent fiscal half-year that has materially affected, or is reasonably likely to materially affect, the company's internal control over financial reporting.

- *Paragraph (5) of the certification of Item 10(a)(2) of Form N-CSR.* The amendments require the signing officers to state that they have disclosed to the investment company's auditors and the audit committee all significant deficiencies and material weaknesses in the design or operation of internal control over financial reporting which are reasonably likely to adversely affect the investment company's ability to record, process, summarize, and report financial information.

We are not, however, adopting proposed amendments that would have required the evaluation by an investment company's management of the effectiveness of its disclosure controls and procedures to be as of the end of the period covered by each report on Form N-CSR, rather than within 90 days prior to the filing date of the report, as our certification rules currently require.[125] Commenters noted that this would require investment company complexes that have funds with staggered fiscal year ends to perform evaluations of their disclosure controls and procedures as many as twelve times per year. They argued that requiring such frequent evaluations would be extremely costly, inefficient, and operationally disruptive, and would not provide any benefits to shareholders.[126] We agree that the costs of requiring investment company complexes to perform evaluations of their disclosure controls and procedures twelve times per year would outweigh the benefits to investors. The certification rules we are adopting will require an investment company complex to perform at most four such evaluations per year.[127]

Transition Period for Registered Investment Companies

Registered investment companies must comply with the rule and form amendments applicable to them on and after August 14, 2003, except as follows. Registered investment companies must comply with the amendments to Exchange Act Rules 13a-15(a) and 15d-15(a) and Investment Company Act Rule 30a-3(a) that require them to maintain internal control over financial reporting with respect to fiscal years ending on or after June 15, 2004. In addition, registered investment companies must comply with the portion of the introductory language in paragraph 4 of the certification in Item 10(a)(2) of Form N-CSR that refers to the certifying officers' responsibility for establishing and maintaining internal control over financial reporting, as well as paragraph 4(b) of the certification, beginning with the first annual report filed on Form N-CSR for a fiscal year ending on or after June 15, 2004.

J. Transition Period

We received a number of comments urging us to adopt an extended transition period for compliance with the new disclosure requirements.[128] We have decided to delay the compliance date of the requirement to provide a management report assessing the effectiveness of internal control over financial reporting and an auditor's attestation to, and report on, that assessment beyond that in the Proposing Release so that companies and their auditors will have time to prepare and satisfy the new requirements. These compliance dates do not apply to registered investment companies, which are not required to provide the management report assessing the effectiveness of internal control over financial reporting and the related auditor's attestation.[129] A company that is an "accelerated filer," as defined in Exchange Act Rule 12b-2, as of the end of its first fiscal year ending on or after June 15, 2004, must begin to comply with the management report on internal control over financial reporting disclosure requirements promulgated under Section 404 of the Sarbanes-Oxley

---

125. Proposed Exchange Act Rules 13a-15(c) and 15d-15(c), proposed Investment Company Act Rule 30a-2(b)(4)(iii), and proposed Investment Company Act Rule 30a-3(b).

126. *See* letters regarding File No. S7-40-02 of: D&T; ICI; Ogg; and Oppenheimer.

127. *See* Release No. IC-25914 (Jan. 27, 2003) [68 FR 5348, 5352 n. 43] (noting that in the case of a series fund or family of investment companies in which the disclosure controls and procedures for each fund in the series or family are the same, a single evaluation of the effectiveness of the disclosure controls and procedures for the series or family could be used in multiple certifications for the funds in the series or family, as long as the evaluation has been performed within 90 days of the report on Form N-CSR).

128. *See*, for example, the letters regarding File No. S7-40-02 of: AICPA; D&T; CSC; E&Y; and Association of the Bar of the City of New York, Committee on Securities Regulation ("NYCB-CSR").

129. *See* Section II. I., above, for compliance dates applicable to registered investment companies.

Act in its annual report for that fiscal year. We recognize that non-accelerated filers, including smaller companies and foreign private issuers, may have greater difficulty in preparing the management report on internal control over financial reporting. Therefore, these types of companies must begin to comply with the disclosure requirements in annual reports for their first fiscal year ending on or after April 15, 2005. A company must begin to comply with the quarterly evaluation of changes to internal control over financial reporting requirements for its first periodic report due after the first annual report that must include management's report on internal control over financial reporting. We believe that the transition period is appropriate in light of both the substantial time and resources needed to properly implement the rules[130] and the corresponding benefit to investors that will result. In addition, the transition period will provide additional time for the PCAOB to consider relevant factors in determining and implementing any new attestation standard as it finds appropriate, subject to our approval.

Consistent with this extended compliance period for management's internal control report and the related attestation, and for the subsequent evaluation of changes in internal control over financial reporting, the following provisions of the rules adopted today are subject to the extended compliance period:

- The provisions of Items 308(a) and (b) of Regulations S-K and S-B and the comparable provisions of Forms 20-F and 40-F requiring management's internal control report and the related attestation;
- The amendments to Rules 13a-15(a) and 15d-15(a) under the Exchange Act relating to maintenance of internal control over financial reporting; and
- The provisions of Rules 13a-15(c) and (d) and 15d-15(c) and (d) under the Exchange Act requiring evaluations of internal control over financial reporting and changes thereto.

The extended compliance period does not in any way affect the provisions of our other rules and regulations regarding internal controls that are in effect, including, without limitation, Rule 13b-2 under the Exchange Act.

Other rules relating to evaluation and disclosure adopted today are effective on August 14, 2003. These other rules include amendments to Items 308(c) of Regulations S-K and S-B and the comparable provisions of Forms 20-F and 40-F requiring disclosure regarding certain changes in internal control over financial reporting. These amendments modify existing requirements regarding disclosure of changes in internal control over financial reporting, are related to statements made in the Section 302 certifications of principal executive and financial officers, and provide clarifications that are beneficial and whose implementation need not be delayed. These other rules that are effective on August 14, 2003 also include amendments relating to disclosure controls and procedures.

III. Discussion of Amendments Related to Certifications

A. Proposed Rules

We proposed to amend our rules and forms to require companies to file the certifications required by Section 302 of the Sarbanes-Oxley Act as an exhibit to the periodic reports to which they relate. Specifically, we proposed to amend the exhibit requirements of Forms 20-F and 40-F and Item 601 of Regulations S-B and S-K to add the Section 302 certifications to the list of required exhibits. In addition, we proposed to amend Exchange Act Rules 13a-14 and 15d-14 to require that Section 906 certifications accompany the periodic reports to which they relate, and to amend Forms 20-F and 40-F and Item 601 of Regulations S-B and S-K to add Section 906 certifications to the list of required exhibits. We also proposed to amend Investment Company Act Rule 30a-2 to require that Section 906 certifications accompany the periodic reports on Form N-CSR to which they relate and Item 10 of Form N-CSR to add the Section 906 certifications as a required exhibit.

We received eight comment letters in response to the proposals.[131] The primary topic addressed by the commenters was whether Section 906 of the Sarbanes-Oxley Act applied to annual reports

---

130. *See* Section V. below.
131. *See* letters regarding File No. S7-06-03 of: ABA; Cleary, Gottlieb, Steen & Hamilton ("Cleary"); Prof. Paul A. Griffin ("Griffin"); Intel Corporation ("Intel"); ICI; PwC; John Stalnaker and Patrick Derksen ("Stalnaker"); and Rooks Pitts ("Rooks").

filed on Form 11-K. Most of the commenters believed that issuers required to file annual reports on Form 11-K should be exempt from the requirement to furnish a Section 906 certification as an exhibit.[132] Two commenters noted that the language of Section 906 that requires certification of the chief executive officer and chief financial officer (or equivalent thereof) is inconsistent with the actual administration of employee benefit plans because such plans do not have individuals acting as chief executive officer and chief financial officer.[133] Those commenters noted that employee benefit plans are typically administered through one or more committees that are appointed as the plan's named fiduciaries to administer the plan and oversee investments.[134] In addition, some commenters believed that we should provide an exemption for Form 11-K because employee benefit plans are already subject to extensive regulation under the Employee Retirement Income Security Act of 1974 ("ERISA"),[135] which includes a requirement for the plan administrator to certify, under penalties of perjury and other criminal and administrative penalties, the accuracy of the plan's disclosures under ERISA.[136]

Commenters also addressed other topics related to Section 906. One commenter requested that the Commission allow Section 906 certifications to remain confidential.[137] That commenter expressed concern that a plaintiff could use a Section 906 certification to create a basis for liability that did not otherwise exist.[138] One commenter objected to the proposal to deem Section 906 certifications as "furnished," rather than as "filed."[139] After considering all of the comments, we are adopting the proposals substantially as proposed.

On April 11, 2003, U.S. Senator Joseph Biden introduced a statement into the Congressional Record that discusses Section 906.[140] The statement asserts that Section 906 "is intended to apply to any financial statement filed by a publicly-traded company, upon which the investing public will rely to gauge the financial health of the company," which includes financial statements included in current reports on Forms 6-K and 8-K and annual reports on Form 11-K.[141] The language added to Title 18 by Section 906 refers to "periodic reports containing financial statements," and our proposals to require companies to furnish Section 906 certifications as exhibits applied to periodic (annual, semi-annual and quarterly) reports but did not address current reports on Forms 6-K and 8-K.[142] One commenter addressed the statement in the Congressional Record, indicating that the suggested requirements would create substantial practical burdens for companies to provide Section 906 certifications in current reports filed on Forms 6-K or 8-K.[143] We are also concerned that extending Section 906 certifications to Forms 6-K or 8-K could potentially chill the disclosure of information by companies. As noted above, four commenters argued that Section 906 should not apply to Form 11-K.[144] In light of these developments, we are considering, in consultation with the Department of Justice, the application of Section 906 to current reports on Forms 6-K and 8-K and annual reports on Form 11-K and the possibility of taking additional action.

B. Final Rules

We are amending the exhibit requirements of Forms 20-F and 40-F and Item 601 of Regulations S-B and S-K to add the Section 302 certifications to the list of required exhibits.[145] In the final rules, the specific form and content of the required certifications is set forth in the applicable exhibit filing requirement.[146] To coordinate the rules requiring an evaluation of "disclosure controls

---

132. *See* letters regarding File No. S7-06-03 of: ABA; Cleary; Intel; and PwC.
133. *See* letters File No. S7-06-03 of ABA and Cleary.
134. *Id.*
135. Pub. L. No. 83-406, 88 Stat. 129 (1974).
136. *See* letters regarding File No. S7-06-03 of: ABA; Cleary; and PwC.
137. *See* ABA letter regarding File No. S7-06-03.
138. *Id.*
139. *See* Stalnaker letter regarding File No. S7-06-03.
140. *See* 149 Cong. Rec. S5325 (daily ed. Apr. 11, 2003).
141. *Id.* at S5331.
142. *See* Release No. 33-8212 (Mar. 21, 2003) [68 FR 15600] at fn. 37.
143. *See* ABA letter regarding File No. S7-06-03.
144. *See* letters regarding File No. S7-06-03 of: ABA; Cleary; Intel; and PwC.
145. We recently adopted Form N-CSR, to be used by registered management investment companies to file certified shareholder reports with the Commission. *See* Release No. IC-25914 (Jan. 27, 2003) [68 FR 5348]. As adopted, Form N-CSR requires the Section 302 certifications to be filed as an exhibit to a report on Form N-CSR. Item 10(b) of Form N-CSR.
146. Accordingly, we are revising Exchange Act Rules 13a-14 and 15d-14 to delete from those rules the detailed description of the contents of the required certifications and to revise the instructions to Forms 10-Q, 10-QSB, 10-K, and 10-KSB to delete the references to the Section 302 certification requirements. We are also adopting similar changes to Investment Company Act Rule 30a-2 and Form N-CSR.

and procedures" and "internal control over financial reporting," we are moving the definition of the term "disclosure controls and procedures" from Exchange Act Rules 13a-14(c) and 15d-14(c) and Investment Company Act Rule 30a-2(c) to new Exchange Act Rules 13a-15(c) and 15d-15(c) and Investment Company Act Rule 30a-3(c), respectively.

We are amending Exchange Act Rules 13a-14 and 15d-14 and Investment Company Act Rule 30a-2 to require the Section 906 certifications to accompany periodic reports containing financial statements as exhibits. We also are amending the exhibit requirements in Forms 20-F, 40-F and Item 601 of Regulations S-B and S-K to add the Section 906 certifications to the list of required exhibits to be included in reports filed with the Commission. In addition, we are amending Item 10 of Form N-CSR to add the Section 906 certifications as a required exhibit. Because the Section 906 certification requirement applies to periodic reports containing financial statements that are filed by an issuer pursuant to Section 13(a) or 15(d) of the Exchange Act, the exhibit requirement will only apply to reports on Form N-CSR filed under these sections and not to reports on Form N-CSR that are filed under the Investment Company Act only.[147] A failure to furnish the Section 906 certifications would cause the periodic report to which they relate to be incomplete, thereby violating Section 13(a) of the Exchange Act.[148] In addition, referencing the Section 906 certifications in Exchange Act Rules 13a-14 and 15d-14 and Investment Company Act Rule 30a-2 subjects these certifications to the signature requirements of Rule 302 of Regulation S-T.[149]

Section 906 requires that the certifications "accompany" the periodic report to which they relate. This is in contrast to Section 302, which requires the certifications to be included "in" the periodic report. In recognition of this difference, we are permitting companies to "furnish," rather than "file," the Section 906 certifications with the Commission.[150] Thus, the certifications would not be subject to liability under Section 18 of the Exchange Act.[151] Moreover, the certifications would not be subject to automatic incorporation by reference into a company's Securities Act registration statements, which are subject to liability under Section 11 of the Securities Act,[152] unless the issuer takes steps to include the certifications in a registration statement.

Although Section 906 does not explicitly require the certifications to be made public, we believe that it is appropriate to require certifications that "accompany" a publicly filed periodic report to be provided publicly in this manner. We believe that Congress intended for Section 906 certifications to be publicly provided. Civil liability already exists under our signature requirements and the Section 302 certifications. In addition, any Section 906 certification submitted to the Commission as correspondence is subject to the Freedom of Information Act.[153] Finally, the requirement to furnish Section 906 certifications as exhibits serves a number of important functions. First, the exhibit requirement enhances compliance by allowing the Commission, the Department of Justice and the public to monitor the certifications effectively. Second, by subjecting the Section 906 certifications to the signature requirements of Regulation S-T, companies are required to retain a manually signed signature page or other authenticating document for a five-year period. This requirement helps to preserve evidential matter in the event of prosecution.

There are important distinctions to be made between Sections 302 and 906 of the Sarbanes-Oxley Act. Unlike the Section 302 certifications, the Section 906 certifications are required only in periodic reports that contain financial statements. Therefore, amendments to periodic reports that

---

147. *See* General Instruction A of Form N-CSR (Form N-CSR is a combined reporting form to be used for reports of registered management investment companies under Section 30(b)(2) of the Investment Company Act and Sections 13(a) or 15(d) of the Exchange Act); n. 28 above (discussing issuers covered by Sections 13(a) and 15(d) of the Exchange Act). Registered management investment companies that are required to file reports on Form N-CSR pursuant to Section 13(a) or 15(d) of the Exchange Act will be required to provide the Section 906 certifications under Exchange Act Rules 13a-14(b) and 15d-14(b) as well as Investment Company Act Rule 30a-2(b). By contrast, registered management investment companies that are required to file reports on Form N-CSR are required to provide the Section 302 certifications solely under Investment Company Act Rule 30a-2(a), which was adopted under Sections 13(a) and 15(d) of the Exchange Act as well as the Investment Company Act. Release No. 33-8124 (Aug. 28, 2002) [67 FR 57276, 57295]; Release No. IC-25914 (Jan. 27, 2003) [68 FR 5348, 5365].

148. *See also* Section 3(b)(1) of the Sarbanes-Oxley Act, which provides that "[a] violation by any person of this Act * * * shall be treated for all purposes in the same manner as a violation of the Securities Exchange Act of 1934 * * * and any such person shall be subject to the same penalties, and to the same extent, as for a violation of that Act * * * ."

149. *See* Rule 302(b) of Regulation S-T [17 CFR 232.302(b)]. Among other things, this rule requires that an issuer maintain manually signed certifications or other authenticating documents.

150. *See*, for example, Item 601(b)(32)(ii) of Regulation S-K.

151. 15 U.S.C. 78r.

152. 15 U.S.C. 77k.

153. 5 U.S.C. 552 *et seq.*

do not contain financial statements would not require a new Section 906 certification, but would require a new Section 302 certification to be filed with the amendment.[154] In addition, unlike the Section 302 certifications, the Section 906 certifications may take the form of a single statement signed by a company's chief executive and financial officers.[155]

C. Effect on Interim Guidance Regarding Filing Procedures

We provided interim guidance regarding voluntary filing procedures for Section 906 certifications.[156] That guidance encouraged issuers to submit their Section 906 certifications as exhibits to the periodic reports to which they relate.[157] For issuers that are not investment companies, that interim voluntary guidance shall remain in effect until the rules become effective. In the event that the EDGAR system is not updated by the effective date, companies should submit the required certifications as Exhibit 99.[158] For registered investment companies, the interim guidance shall remain in effect until the rules become effective.[159]

D. Form of Section 302 Certifications

We proposed several amendments to the form of certifications to be provided pursuant to Section 302 of the Sarbanes-Oxley Act. In particular, we proposed the following:

- The addition of a statement that principal executive and financial officers are responsible for designing internal controls and procedures for financial reporting or having such controls and procedures designed under their supervision;

- The clarification that disclosure controls and procedures may be designed under the supervision of principal executive and financial officers; and

- The revision of the statement as to the effectiveness of disclosure controls and procedures and internal controls and procedures for financial reporting would be as of the end of the period.

We have adopted the proposals referred to above substantially as proposed. In addition, we have made the following changes:

- We have incorporated the term "internal control over financial reporting" into the certification;

- We have amended the provision of the certification relating to changes in internal control over financial reporting, consistent with the final rules discussed above regarding evaluation and disclosure, so that it refers to changes that have materially affected or are reasonably likely to materially affect internal control over financial reporting;

- We have clarified that the statement as effectiveness of disclosure controls and procedures be as of the end of the period, but that the date of the evaluation is not specified; and

- We have made minor changes in the organization of the certification.

E. Transition Period

---

154. *See* Exchange Act Rule 12b-15 [17 CFR 240.12b-15] and Investment Company Act Rule 8b-15 [17 CFR 270.8b-15]. Depending on the contents of the amendment, the form of certification required to be included may be subject to modification.

155. *See* Exchange Act Rules 13a-14(b) and 15d-14(b) [17 CFR 240.13a-14(b) and 240.15d-14(b)] and Investment Company Act Rule 30a-2(b) [17 CFR 270.30a-2(b)].

156. *See* Release No. 33-8212 (Mar. 21, 2003) [68 FR 15600] at Section III.

157. We are modifying that interim guidance, however, to more closely parallel the provisions of Section 302 of Regulation S-T that require retention of manual signatures for electronically filed signed statements. Issuers furnishing Section 906 certifications to the Commission as an exhibit to the periodic reports to which they relate during the period covered by the interim guidance should insert the following legend after the text of each certification: "A signed original of this written statement required by Section 906, or other document authenticating, acknowledging, or otherwise adopting the signature that appears in typed form within the electronic version of this written statement required by Section 906, has been provided to [name of issuer] and will be retained by [name of issuer] and furnished to the Securities and Exchange Commission or its staff upon request."

158. Use of Exhibit 99 for this purpose will remain in effect until we announce that our EDGAR system permits registrants to file or furnish exhibits 31 and 32 for Section 302 and 906 certifications. We will issue a statement and post it on the Commission's website to announce this date as soon as it becomes known.

159. For a registered management investment company filing reports on Form N-CSR, the EDGAR document type should be EX-99.906CERT for the Section 906 certifications.

The final rules regarding filing of certifications under Sections 302 and 906, for companies other than registered investment companies, will be effective on August 14, 2003. The compliance dates applicable to registered investment companies are described in Section II. I., above.

We believe that changes in the form of Section 302 certification described above are beneficial to both registrants and investors because they clarify the provisions of the certification. With one exception, discussed below, the changes are also not related to our new requirements regarding management's internal control report. With that one exception, appropriateness of the modified certification is thus not affected by the extended compliance period we are providing in connection with management's internal control report and the related attestation. Our rules adopted today also therefore provide that the form of Section 302 certification will be modified, with that one exception, in accordance with these rules effective on August 14, 2003.

We are applying the extended compliance period to the portion of the introductory language in paragraph 4 of the Section 302 certification that refers to the certifying officers' responsibility for establishing and maintaining internal control over financial reporting for the company, as well as paragraph 4(b), which must be provided in the first annual report required to contain management's internal control report and thereafter. As noted above, this extended compliance period does not in any way affect the provisions of our other rules and regulations regarding internal controls that are in effect.

IV. Paperwork Reduction Act

A. Background

Certain provisions of our final amendments contain "collection of information" requirements within the meaning of the Paperwork Reduction Act of 1995 ("PRA").[160] We published a notice requesting comment on the collection of information requirements in the proposing release for the rule amendments, and we submitted these requirements to the Office of Management and Budget ("OMB") for review in accordance with the PRA.[161] The titles for the collection of information are:

(1) "Form 10-Q" (OMB Control No. 3235-0070);

(2) "Form 10-QSB" (OMB Control No. 3235-0416);

(3) "Form 10-K" (OMB Control No. 3235-0063);

(4) "Form 10-KSB" (OMB Control No. 3235-0420);

(5) "Form 20-F" (OMB Control No. 3235-0288);

(6) "Form 40-F" (OMB Control No. 3235-0381);

(7) "Regulation S-X" (OMB Control No. 3235-0009);

(8) "Regulation S-K" (OMB Control No. 3235-0071);

(9) "Regulation S-B" (OMB Control No. 3235-0417); and

(10) "Form N-CSR" (OMB Control No. 3235-0570).

The forms are periodic reports adopted under the Exchange Act and the Investment Company Act. The regulations set forth the disclosure requirements for periodic reports, registration statements and proxy and information statements filed by companies to ensure that investors are informed. The hours and costs associated with preparing, filing and sending these forms constitute reporting and cost burdens imposed by each collection of information. An agency may not conduct or sponsor, and a person is not required to respond to, a collection of information unless it displays a currently valid OMB control number. Compliance with the requirements is mandatory. Under our rules for the retention of manual signatures,[162] companies must retain, for a period of five years, an original signature page or other document authenticating, acknowledging or otherwise adopting the certifying officers' signatures that appear in their electronically filed periodic reports. Responses to the information collections are not kept confidential.

---

160. 44 U.S.C. 3501 *et seq.*
161. 44 U.S.C. 3507(d) and 5 CFR 1320.11.
162. *See* Rule 302 of Regulation S-T [17 CFR 232.302].

B. Summary of the Final Rules

The final rules require the annual report of every company that files periodic reports under Section 13(a) or 15(d) of the Exchange Act, other than reports by registered investment companies, to contain a report of management that includes:

- A statement of management's responsibility for establishing and maintaining adequate internal control over financial reporting for the company;

- A statement identifying the framework used by management to evaluate the effectiveness of the company's internal control over financial reporting;

- Management's assessment of the effectiveness of the company's internal control over financial reporting, as of the end of the most recent fiscal year; and

- A statement that the registered public accounting firm that audited the financial statements included in the annual report has issued an attestation report on management's evaluation of the company's internal control over financial reporting.

We are adding these requirements pursuant to the legislative mandate in Section 404 of the Sarbanes-Oxley Act. Under our final rules, a company also will be required to evaluate and disclose any change in its internal control over financial reporting that occurred during the fiscal quarter that has materially affected, or is reasonably likely to materially affect, the company's internal control over financial reporting.

We are also adopting amendments to require companies to file the certifications mandated by Sections 302 and 906 of the Sarbanes-Oxley Act as exhibits to their annual, semi-annual and quarterly reports. These amendments will enhance the ability of investors, the Commission staff, the Department of Justice and other interested parties to easily and efficiently access the certifications through our Electronic Data Gathering, Analysis and Retrieval ("EDGAR") system and facilitate better monitoring of a company's compliance with the certification requirements.

C. Summary of Comment Letters and Revisions to Proposals

We requested comment on the PRA analysis contained in the proposing releases addressing Section 404 and Sections 302 and 906 of the Sarbanes-Oxley Act.[163] We received no comments on our PRA estimates for the certification requirements. With respect to our PRA estimates for the rules implementing Section 404 of the Sarbanes-Oxley Act, eight commenters thought that our PRA estimates significantly understated the actual time and costs that companies would have to expend evaluating and reporting on their internal control over financial reporting.[164] However, few of these commenters provided actual alternative cost estimates, and none provided estimates that could be applied generally to all types and sizes of companies. One commenter believed that, based on its experience, we understated the burden estimate by at least a factor of 100.[165] In response to these commenters, and based on follow-up conversations with several of the commenters who expressed a view on our burden and cost estimates, we have revised our estimates as discussed more fully in Section IV.D below.

We have made a substantive modification to the proposed rules in response to the cost concerns expressed by commenters. Specifically, the final rules require companies to undertake a quarterly evaluation only of any change occurring during the fiscal quarter that has materially affected, or is reasonably likely to materially affect, the company's internal control over financial reporting. This change should substantially mitigate some of the costs and burdens associated with the proposed requirements.

We have made additional substantive changes to the proposed rule as well. First, the final rules require management to evaluate the company's internal control over financial reporting using a suitable framework, such as the COSO Framework. Second, the final rules expand the list of information that must be included in the management report and specify that management cannot conclude that a company's internal control over financial reporting is effective if there are one or more material weaknesses in such control. Under the final rules, management must identify the frame-

---

163. See Release No. 33-8138 (Oct. 22, 2002) [67 FR 66208] and Release No. 33-8212 (Mar. 21, 2003) [68 FR 15600].
164. See letters regarding File No. S7-40-02 of: AICPA; BDO; D&T; Emerson; E&Y; IPC; Intel; and NYCB-CCL.
165. See Intel letter regarding File No. S7-40-02.

work used to evaluate the company's internal control over financial reporting and disclose any material weaknesses in the company's internal control over financial reporting discovered through the evaluation. We do not believe that these changes significantly alter the burdens imposed on companies resulting from the required assessment of internal control over financial reporting.

D. Revisions to PRA Reporting and Cost Burden Estimates

As discussed above, in consideration of commenters' remarks, we are revising our PRA burden and cost estimates for the rules pertaining to Section 404 that we originally submitted to the OMB in connection with the proposed rules.

We derived our new burden hour estimates for the annual report forms by estimating the total amount of time that it will take a company's management to conduct the annual evaluation of its internal control over financial reporting and to prepare the required management report.[166] Our annual burden estimate is based on several assumptions. First, we assumed that the annual number of responses for each form would be consistent with the number of filings that we received in fiscal year 2002.[167] Second, we assumed that there is a direct correlation between the extent of the burden and the size of the reporting company, with the burden increasing commensurate with the size of the company. We believe that there will be a marked disparity of burdens and costs resulting from the new internal control requirements between the largest and smallest reporting companies. Our estimates reflect an average burden for all sizes of companies. Third, we assumed that the first-year burden would be greater than that for subsequent years, as a portion of the costs will reflect one-time expenditures associated with complying with the rule, such as compiling documentation, implementing new processes, and training staff. We also adjusted the second and third year estimates to account for the fact that management should become more efficient at conducting its internal control assessment and preparing the disclosure after the first year as the process becomes more routine.[168] Under these assumptions, we estimate that the average incremental burden for an annual filing will be 383 hours per company and the portion of that burden that is reflected as the cost associated with outside professionals is approximately $34,300 per company. For large corporations, we expect that this burden will be substantially higher. Indeed, we received estimates in the thousands of hours for some large and complex companies. Conversely, we expect small companies to find their burden to be less than this average. We also believe that many companies will experience costs well in excess of this average in the first year of compliance with the final rules. We believe that costs will decrease in subsequent years. This burden will also vary among companies based on the complexity of their organization and the nature of their current internal control procedures. We therefore calculated our estimates by averaging the estimated burdens over a three-year period.

We derived our burden estimates for the quarterly report forms by estimating the total amount of time that it will take a company's management to conduct the quarterly evaluation of material changes to the company's internal control over financial reporting and for the company to prepare the required disclosure about such changes. We believe that these quarterly evaluations will impose little additional burden, as much of the structure to conduct these evaluations will be established in connection with the annual evaluations. We estimate that the quarterly reporting will impose an additional burden of five hours per company in connection with each quarterly report. Accordingly, we did not revise our original burden hour estimates for the quarterly report forms.

We estimate the total annual incremental burden (for annual and quarterly reports) associated with the new internal control evaluation and disclosure requirements for all companies to be approximately 3,792,888 hours of company personnel time and a cost of $481,013,550 for the services of outside professionals.[169]

---

166. Our estimates are based on information from with several large and small firms, accounting firms and trade and professional associations.
167. The estimates used in the releases proposing these rules were based on the number of filings that we received in fiscal year 2001.
168. We assumed the estimated burdens in the second and third years would decline by 75% from the first year estimate.
169. Our PRA estimates do not include any additional burdens or costs that a company will incur as a result of having to obtain an auditor's attestation report on management's internal control report because the PCAOB, rather than the Commission, is responsible for establishing the attestation standards and the Sarbanes-Oxley Act itself requires companies to obtain such an attestation. We have, however, included an estimated 0.5 hour burden in our revised annual burden estimates to account for the filing by the company of the attestation report.

Table 1 below presents these burdens and costs for each form affected by the final rules implementing Section 404 of Sarbanes-Oxley. We calculated the burden by multiplying the estimated number of affected responses by the estimated average number of hours that management will spend conducting its assessment of the company's internal control over financial reporting and preparing the related disclosure. For Exchange Act annual reports, we estimate that 75% of the burden of preparation is carried by the company internally and that 25% of the burden of preparation is carried by outside professionals retained by the company at an average cost of $300 per hour.[170] The portion of the burden carried by outside professionals is reflected as a cost, while the portion of the burden carried by the company internally is reflected in hours. There is no change to the estimated burden of the collections of information entitled "Regulation S-K," "Regulation S-B" and "Regulation S-X" because the burdens that these regulations impose are reflected in our revised estimates for the forms.

Table 1: Incremental Paperwork Burden for the Rules Implementing Section 404

	Annual Responses (A)	Incremental Hours/Form (B)	Total Burden (C)=(A)*(B)	75% Company (D)=(C)*0.75	25% Professional (E)=(C)*0.25	Professional Costs (F)=(E)*$300
10-K	8,484	383	3,249,372	2,437,029	812,343	243,702,900
10-KSB	3,820	383	1,463,606	1,097,295	365,765	109,729,500
20-F	1,194	383	457,302	114,326	342,977	102,892,950
40-F	134	383	51,322	12,831	37,989	11,547,450
10-Q	23,743	5	118,715	89,036	29,679	8,903,625
10-QSB	11,299	5	56,495	42,371	14,124	4,237,125
Reg. S-K . . .	N/A	1	1	N/A	N/A	N/A
Reg. S-B . . .	N/A	1	1	N/A	N/A	N/A
Reg. S-X . . .	N/A	1	1	N/A	N/A	N/A
Total				3,792,888	. . . .	$481,013,550

170. The burden allocation for Forms 20-F and 40-F, however, use a 25% internal to 75% outside professional allocation to reflect the fact that foreign private issuers rely more heavily on outside professionals for the preparation of these forms.

We do not believe that the amendments with respect to the Section 302 certifications result in a need to alter the burden estimates that we previously submitted to OMB because they merely relocate the certifications from the text of quarterly and annual reports filed or submitted under Section 13(a) or 15(d) of the Exchange Act to the "Exhibits" section of the reports. We are, however, revising the burden estimates for quarterly and annual reports and for Form N-CSR based on the amendment with respect to the Section 906 certification.[171] The PRA estimates for these amendments do not reflect a cost because we believe that the entire burden will be borne by company personnel. With respect to semi-annual reports on Form N-CSR, because the financial statements of registered management investment companies are not as complex as those of operating companies, we estimate that the amendments relating to the Section 906 certifications would result in an increase of one burden hour per portfolio.[172] We estimate that there are approximately 3,700 registered management investment companies that are required to file reports on Form N-CSR, containing 9,850 portfolios. The following table illustrates the incremental PRA estimates for the new Section 906 certification[173] requirements:

171. While Section 906 of the Sarbanes-Oxley Act requires that certifications must accompany a periodic report, we are increasing our PRA burdens in view of the fact that the amendments explicitly require companies to furnish Section 906 certifications as exhibits to these reports. To date, companies have used various methods to fulfill their obligations under Section 906, and have not consistently submitted the certifications as part of the report.

172. Many registered management investment companies have multiple portfolios. However, they prepare separate financial statements for each portfolio. Thus, the burden of the Section 906 certifications is estimated on a portfolio basis rather than a registered management investment company basis.

173. This number represents the burden associated with the average number of portfolios per form. This number will vary for each registered management investment company depending on the number of portfolios. We estimate that the paperwork burden for each portfolio is one hour.

Table 2: Incremental Paperwork Burden for Certification Requirements

Form	Annual Responses	Hours/Form	Total Hours Added
20-F	1,194	2	2,388
40-F	134	2	268
10-K	8,484	2	16,968
10-KSB	3,820	2	7,640
10-Q	23,743	2	47,486
10-QSB	11,299	2	22,598
N-CSR	7,400	2.66[173]	19,700
Total			117,048

173. This number represents the burden associated with the average number of portfolios per form. This number will vary for each registered management investment company depending on the number of portfolios. We estimate that the paperwork burden for each portfolio is one hour.

V. Cost-Benefit Analysis

The amendments implementing Section 404 of the Sarbanes-Oxley Act are congressionally mandated. We recognize that implementation of the Sarbanes-Oxley Act will likely result in costs and benefits to the economy. We are sensitive to the costs and benefits imposed by our rules, and we have considered costs and benefits of our amendments.

A. Benefits

One of the main goals of the Sarbanes-Oxley Act is to enhance the quality of reporting and increase investor confidence in the financial markets. Recent market events have evidenced a need to provide investors with a clearer understanding of the processes that surround the preparation and presentation of financial information. These amendments are intended to accomplish the Act's goals by improving public company disclosure to investors about the extent of management's responsibility for the company's financial statements and internal control over financial reporting and the means by which management discharges its responsibility. The establishment and maintenance of internal control over financial reporting has always been an important responsibility of management. An effective system of internal control over financial reporting is necessary to produce reliable financial statements and other financial information used by investors. By requiring a report of management stating management's responsibility for the company's financial statements and internal control over financial reporting and management's assessment regarding the effectiveness of such control, investors will be able to better evaluate management's performance of its stewardship responsibilities and the reliability of a company's financial statements and other unaudited financial information.

The required annual evaluation of internal control over financial reporting will encourage companies to devote adequate resources and attention to the maintenance of such control. Additionally, the required evaluation should help to identify potential weaknesses and deficiencies in advance of a system breakdown, thereby facilitating the continuous, orderly and timely flow of information within the company and, ultimately, to investors and the marketplace. Improved disclosure may help companies detect fraudulent financial reporting earlier and perhaps thereby deter financial fraud or minimize its adverse effects. All of these benefits will increase market efficiency by improving investor confidence in the reliability of a company's financial disclosure and system of internal control over financial reporting. These benefits are not readily quantifiable. Commenters overwhelmingly supported the benefits of the amendments.

The amendments related to Section 302 of the Sarbanes-Oxley Act relocate the certifications required by Exchange Act Rules 13a-14 and 15d-14 from the text of quarterly and annual reports filed or submitted under Section 13(a) or 15(d) of the Exchange Act to the "Exhibits" section of these reports. The amendments related to Section 906 of the Sarbanes-Oxley Act require that the certifications required by Section 1350 of Title 18 of the United States Code, added by Section 906 of the Act, accompany the periodic reports to which they relate as exhibits. These changes will enhance the ability of investors and the Commission staff to verify that the certifications have, in fact, been submitted with the Exchange Act reports to which they relate and to review the contents of the certifications to ensure compliance with the applicable requirements. In addition, the changes will enable the Department of Justice, which has responsibility for enforcing Section 906, to review effectively the form and content of the certifications required by that section.

B. Costs

The final rules related to Section 404 of the Sarbanes-Oxley Act require companies, other than registered investment companies, to include in their annual reports a report of management on the company's internal control over financial reporting. The management report on internal control over financial reporting must include: a statement of management's responsibility for establishing and maintaining adequate internal control over financial reporting; a statement identifying the framework used to evaluate the effectiveness of the company's internal control over financial reporting; management's assessment of the effectiveness of the company's internal control over financial reporting as of the end of the company's most recent fiscal year; and a statement that the registered public accounting firm that audited the company's financial statements included in the annual report has issued an attestation report on management's evaluation of the company's internal control over financial reporting. The final rules will increase costs for all reporting companies. These costs are mitigated somewhat because companies have an existing obligation to maintain an adequate system of internal accounting control under the FCPA. Moreover, one commenter noted that some companies already voluntarily include management reports on their internal controls in their annual reports. The preparation of the management report on internal control over financial reporting will likely involve multiple parties, including senior management, internal auditors, in-house counsel, outside counsel and audit committee members.

Many commenters believed that our proposal to require quarterly evaluations of a company's internal control over financial reporting would significantly increase the costs of preparing periodic reports. Several commenters also were concerned that the proposals would result in increased audit fees. We have limited data on which to base cost estimates of the final rules.

Using our PRA burden estimates, we estimate the aggregate annual costs of implementing Section 404(a) of the Sarbanes-Oxley Act to be around $1.24 billion (or $91,000 per company).[174] We recognize the magnitude of the cost burdens and we are making several accommodations to address commenters' concerns and to ease compliance, including:

- Requiring quarterly disclosure only of any change that has materially affected, or is reasonably likely to materially affect, a company's internal control over financial reporting; and
- An extended transition period for the new internal control reporting requirements.

We originally proposed to require a company to include an internal control report in its annual report for fiscal years ending on or after September 15, 2003. Under the final rules, a company that is an "accelerated filer" under the definition in Exchange Act Rule 12b-2 must begin to comply with the internal control report requirement in its annual report for its first fiscal year ending on or after June 15, 2004. All other companies must begin to comply with the requirement in their annual reports for their first fiscal year ending on or after April 15, 2005.

A longer transition period will help to alleviate the immediate impact of any costs and burdens imposed on companies. A longer transition period may even help to reduce costs as companies will have additional time to develop best practices, long-term processes and efficiencies in preparing management reports. Also, a longer transition period will expand the period of availability of outside professionals that some companies may wish to retain as they prepare to comply with the new requirements.

The PRA burden estimate, however, excludes several costs attributable to Section 404. The estimate does not include the costs associated with the auditor's attestation report, which many commenters have suggested might be substantial. It also excludes estimates of likely "indirect" costs

---

174.   This estimate is based on the estimated total burden hours of 5,396,266, an assumed 75%/25% split of the burden hours between internal staff and external professionals, and an hourly rate of $200 for internal staff time and $300 for external professionals. The hourly cost estimate is based on consultations with several registrants and law firms and other persons who regularly assist registrants in preparing and filing periodic reports with the Commission. Our PRA estimate does not reflect any additional cost burdens that a company will incur as a result of having to obtain an auditor's attestation on management's internal control report.

of the final rules. For instance, the final rules increase the cost of being a public company; therefore the final rules may discourage some companies from seeking capital from the public markets. Moreover, the final rules may also discourage non-U.S. firms from seeking capital in the United States.

The incremental costs of the amendments related to Section 302 of the Sarbanes-Oxley Act are minimal. Since companies must already include the certifications required by Exchange Act Rules 13a-14 and 15d-14 in their quarterly and annual reports, there should be no incremental cost to relocating the certifications from the text of the reports to the "Exhibits" section of these reports. Requiring the Section 906 certifications to be included as an exhibit to the periodic reports to which they relate will lead to some additional costs for companies that currently are submitting the certifications to the Commission in some other manner. While these costs are difficult to quantify, we estimate that the annual paperwork burden of the amendments will be approximately $23.4 million.[175]

One commenter has expressed concern that companies may assume greater legal risk by making their Section 906 certifications publicly available.[176] To the extent that companies may assume greater legal risk by including the Section 906 certifications as part of their periodic reports filed pursuant to the Exchange Act where these reports are incorporated by reference into Securities Act registration statements, we address this risk by requiring companies to "furnish," rather than "file," the certifications with the Commission for purposes of Section 18 of the Exchange Act or incorporation by reference into other filings. Thus, the amendments should mitigate this potential indirect cost of compliance. We believe that it is appropriate to require the certifications that accompany a periodic report to be publicly available. We believe that Congress intended for Section 906 certifications to be publicly available. Civil liability already exists by virtue of the pre-existing signature requirements and Section 302 certifications. In addition, any Section 906 certification submitted to the Commission as correspondence is subject to the Freedom of Information Act.[177]

VI. Effect on Efficiency, Competition and Capital Formation

Section 23(a)(2) of the Exchange Act[178] requires us to consider the anti-competitive effects of any rules that we adopt under the Exchange Act. In addition, Section 23(a)(2) prohibits us from adopting any rule that would impose a burden on competition not necessary or appropriate in furtherance of the purposes of the Exchange Act. The amendments related to Section 404 of the Sarbanes-Oxley Act represent the implementation of a congressional mandate. The final rules require management reports that improve investors' understanding of management's responsibility for the preparation of reliable financial information and maintaining adequate internal control over financial reporting. We anticipate that these requirements will enhance the proper functioning of the capital markets by increasing the quality and accountability of financial reporting and restoring investor confidence.

Section 2(b) of the Securities Act,[179] Section 3(f) of the Exchange Act[180] and Section 2(c) of the Investment Company Act[181] require us, when engaging in rulemaking to consider or determine whether an action is necessary or appropriate in the public interest, and consider whether the action will promote efficiency, competition, and capital formation. The amendments related to Section 404 are designed to enhance the quality and accountability of the financial reporting process and may help increase investor confidence, which implies increased efficiency and competitiveness of the U.S. capital markets. Increased market efficiency and investor confidence also may encourage more efficient capital formation. We requested comments on the effect of these amendments on efficiency, competition and capital formation analyses in the proposing release addressing Section 404. We received no comments in response to these requests.

---

175. This calculation is based on an estimate of burden hours multiplied by a cost of $200.00 per hour. (117,048 hours multiplied by $200.00 per hour). The hourly cost estimate is based on consultations with several registrants and law firms and other persons who regularly assist registrants in preparing and filing periodic reports with the Commission.
176. *See* ABA letter regarding File No. S7-06-03.
177. 5 U.S.C. 552 *et seq.*
178. 15 U.S.C. 78w(a)(2).
179. 15 U.S.C 77b(b).
180. 15 U.S.C. 78c(f).
181. 15 U.S.C. 80a-2(c).

The amendments related to Section 302 of the Sarbanes-Oxley Act would relocate the certifications required by Exchange Act Rules 13a-14 and 15d-14 from the text of quarterly and annual reports filed or submitted under Section 13(a) or 15(d) of the Exchange Act to the "Exhibits" section of these reports. This relocation will enhance the ability of investors and the Commission staff to verify that the certifications have, in fact, been submitted with the Exchange Act reports to which they relate and to review the contents of the certifications to ensure compliance with the applicable requirements. The amendments related to Section 906 of the Sarbanes-Oxley Act also will streamline compliance with Section 1350 of Title 18 of the United States Code, added by Section 906 of the Act, and will enable investors, the Commission staff and the Department of Justice, which has responsibility for enforcing Section 1350, to verify submission and efficiently review the form and content of the certifications required by that provision.

We do not believe that the amendments related to certifications will impose any burden on competition, nor are we aware of any impact on capital formation that would result from the amendments. Depending on how an issuer's principal executive and principal financial officers presently satisfy the Section 906 certification requirements, issuers may incur some additional costs in submitting these certifications as an exhibit to their periodic reports. While these costs are difficult to quantify, we believe that they would be nominal. We requested comment on whether the amendments would affect competition, efficiency and capital formation. We received no comments in response to this request.

VII. Final Regulatory Flexibility Analysis

This Final Regulatory Flexibility Analysis ("FRFA") has been prepared in accordance with the Regulatory Flexibility Act.[182] This FRFA relates to new rules and amendments that require Exchange Act companies, other than registered investment companies, to include in their annual reports a report of management on the company's internal control over financial reporting. The management report on internal control over financial reporting must include: a statement of management's responsibility for establishing and maintaining adequate internal control over financial reporting; a statement identifying the framework used to evaluate the effectiveness of the company's internal control over financial reporting; management's assessment of the effectiveness of the company's internal control over financial reporting as of the end of the company's most recent fiscal year; and a statement that the registered public accounting firm that audited the company's financial statements included in the annual report has issued an attestation report on management's evaluation of the company's internal control over financial reporting. This FRFA also addresses new rules and amendments that require companies to file the certifications mandated by Sections 302 and 906 of the Sarbanes-Oxley Act as exhibits to their periodic reports. An Initial Regulatory Flexibility Analysis ("IRFA") was prepared in accordance with the Regulatory Flexibility Act in conjunction with each of the releases proposing these rules.[183] The proposing releases solicited comments on these analyses.

A. Need for the Amendments

We are adopting these disclosure requirements to comply with the mandate of, and to fulfill the purposes underlying the provisions of, the Sarbanes-Oxley Act of 2002. The new evaluation and disclosure requirements regarding a company's internal control over financial reporting are intended to enhance the quality of reporting and increase investor confidence in the fairness and integrity of the securities markets by making it clear that a company's management is responsible for maintaining and annually assessing such controls. The amendments related to Sections 302 and 906 of the Sarbanes-Oxley Act will enhance the ability of investors and the Commission staff to verify that the certifications have, in fact, been submitted with the Exchange Act reports to which they relate and to review the contents of the certifications to ensure compliance with the applicable requirements. The amendments also will streamline compliance with Section 1350 of Title 18 of the United States Code and will enable investors, the Commission staff and the Department of Justice, which has responsibility for enforcing Section 1350, to verify a company's submission of the Section 906 certification and efficiently review the form and content of the certifications.

B. Significant Issues Raised by Public Comment

182. 5 U.S.C. 601.
183. 5 U.S.C. 603.

In the Proposing Releases, we requested comment on any aspect of the IRFA, including the number of small entities that would be affected by the proposals, and both quantitative and qualitative nature of the impact. Several commenters expressed concern that small business issuers, including small entities, would be particularly disadvantaged by our proposal to require quarterly evaluations of internal control over financial reporting. We received no commentary on the impact on small entities of the new certification requirements.

C. Small Entities Subject to the Amendments

The new disclosure items affect issuers that are small entities. Exchange Act Rule 0-10(a)[184] defines an issuer, other than an investment company, to be a "small business" or "small organization" if it had total assets of $5 million or less on the last day of its most recent fiscal year. We estimate that there are approximately 2,500 issuers, other than investment companies, that may be considered small entities. For purposes of the Regulatory Flexibility Act, an investment company is a "small entity" if it, together with other investment companies in the same group of related investment companies, has net assets of $50 million or less as of the end of its most recent fiscal year.[185] We estimate that there are approximately 190 registered management investment companies that, together with other investment companies in the same group of related investment companies, have net assets of $50 million or less as of the end of the most recent fiscal year.[186]

The new disclosure items with respect to management's report on internal control over financial reporting and the registered public accounting firm's attestation report apply to any small entity, other than a registered investment company, that is subject to Exchange Act reporting requirements. The new certification requirements apply to any small entity that is subject to Exchange Act reporting requirements.

D. Reporting, Recordkeeping and Other Compliance Requirements

The amendments require a company's management to disclose information regarding the company's internal control over financial reporting, including management's assessment of the effectiveness of the company's internal control over financial reporting. All small entities that are subject to the reporting requirements of Section 13(a) or 15(d) of the Exchange Act, other than registered investment companies, are subject to these evaluation and disclosure requirements. Because reporting companies already file the forms being amended, no additional professional skills beyond those currently possessed by these filers necessarily are required to prepare the new disclosure, although some companies may choose to engage outside professionals to assist them in complying with the new requirements. We expect that these new disclosure items will increase compliance costs incurred by small entities. We have calculated for purposes of the Paperwork Reduction Act that each company would be subject to an added annual reporting burden of approximately 398 hours and the portion of that burden that is reflected as the cost associated with outside professionals is approximately $35,286.[187] We believe, however, that the annual average burden and costs for small issuers are much lower.[188] For the new certification requirements, we estimate that a company, including a small entity, will be subject to an additional reporting burden of eight hours per year.[189] These burden estimates reflect only the burden and cost of the required collection of information.

E. Agency Action to Minimize Effect on Small Entities

The Regulatory Flexibility Act directs us to consider alternatives that would accomplish our stated objectives, while minimizing any significant adverse impact on small entities. In connection with the amendments, we considered the following alternatives:

- Establishing different compliance or reporting requirements or timetables that take into account the resources available to small entities;

---

184. 17 CFR 240.0-10(a).
185. 17 CFR 270.0-10.
186. This estimate is based on figures compiled by the Commission staff regarding investment companies registered on Forms N-1A, N-2 and N-3, which are required to file reports on Form N-CSR.
187. This estimate includes the burden for one annual report and three quarterly reports.
188. Under the method we used to estimate the PRA burdens associated with the Section 404 rules, we estimated that companies with less than $100 million in revenues would be subject to an added annual reporting burden of approximately 100 hours.
189. The estimated burden for one annual report and three quarterly reports.

- Clarifying, consolidating or simplifying compliance and reporting requirements under the rules for small entities;
- Using performance rather than design standards; and
- Exempting small entities from all or part of the requirements.

Several of these alternatives were considered but rejected, while other alternatives were taken into account in the final rules. We believe the final rules fulfill the intent of the Sarbanes-Oxley Act of enhancing the quality of reporting and increasing investor confidence in the fairness and integrity of the securities markets.

Sections 302, 404 and 906 of the Sarbanes-Oxley Act make no distinction based on a company's size. We think that improvements in the financial reporting process for all companies are important for promoting investor confidence in our markets. For example, a 1999 report commissioned by the organizations that sponsored the Treadway Commission found that the incidence of financial fraud was greater in small companies.[190] However, we are sensitive to the costs and burdens that small entities will face. The final rules require only a quarterly evaluation of material changes to a company's internal control over financial reporting, unlike the proposed rules that would have required management to evaluate the effectiveness of a company's internal control over financial reporting on a quarterly basis. In response to comments, including comments submitted by the Small Business Administration, we have decided not to adopt this proposal.

We believe that a blanket exemption for small entities from coverage of the requirements is not appropriate and would be inconsistent with the policies underlying the Sarbanes-Oxley Act. However, we have provided an extended transition period for companies that do not meet the definition in Exchange Act Rule 12b-2[191] of an "accelerated filer" for the rules implementing Section 404 of the Sarbanes-Oxley Act. Under the adopted rules, non-accelerated filers, including small business issuers, need not prepare the management report on internal control over financial reporting until they file their annual reports for fiscal years ending on or after April 15, 2005. This deferral provides non-accelerated filers more time to develop structured and formal systems of internal control over financial reporting.

We believe that the new disclosure and certification requirements are clear and straightforward. The amendments require only brief disclosure. An effective system of internal control over financial reporting has always been necessary to produce reliable financial statements and other financial information. Our amendments do not specify any particular controls that a company's internal control over financial reporting should include. Each company is afforded the flexibility to design its internal control over financial reporting according to its own set of circumstances. This flexibility should enable companies to keep costs of compliance as low as possible. Therefore, it does not seem necessary to develop separate requirements for small entities.

The final rules impose both design and performance standards regarding disclosure of management's responsibility for establishing and maintaining adequate internal control over financial reporting for the company and management's assessment of the effectiveness of such controls. The rules do, however, afford a company the flexibility to design its internal control over financial reporting to fit its particular circumstances. We believe that it would be inconsistent with the purposes of the Sarbanes-Oxley Act to specify different requirements for small entities.

VIII. Statutory Authority and Text of Rule Amendments

The amendments described in this release are being adopted under the authority set forth in Sections 5, 6, 7, 10, 17 and 19 of the Securities Act, as amended, Sections 12, 13, 15, 23 and 36 of the Exchange Act, Sections 8, 30, 31 and 38 of the Investment Company Act, as amended and Sections 3(a), 302, 404, 405 and 906 of the Sarbanes-Oxley Act.

List of Subjects

17 CFR Part 210

---

190. *See* Beasley, Carcello and Hermanson, Fraudulent Financial Reporting: 1987-1997, *An Analysis of U.S. Public Companies* (Mar. 1999) (study commissioned by the Committee of Sponsoring Organizations of the Treadway Commission).
191. 17 CFR 240.12b-2.

Accountants, Accounting, Reporting and recordkeeping requirements, Securities.

17 CFR Part 228

Reporting and recordkeeping requirements, Securities, Small businesses.

17 CFR Parts 229, 240 and 249

Reporting and recordkeeping requirements, Securities.

17 CFR Parts 270 and 274

Investment companies, Reporting and recordkeeping requirements, Securities.

Text of Amendments

For the reasons set out in the preamble, the Commission amends title 17, chapter II, of the Code of Federal Regulations as follows:

PART 210—FORM AND CONTENT OF AND REQUIREMENTS FOR FINANCIAL STATEMENTS, SECURITIES ACT OF 1933, SECURITIES EXCHANGE ACT OF 1934, PUBLIC UTILITY HOLDING COMPANY ACT OF 1935, INVESTMENT COMPANY ACT OF 1940, INVESTMENT ADVISERS ACT OF 1940, AND ENERGY POLICY AND CONSERVATION ACT OF 1975

1. The authority citation for Part 210 is revised to read as follows:

Authority: 15 U.S.C. 77f, 77g, 77h, 77j, 77s, 77z-2, 77z-3, 77aa(25), 77aa(26), 78c, 78j-1, 78l, 78m, 78n, 78o(d), 78q, 78u-5, 78w(a), 78ll, 78mm, 79e(b), 79j(a), 79n, 79t(a), 80a-8, 80a-20, 80a-29, 80a-30, 80a-31, 80a-37(a), 80b-3, 80b-11, 7202 and 7262, unless otherwise noted.

2. Section 210.1-02 is amended by:

a. Removing the authority citation following Sec. 210.1-02;

b. Redesignating paragraph (a) as paragraph (a)(1); and

c. Adding paragraph (a)(2).

The revisions read as follows:

Sec. 210.1-02 Definitions of terms used in Regulation S-X (17 CFR part 210).

* * * * *

(a)(1) Accountant's report. The term accountant's report, when used in regard to financial statements, means a document in which an independent public or certified public accountant indicates the scope of the audit (or examination) which he has made and sets forth his opinion regarding the financial statements taken as a whole, or an assertion to the effect that an overall opinion cannot be expressed. When an overall opinion cannot be expressed, the reasons therefor shall be stated.

(2) Attestation report on management's assessment of internal control over financial reporting. The term attestation report on management's assessment of internal control over financial reporting means a report in which a registered public accounting firm expresses an opinion, or states that an opinion cannot be expressed, concerning management's assessment of the effectiveness of the registrant's internal control over financial reporting (as defined in Sec. 240.13a-15(f) or 240.15d-15(f) of this chapter) in accordance with standards on attestation engagements. When an overall opinion cannot be expressed, the registered public accounting firm must state why it is unable to express such an opinion.

(b) Affiliate. An affiliate of, or a person affiliated with, a specific person is a person that directly, or indirectly through one or more intermediaries, controls, or is controlled by, or is under common control with, the person specified.

(c) **Amount.** The term amount, when used in regard to securities, means the principal amount if relating to evidences of indebtedness, the number of shares if relating to shares, and the number of units if relating to any other kind of security.

(d) **Audit (or examination).** The term *audit (or examination)*, when used in regard to financial statements, means an examination of the financial statements by an independent accountant in accordance with generally accepted auditing standards, as may be modified or supplemented by the Commission, for the purpose of expressing an opinion thereon.

(e) **Bank holding company.** The term bank holding company means a person which is engaged, either directly or indirectly, primarily in the business of owning securities of one or more banks for the purpose, and with the effect, of exercising control.

(f) **Certified.** The term certified, when used in regard to financial statements, means examined and reported upon with an opinion expressed by an independent public or certified public accountant.

(g) **Control.** The term control (including the terms controlling, controlled by and under common control with) means the possession, direct or indirect, of the power to direct or cause the direction of the management and policies of a person, whether through the ownership of voting shares, by contract, or otherwise.

(h) **Development stage company.** A company shall be considered to be in the development stage if it is devoting substantially all of its efforts to establishing a new business and either of the following conditions exists:

(1) Planned principal operations have not commenced.

(2) Planned principal operations have commenced, but there has been no significant revenue therefrom.

(i) **Equity security.** The term equity security means any stock or similar security; or any security convertible, with or without consideration, into such a security, or carrying any warrant or right to subscribe to or purchase such a security; or any such warrant or right.

(j) **Fifty-percent-owned person.** The term 50-percent-owned person, in relation to a specified person, means a person approximately 50 percent of whose outstanding voting shares is owned by the specified person either directly, or indirectly through one or more intermediaries.

(k) **Fiscal year.** The term fiscal year means the annual accounting period or, if no closing date has been adopted, the calendar year ending on December 31.

(l) **Foreign business.** A business that is majority owned by persons who are not citizens or residents of the United States and is not organized under the laws of the United States or any state thereof, and either:

(1) More than 50 percent of its assets are located outside the United States; or

(2) The majority of its executive officers and directors are not United States citizens or residents.

(m) **Insurance holding company.** The term insurance holding company means a person which is engaged, either directly or indirectly, primarily in the business of owning securities of one or more insurance companies for the purpose, and with the effect, of exercising control.

(n) **Majority-owned subsidiary.** The term majority-owned subsidiary means a subsidiary more than 50 percent of whose outstanding voting shares is owned by its parent and/or the parent's other majority-owned subsidiaries.

(o) **Material.** The term material, when used to qualify a requirement for the furnishing of information as to any subject, limits the information required to those matters about which an average prudent investor ought reasonably to be informed.

(p) **Parent.** A parent of a specified person is an affiliate controlling such person directly, or indirectly through one or more intermediaries.

(q) Person. The term person means an individual, a corporation, a partnership, an association, a joint-stock company, a business trust, or an unincorporated organization.

(r) Principal holder of equity securities. The term principal holder of equity securities, used in respect of a registrant or other person named in a particular statement or report, means a holder of record or a known beneficial owner of more than 10 percent of any class of equity securities of the registrant or other person, respectively, as of the date of the related balance sheet filed.

(s) Promoter. The term promoter includes:

(1) Any person who, acting alone or in conjunction with one or more other persons, directly or indirectly takes initiative in founding and organizing the business or enterprise of an issuer;

(2) Any person who, in connection with the founding and organizing of the business or enterprise of an issuer, directly or indirectly receives in consideration of services or property, or both services and property, 10 percent or more of any class of securities of the issuer or 10 percent or more of the proceeds from the sale of any class of securities. However, a person who receives such securities or proceeds either solely as underwriting commissions or solely in consideration of property shall not be deemed a promoter within the meaning of this paragraph if such person does not otherwise take part in founding and organizing the enterprise.

(t) Registrant. The term registrant means the issuer of the securities for which an application, a registration statement, or a report is filed.

(u) Related parties. The term related parties is used as that term is defined in the Glossary to Statement of Financial Accounting Standards No. 57, "Related Party Disclosures."

(v) Share. The term share means a share of stock in a corporation or unit of interest in an unincorporated person.

(w) Significant subsidiary. The term significant subsidiary means a subsidiary, including its subsidiaries, which meets any of the following conditions:

(1) The registrant's and its other subsidiaries' investments in and advances to the subsidiary exceed 10 percent of the total assets of the registrant and its subsidiaries consolidated as of the end of the most recently completed fiscal year (for a proposed business combination to be accounted for as a pooling of interests, this condition is also met when the number of common shares exchanged or to be exchanged by the registrant exceeds 10 percent of its total common shares outstanding at the date the combination is initiated); or

(2) The registrant's and its other subsidiaries' proportionate share of the total assets (after intercompany eliminations) of the subsidiary exceeds 10 percent of the total assets of the registrants and its subsidiaries consolidated as of the end of the most recently completed fiscal year; or

(3) The registrant's and its other subsidiaries' equity in the income from continuing operations before income taxes, extraordinary items and cumulative effect of a change in accounting principle of the subsidiary exceeds 10 percent of such income of the registrant and its subsidiaries consolidated for the most recently completed fiscal year.

Computational note: For purposes of making the prescribed income test the following guidance should be applied:

1. When a loss has been incurred by either the parent and its subsidiaries consolidated or the tested subsidiary, but not both, the equity in the income or loss of the tested subsidiary should be excluded from the income of the registrant and its subsidiaries consolidated for purposes of the computation.

2. If income of the registrant and its subsidiaries consolidated for the most recent fiscal year is at least 10 percent lower than the average of the income for the last five fiscal years, such average income should be substituted for purposes of the computation. Any loss years should be omitted for purposes of computing average income.

3. Where the test involves combined entities, as in the case of determining whether summarized financial data should be presented, entities reporting losses shall not be aggregated with entities reporting income.

(x) Subsidiary. A subsidiary of a specified person is an affiliate controlled by such person directly, or indirectly through one or more intermediaries.

(y) Totally held subsidiary. The term totally held subsidiary means a subsidiary—

(1) substantially all of whose outstanding equity securities are owned by its parent and/or the parent's other totally held subsidiaries, and

(2) which is not indebted to any person other than its parent and/or the parent's other totally held subsidiaries, in an amount which is material in relation to the particular subsidiary, excepting indebtedness incurred in the ordinary course of business which is not overdue and which matures within 1 year from the date of its creation, whether evidenced by securities or not. Indebtedness of a subsidiary which is secured by its parent by guarantee, pledge, assignment, or otherwise is to be excluded for purposes of paragraph (x)(2) of this section.

(z) Voting shares. The term voting shares means the sum of all rights, other than as affected by events of default, to vote for election of directors and/or the sum of all interests in an unincorporated person.

(aa) Wholly owned subsidiary. The term wholly owned subsidiary means a subsidiary substantially all of whose outstanding voting shares are owned by its parent and/or the parent's other wholly owned subsidiaries.

(bb) Summarized financial information. (1) Except as provided in paragraph (aa)(2), summarized financial information referred to in this regulation shall mean the presentation of summarized information as to the assets, liabilities and results of operations of the entity for which the information is required. Summarized financial information shall include the following disclosures:

(i) Current assets, noncurrent assets, current liabilities, noncurrent liabilities, and, when applicable, redeemable preferred stocks (see §210.5-02.28) and minority interests (for specialized industries in which classified balance sheets are normally not presented, information shall be provided as to the nature and amount of the major components of assets and liabilities);

(ii) Net sales or gross revenues, gross profit (or, alternatively, costs and expenses applicable to net sales or gross revenues), income or loss from continuing operations before extraordinary items and cumulative effect of a change in accounting principle, and net income or loss (for specialized industries, other information may be substituted for sales and related costs and expenses if necessary for a more meaningful presentation); and

(2) Summarized financial information for unconsolidated subsidiaries and 50 percent or less owned persons referred to in and required by §210.10-01(b) for interim periods shall include the information required by paragraph (aa)(1)(ii) of this section.

* * * * *

3. Amend Sec. 210.2-02 by:

a. Revising the section heading;

b. Revising the headings of paragraphs (a), (b), (c) and (d); and

c. Adding paragraph (f).

The addition and revisions read as follows.

Sec. 210.2-02 Accountants' reports and attestation reports on management's assessment of internal control over financial reporting.

(a) Technical requirements for accountants' reports. The accountant's report:

(1) Shall be dated;

(2) shall be signed manually;

(3) shall indicate the city and State where issued; and

(4) shall identify without detailed enumeration the financial statements covered by the report.

(b) Representations as to the audit included in accountants' reports. The accountant's report:

(1) Shall state whether the audit was made in accordance with generally accepted auditing standards; and

(2) shall designate any auditing procedures deemed necessary by the accountant under the circumstances of the particular case, which have been omitted, and the reasons for their omission. Nothing in this rule shall be construed to imply authority for the omission of any procedure which independent accountants would ordinarily employ in the course of an audit made for the purpose of expressing the opinions required by paragraph (c) of this section.

(c) Opinions to be expressed in accountants' reports. The accountant's report shall state clearly:

(1) The opinion of the accountant in respect of the financial statements covered by the report and the accounting principles and practices reflected therein; and

(2) the opinion of the accountant as to the consistency of the application of the accounting principles, or as to any changes in such principles which have a material effect on the financial statements.

(d) Exceptions identified in accountants' reports. Any matters to which the accountant takes exception shall be clearly identified, the exception thereto specifically and clearly stated, and, to the extent practicable, the effect of each such exception on the related financial statements given. (See section 101 of the Codification of Financial Reporting Policies.)

(e) Paragraph (e) of this section applies only to registrants that are providing financial statements in a filing for a period with respect to which Arthur Andersen LLP or a foreign affiliate of Arthur Andersen LLP ("Andersen") issued an accountants' report. Notwithstanding any other Commission rule or regulation, a registrant that cannot obtain an accountants' report that meets the technical requirements of paragraph (a) of this section after reasonable efforts may include in the document a copy of the latest signed and dated accountants' report issued by Andersen for such period in satisfaction of that requirement, if prominent disclosure that the report is a copy of the previously issued Andersen accountants' report and that the report has not been reissued by Andersen is set forth on such copy.

(f) Attestation report on management's assessment of internal control over financial reporting. Every registered public accounting firm that issues or prepares an accountant's report for a registrant, other than an investment company registered under section 8 of the Investment Company Act of 1940 (15 U.S.C. 80a-8), that is included in an annual report required by section 13(a) or 15(d) of the Securities Exchange Act of 1934 (15 U.S.C. 78a *et seq.*) containing an assessment by management of the effectiveness of the registrant's internal control over financial reporting must attest to, and report on, such assessment. The attestation report on management's assessment of internal control over financial reporting shall be dated, signed manually, identify the period covered by the report and clearly state the opinion of the accountant as to whether management's assessment of the effectiveness of the registrant's internal control over financial reporting is fairly stated in all material respects, or must include an opinion to the effect that an overall opinion cannot be expressed. If an overall opinion cannot be expressed, explain why. The attestation report on management's assessment of internal control over financial reporting may be separate from the accountant's report.

PART 228—INTEGRATED DISCLOSURE SYSTEM FOR SMALL BUSINESS ISSUERS

4. The general authority citation for Part 228 is revised to read as follows:

Authority: 15 U.S.C. 77e, 77f, 77g, 77h, 77j, 77k, 77s, 77z-2, 77z-3, 77aa(25), 77aa(26), 77ddd, 77eee, 77ggg, 77hhh, 77jjj, 77nnn, 77sss, 78l, 78m, 78n, 78o, 78u-5, 78w, 78ll, 78mm, 80a-8, 80a-29, 80a-30, 80a-37, 80b-11, 7202, 7241, and 7262; and 18 U.S.C. 1350, unless otherwise noted.

* * * * *

5. Revise Sec. 228.307 to read as follows:

Sec. 228.307 (Item 307) Disclosure controls and procedures.

Disclose the conclusions of the small business issuer's principal executive and principal financial officers, or persons performing similar functions, regarding the effectiveness of the small business issuer's disclosure controls and procedures (as defined in Sec. 240.13a-15(e) or 240.15d-15(e) of this chapter) as of the end of the period covered by the report, based on the evaluation of these controls and procedures required by paragraph (b) of Sec. 240.13a-15 or 240.15d-15 of this chapter.

6. Add Sec. 228.308 to read as follows:

Sec. 228.308 (Item 308) Internal control over financial reporting.

(a) Management's annual report on internal control over financial reporting. Provide a report of management on the small business issuer's internal control over financial reporting (as defined in Sec. 240.13a-15(f) or 240.15d-15(f) of this chapter) that contains:

(1) A statement of management's responsibility for establishing and maintaining adequate internal control over financial reporting for the small business issuer;

(2) A statement identifying the framework used by management to evaluate the effectiveness of the small business issuer's internal control over financial reporting as required by paragraph (c) of Sec. 240.13a-15 or 240.15d-15 of this chapter;

(3) Management's assessment of the effectiveness of the small business issuer's internal control over financial reporting as of the end of the small business issuer's most recent fiscal year, including a statement as to whether or not internal control over financial reporting is effective. This discussion must include disclosure of any material weakness in the small business issuer's internal control over financial reporting identified by management. Management is not permitted to conclude that the small business issuer's internal control over financial reporting is effective if there are one or more material weaknesses in the small business issuer's internal control over financial reporting; and

(4) A statement that the registered public accounting firm that audited the financial statements included in the annual report containing the disclosure required by this Item has issued an attestation report on management's assessment of the small business issuer's internal control over financial reporting.

(b) Attestation report of the registered public accounting firm. Provide the registered public accounting firm's attestation report on management's assessment of the small business issuer's internal control over financial reporting in the small business issuer's annual report containing the disclosure required by this Item.

(c) Changes in internal control over financial reporting. Disclose any change in the small business issuer's internal control over financial reporting identified in connection with the evaluation required by paragraph (d) of Sec. 240.13a-15 or 240.15d-15 of this chapter that occurred during the small business issuer's last fiscal quarter (the small business issuer's fourth fiscal quarter in the case of an annual report) that has materially affected, or is reasonably likely to materially affect, the small business issuer's internal control over financial reporting.

Instructions to Item 308

1. The small business issuer must maintain evidential matter, including documentation, to provide reasonable support for management's assessment of the effectiveness of the small business issuer's internal control over financial reporting.

2. A small business issuer that is an Asset-Backed Issuer (as defined in Sec. 240.13a-14(g) and Sec. 240.15d-14(g) of this chapter) is not required to disclose the information required by this Item.

Sec. 228.401 [Amended]

7. Amend Sec. 228.401 by removing the phrase "internal controls and procedures for financial reporting" in paragraph (e)(2)(iv) of Item 401 and adding, in its place, the phrase "internal control over financial reporting".

Sec. 228.401. Directors, executive officers, promoters and control persons.

(a) Identify directors and executive officers.

(1) List the names and ages of all directors and executive officers and all persons nominated or chosen to become such;

(2) List the positions and offices that each such person held with the small business issuer;

(3) Give the person's term of office as a director and the period during which the person has served;

(4) Briefly describe the person's business experience during the past five years; and

(5) If a director, identify other directorships held in reporting companies naming each company.

(b) Identify significant employees. Give the information specified in paragraph (a) of this Item for each person who is not an executive officer but who is expected by the small business issuer to make a significant contribution to the business.

(c) Family relationships. Describe any family relationships among directors, executive officers, or persons nominated or chosen by the small business issuer to become directors or executive officers.

(d) Involvement in certain legal proceedings. Describe any of the following events that occurred during the past five years that are material to an evaluation of the ability or integrity of any director, person nominated to become a director, executive officer, promoter or control person of the small business issuer:

(1) Any bankruptcy petition filed by or against any business of which such person was a general partner or executive officer either at the time of the bankruptcy or within two years prior to that time;

(2) Any conviction in a criminal proceeding or being subject to a pending criminal proceeding (excluding traffic violations and other minor offenses);

(3) Being subject to any order, judgment, or decree, not subsequently reversed, suspended or vacated, of any court of competent jurisdiction, permanently or temporarily enjoining, barring, suspending or otherwise limiting his involvement in any type of business, securities or banking activities; and

(4) Being found by a court of competent jurisdiction (in a civil action), the Commission or the Commodity Futures Trading Commission to have violated a federal or state securities or commodities law, and the judgment has not been reversed, suspended, or vacated.

(e) Audit committee financial expert. (1) (i) Disclose that the small business issuer's board of directors has determined that the small business issuer either:

(A) Has at least one audit committee financial expert serving on its audit committee; or

(B) Does not have an audit committee financial expert serving on its audit committee.

(ii) If the small business issuer provides the disclosure required by paragraph (e)(1)(i)(A) of this Item, it must disclose the name of the audit committee financial expert and whether that person is independent, as that term is used in Item 7(d)(3)(iv) of Schedule 14A (240.14a-101 of this chapter) under the Exchange Act.

(iii) If the small business issuer provides the disclosure required by paragraph (e)(1)(i)(B) of this Item, it must explain why it does not have an audit committee financial expert.

Instruction to paragraph (e)(1) of Item 401

If the small business issuer's board of directors has determined that the small business issuer has more than one audit committee financial expert serving on its audit committee, the small business issuer may, but is not required to, disclose the names of those additional persons. A small business issuer choosing to identify such persons must indicate whether they are independent pursuant to Item 401(e)(1)(ii).

(2) For purposes of this Item, an audit committee financial expert means a person who has the following attributes:

(i) An understanding of generally accepted accounting principles and financial statements;

(ii) The ability to assess the general application of such principles in connection with the accounting for estimates, accruals and reserves;

(iii) Experience preparing, auditing, analyzing or evaluating financial statements that present a breadth and level of complexity of accounting issues that are generally comparable to the breadth and complexity of issues that can reasonably be expected to be raised by the small business issuer's financial statements, or experience actively supervising one or more persons engaged in such activities;

(iv) An understanding of internal control over financial reporting; and

(v) An understanding of audit committee functions.

(3) A person shall have acquired such attributes through:

(i) Education and experience as a principal financial officer, principal accounting officer, controller, public accountant or auditor or experience in one or more positions that involve the performance of similar functions;

(ii) Experience actively supervising a principal financial officer, principal accounting officer, controller, public accountant, auditor or person performing similar functions;

(iii) Experience overseeing or assessing the performance of companies or public accountants with respect to the preparation, auditing or evaluation of financial statements; or

(iv) Other relevant experience.

(4) Safe Harbor. (i) A person who is determined to be an audit committee financial expert will not be deemed an expert for any purpose, including without limitation for purposes of section 11 of the Securities Act of 1933 (15 U.S.C. 77k), as a result of being designated or identified as an audit committee financial expert pursuant to this Item 401.

(ii) The designation or identification of a person as an audit committee financial expert pursuant to this Item 401 does not impose on such person any duties, obligations or liability that are greater than the duties, obligations and liability imposed on such person as a member of the audit committee and board of directors in the absence of such designation or identification.

(iii) The designation or identification of a person as an audit committee financial expert pursuant to this Item 401 does not affect the duties, obligations or liability of any other member of the audit committee or board of directors.

Instructions to Item 401(e)

1. The disclosure under Item 401(e) is required only in a small business issuer's annual report. The small business issuer need not provide the disclosure required by this Item 401(e) in a proxy or information statement unless that small business issuer is electing to incorporate this information by reference from the proxy or information statement into its annual report pursuant to general instruction E(3) to Form 10-KSB.

2. If a person qualifies as an audit committee financial expert by means of having held a position described in paragraph (e)(3)(iv) of this Item, the small business issuer shall provide a brief listing of that person's relevant experience. Such disclosure may be made by reference to disclosures required under paragraph (a)(4) of this Item 401 (§229.401(a)(4) or this chapter).

3. In the case of a foreign private issuer with a two-tier board of directors, for purposes of this Item 401(e), the term board of directors means the supervisory or non-management board. Also, in the case of a foreign private issuer, the term generally accepted accounting principles in paragraph (e)(2)(i) of this Item means the body of generally accepted accounting principles used by that issuer in its primary financial statements filed with the Commission.

4. A small business issuer that is an Asset-Backed Issuer (as defined in §240.13a-14(g) and §240.15d-14(g) of this chapter) is not required to disclose the information required by this Item 401(e).

5. Following the effective date of the first registration statement filed under the Securities Act (15 U.S.C. 77a *et seq.*) or Securities Exchange Act (15 U.S.C. 78a *et seq.*) by a small business issuer, the small business issuer or successor issuer need not make the disclosures required by this Item in its first annual report filed pursuant to Section 13(a) or 15(d) (15 U.S.C. 78m(a) or 78o(d)) of the Exchange Act after effectiveness.

(f) Identification of the audit committee. (1) If you meet the following requirements, provide the disclosure in paragraph (f)(2) of this section:

(i) You are a listed issuer, as defined in §240.10A-3 of this chapter;

(ii) You are filing either an annual report on Form 10-KSB (17 CFR 249.310b), or a proxy statement or information statement pursuant to the Exchange Act (15 U.S.C. 78a *et seq.*) if action is to be taken with respect to the election of directors; and

(iii) You are neither:

(A) A subsidiary of another listed issuer that is relying on the exemption in §240.10A-3(c)(2) of this chapter; nor

(B) Relying on any of the exemptions in §240.10A-3(c)(4) through (c)(7) of this chapter.

(2) (i) State whether or not the small business issuer has a separately-designated standing audit committee established in accordance with section 3(a)(58)(A) of the Exchange Act (15 U.S.C. 78c(a)(58)(A)), or a committee performing similar functions. If the small business issuer has such a committee, however designated, identify each committee member. If the entire board of directors is acting as the small business issuer's audit committee as specified in section 3(a)(58)(B) of the Exchange Act (15 U.S.C. 78c(a)(58)(B)), so state.

(ii) If applicable, provide the disclosure required by §240.10A-3(d) of this chapter regarding an exemption from the listing standards for audit committees.

8. Amend Sec. 228.601 by:

a. Removing the last sentence of paragraph (a)(1);

b. Revising the Exhibit Table;

c. Revising paragraph (b)(7) to read "No exhibit required.";

d. Revising the heading in paragraph (b)(11) to read "Statement re: computation of per share earnings"; and

e. Revising paragraphs (b)(27) through (b)(98).

The revisions read as follows.

Sec. 228.601 (Item 601) Exhibits.

* * * * *

[*Editor's Note:* Sec. 228.601 was further revised at 69 Fed. Reg. 15593, 15615, dated 3/25/2004.]

Exhibit Table

		Securities Act Forms					Exchange Act Forms			
		SB-2	S-2	S-3	S-4***	S-8	10-SB	8-K*****	10-QSB	10-KSB
(1)	Underwriting agreement	x	x	x	x	...	...	x	...	...
(2)	Plan of purchase, sale, reorganization, arrangement, liquidation, or succession	x	x	x	x	...	x	x	x	x
(3)(i)	Articles of incorporation	x	...	...	x	...	x	x	x	x
(ii)	By-laws	x	...	...	x	...	x	x	x	x
(4)	Instruments defining the rights of security holders, incl. indentures	x	x	x	x	x	x	x	x	x
(5)	Opinion on legality	x	x	x	x	x	...	...	...	...
(6)	No exhibit required	N/A	N/A	N/A	N/A	N/A	N/A	N/A	N/A	N/A
(7)	Correspondence from an independent accountant regarding non-reliance upon a previously issued audit report or completed interim review	...	...	...	...	...	...	x	...	...
(8)	Opinion on tax matters	x	x	x	x	...	...	...	...	...
(9)	Voting trust agreement and amendments	x	...	...	x	...	x	...	...	x
(10)	Material contracts	x	x	...	x	...	x	...	x	x
(11)	Statement re: computation of per share earnings	x	x	...	x	...	x	...	x	x
(12)	No exhibit required	N/A	N/A	N/A	N/A	N/A	N/A	N/A	N/A	N/A
(13)	Annual report to security holders for the last fiscal year, Form 10-Q or 10-QSB or quarterly report to security holders*	x	x	...	x	...	...	...	...	x
(14)	Code of ethics							x		x
(15)	Letter on unaudited interim financial information	x	x	x	x	x	...	...	x	...

(16)	Letter on change in certifying accountant****	x	x	...	x	...	x	x	...	x
(17)	Letter on departure of director	...	...	...	...	...	...	x	...	...
(18)	Letter on change in accounting principles	...	...	...	...	...	...	...	x	x
(19)	Reports furnished to security-holders	...	...	...	...	...	...	...	x	...
(20)	Other documents or statements to security holders or any document incorporated by reference	...	...	...	...	...	...	...	x	x
(21)	Subsidiaries of the small business issuer	x	...	...	x	...	x	...	...	x
(22)	Published report regarding matters submitted to vote of security holders	...	...	...	...	...	...	...	x	x
(23)	Consents of experts and counsel	x	x	x	x	x	...	x**	x**	x**
(24)	Power of attorney	x	x	x	x	x	x	x	x	x
(25)	Statement of eligibility of trustee	x	x	x	x	...	...	...	...	...
(26)	Invitations for competitive bids	...	x	x	x	x	...	...	...	...
(27)-(30)	[Reserved]	...	...	...	...	...	...	...	...	...
(31)	Rule 13a-14(a)/15d-14(a) Certifications	...	...	...	...	...	...	...	x	x
(32)	Section 1350 Certifications	...	...	...	...	...	...	...	x	x
(33) through (98)	[Reserved]	...	...	...	...	...	...	...	...	...
(99)	Additional exhibits	x	x	x	x	x	x	x	x	x

* Only if incorporated by reference into a prospectus and delivered to holders along with the prospectus as permitted by the registration statement; or in the case of a Form 10-KSB, where the annual report is incorporated by reference into the text of the Form 10-KSB.

** Where the opinion of the expert or counsel has been incorporated by reference into a previously filed Securities Act registration statement.

*** An issuer need not provide an exhibit if: (1) an election was made under Form S-4 to provide S-2 or S-3 disclosure; and (2) the form selected (S-2 or S-3) would not require the company to provide the exhibit.

**** If required under Item 304 of Regulation S-B.

***** A Form 8-K exhibit is required only if relevant to the subject matter reported on the Form 8-K report. For example, if the Form 8-K pertains to the departure of a director, only the exhibit described in paragraph (b)(17) of this section need be filed. A required exhibit may be incorporated by reference from a previous filing.

(b) Description of exhibits. * * *

(27) through (30) [Reserved]

(31) Rule 13a-14(a)/15d-14(a) Certifications. The certifications required by Rule 13a-14(a) (17 CFR 240.13a-14(a)) or Rule 15d-14(a) (17 CFR 240.15d-14(a)) exactly as set forth below:

Certifications *

I, [identify the certifying individual], certify that:

1. I have reviewed this [specify report] of [identify small business issuer];

2. Based on my knowledge, this report does not contain any untrue statement of a material fact or omit to state a material fact necessary to make the statements made, in light of the circumstances under which such statements were made, not misleading with respect to the period covered by this report;

3. Based on my knowledge, the financial statements, and other financial information included in this report, fairly present in all material respects the financial condition, results of operations and cash flows of the small business issuer as of, and for, the periods presented in this report;

4. The small business issuer's other certifying officer(s) and I are responsible for establishing and maintaining disclosure controls and procedures (as defined in Exchange Act Rules 13a-15(e) and 15d-15(e)) and internal control over financial reporting (as defined in Exchange Act Rules 13a-15(f) and 15d-15(f)) for the small business issuer and have:

(a) Designed such disclosure controls and procedures, or caused such disclosure controls and procedures to be designed under our supervision, to ensure that material information relating to the small business issuer, including its consolidated subsidiaries, is made known to us by others within those entities, particularly during the period in which this report is being prepared;

(b) Designed such internal control over financial reporting, or caused such internal control over financial reporting to be designed under our supervision, to provide reasonable assurance regarding the reliability of financial reporting and the preparation of financial statements for external purposes in accordance with generally accepted accounting principles;

(c) Evaluated the effectiveness of the small business issuer's disclosure controls and procedures and presented in this report our conclusions about the effectiveness of the disclosure controls and procedures, as of the end of the period covered by this report based on such evaluation; and

(d) Disclosed in this report any change in the small business issuer's internal control over financial reporting that occurred during the small business issuer's most recent fiscal quarter (the small business issuer's fourth fiscal quarter in the case of an annual report) that has materially affected, or is reasonably likely to materially affect, the small business issuer's internal control over financial reporting; and

5. The small business issuer's other certifying officer(s) and I have disclosed, based on our most recent evaluation of internal control over financial reporting, to the small business issuer's auditors and the audit committee of the small business issuer's board of directors (or persons performing the equivalent functions):

(a) All significant deficiencies and material weaknesses in the design or operation of internal control over financial reporting which are reasonably likely to adversely affect the small business issuer's ability to record, process, summarize and report financial information; and

(b) Any fraud, whether or not material, that involves management or other employees who have a significant role in the small business issuer's internal control over financial reporting.

Date:

[Signature]

[Title]

Provide a separate certification for each principal executive officer and principal financial officer of the small business issuer. See Rules 13a-14(a) and 15d-14(a)

(32) Section 1350 Certifications.

(i) The certifications required by Rule 13a-14(b) (17 CFR 240.13a-14(b)) or Rule 15d-14(b) (17 CFR 240.15d-14(b)) and Section 1350 of Chapter 63 of Title 18 of the United States Code (18 U.S.C. 1350).

(ii) A certification furnished pursuant to this Item will not be deemed "filed" for purposes of section 18 of the Exchange Act (15 U.S.C. 78r), or otherwise subject to the liability of that section. Such certification will not be deemed to be incorporated by reference into any filing under the Securities Act or the Exchange Act, except to the extent that the small business issuer specifically incorporates it by reference.

(33) through (98) [Reserved]

* * * * *

PART 229—STANDARD INSTRUCTIONS FOR FILING FORMS UNDER SECURITIES ACT OF 1933, SECURITIES EXCHANGE ACT OF 1934 AND ENERGY POLICY AND CONSERVATION ACT OF 1975—REGULATION S-K

9. The general authority citation for Part 229 is revised to read as follows:

Authority: 15 U.S.C. 77e, 77f, 77g, 77h, 77j, 77k, 77s, 77z-2, 77z-3, 77aa(25), 77aa(26), 77ddd, 77eee, 77ggg, 77hhh, 77iii, 77jjj, 77nnn, 77sss, 78c, 78i, 78j, 78l, 78m, 78n, 78o, 78u-5, 78w, 78ll, 78mm, 79e, 79j, 79n, 79t, 80a-8, 80a-9, 80a-20, 80a-29, 80a-30, 80a-31(c), 80a-37, 80a-38(a), 80a-39, 80b-11, 7202, 7241, and 7262; and 18 U.S.C. 1350, unless otherwise noted.

* * * * *

10. By revising Sec. 229.307 to read as follows:

Sec. 229.307 (Item 307) Disclosure controls and procedures.

Disclose the conclusions of the registrant's principal executive and principal financial officers, or persons performing similar functions, regarding the effectiveness of the registrant's disclosure controls and procedures (as defined in Sec. 240.13a-15(e) or 240.15d-15(e) of this chapter) as of the end of the period covered by the report, based on the evaluation of these controls and procedures required by paragraph (b) of Sec. 240.13a-15 or 240.15d-15 of this chapter.

11. By adding Sec. 229.308 to read as follows:

Sec. 229.308 (Item 308) Internal control over financial reporting.

(a) Management's annual report on internal control over financial reporting. Provide a report of management on the registrant's internal control over financial reporting (as defined in Sec. 240.13a-15(f) or 240.15d-15(f) of this chapter) that contains:

(1) A statement of management's responsibility for establishing and maintaining adequate internal control over financial reporting for the registrant;

(2) A statement identifying the framework used by management to evaluate the effectiveness of the registrant's internal control over financial reporting as required by paragraph (c) of Sec. 240.13a-15 or 240.15d-15 of this chapter;

(3) Management's assessment of the effectiveness of the registrant's internal control over financial reporting as of the end of the registrant's most recent fiscal year, including a statement as to whether or not internal control over financial reporting is effective. This discussion must include disclosure of any material weakness in the registrant's internal control over financial reporting identified by management. Management is not permitted to conclude that the registrant's internal control over financial reporting is effective if there are one or more material weaknesses in the registrant's internal control over financial reporting; and

(4) A statement that the registered public accounting firm that audited the financial statements included in the annual report containing the disclosure required by this Item has issued an attestation report on management's assessment of the registrant's internal control over financial reporting.

(b) Attestation report of the registered public accounting firm. Provide the registered public accounting firm's attestation report on management's assessment of the registrant's internal control over financial reporting in the registrant's annual report containing the disclosure required by this Item.

(c) Changes in internal control over financial reporting. Disclose any change in the registrant's internal control over financial reporting identified in connection with the evaluation required by paragraph (d) of Sec. 240.13a-15 or 240.15d-15 of this chapter that occurred during the registrant's last fiscal quarter (the registrant's fourth fiscal quarter in the case of an annual report) that has materially affected, or is reasonably likely to materially affect, the registrant's internal control over financial reporting.

Instructions to Item 308

1. The registrant must maintain evidential matter, including documentation, to provide reasonable support for management's assessment of the effectiveness of the registrant's internal control over financial reporting.

2. A registrant that is an Asset-Backed Issuer (as defined in Sec. 240.13a-14(g) and Sec. 240.15d-14(g) of this chapter) is not required to disclose the information required by this Item.

Sec. 229.401 [Amended]

12. By amending Sec. 229.401 by removing the phrase "internal controls and procedures for financial reporting" in paragraph (h)(2)(iv) of Item 401 and adding, in its place, the phrase "internal control over financial reporting".

Sec. 229.401. Directors, executive officers, promoters and control persons.

(a) Identification of directors. List the names and ages of all directors of the registrant and all persons nominated or chosen to become directors; indicate all positions and offices with the registrant held by each such person; state his term of office as director and any period(s) during which he has served as such; describe briefly any arrangement or understanding between him and any other person(s) (naming such person(s)) pursuant to which he was or is to be selected as a director or nominee.

Instructions to Paragraph (a) of Item 401

1. Do not include arrangements or understandings with directors or officers of the registrant acting solely in their capacities as such.

2. No nominee or person chosen to become a director who has not consented to act as such shall be named in response to this Item. In this regard, with respect to proxy statements, see Rule 14a-4(d) under the Exchange Act (§240.14a-4(d) of this chapter).

3. If the information called for by this paragraph (a) is being presented in a proxy or information statement, no information need be given respecting any director whose term of office as a director will not continue after the meeting to which the statement relates.

4. With regard to proxy statements in connection with action to be taken concerning the election of directors, if fewer nominees are named than the number fixed by or pursuant to the governing instruments, state the reasons for this procedure and that the proxies cannot be voted for a greater number of persons than the number of nominees named.

5. With regard to proxy statements in connection with action to be taken concerning the election of directors, if the solicitation is made by persons other than management, information shall be given as to nominees of the persons making the solicitation. In all other instances, information

shall be given as to directors and persons nominated for election or chosen by management to become directors.

(b) Identification of executive officers. List the names and ages of all executive officers of the registrant and all persons chosen to become executive officers; indicate all positions and offices with the registrant held by each such person; state his term of office as officer and the period during which he has served as such and describe briefly any arrangement or understanding between him and any other person(s) (naming such person) pursuant to which he was or is to be selected as an officer.

Instructions to Paragraph (b) of Item 401

1. Do not include arrangements or understandings with directors or officers of the registrant acting solely in their capacities as such.

2. No person chosen to become an executive officer who has not consented to act as such shall be named in response to this Item.

3. The information regarding executive officers called for by this Item need not be furnished in proxy or information statements prepared in accordance with Schedule 14A under the Exchange Act (§240.14a-101 of this chapter) by those registrants relying on General Instruction G of Form 10-K and Form 10-KSB under the Exchange Act (§249.310 of this chapter), Provided, That such information is furnished in a separate item captioned Executive officers of the registrant and included in Part I of the registrant's annual report on Form 10-K and Form 10-KSB.

(c) Identification of certain significant employees. Where the registrant employs persons such as production managers, sales managers, or research scientists who are not executive officers but who make or are expected to make significant contributions to the business of the registrant, such persons shall be identified and their background disclosed to the same extent as in the case of executive officers. Such disclosure need not be made if the registrant was subject to section 13(a) or 15(d) of the Exchange Act or was exempt from section 13(a) by section 12(g)(2)(G) of such Act immediately prior to the filing of the registration statement, report, or statement to which this Item is applicable.

(d) Family relationships. State the nature of any family relationship between any director, executive officer, or person nominated or chosen by the registrant to become a director or executive officer.Instruction to Paragraph 401(d) The term family relationship means any relationship by blood, marriage, or adoption, not more remote than first cousin.

(e) Business experience. (1) Background. Briefly describe the business experience during the past five years of each director, executive officer, person nominated or chosen to become a director or executive officer, and each person named in answer to paragraph (c) of Item 401, including: Each person's principal occupations and employment during the past five years; the name and principal business of any corporation or other organization in which such occupations and employment were carried on; and whether such corporation or organization is a parent, subsidiary or other affiliate of the registrant. When an executive officer or person named in response to paragraph (c) of Item 401 has been employed by the registrant or a subsidiary of the registrant for less than five years, a brief explanation shall be included as to the nature of the responsibility undertaken by the individual in prior positions to provide adequate disclosure of his prior business experience. What is required is information relating to the level of his professional competence, which may include, depending upon the circumstances, such specific information as the size of the operation supervised.

(2) Directorships. Indicate any other directorships held by each director or person nominated or chosen to become a director in any company with a class of securities registered pursuant to section 12 of the Exchange Act or subject to the requirements of section 15(d) of such Act or any company registered as an investment company under the Investment Company Act of 1940, 15 U.S.C. 80a-1, et seq., as amended, naming such company.Instruction to Paragraph (e) of Item 401. For the purposes of paragraph (e)(2), where the other directorships of each director or person nominated or chosen to become a director include directorships of two or more registered investment companies that are part of a fund complex as that term is defined in Item 22(a) of Schedule 14A under the Exchange Act (§240.14a 101 of this chapter), the registrant may, rather than listing each such investment company, identify the fund complex and provide the number of investment company directorships held by the director or nominee in such fund complex.

(f) Involvement in certain legal proceedings. Describe any of the following events that occurred during the past five years and that are material to an evaluation of the ability or integrity of any director, person nominated to become a director or executive officer of the registrant:

(1) A petition under the Federal bankruptcy laws or any state insolvency law was filed by or against, or a receiver, fiscal agent or similar officer was appointed by a court for the business or property of such person, or any partnership in which he was a general partner at or within two years before the time of such filing, or any corporation or business association of which he was an executive officer at or within two years before the time of such filing;

(2) Such person was convicted in a criminal proceeding or is a named subject of a pending criminal proceeding (excluding traffic violations and other minor offenses);

(3) Such person was the subject of any order, judgment, or decree, not subsequently reversed, suspended or vacated, of any court of competent jurisdiction, permanently or temporarily enjoining him from, or otherwise limiting, the following activities:

(i) Acting as a futures commission merchant, introducing broker, commodity trading advisor, commodity pool operator, floor broker, leverage transaction merchant, any other person regulated by the Commodity Futures Trading Commission, or an associated person of any of the foregoing, or as an investment adviser, underwriter, broker or dealer in securities, or as an affiliated person, director or employee of any investment company, bank, savings and loan association or insurance company, or engaging in or continuing any conduct or practice in connection with such activity;

(ii) Engaging in any type of business practice; or

(iii) Engaging in any activity in connection with the purchase or sale of any security or commodity or in connection with any violation of Federal or State securities laws or Federal commodities laws;

(4) Such person was the subject of any order, judgment or decree, not subsequently reversed, suspended or vacated, of any Federal or State authority barring, suspending or otherwise limiting for more than 60 days the right of such person to engage in any activity described in paragraph (f)(3)(i) of this section, or to be associated with persons engaged in any such activity; or

(5) Such person was found by a court of competent jurisdiction in a civil action or by the Commission to have violated any Federal or State securities law, and the judgment in such civil action or finding by the Commission has not been subsequently reversed, suspended, or vacated.

(6) Such person was found by a court of competent jurisdiction in a civil action or by the Commodity Futures Trading Commission to have violated any Federal commodities law, and the judgment in such civil action or finding by the Commodity Futures Trading Commission has not been subsequently reversed, suspended or vacated.

Instructions to Paragraph (f) of Item 401

1. For purposes of computing the five year period referred to in this paragraph, the date of a reportable event shall be deemed the date on which the final order, judgment or decree was entered, or the date on which any rights of appeal from preliminary orders, judgments, or decrees have lapsed. With respect to bankruptcy petitions, the computation date shall be the date of filing for uncontested petitions or the date upon which approval of a contested petition became final.

2. If any event specified in this paragraph (f) has occurred and information in regard thereto is omitted on the grounds that it is not material, the registrant may furnish to the Commission, at time of filing (or at the time preliminary materials are filed, or ten days before definitive materials are filed in preliminary filing is not required, pursuant to Rule 14a-6 or 14c-5 under the Exchange Act (§§ 240.14a-6 and 240-14c-5 of this chapter)), as supplemental information and not as part of the registration statement, report, or proxy or information statement, materials to which the omission relates, a description of the event and a statement of the reasons for the omission of information in regard thereto.

3. The registrant is permitted to explain any mitigating circumstances associated with events reported pursuant to this paragraph.

4. If the information called for by this paragraph (f) is being presented in a proxy or information statement, no information need be given respecting any director whose term of office as a director will not continue after the meeting to which the statement relates.

(g) Promoters and control persons. (1) Registrants, which have not been subject to the reporting requirements of section 13(a) or 15(d) of the Exchange Act for the twelve months immediately prior to the filing of the registration statement, report, or statement to which this Item is applicable, and which were organized within the last five years, shall describe with respect to any promoter, any of the events enumerated in paragraphs (f)(1) through (f)(6) of this section that occurred during the past five years and that are material to a voting or investment decision.

(2) Registrants, which have not been subject to the reporting requirements of section 13(a) or 15(d) of the Exchange Act for the twelve months immediately prior to the filing of the registration statement, report, or statement to which this Item is applicable, shall describe with respect to any control person, any of the events enumerated in paragraphs (f)(1) through (f)(6) of this section that occurred during the past five years and that are material to a voting or investment decision.

Instructions to Paragraph (g) of Item 401

1. Instructions 1. through 3. to paragraph (f) shall apply to this paragraph (g).

2. Paragraph (g) shall not apply to any subsidiary of a registrant which has been reporting pursuant to Section 13(a) or 15(d) of the Exchange Act for the twelve months immediately prior to the filing of the registration statement, report or statement.

(h) Audit committee financial expert. (1) (i) Disclose that the registrant's board of directors has determined that the registrant either:

(A) Has at least one audit committee financial expert serving on its audit committee; or

(B) Does not have an audit committee financial expert serving on its audit committee.

(ii) If the registrant provides the disclosure required by paragraph (h)(1)(i)(A) of this Item, it must disclose the name of the audit committee financial expert and whether that person is independent, as that term is used in Item 7(d)(3)(iv) of Schedule 14A (240.14a-101 of this chapter) under the Exchange Act.

(iii) If the registrant provides the disclosure required by paragraph (h)(1)(i)(B) of this Item, it must explain why it does not have an audit committee financial expert.

Instruction to paragraph (h)(1) of Item 401

If the registrant's board of directors has determined that the registrant has more than one audit committee financial expert serving on its audit committee, the registrant may, but is not required to, disclose the names of those additional persons. A registrant choosing to identify such persons must indicate whether they are independent pursuant to Item 401(h)(1)(ii).

(2) For purposes of this Item, an audit committee financial expert means a person who has the following attributes:

(i) An understanding of generally accepted accounting principles and financial statements;

(ii) The ability to assess the general application of such principles in connection with the accounting for estimates, accruals and reserves;

(iii) Experience preparing, auditing, analyzing or evaluating financial statements that present a breadth and level of complexity of accounting issues that are generally comparable to the breadth and complexity of issues that can reasonably be expected to be raised by the registrant's financial statements, or experience actively supervising one or more persons engaged in such activities;

(iv) An understanding of internal control over financial reporting; and

(v) An understanding of audit committee functions.

(3) A person shall have acquired such attributes through:

(i) Education and experience as a principal financial officer, principal accounting officer, controller, public accountant or auditor or experience in one or more positions that involve the performance of similar functions;

(ii) Experience actively supervising a principal financial officer, principal accounting officer, controller, public accountant, auditor or person performing similar functions;

(iii) Experience overseeing or assessing the performance of companies or public accountants with respect to the preparation, auditing or evaluation of financial statements; or

(iv) Other relevant experience.

(4) Safe Harbor. (i) A person who is determined to be an audit committee financial expert will not be deemed an expert for any purpose, including without limitation for purposes of section 11 of the Securities Act of 1933 (15 U.S.C. 77k), as a result of being designated or identified as an audit committee financial expert pursuant to this Item 401.

(ii) The designation or identification of a person as an audit committee financial expert pursuant to this Item 401 does not impose on such person any duties, obligations or liability that are greater than the duties, obligations and liability imposed on such person as a member of the audit committee and board of directors in the absence of such designation or identification.

(iii) The designation or identification of a person as an audit committee financial expert pursuant to this Item 401 does not affect the duties, obligations or liability of any other member of the audit committee or board of directors.

Instructions to Item 401(h)

1. The disclosure under Item 401(h) is required only in a registrant's annual report. The registrant need not provide the disclosure required by this Item 401(h) in a proxy or information statement unless that registrant is electing to incorporate this information by reference from the proxy or information statement into its annual report pursuant to general instruction G(3) to Form 10-K.

2. If a person qualifies as an audit committee financial expert by means of having held a position described in paragraph (h)(3)(iv) of this Item, the registrant shall provide a brief listing of that person's relevant experience. Such disclosure may be made by reference to disclosures required under paragraph (e) of this Item 401 (§229.401(e) or this chapter).

3. In the case of a foreign private issuer with a two-tier board of directors, for purposes of this Item 401(h), the term board of directors means the supervisory or non-management board. In the case of a foreign private issuer meeting the requirements of §240.10A-3(c)(3), for purposes of this Item 401(h), the term board of directors means the issuer's board of auditors (or similar body) or statutory auditors, as applicable. Also, in the case of a foreign private issuer, the term generally accepted accounting principles in paragraph (h)(2)(i) of this Item means the body of generally accepted accounting principles used by that issuer in its primary financial statements filed with the Commission.

4. A registrant that is an Asset-Backed Issuer (as defined in §240.13a-14(g) and §240.15d-14(g) of this chapter) is not required to disclose the information required by this Item 401(h).

(i) Identification of the audit committee. (1) If you meet the following requirements, provide the disclosure in paragraph (i)(2) of this section:

(i) You are a listed issuer, as defined in §240.10A-3 of this chapter;

(ii) You are filing either an annual report on Form 10-K or 10-KSB (17 CFR 249.310 or 17 CFR 249.310b), or a proxy statement or information statement pursuant to the Exchange Act (15 U.S.C. 78a et seq.) if action is to be taken with respect to the election of directors; and

(iii) You are neither:

(A) A subsidiary of another listed issuer that is relying on the exemption in §240.10A-3(c)(2) of this chapter; nor

(B) Relying on any of the exemptions in §240.10A-3(c)(4) through (c)(7) of this chapter.

(2) (i) State whether or not the registrant has a separately-designated standing audit committee established in accordance with section 3(a)(58)(A) of the Exchange Act (15 U.S.C. 78c(a)(58)(A)), or a committee performing similar functions. If the registrant has such a committee, however designated, identify each committee member. If the entire board of directors is acting as the registrant's audit committee as specified in section 3(a)(58)(B) of the Exchange Act (15 U.S.C. 78c(a)(58)(B)), so state.

(ii) If applicable, provide the disclosure required by §240.10A-3(d) of this chapter regarding an exemption from the listing standards for audit committees.

13. By amending Sec. 229.601 by:

a. Removing the second and third sentences of paragraph (a)(1);

b. Revising the Exhibit Table which follows the Instructions to the Exhibit Table; and

c. Revising paragraphs (b)(27) through (b)(98).

The revisions read as follows:

Sec. 229.601 (Item 601) Exhibits.

(a) Exhibits and index required.

(1) Subject to Rule 411(c) (§230.411(c) of this chapter) under the Securities Act and Rule 12b-32 (§240.12b-32 of this chapter) under the Exchange Act regarding incorporation of exhibits by reference, the exhibits required in the exhibit table shall be filed as indicated, as part of the registration statement or report.

(2) Each registration statement or report shall contain an exhibit index, which shall precede immediately the exhibits filed with such registration statement. For convenient reference, each exhibit shall be listed in the exhibit index according to the number assigned to it in the exhibit table. The exhibit index shall indicate, by handwritten, typed, printed, or other legible form of notation in the manually signed original registration statement or report, the page number in the sequential numbering system where such exhibit can be found. Where exhibits are incorporated by reference, this fact shall be noted in the exhibit index referred to in the preceding sentence. Further, the first page of the manually signed registration statement shall list the page in the filing where the exhibit index is located. For a description of each of the exhibits included in the exhibit table, see paragraph (b) of this section.

(3) This Item applies only to the forms specified in the exhibit table. With regard to forms not listed in that table, reference shall be made to the appropriate form for the specific exhibit filing requirements applicable thereto.

(4) If a material contract or plan of acquisition, reorganization, arrangement, liquidation or succession is executed or becomes effective during the reporting period reflected by a Form 10-Q and Form 10-QSB or Form 10-K and Form 10-KSB, it shall be filed as an exhibit to the Form 10-Q and Form 10-QSB or Form 10-K and Form 10-KSB filed for the corresponding period. Any amendment or modification to a previously filed exhibit to a Form 10 and Form 10-SB, 10-K or 10-Q document shall be filed as an exhibit to a Form 10-Q and Form 10-QSB or Form 10-K and Form 10-KSB. Such amendment or modification need not be filed where such previously filed exhibit would not be currently required.

Instructions to Item 601

1. If an exhibit to a registration statement (other than an opinion or consent), filed in preliminary form, has been changed only (A) to insert information as to interest, dividend or conversion rates, redemption or conversion prices, purchase or offering prices, underwriters' or dealers" commissions, names, addresses or participation of underwriters or similar matters, which information appears elsewhere in an amendment to the registration statement or a prospectus filed pursuant to Rule 424(b) under the Securities Act (§230.424(b) of this chapter), or (B) to correct typographical errors, insert signatures or make other similar immaterial changes, then, notwithstanding any con-

trary requirement of any rule or form, the registrant need not refile such exhibit as so amended. Any such incomplete exhibit may not, however, be incorporated by reference in any subsequent filing under any Act administered by the Commission.

2. In any case where two or more indentures, contracts, franchises, or other documents required to be filed as exhibits are substantially identical in all material respects except as to the parties thereto, the dates of execution, or other details, the registrant need file a copy of only one of such documents, with a schedule identifying the other documents omitted and setting forth the material details in which such documents differ from the document a copy of which is filed. The Commission may at any time in its discretion require filing of copies of any documents so omitted.

3. Only copies, rather than originals, need be filed of each exhibit required except as otherwise specifically noted.

4. Electronic filings. Whenever an exhibit is filed in paper pursuant to a hardship exemption (§§ 232.201 and 232.202 of this chapter), the letter "P" (paper) shall be placed next to the exhibit in the list of exhibits required by Item 601(a)(2) of this Rule. Whenever an electronic confirming copy of an exhibit is filed pursuant to a hardship exemption (§232.201 or §232.202(d) of this chapter), the exhibit index should specify where the confirming electronic copy can be located; in addition, the designation "CE" (confirming electronic) should be placed next to the listed exhibit in the exhibit index.

EXHIBIT TABLE

Instructions to the Exhibit Table

1. The exhibit table indicates those documents that must be filed as exhibits to the respective forms listed.

2. The "X" designation indicates the documents which are required to be filed with each form even if filed previously with another document, Provided, However, that such previously filed documents may be incorporated by reference to satisfy the filing requirements.

3. The number used in the far left column of the table refers to the appropriate subsection in paragraph (b) where a description of the exhibit can be found. Whenever necessary, alphabetical or numerical subparts may be used.

Exhibit Table

		Securities Act Forms										Exchange Act Forms			
		S-1	S-2	S-3	S-4***	S-8	S-11	F-1	F-2	F-3	F-4***	10	8-K	10-Q	10-K
(1)	Underwriting agreement	X	X	X	X	...	X	X	X	X	X	...	X	...	...
(2)	Plan of acquisition, reorganization, arrangement, liquidation, or succession	X	X	X	X	...	X	X	X	X	X	X	X	X	X
(3)(i)	Articles of incorporation	X	...	...	X	...	X	X	...	...	X	X	...	X	X
(ii)	By-laws	X	...	...	X	...	X	X	...	...	X	X	...	X	X
(4)	Instruments defining the rights of security holders, incl. indentures	X	X	X	X	X	X	X	X	X	X	X	X	X	X
(5)	Opinion re: legality	X	X	X	X	X	X	X	X	X	X	...	...	...	...
(6)	Reserved	N/A	N/A	N/A	N/A	N/A	N/A	N/A	N/A	N/A	N/A	N/A	N/A	N/A	N/A
(7)	Reserved	N/A	N/A	N/A	N/A	N/A	N/A	N/A	N/A	N/A	N/A	N/A	N/A	N/A	N/A

(8)	Opinion re: tax matters	X	X	X	X	...	X	X	X	X	X	...	...	...	...
(9)	Voting trust agreement	X	X	X.	X	X	X	X	X	X	X	X	X	X	X
(10)	Material contracts	X	X	...	X	...	X	X	X	...	X	X	...	X	X
(11)	Statement re: computation of per share earnings	X	X	...	X	...	X	X	X	...	X	X	...	X	X
(12)	Statements re: computation of ratios	X	X	X	X	...	X	X	X	...	X	X	...	...	X
(13)	Annual report to security holders, Form 10-Q and 10-QSB, or quarterly report to security holders*	...	X	...	X	...	...	...	...	...	...	...	...	...	X
(14)	Code of ethics														X
(15)	Letter re: unaudited interim financial information	X	X	X	X	X	X	X	X	X	X	...	...	X	...
(16)	Letter re: change in certifying accountant****	X	X	...	X	...	X	...	...	...	...	X	X	...	X
(17)	Letter re: director resignation	...	...	...	...	...	...	...	...	...	...	...	X	...	...
(18)	Letter re change in accounting principles	...	...	...	...	...	...	...	...	...	...	...	...	X	X
(19)	Report furnished to security holders	...	...	...	...	...	...	...	...	...	...	...	...	X	...
(20)	Other documents or statements to security holders	...	...	...	...	...	...	...	...	...	...	...	X	...	...
(21)	Subsidiaries of the registrant	X	...	...	X	...	X	X	...	...	X	X	...	...	X
(22)	Published report regarding matters submitted to vote of security holders	...	...	...	...	...	...	...	...	...	...	...	...	X	X
(23)	Consent of experts and counsel	X	X	X	X	X	X	X	X	X	X	...	X **	X **	X **
(24)	Power of attorney	X	X	X	X	X	X	X	X	X	X	X	X	X	X
(25)	Statement of eligibility of trustee	X	X	X	X	...	X	X	X	X	X	...	...	...	...
(26)	Invitations for competitive bids	X	X	X	X	...	...	X	X	X	X	...	...	...	...

(27)- (30)	[Reserved]														
(31)	Rule 13a-14(a)/15d-14(a) Certifications	...	...	...	...	...	...	...	...	...	...	...	...	x	x
(32)	Section 1350 Certifications	...	...	...	...	...	...	...	...	...	...	...	...	x	x
(33) through (98)	[Reserved]	N/A	N/A	N/A	N/A	N/A	N/A	N/A	N/A	N/A	N/A	N/A	N/A	N/A	N/A
(99)	Additional exhibits	x	x	x	x	x	x	x	x	x	x	x	x	x	x

* Where incorporated by reference into the text of the prospectus and delivered to security holders along with the prospectus as permitted by the registration statement; or, in the case of the Form 10-K, where the annual report to security holders is incorporated by reference into the text of the Form 10-K.

** Where the opinion of the expert or counsel has been incorporated by reference into a previously filed Securities Act registration statement.

*** An exhibit need not be provided about a company if: (1) With respect to such company an election has been made under Form S-4 or F-4 to provide information about such company at a level prescribed by Forms S-2, S-3, F-2 or F-3 and (2) the form, the level of which has been elected under Forms S- 4 or F-4, would not require such company to provide such exhibit if it were registering a primary offering.

**** If required pursuant to Item 304 of Regulation S-K.

(b) **Description of exhibits.** Set forth below is a description of each document listed in the exhibit tables.

(1) **Underwriting agreement.** Each underwriting contract or agreement with a principal underwriter pursuant to which the securities being registered are to be distributed; if the terms of such documents have not been determined, the proposed forms thereof. Such agreement may be filed as an exhibit to a report on Form 8-K (§249.308 of this chapter) which is incorporated by reference into a registration statement subsequent to its effectiveness.

(2) **Plan of acquisition, reorganization, arrangement, liquidation or succession.** Any material plan of acquisition, disposition, reorganization, readjustment, succession, liquidation or arrangement and any amendments thereto described in the statement or report. Schedules (or similar attachments) to these exhibits shall not be filed unless such schedules contain information which is material to an investment decision and which is not otherwise disclosed in the agreement or the disclosure document. The plan filed shall contain a list briefly identifying the contents of all omitted schedules, together with an agreement to furnish supplementally a copy of any omitted schedule to the Commission upon request.

(3) (i) Articles of incorporation. The articles of incorporation of the registrant or instruments corresponding thereto as currently in effect and any amendments thereto. Whenever amendments to articles of incorporation are filed, a complete copy of the articles as amended shall be filed. Where it is impracticable for the registrant to file a charter amendment authorizing new securities with the appropriate state authority prior to the effective date of the registration statement registering such securities, the registrant may file as an exhibit to the registration statement the form of amendment to be filed with the state authority; and in such a case, if material changes are made after the copy is filed, the registrant must also file the changed copy.

(ii) By-laws. The by-laws of the registrant or instruments corresponding thereto as currently in effect and any amendments thereto. Whenever amendments to the by-laws are filed, a complete copy of the by-laws as amended shall be filed.

(4) **Instruments defining the rights of security holders, including identures.** (i) All instruments defining the rights of holders of the equity or debt securities being registered including, where applicable, the relevant portion of the articles of incorporation or by-laws of the registrant.

(ii) Except as set forth in paragraph (b)(4)(iii) of this section for filings on Forms S-1, S-4, S-11, S-14 and F-4 under the Securities Act (§§ 239.1, and 25, 18, 23 and 34 of this chapter) and Forms 10 and Form 10-SB and 10-K and Form 10-KSB (§§ 249.210 and 310 of this chapter) under the Exchange Act all instruments defining the rights of holders of long-term debt of the registrant and its consolidated subsidiaries and for any of its unconsolidated subsidiaries for which financial statements are required to be filed.

(iii) Where the instrument defines the rights of holders of long-term debt of the registrant and its consolidated subsidiaries and for any of its unconsolidated subsidiaries for which financial statements are required to be filed, there need not be filed:

(A) Any instrument with respect to long-term debt not being registered if the total amount of securities authorized thereunder does not exceed 10 percent of the total assets of the registrant and its subsidiaries on a consolidated basis and if there is filed an agreement to furnish a copy of such agreement to the Commission upon request;

(B) Any instrument with respect to any class of securities if appropriate steps to assure the redemption or retirement of such class will be taken prior to or upon delivery by the registrant of the securities being registered; or

(C) Copies of instruments evidencing scrip certificates for fractions of shares.

(iv) If any of the securities being registered are, or will be, issued under an indenture to be qualified under the Trust Indenture Act, the copy of such indenture which is filed as an exhibit shall include or be accompanied by:

(A) A reasonably itemized and informative table of contents; and

(B) A cross-reference sheet showing the location in the indenture of the provisions inserted pursuant to sections 310 through 318(a) inclusive of the Trust Indenture Act of 1939.

(v) With respect to Forms 8-K and 10-Q and 10-QSB under the Exchange Act which are filed and which disclose, in the text of the Form 10-Q and Form 10-QSB, the interim financial statements, or the footnotes thereto the creation of a new class of securities or indebtedness or the modification of existing rights of security holders, file all instruments defining the rights of holders of these securities or indebtedness. However, there need not be filed any instrument with respect to long-term debt not being registered which meets the exclusion set forth above in paragraph (b)(4)(iii)(A).

Instruction 1 to paragraph (b)(4). There need not be filed any instrument which defines the rights of participants (not as security holders) pursuant to an employee benefit plan.

Instruction 2 to paragraph (b)(4) (for electronic filings). If the instrument defining the rights of security holders is in the form of a certificate, the text appearing on the certificate shall be reproduced in an electronic filing together with a description of any other graphic and image material appearing on the certificate, as provided in Rule 304 of Regulation S T (§232.304 of this chapter).

(5) Opinion re legality. (i) Opinion re legality. An opinion of counsel as to the legality of the securities being registered, indicating whether they will, when sold, be legally issued, fully paid and non-assessable, and, if debt securities, whether they will be binding obligations of the registrant.

(ii) If the securities being registered are issued under a plan and the plan is subject to the requirements of ERISA furnish either:

(A) An opinion of counsel which confirms compliance of the provisions of the written documents constituting the plan with the requirements of ERISA pertaining to such provisions; or

(B) A copy of the Internal Revenue Service determination letter that the plan is qualified under section 401 of the Internal Revenue Code; or

(iii) If the securities being registered are issued under a plan which is subject to the requirements of ERISA and the plan has been amended subsequent to the filing of paragraph (b)(5)(ii)(A) or (B) above, furnish either:

(A) An opinion of counsel which confirms compliance of the amended provisions of the plan with the requirements of ERISA pertaining to such provisions; or

(B) A copy of the Internal Revenue Service determination letter that the amended plan is qualified under section 401 of the Internal Revenue Code.

Note: Attention is directed to Item 8 of Form S-8 for exemptions to this exhibit requirement applicable to that Form.

(6) [Reserved]

(7) [Reserved]

(8) Opinion re tax matters. For filings on Form S-11 under the Securities Act (§239.18) or those to which Securities Act Industry Guide 5 applies, an opinion of counsel or of an independent public or certified public accountant or, in lieu thereof, a revenue ruling from the Internal Revenue Service, supporting the tax matters and consequences to the shareholders as described in the filing when such tax matters are material to the transaction for which the registration statement is being filed. This exhibit otherwise need only be filed with the other applicable registration forms where the tax consequences are material to an investor and a representation as to tax consequences is set forth in the filing. If a tax opinion is set forth in full in the filing, an indication that such is the case may be made in lieu of filing the otherwise required exhibit. Such tax opinions may be conditioned or may be qualified, so long as such conditions and qualifications are adequately described in the filing.

(9) Voting trust agreement. Any voting trust agreements and amendments thereto.

(10) Material contracts. (i) Every contract not made in the ordinary course of business which is material to the registrant and is to be performed in whole or in part at or after the filing of the registration statement or report or was entered into not more than two years before such filing. Only contracts need be filed as to which the registrant or subsidiary of the registrant is a party or has succeeded to a party by assumption or assignment or in which the registrant or such subsidiary has a beneficial interest.

(ii) If the contract is such as ordinarily accompanies the kind of business conducted by the registrant and its subsidiaries, it will be deemed to have been made in the ordinary course of business and need not be filed unless it falls within one or more of the following categories, in which case it shall be filed except where immaterial in amount or significance:

(A) Any contract to which directors, officers, promoters, voting trustees, security holders named in the registration statement or report, or underwriters are parties other than contracts involving only the purchase or sale of current assets having a determinable market price, at such market price;

(B) Any contract upon which the registrant's business is substantially dependent, as in the case of continuing contracts to sell the major part of registrant's products or services or to purchase the major part of registrant's requirements of goods, services or raw materials or any franchise or license or other agreement to use a patent, formula, trade secret, process or trade name upon which registrant's business depends to a material extent;

(C) Any contract calling for the acquisition or sale of any property, plant or equipment for a consideration exceeding 15 percent of such fixed assets of the registrant on a consolidated basis; or

(D) Any material lease under which a part of the property described in the registration statement or report is held by the registrant.

(iii)(A) Any management contract or any compensatory plan, contract or arrangement, including but not limited to plans relating to options, warrants or rights, pension, retirement or deferred compensation or bonus, incentive or profit sharing (or if not set forth in any formal document, a written description thereof) in which any director or any of the named executive officers of the registrant, as defined by Item 402(a)(3) (§229.402(a)(3)), participates shall be deemed material and shall be filed; and any other management contract or any other compensatory plan, contract, or arrangement in which any other executive officer of the registrant participates shall be filed unless immaterial in amount or significance.

(B) Any compensatory plan, contract or arrangement adopted without the approval of security holders pursuant to which equity may be awarded, including, but not limited to, options, warrants or rights (or if not set forth in any formal document, a written description thereof), in which any employee (whether or not an executive officer of the registrant) participates shall be filed unless immaterial in amount or significance. A compensation plan assumed by a registrant in connection with a merger, consolidation or other acquisition transaction pursuant to which the registrant may make further grants or awards of its equity securities shall be considered a compensation plan of the registrant for purposes of the preceding sentence.

(C) Notwithstanding paragraph (b)(10)(iii)(A) above, the following management contracts or compensatory plans, contracts or arrangements need not be filed:

(1) Ordinary purchase and sales agency agreements.

(2) Agreements with managers of stores in a chain organization or similar organization.

(3) Contracts providing for labor or salesmen's bonuses or payments to a class of security holders, as such.

(4) Any compensatory plan, contract or arrangement which pursuant to its terms is available to employees, officers or directors generally and which in operation provides for the same method of allocation of benefits between management and nonmanagement participants.

(5) Any compensatory plan, contract or arrangement if the registrant is a foreign private issuer that furnishes compensatory information on an aggregate basis as permitted by General Instruction 1 to Item 402 (§229.402) or by Item 6.B. of Form 20-F (§249.220f of this chapter).

(6) Any compensatory plan, contract, or arrangement if the registrant is a wholly owned subsidiary of a company that has a class of securities registered pursuant to section 12 or files reports pursuant to section 15(d) of the Exchange Act and is filing a report on Form 10-K and Form 10-KSB or registering debt instruments or preferred stock which are not voting securities on Form S-2.

Instruction 1 to paragraph (b)(10). With the exception of management contracts, in order to comply with paragraph (iii) above, registrants need only file copies of the various compensatory plans and need not file each individual director's or executive officer's personal agreement under the plans unless there are particular provisions in such personal agreements whose disclosure in an exhibit is necessary to an investor's understanding of that individual's compensation under the plan.

Instruction 2 to paragraph (b)(10). If a material contract is executed or becomes effective during the reporting period reflected by a Form 10-Q or Form 10-K, it shall be filed as an exhibit to the Form 10-Q or Form 10-K filed for the corresponding period. See paragraph (a)(4) of this Item. With respect to quarterly reports on Form 10-Q, only those contracts executed or becoming effective during the most recent period reflected in the report shall be filed.

(11) Statement re computation of per share earnings. A statement setting forth in reasonable detail the computation of per share earnings, unless the computation can be clearly determined from the material contained in the registration statement or report. The information with respect to the computation of per share earnings on both primary and fully diluted basis, presented by exhibit or otherwise, must be furnished even though the amounts of per share earnings on the fully diluted bases are not required to be presented in the income statement under the provisions of Accounting Principles Board Opinion No. 15. That Opinion provides that any reduction of less than 3% need not be considered as dilution (see footnote to paragraph 14 of the Opinion) and that a computation on the fully diluted basis which results in improvement of earnings per share not be taken into account (see paragraph 40 of the Opinion).

(12) Statements re computation of ratios. A statement setting forth in reasonable detail the computation of any ratio of earnings to fixed charges, any ratio of earnings to combined fixed charges and preferred stock dividends or any other ratios which appear in the registration statement or report. See Item 503(d) of Regulation S-K (§229.503(d)).

(13) Annual report to security holders, Form 10-Q and Form 10-QSB or quarterly report to security holders. (i) The registrant's annual report to security holders for its last fiscal year, its Form 10-Q and Form 10-QSB (if specifically incorporated by reference in the prospectus) or its quarterly report to security holders, if all or a portion thereof is incorporated by reference in the filing. Such report, except for those portions thereof which are expressly incorporated by reference in the filing, is to be furnished for the information of the Commission and is not to be deemed "filed" as part of the filing. If the financial statements in the report have been incorporated by reference in the filing, the accountant's certificate shall be manually signed in one copy. See Rule 411(b) (§230.411(b) of this chapter).

(ii) Electronic filings. If all, or any portion, of the annual or quarterly report to security holders is incorporated by reference into any electronic filing, all, or such portion of the annual or quarterly report to security holders so incorporated, shall be filed in electronic format as an exhibit to the filing.

(14) Code of ethics. Any code of ethics, or amendment thereto, that is the subject of the disclosure required by Item 406 of Regulation S-K (§229.406) or Item 10 of Form 8-K (§249.308 of this chapter), to the extent that the registrant intends to satisfy the Item 406 or Item 10 requirements through filing of an exhibit.

(15) Letter re unaudited interim financial information. A letter, where applicable, from the independent accountant which acknowledges awareness of the use in a registration statement of a report on unaudited interim financial information which pursuant to Rule 436(c) under the Securities Act (§230.436(c) of this chapter) is not considered a part of a registration statement prepared or certified by an accountant or a report prepared or certified by an accountant within the meaning of sections 7 and 11 of that Act. Such letter may be filed with the registration statement, an amendment thereto, or a report on Form 10-Q and Form 10-QSB which is incorporated by reference into the registration statement.

(16) Letter re change in certifying accountant. A letter from the registrant's former independent accountant regarding its concurrence or disagreement with the statements made by the registrant in the current report concerning the resignation or dismissal as the registrant's principal accountant.

(17) Letter re director resignation. Any letter from a former director which sets forth a description of a disagreement with the registrant that led to the director's resignation or refusal to stand for re-election and which requests that the matter be disclosed.

(18) Letter re change in accounting principles. Unless previously filed, a letter from the registrant's independent accountant indicating whether any change in accounting principles or practices followed by the registrant, or any change in the method of applying any such accounting principles or practices, which affected the financial statements being filed with the Commission in the report or which is reasonably certain to affect the financial statements of future fiscal years is to an alternative principle which in his judgment is preferable under the circumstances. No such letter need be filed when such change is made in response to a standard adopted by the Financial Accounting Standards Board that creates a new accounting principle, that expresses a preference for an accounting principle, or that rejects a specific accounting principle.

(19) Report furnished to security holders. If the registrant makes available to its stockholders or otherwise publishes, within the period prescribed for filing the report, a document or statement containing information meeting some or all of the requirements of Part I of Form 10-Q and Form 10-QSB, the information called for may be incorporated by reference to such published document or statement provided copies thereof are included as an exhibit to the registration statement or to Part I of the Form 10-Q and Form 10-QSB report.

(20) Other documents or statements to security holders. If the registrant makes available to its stockholders or otherwise publishes, within the period prescribed for filing the report, a document or statement containing information meeting some or all of the requirements of this form the information called for may be incorporated by reference to such published document or statement provided copies thereof are filed as an exhibit to the report on this form.

(21) Subsidiaries of the registrant. (i) List all subsidiaries of the registrant, the state or other jurisdiction of incorporation or organization of each, and the names under which such subsidiaries do business. This list may be incorporated by reference from a document which includes a complete and accurate list.

(ii) The names of particular subsidiaries may be omitted if the unnamed subsidiaries, considered in the aggregate as a single subsidiary, would not constitute a significant subsidiary as of the end of the year covered by this report. (See the definition of "significant subsidiary" in Rule 1-02(w) (17 CFR 210.1-02(w)) of Regulation S-X.) The names of consolidated wholly-owned multiple subsidiaries carrying on the same line of business, such as chain stores or small loan companies, may be omitted, provided the name of the immediate parent, the line of business, the number of omitted subsidiaries operating in the United States and the number operating in foreign countries are given. This instruction shall not apply, however, to banks, insurance companies, savings and loan associations or to any subsidiary subject to regulation by another Federal agency.

(22) Published report regarding matters submitted to vote of security holders. Published reports containing all of the information called for by Item 4 of Part II of Form 10-Q and Form 10-QSB or Item 4 of Part I of Form 10-K and Form 10-KSB which is referred to therein in lieu of providing disclosure in Form 10-Q and Form 10-QSB or 10-K and Form 10-KSB, which are required to be filed as exhibits by Rule 12b-23(a)(3) under the Exchange Act (§240.12b-23(a)(3) of this chapter).

(23) Consents of experts and counsel. (i) Securities Act filings. All written consents required to be filed shall be dated and manually signed. Where the consent of an expert or counsel is contained in his report or opinion or elsewhere in the registration statement or document filed therewith, a reference shall be made in the index to the report, the part of the registration statement or document or opinion, containing the consent.

(ii) Exchange Act reports. Where the filing of a written consent is required with respect to material incorporated by reference in a previously filed registration statement under the Securities Act, such consent may be filed as exhibit to the material incorporated by reference. Such consents shall be dated and manually signed.

(24) Power of attorney. If any name is signed to the registration statement or report pursuant to a power of attorney, manually signed copies of such power of attorney shall be filed. Where the power of attorney is contained elsewhere in the registration statement or documents filed therewith a reference shall be made in the index to the part of the registration statement or document containing such power of attorney. In addition, if the name of any officer signing on behalf of the registrant is signed pursuant to a power of attorney, certified copies of a resolution of the registrant's board of directors authorizing such signature shall also be filed. A power of attorney that is filed with the Commission shall relate to a specific filing or an amendment thereto, provided, however, that a power of attorney relating to a registration statement under the Securities Act or an amendment thereto also may relate to any registration statement for the same offering that is to be effective upon filing pursuant to Rule 462(b) under the Securities Act (§230.462(b) of this chapter). A power of attorney that confers general authority shall not be filed with the Commission.

(25) Statement of eligibility of trustee. (i) A statement of eligibility and qualification of each person designated to act as trustee under an indenture to be qualified under the Trust Indenture Act of 1939. Such statement of eligibility shall be bound separately from the other exhibits.

(ii) Electronic filings. The requirement to bind separately the statement of eligibility and qualification of each person designated to act as a trustee under the Trust Indenture Act of 1939 from other exhibits shall not apply to statements submitted in electronic format. Rather, such statements must be submitted as exhibits in the same electronic submission as the registration statement to which they relate, or in an amendment thereto, except that electronic filers that rely on Trust Indenture Act Section 305(b)(2) for determining the eligibility of the trustee under indentures for securities to be issued, offered or sold on a delayed basis by or on behalf of the registrant shall file such statements separately in the manner prescribed by §260.5b-1 through §260.5b-3 of this chapter and by the EDGAR Filer Manual.

(26) Invitations for competitive bids. If the registration statement covers securities to be offered at competitive bidding, any form of communication which is an invitation for competitive bid which will be sent or given to any person shall be filed.

(27) - (30) [Reserved]

(31) Rule 13a-14(a)/15d-14(a) Certifications. The certifications required by Rule 13a-14(a) (17 CFR 240.13a-14(a)) or Rule 15d-14(a) (17 CFR 240.15d-14(a)) exactly as set forth below:

CERTIFICATIONS*

I, [identify the certifying individual], certify that:

1. I have reviewed this [specify report] of [identify registrant];

2. Based on my knowledge, this report does not contain any untrue statement of a material fact or omit to state a material fact necessary to make the statements made, in light of the circumstances under which such statements were made, not misleading with respect to the period covered by this report;

3. Based on my knowledge, the financial statements, and other financial information included in this report, fairly present in all material respects the financial condition, results of operations and cash flows of the registrant as of, and for, the periods presented in this report;

4. The registrant's other certifying officer(s) and I are responsible for establishing and maintaining disclosure controls and procedures (as defined in Exchange Act Rules 13a-15(e) and 15d-15(e)) and internal control over financial reporting (as defined in Exchange Act Rules 13a-15(f) and 15d-15(f)) for the registrant and have:

(a) Designed such disclosure controls and procedures, or caused such disclosure controls and procedures to be designed under our supervision, to ensure that material information relating to the registrant, including its consolidated subsidiaries, is made known to us by others within those entities, particularly during the period in which this report is being prepared;

(b) Designed such internal control over financial reporting, or caused such internal control over financial reporting to be designed under our supervision, to provide reasonable assurance regarding the reliability of financial reporting and the preparation of financial statements for external purposes in accordance with generally accepted accounting principles;

(c) Evaluated the effectiveness of the registrant's disclosure controls and procedures and presented in this report our conclusions about the effectiveness of the disclosure controls and procedures, as of the end of the period covered by this report based on such evaluation; and

(d) Disclosed in this report any change in the registrant's internal control over financial reporting that occurred during the registrant's most recent fiscal quarter (the registrant's fourth fiscal quarter in the case of an annual report) that has materially affected, or is reasonably likely to materially affect, the registrant's internal control over financial reporting; and

5. The registrant's other certifying officer(s) and I have disclosed, based on our most recent evaluation of internal control over financial reporting, to the registrant's auditors and the audit committee of the registrant's board of directors (or persons performing the equivalent functions):

(a) All significant deficiencies and material weaknesses in the design or operation of internal control over financial reporting which are reasonably likely to adversely affect the registrant's ability to record, process, summarize and report financial information; and

(b) Any fraud, whether or not material, that involves management or other employees who have a significant role in the registrant's internal control over financial reporting.

Date: ....

_____ [Signature] [Title]

* Provide a separate certification for each principal executive officer and principal financial officer of the registrant. See Rules 13a-14(a) and 15d-14(a).

(32) Section 1350 Certifications. (i) The certifications required by Rule 13a-14(b) (17 CFR 240.13a-14(b)) or Rule 15d-14(b) (17 CFR 240.15d-14(b)) and Section 1350 of Chapter 63 of Title 18 of the United States Code (18 U.S.C. 1350).

(ii) A certification furnished pursuant to this item will not be deemed "filed" for purposes of Section 18 of the Exchange Act (15 U.S.C. 78r), or otherwise subject to the liability of that section. Such certification will not be deemed to be incorporated by reference into any filing under the Securities Act or the Exchange Act, except to the extent that the registrant specifically incorporates it by reference.

(33) - (98) [Reserved]

(99) Additional exhibits. (i) Any additional exhibits which the registrant may wish to file shall be so marked as to indicate clearly the subject matters to which they refer.

(ii) Any document (except for an exhibit) or part thereof which is incorporated by reference in the filing and is not otherwise required to be filed by this Item or is not a Commission filed document incorporated by reference in a Securities Act registration statement.

(iii) If pursuant to Section 11(a) of the Securities Act (15 U.S.C. 77k(a)) an issuer makes generally available to its security holders an earnings statement covering a period of at least 12 months beginning after the effective date of the registration statement, and if such earnings statement is made available by "other methods" than those specified in paragraphs (a) or (b) of §230.158 of this chapter, it must be filed as an exhibit to the Form 10-Q or the Form 10-K, as appropriate, covering the period in which the earnings statement was released.

(c) [Removed]

PART 240—GENERAL RULES AND REGULATIONS, SECURITIES EXCHANGE ACT OF 1934

14. The general authority citation for Part 240 is revised to read as follows:

Authority: 15 U.S.C. 77c, 77d, 77g, 77j, 77s, 77z-2, 77z-3, 77eee, 77ggg, 77nnn, 77sss, 77ttt, 78c, 78d, 78e, 78f, 78g, 78i, 78j, 78j-1, 78k, 78k-1, 78l, 78m, 78n, 78o, 78p, 78q, 78s, 78u-5, 78w, 78x, 78ll, 78mm, 79q, 79t, 80a-20, 80a-23, 80a-29, 80a-37, 80b-3, 80b-4, 80b-11, 7202, 7241, 7262, and 7263; and 18 U.S.C. 1350, unless otherwise noted.

* * * * *

15. By revising Sec. 240.12b-15 to read as follows:

Sec. 240.12b-15 Amendments.

All amendments must be filed under cover of the form amended, marked with the letter "A" to designate the document as an amendment, e.g., "10-K/A," and in compliance with pertinent requirements applicable to statements and reports. Amendments filed pursuant to this section must set forth the complete text of each item as amended. Amendments must be numbered sequentially and be filed separately for each statement or report amended. Amendments to a statement may be filed either before or after registration becomes effective. Amendments must be signed on behalf of the registrant by a duly authorized representative of the registrant. An amendment to any report required to include the certifications as specified in Sec. 240.13a-14(a) or Sec. 240.15d-14(a) must include new certifications by each principal executive and principal financial officer of the registrant, and an amendment to any report required to be accompanied by the certifications as specified in Sec. 240.13a-14(b) or Sec. 240.15d-14(b) must be accompanied by new certifications by each principal executive and principal financial officer of the registrant. The requirements of the form being amended will govern the number of copies to be filed in connection with a paper format amendment. Electronic filers satisfy the provisions dictating the number of copies by filing one copy of the amendment in electronic format. See Sec. 232.309 of this chapter (Rule 309 of Regulation S-T).

16. By amending Sec. 240.13a-14 by:

a. Revising paragraphs (a) and (b);

b. Removing paragraph (c);

c. Redesignating paragraphs (d), (e) and (f) as paragraphs (c), (d) and (e);

d. Revising newly redesignated paragraph (c), the introductory text of newly redesignated paragraph (d) and newly redesignated paragraph (e); and

e. Adding and reserving new paragraph (f).

The revisions read as follows:

Sec. 240.13a-14 Certification of disclosure in annual and quarterly reports.

(a) Each report, including transition reports, filed on Form 10-Q, Form 10-QSB, Form 10-K, Form 10-KSB, Form 20-F or Form 40-F (§§ 249.308a, 249.308b, 249.310, 249.310b, 249.220f or 249.240f of this chapter) under section 13(a) of the Act (15 U.S.C. 78m(a)), other than a report filed by an Asset-Backed Issuer (as defined in paragraph (g) of this section), must include certifications in the form specified in the applicable exhibit filing requirements of such report and such certifications must be filed as an exhibit to such report. Each principal executive and principal financial officer of the issuer, or persons performing similar functions, at the time of filing of the report must sign a certification.

(b) Each periodic report containing financial statements filed by an issuer pursuant to section 13(a) of the Act (15 U.S.C. 78m(a)) must be accompanied by the certifications required by Section 1350 of Chapter 63 of Title 18 of the United States Code (18 U.S.C. 1350) and such certifications must be furnished as an exhibit to such report as specified in the applicable exhibit requirements for such report. Each principal executive and principal financial officer of the issuer (or equivalent thereof) must sign a certification. This requirement may be satisfied by a single certification signed by an issuer's principal executive and principal financial officers.

(c) A person required to provide a certification specified in paragraph (a) or (b) of this section may not have the certification signed on his or her behalf pursuant to a power of attorney or other form of confirming authority.

(d) Each annual report filed by an Asset-Backed Issuer (as defined in paragraph (g) of this section) under section 13(a) of the Act (15 U.S.C. 78m(a)) must include a certification addressing the following items:

(1) Review by the certifying officer of the annual report and other reports containing distribution information for the period covered by the annual report;

(2) The absence in these reports, to the best of the certifying officer's knowledge, of any untrue statement of material fact or omission of a material fact necessary to make the statements made, in light of the circumstances under which such statements were made, not misleading;

(3) The inclusion in these reports, to the best of the certifying officer's knowledge, of the financial information required to be provided to the trustee under the governing documents of the issuer; and

(4) Compliance by the servicer with its servicing obligations and minimum servicing standards.

(e) With respect to Asset-Backed Issuers, the certification required by paragraph (d) of this section must be signed by the trustee of the trust (if the trustee signs the annual report) or the senior officer in charge of securitization of the depositor (if the depositor signs the annual report). Alternatively, the senior officer in charge of the servicing function of the master servicer (or entity performing the equivalent functions) may sign the certification.

(f) [Reserved]

* * * * *

17. Section 240.13a-15 is revised to read as follows:

Sec. 240.13a-15 Controls and procedures.

(a) Every issuer that has a class of securities registered pursuant to section 12 of the Act (15 U.S.C. 78l), other than an Asset-Backed Issuer (as defined in §240.13a-14(g)), a small business investment company registered on Form N-5 (§§ 239.24 and 274.5 of this chapter), or a unit investment trust as defined by section 4(2) of the Investment Company Act of 1940 (15 U.S.C. 80a-4(2)), must maintain disclosure controls and procedures (as defined in paragraph (e) of this section) and internal control over financial reporting (as defined in paragraph (f) of this section).

(b) Each such issuer's management must evaluate, with the participation of the issuer's principal executive and principal financial officers, or persons performing similar functions, the effectiveness of the issuer's disclosure controls and procedures, as of the end of each fiscal quarter, except that management must perform this evaluation:

(1) In the case of a foreign private issuer (as defined in § 240.3b-4) as of the end of each fiscal year; and

(2) In the case of an investment company registered under section 8 of the Investment Company Act of 1940 (15 U.S.C. 80a-8), within the 90-day period prior to the filing date of each report requiring certification under §270.30a-2 of this chapter.

(c) The management of each such issuer, other than an investment company registered under section 8 of the Investment Company Act of 1940, must evaluate, with the participation of the issuer's principal executive and principal financial officers, or persons performing similar functions, the effectiveness, as of the end of each fiscal year, of the issuer's internal control over financial reporting. The framework on which management's evaluation of the issuer's internal control over financial reporting is based must be a suitable, recognized control framework that is established by a body or group that has followed due-process procedures, including the broad distribution of the framework for public comment.

(d) The management of each such issuer, other than an investment company registered under section 8 of the Investment Company Act of 1940, must evaluate, with the participation of the issuer's principal executive and principal financial officers, or persons performing similar functions, any change in the issuer's internal control over financial reporting, that occurred during each of the issuer's fiscal quarters, or fiscal year in the case of a foreign private issuer, that has materially affected, or is reasonably likely to materially affect, the issuer's internal control over financial reporting.

(e) For purposes of this section, the term disclosure controls and procedures means controls and other procedures of an issuer that are designed to ensure that information required to be disclosed by the issuer in the reports that it files or submits under the Act (15 U.S.C. 78a et seq.) is recorded, processed, summarized and reported, within the time periods specified in the Commission's rules and forms. Disclosure controls and procedures include, without limitation, controls and procedures designed to ensure that information required to be disclosed by an issuer in the reports that it files or submits under the Act is accumulated and communicated to the issuer's management, including its principal executive and principal financial officers, or persons performing similar functions, as appropriate to allow timely decisions regarding required disclosure.

(f) The term internal control over financial reporting is defined as a process designed by, or under the supervision of, the issuer's principal executive and principal financial officers, or persons performing similar functions, and effected by the issuer's board of directors, management and other personnel, to provide reasonable assurance regarding the reliability of financial reporting and the preparation of financial statements for external purposes in accordance with generally accepted accounting principles and includes those policies and procedures that:

(1) Pertain to the maintenance of records that in reasonable detail accurately and fairly reflect the transactions and dispositions of the assets of the issuer;

(2) Provide reasonable assurance that transactions are recorded as necessary to permit preparation of financial statements in accordance with generally accepted accounting principles, and that receipts and expenditures of the issuer are being made only in accordance with authorizations of management and directors of the issuer; and

(3) Provide reasonable assurance regarding prevention or timely detection of unauthorized acquisition, use or disposition of the issuer's assets that could have a material effect on the financial statements.

18. Amending Sec. 240.15d-14 by:

a. Revising paragraphs (a) and (b);

b. Removing paragraph (c);

c. Redesignating paragraphs (d), (e) and (f) as paragraphs (c), (d) and (e);

d. Revising newly redesignated paragraph (c), the introductory text of newly redesignated paragraph (d) and newly redesignated paragraph (e); and

e. Adding and reserving new paragraph (f).

The revisions read as follows:

Sec. 240.15d-14 Certification of disclosure in annual and quarterly reports.

(a) Each report, including transition reports, filed on Form 10-Q, Form 10-QSB, Form 10-K, Form 10-KSB, Form 20-F or Form 40-F (§§ 249.308a, 249.308b, 249.310, 249.310b, 249.220f or 249.240f of this chapter) under section 15(d) of the Act (15 U.S.C. 78o(d)), other than a report filed by an Asset-Backed Issuer (as defined in paragraph (g) of this section), must include certifications in the form specified in the applicable exhibit filing requirements of such report and such certifications must be filed as an exhibit to such report. Each principal executive and principal financial officer of the issuer, or persons performing similar functions, at the time of filing of the report must sign a certification.

(b) Each periodic report containing financial statements filed by an issuer pursuant to section 15(d) of the Act (15 U.S.C. 78o(d)) must be accompanied by the certifications required by Section 1350 of Chapter 63 of Title 18 of the United States Code (18 U.S.C. 1350) and such certifications must be furnished as an exhibit to such report as specified in the applicable exhibit requirements for such report. Each principal executive and principal financial officer of the issuer (or equivalent thereof) must sign a certification. This requirement may be satisfied by a single certification signed by an issuer's principal executive and principal financial officers.

(c) A person required to provide a certification specified in paragraph (a) or (b) of this section may not have the certification signed on his or her behalf pursuant to a power of attorney or other form of confirming authority.

(d) Each annual report filed by an Asset-Backed Issuer (as defined in paragraph (g) of this section) under section 15(d) of the Act (15 U.S.C. 78o(d)), must include a certification addressing the following items:

(1) Review by the certifying officer of the annual report and other reports containing distribution information for the period covered by the annual report;

(2) The absence in these reports, to the best of the certifying officer's knowledge, of any untrue statement of material fact or omission of a material fact necessary to make the statements made, in light of the circumstances under which such statements were made, not misleading;

(3) The inclusion in these reports, to the best of the certifying officer's knowledge, of the financial information required to be provided to the trustee under the governing documents of the issuer; and

(4) Compliance by the servicer with its servicing obligations and minimum servicing standards.

(e) With respect to Asset-Backed Issuers, the certification required by paragraph (d) of this section must be signed by the trustee of the trust (if the trustee signs the annual report) or the senior officer in charge of securitization of the depositor (if the depositor signs the annual report). Alternatively, the senior officer in charge of the servicing function of the master servicer (or entity performing the equivalent functions) may sign the certification.

(f) [Reserved]

* * * * *

19. Section 240.15d-15 is revised to read as follows:

Sec. 240.15d-15 Controls and procedures.

(a) Every issuer that files reports under section 15(d) of the Act (15 U.S.C. 78o(d)), other than an Asset-Backed Issuer (as defined in Sec. 240.15d-14(g) of this chapter), a small business investment company registered on Form N-5 (§§ 239.24 and 274.5 of this chapter), or a unit investment trust as defined in section 4(2) of the Investment Company Act of 1940 (15 U.S.C. 80a-4(2)), must maintain disclosure controls and procedures (as defined in paragraph (e) of this section) and internal control over financial reporting (as defined in paragraph (f) of this section).

(b) Each such issuer's management must evaluate, with the participation of the issuer's principal executive and principal financial officers, or persons performing similar functions, the effectiveness of the issuer's disclosure controls and procedures, as of the end of each fiscal quarter, except that management must perform this evaluation:

(1) In the case of a foreign private issuer (as defined in § 240.3b-4) as of the end of each fiscal year; and

(2) In the case of an investment company registered under section 8 of the Investment Company Act of 1940 (15 U.S.C. 80a-8), within the 90-day period prior to the filing date of each report requiring certification under § 270.30a-2 of this chapter.

(c) The management of each such issuer, other than an investment company registered under section 8 of the Investment Company Act of 1940, must evaluate, with the participation of the issuer's principal executive and principal financial officers, or persons performing similar functions, the effectiveness, as of the end of each fiscal year, of the issuer's internal control over financial reporting. The framework on which management's evaluation of the issuer's internal control over financial reporting is based must be a suitable, recognized control framework that is established by a body or group that has followed due-process procedures, including the broad distribution of the framework for public comment.

(d) The management of each such issuer, other than an investment company registered under section 8 of the Investment Company Act of 1940, must evaluate, with the participation of the issuer's principal executive and principal financial officers, or persons performing similar functions, any change in the issuer's internal control over financial reporting, that occurred during each of the issuer's fiscal quarters, or fiscal year in the case of a foreign private issuer, that has materially affected, or is reasonably likely to materially affect, the issuer's internal control over financial reporting.

(e) For purposes of this section, the term disclosure controls and procedures means controls and other procedures of an issuer that are designed to ensure that information required to be disclosed by the issuer in the reports that it files or submits under the Act (15 U.S.C. 78a et seq.) is recorded, processed, summarized and reported, within the time periods specified in the Commission's rules and forms. Disclosure controls and procedures include, without limitation, controls and procedures designed to ensure that information required to be disclosed by an issuer in the reports that it files or submits under the Act is accumulated and communicated to the issuer's management, including its principal executive and principal financial officers, or persons performing similar functions, as appropriate to allow timely decisions regarding required disclosure.

(f) The term internal control over financial reporting is defined as a process designed by, or under the supervision of, the issuer's principal executive and principal financial officers, or persons performing similar functions, and effected by the issuer's board of directors, management and other personnel, to provide reasonable assurance regarding the reliability of financial reporting and the preparation of financial statements for external purposes in accordance with generally accepted accounting principles and includes those policies and procedures that:

(1) Pertain to the maintenance of records that in reasonable detail accurately and fairly reflect the transactions and dispositions of the assets of the issuer;

(2) Provide reasonable assurance that transactions are recorded as necessary to permit preparation of financial statements in accordance with generally accepted accounting principles, and that receipts and expenditures of the issuer are being made only in accordance with authorizations of management and directors of the issuer; and

(3) Provide reasonable assurance regarding prevention or timely detection of unauthorized acquisition, use or disposition of the issuer's assets that could have a material effect on the financial statements.

PART 249—FORMS, SECURITIES EXCHANGE ACT OF 1934

20. The general authority citation for Part 249 and the subauthority citation for "Section 249.331" are revised to read as follows:

Authority: 15 U.S.C. 78a et seq., 7202, 7233, 7241, 7262, 7264, and 7265; and 18 U.S.C. 1350, unless otherwise noted.

* * * * *

Section 249.331 is also issued under 15 U.S.C. 78j-1, 7202, 7233, 7241, 7264, 7265; and 18 U.S.C. 1350.

* * * * *

21. By amending Form 10-Q (referenced in Sec. 249.308a) by:

a. Removing the last sentence of General Instruction G;

b. Revising Item 4 to "Part I—Financial Information;" and

c. Removing the "Certifications" section after the "Signatures" section.

The revision reads as follows.

Note: The text of Form 10-Q does not, and this amendment will not, appear in the Code of Federal Regulations.

Form 10-Q

* * * * *

Part I—Financial Information

* * * * *

Item 4. Controls and Procedures.

Furnish the information required by Items 307 of Regulation S-K (17 CFR 229.307) and 308(c) of Regulation S-K (17 CFR 229.308(c)).

* * * * *

22. By amending Form 10-QSB (referenced in Sec. 249.308b) by:

a. Removing the last sentence of paragraph 2 of General Instruction F;

b. Revising Item 3 to "Part I—Financial Information;" and

c. Removing the "Certifications" section after the "Signatures" section.

The revision reads as follows.

Note: The text of Form 10-QSB does not, and this amendment will not, appear in the Code of Federal Regulations.

Form 10-QSB

* * * * *

Part I—Financial Information

* * * * *

Item 3. Controls and Procedures.

Furnish the information required by Items 307 of Regulation S-B (17 CFR 228.307) and 308(c) of Regulation S-B (17 CFR 228.308(c)).

* * * * *

23. By amending Form 10-K (referenced in Sec. 249.310) by:

a. Removing the phrase "(who also must provide the certification required by Rule 13a-14 (17 CFR 240.13a-14) or Rule 15d-14 (17 CFR 240.15d-14) exactly as specified in this form)" each time it appears in the first sentence of paragraph (2)(a) of General Instruction D.;

b. Removing the phrase "(Items 1 through 9 or any portion thereof)" and adding, in its place, the phrase "(Items 1 through 9A or any portion thereof)" in the first sentence of paragraph (2) of General Instruction G.;

c. Removing the phrase "(Items 10, 11, 12 and 13)" and adding, in its place, the phrase "(Items 10, 11, 12, 13 and 14)" in the first sentence of paragraph (3) of General Instruction G.;

d. Removing the phrase "(Items 1 through 9)" in the third sentence of paragraph (4) of General Instruction G and adding, in its place, the phrase "(Items 1 through 9A)";

e. Removing the phrase "(Items 10 through 13)" in the third sentence of paragraph (4) of General Instruction G and adding, in its place, the phrase "(Items 10 through 14)";

f. Redesignating Item 14 of Part III as Item 9A of Part II and revising newly redesignated Item 9A;

g. Redesignating Item 15 in Part III as Item 14;

h. "Instruction to Item 15" is corrected to read "Instruction to Item 14";

i. Redesignating Item 16 in Part IV as Item 15;

j. Removing the "Certifications" section after the "Signatures" section and before the reference to "Supplemental Information to be Furnished With Reports Filed Pursuant to Section 15(d) of the Act by Issuers Which Have Not Registered Securities Pursuant to Section 12 of the Act."

The revision reads as follows.

Note: The text of Form 10-K does not, and this amendment will not, appear in the Code of Federal Regulations.

Form 10-K

* * * * *

Part II

* * * * *

Item 9A. Controls and procedures.

Furnish the information required by Items 307 and 308 of Regulation S-K (17 CFR 229.307 and 229.308).

24. By amending Form 10-KSB (referenced in Sec. 249.310b) by:

a. Removing the phrase "(who also must provide the certification required by Rule 13a-14 (17 CFR 240.13a-14) or Rule 15d-14 (17 CFR 240.15d-14) exactly as specified in this form)" each time it appears in the first sentence of paragraph 2 of General Instruction C.;

b. Redesignating Item 14 of Part III as Item 8A of Part II and revising newly redesignated Item 8A;

c. Redesignating Item 15 of Part III as Item 14;

d. "Instruction to Item 15" is corrected to read "Instruction to Item 14";

e. Revising Item 2 of Part III of "INFORMATION REQUIRED IN ANNUAL REPORT OF TRANSITIONAL SMALL BUSINESS ISSER"; and

f. Removing the "Certifications" section after the "Signatures" section and before the reference to "Supplemental Information to be Furnished With Reports Filed Pursuant to Section 15(d) of the Exchange Act By Non-reporting Issuers."

Note: The text of Form 10-KSB does not, and this amendment will not, appear in the Code of Federal Regulations.

Form 10-KSB

* * * * *

PART II

* * * * *

Item 8A. Controls and Procedures

Furnish the information required by Items 307 of Regulation S-B (17 CFR 228.307) and 308 of Regulation S-B (17 CFR 228.308).

* * * * *

Information Required in Annual Report of Transitional Small Business isser

* * * * *

PART III

* * * * *

Item 2. Description of Exhibits.

As appropriate, the issuer should file those documents required to be filed as Exhibit Number 2, 3, 5, 6, and 7 in Part III of Form 1-A. The registrant also shall file:

(12) Additional exhibits—Any additional exhibits which the issuer may wish to file, which shall be so marked as to indicate clearly the subject matters to which they refer.

(13) Form F-X—Canadian issuers shall file a written irrevocable consent and power of attorney on Form F-X.

(31) The exhibit described in paragraph (b)(31) of Item 601 of Regulation S-B.

(32) The exhibit described in paragraph (b)(32) of Item 601 of Regulation S-B.

25. By amending Form 20-F (referenced in Sec. 249.220f) by:

a. Revising paragraph (e) to General Instruction B;

b. Revising Item 15 of Part II;

c. Removing the phrase "internal controls and procedures for financial reporting" in paragraph (b)(4) of Item 16A of Part II and adding, in its place, the phrase "internal control over financial reporting";

d. Removing the "Certifications" section after the "Signatures" section and before the section referencing "Instructions as to Exhibits"; and

e. In the "Instruction as to Exhibits" section, redesignate paragraph 12 as paragraph 14 and add new paragraph 12 and paragraph 13.

The revisions and addition read as follows.

Note: The text of Form 20-F does not, and this amendment will not, appear in the Code of Federal Regulations.

Form 20-F

* * * * *

General Instructions

* * * * *

B. General Rules and Regulations That Apply to this Form.

* * * * *

(e) Where the Form is being used as an annual report filed under Section 13(a) or 15(d) of the Exchange Act, provide the certifications required by Rule 13a-14 (17 CFR 240.13a-14) or Rule 15d-14 (17 CFR 240.15d-14).

* * * * *

Part II

* * * * *

Item 15. Controls and Procedures.

(a) **Disclosure Controls and Procedures.** Where the Form is being used as an annual report filed under Section 13(a) or 15(d) of the Exchange Act, disclose the conclusions of the issuer's principal executive and principal financial officers, or persons performing similar functions, regarding the effectiveness of the issuer's disclosure controls and procedures (as defined in 17 CFR 240.13a-15(e) or 240.15d-15(e)) as of the end of the period covered by the report, based on the evaluation of these controls and procedures required by paragraph (b) of 17 CFR 240.13a-15 or 240.15d-15.

(b) **Management's annual report on internal control over financial reporting.** Where the Form is being used as an annual report filed under Section 13(a) or 15(d) of the Exchange Act, provide a report of management on the issuer's internal control over financial reporting (as defined in 17 CFR 240.13a-15(f) or 240.15d-15(f)) that contains:

(1) A statement of management's responsibility for establishing and maintaining adequate internal control over financial reporting for the issuer;

(2) A statement identifying the framework used by management to evaluate the effectiveness of the issuer's internal control over financial reporting as required by paragraph (c) of 17 CFR 240.13a-15 or 240.15d-15;

(3) Management's assessment of the effectiveness of the issuer's internal control over financial reporting as of the end of the issuer's most recent fiscal year, including a statement as to whether or not internal control over financial reporting is effective. This discussion must include disclosure of any material weakness in the issuer's internal control over financial reporting identified by management. Management is not permitted to conclude that the issuer's internal control over financial reporting is effective if there are one or more material weaknesses in the issuer's internal control over financial reporting; and

(4) A statement that the registered public accounting firm that audited the financial statements included in the annual report containing the disclosure required by this Item has issued an attestation report on management's assessment of the issuer's internal control over financial reporting.

(c) **Attestation report of the registered public accounting firm.** Where the Form is being used as an annual report filed under Section 13(a) or 15(d) of the Exchange Act, provide the registered public accounting firm's attestation report on management's assessment of the issuer's internal control over financial reporting in the issuer's annual report containing the disclosure required by this Item.

(d) **Changes in internal control over financial reporting.** Disclose any change in the issuer's internal control over financial reporting identified in connection with the evaluation required by paragraph (d) of 17 CFR 240.13a-15 or 240.15d-15 that occurred during the period covered by the annual report that has materially affected, or is reasonably likely to materially affect, the issuer's internal control over financial reporting.

Instructions to Item 15.

1. The issuer must maintain evidential matter, including documentation, to provide reasonable support for management's assessment of the effectiveness of the issuer's internal control over financial reporting.

2. An issuer that is an Asset-Backed Issuer (as defined in 17 CFR 240.13a-14(g) and 17 CFR 240.15d-14(g)) is not required to disclose the information required by this Item.

* * * * *

Instructions as to Exhibits

* * * * *

12. The certifications required by Rule 13a-14(a) (17 CFR 240.13a-14(a)) or Rule 15d-14(a) (17 CFR 240.15d-14(a)) exactly as set forth below:

Certifications*

I, [identify the certifying individual], certify that:

1. I have reviewed this annual report on Form 20-F of [identify company];

2. Based on my knowledge, this report does not contain any untrue statement of a material fact or omit to state a material fact necessary to make the statements made, in light of the circumstances under which such statements were made, not misleading with respect to the period covered by this report;

3. Based on my knowledge, the financial statements, and other financial information included in this report, fairly present in all material respects the financial condition, results of operations and cash flows of the company as of, and for, the periods presented in this report;

4. The company's other certifying officer(s) and I are responsible for establishing and maintaining disclosure controls and procedures (as defined in Exchange Act Rules 13a-15(e) and 15d-15(e)) and internal control over financial reporting (as defined in Exchange Act Rules 13a-15(f) and 15d-15(f)) for the company and have:

(a) Designed such disclosure controls and procedures, or caused such disclosure controls and procedures to be designed under our supervision, to ensure that material information relating to the company, including its consolidated subsidiaries, is made known to us by others within those entities, particularly during the period in which this report is being prepared;

(b) Designed such internal control over financial reporting, or caused such internal control over financial reporting to be designed under our supervision, to provide reasonable assurance regarding the reliability of financial reporting and the preparation of financial statements for external purposes in accordance with generally accepted accounting principles;

(c) Evaluated the effectiveness of the company's disclosure controls and procedures and presented in this report our conclusions about the effectiveness of the disclosure controls and procedures, as of the end of the period covered by this report based on such evaluation; and

(d) Disclosed in this report any change in the company's internal control over financial reporting that occurred during the period covered by the annual report that has materially affected, or is reasonably likely to materially affect, the company's internal control over financial reporting; and

5. The company's other certifying officer(s) and I have disclosed, based on our most recent evaluation of internal control over financial reporting, to the company's auditors and the audit committee of the company's board of directors (or persons performing the equivalent functions):

---

*. Provide a separate certification for each principal executive officer and principal financial officer of the company. See Rules 13a-14(a) and 15d-14(a).

(a) All significant deficiencies and material weaknesses in the design or operation of internal control over financial reporting which are reasonably likely to adversely affect the company's ability to record, process, summarize and report financial information; and

(b) Any fraud, whether or not material, that involves management or other employees who have a significant role in the company's internal control over financial reporting.

Date:

[Signature]

[Title]

13. (a) The certifications required by Rule 13a-14(b) (17 CFR 240.13a-14(b)) or Rule 15d-14(b) (17 CFR 240.15d-14(b)) and Section 1350 of Chapter 63 of Title 18 of the United States Code (18 U.S.C. 1350).

(b) A certification furnished pursuant to Rule 13a-14(b) (17 CFR 240.13a-14(b)) or Rule 15d-14(b) (17 CFR 240.15d-14(b)) and Section 1350 of Chapter 63 of Title 18 of the United States Code (18 U.S.C. 1350) will not be deemed "filed" for purposes of Section 18 of the Exchange Act [15 U.S.C. 78r], or otherwise subject to the liability of that section. Such certification will not be deemed to be incorporated by reference into any filing under the Securities Act or the Exchange Act, except to the extent that the company specifically incorporates it by reference.

26. By amending Form 40-F (referenced in Sec. 249.240f) by:

a. Revising paragraph (6) to General Instruction B; and

b. Removing the phrase "internal controls and procedures for financial reporting" and adding, in its place, the phrase "internal control over financial reporting" in paragraph (8)(b)(4) of General Instruction B; and

c. Removing the "Certifications" section after the "Signatures" section.

The revision reads as follows.

Note: The text of Form 40-F does not, and this amendment will not, appear in the Code of Federal Regulations.

FORM 40-F

* * * * *

General Instructions

* * * * *

B. Information To Be Filed on this Form

* * * * *

(6) Where the Form is being used as an annual report filed under Section 13(a) or 15(d) of the Exchange Act:

(a) (1) Provide the certifications required by Rule 13a-14(a) (17 CFR 240.13a-14(a)) or Rule 15d-14(a) (17 CFR 240.15d-14(a)) as an exhibit to this report exactly as set forth below.

Certifications*

I, [identify the certifying individual], certify that:

1. I have reviewed this annual report on Form 40-F of [identify issuer];

2. Based on my knowledge, this report does not contain any untrue statement of a material fact or omit to state a material fact necessary to make the statements made, in light of the circum-

---

*. Provide a separate certification for each principal executive officer and principal financial officer of the issuer. See Rules 13a-14(a) and 15d-14(a).

stances under which such statements were made, not misleading with respect to the period covered by this report;

3. Based on my knowledge, the financial statements, and other financial information included in this report, fairly present in all material respects the financial condition, results of operations and cash flows of the issuer as of, and for, the periods presented in this report;

4. The issuer's other certifying officer(s) and I are responsible for establishing and maintaining disclosure controls and procedures (as defined in Exchange Act Rules 13a-15(e) and 15d-15(e)) and internal control over financial reporting (as defined in Exchange Act Rules 13a-15(f) and 15d-15(f)) for the issuer and have:

(a) Designed such disclosure controls and procedures, or caused such disclosure controls and procedures to be designed under our supervision, to ensure that material information relating to the issuer, including its consolidated subsidiaries, is made known to us by others within those entities, particularly during the period in which this report is being prepared;

(b) Designed such internal control over financial reporting, or caused such internal control over financial reporting to be designed under our supervision, to provide reasonable assurance regarding the reliability of financial reporting and the preparation of financial statements for external purposes in accordance with generally accepted accounting principles;

(c) Evaluated the effectiveness of the issuer's disclosure controls and procedures and presented in this report our conclusions about the effectiveness of the disclosure controls and procedures, as of the end of the period covered by this report based on such evaluation; and

(d) Disclosed in this report any change in the issuer's internal control over financial reporting that occurred during the period covered by the annual report that has materially affected, or is reasonably likely to materially affect, the issuer's internal control over financial reporting; and

5. The issuer's other certifying officer(s) and I have disclosed, based on our most recent evaluation of internal control over financial reporting, to the issuer's auditors and the audit committee of the issuer's board of directors (or persons performing the equivalent functions):

(a) All significant deficiencies and material weaknesses in the design or operation of internal control over financial reporting which are reasonably likely to adversely affect the issuer's ability to record, process, summarize and report financial information; and

(b) Any fraud, whether or not material, that involves management or other employees who have a significant role in the issuer's internal control over financial reporting.

Date:

[Signature]

[Title]

(2) (i) Provide the certifications required by Rule 13a-14(b) (17 CFR 240.13a-14(b)) or Rule 15d-14(b) (17 CFR 240.15d-14(b)) and Section 1350 of Chapter 63 of Title 18 of the United States Code (18 U.S.C. 1350) as an exhibit to this report.

(ii) A certification furnished pursuant to Rule 13a-14(b) (17 CFR 240.13a-14(b)) or Rule 15d-14(b) (17 CFR 240.15d-14(b)) and Section 1350 of Chapter 63 of Title 18 of the United States Code (18 U.S.C. 1350) will not be deemed "filed" for purposes of Section 18 of the Exchange Act [15 U.S.C. 78r], or otherwise subject to the liability of that section. Such certification will not be deemed to be incorporated by reference into any filing under the Securities Act or the Exchange Act, except to the extent that the issuer specifically incorporates it by reference.

(b) Disclosure Controls and Procedures. Where the Form is being used as an annual report filed under Section 13(a) or 15(d) of the Exchange Act, disclose the conclusions of the issuer's principal executive and principal financial officers, or persons performing similar functions, regarding the effectiveness of the issuer's disclosure controls and procedures (as defined in 17 CFR 240.13a-15(e) or 240.15d-15(e)) as of the end of the period covered by the report, based on the evaluation of these controls and procedures required by paragraph (b) of 17 CFR 240.13a-15 or 240.15d-15.

(c) Management's annual report on internal control over financial reporting. Where the Form is being used as an annual report filed under Section 13(a) or 15(d) of the Exchange Act, provide a report of management on the issuer's internal control over financial reporting (as defined in 17 CFR 240.13a-15(f) or 240.15d-15(f)) that contains:

(1) A statement of management's responsibility for establishing and maintaining adequate internal control over financial reporting for the issuer;

(2) A statement identifying the framework used by management to evaluate the effectiveness of the issuer's internal control over financial reporting as required by paragraph (c) of 17 CFR 240.13a-15 or 240.15d-15;

(3) Management's assessment of the effectiveness of the issuer's internal control over financial reporting as of the end of the issuer's most recent fiscal year, including a statement as to whether or not internal control over financial reporting is effective. This discussion must include disclosure of any material weakness in the issuer's internal control over financial reporting identified by management. Management is not permitted to conclude that the issuer's internal control over financial reporting is effective if there are one or more material weaknesses in the issuer's internal control over financial reporting; and

(4) A statement that the registered public accounting firm that audited the financial statements included in the annual report containing the disclosure required by this Item has issued an attestation report on management's assessment of the issuer's internal control over financial reporting.

(d) Attestation report of the registered public accounting firm. Where the Form is being used as an annual report filed under Section 13(a) or 15(d) of the Exchange Act, provide the registered public accounting firm's attestation report on management's assessment of internal control over financial reporting in the annual report containing the disclosure required by this Item.

(e) Changes in internal control over financial reporting. Disclose any change in the issuer's internal control over financial reporting identified in connection with the evaluation required by paragraph (d) of 17 CFR 240.13a-15 or 240.15d-15 that occurred during the period covered by the annual report that has materially affected, or is reasonably likely to materially affect, the issuer's internal control over financial reporting.

Instructions to paragraphs (b), (c), (d) and (e) of General Instruction B. 6.

1. The issuer must maintain evidential matter, including documentation, to provide reasonable support for management's assessment of the effectiveness of the issuer's internal control over financial reporting.

2. An issuer that is an Asset-Backed Issuer (as defined in 17 CFR 240.13a-14(g) and 240.15d-14(g)) is not required to disclose the information required by this Item.

* * * * *

PART 270—RULES AND REGULATIONS, INVESTMENT COMPANY ACT OF 1940

27. The authority citation for Part 270 is amended by revising the subauthority citation for "Section 270.30a-2" to read as follows:

Authority: 15 U.S.C. 80a-1 et seq., 80a-34(d), 80a-37, and 80a-39, unless otherwise noted.

* * * * *

Section 270.30a-2 is also issued under 15 U.S.C. 78m, 78o(d), 80a-8, 80a-29, 7202, and 7241; and 18 U.S.C. 1350, unless otherwise noted.

* * * * *

28. By revising the last sentence of Sec. 270.8b-15 to read as follows:

Sec. 270.8b-15 Amendments.

All amendments shall be filed under cover of the facing sheet of the appropriate form, shall be clearly identified as amendments, and shall comply with all pertinent requirements applicable to registration statements and reports. Amendments shall be filed separately for each separate registration or report amended. Except as permitted under rule 102(b) of Regulation S-T (§232.102(b) of this chapter), any amendment filed under this section shall state the complete text of each item amended. An amendment to any report required to include the certifications as specified in §270.30a-2(a) must include new certifications by each principal executive and principal financial officer of the registrant, and an amendment to any report required to be accompanied by the certifications as specified in §240.13a-14(b) or §240.15d-14(b) and §270.30a-2(b) must be accompanied by new certifications by each principal executive and principal financial officer of the registrant.

29. Section 270.30a-2 is revised to read as follows:

Sec. 270.30a-2 Certification of Form N-CSR.

(a) Each report filed on Form N-CSR (Sec. Sec. 249.331 and 274.128 of this chapter) by a registered management investment company must include certifications in the form specified in Item 10(a)(2) of Form N-CSR and such certifications must be filed as an exhibit to such report. Each principal executive and principal financial officer of the investment company, or persons performing similar functions, at the time of filing of the report must sign a certification.

(b) Each report on Form N-CSR filed by a registered management investment company under Section 13(a) or 15(d) of the Securities Exchange Act of 1934 (15 U.S.C. 78m(a) or 78o(d)) and that contains financial statements must be accompanied by the certifications required by Section 1350 of Chapter 63 of Title 18 of the United States Code (18 U.S.C. 1350) and such certifications must be furnished as an exhibit to such report as specified in Item 10(b) of Form N-CSR. Each principal executive and principal financial officer of the investment company (or equivalent thereof) must sign a certification. This requirement may be satisfied by a single certification signed by an investment company's principal executive and principal financial officers.

(c) A person required to provide a certification specified in paragraph (a) or (b) of this section may not have the certification signed on his or her behalf pursuant to a power of attorney or other form of confirming authority.

30. By revising Sec. 270.30a-3 to read as follows:

Sec. 270.30a-3 Controls and procedures.

(a) Every registered management investment company, other than a small business investment company registered on Form N-5 (Sec. Sec. 239.24 and 274.5 of this chapter), must maintain disclosure controls and procedures (as defined in paragraph (c) of this section) and internal control over financial reporting (as defined in paragraph (d) of this section).

(b) Each such registered management investment company's management must evaluate, with the participation of the company's principal executive and principal financial officers, or persons performing similar functions, the effectiveness of the company's disclosure controls and procedures, within the 90-day period prior to the filing date of each report on Form N-CSR (Sec. Sec. 249.331 and 274.128 of this chapter).

(c) For purposes of this section, the term disclosure controls and procedures means controls and other procedures of a registered management investment company that are designed to ensure that information required to be disclosed by the investment company on Form N-CSR (Sec. Sec. 249.331 and 274.128 of this chapter) is recorded, processed, summarized, and reported within the time periods specified in the Commission's rules and forms. Disclosure controls and procedures include, without limitation, controls and procedures designed to ensure that information required to be disclosed by an investment company in the reports that it files or submits on Form N-CSR is accumulated and communicated to the investment company's management, including its principal executive and principal financial officers, or persons performing similar functions, as appropriate to allow timely decisions regarding required disclosure.

(d) The term internal control over financial reporting is defined as a process designed by, or under the supervision of, the registered management investment company's principal executive and principal financial officers, or persons performing similar functions, and effected by the company's board of directors, management, and other personnel, to provide reasonable assurance regarding the reliability of financial reporting and the preparation of financial statements for external purposes in accordance with generally accepted accounting principles and includes those policies and procedures that:

(1) Pertain to the maintenance of records that in reasonable detail accurately and fairly reflect the transactions and dispositions of the assets of the investment company;

(2) Provide reasonable assurance that transactions are recorded as necessary to permit preparation of financial statements in accordance with generally accepted accounting principles, and that receipts and expenditures of the investment company are being made only in accordance with authorizations of management and directors of the investment company; and

(3) Provide reasonable assurance regarding prevention or timely detection of unauthorized acquisition, use, or disposition of the investment company's assets that could have a material effect on the financial statements.

PART 274—FORMS PRESCRIBED UNDER THE INVESTMENT COMPANY ACT OF 1940

31. The authority citation for Part 274 is amended by revising the authority citation for "Section 274.128" to read as follows:

Authority: 15 U.S.C. 77f, 77g, 77h, 77j, 77s, 78c(b), 78l, 78m, 78n, 78o(d), 80a-8, 80a-24, 80a-26, and 80a-29, unless otherwise noted.

* * * * *

Section 274.128 is also issued under 15 U.S.C. 78j-1, 7202, 7233, 7241, 7264, and 7265; and 18 U.S.C. 1350.

32. Form N-SAR (referenced in Sec. Sec. 249.330 and 274.101) is amended by revising the reference "internal controls and procedures for financial reporting" in paragraph (b)(6)(iv) of the Instruction to Sub-Item 102P3 to read "internal control over financial reporting".

33. Form N-CSR (referenced in Sec. Sec. 249.331 and 274.128) is amended by:

a. In General Instruction D, revising the reference "Items 4, 5, and 10(a)" to read "Items 4, 5, and 10(a)(1)";

b. Revising paragraph 2.(a) of General Instruction F;

c. In paragraph (c) of Item 2, revising the reference "Item 10(a)" to read "Item 10(a)(1)";

d. In paragraph (f)(1) of Item 2, revising the reference "Item 10(a)" to read "Item 10(a)(1)";

e. In paragraph (b)(4) of Item 3, revising the reference "internal controls and procedures for financial reporting" to read "internal control over financial reporting";

f. Revising Item 9; and

g. In Item 10:

(i) The introductory text and paragraphs (a) and (b) are redesignated as paragraphs (a), (a)(1) and (a)(2), respectively;

(ii) Revising newly redesignated paragraph (a) and newly redesignated paragraph (a)(2); and

(iii) Adding new paragraph (b) and an Instruction to Item 10.

The revisions and additions read as follows.

Note: The text of Form N-CSR does not, and these amendments will not, appear in the Code of Federal Regulations.

FORM N-CSR

* * * * *

General Instructions

* * * * *

F. Signature and Filing of Report.

* * * * *

2. (a) The report must be signed by the registrant, and on behalf of the registrant by its principal executive and principal financial officers.

* * * * *

Item 9. Controls and Procedures.

(a) Disclose the conclusions of the registrant's principal executive and principal financial officers, or persons performing similar functions, regarding the effectiveness of the registrant's disclosure controls and procedures (as defined in Rule 30a-3(c) under the Act (17 CFR 270.30a-3(c))) as of a date within 90 days of the filing date of the report that includes the disclosure required by this paragraph, based on the evaluation of these controls and procedures required by Rule 30a-3(b) under the Act (17 CFR 270.30a-3(b)) and Rules 13a-15(b) or 15d-15(b) under the Exchange Act (17 CFR 240.13a-15(b) or 240.15d-15(b)).

(b) Disclose any change in the registrant's internal control over financial reporting (as defined in Rule 30a-3(d) under the Act (17 CFR 270.30a-3(d)) that occurred during the registrant's last fiscal half-year (the registrant's second fiscal half-year in the case of an annual report) that has materially affected, or is reasonably likely to materially affect, the registrant's internal control over financial reporting.

Item 10. Exhibits.

(a) File the exhibits listed below as part of this Form.

* * * * *

(a)(2) A separate certification for each principal executive and principal financial officer of the registrant as required by Rule 30a-2(a) under the Act (17 CFR 270.30a-2(a)), exactly as set forth below:

Certifications

I, [identify the certifying individual], certify that:

1. I have reviewed this report on Form N-CSR of [identify registrant];

2. Based on my knowledge, this report does not contain any untrue statement of a material fact or omit to state a material fact necessary to make the statements made, in light of the circumstances under which such statements were made, not misleading with respect to the period covered by this report;

3. Based on my knowledge, the financial statements, and other financial information included in this report, fairly present in all material respects the financial condition, results of operations, changes in net assets, and cash flows (if the financial statements are required to include a statement of cash flows) of the registrant as of, and for, the periods presented in this report;

4. The registrant's other certifying officer(s) and I are responsible for establishing and maintaining disclosure controls and procedures (as defined in Rule 30a-3(c) under the Investment Company Act of 1940) and internal control over financial reporting (as defined in Rule 30a-3(d) under the Investment Company Act of 1940) for the registrant and have:

(a) Designed such disclosure controls and procedures, or caused such disclosure controls and procedures to be designed under our supervision, to ensure that material information relating to the registrant, including its consolidated subsidiaries, is made known to us by others within those entities, particularly during the period in which this report is being prepared;

(b) Designed such internal control over financial reporting, or caused such internal control over financial reporting to be designed under our supervision, to provide reasonable assurance regarding the reliability of financial reporting and the preparation of financial statements for external purposes in accordance with generally accepted accounting principles;

(c) Evaluated the effectiveness of the registrant's disclosure controls and procedures and presented in this report our conclusions about the effectiveness of the disclosure controls and procedures, as of a date within 90 days prior to the filing date of this report based on such evaluation; and

(d) Disclosed in this report any change in the registrant's internal control over financial reporting that occurred during the registrant's most recent fiscal half-year (the registrant's second fiscal half-year in the case of an annual report) that has materially affected, or is reasonably likely to materially affect, the registrant's internal control over financial reporting; and

5. The registrant's other certifying officer(s) and I have disclosed to the registrant's auditors and the audit committee of the registrant's board of directors (or persons performing the equivalent functions):

(a) All significant deficiencies and material weaknesses in the design or operation of internal control over financial reporting which are reasonably likely to adversely affect the registrant's ability to record, process, summarize, and report financial information; and

(b) Any fraud, whether or not material, that involves management or other employees who have a significant role in the registrant's internal control over financial reporting.

Date:

[Signature]

[Title]

(b) If the report is filed under Section 13(a) or 15(d) of the Exchange Act, provide the certifications required by Rule 30a-2(b) under the Act (17 CFR 270.30a-2(b)), Rule 13a-14(b) or Rule 15d-14(b) under the Exchange Act (17 CFR 240.13a-14(b) or 240.15d-14(b)), and Section 1350 of Chapter 63 of Title 18 of the United States Code (18 U.S.C. 1350) as an exhibit. A certification furnished pursuant to this paragraph will not be deemed "filed" for purposes of Section 18 of the Exchange Act (15 U.S.C. 78r), or otherwise subject to the liability of that section. Such certification will not be deemed to be incorporated by reference into any filing under the Securities Act of 1933 or the Exchange Act, except to the extent that the registrant specifically incorporates it by reference.

Instruction to Item 10.

Letter or number the exhibits in the sequence that they appear in this item.

* * * * *

By the Commission.

Dated: June 5, 2003.

J. Lynn Taylor,

Assistant Secretary.

[FR Doc. 03-14640 Filed 6-13-03; 8:45 am]

BILLING CODE 8010-01-P

¶ 1100. Management's Report on Internal Control Over Financial Reporting and Certification of Disclosure in Exchange Act Periodic Reports; Final Rule

SECURITIES AND EXCHANGE COMMISSION

17 CFR Parts 210, 228, 229, 240, 249, 270, and 274

[Release Nos. 33-8392; 34-49313; IC-26357; File Nos. S7-40-02; S7-06-03]

RIN 3235-AI66 and 3235-AI79

Management's Report on Internal Control Over Financial Reporting and Certification of Disclosure in Exchange Act Periodic Reports

AGENCY: Securities and Exchange Commission.

ACTION: Final rule; extension of compliance dates.

SUMMARY: We are extending the compliance dates that were published on June 18, 2003, in Release No. 33-8238 (68 FR 36636) for certain amendments to Rules 13a-15 and 15d-15 under the Securities Exchange Act of 1934, items 308(a) and (b) of Regulations S-K and S-B and the corresponding provisions in Forms 20-F and 40-F, that require companies, other than registered investment companies, to include in their annual reports a report of management on the company's internal control over financial reporting, and to evaluate, as of the end of each fiscal period, any change in the company's internal control over financial reporting that occurred during the period that has materially affected, or is reasonably likely to materially affect, the company's internal control over financial reporting. We are also extending the compliance dates for amendments to certain representations that must be included in the certifications required by Exchange Act Rules 13a-14 and 15d-14 and Investment Company Act of 1940 Rule 30a-2, regarding the company's internal control over financial reporting. The companies subject to these certification provisions include registered investment companies. Finally, we are extending the compliance date for an amendment to Investment Company Act Rule 30a-3 regarding the maintenance of internal control over financial reporting.

DATES: *Effective Date:* The effective date published on June 18, 2003, remains August 14, 2003.

Compliance Dates: The compliance dates are extended as follows: A company that is an "accelerated filer," as defined in Exchange Act Rule 12b-2, must begin to comply with the management report on internal control over financial reporting requirement and the related registered public accounting firm report requirement in items 308(a) and (b) of Regulations S-K and S-B for its first fiscal year ending on or after November 15, 2004. A non-accelerated filer must begin to comply with these requirements for its first fiscal year ending on or after July 15, 2005. A foreign private issuer that files its annual report on Form 20-F or Form 40-F must begin to comply with the corresponding requirements in these forms for its first fiscal year ending on or after July 15, 2005.

A company must begin to comply with the provisions of Exchange Act Rule 13a-15(d) or 15d-15(d), whichever applies, requiring an evaluation of changes to internal control over financial reporting requirements with respect to the company's first periodic report due after the first annual report that must include management's report on internal control over financial reporting.

In addition, we are applying the extended compliance period to the amended portion of the introductory language in paragraph 4 of the certification required by Exchange Act Rules 13a-14(a) and 15d-14(a) that refers to the certifying officers' responsibility for establishing and maintaining internal control over financial reporting for the company, as well as paragraph 4(b). The amended language must be provided in the first annual report required to contain management's internal control report and in all periodic reports filed thereafter. The extended compliance dates also apply to the amendments of Exchange Act Rules 13a-15(a) and 15d-15(a) relating to the maintenance of internal control over financial reporting.

We are also extending the compliance period for registered investment companies to comply with the amended portion of the introductory language in paragraph 4 of the certification in Form

N-CSR required by Investment Company Act Rule 30a-2(a) that refers to the certifying officers' responsibility for establishing and maintaining internal control over financial reporting for the company, as well as paragraph 4(b) of the certification in Form N-CSR. The amended language must be provided beginning with the first annual report filed on Form N-CSR for a fiscal year ending on or after November 15, 2004.[1] Registered investment companies must comply with the amendment to Investment Company Act Rule 30a-3(a) relating to the maintenance of internal control over financial reporting with respect to fiscal years ending on or after November 15, 2004.

The extended compliance period does not in any way affect the provisions of our other rules and regulations regarding internal controls that are in effect, including, without limitation, Exchange Act Rule 13b2-2.

FOR FURTHER INFORMATION CONTACT: Sean Harrison, Special Counsel, Division of Corporation Finance, at (202) 942-2910, or with respect to registered investment companies, Christian Broadbent, Senior Counsel, Division of Investment Management, at (202) 942-0721, U.S. Securities and Exchange Commission, 450 Fifth Street, NW., Washington, DC 20549.

SUPPLEMENTARY INFORMATION: On June 5, 2003,[2] the Commission adopted amendments to Items 307, 401 and 601 of Regulations S-B[3] and S-K;[4] added new Item 308 to Regulations S-B and S-K; amended Form 10-K,[5] Form 10-KSB,[6] Form 10-Q,[7] Form 10-QSB,[8] Form 20-F,[9] Form 40-F,[10] Rule 12b-15,[11] Rule 13a-14,[12] Rule 13a-15,[13] Rule 15d-14[14] and Rule 15d-15[15] under the Securities Exchange Act of 1934;[16] amended Rules 1-02 and 2-02[17] of Regulation S-X;[18] amended Rules 8b-15,[19] 30a-2[20] and 30a-3[21] under the Investment Company Act of 1940;[22] and amended Forms N-CSR[23] and N-SAR[24] under the Exchange Act and the Investment Company Act. Among other things, these amendments require companies, other than registered investment companies, to include in their annual reports a report of management on the company's internal control over financial reporting, and to evaluate, as of the end of each fiscal quarter, or year in the case of a foreign private issuer filing its annual report on Form 20-F or 40-F, any change in the company's internal control over financial reporting that occurred during the period that has materially affected, or is reasonably likely to materially affect, the company's internal control over financial reporting.

In our June 2003 Adopting Release, we decided to provide a lengthy compliance period for the amendments requiring a report by management on a company's internal control over financial reporting. Specifically, we provided that a company that was an accelerated filer would have to begin complying with the new amendments in its annual report for its first fiscal year ending on or after June 15, 2004, and that a non-accelerated filer would have to begin complying in its annual report for its first fiscal year ending on or after April 15, 2005. We stated that a longer transition period was appropriate in light of both the substantial time and resources needed by companies to properly implement the rules, and the corresponding benefit to investors that would result from

---

1. The amended language must also be provided in reports on Form N-Q following this report on Form N-CSR. On February 11, 2004, the Commission indicated that it would issue a release adopting rules that will require a registered management investment company to file its portfolio holdings with the Commission on Form N-Q not later than 60 days after the close of the first and third quarters of each fiscal year.
2. See Release No. 33-8238 (June 5, 2003) (68 FR 36636) (the "Adopting Release").
3. 17 CFR 228.10 et seq.
4. 17 CFR 229.10 et seq.
5. 17 CFR 249.310.
6. 17 CFR 249.310b.
7. 17 CFR 249.308a.
8. 17 CFR 249.308b.
9. 17 CFR 249.220f.
10. 17 CFR 249.240f.
11. 17 CFR 240.12b-15.
12. 17 CFR 240.13a-14.
13. 17 CFR 240.13a-15.
14. 17 CFR 140.15d-14.
15. 17 CFR 240.15d-15.
16. 15 U.S.C. 78a et seq.
17. 17 CFR 210.1-02 and 2-02.
18. 17 CFR 210.1-01 et seq.
19. 17 CFR 270.8b-15.
20. 17 CFR 270.30a-2.
21. 17 CFR 270.30a-3.
22. 15 U.S.C. 80a-1 et seq.
23. 17 CFR 249.331; 17 CFR 274.128.
24. 17 CFR 249.330; 17 CFR 274.101.

companies' proper implementation of the new requirements. We further noted that a longer transition period would provide additional time for the Public Company Accounting Oversight Board (the "PCAOB") to consider relevant factors in determining and implementing new standards for registered public accounting firms.[25] The PCAOB made a determination to set new standards and has been working expeditiously to do so. It held a public roundtable in July 2003 to discuss significant issues associated with the establishment of a new standard and issued a proposed standard on October 7, 2003.[26] The PCAOB received nearly 200 comment letters on the proposals and has completed its review and analysis of the public comment.

On January 23, 2004, representatives of five companies requested that the Commission extend the June 15, 2004, compliance date for accelerated filers.[27] In their request, these companies argued that it would be extremely difficult for companies to properly prepare for compliance with the new internal control over financial reporting requirements, and for auditors to properly implement a new standard that has not yet been finalized, for a fiscal year that is nearly complete. They further asserted that companies with June, July and August fiscal year ends that are in the process of documenting and evaluating controls have based these processes on the PCAOB's proposed standard. Several commenters on the PCAOB's proposed standard expressed similar concerns and requested that the Commission and the PCAOB provide additional time for compliance.[28]

We believe that an extension of compliance dates for the internal control reporting over financial reporting requirements is appropriate. We believe that the extension will benefit investors because this will help ensure that appropriate controls are in place for the first reporting process. Moreover, an extension will minimize the cost and disruption of implementing a new disclosure requirement under a current standard that will soon be superseded, and will provide companies and their auditors with a sufficient amount of time to perform additional testing or remediation of controls based on the final standard. We also, for good cause, find that, based on the reasons cited above, notice and solicitation of comment regarding extension of the compliance dates is impracticable, unnecessary, and contrary to the public interest.[29] In addition, for good cause and because the extension will relieve a restriction, the extension will be effective on March 1, 2004.

By the Commission.

Dated: February 24, 2004.

Margaret H. McFarland,

Deputy Secretary.

[FR Doc. 04-4425 Filed 2-27-04; 8:45 am]

---

25. Under the Sarbanes-Oxley Act, the PCAOB was granted authority to set auditing and attestation standards for registered public accounting firms to use in the preparation and issuance of audit reports on the financial statements of issuers. Under section 404(b) of the Act, the PCAOB is required to set standards for registered public accounting firms' attestations to, and reports on, management's assessment regarding its internal control over financial reporting.
26. See PCAOB Release No. 2003-017, PCAOB Rulemaking Docket Matter No. 008.
27. See letter to Mr. William H. Donaldson, Chairman of the Securities and Exchange Commission, and Mr. William J. McDonough, Chairman of the Public Company Accounting Oversight Board, from John G. Connors, Sr., Vice President and Chief Financial Officer, Microsoft Corporation, on behalf of Clayton C. Daley Jr., Chief Financial Officer, Proctor & Gamble; Richard J. Miller, Executive Vice President and Chief Financial Officer, Cardinal Health Corporation; Richard A. Galanti, Executive Vice President and Chief Financial Officer, Costco Wholesale Corporation and Michael J. Irwin, Executive Vice President and Chief Financial Officer, WD-40 Company, dated January 23, 2004.
28. See letters regarding PCAOB Rulemaking Docket Matter No. 008 of: the American Institute of Certified Public Accountants, Deloitte & Touche LLP, PricewaterhouseCoopers LLP, Walt Disney Corporation and H.W. Willoughby. These letters are available at http://www.pcaobus.org.
29. See Section 553(b)(3)(B) of the Administrative Procedure Act (5 U.S.C. 55s(b)(3)(B)) (an agency may dispense with prior notice and comment when it finds, for good cause, that notice and comment are "impracticable, unnecessary, or contrary to the public interest").

Sarbanes-Oxley Act of 2002
P.L. 107-204
One Hundred Seventh Congress
2nd Session

This section reproduces the complete text of the Sarbanes-Oxley Act of 2002, P.L. 107-204.

[¶ 1200] Sec. 1. Short title; table of contents.

(a) Short title. This Act may be cited as the "Sarbanes-Oxley Act of 2002".

(b) Table of contents. The table of contents for this Act is as follows:

[¶ 1201] Sec. 2. Definitions.

(a) **In general.** In this Act, the following definitions shall apply:

(1) **Appropriate State regulatory authority.** The term "appropriate State regulatory authority" means the State agency or other authority responsible for the licensure or other regulation of the practice of accounting in the State or States having jurisdiction over a

registered public accounting firm or associated person thereof, with respect to the matter in question.

(2) Audit. The term "audit" means an examination of the financial statements of any issuer by an independent public accounting firm in accordance with the rules of the Board or the Commission (or, for the period preceding the adoption of applicable rules of the Board under section 103, in accordance with then-applicable generally accepted auditing and related standards for such purposes), for the purpose of expressing an opinion on such statements.

(3) Audit committee. The term "audit committee" means—

(A) a committee (or equivalent body) established by and amongst the board of directors of an issuer for the purpose of overseeing the accounting and financial reporting processes of the issuer and audits of the financial statements of the issuer; and

(B) if no such committee exists with respect to an issuer, the entire board of directors of the issuer.

(4) Audit report. The term "audit report" means a document or other record—

(A) prepared following an audit performed for purposes of compliance by an issuer with the requirements of the securities laws; and

(B) in which a public accounting firm either—

(i) sets forth the opinion of that firm regarding a financial statement, report, or other document; or

(ii) asserts that no such opinion can be expressed.

(5) Board. The term "Board" means the Public Company Accounting Oversight Board established under section 101.

(6) Commission. The term "Commission" means the Securities and Exchange Commission.

(7) Issuer. The term "issuer" means an issuer (as defined in section 3 of the Securities Exchange Act of 1934 (15 U.S.C. 78c)), the securities of which are registered under section 12 of that Act (15 U.S.C. 78l), or that is required to file reports under section 15(d) (15 U.S.C. 78o(d)), or that files or has filed a registration statement that has not yet become effective under the Securities Act of 1933 (15 U.S.C. 77a et seq.), and that it has not withdrawn.

(8) Non-audit services. The term "non-audit services" means any professional services provided to an issuer by a registered public accounting firm, other than those provided to an issuer in connection with an audit or a review of the financial statements of an issuer.

(9) Person associated with a public accounting firm.

(A) In general. The terms "person associated with a public accounting firm" (or with a "registered public accounting firm") and "associated person of a public accounting firm" (or of a "registered public accounting firm") mean any individual proprietor, partner, shareholder, principal, accountant, or other professional employee of a public accounting firm, or any other independent contractor or entity that, in connection with the preparation or issuance of any audit report—

(i) shares in the profits of, or receives compensation in any other form from, that firm; or

(ii) participates as agent or otherwise on behalf of such accounting firm in any activity of that firm.

(B) Exemption authority. The Board may, by rule, exempt persons engaged only in ministerial tasks from the definition in subparagraph (A), to the extent that the Board determines that any such exemption is consistent with the purposes of this Act, the public interest, or the protection of investors.

(10) Professional standards. The term "professional standards" means—

(A) accounting principles that are—

(i) established by the standard setting body described in section 19(b) of the Securities Act of 1933, as amended by this Act, or prescribed by the Commission under section

19(a) of that Act (15 U.S.C. 17a(s)) or section 13(b) of the Securities Exchange Act of 1934 (15 U.S.C. 78a(m)); and

(ii) relevant to audit reports for particular issuers, or dealt with in the quality control system of a particular registered public accounting firm; and

(B) auditing standards, standards for attestation engagements, quality control policies and procedures, ethical and competency standards, and independence standards (including rules implementing title II) that the Board or the Commission determines—

(i) relate to the preparation or issuance of audit reports for issuers; and

(ii) are established or adopted by the Board under section 103(a), or are promulgated as rules of the Commission.

(11) Public accounting firm. The term "public accounting firm" means—

(A) a proprietorship, partnership, incorporated association, corporation, limited liability company, limited liability partnership, or other legal entity that is engaged in the practice of public accounting or preparing or issuing audit reports; and

(B) to the extent so designated by the rules of the Board, any associated person of any entity described in subparagraph (A).

(12) Registered public accounting firm. The term "registered public accounting firm" means a public accounting firm registered with the Board in accordance with this Act.

(13) Rules of the Board. The term "rules of the Board" means the bylaws and rules of the Board (as submitted to, and approved, modified, or amended by the Commission, in accordance with section 107), and those stated policies, practices, and interpretations of the Board that the Commission, by rule, may deem to be rules of the Board, as necessary or appropriate in the public interest or for the protection of investors.

(14) Security. The term "security" has the same meaning as in section 3(a) of the Securities Exchange Act of 1934 (15 U.S.C. 78c(a)).

(15) Securities laws. The term "securities laws" means the provisions of law referred to in section 3(a)(47) of the Securities Exchange Act of 1934 (15 U.S.C. 78c(a)(47)), as amended by this Act, and includes the rules, regulations, and orders issued by the Commission thereunder.

(16) State. The term "State" means any State of the United States, the District of Columbia, Puerto Rico, the Virgin Islands, or any other territory or possession of the United States.

(b) Conforming amendment. Section 3(a)(47) of the Securities Exchange Act of 1934 (15 U.S.C. 78c(a)(47)) is amended by inserting "the Sarbanes-Oxley Act of 2002," before "the Public".

[¶ 1202] Sec. 3. Commission rules and enforcement.

(a) Regulatory action. The Commission shall promulgate such rules and regulations, as may be necessary or appropriate in the public interest or for the protection of investors, and in furtherance of this Act.

(b) Enforcement.

(1) In general. A violation by any person of this Act, any rule or regulation of the Commission issued under this Act, or any rule of the Board shall be treated for all purposes in the same manner as a violation of the Securities Exchange Act of 1934 (15 U.S.C. 78a et seq.) or the rules and regulations issued thereunder, consistent with the provisions of this Act, and any such person shall be subject to the same penalties, and to the same extent, as for a violation of that Act or such rules or regulations.

(2) Investigations, injunctions, and prosecution of offenses. Section 21 of the Securities Exchange Act of 1934 (15 U.S.C. 78u) is amended—

(A) in subsection (a)(1), by inserting "the rules of the Public Company Accounting Oversight Board, of which such person is a registered public accounting firm or a person associated with such a firm," after "is a participant,";

(B) in subsection (d)(1), by inserting "the rules of the Public Company Accounting Oversight Board, of which such person is a registered public accounting firm or a person associated with such a firm," after "is a participant,";

(C) in subsection (e), by inserting "the rules of the Public Company Accounting Oversight Board, of which such person is a registered public accounting firm or a person associated with such a firm," after "is a participant,"; and

(D) in subsection (f), by inserting "or the Public Company Accounting Oversight Board" after "self-regulatory organization" each place that term appears.

(3) Cease-and-desist proceedings. Section 21C(c)(2) of the Securities Exchange Act of 1934 (15 U.S.C. 78u-3(c)(2)) is amended by inserting "registered public accounting firm (as defined in section 2 of the Sarbanes-Oxley Act of 2002)," after "government securities dealer,".

(4) Enforcement by Federal banking agencies. Section 12(i) of the Securities Exchange Act of 1934 (15 U.S.C. 78l(i)) is amended by —

(A) striking "sections 12," each place it appears and inserting "sections 10A(m), 12,"; and

(B) striking "and 16," each place it appears and inserting "and 16 of this Act, and sections 302, 303, 304, 306, 401(b), 404, 406, and 407 of the Sarbanes-Oxley Act of 2002,".

(c) Effect on Commission authority. Nothing in this Act or the rules of the Board shall be construed to impair or limit—

(1) the authority of the Commission to regulate the accounting profession, accounting firms, or persons associated with such firms for purposes of enforcement of the securities laws;

(2) the authority of the Commission to set standards for accounting or auditing practices or auditor independence, derived from other provisions of the securities laws or the rules or regulations thereunder, for purposes of the preparation and issuance of any audit report, or otherwise under applicable law; or

(3) the ability of the Commission to take, on the initiative of the Commission, legal, administrative, or disciplinary action against any registered public accounting firm or any associated person thereof.

TITLE I— PUBLIC COMPANY ACCOUNTING OVERSIGHT BOARD

[¶ 1203] Sec. 101. Establishment; administrative provisions.

(a) Establishment of Board. There is established the Public Company Accounting Oversight Board, to oversee the audit of public companies that are subject to the securities laws, and related matters, in order to protect the interests of investors and further the public interest in the preparation of informative, accurate, and independent audit reports for companies the securities of which are sold to, and held by and for, public investors. The Board shall be a body corporate, operate as a nonprofit corporation, and have succession until dissolved by an Act of Congress.

(b) Status. The Board shall not be an agency or establishment of the United States Government, and, except as otherwise provided in this Act, shall be subject to, and have all the powers conferred upon a nonprofit corporation by, the District of Columbia Nonprofit Corporation Act. No member or person employed by, or agent for, the Board shall be deemed to be an officer or employee of or agent for the Federal Government by reason of such service.

(c) Duties of the Board. The Board shall, subject to action by the Commission under section 107, and once a determination is made by the Commission under subsection (d) of this section—

(1) register public accounting firms that prepare audit reports for issuers, in accordance with section 102;

(2) establish or adopt, or both, by rule, auditing, quality control, ethics, independence, and other standards relating to the preparation of audit reports for issuers, in accordance with section 103;

(3) conduct inspections of registered public accounting firms, in accordance with section 104 and the rules of the Board;

(4) conduct investigations and disciplinary proceedings concerning, and impose appropriate sanctions where justified upon, registered public accounting firms and associated persons of such firms, in accordance with section 105;

(5) perform such other duties or functions as the Board (or the Commission, by rule or order) determines are necessary or appropriate to promote high professional standards among, and improve the quality of audit services offered by, registered public accounting firms and associated persons thereof, or otherwise to carry out this Act, in order to protect investors, or to further the public interest;

(6) enforce compliance with this Act, the rules of the Board, professional standards, and the securities laws relating to the preparation and issuance of audit reports and the obligations and liabilities of accountants with respect thereto, by registered public accounting firms and associated persons thereof; and

(7) set the budget and manage the operations of the Board and the staff of the Board.

(d) Commission determination. The members of the Board shall take such action (including hiring of staff, proposal of rules, and adoption of initial and transitional auditing and other professional standards) as may be necessary or appropriate to enable the Commission to determine, not later than 270 days after the date of enactment of this Act, that the Board is so organized and has the capacity to carry out the requirements of this title, and to enforce compliance with this title by registered public accounting firms and associated persons thereof. The Commission shall be responsible, prior to the appointment of the Board, for the planning for the establishment and administrative transition to the Board's operation.

(e) Board membership.

(1) **Composition.** The Board shall have 5 members, appointed from among prominent individuals of integrity and reputation who have a demonstrated commitment to the interests of investors and the public, and an understanding of the responsibilities for and nature of the financial disclosures required of issuers under the securities laws and the obligations of accountants with respect to the preparation and issuance of audit reports with respect to such disclosures.

(2) **Limitation.** Two members, and only 2 members, of the Board shall be or have been certified public accountants pursuant to the laws of 1 or more States, provided that, if 1 of those 2 members is the chairperson, he or she may not have been a practicing certified public accountant for at least 5 years prior to his or her appointment to the Board.

(3) **Full-time independent service.** Each member of the Board shall serve on a full-time basis, and may not, concurrent with service on the Board, be employed by any other person or engage in any other professional or business activity. No member of the Board may share in any of the profits of, or receive payments from, a public accounting firm (or any other person, as determined by rule of the Commission), other than fixed continuing payments, subject to such conditions as the Commission may impose, under standard arrangements for the retirement of members of public accounting firms.

(4) **Appointment of Board members.**

(A) Initial Board. Not later than 90 days after the date of enactment of this Act, the Commission, after consultation with the Chairman of the Board of Governors of the Federal Reserve System and the Secretary of the Treasury, shall appoint the chairperson and other initial members of the Board, and shall designate a term of service for each.

(B) Vacancies. A vacancy on the Board shall not affect the powers of the Board, but shall be filled in the same manner as provided for appointments under this section.

(5) Term of service.

(A) In general. The term of service of each Board member shall be 5 years, and until a successor is appointed, except that—

(i) the terms of office of the initial Board members (other than the chairperson) shall expire in annual increments, 1 on each of the first 4 anniversaries of the initial date of appointment; and

(ii) any Board member appointed to fill a vacancy occurring before the expiration of the term for which the predecessor was appointed shall be appointed only for the remainder of that term.

(B) Term limitation. No person may serve as a member of the Board, or as chairperson of the Board, for more than 2 terms, whether or not such terms of service are consecutive.

(6) Removal from office. A member of the Board may be removed by the Commission from office, in accordance with section 107(d)(3), for good cause shown before the expiration of the term of that member.

(f) Powers of the Board. In addition to any authority granted to the Board otherwise in this Act, the Board shall have the power, subject to section 107—

(1) to sue and be sued, complain and defend, in its corporate name and through its own counsel, with the approval of the Commission, in any Federal, State, or other court;

(2) to conduct its operations and maintain offices, and to exercise all other rights and powers authorized by this Act, in any State, without regard to any qualification, licensing, or other provision of law in effect in such State (or a political subdivision thereof);

(3) to lease, purchase, accept gifts or donations of or otherwise acquire, improve, use, sell, exchange, or convey, all of or an interest in any property, wherever situated;

(4) to appoint such employees, accountants, attorneys, and other agents as may be necessary or appropriate, and to determine their qualifications, define their duties, and fix their salaries or other compensation (at a level that is comparable to private sector self-regulatory, accounting, technical, supervisory, or other staff or management positions);

(5) to allocate, assess, and collect accounting support fees established pursuant to section 109, for the Board, and other fees and charges imposed under this title; and

(6) to enter into contracts, execute instruments, incur liabilities, and do any and all other acts and things necessary, appropriate, or incidental to the conduct of its operations and the exercise of its obligations, rights, and powers imposed or granted by this title.

(g) Rules of the Board. The rules of the Board shall, subject to the approval of the Commission—

(1) provide for the operation and administration of the Board, the exercise of its authority, and the performance of its responsibilities under this Act;

(2) permit, as the Board determines necessary or appropriate, delegation by the Board of any of its functions to an individual member or employee of the Board, or to a division of the Board, including functions with respect to hearing, determining, ordering, certifying, reporting, or otherwise acting as to any matter, except that—

(A) the Board shall retain a discretionary right to review any action pursuant to any such delegated function, upon its own motion;

(B) a person shall be entitled to a review by the Board with respect to any matter so delegated, and the decision of the Board upon such review shall be deemed to be the action of the Board for all purposes (including appeal or review thereof); and

(C) if the right to exercise a review described in subparagraph (A) is declined, or if no such review is sought within the time stated in the rules of the Board, then the action taken by the holder of such delegation shall for all purposes, including appeal or review thereof, be deemed to be the action of the Board;

(3) establish ethics rules and standards of conduct for Board members and staff, including a bar on practice before the Board (and the Commission, with respect to Board-related matters) of 1 year for former members of the Board, and appropriate periods (not to exceed 1 year) for former staff of the Board; and

(4) provide as otherwise required by this Act.

(h) Annual report to the Commission. The Board shall submit an annual report (including its audited financial statements) to the Commission, and the Commission shall transmit a copy of that report to the Committee on Banking, Housing, and Urban Affairs of the Senate, and the Committee on Financial Services of the House of Representatives, not later than 30 days after the date of receipt of that report by the Commission.

[¶ 1204] Sec. 102. Registration with the Board.

(a) Mandatory registration. Beginning 180 days after the date of the determination of the Commission under section 101(d), it shall be unlawful for any person that is not a registered public accounting firm to prepare or issue, or to participate in the preparation or issuance of, any audit report with respect to any issuer.

(b) Applications for registration.

(1) Form of application. A public accounting firm shall use such form as the Board may prescribe, by rule, to apply for registration under this section.

(2) Contents of applications. Each public accounting firm shall submit, as part of its application for registration, in such detail as the Board shall specify—

(A) the names of all issuers for which the firm prepared or issued audit reports during the immediately preceding calendar year, and for which the firm expects to prepare or issue audit reports during the current calendar year;

(B) the annual fees received by the firm from each such issuer for audit services, other accounting services, and non-audit services, respectively;

(C) such other current financial information for the most recently completed fiscal year of the firm as the Board may reasonably request;

(D) a statement of the quality control policies of the firm for its accounting and auditing practices;

(E) a list of all accountants associated with the firm who participate in or contribute to the preparation of audit reports, stating the license or certification number of each such person, as well as the State license numbers of the firm itself;

(F) information relating to criminal, civil, or administrative actions or disciplinary proceedings pending against the firm or any associated person of the firm in connection with any audit report;

(G) copies of any periodic or annual disclosure filed by an issuer with the Commission during the immediately preceding calendar year which discloses accounting disagreements between such issuer and the firm in connection with an audit report furnished or prepared by the firm for such issuer; and

(H) such other information as the rules of the Board or the Commission shall specify as necessary or appropriate in the public interest or for the protection of investors.

(3) Consents. Each application for registration under this subsection shall include—

(A) a consent executed by the public accounting firm to cooperation in and compliance with any request for testimony or the production of documents made by the Board in the furtherance of its authority and responsibilities under this title (and an agreement to secure and enforce similar consents from each of the associated persons of the public accounting firm as a condition of their continued employment by or other association with such firm); and

(B) a statement that such firm understands and agrees that cooperation and compliance, as described in the consent required by subparagraph (A), and the securing and enforcement of such consents from its associated persons, in accordance with the rules of the Board, shall be a condition to the continuing effectiveness of the registration of the firm with the Board.

(c) Action on applications.

(1) Timing. The Board shall approve a completed application for registration not later than 45 days after the date of receipt of the application, in accordance with the rules of the Board, unless the Board, prior to such date, issues a written notice of disapproval to, or requests more information from, the prospective registrant.

(2) Treatment. A written notice of disapproval of a completed application under paragraph (1) for registration shall be treated as a disciplinary sanction for purposes of sections 105(d) and 107(c).

(d) Periodic reports. Each registered public accounting firm shall submit an annual report to the Board, and may be required to report more frequently, as necessary to update the information contained in its application for registration under this section, and to provide to the Board such additional information as the Board or the Commission may specify, in accordance with subsection (b)(2).

(e) Public availability. Registration applications and annual reports required by this subsection, or such portions of such applications or reports as may be designated under rules of the Board, shall be made available for public inspection, subject to rules of the Board or the Commission, and to applicable laws relating to the confidentiality of proprietary, personal, or other information contained in such applications or reports, provided that, in all events, the Board shall protect from public disclosure information reasonably identified by the subject accounting firm as proprietary information.

(f) Registration and annual fees. The Board shall assess and collect a registration fee and an annual fee from each registered public accounting firm, in amounts that are sufficient to recover the costs of processing and reviewing applications and annual reports.

[¶ 1205] Sec. 103. Auditing, quality control, and independence standards and rules.

(a) Auditing, quality control, and ethics standards.

(1) In general. The Board shall, by rule, establish, including, to the extent it determines appropriate, through adoption of standards proposed by 1 or more professional groups of accountants designated pursuant to paragraph (3)(A) or advisory groups convened pursuant to paragraph (4), and amend or otherwise modify or alter, such auditing and related attestation standards, such quality control standards, and such ethics standards to be used by registered public accounting firms in the preparation and issuance of audit reports, as required by this Act or the rules of the Commission, or as may be necessary or appropriate in the public interest or for the protection of investors.

(2) Rule requirements. In carrying out paragraph (1), the Board—

(A) shall include in the auditing standards that it adopts, requirements that each registered public accounting firm shall—

(i) prepare, and maintain for a period of not less than 7 years, audit work papers, and other information related to any audit report, in sufficient detail to support the conclusions reached in such report;

(ii) provide a concurring or second partner review and approval of such audit report (and other related information), and concurring approval in its issuance, by a qualified person (as prescribed by the Board) associated with the public accounting firm, other than the person in charge of the audit, or by an independent reviewer (as prescribed by the Board); and

(iii) describe in each audit report the scope of the auditor's testing of the internal control structure and procedures of the issuer, required by section 404(b), and present (in such report or in a separate report)—

> (I) the findings of the auditor from such testing;
> (II) an evaluation of whether such internal control structure and procedures—
>> (aa) include maintenance of records that in reasonable detail accurately and fairly reflect the transactions and dispositions of the assets of the issuer;
>> (bb) provide reasonable assurance that transactions are recorded as necessary to permit preparation of financial statements in accordance with generally accepted accounting principles, and that receipts and expenditures of the issuer are being made only in accordance with authorizations of management and directors of the issuer; and
> (III) a description, at a minimum, of material weaknesses in such internal controls, and of any material noncompliance found on the basis of such testing.

(B) shall include, in the quality control standards that it adopts with respect to the issuance of audit reports, requirements for every registered public accounting firm relating to—

(i) monitoring of professional ethics and independence from issuers on behalf of which the firm issues audit reports;

(ii) consultation within such firm on accounting and auditing questions;

(iii) supervision of audit work;

(iv) hiring, professional development, and advancement of personnel;

(v) the acceptance and continuation of engagements;

(vi) internal inspection; and

(vii) such other requirements as the Board may prescribe, subject to subsection (a)(1).

(3) Authority to adopt other standards.

(A) In general. In carrying out this subsection, the Board—

(i) may adopt as its rules, subject to the terms of section 107, any portion of any statement of auditing standards or other professional standards that the Board determines satisfy the requirements of paragraph (1), and that were proposed by 1 or more professional groups of accountants that shall be designated or recognized by the Board, by rule, for such purpose, pursuant to this paragraph or 1 or more advisory groups convened pursuant to paragraph (4); and

(ii) notwithstanding clause (i), shall retain full authority to modify, supplement, revise, or subsequently amend, modify, or repeal, in whole or in part, any portion of any statement described in clause (i).

(B) Initial and transitional standards. The Board shall adopt standards described in subparagraph (A)(i) as initial or transitional standards, to the extent the Board determines necessary, prior to a determination of the Commission under section 101(d), and such standards shall be separately approved by the Commission at the time of that determination, without regard to the procedures required by section 107 that otherwise would apply to the approval of rules of the Board.

(4) Advisory groups. The Board shall convene, or authorize its staff to convene, such expert advisory groups as may be appropriate, which may include practicing accountants and other experts, as well as representatives of other interested groups, subject to such rules as the Board may prescribe to prevent conflicts of interest, to make recommendations concerning the content (including proposed drafts) of auditing, quality control, ethics, independence, or other standards required to be established under this section.

(b) Independence standards and rules. The Board shall establish such rules as may be necessary or appropriate in the public interest or for the protection of investors, to implement, or as authorized under, title II of this Act.

(c) Cooperation with designated professional groups of accountants and advisory groups.
   (1) In general. The Board shall cooperate on an ongoing basis with professional groups of accountants designated under subsection (a)(3)(A) and advisory groups convened under subsection (a)(4) in the examination of the need for changes in any standards subject to its authority under subsection (a), recommend issues for inclusion on the agendas of such designated professional groups of accountants or advisory groups, and take such other steps as it deems appropriate to increase the effectiveness of the standard setting process.
   (2) Board responses. The Board shall respond in a timely fashion to requests from designated professional groups of accountants and advisory groups referred to in paragraph (1) for any changes in standards over which the Board has authority.

(d) Evaluation of standard setting process. The Board shall include in the annual report required by section 101(h) the results of its standard setting responsibilities during the period to which the report relates, including a discussion of the work of the Board with any designated professional groups of accountants and advisory groups described in paragraphs (3)(A) and (4) of subsection (a), and its pending issues agenda for future standard setting projects.

[¶ 1206] Sec. 104. Inspections of registered public accounting firms.

(a) In general. The Board shall conduct a continuing program of inspections to assess the degree of compliance of each registered public accounting firm and associated persons of that firm with this Act, the rules of the Board, the rules of the Commission, or professional standards, in connection with its performance of audits, issuance of audit reports, and related matters involving issuers.

(b) Inspection frequency.
   (1) In general. Subject to paragraph (2), inspections required by this section shall be conducted—
      (A) annually with respect to each registered public accounting firm that regularly provides audit reports for more than 100 issuers; and
      (B) not less frequently than once every 3 years with respect to each registered public accounting firm that regularly provides audit reports for 100 or fewer issuers.
   (2) Adjustments to schedules. The Board may, by rule, adjust the inspection schedules set under paragraph (1) if the Board finds that different inspection schedules are consistent with the purposes of this Act, the public interest, and the protection of investors. The Board may conduct special inspections at the request of the Commission or upon its own motion.

(c) Procedures. The Board shall, in each inspection under this section, and in accordance with its rules for such inspections—
   (1) identify any act or practice or omission to act by the registered public accounting firm, or by any associated person thereof, revealed by such inspection that may be in violation of this Act, the rules of the Board, the rules of the Commission, the firm's own quality control policies, or professional standards;
   (2) report any such act, practice, or omission, if appropriate, to the Commission and each appropriate State regulatory authority; and

(3) begin a formal investigation or take disciplinary action, if appropriate, with respect to any such violation, in accordance with this Act and the rules of the Board.

(d) Conduct of inspections. In conducting an inspection of a registered public accounting firm under this section, the Board shall—

(1) inspect and review selected audit and review engagements of the firm (which may include audit engagements that are the subject of ongoing litigation or other controversy between the firm and 1 or more third parties), performed at various offices and by various associated persons of the firm, as selected by the Board;

(2) evaluate the sufficiency of the quality control system of the firm, and the manner of the documentation and communication of that system by the firm; and

(3) perform such other testing of the audit, supervisory, and quality control procedures of the firm as are necessary or appropriate in light of the purpose of the inspection and the responsibilities of the Board.

(e) Record retention. The rules of the Board may require the retention by registered public accounting firms for inspection purposes of records whose retention is not otherwise required by section 103 or the rules issued thereunder.

(f) Procedures for review. The rules of the Board shall provide a procedure for the review of and response to a draft inspection report by the registered public accounting firm under inspection. The Board shall take such action with respect to such response as it considers appropriate (including revising the draft report or continuing or supplementing its inspection activities before issuing a final report), but the text of any such response, appropriately redacted to protect information reasonably identified by the accounting firm as confidential, shall be attached to and made part of the inspection report.

(g) Report. A written report of the findings of the Board for each inspection under this section, subject to subsection (h), shall be—

(1) transmitted, in appropriate detail, to the Commission and each appropriate State regulatory authority, accompanied by any letter or comments by the Board or the inspector, and any letter of response from the registered public accounting firm; and

(2) made available in appropriate detail to the public (subject to section 105(b)(5)(A), and to the protection of such confidential and proprietary information as the Board may determine to be appropriate, or as may be required by law), except that no portions of the inspection report that deal with criticisms of or potential defects in the quality control systems of the firm under inspection shall be made public if those criticisms or defects are addressed by the firm, to the satisfaction of the Board, not later than 12 months after the date of the inspection report.

(h) Interim Commission review.

(1) **Reviewable matters.** A registered public accounting firm may seek review by the Commission, pursuant to such rules as the Commission shall promulgate, if the firm—

(A) has provided the Board with a response, pursuant to rules issued by the Board under subsection (f), to the substance of particular items in a draft inspection report, and disagrees with the assessments contained in any final report prepared by the Board following such response; or

(B) disagrees with the determination of the Board that criticisms or defects identified in an inspection report have not been addressed to the satisfaction of the Board within 12 months of the date of the inspection report, for purposes of subsection (g)(2).

(2) **Treatment of review.** Any decision of the Commission with respect to a review under paragraph (1) shall not be reviewable under section 25 of the Securities Exchange Act of 1934 (15 U.S.C. 78y), or deemed to be "final agency action" for purposes of section 704 of title 5, United States Code.

(3) Timing. Review under paragraph (1) may be sought during the 30-day period following the date of the event giving rise to the review under subparagraph (A) or (B) of paragraph (1).

[¶ 1207] Sec. 105. Investigations and disciplinary proceedings.

(a) In general. The Board shall establish, by rule, subject to the requirements of this section, fair procedures for the investigation and disciplining of registered public accounting firms and associated persons of such firms.

(b) Investigations.
   (1) Authority. In accordance with the rules of the Board, the Board may conduct an investigation of any act or practice, or omission to act, by a registered public accounting firm, any associated person of such firm, or both, that may violate any provision of this Act, the rules of the Board, the provisions of the securities laws relating to the preparation and issuance of audit reports and the obligations and liabilities of accountants with respect thereto, including the rules of the Commission issued under this Act, or professional standards, regardless of how the act, practice, or omission is brought to the attention of the Board.
   (2) Testimony and document production. In addition to such other actions as the Board determines to be necessary or appropriate, the rules of the Board may—
     (A) require the testimony of the firm or of any person associated with a registered public accounting firm, with respect to any matter that the Board considers relevant or material to an investigation;
     (B) require the production of audit work papers and any other document or information in the possession of a registered public accounting firm or any associated person thereof, wherever domiciled, that the Board considers relevant or material to the investigation, and may inspect the books and records of such firm or associated person to verify the accuracy of any documents or information supplied;
     (C) request the testimony of, and production of any document in the possession of, any other person, including any client of a registered public accounting firm that the Board considers relevant or material to an investigation under this section, with appropriate notice, subject to the needs of the investigation, as permitted under the rules of the Board; and
     (D) provide for procedures to seek issuance by the Commission, in a manner established by the Commission, of a subpoena to require the testimony of, and production of any document in the possession of, any person, including any client of a registered public accounting firm, that the Board considers relevant or material to an investigation under this section.
   (3) Noncooperation with investigations.
     (A) In general. If a registered public accounting firm or any associated person thereof refuses to testify, produce documents, or otherwise cooperate with the Board in connection with an investigation under this section, the Board may—
       (i) suspend or bar such person from being associated with a registered public accounting firm, or require the registered public accounting firm to end such association;
       (ii) suspend or revoke the registration of the public accounting firm; and
       (iii) invoke such other lesser sanctions as the Board considers appropriate, and as specified by rule of the Board.
     (B) Procedure. Any action taken by the Board under this paragraph shall be subject to the terms of section 107(c).
   (4) Coordination and referral of investigations.
     (A) Coordination. The Board shall notify the Commission of any pending Board investigation involving a potential violation of the securities laws, and thereafter coordinate its work with the work of the Commission's Division of Enforcement, as necessary to protect an ongoing Commission investigation.

(B) Referral. The Board may refer an investigation under this section—

(i) to the Commission;

(ii) to any other Federal functional regulator (as defined in section 509 of the Gramm-Leach-Bliley Act (15 U.S.C. 6809)), in the case of an investigation that concerns an audit report for an institution that is subject to the jurisdiction of such regulator; and

(iii) at the direction of the Commission, to—

(I) the Attorney General of the United States;

(II) the attorney general of 1 or more States; and

(III) the appropriate State regulatory authority.

(5) Use of documents.

(A) Confidentiality. Except as provided in subparagraph (B), all documents and information prepared or received by or specifically for the Board, and deliberations of the Board and its employees and agents, in connection with an inspection under section 104 or with an investigation under this section, shall be confidential and privileged as an evidentiary matter (and shall not be subject to civil discovery or other legal process) in any proceeding in any Federal or State court or administrative agency, and shall be exempt from disclosure, in the hands of an agency or establishment of the Federal Government, under the Freedom of Information Act (5 U.S.C. 552a), or otherwise, unless and until presented in connection with a public proceeding or released in accordance with subsection (c).

(B) Availability to government agencies. Without the loss of its status as confidential and privileged in the hands of the Board, all information referred to in subparagraph (A) may—

(i) be made available to the Commission; and

(ii) in the discretion of the Board, when determined by the Board to be necessary to accomplish the purposes of this Act or to protect investors, be made available to—

(I) the Attorney General of the United States;

(II) the appropriate Federal functional regulator (as defined in section 509 of the Gramm-Leach-Bliley Act (15 U.S.C. 6809)), other than the Commission, with respect to an audit report for an institution subject to the jurisdiction of such regulator;

(III) State attorneys general in connection with any criminal investigation; and

(IV) any appropriate State regulatory authority, each of which shall maintain such information as confidential and privileged.

(6) Immunity. Any employee of the Board engaged in carrying out an investigation under this Act shall be immune from any civil liability arising out of such investigation in the same manner and to the same extent as an employee of the Federal Government in similar circumstances.

(c) Disciplinary procedures.

(1) Notification; recordkeeping. The rules of the Board shall provide that in any proceeding by the Board to determine whether a registered public accounting firm, or an associated person thereof, should be disciplined, the Board shall—

(A) bring specific charges with respect to the firm or associated person;

(B) notify such firm or associated person of, and provide to the firm or associated person an opportunity to defend against, such charges; and

(C) keep a record of the proceedings.

(2) Public hearings. Hearings under this section shall not be public, unless otherwise ordered by the Board for good cause shown, with the consent of the parties to such hearing.

(3) Supporting statement. A determination by the Board to impose a sanction under this subsection shall be supported by a statement setting forth—

(A) each act or practice in which the registered public accounting firm, or associated person, has engaged (or omitted to engage), or that forms a basis for all or a part of such sanction;

(B) the specific provision of this Act, the securities laws, the rules of the Board, or professional standards which the Board determines has been violated; and

(C) the sanction imposed, including a justification for that sanction.

(4) Sanctions. If the Board finds, based on all of the facts and circumstances, that a registered public accounting firm or associated person thereof has engaged in any act or practice, or omitted to act, in violation of this Act, the rules of the Board, the provisions of the securities laws relating to the preparation and issuance of audit reports and the obligations and liabilities of accountants with respect thereto, including the rules of the Commission issued under this Act, or professional standards, the Board may impose such disciplinary or remedial sanctions as it determines appropriate, subject to applicable limitations under paragraph (5), including—

(A) temporary suspension or permanent revocation of registration under this title;

(B) temporary or permanent suspension or bar of a person from further association with any registered public accounting firm;

(C) temporary or permanent limitation on the activities, functions, or operations of such firm or person (other than in connection with required additional professional education or training);

(D) a civil money penalty for each such violation, in an amount equal to—

(i) not more than $100,000 for a natural person or $2,000,000 for any other person; and

(ii) in any case to which paragraph (5) applies, not more than $750,000 for a natural person or $15,000,000 for any other person;

(E) censure;

(F) required additional professional education or training; or

(G) any other appropriate sanction provided for in the rules of the Board.

(5) Intentional or other knowing conduct. The sanctions and penalties described in subparagraphs (A) through (C) and (D)(ii) of paragraph (4) shall only apply to—

(A) intentional or knowing conduct, including reckless conduct, that results in violation of the applicable statutory, regulatory, or professional standard; or

(B) repeated instances of negligent conduct, each resulting in a violation of the applicable statutory, regulatory, or professional standard.

(6) Failure to supervise.

(A) In general. The Board may impose sanctions under this section on a registered accounting firm or upon the supervisory personnel of such firm, if the Board finds that—

(i) the firm has failed reasonably to supervise an associated person, either as required by the rules of the Board relating to auditing or quality control standards, or otherwise, with a view to preventing violations of this Act, the rules of the Board, the provisions of the securities laws relating to the preparation and issuance of audit reports and the obligations and liabilities of accountants with respect thereto, including the rules of the Commission under this Act, or professional standards; and

(ii) such associated person commits a violation of this Act, or any of such rules, laws, or standards.

(B) Rule of construction. No associated person of a registered public accounting firm shall be deemed to have failed reasonably to supervise any other person for purposes of subparagraph (A), if—

(i) there have been established in and for that firm procedures, and a system for applying such procedures, that comply with applicable rules of the Board and that would reasonably be expected to prevent and detect any such violation by such associated person; and

(ii) such person has reasonably discharged the duties and obligations incumbent upon that person by reason of such procedures and system, and had no reasonable cause to believe that such procedures and system were not being complied with.

(7) Effect of suspension.

(A) Association with a public accounting firm. It shall be unlawful for any person that is suspended or barred from being associated with a registered public accounting firm under this subsection willfully to become or remain associated with any registered public accounting firm, or for any registered public accounting firm that knew, or, in the exercise of reasonable care should have known, of the suspension or bar, to permit such an association, without the consent of the Board or the Commission.

(B) Association with an issuer. It shall be unlawful for any person that is suspended or barred from being associated with an issuer under this subsection willfully to become or remain associated with any issuer in an accountancy or a financial management capacity, and for any issuer that knew, or in the exercise of reasonable care should have known, of such suspension or bar, to permit such an association, without the consent of the Board or the Commission.

(d) Reporting of sanctions.

(1) Recipients. If the Board imposes a disciplinary sanction, in accordance with this section, the Board shall report the sanction to—

(A) the Commission;

(B) any appropriate State regulatory authority or any foreign accountancy licensing Board with which such firm or person is licensed or certified; and

(C) the public (once any stay on the imposition of such sanction has been lifted).

(2) Contents. The information reported under paragraph (1) shall include—

(A) the name of the sanctioned person;

(B) a description of the sanction and the basis for its imposition; and

(C) such other information as the Board deems appropriate.

(e) Stay of sanctions.

(1) In general. Application to the Commission for review, or the institution by the Commission of review, of any disciplinary action of the Board shall operate as a stay of any such disciplinary action, unless and until the Commission orders (summarily or after notice and opportunity for hearing on the question of a stay, which hearing may consist solely of the submission of affidavits or presentation of oral arguments) that no such stay shall continue to operate.

(2) Expedited procedures. The Commission shall establish for appropriate cases an expedited procedure for consideration and determination of the question of the duration of a stay pending review of any disciplinary action of the Board under this subsection.

[¶ 1208] Sec. 106. Foreign public accounting firms.

(a) Applicability to certain foreign firms.

(1) In general. Any foreign public accounting firm that prepares or furnishes an audit report with respect to any issuer, shall be subject to this Act and the rules of the Board and the Commission issued under this Act, in the same manner and to the same extent as a public accounting firm that is organized and operates under the laws of the United States or any State, except that registration pursuant to section 102 shall not by itself provide a basis for subjecting such a foreign public accounting firm to the jurisdiction of the Federal or State courts, other than with respect to controversies between such firms and the Board.

(2) Board authority. The Board may, by rule, determine that a foreign public accounting firm (or a class of such firms) that does not issue audit reports nonetheless plays such a substantial role in the preparation and furnishing of such reports for particular issuers, that it is necessary or appropriate, in light of the purposes of this Act and in the public interest or for the protection of investors, that such firm (or class of firms) should be treated as a public accounting firm (or firms) for purposes of registration under, and oversight by the Board in accordance with, this title.

(b) Production of audit workpapers.

(1) Consent by foreign firms. If a foreign public accounting firm issues an opinion or otherwise performs material services upon which a registered public accounting firm relies in issuing all or part of any audit report or any opinion contained in an audit report, that foreign public accounting firm shall be deemed to have consented—

(A) to produce its audit workpapers for the Board or the Commission in connection with any investigation by either body with respect to that audit report; and

(B) to be subject to the jurisdiction of the courts of the United States for purposes of enforcement of any request for production of such workpapers.

(2) Consent by domestic firms. A registered public accounting firm that relies upon the opinion of a foreign public accounting firm, as described in paragraph (1), shall be deemed—

(A) to have consented to supplying the audit workpapers of that foreign public accounting firm in response to a request for production by the Board or the Commission; and

(B) to have secured the agreement of that foreign public accounting firm to such production, as a condition of its reliance on the opinion of that foreign public accounting firm.

(c) Exemption authority. The Commission, and the Board, subject to the approval of the Commission, may, by rule, regulation, or order, and as the Commission (or Board) determines necessary or appropriate in the public interest or for the protection of investors, either unconditionally or upon specified terms and conditions exempt any foreign public accounting firm, or any class of such firms, from any provision of this Act or the rules of the Board or the Commission issued under this Act.

(d) Definition. In this section, the term "foreign public accounting firm" means a public accounting firm that is organized and operates under the laws of a foreign government or political subdivision thereof.

[¶ 1209] Sec. 107. Commission oversight of the Board.

(a) General oversight responsibility. The Commission shall have oversight and enforcement authority over the Board, as provided in this Act. The provisions of section 17(a)(1) of the Securities Exchange Act of 1934 (15 U.S.C. 78q(a)(1)), and of section 17(b)(1) of the Securities Exchange Act of 1934 (15 U.S.C. 78q(b)(1)) shall apply to the Board as fully as if the Board were a "registered securities association" for purposes of those sections 17(a)(1) and 17(b)(1).

(b) Rules of the Board.

(1) Definition. In this section, the term "proposed rule" means any proposed rule of the Board, and any modification of any such rule.

(2) Prior approval required. No rule of the Board shall become effective without prior approval of the Commission in accordance with this section, other than as provided in section 103(a)(3)(B) with respect to initial or transitional standards.

(3) Approval criteria. The Commission shall approve a proposed rule, if it finds that the rule is consistent with the requirements of this Act and the securities laws, or is necessary or appropriate in the public interest or for the protection of investors.

(4) Proposed rule procedures. The provisions of paragraphs (1) through (3) of section 19(b) of the Securities Exchange Act of 1934 (15 U.S.C. 78s(b)) shall govern the proposed rules of the Board, as fully as if the Board were a "registered securities association" for purposes of that section 19(b), except that, for purposes of this paragraph—

(A) the phrase "consistent with the requirements of this title and the rules and regulations thereunder applicable to such organization" in section 19(b)(2) of that Act shall be deemed to read "consistent with the requirements of title I of the Sarbanes-Oxley Act of 2002, and the rules and regulations issued thereunder applicable to such organization, or as necessary or appropriate in the public interest or for the protection of investors"; and

(B) the phrase "otherwise in furtherance of the purposes of this title" in section 19(b)(3)(C) of that Act shall be deemed to read "otherwise in furtherance of the purposes of title I of the Sarbanes-Oxley Act of 2002".

(5) Commission authority to amend rules of the Board. The provisions of section 19(c) of the Securities Exchange Act of 1934 (15 U.S.C. 78s(c)) shall govern the abrogation, deletion, or addition to portions of the rules of the Board by the Commission as fully as if the Board were a "registered securities association" for purposes of that section 19(c), except that the phrase "to conform its rules to the requirements of this title and the rules and regulations thereunder applicable to such organization, or otherwise in furtherance of the purposes of this title" in section 19(c) of that Act shall, for purposes of this paragraph, be deemed to read "to assure the fair administration of the Public Company Accounting Oversight Board, conform the rules promulgated by that Board to the requirements of title I of the Sarbanes-Oxley Act of 2002, or otherwise further the purposes of that Act, the securities laws, and the rules and regulations thereunder applicable to that Board".

(c) Commission review of disciplinary action taken by the Board.

(1) Notice of sanction. The Board shall promptly file notice with the Commission of any final sanction on any registered public accounting firm or on any associated person thereof, in such form and containing such information as the Commission, by rule, may prescribe.

(2) Review of sanctions. The provisions of sections 19(d)(2) and 19(e)(1) of the Securities Exchange Act of 1934 (15 U.S.C. 78s(d)(2) and (e)(1)) shall govern the review by the Commission of final disciplinary sanctions imposed by the Board (including sanctions imposed under section 105(b)(3) of this Act for noncooperation in an investigation of the Board), as fully as if the Board were a self-regulatory organization and the Commission were the appropriate regulatory agency for such organization for purposes of those sections 19(d)(2) and 19(e)(1), except that, for purposes of this paragraph—

(A) section 105(e) of this Act (rather than that section 19(d)(2)) shall govern the extent to which application for, or institution by the Commission on its own motion of, review of any disciplinary action of the Board operates as a stay of such action;

(B) references in that section 19(e)(1) to "members" of such an organization shall be deemed to be references to registered public accounting firms;

(C) the phrase "consistent with the purposes of this title" in that section 19(e)(1) shall be deemed to read "consistent with the purposes of this title and title I of the Sarbanes-Oxley Act of 2002";

(D) references to rules of the Municipal Securities Rulemaking Board in that section 19(e)(1) shall not apply; and

(E) the reference to section 19(e)(2) of the Securities Exchange Act of 1934 shall refer instead to section 107(c)(3) of this Act.

(3) Commission modification authority. The Commission may enhance, modify, cancel, reduce, or require the remission of a sanction imposed by the Board upon a registered public accounting firm or associated person thereof, if the Commission, having due regard for the public interest and the protection of investors, finds, after a proceeding in accordance with this subsection, that the sanction—

(A) is not necessary or appropriate in furtherance of this Act or the securities laws; or

(B) is excessive, oppressive, inadequate, or otherwise not appropriate to the finding or the basis on which the sanction was imposed.

(d) Censure of the Board; other sanctions.

(1) Rescission of Board authority. The Commission, by rule, consistent with the public interest, the protection of investors, and the other purposes of this Act and the securities laws, may relieve the Board of any responsibility to enforce compliance with any provision of this Act, the securities laws, the rules of the Board, or professional standards.

(2) Censure of the Board; limitations. The Commission may, by order, as it determines necessary or appropriate in the public interest, for the protection of investors, or otherwise in furtherance of the purposes of this Act or the securities laws, censure or impose limitations upon the activities, functions, and operations of the Board, if the Commission finds, on the record, after notice and opportunity for a hearing, that the Board—

(A) has violated or is unable to comply with any provision of this Act, the rules of the Board, or the securities laws; or

(B) without reasonable justification or excuse, has failed to enforce compliance with any such provision or rule, or any professional standard by a registered public accounting firm or an associated person thereof.

(3) Censure of Board members; removal from office. The Commission may, as necessary or appropriate in the public interest, for the protection of investors, or otherwise in furtherance of the purposes of this Act or the securities laws, remove from office or censure any member of the Board, if the Commission finds, on the record, after notice and opportunity for a hearing, that such member—

(A) has willfully violated any provision of this Act, the rules of the Board, or the securities laws;

(B) has willfully abused the authority of that member; or

(C) without reasonable justification or excuse, has failed to enforce compliance with any such provision or rule, or any professional standard by any registered public accounting firm or any associated person thereof.

[¶ 1210] Sec. 108. Accounting standards.

(a) Amendment to Securities Act of 1933. Section 19 of the Securities Act of 1933 (15 U.S.C. 77s) is amended—

(1) by redesignating subsections (b) and (c) as subsections (c) and (d), respectively; and

(2) by inserting after subsection (a) the following:

"(b) RECOGNITION OF ACCOUNTING STANDARDS—

"(1) IN GENERAL- In carrying out its authority under subsection (a) and under section 13(b) of the Securities Exchange Act of 1934, the Commission may recognize, as 'generally accepted' for purposes of the securities laws, any accounting principles established by a standard setting body—

"(A) that—

"(i) is organized as a private entity;

"(ii) has, for administrative and operational purposes, a board of trustees (or equivalent body) serving in the public interest, the majority of whom are not, concurrent with their service on such Board, and have not been during the 2-year period preceding such service, associated persons of any registered public accounting firm;

"(iii) is funded as provided in section 109 of the Sarbanes-Oxley Act of 2002;

"(iv) has adopted procedures to ensure prompt consideration, by majority vote of its members, of changes to accounting principles necessary to reflect emerging accounting issues and changing business practices; and

"(v) considers, in adopting accounting principles, the need to keep standards current in order to reflect changes in the business environment, the extent to which international convergence on high quality accounting standards is necessary or appropriate in the public interest and for the protection of investors; and

"(B) that the Commission determines has the capacity to assist the Commission in fulfilling the requirements of subsection (a) and section 13(b) of the Securities Exchange Act of

1934, because, at a minimum, the standard setting body is capable of improving the accuracy and effectiveness of financial reporting and the protection of investors under the securities laws.

"(2) ANNUAL REPORT- A standard setting body described in paragraph (1) shall submit an annual report to the Commission and the public, containing audited financial statements of that standard setting body.".

(b) Commission authority. The Commission shall promulgate such rules and regulations to carry out section 19(b) of the Securities Act of 1933, as added by this section, as it deems necessary or appropriate in the public interest or for the protection of investors.

(c) No effect on Commission powers. Nothing in this Act, including this section and the amendment made by this section, shall be construed to impair or limit the authority of the Commission to establish accounting principles or standards for purposes of enforcement of the securities laws.

(d) Study and report on adopting principles-based accounting.
  (1) Study.
    (A) In general. The Commission shall conduct a study on the adoption by the United States financial reporting system of a principles-based accounting system.
    (B) Study topics. The study required by subparagraph (A) shall include an examination of—
      (i) the extent to which principles-based accounting and financial reporting exists in the United States;
      (ii) the length of time required for change from a rules-based to a principles-based financial reporting system;
      (iii) the feasibility of and proposed methods by which a principles-based system may be implemented; and
      (iv) a thorough economic analysis of the implementation of a principles-based system.
  (2) Report. Not later than 1 year after the date of enactment of this Act, the Commission shall submit a report on the results of the study required by paragraph (1) to the Committee on Banking, Housing, and Urban Affairs of the Senate and the Committee on Financial Services of the House of Representatives.

[¶ 1211] Sec. 109. Funding.

(a) In general. The Board, and the standard setting body designated pursuant to section 19(b) of the Securities Act of 1933, as amended by section 108, shall be funded as provided in this section.

(b) Annual budgets. The Board and the standard setting body referred to in subsection (a) shall each establish a budget for each fiscal year, which shall be reviewed and approved according to their respective internal procedures not less than 1 month prior to the commencement of the fiscal year to which the budget pertains (or at the beginning of the Board's first fiscal year, which may be a short fiscal year). The budget of the Board shall be subject to approval by the Commission. The budget for the first fiscal year of the Board shall be prepared and approved promptly following the appointment of the initial five Board members, to permit action by the Board of the organizational tasks contemplated by section 101(d).

(c) Sources and uses of funds.
  (1) Recoverable budget expenses. The budget of the Board (reduced by any registration or annual fees received under section 102(e) for the year preceding the year for which the budget is being computed), and all of the budget of the standard setting body referred to in subsection (a), for each fiscal year of each of those 2 entities, shall be payable from annual accounting support fees, in accordance with subsections (d) and (e). Accounting support

fees and other receipts of the Board and of such standard-setting body shall not be considered public monies of the United States.

(2) Funds generated from the collection of monetary penalties. Subject to the availability in advance in an appropriations Act, and notwithstanding subsection (i), all funds collected by the Board as a result of the assessment of monetary penalties shall be used to fund a merit scholarship program for undergraduate and graduate students enrolled in accredited accounting degree programs, which program is to be administered by the Board or by an entity or agent identified by the Board.

(d) Annual accounting support fee for the Board.

(1) Establishment of fee. The Board shall establish, with the approval of the Commission, a reasonable annual accounting support fee (or a formula for the computation thereof), as may be necessary or appropriate to establish and maintain the Board. Such fee may also cover costs incurred in the Board's first fiscal year (which may be a short fiscal year), or may be levied separately with respect to such short fiscal year.

(2) Assessments. The rules of the Board under paragraph (1) shall provide for the equitable allocation, assessment, and collection by the Board (or an agent appointed by the Board) of the fee established under paragraph (1), among issuers, in accordance with subsection (g), allowing for differentiation among classes of issuers, as appropriate.

(e) Annual accounting support fee for standard setting body. The annual accounting support fee for the standard setting body referred to in subsection (a)—

(1) shall be allocated in accordance with subsection (g), and assessed and collected against each issuer, on behalf of the standard setting body, by 1 or more appropriate designated collection agents, as may be necessary or appropriate to pay for the budget and provide for the expenses of that standard setting body, and to provide for an independent, stable source of funding for such body, subject to review by the Commission; and

(2) may differentiate among different classes of issuers.

(f) Limitation on fee. The amount of fees collected under this section for a fiscal year on behalf of the Board or the standards setting body, as the case may be, shall not exceed the recoverable budget expenses of the Board or body, respectively (which may include operating, capital, and accrued items), referred to in subsection (c)(1).

(g) Allocation of accounting support fees among issuers. Any amount due from issuers (or a particular class of issuers) under this section to fund the budget of the Board or the standard setting body referred to in subsection (a) shall be allocated among and payable by each issuer (or each issuer in a particular class, as applicable) in an amount equal to the total of such amount, multiplied by a fraction—

(1) the numerator of which is the average monthly equity market capitalization of the issuer for the 12-month period immediately preceding the beginning of the fiscal year to which such budget relates; and

(2) the denominator of which is the average monthly equity market capitalization of all such issuers for such 12-month period.

(h) Conforming amendments. Section 13(b)(2) of the Securities Exchange Act of 1934 (15 U.S.C. 78m(b)(2)) is amended—

(1) in subparagraph (A), by striking "and" at the end; and

(2) in subparagraph (B), by striking the period at the end and inserting the following: "; and

"(C) notwithstanding any other provision of law, pay the allocable share of such issuer of a reasonable annual accounting support fee or fees, determined in accordance with section 109 of the Sarbanes-Oxley Act of 2002.".

(i) Rule of construction. Nothing in this section shall be construed to render either the Board, the standard setting body referred to in subsection (a), or both, subject to procedures in Congress to authorize or appropriate public funds, or to prevent such organization from utilizing additional sources of revenue for its activities, such as earnings from publication sales, provided that each additional source of revenue shall not jeopardize, in the judgment of the Commission, the actual and perceived independence of such organization.

(j) Start-up expenses of the Board. From the unexpended balances of the appropriations to the Commission for fiscal year 2003, the Secretary of the Treasury is authorized to advance to the Board not to exceed the amount necessary to cover the expenses of the Board during its first fiscal year (which may be a short fiscal year).

TITLE II— AUDITOR INDEPENDENCE

[¶ 1212] Sec. 201. Services outside the scope of practice of auditors.

(a) Prohibited activities. Section 10A of the Securities Exchange Act of 1934 (15 U.S.C. 78j-1) is amended by adding at the end the following:

"(g) PROHIBITED ACTIVITIES- Except as provided in subsection (h), it shall be unlawful for a registered public accounting firm (and any associated person of that firm, to the extent determined appropriate by the Commission) that performs for any issuer any audit required by this title or the rules of the Commission under this title or, beginning 180 days after the date of commencement of the operations of the Public Company Accounting Oversight Board established under section 101 of the Sarbanes-Oxley Act of 2002 (in this section referred to as the 'Board'), the rules of the Board, to provide to that issuer, contemporaneously with the audit, any non-audit service, including—

"(1) bookkeeping or other services related to the accounting records or financial statements of the audit client;

"(2) financial information systems design and implementation;

"(3) appraisal or valuation services, fairness opinions, or contribution-in-kind reports;

"(4) actuarial services;

"(5) internal audit outsourcing services;

"(6) management functions or human resources;

"(7) broker or dealer, investment adviser, or investment banking services;

"(8) legal services and expert services unrelated to the audit; and

"(9) any other service that the Board determines, by regulation, is impermissible.

"(h) PREAPPROVAL REQUIRED FOR NON-AUDIT SERVICES- A registered public accounting firm may engage in any non-audit service, including tax services, that is not described in any of paragraphs (1) through (9) of subsection (g) for an audit client, only if the activity is approved in advance by the audit committee of the issuer, in accordance with subsection (i).".

(b) Exemption authority. The Board may, on a case by case basis, exempt any person, issuer, public accounting firm, or transaction from the prohibition on the provision of services under section 10A(g) of the Securities Exchange Act of 1934 (as added by this section), to the extent that such exemption is necessary or appropriate in the public interest and is consistent with the protection of investors, and subject to review by the Commission in the same manner as for rules of the Board under section 107.

[¶ 1213] Sec. 202. Preapproval requirements. Section 10A of the Securities Exchange Act of 1934 (15 U.S.C. 78j-1), as amended by this Act, is amended by adding at the end the following:

"(i) PREAPPROVAL REQUIREMENTS—

"(1) IN GENERAL—

"(A) AUDIT COMMITTEE ACTION- All auditing services (which may entail providing comfort letters in connection with securities underwritings or statutory audits required for insurance companies for purposes of State law) and non-audit services, other than as provided in subparagraph (B), provided to an issuer by the auditor of the issuer shall be preapproved by the audit committee of the issuer.

"(B) DE MINIMUS EXCEPTION- The preapproval requirement under subparagraph (A) is waived with respect to the provision of non-audit services for an issuer, if—

"(i) the aggregate amount of all such non-audit services provided to the issuer constitutes not more than 5 percent of the total amount of revenues paid by the issuer to its auditor during the fiscal year in which the nonaudit services are provided;

"(ii) such services were not recognized by the issuer at the time of the engagement to be non-audit services; and

"(iii) such services are promptly brought to the attention of the audit committee of the issuer and approved prior to the completion of the audit by the audit committee or by 1 or more members of the audit committee who are members of the Board of directors to whom authority to grant such approvals has been delegated by the audit committee.

"(2) DISCLOSURE TO INVESTORS- Approval by an audit committee of an issuer under this subsection of a non-audit service to be performed by the auditor of the issuer shall be disclosed to investors in periodic reports required by section 13(a).

"(3) DELEGATION AUTHORITY- The audit committee of an issuer may delegate to 1 or more designated members of the audit committee who are independent directors of the Board of directors, the authority to grant preapprovals required by this subsection. The decisions of any member to whom authority is delegated under this paragraph to preapprove an activity under this subsection shall be presented to the full audit committee at each of its scheduled meetings.

"(4) APPROVAL OF AUDIT SERVICES FOR OTHER PURPOSES- In carrying out its duties under subsection (m)(2), if the audit committee of an issuer approves an audit service within the scope of the engagement of the auditor, such audit service shall be deemed to have been preapproved for purposes of this subsection.".

[¶ 1214] Sec. 203. Audit partner rotation. Section 10A of the Securities Exchange Act of 1934 (15 U.S.C. 78j-1), as amended by this Act, is amended by adding at the end the following:

"(j) AUDIT PARTNER ROTATION- It shall be unlawful for a registered public accounting firm to provide audit services to an issuer if the lead (or coordinating) audit partner (having primary responsibility for the audit), or the audit partner responsible for reviewing the audit, has performed audit services for that issuer in each of the 5 previous fiscal years of that issuer.".

[¶ 1215] Sec. 204. Auditor reports to audit committees. Section 10A of the Securities Exchange Act of 1934 (15 U.S.C. 78j-1), as amended by this Act, is amended by adding at the end the following:

"(k) REPORTS TO AUDIT COMMITTEES- Each registered public accounting firm that performs for any issuer any audit required by this title shall timely report to the audit committee of the issuer—

"(1) all critical accounting policies and practices to be used;

"(2) all alternative treatments of financial information within generally accepted accounting principles that have been discussed with management officials of the issuer, ramifications of the use of such alternative disclosures and treatments, and the treatment preferred by the registered public accounting firm; and

"(3) other material written communications between the registered public accounting firm and the management of the issuer, such as any management letter or schedule of unadjusted differences.".

[¶ 1216] Sec. 205. Conforming amendments.

(a) Definitions. Section 3(a) of the Securities Exchange Act of 1934 (15 U.S.C. 78c(a)) is amended by adding at the end the following:

"(58) AUDIT COMMITTEE- The term 'audit committee' means—

"(A) a committee (or equivalent body) established by and amongst the board of directors of an issuer for the purpose of overseeing the accounting and financial reporting processes of the issuer and audits of the financial statements of the issuer; and

"(B) if no such committee exists with respect to an issuer, the entire board of directors of the issuer.

"(59) REGISTERED PUBLIC ACCOUNTING FIRM- The term 'registered public accounting firm' has the same meaning as in section 2 of the Sarbanes-Oxley Act of 2002.".

(b) Auditor requirements. Section 10A of the Securities Exchange Act of 1934 (15 U.S.C. 78j-1) is amended—

(1) by striking "an independent public accountant" each place that term appears and inserting "a registered public accounting firm";

(2) by striking "the independent public accountant" each place that term appears and inserting "the registered public accounting firm";

(3) in subsection (c), by striking "No independent public accountant" and inserting "No registered public accounting firm"; and

(4) in subsection (b)—

(A) by striking "the accountant" each place that term appears and inserting "the firm";

(B) by striking "such accountant" each place that term appears and inserting "such firm"; and

(C) in paragraph (4), by striking "the accountant's report" and inserting "the report of the firm".

(c) Other references. The Securities Exchange Act of 1934 (15 U.S.C. 78a et seq.) is amended—

(1) in section 12(b)(1) (15 U.S.C. 78l(b)(1)), by striking "independent public accountants" each place that term appears and inserting "a registered public accounting firm"; and

(2) in subsections (e) and (i) of section 17 (15 U.S.C. 78q), by striking "an independent public accountant" each place that term appears and inserting "a registered public accounting firm".

(d) Conforming amendment. Section 10A(f) of the Securities Exchange Act of 1934 (15 U.S.C. 78k(f)) is amended—

(1) by striking "DEFINITION" and inserting "DEFINITIONS"; and

(2) by adding at the end the following: "As used in this section, the term 'issuer' means an issuer (as defined in section 3), the securities of which are registered under section 12, or that is required to file reports pursuant to section 15(d), or that files or has filed a registration statement that has not yet become effective under the Securities Act of 1933 (15 U.S.C. 77a et seq.), and that it has not withdrawn.".

[¶ 1217] Sec. 206. Conflicts of interest. Section 10A of the Securities Exchange Act of 1934 (15 U.S.C. 78j-1), as amended by this Act, is amended by adding at the end the following:

"(l) CONFLICTS OF INTEREST- It shall be unlawful for a registered public accounting firm to perform for an issuer any audit service required by this title, if a chief executive officer, controller, chief financial officer, chief accounting officer, or any person serving in an equivalent position for the issuer, was employed by that registered independent public accounting firm and participated in any capacity in the audit of that issuer during the 1-year period preceding the date of the initiation of the audit.".

[¶ 1218] Sec. 207. Study of mandatory rotation of registered public accounting firms.

(a) Study and review required. The Comptroller General of the United States shall conduct a study and review of the potential effects of requiring the mandatory rotation of registered public accounting firms.

(b) Report required. Not later than 1 year after the date of enactment of this Act, the Comptroller General shall submit a report to the Committee on Banking, Housing, and Urban Affairs of the Senate and the Committee on Financial Services of the House of Representatives on the results of the study and review required by this section.

(c) Definition. For purposes of this section, the term "mandatory rotation" refers to the imposition of a limit on the period of years in which a particular registered public accounting firm may be the auditor of record for a particular issuer.

[¶ 1219] Sec. 208. Commission authority.

(a) Commission regulations. Not later than 180 days after the date of enactment of this Act, the Commission shall issue final regulations to carry out each of subsections (g) through (l) of section 10A of the Securities Exchange Act of 1934, as added by this title.

(b) Auditor independence. It shall be unlawful for any registered public accounting firm (or an associated person thereof, as applicable) to prepare or issue any audit report with respect to any issuer, if the firm or associated person engages in any activity with respect to that issuer prohibited by any of subsections (g) through (l) of section 10A of the Securities Exchange Act of 1934, as added by this title, or any rule or regulation of the Commission or of the Board issued thereunder.

[¶ 1220] Sec. 209. Considerations by appropriate State regulatory authorities. In supervising nonregistered public accounting firms and their associated persons, appropriate State regulatory authorities should make an independent determination of the proper standards applicable, particularly taking into consideration the size and nature of the business of the accounting firms they supervise and the size and nature of the business of the clients of those firms. The standards applied by the Board under this Act should not be presumed to be applicable for purposes of this section for small and medium sized nonregistered public accounting firms.

TITLE III— CORPORATE RESPONSIBILITY

[¶ 1221] Sec. 301. Public company audit committees. Section 10A of the Securities Exchange Act of 1934 (15 U.S.C. 78f [sic 78j-1]) is amended by adding at the end the following:

"(m) STANDARDS RELATING TO AUDIT COMMITTEES—

"(1) COMMISSION RULES—

"(A) IN GENERAL- Effective not later than 270 days after the date of enactment of this subsection, the Commission shall, by rule, direct the national securities exchanges and national securities associations to prohibit the listing of any security of an issuer that is not in compliance with the requirements of any portion of paragraphs (2) through (6).

"(B) OPPORTUNITY TO CURE DEFECTS- The rules of the Commission under subparagraph (A) shall provide for appropriate procedures for an issuer to have an opportunity to cure any defects that would be the basis for a prohibition under subparagraph (A), before the imposition of such prohibition.

"(2) RESPONSIBILITIES RELATING TO REGISTERED PUBLIC ACCOUNTING FIRMS- The audit committee of each issuer, in its capacity as a committee of the board of directors, shall be directly responsible for the appointment, compensation, and oversight of the work of any registered public accounting firm employed by that issuer (including resolution of disagreements between management and the auditor regarding financial reporting) for the purpose of preparing or issuing an audit report or related work, and each such registered public accounting firm shall report directly to the audit committee.

"(3) INDEPENDENCE—

"(A) IN GENERAL- Each member of the audit committee of the issuer shall be a member of the board of directors of the issuer, and shall otherwise be independent.

"(B) CRITERIA- In order to be considered to be independent for purposes of this paragraph, a member of an audit committee of an issuer may not, other than in his or her capacity as a member of the audit committee, the board of directors, or any other board committee—

"(i) accept any consulting, advisory, or other compensatory fee from the issuer; or

"(ii) be an affiliated person of the issuer or any subsidiary thereof.

"(C) EXEMPTION AUTHORITY- The Commission may exempt from the requirements of subparagraph (B) a particular relationship with respect to audit committee members, as the Commission determines appropriate in light of the circumstances.

"(4) COMPLAINTS- Each audit committee shall establish procedures for—

"(A) the receipt, retention, and treatment of complaints received by the issuer regarding accounting, internal accounting controls, or auditing matters; and

"(B) the confidential, anonymous submission by employees of the issuer of concerns regarding questionable accounting or auditing matters.

"(5) AUTHORITY TO ENGAGE ADVISERS- Each audit committee shall have the authority to engage independent counsel and other advisers, as it determines necessary to carry out its duties.

"(6) FUNDING- Each issuer shall provide for appropriate funding, as determined by the audit committee, in its capacity as a committee of the board of directors, for payment of compensation—

"(A) to the registered public accounting firm employed by the issuer for the purpose of rendering or issuing an audit report; and

"(B) to any advisers employed by the audit committee under paragraph (5).".

[¶ 1222] Sec. 302. Corporate responsibility for financial reports.

(a) Regulations required. The Commission shall, by rule, require, for each company filing periodic reports under section 13(a) or 15(d) of the Securities Exchange Act of 1934 (15 U.S.C. 78m, 78o(d)), that the principal executive officer or officers and the principal financial officer or officers, or persons performing similar functions, certify in each annual or quarterly report filed or submitted under either such section of such Act that—

(1) the signing officer has reviewed the report;

(2) based on the officer's knowledge, the report does not contain any untrue statement of a material fact or omit to state a material fact necessary in order to make the statements made, in light of the circumstances under which such statements were made, not misleading;

(3) based on such officer's knowledge, the financial statements, and other financial information included in the report, fairly present in all material respects the financial condition and results of operations of the issuer as of, and for, the periods presented in the report;

(4) the signing officers—

(A) are responsible for establishing and maintaining internal controls;

(B) have designed such internal controls to ensure that material information relating to the issuer and its consolidated subsidiaries is made known to such officers by others within those entities, particularly during the period in which the periodic reports are being prepared;

(C) have evaluated the effectiveness of the issuer's internal controls as of a date within 90 days prior to the report; and

WG
          &L Warren, Gorham & Lamont

(D) have presented in the report their conclusions about the effectiveness of their internal controls based on their evaluation as of that date;

(5) the signing officers have disclosed to the issuer's auditors and the audit committee of the board of directors (or persons fulfilling the equivalent function)—

(A) all significant deficiencies in the design or operation of internal controls which could adversely affect the issuer's ability to record, process, summarize, and report financial data and have identified for the issuer's auditors any material weaknesses in internal controls; and

(B) any fraud, whether or not material, that involves management or other employees who have a significant role in the issuer's internal controls; and

(6) the signing officers have indicated in the report whether or not there were significant changes in internal controls or in other factors that could significantly affect internal controls subsequent to the date of their evaluation, including any corrective actions with regard to significant deficiencies and material weaknesses.

(b) Foreign reincorporations have no effect. Nothing in this section 302 shall be interpreted or applied in any way to allow any issuer to lessen the legal force of the statement required under this section 302, by an issuer having reincorporated or having engaged in any other transaction that resulted in the transfer of the corporate domicile or offices of the issuer from inside the United States to outside of the United States.

(c) Deadline. The rules required by subsection (a) shall be effective not later than 30 days after the date of enactment of this Act.

[¶ 1223] Sec. 303. Improper influence on conduct of audits.

(a) Rules to prohibit. It shall be unlawful, in contravention of such rules or regulations as the Commission shall prescribe as necessary and appropriate in the public interest or for the protection of investors, for any officer or director of an issuer, or any other person acting under the direction thereof, to take any action to fraudulently influence, coerce, manipulate, or mislead any independent public or certified accountant engaged in the performance of an audit of the financial statements of that issuer for the purpose of rendering such financial statements materially misleading.

(b) Enforcement. In any civil proceeding, the Commission shall have exclusive authority to enforce this section and any rule or regulation issued under this section.

(c) No preemption of other law. The provisions of subsection (a) shall be in addition to, and shall not supersede or preempt, any other provision of law or any rule or regulation issued thereunder.

(d) Deadline for rulemaking. The Commission shall—

(1) propose the rules or regulations required by this section, not later than 90 days after the date of enactment of this Act; and

(2) issue final rules or regulations required by this section, not later than 270 days after that date of enactment.

[¶ 1224] Sec. 304. Forfeiture of certain bonuses and profits.

(a) Additional compensation prior to noncompliance with Commission financial reporting requirements. If an issuer is required to prepare an accounting restatement due to the material noncompliance of the issuer, as a result of misconduct, with any financial reporting requirement under the securities laws, the chief executive officer and chief financial officer of the issuer shall reimburse the issuer for—

(1) any bonus or other incentive-based or equity-based compensation received by that person from the issuer during the 12-month period following the first public issuance or filing with the Commission (whichever first occurs) of the financial document embodying such financial reporting requirement; and

(2) any profits realized from the sale of securities of the issuer during that 12-month period.

(b) Commission exemption authority. The Commission may exempt any person from the application of subsection (a), as it deems necessary and appropriate.

[¶ 1225] Sec. 305. Officer and director bars and penalties.

(a) Unfitness standard.

(1) Securities Exchange Act of 1934. Section 21(d)(2) of the Securities Exchange Act of 1934 (15 U.S.C. 78u(d)(2)) is amended by striking "substantial unfitness" and inserting "unfitness".

(2) Securities Act of 1933. Section 20(e) of the Securities Act of 1933 (15 U.S.C. 77t(e)) is amended by striking "substantial unfitness" and inserting "unfitness".

(b) Equitable relief. Section 21(d) of the Securities Exchange Act of 1934 (15 U.S.C. 78u(d)) is amended by adding at the end the following:

"(5) EQUITABLE RELIEF- In any action or proceeding brought or instituted by the Commission under any provision of the securities laws, the Commission may seek, and any Federal court may grant, any equitable relief that may be appropriate or necessary for the benefit of investors.".

[¶ 1226] Sec. 306. Insider trades during pension fund blackout periods.

(a) Prohibition of insider trading during pension fund blackout periods.

(1) In general. Except to the extent otherwise provided by rule of the Commission pursuant to paragraph (3), it shall be unlawful for any director or executive officer of an issuer of any equity security (other than an exempted security), directly or indirectly, to purchase, sell, or otherwise acquire or transfer any equity security of the issuer (other than an exempted security) during any blackout period with respect to such equity security if such director or officer acquires such equity security in connection with his or her service or employment as a director or executive officer.

(2) Remedy.

(A) In general. Any profit realized by a director or executive officer referred to in paragraph (1) from any purchase, sale, or other acquisition or transfer in violation of this subsection shall inure to and be recoverable by the issuer, irrespective of any intention on the part of such director or executive officer in entering into the transaction.

(B) Actions to recover profits. An action to recover profits in accordance with this subsection may be instituted at law or in equity in any court of competent jurisdiction by the issuer, or by the owner of any security of the issuer in the name and in behalf of the issuer if the issuer fails or refuses to bring such action within 60 days after the date of request, or fails diligently to prosecute the action thereafter, except that no such suit shall be brought more than 2 years after the date on which such profit was realized.

(3) Rulemaking authorized. The Commission shall, in consultation with the Secretary of Labor, issue rules to clarify the application of this subsection and to prevent evasion thereof. Such rules shall provide for the application of the requirements of paragraph (1) with respect to entities treated as a single employer with respect to an issuer under section 414(b), (c), (m), or (o) of the Internal Revenue Code of 1986 to the extent necessary to clarify the application of such requirements and to prevent evasion thereof. Such rules may also provide for appropriate exceptions from the requirements of this subsection, including exceptions for purchases pursuant to an automatic dividend reinvestment program or purchases or sales made pursuant to an advance election.

(4) Blackout period. For purposes of this subsection, the term "blackout period", with respect to the equity securities of any issuer—

(A) means any period of more than 3 consecutive business days during which the ability of not fewer than 50 percent of the participants or beneficiaries under all individual account plans maintained by the issuer to purchase, sell, or otherwise acquire or transfer an interest in any equity of such issuer held in such an individual account plan is temporarily suspended by the issuer or by a fiduciary of the plan; and

(B) does not include, under regulations which shall be prescribed by the Commission—

(i) a regularly scheduled period in which the participants and beneficiaries may not purchase, sell, or otherwise acquire or transfer an interest in any equity of such issuer, if such period is—

(I) incorporated into the individual account plan; and

(II) timely disclosed to employees before becoming participants under the individual account plan or as a subsequent amendment to the plan; or

(ii) any suspension described in subparagraph (A) that is imposed solely in connection with persons becoming participants or beneficiaries, or ceasing to be participants or beneficiaries, in an individual account plan by reason of a corporate merger, acquisition, divestiture, or similar transaction involving the plan or plan sponsor.

(5) Individual account plan. For purposes of this subsection, the term "individual account plan" has the meaning provided in section 3(34) of the Employee Retirement Income Security Act of 1974 (29 U.S.C. 1002(34), except that such term shall not include a one-participant retirement plan (within the meaning of section 101(i)(8)(B) of such Act (29 U.S.C. 1021(i)(8)(B))).

(6) Notice to directors, executive officers, and the Commission. In any case in which a director or executive officer is subject to the requirements of this subsection in connection with a blackout period (as defined in paragraph (4)) with respect to any equity securities, the issuer of such equity securities shall timely notify such director or officer and the Securities and Exchange Commission of such blackout period.

(b) Notice requirements to participants and beneficiaries under ERISA.

(1) In general. Section 101 of the Employee Retirement Income Security Act of 1974 (29 U.S.C. 1021) is amended by redesignating the second subsection (h) as subsection (j), and by inserting after the first subsection (h) the following new subsection:

"(i) NOTICE OF BLACKOUT PERIODS TO PARTICIPANT OR BENEFICIARY UNDER INDIVIDUAL ACCOUNT PLAN—

"(1) DUTIES OF PLAN ADMINISTRATOR- In advance of the commencement of any blackout period with respect to an individual account plan, the plan administrator shall notify the plan participants and beneficiaries who are affected by such action in accordance with this subsection.

"(2) NOTICE REQUIREMENTS—

"(A) IN GENERAL- The notices described in paragraph (1) shall be written in a manner calculated to be understood by the average plan participant and shall include—

"(i) the reasons for the blackout period,

"(ii) an identification of the investments and other rights affected,

"(iii) the expected beginning date and length of the blackout period,

"(iv) in the case of investments affected, a statement that the participant or beneficiary should evaluate the appropriateness of their current investment decisions in light of their inability to direct or diversify assets credited to their accounts during the blackout period, and

"(v) such other matters as the Secretary may require by regulation.

"(B) NOTICE TO PARTICIPANTS AND BENEFICIARIES- Except as otherwise provided in this subsection, notices described in paragraph (1) shall be furnished to all participants and beneficiaries under the plan to whom the blackout period applies at least 30 days in advance of the blackout period.

"(C) EXCEPTION TO 30-DAY NOTICE REQUIREMENT- In any case in which—

"(i) a deferral of the blackout period would violate the requirements of subparagraph (A) or (B) of section 404(a)(1), and a fiduciary of the plan reasonably so determines in writing, or

"(ii) the inability to provide the 30-day advance notice is due to events that were unforeseeable or circumstances beyond the reasonable control of the plan administrator, and a fiduciary of the plan reasonably so determines in writing, subparagraph (B) shall not apply, and the notice shall be furnished to all participants and beneficiaries under the plan to whom the blackout period applies as soon as reasonably possible under the circumstances unless such a notice in advance of the termination of the blackout period is impracticable.

"(D) WRITTEN NOTICE- The notice required to be provided under this subsection shall be in writing, except that such notice may be in electronic or other form to the extent that such form is reasonably accessible to the recipient.

"(E) NOTICE TO ISSUERS OF EMPLOYER SECURITIES SUBJECT TO BLACKOUT PERIOD- In the case of any blackout period in connection with an individual account plan, the plan administrator shall provide timely notice of such blackout period to the issuer of any employer securities subject to such blackout period.

"(3) EXCEPTION FOR BLACKOUT PERIODS WITH LIMITED APPLICABILITY- In any case in which the blackout period applies only to 1 or more participants or beneficiaries in connection with a merger, acquisition, divestiture, or similar transaction involving the plan or plan sponsor and occurs solely in connection with becoming or ceasing to be a participant or beneficiary under the plan by reason of such merger, acquisition, divestiture, or transaction, the requirement of this subsection that the notice be provided to all participants and beneficiaries shall be treated as met if the notice required under paragraph (1) is provided to such participants or beneficiaries to whom the blackout period applies as soon as reasonably practicable.

"(4) CHANGES IN LENGTH OF BLACKOUT PERIOD- If, following the furnishing of the notice pursuant to this subsection, there is a change in the beginning date or length of the blackout period (specified in such notice pursuant to paragraph (2)(A)(iii)), the administrator shall provide affected participants and beneficiaries notice of the change as soon as reasonably practicable. In relation to the extended blackout period, such notice shall meet the requirements of paragraph (2)(D) and shall specify any material change in the matters referred to in clauses (i) through (v) of paragraph (2)(A).

"(5) REGULATORY EXCEPTIONS- The Secretary may provide by regulation for additional exceptions to the requirements of this subsection which the Secretary determines are in the interests of participants and beneficiaries.

"(6) GUIDANCE AND MODEL NOTICES- The Secretary shall issue guidance and model notices which meet the requirements of this subsection.

"(7) BLACKOUT PERIOD- For purposes of this subsection—

"(A) IN GENERAL- The term 'blackout period' means, in connection with an individual account plan, any period for which any ability of participants or beneficiaries under the plan, which is otherwise available under the terms of such plan, to direct or diversify assets credited to their accounts, to obtain loans from the plan, or to obtain distributions from the plan is temporarily suspended, limited, or restricted, if such suspension, limitation, or restriction is for any period of more than 3 consecutive business days.

"(B) EXCLUSIONS- The term 'blackout period' does not include a suspension, limitation, or restriction—

"(i) which occurs by reason of the application of the securities laws (as defined in section 3(a)(47) of the Securities Exchange Act of 1934),

"(ii) which is a change to the plan which provides for a regularly scheduled suspension, limitation, or restriction which is disclosed to participants or beneficiaries through any summary of material modifications, any materials describing specific investment alternatives under the plan, or any changes thereto, or

"(iii) which applies only to 1 or more individuals, each of whom is the participant, an alternate payee (as defined in section 206(d)(3)(K)), or any other beneficiary pursuant to a qualified domestic relations order (as defined in section 206(d)(3)(B)(i)).

"(8) INDIVIDUAL ACCOUNT PLAN—

"(A) IN GENERAL- For purposes of this subsection, the term 'individual account plan' shall have the meaning provided such term in section 3(34), except that such term shall not include a one-participant retirement plan.

"(B) ONE-PARTICIPANT RETIREMENT PLAN- For purposes of subparagraph (A), the term 'one-participant retirement plan' means a retirement plan that—

"(i) on the first day of the plan year—

"(I) covered only the employer (and the employer's spouse) and the employer owned the entire business (whether or not incorporated), or

"(II) covered only one or more partners (and their spouses) in a business partnership (including partners in an S or C corporation (as defined in section 1361(a) of the Internal Revenue Code of 1986)),

"(ii) meets the minimum coverage requirements of section 410(b) of the Internal Revenue Code of 1986 (as in effect on the date of the enactment of this paragraph) without being combined with any other plan of the business that covers the employees of the business,

"(iii) does not provide benefits to anyone except the employer (and the employer's spouse) or the partners (and their spouses),

"(iv) does not cover a business that is a member of an affiliated service group, a controlled group of corporations, or a group of businesses under common control, and

"(v) does not cover a business that leases employees.".

(2) Issuance of initial guidance and model notice. The Secretary of Labor shall issue initial guidance and a model notice pursuant to section 101(i)(6) of the Employee Retirement Income Security Act of 1974 (as added by this subsection) not later than January 1, 2003. Not later than 75 days after the date of the enactment of this Act, the Secretary shall promulgate interim final rules necessary to carry out the amendments made by this subsection.

(3) Civil penalties for failure to provide notice. Section 502 of such Act (29 U.S.C. 1132) is amended—

(A) in subsection (a)(6), by striking "(5), or (6)" and inserting "(5), (6), or (7)";

(B) by redesignating paragraph (7) of subsection (c) as paragraph (8); and

(C) by inserting after paragraph (6) of subsection (c) the following new paragraph:

"(7) The Secretary may assess a civil penalty against a plan administrator of up to $100 a day from the date of the plan administrator's failure or refusal to provide notice to participants and beneficiaries in accordance with section 101(i). For purposes of this paragraph, each violation with respect to any single participant or beneficiary shall be treated as a separate violation.".

(3) Plan amendments. If any amendment made by this subsection requires an amendment to any plan, such plan amendment shall not be required to be made before the first plan year beginning on or after the effective date of this section, if—

(A) during the period after such amendment made by this subsection takes effect and before such first plan year, the plan is operated in good faith compliance with the requirements of such amendment made by this subsection, and

(B) such plan amendment applies retroactively to the period after such amendment made by this subsection takes effect and before such first plan year.

(c) Effective date. The provisions of this section (including the amendments made thereby) shall take effect 180 days after the date of the enactment of this Act. Good faith compliance with the requirements of such provisions in advance of the issuance of applicable regulations thereunder shall be treated as compliance with such provisions.

[¶ 1227] Sec. 307. Rules of professional responsibility for attorneys. Not later than 180 days after the date of enactment of this Act, the Commission shall issue rules, in the public interest and for the protection of investors, setting forth minimum standards of professional conduct for attorneys appearing and practicing before the Commission in any way in the representation of issuers, including a rule—

(1) requiring an attorney to report evidence of a material violation of securities law or breach of fiduciary duty or similar violation by the company or any agent thereof, to the chief legal counsel or the chief executive officer of the company (or the equivalent thereof); and

(2) if the counsel or officer does not appropriately respond to the evidence (adopting, as necessary, appropriate remedial measures or sanctions with respect to the violation), requiring the attorney to report the evidence to the audit committee of the board of directors of the issuer or to another committee of the board of directors comprised solely of directors not employed directly or indirectly by the issuer, or to the board of directors.

[¶ 1228] Sec. 308. Fair funds for investors.

(a) Civil penalties added to disgorgement funds for the relief of victims. If in any judicial or administrative action brought by the Commission under the securities laws (as such term is defined in section 3(a)(47) of the Securities Exchange Act of 1934 (15 U.S.C. 78c(a)(47)) the Commission obtains an order requiring disgorgement against any person for a violation of such laws or the rules or regulations thereunder, or such person agrees in settlement of any such action to such disgorgement, and the Commission also obtains pursuant to such laws a civil penalty against such person, the amount of such civil penalty shall, on the motion or at the direction of the Commission, be added to and become part of the disgorgement fund for the benefit of the victims of such violation.

(b) Acceptance of additional donations. The Commission is authorized to accept, hold, administer, and utilize gifts, bequests and devises of property, both real and personal, to the United States for a disgorgement fund described in subsection (a). Such gifts, bequests, and devises of money and proceeds from sales of other property received as gifts, bequests, or devises shall be deposited in the disgorgement fund and shall be available for allocation in accordance with subsection (a).

(c) Study required.

　(1) Subject of study. The Commission shall review and analyze—

　　(A) enforcement actions by the Commission over the five years preceding the date of the enactment of this Act that have included proceedings to obtain civil penalties or disgorgements to identify areas where such proceedings may be utilized to efficiently, effectively, and fairly provide restitution for injured investors; and

　　(B) other methods to more efficiently, effectively, and fairly provide restitution to injured investors, including methods to improve the collection rates for civil penalties and disgorgements.

　(2) Report required. The Commission shall report its findings to the Committee on Financial Services of the House of Representatives and the Committee on Banking, Housing, and Urban Affairs of the Senate within 180 days after of the date of the enactment of this Act, and shall use such findings to revise its rules and regulations as necessary. The report shall include a discussion of regulatory or legislative actions that are recommended or that may be necessary to address concerns identified in the study.

(d) Conforming amendments. Each of the following provisions is amended by inserting ", except as otherwise provided in section 308 of the Sarbanes-Oxley Act of 2002" after "Treasury of the United States":

(1) Section 21(d)(3)(C)(i) of the Securities Exchange Act of 1934 (15 U.S.C. 78u(d)(3)(C)(i)).

(2) Section 21A(d)(1) of such Act (15 U.S.C. 78u-1(d)(1)).

(3) Section 20(d)(3)(A) of the Securities Act of 1933 (15 U.S.C. 77t(d)(3)(A)).

(4) Section 42(e)(3)(A) of the Investment Company Act of 1940 (15 U.S.C. 80a-41(e)(3)(A)).

(5) Section 209(e)(3)(A) of the Investment Advisers Act of 1940 (15 U.S.C. 80b-9(e)(3)(A)).

(e) Definition. As used in this section, the term "disgorgement fund" means a fund established in any administrative or judicial proceeding described in subsection (a).

TITLE IV— ENHANCED FINANCIAL DISCLOSURES

[¶ 1229] Sec. 401. Disclosures in periodic reports.

(a) Disclosures required. Section 13 of the Securities Exchange Act of 1934 (15 U.S.C. 78m) is amended by adding at the end the following:

"(i) ACCURACY OF FINANCIAL REPORTS- Each financial report that contains financial statements, and that is required to be prepared in accordance with (or reconciled to) generally accepted accounting principles under this title and filed with the Commission shall reflect all material correcting adjustments that have been identified by a registered public accounting firm in accordance with generally accepted accounting principles and the rules and regulations of the Commission.

"(j) OFF-BALANCE SHEET TRANSACTIONS- Not later than 180 days after the date of enactment of the Sarbanes-Oxley Act of 2002, the Commission shall issue final rules providing that each annual and quarterly financial report required to be filed with the Commission shall disclose all material off-balance sheet transactions, arrangements, obligations (including contingent obligations), and other relationships of the issuer with unconsolidated entities or other persons, that may have a material current or future effect on financial condition, changes in financial condition, results of operations, liquidity, capital expenditures, capital resources, or significant components of revenues or expenses.".

(b) Commission rules on pro forma figures. Not later than 180 days after the date of enactment of the Sarbanes-Oxley Act fo [sic] 2002, the Commission shall issue final rules providing that pro forma financial information included in any periodic or other report filed with the Commission pursuant to the securities laws, or in any public disclosure or press or other release, shall be presented in a manner that—

(1) does not contain an untrue statement of a material fact or omit to state a material fact necessary in order to make the pro forma financial information, in light of the circumstances under which it is presented, not misleading; and

(2) reconciles it with the financial condition and results of operations of the issuer under generally accepted accounting principles.

(c) Study and report on special purpose entities.

(1) Study required. The Commission shall, not later than 1 year after the effective date of adoption of off-balance sheet disclosure rules required by section 13(j) of the Securities Exchange Act of 1934, as added by this section, complete a study of filings by issuers and their disclosures to determine—

(A) the extent of off-balance sheet transactions, including assets, liabilities, leases, losses, and the use of special purpose entities; and

(B) whether generally accepted accounting rules result in financial statements of issuers reflecting the economics of such off-balance sheet transactions to investors in a transparent fashion.

(2) Report and recommendations. Not later than 6 months after the date of completion of the study required by paragraph (1), the Commission shall submit a report to the President, the Committee on Banking, Housing, and Urban Affairs of the Senate, and the Committee on Financial Services of the House of Representatives, setting forth—

(A) the amount or an estimate of the amount of off-balance sheet transactions, including assets, liabilities, leases, and losses of, and the use of special purpose entities by, issuers filing periodic reports pursuant to section 13 or 15 of the Securities Exchange Act of 1934;

(B) the extent to which special purpose entities are used to facilitate off-balance sheet transactions;

(C) whether generally accepted accounting principles or the rules of the Commission result in financial statements of issuers reflecting the economics of such transactions to investors in a transparent fashion;

(D) whether generally accepted accounting principles specifically result in the consolidation of special purpose entities sponsored by an issuer in cases in which the issuer has the majority of the risks and rewards of the special purpose entity; and

(E) any recommendations of the Commission for improving the transparency and quality of reporting off-balance sheet transactions in the financial statements and disclosures required to be filed by an issuer with the Commission.

[¶ 1230] Sec. 402. Enhanced conflict of interest provisions.

(a) Prohibition on personal loans to executives. Section 13 of the Securities Exchange Act of 1934 (15 U.S.C. 78m), as amended by this Act, is amended by adding at the end the following:

"(k) PROHIBITION ON PERSONAL LOANS TO EXECUTIVES—

"(1) IN GENERAL- It shall be unlawful for any issuer (as defined in section 2 of the Sarbanes-Oxley Act of 2002), directly or indirectly, including through any subsidiary, to extend or maintain credit, to arrange for the extension of credit, or to renew an extension of credit, in the form of a personal loan to or for any director or executive officer (or equivalent thereof) of that issuer. An extension of credit maintained by the issuer on the date of enactment of this subsection shall not be subject to the provisions of this subsection, provided that there is no material modification to any term of any such extension of credit or any renewal of any such extension of credit on or after that date of enactment.

"(2) LIMITATION- Paragraph (1) does not preclude any home improvement and manufactured home loans (as that term is defined in section 5 of the Home Owners' Loan Act (12 U.S.C. 1464)), consumer credit (as defined in section 103 of the Truth in Lending Act (15 U.S.C. 1602)), or any extension of credit under an open end credit plan (as defined in section 103 of the Truth in Lending Act (15 U.S.C. 1602)), or a charge card (as defined in section 127(c)(4)(e) of the Truth in Lending Act (15 U.S.C. 1637(c)(4)(e)), or any extension of credit by a broker or dealer registered under section 15 of this title to an employee of that broker or dealer to buy, trade, or carry securities, that is permitted under rules or regulations of the Board of Governors of the Federal Reserve System pursuant to section 7 of this title (other than an extension of credit that would be used to purchase the stock of that issuer), that is—

"(A) made or provided in the ordinary course of the consumer credit business of such issuer;

"(B) of a type that is generally made available by such issuer to the public; and

"(C) made by such issuer on market terms, or terms that are no more favorable than those offered by the issuer to the general public for such extensions of credit.

"(3) RULE OF CONSTRUCTION FOR CERTAIN LOANS- Paragraph (1) does not apply to any loan made or maintained by an insured depository institution (as defined in section 3 of the Federal Deposit Insurance Act (12 U.S.C. 1813)), if the loan is subject to the insider lending restrictions of section 22(h) of the Federal Reserve Act (12 U.S.C. 375b).".

[¶ 1231] Sec. 403. Disclosures of transactions involving management and principal stockholders.

(a) Amendment. Section 16 of the Securities Exchange Act of 1934 (15 U.S.C. 78p) is amended by striking the heading of such section and subsection (a) and inserting the following:

"SEC. 16. DIRECTORS, OFFICERS, AND PRINCIPAL STOCKHOLDERS.

"(a) DISCLOSURES REQUIRED—

"(1) DIRECTORS, OFFICERS, AND PRINCIPAL STOCKHOLDERS REQUIRED TO FILE- Every person who is directly or indirectly the beneficial owner of more than 10 percent of any class of any equity security (other than an exempted security) which is registered pursuant to section 12, or who is a director or an officer of the issuer of such security, shall file the statements required by this subsection with the Commission (and, if such security is registered on a national securities exchange, also with the exchange).

"(2) TIME OF FILING- The statements required by this subsection shall be filed—

"(A) at the time of the registration of such security on a national securities exchange or by the effective date of a registration statement filed pursuant to section 12(g);

"(B) within 10 days after he or she becomes such beneficial owner, director, or officer;

"(C) if there has been a change in such ownership, or if such person shall have purchased or sold a security-based swap agreement (as defined in section 206(b) of the Gramm-Leach-Bliley Act (15 U.S.C. 78c note)) involving such equity security, before the end of the second business day following the day on which the subject transaction has been executed, or at such other time as the Commission shall establish, by rule, in any case in which the Commission determines that such 2-day period is not feasible.

"(3) CONTENTS OF STATEMENTS- A statement filed—

"(A) under subparagraph (A) or (B) of paragraph (2) shall contain a statement of the amount of all equity securities of such issuer of which the filing person is the beneficial owner; and

"(B) under subparagraph (C) of such paragraph shall indicate ownership by the filing person at the date of filing, any such changes in such ownership, and such purchases and sales of the security-based swap agreements as have occurred since the most recent such filing under such subparagraph.

"(4) ELECTRONIC FILING AND AVAILABILITY- Beginning not later than 1 year after the date of enactment of the Sarbanes-Oxley Act of 2002—

"(A) a statement filed under subparagraph (C) of paragraph (2) shall be filed electronically;

"(B) the Commission shall provide each such statement on a publicly accessible Internet site not later than the end of the business day following that filing; and

"(C) the issuer (if the issuer maintains a corporate website) shall provide that statement on that corporate website, not later than the end of the business day following that filing.".

(b) Effective date. The amendment made by this section shall be effective 30 days after the date of the enactment of this Act.

[¶ 1232] Sec. 404. Management assessment of internal controls.

(a) Rules required. The Commission shall prescribe rules requiring each annual report required by section 13(a) or 15(d) of the Securities Exchange Act of 1934 (15 U.S.C. 78m or 78o(d)) to contain an internal control report, which shall—

(1) state the responsibility of management for establishing and maintaining an adequate internal control structure and procedures for financial reporting; and

(2) contain an assessment, as of the end of the most recent fiscal year of the issuer, of the effectiveness of the internal control structure and procedures of the issuer for financial reporting.

(b) Internal control evaluation and reporting. With respect to the internal control assessment required by subsection (a), each registered public accounting firm that prepares or issues the audit report for the issuer shall attest to, and report on, the assessment made by the management of the issuer. An attestation made under this subsection shall be made in accordance with standards for attestation engagements issued or adopted by the Board. Any such attestation shall not be the subject of a separate engagement.

[¶ 1233] Sec. 405. Exemption. Nothing in section 401, 402, or 404, the amendments made by those sections, or the rules of the Commission under those sections shall apply to any investment company registered under section 8 of the Investment Company Act of 1940 (15 U.S.C. 80a-8).

[¶ 1234] Sec. 406. Code of ethics for senior financial officers.

(a) Code of ethics disclosure. The Commission shall issue rules to require each issuer, together with periodic reports required pursuant to section 13(a) or 15(d) of the Securities Exchange Act of 1934, to disclose whether or not, and if not, the reason therefor, such issuer has adopted a code of ethics for senior financial officers, applicable to its principal financial officer and comptroller or principal accounting officer, or persons performing similar functions.

(b) Changes in codes of ethics. The Commission shall revise its regulations concerning matters requiring prompt disclosure on Form 8-K (or any successor thereto) to require the immediate disclosure, by means of the filing of such form, dissemination by the Internet or by other electronic means, by any issuer of any change in or waiver of the code of ethics for senior financial officers.

(c) Definition. In this section, the term "code of ethics" means such standards as are reasonably necessary to promote—
　(1) honest and ethical conduct, including the ethical handling of actual or apparent conflicts of interest between personal and professional relationships;
　(2) full, fair, accurate, timely, and understandable disclosure in the periodic reports required to be filed by the issuer; and
　(3) compliance with applicable governmental rules and regulations.

(d) Deadline for rulemaking. The Commission shall—
　(1) propose rules to implement this section, not later than 90 days after the date of enactment of this Act; and
　(2) issue final rules to implement this section, not later than 180 days after that date of enactment.

[¶ 1235] Sec. 407. Disclosure of audit committee financial expert.

(a) Rules defining "financial expert". The Commission shall issue rules, as necessary or appropriate in the public interest and consistent with the protection of investors, to require each issuer, together with periodic reports required pursuant to sections 13(a) and 15(d) of the Securities Exchange Act of 1934, to disclose whether or not, and if not, the reasons therefor, the audit committee of that issuer is comprised of at least 1 member who is a financial expert, as such term is defined by the Commission.

(b) Considerations. In defining the term "financial expert" for purposes of subsection (a), the Commission shall consider whether a person has, through education and experience as a public accountant or auditor or a principal financial officer, comptroller, or principal accounting officer of an issuer, or from a position involving the performance of similar functions—
　(1) an understanding of generally accepted accounting principles and financial statements;
　(2) experience in—

(A) the preparation or auditing of financial statements of generally comparable issuers; and

(B) the application of such principles in connection with the accounting for estimates, accruals, and reserves;

(3) experience with internal accounting controls; and

(4) an understanding of audit committee functions.

(c) **Deadline for rulemaking.** The Commission shall—

(1) propose rules to implement this section, not later than 90 days after the date of enactment of this Act; and

(2) issue final rules to implement this section, not later than 180 days after that date of enactment.

[¶ 1236] Sec. 408. Enhanced review of periodic disclosures by issuers.

(a) **Regular and systematic review.** The Commission shall review disclosures made by issuers reporting under section 13(a) of the Securities Exchange Act of 1934 (including reports filed on Form 10-K), and which have a class of securities listed on a national securities exchange or traded on an automated quotation facility of a national securities association, on a regular and systematic basis for the protection of investors. Such review shall include a review of an issuer's financial statement.

(b) **Review criteria.** For purposes of scheduling the reviews required by subsection (a), the Commission shall consider, among other factors—

(1) issuers that have issued material restatements of financial results;

(2) issuers that experience significant volatility in their stock price as compared to other issuers;

(3) issuers with the largest market capitalization;

(4) emerging companies with disparities in price to earning ratios;

(5) issuers whose operations significantly affect any material sector of the economy; and

(6) any other factors that the Commission may consider relevant.

(c) **Minimum review period.** In no event shall an issuer required to file reports under section 13(a) or 15(d) of the Securities Exchange Act of 1934 be reviewed under this section less frequently than once every 3 years.

[¶ 1237] Sec. 409. Real time issuer disclosures. Section 13 of the Securities Exchange Act of 1934 (15 U.S.C. 78m), as amended by this Act, is amended by adding at the end the following:

"(l) REAL TIME ISSUER DISCLOSURES- Each issuer reporting under section 13(a) or 15(d) shall disclose to the public on a rapid and current basis such additional information concerning material changes in the financial condition or operations of the issuer, in plain English, which may include trend and qualitative information and graphic presentations, as the Commission determines, by rule, is necessary or useful for the protection of investors and in the public interest.".

TITLE V— ANALYST CONFLICTS OF INTEREST

[¶ 1238] Sec. 501. Treatment of securities analysts by registered securities associations and national securities exchanges.

(a) **Rules regarding securities analysts.** The Securities Exchange Act of 1934 (15 U.S.C. 78a et seq.) is amended by inserting after section 15C the following new section:

"SEC. 15D. SECURITIES ANALYSTS AND RESEARCH REPORTS.

"(a) ANALYST PROTECTIONS- The Commission, or upon the authorization and direction of the Commission, a registered securities association or national securities exchange, shall have adopted, not later than 1 year after the date of enactment of this section, rules reasonably designed to address conflicts of interest that can arise when securities analysts recommend equity securities in research reports and public appearances, in order to improve the objectivity of research and provide investors with more useful and reliable information, including rules designed—

"(1) to foster greater public confidence in securities research, and to protect the objectivity and independence of securities analysts, by—

"(A) restricting the prepublication clearance or approval of research reports by persons employed by the broker or dealer who are engaged in investment banking activities, or persons not directly responsible for investment research, other than legal or compliance staff;

"(B) limiting the supervision and compensatory evaluation of securities analysts to officials employed by the broker or dealer who are not engaged in investment banking activities; and

"(C) requiring that a broker or dealer and persons employed by a broker or dealer who are involved with investment banking activities may not, directly or indirectly, retaliate against or threaten to retaliate against any securities analyst employed by that broker or dealer or its affiliates as a result of an adverse, negative, or otherwise unfavorable research report that may adversely affect the present or prospective investment banking relationship of the broker or dealer with the issuer that is the subject of the research report, except that such rules may not limit the authority of a broker or dealer to discipline a securities analyst for causes other than such research report in accordance with the policies and procedures of the firm;

"(2) to define periods during which brokers or dealers who have participated, or are to participate, in a public offering of securities as underwriters or dealers should not publish or otherwise distribute research reports relating to such securities or to the issuer of such securities;

"(3) to establish structural and institutional safeguards within registered brokers or dealers to assure that securities analysts are separated by appropriate informational partitions within the firm from the review, pressure, or oversight of those whose involvement in investment banking activities might potentially bias their judgment or supervision; and

"(4) to address such other issues as the Commission, or such association or exchange, determines appropriate.

"(b) DISCLOSURE- The Commission, or upon the authorization and direction of the Commission, a registered securities association or national securities exchange, shall have adopted, not later than 1 year after the date of enactment of this section, rules reasonably designed to require each securities analyst to disclose in public appearances, and each registered broker or dealer to disclose in each research report, as applicable, conflicts of interest that are known or should have been known by the securities analyst or the broker or dealer, to exist at the time of the appearance or the date of distribution of the report, including—

"(1) the extent to which the securities analyst has debt or equity investments in the issuer that is the subject of the appearance or research report;

"(2) whether any compensation has been received by the registered broker or dealer, or any affiliate thereof, including the securities analyst, from the issuer that is the subject of the appearance or research report, subject to such exemptions as the Commission may determine appropriate and necessary to prevent disclosure by virtue of this paragraph of material nonpublic information regarding specific potential future investment banking transactions of such issuer, as is appropriate in the public interest and consistent with the protection of investors;

"(3) whether an issuer, the securities of which are recommended in the appearance or research report, currently is, or during the 1-year period preceding the date of the appearance or date of distribution of the report has been, a client of the registered broker or dealer, and if so, stating the types of services provided to the issuer;

"(4) whether the securities analyst received compensation with respect to a research report, based upon (among any other factors) the investment banking revenues (either generally or specifically earned from the issuer being analyzed) of the registered broker or dealer; and

"(5) such other disclosures of conflicts of interest that are material to investors, research analysts, or the broker or dealer as the Commission, or such association or exchange, determines appropriate.

"(c) DEFINITIONS- In this section—

"(1) the term 'securities analyst' means any associated person of a registered broker or dealer that is principally responsible for, and any associated person who reports directly or indirectly to a securities analyst in connection with, the preparation of the substance of a research report, whether or not any such person has the job title of 'securities analyst'; and

"(2) the term 'research report' means a written or electronic communication that includes an analysis of equity securities of individual companies or industries, and that provides information reasonably sufficient upon which to base an investment decision.".

(b) Enforcement. Section 21B(a) of the Securities Exchange Act of 1934 (15 U.S.C. 78u-2(a)) is amended by inserting "15D," before "15B".

(c) Commission authority. The Commission may promulgate and amend its regulations, or direct a registered securities association or national securities exchange to promulgate and amend its rules, to carry out section 15D of the Securities Exchange Act of 1934, as added by this section, as is necessary for the protection of investors and in the public interest.

TITLE VI— COMMISSION RESOURCES AND AUTHORITY

[¶ 1239] Sec. 601. Authorization of appropriations. Section 35 of the Securities Exchange Act of 1934 (15 U.S.C. 78kk) is amended to read as follows:

"SEC. 35. AUTHORIZATION OF APPROPRIATIONS.

"In addition to any other funds authorized to be appropriated to the Commission, there are authorized to be appropriated to carry out the functions, powers, and duties of the Commission, $776,000,000 for fiscal year 2003, of which—

"(1) $102,700,000 shall be available to fund additional compensation, including salaries and benefits, as authorized in the Investor and Capital Markets Fee Relief Act (Public Law 107-123; 115 Stat. 2390 et seq.);

"(2) $108,400,000 shall be available for information technology, security enhancements, and recovery and mitigation activities in light of the terrorist attacks of September 11, 2001; and

"(3) $98,000,000 shall be available to add not fewer than an additional 200 qualified professionals to provide enhanced oversight of auditors and audit services required by the Federal securities laws, and to improve Commission investigative and disciplinary efforts with respect to such auditors and services, as well as for additional professional support staff necessary to strengthen the programs of the Commission involving Full Disclosure and Prevention and Suppression of Fraud, risk management, industry technology review, compliance, inspections, examinations, market regulation, and investment management.".

[¶ 1240] Sec. 602. Appearance and practice before the Commission. The Securities Exchange Act of 1934 (15 U.S.C. 78a et seq.) is amended by inserting after section 4B the following:

"SEC. 4C. APPEARANCE AND PRACTICE BEFORE THE COMMISSION.

"(a) AUTHORITY TO CENSURE- The Commission may censure any person, or deny, temporarily or permanently, to any person the privilege of appearing or practicing before the Commission in any way, if that person is found by the Commission, after notice and opportunity for hearing in the matter—

"(1) not to possess the requisite qualifications to represent others;

"(2) to be lacking in character or integrity, or to have engaged in unethical or improper professional conduct; or

"(3) to have willfully violated, or willfully aided and abetted the violation of, any provision of the securities laws or the rules and regulations issued thereunder.

"(b) DEFINITION- With respect to any registered public accounting firm or associated person, for purposes of this section, the term 'improper professional conduct' means—

"(1) intentional or knowing conduct, including reckless conduct, that results in a violation of applicable professional standards; and

"(2) negligent conduct in the form of—

"(A) a single instance of highly unreasonable conduct that results in a violation of applicable professional standards in circumstances in which the registered public accounting firm or associated person knows, or should know, that heightened scrutiny is warranted; or

"(B) repeated instances of unreasonable conduct, each resulting in a violation of applicable professional standards, that indicate a lack of competence to practice before the Commission.".

[¶ 1241] Sec. 603. Federal court authority to impose penny stock bars.

(a) Securities Exchange Act of 1934. Section 21(d) of the Securities Exchange Act of 1934 (15 U.S.C. 78u(d)), as amended by this Act, is amended by adding at the end the following:

"(6) AUTHORITY OF A COURT TO PROHIBIT PERSONS FROM PARTICIPATING IN AN OFFERING OF PENNY STOCK—

"(A) IN GENERAL- In any proceeding under paragraph (1) against any person participating in, or, at the time of the alleged misconduct who was participating in, an offering of penny stock, the court may prohibit that person from participating in an offering of penny stock, conditionally or unconditionally, and permanently or for such period of time as the court shall determine.

"(B) DEFINITION- For purposes of this paragraph, the term 'person participating in an offering of penny stock' includes any person engaging in activities with a broker, dealer, or issuer for purposes of issuing, trading, or inducing or attempting to induce the purchase or sale of, any penny stock. The Commission may, by rule or regulation, define such term to include other activities, and may, by rule, regulation, or order, exempt any person or class of persons, in whole or in part, conditionally or unconditionally, from inclusion in such term.".

(b) Securities Act of 1933. Section 20 of the Securities Act of 1933 (15 U.S.C. 77t) is amended by adding at the end the following:

"(g) AUTHORITY OF A COURT TO PROHIBIT PERSONS FROM PARTICIPATING IN AN OFFERING OF PENNY STOCK—

"(1) IN GENERAL- In any proceeding under subsection (a) against any person participating in, or, at the time of the alleged misconduct, who was participating in, an offering of penny stock, the court may prohibit that person from participating in an offering of penny stock, conditionally or unconditionally, and permanently or for such period of time as the court shall determine.

"(2) DEFINITION- For purposes of this subsection, the term 'person participating in an offering of penny stock' includes any person engaging in activities with a broker, dealer, or issuer for purposes of issuing, trading, or inducing or attempting to induce the purchase or sale of, any penny stock. The Commission may, by rule or regulation, define such term to include other activities, and may, by rule, regulation, or order, exempt any person or class of persons, in whole or in part, conditionally or unconditionally, from inclusion in such term.".

[¶ 1242] Sec. 604. Qualifications of associated persons of brokers and dealers.

(a) Brokers and dealers. Section 15(b)(4) of the Securities Exchange Act of 1934 (15 U.S.C. 78o) is amended—

(1) by striking subparagraph (F) and inserting the following:

"(F) is subject to any order of the Commission barring or suspending the right of the person to be associated with a broker or dealer;"; and

(2) in subparagraph (G), by striking the period at the end and inserting the following: "; or

"(H) is subject to any final order of a State securities Commission (or any agency or officer performing like functions), State authority that supervises or examines banks, savings associations, or credit unions, State insurance Commission (or any agency or office performing like functions), an appropriate Federal banking agency (as defined in section 3 of the Federal Deposit Insurance Act (12 U.S.C. 1813(q))), or the National Credit Union Administration, that—

"(i) bars such person from association with an entity regulated by such Commission, authority, agency, or officer, or from engaging in the business of securities, insurance, banking, savings association activities, or credit union activities; or

"(ii) constitutes a final order based on violations of any laws or regulations that prohibit fraudulent, manipulative, or deceptive conduct.".

(b) Investment advisers. Section 203(e) of the Investment Advisers Act of 1940 (15 U.S.C. 80b-3(e)) is amended—

(1) by striking paragraph (7) and inserting the following:

"(7) is subject to any order of the Commission barring or suspending the right of the person to be associated with an investment adviser;";

(2) in paragraph (8), by striking the period at the end and inserting "; or"; and

(3) by adding at the end the following:

"(9) is subject to any final order of a State securities Commission (or any agency or officer performing like functions), State authority that supervises or examines banks, savings associations, or credit unions, State insurance Commission (or any agency or office performing like functions), an appropriate Federal banking agency (as defined in section 3 of the Federal Deposit Insurance Act (12 U.S.C. 1813(q))), or the National Credit Union Administration, that—

"(A) bars such person from association with an entity regulated by such Commission, authority, agency, or officer, or from engaging in the business of securities, insurance, banking, savings association activities, or credit union activities; or

"(B) constitutes a final order based on violations of any laws or regulations that prohibit fraudulent, manipulative, or deceptive conduct.".

(c) Conforming amendments.

(1) Securities Exchange Act of 1934. The Securities Exchange Act of 1934 (15 U.S.C. 78a et seq.) is amended—

(A) in section 3(a)(39)(F) (15 U.S.C. 78c(a)(39)(F))—

(i) by striking "or (G)" and inserting "(H), or (G)"; and

(ii) by inserting ", or is subject to an order or finding," before "enumerated";

(B) in each of section 15(b)(6)(A)(i) (15 U.S.C. 78o(b)(6)(A)(i)), paragraphs (2) and (4) of section 15B(c) (15 U.S.C. 78o-4(c)), and subparagraphs (A) and (C) of section 15C(c)(1) (15 U.S.C. 78o-5(c)(1))—

(i) by striking "or (G)" each place that term appears and inserting "(H), or (G)"; and

(ii) by striking "or omission" each place that term appears, and inserting ", or is subject to an order or finding,"; and

(C) in each of paragraphs (3)(A) and (4)(C) of section 17A(c) (15 U.S.C. 78q-1(c))—

(i) by striking "or (G)" each place that term appears and inserting "(H), or (G)"; and

(ii) by inserting ", or is subject to an order or finding," before "enumerated" each place that term appears.

(2) Investment Advisers Act of 1940. Section 203(f) of the Investment Advisers Act of 1940 (15 U.S.C. 80b-3(f)) is amended—

(A) by striking "or (8)" and inserting "(8), or (9)"; and

(B) by inserting "or (3)" after "paragraph (2)".

TITLE VII— STUDIES AND REPORTS

[¶ 1243] Sec. 701. GAO study and report regarding consolidation of public accounting firms.

(a) Study required. The Comptroller General of the United States shall conduct a study—
(1) to identify—
(A) the factors that have led to the consolidation of public accounting firms since 1989 and the consequent reduction in the number of firms capable of providing audit services to large national and multi-national business organizations that are subject to the securities laws;
(B) the present and future impact of the condition described in subparagraph (A) on capital formation and securities markets, both domestic and international; and
(C) solutions to any problems identified under subparagraph (B), including ways to increase competition and the number of firms capable of providing audit services to large national and multinational business organizations that are subject to the securities laws;
(2) of the problems, if any, faced by business organizations that have resulted from limited competition among public accounting firms, including—
(A) higher costs;
(B) lower quality of services;
(C) impairment of auditor independence; or
(D) lack of choice; and
(3) whether and to what extent Federal or State regulations impede competition among public accounting firms.

(b) Consultation. In planning and conducting the study under this section, the Comptroller General shall consult with—
(1) the Commission;
(2) the regulatory agencies that perform functions similar to the Commission within the other member countries of the Group of Seven Industrialized Nations;
(3) the Department of Justice; and
(4) any other public or private sector organization that the Comptroller General considers appropriate.

(c) Report required. Not later than 1 year after the date of enactment of this Act, the Comptroller General shall submit a report on the results of the study required by this section to the Committee on Banking, Housing, and Urban Affairs of the Senate and the Committee on Financial Services of the House of Representatives.

[¶ 1244] Sec. 702. Commission study and report regarding credit rating agencies.

(a) Study required.
(1) **In general.** The Commission shall conduct a study of the role and function of credit rating agencies in the operation of the securities market.
(2) **Areas of consideration.** The study required by this subsection shall examine—
(A) the role of credit rating agencies in the evaluation of issuers of securities;
(B) the importance of that role to investors and the functioning of the securities markets;
(C) any impediments to the accurate appraisal by credit rating agencies of the financial resources and risks of issuers of securities;
(D) any barriers to entry into the business of acting as a credit rating agency, and any measures needed to remove such barriers;
(E) any measures which may be required to improve the dissemination of information concerning such resources and risks when credit rating agencies announce credit ratings; and

(F) any conflicts of interest in the operation of credit rating agencies and measures to prevent such conflicts or ameliorate the consequences of such conflicts.

(b) Report required. The Commission shall submit a report on the study required by subsection (a) to the President, the Committee on Financial Services of the House of Representatives, and the Committee on Banking, Housing, and Urban Affairs of the Senate not later than 180 days after the date of enactment of this Act.

[¶ 1245] Sec. 703. Study and report on violators and violations.

(a) Study. The Commission shall conduct a study to determine, based upon information for the period from January 1, 1998, to December 31, 2001—

(1) the number of securities professionals, defined as public accountants, public accounting firms, investment bankers, investment advisers, brokers, dealers, attorneys, and other securities professionals practicing before the Commission—

(A) who have been found to have aided and abetted a violation of the Federal securities laws, including rules or regulations promulgated thereunder (collectively referred to in this section as "Federal securities laws"), but who have not been sanctioned, disciplined, or otherwise penalized as a primary violator in any administrative action or civil proceeding, including in any settlement of such an action or proceeding (referred to in this section as "aiders and abettors"); and

(B) who have been found to have been primary violators of the Federal securities laws;

(2) a description of the Federal securities laws violations committed by aiders and abettors and by primary violators, including—

(A) the specific provision of the Federal securities laws violated;

(B) the specific sanctions and penalties imposed upon such aiders and abettors and primary violators, including the amount of any monetary penalties assessed upon and collected from such persons;

(C) the occurrence of multiple violations by the same person or persons, either as an aider or abettor or as a primary violator; and

(D) whether, as to each such violator, disciplinary sanctions have been imposed, including any censure, suspension, temporary bar, or permanent bar to practice before the Commission; and

(3) the amount of disgorgement, restitution, or any other fines or payments that the Commission has assessed upon and collected from, aiders and abettors and from primary violators.

(b) Report. A report based upon the study conducted pursuant to subsection (a) shall be submitted to the Committee on Banking, Housing, and Urban Affairs of the Senate, and the Committee on Financial Services of the House of Representatives not later than 6 months after the date of enactment of this Act.

[¶ 1246] Sec. 704. Study of enforcement actions.

(a) Study required. The Commission shall review and analyze all enforcement actions by the Commission involving violations of reporting requirements imposed under the securities laws, and restatements of financial statements, over the 5-year period preceding the date of enactment of this Act, to identify areas of reporting that are most susceptible to fraud, inappropriate manipulation, or inappropriate earnings management, such as revenue recognition and the accounting treatment of off-balance sheet special purpose entities.

(b) Report required. The Commission shall report its findings to the Committee on Financial Services of the House of Representatives and the Committee on Banking, Housing, and Urban Affairs of the Senate, not later than 180 days after the date of enactment of this Act, and shall use such findings to revise its rules and regulations, as necessary. The report shall include a discussion of regulatory or legislative steps that are recommended or that may be necessary to address concerns identified in the study.

[¶ 1247] Sec. 705. Study of investment banks.

(a) GAO study. The Comptroller General of the United States shall conduct a study on whether investment banks and financial advisers assisted public companies in manipulating their earnings and obfuscating their true financial condition. The study should address the rule of investment banks and financial advisers—

(1) in the collapse of the Enron Corporation, including with respect to the design and implementation of derivatives transactions, transactions involving special purpose vehicles, and other financial arrangements that may have had the effect of altering the company's reported financial statements in ways that obscured the true financial picture of the company;

(2) in the failure of Global Crossing, including with respect to transactions involving swaps of fiberoptic cable capacity, in the designing transactions that may have had the effect of altering the company's reported financial statements in ways that obscured the true financial picture of the company; and

(3) generally, in creating and marketing transactions which may have been designed solely to enable companies to manipulate revenue streams, obtain loans, or move liabilities off balance sheets without altering the economic and business risks faced by the companies or any other mechanism to obscure a company's financial picture.

(b) Report. The Comptroller General shall report to Congress not later than 180 days after the date of enactment of this Act on the results of the study required by this section. The report shall include a discussion of regulatory or legislative steps that are recommended or that may be necessary to address concerns identified in the study.

TITLE VIII— CORPORATE AND CRIMINAL FRAUD ACCOUNTABILITY

[¶ 1248] Sec. 801. Short title. This title may be cited as the "Corporate and Criminal Fraud Accountability Act of 2002".

[¶ 1249] Sec. 802. Criminal penalties for altering documents.

(a) In general. Chapter 73 of title 18, United States Code, is amended by adding at the end the following:

"Sec. 1519. Destruction, alteration, or falsification of records in Federal investigations and bankruptcy

"Whoever knowingly alters, destroys, mutilates, conceals, covers up, falsifies, or makes a false entry in any record, document, or tangible object with the intent to impede, obstruct, or influence the investigation or proper administration of any matter within the jurisdiction of any department or agency of the United States or any case filed under title 11, or in relation to or contemplation of any such matter or case, shall be fined under this title, imprisoned not more than 20 years, or both.

"Sec. 1520. Destruction of corporate audit records

"(a)(1) Any accountant who conducts an audit of an issuer of securities to which section 10A(a) of the Securities Exchange Act of 1934 (15 U.S.C. 78j-1(a)) applies, shall maintain all audit or review workpapers for a period of 5 years from the end of the fiscal period in which the audit or review was concluded.

"(2) The Securities and Exchange Commission shall promulgate, within 180 days, after adequate notice and an opportunity for comment, such rules and regulations, as are reasonably necessary, relating to the retention of relevant records such as workpapers, documents that form the basis of an audit or review, memoranda, correspondence, communications, other documents, and records (including electronic records) which are created, sent, or received in connection with an audit or review and contain conclusions, opinions, analyses, or financial data relating to such an audit or review, which is conducted by any accountant who conducts an audit of an issuer of securities to which section 10A(a) of the Securities Exchange Act of 1934 (15 U.S.C. 78j-1(a)) applies. The Commission may, from time to time, amend or supplement the rules and regulations that it is required to promulgate under this section, after adequate notice and an opportunity for comment, in order to ensure that such rules and regulations adequately comport with the purposes of this section.

"(b) Whoever knowingly and willfully violates subsection (a)(1), or any rule or regulation promulgated by the Securities and Exchange Commission under subsection (a)(2), shall be fined under this title, imprisoned not more than 10 years, or both.

"(c) Nothing in this section shall be deemed to diminish or relieve any person of any other duty or obligation imposed by Federal or State law or regulation to maintain, or refrain from destroying, any document.".

(b) Clerical amendment. The table of sections at the beginning of chapter 73 of title 18, United States Code, is amended by adding at the end the following new items:

"1519. Destruction, alteration, or falsification of records in Federal investigations and bankruptcy.

"1520. Destruction of corporate audit records.".

[¶ 1250] Sec. 803. Debts nondischargeable if incurred in violation of securities fraud laws. Section 523(a) of title 11, United States Code, is amended—

(1) in paragraph (17), by striking "or" after the semicolon;

(2) in paragraph (18), by striking the period at the end and inserting "; or"; and

(3) by adding at the end, the following:

"(19) that—

"(A) is for—

"(i) the violation of any of the Federal securities laws (as that term is defined in section 3(a)(47) of the Securities Exchange Act of 1934), any of the State securities laws, or any regulation or order issued under such Federal or State securities laws; or

"(ii) common law fraud, deceit, or manipulation in connection with the purchase or sale of any security; and

"(B) results from—

"(i) any judgment, order, consent order, or decree entered in any Federal or State judicial or administrative proceeding;

"(ii) any settlement agreement entered into by the debtor; or

"(iii) any court or administrative order for any damages, fine, penalty, citation, restitutionary payment, disgorgement payment, attorney fee, cost, or other payment owed by the debtor.".

[¶ 1251] Sec. 804. Statute of limitations for securities fraud.

(a) In general. Section 1658 of title 28, United States Code, is amended—

(1) by inserting "(a)" before "Except"; and

(2) by adding at the end the following:

"(b) Notwithstanding subsection (a), a private right of action that involves a claim of fraud, deceit, manipulation, or contrivance in contravention of a regulatory requirement concerning the securities laws, as defined in section 3(a)(47) of the Securities Exchange Act of 1934 (15 U.S.C. 78c(a)(47)), may be brought not later than the earlier of—

"(1) 2 years after the discovery of the facts constituting the violation; or

"(2) 5 years after such violation.".

(b) Effective date. The limitations period provided by section 1658(b) of title 28, United States Code, as added by this section, shall apply to all proceedings addressed by this section that are commenced on or after the date of enactment of this Act.

(c) No creation of actions. Nothing in this section shall create a new, private right of action.

[¶ 1252] Sec. 805. Review of Federal Sentencing Guidelines for obstruction of justice and extensive criminal fraud.

(a) Enhancement of fraud and obstruction of justice sentences. Pursuant to section 994 of title 28, United States Code, and in accordance with this section, the United States Sentencing Commission shall review and amend, as appropriate, the Federal Sentencing Guidelines and related policy statements to ensure that—

(1) the base offense level and existing enhancements contained in United States Sentencing Guideline 2J1.2 relating to obstruction of justice are sufficient to deter and punish that activity;

(2) the enhancements and specific offense characteristics relating to obstruction of justice are adequate in cases where—

(A) the destruction, alteration, or fabrication of evidence involves—

(i) a large amount of evidence, a large number of participants, or is otherwise extensive;

(ii) the selection of evidence that is particularly probative or essential to the investigation; or

(iii) more than minimal planning; or

(B) the offense involved abuse of a special skill or a position of trust;

(3) the guideline offense levels and enhancements for violations of section 1519 or 1520 of title 18, United States Code, as added by this title, are sufficient to deter and punish that activity;

(4) a specific offense characteristic enhancing sentencing is provided under United States Sentencing Guideline 2B1.1 (as in effect on the date of enactment of this Act) for a fraud offense that endangers the solvency or financial security of a substantial number of victims; and

(5) the guidelines that apply to organizations in United States Sentencing Guidelines, chapter 8, are sufficient to deter and punish organizational criminal misconduct.

(b) Emergency authority and deadline for Commission action. The United States Sentencing Commission is requested to promulgate the guidelines or amendments provided for under this section as soon as practicable, and in any event not later than 180 days after the date of enactment of this Act, in accordance with the prcedures [sic] set forth in section 219(a) of the Sentencing Reform Act of 1987, as though the authority under that Act had not expired.

[¶ 1253] Sec. 806. Protection for employees of publicly traded companies who provide evidence of fraud.

(a) In general. Chapter 73 of title 18, United States Code, is amended by inserting after section 1514 the following:

"Sec. 1514A. Civil action to protect against retaliation in fraud cases

"(a) WHISTLEBLOWER PROTECTION FOR EMPLOYEES OF PUBLICLY TRADED COMPANIES- No company with a class of securities registered under section 12 of the Securities Exchange Act of 1934 (15 U.S.C. 78l), or that is required to file reports under section 15(d) of the Securities Exchange Act of 1934 (15 U.S.C. 78o(d)), or any officer, employee, contractor, subcontractor, or agent of such company, may discharge, demote, suspend, threaten, harass, or in any other manner discriminate against an employee in the terms and conditions of employment because of any lawful act done by the employee—

"(1) to provide information, cause information to be provided, or otherwise assist in an investigation regarding any conduct which the employee reasonably believes constitutes a violation of section 1341, 1343, 1344, or 1348, any rule or regulation of the Securities and Exchange Commission, or any provision of Federal law relating to fraud against shareholders, when the information or assistance is provided to or the investigation is conducted by—

"(A) a Federal regulatory or law enforcement agency;

"(B) any Member of Congress or any committee of Congress; or

"(C) a person with supervisory authority over the employee (or such other person working for the employer who has the authority to investigate, discover, or terminate misconduct); or

"(2) to file, cause to be filed, testify, participate in, or otherwise assist in a proceeding filed or about to be filed (with any knowledge of the employer) relating to an alleged violation of section 1341, 1343, 1344, or 1348, any rule or regulation of the Securities and Exchange Commission, or any provision of Federal law relating to fraud against shareholders.

"(b) ENFORCEMENT ACTION—

"(1) IN GENERAL- A person who alleges discharge or other discrimination by any person in violation of subsection (a) may seek relief under subsection (c), by—

"(A) filing a complaint with the Secretary of Labor; or

"(B) if the Secretary has not issued a final decision within 180 days of the filing of the complaint and there is no showing that such delay is due to the bad faith of the claimant, bringing an action at law or equity for de novo review in the appropriate district court of the United States, which shall have jurisdiction over such an action without regard to the amount in controversy.

"(2) PROCEDURE—

"(A) IN GENERAL- An action under paragraph (1)(A) shall be governed under the rules and procedures set forth in section 42121(b) of title 49, United States Code.

"(B) EXCEPTION- Notification made under section 42121(b)(1) of title 49, United States Code, shall be made to the person named in the complaint and to the employer.

"(C) BURDENS OF PROOF- An action brought under paragraph (1)(B) shall be governed by the legal burdens of proof set forth in section 42121(b) of title 49, United States Code.

"(D) STATUTE OF LIMITATIONS- An action under paragraph (1) shall be commenced not later than 90 days after the date on which the violation occurs.

"(c) REMEDIES—

"(1) IN GENERAL- An employee prevailing in any action under subsection (b)(1) shall be entitled to all relief necessary to make the employee whole.

"(2) COMPENSATORY DAMAGES- Relief for any action under paragraph (1) shall include—

"(A) reinstatement with the same seniority status that the employee would have had, but for the discrimination;

"(B) the amount of back pay, with interest; and

"(C) compensation for any special damages sustained as a result of the discrimination, including litigation costs, expert witness fees, and reasonable attorney fees.

"(d) RIGHTS RETAINED BY EMPLOYEE- Nothing in this section shall be deemed to diminish the rights, privileges, or remedies of any employee under any Federal or State law, or under any collective bargaining agreement.".

(b) Clerical amendment. The table of sections at the beginning of chapter 73 of title 18, United States Code, is amended by inserting after the item relating to section 1514 the following new item:

"1514A. Civil action to protect against retaliation in fraud cases.".

[¶ 1254] Sec. 807. Criminal penalties for defrauding shareholders of publicly traded companies.

(a) In general. Chapter 63 of title 18, United States Code, is amended by adding at the end the following:

"Sec. 1348. Securities fraud

"Whoever knowingly executes, or attempts to execute, a scheme or artifice—

"(1) to defraud any person in connection with any security of an issuer with a class of securities registered under section 12 of the Securities Exchange Act of 1934 (15 U.S.C. 78l) or that is required to file reports under section 15(d) of the Securities Exchange Act of 1934 (15 U.S.C. 78o(d)); or

"(2) to obtain, by means of false or fraudulent pretenses, representations, or promises, any money or property in connection with the purchase or sale of any security of an issuer with a class of securities registered under section 12 of the Securities Exchange Act of 1934 (15 U.S.C. 78l) or that is required to file reports under section 15(d) of the Securities Exchange Act of 1934 (15 U.S.C. 78o(d)); shall be fined under this title, or imprisoned not more than 25 years, or both.".

(b) Clerical amendment. The table of sections at the beginning of chapter 63 of title 18, United States Code, is amended by adding at the end the following new item:

"1348. Securities fraud.".

TITLE IX— WHITE-COLLAR CRIME PENALTY ENHANCEMENTS

[¶ 1255] Sec. 901. Short title. This title may be cited as the "White-Collar Crime Penalty Enhancement Act of 2002".

[¶ 1256] Sec. 902. Attempts and conspiracies to commit criminal fraud offenses.

(a) In general. Chapter 63 of title 18, United States Code, is amended by inserting after section 1348 as added by this Act the following:

"Sec. 1349. Attempt and conspiracy

"Any person who attempts or conspires to commit any offense under this chapter shall be subject to the same penalties as those prescribed for the offense, the Commission of which was the object of the attempt or conspiracy."

(b) Clerical amendment. The table of sections at the beginning of chapter 63 of title 18, United States Code, is amended by adding at the end the following new item:

"1349. Attempt and conspiracy.".

[¶ 1257] Sec. 903. Criminal penalties for mail and wire fraud.

(a) Mail fraud. Section 1341 of title 18, United States Code, is amended by striking "five" and inserting "20".

(b) Wire fraud. Section 1343 of title 18, United States Code, is amended by striking "five" and inserting "20".

[¶ 1258] Sec. 904. Criminal penalties for violations of the Employee Retirement Income Security Act of 1974. Section 501 of the Employee Retirement Income Security Act of 1974 (29 U.S.C. 1131) is amended—

(1) by striking "$5,000" and inserting "$100,000";

(2) by striking "one year" and inserting "10 years"; and

(3) by striking "$100,000" and inserting "$500,000".

[¶ 1259] Sec. 905. Amendment to sentencing guidelines relating to certain white-collar offenses.

(a) Directive to the United States Sentencing Commission. Pursuant to its authority under section 994(p) of title 18, United States Code, and in accordance with this section, the United States Sentencing Commission shall review and, as appropriate, amend the Federal Sentencing Guidelines and related policy statements to implement the provisions of this Act.

(b) Requirements. In carrying out this section, the Sentencing Commission shall—
(1) ensure that the sentencing guidelines and policy statements reflect the serious nature of the offenses and the penalties set forth in this Act, the growing incidence of serious fraud offenses which are identified above, and the need to modify the sentencing guidelines and policy statements to deter, prevent, and punish such offenses;
(2) consider the extent to which the guidelines and policy statements adequately address whether the guideline offense levels and enhancements for violations of the sections amended by this Act are sufficient to deter and punish such offenses, and specifically, are adequate in view of the statutory increases in penalties contained in this Act;
(3) assure reasonable consistency with other relevant directives and sentencing guidelines;
(4) account for any additional aggravating or mitigating circumstances that might justify exceptions to the generally applicable sentencing ranges;
(5) make any necessary conforming changes to the sentencing guidelines; and
(6) assure that the guidelines adequately meet the purposes of sentencing, as set forth in section 3553(a)(2) of title 18, United States Code.

(c) Emergency authority and deadline for Commission action. The United States Sentencing Commission is requested to promulgate the guidelines or amendments provided for under this section as soon as practicable, and in any event not later than 180 days after the date of enactment of this Act, in accordance with the procedures set forth in section 219(a) of the Sentencing Reform Act of 1987, as though the authority under that Act had not expired.

[¶ 1260] Sec. 906. Corporate responsibility for financial reports.

(a) In general. Chapter 63 of title 18, United States Code, is amended by inserting after section 1349, as created by this Act, the following:
"Sec. 1350. Failure of corporate officers to certify financial reports
"(a) CERTIFICATION OF PERIODIC FINANCIAL REPORTS. Each periodic report containing financial statements filed by an issuer with the Securities Exchange Commission pursuant to section 13(a) or 15(d) of the Securities Exchange Act of 1934 (15 U.S.C. 78m(a) or 78o(d)) shall be accompanied by a written statement by the chief executive officer and chief financial officer (or equivalent thereof) of the issuer.
"(b) CONTENT- The statement required under subsection (a) shall certify that the periodic report containing the financial statements fully complies with the requirements of section 13(a) or 15(d) of the Securities Exchange Act pf [sic] 1934 (15 U.S.C. 78m or 78o(d)) and that information contained in the periodic report fairly presents, in all material respects, the financial condition and results of operations of the issuer.
"(c) CRIMINAL PENALTIES- Whoever—
"(1) certifies any statement as set forth in subsections (a) and (b) of this section knowing that the periodic report accompanying the statement does not comport with all the requirements set forth in this section shall be fined not more than $1,000,000 or imprisoned not more than 10 years, or both; or
"(2) willfully certifies any statement as set forth in subsections (a) and (b) of this section knowing that the periodic report accompanying the statement does not comport with all the requirements set forth in this section shall be fined not more than $5,000,000, or imprisoned not more than 20 years, or both.".

(b) Clerical amendment. The table of sections at the beginning of chapter 63 of title 18, United States Code, is amended by adding at the end the following:
"1350. Failure of corporate officers to certify financial reports.".

TITLE X— CORPORATE TAX RETURNS

[¶ 1261] Sec. 1001. Sense of the Senate regarding the signing of corporate tax returns by chief executive officers. It is the sense of the Senate that the Federal income tax return of a corporation should be signed by the chief executive officer of such corporation.

TITLE XI— CORPORATE FRAUD ACCOUNTABILITY

[¶ 1262] Sec. 1101. Short title. This title may be cited as the "Corporate Fraud Accountability Act of 2002".

[¶ 1263] Sec. 1102. Tampering with a record or otherwise impeding an official proceeding. Section 1512 of title 18, United States Code, is amended—

(1) by redesignating subsections (c) through (i) as subsections (d) through (j), respectively; and

(2) by inserting after subsection (b) the following new subsection:

"(c) Whoever corruptly—

"(1) alters, destroys, mutilates, or conceals a record, document, or other object, or attempts to do so, with the intent to impair the object's integrity or availability for use in an official proceeding; or

"(2) otherwise obstructs, influences, or impedes any official proceeding, or attempts to do so,

shall be fined under this title or imprisoned not more than 20 years, or both.'.

[¶ 1264] Sec. 1103. Temporary freeze authority for the Securities and Exchange Commission.

(a) In general. Section 21C(c) of the Securities Exchange Act of 1934 (15 U.S.C. 78u-3(c)) is amended by adding at the end the following:

"(3) TEMPORARY FREEZE—

"(A) IN GENERAL—

"(i) ISSUANCE OF TEMPORARY ORDER- Whenever, during the course of a lawful investigation involving possible violations of the Federal securities laws by an issuer of publicly traded securities or any of its directors, officers, partners, controlling persons, agents, or employees, it shall appear to the Commission that it is likely that the issuer will make extraordinary payments (whether compensation or otherwise) to any of the foregoing persons, the Commission may petition a Federal district court for a temporary order requiring the issuer to escrow, subject to court supervision, those payments in an interest-bearing account for 45 days.

"(ii) STANDARD- A temporary order shall be entered under clause (i), only after notice and opportunity for a hearing, unless the court determines that notice and hearing prior to entry of the order would be impracticable or contrary to the public interest.

"(iii) EFFECTIVE PERIOD- A temporary order issued under clause (i) shall—

"(I) become effective immediately;

"(II) be served upon the parties subject to it; and

"(III) unless set aside, limited or suspended by a court of competent jurisdiction, shall remain effective and enforceable for 45 days.

"(iv) EXTENSIONS AUTHORIZED- The effective period of an order under this subparagraph may be extended by the court upon good cause shown for not longer than 45 additional days, provided that the combined period of the order shall not exceed 90 days.

"(B) PROCESS ON DETERMINATION OF VIOLATIONS—

"(i) VIOLATIONS CHARGED- If the issuer or other person described in subparagraph (A) is charged with any violation of the Federal securities laws before the expiration of the effective period of a temporary order under subparagraph (A) (including any applicable extension period), the order shall remain in effect, subject to court approval, until the conclusion of any legal proceedings related thereto, and the affected issuer or other person, shall have the right to petition the court for review of the order.

"(ii) VIOLATIONS NOT CHARGED- If the issuer or other person described in subparagraph (A) is not charged with any violation of the Federal securities laws before the expiration of the effective period of a temporary order under subparagraph (A) (including any applicable extension period), the escrow shall terminate at the expiration of the 45-day effective period (or the expiration of any extension period, as applicable), and the disputed payments (with accrued interest) shall be returned to the issuer or other affected person.".

(b) Technical amendment. Section 21C(c)(2) of the Securities Exchange Act of 1934 (15 U.S.C. 78u-3(c)(2)) is amended by striking "This" and inserting "paragraph (1)".

[¶ 1265] Sec. 1104. Amendment to the Federal sentencing guidelines.

(a) Request for immediate consideration by the United States Sentencing Commission. Pursuant to its authority under section 994(p) of title 28, United States Code, and in accordance with this section, the United States Sentencing Commission is requested to—

   (1) promptly review the sentencing guidelines applicable to securities and accounting fraud and related offenses;

   (2) expeditiously consider the promulgation of new sentencing guidelines or amendments to existing sentencing guidelines to provide an enhancement for officers or directors of publicly traded corporations who commit fraud and related offenses; and

   (3) submit to Congress an explanation of actions taken by the Sentencing Commission pursuant to paragraph (2) and any additional policy recommendations the Sentencing Commission may have for combating offenses described in paragraph (1).

(b) Considerations in review. In carrying out this section, the Sentencing Commission is requested to—

   (1) ensure that the sentencing guidelines and policy statements reflect the serious nature of securities, pension, and accounting fraud and the need for aggressive and appropriate law enforcement action to prevent such offenses;

   (2) assure reasonable consistency with other relevant directives and with other guidelines;

   (3) account for any aggravating or mitigating circumstances that might justify exceptions, including circumstances for which the sentencing guidelines currently provide sentencing enhancements;

   (4) ensure that guideline offense levels and enhancements for an obstruction of justice offense are adequate in cases where documents or other physical evidence are actually destroyed or fabricated;

   (5) ensure that the guideline offense levels and enhancements under United States Sentencing Guideline 2B1.1 (as in effect on the date of enactment of this Act) are sufficient for a fraud offense when the number of victims adversely involved is significantly greater than 50;

   (6) make any necessary conforming changes to the sentencing guidelines; and

   (7) assure that the guidelines adequately meet the purposes of sentencing as set forth in section 3553 (a)(2) of title 18, United States Code.

(c) Emergency authority and deadline for Commission action. The United States Sentencing Commission is requested to promulgate the guidelines or amendments provided for under this section as soon as practicable, and in any event not later than the 180 days after the date of enactment of this Act, in accordance with the procedures sent forth in section 21(a) of the Sentencing Reform Act of 1987, as though the authority under that Act had not expired.

[¶ 1266] Sec. 1105. Authority of the Commission to prohibit persons from serving as officers or directors.

(a) Securities Exchange Act of 1934. Section 21C of the Securities Exchange Act of 1934 (15 U.S.C. 78u-3) is amended by adding at the end the following:

"(f) AUTHORITY OF THE COMMISSION TO PROHIBIT PERSONS FROM SERVING AS OFFICERS OR DIRECTORS- In any cease-and-desist proceeding under subsection (a), the Commission may issue an order to prohibit, conditionally or unconditionally, and permanently or for such period of time as it shall determine, any person who has violated section 10(b) or the rules or regulations thereunder, from acting as an officer or director of any issuer that has a class of securities registered pursuant to section 12, or that is required to file reports pursuant to section 15(d), if the conduct of that person demonstrates unfitness to serve as an officer or director of any such issuer.".

(b) Securities Act of 1933. Section 8A of the Securities Act of 1933 (15 U.S.C. 77h-1) is amended by adding at the end of the following:

"(f) AUTHORITY OF THE COMMISSION TO PROHIBIT PERSONS FROM SERVING AS OFFICERS OR DIRECTORS- In any cease-and-desist proceeding under subsection (a), the Commission may issue an order to prohibit, conditionally or unconditionally, and permanently or for such period of time as it shall determine, any person who has violated section 17(a)(1) or the rules or regulations thereunder, from acting as an officer or director of any issuer that has a class of securities registered pursuant to section 12 of the Securities Exchange Act of 1934, or that is required to file reports pursuant to section 15(d) of that Act, if the conduct of that person demonstrates unfitness to serve as an officer or director of any such issuer.".

[¶ 1267] Sec. 1106. Increased criminal penalties under Securities Exchange Act of 1934. Section 32(a) of the Securities Exchange Act of 1934 (15 U.S.C. 78ff(a)) is amended—

(1) by striking "$1,000,000, or imprisoned not more than 10 years" and inserting "$5,000,000, or imprisoned not more than 20 years"; and

(2) by striking "$2,500,000" and inserting "$25,000,000".

[¶ 1268] Sec. 1107. Retaliation against informants.

(a) In general. Section 1513 of title 18, United States Code, is amended by adding at the end the following:

"(e) Whoever knowingly, with the intent to retaliate, takes any action harmful to any person, including interference with the lawful employment or livelihood of any person, for providing to a law enforcement officer any truthful information relating to the commission or possible commission of any Federal offense, shall be fined under this title or imprisoned not more than 10 years, or both.".

INDEX

References are to paragraph numbers

WG
&L Warren, Gorham & Lamont